CAMBRIDGE

Higher

MATHEMATICS
GCSE for AQA
Student Book

Karen Morrison, Julia Smith, Pauline McLean, Rachael Horsman and Nick Asker

CAMBRIDGE
UNIVERSITY PRESS

University Printing House, Cambridge CB2 8BS, United Kingdom

Cambridge University Press is part of the University of Cambridge.

It furthers the University's mission by disseminating knowledge in the pursuit of education, learning and research at the highest international levels of excellence.

www.cambridge.org

Information on this title:
www.cambridge.org/9781107448032 (Paperback)
www.cambridge.org/9781107449800 (1 Year Online Subscription)
www.cambridge.org/9781107449770 (2 year Online Subscription)
www.cambridge.org/9781107447943 (Paperback + Online Subscription)

© Cambridge University Press 2015

First published 2015

Printed in Dubai by Oriental Press

A catalogue record for this publication is available from the British Library

ISBN 978-1-107-44803-2 Paperback
ISBN 978-1-107-44980-0 (1 Year Online Subscription)
ISBN 978-1-107-44977-0 (2 Year Online Subscription)
ISBN 978-1-107-44794-3 Paperback + Online Subscription

Additional resources for this publication at www.cambridge.org/ukschools

Cambridge University Press has no responsibility for the persistence or accuracy of URLs for external or third-party internet websites referred to in this publication, and does not guarantee that any content on such websites is, or will remain, accurate or appropriate. Information regarding prices, travel timetables, and other factual information given in this work is correct at the time of first printing but Cambridge University Press does not guarantee the accuracy of such information thereafter.

Approval message from AQA

This textbook has been approved by AQA for use with our qualification. This means that we have checked that it broadly covers the specification and we are satisfied with the overall quality. Full details of our approval process can be found on our website.

We approve textbooks because we know how important it is for teachers and students to have the right resources to support their teaching and learning. Please note, however, that the publisher is ultimately responsible for the editorial control and quality of this book.

Please note that when teaching the GCSE Mathematics (8300) course, you must refer to AQA's specification as your definitive source of information. While this book has been written to match the specification, it cannot provide complete coverage of every aspect of the course.

A wide range of other useful resources can be found on the relevant subject pages of our website: www.aqa.org.uk

Contents

Note

The colour of each chapter corresponds to the area of maths that it covers:

- Number
- Algebra
- Ratio, proportion and rates of change
- Geometry and measures
- Probability
- Statistics

Introduction

This book has been written by experienced teachers to help build your understanding and enjoyment of the maths you will meet at GCSE.

Each chapter opens with a list of skills that are covered in the chapter. The **real-life applications** section describes an example of how the maths is used in real life.

All chapters build on knowledge that you will have learned in previous years. You may need to revise some topics before starting a chapter. To check your knowledge, answer the questions in the **Before you start …** table. You can check your answers using the free answer booklet available at **www.cambridge.org/ukschools/gcsemaths-studentbookanswers**. If you answer any questions incorrectly, you may need to revise the topic from your work in earlier years.

The chapters are divided into sections, each covering a single topic. Some chapters may cover topics that you already know and understand. You can use the **Launchpad** to identify the best section for you to start with. Answer the questions in each step. If you find a question difficult to answer correctly, the step suggests the section that you should look at.

Throughout the book, there are features to help you build knowledge and improve your skills:

- This means you may need a calculator to work through a question.
- This means you should work through a question without using a calculator.
- This shows the question is from a past exam paper.

Tip

Tip boxes provide helpful hints.

Calculator tip

Calculator tips help you to use your calculator.

Learn this formula

Learn this formula boxes contain formulae that you need to know.

Key vocabulary

Important maths terms are written in **green**. You can find what they mean in **Key vocabulary** boxes and also in the **Glossary** at the back of the book.

Did you know?

Did you know? boxes contain interesting maths facts.

WORK IT OUT

Work it out boxes contain a question with several worked solutions. Some of the solutions contain common mistakes. Try to spot the correct solution and check the free answer booklet available at **www.cambridge.org/ukschools/gcsemaths-studentbookanswers** to see if you're right.

WORKED EXAMPLE

Worked examples guide you through model answers to help you understand methods of answering questions.

Some chapters contain a **Problem-solving framework**, which sets a problem and then shows how you can go about answering it.

Checklist of learning and understanding

At the end of a chapter, use the **Checklist of learning and understanding** to check whether you have covered everything you need to know.

Chapter review

You can check whether you have understood the topics using the **Chapter review,** which contains questions from the whole chapter.

A booklet containing answers to all exercises is free to download from the maths pages at **www.cambridge.org/ukschools/gcsemaths-studentbookanswers**.

You can find more resources, including interactive widgets, games and quizzes on **GCSE Mathematics Online**.

1 Working with integers

In this chapter you will learn how to …

- use formal written methods to calculate with positive and negative integers.
- perform operations in the correct order based on mathematical conventions.
- recognise inverse operations and use them to simplify and check calculations.

For more resources relating to this chapter, visit GCSE Mathematics Online.

Using mathematics: real-life applications

Everyone uses numbers on a daily basis often without really thinking about them. Shopping, cooking, working out bills, paying for transport and measuring, all rely on a good understanding of numbers and calculation skills.

Tip

You probably already know most of the concepts in this chapter. They have been included so that you can revise them if you need to and check that you know them well.

"Number puzzles and games are very popular and there are mobile apps and games available for all age groups. I use an app with my GCSE classes where they have to work in the correct order to solve different number puzzles."

(Secondary school teacher)

Before you start …

KS3	You should be able to add, subtract, multiply and divide positive and negative numbers.	**1**	Copy and complete each statement to make it true. Use only <, = or >. **a** $2 + 3 \,\square\, 4 - 7$ **b** $-3 + 6 \,\square\, 4 - 7$ **c** $-1 - 4 \,\square\, 20 \div -4$ **d** $-6 \times 2 \,\square\, -7 - (-5)$
KS3	You should know the rules for working when more than one operation is involved in a calculation (BODMAS).	**2**	Spot the mistake in each calculation and correct the answers. **a** $3 + 8 + 3 \times 4 = 56$ **b** $\quad 3 + 8 \times 3 + 4 = 37$ **c** $3 \times (8 + 3) \times 4 = 130$

KS3	You should understand that addition and subtraction, and multiplication and division are inverse operations.	**3**	Identify the inverse operation by choosing the correct option.
			 a $14 \times 4 = 56$
			    A $56 \times 4 = 14$ B $14 \div 4 = 56$ C $56 \div 4 = 14$
			 b $200 \div 10 = 20$
			    A $200 \div 20 = 10$ B $200 = 10 \times 20$ C $10 \times 200 = 2000$
			 c $27 + 53 = 80$
			    A $80 = 4 \times 20$ B $80 - 27 = 53$ C $80 + 27 = 107$

Find answers at: cambridge.org/ukschools/gcsemaths-studentbookanswers

Assess your starting point using the Launchpad

STEP 1

1 Calculate without using a calculator and show your working.

a 647 + 786 **b** 1406 − 289

c 45 × 19 **d** 414 ÷ 23

GO TO
Section 1:
Basic calculations

STEP 2

2 Choose the correct answer.

a 9 ÷ (2 + 1) − 2

A 9 B $3\frac{1}{2}$ C 1 D 0

b (3 × 8) ÷ 4 + 8

A 2 B 30 C 16 D 14

c 12 − 6 × 2 + 11

A 78 B 23 C 1 D 11

d [5 × (9 + 1)] − 3

A 53 B 47 C 40 D 43

e (6 + 5) × 2 + (15 − 2 × 3) − 6

A 40 B 20 C 32 D 25

GO TO
Section 2:
Order of operations

STEP 3

3 The perimeter of a square is equal to four times the length of a side.

If the perimeter is 128 cm, what is the length of a side?

4 What should you add to 342 to get 550?

5 A number divided by 45 is 30.

What is the number?

GO TO
Section 3:
Inverse operations

GO TO
Chapter review

Section 1: Basic calculations

You will not always have a calculator so it is useful to know how to do calculations using mental and written strategies.

It is best to use a method that you are confident with and always **show your working**.

When a question asks you to find the:

- **sum**, you need to add
- **difference**, you need to subtract the smaller number from the larger number
- **product**, you need to multiply ✓
- **quotient**, you need to divide. ✓

Tip

Some examination papers will not allow you to use your calculator. In this book the past paper questions that you are not allowed to use your calculator for are marked with a 🝙 symbol.

WORK IT OUT 1.1

Look at these calculations carefully.

Discuss with a partner what methods these students have used to find the answer.

Which method would you use to do each of these calculations? Why?

① $489 + 274$

$$400 + 200 \rightarrow 600$$
$$80 + 70 \rightarrow 150$$
$$9 + 4 \rightarrow \underline{\ \ 13}$$
$$\overline{763}$$

② $284 - 176$

$$\begin{array}{r} 2\overset{7}{\cancel{8}}\overset{1}{4} \\ -\ 176 \\ \hline 108 \end{array}$$

③ 29×17

$$= 30 \times 17 - 17$$
$$= 3 \times 170 - 17$$
$$= 510 - 17$$
$$= 493$$

④ 15×62

$$\begin{array}{ll} = 30 \times 31 & 310 \\ = 930 & 310 \\ = 3 \times 310 & \underline{310} \\ & 930 \end{array}$$

⑤ 207×47

×	200	0	7
40	8000	0	280
7	1400	0	49

$$9400 + 0 + 329$$
$$= 9729$$

⑥ $2394 \div 42$

$$\begin{array}{r} 2394 \\ -\ 1680 \quad \textcircled{40} \\ \hline 714 \\ -\ 420 \quad \textcircled{10} \\ \hline 294 \\ -\ 210 \quad \textcircled{5} \\ \hline 84 \\ -\ 84 \quad \textcircled{2} \\ \hline 0 \quad 57 \end{array}$$

$$42 \times 10 = 420$$
$$42 \times 20 = 840$$
$$42 \times 40 = 1680$$
$$42 \times 5 = 210$$
$$42 \times 2 = 84$$

Find answers at: cambridge.org/ukschools/gcsemaths-studentbookanswers

Problem-solving strategies

The Problem-solving framework below outlines the steps that you can take to break down most problems to help you solve them.

Follow these steps each time you are faced with a problem to help you become more skilled at problem-solving and more able to self-check.

These are important skills both for your GCSE courses and for everyday life.

Problem-solving framework

Sally had a budget of £60 to buy items.
Sally bought:

a table for £32 and

a bench for £18.

She spent £12 to repair them.

She then sold the two items for £69.

How much profit did she make?

Steps for solving problems	What you would do for this example
Step 1: Work out what you have to do. Start by reading the question carefully.	Find the profit.
Step 2: What information do you need? Have you got it all?	Cost of items = £32 + £18 Cost of repairs = £12 Selling price = £69 Yes
Step 3: Is there any information that you don't need?	You don't need to know her budget. You just need to know how much she spent. Many problems contain extra information that you don't need to test your understanding.
Step 4: Decide what maths you can do.	Profit = selling price – cost
Step 5: Set out your solution clearly. Check your working and make sure your answer is reasonable.	Cost = £32 + £18 + £12 = £62 Profit = £69 – £62 = £7 Sally made £7 profit.
Step 6: Check that you have answered the question.	Yes. You needed to find the profit and you have found it.

EXERCISE 1A

Solve these problems using written methods.

You **must** show your working.

1 A pack of pens cost £3.90 for three.
Nola bought fifteen pens.

   a i How much did she pay in total?

     ii What is the cost per pen?

   b How many packs of pens did Nola buy? Why do you need to know this?

   c What operation would you do to find the total cost? Why?

   d How would you work out the cost per pen?

   e Does a price of £1.50 per pen seem reasonable?

2 A pair of jeans costs £34.
A scarf costs £9.50.
A top costs £20.

  Sandra saved £100 to buy these items.
How much money did she have left?

3 How many 16-page brochures can you make from 1030 pages?

4 Jason can type 48 words per minute.

   a How many words can he type in an hour and a half?

   b Approximately how long would it take him to type 2000 words?

5 At the start of a year the population of Greenside Village was 56 309.

During the year:

617 people died,

1835 babies were born,

4087 people left the village

and 3099 people moved into the village.

What was the population at the end of the year?

6 The Amazon River is 6448 km long.

The Nile River is 6670 km.

The Severn River is 354 km long.

   a How much longer is the Nile River than the Amazon River?

   b How much shorter is the Severn River than the Amazon River?

7 What is the result when you add the sum of 132 and 99 to the product of 36 and 127?

8 Find the result when the difference between 8765 and 3087 is added to the result of 1206 divided by 18.

Tip

You don't always need to write something for the first few steps in the Problem-solving framework, but you should still consider these steps mentally when approaching a problem in order to help you decide what to do. You should **always** show how you worked out the problem.

Did you know?

The Severn is the longest river in the UK.

Working with positive and negative integers

When doing calculations involving positive and negative **integers**, you need to remember the following:

- Adding a negative number is the same as subtracting the number:
  $4 + -3 = 1$
- Subtracting a negative number is the same as adding a positive number:
  $5 - -3 = 8$
- Multiplying or dividing the same signs gives a positive answer:
  $-4 \times -2 = 8$ and $\frac{-4}{-2} = 2$
- Multiplying or dividing different signs gives a negative answer:
  $4 \times -2 = -8$ and $\frac{4}{-2} = -2$

EXERCISE 1B

1 What would you add to each number to get a result of 5?

    a 7   **b** 3   **c** −1   **d** −4   **e** −24

2 What would you subtract from each number to get a result of −8?

    a 7   **b** 3   **c** −1   **d** −4   **e** −24

3 −4 is multiplied by another number to get each result.

Work out what the other number is in each case.

    a 12   **b** −100   **c** −36   **d** 504   **e** 0

4 By what would you divide −64 to get the following results?

    a 8   **b** −8   **c** 2   **d** $-\frac{1}{2}$ **e** −256

5 Here is a set of integers: {−8, −6, −3, 1, 3, 7}

From the numbers in this set:

    a Write down two numbers with a difference of 9.

    b Write down three numbers with a sum of 1.

    c Write down two numbers whose product is −3.

    d Write down two numbers that, when divided, will give an answer of −6.

6 One more than −6 is added to the product of 7 and 6 less than 3.

What is the result?

7 Saleem has a container of wooden dowels.

Some are 5 cm long and some are 7 cm long.

If the dowels are joined end to end, investigate what lengths between 5 cm and 150 cm **cannot** be made.

Section 2: Order of operations

Jose posted this calculation on his wall on social media.

JOSE:
$24 + 6 \div 2 - 1 \times 4 = ?$

💬 COMMENT ✓ LIKE ↷ SHARE

JOANNA: 56

PETER: 11

LUCIA: 23

DIPAK: 104

Which one of Jose's friends (if any) do you think is correct? Why?

There is a set of rules that tell you the order in which you need to work when there is more than one operation.

The order of operations is:

1 Do any operations in brackets first.
2 If there are any '**powers of**' or '**fractions of**' in the calculation, do them next.
3 Do division and multiplication next, working from left to right.
4 Do addition and subtraction last, working from left to right.

Brackets

Brackets are used to group operations. For example:

$(3 + 7) \times (30 \div 2)$

When there is more than one set of brackets, work from the **innermost set** to the **outermost set**.

Different styles of bracket can be used to make it easier to identify each pair.

> **Tip**
>
> Many people remember these rules using the letters **BODMAS** (or sometimes BIDMAS).
>
> **B**rackets
> **O**f ('powers of' or 'fractions of'; in BIDMAS I stands for indices)
> **D**ivide and/or **M**ultiply
> **A**dd and/or **S**ubtract

WORKED EXAMPLE 1

Work out $2((4 + 2) \times 2 - 3(1 - 3) - 10)$.

$2((4 + 2) \times 2 - 3(1 - 3) - 10)$

Highlight the different pairs of brackets to help if you need to.

$2((4 + 2) \times 2 - 3(1 - 3) - 10)$
$= 2((6) \times 2 - 3(-2) - 10)$
$= 2(6 \times 2 - 3 \times -2 - 10)$

The red brackets are the innermost, so do the calculations inside these brackets first. There are two lots, so work from left to right. **Note** that you can leave −2 inside brackets if you prefer because 3(−2) is the same as 3 × −2.

$2(6 \times 2 - 3 \times -2 - 10)$
$= 2(12 - -6 - 10)$
$= 2(8)$
$= 2 \times 8$
$= 16$

Blue brackets are next. Do the multiplications first from left to right, then the subtractions from left to right.

For example, the following different types of brackets have been used below: ( ), [ ], { }.

$$\{2 - [4(2 - 7) - 4(3 + 8)] - 2\} \times 8$$

Other symbols can also be used to group operations.

For example:

Fraction bars: $\dfrac{5 - 12}{3 - 8}$

Roots: $\sqrt{16 + 9}$

These symbols are treated like brackets when you do a calculation.

Tip

$\dfrac{5 - 12}{3 - 8}$ is the same calculation as $(5 - 12) \div (3 - 8)$.

Calculator tip

Most modern calculators are programmed to use the correct order of operations. Check your calculator by entering $2 + 3 \times 4$. You should get 14.

If a calculation is written with brackets, you need to enter the brackets into the calculator to make sure it does these first.

WORK IT OUT 1.2

Which of the solutions is correct in each case?

Find the mistakes in the incorrect option.

	Option A	Option B
1	$7 \times 3 + 4$ $= 21 + 4$ $= 25$	$7 \times 3 + 4$ $= 7 \times 7$ $= 49$
2	$(10 - 4) \times (4 + 9)^2$ $= 6 \times 16 + 81$ $= 96 + 81$ $= 177$	$(10 - 4) \times (4 + 9)^2$ $= 6 \times (13)^2$ $= 6 \times 169$ $= 1014$
3	$45 - [20 \times (4 - 3)]$ $= 45 - [20 \times 1]$ $= 45 - 21$ $= 24$	$45 - [20 \times (4 - 3)]$ $= 45 - 20 \times 1$ $= 45 - 20$ $= 25$
4	$30 - 4 \div 2 + 2$ $= 26 \div 2 + 2$ $= 13 + 2$ $= 15$	$30 - 4 \div 2 + 2$ $= 30 - 2 + 2$ $= 30$
5	$\dfrac{18 - 4}{4 - 2}$ $= \dfrac{18}{2}$ $= 9$	$\dfrac{18 - 4}{4 - 2}$ $= \dfrac{14}{2}$ $= 7$
6	$\sqrt{36 \div 4} + 40 \div 4 + 1$ $= \sqrt{9} + 10 + 1$ $= 3 + 11$ $= 14$	$\sqrt{36 \div 4} + 40 \div 4 + 1$ $= \sqrt{9} + 40 \div 5$ $= 3 + 8$ $= 11$

EXERCISE 1C

1 Check whether these answers are correct.

If not, work out the correct answer.

a $12 \times 4 + 76 = 124$ **b** $8 + 75 \times 8 = 698$

c $12 \times 18 - 4 \times 23 = 124$ **d** $(16 \div 4) \times (7 + 3 \times 4) = 76$

e $(82 - 36) \times (2 + 6) = 16$ **f** $(3 \times 7 - 4) - (4 + 6 \div 2) = 12$

2 Use the numbers listed to make each number sentence true.

a $\square - \square \div \square = \square$ 9, 11, 13, 18

b $\square \div (\square - \square) - \square = \square$ 1, 3, 8, 14, 16

c $(\square + \square) - (\square - \square) = \square$ 4, 5, 6, 9, 12

3 Insert brackets into each calculation, if necessary, to make it true.

a $3 \times 4 + 6 = 30$ **b** $25 - 15 \times 9 = 90$ **c** $40 - 10 \times 3 = 90$

d $14 - 9 \times 2 = 10$ **e** $12 + 3 \div 5 = 3$ **f** $19 - 9 \times 15 = 150$

g $10 + 10 \div 6 - 2 = 5$ **h** $3 + 8 \times 15 - 9 = 66$ **i** $9 - 4 \times 7 + 2 = 45$

j $10 - 4 \times 5 = 30$ **k** $6 \div 3 + 3 \times 5 = 5$ **l** $15 - 6 \div 2 = 12$

m $1 + 4 \times 20 \div 5 = 20$ **n** $8 + 5 - 3 \times 2 = 20$ **o** $36 \div 3 \times 3 - 3 = 6$

p $3 \times 4 - 2 \div 6 = 1$ **q** $40 \div 4 + 1 = 11$ **r** $6 + 2 \times 8 + 2 = 24$

4 Each $\bigcirc$ represents an operation.

Fill in the missing operations to make these calculations true.

a $12 \bigcirc (28 \bigcirc 24) = 3$ **b** $88 \bigcirc 10 \bigcirc 8 = 8$

c $40 \bigcirc 5 \bigcirc (7 \bigcirc 5) = 4$ **d** $9 \bigcirc 15 \bigcirc (3 \bigcirc 2) = 12$

5 Calculate:

a $\dfrac{7 \times \sqrt{16}}{2^3 + 7^{(2-1)}}$

b $\dfrac{5^2 \times \sqrt{4}}{1 + 6^2 - 12}$

c $\dfrac{2 + 3^2}{5^2 + 4 \times 10 - \sqrt{25}}$

d $\dfrac{6^2 - 11}{2(17 + 2 \times 4)}$

e $\dfrac{3^2 - 3}{2 \times \sqrt{81}}$

f $\dfrac{3^2 - 5 + 6}{\sqrt{4} \times 5}$

g $\dfrac{36 - 3 \times \sqrt{16}}{15 - 3^2 \div 3}$

h $\dfrac{-30 + [18 \div (3 - 12) + 24]}{5 - 8 - 3^2}$

6 Work with a partner.

a Find a quick method for adding a set of consecutive whole numbers.

b Give a reason why your method works.

c Test your method on a set of consecutive negative integers.

d Does it work? Give a reason why or why not.

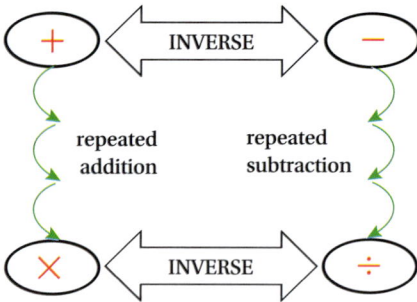

Section 3: Inverse operations

The four operations, add, subtract, multiply and divide, are related to each other.

Operations are inverses of each other if one undoes (cancels out) the effect of the other.

- Adding is the inverse of subtracting, for example, add 5 is undone by subtract 5.
- Multiplying is the inverse of dividing, for example, multiply by 2 is undone by divide by 2.
- Taking a square root is the inverse of squaring a number, for example, 4^2 is undone by $\sqrt{16}$.
- Taking the cube root is the inverse of cubing a number, for example, 2^3 is undone by $\sqrt[3]{8}$.

Inverse operations are useful for checking the results of your calculations.

For example, is $4320 - 500 = 3820$ correct?

Check by adding 500 back to the result (that is, by doing the inverse operation) to see whether it gives you 4320.

$3820 + 500 = 4320$, so it is correct.

When there is more than one operation involved, you have to reverse the order of the inverse operations to return to the starting number.

For example, is $(50 + 62) \div 8 = 14$?

Check by working backwards and applying inverse operations:

$14 \times 8 - 62 = 50$, so it is correct.

> **Tip**
>
> You will use inverse operations to solve equations and to deal with functions, so it is important that you understand how they work.

EXERCISE 1D

1 Use inverse operations to find the missing values in each of these calculations.

- **a** $\square + 217 = 529$
- **b** $\square + 388 = 490$
- **c** $\square - 218 = 182$
- **d** $121 \times \square = -605$
- **e** $-6 \times \square = 870$
- **f** $\square \div 40 = 5400$

2 Use inverse operations to check these calculations.

- **a** $45 \times 5 - 8 = 217$
- **b** $14 + 5 \times 9 - 9 = 50$
- **c** $(23 + 48) \times 4 = 284$
- **d** $(412 - 128) \div 4 = 71$

3 The formula for finding the area of a triangle is $A = \dfrac{bh}{2}$, where b is the base length and h is the height.

- **a** Find the height of a triangle with an area of $54\,\text{cm}^2$ and a base of length $9\,\text{cm}$.
- **b** A triangle has an area of $64\,\text{cm}^2$.

  Find the height and the length of the base if the base is twice the height.

4 Here is an expression: $1 - \left(\dfrac{2}{3}(4 + 5) + 6\right) \times 7$

- **a** Calculate the value of the expression.
- **b** Keep the numbers in order (from 1 to 7) but change the operations as necessary to find:

  i the highest possible answer   **ii** the lowest possible answer.

- **c** Comment on how changing the operations affected your results.

Checklist of learning and understanding

Basic calculations

- Written methods are important when you do not have a calculator.
- You can use any method as long as you show your working.
- Negative and positive numbers can be added, subtracted, multiplied and divided as long as you apply the rules to get the correct sign in the answer.

Order of operations

- In maths there is a conventional order for working when there is more than one operation:
  - Always work out brackets (or other grouping symbols) first,
  - then powers and fractions,
  - multiply and/or divide next,
  - then add and/or subtract.

Inverse operations

- An inverse operation undoes the previous operation:
- Addition and subtraction are the inverse of each other.
- Multiplication and division are the inverse of each other.
- Squaring and taking the square root are the inverse of each other.

Chapter review

For additional questions on the topics in this chapter, visit GCSE Mathematics Online.

1 Choose the correct answer.

a What is the first operation you would do in this calculation:
$4 \times [20 \div (5 - 3)] - 8 + 2$?

A +   B −   C ×   D ÷

b To make the statement $5 - 3 \times 8 - 6 \div 2 = 2$ correct, you would need to insert brackets as follows:

A $5 - (3 \times 8) - 6 \div 2 = 2$ B $5 [- 3 \times (8 - 6)] \div 2 = 2$

C $(5 - 3) \times 8 - 6 \div 2 = 2$ D $(5 - 3) \times (8 - 6) \div 2 = 2$

2 These are the solutions to a cross-number puzzle.

The clues are all calculations that involve using the correct order of operations.

Write a set of clues that would give these results. Use at least **two** operations for each clue.

3 Use integers and operations to write ten different questions that give an answer of −17.

4 On a page of a magazine there are three columns of text.

Each column contains 42 rows.

In each column row there is an average of 32 letters.

Approximately how many letters are there on a page?

5 A stadium has seats for 32 000 people.

There are 125 seats in a row.

How many rows are there in the stadium?

6 This grid follows two rules.

Rule 1: The sums of each row are equal.

Rule 2: The products of each column are equal.

			Sum of rows
5	32	80	117
96	15	6	117

Product of columns: 480 | 480 | 480

The grid below follows the same two rules.

Work out the missing numbers.

			Sum of rows
	5	6	

Product of columns: 60 | | |

(3 marks)

© AQA 2013

7 Two numbers have a sum of −15 and a product of −100.

What are the numbers?

8 The sum of two numbers is 1, and their product is −20.

What are the numbers?

9 Jenna's bank account was overdrawn.

Then she deposited £1000.

Her new balance is £432.

By how much was her account overdrawn to start with?

10 You can use the formula $F = 2C + 32$ to approximately convert temperatures from Celsius to Fahrenheit.

Find the approximate temperature in degrees Celsius when it is:

a 68 °F   **b** 100 °F

2 Collecting, interpreting and representing data

In this chapter you will learn how to ...

- work out the properties of a large set of data from a sample of the data, and understand the limitations of sampling.
- interpret and construct appropriate tables, charts and graphs.
- choose the best form of representation for data and understand the appropriate use of different graphs.

For more resources relating to this chapter, visit GCSE Mathematics Online.

Using mathematics: real-life applications

We live in a very information-rich world. Knowing how to construct accurate graphs and how to interpret the graphs we see is important. Many graphs in print and other media are carefully designed to influence what we think by displaying the data in particular ways.

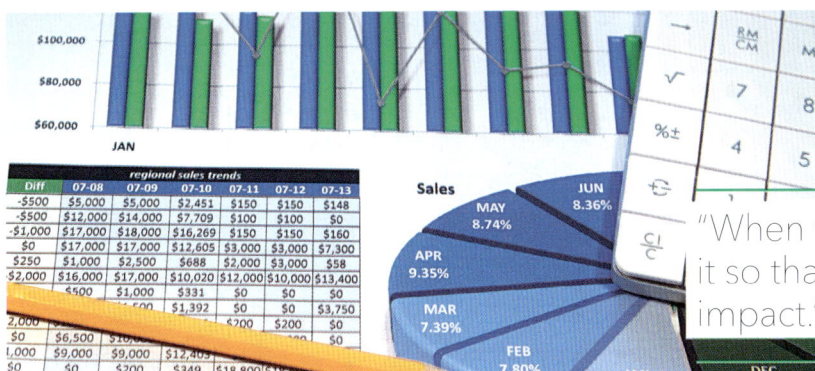

"When we have data, we need to display it so that our message has the maximum impact."

(Newspaper editor)

Before you start ...

KS3	You need to be able to sort and categorise data.	**1**	What would be suitable categories for a set of adult heights ranging from 1.39 m to 1.85 m?
KS3	You need to be able to use scales properly.	**2**	**a** What is each division on this scale: 200 — 300 **b** A scale between 0 and 100 has four divisions. Which numbers should go alongside each division?
KS3	You need to be able to measure and draw angles to create pie charts.	**3**	**a** Measure these angles: **b** Draw an angle of 72° accurately.

Find answers at: cambridge.org/ukschools/gcsemaths-studentbookanswers

Assess your starting point using the Launchpad

STEP 1

1 You want to find out what the most popular music in the school is, but you don't have time to ask everybody.

How can you do this and make sure your data is reliable?

?

GO TO
Section 1:
Populations and samples

✓

STEP 2

2 **a** Who scored the fewest goals in qualifying for the 2014 football World Cup tournament?

b Which teams scored the same number of goals?

Goals scored in qualifying for 2014 World Cup

[Bar chart: Number of goals (y-axis, 0 to 40) vs Country (x-axis). Belgium 18, Croatia 12, Italy 19, Germany 36, Holland 34, Switzerland 17, Russia 20, Portugal 20, Bosnia 30, Greece 12, England 31, Spain 14, France 15]

?

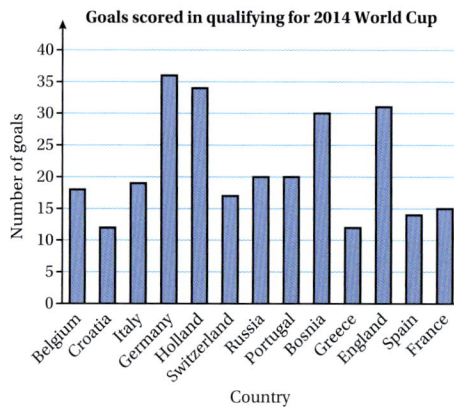

GO TO
Section 2:
Tables and charts

✓

STEP 3

3 Study the pie chart.

a Which age group had the biggest proportion of participants in a cycle event?

b There were 200 participants in total. How many of them were under 21?

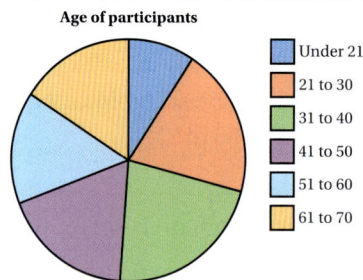

Age of participants

[Pie chart with legend: Under 21, 21 to 30, 31 to 40, 41 to 50, 51 to 60, 61 to 70]

?

GO TO
Section 3:
Pie charts

✓

GO TO
Step 4:
The Launchpad continues on the next page …

Launchpad continued …

STEP 4

4 **a** Why are the bars different widths on this graph?

b What is the class interval for the yellow bar?

c State how many students are between 11 and 16.

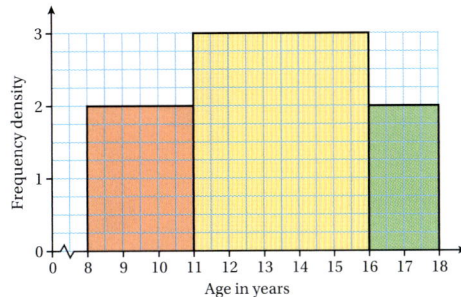

GO TO
Section 4: Cumulative frequency graphs and histograms
Section 5: Line graphs for time-series data

GO TO
Chapter review

Section 1: Populations and samples

A statistical **population** is a set of individuals or objects of interest.

For example, a school wants to find the mean height of students to decide what size of equipment to buy for the gymnasium.

In this example, the population would be all the students in the school.

In a large school it would be impractical to measure each student's height. It is more likely that the researcher would choose some of the students as a **sample** of the population.

The sample needs to be a **representative sample** to provide useful data.

A representative sample would come from measuring a mix of male and female students from different years, to get a good spread of the data.

It would not be a good idea to measure just the Year 7 students or just the Year 11 students because the sample would only be the shortest or tallest students.

A representative sample can be created by taking a factor that is unrelated to age and using it to select the students. This can be done, for example, by surveying all the students whose first name begins with a letter drawn at random.

Key vocabulary

population: the name given to a data set

sample: a small set of data from a population

representative sample: a small quantity of data that represents the characteristics of a larger population

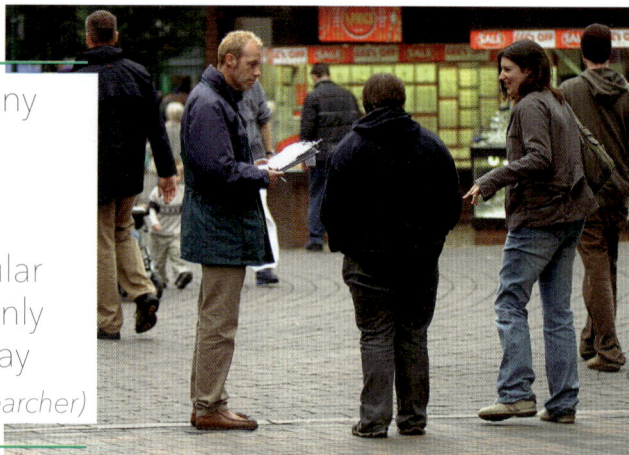

"I collect data on behalf of my company so that they can find out how likely people are to buy new products. We use quota sampling in our work. This involves choosing people with particular characteristics. For example, I might only be interested in teenage boys who play video games."

(Market researcher)

WORK IT OUT 2.1

A market researcher has been asked to conduct a sample of shoppers at a shopping centre. She suggests the following four options.

Option A	Option B	Option C	Option D
Ask all the women with children.	Ask people between 8 am and 8.30 am.	Stand outside a book shop and ask everyone who comes out.	Stop and ask every 10th person who walks past her.

What would be a sensible way to collect the sample? Give reasons for your answer.

EXERCISE 2A

1 Which of these would be a good way to collect a sample? Give reasons for your answers.

  A Selecting all the odd numbered houses in a street.

  B Calling people on their home telephones during the day.

  C Selecting everybody who is wearing trainers.

  D Calling the person whose name is at the top of each page of the phone book.

  E Drawing a series of names from a hat.

2 A market research company wants to find out how many people are likely to buy a new baby food.

  a Suggest a good place to conduct a survey of young parents.

  b Of the people asked, 35 of the 50 parents said they would be interested.

    How many parents would you expect to be interested in a population of 1000 parents?

3 A gym owner wants to know how many treadmills to buy.

She asks every member whose surname begins with 'S' whether they will use a treadmill.

a In her sample of 28, 15 members say, 'Yes'.

There are 300 members overall.

What is a sensible number of machines to buy?

b Does she really need this many machines?

c Suggest a better way of sampling her members to make sure she gets a realistic number of machines.

4 At the end of 2012 there were 28.7 million cars on the roads of Great Britain.

Surjay and his friends conduct a survey of the cars passing the school.

They discover that of the 50 cars recorded, 3 had a sun roof, 1 had a faulty exhaust and 4 had chips on the windscreen.

Use this information to estimate how many cars in Great Britain have:

a sun roofs　　**b** faulty exhausts　　**c** chips on the windscreen.

Section 2: Tables and charts

Using tables to organise data

A frequency table is used to organise data and show the 'frequency' of an event, or how often it happens.

For example, the number of goals scored by each of the 20 Premiership teams one weekend was as follows:

| 5 | 1 | 3 | 0 | 1 | 2 | 4 | 1 | 1 | 2 |
| 0 | 3 | 1 | 0 | 0 | 4 | 0 | 1 | 3 | 0 |

In a frequency table these results would look like this:

Number of goals scored	Tally	Frequency
0	JHT I	6
1	JHT I	6
2	II	2
3	III	3
4	II	2
5	I	1

Using bar charts to display data

The data in the previous frequency table can be shown on a bar chart.

Number of goals scored by each team

The chart has a title, a scale on the left and accurately drawn bars.

There is a gap between each bar and each one is labelled.

Bar charts are used to display **discrete data**.

The number of goals scored by each team is discrete data because it can only have certain values. It must be a whole number as you can't score $\frac{1}{2}$ a goal or 2.34 goals.

Sometimes it is helpful to sort data into categories.

For example, pairs of shoes in a cupboard could be categorised into 'brown shoes', 'black shoes', etc. Each piece of data can only be in one category. This is known as **categorical data**.

A vertical line chart is very similar to a bar chart but the number of pieces of data in each category is represented by a line rather than a bar.

Number of goals scored by each team

Key vocabulary

discrete data: data that can be counted and that can only have certain values

categorical data: data that has been arranged in categories

WORK IT OUT 2.2

Ramiz records the number of mistakes he makes in a series of maths tests.

2 3 1 3 4 2 0 3 2 6 1 1 3 2 4 2

Which graph or chart best shows this data? What is wrong with the other two?

Option A	Option B	Option C
Number of mistakes in each test 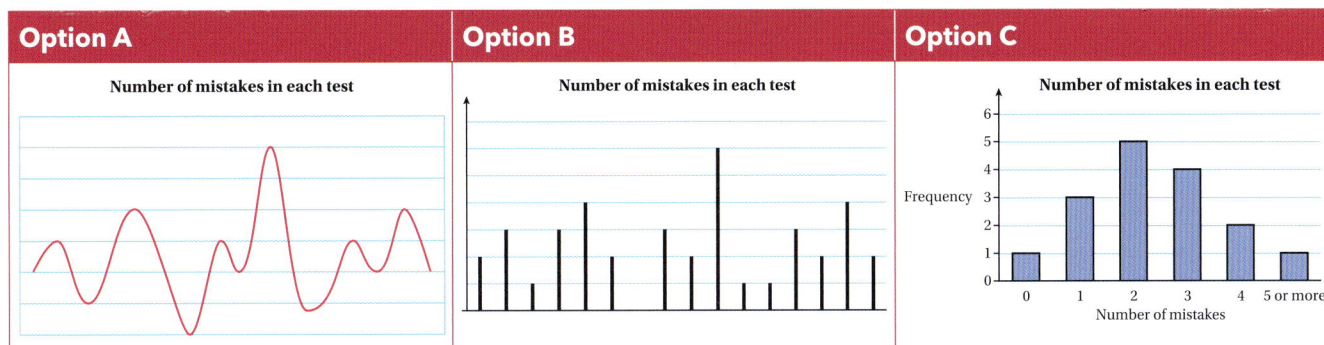	Number of mistakes in each test	Number of mistakes in each test

It is not always possible to say that one type of graph is better than another. The type of graph you draw depends on what data you have collected.

These guidelines might help you choose an appropriate graph for different kinds of data.

- Use bar charts or vertical line charts for discrete data that can be categorised.
- Use a pie chart or a composite bar chart if you want to compare different parts of the whole or show proportions in the data.
- Use a line graph for numerical data when you want to show trends (changes over time).
- Use histograms for continuous data with equal or unequal class intervals (you will deal with these in Section 4).

Tip

In Chapter 3, you will learn about scatter diagrams. Scatter diagrams are useful for showing relationships between different sets of data.

EXERCISE 2B

1 In an extended family of 30 members, 10 have blond hair, 9 have black hair, 6 have brown hair and 5 have grey hair.

Draw a vertical line graph to show this information.

2 30 students were asked how many times in the last week they had visited the snack shop. Their responses were:

1 2 1 2 1 5 1 3 2 1 2 1 3 2 1 2 0 2 3 2 0 2 0 1 2 0 0 3 1 2

a Draw a frequency table for this data.

b Present this information on a suitable graph.

3 This table shows the number of people who chose these countries as their favourite holiday destination.

Favourite holiday destination	UK	Spain	France	USA	Greece
Frequency	9	15	17	12	8

a Construct a bar chart showing the data in the table.

b Jack says that 25% more people chose Spain than the USA. Show that he is correct.

4 The graph shows the number of goals scored in football matches.

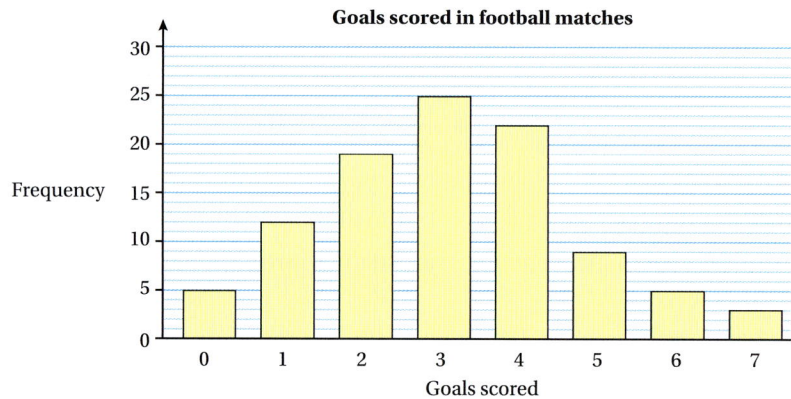

Goals scored in football matches

a What is the total number of games played?

Choose from the options below.

A 90   B 95   C 100   D 110

b In what percentage of the games were more than 4 goals scored?

c 5 of the scores were 1-0, how many were 0-1?

d In one game a team scored 3 goals and lost. What was the final score?

5 The chart below shows the monthly rainfall in Lowestoft in 2012.

Monthly rainfall for Lowestoft

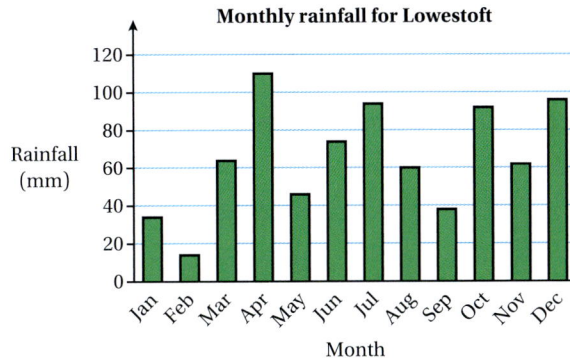

a State which month had the heaviest rainfall.

b Estimate the amount of rain that fell in April.

c State which month was the driest.

d Spring is March, April and May. Estimate how much rain fell during spring.

e The average annual rainfall for Lowestoft is approximately 575 mm.

Was 2012 a wetter or drier year than average? Give a reason for your answer.

6 Jenny is carrying out a survey of the sort of snacks bought from a shop outside her school.

She writes down the items that people buy:

Chocobar	Apple	NRG drink	Juicebar	Crisps	NRG drink	Chocobar	NRG drink	Juicebar
Juicebar	Crisps	Cheese puffs	Gum	Cheese puffs	Fruit chews	NRG drink	NRG drink	Chocobar
Chocobar	Juicebar	Chocobar	Crisps	Chocobar	Gum	Chocobar	Cheese puffs	Crisps
Cheese puffs	Crisps	NRG drink	Fruit chews	NRG drink	Cheese puffs	NRG drink	Juicebar	Gum
NRG drink	Chocobar	Apple	NRG drink	Chocobar	Juicebar	Crisps	Chocobar	Cheese puffs
Gum	Fruit chews	Gum	Crisps	Apple	Crisps	Fruit chews	Fruit chews	Fruit chews
Juicebar	Crisps	Cheese puffs	Fruit chews	Gum	Cheese puffs	Fruit chews	Crisps	Cheese puffs

a Suggest how Jenny could have been better organised before she started her survey.

b Use Jenny's data to create a table to show what was bought in the shop.

c Jenny gets extra marks if she categorises her data.

Adjust your table so that the data is classified in an appropriate way.

Multiple and composite bar charts

A multiple bar chart is useful when you want to compare data for two or more groups.

For example, this chart compares shoe sizes of male and female students in Year 9. The chart shows the data for male and female students in pairs.

Shoe size of Year 9 students

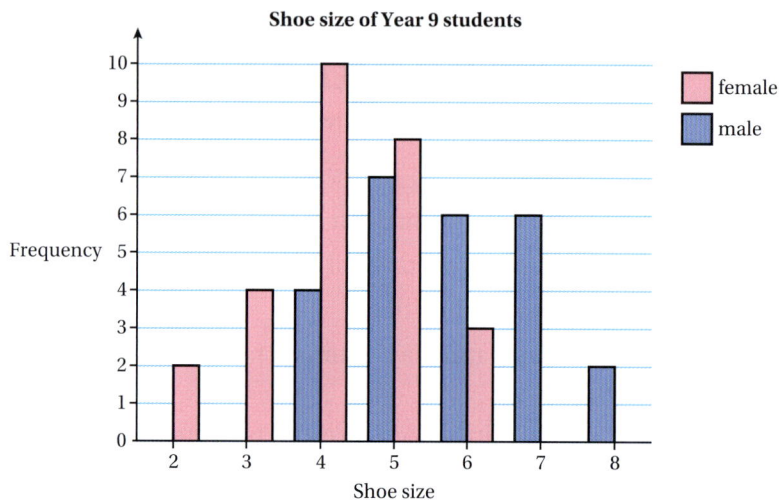

Notice that:

- the chart has a key to show what each colour bar represents
- the two bars for male and female students who wear each size touch each other, but there is an equal space between each pair of bars.

Composite bar charts are used to show parts of a whole.

The total height of each bar represents a total amount. The length of the bar is divided into parts that show each category's share of the total amount.

To interpret a composite bar chart you need to work out what each bar represents and then do a calculation to find the fraction or percentage of the total that each part represents.

This composite bar chart shows the amount of water used by three different households over a four-month period.

Water use by household

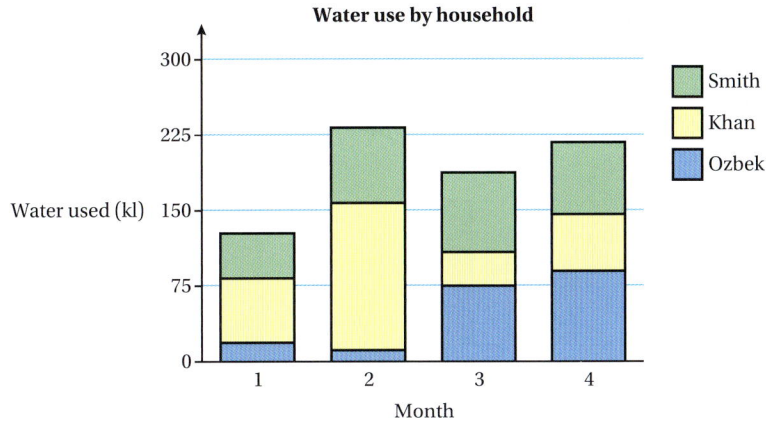

EXERCISE 2C

1 Study the bar chart.

Time spent watching television and doing homework

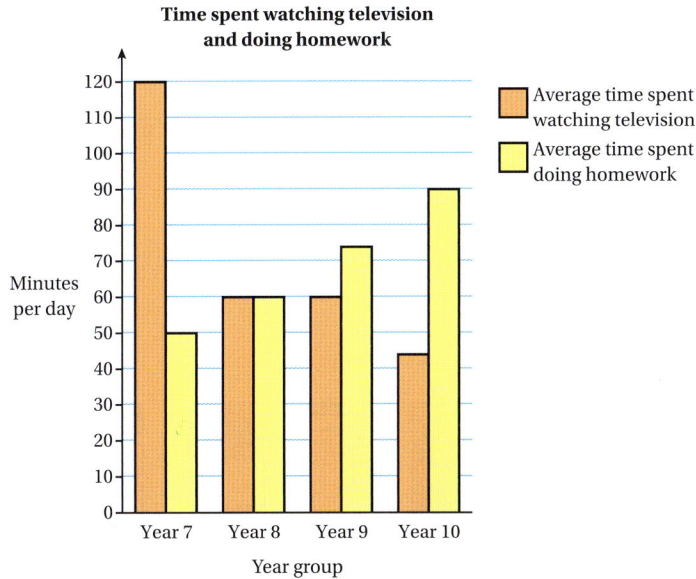

a What two sets of data are shown on this chart?

b Describe the trend in the amount of time spent watching TV as students move into higher grades.

c Describe what happens to the amount of time spent on homework as TV watching time decreases.

d How much time do Year 10 students spend on average each day:

i doing homework?   ii watching TV?

2 Naresh runs a computer company. He keeps a record of his costs and his income for four large projects in a year.

He drew this chart to compare his costs and his income for each project.

Cost and income by project

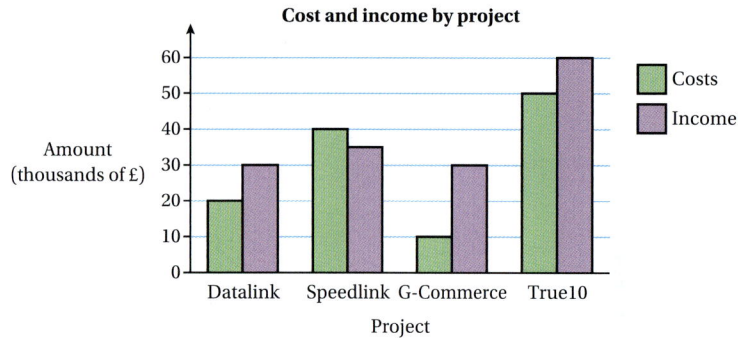

a Which project brought in most money?

b Which project brought in least money?

c Which project had the highest costs?

d Which project had the lowest costs?

e Which project gave Naresh the biggest profit? (Remember, profit = income − cost)

f On which project did Naresh lose money? Give a reason for your answer.

g How much profit did Naresh make altogether?

3 This composite bar chart shows the proportions in sales for four different companies.

Number of sales

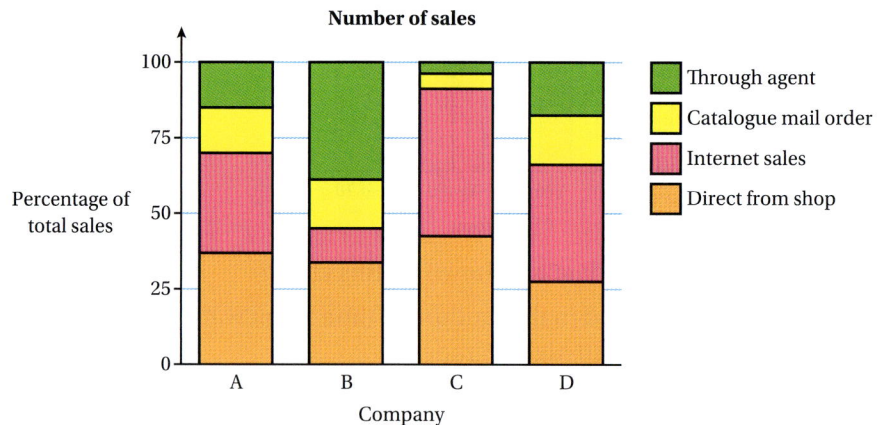

a Can you work out the value of each company's total sales from this chart? Give a reason for your answer.

b State which company does most of its sales direct from the shop.

c State which company makes the least of its sales through agents.

d State which company makes almost half of its sales over the internet.

e State what fraction of Company A's sales are done over the internet.

f Describe the breakdown of sales by type for Company D.

4 The bar chart shows the results in geography for six students in their mock and actual exams.

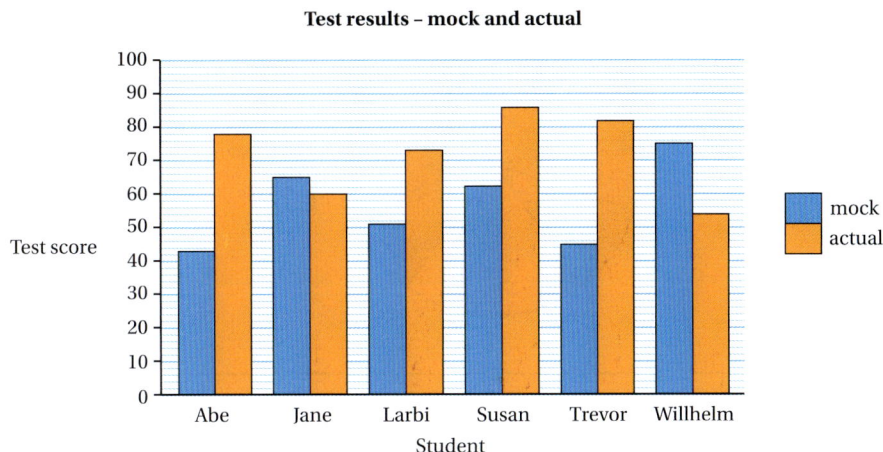

Test results – mock and actual

a Who achieved the highest score on their mock exam?

b Who achieved the highest score on their actual exam?

c Who made the biggest improvement from the mock to the actual exam?

d What was similar about Jane and Willhelm's results in these exams?.

Section 3: Pie charts

A pie chart is useful for displaying data when you are interested in the relative sizes or the proportions of the data.

Pie charts are always circular, so the sum of the angles at the centre must always be 360°.

When drawing pie charts that have data as percentages, each 1% will be represented by 3.6° because 360° ÷ 100 = 3.6°.

In this example, data has been collected that shows where students in a class live:

Area where students live	Frequency	Percentage (%)
Reepham	12	40.0
Whitwell	6	20.0
Booton	3	10.0
Cawston	2	6.7
Salle	7	23.3

There are 30 students altogether.

Each percentage is worked out by dividing the number of students by the total number of students and multiplying by 100. For example, for Reepham,

$\frac{12}{30} \times 100 = 40\%$.

The pie chart below shows this data:

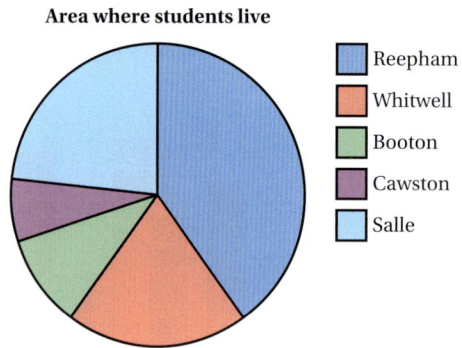

Area where students live

- Reepham
- Whitwell
- Booton
- Cawston
- Salle

WORK IT OUT 2.3

These are the results from a survey of how many minutes late 20 trains were on a particular day:

1 0 2 0 3 1 5 4 1 3 6 4 3 5 2 4 3 2 2 4

Which of the pie charts best shows this information? Write down what is wrong with the other two pie charts.

Option A	Option B	Option C
Train punctuality	**Train punctuality**	**Train punctuality**

Option B legend:
- On time
- One minute
- Two minutes
- Three minutes
- Four minutes
- Five minutes
- Six minutes

Option C legend:
- On time
- Up to 1
- Up to 2
- Up to 3
- Up to 4
- Up to 5
- Up to 6

EXERCISE 2D

1 Draw a pie chart to represent this data:

Electricity generation	Proportion used (%)
gas	28.0
other fuels	2.6
coal	39.0
nuclear	19.0
renewables	11.4

2 The pie charts below show the population of two different countries by age.

Greece   Ireland

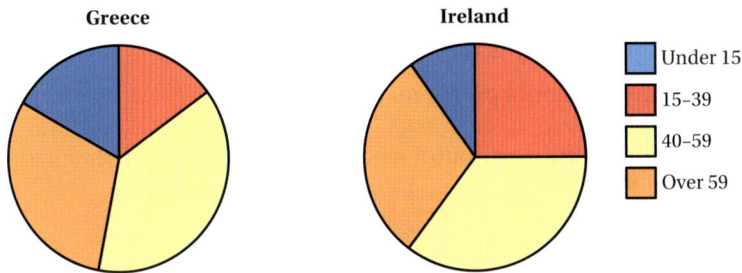

- Under 15
- 15–39
- 40–59
- Over 59

a Write down two differences between Greece and Ireland.

b Which country has the biggest number of over 59s?

c There are more under 15s in Ireland than Greece.

Is this statement true or false?

3 The Department for Transport maintains data for the different types of vehicles on the road in the UK. Data for vehicles other than cars is shown for 1994 and 2013.

Vehicles on the road other than cars in 1994   Vehicles on the road other than cars in 2013

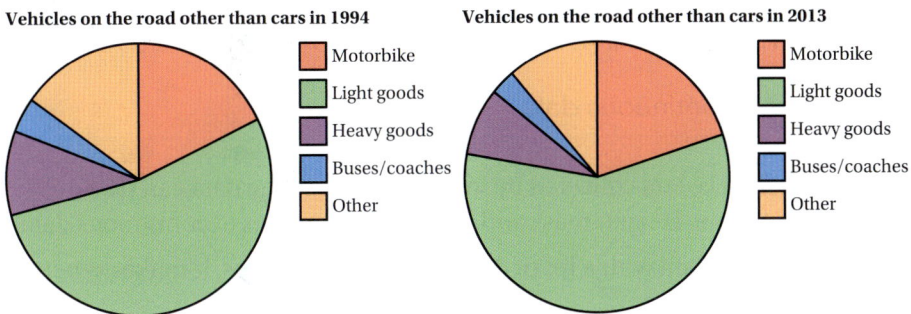

- Motorbike
- Light goods
- Heavy goods
- Buses/coaches
- Other

a Write down two differences between the proportions for 1994 and 2013.

b There were 6.075 million vehicles other than cars on the road in 2013.

Calculate the number of light goods vehicles there were.

c In 2013, what percentage of vehicles other than cars were motorbikes?

d Which of the following statements is true?

  A   There were more motorbikes on the road in 1994.

  B   The proportion of heavy goods vehicles was greater in 1994 than in 2013.

  C   Buses and coaches were a bigger proportion of vehicles other than cars in 2013 than in 1994.

  D   There were more buses and coaches on the road in 1994 than in 2013.

Leisure activities

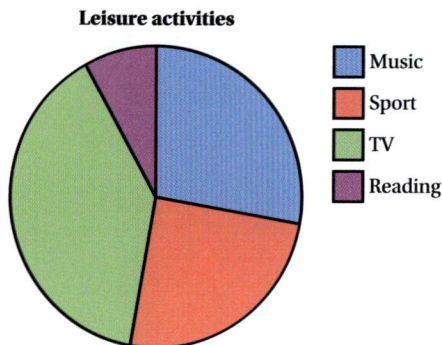

- Music
- Sport
- TV
- Reading

4 This pie chart shows the favourite leisure activity of 72 students.

  a Use a protractor to measure the sector for music. Use this measurement to work out how many students prefer music.

  b State which activity is the most popular.

  c How many students prefer reading?

5 This data shows the destinations of students leaving a sixth-form college:

Destination	College A	College B
higher education	32	46
further education	45	72
employment	28	31
gap year	12	24
unemployment	15	22

Create two pie charts and use them to argue that one college is more successful than the other.

Section 4: Cumulative frequency graphs and histograms

Grouped and continuous data

Continuous data is data collected by measurement, so the data can take on any fractional value. Height, mass and age are all examples of continuous data.

When you collect data with a lot of different possible values, it makes sense to group the values.

For example, if you are collecting test percentages the data values could range from 0 to 100. In this case you might group the data in tens, listing scores from 0 to 10, more than 10 to 20 and so on.

The groups are called **class intervals**. The maximum value in each interval is called the upper class boundary.

Generally, class intervals are equal and they do not overlap.

For discrete data the intervals may be given in the form of a range such as 11 to 20.

For continuous data the interval is often given in inequality notation.

For example, heights (h) between 10 and 15 metres might be given as $10 \leqslant h < 15$.

The class size is normally chosen to give between 5 and 10 class intervals in the data set.

Key vocabulary

continuous data: data that can have any value

class intervals: the sizes of the groups that data has been grouped into

Cumulative frequency

Questions like these can be answered using cumulative frequencies:

How many cars were travelling above 30 miles per hour?

How many students scored higher than 60% on a test?

How many of the strawberries in your garden weighed at least 24 grams?

A cumulative frequency is a running total of the frequencies for each class interval.

Adding the frequencies up to a particular value allows you to work out how many values are below or above that level.

The frequency table below shows the masses of strawberries picked from a garden.

Mass, m (g)	Frequency	Cumulative frequency
$12 \leqslant m < 16$	3	3
$16 \leqslant m < 20$	5	$3 + 5 = 8$
$20 \leqslant m < 24$	9	$3 + 5 + 9 = 17$
$24 \leqslant m < 28$	7	24
$28 \leqslant m < 31$	2	26

The data has been **grouped** into classes, and the **cumulative frequency** calculated as a 'running total'.

Now you can see quite quickly that 17 strawberries have a mass of less than 24 grams.

Cumulative frequencies can be plotted against the upper boundaries of each class interval to produce a curved graph.

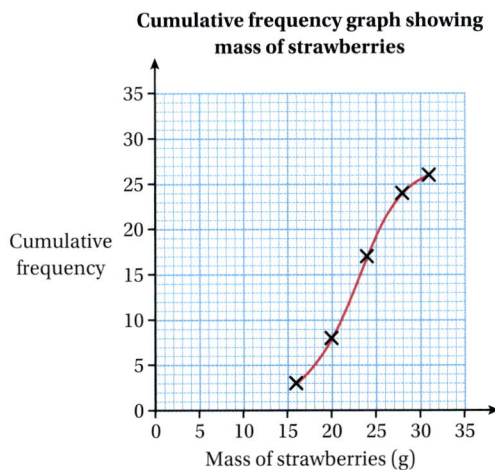

Cumulative frequency graph showing mass of strawberries

Key vocabulary

grouped data: data that has been put into groups

cumulative frequency: the sum total of all the frequencies up to a given value

Tip

You plot the point for each cumulative frequency at the upper end of the class interval. The graphs are curves, so you must join them with a smooth curved line and not broken straight lines.

Histograms

Grouped continuous data can also be plotted on a graph called a **histogram**.

This histogram shows the ages of members visiting a gym:

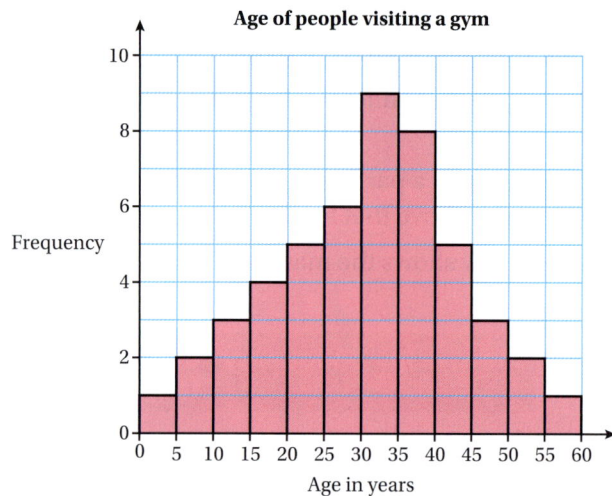

Age of people visiting a gym

Histograms look like bar charts but there are important differences between them:

- The horizontal scale is continuous and each 'bar' is drawn above a particular class interval. For example, the first bar shows ages from 0 to 5.
- The frequency of the data is shown by the **area** of the bars.
- There are no spaces between the bars because the horizontal scale is continuous.

In this example, the class intervals are equal so the bars are the same width.

When the class intervals are equal you can read the frequency off the vertical axis and you do not need to work out the area of the bars.

Histograms with unequal class intervals

When the class intervals in the data are not the same you cannot use the height of the bars to give the frequency.

Instead, the vertical scale is used to give frequency density.

$$\text{Frequency density} = \frac{\text{frequency } (f)}{\text{class width}}$$

WORKED EXAMPLE 2

The ages of young people visiting a park are shown in the frequency table.

Draw a histogram to show these results.

Age	Frequency
5–9	10
10–15	24
16–17	6
> 18	0

Class boundaries are:
5, 10, 16 and 18

These are the lowest values that could be in each class, for example, the first class covers children from 5 to 9 so the lowest value that can be in that class is 5. The other class boundaries are therefore 10, 16 and 18.

Class widths are:
10 – 5 = 5
16 – 10 = 6
18 – 16 = 2

Work out the class widths by subtracting the lower boundary from the upper boundary.

Frequency densities for each class are:
10 ÷ 5 = 2
24 ÷ 6 = 4
6 ÷ 2 = 3

Divide the frequency for each class by the class width to find the frequency density.

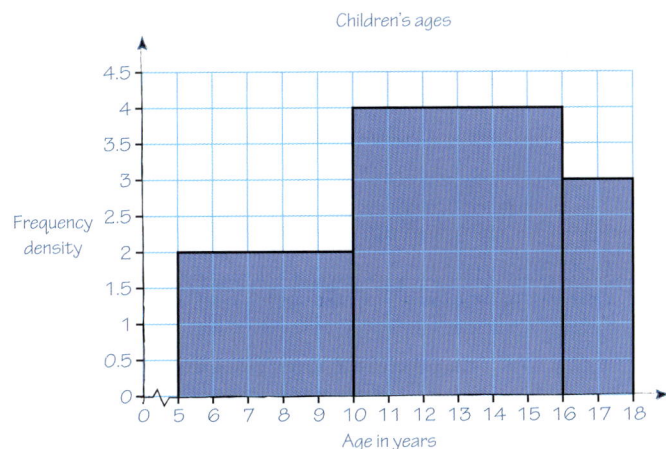

Children's ages

Vertical scale is 'Frequency density'.

Horizontal scale is continuous.

In the histogram, the area of each block should be the same as the frequency.

As there are 24 children in the group 10–15, the density is 4 because 4 × 6 (class width) = 24 (frequency).

Problem-solving framework

The heights of sunflowers grown by a class of children are measured and recorded in centimetres:

85.4	114.9	99.6	81.6	105.0	114.7	88.0	99.2	107.0	123.8
104.5	121.4	116.7	79.4	118.5	115.8	103.8	113.6	77.5	89.9
113.6	110.7	120.3	103.5	75.9	99.0	104.1	99.0	101.8	98.7

Group the data into suitable class intervals and draw a cumulative frequency graph and a histogram to represent the data.

Steps for solving problems	What you would do for this example
Step 1: Choose a class interval that allows for between 5 and 10 classes. Put the data into a frequency table.	<table><thead><tr><th>Class interval (cm)</th><th>Frequency</th></tr></thead><tbody><tr><td>75–95</td><td>7</td></tr><tr><td>95.1–105</td><td>11</td></tr><tr><td>105.1–115</td><td>6</td></tr><tr><td>115.1–120</td><td>3</td></tr><tr><td>120.1–125</td><td>3</td></tr></tbody></table>
Step 2: Identify what you have to do.	You need to choose a suitable means of displaying the data and then draw it. As you have grouped data, either a cumulative frequency graph or a histogram would be appropriate. You need a cumulative frequency table.
Step 3: Start working on the problem using what you know.	<table><thead><tr><th>Class interval (cm)</th><th>Frequency</th><th>Cumulative frequency</th></tr></thead><tbody><tr><td>75–95</td><td>7</td><td>7</td></tr><tr><td>95.1–105</td><td>11</td><td>18</td></tr><tr><td>105.1–115</td><td>6</td><td>24</td></tr><tr><td>115.1–120</td><td>3</td><td>27</td></tr><tr><td>120.1–125</td><td>3</td><td>30</td></tr></tbody></table> Construct a cumulative frequency graph remembering to use the upper boundary of each class interval. Cumulative frequency graph showing sunflower heights

Continues on next page …

The histogram is plotted using the area of each rectangle to represent the frequency, and will look like this:

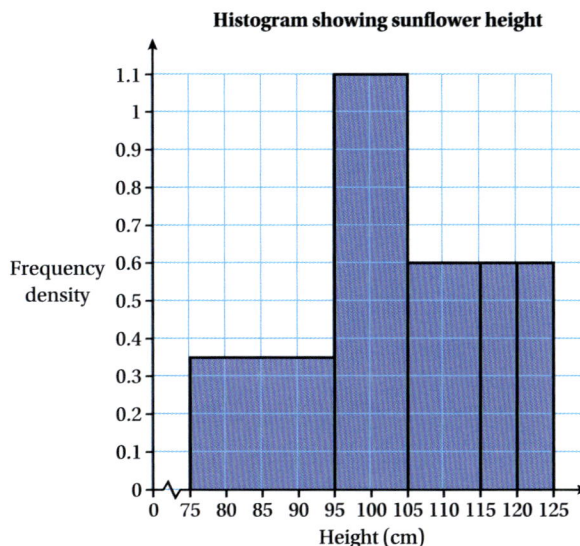

Histogram showing sunflower height

Step 4: Check your working and that your answer is reasonable.	Check the shape of the graphs. Does the cumulative frequency graph resemble a curve? Do the areas of the rectangles match the numbers in each class interval?
Step 5: Have you answered the question?	Yes, the data is correctly displayed.

EXERCISE 2E

1 The number of ice creams sold on a series of days is recorded as follows:

193	210	265	203	246	216	236
343	242	208	294	229	287	266
343	223	308	235	166	231	241
255	196	230	276	247	296	266

Group the data into suitable equal-sized class intervals, and draw a cumulative frequency graph.

Use your graph to estimate:

a on how many days fewer than 230 ice creams were sold.

b on how many days more than 300 ice creams were sold.

> **Tip**
>
> Too few class intervals can oversimplify, and too many can negate the effect of grouping. Aim for between 5 and 10 groups.

2 The maximum daily temperature is measured every day for 25 days.
The results are as follows:

18.5	19.6	18.6	23.5	17.2
19	17.1	23	17.5	15
22.4	24.6	24.1	15.3	18.3
15.1	19.7	19.3	17.9	20.5
16	18.5	18.3	15.8	15.3

Group the data into suitable equal-sized class intervals, and draw a cumulative frequency graph.

Use your graph to estimate:

a how many days the temperature was less than 20 °C.

b how many days the temperature was above 22 °C.

c how many days the temperature was between 20 °C and 22 °C.

3 The timed results from a 5 km race are given below:

20:48	18:39	26:09	23:36	21:20	26:07
23:46	23:31	20:03	21:45	23:20	22:55
24:38	25:16	22:24	18:26	21:27	21:04
17:33	22:14	20:57	24:00	19:14	24:38
19:32	26:39	17:31	23:25	22:50	21:27
25:08	22:57	23:55	20:25	25:30	24:45
21:43	19:04	18:19	17:36	22:31	25:14
22:40	21:07	24:11	21:34	25:41	23:45
25:42	24:01	20:19	26:17	20:13	25:10
20:14	24:44	26:21	23:48	22:52	24:14

Group the data into suitable equal-sized class intervals, and draw a cumulative frequency graph.

Use your graph to estimate:

a how many runners completed the course in more than 25 minutes.

b how many completed the course in less than 20 minutes.

c how many runners finished in less than 19 minutes.

4 The frequency table shown gives the test results of a group of 23 students.

Present this information in a histogram.

Score	Frequency
15–19	1
20–24	3
25–29	5
30–34	2
35–39	6
40–44	3
45–49	3

5 A group of students measured the distance from their hip to their heel.

The measurements were made correct to the nearest centimetre.

The results were as follows:

85   86   91   87   77   88   83   86   74   89   85   85   80

94   82   84   89   84   94   84   76   93   86   84   94   84

Present this information in a histogram using the classes:

a 70–79, 80–89, 90–99   **b** 70–74, 75–79, 80–84, 85–89, 90–94

6 The histogram below gives information about the results of Year 9 students in a history examination.

Histogram showing exam marks

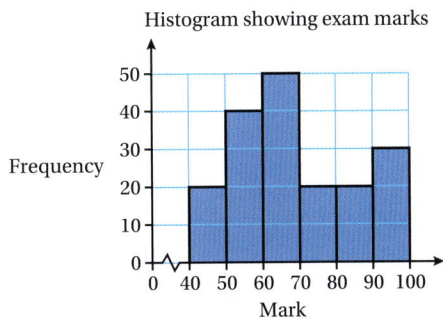

a How many students sat for the examination?

b The pass mark was 60. How many students passed?

c State the percentage of students who obtained 90 or more.

d State the percentage of students who obtained less than 70.

Section 5: Line graphs for time-series data

Line graphs are useful for showing how data changes over time.

When time is one of the variables it is always plotted on the horizontal axis of the graph.

For example, the temperature at a weather station is recorded at midday every day. Data showing change over time like this is called time-series data.

Daily temperature at midday

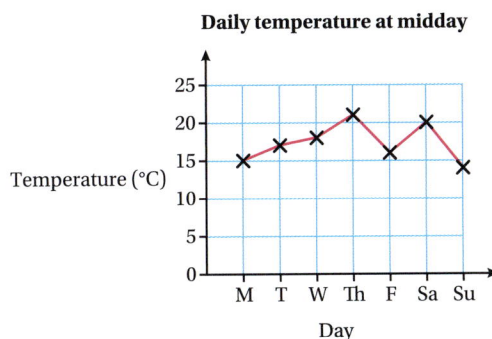

Weekday	Temperature (°C)
Monday	15
Tuesday	17
Wednesday	18
Thursday	21
Friday	16
Saturday	20
Sunday	14

Find answers at: cambridge.org/ukschools/gcsemaths-studentbookanswers

Each of the points on the line (for example, Mon, 15 °C) is joined to the point next to it by a straight line.

This type of graph is used when you want to show trends over time.

Problem-solving framework

The average temperature each month in Alicante is as follows:

| Jan 17 °C | Feb 18 °C | Mar 20 °C | Apr 21 °C | May 24 °C | Jun 28 °C |
| Jul 30 °C | Aug 31 °C | Sep 29 °C | Oct 25 °C | Nov 20 °C | Dec 18 °C |

Display this data to show how the temperature changes through the year.

Steps for solving problems	What you would do for this example
Step 1: If it is useful to have a table, draw one.	<table><tr><th>J</th><th>F</th><th>M</th><th>A</th><th>M</th><th>J</th><th>J</th><th>A</th><th>S</th><th>O</th><th>N</th><th>D</th></tr><tr><td>17 °C</td><td>18 °C</td><td>20 °C</td><td>21 °C</td><td>24 °C</td><td>28 °C</td><td>30 °C</td><td>31 °C</td><td>29 °C</td><td>25 °C</td><td>20 °C</td><td>18 °C</td></tr></table>
Step 2: Identify what you have to do.	We need to choose a suitable means of displaying the data and then draw it.
Step 3: Start working on the problem using what you know.	We know that a time-series graph shows changes over time, so will be a good visual way of showing how the temperature varies. Choose a suitable scale and plot each point on the axes using the table. Join the points to make a line. **Monthly average temperature for Alicante**
Step 4: Check your working and that your answer is reasonable.	Check the shape of the graph. Does it get warmer in the summer and colder in the winter? Are there any unexpected sharp increases or decreases?
Step 5: Have you answered the question?	Yes, the graph shows how the temperature changes through the year.

EXERCISE 2F

1 **a** Construct a time-series graph for the average temperature (in °C) in a
particular city, from the data given in the table below.

Month	Jan	Feb	Mar	Apr	May	Jun	Jul	Aug	Sep	Oct	Nov	Dec
Average temp (°C)	15.2	16.5	17.2	19.1	19.6	20.1	22.2	24.1	21.3	19.3	17.6	16.6

   b Use the time-series graph to write a brief description of how the
average temperature varies in this particular city.

2 The table below gives the annual profit (in £million) of a company over
a ten-year period. Construct a time-series graph of the information.

Year	Year 1	Year 2	Year 3	Year 4	Year 5	Year 6	Year 7	Year 8	Year 9	Year 10
Profit (£million)	2.2	1.8	2.3	1.2	0.6	1.1	2.2	3.1	3.7	4.2

3 The table below gives the number of teeth extracted at a dentist's
surgery each month for a year.

Month	Jan	Feb	Mar	Apr	May	Jun	Jul	Aug	Sep	Oct	Nov	Dec
Number of teeth	54	47	49	60	41	45	36	11	38	42	32	22

   a Represent this information on a time-series graph.

   b Briefly describe how the number of teeth extracted each month
changed over the year.

   c Why might the number of teeth extracted fall during August?

4 The table below gives the position of a particular five-a-side football
team in a league of 10 teams at the completion of each week throughout
the season.

Round	1	2	3	4	5	6	7	8	9
Position	2	3	5	7	6	5	6	7	5
Round	12	13	14	15	16	17	18	10	11
Position	5	3	4	3	3	4	3	5	4

   a Represent this information on a time-series graph.

   b Describe the progress of the team throughout the season.

Sales quarter	Sales (£thousand)
Quarter 1	64
Quarter 2	82
Quarter 3	83
Quarter 4	65
Quarter 5	77
Quarter 6	89
Quarter 7	96
Quarter 8	58
Quarter 9	79
Quarter 10	92
Quarter 11	101
Quarter 12	66

5 The data in the table shows the value of sales at a service station on a main road over a period of three years. Each quarter represents three months (a quarter) of the year. The quarters are labelled 1 to 12 in the corresponding time-series graph shown below.

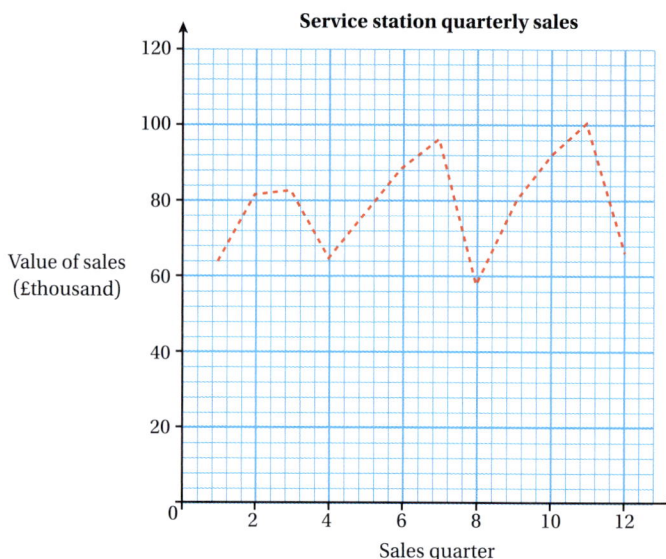

Service station quarterly sales

a In which quarter of each year is the value of sales highest?

b In which quarter of each year is the value of sales lowest?

c Compare the sales figures for the first quarter of each year. Are the sales figures improving from one year to the next?

6 The table below gives the numbers of garden sheds sold each quarter during 2012–2014.

Number of sales

Year \ Quarter	Q1	Q2	Q3	Q4
2012	27	32	56	41
2013	33	35	65	45
2014	38	41	72	51

a Represent this information on a time series graph.

b Describe how the shed sales have altered over the given time period.

c Does it appear that sheds sales are seasonal?

7 Study the following graph.

**Road traffic by vehicle type (commercial and public service vehicles)
in Great Britain, from 2002 (Table TRA0101)**

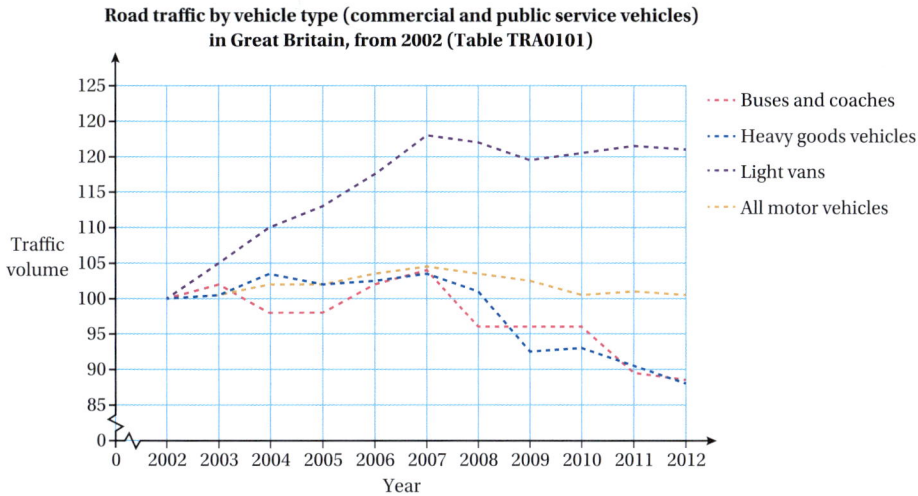

a Describe the trend in numbers of light vans.

b Describe what has happened to the total number of motor vehicles.

c Suggest why the number of heavy goods vehicles might have decreased. Can this be answered by just using the graph?

8 This graph shows how the water level in a pond varies from month to month.

Depth of water in a garden pond

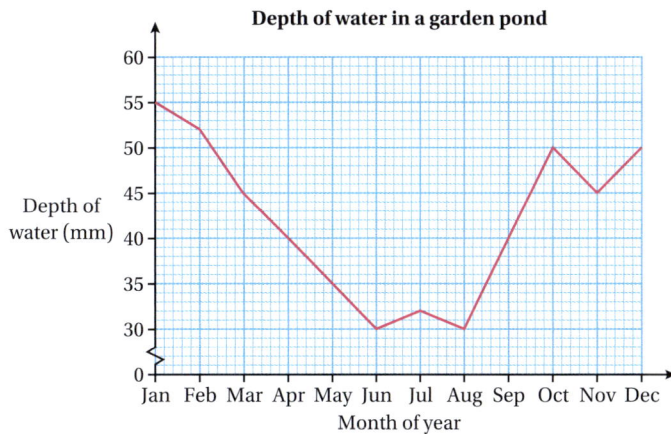

a When is the lowest depth of water?

b Suggest what might have happened in July.

c When does the water level drop most rapidly?

d How much water is in the pond in May?

e Find the difference in depth between August and September.

Find answers at: cambridge.org/ukschools/gcsemaths-studentbookanswers

Checklist of learning and understanding

Sampling

- A sample is a representative group chosen from a population.

Tables and charts

- A frequency table is a method of organising data by showing how often a result appears in the data.
- Data can be displayed using a number of different charts and graphs.
- All charts and graphs should be clearly labelled and scaled, and have a title.
- Vertical line charts and bar charts are a good way of showing discrete data, where the height of each bar or line indicates the frequency.
- Pie charts are used to compare categories of the same data set.

Cumulative frequency graphs and histograms

- Cumulative frequency graphs are used to display grouped continuous numerical data.
- Histograms are specialised bar graphs that are used to show grouped continuous data for equal and unequal class intervals. There are no gaps between the bars and the area of each bar gives the frequency density of the data.

Line graphs

- Line graphs for time-series data show trends and changes over time.

For additional questions on the topics in this chapter, visit GCSE Mathematics Online.

Chapter review

1 Bonita takes a representative sample to find out how students travel to school.

a Suggest two ways in which she could do this.

b Bonita asks a representative sample of 50 students and gets the following results:

car	15
walk	17
bus	6
taxi	7
bike	5

There are 600 students in the school in total. What is a sensible estimate of the total number of students who walk to school?

2 Josh and Ben are comparing how much money they spend each month.

Expenditure per month (£)	Josh	Ben
rent	840	450
food	250	300
transport	350	160
savings	250	40
entertainment	110	250

a Draw suitable charts of the data to compare the amounts of money they spend.

b Write two sentences comparing their spending habits.

3 The table shows the profits for two companies for each quarter of a two-year period.

Company profits (£)	Company A	Company B
1st quarter 2013	134 820	125 912
2nd quarter 2013	138 429	189 355
3rd quarter 2013	140 721	130 969
4th quarter 2013	131 717	156 548
1st quarter 2014	103 746	219 357
2nd quarter 2014	197 028	151 296
3rd quarter 2014	187 883	249 216
4th quarter 2014	168 414	102 158

a Use the data to plot a suitable graph to compare how the profits change.

b Which company is the most successful?

c Which is the biggest change between quarters?

d Which of the following statements is true?

A   Company B's sales are always better than Company A's.

B   Company A's sales never exceed £198 000.

C   Company B's sales are more consistent than Company A's.

D   Both companies' sales are better in the 4th quarter of 2014 than in the 1st quarter of 2013.

4 a The table shows information about the travel expenses of employees at a company.

Minimum	Lower quartile	Median	Upper quartile	Maximum
9	18	23	30	45

All amounts are in £.

Copy this graph grid and draw a box plot to show this information.

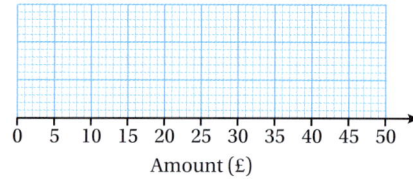

(2 marks)

b The table shows information about the distances the employees travel to work.

Distance, D (km)	Frequency
$0 < D \leqslant 10$	17
$10 < D \leqslant 15$	12
$15 < D \leqslant 30$	3
$30 < D \leqslant 60$	9

Copy this graph grid and draw a histogram to show this information.

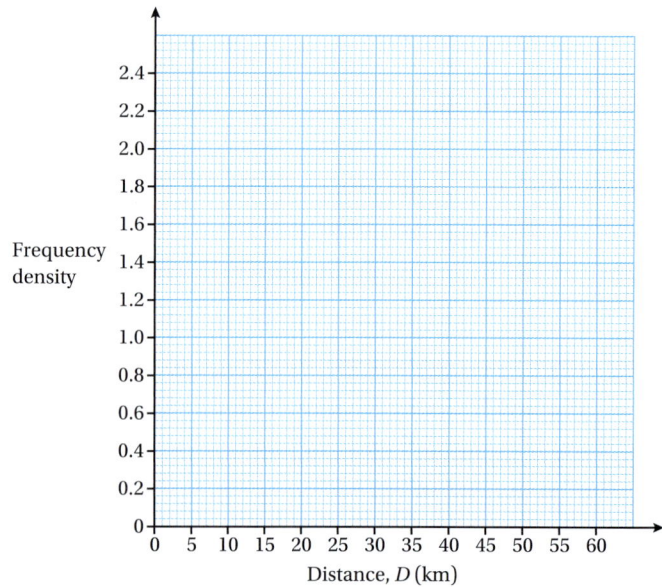

(3 marks)

© AQA 2013

5 Two machines are used in a factory to pack crisps into packets of 65 g.
A sample of the mass of 30 bags packed by each machine is given in the
tables below:

Machine A				
65.4	64.8	65.4	64.3	64.2
64.4	65.3	65.1	64.7	64.7
64.6	65.0	65.5	64.1	65.0
64.9	64.5	64.6	64.2	64.7
65.3	64.9	64.5	64.6	65.4
65.5	64.5	65.5	64.6	64.2

Machine B				
64.0	65.5	63.6	63.9	65.8
64.3	65.2	64.7	64.7	64.4
65.4	64.2	65.7	65.2	63.9
64.4	65.6	63.9	65.9	65.0
65.6	65.7	64.0	64.2	66.0
65.0	65.7	64.8	64.8	64.7

a Use class intervals of 0.5 g and draw a histogram for each machine.

b Which machine is the most reliable? Give a reason for your answer.

Find answers at: cambridge.org/ukschools/gcsemaths-studentbookanswers

3 Analysing data

In this chapter you will learn how to ...

- calculate and compare summary statistics for ungrouped and grouped data and compare distributions.
- draw and interpret box plots.
- recognise when data is being misrepresented.
- plot and interpret scatter diagrams and use them to describe correlation and predict results.
- identify outliers.

For more resources relating to this chapter, visit GCSE Mathematics Online.

Using mathematics: real-life applications

Analysing large sets of data enables financial and insurance companies to make predictions about what might happen in the future. Car insurance premiums are worked out according to typical or 'average' behaviour of large groups of people.

> **Tip**
>
> Knowing how to calculate averages and measures of spread gives us tools to compare different sets of data. Make sure you know what these are and when to use the different measures.

"We group drivers together by age and gender and use statistics to find typical driving behaviour for each group. Young drivers have more accidents, so their insurance costs more." *(Insurance broker)*

Before you start ...

KS3	You should remember how to find the mean, median, mode and range of a set of data.	**1** Find the mean, median, mode and range of the following sets of data. Give your answers to one decimal place. **a** 2, 4, 2, 7, 3, 5, 4, 2, 3, 1 **b** 40, 20, 30, 60, 50, 10
KS3	You should be able to plot coordinates on a set of axes.	**2** Write down the coordinates of points A, B and C on the line.
KS3	You should be able to recognise whether a gradient is positive or negative.	**3** Look at the graph in question 2. **a** What is the gradient of the graph? **b** What is the equation of the line?

Assess your starting point using the Launchpad

STEP 1

1 The table shows how many cups of coffee a group of office workers drank in one week.

Number of cups of coffee	Frequency
0–5	16
6–10	5
11–15	5
16–20	4
21–25	5
26–30	3

a What is the modal class of the data?

b Estimate the median number of cups consumed per week.

c Estimate the mean number of cups of coffee consumed per week.

d How many people drink 10 or fewer cups of coffee per week.

2 These box plots compare the distribution of a class's marks in March and June of the same year.

a Comment on the differences in the data.

b Did the class's performance improve in June?

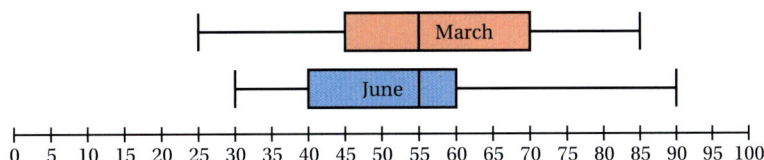

GO TO
Section 1:
Summary statistics

STEP 2

3 This graph appeared in a newspaper article. Give a reason why this graph could be misleading.

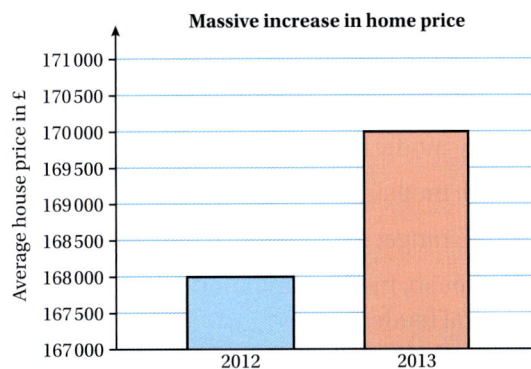

GO TO
Section 2:
Misleading graphs

GO TO
Step 3:
The Launchpad continues on the next page ...

Find answers at: cambridge.org/ukschools/gcsemaths-studentbookanswers

Launchpad continued …

STEP 3

4 Study the scatter diagram carefully.

a Describe the correlation on the graph.

b What does this suggest about the relationship between smoking and life expectancy?

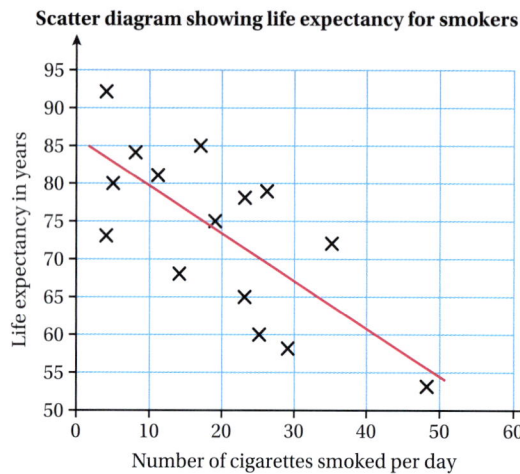

Scatter diagram showing life expectancy for smokers

GO TO
Section 3:
Scatter diagrams

GO TO
Chapter review

Section 1: Summary statistics

In statistics you are often asked to give a single value that summarises the data and tells you something about it.

Four different values are used to summarise data, as follows:

- the mean: $\dfrac{\text{sum of values}}{\text{number of values}}$
- the mode: the value with the highest frequency
- the median: the middle value when the values are arranged in size order
- the range: the difference between the highest value and the lowest value.

The mean, median and mode are all types of averages, or measures of central tendency.

The range is a measure of spread or dispersion. The range is useful for finding out whether the mean is distorted or not.

To describe and compare two sets of data, calculate the averages and range and write a few sentences to summarise what you notice.

Tip

The mode can also be referred to as the modal value.

Choosing the correct type of average

The type of average that you choose depends on the situation and what you want to know.

The mean is useful when you want to know a typical value. If the data values are very spread out (they have a big range) then the mean will not be typical.

For example, the manager in a company earns £20 000 per month. Her nine employees earn £2000 each per month. This gives a mean salary of £3800, which is not typical.

In this situation, the median salary is £2000 and the modal salary is £2000. Both are more representative than the mean.

When the data is not numerical, you have to use the mode as the average.

The mode is most useful when you need to know which item is most common or most popular.

You would use the mode when you wanted to show:
- which clothing size was bought most often
- what shoe size is most common
- what brand of mobile phone is the most popular.

The type of average you choose can affect how you see the data.

Tip

Modal salary means the salary which is the mode, or the one that occurs most often.

Quartiles and interquartile range

Quartiles and the interquartile range are summary statistics that give more information about the spread of data.

The median is the middle data item in an ordered set of data values, and divides the data into two halves.

The quartiles divide an ordered data set into quarters. You work out the value of the quartiles in a similar way to the median.

The first quartile (Q_1) is the data value one quarter of the way along the data set. This can also be called the lower quartile.

So 25% of the values are smaller than the first quartile, and three quarters are larger than the first quartile.

The second quartile (Q_2) is the same as the median.

The third quartile (Q_3) is the value that lies three quarters of the way along the data set. So 75% of the values are smaller than this value. This can also be called the upper quartile.

The interquartile range (IQR) is the difference between the values of the upper and lower quartiles.

    IQR = third quartile – first quartile

The IQR tells us where the middle 50% of the data occurs.

This is important to know because it gives us information about whether the data is spread out far away from the median, or clustered close to the median value.

	Q_1	Q_2	Q_3	
25%	25%	25%	25%

Interquartile Range
= $Q_3 - Q_1$

Median = 32

| 23 | 23 | 24 | 31 | 32 | 37 | 37 | 42 | 42 |

Lower quartile

IQR: 39.5 − 23.5 = 16

Upper quartile

$$Q_1 = \frac{(23 + 24)}{2} = 23.5$$

$$Q_3 = \frac{(37 + 42)}{2} = 39.5$$

WORKED EXAMPLE 1

Babak has developed a website and is monitoring how many hits it receives per hour.

In the first 48 hours it receives the following numbers of hits per hour (arranged in numerical order):

100	105	106	106	107	107	108	110	117	118
135	137	145	148	148	148	153	155	157	159
162	171	171	179	183	183	185	185	189	199
201	203	204	209	216	220	223	224	224	227
229	230	231	233	234	235	237	238		

1 Find the following summary statistics:

   a the mean, the median and the mode   **b** the range.

   a Mean of the data:

      $\frac{8394}{48} = 174.88$ hits

> Find the mean of the data by finding the total number of hits, then dividing this total by the number of hours.

      Median of the data is halfway between the 24th and the 25th data values

      $= \frac{179 + 183}{2} = 181$ hits

> Arrange all the data values in numerical order and the median is the middle value if you have an odd number of data values, or halfway between the two middle values if you have an even number of data values.

      The value 148 is the mode because it occurs three times.

> Find the mode by identifying the piece of data that appears most often.

   b The range = 238 − 100 = 138

> Calculate the range by subtracting the smallest data value from the largest data value.

2 Babak is trying to sell advertising on his website.

Write a sentence he could use about the number of hits his site is receiving.

   There is a consistent hit rate of over 100 hits per hour with 175 hits per hour on average.

> Write a sentence that summarises the key data.

3 Babak compares his data to a similar website run by his colleague Delia.

Delia's data set has the following data values:

mean = 180 hits   median = 140 hits   mode = 135 hits   range = 200.

What can Babak say to compare the two sets?

   Although the mean of the hits is a bit higher for Delia's set, the median is much lower.
   This shows that the mean of Delia's hits is influenced by a few high values, but usually the number of hits is lower.

> Compare and contrast the two data sets, looking for differences and similarities.

   Delia's data show a wider range, which means that the data is more spread out and therefore less consistent.

> Make a statement about how spread out or consistent the data is.

Analysing grouped data

Data is sometimes grouped together before it is analysed.

The groups are known as class intervals. They do not overlap.

For example:

When you have grouped data in a frequency table, it is not possible to calculate exact values for the mean, median, mode and range because you don't know the individual values.

However, you can identify the modal and median classes from the table.

Marks scored	Frequency
0–9	6
10–19	6
20–29	4
30–39	5
40–50	9
Total	30

- The modal class is the class interval that has the most elements, not the individual value that appears the most. In the table above, the modal class is 40–50 marks.

- To estimate the median of grouped data, find the class interval in which the middle value occurs. It is only possible to say that the median is within that group. In the table there are 30 values and the middle value is between the 15th and 16th values, so it must fall in the class 20–29 marks.

Estimating the mean of a frequency distribution

To estimate the mean of grouped data, first find the midpoint of each class interval.

The midpoint is found by adding the lowest and highest possible values for each class interval and dividing by 2.

Multiply each midpoint by the frequency for each class interval.

Find the total of these values, and divide by the total number of values you have.

WORKED EXAMPLE 2

Ben goes fishing and records the masses of the fish he catches in the table below:

a Complete the table.

b Find the modal class.

c Estimate the mean, the median and the range.

Mass, m (kg)	Frequency	Midpoint	Midpoint × frequency
$2 \leqslant m < 4$	5		
$4 \leqslant m < 6$	8		
$6 \leqslant m < 8$	4		
$8 \leqslant m < 10$	9		
$10 \leqslant m < 12$	3		

Continues on next page …

a Completed table:

Mass, m (kg)	Frequency	Midpoint	Midpoint × frequency
$2 \leqslant m < 4$	5	3	15
$4 \leqslant m < 6$	8	5	40
$6 \leqslant m < 8$	4	7	28
$8 \leqslant m < 10$	9	9	81
$10 \leqslant m < 12$	3	11	33

Find the midpoint between the upper and lower value in each class interval.

Multiply this number by the frequency to complete the right-hand column of the table.

b The modal class is $8\,\text{kg} \leqslant m < 10\,\text{kg}$.

The modal class is the one that has the largest frequency.

c The mean:
Total of midpoint × frequency values is 197.
The sum of the frequencies is 29. So the estimated mean
is $\frac{197}{29} = 6.79\,\text{kg}$

The mean is an estimate because you have used an approximate value, the midpoint.

The median class: there are 29 values, so the middle value is value number 15.
The median value falls in the class $6\,\text{kg} \leqslant m < 8\,\text{kg}$.
The range: $12 - 2 = 10\,\text{kg}$.

The median class is found by finding the class in which the median value sits.

EXERCISE 3A

1 A small set of data has a mean of 5, a mode of 5 and a median of 5.
Which of these data sets would give this result?

A 3, 4, 5, 6, 7   B 5, 4, 3, 5, 5,6

C 5, 4, 3, 6, 7, 5   D 1, 2, 5, 5, 1, 6, 8

2 A company keeps a record of how many days each employee is absent from work each year.
The results are in the table below.

Days absent, d	Frequency	Midpoint	Midpoint × frequency
$0 \leqslant d < 5$	15		
$5 \leqslant d < 10$	23		
$10 \leqslant d < 15$	19		
$15 \leqslant d < 20$	12		
$20 \leqslant d < 25$	6		
Total			

a Copy and complete the table.

b Use the information to find the modal class.

c Estimate the mean, the median and the range.

3 The scores from a game of darts are given in the table.

89	11	57	25	55	78
28	35	15	90	83	38
57	37	28	14	36	40
74	59	57	9	18	70
25	18	22	2	37	53
74	61	79	53	87	46
30	29	4	90	83	77

a Choose suitable class intervals and group the data.

b Using your work in part **a**, estimate the mean, the median and the range of the scores.

c Is it sensible to estimate the range?

d What is the modal group?

4 The heights, in centimetres, of some members of a club are given in the table.

1.68	1.68	1.58	1.72	1.58	1.75	1.89
1.84	1.55	1.65	1.66	1.84	1.55	1.81
1.47	1.55	1.58	1.66	1.55	1.61	1.68
1.57	1.57	1.69	1.65	1.75	1.55	1.73
1.64	1.85	1.53	1.65	1.77	1.66	1.75
1.75	1.59	1.88	1.82	1.62	1.69	1.67
1.63	1.66	1.84	1.77	1.52	1.84	1.53

a Use group intervals of every 5 cm, starting with the group $1.45\,\text{cm} \leqslant h < 1.50\,\text{cm}$, to draw a grouped frequency table.

Estimate the mean and the median.

b What is the modal class?

c Use class intervals of every 10 cm, starting with the class $1.40\,\text{cm} \leqslant h < 1.50\,\text{cm}$, to draw a new grouped frequency table. Estimate the mean and the median.

Write down the effect that the new group intervals have on your estimates of the mean and the median.

5 Thirty runners complete a marathon race. Their times are given below (to the nearest minute):

2 hours 45 minutes, 3 hours 25 minutes, 3 hours 46 minutes, 4 hours 15 minutes, 5 hours 8 minutes, 4 hours 49 minutes, 4 hours 18 minutes, 3 hours 38 minutes, 3 hours 43 minutes, 3 hours 5 minutes, 2 hours 55 minutes, 4 hours 23 minutes, 4 hours 25 minutes, 3 hours 39 minutes, 3 hours 20 minutes, 4 hours 1 min, 3 hours 33 minutes, 4 hours 6 minutes, 5 hours 11 minutes, 2 hours 51 minutes, 4 hours 35 minutes, 3 hours 19 minutes, 4 hours 47 minutes, 4 hours 28 minutes, 5 hours 5 minutes, 4 hours 19 minutes, 2 hours 46 minutes, 3 hours 18 minutes, 3 hours 53 minutes, 4 hours 35 minutes.

a Group the data into suitable class intervals.

b Find the modal class.

c Estimate the mean, the median and the range.

6 The mass of fruit produced by a farm is recorded in the table below.

Mass of produce, m (kg)	Frequency	Midpoint of class interval	Midpoint × frequency
$200 \leqslant m < 250$	15		
$250 \leqslant m < 300$	10		
$300 \leqslant m < 350$	13		
$350 \leqslant m < 400$	7		
$400 \leqslant m < 450$	2		
$450 \leqslant m < 500$	2		
$500 \leqslant m < 550$	2		
Total			

a Calculate an estimate of the mean mass of the fruit.

b In which interval does the median lie?

c In which interval does the third quartile lie?

Estimating values from cumulative frequency graphs

It is possible to find further summary statistics about grouped data from a cumulative frequency graph.

Remember that cumulative frequency graphs are drawn from grouped data and are plotted at the upper end of the class interval.

In the graph shown there are 32 pieces of data, as the maximum cumulative frequency is 32.

Draw a line across to the curve and down to the horizontal scale giving the value of:

- 14 as an estimate of the median (as the data is grouped)

- 12 as an estimate of the lower quartile ($\frac{1}{4}$ of the total frequency)

- 17 as an estimate of the upper quartile ($\frac{3}{4}$ of the total frequency)

The interquartile range is upper quartile – lower quartile, and is a way of measuring how spread out the middle 50% of the data values are.

In this example the interquartile range (IQR) is 17 – 12 = 5 (although this is an estimate).

The lower quartile is sometimes referred to as Q^1, and the upper quartile Q^3.

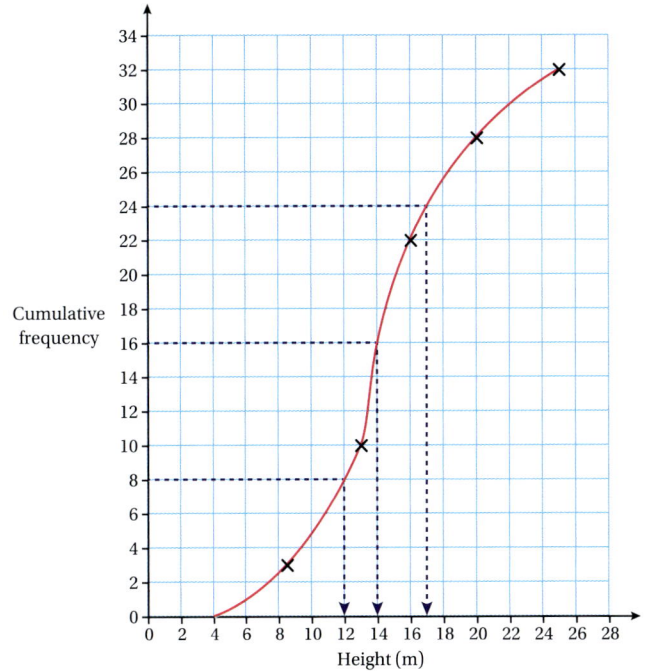

EXERCISE 3B

1 The graph below shows the cumulative frequency of the ages of 30 members of a bingo club.

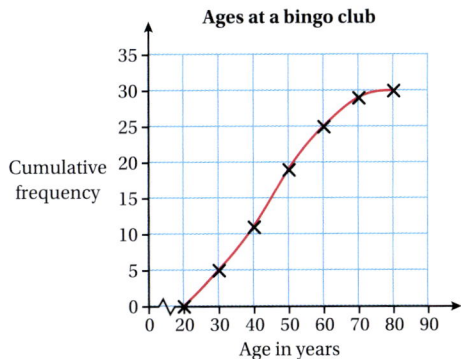

Use the graph to estimate the median and interquartile range of the ages.

2 The graph below shows the prices of 25 cars in a second-hand car shop.

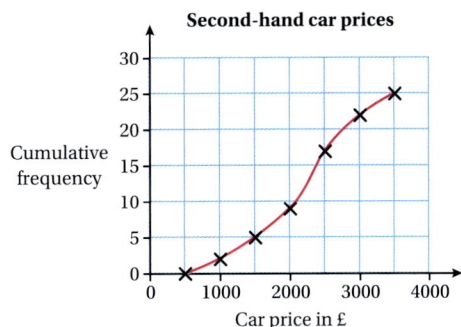

Use the graph to estimate the median and the interquartile range of the prices.

Find answers at: cambridge.org/ukschools/gcsemaths-studentbookanswers

3 The graph below shows the time taken for the same train journey on 32 different occasions.

Journey times

Cumulative frequency

Journey time in minutes

Use the graph to estimate the median and the interquartile range of the journey times.

Using box plots to compare two sets of data

A **box plot** is a way of displaying data that also shows these summary statistics:

- the lowest and highest values (range)
- the first and third quartiles (the interquartile range)
- the median.

The box plot gives an instant impression of how the data set is distributed.

It is especially useful for comparing data for two different populations, by aligning the box plots on the same number line.

Tip

When comparing box plots, plot them on the same scale so that you can compare the IQR, median and range.

WORKED EXAMPLE 3

The masses in kilograms of 20 students are (in order): 47, 48, 52, 54, 55, 58, 58, 61, 62, 63, 63, 64, 65, 66, 66, 67, 69, 70, 72, 79. Draw a box plot for this data.

47, 48, 52, 54, 55, 58, 58, 61, 62, 63, 63, 64, 65, 66, 66, 67, 69, 70, 72, 79

Make sure the data is arranged in numerical order.

Finding the median value
47, 48, 52, 54, 55, 58, 58, 61, 62, (63, 63) 64, 65, 66, 66, 67, 69, 70, 72, 79

There are 20 data values so the median will be halfway between the 10th and 11th data values. As these are both 63, the median is 63 kg.

Finding Q^1
47, 48, 52, 54, 55, (58, 58) 61, 62, 63
$$\frac{55+58}{2} = 56.5$$
$$Q^1 = 56.5 \text{ kg}$$

Q^1 is the first quartile, so find the middle value of the lower half of the data.

There are 10 pieces of data in the lower half, so the median is between the 5th and 6th values.

Continues on next page …

Finding Q^3
63, 64, 65, 66, (66, 67) 69, 70, 72, 79
$\frac{66 + 67}{2} = 66.5$
$Q^3 = 66.5$ kg

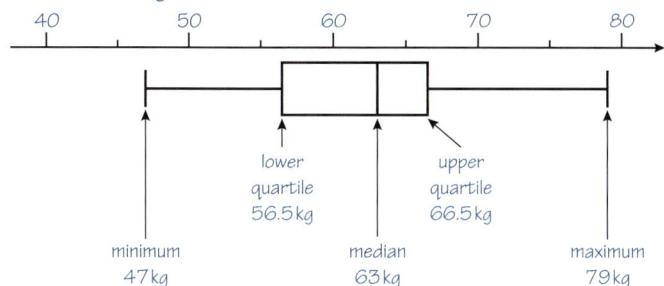

Q^3 is the upper quartile, so find it in the same way as Q^1 using the upper half of the data, between the 15th and 16th data values.

Use a horizontal scale that allows the minimum and maximum values to be shown.

Draw a rectangle with Q^1 and Q^3 as two opposite sides.

Draw a straight line to the minimum and maximum value.

Mark the median with a line parallel to Q^1 and Q^3.

lower quartile 56.5 kg
upper quartile 66.5 kg
minimum 47 kg
median 63 kg
maximum 79 kg

WORKED EXAMPLE 4

There are 10 boys and 10 girls in a Year 7 class.
Their heights (in cm) are:

| G | 137 | 133 | 141 | 137 | 138 | 134 | 149 | 144 | 144 | 131 |
| B | 145 | 142 | 146 | 139 | 138 | 148 | 138 | 147 | 142 | 146 |

a Use calculations of the mean, median and range to describe and compare these populations.

b Draw a box plot for both sets of data, and compare the interquartile ranges.

a Arranging data in order:
Girls: 131   133   134   137   137   138   141   144   144   149
Girls: mean = 138.8 cm, median = 137.5 cm and range = 18 cm.
Boys: 138   138   139   142   142   145   146   146   147   148
Boys: mean = 143.1 cm, median = 143.5 cm and range = 10 cm.
The girls' heights are fairly widely spread. The boys are generally taller than the girls, but their heights are less spread out. For both boys and girls the median is not far from the mean, but the two are closer for the boys; this indicates that there are no really exceptional heights greatly affecting either mean, but that there are one or two slightly unusual ones among the girls (in this case the girl of height 149 cm).

b Box plot:
For girls' data
Find Q^1
131   133   (134)   137   137
$Q^1 = 134$ cm

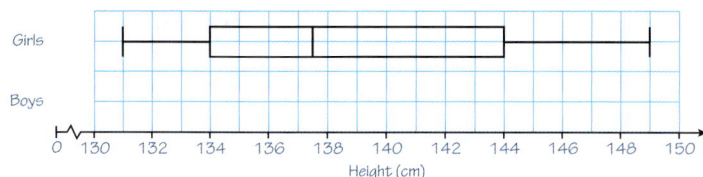

Q^1 is the first quartile, so find the middle value of the lower half of the data.

There are five pieces of data in the lower half, so the middle value is the third value.

Find Q^3
138   141   (144)   144   149
$Q^3 = 144$ cm

Q^3 is the upper quartile, so find it in the same way as Q^1 using the upper half of the data.

Girls
Boys
Height (cm)

Use a horizontal scale that allows the minimum and maximum values.

Continues on next page ...

Find answers at: cambridge.org/ukschools/gcsemaths-studentbookanswers

55

For boys' data

Find Q^1

138   138   (139)   142   142

$Q^1 = 139$ cm

> Q^1 is the first quartile, so find the middle value of the lower half of the data.
>
> There are five pieces of data in the lower half, so the median is the third value.

Find Q^3

145   146   (146)   147   148

$Q^3 = 146$ cm

> Q^3 is the upper quartile, so find it in the same way as Q^1 using the upper half of the data.

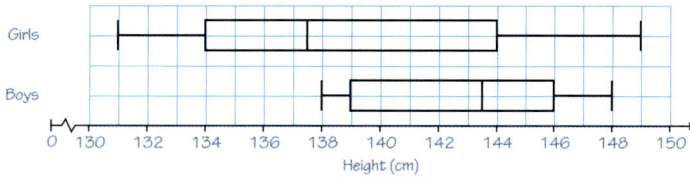

The IQR for girls (10 cm) is wider than that for boys (7 cm), showing that the data is more varied and spread out.

EXERCISE 3C

1 The results from two maths tests are given.

A	35	68	55	52	49	63	61	69	35	53
B	47	34	71	41	60	44	57	74	67	64

a For each test, calculate the mean, median and range to compare the two sets of data.

b Draw a box plot for both sets of data, and compare the interquartile ranges.

2 Two cricketers are having an argument about who has had the best season.

They have both batted 16 times, and the number of runs they have scored in each innings is given in the table.

Ahmed	27	16	36	27	55	35	51	38	44	17	41	53	7	43	48	49
Bill	2	30	44	11	26	32	13	46	40	44	0	45	15	34	14	24

a Compare and describe their records.

b Who do you think has had the best season? Write down your reasons.

3 Yusuf has recorded the time it takes him to get home on two different buses. His results are given in the table.

Bus 127	17	17	21	23	19	20	19	18	21	22	19	22	21	20
Bus 362	23	26	20	15	15	20	26	19	18	15	16			

Which bus route should he use? Give reasons for your answer.

Does it matter that he has more data about the 127 bus?

4 A factory needs to choose between two machines for bottling soft drinks.

Data about how many bottles each machine fills per hour is given in the table.

Machine A	Bottles, b	Frequency	Machine B	Bottles, b	Frequency
	$200 \leqslant b < 250$	36		$200 \leqslant b < 250$	16
	$250 \leqslant b < 300$	48		$250 \leqslant b < 300$	58
	$300 \leqslant b < 350$	59		$300 \leqslant b < 350$	63
	$350 \leqslant b < 400$	61		$350 \leqslant b < 400$	78
	$400 \leqslant b < 450$	21		$400 \leqslant b < 450$	15

Use estimates of the mean, the median and the range along with the modal group to decide which machine the factory should choose.

5 According to the Office for National Statistics, the 'average' price of a house in the UK in July 2014 was £272 000.

a What would be the best type of average to measure house prices?

Give a reason for your answer.

b Give an example of when using the mean as a measure of central tendency would be the most useful.

c Give two examples when using the mode as a measure of central tendency is the most useful.

6 The heights, measured in centimetres, of 25 students in a class are:

170   175   133   153   164   189   143   133   167   145

150   164   169   159   177   186   173   164   177   168

142   155   153   167   166

a Find Q^1, the median and Q^3.

b Find the interquartile range.

c Draw a box plot to display the data.

Find answers at: cambridge.org/ukschools/gcsemaths-studentbookanswers

7 The annual incomes of 30 people, given to the nearest £1000, are:

54 000	67 000	92 000	78 000	54 000	87 000
102 000	112 000	132 000	45 000	256 000	89 000
78 000	98 000	34 000	75 000	65 000	100 000
34 000	68 000	79 000	81 000	82 000	103 000
21 000	345 000	98 000	67 000	105 000	98 000

a Find Q^1, the median and Q^3.

b Find the interquartile range.

c Draw a box plot to display the data.

8 Two teams of friends have recorded their scores on a game and created a pair of box plots.

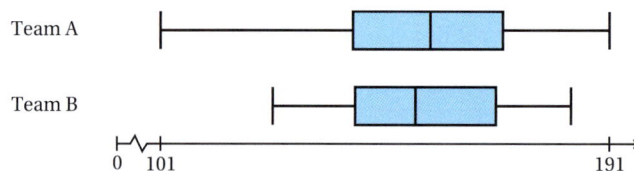

a What is the interquartile range for Team A?

b What is the interquartile range for Team B?

c Which team has the most consistent scores?

d To stay in the game you must score at least 120.

Which team seems most likely to stay in?

e Which team gets the highest scores?

f Give your reasons for your answer to part **e**.

Section 2: Misleading graphs

One of the advantages of using graphs is that they show information quickly and visually.

Graphs can also be misleading because most people don't look at them very closely.

When you look carefully at a graph you might find that it has been drawn in a way that gives a misleading impression.

When you look at a graph, think about:

- the scale and whether or not it has been exaggerated in any way to give a particular impression
- whether or not the scale starts at 0, as this can affect the information shown and give us a misleading impression
- whether bars or pie charts have 3D sections which make some parts look much bigger than others
- whether the scales are labelled and whether or not the graph has a title
- whether the source of the data is given.

Here are some examples of misleading graphs.

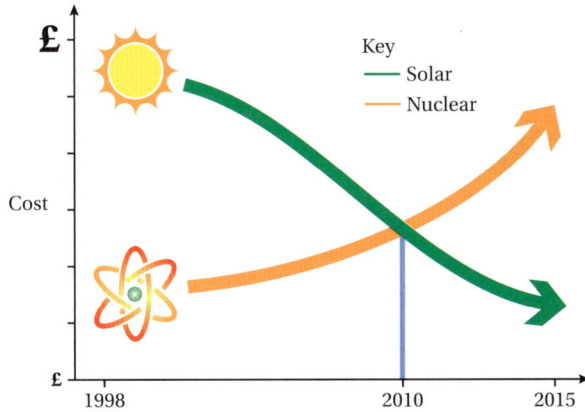

This graph seems to suggest that the price of solar energy is dropping quickly while the cost of nuclear power is increasing.

There are no values on the cost scale, so it is not possible to decide whether that is really true.

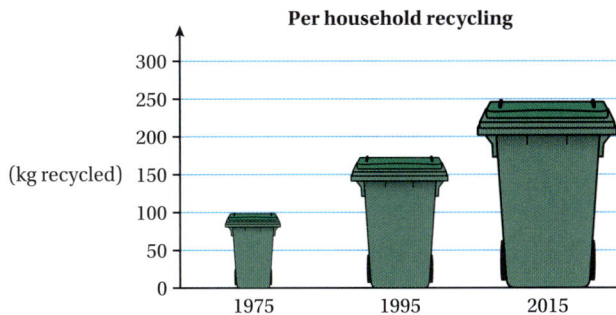

This graph of household recycling uses proportion to mislead.

The scale shows that the amount of recycled material has increased from 100 kg to 250 kg, so 2.5 times more material is recycled.

The bin for 2015 is about six times bigger, so it makes it look like much more is recycled.

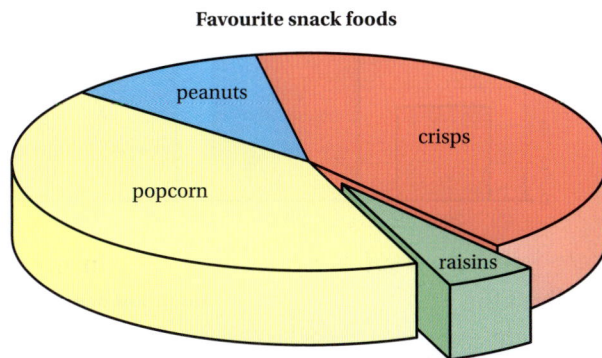

Drawing the pie chart in this orientation and with the sectors 3D makes it look like raisins are just as popular as peanuts and that popcorn is more popular than crisps.

The real figures show that 5% chose raisins and 11% chose peanuts, so the green sector represents less than half of the blue sector.

The other two sectors each represent 42% but they don't look the same size in the pie chart.

Find answers at: cambridge.org/ukschools/gcsemaths-studentbookanswers

EXERCISE 3D

1 Identify the errors in this graph.

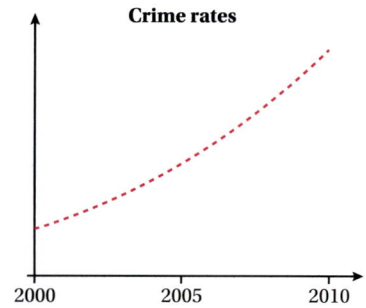

Crime rates

2 Write down reasons why this graph is misleading.

Suggest why someone might have drawn the graph like this.

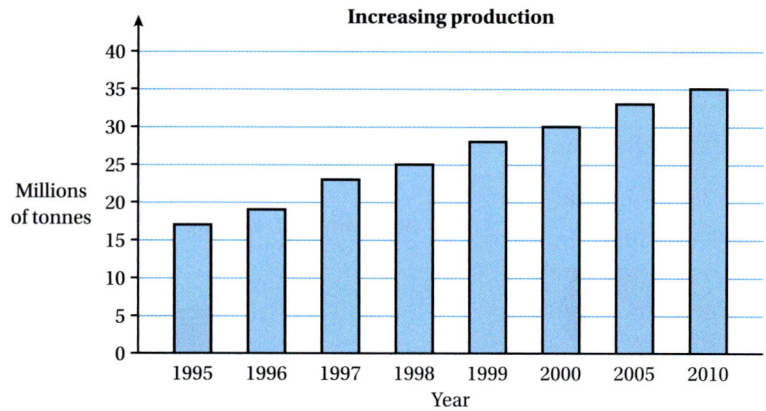

3 Write down what is wrong with the crisp sales graph in the margin.

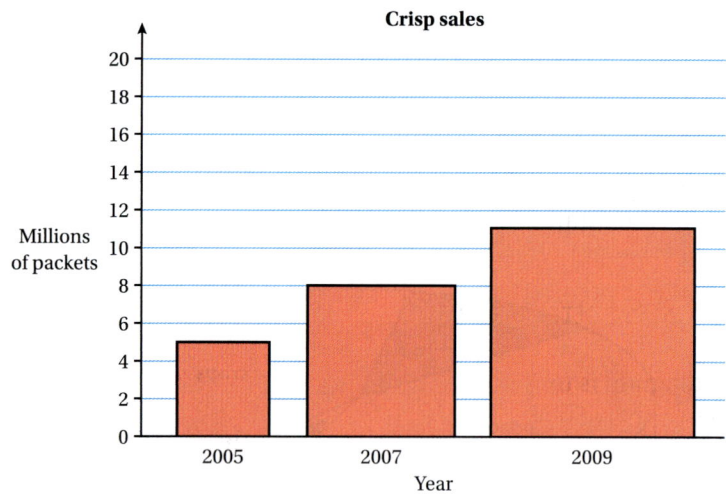

4 Look carefully at the graph on the right.

  a What is misleading about this graph?

  b Suggest why it might have been drawn this way.

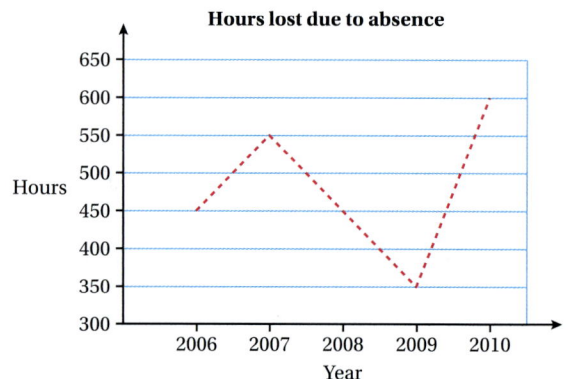

5 The same data as in question 4 have been presented in this 3D graph.

Hours lost due to absence

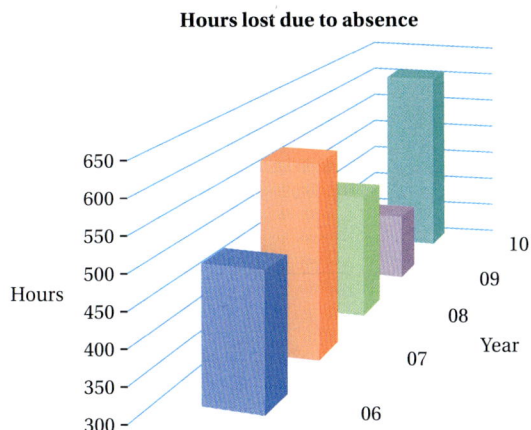

a Which year has the most days lost, 2006 or 2008?

b Why is it hard to tell?

6 The following data shows viewing figures for different TV programmes (in millions).

Week beginning	Britain's Got Talent	The Crimson Field	Gogglebox
07/04/14	10.03	6.89	2.75
14/04/14	8.45	6.31	3.37
21/04/14	8.63	6.25	3.48
28/04/14	8.45	6.01	3.47
05/05/14	8.58	6.33	3.54

Choose one of the TV programmes and create a graph that shows how well it has performed. You can use any type of graph, but you must not change the numbers.

Section 3: Scatter diagrams

A scatter diagram is used to show whether or not there is a relationship between two sets of data collected in pairs. Data that is collected in pairs is called **bivariate data**.

For example, you could record the number of hours different students spend studying and the results they get in a test.

This would give two pieces of data for each student: time spent studying and their result.

In bivariate data, both sets of data are numerical, so each pair of data can be plotted as a point using coordinates on a pair of axes, (x, y).

Once you have plotted the data, you can look for a pattern to see whether there is a **correlation** between the two variables.

Key vocabulary

bivariate data: data that is collected in pairs
correlation: a relationship or connection between data items

These diagrams show the typical patterns of correlation and what they mean.

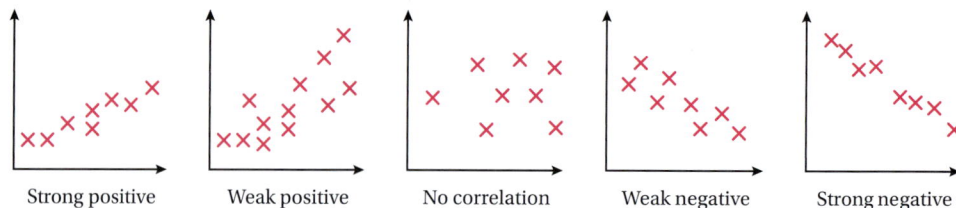

| Strong positive | Weak positive | No correlation | Weak negative | Strong negative |

WORKED EXAMPLE 5

Nick says people who are good at maths are also good at science.

Use this data to draw a scatter diagram and comment on whether the graph supports Nick.

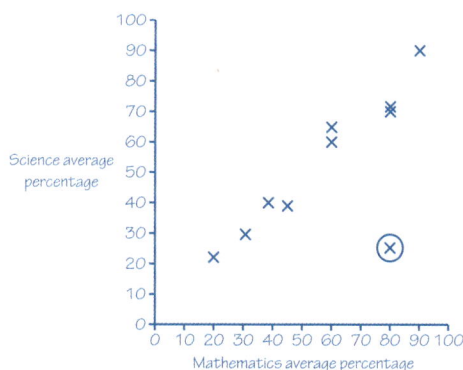

Look at the distribution of the points to see if there is a general pattern.

The points slope up towards the right, so there is a positive correlation between maths achievement and science achievement. The graph seems to support Nick.

Decide whether there is a positive correlation (as one quantity increases, so does the other) or a negative correlation (as one quantity increases the other decreases).

Maths average (%)	Science average (%)
20	22
32	30
45	39
38	40
60	60
80	70
80	72
90	90
80	25
60	65

Key vocabulary

dependent variable: the variable that is being measured in an experiment

outlier: data value that is much larger or smaller than others in the same data set

In the graph from Worked Example 5, maths is on the horizontal axis and science is on the vertical axis.

Science is the **dependent variable** in this case.

Nick's statement is that science achievement is dependent on whether or not you are good at maths. Maths is the independent variable so it goes on the horizontal axis.

One dot (circled on the graph) is far away from the others and doesn't seem to fit the pattern.

It shows a student with a high mark for maths but a low mark for science.

This point is an **outlier** in this set of data.

It is important to understand that *correlation is not causation*. This means that although there might be a relationship between two variables, you cannot be certain that the change in one is the reason for the change in the other. One does not necessarily cause the other.

Lines of best fit

A line of best fit is used to show a general trend on a scatter diagram.

This is a straight line drawn on the graph passing as close to as many points as possible.

This is the line of best fit for the scatter diagram in Worked Example 5. Note that the circled point, which is an outlier, has not been included in the plotting of this line.

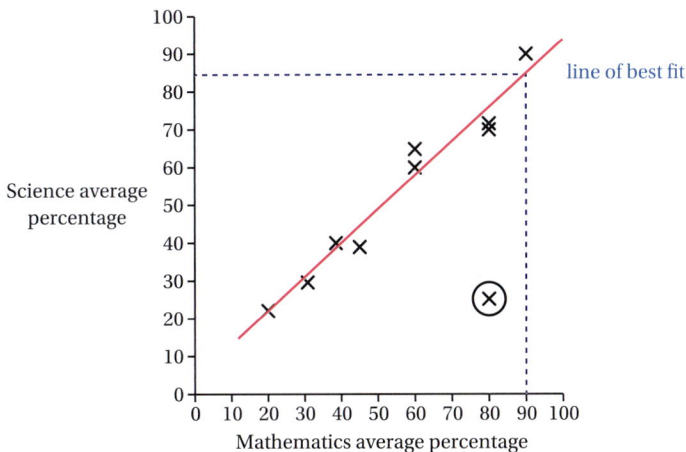

You can use the line of best fit to make predictions based on the data collected.

For example, if you wanted to predict the science results for a student who got 90% for maths, by using the line you find this is 84%. This is shown by the dotted line on the diagram. The same method can be used to predict the maths score for any other desired science score.

EXERCISE 3E

1 Draw a scatter diagram for the following data and draw a line of best fit.

Time spent on homework (min)	10	25	38	65	84	105	135	158
TV viewing time (min)	60	55	50	20	30	15	10	8

State the type of correlation.

2 Draw a scatter diagram to show the relationship between car engine size and fuel economy (miles per gallon):

Car fuel economy (miles per gallon)	64	60	59	58	55	49	47	42
Car engine size (litres)	1.1	1.3	1.4	1.6	1.8	2.0	2.5	3.0

3 Mike writes down the number of ice creams he sells and the maximum temperature each day for a week.

Ice creams sold	86	89	45	69	84	25	78
Maximum temperature (°C)	25	26	19	23	25	15	21

a Draw a scatter diagram to show the correlation between ice cream sales and the temperature.

b Suggest any other factors that might affect sales of ice cream.

4 During a census the number of people living in each house on a street is recorded.

House number	1	3	5	7	9	11	13	15	17	19	21
Number of residents	1	5	1	4	2	5	6	3	5	3	6

a Draw a scatter diagram to show this data.

b State what kind of correlation this shows.

5 The table below shows the athlete's height and the height jumped by the last 10 men's high jump world record holders.

	Athlete height (m)	Height jumped (m)
Sötomayor	1.95	2.45
Sjöberg	2.00	2.42
Paklin	1.91	2.41
Povarnitsyn	2.01	2.40
Jianhua	1.93	2.39
Wessig	2.00	2.36
Mögenburg	2.01	2.35
Wszola	1.90	2.35
Yashchenko	1.93	2.34
Stones	1.96	2.32

a Draw a scatter diagram showing this data.

b Is there a correlation between the height of the jumper and the height he jumped?

c Which one of the following statements is true?

A The shortest man jumps the smallest height.

B The tallest man jumps the greatest height.

C All men over 2 m tall can jump higher than those under 2 m tall.

D Paklin can jump the same distance above his own height as Sötomayor.

Outliers

Outliers are data values that lie outside the normal range for a set of data.

It can be difficult to decide when it is reasonable to disregard an outlier, but if it is an obvious error then the value is usually just ignored.

However, outliers can't be ignored just because they spoil a pattern.

Outliers will have an impact on calculating the mean and the range of a set of data, but less so when finding the median and the mode.

On a scatter diagram an outlier will be a point that is away from the main scatter of points, or might fit the line of best fit but be at an extreme value.

WORKED EXAMPLE 6

A coach records the 100-metre times of her 10 athletes at the start and the end of a week of intense training.

Nine of the athletes improve by a mean of 0.2 seconds, but one athlete is 2 seconds slower.

Can the coach claim to be making an impact on her athletes?

Yes, the coach is making an impact on the athletes. The mean would show a reduced performance, because the single athlete's performance has reduced by much more than the others have improved. The athlete with reduced performance is an outlier, and her performance might be affected by ill health.

Answer the question directly – is the coach making an impact?

Give reasons and justify why this is the case.

Suggest an explanation for the outlier.

EXERCISE 3F

1 Which one of the following statements is correct?

A An outlier is the biggest number in a data set.

B An outlier is a value that is significantly different from the rest in a data set.

C An outlier is the smallest number in a data set.

D In the data set 5, 6, 7, 10, 12, 15, the value 15 is an outlier.

2 Some students' scores in a test are given below:

54 50 47 42 54 44 36 37 45 36 55 55 52 85 39

a Work out the mean score in the test.

b Work out the range.

c What is the median score?

d What is the median without the outlier?

e Work out the mean without the outlier.

3 The maths and English exam scores for a set of students are given below:

English	49	42	46	44	53	41	64	14	44	53	55	42
Maths	46	47	43	45	49	48	69	39	33	46	53	44

a Plot the scores on a scatter diagram.

b Draw a line of best fit on your scatter diagram.

c Identify any outliers.

4 The time taken to travel by train from Norwich to London in minutes is recorded for 20 journeys:

109	129	98	106	109	156	128	98	99	113
126	99	105	110	126	98	106	114	122	107

On a normal day the journey should take between 95 and 115 minutes, depending on the number of stops at stations.

a Work out the mean journey time.

b The train company claim that the mean journey time is 111 minutes on a normal day.

Is this right?

Checklist of learning and understanding

Summary statistics

- The mean, the median and the mode are all measures of central tendency. They can be found precisely for populations that are ungrouped and have to be estimated for grouped data.
- The range is a measure of spread. It can be found precisely for ungrouped data and has to be estimated for grouped data.
- Quartiles are the values that divide an ordered set of data into quarters.
- The interquartile range is the range between the upper and lower quartiles, and is a measure of spread.
- Box plots show the range, the quartiles and the median value and are a good way of comparing data sets.

Misleading graphs

- The way that data is presented in graphs can be misleading. Watch out for uneven scales and for graphs that show increases by using areas that exaggerate those increases.

Scatter diagrams and correlation

- Scatter diagrams can be used to look for correlations in bivariate data. A correlation is a relationship, for example, one quantity increasing as another decreases. Some bivariate data has no correlation.
- Correlation does not mean causation. In other words, identifying a relationship does not necessarily mean that a change in one data set is causing the change in the other.
- Outliers are pieces of data that sit outside the pattern or expected result. They can be ignored if they are an obvious error, but otherwise should be considered and reasons given.

Chapter review

For additional questions on the topics in this chapter, visit GCSE Mathematics Online.

1 A learner windsurfer would typically sail in a wind speed of 7–18 knots, but an expert would prefer to sail at wind speeds above 30 knots.

a The data below is wind speed in knots measured at the same time each day for two lakes. From the data, decide which lake is best for beginners and which is best for experts.

Use measures of central tendency and spread to support your argument.

Wind speed on first lake (knots)	0	21	33	13	20	11	35	3	5	3	31
	28	19	19	22	26	40	40	4	25	21	26
Wind speed on second lake (knots)	15	11	19	11	10	19	23	25	10	18	10
	16	23	15	15	20	22	10	13	11	18	18

b Which of these statements is true about the data?

A 0 is an outlier.

B We can ignore values above 35 knots as they are outliers.

C All data must be considered to support the argument.

D The second lake is always windier than the first lake.

2 The box plot shows the height of 30 Year 10 students in centimetres.

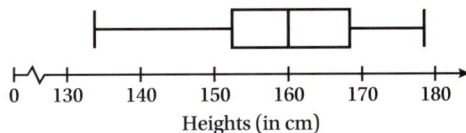

Heights (in cm)

a What information is shown on the box plot?

b How does this help you make sense of the data?

3 Chen records his journey times to college as shown in the table.

a Calculate an estimate of his mean journey time.   *(4 marks)*

b Explain why your answer to part **a** is an estimate.   *(1 mark)*

c The frequency polygon shows Lee's journey times to college.

Time, t (minutes)	Frequency
$25 < m \leqslant 30$	12
$30 < m \leqslant 35$	18
$35 < m \leqslant 40$	24
$40 < m \leqslant 45$	6
Total	60

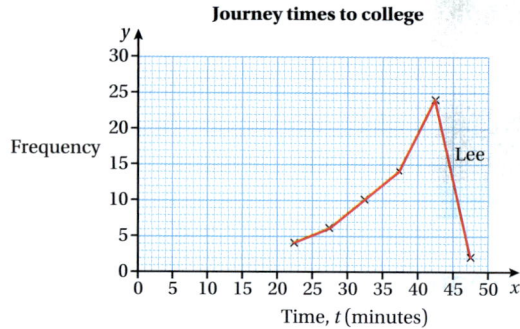

Journey times to college

On a copy of the grid, draw a frequency polygon for Chen's journey times.   *(2 marks)*

d An estimate of Lee's mean journey time is 37 minutes.

Compare the journey times for Lee and Chen.   *(2 marks)*

© AQA 2013

4 Study the two line graphs.

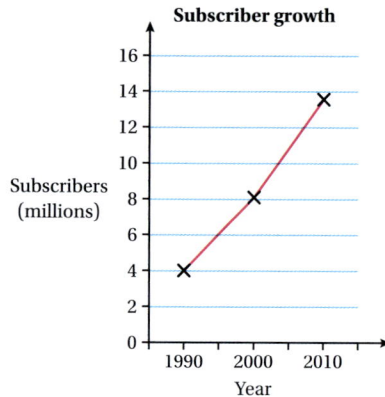

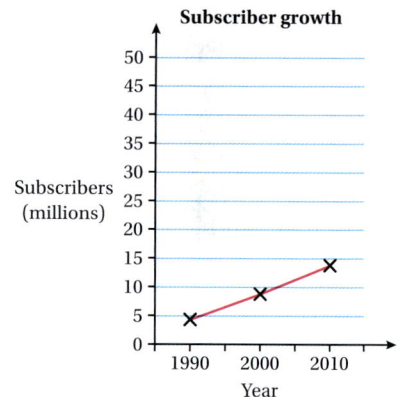

a These two graphs show the same data. Give reasons why they look different.

b Which graph would you use if you were a mobile phone service provider who wanted to suggest that there had been a huge increase in subscribers over this period? Give reasons for your answer.

c Who might find the other graph useful? Why?

5 Data for the price of chocolate bars and their mass is given in the table.

Price of chocolate bar	45p	80p	£1.50	£3.00	£5.00	£10
Mass of bar	35 g	80 g	175 g	320 g	540 g	1 kg

a Plot the data on a scatter diagram and draw a line of best fit.

b State what type of correlation there is.

4 Properties of integers

Using mathematics: real-life applications

People use numbers and basic calculations on a daily basis. A market stall holder has to quickly calculate the cost of a customer's order; a logistics manager has to order stock and divide the supplies so that they are never over or under stocked. There are many applications of basic calculation.

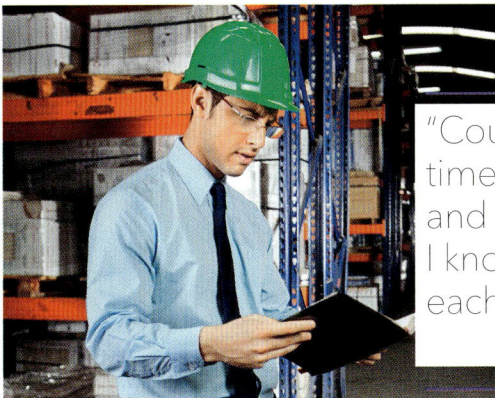

"Counting in multiples saves quite a bit of time. If I know that each shelf has 15 boxes and each box contains 5 reams of paper, then I know straightaway that I have 75 reams on each shelf without having to count each ream."

(Logistics manager)

Before you start …

KS3	You should be able to recognise and find the factors of a number and to list multiples of a number.	**1** If these are the factors, what is the number? **a** 1, 5, 25 **b** 1, 2, 3, 6 **c** 1, 11 **2** If these are all multiples of a number, what is the number? **a** 8, 10, 12, 14 **b** 18, 21, 27, 33 **c** 5, 20, 35, 60	
KS3	You should know the first few prime numbers, square numbers and cube numbers.	**3** Which of the numbers in the box are: **a** prime numbers? **b** square numbers? **c** cube numbers?	0, 1, 2, 3, 4, 5, 6, 7, 8, 9, 10, 11, 12, 13, 14, 15, 16, 17, 18, 19, 20
KS3	You will need to be able to express a number as a product of its prime factors.	**4** Match each number to the product of its prime factors. **a** 450 **b** 180 **c** 120 **d** 72 A $2^3 \times 3^2$ B $2^2 \times 3^2 \times 5$ C $2^3 \times 3 \times 5$ D $2 \times 3^2 \times 5^2$	

Assess your starting point using the Launchpad

STEP 1

1 True or false?

a 1 is the smallest prime number.

b If you square 7 you get 14.

c 8 is the cube of 2.

d Any whole number that ends in 1 is an odd number.

e 33, 43 and 53 are prime numbers.

f 7, 14 and 21 are factors of 7.

2 There is one incorrect number in each set.

Work out what the set is and find the incorrect number.

a 20, 22, 24, 26, 28, 29, 30   **b** 11, 22, 33, 44, 56, 66

c 1, 2, 3, 4, 8, 12   **d** 27, 30, 33, 36, 39, 41

e 1, 2, 3, 4, 6, 9, 12, 18, 24, 36   **f** 12, 24, 48, 60, 72, 86

g 2, 3, 5, 7, 9, 11, 13, 17, 19

GO TO
Section 1:
Review of number properties

STEP 2

3 Choose the correct product of prime factors for each number.

a 48   A $2 \times 2 \times 2 \times 3 \times 3$ B $2 \times 2 \times 2 \times 2 \times 3$

b 100   A $2 \times 2 \times 5 \times 5$ B $2 \times 5 \times 5$

GO TO
Section 2:
Prime factors

STEP 3

4 Given that $72 = 2 \times 2 \times 2 \times 3 \times 3$ and $120 = 2 \times 2 \times 2 \times 3 \times 5$, choose the correct answers.

a The HCF of 72 and 120 is:

A 360   B 12   C 24   D 5

b The LCM of 72 and 120 is:

A 30   B 2   C 120   D 360

GO TO
Section 3:
Multiples and factors

GO TO

Chapter review

Section 1: Review of number properties

Defining mathematical terms

Make sure you remember the correct mathematical terms for the different types of numbers shown in the table.

Mathematical term	Definition	Example
odd number	A whole number that cannot be divided exactly by 2; it has a remainder of 1.	1, 3, 5, 7, ...
even number	A whole number that can be divided exactly by 2 (no remainder).	0, 2, 4, 6, 8, ...
prime number	A whole number greater than 1 that can only be divided exactly by itself and by 1. (It has only two factors.)	2, 3, 5, 7, 11, 13, 17, 19, ...
square number	The product when an integer is multiplied by itself. For example, $2 \times 2 = 4$, so 4 is a square number.	1, 4, 9, 16, ...
cubed number	The product when an integer is multiplied by itself twice. For example, $2 \times 2 \times 2 = 8$, so 8 is a cube number.	1, 8, 27, 64, ...
root	The number that produces a square number when it is multiplied by itself is a square root. The number that produces a cube number when it is multiplied by itself and then by itself again is a cube root.	The square root of 25 is 5. $\sqrt{25} = 5$ $(5 \times 5 = 25)$ The cube root of 8 is 2. $\sqrt[3]{8} = 2$ $(2 \times 2 \times 2 = 8)$
factor (also called divisor)	A number that divides exactly into another number, without a remainder.	Factors of 6 are 1, 2, 3 and 6. Factors of 7 are 1 and 7. Factors of 25 are 1, 5 and 25.
multiple	A multiple of a number is found when you multiply that number by a whole number. Your times tables are really just lists of multiples.	Multiples of 3 are 3, 6, 9, 12, ... Multiples of 7 are 7, 14, 21, ...
common factor	A common factor is a factor shared by two or more numbers. The number 1 is a common factor of all numbers.	Factors of 6 are 1, 2, 3 and 6. Factors of 12 are 1, 2, 3, 4, 6 and 12. 1, 2, 3 and 6 are common factors of 6 and 12.
common multiple	A common multiple is a multiple shared by two or more numbers.	Multiples of 2 are 2, 4, 6, 8, 10, 12, ... Multiples of 3 are 3, 6, 9, 12, ... 6 and 12 are common multiples of 2 and 3.

i Did you know?

Mathematicians use the following arguments to define zero as an even number:

- When zero is divided by two, the result is a whole number (zero) with no remainder.
- In a list of consecutive numbers, an even number has an odd number before and after it, i.e. −1 and 1 are either side of zero.
- When an even number is added to another even number it will give an even result, but when added to an odd number it will give an odd result. When zero is added to any number, the result is the number you started with.
- Numbers that end in 0 are even.
- It is the next number in this pattern of even numbers: 8, 6, 4, 2, …

EXERCISE 4A

1 Here is a set of numbers.

1	2	3	4	5	6	7	8	9	10
11	12	13	14	15	16	17	18	19	20
21	22	23	24	25	26	27	28	29	30

Write down the numbers from the box that are:

a odd   **b** even   **c** prime

d square   **e** cube   **f** factors of 24

g multiples of 3   **h** common factors of 8 and 12

i common multiples of 3 and 4.

2 Which of the following options is both a prime **and** a factor of 12?

A 2   B 4   C 6   D 12

3 Write down:

a the next four odd numbers after 207

b four **consecutive** even numbers between 500 and 540

c the square numbers between 20 and 70

d the factors of 23

e four prime numbers greater than 15

f the first ten cube numbers

g the first five multiples of 8

h the factors of 36.

Key vocabulary

consecutive: following each other in order and without a gap. For example, 1, 2, 3 or 35, 36, 37

4 Write down whether the following results will be odd or even.

a The sum of two odd numbers.

b The sum of two even numbers.

c The difference between two even numbers.

d The square of an odd number.

e The product of an odd number and an even number.

f The cube of an odd number.

Place value

Consider the number 222 222.

Each of the 2s in the number has a different place value.

The place value tells you the value of the digit. The underlined 2 in the number above has a value of 2 thousands or 2000.

Hundred thousands 100 000	Ten thousands 10 000	Thousands 1000	Hundreds 100	Tens 10	Ones/units 1
2	2	2	2	2	2

Each column in the place-value table is ten times the value of the place to the right of it.

EXERCISE 4B

1 For each set of numbers, rewrite the numbers in order from smallest to largest.

   a 432   456   348   843   654

   b 606   660   607   670   706

   c 123   1231   312   1321   231

   d 12 700   71 200   21 700   21 007

2 Write down the value of the 5 in each of these numbers.

   a 35   **b** 534   **c** 256

   d 25 876   **e** 50 346 987   **f** 1 532 980

   g 5 678 432   **h** 356 432   **i** 56 987 089

3 What is the value of 7 in the number 307 642?

   Choose from the following options.

   A 70 000   B 7000   C 700   D 7

4 For each set of digits, write down:

   i the biggest number you can make

   ii the smallest number you can make.

   Use each digit only once in each number. Do not begin any of your numbers with zero.

   a 4, 0 and 6   **b** 5, 7, 3 and 1   **c** 1, 0, 3, 4, 6 and 2

Section 2: Prime factors

If a factor of a number is a prime number it is called a **prime factor**.

Every integer greater than 1 can be written as a product of its prime factors.

Finding the prime numbers that multiply together to make a given number is known as **prime factorisation**.

You can find the prime factors of a number by **repeatedly dividing by prime numbers**, or by using **factor trees**.

> **Key vocabulary**
>
> **prime factor**: a factor that is also a prime number

> **Tip**
>
> Remember that 1 is **not** a prime number because it only has one factor, and 2 is the only **even** prime number. It will help you to work faster if you learn to recognise all the prime numbers up to 100.

WORKED EXAMPLE 1

Express 48 as a product of its prime factors:

a by division   **b** by using a factor tree.

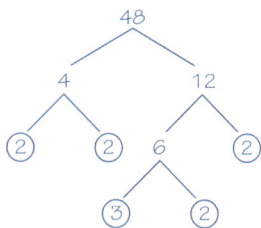

a

```
2 | 48
2 | 24
2 | 12
2 |  6
3 |  3
```

$2 \times 2 \times 2 \times 2 \times 3$

> Divide by prime numbers.
>
> Start with the lowest divisor that is prime; always try 2 first. Continue dividing, moving to higher prime numbers as necessary.

b

$2 \times 2 \times 2 \times 2 \times 3$

> Write the number as a product of any two of its factors. Keep doing this for the factors until you cannot divide a factor anymore, that is, until you get to a prime factor.

Even if you do the division in a different order and split the factors differently in the factor tree, you will always get the same result for a given number.

You get the same result with both methods because a whole number can only be expressed in terms of its prime factors in one way. This is called the **unique factorisation theorem**.

Here are three ways of finding the prime factors of 280.

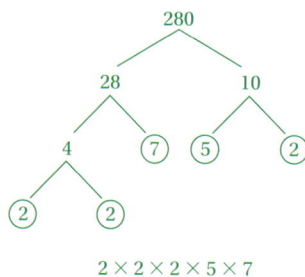

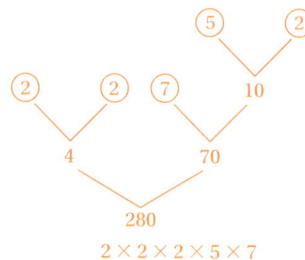

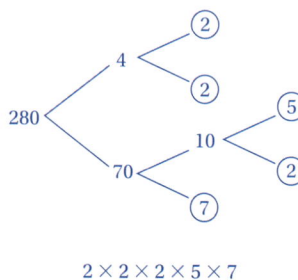

$2 \times 2 \times 2 \times 5 \times 7$

$2 \times 2 \times 2 \times 5 \times 7$

$2 \times 2 \times 2 \times 5 \times 7$

Tip

The **unique factorisation theorem** in mathematics states that each number can be written as a product of prime factors in one way only. It means that different numbers cannot have the same product of prime factors.

$2 \times 2 \times 2 \times 5 \times 7 = 2^3 \times 5 \times 7$

expanded form   index form

Writing a number as a product of its prime factors is known as **prime factor decomposition**.

You have seen the product of factors in expanded form, but you can write them in a more efficient way using powers, called the index form, as shown in the margin.

EXERCISE 4C

1 Write down the prime numbers in each set.

  a 1, 2, 3, 4, 5, 6, 7, 8, 9, 10

  b 50, 51, 52, 53, 54, 55, 56, 57, 58, 59, 60

  c 95, 96, 97, 98, 99, 100, 101, 102, 103, 104, 105

2 How should you express 96 as a product of its prime factors?

  Choose from the following options.

  A 32×3 B 3×2^5 C 2×48 D $1 \times 2^5 \times 3$

3 Express each of the following numbers as a product of its prime factors.

  Write your final answers in index form.

  a 36   **b** 65   **c** 64   **d** 84

  e 80   **f** 1000   **g** 1270   **h** 1963

4 A number is expressed as $2^3 \times 3^3 \times 5$.

  a What is the number?

  b Could it be any other number?

    Give a reason for your answer.

5 Research the 'sieve of Eratosthenes' and show how it can be used to identify prime numbers up to 100.

6 The number $(2^{(57\,885\,161)} - 1)$ is a prime number with 17 425 170 digits.

  This is a 'Mersenne prime'.

  a Research Marin Mersenne and why prime numbers in the form of $(2^p - 1)$ are known as Mersenne primes.

  b The Great Internet Mersenne Prime Search (GIMPS) is a project that anyone can join.

    Find out what it aims to do and whether or not any new primes have been discovered since 2013. (www.mersenne.org is a good starting point.)

7 There are four prime numbers between 10 and 20.

  a Find two other sets of four prime numbers between two consecutive multiples of 10.

  b Give a reason why you cannot expect to find four prime numbers between most other consecutive multiples of 10.

Section 3: Multiples and factors

The lowest common multiple (LCM)

The lowest common multiple (LCM) of two or more numbers is the smallest number that is a multiple of all the given numbers.

To find the LCM, list the multiples of the given numbers until you find the first multiple that appears in all the lists.

Tip

The notation M_4 means multiples of 4.

F_4 means factors of 4.

WORKED EXAMPLE 2

Find the LCM of 4 and 7.

$M_4 = 4, 8, 12, 16, 20, 24, 28, 32, \ldots$ ◄ List the multiples of 4.

$M_7 = 7, 14, 21, 28, \ldots$ ◄ List the multiples of 7.
Stop listing at 28 as it appears in both the lists.

LCM of 4 and 7 is 28.

The highest common factor (HCF)

The highest common factor of two or more numbers is the largest number that is a factor of all the given numbers.

To find the HCF, list all the factors in each number, and pick out the highest number that appears in all the lists.

Tip

The LCM is used to find the lowest common denominator when you add or subtract fractions.

The HCF is useful for cancelling fractions. You will use these terms again in Chapter 7 to factorise algebraic expressions.

WORKED EXAMPLE 3

Find the HCF of 8 and 24.

$F_8 = \underline{1}, \underline{2}, \underline{4}, \underline{8}$ ◄ List the factors of 8.

$F_{24} = \underline{1}, \underline{2}, 3, \underline{4}, 6, \underline{8}, 12, 24$ ◄ List the factors of 24.
Underline the common factors.

HCF of 8 and 24 is 8. ◄ The highest underlined number in both lists is the HCF.

With word problems, you need to work out whether to use the LCM or HCF to find the answers.

- Problems involving the LCM usually include repeating events. You might be asked how many items you need to 'have enough' or when something will happen again at the same time.
- Problems involving the HCF usually involve splitting things into smaller pieces or arranging things in equal groups or rows.

Finding the HCF and LCM using prime factors

Tip

Use the letters to help you remember what to do. LCM requires the **L**argest set of **M**ultiples.

When you work with larger numbers you can find the HCF and LCM by writing the numbers as products of prime factors, that is, by prime factorisation.

Once you have done that you can use the factors to quickly find the HCF and LCM.

WORKED EXAMPLE 4

Find the HCF and LCM of 72 and 120.

a HCF of 72 and 120.
$72 = \underline{2} \times \underline{2} \times \underline{2} \times \underline{3} \times 3$
$120 = \underline{2} \times \underline{2} \times \underline{2} \times \underline{3} \times 5$

First express each number as a product of prime factors. Underline the common factors.

$2 \times 2 \times 2 \times 3 = 24$
HCF of 72 and 120 is 24.

Write down the common factors and multiply them out.

b LCM of 72 and 120.
$72 = \underline{2} \times \underline{2} \times \underline{2} \times \underline{3} \times \underline{3}$
$120 = 2 \times 2 \times 2 \times 3 \times \underline{5}$

First express each number as a product of prime factors. Underline the largest set of multiples of each factor across **both** lists. Here, 2 appears three times in each list, so underline one set of them. 3 appears twice in the first list, but only once in the second, so underline the top set of 3s. 5 only appears in the bottom list, so underline it there.

$2 \times 2 \times 2 \times 3 \times 3 \times 5 = 360$
LCM of 72 and 120 is 360.

Write down each set of underlined multiples and multiply them out.

EXERCISE 4D

1 **a** What is the LCM of 5, 3 and 2?
Choose from the following options.
  A 30   B 15   C 10   D 6

b Which number is not a factor of 42?
Choose from the following options.
  A 6   B 7   C 8   D 14

2 Find the LCM of the numbers given.
  a 9 and 18   **b** 12 and 18   **c** 15 and 18   **d** 24 and 12
  e 36 and 9   **f** 4, 12 and 8   **g** 3, 9 and 24   **h** 12, 16 and 32

3 $50 = 2 \times 5^2$ and $36 = 2^2 \times 3^2$.
What is the LCM of 50 and 36?
Choose from the following options.
  A $2 \times 3 \times 5$ B $2 \times 2^2 \times 3^2 \times 5^2$
  C $2^2 \times 3^2 \times 5^2$ D $3^2 \times 5^2$

4 Find the LCM and the HCF of the following numbers by using prime factors.
  a 27 and 14   **b** 85 and 15   **c** 96 and 27   **d** 53 and 16
  e 674 and 72   **f** 234 and 66   **g** 550 and 128   **h** 315 and 275

5 A roll of red fabric is 72 metres long.
A roll of yellow fabric is 90 metres long.
Sian wants to cut equal lengths of red and yellow fabric with as little waste as possible.

What is the longest possible length the pieces can be?

Find answers at: cambridge.org/ukschools/gcsemaths-studentbookanswers

6 Every 30th shopper gets a £10 voucher.
Every 120th shopper gets a free meal.

How many shoppers must there be before one receives both a voucher and a free meal?

7 Amanda has 40 pieces of fruit and 100 sweets.
She gives each student an equal number of pieces of fruit and an equal number of sweets.

What is the largest possible number of students in her class?

8 Samir and Li walk in opposite directions around a track.
They start at the same point at the same time.
It takes Samir 5 minutes to walk round the track.
It takes Li 4 minutes.

How long will it be before they meet again at the starting point?

9 Lana cycles every 2nd day.
Pete cycles every 3rd day.
Karen cycles every 4th day.
Anna cycles every 5th day.

They all cycle on 1 January this year.

a After how many days will they all cycle on the same day again?

b How many times a year will they all cycle on the same day?

10 Mr Abbot has three pieces of ribbon of different lengths:

2.4 m   3.18 m   4.26 m

He wants to cut the ribbons into pieces that are all the same length, with the least possible waste.

What is the greatest possible length for the pieces?

11 One warning light flashes every 20 seconds.
Another warning light flashes every 30 seconds.
They flash together at 4.30 pm.

When will they next flash at the same time?

12 Fran cycles round a track and completes a lap in 20 seconds.
Ayuba runs and completes a lap in 84 seconds.
Claire goes round the track in her wheelchair, taking 105 seconds.

They start at the same place at the same time.

a How long will it take for all three athletes to be at the same point again?

b How many laps will they each have completed?

13 Mr Smith tiles a rectangular floor with dimensions 4.2 m × 8.1 m.
He uses a whole number of identical square tiles.
He wants the tiles to be as large as possible.

a Find the area of the largest possible tile in cm².

b How many of these tiles will Mr Smith need to tile the floor?

14 At a relief centre, supplies are handed out equally to a number of people. On one day, 284 items of clothing, 426 food packets and 710 bottles of water are handed out.

How many people were in the relief centre on that day?

Checklist of learning and understanding

Types of numbers

- Even numbers are multiples of 2; odd numbers are not.
- Factors are numbers that divide exactly into a number.
- Prime numbers have only two factors: 1 and the number itself.
- Square numbers are the product of a number and itself ($n \times n$).
- Cube numbers are the product of a number multiplied by itself twice ($n \times n \times n$).
- The value of a digit depends on its place in the number.

Prime numbers

- If a factor is a prime number it is called a prime factor.
- Whole numbers can be written as the product of their prime factors.
- The prime factors are found by:
  - repeated division by prime numbers (starting from 2 and working upwards)
  - using a factor tree and breaking down factors until they are all prime factors.

Multiples and factors

- The lowest common multiple (LCM) of two numbers can be found by:
  - listing the multiples of both numbers and selecting the lowest multiple that appears in both lists
  - finding the largest set of multiples of each of the prime factors and multiplying them together.
- The highest common factor (HCF) of two numbers can be found by:
  - listing the factors of both numbers and selecting the highest factor that appears in both lists
  - finding the common prime factors and multiplying them together.

Chapter review

For additional questions on the topics in this chapter, visit GCSE Mathematics Online.

1 Is 149 a prime number?

Give reasons for your answer.

2 Which number is both a factor and a multiple of 12?

Choose from the following options.

A 12   B 24   C 4   D 3

3 Complete the crossword puzzle provided by your teacher.

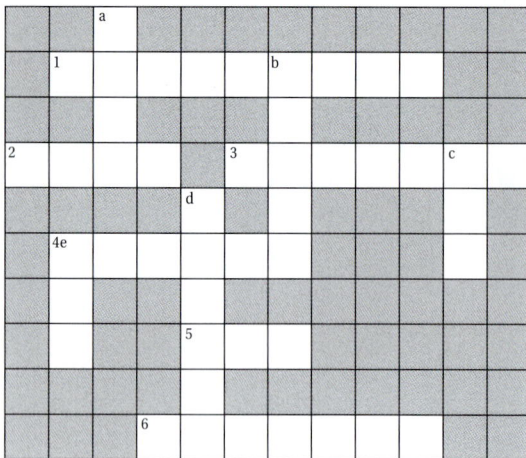

Clues

Across

1 The times tables are examples of these.

2 Whole numbers divisible by 2.

3 Another word used for factor.

4 Numbers in the sequence 1, 4, 9, 16, ...

5 An even prime number.

6 The result of a multiplication.

Down

a $n \times n \times n$ is the __ of n.

b Numbers with only two factors.

c Whole numbers that are not exactly divisible by 2.

d Number that divides into another with no remainder.

e HCF of 12 and 18.

4 Find the HCF and the LCM of 20 and 35 by listing the factors and multiples.

5 a Write 36 as the product of prime factors.

Give your answer in index form. *(3 marks)*

b Work out the Highest Common Factor (HCF) of 36 and 81. *(2 marks)*

© AQA 2013

6 Express 800 as a product of prime factors.

Give your final answer in index form.

7 Work out the HCF and LCM of the following by prime factorisation.

a 72 and 108

b 84 and 60

8 Jo jumped 2 steps at a time on a flight of stairs.

Mo jumped 3 steps at a time.

Jenny jumped 4 steps at a time.

They started together on the bottom step.

What is the first step they will **all** jump on together?

9 Nick starts an exercise programme on 3 March.

He decides to swim every third day and to cycle every fourth day.

On which dates in March will he swim and cycle on the same day?

10 32 boys and 52 girls arrive for a Year 10 sports lesson.

The teacher wants to divide the students into the greatest possible number of groups.

He also wants to make sure that the boys and girls are equally spread out among the groups.

How many boys and girls are in each group?

5 Working with fractions

In this chapter you will learn how to ...

- recognise equivalence between fractions and mixed numbers.
- carry out the four basic operations on fractions and mixed numbers.
- express one quantity as a fraction of another.

For more resources relating to this chapter, visit GCSE Mathematics Online.

Using mathematics: real-life applications

Nurses and other medical support staff work with fractions, decimals, percentages, rates and ratios every day. They calculate medicine doses, convert between different systems of measurement and set the patients' drips to supply the correct amount of fluid per hour.

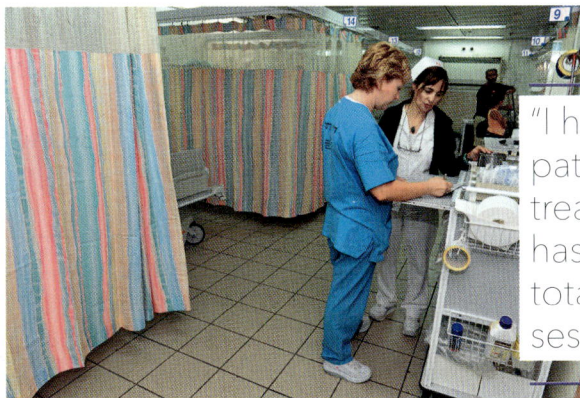

"I have to work out a treatment plan for patients who are going to have radiation treatment for various cancers. The patient has to receive a certain fraction of the total dose of radiation at each treatment session."

(Oncologist)

Before you start ...

KS3 Ch 4	Check that you can find common factors of sets of numbers.	**1** From this set of numbers, choose numbers that have: 18 24 27 28 30 32 36 **a** a common factor of 9 **b** common factors 2 and 3 **c** common factors 3, 4, and 12 **d** common factors of 3 and 6.
KS3 Ch 4	Find the lowest common multiple of sets of numbers.	**2** Choose the lowest common multiple of each set of numbers. **a** 5 and 10 A 15 B 50 C 10 D 20 **b** 8 and 12 A 12 B 96 C 36 D 24 **c** 2, 3 and 5 A 1 B 30 C 10 D 6
KS3 Ch 1	Know the correct order for performing operations. (BODMAS)	**3** Which calculation is correct in each pair? Why?

	Student A	Student B
a	$-3 - 2 \times -6 - 4 = 5$	$-3 - 2 \times -6 - 4 = 50$
b	$-60 \div 5 + 3 \times -4 - 8 = 28$	$-60 \div 5 + 3 \times -4 - 8 = -32$
c	$13 - 2 \times -6 - 5 \times 4 = 80$	$13 - 2 \times -6 - 5 \times 4 = 5$

Find answers at: cambridge.org/ukschools/gcsemaths-studentbookanswers

Assess your starting point using the Launchpad

STEP 1

1 Which fraction does not belong in each set?

a $\dfrac{3}{15}, \dfrac{1}{5}, \dfrac{6}{30}, \dfrac{5}{35}, \dfrac{4}{20}$ **b** $\dfrac{4}{7}, \dfrac{8}{14}, \dfrac{12}{21}, \dfrac{9}{16}, \dfrac{52}{91}$

c $\dfrac{22}{10}, \dfrac{11}{4}, 2\dfrac{3}{4}, \dfrac{33}{12}, 2\dfrac{18}{24}$

GO TO
Section 1:
Equivalent fractions

STEP 2

2 Each calculation contains a mistake.
Find the mistake and write the correct answer.

a $\dfrac{2}{3} + \dfrac{3}{4} = \dfrac{5}{7}$ **b** $\dfrac{4}{5} - \dfrac{9}{10} = \dfrac{1}{10}$

c $\dfrac{2}{7} \times \dfrac{4}{5} = \dfrac{6}{35}$ **d** $30 \div \dfrac{1}{2} = 15$

GO TO
Section 2:
Using the four operations
with fractions

STEP 3

3 Which is greater in each pair?

a $\dfrac{5}{8}$ of 40 or $\dfrac{3}{5}$ of 60   **b** $\dfrac{3}{4}$ of 240 or $\dfrac{7}{10}$ of 300

c $\dfrac{1}{4}$ of $\dfrac{1}{2}$ or $\dfrac{1}{2}$ of $\dfrac{3}{4}$

4 Sammy read 45 pages of a 240 page book.
What fraction of the book remains unread?

5 What fraction of 30 minutes is 45 seconds?

GO TO
Section 3:
Finding fractions of a
quantity

GO TO

Chapter review

Section 1: Equivalent fractions

Equivalent fractions are equal in value.

For example, $\frac{1}{4}$, $\frac{2}{8}$ and $\frac{16}{64}$ are equivalent.

You can find equivalent fractions by multiplying the numerator and denominator by the same number.

You can also find equivalent fractions by dividing the numerator and denominator by the same number (cancelling).

This is known as simplifying, or reducing the fraction to simplest terms.

When you give an answer in the form of a fraction, you usually give it in simplest form.

$$\frac{6}{18} = \frac{1}{3} \qquad \frac{12}{27} = \frac{4}{9} \qquad 3\frac{5}{50} = 3\frac{1}{6}$$

When you are asked to compare fractions that look different, you can write them both with the same denominators so that you can compare them by size, or you can cross multiply to find out whether they are equivalent or not.

WORKED EXAMPLE 1

Are the following pairs of fractions equivalent or not?

a $\frac{5}{6}$ and $\frac{7}{8}$ b $3\frac{3}{4}$ and $\frac{45}{12}$

Method 1: Using common denominators

a $\frac{5}{6} = \frac{20}{24}$ and $\frac{7}{8} = \frac{21}{24}$ — Write both fractions with the same denominator.

$\frac{5}{6} \neq \frac{7}{8}$ — When the fractions have the same denominator it is easy to see whether they are equivalent or not.

It is also easy to compare them by size.

b $3\frac{3}{4} = \frac{15}{4}$ — Write the mixed number as an improper fraction.

$\frac{15}{4} = \frac{45}{12}$ — Write $\frac{15}{4}$ with a denominator of 12, or write $\frac{45}{12}$ with a denominator of 4.

So the fractions are equivalent.

Method 2: By cross multiplying

a $\frac{5}{6} \times \frac{7}{8}$

$5 \times 8 = 40$

$6 \times 7 = 42$

$40 \neq 42$

$\therefore$ the fractions are not equivalent.

40 is also smaller than 42, so $\frac{5}{6} < \frac{7}{8}$

This is a useful strategy for comparing the size of fractions.

b $3\frac{3}{4} = \frac{15}{4}$ — Write the mixed number as an improper fraction.

$\frac{15}{4} \times \frac{45}{12}$

$15 \times 12 = 120 + 60 = 180$

$4 \times 45 = 2 \times 90 = 180$

$180 = 180$ — $\therefore$ the fractions are equivalent.

Key vocabulary

common denominator: a number into which all the denominators of a set of fractions divide exactly

Tip

You can use the LCM of the denominators to find a common denominator, but any common denominator works (not just the lowest).

Find answers at: cambridge.org/ukschools/gcsemaths-studentbookanswers

EXERCISE 5A

1 **a** Which fraction is greater than $\frac{5}{8}$?

Choose from the following options.

   A $\frac{1}{2}$ B $\frac{2}{3}$ C $\frac{5}{9}$ D $\frac{6}{12}$

b Which fraction is smaller than $\frac{2}{3}$?

Choose from the following options.

   A $\frac{3}{2}$ B $\frac{3}{4}$ C $\frac{2}{5}$ D $\frac{20}{30}$

c What is the simplest form of $\frac{28}{32}$?

Choose from the following options.

   A $\frac{2}{3}$ B $\frac{6}{5}$ C $\frac{7}{8}$ D $\frac{14}{16}$

2 Work out whether the following pairs of fractions are equivalent (=) or not (≠).

  a $\frac{2}{5}$ and $\frac{3}{4}$ **b** $\frac{2}{3}$ and $\frac{3}{4}$ **c** $\frac{3}{8}$ and $\frac{5}{12}$ **d** $\frac{2}{11}$ and $\frac{1}{10}$

  e $\frac{3}{5}$ and $\frac{9}{15}$ **f** $\frac{10}{25}$ and $\frac{4}{10}$ **g** $\frac{6}{24}$ and $\frac{5}{20}$ **h** $\frac{11}{9}$ and $\frac{121}{99}$

3 Find the equivalent fractions of $\frac{1}{4}$ with:

  a denominator 32   **b** numerator 48

  c numerator 27   **d** denominator 52.

4 How could you find the missing values in examples like these?

  a $\frac{3}{5} = \frac{18}{x}$ **b** $\frac{y}{51} = \frac{2}{17}$

5 Reduce the following fractions to their simplest form.

  a $\frac{3}{15}$ **b** $\frac{4}{6}$ **c** $\frac{25}{100}$ **d** $\frac{5}{10}$

  e $\frac{4}{12}$ **f** $\frac{-7}{21}$ **g** $\frac{36}{-24}$ **h** $\frac{60}{100}$

  i $\frac{-14}{-21}$ **j** $\frac{18}{27}$ **k** $\frac{15}{21}$ **l** $\frac{-18}{-42}$

6 Write each set of fractions in ascending order.

  a $\frac{3}{5}, \frac{1}{4}, \frac{9}{4}, 1\frac{3}{4}, \frac{4}{7}$ **b** $\frac{5}{6}, \frac{3}{4}, \frac{11}{3}, \frac{19}{24}, 2\frac{2}{3}$ **c** $2\frac{3}{7}, \frac{1}{7}, \frac{7}{7}, \frac{8}{14}, \frac{10}{21}, \frac{13}{7}$

EXERCISE 5B

A mediant fraction is a fraction that lies between two other fractions.

They follow the general rule:

If $\frac{a}{b}$ and $\frac{c}{d}$ are two fractions, then the fraction $\frac{a+c}{b+d}$ lies between them such that

$$\frac{a}{b} < \frac{a+c}{b+d} < \frac{c}{d}$$

1 Use this general rule to find a fraction between:

    a $\frac{1}{4}$ and $\frac{3}{5}$ **b** $\frac{4}{5}$ and $\frac{9}{11}$

2 Show how you could apply the rule to find three fractions between $\frac{1}{3}$ and $\frac{3}{4}$

3 Test your results to show that the answers are correct.

4 How does this work?

    Find out what you can and try to write down the general rule in simple terms.

> **Tip**
>
> Mediant fractions should not be confused with the median value in a set of data. These concepts are not related.

Section 2: Using the four operations with fractions

Multiplying fractions

To multiply fractions, multiply the numerators and then multiply the denominators.

WORKED EXAMPLE 2

Calculate   **a** $\frac{3}{4} \times \frac{2}{7}$ **b** $\frac{5}{7} \times 3$ **c** $\frac{3}{8} \times 4\frac{1}{2}$

a $\frac{3}{4} \times \frac{2}{7} = \frac{3 \times 2}{4 \times 7}$ Multiply numerators by numerators and denominators by denominators.

$= \frac{6}{28}$

$= \frac{3}{14}$ Give the answer in its simplest form.

b $\frac{5}{7} \times 3 = \frac{5 \times 3}{7 \times 1}$ Think of a whole number as a fraction with a denominator of 1.

$= \frac{15}{7}$ $\frac{15}{7}$ cannot be simplified further but it can be written as a mixed number.

$= 2\frac{1}{7}$

c $\frac{3}{8} \times 4\frac{1}{2} = \frac{3}{8} \times \frac{9}{2}$ Rewrite the mixed number as an improper fraction.

$= \frac{27}{16}$ $\frac{27}{16}$ cannot be simplified but it can be written as a mixed number.

$= 1\frac{11}{16}$

> **Tip**
>
> You can cancel before you multiply to make it easier to work out the answers.

If possible, cancel before you multiply to make the calculations easier.

Adding and subtracting fractions

To add or subtract fractions they must have the same denominators.

Find a common denominator and then find the equivalent fractions before you add or subtract the numerators.

Tip

Think of $\frac{3}{7}$ and $\frac{2}{7}$ as 3 lots of 7ths and 2 lots of 7ths. If you combine them, you have 5 lots of 7ths, or $\frac{5}{7}$

You never add the denominators.

WORKED EXAMPLE 3

Simplify **a** $\frac{1}{2}+\frac{1}{4}$ **b** $2\frac{1}{2}+\frac{5}{6}$ **c** $2\frac{3}{4}-1\frac{5}{7}$

a $\frac{1}{2}+\frac{1}{4}$

$=\frac{2}{4}+\frac{1}{4}$ Write $\frac{1}{2}$ as its equivalent of $\frac{2}{4}$. Use 4 as a common denominator.

$=\frac{3}{4}$ Add the numerators.

b $2\frac{1}{2}+\frac{5}{6}$

$=\frac{5}{2}+\frac{5}{6}$ Rewrite mixed number as improper fraction.

$=\frac{15}{6}+\frac{5}{6}$ Find a common denominator.

$=\frac{20}{6}$ Add the numerators.

$=\frac{10}{3}$ or $3\frac{1}{3}$ Simplify the answer.

c $2\frac{3}{4}-1\frac{5}{7}$

$=\frac{11}{4}-\frac{12}{7}$ Rewrite mixed numbers as improper fractions.

Find a common denominator.

$=\frac{77}{28}-\frac{48}{28}$ Subtract the numerators.

$=\frac{29}{28}$ or $1\frac{1}{28}$ Simplify the answer.

Dividing fractions

To divide one fraction by another fraction you multiply the first fraction by the **reciprocal** of the second fraction.

To find the reciprocal of a fraction you invert it.

So, the reciprocal of $\frac{3}{4}$ is $\frac{4}{3}$ and the reciprocal of $\frac{7}{4}$ is $\frac{4}{7}$

The reciprocal of a whole number is a unit fraction.

For example, the reciprocal of 3 is $\frac{1}{3}$ and the reciprocal of 12 is $\frac{1}{12}$

Key vocabulary

reciprocal: the value obtained by inverting a fraction. Any number multiplied by its reciprocal is 1.

WORKED EXAMPLE 4

Simplify   **a** $\frac{3}{4} \div \frac{1}{2}$ **b** $1\frac{3}{4} \div 2\frac{1}{3}$ **c** $\frac{6}{7} \div 3$

a $\frac{3}{4} \div \frac{1}{2}$

$= \frac{3}{4} \times \frac{2}{1}$ Multiply by the reciprocal of $\frac{1}{2}$.

$= \frac{6}{4}$

$= \frac{3}{2}$ or $1\frac{1}{2}$

Simplify the answer.

b $1\frac{3}{4} \div 2\frac{1}{3}$

$= \frac{7}{4} \div \frac{7}{3}$ Convert mixed numbers to improper fractions.

$= \frac{7}{4} \times \frac{3}{7}$ Multiply by the reciprocal of $\frac{7}{3}$.
Cancel the 7s.

$= \frac{3}{4}$

c $\frac{6}{7} \div 3$

$= \frac{6}{7} \times \frac{1}{3}$ Multiply by the reciprocal of 3.

$= \frac{6}{21}$

$= \frac{2}{7}$ Simplify the answer.

The rules for order of operations and negative and positive signs also apply to calculations with fractions.

EXERCISE 5C

1 Simplify:

a $\frac{3}{4} \times \frac{2}{5}$ **b** $\frac{1}{5} \times \frac{1}{9}$ **c** $\frac{5}{7} \times \frac{1}{5}$

d $\frac{7}{10} \times \frac{2}{3}$ **e** $\frac{1}{5} \times \frac{3}{8} \times \frac{-5}{9}$ **f** $\frac{2}{3} \times \frac{-3}{4} \times \frac{-4}{5}$

g $\frac{1}{2} \times \frac{2}{3} \times \frac{4}{11}$ **h** $\frac{5}{8} \times \frac{3}{7} \times \frac{2}{3}$ **i** $\frac{4}{25} \times \frac{-3}{5} \times \frac{-7}{8}$

j $\frac{9}{20} \times \frac{10}{11} \times \frac{1}{12}$ **k** $1\frac{2}{9} \times 1\frac{5}{22} \times 1\frac{1}{6}$ **l** $\frac{2}{7} + \frac{1}{2}$

m $\frac{1}{2} + \frac{1}{4}$ **n** $\frac{5}{8} - \frac{1}{4}$ **o** $\frac{7}{9} - \frac{1}{3}$

p $4\frac{3}{4} + \frac{15}{6}$ **q** $8\frac{2}{5} - 3\frac{1}{2}$ **r** $7\frac{1}{4} - 2\frac{9}{10}$

s $9\frac{3}{7} - 2\frac{4}{5}$ **t** $\frac{1}{4} \div \frac{1}{4}$ **u** $\frac{1}{8} \div \frac{7}{9}$

v $\frac{2}{11} \div \frac{-3}{5}$ **w** $3\frac{1}{5} \div 2\frac{1}{2}$ **x** $1\frac{7}{8} \div 2\frac{3}{4}$

Find answers at: cambridge.org/ukschools/gcsemaths-studentbookanswers

2 **a** Which expression is equivalent to $\frac{2}{3} \div \frac{1}{4}$?

Choose your answer from the following options.

A $\frac{2}{3} \times \frac{1}{4}$ B $\frac{3}{2} \times \frac{1}{4}$ C $\frac{2}{3} \times \frac{4}{1}$ D $\frac{3}{2} \times \frac{4}{1}$

b Which expression is equivalent to $\frac{5}{8} \div 3\frac{3}{4}$?

Choose the correct answer from the options below.

A $\frac{1}{8}$ B $\frac{1}{6}$ C $\frac{1}{4}$ D $\frac{1}{3}$

3 What should be added to $4\frac{3}{5}$ to get $9\frac{7}{20}$?

4 What should be subtracted from $13\frac{3}{4}$ to get $5\frac{1}{3}$?

5 Subtract the product of $\frac{1}{6}$ and $20\frac{4}{7}$ from the sum of $4\frac{7}{9}$ and $5\frac{5}{18}$.

6 Simplify:

a $4 + \frac{2}{3} \times \frac{1}{3}$

b $2\frac{1}{8} - (2\frac{1}{5} - \frac{7}{8})$

c $\frac{3}{7} \times (\frac{2}{3} + 6 \div \frac{2}{3}) + 5 \times \frac{2}{7}$

d $2\frac{7}{8} + (8\frac{1}{4} - 6\frac{3}{8})$

e $\frac{5}{6} \times \frac{1}{4} + \frac{5}{8} \times \frac{1}{3}$

f $(5 \div \frac{3}{11} - \frac{5}{12}) \times \frac{1}{6}$

g $(\frac{5}{8} \div \frac{15}{4}) - (\frac{5}{6} \times \frac{1}{5})$

h $(2\frac{2}{3} \div 4 - \frac{3}{10}) \times \frac{3}{17}$

i $(7 \div \frac{2}{9} - \frac{1}{3}) \times \frac{2}{3}$

j $(\frac{5}{9} \times \frac{27}{35}) \div \frac{6}{9} + \frac{2}{3}$

k $1\frac{2}{3} \div \frac{5}{6} \times \frac{24}{35} \times \frac{1}{3}$

l $2\frac{1}{9} + [3\frac{20}{27} + \{\frac{5}{14} - (\frac{3}{35} - \frac{3}{7}) - \frac{1}{5}\} \times \frac{7}{9}]$

EXERCISE 5D

1 A petrol tank with a capacity of 55 litres is $\frac{3}{4}$ full.

How many litres are there in the tank at present?

Choose your answer from the options below.

A $13\frac{3}{4}$ B $18\frac{1}{3}$ C $41\frac{1}{4}$ D $73\frac{1}{3}$

2 Kevin is a deep-sea diver.

He spends:

$9\frac{3}{4}$ minutes swimming to a wreck;

$12\frac{5}{6}$ minutes exploring the wreck;

and $3\frac{5}{6}$ minutes examining corals.

How much time has he spent underwater in total?

Tip

Remember that addition and subtraction are inverse operations.

Tip

Remember that the rules for order of operations apply to fractions as well. Simplify brackets first, then powers, then multiplication and/or division, then addition and/or subtraction. When there is more than one set of brackets, work from the inner ones to the outer ones.

3 In a public park:

$\frac{2}{3}$ of the area is grassed;

$\frac{1}{5}$ is taken up by flower beds;

and the rest is paved.

How much of the park area is paved?

4 The perimeter of a quadrilateral is $18\frac{23}{60}$ m.

The lengths of three sides are $6\frac{1}{6}$ m, $7\frac{2}{3}$ m and $1\frac{2}{15}$ m.

Find the length of the other side.

5 A tank contains $\frac{7}{30}$ of a litre of water.

The water is removed at a rate of $\frac{3}{5}$ of a litre per minute.

How long will it take to remove all the water?

6 There are $1\frac{3}{4}$ cakes left over after a party.

These are shared out equally amongst six people.

What fraction of a cake does each person get?

7 A container holds $5\frac{2}{3}$ litres of juice.

A set of cups hold $\frac{2}{15}$ of a litre each.

How many cups will the container fill?

8 Nico buys six trays of chicken pieces for his restaurant.

Each tray contains $2\frac{1}{2}$ kg of chicken.

Each chicken meal served uses $\frac{3}{8}$ kg of chicken.

How many meals can he serve?

9 A mountaineer inserts a bolt into the rock face every $5\frac{3}{4}$ metres she climbs.

She uses 32 bolts.

What is the maximum height she has climbed?

10 Ted has marked out three lengths of wood.

Length C is $\frac{2}{3}$ of the length of B.

Length B is $1\frac{1}{3}$ times as long as A.

A is $\frac{97}{3}$ m long.

What is the length of piece C?

Find answers at: cambridge.org/ukschools/gcsemaths-studentbookanswers

11 Triangle ABC is isosceles with a perimeter of $12\frac{3}{4}$ cm.

BC is $2\frac{11}{12}$ cm.

Find the length of sides AB and AC.

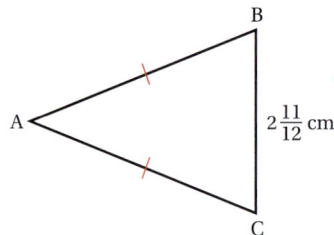

12 What is the length of the side of a square of perimeter $9\frac{3}{7}$ m?

13 Salma read $\frac{2}{9}$ of her book on Saturday, $\frac{1}{6}$ on Sunday and $\frac{5}{12}$ on Monday.

  a What fraction of the book does she still have to read?

  b If there are still 49 pages left for her to read, how many pages in total are in the book?

Section 3: Finding fractions of a quantity

Expressing one quantity as a fraction of another

The numerator in a fraction tells you how many parts of the whole quantity you are dealing with.

The denominator represents the whole quantity.

So, the fraction $\frac{3}{5}$ means you are dealing with 3 parts of the 5 parts that make up the whole.

To write a quantity as a fraction of another quantity make sure the two quantities are in the same units and then write them as a fraction and simplify.

WORKED EXAMPLE 5

a What fraction is 20 minutes of 1 hour?

b Express 35 centimetres as a fraction of a metre.

a 20 minutes is the part of the whole, so it is the numerator.

The hour is the whole, so it is the denominator.

20 minutes is part of 60 minutes: $\frac{20}{60} = \frac{2}{6} = \frac{1}{3}$

20 minutes is $\frac{1}{3}$ of an hour.

Decide which time is the numerator and which is the denominator.

You cannot form a fraction using one unit for the numerator and another for the denominator, so you need to convert the hour to minutes.

b 35 cm is the part of the whole, so it is the numerator.

The metre is the whole, so it is the denominator.

35 cm is part of 100 cm: $\frac{35}{100} = \frac{7}{20}$

35 cm is $\frac{7}{20}$ of a metre.

You cannot use centimetres and metres in the same fraction, so you convert 1 m to 100 cm.

EXERCISE 5E

1 Calculate:

a $\frac{3}{8}$ of 144 **b** $\frac{4}{5}$ of 180 **c** $\frac{1}{2}$ of $\frac{3}{4}$ **d** $\frac{1}{3}$ of $\frac{3}{10}$

e $\frac{4}{9}$ of $\frac{3}{14}$ **f** $\frac{1}{4}$ of $2\frac{1}{2}$ **g** $\frac{3}{4}$ of $2\frac{1}{3}$ **h** $\frac{5}{6}$ of $3\frac{1}{2}$

2 Choose your answer from the options given.

a What is $\frac{7}{12}$ of 768?

  A 64 B $109\frac{7}{12}$ C 448 D $537\frac{1}{2}$

b How many minutes is $\frac{3}{2}$ of $2\frac{3}{10}$ hours?

  A 204 min B 205 min C 206 min D 207 min

3 Calculate the following quantities.

a $\frac{1}{2}$ of $1\frac{1}{2}$ cups of sugar **b** $\frac{3}{4}$ of $2\frac{1}{3}$ cups of flour **c** $\frac{2}{3}$ of $1\frac{1}{2}$ cups of sugar

d $\frac{2}{3}$ of 4 hours **e** $\frac{1}{3}$ of $2\frac{1}{2}$ hours **f** $\frac{3}{4}$ of 5 hours

g $\frac{1}{3}$ of $\frac{3}{4}$ of an hour **h** $\frac{2}{3}$ of $3\frac{1}{2}$ minutes **i** $\frac{3}{15}$ of a minute

4 Express the first quantity as a fraction of the second.

a 12p of every £1 **b** 35 cm of a 2 m length

c 12 mm of 30 cm **d** 45 minutes per 8 hour shift

e 5 minutes per hour **f** 150 m of a kilometre

g 45 seconds of 30 minutes **h** 575 ml of 4 litres

5 In a Year 10 group, $\frac{1}{3}$ of the students like maths. Of those who like maths, $\frac{1}{3}$ also like music.

What fraction of the Year 10 group likes both maths and music?

6 Jess spent $1\frac{3}{5}$ hours online in four days.

If she spends the same amount of time online each day, how many minutes does she spend online?

7 The area of the floor in a room is 12 m².

Pete buys a rug that is 110 cm wide and 160 cm long.

What fraction of the area of the floor will be covered by this rug?

8 A technical college has 8400 books in their library.

$\frac{1}{7}$ are general reference books, $\frac{3}{7}$ are technology related and $\frac{4}{35}$ are engineering related. The rest are computer related.

Find the total number of books in each category.

9 A section of road $1\frac{1}{2}$ km long is to be tarred.

$\frac{1}{6}$ is tarred in Week 1, and $\frac{3}{5}$ is tarred in Week 2.

The rest is completed in Week 3.

Calculate the length of road tarred in each week.

Find answers at: cambridge.org/ukschools/gcsemaths-studentbookanswers

10 60 000 people pass through an airport in one week.

$\frac{1}{6}$ are travelling first class, $\frac{1}{4}$ are travelling business class, and

$\frac{3}{8}$ are travelling in economy class.

The rest are using low-cost tickets.

Work out the number of people travelling in each class.

EXERCISE 5F

The Ancient Egyptians believed that anything other than a unit fraction was unacceptable (a unit fraction has a numerator of 1).

So they wrote all fractions as the sum or difference of unit fractions.

The sum or difference always started with the largest possible unit fraction and they did not allow repetition.

For example, $\frac{2}{3}$ would be written as $\frac{1}{2} + \frac{1}{6}$ and not as $\frac{1}{3} + \frac{1}{3}$

1 Write each of the following as the sum or difference of unit fractions:

a $\frac{5}{8}$ **b** $\frac{3}{5}$ **c** $\frac{2}{7}$ **d** $\frac{2}{9}$ **e** $\frac{3}{10}$

2 Find three unit fractions that have a sum of $\frac{2}{5}$ when added together.

3 Find a unit fraction:
- greater than $\frac{1}{9}$
- with a denominator that is a multiple of 4; and
- which has three other factors.

4 Can all fractions be written as the sum or difference of unit fractions?

Justify your answer.

Checklist of learning and understanding

Equivalent fractions
- Fractions that represent the same amount are called equivalent fractions.
- You can change fractions to their equivalents by multiplying the numerator and denominator by the same value or by dividing the numerator and denominator by the same value (simplifying).

Operations on fractions
- To add or subtract fractions, find equivalent fractions with the same denominator.
- Add or subtract the numerators once the denominators are the same. Do not add or subtract denominators.
- To multiply fractions, multiply numerators by numerators and denominators by denominators.
- To divide fractions, multiply by the reciprocal of the divisor.

Fractions of a quantity
- The word 'of' means multiply.
- A quantity can be written as a fraction of another as long as they are in the same units. Write one quantity as the numerator and the other as the denominator and simplify.

Chapter review

For additional questions on the topics in this chapter, visit GCSE Mathematics Online.

1 What fraction is equivalent to $3\frac{60}{72}$?

Choose your answer from the options below.

A $\frac{138}{72}$ B $\frac{180}{72}$ C $\frac{23}{60}$ D $\frac{23}{6}$

2 Simplify:

a $\frac{15}{90}$ **b** $\frac{195}{230}$ **c** $4\frac{18}{48}$

3 Write each set of fractions in ascending order.

a $\frac{8}{9}, \frac{4}{5}, \frac{5}{6}, \frac{3}{7}$ **b** $2\frac{2}{5}, \frac{23}{7}, 1\frac{3}{5}, \frac{16}{9}$

4 Evaluate:

a $\frac{7}{5} + \frac{3}{8} - \frac{1}{2}$ **b** $\frac{7}{5} \times \frac{3}{8} + \frac{1}{2}$ **c** $\frac{7}{5} \div \frac{3}{8} \times 3$

d $3\frac{1}{17} + 2\frac{2}{5}$ **e** $3\frac{1}{15} - 1\frac{3}{5}$ **f** $\frac{1}{7}$ of $3\frac{3}{4} + \frac{3}{4}$

g $\frac{2}{7} \times \frac{8}{18} \div 3$ **h** $28 \div \frac{3}{4} - \frac{5}{7}$ **i** $\frac{2}{9}$ of $\frac{3}{4} - \frac{1}{8}$

5 Use a calculator to work out the perimeter of the rectangle.

Give your answer as a mixed fraction.

6 Simplify:

a $(\frac{3}{8} \div \frac{13}{4}) + (\frac{5}{9} \times \frac{3}{5})$ **b** $2\frac{2}{3} \times (8 \div \frac{4}{7} + \frac{7}{8})$

c $4\frac{2}{5} + 3\frac{1}{2} + 5\frac{5}{6} - 4\frac{11}{12} + 2\frac{7}{9}$ **d** $(7 \div \frac{2}{9} - \frac{1}{3}) \times \frac{2}{3}$

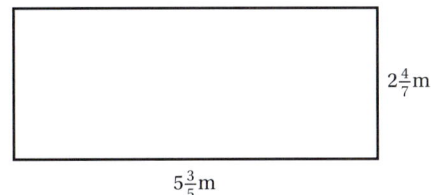

$2\frac{4}{7}$ m

$5\frac{3}{5}$ m

(2 marks)

© AQA 2013

7 Express 425 g as a fraction of $2\frac{1}{2}$ kg.

8 Sandy has $12\frac{1}{2}$ litres of water.

How many bottles containing $\frac{3}{4}$ litre can she fill?

9 A surveyor has to divide a 15 km² area of land into equal plots each measuring $\frac{1}{2}$ km².

How many plots can she make?

10 A ladder $7\frac{2}{10}$ m long is lowered into a manhole.

$\frac{15}{32}$ parts of the ladder are outside the manhole when the bottom of the ladder touches the ground.

How deep is the manhole?

11 Andy uses 2 cups of flour to make 12 muffins.

How many cups of flour would he need to make 20 muffins?

Find answers at: cambridge.org/ukschools/gcsemaths-studentbookanswers

6 Working with decimals

In this chapter you will learn how to ...

- express decimals as fractions and fractions as decimals.
- convert decimals to fractions and fractions to decimals.
- order fractions and decimals.
- carry out the four basic operations on decimals without using a calculator.
- solve problems involving decimal quantities.

For more resources relating to this chapter, visit GCSE Mathematics Online.

Using mathematics: real-life applications

Food technologists analyse the contents of different raw and prepared foods to work out what they contain and how much there is of each ingredient. For example, how much water, protein and fat there is in a cut of meat. They use decimal fractions to give the quantities correct to tenths, hundredths or even smaller parts of a gram.

> **Tip**
>
> You might already know most of the concepts in this chapter. They have been included so that you can revise concepts if you need to and check that you know them well.

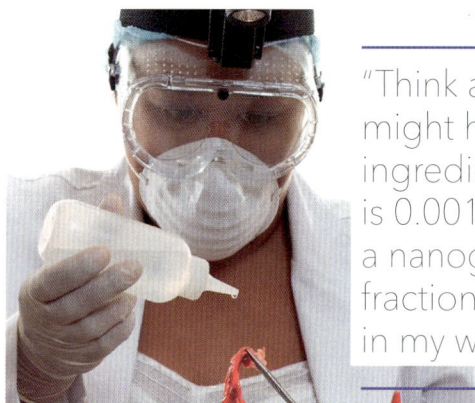

"Think about a product like a vitamin pill. We might have to list the mass of 30 different ingredients in fractions of milligrams. A milligram is 0.001 grams, a microgram (μg) is 0.001 mg and a nanogram (ng) is 0.000 001 mg, so decimal fractions (and negative indices) are very important in my work."

(Food technologist)

Before you start ...

KS3	You need to be able to work confidently with place value.	1	130.098 0.0398 300.098 0.98308 19.308 Choose the number from the box that has a 3 in the: **a** hundreds position **b** hundredths position **c** tenths position **d** thousandths position **e** tens position.
KS3	Check that you can compare decimal fractions and order them by size.	2	Fill in <, = or > between each pair of decimal fractions. **a** 0.65 ☐ 0.7 **b** 0.08 ☐ 0.01 **c** 0.8 ☐ 0.85 **d** 2.87 ☐ 0.99 **e** 4.230 ☐ 4.23
KS3	You need to know the fractional equivalents of some common decimals.	3	Make equivalent pairs by matching the decimals in the top row with the fractions in the bottom row. 	**a** 0.25	**b** 0.375	**c** 0.4	**d** 0.75	**e** 0.5	**f** 0.025	 | $\frac{2}{5}$ | $\frac{3}{4}$ | $\frac{45}{90}$ | $\frac{1}{40}$ | $\frac{4}{16}$ | $\frac{3}{8}$ |

Assess your starting point using the Launchpad

STEP 1

1 Write a decimal that is between:

    a 2.15 and 2.16   **b** 2.155 and 2.156   **c** 0.6753 and 0.6754

2 Write the red digit in each number as a fraction with a denominator of 10, 100 or 1000.

    a 3.0987   **b** 12.342   **c** 0.8865

3 Which is greater in each pair?

    a 3.14 or $3\frac{1}{4}$ **b** 0.78 or $\frac{8}{9}$ **c** $\frac{10}{11}$ or 0.99

GO TO
Section 1:
Review of decimals and fractions

STEP 2

4 Choose the correct answer for each calculation.

Calculation	Possible answers		
a 24 − 2.35	A 2.165	B 216.5	C 21.65
b 19.5 − 3.45	A 16.5	B 1.605	C 16.05
c 2.25 × 3	A 675	B 67.5	C 6.75
d 18.32 × 4	A 732.8	B 73.28	C 7.328
e 7.488 ÷ 6	A 1.248	B 12.48	C 124.8
f 58.35 ÷ 3	A 0.1945	B 1.945	C 19.45

GO TO
Section 2:
Calculating with decimals

STEP 3

5 Convert each of these recurring decimals to an exact fraction in simplest terms.

    a $0.\dot{2}$ **b** $0.1\dot{8}$ **c** $1.2\dot{1}$

GO TO
Section 3:
Converting recurring decimals to exact fractions

GO TO
Chapter review

Find answers at: cambridge.org/ukschools/gcsemaths-studentbookanswers

Section 1: Review of decimals and fractions

The table shows the results of the men's 4 × 100 m relay final at the 2010 Commonwealth Games in New Delhi.

Five teams completed the race.

Team	Time (seconds)
Australia	39.14
Bahamas	39.27
England	38.74
India	38.89
Jamaica	38.79

Comparing decimals

To write the times in order from fastest to slowest, compare the whole number parts of each time first. If those are the same, compare the decimal parts.

England, India and Jamaica ran the relay in 38 seconds and a fraction of a second.

To decide first, second and third places, you need to look at the decimal parts.

Here are the times written in a place value table.

	Tens	Ones/units	.	Tenths	Hundredths
England	3	8	.	7	4
India	3	8	.	8	9
Jamaica	3	8	.	7	9

Start by comparing the tenths, and then the hundredths.

India has the highest number in the tenths place so India came third.

England and Jamaica both have 7 in the tenths place so compare the hundredths.

England has 4 in the hundredths and Jamaica has 9. This means that England was faster.

The places were: England (1st), Jamaica (2nd) and India (3rd), followed by Australia then the Bahamas.

Tip

Remember you are comparing winning times, so you are looking for the smallest fraction of a second as this is the fastest time. The greater the fraction, the slower the team ran.

Converting decimals to fractions

England ran the relay in 38 seconds and $\frac{74}{100}$ of a second.

Tens	Ones/units	.	Tenths	Hundredths
3	8	.	7	4

The fraction can be simplified further: $\frac{74}{100} = \frac{37}{50}$

Any decimal can be converted to a fraction in this way. For example:

$$0.6 = \frac{6}{10} = \frac{3}{5} \qquad 0.25 = \frac{25}{100} = \frac{1}{4} \qquad 0.375 = \frac{375}{1000} = \frac{3}{8}$$

Converting fractions to decimals

Fractions can be converted to decimals. There are different methods of doing this and you should choose the method that is easiest for the fraction involved.

Method 1: Equivalent fractions with denominators of 10, 100, 1000, and so on.	Method 2: Pen and paper division.	Method 3: Calculator division.
Express $\frac{61}{125}$ as a decimal. $\frac{61}{125} = \frac{122}{250} = \frac{244}{500} = \frac{488}{1000}$ $\frac{61}{125} = 0.488$ This method works well if the denominator is a factor of 10, 100 or 1000.	Express $\frac{5}{8}$ as a decimal. Work out $5 \div 8$ using division. insert decimal point so that it aligns with the decimal point in the number you are dividing $\begin{array}{r} 0.625 \\ 8\overline{)5.0} \\ \underline{4.8} \quad 0.6 \times 8 \\ 0.20 \\ \underline{0.16} \quad 0.02 \times 8 \\ 0.040 \\ \underline{0.040} \quad 0.005 \times 8 \\ 0.00 \end{array}$	Express $\frac{2}{3}$ as a decimal. Input $2 \div 3$ on your calculator. [2] [÷] [3] [=] 0.666666666 The 6s continue forever (they recur) show this by writing the answer as $0.\dot{6}$. **Tip** Remember you write a dot above the first and last digit of the recurring numbers if more than one digit recurs.

Tip

When you have to compare and order ordinary fractions you can convert them all to decimals and compare them easily using place value. This is often quicker than changing them all into equivalent fractions with a common denominator.

EXERCISE 6A

1 Which of the following decimals is equivalent to $\frac{6}{24}$?

    A 0.12   B 0.25   C 0.3   D 0.144

2 Write each of the following decimals as a fraction in its simplest form.

    a 0.6   **b** 0.84   **c** 1.64   **d** 0.385   **e** 0.125

    f 1.08   **g** 0.875   **h** 0.008   **i** 3.064   **j** 0.333

3 Convert the following fractions to decimals without using a calculator.

    a $\frac{3}{5}$ **b** $\frac{3}{4}$ **c** $\frac{18}{25}$ **d** $\frac{19}{20}$ **e** $\frac{34}{50}$

    f $\frac{110}{250}$ **g** $\frac{89}{200}$ **h** $\frac{76}{500}$ **i** $\frac{185}{20}$ **j** $\frac{145}{50}$

    k $\frac{11}{6}$ **l** $\frac{3}{8}$ **m** $\frac{9}{4}$ **n** $\frac{8}{9}$ **o** $\frac{19}{8}$

4 Use a calculator to convert the fractions from $\frac{1}{9}$ to $\frac{8}{9}$ into decimal.

    a What pattern do you notice?

    b What is the mathematical name for this type of decimal?

    c Repeat this for the fractions from $\frac{1}{6}$ to $\frac{5}{6}$.

    d Convert $\frac{1}{11}$ and $\frac{2}{11}$ to decimals.

    e Predict what $\frac{3}{11}$ and $\frac{4}{11}$ will be if you convert them to decimals. Check your prediction using a calculator.

5 Arrange the following sets of numbers in order from largest to smallest.

    a 5.2, 5.29, 8.62, 4.92, 4.09   **b** 7.42, 0.76, 0.742, 0.421, 3.219

    c 14.3, 14.72, 14.07, 14.89, 14.009   **d** 0.23, 0.26, 0.273, 0.287, 0.206

    e 0.403, $\frac{1}{2}$, $\frac{2}{3}$, 0.68, 0.45, $\frac{5}{11}$ **f** $\frac{7}{9}$, $\frac{3}{8}$, 0.625, 0.88, 0.718

6 Copy and fill in the boxes using < , = or > to make each statement true.

    a 13.098 ☐ 13.099   **b** 0.312 ☐ 0.322   **c** $\frac{5}{6}$ ☐ 0.84

    d 0.375 ☐ $\frac{3}{8}$ **e** 2.05 ☐ $\frac{205}{1000}$ **f** $\frac{3}{5}$ ☐ 0.7

    g $\frac{2}{5}$ ☐ 0.35   **h** $\frac{18}{25}$ ☐ 0.67   **i** $\frac{1}{3}$ ☐ 0.37

7 Write a decimal fraction that is between each pair of decimals.

    a 3.135 and 3.136   **b** 0.6645 and 06646   **c** 4.998 and 4.999

8   The lengths of some roller coaster rides are given in the table.

Roller coaster	Length of ride (km)
The Beast	2.243
California Screaming	1.851
Formula Rossa	2.0
Fujiyama	2.045
Steel Dragon	2.479
The Ultimate	2.268

a   Which is the longest roller coaster?

b   Which is the shortest roller coaster?

c   Is the Steel Dragon longer or shorter than $2\frac{1}{2}$ km?

d   Which roller coasters are longer than $2\frac{1}{4}$ km?

e   Write the lengths in order from longest to shortest.

Section 2: Calculating with decimals

You need to be able to add, subtract, multiply and divide decimals without using a calculator.

When you calculate with decimals it is useful to estimate the answer so that you can tell whether your solution is reasonable and whether you have the decimal point in the correct place.

Adding and subtracting decimals

Add or subtract decimals in columns by lining up the places and the decimal points.

WORKED EXAMPLE 1

Calculate:

a $12.7 + 18.34 + 3.087$ b $399.65 - 245.175$

a
```
   12.7
   18.34
 +  3.087
   34.127
```
Make sure you line up the decimal points and the place values correctly or you will get the wrong answer.

b
```
   399.650
 - 245.175
   154.475
```
Write a 0 as a place holder here.

Multiplying and dividing decimals

Andy made the following notes about multiplying and dividing decimals when he was studying for exams at the end of last year.

- When multiplying or dividing by a power of 10 (10, 100, 1000, etc):

  Move the digits as many places to the left as the number of zeros when multiplying.

  Move the digits as many places to the right as the number of zeros when dividing.

- When multiplying decimal fractions by decimal fractions:

  Ignore the decimal points and multiply the numbers.

  Place the decimal point in the answer so it has the same name number of digits after the decimal point as there were altogether in the multiplication problem.

- When dividing by a decimal:

  Make the divisor a whole number by multiplying the divisor and the dividend (the number you are dividing into) by the same power of 10.

  Then divide as normal, keeping the decimal point in the answer directly above the decimal point in the number you are dividing.

EXERCISE 6B

1 Work with a partner.

  a Read through Andy's summary notes.

  b Provide one or two examples for each summary point using numbers to show what he means.

  c Write your own summary point for dividing a decimal by a whole number.

  Include two examples that show what you mean.

2 Use a place value chart and provide some examples to show why you can multiply and divide decimals in the way Andy has summarised.

EXERCISE 6C

1 Which of the following is a sensible estimate for the calculation 16.34×1.8?

  A 24.75　　　　B 30　　　　C 35　　　　D 40

2 Estimate the answer then calculate:

  a $0.8 + 0.78$ 　　**b** $12.8 - 11.13$ 　　**c** $0.8 + 0.9$

  d $15.31 - 1.96$ 　　**e** 2.77×8.2 　　**f** 9.81×3.5

3 Evaluate without a calculator:

  a $12.7 + 18.34 + 35.01$ 　　**b** $12.35 + 8.5 + 2.91$ 　　**c** $6.89 - 3.28$

  d $34.45 - 12.02$ 　　**e** $345.297 - 12.39$ 　　**f** $56 + 8.345 - 34.65$

  g $27.4 + 9.01 - 12.451$ 　　**h** 0.786×100 　　**i** 54.76×2000

  j 1.234×0.65 　　**k** 87.87×2.34 　　**l** $1.83 \div 61$

  m $0.358 \div 4$ 　　**n** $5.053 \div 0.62$ 　　**o** $31.72 \div 0.04$

4 The world record for the men's 4 × 100 m relay is 36.84 seconds (Jamaica, 2012).

The Commonwealth Games record is 37.58 seconds (Jamaica, 2014).

a What is the time difference between the world record and the Commonwealth Games record?

b In the 2014 Commonwealth Games, the English team won silver and ran the relay in 38.02 seconds.

How much slower is this than the Commonwealth record?

c Each of the four runners in a relay runs 100 m.

Calculate the average time taken to run 100 m during the world record winning race.

d Does each runner take the same amount of time? Give reasons for your answer.

5 Nadia makes a dish that requires 1.5 litres of cream.

She has four 0.385 litre cartons of cream.

Does she have enough cream?

6 Jai takes a multivitamin every morning.

He calculates that if he takes one tablet every day for a week he will take in:

1166.69 g of vitamin C,

54.6 mg of boron, and

257.95 mg of calcium.

Work out how much of each ingredient there is in a tablet.

7 The Chetty household uses about 25.75 kilowatt-hours of electricity per day.

Calculate how much they will use in:

a one week   **b** one year (not a leap year).

EXERCISE 6D

You may use a calculator in this exercise.

1 Sandra has £87.50 in her purse.

She buys two jumpers that cost £32.99 each.

How much money does she have left? Choose from the options below.

A £21.52   B £30.00   C £54.51   D £153.48

2 George travels from York to Oxford by car.

His odometer reads 123 456.8 km when he leaves York and 123 642.7 km when he arrives in Oxford.

How far did he travel? Give your answer in km.

3 A container holds 5.67 litres of juice.

How many cups containing $\frac{2}{15}$ of a litre each does this fill?

4 Find 0.75 of 2400.

5 Sheldon wants to place fence posts 0.84 m apart along his boundary fence.

The fence is 60 metres long.

How many posts does he need?

6 Jamil bought 6.65 litres of petrol at £1.29 per litre.

What is the total cost of the petrol?

7 Toni earns £28 650 per year.

   a How much is this per day? Remember there are 365.25 days in a year.

   b How much is this per five-day week? Give your answer to two decimal places.

   c If Toni is paid the amount in part **b** every week for 52 weeks of a year, will she earn more or less than the original total? Give reasons for your answer.

Section 3: Converting recurring decimals to exact fractions

There are three types of decimal:
- exact or terminating decimals such as 0.25 and 0.375
- non-terminating and recurring decimals in which a set of digits repeats to infinity
- other decimals that are non-terminating and non-recurring (irrational numbers) such as π (3.141592654...) and $\sqrt{2}$ (1.414213562...).

EXERCISE 6E

How do you know whether a fraction will give you a terminating or recurring decimal?

1 Nazeem says you can work this out by writing the denominator of the fraction as the product of its prime factors.

Any denominator that has only 2s and/or 5s as prime factors will produce a terminating decimal.

All the others will produce recurring decimals.

Do you agree?

Test Nazeem's hypothesis and state whether it is correct or not.

2 Andy says Nazeem is wrong and he uses sixths to show this:

$6 = 2 \times 3$, so it should produce recurring decimals according to Nazeem. But $\frac{3}{6}$ gives an exact decimal of 0.5, so Nazeem is wrong.

Consider Andy's argument and use it to adapt Nazeem's hypothesis so that it holds for fractions such as $\frac{3}{6}$ as well.

Writing decimals as fractions in the form $\frac{a}{b}$

Exact and recurring decimals can be written as fractions in the form $\frac{a}{b}$, so that they are rational numbers.

You cannot convert a recurring decimal to a fraction by writing it with a denominator that is a power of 10.

You cannot give it a denominator with an infinite number of zeros.

To convert a recurring decimal to an exact fraction you can set up a pair of equations using the decimal and then use algebra to solve for x.

WORKED EXAMPLE 2

Convert each of the following recurring decimals to fractions:

a $0.\dot{4}$ **b** $0.\dot{2}\dot{4}$ **c** $0.2\dot{3}$

a Let $x = 0.444...$ (1)
Then $10x = 4.444...$ (2)
Subtract (1) from (2).
$10x - x = 4.444 - 0.444$
$9x = 4$
Divide both sides by 9 to get x.
So, $x = \frac{4}{9}$

> This gets rid of the recurring digits.

b Let $x = 0.\dot{2}\dot{4}$ (1)
Then $100x = 24.\dot{2}\dot{4}$ (2)
Subtract (1) from (2).
$99x = 24.\dot{2}\dot{4} - 0.\dot{2}\dot{4}$
$99x = 24$
So, $x = \frac{24}{99} = \frac{8}{33}$

c Let $x = 0.2\dot{3}$ (1)
Then $10x = 2.\dot{3}$ (2)
And $100x = 23.\dot{3}$ (3)
Subtract (2) from (3).
$100x - 10x = 23.\dot{3} - 2.\dot{3}$
$90x = 21$
So, $x = \frac{21}{90} = \frac{7}{30}$

> Note that you need three equations here to get the recurring part on its own after the decimal point.

When you convert recurring decimals:

- Multiply by 10^n, where n = the number of recurring decimals, to find the second equation.
- Always give your answer in the simplest form.

EXERCISE 6F

1 Express each rational number as a decimal:

a $\frac{3}{8}$ b $\frac{5}{16}$ c $\frac{5}{11}$ d $\frac{4}{9}$

e $\frac{18}{7}$ f $\frac{7}{15}$ g $\frac{32}{7}$ h $\frac{11}{7}$

2 Express each decimal as a rational number:

a 0.888...   b 2.777...   c 0.812 812...   d 3.454 545...

e 1.999...   f 0.6565...   g 0.277 777...   h 2.499 999...

3 Write each of the following as an exact fraction in its simplest form:

a $0.\dot{4}$ b $0.7\dot{4}$ c $0.8\dot{7}$ d $0.11\dot{4}$

e $0.94\dot{3}$ f $0.\dot{1}85\dot{7}$ g $4.\dot{5}6\dot{7}$ h $0.11\dot{3}$

4 What is the exact length of line AC in this diagram?

EXERCISE 6G

1 Write the following pairs of decimals as pairs of fractions in the form $\frac{a}{b}$:

a 0.3 and $0.\dot{3}$ b 0.17 and $0.1\dot{7}$ c 0.173 and $0.1\dot{7}\dot{3}$

2 Use your results to make a rule for writing recurring decimals as fractions.

3 Test your rule using a few examples of your own.

Comment on what you find.

Calculator tip

Most calculators cannot deal with recurring fractions such as $0.\dot{1}$ (although they can easily deal with 0.1), so you have to know how to convert these to exact fractions using algebra.

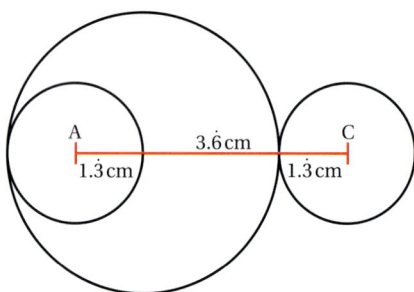

A —— 3.6 cm —— C, 1.3 cm and 1.3 cm

Checklist of learning and understanding

Decimals and fractions

- You can express decimals as fractions by writing them with a denominator that is a power of ten and then simplifying them. For example, $0.4 = \frac{4}{10} = \frac{2}{5}$
- You can change fractions to decimals by dividing the numerator by the denominator. For example, $\frac{3}{4} = 3 \div 4 = 0.75$
- Changing ordinary fractions to decimals makes it easier to compare their sizes using place value.

Calculations with decimals

- Pen and paper methods are important in the non-calculator exam paper.
- You can use any method as long as you show your working.
- Decimals can be added and subtracted by lining up the places and the decimal points.
- Decimals can be multiplied like whole numbers. You need to insert the decimal point so there are the same number of decimal places in the answer as there were altogether in the numbers being multiplied.
- Decimals can be divided by making the divisor a whole number (multiply both numbers by a power of ten to do this). Then divide as normal, keeping the decimal point in the answer directly above the decimal point in the number you are dividing.

Recurring decimals

- Recurring decimals can be written as fractions in the form $\frac{a}{b}$. To do this, set up a pair of equations and subtract to get rid of the recurring digits, then simplify to get an answer.

Chapter review

For additional questions on the topics in this chapter, visit GCSE Mathematics Online.

1 Arrange each set of numbers in order from smallest to largest.

   a 4.2, 4.8, 4.22, 4.97, 4.08

   b 2.96, 2.955, $2\frac{46}{50}$, $2\frac{9}{25}$, 2.12

   c $\frac{3}{4}$, 0.86, $\frac{4}{5}$, 0.78, $\frac{5}{6}$, 0.91

2 Here are four rods.

A	B	C	D
3.4 m	$3\frac{1}{4}$ m	3.35 m	3.1 m

Not drawn accurately

   a Which rod is the longest? *(1 mark)*

   b Work out the total length of rod C and rod D. *(1 mark)*

   c Which three rods have a total length of 10 metres? *(2 marks)*

   © AQA 2013

3 Convert each fraction to a decimal and insert <, = or > to compare the fractions.

   a $\frac{3}{5} \square \frac{12}{30}$ **b** $\frac{5}{6} \square \frac{7}{11}$ **c** $\frac{2}{9} \square \frac{1}{3}$

4 Write each as a fraction in its simplest form.

   a 0.88   **b** 2.75   **c** 0.008

5 **a** Increase $\frac{2}{5}$ by 2.75   **b** Reduce 91.07 by half of 42.8

   c Divide 4 by 0.125   **d** Multiply 0.4 by 0.8

6 **a** Add 4.726 and 3.09   **b** Subtract 2.916 from 4.008

   c Multiply 8.76 by 100   **d** Divide 18.07 by 1000

   e Multiply 4.12 by 0.7   **f** Simplify $\frac{32.64}{2.4}$

7 Mike had a 0.75 litre tin of varnish. He used half of the tin on his desk and 0.3 of the tin on a small table.

   What fraction of the varnish was left over?

8 Jarryd and Kate have £16 each. Jarryd spends 0.416 of his money and Kate spends $\frac{4}{15}$ of hers.

   Who has the most money left? How much more?

9 Convert each recurring decimal to a fraction in its simplest form:

   a $0.\dot{2}$ **b** $0.5\dot{4}$ **c** $4.8\dot{5}$ **d** $2.4\dot{3}\dot{8}$

Find answers at: cambridge.org/ukschools/gcsemaths-studentbookanswers

7 Basic algebra

In this chapter you will learn how to ...

- use algebraic notation and write algebraic expressions.
- simplify and manipulate algebraic expressions.
- use common factors to factorise expressions.
- use algebra to solve problems in different contexts.

For more resources relating to this chapter, visit GCSE Mathematics Online.

Using mathematics: real-life applications

Algebra lets you describe and represent patterns using concise mathematical language.

This is useful in many different careers including accounting, navigation, building, plumbing, health, medicine, science and computing.

"You are unlikely to think about algebra when you watch cartoons or play video games, but animators use complex algebra to program the characters and make objects move." *(Games designer)*

Before you start ...

KS3	You need to understand the basic conventions of algebra.	**1** Choose the correct way to write each of these.
		
		 a $n \times n$ A $2n$ B n^2 C 2^n D $2(n)$
		
		 b c multiplied by 3 and then added to 5
		    A $3c + 5$ B $3(c + 5)$ C $c + 15$
		
		 c n squared and then multiplied by 2
		    A $2n^2$ B $(2n)^2$ C $4n^2$

KS3	You should be able to substitute numbers for letters and evaluate expressions.	**2 a** Evaluate the following expressions for $n = 5$ and $n = -5$. **i** $3n + 4$ **ii** $3(n + 4)$ **b** What is the value of $\dfrac{(2 + 4)^2}{6}$?

Ch 4	You should be able to find the highest common factor in a group of terms.	**3** Write down the HCF of:
		    a $12xy$ and $18y^2$
		    b $45x$ and $50xy$

	You need to know how to apply the rules of indices to simplify expressions.	**4** Match the simplified expressions (**A–D**) to the mathematical statements **a–d**:
		    a $a^m \times a^n$ **b** $a^m \div a^n$ **c** $(a^m)^n$ **d** a^0
		    A 1 **B** a^{m-n} **C** a^{m+n} **D** $a^{m \times n}$

Assess your starting point using the Launchpad

STEP 1

1 Use the correct notation and conventions to write each statement as an algebraic expression.

a Multiply n by 3 and add 4 to the result.

b Subtract 4 from n and multiply the result by 3.

c Multiply n squared by 4, add 3 and divide the result by 2.

?

GO TO
Section 1:
Algebraic notation

STEP 2

2 Simplify these expressions by collecting like terms.

a $3a + 2b + 2a - b$ **b** $4x + 7 + 3x - 3 - x$

c $4a^2 + 8ab - 10a^2 - 5ab$

?

GO TO
Section 2:
Simplifying expressions

STEP 3

3 Expand and simplify:

a $m(n - p)$ **b** $3(x + 5) + 4(x + 2)$ **c** $2z(z + 4) - z(z + 5)$

?

GO TO
Section 3:
Expanding brackets

STEP 4

4 Complete the following.

a $3x + 12 = \boxed{}(x + 4)$ **b** $5x + 10y = \boxed{}(x + 2y)$

c $x^2 - 3x = \boxed{}(x - 3)$ **d** $ab - ac = a(\boxed{} - \boxed{})$

e $-x + 7x^2 = -x(\boxed{}\boxed{}\boxed{})$

5 Factorise each expression.

a $2x + 4y$ **b** $-3x - 9$ **c** $5x + 5y$

?

GO TO
Section 4:
Factorising expressions
Section 5:
Solving problems using algebra

GO TO
Chapter review

Find answers at: cambridge.org/ukschools/gcsemaths-studentbookanswers

Section 1: Algebraic notation

In algebra you use letters to represent unknown numbers.

For example: $x + y = 20$

The letters can represent many different values so they are called **variables**.

Letters and numbers can be combined and linked together with operation signs to form **expressions** such as $5a^3 - 2xy + 3$.

This expression has three **terms**.

The sign belongs with the term that follows it.

Terms should always be written in the simplest way:

You write $a \times b$ as ab and $5 \times z$ as $5z$

$2 \times h$ is written as $2h$

$x \times x \times y$ is written as x^2y

$4x \div 3$ is written as $\dfrac{4x}{3}$

$(x + 4) \div 2$ is written as $\dfrac{x + 4}{2}$

The symbol $\equiv$ means exactly the same as, or identical to. The following are examples of **identities**.

$a \times b \equiv ab$ and $5 \times z \equiv 5z$

$a \div b \equiv \dfrac{a}{b}$ and $5 \div z \equiv \dfrac{5}{z}$

EXERCISE 7A

1 Write the algebraic expression for:

  a x multiplied by 3 and added to y multiplied by 7.

  b 4 subtracted from x squared and the result multiplied by 5.

  c x cubed added to y squared and the result divided by 4.

  d 6 added to x and the result multiplied by 4, then minus y.

  e x multiplied by itself and then divided by 2.

  f Five less than three-fifths of a number.

2 A number x is divided by 3 and the answer is squared.

  Choose the correct expression from the following options.

  A $\dfrac{x^2}{3}$ B $\dfrac{x}{9}$ C $\dfrac{x^2}{9}$ D $9x^2$

3 Use algebraic notation to write simply each of the following in its simplest form:

  a $2 \times 3a$ **b** $4b \times 5$ **c** $d \times (-9)$

  d $4a \times 3b$ **e** $5c \times 2d$ **f** $-3m \times 4n$

  g $-2p \times (-3q)$ **h** $a \times a$ **i** $m \times m$

  j $2a \times 4a$ **k** $-3a \times 5a$ **l** $-2m \times (-4m)$

  m $7a \times 8ab$ **n** $-6cd \times (-2de)$ **o** $2a \times 2a \times 2a$

Key vocabulary

variable: a letter representing an unknown number

expression: a group of numbers and letters linked by operation signs

term: a combination of letters and/or numbers. Each number in a sequence is called a term.

identity: an equation that is true no matter what values are chosen for the variables

Tip

When you have numbers and letters in a term, the number is written first and the letters are usually written in alphabetical order.

So, you write $5x$ not $x5$ and $3xy$ not $3yx$.

4 Match the statements (**a–i**) to their correct algebraic expression from (**A–I**).

a Take a number and multiply it by 3, then add 2 to it.	**A** $\dfrac{6x+2}{3}$
b Take a number and add 3 to it, then double it.	**B** $3x+2$
c Take a number and multiply it by itself, then add three to it.	**C** $5(x-4)$
d Add 6 to a number, then divide it by 2.	**D** $(3x)^2$
e Take 4 away from a number all multiplied by 5.	**E** $x^{\frac{2}{3}}$
f Square a number, then multiply by 9.	**F** $2x^2-3x^3$
g Square a number and multiply by 2 and subtract the number cubed multiplied by 3.	**G** $2(x+3)$
h Twice the sum of one third and a number.	**H** $\dfrac{6+x}{2}$
i The cube root of a number multiplied by the square of a number.	**I** x^2+3

5 Write each of the following divisions as simply as possible in its simplest form:

a $15x \div 5$ **b** $27y \div 3$ **c** $24a^2 \div 8$

d $7 \times 15p \div 21$ **e** $24x \div (8 \times 3)$ **f** $18y \div (6 \times 2)$

g $-18x^2 \div 9$ **h** $-16a^2 \div (-4)$ **i** $15 \div (3 \times n \times n)$

6 Simplify:

a $x^6 \times x^7$ **b** $y^4 \times y^9$ **c** $3a^4 \times 5a^5$

d $2x^3 \times 5x^6$ **e** $a^2 \div a^4$ **f** $\dfrac{12b^7}{6b^2}$

g $\dfrac{18p^{10}}{9p^{11}}$ **h** $(x^4)^3$ **i** $(2a^7)^3$

j $4x^2y^3 \times 5xy^4 \div 2x^5y^3$ **k** $5x^0$

> **Tip**
>
> Use the laws of indices for this question:
>
> $a^m \times a^n = a^{m+n}$
>
> $a^m \div a^n = a^{m-n}$
>
> $(a^m)^n = a^{m \times n}$
>
> $a^0 = 1$

7 Simplify $(x^3 \times y^7)^0$.

Choose your answer from the following options.

A xy^{10} B x^3y^7 C 1   D xy^4

8 Write expressions to represent the perimeter and area of each shape:

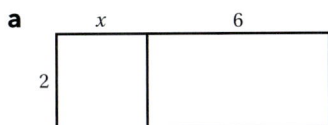

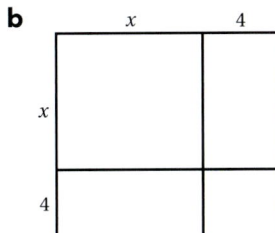

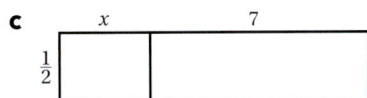

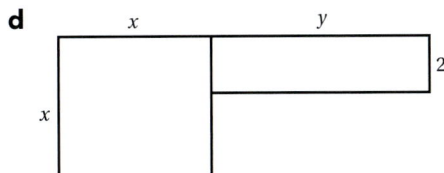

a

b

c

d

9 A man is x years old.

    a How old will he be ten years from now?

    b How old was he ten years ago?

    c His daughter is a third of his age.

       How old is his daughter?

10 A CD and a DVD together cost C pounds.

    a If the CD cost £5, what did the DVD cost?

    b If the DVD cost twice as much as the CD, what did the CD cost?

    c If the CD cost £$(C - 15)$, what did the DVD cost?

Substituting values for unknowns

You can work out the value of an expression if you are told what the letters represent. Working out the value of an expression is called evaluating.

For example, if you know that $x = -2$, then you can work out that:

$$2x + 1 = 2 \times -2 + 1 = -4 + 1 = -3$$

> **Tip**
>
> When you substitute values into a term, such as $2y$, you need to remember that $2y$ means $2 \times y$.
>
> So, if $y = 6$, you need to write $2y$ as 2×6 and not as 26.

> **Tip**
>
> Evaluate means to calculate the value of. This word is often used in examination questions.

> **Tip**
>
> Substitution is an important skill. You will need to substitute values for letters when you work with formulae for perimeter, areas and volumes of shapes and when you solve problems involving Pythagoras' theorem.

WORKED EXAMPLE 1

Given that $a = -2$ and $b = 8$, evaluate:

a ab **b** $3b - 2a$ **c** $2a^3$ **d** $2(a + b)$

a $ab = a \times b$
$= -2 \times 8$
$= -16$

> In algebra ab is the way we write $a \times b$. To evaluate, replace the letters with the values given and complete the calculation.
>
> Be careful to make sure that the sign of the final answer is correct.

b $3b - 2a = 3 \times b - 2 \times a$
$= 3 \times 8 - 2 \times -2$
$= 24 - (-4)$
$= 28$

> Expand the expression and evaluate by substituting values given for the letters a and b.
>
> Be careful with negative signs:
>
> $2 \times -2 = -4$
>
> $-(-4) = 4$
>
> The final answer is $24 + 4 = 28$

c $2a^3 = 2 \times a^3$
$= 2 \times (-2)^3$
$= 2 \times -8$
$= -16$

> Expand the expression and make the given substitution for the value of a.
>
> Be careful when cubing a negative value:
>
> $(-2)^3 = -2 \times -2 \times -2 = 4 \times -2 = -8$

d $2(a + b) = 2 \times (a + b)$
$= 2 \times (-2 + 8)$
$= 2 \times 6$
$= 12$

> Remember to do the calculation in brackets first.

EXERCISE 7B

1 Given that $x = 3$ and $y = 6$, evaluate these expressions.

    a $2x + 3y$ **b** $3x + 2y$ **c** $10y - 2x$ **d** $x + 2y$

    e $6x + y$ **f** $5x - 5y$ **g** $2xy$ **h** $\frac{1}{2}xy$

2 Find the value of each expression when $a = -2$ and $b = 5$.

    a $-5ab + 10$ **b** $-3ab - 6$ **c** $\frac{10}{b}$ **d** $\frac{400}{a}$

    e $\frac{6}{a} - \frac{15}{b}$ **f** $\frac{15}{b} - \frac{24}{2a}$ **g** $8 - 2a + 2b$ **h** $7a - 4 + 2b$

    i $-3a^2$ **j** $4 - 3(ab)^3$ **k** $\frac{3a^2b^4}{2b^3}$ **l** $-12a^2b \div -2ab^2$

3 An expression has two terms. One term is a number and the letter x and the other term a number and the letter y.

    Write two different expressions in x and y, with two terms that evaluate to 37 for given values for x and y. Show by substitution:

    a That the values for x and y can be both positive.

    b That the values for x and y can be both negative.

Section 2: Simplifying expressions

Adding and subtracting like terms

Like terms have exactly the same letters or combination of letters and powers.

You can simplify expressions by adding or subtracting like terms.

$3a$ and $4a$ are **like** terms.

    $3a + 4a = 7a$

$7xy$ and $2xy$ are **like** terms.

    $7xy - 2xy = 5xy$

$5x^2$ and $3x^2$ are **like** terms.

    $5x^2 - 3x^2 = 2x^2$

$5ab^2$ and $2a^2b$ are **not** like terms so $5ab^2 - 2a^2b$ cannot be simplified further.

When an expression contains many different terms you might be able to simplify it by collecting and combining like terms.

> **Tip**
>
> You should always give an answer in its simplest form, even if the question does not ask you to.

WORKED EXAMPLE 2

Simplify $2x - 4y + 3x + y$

$2x - 4y + 3x + y = 2x + 3x - 4y + y$ Rearrange the terms so like terms are together.

Keep the signs with the terms they belong to.

$= 5x - 3y$ Combine the like terms. Remember $y = 1y$.

Find answers at: cambridge.org/ukschools/gcsemaths-studentbookanswers

Multiplication and division

WORKED EXAMPLE 3

Simplify **a** $5 \times 4a$ **b** $2x \times 6y$ **c** $2a^2 \times 7ab$ **d** $12a \div -4$

e $\dfrac{6x^2}{2}$ **f** $\dfrac{-8xy}{-16}$ **g** $\dfrac{12ab^2}{36ab}$

a $5 \times 4a = 20a$

b $2x \times 6y = 12xy$

> Multiply numbers by numbers and write letters in alphabetical order.

c $2a^2 \times 7ab = 14a^3b$

> $a^2 = a \times a$, so $a^2 \times a = a \times a \times a = a^3$

d $12a \div -4 = \dfrac{12a}{-4} = -3a$

> Write the division as a fraction and reduce it to its lowest terms.

e $\dfrac{6x^2}{2} = 3x^2$

> Reduce to lowest terms.

f $\dfrac{-8xy}{-16} = \dfrac{xy}{2}$

> Reduce to lowest terms.

g $\dfrac{12ab^2}{36ab} = \dfrac{b}{3}$

> Write the numerator as b not $1b$ by convention.

EXERCISE 7C

1 Say whether each of these are like or unlike terms.

   a $4a$ and $3b$ **b** $5b$ and $-3b$ **c** $3b$ and $9b$

   d $4p$ and $6p$ **e** $8p$ and $-4q$ **f** $5a$ and $6b$

   g $7mn$ and $3mn$ **h** $4ab$ and $-2ab$ **i** $-6xy$ and $-7x$

   j $9ab$ and $3a$ **k** $9x^2$ and $6x^2$ **l** $6a^2$ and $-7a^2$

2 Simplify:

   a $9x + 4y - 4y - 3x + 5y$ **b** $3c + 6d - 6c - 4d$

   c $2xy + 3y^2 - 5xy - 4y^2$ **d** $2a^2 - ab^2 + 3ab^2 + 2ab$

   e $5f - 7g - 6f + 9g$ **f** $7a^2b + 3a^2b - 4a^2b$

   g $6mn^3 - 2mn^3 + 8mn^3$

3 Copy and complete:

   a $2a + \square = 7a$ **b** $5b - \square = 2b$

   c $8mn + \square = 12mn$ **d** $11pq - \square = 6pq$

   e $4x^2 + \square = 7x^2$ **f** $6m^2 - \square = m^2$

   g $8ab - \square = -2ab$ **h** $-3st + \square = 5st$

4 **a** Simplify $3a + 4b + 4a - 3b$.

Choose your answer from the following options.

A $7ab + 8ba$ B $7a + b$ C $6a + 8b$ D $7a + 7b$

b Simplify $7ab \times 2a$.

Choose your answer from the following options.

A $14ab$ B $9a^2b$ C $14ab^2$ D $14a^2b$

c Simplify $\dfrac{6ab}{4b^2}$

Choose your answer from the following options.

A $3ab$ B $3b$ C $3ab^2$ D $\dfrac{3a}{2b}$

d Simplify $2x^2 + 3xy - -4y^2 + 2xy - -3x^2 + y^2$.

Choose from the following options.

A $5x^2 + 5xy + 5y^2$ B $5xy - -3y^2 + 5x^2$

C $x^2 + y^2 + 5xy$ D $5xy - -x^2 - -3y^2$

5 Copy and complete:

a $8a \times \square = 16a$ **b** $9b \times \square = 18b$

c $8a \times \square = 16ab$ **d** $5m \times \square = 15mn$

e $3a \times \square = 12a^2$ **f** $6p \times \square = 30p^2$

g $-5b \times \square = 10b^2$ **h** $4m \times \square = 12m^2n$

6 Rewrite each expression in its simplest form.

a $7 \times 2x \times -2$ **b** $4x \times 2y \times 2z$ **c** $2a \times 5 \times a$

d $ab \times bc \times cd$ **e** $-4x \times 2x \times -3y$ **f** $\dfrac{1}{4x} \times 4y \times -y$

g $-9x \div 3$ **h** $-24y \div 2x$ **i** $18x^2 \div 6$

7 Simplify:

a $\dfrac{4x}{6}$ **b** $\dfrac{3a}{9}$ **c** $\dfrac{-12m}{18}$ **d** $\dfrac{14p}{21}$

e $\dfrac{22x^2}{33}$ **f** $\dfrac{15xy}{20}$ **g** $\dfrac{12ab}{a}$ **h** $\dfrac{2xy}{6xy}$

Section 3: Expanding brackets

You might need to multiply to remove brackets before you can simplify an expression.

Removing brackets is called **expanding** the expression.

$$2(a + b) = 2 \times a + 2 \times b$$
$$= 2a + 2b$$

To expand an expression such as $2(a + b)$ you multiply each term inside the bracket by the value outside the bracket.

$$-2(a + b) = -2 \times a + (-2 \times b)$$
$$= -2a - 2b$$

Key vocabulary

expanding: multiplying out an expression to get rid of the brackets

Tip

Remember that $2(a + b)$ means $2 \times (a + b)$.

In algebraic notation you don't write the multiplication sign.

Tip

Pay careful attention to the rules for multiplying negative and positive numbers when you multiply out.

Find answers at: cambridge.org/ukschools/gcsemaths-studentbookanswers

WORKED EXAMPLE 4

Expand   **a** $3x(y + 2z)$ **b** $-2x(4 + y)$ **c** $-(3x - 2)$

a $3x(y + 2z) = 3x \times y + 3x \times 2z$

> Remove the brackets and multiply each of the terms inside the brackets by $3x$.

$= 3xy + 6xz$

> Write each of the two terms in the standard simplified form. In algebra we write number and letters next to each other to mean multiplication.

b $-2x(4 + y) = -2x \times 4 + (-2x \times y)$
$= -8x - 2xy$

> Expand the brackets and multiply out the two terms formed.
> Remember the rules for multiplying different signs.

c $-(3x - 2) = -1 \times 3x + (-1 \times -2)$
$= -3x + 2$

> The value in front of this bracket is -1 so each term in the bracket is multiplied by -1 when the brackets are removed.
> Remember the rules for multiplying different signs.

The distributive law states that

$$a(b + c) \equiv ab + ac$$

So:

$$3(2x - 4) \equiv 6x - 12$$

and

$$2x(x - 5) \equiv 2x^2 - 10x$$

Both sides of these expressions are identical no matter what the value of the variable so you can use the $\equiv$ symbol.

If two algebraic expressions are identical, the values calculated will be equal for any numbers substituted for the variables.

Identical expressions are called identities. See key vocabulary in Section 1.

Tip

Remember an identity is true for all values.

WORKED EXAMPLE 5

Use substitution to work out if $(a + b)^2 \equiv a^2 + b^2$ is an identity.

Let $a = 1$ and $b = 2$.

> Choose small values to make your calculations as simple as possible.

$(a + b)^2 = (1 + 2)^2 = (3)^2 = 9$

> Substitute a and b into the left-hand side of the identity.

$a^2 + b^2 = 1^2 + 2^2 = 1 + 4 = 5$

> Substitute a and b into the right-hand side of the identity.

$9 \neq 5$

> The expressions are not identical.

Expanding and simplifying

When you have expanded an expression it might contain like terms.

Add or subtract like terms to simplify the expression further.

You should always give an answer in its simplest form.

EXERCISE 7D

1 Which identity is correct? Choose from these options.

A $2(y-1) - y \equiv 3y - 2$

B $2(y-1) - y \equiv 2y - 2$

C $2(y-1) - y \equiv y - 2$

D $2(y-1) - y \equiv y - 1$

2 Some of these expansions are incorrect.

Check each one and correct those that are wrong.

a $4(a + b) = 4a + b$

b $5(a + 1) = 5a + 6$

c $8(p - 7) = 8p - 56$

d $-3(p - 5) = -3p - 15$

e $a(a + b) = 2a + ab$

f $2m(3m + 5) = 6m^2 + 10m$

g $-6(x - 5) = 6x + 30$

h $3a(4a - 7) = 12a^2 - 7$

i $4a(3a + 5) = 12a^2 + 20a$

j $3x(2x - 7y) = 6x^2 - 21y$

3 Expand and simplify:

a $2(c + 7) - 9$

b $(a + 2) + 7$

c $5(b + 3) + 10$

d $2(e - 5) + 15$

e $3(f - 4) - 6$

f $2a(4a + 3) + 7a$

g $5b(2b - 3) + 6b$

h $2a(4a + 3) + 7a^2$

i $3b(3b - 5) - 7b^2$

4 Expand and simplify:

a $2(y + 1) + 3(y + 4)$

b $2(3b - 2) + 5(2b - 1)$

c $3(a + 5) - 2(a + 7)$

d $5(b - 2) - 4(b + 3)$

e $x(x - 2) + 3(x - 2)$

f $2p(p + 1) - 5(p + 1)$

g $3z(z + 4) - z(3z + 2)$

h $3y(y - 4) + y(y - 4)$

5 The expression in each box is obtained by adding the expressions in the two boxes directly below it.

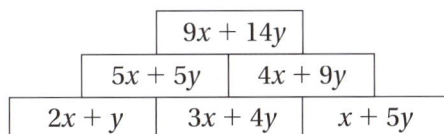

```
                    9x + 14y
             5x + 5y      4x + 9y
        2x + y      3x + 4y      x + 5y
```

Copy and complete these two pyramids.

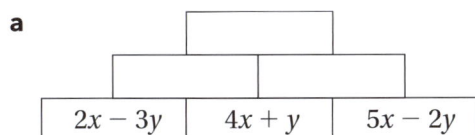

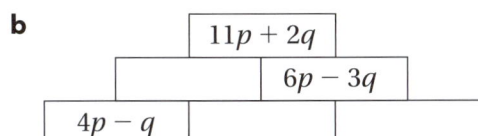

a

```
              _____
         ____       ____
    2x − 3y    4x + y    5x − 2y
```

b

```
         11p + 2q
    ____       6p − 3q
4p − q    ____
```

6 Show that the following expressions are **not** identities.

a $a + a$ and a^2

b $3x + 4 - x + 2$ and $2x + 2$

c $(m + 2)^2$ and $m^2 + 4$

d $\dfrac{x + 4}{3}$ and $x + 1$

Section 4: Factorising expressions

Factorising is the inverse of expanding.

When you factorise an expression you use brackets to write it as a product of its factors.

To factorise $5x + 35$ you find the highest common factor of the terms.

The highest common factor (HCF) of $5x$ and 35 is 5.

The number 5 is written outside the brackets and the remaining factors are written in the brackets:

Multiply out
to expand

$5(x + 7)$ $5x + 35$

Remove the
HCF to factorise

> **Tip**
>
> The highest common factor (HCF) can be a number or a variable. It might also be a negative quantity.

WORKED EXAMPLE 6

Factorise each expression.

a $10a + 15b$ **b** $-2x - 8$ **c** $3x^2 - 6xy$ **d** $3(m + 2) - n(m + 2)$

a $10a + 15b = 5(2a + 3b)$

> HCF of 10 and 15 is 5. There are no common variables.

b $-2x - 8 = -2(x + 4)$

> HCF of −2 and −8 is −2.

c $3x^2 - 6xy = 3x(x - 2y)$

> HCF is $3x$.

d $3(m + 2) - n(m + 2) = (m + 2)(3 - n)$

> This looks like an expansion, but you are asked to factorise!
> $(m + 2)$ is common to both terms, so it is the HCF.

EXERCISE 7E

1 Factorise each expression.

a $2x + 4$

b $12m - 18n$

c $3a - 3b - 6$

d $xy - xz$

e $5xy - 15xyz$

f $14ab - 21bc$

g $pq - pr$

h $x^2 - x$

i $18abc - 12ac$

j $2x^2 - 4xy$

k $2x^2y - 4xy^2$

l $-6a - 12$

m $-3a - 9$

n $-xy - 5x$

o $-x^2 + 6x$

2 Factorise:

a $7x - xy + x^2$ **b** $2xy + 4xz + 10x$ **c** $10x - 5y + 15z$

d $x(x - 2) + 5(x - 2)$ **e** $a(a - 7) - (a - 7)$ **f** $(x - 3) - 3(x - 3)$

g $3x^2y + 6xy^2$ **h** $36x^2 - \frac{1}{4}x^4$ **i** $-ax^2 - ay^2$

> **Tip**
>
> You will learn other methods of factorising expressions in Chapter 16 when you deal with binomials and quadratic equations.

Section 5: Solving problems using algebra

Read through this example to see how algebra can be used to generalise situations and solve problems.

WORKED EXAMPLE 7

Write down an expression for the sum of any three consecutive numbers.

Let the first number be n.
The next number must be 1 more than n, so let it be $n + 1$
The third number is 1 more than $n + 1$, so let it be $n + 1 + 1 = n + 2$
Sum of three consecutive numbers
$= n + n + 1 + n + 2$
$= 3n + 3$

This gives you a general rule for finding the sum of any three consecutive numbers, when the first number, n, is known.

Try it out.

What is the sum of the three consecutive numbers starting at 205?

$3 \times 205 + 3 = 615 + 3 = 618$

Substitute 205 for n in $3n + 3$.

Check: $205 + 206 + 207 = 618$

Check your answer.

Expressions like this are very useful for programmed operations and repeated calculations involving different starting numbers.

EXERCISE 7F

1 Write down whether the following statements are true or false.

a The expression $3z^2 + 5yx - z^2 - 6yx$ simplified is $2z^2 - 11xy$.

b If you expand the brackets $2p(3p + q)$ you get the expression $6p^2 + 2pq$.

c This is a correct use of the identity symbol: $4(a + 1) \equiv 4a + 4$.

d $\frac{4}{x}$ always has the same value as $\frac{x}{4}$.

e x squared and added to 7 with the result divided by 3 is $\frac{x^2 + 7}{3}$.

2 In a magic square the sum of each row, column and diagonal is the same.

State whether the following is a magic square. You must show your working.

$m - p$	$m + p - q$	$m + q$
$m + p + q$	m	$m - p - q$
$m - q$	$m - p + q$	$m + p$

3 **a** Write an expression for each missing length in this rectangle.

b Write an expression for P, the perimeter of the rectangle.

c Given that $a = 2.1$ and $b = 4.5$, calculate the area of the rectangle. (Area = length × breadth)

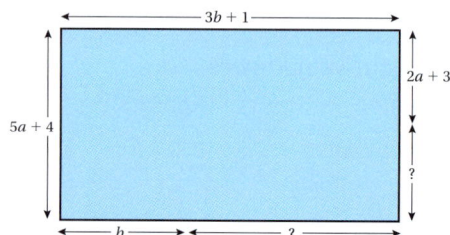

4 **a** The area of a rectangle is $2x^2 + 4x$.

Suggest possible lengths for its sides.

b The perimeter of a rectangle is $2x^2 + 4$.

Suggest possible lengths for its sides.

5 Draw two diagrams representing areas to prove that $(3x)^2$ and $3x^2$ are different.

6 The diagram represents a room with an area of floor covered by carpet (shaded).

Write down different expressions for the floor area that is not covered by carpet.

Multiply out the expressions to confirm that they are equivalent.

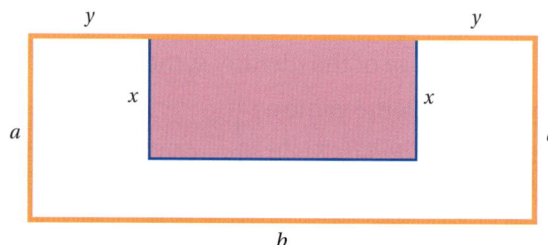

7 In the following pyramids, the number in each cell is made by adding the numbers in the two cells beneath it.

Copy and complete the diagrams.

Write each expression as simply as possible. The first entry in part **a** has been completed in red.

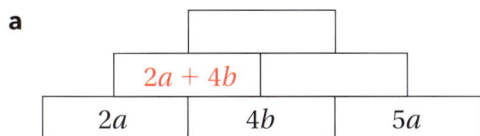

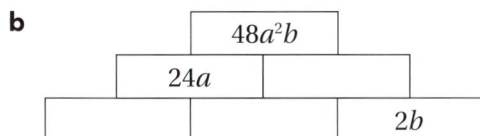

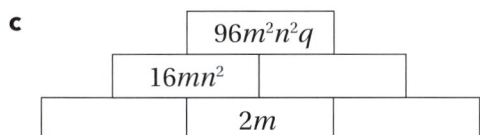

a

$2a + 4b$

| $2a$ | $4b$ | $5a$ |

b

$48a^2b$

$24a$

| | | $2b$ |

c

$96m^2n^2q$

$16mn^2$

| | $2m$ | |

8 **a** Paul plays a 'think of a number game' with his friends.

He predicts what their answer will be.

These are the steps he tells his friends to follow:

Think of a number.

Double it.

Add 6.

Halve it.

Take away the number you first thought of.

Paul then guesses that the answer is 3.

Use algebra to show why Paul will always guess correctly.

b Make up a 'think of a number' problem of your own.

Use algebra to check that it will work and to see which number you end up with.

Try it out with another student to check that it works.

9 The expression $7(x + 4) - 3(x - 2)$ simplifies to $a(2x + b)$.

Work out the values of a and b.

10 Check whether each expression has been fully simplified.

If not, rewrite it in its simplest form.

a $5(g + 2) + 8g = 5g + 10 + 8g$ **b** $4z(4z - 2) - z(z + 2) = 15z^2 - 10z$

c $-5ab \times (-3bc) = 15ab^2c$ **d** $\dfrac{18x^3}{3x} = \dfrac{6x^3}{x}$

e $\dfrac{(x^5 \times x^7)}{x^4} = \dfrac{x^{12}}{x^4}$

11 Simplify:

a $\dfrac{2x}{y^3} + \dfrac{7x}{3y^3}$

b $\dfrac{3a}{b} + \dfrac{5}{2b}$

c $-\dfrac{1}{4}(80x - 320)$

d $-\dfrac{3}{5}\left(\dfrac{a}{3} - \dfrac{2}{3}\right)$

12 Simplify:

a $\dfrac{6x^3y^3}{xy} + \dfrac{2x^3y^2}{y^2} - \dfrac{14x^5y}{2x^2y} + \dfrac{12x^4y^2}{3x^2}$

b $\dfrac{4p^2q^3}{2pq} + 3p^2 - \dfrac{6p^5q^2}{3pq^2} + 5pq^2$

Checklist of learning and understanding

Algebraic notation

- You can use letters (called variables) in place of unknown quantities in algebra.
- An expression is a collection of numbers, operation signs and at least one variable.
- Each part of an expression is called a term.
- To evaluate an expression you substitute numbers in place of the variables.

Simplifying expressions

- Like terms have exactly the same variables.
- Expressions can be simplified by adding or subtracting like terms.

Expanding brackets

- You can multiply and divide unlike terms.
- If an expression contains brackets you multiply them out and then add or subtract like terms to simplify it further.

Factorising

- Factorising involves putting brackets back into an expression.
- If terms have a common factor, write it in front of the bracket and write the remaining terms in the bracket as a factor. You can check by multiplying out.

Solving problems

- Algebra allows you to make general rules that apply to any number. This is useful in problem solving.

Chapter review

For additional questions on the topics in this chapter, visit GCSE Mathematics Online.

1 Expand and simplify:

   a $3b(3b - 5) - 7b^2$

   b $2x(5x + 4) - 6x(3x - 7)$

   c $\frac{3}{4}(p + 2) + \frac{1}{2}(p - 1)$

   d $\frac{2y}{3}(y + 5) + \frac{y}{3}(y - 4)$

2 Two of these expressions have been incorrectly simplified.

Find them and correct them.

   a $2x \times 6y = 12xy$

   b $2a^2 \times 7ab = 14a^3b$

   c $\frac{12a}{4} = 3a$

   d $\frac{6x^2}{2} = 3x^2$

   e $\frac{8xy}{16} = \frac{xy}{4}$

   f $\frac{12ab^2}{36ab} = \frac{b}{3}$

   g $\frac{15}{2x} \times \frac{2}{3x} = \frac{10}{x^2}$

   h $\frac{6a}{7b} \div \frac{2ab}{3} = \frac{9}{7b^2}$

3 Work out by substitution whether the following pairs of expressions are identities. For those that you think are identities, show that the left-hand side is identical to the right-hand side.

   a $5(x + 3)$ and $5x + 3$

   b $-3(m - 2)$ and $-3m - 6$

   c $4(y - 3) + 2(y + 4)$ and $6y - 4$

4 The general rule for adding or subtracting fractions states that:

$$\frac{a}{b} \pm \frac{c}{d} = \frac{(ad \pm bc)}{bd}$$

A student wrote the following:

$$\frac{1}{t} + \frac{1}{w} = \frac{2}{(t + w)}$$

Show that this is incorrect.

5 Prove, using algebra, that the sum of two consecutive whole numbers is always an odd number.

6 Prove algebraically that the difference between the squares of any two consecutive integers is equal to the sum of these two integers.

7 Show that all sides of this quadrilateral could be equal.

(5 marks)

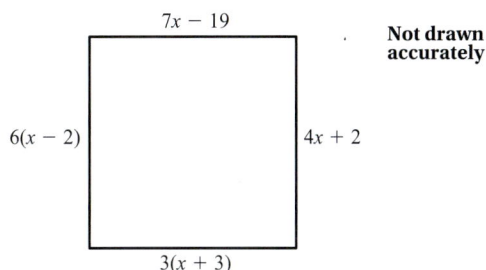

7x − 19

Not drawn accurately

6(x − 2)

4x + 2

3(x + 3)

© AQA 2013

8 Properties of polygons and 3D objects

In this chapter you will learn how to …

- use the correct geometrical terms to talk about lines, angles and shapes.
- recognise and name common 2D shapes and 3D objects.
- describe the symmetrical properties of various polygons.
- classify triangles and quadrilaterals and use their properties to identify them.

For more resources relating to this chapter, visit GCSE Mathematics Online.

Using mathematics: real-life applications

Many people use geometry in their jobs and daily lives. Artists, craftspeople, builders, designers, architects and engineers use shape and space in their jobs, but almost everyone uses lines, angles, patterns and shapes in different ways every day.

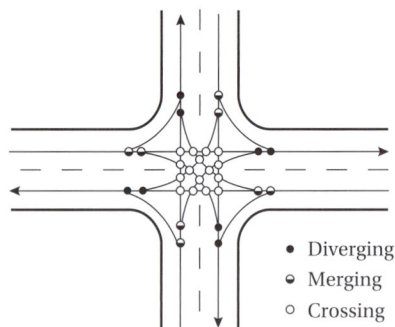

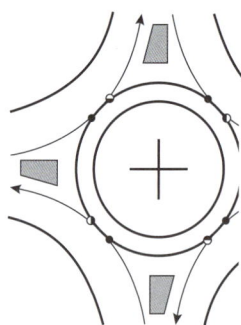

- Diverging
- Merging
- Crossing

"I use a CAD package to plot lines and angles and show the direction of traffic flow when I design new road junctions."

(Civil engineer)

Before you start …

| KS3 | You should be able to use geometrical terms correctly. | **1** Choose the correct labels for each diagram.

base   vertex   acute angle   point

edge   right angle   height   face |
|---|---|---|
| KS3 | You need to be able to recognise and name different types of shapes. | **2 a** Identify three different shapes in this diagram and use letters to name them correctly.

b ABCE is one face of a solid with 8 faces. What type of solid could it be? |

122

Assess your starting point using the Launchpad

STEP 1

1 Look at the shape.

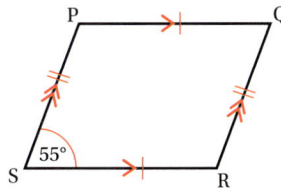

  a What is the mathematical name for this shape?

  b What do the arrow markings on the lines mean?

  c Complete the statement PQ // ☐.

  d Correctly name the angle labelled 55°.

GO TO
Section 1:
Types of shapes

STEP 2

2 How many lines of reflective and rotational symmetry does the capital letter H have?

GO TO
Section 2:
Symmetry

STEP 3

3 Choose the correct terms to name each triangle as accurately as possible.

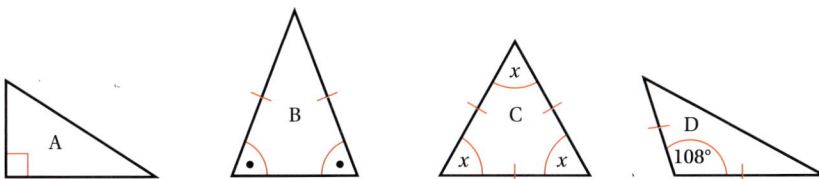

scalene	isosceles	equilateral
right-angled	acute-angled	obtuse-angled

GO TO
Section 3:
Triangles

GO TO
Step 4:
The Launchpad continues on the next page …

Find answers at: cambridge.org/ukschools/gcsemaths-studentbookanswers

Launchpad continued ...

STEP 4

4 Write down the name of a 4-sided shape that has:

a opposite sides equal   **b** all sides equal

c two pairs of parallel sides   **d** four equal angles

e one pair of parallel sides only   **f** no parallel sides.

?

GO TO
Section 4:
Quadrilaterals

STEP 5

5 Copy and complete this table.

Solid	Mathematical name	Number of faces	Number of edges	Number of vertices
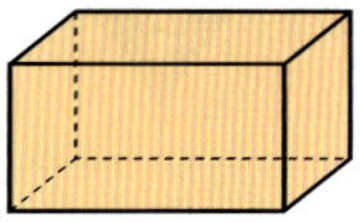				
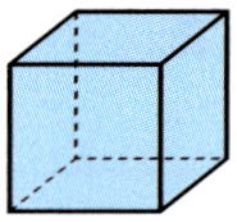				
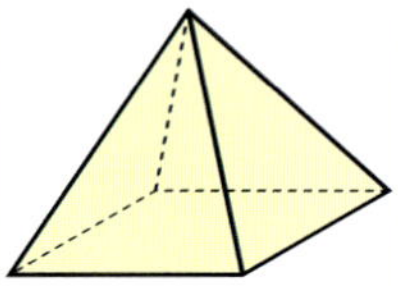				

?

GO TO
Section 5:
Properties of 3D objects

GO TO
Chapter review

Section 1: Types of shapes

Flat shapes are called **plane shapes** or two-dimensional (2D) shapes.

A **polygon** is a closed plane shape with three or more straight sides.

Circles and ellipses (ovals) are plane shapes, but they do not have straight sides, so they are not classified as polygons.

A **regular polygon** has:

- all sides of equal length
- all interior angles of equal size
- all exterior angles of equal size.

The equilateral triangle above is a regular polygon.

If a polygon does not have equal sides and equal angles it is called an **irregular polygon**.

The rectangle above is an irregular polygon because its sides are not all equal in length.

Polygons

Polygons can be named according to the number of sides they have:

Name of polygon	Number of sides	Regular polygon	Irregular polygon
triangle	3		
quadrilateral	4		
pentagon	5		
hexagon	6		
heptagon	7		
octagon	8		
nonagon	9		
decagon	10		

Find answers at: cambridge.org/ukschools/gcsemaths-studentbookanswers

Solids

Solids are three-dimensional (3D) shapes with length, breadth and height.

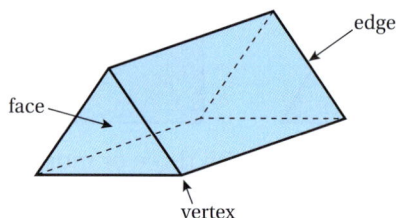

A solid such as the triangular prism above can also be called a **polyhedron**.

Polyhedra are solid shapes with flat faces that are polygons.

Cylinders, spheres and cones are not polyhedra. They are solids with a curved surface.

EXERCISE 8A

1 Write down the mathematical name for each of the following shapes.

   a A plane shape with three equal sides

   b A polygon with five equal sides

   c A polygon with six vertices and six equal angles

   d A plane shape with eight equal sides and eight equal internal angles

2 Give a real-life example of where you might find each of the following.

   a A regular octagon   **b** A cube.

   c A regular quadrilateral   **d** An irregular pentagon

Perpendicular and parallel lines

Perpendicular lines meet at right angles (90°).

The symbol ⊥ means 'perpendicular to'.

In the diagram, AB ⊥ CD.

The shortest distance from a point to a line is the perpendicular distance between them.

Lines are parallel if they are equidistant along their length.

The symbol // means 'parallel to'.

Small arrow symbols are drawn on lines to indicate that they are parallel to each other.

When there is more than one pair of parallel lines in a diagram, each pair is usually given a different set of arrow markings.

In this diagram, AB // DC, AD // HG and EF // HC.

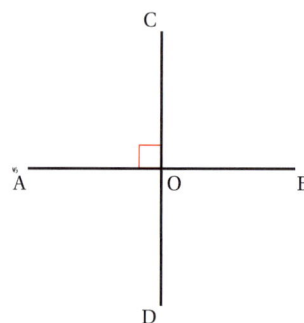

Perpendicular Lines

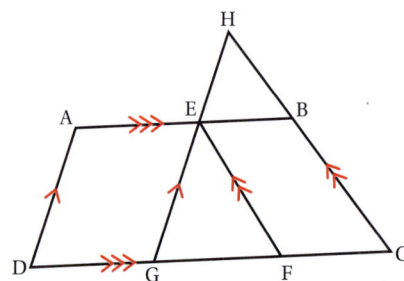

Sides and angles

Shapes are labelled using capital letters on each vertex.

The letters are usually written in alphabetical order as you move round the shape.

This shape would be called △ABC.

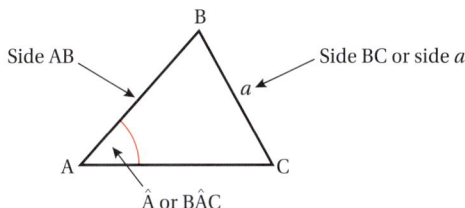

Each side of this triangle can be named using the capital letters on the vertices: AB, BC and CA.

The angles can be named in different ways.

The angle at vertex A can be named A, BAC or CAB.

Symbols can be used to label angles. For example, ∠BAC or BÂC.

Sometimes single letters are used to name the sides.

In this example, side BC can also be called side *a* because it is opposite to angle A.

This convention is often used when you work with Pythagoras' theorem and in trigonometry that both explore angle sizes and lengths of sides in triangles.

Tip

Greek letters are sometimes used to label angles. Don't be surprised to see α (alpha), β (beta), γ (gamma), δ (delta), and θ (theta) used to label angles, particularly in trigonometry.

Marking equal sides and angles

Small lines can be drawn on the sides of a shape to show whether the sides are equal or not.

Sides that have the same markings are equal in length.

Curved lines and symbols such as dots or letters can be used to show whether angles are equal or not.

Angles that are equal have the same marking, symbol or letter.

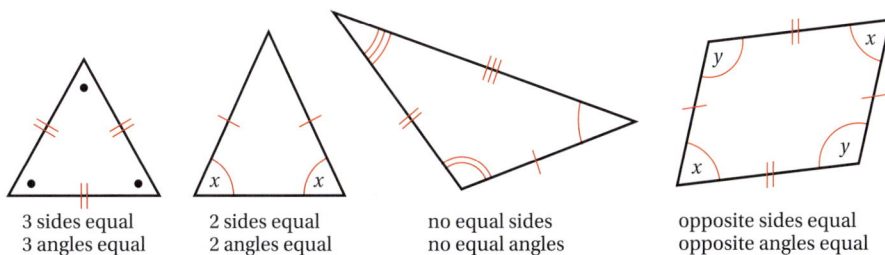

3 sides equal
3 angles equal

2 sides equal
2 angles equal

no equal sides
no equal angles

opposite sides equal
opposite angles equal

EXERCISE 8B

1 Read each clue in Column A. Match it to a term in Column B.

	Column A	Column B
a	A shape that has two fewer sides than an octagon.	decagon
b	A shape that has two sides more than a triangle.	hexagon
c	A shape with four sides.	equilateral triangle
d	An 8-sided shape.	two-dimensional
e	A figure that has length and height.	pentagon
f	A closed plane shape with all sides x cm long and all angles the same size.	quadrilateral
g	A 10-sided figure.	square
h	Another name for a regular 4-sided polygon.	regular polygon
i	The more common name for a regular 3-sided polygon.	octagon

2 Look at this diagram.

Write down whether the following statements are true or false.

a AF // EC.

b △BFD is equilateral.

c CE ⊥ BC.

d AE // BD.

e ABCE is a regular polygon.

f GB // BC.

g In △DHJ, angle H = angle J = angle D.

h △GHJ is a regular polygon.

3 Draw and correctly label a sketch of each of the following shapes.

a A triangle ABC, with angle B = angle C and side AB ⊥ AC.

b A regular four-sided polygon DEFG.

c Quadrilateral PQRS such that PQ // SR but PQ ≠ SR and ∠PSR = ∠QRS.

4 A quadrilateral has both pairs of opposite sides parallel.

Use mathematical reasoning to say why the opposite sides of the shape must also be equal in length.

Section 2: Symmetry

Reflection symmetry

If you can fold a shape in half to create a mirror image (**reflection**) on either side of the fold the shape has reflection symmetry.

The fold is known as the **line of symmetry**.

Each half of the shape is a reflection of the other half so this type of symmetry is also called line symmetry.

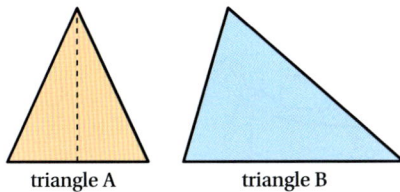

triangle A   triangle B

Triangle A has reflection symmetry. The dotted line is the line of symmetry.

Triangle B is not symmetrical. You cannot draw a line to divide it into two identical parts.

A shape can have more than one line of symmetry.

For example, a regular pentagon has five lines of symmetry.

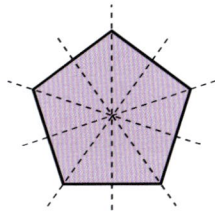

Lines of symmetry can be horizontal, vertical or diagonal.

Rotation symmetry

A shape has **rotation symmetry** if you rotate it around a fixed point and it looks identical in different positions.

The order of rotation symmetry tells you how many times the shape will look identical before it returns to the starting point.

If you have to rotate the shape a full 360° before it appears identical again then it does **not** have rotation symmetry.

> **Key vocabulary**
>
> **reflection**: an exact image of a shape about a line of symmetry (mirror line)
>
> **line of symmetry**: a line that divides a plane shape into two identical halves, each the reflection of the other

> **Tip**
>
> The line of symmetry is sometimes called the mirror line. If you place a small mirror on the line of symmetry you will see the whole shape reflected in the mirror.

> **Key vocabulary**
>
> **rotation symmetry**: symmetry by turning a shape around a fixed point so that it looks the same from different positions

Tip

You will deal with reflections in mirror lines and rotations about a fixed point again in Chapter 33 when you deal with transformations using coordinates.

A square has an order of rotation symmetry of 4 around its centre.

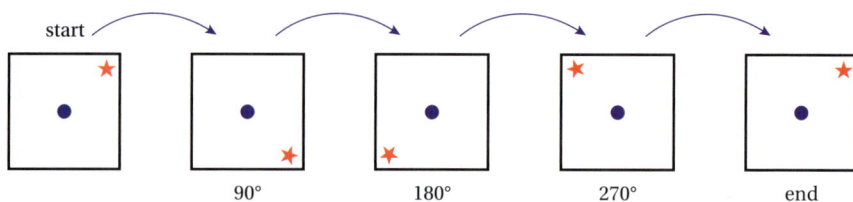

The star shows the position of one vertex of the square as it rotates.

This symbol is the national symbol for the Isle of Man.

It has an order of rotation symmetry of 3 about its centre.

EXERCISE 8C

1 Write down which of the dotted lines in each figure are lines of symmetry.

a

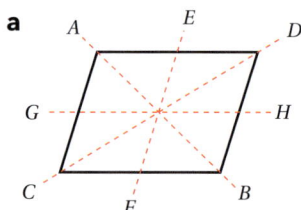

b

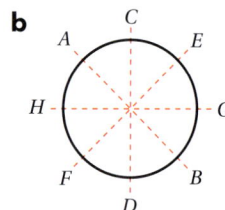

c

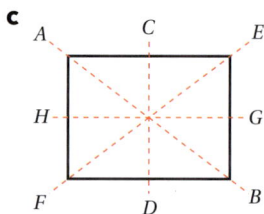

d

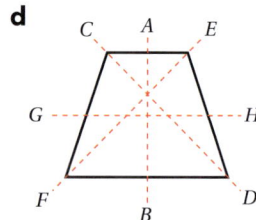

2 How many lines of reflective symmetry does an equilateral triangle have?

Choose from the following options.

A 0   B 3   C 1   D 2

3 Investigate and work out the number of lines of symmetry and the order of rotation symmetry of each shape.

Copy and complete the table to summarise your results.

Shape	Number of lines of symmetry	Order of rotation symmetry
square		
rectangle		
isosceles triangle		
equilateral triangle		
parallelogram		
regular hexagon		
regular octagon		
regular decagon		

4 Give an example of a shape that has rotation symmetry of order 3 but which is not a triangle.

5 Write down which of the following letters has rotation symmetry.

C   H   A   R

6 Describe the symmetry in this design in as much detail as possible.

7 Find and draw five examples of metal alloy rim designs for cars.

For each one, state its order of rotation symmetry.

8 Find and sketch five different symmetrical designs or logos that you can find in your environment.

Label your sketches to indicate how the design is symmetrical.

Section 3: Triangles

The table below summarises the properties of different types of triangles.

Type of triangle	Properties
Scalene	No equal sides. No equal angles. No line of symmetry. No rotation symmetry (or rotation symmetry of order 1).
Isosceles	Two equal sides. Angles at base of equal sides are equal. One line of symmetry. Line of symmetry is perpendicular height. No rotational symmetry (or rotation symmetry of order 1).
Equilateral	All sides equal. Three equal angles, each of 60°. Three lines of symmetry. Rotation symmetry of order 3.
Acute-angled	All angles are less than 90° (acute).
Right-angled	One angle is a right angle (90°).
Obtuse-angled	One angle is greater than 90° (obtuse).

Triangles can be more than one type.

For example, triangle MNO below is right-angled and an isosceles triangle.

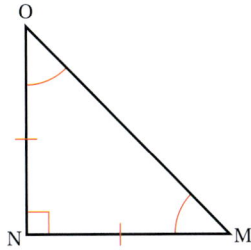

You will need to know and apply the basic properties of triangles when you work with theorems and proofs.

For example, you will use triangle properties extensively when you deal with circle theorems in Chapter 31.

Angle properties of triangles

The angles inside a triangle are called interior angles.

The three interior angles of any triangle always add up to 180°.

If you extend the length of one side of a triangle you form another angle outside the triangle.

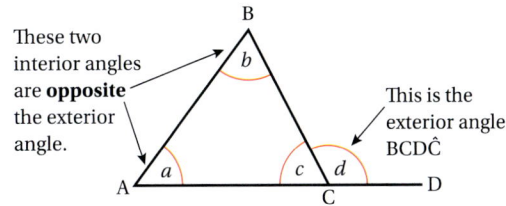

These two interior angles are **opposite** the exterior angle.

This is the exterior angle BCD$\hat{C}$

Tip

You will learn how to prove these properties using mathematical principles in Chapter 9.

Angles formed outside the triangle are called exterior angles.

The exterior angle is equal to the sum of the two interior angles that are opposite it.

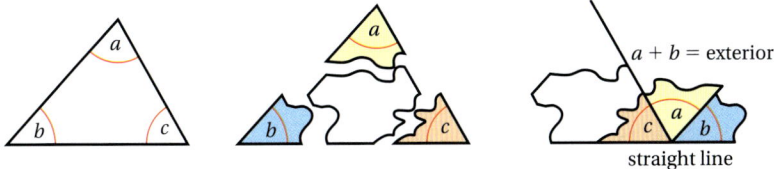

$a + b =$ exterior

straight line

Using the properties of triangles to solve problems

You can use the properties of triangles to solve problems involving unknown angles and lengths of sides.

Problem-solving framework

Triangle ABC is isosceles with perimeter 85 mm.

AB = BC and AC = 25 mm. Angle ABC = 48°.

Find:

a the length of each equal side

b the size of each equal angle.

Steps for solving problems	What you would do for this example
Step 1: Work out what you have to do. Start by reading the question carefully.	You need to use the properties of isosceles triangles and the given information to find the length of two sides and the size of two angles.
Step 2: What information do you need? Have you got it all?	Draw a labelled sketch to see whether you have the information you need.
Step 3: Decide what maths you can use.	Use the values you already have to make equations to find the missing values.
Step 4: Set out your solution clearly. Check your working and that your answer is reasonable.	**a** Perimeter = AC + AB + BC $\qquad\qquad$ = 85 mm So, 85 = 25 + AB + BC 85 − 25 = AB + BC 60 = AB + BC But AB = BC, so AB = BC = 30 mm Check: 30 + 30 + 25 = 85	**b** Let each equal angle be x. 48° + 2x = 180° (angle sum of triangle) 2x = 180° − 48° 2x = 132° x = 66° Check: 66 + 66 + 48 = 180
Step 5: Check that you've answered the question.	Each equal side is 30 mm long. Each equal angle is 66°.	

Tip

You will use these properties often when you deal with trigonometry in Chapter 38.

In many questions you will have to find the size of unknown angles before you can move on and solve the problem.

EXERCISE 8D

1 Without measuring, write down the type of triangle in the diagram.
Give a reason for your answer.

2 Choose the correct type of triangle
from the options given.

A obtuse-angled scalene

B right-angled isosceles

C acute-angled isosceles

D obtuse-angled isosceles

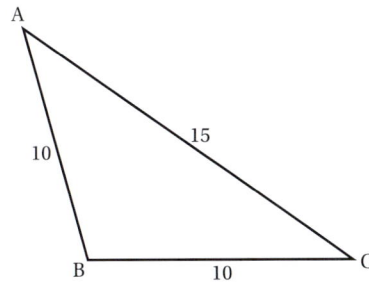

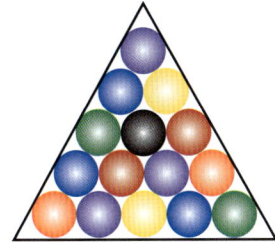

3 Identify which of these triangles are not possible.
Give reasons for your answers.

a An isosceles triangle with an obtuse angle.

b A scalene triangle with two angles > 90°.

c A scalene triangle with three angles, 34°, 64° and 92°.

d An obtuse-angled equilateral triangle.

e An isosceles triangle with side lengths 6.5 cm, 7 cm and 7.5 cm.

4 Two angles in a triangle are 67° and 45°.
What is the size of the third angle?

A 68°   B 136°   C 90°   D 112°

5 A triangle has two angles of 38° and 104°.

a What is the size of the third angle?

b What type of triangle is it?

6 Find the size of the unknown angles in the following diagrams.
Show your working and give mathematical reasons for any deductions
you make.

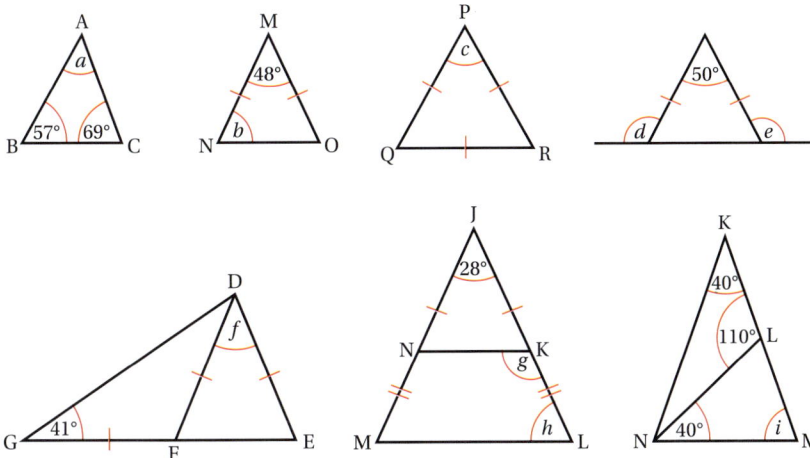

7 The isosceles triangle DEF with DE = EF has a perimeter of 50 mm.
Find the length of EF if:

a DF = 15 mm   b DF = $\sqrt{130}$ c DE = $(3x + 2)$ and DF = $(x + 4)$

Section 4: Quadrilaterals

You need to know the names and basic properties of the quadrilaterals shown in the table.

<table>
<tr><th>Quadrilateral</th><th colspan="2">Properties</th></tr>
<tr>
<td>trapezium</td>
<td></td>
<td><ul><li>One pair of opposite sides are parallel.</li></ul></td>
</tr>
<tr>
<td>kite</td>
<td></td>
<td><ul><li>Two pairs of adjacent sides are equal.</li><li>Diagonals are perpendicular.</li><li>One diagonal bisects the other.</li><li>One diagonal bisects the angles.</li></ul></td>
</tr>
<tr>
<td>parallelogram</td>
<td></td>
<td><ul><li>Both pairs of opposite sides are parallel.</li><li>Both pairs of opposite sides are equal.</li><li>Both pairs of opposite angles are equal.</li><li>Diagonals bisect each other.</li></ul></td>
</tr>
<tr>
<td>rhombus</td>
<td></td>
<td>As for parallelogram, plus:<ul><li>All sides are equal.</li><li>Diagonals bisect at right angles.</li><li>Diagonals bisect the angles.</li></ul></td>
</tr>
<tr>
<td>rectangle</td>
<td></td>
<td>As for parallelogram, plus:<ul><li>All angles are 90°.</li><li>Diagonals are equal in length.</li></ul></td>
</tr>
<tr>
<td>square</td>
<td></td>
<td>As for a rectangle, plus:<ul><li>All sides are equal.</li><li>Diagonals bisect at right angles.</li><li>Diagonals bisect the angles.</li></ul></td>
</tr>
</table>

Key vocabulary

adjacent: next to each other. In shapes, sides that intersect each other are adjacent.

bisect: to divide exactly into two halves

Using the properties of quadrilaterals to solve problems

You can use the given or marked properties of a quadrilateral to identify and name it.

You should always state what properties you are using to justify your answer.

> **WORKED EXAMPLE 1**
>
> A plane shape has two diagonals.
>
> The diagonals are perpendicular.
>
> **a** Write down what shape(s) this could be.
>
> **b** The diagonals are not the same length. Write down what shape(s) it could not be.
>
> **a** Two diagonals means that the shape is a quadrilateral.
> Only the square, rhombus and kite have diagonals that intersect at 90°.
> The shape could be a square, a rhombus or a kite.
>
> **b** Of the three shapes, only the square has diagonals that are equal in length.
> Therefore the shape could not be a square.
>
> Take a systematic approach by working through the properties of quadrilaterals. By a process of elimination you can work through to identify which shape it might be.

The angle sum of quadrilaterals

All quadrilaterals have only two diagonals. If you draw in one diagonal you divide the quadrilateral into two triangles.

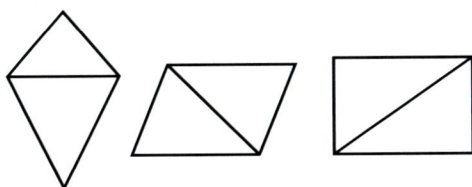

The interior angles of a triangle add up to 180°.

Therefore, the interior angles of a quadrilateral are equal to $2 \times 180° = 360°$.

You can use this property together with the other properties of quadrilaterals to find the size of unknown angles.

WORK IT OUT 8.1

Find the sizes of the missing angles.

Identify the correct solution.

Find the error in the other two.

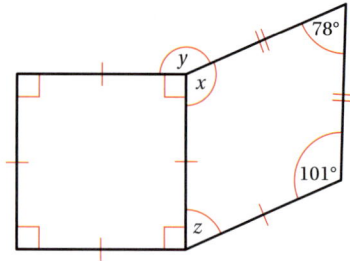

Option A	Option B	Option C
$x = 180° - 78° = 102°$ (angles on a straight line = 180°)	$x = 101°$ as the shape is a kite and opposite angles are equal	The shape is a square and a rhombus
$x + 90° + y = 360°$	If $x = 101°$ then the angles in any quadrilateral = 360°	Angle $x = 101°$
$192° + y = 360°$	$z = 360° - 78° - 101° - 101° = 80°$	Angle $z = 78°$
$y = 360° - 192° = 168°$ (angles in a quadrilateral add to 360°)	Angles round a point add to 360°	Angle $y = 360° - 101° - 90°$
$x + 78° + 101° + z = 360°$	$x + y + 90° = 360°$	$y = 360° - 192°$
$102° + 78° + 101° + z = 360°$	$360° - 90° - 101° = y$	$y = 168°$
$281° + z = 360°$	$y = 169°$	
$z = 360° - 281° = 79°$		

EXERCISE 8E

1 A quadrilateral has:
- two pairs of equal parallel lines
- opposite angles are equal, and
- the diagonals bisect each other at right angles.

Name the shape from the options below.

A Rhombus   B Kite   C Trapezium   D Parallelogram

2 Identify the quadrilateral(s) from the description in each part.

   a All angles are equal.

   b Diagonals are equal in length.

   c Two pairs of sides are equal and parallel.

   d No sides are parallel.

   e The only regular quadrilateral.

   f Diagonals bisect each other.

3 You can identify a quadrilateral by considering its diagonals.

Copy and complete this table.

Shape	Diagonals are equal in length	Diagonals bisect each other	Diagonals are perpendicular
rhombus			
parallelogram			
square			
kite			
rectangle			

4 What is the most obvious difference between a square and a rhombus?

5 Millie says that quadrilateral ABCD has all four sides the same length.

Elizabeth says it must be a square.

Is Elizabeth correct? Give a reason for your answer.

6 A kite has one angle of 47° and one of 133°. What sizes are the other two angles?

7 State whether each statement is always true, sometimes true or never true.

Give a reason for each of your answers.

a A square is a rectangle.   **b** A rectangle is a square.

c A rectangle is a rhombus.   **d** A rhombus is a parallelogram.

e A parallelogram is a rhombus.

8 Quadrilateral ABCD is a rhombus.

State which of the following statements are true. Justify your answers.

a AMB = 90°

b DB = AC

c ∠BDC + ∠ACD = 180°

d ∠ABC = ∠ADC

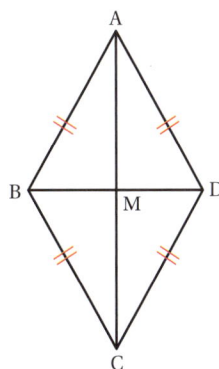

9 Calculate the value of x in rhombus ABCD.

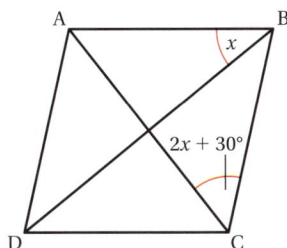

x

$2x + 30°$

10 In rhombus ABCD, AB = 26 mm and diagonal BD = 48 mm.

Calculate the length of diagonal AC.

Tip

Use the Problem-solving framework and think carefully about what other mathematics you can use to solve this problem.

Find answers at: cambridge.org/ukschools/gcsemaths-studentbookanswers

139

11 In this figure ABCD and ADEF are parallelograms.

Show that FECB is a parallelogram.

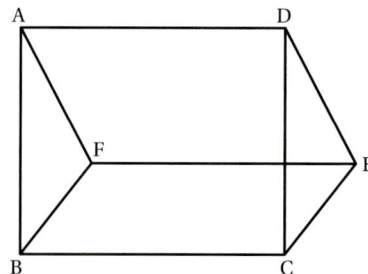

12 Jason says that if two opposite sides of a quadrilateral are equal in length and are almost parallel then the quadrilateral must be a parallelogram.

Is he correct? Give reasons for your answer.

Section 5: Properties of 3D objects

The flat surfaces of a solid are called faces. Two faces meet at the edge of a solid.

Three or more faces meet at a point called a vertex. (The plural of vertex is vertices.)

A solid with flat faces and straight edges is a polyhedron.

Cubes, cuboids, prisms and pyramids are all types of polyhedra.

Cubes and cuboids

Cubes and cuboids are box-shaped polyhedra.

They have six faces, twelve edges and eight vertices.

A cube has **congruent** square faces.

A cuboid has rectangular faces.

All cubes are cuboids, but not all cuboids are cubes.

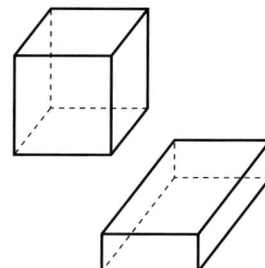

Prisms

A prism is a 3D shape with two congruent, parallel faces.

If the prism is sliced parallel to one of these faces the cross-section will always be the same shape.

The parallel faces of a prism can be any shape.

If the prism is a polyhedron all of the other faces are rectangular.

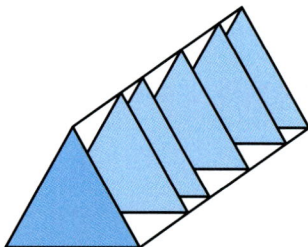

Tip

You need to know the properties of the basic polyhedra and other 3D solids.

You will use these properties to draw plans, elevations and nets of solids in Chapter 21 and you will apply them when you solve problems relating to volume and surface area in Chapter 24.

Key vocabulary

congruent: identical in shape and size

Prisms are named according to the shape of their parallel faces.

Pentagonal prism

2 pentagonal faces

5 rectangular faces

Hexagonal prism

2 hexagonal faces

6 rectangular faces

Octagonal prism

2 octagonal faces

8 rectangular faces

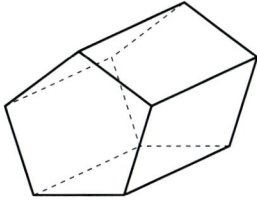 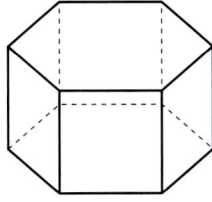 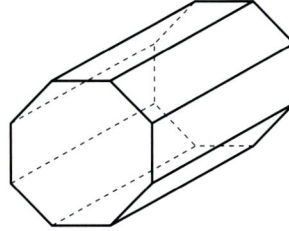

A cube is a square prism and a cuboid is a rectangular prism.

Pyramids

A pyramid is a polyhedron with a base and triangular faces that meet at a vertex (sometimes called the apex of the pyramid).

Pyramids are named according to the shape of their base.

Triangular pyramid   **Square pyramid**   **Pentagonal pyramid**   **Hexagonal pyramid**

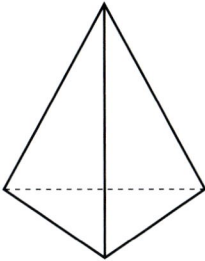 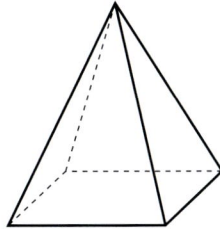 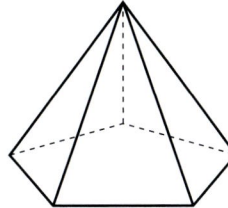 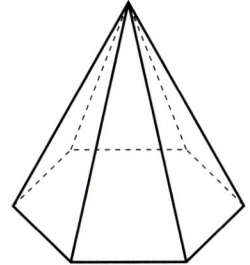

The number of sides of the base tells you how many triangular faces the pyramid has.

Other solids

Cylinders, cones and spheres are also 3D shapes.

They do not have straight edges or flat faces that are polygons so they are not polyhedral.

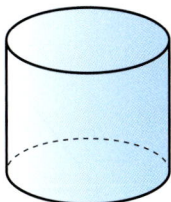 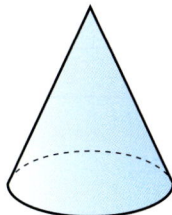 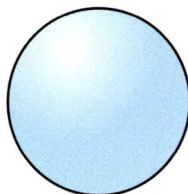

cylinder   cone   sphere

EXERCISE 8F

1 Sketch a possible solid you could make by combining the given solids.

For each one, state whether it is a polyhedron and how many faces, vertices and edges it would have.

a A large and a small cylinder

b A cube and a square pyramid

c Two identical pentagonal pyramids

d A triangular prism and a cuboid

2 Copy and complete the table.

3D Shape	Number of faces (F)	Number of vertices (V)	Number of edges (E)
cube			
cuboid			
triangular pyramid			
square pyramid			
triangular prism			
hexagonal prism			

a Write an expression to show the relationship between F, V and E in these solids.

b Use your expression to find the number of faces in a polyhedron with 12 vertices and 30 edges.

c Show whether your expression works for each of the following solids.

If it doesn't work, suggest a reason for this.

d Is it possible to have a polyhedron with 25 faces, 45 edges and 30 vertices?

Justify your answer.

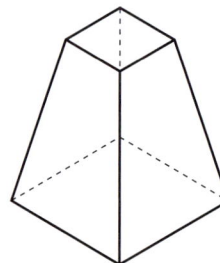 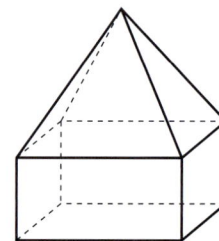

3 Janice is building wire models of 3D objects for a school project.

How much wire would she need to build each of these shapes?

Assume there is no overlap at the vertices or joins.

a

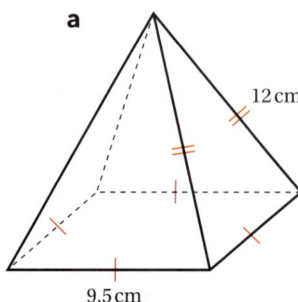

12 cm

9.5 cm

b

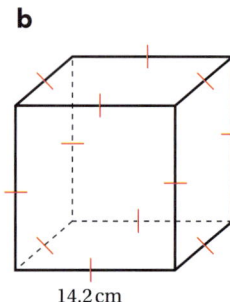

14.2 cm

c

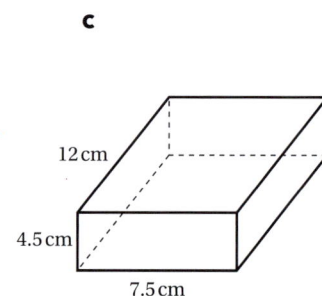

12 cm

4.5 cm

7.5 cm

Checklist of learning and understanding

Types of shapes
- Polygons are closed plane shapes with straight sides.
- Triangles, quadrilaterals, pentagons and hexagons are all polygons.
- Circles and ovals are plane shapes, but they are not polygons.

Symmetry
- Shapes have reflection symmetry if they can be folded along a line of symmetry to produce two identical mirror images.
- Shapes have rotation symmetry if they fit on to themselves more than once during a 360° rotation.

Triangles
- Triangles are 3-sided polygons.
- Triangles can be classified and named using their side and angle properties.
- The sum of the interior angles of a triangle is 180°.

Quadrilaterals
- Quadrilaterals are 4-sided polygons.
- Quadrilaterals can be classified and named using their side, angle and diagonal properties.
- The sum of the interior angles of a quadrilateral is 360°.

Properties of 3D objects
- 3D shapes are solids with length, breadth and height.
- Polyhedra are solids with flat faces and straight edges.
- Prisms and pyramids are polyhedral.
- Cylinders, cones and spheres are 3D shapes but they are not polyhedral.

Chapter review

> For additional questions on the topics in this chapter, visit GCSE Mathematics Online.

1 Write down whether the following statements are true or false.
   a A slice of pizza can be accurately described as a triangle.
   b A triangular pyramid has 4 vertices, 4 faces and 6 edges.
   c A pair of lines that are equidistant and never meet are described as being perpendicular.
   d A pyramid with a polygon base of n sides will have $n + 1$ vertices.
   e A cylinder has a uniform circular cross-section.

2 Describe the symmetrical features of a regular hexagon as fully as possible.

3 Find the missing angles in this trapezium.

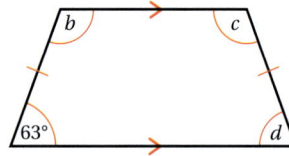

4 Decide whether the missing angle in the diagram is a right angle.
Give a reason for your answer.

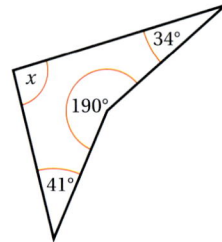

5 Find the unknown angles.

a

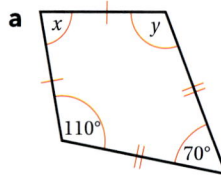

b

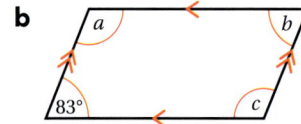

6 Is this quadrilateral a parallelogram?

Justify your answer.

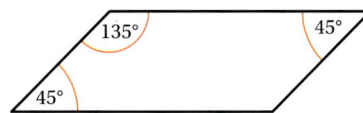

7 Niresh states that if the diagonals of a quadrilateral intersect at right angles, the quadrilateral must be a square.

Is he correct?

Justify your answer.

8 Spot the mistakes in this table and correct them.

3D shape	Faces	Edges	Vertices
a square-based pyramid	5	5	5
b triangular prism	9	9	9
c cube	12	6	8
d sphere	2	2	1

9 Look at the shape in the margin.

Complete the sentences by choosing the correct words from the box.

parallel	perpendicular	reciprocal	acute	congruent
reflective symmetry	reflex	obtuse	parallelogram	obtuse
trapezium	kite	right angle	rotational symmetry

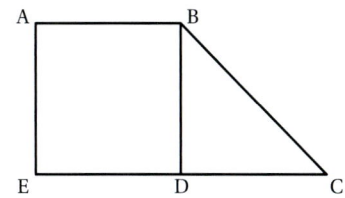

a AB is _____ to DC

b AE is _____ to AB

c ABCE is called a _____

d Angle EDB is a _____

e Angle ABC is _____

f Shape ABCE has no lines of _____

10 Look at the diagram of the building in the margin.

a Which side lengths are parallel?

b Which side lengths are perpendicular?

c How many lines of reflective symmetry does this shape have?

d What rotational symmetry does it have?

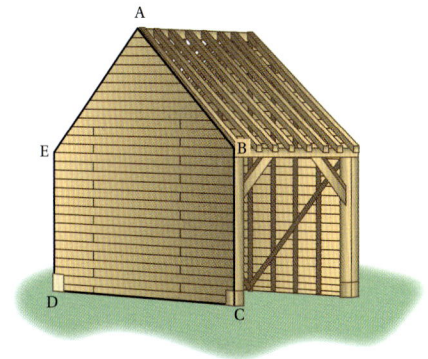

11 Look at the diagram of the rhombus below.

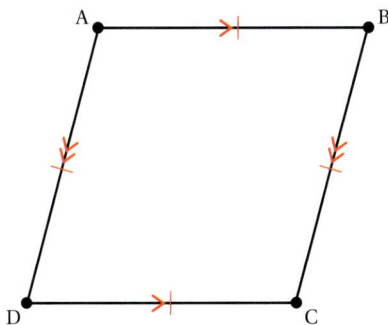

a How many lines of symmetry does it have?

b What rotational symmetry does it have?

c At what angle do the diagonals cross each other?

d What do the angles ABC and BCD add up to?

12 Jack is making spheres out of clay.

A box of clay contains 25 packs.

Each pack is a cuboid measuring 10 cm by 10 cm by 4 cm.

a How many spheres of radius 6 cm can Jack make from a box of clay?

(6 marks)

b A pack of clay has a mass of 500 grams.

Work out the density of the clay. *(2 marks)*

© AQA 2012

9 Angles

Using mathematics: real-life applications

People who work in many varied and unrelated jobs rely on an understanding of angles and how shapes fit with others in their daily work. These include designers, architects, opticians and tree surgeons among others.

"I had to work quite carefully with the 360 degrees around the centre to place each of the 32 pods correctly on the London Eye."   *(Structural engineer)*

Before you start …

KS3 Ch 1	You should be able to use inverse operations to make 180° and 360°.	**1** Copy and complete. **a** $180° - 96° = \square$ **b** $180° - 116° = \square$ **c** $360° - 173° = \square$ **d** $360° - 55° - 97° = \square$
KS3 Ch 8	You need to know and apply the basic properties of triangles and quadrilaterals.	**2** Use the marked properties to name each polygon as accurately as possible. **a** (45°, 45°) **b** **c** (x, y) **3** What can you say about angles x and y in **c**? Why?
KS3 Ch 31	You need to know how to use a protractor to measure angles.	**4** Measure the following angles. **a** **b**

Assess your starting point using the Launchpad

STEP 1

1 Work out the size of angles *a*, *b* and *c* in the diagrams below without measuring them. Give a reason for each answer.

a
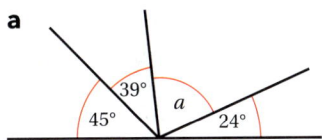

b
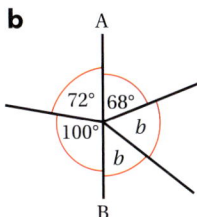

c
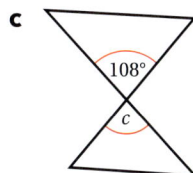

2 Is it possible for AB to be a straight line in diagram **b**? Give a reason for your answer.

GO TO
Section 1:
Angle facts

STEP 2

3 List three pairs of equal angles in this diagram.

4 Under what conditions would angle *c* = *f*?

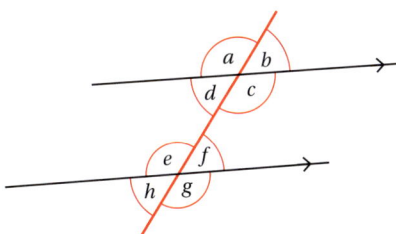

GO TO
Section 2:
Parallel lines and angles

STEP 3

5 Find the size of angle *x*. Give reasons for your answers.

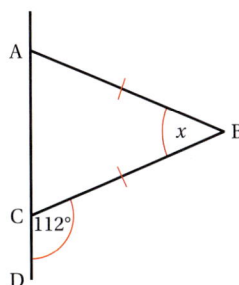

GO TO
Section 3:
Angles in triangles
Section 4:
Angles in polygons

GO TO
Chapter review

Section 1: Angle facts

Angles around a point

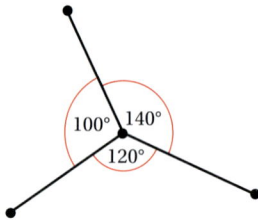

- There are 360° around a point. One 90° angle is one quarter turn, two 90° angles are half a turn, and so on.
- There are four quarter turns around a point. $4 \times 90° = 360°$
- This rule applies to any point. The sum of angles around a point is 360°.

WORKED EXAMPLE 1

Find the size of x.

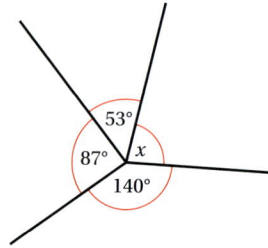

$87° + 53° + x + 140° = 360°$ ◀ Angles round a point add up to 360°.

$x = 360° - 140° - 53° - 87°$ ◀ Make x the subject of the equation
$\quad = 360° - 280°$ and then work out its value.
$\quad = 80°$

Angles on a straight line

Angles on a straight line add up to 180°.

This is true for any number of angles that meet at a point on a line.

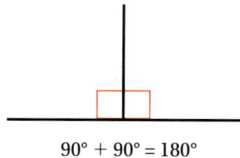

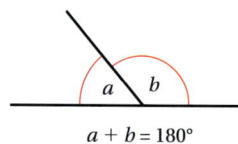

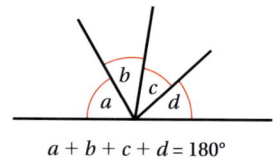

$90° + 90° = 180°$ $\qquad$ $a + b = 180°$ $\qquad$ $a + b + c + d = 180°$

WORKED EXAMPLE 2

Work out the size of x.

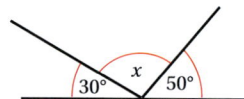

$30° + x + 50° = 180°$ ◀ Angles on a line add up to 180°.

$x = 180° - 30° - 50°$ ◀ Make x the subject of the equation and
$\quad = 100°$ then work out its value.

Vertically opposite angles

When two lines cross, or intersect, they form four angles.

The angles a and b are vertically opposite each other and the angles x and y are vertically opposite each other.

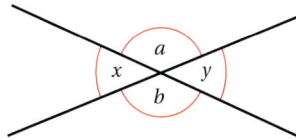

Vertically opposite angles are equal.

$a = b$

$x = y$

EXERCISE 9A

1 Three angles meet at a point.
Two angles are obtuse and are 120° and 96° respectively.
Choose the correct option for the size and type of the third angle.

    A Obtuse angle of 144°   B Acute angle of 36°

    C Reflex angle of 216°   D Obtuse angle of $\sqrt{144°}$

2 Which of the following statements is correct?

    A Angles around a point always add up to 180°.

    B Angles on a straight line always add up to 180°.

    C Vertically opposite angles always add up to 180°.

3 Calculate the size of the angles marked x.

a 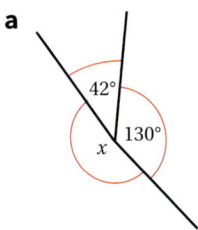   **b** 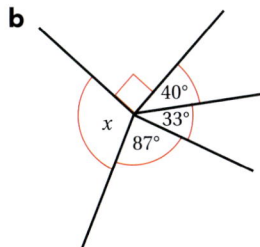   **c**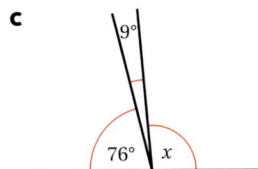

    d What type of angle is x in each case?

4 Find the marked angles in each diagram. Give reasons for any deductions you make.

    a Find x and y.   **b** Find x.   **c** Find p.

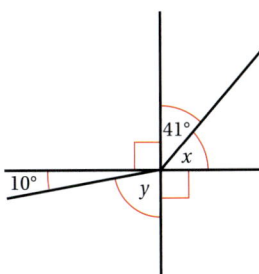   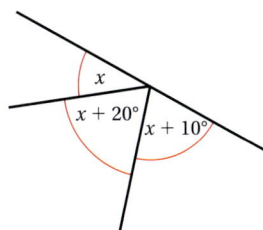   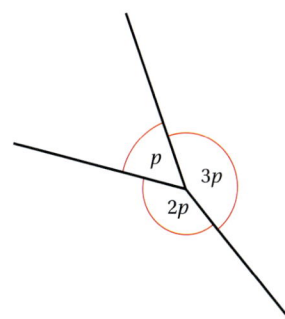

5 Give a reason why AE cannot be a straight line.

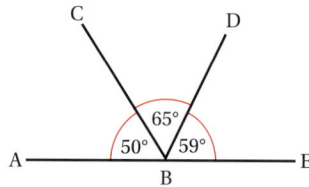

6 Calculate the size of the marked angles in each figure.

The lines are straight lines but the diagrams are not to scale.

Show your working and give reasons for any deductions you make.

a

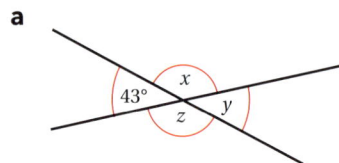

b

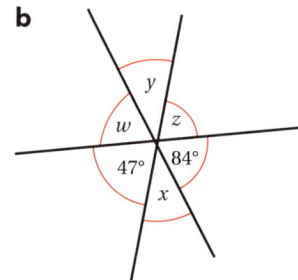

7 In the diagram, $x = 50°$.

Find the size of angle z.

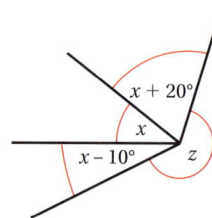

8 Calculate the size of each angle in the diagram when:

a $x = 69°$ **b** $x = b$

c $2b = 112°$ **d** $a = 2x$

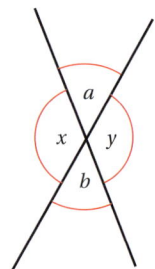

9 Three angles meet at a point.

a What is the size of the acute angle?

b What is the size of the reflex angle?

c What is the size of the obtuse angle?

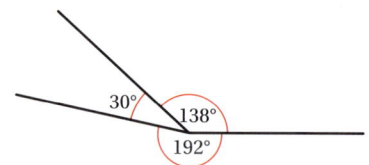

10 Millie has measured an obtuse angle with a protractor. She says that it is 42°.

a What has she done wrong with the protractor?

b What should the size of the angle be?

11 Find the value of the variables in each diagram.

Give reasons for your answers.

a

b

c

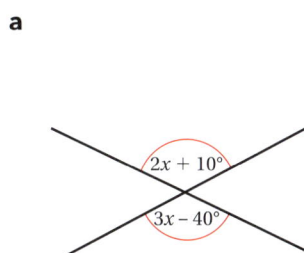

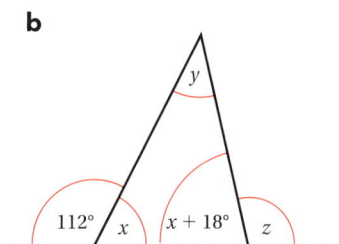

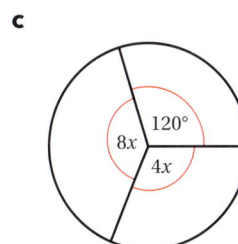

"When I'm designing and making clothes I need to be able to cut on the bias (at a given angle) and also bisect angles to add darts and fit sleeves." *(Fashion designer)*

Section 2: Parallel lines and angles

A line intersecting two or more parallel lines is called a **transversal**.

When a transversal intersects with parallel lines, it creates pairs of angles.

Corresponding angles

Corresponding angles formed between a transversal and each parallel line are equal.

When a transversal crosses two parallel lines, there are four pairs of corresponding angles.

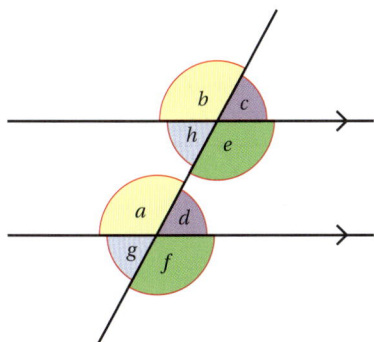

The corresponding angle pairs are:

$a = b$ $c = d$ $e = f$ $g = h$

Key vocabulary

transversal: a straight line that crosses a pair of parallel lines

corresponding angles: angles that are created at the same point of the intersection when a transversal crosses a pair of parallel lines

Alternate angles

Key vocabulary

alternate angles: the angles on parallel lines on opposite sides of a transversal

Alternate angles on opposite sides of the transversal on parallel lines are equal.

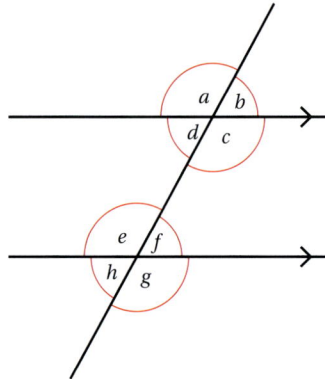

The alternate angle pairs are:

$$a = g \qquad b = h \qquad c = e \qquad d = f$$

Co-interior or allied angles

Key vocabulary

co-interior angles: the angles within the parallel lines on the same side of the transversal

The angles inside the parallel lines and on the same side of the transversal are called **co-interior angles**. They add to 180°. You might also see them referred to as **allied angles**.

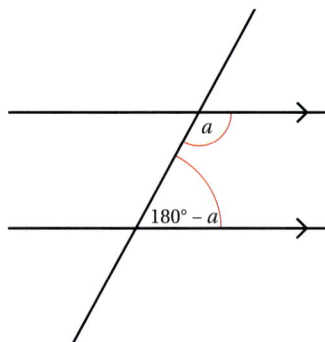

Key vocabulary

supplementary angles: two angles are supplementary angles if they add up to 180°

Co-interior angles are **supplementary**. Read through this proof to see why.

Prove that $\angle BEF + \angle EFD = 180°$

Let $\angle BEF = x$

$\therefore \angle EFC = x$
Alternate angles are equal.

$\angle EFC + \angle EFD = 180°$
Angles on a line sum to 180°.

$\therefore \angle EFD = 180° - x$

$\angle BEF + \angle EFD = x + 180° - x = 180°$

So, $\angle BEF + \angle EFD = 180°$

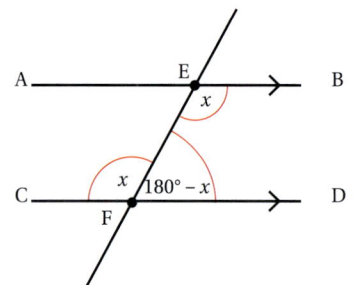

This table summarises the facts you need to know about the angles associated with parallel lines.

Alternate angles are equal.	Corresponding angles are equal.	Co-interior angles are supplementary. They add to 180°.

EXERCISE 9B

1 Which of the following is the correct definition of a transversal?

A a pair of lines that are always an equal distance apart and never meet

B a pair of lines that meet at a right angle

C a straight line that crosses a pair of parallel lines

D a straight line that bisects a set of perpendicular lines

2 Find the size of the missing angles a, b, c and d.

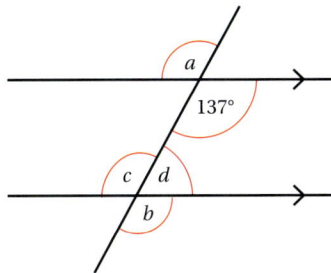

3 Find the sizes of the angles marked x and y.

Choose the correct answer from the following options.

A $x = 130°$ and $y = 130°$ B $x = 130°$ and $y = 50°$

C $x = 50°$ and $y = 130°$ D $x = 50°$ and $y = 50°$

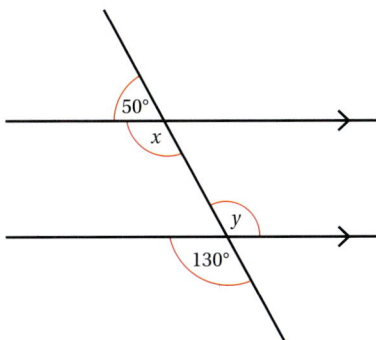

4 In the diagram, the two poles are parallel to each other. Find the angle x.

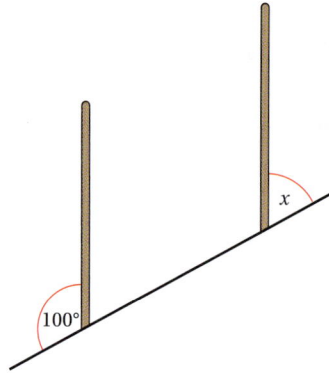

5 Find the size of the missing angles a, b and c.

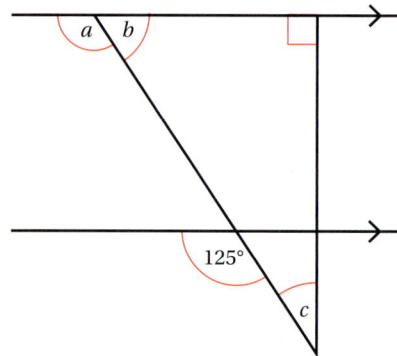

6 Find the size of angles x and y.

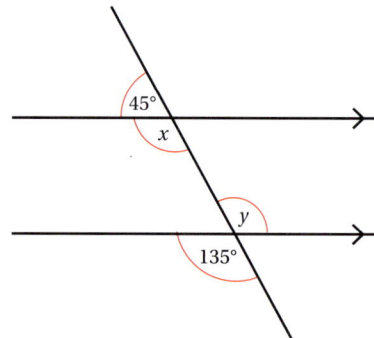

7 Find the size of the missing angles.

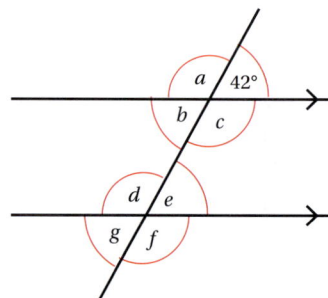

8 Find the size of ∠CEG.

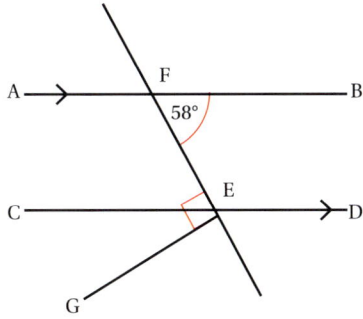

9 Find the size of ∠DCF.

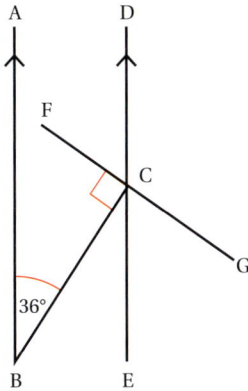

10 Find the value of *x*.

a

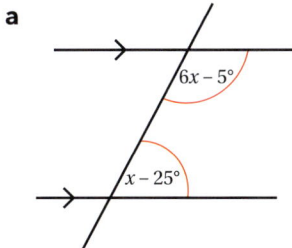

b

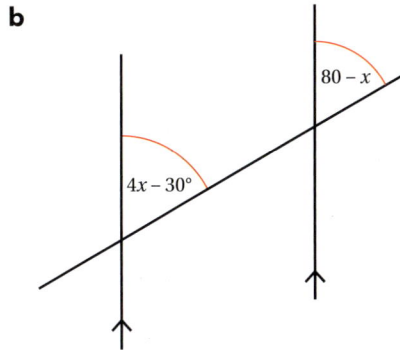

11 State whether AB//DC in each of the following. Give a reason for your answer.

a

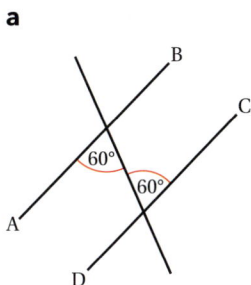

b

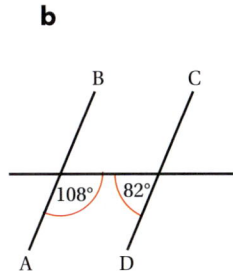

c

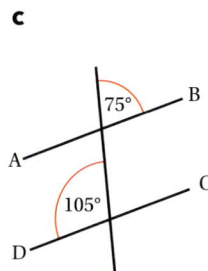

Section 3: Angles in triangles

Angle sum of a triangle

In the diagram, a line parallel to one side of the triangle has been drawn.

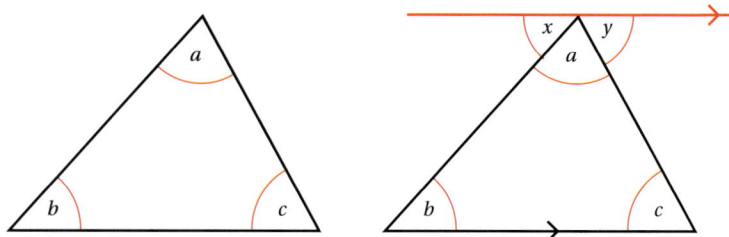

Using the properties of angles and parallel lines, you can prove that
$a + b + c = 180°$

$x + a + y = 180°$ (Angles on a line sum to 180°.)

But: $x = b$ and $y = c$ (Alternate angles are equal.)

Substitute b for x and c for y and you prove that $a + b + c = 180°$.

The angle sum of a triangle is 180°.

The exterior angle is equal to the sum of the opposite interior angles

The exterior angle of a triangle is equal to the sum of the two opposite interior angles.

There are different ways to prove this using mathematical principles.

The worked example shows one way.

WORKED EXAMPLE 3

Show that $a + b = x$, and hence prove that the exterior angle of any triangle is equal to the sum of the opposite interior angles.

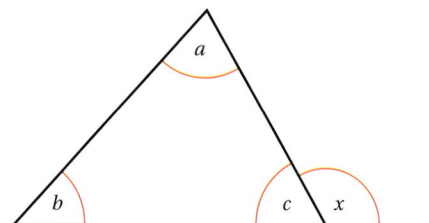

$c + x = 180°$
$\therefore c = 180° - x$ Angles on a line add to 180°.

$a + b + c = 180°$ Angles within a triangle add to 180°.
$\therefore c = 180° - (a + b)$

But, $c = (180° - x)$ Proven above.
So, $180° - (a + b) = 180° - x$
$\therefore a + b = x$

EXERCISE 9C

1 A scalene triangle has two angles of 67° and 73°.

Which of the following is the third angle?

a 70°   **b** 40°   **c** 220°   **d** 67°

2 Calculate the size of the missing angles.

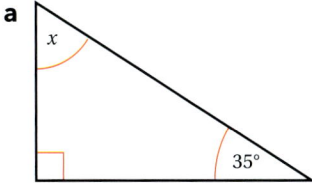

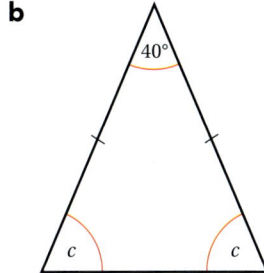

a

b

3 Find the size of the angles marked x and y.

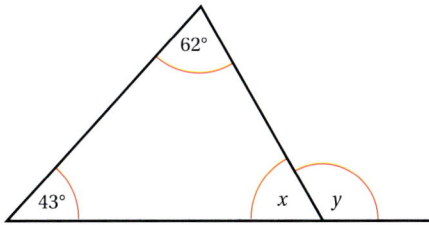

4 Find the size of the angles marked a and b.

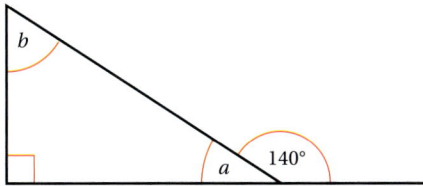

5 Find the size of the angles marked x, y and z.

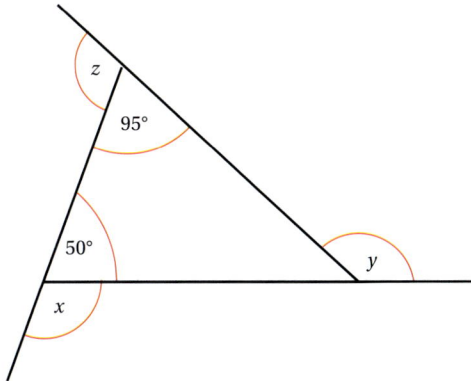

6 Work out the sizes of the angles marked *a*, *b* and *c*. Give reasons to justify your answers.

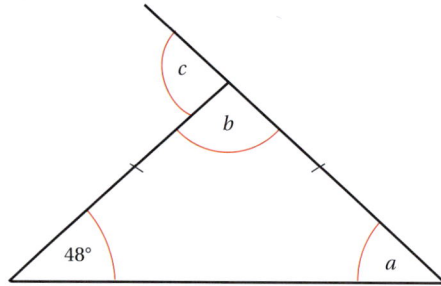

48°

7 Calculate the size of *x*.

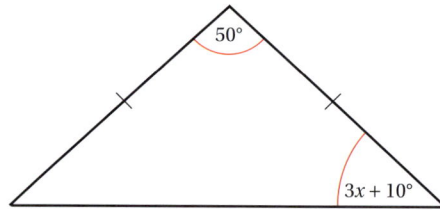

50°

$3x + 10°$

8 An isosceles triangle has one angle of 74°.

What could the size of the other two angles be?

Find both possible answers.

9 With reference to the figure below, show how you can prove that the exterior angle of a triangle is equal to the sum of the opposite interior angles by construction of CE // AB.

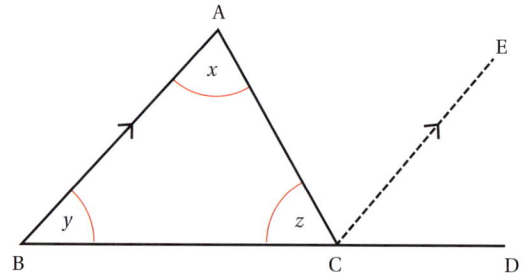

10 Find the size of the angles marked with variables in each diagram. Give reasons.

a

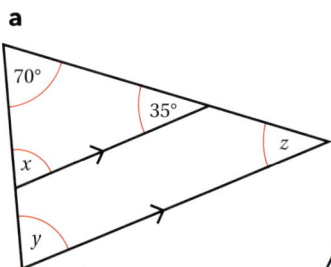

b

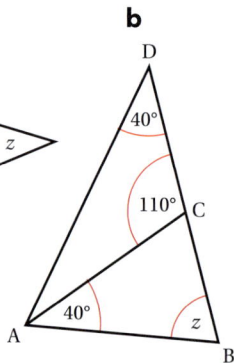

c

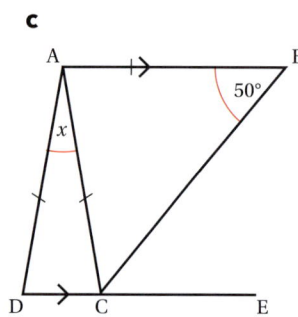

d

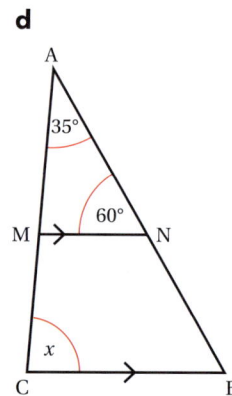

e

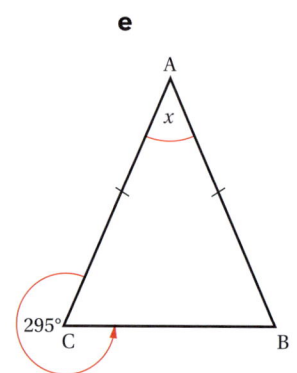

11 In the diagram what are the size of angles marked *x* and *y*? Justify your answer.

Choose the correct answer and reasoning from the following answers.

A *x* = 50° as it is an alternate angle to 50°. *y* = 77° as the other angle in the triangle is 180° − 127°, which is 53°. Three angles in a triangle make 180° so the angle is 77°.

B *x* = 50° as it is a corresponding angle to 50°, *y* = 127° − 50° = 77°.

C *x* = 53° as it is the same size as the angle at PRD as it is an isosceles triangle, *y* = 90° as it hits the parallel line at a right angle.

D *x* = 50° as it is a co-interior angle to 50°, *y* = 73° as the other angle in the triangle is 180° − 127° which is 53°. Three angles in a triangle make 180° so the angle is 73°.

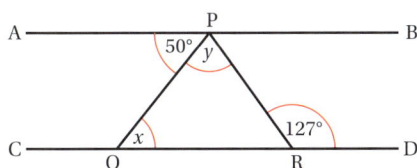

Section 4: Angles in polygons

These basalt columns are formed naturally when lava cools.

The end faces are mostly hexagonal.

> **Tip**
>
> You learned about polygons in Chapter 8. Look back if you need revision.

The angle sum of a polygon

This is a regular hexagon.

It has six **interior angles** that are all equal.

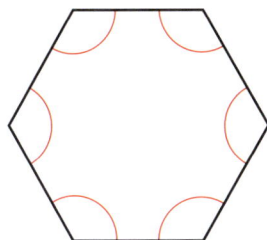

> **Key vocabulary**
>
> **interior angles**: angles inside a two-dimensional shape at the vertices or corners

Find answers at: cambridge.org/ukschools/gcsemaths-studentbookanswers

The diagonals divide the hexagon into four triangles.

So the sum of the interior angles of a hexagon is $4 \times 180° = 720°$.

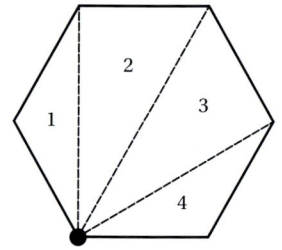

The hexagon is regular, so the six interior angles are equal in size.

$720° \div 6 = 120°$, so each interior angle is 120°.

For any polygon, the sum of the interior angles = $180(n - 2)$, where n is the number of sides.

Work through the investigation in Exercise 9D to understand how this rule is derived.

EXERCISE 9D

1   Draw the following polygons and divide them into triangles by drawing diagonals from one vertex as with the hexagon above.

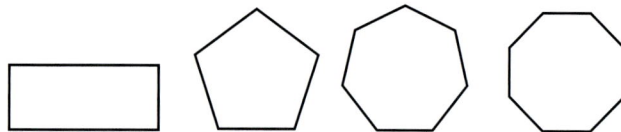

2   Predict how many triangles you could form if you did the same for a ten-sided and twenty-sided polygon.

3   Copy and complete this table using your results.

Number of sides in polygon	3	4	5	6	7	8	10	20
Number of triangles	1			4				
Angle sum of interior angles	180°			720°				

4   What is the relationship between the number of sides in a polygon and the number of triangles you can form in this way?

5   If a polygon has n sides, how many triangles can you form in this way?

6   Write a rule for finding the angle sum of a polygon:

   a   in words

   b   in general algebraic terms for a polygon of n sides.

7   Use your rule to find the angle sum of a polygon with 12 sides.

8   How could you find the size of each angle of a regular 12-sided polygon?

WORK IT OUT 9.1

Three students attempted to calculate the size of the interior angles in a regular pentagon.

Which is the correct solution?

What mistakes have been made by the other students?

Option A	Option B	Option C
There are three triangles within the pentagon. $3 \times 180° = 540°$ Five angles in a pentagon. $540° \div 5 = 108°$ Interior angle = 108°	There are five triangles in a pentagon. $5 \times 180° = 900°$ $900° \div 5 = 180°$ Interior angle = 180°	There is a trapezium and a triangle inside the pentagon. $360° + 180° = 540°$ There are five angles inside the pentagon including the central 360° which gives a total of 900°. Interior angle = $900° \div 5 = 180°$

The sum of exterior angles of a polygon

Each interior angle of a hexagon is 120°.

By extending each side, you can form six **exterior angles**.

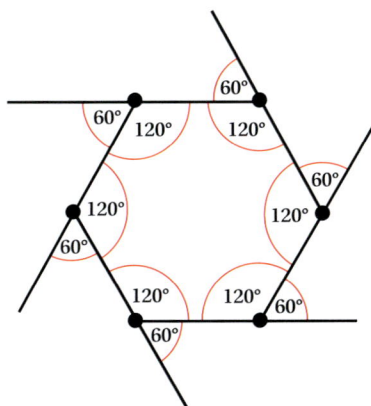

Key vocabulary

exterior angles: angles produced by extending the sides of a polygon

The sum of exterior angles is always 360°. The total of the exterior and interior angles of a polygon is $n \times 180°$ where n is the number of sides of the polygon. Remember that angles on a straight line add to 180° and the exterior and interior angles are supplementary.

In the case of a hexagon this is $6 \times 180° = 1080°$

The sum of the interior angles = $4 \times 180° = 720°$

The difference between the sum of the total angles 1080° less the sum of the interior angles 720° is the sum of the exterior angles. This equals 360°.

Find answers at: cambridge.org/ukschools/gcsemaths-studentbookanswers

To calculate the size of one exterior angle in a regular shape, divide 360° by the number of sides.

Exterior angle of a regular polygon $= \dfrac{360°}{n}$, where n is the number of sides.

In general terms:

Let I be the sum of interior angles.

Let E be the sum of exterior angles.

$I = 180(n - 2)$

$I + E = 180n$

$E = 180n - 180(n - 2)$

$\quad = 180n - 180n + 360$

$\quad = 360$

You can use these rules to find the angle sum of any polygon.

If the polygon is regular, you can also calculate the size of each interior and exterior angle.

WORKED EXAMPLE 4

For a regular ten-sided polygon, find:

a the sum of the interior angles **b** the size of each interior angle.

a Angle sum $= 180(n - 2) = 180(8) = 1440°$

b There are 10 interior angles,

so one angle $= \dfrac{1440}{10} = 144°$

> In a ten-sided figure $n = 10$.

WORKED EXAMPLE 5

A polygon has an angle sum of 2340°. How many sides does it have?

$2340 = 180(n - 2)$

$\dfrac{2340}{180} = n - 2$

$13 = n - 2$

$15 = n$

The polygon has 15 sides.

> Use the angle sum rule.

WORKED EXAMPLE 6

A regular polygon has an exterior angle of 18°. How many sides does it have?

Sum of exterior angles $= 360°$

Number of angles $= \dfrac{360}{18} = 20$

$\therefore$ Number of sides $= 20$

> The number of sides equals the number of angles

EXERCISE 9E

1 In a regular octagon what is the size of each interior angle?
Choose from the following options.
A 110° B 180° C 135° D 120°

2 Calculate the sum of interior angles of a polygon with:
a 9 sides **b** 12 sides **c** 25 sides.

3 A regular polygon has 15 sides. Find:
a the sum of the interior angles **b** the sum of the exterior angles
c the size of an interior angle **d** the size of an exterior angle.

4 A regular polygon has an interior angle that is three times the size of the exterior angle.

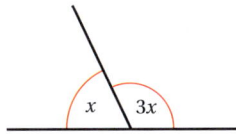

a What is the size of each exterior angle?
b What is the size of each interior angle?
c What is the name of the regular polygon?

5 Find the size of the missing angles x, y and z in this irregular pentagon.

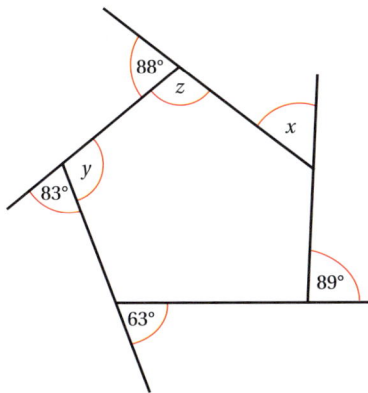

6 A pentagon has three angles that add up to 266°.
The other two angles are equal in size.
Find the size of each of the other two angles.

7 A hexagon has four angles with a sum of 555°.
One of the remaining angles is twice the size of the other.
Find the size of each of the remaining angles.

8 Could a regular polygon have interior angles of 125°?
Give a reason for your answer.

Find answers at: cambridge.org/ukschools/gcsemaths-studentbookanswers

9 How many sides does a polygon have if the sum of interior angles is

    a 1620°?   **b** 3060°?

10 The exterior angle of a regular polygon is 40°.

    What is the sum of its interior angles?

Checklist of learning and understanding

Basic angle facts

- Angles around a point sum to 360°.
- Angles on a straight line sum to 180°.
- Vertically opposite angles are equal.

Angles associated with parallel lines

- Corresponding angles are equal.
- Alternate angles are equal.
- Co-interior angles sum to 180°.

Geometric proofs

- Using properties of alternate and corresponding angles, you can show that the three interior angles of any triangle sum to 180°.
- Using the angle sum of triangles and properties of angles at a line and at a point, you can find the interior and exterior angles of any polygon.

For additional questions on the topics in this chapter, visit GCSE Mathematics Online.

Chapter review

1 Select the correct size for the marked angle in each diagram.

a

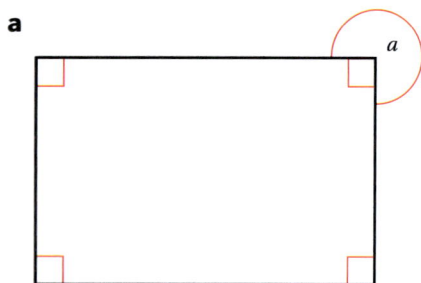

b

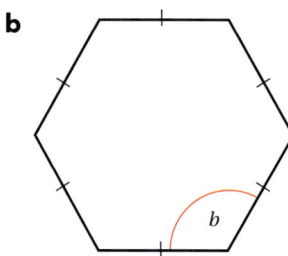

c

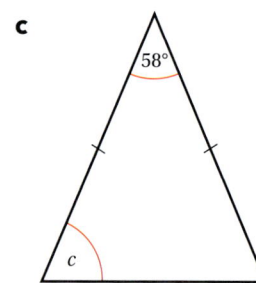

d

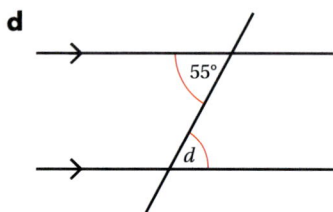

e

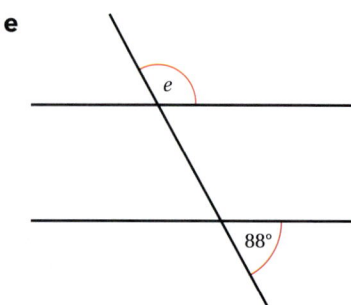

f

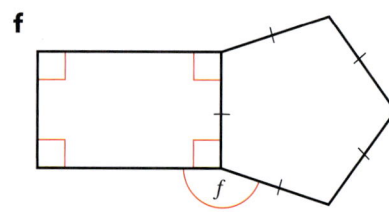

| 270° | 92° | 120° | 162° | 61° | 55° |

2 AB is parallel to CD.

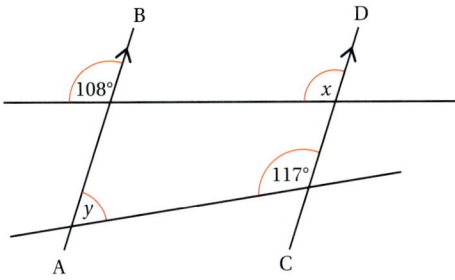

Not drawn accurately

a Write down the size of angle *x*.
Give a reason for your answer. *(2 marks)*

b Work out the size of angle *y*. *(2 marks)*

© AQA 2013

3 The interior angle of a regular polygon is 108°. What type of polygon is it?

4 The angles are marked on the diagram. Calculate $p + q + r + s + t$.

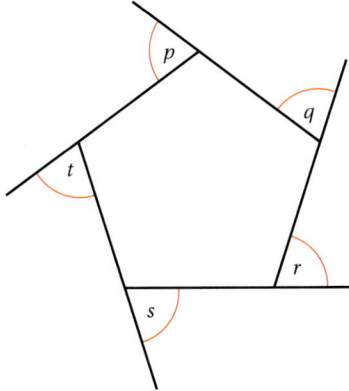

5 Work out the size of angles *x* and *y*.

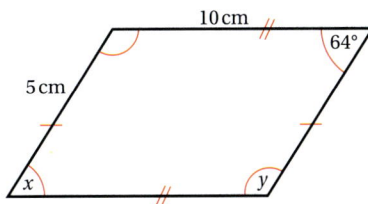

6 In this irregular hexagon, calculate the value of *z*.

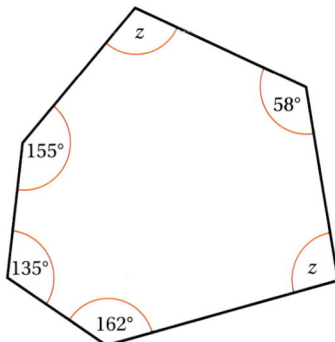

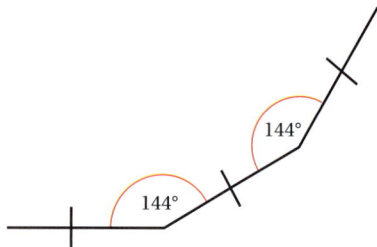

7 The diagram on the left shows part of a regular polygon. The interior angle is 144°.

    a Calculate the number of sides of the polygon.

    b What is the name given to this polygon?

8 Calculate the exterior angles of a regular decagon.

9 Show mathematically why the sum of the exterior angles of any polygon is 360°.

10 Find the values of the angles marked x and y.

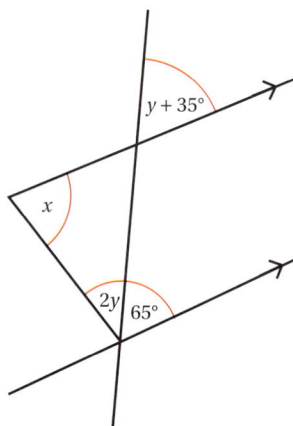

11 Work out the size of angle x.

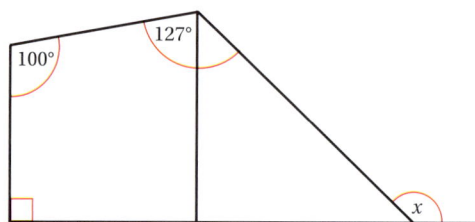

12 Prove that quadrilateral ABCD is a trapezium.

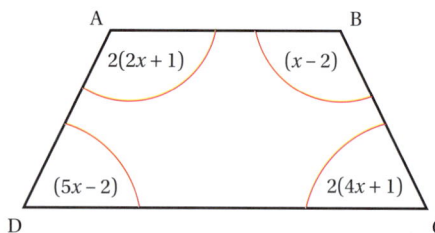

13 The sum of interior angles of an irregular polygon is 3600°.

    a Work out the number of sides.

    b Work out x, if half the angles in the polygon are size x and the other half are size $2x$.

10 Perimeter

In this chapter you will learn how to ...

- calculate the perimeter of simple shapes such as rectangles and triangles.
- find the perimeter of composite shapes.
- calculate the circumference of a circle.
- calculate the perimeter of composite shapes including circles or parts of circles.

> For more resources relating to this chapter, visit GCSE Mathematics Online.

Using mathematics: real-life applications

Working out the amount of fencing needed for a field, or the number of tiles needed to edge a swimming pool, or the number of perimeter security cameras needed to secure an area, all require the calculation of a perimeter.

> "Security cameras in a car park are only effective if they can see all round the perimeter of the car park."
>
> *(Security camera technician)*

Before you start ...

Ch 8	You must be able to recognise and name some common polygons.	1	Match each name to its correct shape. octagon pentagon hexagon **a** **b** **c**
KS3	You must be able to convert between basic metric units.	2	Convert: **a** 5 km into m **b** 12 km into cm **c** 8500 mm into m **d** 4.8 m to mm.
KS3	You need to know and use the correct names of circle parts.	3	True or false? **a** The diameter of a circle is twice the length of the radius. **b** The diameter of a circle is always shorter than the radius. **c** The angles at the centre of a circle add up to 180°.
KS3	You should be able to change the subject of a formula.	4	Make l the subject of the formula $P = 2(l + w)$.
		5	Make r the subject of the formula $P = \pi r + 2r$.

Find answers at: cambridge.org/ukschools/gcsemaths-studentbookanswers

Assess your starting point using the Launchpad

STEP 1

1 A football pitch is 90 m long and 55 m wide.

What is the distance around the pitch?

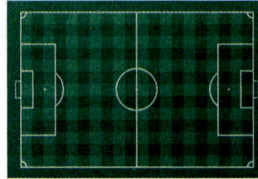

2 Calculate the perimeter of each shape.

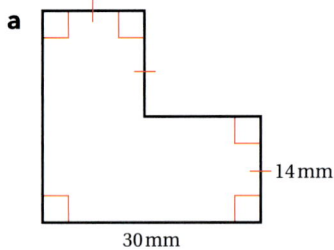

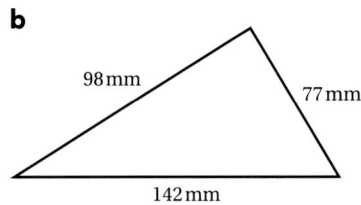

a

30 mm

14 mm

b

98 mm

77 mm

142 mm

3 A square has a perimeter of 169 mm. What is the length of a side?

4 A rectangle with a length of 4 cm, has a perimeter of 150 mm. Calculate the width of the rectangle. (Pay attention to the units.)

GO TO
Section 1:
Perimeter of simple and composite shapes

STEP 2

5 Work out the circumference of each circle. Use exact values of π and give your answers to two decimal places.

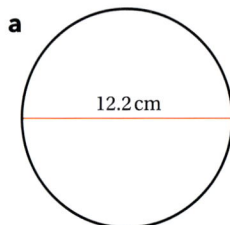

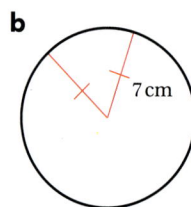

a

12.2 cm

b

7 cm

6 Work out the diameter of a circle to the nearest centimetre, given that its circumference is 37.7 cm (to one decimal place).

7 What is the perimeter of a semicircular rug of radius 1.6 m? Give your answer to two decimal places.

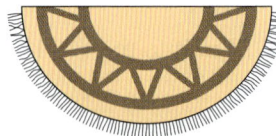

GO TO
Section 2:
Circumference of a circle
Section 3:
Problems involving perimeter and circumference

GO TO
Chapter review

Section 1: Perimeter of simple and composite shapes

The **perimeter** of a shape is the total distance around the boundaries of the shape. To calculate the perimeter of a shape:
- find the lengths of all the sides, making sure they are in the same units
- add the lengths together.

Key vocabulary

perimeter: distance around the boundaries (sides) of a shape

Tip

Composite shapes are shapes that are made up of two or more basic shapes, for example, a rectangle joined to a triangle. Sometimes you will see them referred to as **compound shapes**.

Tip

The perimeter must include **all** the lengths. You can use what you know about the properties of shapes to deduce missing lengths.

WORKED EXAMPLE 1

Find the perimeter (P) of this T-shaped piece of cardboard.

All angles are right angles and all dimensions are in centimetres.

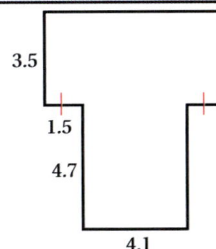

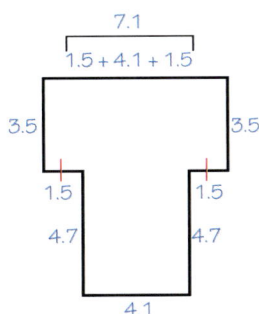

Start by working out the lengths of the missing sides.

$P = 7.1 + 3.5 + 1.5 + 4.7 + 4.1 + 4.7 + 1.5 + 3.5$
$\ = 30.6$

Add up the side lengths.

In shapes with parallel sides:

perimeter = sum of one pair of parallel sides + sum of the other pair of parallel sides,

so you can work it out quickly by finding the total length of each and doubling.

In this example the horizontal sides are 7.1 cm long and the vertical sides are 8.2 cm long, so

$P = 2(7.1 + 8.2) = 30.6$ cm

Using formulae to find perimeter

The properties of different polygons can be used to derive formulae for calculating the perimeter without adding up all the sides.

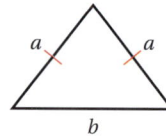

equilateral triangle

$P = 3s$

isosceles triangle

$P = 2a + b$

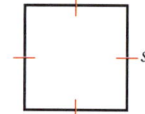

square

$P = 4s$

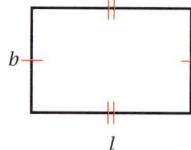

rectangle

$P = 2(l + b)$

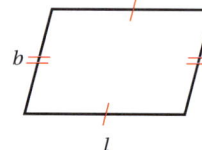

parallelogram

$P = 2(l + b)$

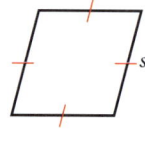

rhombus

$P = 4s$

For **regular polygons** you only need the length of one side to find the perimeter.

Multiply the side length by the number of sides.

Each side length of this regular hexagon is 6 cm so the perimeter is: 6 cm × 6 = 36 cm.

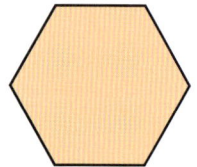

WORKED EXAMPLE 2

Write an expression for the perimeter of this shape in terms of x.

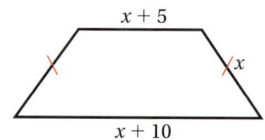

Perimeter $= x + (x + 5) + x + (x + 10)$
$= 4x + 15$

The perimeter is calculated by adding the side lengths around the outside of the shape. In this example the lengths are given in algebraic terms. Add the algebraic terms by collecting like parts.

EXERCISE 10A

1 What is the perimeter of an equilateral triangle of side length 10 cm?

2 A yard is fully enclosed by a fence of lengths 12 m, 4.7 m, 354 cm, 972 cm. What is the perimeter of the yard?

3 The perimeter of a square patio is 64 m.

What length is the side of the patio? Choose your answer from the options below.

A 8 m   B 10 m   C 12 m   D 16 m

4 Write expressions for the perimeter of these shapes.

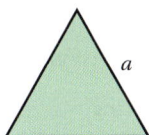

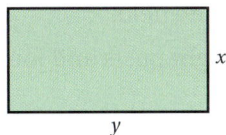

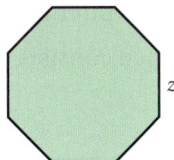

a An equilateral triangle, side length *a*.

b A rectangle, width *x* and length *y*.

c A regular octagon, side length *z*.

5 What is the perimeter of the triangle, in terms of *x*?
Choose from the options below.

A $x^3 + 5$ B $\dfrac{3x + 5}{2}$

C $3x + 5$ D $1.5x + 5$

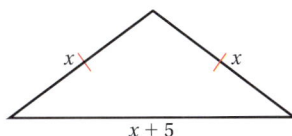

6 Work out the perimeter of this shape.
Each side length is 10 cm.

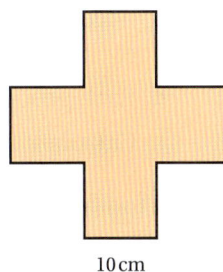

10 cm

7 This pattern is made by joining identical hexagons together.

If the side length of each hexagon is 8 cm, what is the perimeter of this shape?

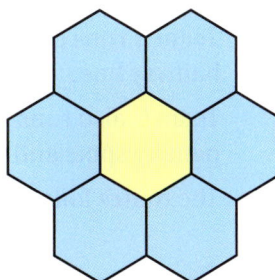

8 Each side length of this tiling pattern is 15 cm.
Work out its perimeter.

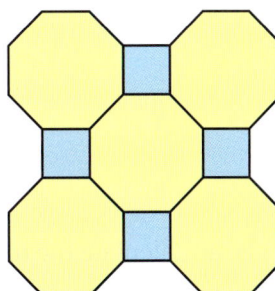

9 **a** Give reasons why the formulae for calculating the perimeter of a rectangle and a parallelogram and those for a square and a rhombus are the same.

b Give a reason why is there no formula for finding the perimeter of a trapezium.

10 A field has dimensions as shown on the diagram.

A fence is put up around the field.

The fence consists of upright posts and four strands of wire, as shown.

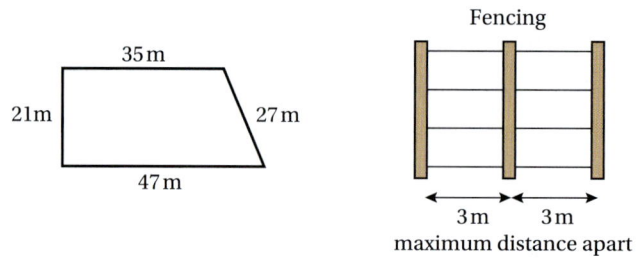

Fencing

35 m

21 m   27 m

47 m

3 m   3 m

maximum distance apart

a Find the total length of wire needed for the fencing.

b The fence posts are placed 2.8 metres apart.

Work out how many posts are needed.

(Assume there is no gate, only a style to get over the fence. You will need to add 4 extra posts as they are unlikely to fit exactly in each corner.)

c Each post costs £2.39 and the wire costs £1.78 per metre.

Calculate the cost of the fencing.

11 A football field is 64 m by 75 m.

Three teams are training on the field.

Team A warms up by running 10 times around the field.

Team B runs round half the field 15 times, cutting across the halfway line.

Team C also runs round half the field 15 times but they cut through the penalty spots and kickoff spot.

The routes followed by each team are shown on the diagram.

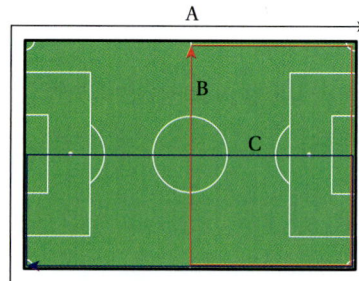

a Calculate the total distance run by each team.

b It takes Team C a quarter of an hour to complete their warm-up laps.

Work out their average running speed in km/h. The formula you need is:

average speed = distance travelled ÷ time taken

Finding lengths when the perimeter is known

You can calculate missing side-lengths of shapes if you know the perimeter and have enough information about the shape.

For example, if you know a regular hexagon has a perimeter of 72 cm, you can deduce that each of the six equal sides is 12 cm long because 72 cm ÷ 6 = 12 cm.

In other shapes you can substitute known values into the formula and solve for the unknown length.

WORKED EXAMPLE 3

What is the length of a rectangle of perimeter 20 cm and width 5.5 cm?

$P = 2(L + W)$
$P = 20, W = 5.5$

> Think about the information you have.

$$20 = 2L + 2(5.5)$$
$$20 = 2L + 11$$
$$20 - 11 = 2L$$
$$9 = 2L$$
$$L = 4.5 \text{ cm}$$

> Substitute the values into the formula and solve for L.

Perimeter of composite shapes

Composite shapes are formed by combining shapes or by removing parts of a shape.

For example, this shape is made up of a rectangle and a triangle.

To find the perimeter, add up the side lengths around the outside boundary of the shape.

The perimeter is: $4 + 3 + 3 + 4 + 3 = 17$ cm

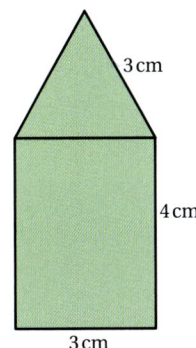

This rectangle has a parallelogram cut out of it.

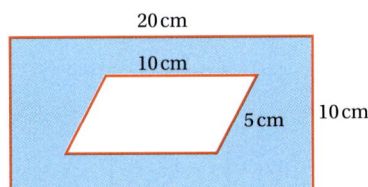

The perimeter of the shape must include all of the boundaries, so in examples like these, you must include the outer and inner boundaries of the shape.

$$P = 2(20 + 10) + 2(10 + 5)$$
$$= 2(30) + 2(15)$$
$$= 60 + 30$$
$$P = 90 \text{ cm}$$

Find answers at: cambridge.org/ukschools/gcsemaths-studentbookanswers

WORK IT OUT 10.1

This shape was made by combining five identical squares with sides of 6.5 cm with four identical equilateral triangles.

Which calculation will result in the correct perimeter? Why?

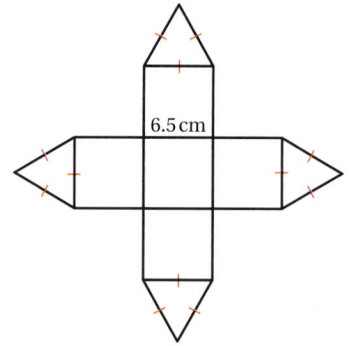

6.5 cm

Option A	Option B	Option C
$P = 16 \times 6.5$	$P = 20 \times 6.5$	$P = 24 \times 6.5$
$= 104$ cm	$= 130$ cm	$= 156$ cm

EXERCISE 10B

1 Copy and complete the table to find the missing values.

Perimeter	Length	Width
rectangle ABCD $P = 242$ mm	77 mm	
parallelogram MNOP $P = 200$ mm		55 mm
rhombus CDEF $P = 12.25$ cm		
square PQRS $P = 47.28$ cm		

2 Calculate the perimeter of each shape.

a

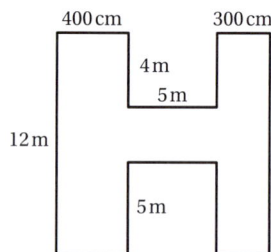

400 cm   300 cm
4 m
5 m
12 m
5 m

b

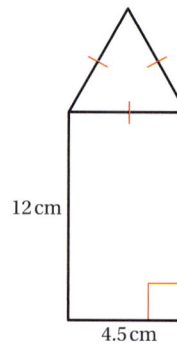

12 cm

4.5 cm

c

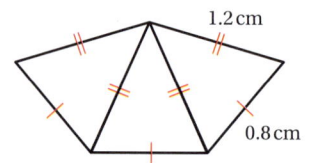

1.2 cm

0.8 cm

d

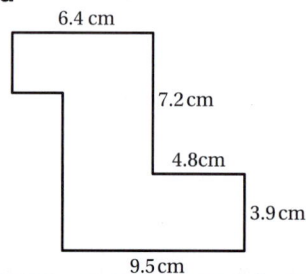

6.4 cm
7.2 cm
4.8 cm
3.9 cm
9.5 cm

e

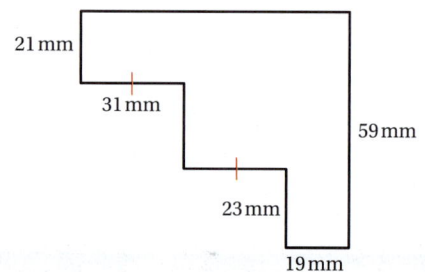

21 mm
31 mm
59 mm
23 mm
19 mm

3 Petra has the following mosaic tiles:

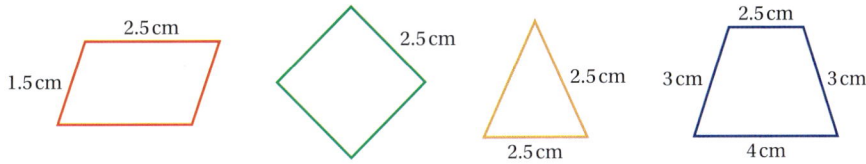

She arranges the tiles to make these shapes.

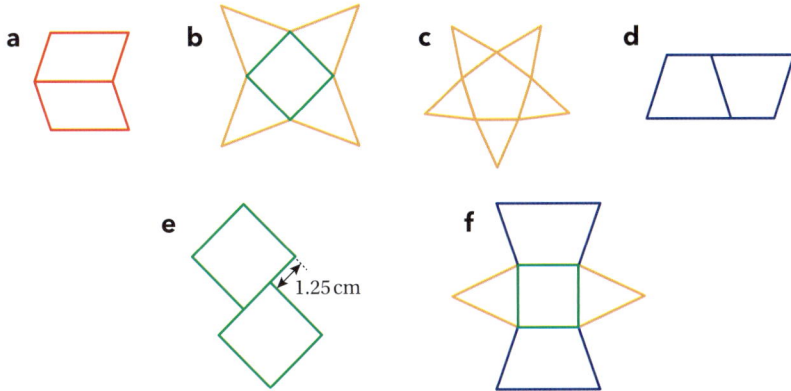

Use the dimensions above to find the perimeter of each shape.

4 The end of a maze consists of a regular pentagon with side length 5 m.

A child runs round this 3 times.

How far has she run in total? Choose from the options below.

A 15 m   B 25 m   C 75 m   D 750 m

5 A rectangular allotment has a perimeter of 25 metres.

The length of one side is 6.8 metres.

How wide is the allotment?

Section 2: Circumference of a circle

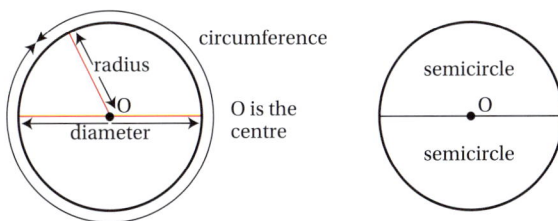

The perimeter of a circle is called its **circumference (C)**.

The radius (r) is the distance from the centre to the circumference.

The diameter (d) is a line through the centre of the circle. The diameter is twice the radius ($2r$).

When you divide the circumference of a circle by its diameter you get a constant ratio of approximately 3.142.

$\pi = \dfrac{C}{d}$ This ratio is called **pi** and the symbol π is used to represent it.

This ratio can be rearranged to give two formulae for finding the circumference of any circle.

Learn this formula

$C = \pi d$

where C = circumference and d = diameter.

Since the diameter is twice the length of the radius, the formula can also be written in terms of r.

$C = 2\pi r$

where r = radius.

Pi has no exact decimal or fractional value (it is an irrational number).

When you do calculations involving pi you might need to give rounded or approximate answers.

Your calculator can work with exact values of π but you might be given an approximate value of pi to use in a problem.

Problem-solving framework

Racing wheelchairs can travel at speeds of up to 45 mph and can cost up to £20 000.

The rear wheels of a chair have a diameter of 70 cm.

The hand wheels have a radius of 20 cm.

a Find the difference in circumference between the two wheels.

b Find the number of revolutions that the rear wheels will make over a 100 m race.

Steps for solving problems	What you would do for this example
Step 1: What have you got to do?	Find the difference in circumference between the two wheels, and find the number of revolutions (turns) that the rear wheels will make over 100 m.
Step 2: What information do you need?	Diameter (d) of rear wheel = 70 cm Radius (r) of hand wheel = 20 cm Length of race = 100 m Circumference formula: $C = \pi d$ or $2\pi r$
Step 3: What information don't you need?	The speed of the wheelchair and its cost are irrelevant.
Step 4: What maths can you use?	Circumference of rear wheel = $\pi d = \pi \times 70 = 219.9$ cm (to 1 dp) Circumference of hand wheel = $2\pi r = 2 \times \pi \times 20 = 125.7$ cm (to 1 dp) Difference in circumference = $219.9 - 125.7 = 94.2$ cm Change the units so that they are the same: 100 m = 100 × 100 cm = 10 000 cm Number of revolutions made by rear wheel = 10 000 ÷ 219.9 = 45.5 (to 1 dp)
Step 5: Have you used all the information? At this point you should check to make sure you have calculated what was asked for in the question.	All relevant information used ✓ Calculated part **a** ✓ Calculated part **b** ✓
Step 6: Is it correct?	Used diameter for rear wheel ✓ Used radius for hand wheel ✓ Converted cm into m correctly ✓

Knowing the circumference of a circle means that you can calculate the diameter and/or the radius.

WORKED EXAMPLE 4

A circle has a circumference of 200 cm.

Calculate the diameter of the circle to one decimal place.

$$C = \pi d$$
$$200 = \pi \times d$$

Using the equation for the circumference of a circle, fill in the parts you are given, using the value of π as 3.14 unless you are told otherwise.

$$200 \div \pi = d$$
$$d = 63.7 \text{ cm (to 1 dp)}$$

Rearrange the formula to find the diameter.

Tip

If you are asked to find r and use $C = \pi d$, remember to divide d by 2 to get r.

EXERCISE 10C

1 Use the π key on your calculator to calculate the circumference of each circle.

Give your answer to two decimal places where necessary.

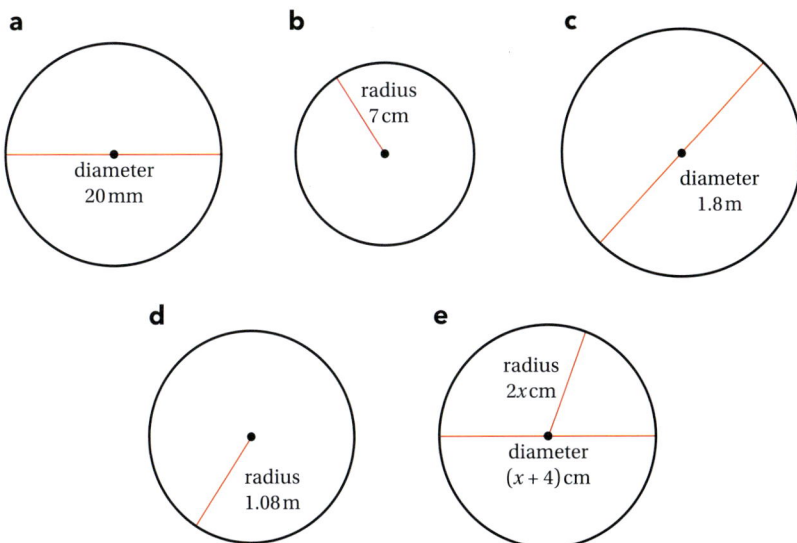

a

diameter 20 mm

b

radius 7 cm

c

diameter 1.8 m

d

radius 1.08 m

e

radius $2x$ cm

diameter $(x + 4)$ cm

2 The circumference of a circle is 94.2 cm.

What is its diameter? Use $\pi = 3.14$

Choose your answer from the following options.

A 295.8 cm   B 60 cm   C 30 cm   D 3.14 cm

3 A car wheel rim has a diameter of 42 cm. Calculate the circumference of the rim.

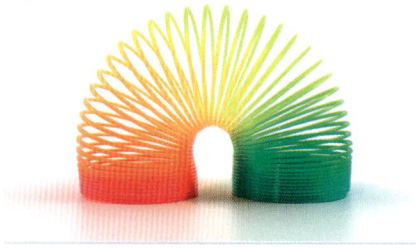

4 A plastic toy consists of 36 coils of plastic.

The diameter of one coil is 55 mm.

What length of plastic is needed to make the toy?

5 Nate has a square piece of metal with sides of 8.5 cm.

He needs to cut out a round disc from the square with a radius of at least 4 cm.

a Draw a rough sketch to show this piece of metal.

b Calculate the circumference of the disc with a radius of 4 cm.

c When he cuts the disc out, Nate finds the diameter is actually 8.3 cm.

What is the circumference of the disc?

d What is the perimeter of the piece of metal left after cutting out a disc of:

i radius 4 cm?   **ii** diameter 8.3 cm?

6 Find the diameter, to two decimal places, of a circle with a circumference of:

a 20 mm   **b** 15.2 cm.

7 A round CD has a circumference of 36.33 cm.

Find the radius of the CD to the nearest millimetre.

8 A round cake has a circumference of 77 cm.

The cake is displayed on a square plate.

What is the smallest possible side length of a plate the cake will fit on, without it hanging over the edge?

9 The minute hand of a clock is 75 mm long.

How far will the tip of the hand travel in one hour?

Give your answer to the nearest centimetre.

Sectors of a circle

A sector is a 'slice' of a circle.

The perimeter of a sector is formed by two radii and a section of the circumference is called an arc.

Perimeter of a sector
= radius + radius + arc length

To find the perimeter of a sector you have to work out the length of the arc.

The angle at the centre of a circle is a fraction of 360°.

You can express this as $\frac{x}{360}$

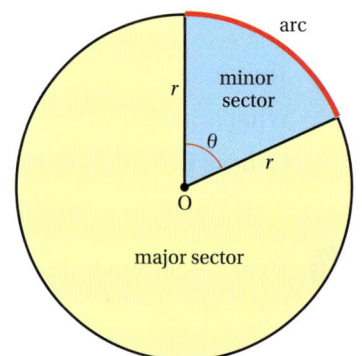

> ### Tip
>
> The term circumference is only used to describe the distance around a whole circle. When you deal with distance around parts of a circle you talk about the perimeter.

The arc length is a fraction of the circumference. To find the length of the arc, use the size of the angle and the circumference of the circle.

$$\text{Arc length} = \frac{x}{360} \times \pi d \qquad \text{or} \qquad \text{Arc length} = \frac{x}{360} \times 2\pi r$$

fraction   circumference   fraction   circumference

The angle θ is said to be **subtended** at the centre.

A subtended angle is one whose sides pass through the ends of an arc (or other curved line).

WORKED EXAMPLE 5

Find the length of the arc in each of these circle sectors.

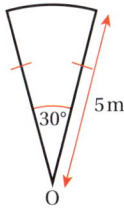

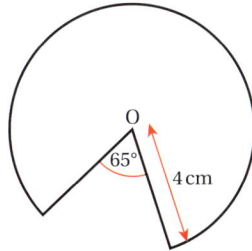

a Arc length $= \frac{30}{360} \times 2\pi r$

> Use $2\pi r$ here as you have been given the radius.

$= \frac{1}{12} \times 2 \times \pi \times 5$

$= 2.62\,\text{m (to 2 dp)}$

b $360° - 65° = 295°$

Arc length $= \frac{295}{360} \times 2 \times \pi \times 4$

> The angle inside the sector is not given. Work it out using angles round a point.

$= 20.59\,\text{cm (to 2 dp)}$

The semicircle and quarter-circle (quadrant) are special cases.

- In a semicircle, the angle at the centre is 180° and the arc length is half the circumference.
- In a quarter-circle, the angle at the centre is 90° and the arc length is a quarter of the circumference.

EXERCISE 10D

1 Find l in each of the following circles.

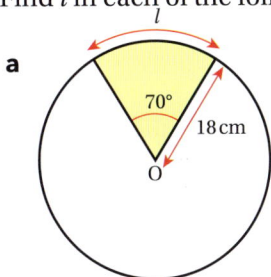

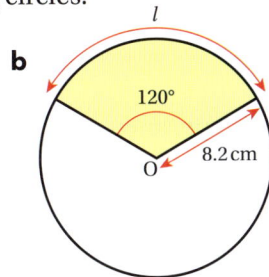

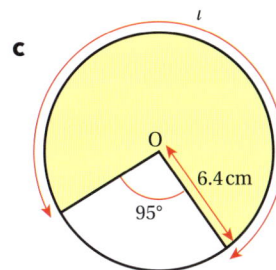

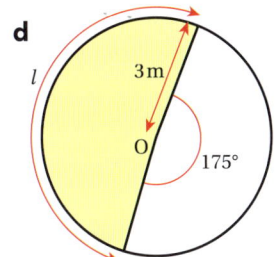

a

b

c

d

2 Find the perimeter of each shape.

a

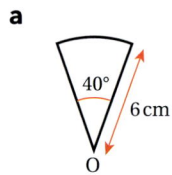
40°
6 cm
O

b

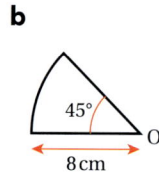
45°
O
8 cm

c

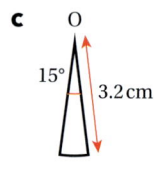
O
15°
3.2 cm

d

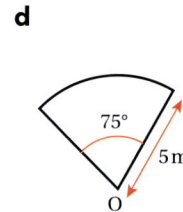
75°
5 m
O

e

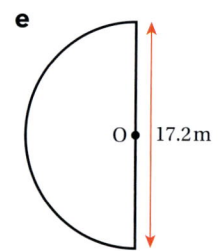
O
17.2 m

f

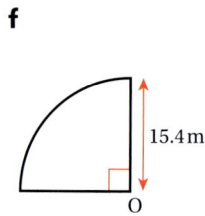
15.4 m
O

g

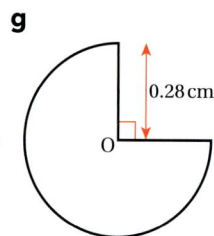
0.28 cm
O

h

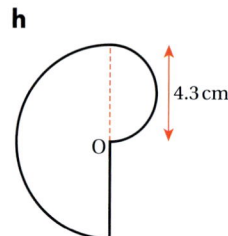
4.3 cm
O

i

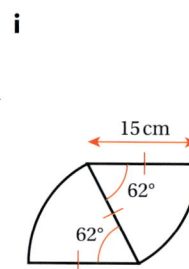
15 cm
62°
62°

j

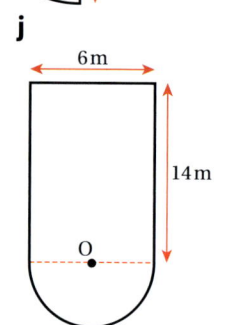
6 m
14 m
O

Section 3: Problems involving perimeter and circumference

In this section you are going to combine what you have learned about perimeter and circumference to solve problems involving composite shapes.

To work with irregular and composite shapes, divide them up into known shapes to make it easier to do the calculations.

WORKED EXAMPLE 6

The diagram shows a baseball field that is $\frac{1}{4}$ of a circle.

Calculate the perimeter of the field to the nearest metre

.

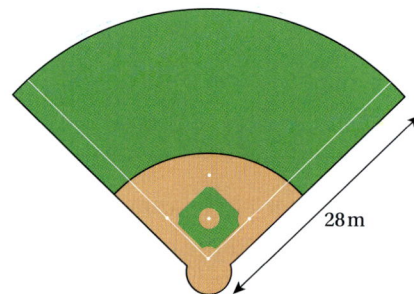
28 m

Circumference of whole circle = $2\pi r = 2 \times \pi \times 28$.

> The basis of this calculation is the formula relating to circles: circumference and arc length.

Arc length of $\frac{1}{4}$ circle $= \frac{C}{4}$
$$= \frac{2 \times \pi \times 28}{4}$$
$$= 43.98 \text{ m}$$

> The arc length is a portion of the circumference of a circle.

Perimeter = $2r$ + arc length
$$= 2 \times 28 + 43.98$$
$$= 56 + 43.98$$
$$= 99.98 \text{ m}$$
Perimeter = 100 m, to the nearest metre

> The perimeter in this case consists of the arc length added to two radii. (Radii is the plural of the radius.)

WORK IT OUT 10.2

This is a plan of a children's play area.

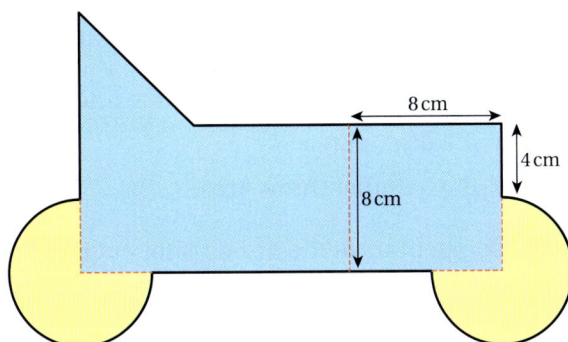

8 cm

4 cm

8 cm

Scale 1:25

Edging is to be placed around the curved edges of the sandpits.

Using π = 3.14, work out the total length of edging required.

Which of the answers below is the correct answer?

What mistakes have been made in the other workings?

Option A	Option B	Option C
Circumference of a circle = $\pi d = 2\pi r$ $r = 4\,cm$	Circumference of a circle = $\pi d = 2\pi r$ $r = 4\,cm$	Circumference of a circle = $2\pi d = \pi r$ $r = 4\,cm$
$C = 2 \times 3.14 \times 4$ $\quad = 3.14 \times 8$ $\quad = 25.12\,cm$	$C = 2 \times 3.14 \times 4$ $\quad = 3.14 \times 8$ $\quad = 25.12\,cm$	$C = 2 \times 3.14 \times 8$ $\quad = 3.14 \times 16$ $\quad = 50.24\,cm$
Scale 1:25 So, actual circumference of circle $= 25.12 \times 25$ $= 628\,cm$ $= 6.28\,m$	Only $\frac{3}{4}$ of the sandpit needs edging: $\frac{3}{4} \times 25.12\,cm = 18.84\,cm$	Only $\frac{3}{4}$ of the sandpit needs edging: $\frac{3}{4} \times 50.24\,cm = 37.68\,cm$
There are two sandpits so total edging required $= 6.28 \times 2 = 12.56\,m$	Two sandpits: $18.84 \times 2 = 37.68\,cm$ of edging Scale 1:25 So actual amount of edging required: $37.68 \times 25 = 942\,cm$ $\qquad\qquad = 9.42\,m$	Two sandpits: $37.68 \times 2 = 75.36\,cm$ of edging Scale 1:25 So actual amount of edging required: $75.36 \times 25 = 1884\,cm$ $\qquad\qquad = 18.84\,m$

💡 **Tip**

Perimeter can be worked out by measuring lengths, or by using lengths from a scale diagram.

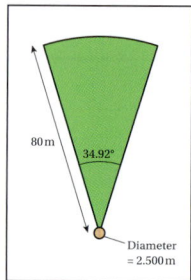

Discus

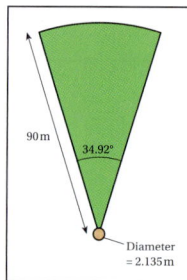

Hammer throw

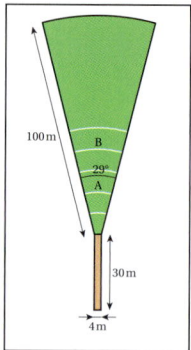

Javelin

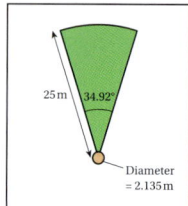

Shot put

EXERCISE 10E

The diagram shows the shape and dimensions of different throwing event field areas used in competitions, such as discus.

Use the information on the diagrams to answer questions 1 to 5.

1 Calculate the length of the white line painted around the outside of:

a the discus area

b the hammer throw area.

2 Competitors in the discus, shot put and hammer throw have to remain inside a marked circle while the equipment is in their hands (before they throw it).

a Which sport has the largest marked circle?

b What is the circumference of the circle in the discus throwing cage?

c In shot put and hammer throw, a raised edge is built around the circumference of the starting circle.

The edge is 10 cm wide.

Calculate its inner and outer circumference.

3 Calculate the perimeter of the event space for javelin.

4 The curved measurement lines on each event space are 10 m apart.

Using the javelin field, calculate the length of the lines marked A and B.

5 The position of a winning discus throw is shown on the field by a red dot.

The angle between its path and the edge of the marked area closest to it is 10°.

Work out how far it is from each edge of the area.

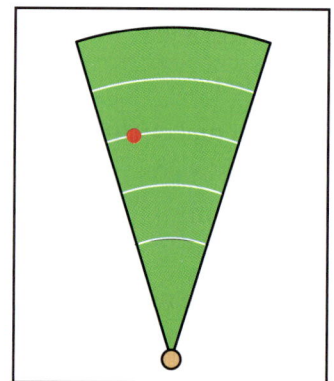

discus

6 The radius of the Earth is approximately 6378.1 km at the Equator.

Calculate the approximate distance around the Equator. Give your answer to two decimal places.

7 A pizza has a circumference of 94 cm.

What is the side length of the smallest cardboard box it will fit into? Choose your answer from the following options.

A 94 cm   B 29.92 cm   C 14.97 cm

8 Find the perimeter of the symmetrical logo shown in the margin.

Use a ruler and protractor to measure and find the dimensions you need.

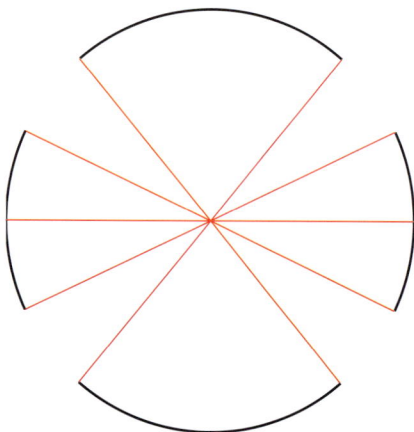

9 The diagram in the margin shows the design of a small stained glass window.

What is the perimeter of the window?

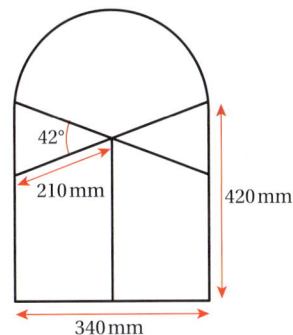

10 The London eye has a diameter of 122 m.

a What is its circumference?

b There are 32 equally spaced pods on the outside of the wheel.

Calculate the curved distance between them.

c The curved boarding platform at the base of the eye is 58 m long.

How far does a capsule travel from where it leaves this platform to where it meets it again after one revolution?

d One capsule takes 30 minutes to make a complete revolution.

What is its speed in metres per second?

e The London Eye rotates 7668 times per year.

How many kilometres does one capsule travel in a year?

f The London Eye opened in 1999. By 2013, 50 million people had ridden it.

i Calculate the mean number of visitors per annum based on these figures.

ii In 2014, the mean ticket price was £26.55.

There was a 10% increase in visitors in 2014 from the mean number of visitors.

Work out the approximate value of ticket sales in 2014.

Checklist of learning and understanding

Perimeter

- Perimeter is the total distance around the boundaries of a shape.
- You can calculate perimeter by adding the lengths of the sides or by applying a formula based on the properties of the shape.

Circumference

- The perimeter of a circle is called its circumference (C).
- $C = \pi d$ or $C = 2\pi r$
- A sector is a part of a circle between two radii. You can find the arc length of a sector by working out what fraction of a circle the sector represents.

For additional questions on the topics in this chapter, visit GCSE Mathematics Online.

Chapter review

1 What is the formula for the circumference of a circle?

Choose from the options below.

A $\frac{1}{2}bh$ B $2\pi r$ C πr^2 D $\frac{4}{3}\pi r^3 h$

2 The perimeters of the two shapes below are equal.

What is the side length of the square?

8 cm

6 cm

3 Drew has a piece of ribbon that is 0.5 m long. She wants to tie a bow around a present in a tube that has a diameter of 10 cm.

Will she have enough ribbon? Use $\pi = 3.14$

4 The perimeter of a regular pentagon is 90 cm.

Work out the length of each side.

5 A rectangular vegetable plot has a perimeter of 50 metres.

The width is 6.5 metres.

What is the length of the plot?

6 John has a new bike with wheels that have diameter 55 cm.

He cycles in a straight line and the wheels turn 25 complete revolutions (turns).

Did he cycle more than 0.5 km? Use $\pi = 3.14$

7 What is the perimeter of this three-quarter circle that is being used in a computer graphic? It has a radius of 50 mm. Use $\pi = 3.14$

8 An irrigator in a field can water a circular area of radius 14.5 m.

What is the circumference of the area that can be irrigated? Use $\pi = 3.14$

9 A pizza has a circumference of 88 cm. It is placed in a cardboard box.

Calculate the perimeter of the smallest box that it will fit into.

10 Calculate the perimeter of the shape shown below.

Give your answer to one decimal place.

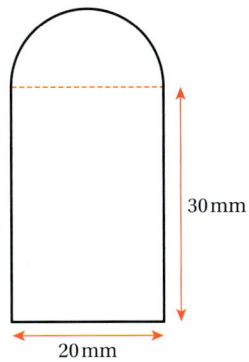

30 mm

20 mm

11 The diagram shows some staging for a concert.

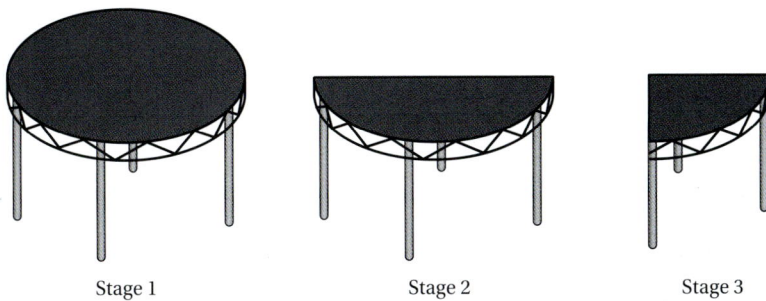

Stage 1   Stage 2   Stage 3

The main stage is a circle of diameter 6 m.

The smaller stages can be made by splitting up a main stage into smaller pieces.

The curved edges of the staging pieces have a patterned edge.

a Work out the length of the patterned edging on the stage sections shown in the diagram.

b A safety rubber strip is to be applied along all the edges of the staging.

Work out the total length of strip required for the three stage sections shown in the diagram.

12 This shape is made from identical quarter circles.

7 cm

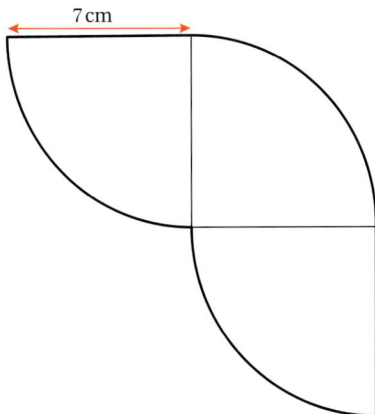

Not drawn accurately

Work out the perimeter of the shape.

(4 marks)

© AQA 2013

11 Area

Using mathematics: real-life applications

Ordering the right quantity of turf for a sports field, preparing detailed floor plans, and working out how much fertiliser is needed to treat a field crop all require knowledge and calculation of areas.

Did you know?

The area of farmland is often given in acres or hectares. An acre was traditionally the area of farmland that could be ploughed in one day by oxen. In the metric system, the acre was replaced by the hectare. 1 hectare = $10\,000\,m^2$

"Fertiliser application rates are normally given in kilograms per hectare. One hectare is an area of $100\,m \times 100\,m$ or $10\,000\,m^2$. Applying too much or too little fertiliser to an area can have disastrous results on the crops."

(Farmer)

Before you start ...

Ch 8	You should remember the properties of quadrilaterals.	**1** Use the marked properties to name the quadrilaterals correctly. **a** **b** **c**

KS3
Ch 4
	You should be familiar with square numbers and square roots.	**2** Calculate:
		  a 5^2 **b** 2×10^2 **c** $3^2 + 4^2$
		
		3 Find the number that is squared to give each of these.
		  a 144 **b** 10 000 **c** 0.25

KS3	You need to be able to convert between square units of measurement.	**4** Complete these: **a** $5\,m^2 = \square\,cm^2$ **b** $\square\,cm^2 = 87\,000\,mm^2$ **c** $4\,km^2 = \square\,m^2$

Assess your starting point using the Launchpad

STEP 1

1 Match each figure to the calculation that will give its area.

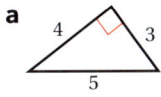

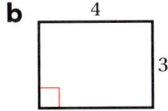

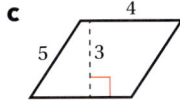

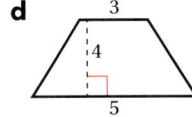

a

b

c

d

e

A $A = 4 \times 3$ B $A = 4 \times 4$ C $A = \dfrac{4 \times 3}{2}$

GO TO
Section 1:
Area of polygons

STEP 2

2 In the formula $A = \pi r^2$:

a what is the subject of the formula?

b what does the symbol π represent?

c what does *r* represent when you are dealing with circles?

3 Calculate the area of this semicircular rug of diameter 3.2 m. Use a value of 3.14 for π and give your answer to two decimal places.

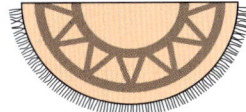

4 Calculate the area of the sector shown. Use a value of 3.14 for π and give your answer to the nearest whole number.

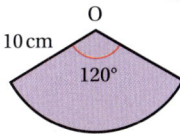

10 cm O 120°

GO TO
Section 2:
Area of circles and sectors

STEP 3

5 Work out the floor area of this stadium.

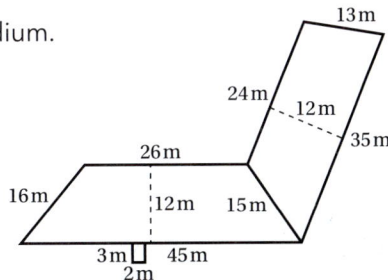

13 m 24 m 12 m 35 m 26 m 16 m 12 m 15 m 3 m 2 m 45 m

GO TO
Section 3:
Area of composite shapes

GO TO
Chapter review

Find answers at: cambridge.org/ukschools/gcsemaths-studentbookanswers

Section 1: Area of polygons

The **area** of a plane shape is the amount of space it takes up.

Area is always given in square units. Common units are mm² (square millimetres), cm² (square centimetres), m² and km².

Area of rectangles and squares

The formula for finding the area of a rectangle is:

area = length × width

$A = lw$

In a square, the length and width are equal, so the formula is:

area of the square = $l \times l = l^2$

$A = l^2$

Area of a triangle

You can show that the area of any triangle is half the area of a rectangle by drawing in a rectangle.

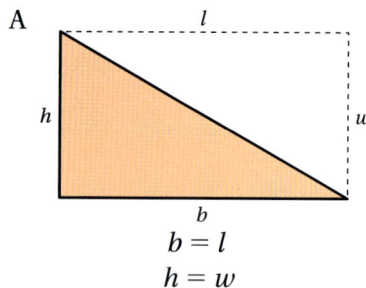

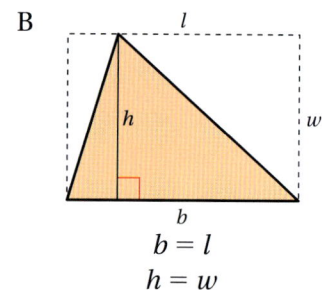

Figure A shows a right-angled triangle. Figure B shows a scalene triangle.

In both diagrams the areas of the shaded and unshaded parts are equal.

Area of rectangle = $l \times w$

Area of triangle = $\frac{1}{2} \times l \times w$

The length l is equal to the base of the triangle and w is equal to the height of the triangle, so

area of triangle = $\frac{1}{2}$ × length of its base × its height

This gives a formula for the area of any triangle.

> **Learn this formula**
>
> Area of a triangle = $\frac{1}{2}$ × base × perpendicular height
> = $\frac{1}{2} \times b \times h$

WORKED EXAMPLE 1

Calculate the area of each triangle.

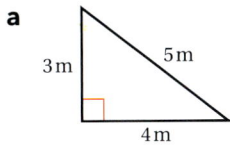

a

3 m, 5 m, 4 m (right-angled triangle)

b

0.9 m, 1.9 m (triangle)

c

30 mm, 170 mm (triangle)

a Area $= \frac{1}{2} \times b \times h$

$= \frac{1}{2} \times 4 \times 3$

$= \frac{1}{2} \times 12$

$= 6 \, m^2$

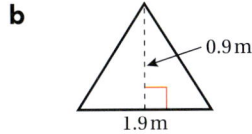

> In a right-angled triangle the two shorter (perpendicular) sides can be used as the base and height.

> Remember to include the units in the answer.

b Area $= \frac{1}{2} \times b \times h$

$= \frac{1}{2} \times 1.9 \times 0.9$

$= \frac{1}{2} \times 1.71$

$= 0.855 \, m^2$

> Use the side marked 1.9 as the base because the height is perpendicular to it.

c Area $= \frac{bh}{2}$

$= \frac{(170 \times 30)}{2}$

$= \frac{5100}{2}$

$= 2550 \, mm^2$

> This is the same formula but expressed differently. Multiplying by $\frac{1}{2}$ is the same as dividing by 2.

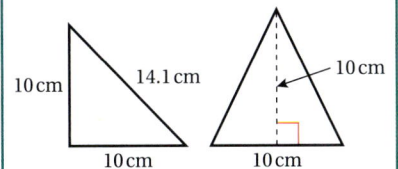

EXERCISE 11A

1 Choose the correct answer from the given options.

a What is the area of a rectangular field with length 24 m and width 17 m?

A 82 m² B 204 m² C 408 m² D 408 m³

b What is the area of a triangle with perpendicular height x cm and base y cm?

A $x^2 y^2$ cm B $(x + y)$ cm² C $\frac{1}{2}(xy)$ cm² D xy cm²

2 Calculate the area of each triangle.

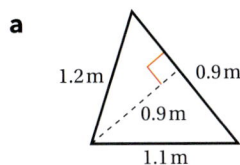

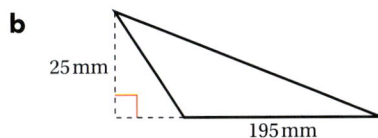

a

1.2 m, 0.9 m, 0.9 m, 1.1 m

b

25 mm, 195 mm

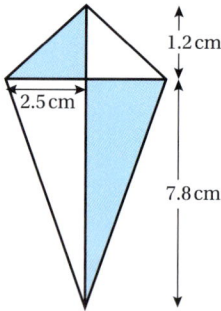

3 The area of a triangle is $36\,m^2$.

Its perpendicular height is $6\,m$.

Work out the length of its base.

4 Work out the total area of the kite shown in the margin.

5 A triangle has a base of $3.6\,m$ and a height of $50\,cm$.

What is its area? Give your answer in square metres.

6 A triangle of area $0.125\,m^2$ has a base $25\,cm$ long.

What is its height in centimetres?

7 The mast on this small boat is $2.7\,m$ tall.

The smaller sail extends $\frac{2}{3}$ of the way up the mast.

Calculate the total area of the sails.

1.5 m   2.2 m

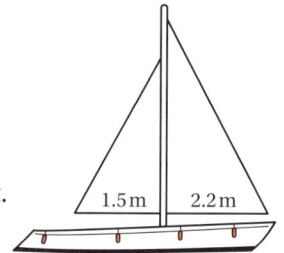

8 The flags of Nepal, Eritrea, Trinidad and Tobago, Antigua and Barbuda, and Guyana were seen at an international convention centre in 2014.

a The flag of Nepal was made up of two triangles, one above the other.

The bottom triangle overlapped the top triangle by $\frac{1}{4}$ of its area.

The dimensions of the top triangle to the bottom one were in the ratio 3 : 4.

The top flag was $84\,cm$ high and $63\,cm$ wide at its base.

What was the area of the whole flag?

b The flag of Eritrea contained three triangles.

The flag dimensions were $1.2\,m$ by $60\,cm$.

Calculate the area of each triangle on the flag.

c The flag of Trinidad and Tobago was $1.3\,m$ by $87\,cm$.

The width of the black and white flash was $32.5\,cm$ along the edges of the flag.

Calculate the area of each red triangle.

d A small decorative flag of Antigua and Barbuda was $210\,mm \times 297\,mm$.

i What is the area of each red triangle?

ii Estimate the area of the white triangle based on these dimensions.

Show how you made your estimate.

e On the flag of Guyana, the point of the black line around the red triangle extended $\frac{4}{9}$ of the length of the flag.

Assuming the flag was $270\,mm$ by $450\,mm$, calculate:

i The area covered by the red and black triangle.

ii The area of each green triangle.

iii The area of the 'golden arrow' made by the yellow and white colour on the flag.

f Investigate the dimensions of the Union Flag. What percentage of the flag area is each colour?

Nepal

Eritea

Trinidad and Tobago

Antigua and Barbuda

Guyana

1.2 cm

2.5 cm

7.8 cm

Area of a parallelogram

The base of this parallelogram is b and the **perpendicular height** is h.

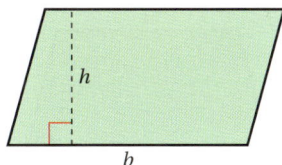

By removing a triangle from one end and joining it to the other end, you can form a rectangle.

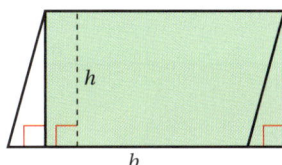

The parallelogram and rectangle have the same area.

Learn this formula

Area of a parallelogram = base × perpendicular height

$$= b \times h$$

Tip

You must use the perpendicular height and not the slant height.

WORKED EXAMPLE 2

Calculate the area of the parallelogram.

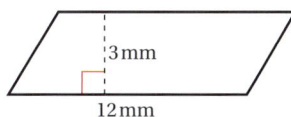

$$Area = b \times h$$
$$= 12 \times 3 = 36\,mm^2$$

Substitute into the area formula.

Don't forget to add the units.

You can use the formula for the area of a triangle to derive the formula for the area of a parallelogram.

A parallelogram can be divided into two triangles.

So, area of parallelogram $= (\frac{1}{2} \times b \times h) + (\frac{1}{2} \times b \times h) = b \times h$

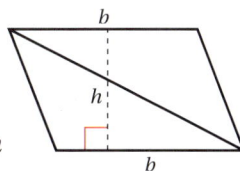

WORK IT OUT 11.1

A parallelogram is made by combining a rectangle and two right-angled triangles like this.

Which of these options will give the correct area?

What is wrong in the other two calculations?

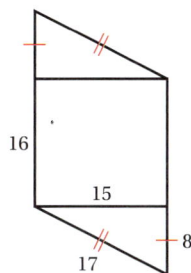

Option A	Option B	Option C
$A = bh$	$A = bh$	$A = bh$
$= 16 \times 17$	$= 24 \times 17$	$= 24 \times 15$

Find answers at: cambridge.org/ukschools/gcsemaths-studentbookanswers

Area of a trapezium

A **trapezium** has parallel sides a and b, and perpendicular height h.

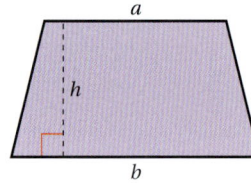

If you join two trapezia you can form a parallelogram.

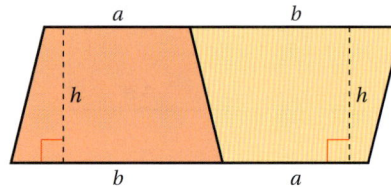

The parallelogram has a base of length $a + b$, and perpendicular height h.

Area of a parallelogram = base × perpendicular height

So area = $(a + b) \times h$

Each trapezium is half the area of the parallelogram.

Learn this formula

Area of a trapezium = $\frac{1}{2} \times (a + b) \times h$, where a and b are the lengths of the parallel sides and h is the perpendicular height

WORK IT OUT 11.2

A solar farm is being built in a field.

Each solar panel measures 98 cm by 150 cm.
A total of 500 panels are installed on the field.
What is the total area of panels being used, in m^2?
(Remember $1\,m^2 = 10\,000\,cm^2$)

Which of the answers below is correct?

What errors were made in each of the others?

Answer A	Answer B	Answer C
Area of one panel:	Area of one panel:	Area of one panel:
$98 \times 150 = 14\,700\,cm^2$	$\frac{1}{2} \times (98 \times 150) = 7350\,cm^2$	$98 \times 150 = 14\,700\,cm^2$
$1\,m^2 = 10\,000\,cm^2$	$1\,m^2 = 10\,000\,cm^2$	$1\,m^2 = 100\,cm^2$
1 panel = $14\,700 \div 10\,000 = 1.47\,m^2$	1 panel = $7350 \div 10\,000 = 0.735\,m^2$	1 panel = $14\,700 \div 100 = 147\,m^2$
500 panels = $1.47\,m^2 \times 500$ $= 735\,m^2$	500 panels = $0.735\,m^2 \times 500$ $= 367.5\,m^2$	500 panels = $147\,m^2 \times 500$ $= 73\,500\,m^2$

EXERCISE 11B

1 Use the formula $A = bh$ to calculate the area of each parallelogram.

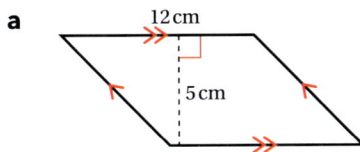

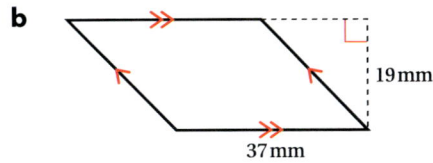

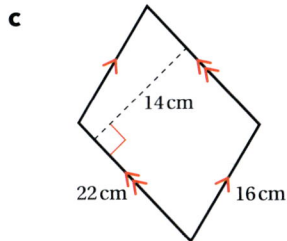

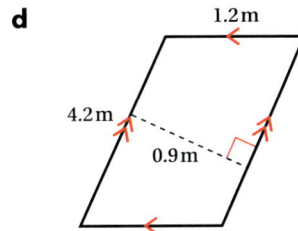

a
12 cm
5 cm

b
37 mm
19 mm

c
14 cm
22 cm
16 cm

d
1.2 m
4.2 m
0.9 m

2 Use the formula $A = \frac{1}{2}(a + b)h$ to calculate the area of each trapezium.

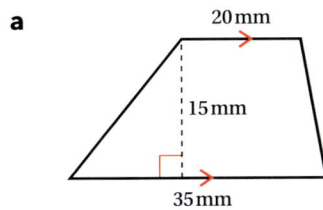

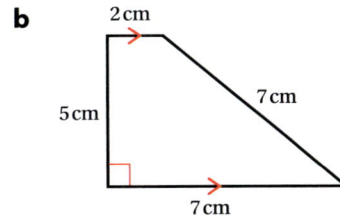

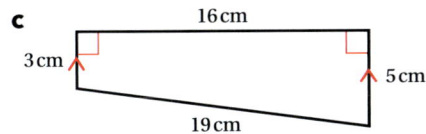

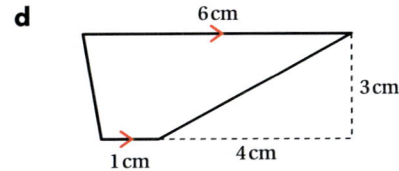

a
20 mm
15 mm
35 mm

b
2 cm
5 cm
7 cm
7 cm

c
16 cm
3 cm
5 cm
19 cm

d
6 cm
3 cm
1 cm
4 cm

3 The area of this rectangle is 96 cm².
Work out its length.

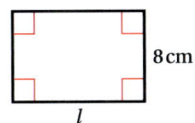

8 cm
l

4 The area of a parallelogram is 40 cm².
Its perpendicular height is 10 cm.
Work out the length of its base. Choose from the options below.

A 2 cm   B 4 cm   C 8 cm   D 10 cm

5 The area and one other measurement is given for each shape.

Use the given information to find the unknown length in each shape.

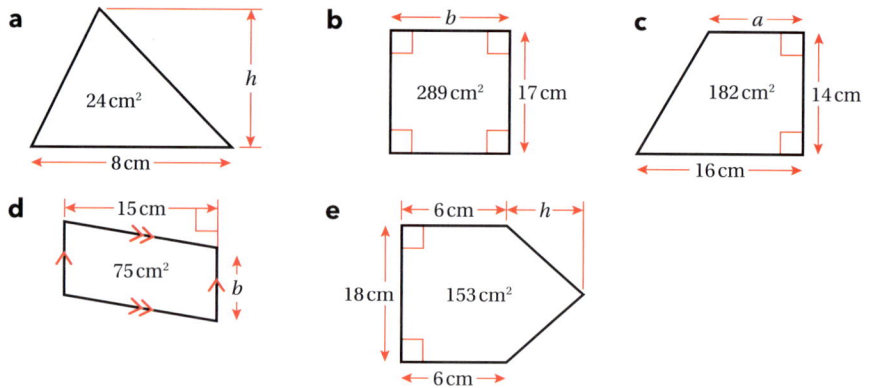

a

$24\,\text{cm}^2$ h $8\,\text{cm}$

b

b $289\,\text{cm}^2$ $17\,\text{cm}$

c

a $182\,\text{cm}^2$ $14\,\text{cm}$ $16\,\text{cm}$

d

$15\,\text{cm}$ $75\,\text{cm}^2$ b

e

$6\,\text{cm}$ h $18\,\text{cm}$ $153\,\text{cm}^2$ $6\,\text{cm}$

6 Amira grows organic vegetables.

The area of land available in one field is shown on the plan.

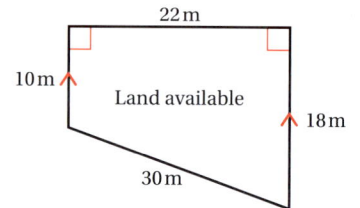

$22\,\text{m}$ $10\,\text{m}$ Land available $18\,\text{m}$ $30\,\text{m}$

a Calculate the area of the available land.

b Amira lays down 25 kg of soil and 10 kg of compost per square metre of land.

Work out how much soil and compost she will need.

c There is a gate 2 m wide along the 22 m boundary.

The rest of the land needs to be fenced.

Work out the total amount of fencing needed.

d Once the first crop is planted an organic fertiliser is mixed with water and applied to the area. The instructions for mixing the powdered fertiliser with water are:

Mix 43 g/litre. The application rate is 125 litres per hectare.

i Work out how many litres are needed for this area. Remember one hectare is $10\,000\,\text{m}^2$.

ii The powder comes in $\frac{1}{2}$ kg tubs.

How many applications can Amira get from one tub?

7 Write an expression in simplest terms for the area of each shape.

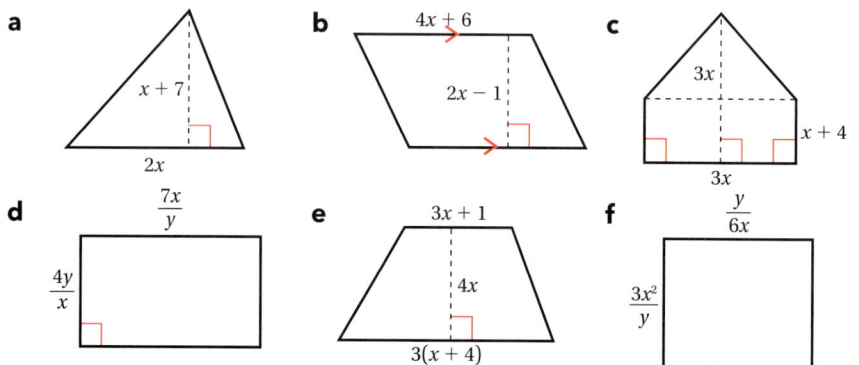

a

$x + 7$ $2x$

b

$4x + 6$ $2x - 1$

c

$3x$ $x + 4$ $3x$

d

$\frac{7x}{y}$ $\frac{4y}{x}$

e

$3x + 1$ $4x$ $3(x + 4)$

f

$\frac{y}{6x}$ $\frac{3x^2}{y}$

Section 2: Area of circles and sectors

Calculator tip

Use the π key of your calculator to find the area and circumference of circles unless you are given an approximate value to use for π.

Leave the value you get on the display for the next step and only round off to the required number of places when you have a final value.

The area of a circle is calculated using the formula:

Learn this formula

Area of a circle, $A = \pi r^2$ where r = radius of the circle

If you are given the diameter, d, of the circle you can still use this formula by remembering that:

$$r = \frac{1}{2}d$$

WORKED EXAMPLE 3

Calculate the area of this circle to two decimal places.

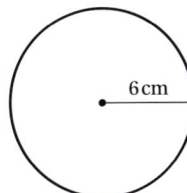

6 cm

$A = \pi r^2$

$= \pi \times 6 \times 6$ Substitute the value for the radius into the formula for the area.

$= 113.0973355 \, \text{cm}^2$ Don't forget to add the units.

$= 113.10 \, \text{cm}^2$ (to 2 dp)   Round to two decimal places.

When you know the area of a circle you can find the length of a radius (or the diameter).

WORKED EXAMPLE 4

Calculate the radius of a circle with area 50 cm².

$A = \pi r^2$

$50 = \pi \times r^2$ Substitute the value for the area into the formula.

$r^2 = \dfrac{50}{\pi}$ Rearrange the equation to make r^2 the subject.

$r = \sqrt{\dfrac{50}{\pi}}$ Solve for r.

$= 3.989422804 \, \text{cm}$ Don't forget to add the units.

$= 3.99 \, \text{cm}$ (to 2 dp)   Round to two decimal places.

Tip

If you are asked to find the diameter (d), remember it is twice the radius ($2 \times r$).

Find answers at: cambridge.org/ukschools/gcsemaths-studentbookanswers

Area of a sector

A sector is a fraction of the area of the whole circle.

To find the area of a sector you need to know what fraction the sector is of the circle.

You find this by dividing the sector angle by 360.

In the diagram the fraction of the area of the whole circle is $\frac{\theta}{360}$.

So, area of sector of circle $= \frac{\theta}{360} \times$ area of circle

Area of a circle $= \pi r^2$

area of sector of circle $= \frac{\theta}{360} \times \pi r^2$

Remember:

A semicircle is half a circle, so its area is half the area of a circle $(\frac{\pi r^2}{2})$.

A quarter-circle is one quarter of a circle, so its area is one quarter of the area of a circle $(\frac{\pi r^2}{4})$.

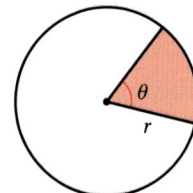

Tip

You also did this to find the arc length in Chapter 10.

WORKED EXAMPLE 5

Calculate the area of the sector shown.

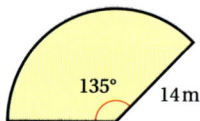

135° 14 m

Area of sector of circle $= \frac{\theta}{360} \times \pi r^2$

$= \frac{135}{360} \times \pi \times r^2$ — Substitute the value of θ into the formula.

$= 0.375 \times \pi \times 14^2$ — Substitute for r.

$= 230.90706 \, m^2$

$= 230.91 \, m^2$ (to 2 dp) — Add the units and round to two decimal places.

EXERCISE 11C

1 Calculate the area of a circle with a diameter of 20 m. Take π as 3.14.
Choose your answer from the options below.
A 314 m²   B 1256 m²   C 62.8 m²   D 31.4 m²

2 Find the area of each circle in the diagram.
Use the value of π from your calculator and give your answers to two decimal places.

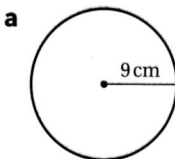

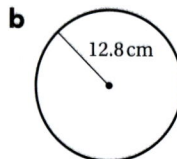

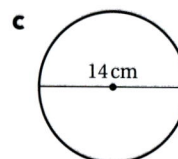

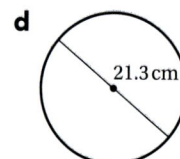

a 9 cm   b 12.8 cm   c 14 cm   d 21.3 cm

3 Use the formula $A = \dfrac{\theta}{360} \times \pi r^2$ to find the area of each sector of these circles.

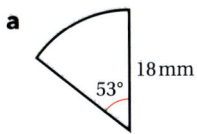

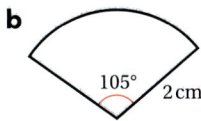

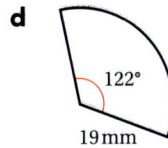

a 18 mm, 53°

b 105°, 2 cm

c 4 m, 28°

d 122°, 19 mm

4 Find the difference in area between these two sectors of a circle.

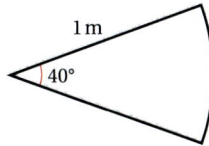

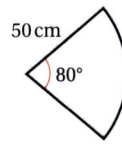

1 m, 40°

50 cm, 80°

5 A pizza has a diameter of 14 cm.
- **a** Calculate the area of the pizza.
- **b** The pizza is served on a round plate with about 1 cm space around the edge.

  Estimate the area of the plate.

6 A pair of sunglasses has circular lenses each 6.4 cm in diameter.
- **a** What is the total area of the tinted surface of the lenses?
- **b** What is the circumference of the smallest round frame that each lens can fit into?

7 The area for discus at an international event has the dimensions shown in the diagram in the margin.
- **a** Calculate the area of the grass in the landing zone.
- **b** Calculate the area of the starting circle in the throwing cage.

Discus throwing cage

34.92°, 80 m, 2.5 m diameter

8 A circular disc has a circumference of 75.398 mm.

Use this information to find the area of the disc.

9 A jeweller is making a tapered tube to set a diamond.

She works out the dimension of the curved piece of metal she needs based on the diameter and depth of the stone.

She draws a rough sketch like this.

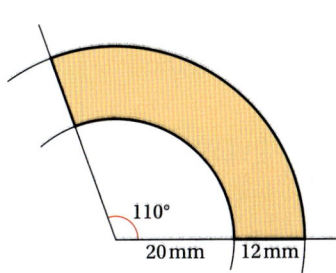

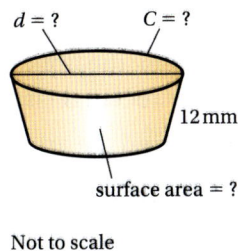

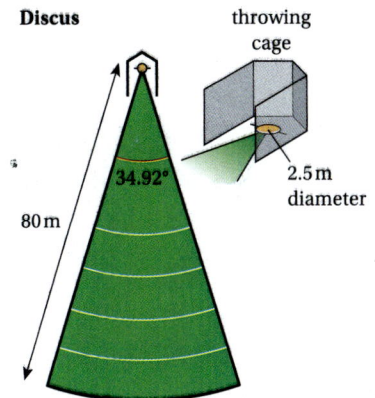

110°, 20 mm, 12 mm

$d = ?$ $C = ?$ 12 mm   surface area = ?   Not to scale

Work out:
- **a** the area of the flat curved section shown on the diagram.
- **b** the diameter and circumference of the top of the finished tube.
- **c** the diameter and circumference of the bottom of the finished tube.

Section 3: Area of composite shapes

You can find the area of composite shapes in different ways.

Addition of parts

- Divide the figure into smaller known shapes whose areas can be found directly.
- Calculate the area of each part separately.
- Add the areas of all the parts to find the total area.

For example:

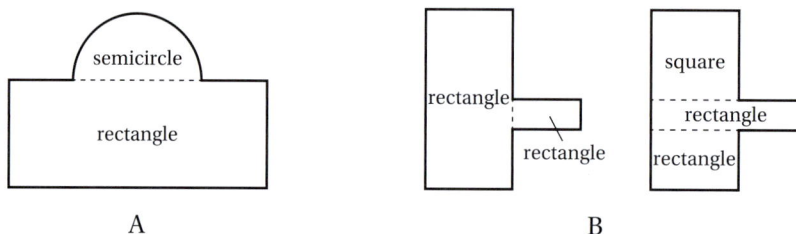

Figure A can be divided into a rectangle and a semicircle.

Figure B can be divided in different ways. The first way requires fewer calculations.

Subtraction of parts

Tip

Some problems can be solved either way. Think carefully about which method will be more efficient before you decide which one to use.

Tip

Copy diagrams into your exercise book so you can draw on them and mark dimensions. This helps you to keep track of your working.

When one figure is 'cut out' of another you have to find the area of the larger figure and subtract the area of the cut-out part.

For example, in the diagram on the right:

shaded area = area of square – area of circle

In some cases, you can find the area by viewing the figure as part of a larger known shape and subtracting the parts that have been 'removed'.

For example , to work out the area of the diagram on the right:

You can work out the area of the large rectangle (made by drawing the dotted line) and subtract the smaller cut-out rectangle from it.

You could also find the area by addition, but you would need to do more calculations.

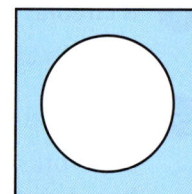

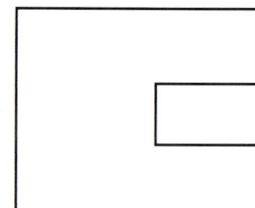

EXERCISE 11D

1 Find the total area of each of these shapes. Show all your working.

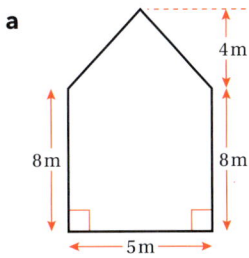

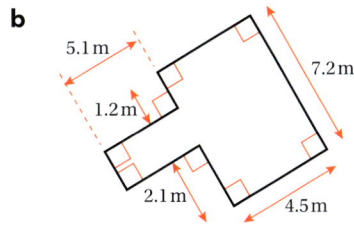

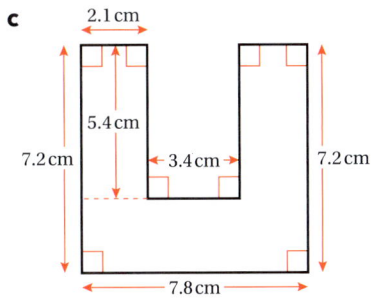

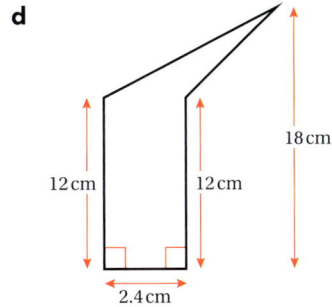

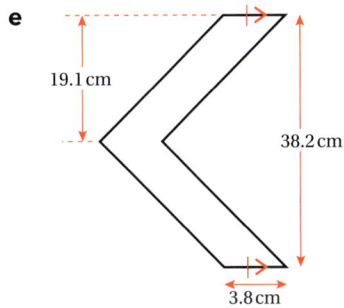

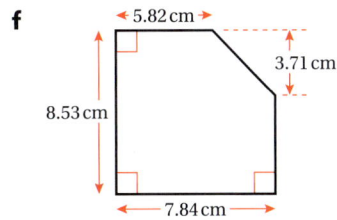

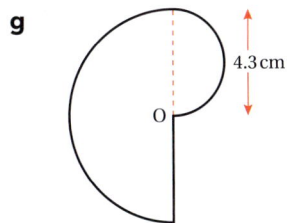

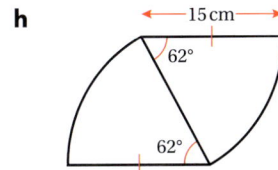

a

4m
8m   8m
5m

b

5.1m
1.2m
7.2m
2.1m
4.5m

c

2.1cm
5.4cm
7.2cm   3.4cm   7.2cm
7.8cm

d

12cm   12cm   18cm
2.4cm

e

19.1cm
38.2cm
3.8cm

f

5.82cm
3.71cm
8.53cm
7.84cm

g

O   4.3cm

h

15cm
62°
62°

2 Find the area of the shaded part of each figure.

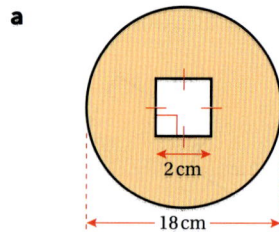

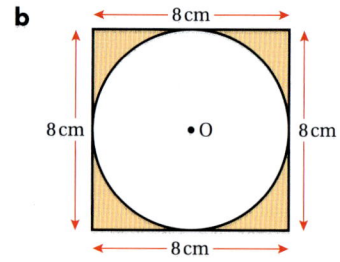

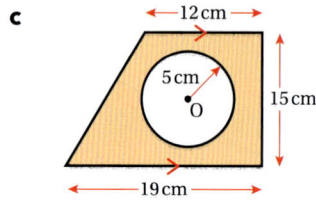

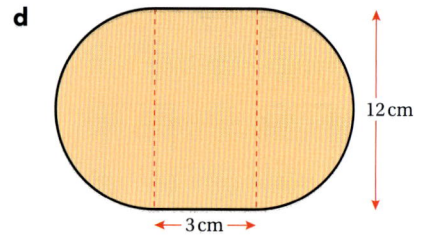

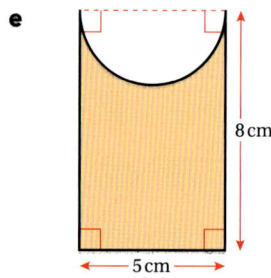

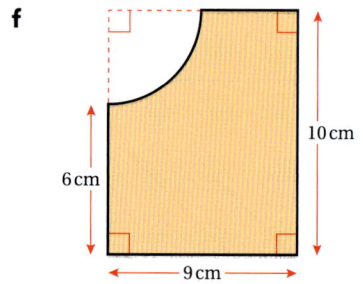

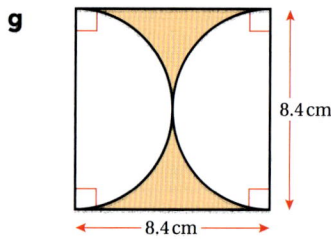

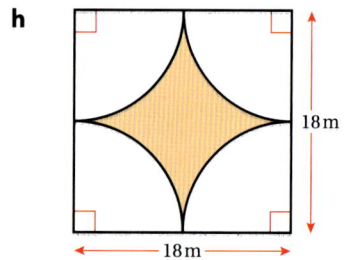

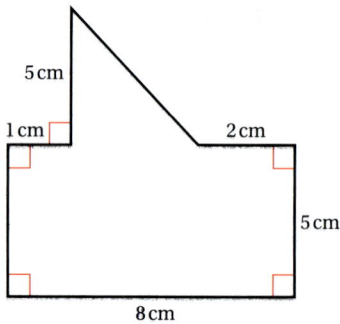

a

2 cm
18 cm

b

8 cm
8 cm
8 cm
•O
8 cm

c

12 cm
5 cm
O
15 cm
19 cm

d

12 cm
3 cm

e

8 cm
5 cm

f

6 cm
10 cm
9 cm

g

8.4 cm
8.4 cm

h

18 m
18 m

5 cm
1 cm
2 cm
5 cm
8 cm

3 Look at the composite shape shown in the margin.

Calculate its area.

Choose the correct answer from the options given below.

A 65 cm²   B 52.5 cm²   C 31 cm²   D 50 cm²

4 Calculate the perimeter and area of the shaded region in each figure.

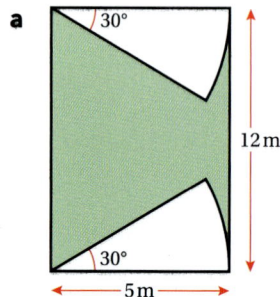

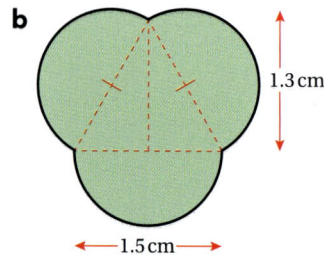

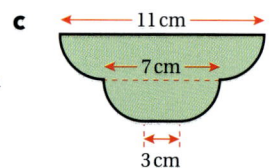

a

30°
12 m
30°
5 m

b

1.3 cm
1.5 cm

c

11 cm
7 cm
3 cm

Problem-solving framework

Perimeter, circumference and area are often combined with other calculations in problem-solving situations.

A garden pond has a radius of 5 m.

a The pond needs netting across the top and some edging all around the water's edge.

  Calculate the quantities of **i** netting and **ii** edging required.

b The pond lies in a rectangular lawned area of width 15 m and length 20 m.

  Grass seed is required for the lawn. What area must the grass seed cover?

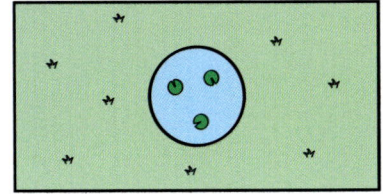

Steps for solving problems	What you would do for this example
Step 1: What have you got to do?	Find: **a i** the area of netting needed for the pond. **ii** the circumference of the pond to work out the amount of edging needed. **b** the area of lawn needing grass seed.
Step 2: What information do you need?	Radius, r, of pond = 5 m Dimensions of lawn: 15 m × 20 m Area of circle, $A = \pi r^2$ Circumference of circle, $C = 2\pi r$ Use 3.14 as the value for π. Area of rectangle = length × width
Step 3: What information don't you need?	The netting will fit exactly on the top of the pond; need to mention that this is the minimum area of netting required.
Step 4: What maths can you use?	Area of pond = πr^2 = 3.14 × 5 × 5 = 78.5 m^2 A minimum of 78.5 m^2 of netting is required. Circumference of pond = $2\pi r$ = 2 × 3.14 × 5 = 31.4 m 31.4 m of edging is required for the pond. Rectangular lawn area = 15 × 20 = 300 m^2 Area for seeding = 300 − 78.5 (area of pond) = 221.5 m^2 Area of lawn needing grass seed is 221.5 m^2.
Step 5: Have you used all the information? At this point you should check to make sure you have calculated what was asked of you.	All information used. ✓ Calculated part **a i**. ✓ Calculated part **a ii**.✓ Calculated part **b**. ✓
Step 6: Is it correct?	Given radius of pond, so used $C = 2\pi r$ to calculate circumference. ✓ Used $A = \pi r^2$ to calculate area of pond. ✓ Squared the radius before multiplying by π. ✓ Used $A = l \times w$ to calculate area of rectangular lawn ✓ The correct units used. ✓

Find answers at: cambridge.org/ukschools/gcsemaths-studentbookanswers

EXERCISE 11E

1 How many rectangular tiles 20 cm by 30 cm would you need to tile the area shown in the margin?

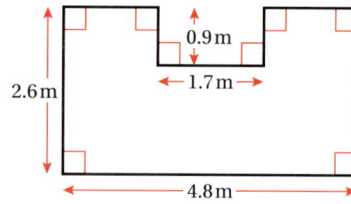

2 The net of a cylinder is shown below.

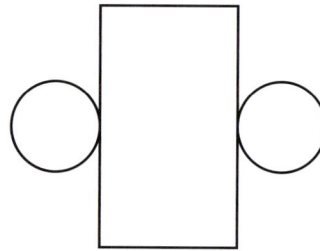

The rectangle has dimensions 10 cm × 16 cm.

Each circle has a radius of 2.55 cm.

Using 3.14 as an approximate value of π, calculate the surface area of the cylinder.

3 The diagram shows a circular mirror that has a mirrored centre and a decorative metal border.

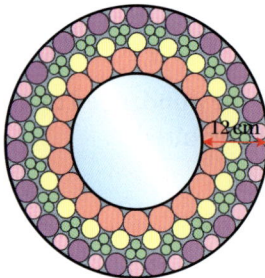

The border measures 12 cm across.

The width of the border is $\frac{4}{5}$ of the radius of the whole mirror.

a Calculate the area of the whole mirror.
(Use 3.14 as an approximate value of π.)

b Calculate the area of the metal border.

4 A piece of icing is rolled out into the shape of a square.

The largest circle that can be cut out of the square has a radius of 11 cm.

Find the difference between the area of the circular icing and the area of the square.

5 The diagram shows a sandpit at the end of a lawn.

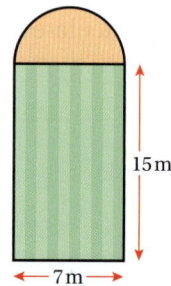

A cover is placed over the sandpit.

What is the area that needs to be covered?

6 A circular photo frame has a plastic surround.

The width of the plastic surround is 8 cm.

The diameter of the complete photo frame is 28 cm.

Calculate the area available for the photo.

7 The shapes below have the same area.

What is the side length of the square?

6 cm · 8 cm · 12 cm

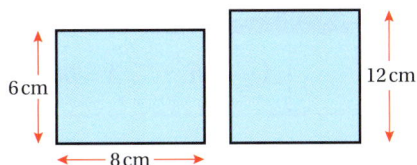

8 Guy is paid £0.15 for every square metre of grass he cuts.

How much would he be paid for cutting the grass in this garden?

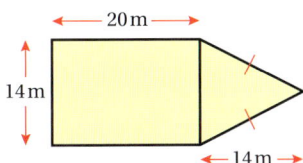

20 m · 14 m · 14 m

9 A stained glass window is a semicircle with radius 30 cm.

Calculate:

a the perimeter of the window

b the area of glass in the window.

10 Car parking bays are either based on rectangles or parallelograms as shown on this model.

a The Department of the Environment's Planning Service specifies the following minimum standing space dimensions for cars and light vans:

Cars   2.4 m × 4.8 m

Vans   2.4 m × 5.5 m

These dimensions do not take into account space between vehicles and space for access and/or unloading.

Based on this, suggest some suitable dimensions for both rectangular and parallelogram parking bays.

b Is it possible for both shapes to have the same area? Give a reason for your answer.

c What are the advantages and disadvantages of using each type of parking bay?

d Given a rectangular area 120 m by 200 m, with access possible from all sides, sketch the parking arrangement you would recommend and justify your choices.

Checklist of learning and understanding

Area of polygons

- Area is the amount of space occupied by a plane shape. Area is always given in square measurements.
- Area can be calculated using formulae.

Rectangle	Square	Triangle	Parallelogram	Trapezium
$A = lw$	$A = l^2$	$A = \frac{1}{2}bh$	$A = bh$	$A = \frac{1}{2}(a + b)h$

Area of circles and sectors

- Area of a circle $= \pi r^2$
- Area of a sector of a circle is a fraction of the area of the whole circle.
- Area of a sector $= \dfrac{\theta}{360} \times \pi r^2$

Composite shapes

- The area of a composite shape can be found by splitting it into known smaller shapes.
- Areas of smaller shapes can be calculated separately and added to find the total area.
- The area of a given shape can be subtracted from the area of a known shape to find the total area.

For additional questions on the topics in this chapter, visit GCSE Mathematics Online.

Chapter review

1. A rectangular vegetable plot has an area of $100\,\text{m}^2$.

   The width is 6.5 m.

   What is the length of the plot?

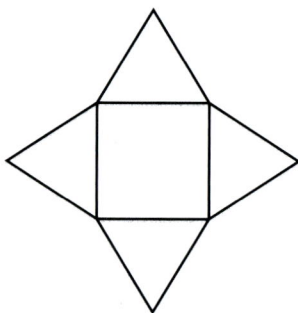

2. The net of a square-based pyramid is shown in the margin.

   The square is of side length 5 cm.

   The triangles have a perpendicular height of 4.3 cm.

   Calculate the surface area of the square-based pyramid.

3. Here is a composite shape.

   Calculate the area of the shaded part. Choose the correct answer from the following options.

   A 8 cm

   B 8 cm^2

   C 12 cm^2

   D 12 cm

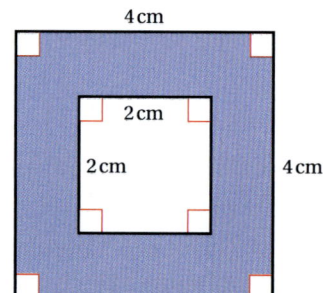

4 A square flower bed has a side length of 3 m.

It sits exactly in the middle of a rectangular lawned area of side length 5 m and width 450 cm.

Calculate the area of lawn.

5 An irrigator in a field waters a circular crop within a radius of 14.5 m.

What is the total area of the crop?

6 Calculate the area of the shape shown below.

Give your answer in cm².

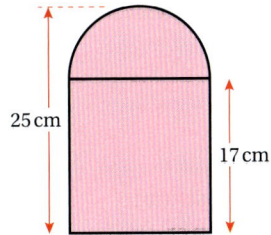

25 cm

17 cm

7 Calculate the area of the shape below.

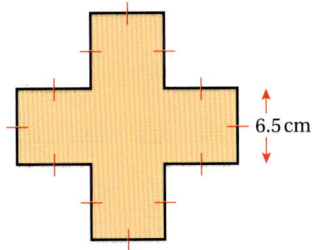

6.5 cm

8 The hexagon is made from a rectangle and two congruent triangles.

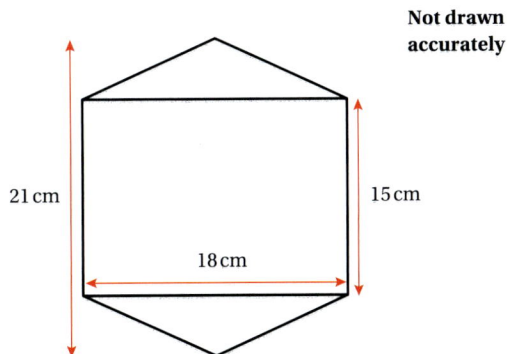

Not drawn accurately

21 cm

15 cm

18 cm

Work out the area of the hexagon.

(5 marks)

© AQA 2013

In this chapter you will learn how to ...

- approximate values by rounding or truncating them to different degrees of accuracy.
- use approximations to estimate and check the results of calculations.
- understand and apply limits of accuracy in numbers and measurements.
- calculate the upper and lower bounds of a calculation (for discrete and continuous quantities).

For more resources relating to this chapter, visit GCSE Mathematics Online.

Using mathematics: real-life applications

When you read that 34 000 people attended a festival, the actual number is likely to be slightly less or slightly more than that. When you roughly estimate what you spent over the weekend, look at an object and guess it is about $2\frac{1}{2}$ m long or say things like, 'I live about 15 kilometres from school' you are estimating and using approximate values.

"I round off the prices to the nearest pound and keep a mental running total of the costs of things I put in my trolley so I know that I am not over-spending."

(Consumer)

Before you start ...

KS3 Ch 1, 4	You should be able to use rounding to quickly estimate the answers to calculations.	**1** Use rounded values to estimate and decide whether each answer is correct without doing the calculation. **a** 312 − 56 = 256 **b** 479 × 17 = 3142 **c** 350 + 351 − 96 = 798
KS3 Ch 6	You should be able to calculate with decimals and estimate to decide whether an answer is reasonable.	**2** State whether each statement is true or false. **a** $5.8 \times 6.72 \approx 42$ **b** $3.789 + 234.6 \approx 4 + 230$ **c** $0.00432 + 3.55 \approx 4$ **d** $4 \times \pi \approx 12$
KS3 Ch 6	You need to be able to work confidently with decimals and place value.	**3** Write the number halfway between: **a** 3.0 and 5.0 **b** 3.5 and 3.6 **c** 0.02 and 0.07

Assess your starting point using the Launchpad

1 Round each value to the degree of accuracy specified.

    a 86 to the nearest 10.   **b** 1565 to the nearest 1000.

    c 134.1234 to 2 decimal places.   **d** 19.999 to 1 decimal place.

    e 1235.26 to 1 significant figure.

    f 234 650 034 to 3 significant figures.

2 The length of a metal component is found to be 0.937 cm.

    What is its length to the nearest millimetre?

3 The cost of a phone call is given as £5.15932.

    a What is this amount truncated to the nearest penny?

    b What is this amount rounded to two decimal places?

GO TO
Section 1:
Approximate values

STEP 2

4 Estimate the cost of 12 packets of seeds at £1.36 each.

5 A litre of petrol costs £1.89.

    Approximately how many litres of petrol can you get for £20?

6 Use rounding to find an approximate answer to each calculation.

    a $\dfrac{784 + 572}{109}$ **b** $(2.099)^2$ **c** $\dfrac{3.802 + 7.52}{3.29}$

GO TO
Section 2:
Approximation and
estimation

STEP 3

7 A piece of wire is 10 m long, to the nearest metre.

    Copy and complete the following statement to show the longest
    and the shortest possible lengths that this wire could be.

    $\square \leqslant 10\,\text{m} < \square$

8 If $a = 3.6$ (to one decimal place) and $b = 14$ (to the nearest whole
number), find the upper and lower bounds of:

    a $a + b$ **b** ab **c** $\dfrac{a + b}{a}$

GO TO
Section 3:
Limits of accuracy

GO TO
Chapter review

Find answers at: cambridge.org/ukschools/gcsemaths-studentbookanswers

Section 1: Approximate values

In daily life we often use approximate values.

For example, you are more likely to say 'about £10' than to say 'exactly £10 and 24 pence'.

Approximation allows you to use numbers in a more convenient form by writing them in a simpler, but less accurate way.

Rounded values

Numbers can be **rounded** to:

- the nearest whole number or place (tens, hundreds or thousands)
- a particular number of decimal places
- a particular number of significant figures.

To round a number to a given place, first find the specified place.

If the digit to the right is 5 or greater, you round up. If it is less than 5, you round down.

This rule applies to whole numbers and decimals whether you are rounding to given places or to significant figures.

Rounding whole numbers

Consider the number 456 744. It can be rounded to different places. Depending on the value of the digit to the right of the digit you are rounding to, the number might be rounded up or down.

To the nearest ten 456 744 rounds down to 456 740.

To the nearest hundred 456 744 rounds down to 456 700.

To the nearest thousand 456 744 rounds up to 457 000.

In a question you might be told to round numbers to a given **degree of accuracy**.

EXERCISE 12A

1 Choose the correct approximation of each animal's weight.

	Weight of an animal		Rounded to	Approximation (choose from A or B)	
a	cow	635 kg	nearest 10 kg	A 630 kg	B 640 kg
b	horse	526 kg	nearest 100 kg	A 500 kg	B 600 kg
c	sheep	96 kg	nearest 10 kg	A 90 kg	B 100 kg
d	dog	32 kg	nearest 10 kg	A 30 kg	B 40 kg
e	cat	5.2 kg	nearest 10 kg	A 0 kg	B 10 kg

2 **a** Round each value to the nearest whole number.

    i 54.8   **ii** 10.6   **iii** 9.4   **iv** 12.3

   b Round each value to the nearest 10.

    i 26   **ii** 57.5   **iii** 111.1   **iv** 35 814

   c Round each value to the nearest 100.

    i 458   **ii** 5732   **iii** 2389   **iv** 35 814

   d Round each value to the nearest 1000.

    i 2590   **ii** 176   **iii** 35 814   **iv** 66 876

   e Round the following to the nearest hundred thousand.

    i 123 456   **ii** 1 234 567   **iii** 12 354 642   **iv** 123 456 789

   f Round the following to the nearest million.

    i 545 000   **ii** 555 000   **iii** 14 354 642   **iv** 546 267 789

3 **a** A food bill is £27.60. How much is this to the nearest pound?

   b There are 27 students in a class. What is this to the nearest ten students?

   c I have £175 saved up. What is this to the nearest £100?

   d A kite is made from 167 cm of material. Approximately how many metres is used?

   e The population of the United Kingdom is 63 793 234.

    Sue says this is 63.7 million to the nearest hundred thousand people.

    She is not correct. What mistake has she made?

4 Between which two integers does $\sqrt{21}$ lie?

Rounding decimals

In calculations you will often get answers with many more decimal places than you need.

You will usually be told to give your answers to a specific number of decimal places.

WORKED EXAMPLE 1

Round:

a 54.149 to one decimal place   **b** 0.8751 to two decimal places   **c** 0.10024 to three decimal places.

a 54.149
    54.1

> There is a 1 in the first decimal place, the next digit is 4, so round down.
> Leave the 1 unchanged and take off the digits to the right of it.

b 0.8751
    0.88

> There is a 7 in the second decimal place, the next digit is 5.
> Round 7 up to 8 and take off the digits to the right of it.

c 0.10024
    0.100

> There is a 0 in the third decimal place, the next digit is 2.
> Leave the 0 unchanged and take off the digits to the right of it.
> The answer 0.100 is the same as 0.1, but you write the two zeros to show that the number is rounded to three decimal places.

Suitable levels of accuracy

Sometimes, you have to decide what to round to.

This will depend on the degree of accuracy required by the situation or problem.

If the situation involves whole quantities, you round to the nearest whole number. It does not make sense to talk about 5.45 bricks or 9.05 tins of paint.

If the question involves money, then you always round to two decimal places. An answer of £4.56896 would be rounded to £4.57.

In mathematical or scientific calculations you usually work to a higher degree of accuracy than when you describe real-life quantities.

If you are working with small values you might round them to tens, if you are working with large numbers you might round to the nearest ten thousand or or the nearest million.

When you calculate with decimals or significant figures you normally round to no more than the number of places in the original values.

EXERCISE 12B

1 Round 13.68952 to one decimal place.

Choose the correct answer from the options below.

A 13.5   B 13.6   C 13.7   D 14

2 Round each number to:

   i 1 dp   **ii** 2 dp   **iii** 3 dp

   a 4.52638   **b** 25.25637   **c** 125.61738

   d 0.537921   **e** 32.3972

3 Write each value to two decimal places.

   a 19.86903   **b** 302.0428   **c** 0.292

   d 0.20528   **e** 21 245.8449   **f** 0.0039

   g 0.0972   **h** 0.9999999   **i** 99.997

4 Round each value to a suitable level of accuracy. Give reasons for your decisions.

   a A large dog weighs 24.4872 kg.

   b To calculate a circumference, I use the value
     $\pi = 3.14159265358979323846\ldots$

   c Dan's car can travel 13.7895 km per 1.0000987 litres of petrol.

   d My share of a phone bill is £14.09876

5 What is $\sqrt{21}$ to 1 dp?

6 The Department of the Environment stated that:

'The total extent of land and sea protected increased from 1 million to 2 million hectares between 2000 and 2013.'

   a What level of accuracy do you think was used in each of these figures?

   b What is the smallest and greatest possible areas that the statement could refer to?

Significant figures

When you work with values with many digits or decimal places it is useful to **round to significant figures (sf)**.

The first **significant figure** in a number is the first non-zero digit when you read the number from left to right. All digits that follow are significant.

For example:

Key vocabulary

round to significant figures (sf): round to a specified level of accuracy from the first significant figure

significant figure: the first non-zero digit when you read a number from left to right

Tip

One significant figure does not mean that you will have only one digit in the answer. The number 12 756 is 10 000 to one significant figure, not 1.

To round a number to a given number of significant figures:
- read the number from left to right and mark the first non-zero digit
- count the required number of significant figures from there to find the rounding place
- look at the digit to the right of this; if it is 5 or more round up, if it is less than 5 leave the digit unchanged
- use 0 as a place holder to fill any gaps between the rounding place and the decimal point (if there is one)
- leave off any digits past your rounding place if they are after the decimal point.

WORKED EXAMPLE 2

Write each number to the given number of significant figures.

a 308 000 000 (to 2 sf)

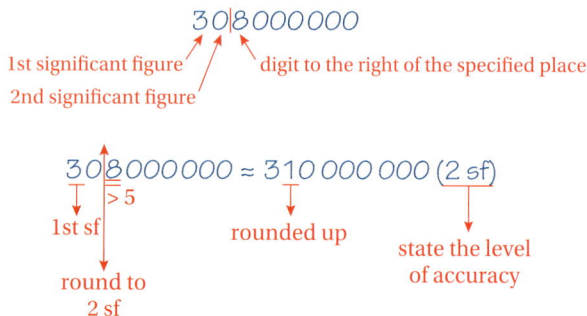

308|000000

1st significant figure / 2nd significant figure / digit to the right of the specified place

$308000000 \approx 310\,000\,000$ (2 sf)

1st sf / >5 / round to 2 sf / rounded up / state the level of accuracy

Include the zeros.

31 is not the same as 310 000 000.

b 476.372 (to 4 sf)

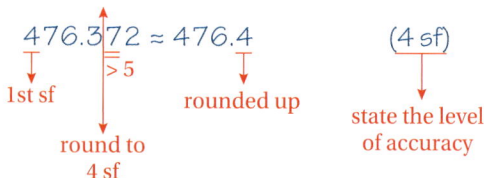

$476.3|72 \approx 476.4$ (4 sf)

1st sf / >5 / round to 4 sf / rounded up / state the level of accuracy

Ignore digits after the specified place if they are decimals.

Continues on next page …

Write each number to the given number of significant figures.

c 2531.8 (to 2 sf)

$25\underset{\text{1st sf}}{3}1.8 \approx 25\underset{\text{leave as it is (rounded down)}}{0}0$ (2 sf)

< 5

round to 2 sf

state the level of accuracy

> Replace digits before the decimal point with zeros.
> Ignore digit after the decimal point.

d 0.00436 (to 1 sf)

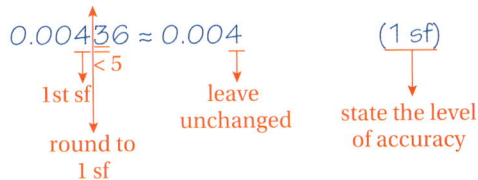

$0.004\underset{\text{1st sf}}{3}6 \approx 0.00\underset{\text{leave unchanged}}{4}$ (1 sf)

< 5

round to 1 sf

state the level of accuracy

> Ignore digits to the right.

EXERCISE 12C

1 a Round each value to one significant figure.

    i 789   **ii** 3874   **iii** 69 356   **iv** 0.0456

   b Write each value to 2 sf.

    i 789   **ii** 3145   **iii** 0.003325   **iv** 0.0007499

   c Express each number to 3 sf.

    i 789   **ii** 46 712   **iii** 0.004214   **iv** 753 413

   d Round each value to 2 sf.

    i 37.673   **ii** −4127   **iii** 3.0392   **iv** 1 999 000

   e Write these to 3 sf.

    i 37.673   **ii** −4127   **iii** 3.0392   **iv** 1 999 000

2 Give reasons why it is more useful to round a value such as 0.000134567 to two significant figures than to two decimal places.

3 a $\pi \approx 3.1415926$

    What is this to 3 sf?

    Choose from the following options.

    A 3.142   B 3.14   C 3.00   D 3.141

   b The density of a gas is 1.234 kg/m^3. What is this to 2 sf?

   c The speed of light is 299 792 458 m/s. What is this to 2 sf?

   d The acceleration due to gravity at the Earth's surface is 9.806 65 m/s^2. What is this to 3 sf?

4 a What is $\sqrt{21}$ to two significant figures?

   b Craig rounded $\sqrt{21}$ to two decimal places in one part of his calculation and to two significant figures in another.

    What difference might this make to the accuracy of Craig's results?

> **Tip**
>
> Rounding numbers to a given number of decimal places means that you start the rounding at the decimal point.
>
> Rounding numbers to significant figures means you start at the first significant figure that can be before or after the decimal point.

Find answers at: cambridge.org/ukschools/gcsemaths-studentbookanswers

Truncation

Truncated means 'cut off'.

A decimal can be **truncated** by cutting off all the digits past a given point without rounding.

You will not generally use truncation to approximate values for calculation. However, you need to be aware that your calculator display will often give you a truncated rather than rounded value.

You can see this if you enter 2 ÷ 3. The display might show 0.66666666666

The fraction $\frac{2}{3}$ can be expressed as the recurring decimal $0.\dot{6}$. So the calculator is showing a truncated value.

If you enter $\frac{20}{3}$ your screen will show either 6.6666666666 or 6.6666666667

The first value is truncated, the second is rounded to 10 decimal places.

EXERCISE 12D

1 Truncate each number after the second decimal place.

   a 37.673   **b** −4.1275   **c** 3.0392   **d** 0.997

2 Truncate each number after the third significant figure.

   a 4.52638   **b** 25.25637   **c** 125.61738

   d 0.537921   **e** 32.397   **f** 200.6127

3 A bill of £20 is split equally between three people.

   What would each person pay? What method of approximation is most useful for deciding?

Section 2: Approximation and estimation

An **estimate** is a very useful tool for checking whether your answer is sensible.

If your estimate and your actual answer are not similar, then you might have made a mistake in your calculation.

For estimating an approximate answer you can generally round to one significant figure (1 sf).

"I estimate measurements and prices to give customers a fairly accurate quote telling them what a building job will cost."

(Builder)

WORKED EXAMPLE 3

Estimate the value of $\dfrac{8.3 \times 536}{2.254 \times 9.612}$

$\dfrac{8.3 \times 536}{2.254 \times 9.612} \approx \dfrac{8 \times 500}{2 \times 10}$ Start off by rounding each number to 1 sf.

$\approx \dfrac{4000}{20}$

≈ 200

If you work out this problem using a calculator, the answer is actually 205.34 (to 2 dp).

Comparing this with your estimate tells you that your calculated answer is reasonable.

Tip

The symbol ≈ means approximately equal to.

WORK IT OUT 12.1

A group of four friends is travelling to a festival. They split the cost of everything between them.

The costs are as follows:

tent hire, £86.50

travel, 140 mile round trip with petrol costing roughly 20p per mile

camping entry at £44 per night for three nights.

Three of them estimate how much they will each have to pay.

Which is the best estimate?
Why is it better than the others?

Estimate A	Estimate B	Estimate C
The cost of tent hire is roughly £90, which is £22.50 per person split between four.	The tent hire is roughly £100 which is £25 per person.	The tent hire is roughly £80, which is £20 each.
Petrol costs roughly £28 (140 × £0.20) which is £7 per person.	The petrol is roughly 150 × £0.20, which is £30, so split four ways this is £7.50.	Petrol is about 100 × £0.20 = £20, so £5 per person.
The camping ticket costs are £44 × three nights or roughly £120, which is £30 per person.	The camping costs about £50 × 3 = £150, which is about £40 each.	Camping cost is about £40 × 3 = £120 for three nights, so about £30 each.
So, total cost per person is £22.50 + £7 + £30 = £59.50	Total cost is approximately £25 + £7.50 + £40 = £72.50	Total cost is approximately £20 + £5 + £30 = £55

EXERCISE 12E

1 Estimate the following by rounding each number to 1 sf.

   a 111.11×3.6 **b** 378×1.07 **c** 0.99×16.7 **d** 13.6×0.48

   e $\pi \times (5.3)^2$ **f** 4.8×12.5 **g** $\dfrac{192}{17.2}$ **h** $\dfrac{58.38}{0.5185}$

2 Estimate the value of 937×26.

Choose your answer from the following options.

   A 2700   B 19 000   C 24 362   D 27 000

3 Which calculation would provide the best estimate? Choose from the options given.

   a 186×9.832 A 200×10 B 190×9 C 190×10

   b $15.76 \div 7.6$ A $15 \div 7$ B $16 \div 8$ C $16 \div 7$

4 Estimate the following by rounding each number to 1 sf.

   a $\dfrac{82.65 \times 0.4654}{42.4 \times 2.53}$ **b** $\dfrac{16.96 + 3.123}{16.9 - 6.432}$

   c $\dfrac{879 \div 43.6}{2.36 \times 0.23}$ **d** $\dfrac{976.9 \div 492.9}{21.6 \div 43.87}$

5 Estimate the following.

   a $\sqrt{\dfrac{3.2 \times 4.05}{0.39 \times 0.29}}$ **b** $\sqrt{\dfrac{4.1 \times 11.9}{7.9 \times 0.25}}$

6 Shafiek runs a cross-country race at an average speed of 6.25 m/s.

   a Estimate how far he will have run after 6 minutes.

   b Assuming he runs at a constant speed, estimate how long it takes him to cover 1467 m.

7 Look at the calculator display answers for each calculation.

Use estimation to state whether the answer is sensible.

   a $3 \times \pi \times 5^2$ `125.6637061`

   b 5×8.9 `445`

   c 50×8.9 `445`

   d 3×192.5 `57.75`

   e $\dfrac{\sqrt{86}}{2.8 \times 16.18}$ `0.204697565`

   f $0.0253 \div 0.45$ `56.222222222`

8 A parallelogram has an area of 54.67 cm².

The base of the parallelogram is 7.9 cm long.

When a student tries to find the height on his calculator, he gets a result of 69 202 531.

This is clearly wrong. Give the correct height, accurate to two significant figures.

9 The square root of 49 is 7 and the square root of 64 is 8.

Using this information, estimate the square root of 50.

10 Given that $\dfrac{0.514 \times 76.3}{2.4^2} = 6.8087$ to 4 dp, work out $\dfrac{51.4 \times 7.63}{24^2}$

11 Find an approximate value of $\dfrac{2876}{31 \times 33}$

Section 3: Limits of accuracy

Even with very accurate measuring instruments, quantities such as mass, length and capacity cannot be measured exactly.

However, the rules of rounding mean the measurement has to fall within certain limits or bounds.

A piece of wood that is 47 cm to the nearest centimetre, could be anything from 46.5 cm up to, but not including 47.5 cm long.

You can see this on the number line:

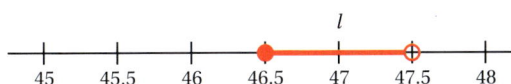

If the length was less than 46.5 cm, it would have been rounded down to 46 cm.

If it was 47.5 cm, it would have been rounded up to 48 cm.

If we let l represent the length of the piece of wood, the possible measurements can be expressed as

$46.5\,\text{cm} \leqslant l < 47.5\,\text{cm}$

This is called inequality notation and it means the length is greater or equal to 46.5 cm and smaller than 47.5 cm.

The smallest value a measurement can take is called the **lower bound** of the measurement.

The largest value it can take is called the **upper bound**.

For any measurement to a given level of accuracy, the exact value lies in a range half a unit below and half a unit above the measurement.

This range of possible values is known as the **error interval**.

Example	Lower and upper bounds	Error interval
0.5 rounded to 1 dp	0.45 and 0.55	$0.45 \leqslant x < 0.55$
0.65 rounded to 2 dp	0.645 and 0.655	$0.645 \leqslant x < 0.655$
0.7663 rounded to 4 dp	0.76625 and 0.76635	$0.76625 \leqslant x < 0.76635$
15 rounded to 2 sf	14.5 and 15.5	$14.5 \leqslant x < 15.5$
320 to 2 sf	315 and 325	$315 \leqslant x < 325$
2.32 rounded to 2 dp	2.315 and 2.325	$2.315 \leqslant x < 2.325$

Tip

It can be helpful to draw a number line to work out the upper and lower bounds of a value.

Tip

$\leqslant$ means 'less than or equal to'
$\geqslant$ means 'greater than or equal to'
$<$ means 'less than'
$>$ means 'greater than'

Key vocabulary

lower bound: the smallest value that a number (given to a specified accuracy) can be

upper bound: the largest value that a number (given to a specified accuracy) can be

error interval: the difference between the upper and lower bounds

EXERCISE 12F

1 Find the lower and upper bound of each value.

  a 96 rounded to 2 sf   **b** 96.0 rounded to 3 sf

  c 96.00 rounded to 4 sf   **d** 0.6 rounded to 1 dp

  e 0.06 rounded to 1 dp   **f** 0.60 rounded to 2 dp

  g 3.142 rounded to 3 dp   **h** 9.9 rounded to 2 sf

  i 3.07 rounded to 3 sf

2 The following lengths were measured to the nearest millimetre.

Write down an error interval for each one using inequality notation. Let the length be L in each case.

  a 4.9 cm   **b** 12.520 m   **c** 43.0 cm   **d** 29 mm

3 **a** There are 36 litres of petrol in a car's tank, to the nearest litre.

What is the least possible volume of petrol in the tank?

Choose from the following options.

A 35 litres   B 35.5 litres   C 36 litres   D 36.5 litres

  b A length of wood is 1.4 m to the nearest centimetre. Is it possible for the wood to be 137 cm long?

  c The weight of a stone is 43.4 kg to the nearest tenth of a kilogram. What is the least and greatest weight it could be?

4 Verna buys 9-carat gold for £10.66 per gram and platinum for £33.46 per gram.

  a Use this information to complete the table.

Mass of a piece of jewellery	Maximum value of gold (to nearest penny)	Maximum value of platinum (to nearest penny)
18 g (to nearest g)		
18.0 g (to nearest 0.1 g)		
18.00 g (to nearest 0.01 g)		

  b Using your data, give reasons why jewellers tend to use scales that are accurate to a hundredth of a gram to weigh the metal they use to make jewellery.

5 Hilal ran 100 m in 15.3 seconds.

The distance is to the nearest metre and the time is to one decimal place.

Write down the upper and lower bounds of:

  a the distance he ran.

  b the actual time taken.

6 The length of a rope is 4.5 metres to the nearest 10 cm.

The actual length of the rope is L metres.

Find the range of possible values for L, giving the answer as an inequality.

The upper and lower bounds of a calculation

Using approximate values in calculations affects the accuracy of the answer.
This usually produces a larger interval of error than for the original values.

WORKED EXAMPLE 4

A rectangle has sides of 10 cm and 6 cm to the nearest centimetre.

Calculate the limits of accuracy of the area of the rectangle.

Possible lengths
$9.5 \leqslant l < 10.5$

10 cm

6 cm   Possible widths
$5.5 \leqslant b < 6.5$

Draw a sketch and find the error interval of each measurement.

From sketch: lowest bound of length = 9.5 cm and
lowest bound of width = 5.5 cm.
So smallest possible area = 5.5 × 9.5 = 52.25 cm.
Upper bound of length = 10.5 cm and upper bound of width = 6.5 cm.
So greatest possible area = 10.5 × 6.5 = 68.25 cm^2.
The limits of accuracy for the area are:
52.25 cm^2 $\leqslant$ Area < 68.25 cm^2.

Tip

In real terms this means that your area calculation could be out by 16 cm^2. If you were coating the area with platinum this could make quite a difference to the amount you needed and the cost.

Discrete and continuous quantities

When working with upper and lower bounds, it is important to understand the difference between **discrete** and **continuous** quantities.

Measurements are continuous quantities. Length, mass, capacity and other measures can take any value between the given points (in the range).

Quantities that can be counted, such as the number of people, number of cars or number of buildings in a given area are discrete values.

When you count people there are no in-between values – there are either 5 or 6 people, never $5\frac{1}{2}$.

The limits of accuracy for discrete values can be expressed in different ways.

For example, the population of a village is 400 to the nearest 100. The number of people that live in the village (n) can be expressed as:

$350 \leqslant n \leqslant 449$ as well as $350 \leqslant n < 450$

n is a discrete variable (there must be a whole number of people). 450 would round to 500 to the nearest 100. So 449 is the greatest number of people.

Key vocabulary

discrete values: counted values where you only count certain values

continuous values: measurements that can take any value in a range

EXERCISE 12G

1 12 kg of sugar is removed from a sack containing 50 kg.

Each measurement is to the nearest kilogram.

Find the upper and lower bounds of the mass of the sugar left in the sack.

2 The dimensions of a rectangle are 3.61 cm and 2.57 cm, each to 3 sf.

a Write down the upper and lower bounds of each measurement.

b Find the upper and lower bounds of the area of the rectangle.

c Write the upper and lower bounds of the area to three significant figures.

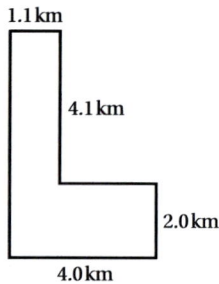

1.1 km

4.1 km

2.0 km

4.0 km

3 In the diagram, the measurements of a piece of land are given to one decimal place.

a Calculate the limits of accuracy of the area of the land.

b A surveyor calculates the area to be 12.51 km².

What is the greatest possible percentage error in taking that value?

c Comment on whether that is a significant error or not, giving reasons for your answer.

4 Henry has £100 to the nearest £1 and he spends £30 to the nearest £1.

What is the least amount of money he can have left?

5 **a** A rectangle has width 5 cm and length 6 cm, both to the nearest cm.

What is the:

i greatest length of perimeter?

ii smallest length of a diagonal?

b Another rectangle measures 3 cm by 7 cm to the nearest cm.

What is its maximum possible area?

6 In order to try to calculate pi (π) John measures a circle.

The circumference (C) is 40 cm to the nearest cm.

The diameter (d) is 12 cm to the nearest cm.

Given that $\pi = \dfrac{C}{d}$, what are the highest and lowest values for John's calculation of π?

7 Mishka runs 100 m in 12.32 seconds, to 2 dp.

Write down the range of values for her average speed.

8 A chocolate manufacturer reduced the weight of its chocolate bar from 49 g to 45 g, to the nearest gram.

What is the maximum weight of chocolate that could have been saved per bar?

9 The velocity of a model car is found using the formula $v = \dfrac{d}{t_2 - t_1}$, where:

d is the distance covered in metres

t_1 is the starting time

t_2 is the finishing time on a stopwatch.

Each time is measured in seconds.

The car travels 1.000 m (to the nearest mm), starting at 0.2 s and ending at 1.4 s (both to the nearest 0.1 second).

Write an inequality to express the values between which v falls.

Checklist of learning and understanding

Approximate values

- When you round to a specified place, if the number following is 5 or above, then the original number goes up to the next number. If it is not more than 5, then the number stays the same.
- Rounding to a given number of significant figures (sf) specifies the number of digits, starting from the first non-zero digit, that is used to express a number. The first significant figure is the first number that is not zero as you read the number from left to right.
- Truncating a decimal number means removing all digits after a specified number of decimal places and expressing the number that remains without rounding.

Estimation

- Complex calculations can be estimated without using a calculator by using approximations of each term in the calculation to make a simple calculation.
- Visual estimation techniques can also be used to approximate sizes and measurements.

Level of accuracy

- Measurement is really approximation within a range of bounds or limits. A measurement can be expressed as a range between upper and lower bounds. It can be expressed using inequality notation ($\leqslant, <, \geqslant, >$).

Chapter review

1 Estimate the value of $\dfrac{6.68^2}{4.76 \times 21.2}$

2 A market trader sells 470 apples for £73.

Roughly how much does an apple cost?

3 If $521 \times 32 = 16\,672$, what is $16\,672 \div 3.2$?

4 Estimate the value of $\dfrac{39.9 + \sqrt{0.934}}{(15.4 - 4.3)^2}$

5 The manager of a theatre records the attendance figure for a show to 2 significant figures.

A newspaper rounds the manager's figure to 1 significant figure.

THEATRE NEWS

500 attend show

What is the lowest and highest possible actual attendance?   *(3 marks)*

© AQA 2013

6 A charity raised £43 000 to the nearest £10.

What is the highest amount of money that they could have raised?

Choose the correct answer from the options below.

A £42 996   B £43 004   C £43 004.99   D £43 005

7 Chocolate bars are supposed to weigh 50 g with a tolerance of 5%.

If they are weighed to the nearest 10 grams, will they be within this tolerance?

8 The potential difference V of an electrical circuit is given by Ohm's law, that has the formula:

$V = IR$ where I is the current in amps and R is the resistance in ohms.

Given that $V = 316$ volts to three significant figures and $R = 19.2$ ohms to three significant figures, calculate the lower bound of I.

9 Quantity x is 45 to the nearest integer.

Quantity y is 98 to the nearest integer.

Calculate upper and lower bounds for x as a percentage of y to one decimal place.

13 Percentages

In this chapter you will learn how to …

- work interchangeably with fractions, decimals and percentages.
- calculate a percentage of an amount.
- express a quantity as a percentage of another.
- increase and decrease amounts by a given percentage.
- solve problems involving percentage change.

For more resources relating to this chapter, visit GCSE Mathematics Online.

Using mathematics: real-life applications

Percentages are often used in daily life to express fractions. For example, you might see adverts claiming that 76% of pets prefer a particular brand of food or that 90% of dentists recommend a particular type of toothpaste. Sale price-reductions, discounts and interest rates are usually given as percentages.

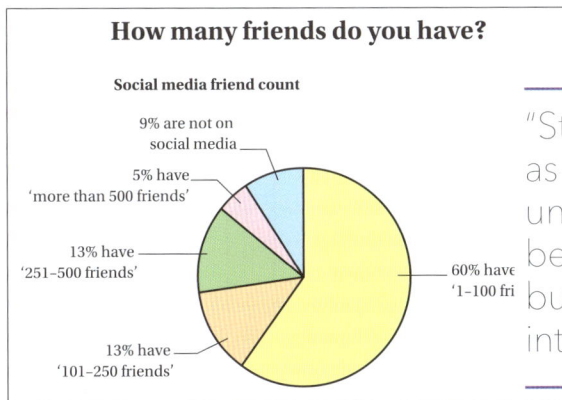

How many friends do you have?

Social media friend count

- 9% are not on social media
- 5% have 'more than 500 friends'
- 13% have '251–500 friends'
- 13% have '101–250 friends'
- 60% have '1–100 fri...'

"Statistics in the media are often reported as percentages. This makes it easier to understand, but percentages can also be misleading – 60% sounds like a lot, but it could just mean 3 out of 5 people interviewed."

(Statistician)

Before you start …

KS3 Ch 6	You need to be able to confidently multiply and divide by 100.	**1**	Where should the decimal place go in each answer? **a** $210 \div 100 = 21$ **b** $21 \div 100 = 21$ **c** $0.24 \times 100 = 24$ **d** $0.024 \times 100 = 24$
Ch 5	You need to be able to cancel to express fractions in simplest terms.	**2**	Match each fraction in box A to its equivalent in box B. **Box A**: $\frac{16}{36}$ $\frac{15}{35}$ $\frac{30}{36}$ $\frac{9}{36}$ $\frac{39}{52}$ $\frac{13}{39}$ **Box B**: $\frac{1}{4}$ $\frac{3}{4}$ $\frac{1}{3}$ $\frac{5}{6}$ $\frac{3}{7}$ $\frac{4}{9}$
KS3 Ch 6	You should be able to express any percentage as a decimal.	**3**	Are the following statements true or false? **a** $20\% = 0.02$ **b** $25\% = 1.4$ **c** $3\% = 0.3$ **d** $12.5\% = 0.125$ **e** $1.25\% = 0.125$

Find answers at: cambridge.org/ukschools/gcsemaths-studentbookanswers

Assess your starting point using the Launchpad

STEP 1

1 Write the following as fractions.

   a 34%   **b** 115%

2 Write these in order from smallest to biggest.

   a 12%, 0.125, $\frac{7}{50}$, $\frac{5}{12}$, 19%

   b $2\frac{3}{4}$, 200%, 2.5%, 12.5%, 1.08, 1.25

GO TO
Section 1:
Review of percentages

STEP 2

3 What is 19 out of 25 marks as a percentage?

4 What is 50% of 128?

5 In a population of 12 500 000 people of working age, 3 400 000 are unemployed.

   What is the unemployment rate as a percentage?

6 Express 25p as a percentage of £7.50.

GO TO
Section 2:
Percentage calculations

STEP 3

7 Increase £20 by 9.5%.

8 Pete wants to buy a secondhand car marked at £2800.

   The dealer offers him a 7.5% discount if he pays cash. What will the cash price be?

9 Mandy bought a book in a 25% off sale for £2.99. What was the original price of the book?

GO TO
Section 3:
Percentage change

GO TO

Chapter review

Section 1: Review of percentages

Per cent means 'number of parts per hundred'.
- 92% means 92 out of every 100.
- 81% means 81 out of every 100.

Percentages, fractions and decimals

Percentages, fractions and decimals are different ways of showing a part of a whole.

$$\frac{5}{100} = 0.05 = 5\% \qquad \qquad \frac{20}{100} = 0.2 = 20\%$$

To convert a percentage to a fraction, write the fraction with a denominator of 100. Then simplify the fraction.

$$92\% = \frac{92}{100} = \frac{23}{25}$$

$$81\% = \frac{81}{100}$$

To change a percentage to a decimal, write it as a fraction with a denominator of 100 and then convert it to a decimal, or use your calculator to divide by 100.

$$92\% = \frac{92}{100} = 0.92 \qquad 92 \div 100 = 0.92$$

$$81\% = \frac{81}{100} = 0.81 \qquad 81 \div 100 = 0.81$$

To change a fraction to a percentage, you can write it as an equivalent fraction with a denominator of 100.

For example:

$$\frac{1}{2} = \frac{50}{100} = 50\%$$

Do not simplify; write the fraction of 100 as a percentage.

You can also use a calculator.

For example:

to convert $\frac{2}{3}$ to a percentage, enter

$$\boxed{2}\ \boxed{\div}\ \boxed{3}\ \boxed{\times}\ \boxed{1}\ \boxed{0}\ \boxed{0}$$

Your display will show 66.666666667

This is the percentage. Write it as 66.67% (to two decimal places) or $66\frac{2}{3}\%$.

> ### 🖩 Calculator tip
>
> When you use a calculator to convert a fraction to a percentage you are actually first changing $\frac{2}{3}$ to a decimal ($2 \div 3 = 0.6666666667$) and then converting the decimal to a percentage. You do not enter the percentage sign in the calculation because the values you are entering are not percentages. The percentage is the answer you get.

Find answers at: cambridge.org/ukschools/gcsemaths-studentbookanswers

To change a decimal to a percentage, write it as a fraction with a denominator of 100 or use your calculator to multiply it by 100.

$$0.3 = \frac{3}{10} = \frac{30}{100} = 30\% \qquad\qquad 0.3 \times 100 = 30\%$$

$$0.025 = \frac{0.25}{10} = \frac{2.5}{100} = 2.5\% \qquad 0.025 \times 100 = 2.5\%$$

$$3.75 = \frac{37.5}{10} = \frac{375}{100} = 375\% \qquad 3.75 \times 100 = 375\%$$

Comparing percentages, fractions and decimals

When you have to compare a mixed set of percentages, fractions and decimals you can compare them by changing them all to percentages.

Some common conversions:

Fraction	Decimal	Percentage
$\frac{1}{2}$	0.5	50%
$\frac{1}{4}$	0.25	25%
$\frac{3}{4}$	0.75	75%
$\frac{1}{3}$	$0.\dot{3}$	$33\frac{1}{3}\%$
$\frac{2}{3}$	$0.\dot{6}$	$66\frac{2}{3}\%$

WORKED EXAMPLE 1

Write the following in ascending order.

$35\%, \frac{1}{3}, 0.38, \frac{2}{5}, \frac{2}{7}$

35%

$\frac{1}{3} \times 100 = 33.33\%$

$0.38 \times 100 = 38\%$

$\frac{2}{5} \times 100 = 40\%$

$\frac{2}{7} \times 100 = 28.57\%$

Convert all the fractions and decimals to percentages. Then put them in order, from the smallest to the largest.

The order is: $\frac{2}{7}, \frac{1}{3}, 35\%, 0.38, \frac{2}{5}$

Remember to use the original fractions when you write the answer, not the percentages you have changed them to.

> **Tip**
>
> You can also change all the values to decimals or equivalent fractions to compare them if the numbers are easier.

EXERCISE 13A

1 **a** Choose the value that is equivalent to $\frac{7}{200}$.

   A 7% B 35% C $\frac{3}{200}$ D $3\frac{1}{2}\%$

   b What is the decimal equivalent of 0.08%?

   Choose from the options below.

   A 80 B 0.08 C 0.008 D 0.0008

   c Which symbol will make this statement true?

   Choose from the options below.

   $\frac{3}{20} \ \square \ 12\%$

   A < B > C = D ≡

2 Express the following as percentages.

Use fractional ($32\frac{1}{2}$%) or decimal (2.5%) percentages where you need to.

a $\frac{5}{100}$ **b** $\frac{27}{50}$ **c** $\frac{11}{25}$ **d** $\frac{17}{20}$

e $\frac{1}{2}$ **f** $\frac{2}{3}$ **g** $\frac{5}{8}$ **h** $\frac{92}{50}$

i 0.3 **j** 0.04 **k** 0.47 **l** 1.12

m 2.07 **n** 2.25 **o** 0.035 **p** 0.007

3 Write each of the following percentages as a common fraction in its simplest terms.

a 25% **b** 80% **c** 90% **d** 12.5%

e 50% **f** 98% **g** 60% **h** 22%

4 Write the decimal equivalent of each percentage.

a 82% **b** 97% **c** 45% **d** 28%

e 0.05% **f** 0.08% **g** 0.006% **h** 0.0007%

i 125% **j** 300% **k** 7.28% **l** 9.007%

5 **a** The percentage of students in a school who have wi-fi at home is 93.5%.

What percentage do not?

b Two-thirds of all the SIM cards sold in a mobile phone shop are pre-paid.

What percentage are not pre-paid?

c The decimal fraction of computer users who back up their work every day is 0.325.

What percentage do not?

6 Zack spends:

- 24.7% of a day playing computer games
- 0.138 of the day doing homework, and
- $\frac{3}{8}$ of the day playing sport.

What percentage of the day does he spend doing all other activities?

7 Write each of the following sets in order from smallest to largest.

a $\frac{1}{20}$, 30%, 0.1, $\frac{3}{5}$, 0.8% **b** 0.75, 57%, 0.88, $\frac{1}{4}$, 0.15

c $\frac{2}{3}$, 0.75, 60%, $\frac{9}{100}$, 0.25 **d** $\frac{3}{7}$, 0.43, 45%, 0.395, $\frac{4}{9}$

e $\frac{5}{6}$, 80%, $\frac{19}{25}$, 55%, 49.3%

8 A media company states that 83.5% of its customers read the news online every day.

What fraction of the customers is this?

9 Lara pays 0.06 as a decimal fraction of her salary into her credit card account.

What percentage of her salary is this?

Find answers at: cambridge.org/ukschools/gcsemaths-studentbookanswers

10 During one shift at work, Sandy spent $\frac{19}{20}$ of his time texting on his phone.

What percentage of the shift was he not texting?

11 Angie gets the following marks for three maths assignments: $\frac{31}{40}$, $\frac{27}{30}$ and $\frac{13}{15}$.

   a In which test did she get the best marks?

   b What is the mean result for the three assignments? Give your answer as a percentage.

Section 2: Percentage calculations

WORK IT OUT 13.1

$9\frac{1}{2}\%$ of 400 is 38.

Which of the following methods will give you the correct answer?

Give reasons why the other methods won't work.

Method A	Method B	Method C	Method D	Method E
$\frac{9}{200} \times 400$	$\frac{19}{200} \times \frac{400}{1}$	$\frac{19}{2} \times 400$	9.5×400	$\frac{9.5}{400} \times 100$

To find a percentage of an amount you have to multiply by the percentage.

Unless you can use a calculator, you have to write the percentage as a fraction of a 100 or a decimal.

WORKED EXAMPLE 2

What is 12% of 700?

Using fractions

$\frac{12}{100} \times \frac{700}{1} = 84$

> Write the percentage as a fraction with a denominator of 100 and then cancel.

Using decimals

$\frac{12}{100} = 0.12$

0.12×700

$\quad = 0.12 \times 100 \times 7$

$\quad = 12 \times 7$

$\quad = 84$

> Divide by 100 to convert the percentage to a decimal and then multiply.

Using a calculator

[1] [2] [%] [×] [7] [0] [0] [=]

Answer is: 84

> Enter the calculation correctly and write the answer.

Calculator tip

Make sure you know how to use the [%] button on your calculator. You might need to enter 12% × 700 or 700 × 12% (some calculators will work both ways). On some calculators you need to press the [=] but on others you might not have to. Check how your calculator works by finding 12% of 350. The answer should be 42.

EXERCISE 13B

1 Calculate:

   a 5% of 250   **b** 9% of 400   **c** 20% of 120

   d 65% of 4500   **e** 12% of 75   **f** 75% of 360

   g 32% of 50   **h** 110% of 60   **i** 150% of 90

2 Calculate, giving your answers as mixed numbers or decimals as necessary.

   a 19% of £50   **b** 60% of 70 kg   **c** 45% of 35 cm

   d 90% of 29 kg   **e** $3\frac{1}{2}$% of £400   **f** 2.6% of 80 minutes

   g 7.4% of £1000   **h** 3.8% of 180 m   **i** $9\frac{2}{3}$% of 600 litres

> **Tip**
>
> Remember your answer will have a unit not a percentage sign. You are not working out a percentage here, you are working out what a given percentage of a quantity is.

3 Anya got 85% for a test that was out of 80 marks.

   What was her mark out of 80?

4 Choose the correct option in each part.

   a A substance is 99.5% fat free. How many grams of fat would there be in 250 g of the substance?

      A 248.75 g   B 125 g   C 12.5 g   D 1.25 g

   b In a crowd of 75 242 people, 62% were female. How many females is this?

      A 4665.4   B 12 136   C 46 650   D 1213.6

5 A salesperson at a mobile phone shop estimates that about 3% of phones come back for some sort of repair in the first week.

   The shop sells 180 phones.

   How many can they expect to come back for repairs in the first week?

6 In an area, 46% of residents do not read the local paper, the rest do read it.

   There are a total of 2450 residents in the area.

   How many people:

   a don't read the paper?   **b** read the paper?

7 Of 240 trains arriving at King's Cross Station, 2.5% arrived early and 13.8% arrived late.

   How many trains were on time?

8 A tablet computer is advertised for sale for £899 excluding VAT.

   VAT was increased from 17.5% to 20% before Narea bought it.

   How much would she have saved if she had bought it when VAT was 17.5%?

9 In a garden 7.5% of the 620 m² area is set aside for growing tulips.

   The rest is used to grow vegetables.

   How many square metres of land is used to grow:

   a tulips?   **b** vegetables?

Find answers at: cambridge.org/ukschools/gcsemaths-studentbookanswers

10 The population of a town increases by about 24.8% each summer.

The population of the town is normally 12 760.

How many people arrive during the summer?

11 Eighteen-carat gold contains 18 parts pure gold per 24 parts.

Nine-carat gold contains 9 parts pure gold per 24 parts.

  a Work out the percentage of pure gold in 9-carat and 18-carat gold.

  b Naz buys an 18-carat gold ring that weighs 7.3 grams.

    How much pure gold does it contain?

  c Vishnu buys a 9-carat gold pendant that has a mass of 16.3 grams.

    How much pure gold does it contain?

  d Is it accurate to label 9-carat gold as gold? Give a reason for your answer.

EXERCISE 13C

Crime statistics are often given as percentages, but these can be misleading.

1 Use the following data to show how expressing values as a percentage increase can be misleading.

Location	Number of violent crimes in Year 1	Number of violent crimes in Year 2	% change in crime rate
village	12	18	50%
town	87	98	12.6%
city	1234	1230	−0.3%

  a Which place looks like it has a high crime rate using percentages? Why?

  b Which place do you think is really the most risky in terms of crime? Give a reason for your answer.

Expressing one quantity as a percentage of another

You write one quantity as a percentage of another quantity by writing the first quantity as a fraction of the other and then multiplying by 100 to get a percentage.

The two quantities must be in the same units before you write them as a fraction.

Tip

You expressed one quantity as a fraction of another in Chapter 5. Read through that work again if you cannot remember how to do this.

WORK IT OUT 13.2

Brian has run 1500 m of a 5 km race when he gets a cramp in his foot.

What percentage of the race has he completed at this stage?

Which of these two students has got the correct answer? Why is the other one wrong?

Student A	Student B
$\dfrac{1500}{5} \times 100$ $= 300 \times 100$ $= 300\%$	$\dfrac{1500}{5000} \times 100$ $= \dfrac{3}{10} \times 100$ $= 30\%$

Tip

When you convert quantities to get them to the same unit you can avoid decimal values by choosing the smaller units (for example, making both units metres in this example rather than making them both kilometres).

EXERCISE 13D

1 In each part, express the first amount as a percentage of the second.

Give your answer to two decimal places (if necessary).

a 400 m of 5 km   b 45 m of 3 km

c 150 m of 1 km   d 8 cm of 2 m

e 14 mm of 4 cm   f 19 cm of 3 m

g 25p of £4   h 66p of £3.50

i 20 seconds of a minute   j 25 seconds of 1.5 minutes

k 750 g of 23 kg   l 800 g of 1.5 kg

m 4 days of a week   n 3 days of 6 weeks

o 800 kg of 3 tonnes   p 8.4 tonnes of 50 000 kg

q 500 mm of 2 m   r 90 mm of 14 cm

s 350 ml of 2 litres   t 5 ml of 0.5 litres

2 What is 30p as a percentage of £2?

Choose from the options below.

A 1500%   B 85%   C 15%   D 6.66%

3 Angelika got 19 out of 24 for an assignment.

Nina got 23 out of 30.

Which of the two girls got the highest percentage mark?

4 In a local election there were 5400 registered voters.

Of these, 3240 voted.

What was the voter turnout? Give your answer as a percentage.

5 Mel improved his running time for the 400 m race by 3 seconds.

His previous running time was 50 seconds.

What is his percentage improvement?

6 Kenny had a box of 40 chocolates.

He ate 32 of them.

What percentage of the chocolates is left?

7 Sylvia keeps a record of how many tennis sets she wins.

In the past month she won 19 out of 27 sets.

What percentage of the sets did she lose?

8 The world record for the longest kiss is 58 hours, 35 minutes and 58 seconds.

It was set at a three-day event.

What percentage of the three-day event was the kiss?

9 Read the label and answer the questions.

a Calculate the combined percentage of fat and sugar in a serving.

b What percentage of a serving is sodium?

10 x is 40% of y.

What percentage of y is x?

11 $2n$ less x% is equivalent to n plus x%.

What is x%?

Nutritional values
(Per 30 g serving)

Carbohydrates	19 g
(of which sugars)	6.2 g
Fat	3.8 g
Sodium	93 mg

Section 3: Percentage change

You will often see changes (increases or decreases) in amounts expressed as percentages.

For example, you might read that the price of petrol is to increase by 5.5% or that the cost of mobile broadband has decreased by 15% over the past year.

Increasing or decreasing an amount by a percentage

WORK IT OUT 13.3

A school population of 650 students increased by 12% last year.

At the same time, the registration fee of £120 decreased by 15%. Work out:

a the new student population   **b** the new registration fee.

Look at these examples to see how different students solved these problems.

Which method seems easiest to you?

Could you use your calculator to do these calculations? How?

Student A	Student B
650 increased by 12% 12% of $650 = \dfrac{12}{100} \times 650$ $\qquad\qquad = 78$ $650 + 78 = 728$ There are now 728 students.	650 increased by 12% Old population = 100% New population = old + increase $= 100\% + 12\% = 112\%$ $112\% = \dfrac{112}{100} = 1.12$ $1.12 \times 650 = 728$ The new student population is 728.
£120 decreased by 15% 15% of $120 = \dfrac{15}{100} \times 120$ $\qquad\qquad = 18$ $£120 - £18 = £102$ The new registration fee is £102.	£120 decreased by 15% $£120 - £18 = £102$ The new registration fee is £102.

For Student B's registration fee calculation:

%	£
10	12
5	6
15	18

Tip

You can express any % increase or decrease as a multiplier.

To increase a number by $x\%$, multiply it by $1 + \dfrac{x}{100}$.

To decrease a number by $x\%$, multiply it by $1 - \dfrac{x}{100}$.

EXERCISE 13E

1 Increase each amount by the given percentage.

  a £48 increased by 14%   **b** £700 increased by 35%

  c £30 increased by 7.6%   **d** £40 000 increased by 0.59%

  e £90 increased by 9.5%   **f** £80 increased by 24.6%

2 The number 1500 is increased by 120%. What is the result?

  Choose from the options below.

  A 300   B 1620   C 1800   D 3300

3 Decrease each amount by the given percentage.

  a £68 decreased by 14%   **b** £800 decreased by 35%

  c £90 decreased by 7.6%   **d** £20 000 decreased by 0.59%

  e £85 decreased by 9.5%   **f** £60 decreased by 24.6%

Find answers at: cambridge.org/ukschools/gcsemaths-studentbookanswers

4 A salesperson earns £130 plus 1.5% of the value of sales.

£20 000 worth of goods were sold.

Calculate the salesperson's earnings.

Choose your answer from the options below.

A $1.5 \times £20\,000$ B $130 + 1.5 \times £20\,000$

C $130 + 0.15 \times £20\,000$ D $130 + 0.015 \times £20\,000$

5 A building cost £125 000 to build.

It increased in value by $3\frac{1}{2}\%$.

What is the building worth now?

6 Jack earns £3125 per month.

He receives a pay increase of 3.8%.

What are his new monthly earnings, to the nearest pound?

7 Sharon earns £25 per shift.

Her boss says she can either have £7 more per shift or a 20% increase.

Which is the bigger increase?

8 The membership of a sports club increased by 26% one year.

There were 284 members the previous year.

How many members do they have now?

9 Sammy bought £2500 worth of shares.

At the end of the first month their value had decreased by 4.25%.

At the end of the second month the value of the shares had gone up 1.5% from the previous month.

Work out the value of the shares at the end of each month.

10 Amira earns £25 000 per year plus 12% commission on sales.

She sells £145 250 worth of goods in one year.

Calculate her annual earnings.

11 An amusement park increased its entry prices by 25% to £15.00.

The number of people entering the park dropped 8% from the previous summer to 25 520.

a What was the entry price the previous summer?

b How many visitors were there the previous summer?

c The running costs of the amusement park remained the same as the previous summer. They made a 30% profit on the entry fees in this summer.

How much was their profit in pounds?

12 The winter of 2014 was 24.5% wetter than an average winter.

Write down what you understand by this and what data you would need to work out how much more rain fell in 2014.

13 A journalist is investigating how the price of a Eurostar train ticket varies depending on whether you buy it in London or Brussels (as a result of exchange rates).

The same ticket costs €240 in London and €225 in Brussels.

Use this information to complete the statement 'Tickets bought in London are ___% more expensive than those bought in Brussels'.

Finding original values

If you know the percentage by which an amount has increased or decreased, you can use it to find the original amount.

Problems involving original values are often called reverse or inverse percentages.

When you work with these problems you need to remember that you are dealing with percentages of the original values.

WORKED EXAMPLE 3

A shop is offering a 10% discount on all sale goods.

Jesse paid £108 for a bike in the sale.

What was the original price of the bike?

90% of $x = £108$

$\therefore \frac{90}{100}x = 108$

$\therefore 90x = 100 \times 108$

$\therefore 90x = 10\,800$

$\therefore x = \frac{10\,800}{90}$

$\therefore x = 120$

If the cost is reduced by 10% then you are actually paying 90%. If you let the original amount be x, you can write an equation and solve it to find x.

The original price was £120.

Check that you have answered the question.

> **Tip**
>
> Undoing a 10% decrease is not the same as just increasing the sale price by 10%. If you add 10% to the sale price of £108 you will get £118.80 which is not the right answer.

WORKED EXAMPLE 4

Sameen sells her shares and receives £3450. This gives her a profit of 15%.

What did she pay for the shares originally?

$1.15x = 3450$

$x = \frac{3450}{1.15}$

$x = 3000$

She paid £3000 for the shares.

15% profit means an increase of 15%, so the selling price = 115% or 1.15 of the cost. If you let the cost price be x, you can write an equation and solve it to find x.

$£3000 \times 1.15 = £3450$

Check this by increasing £3000 by 15%.

Find answers at: cambridge.org/ukschools/gcsemaths-studentbookanswers

EXERCISE 13F

1 Find the original values if:

   a 25% is £30   **b** 8% is 120 grams

   c 120% is 800 kg   **d** 115% is £2000

2 What is the original price of an item sold for £140 in a 25%-off sale?

   Choose your answer from the options below.

   A £175   B £245.50   C £186.67   D £560

3 VAT of 20% is added to most goods before they are sold.

   The prices given here include VAT.

   Work out the net cost of each item (cost before VAT is added).

   a Necklace £1200   **b** Camera £145.50

   c Painting £865   **d** Boots £54.99

4 Misha paid £40 for a DVD box set in a 20%-off sale.

   What was the original price of the DVD set?

5 A camera is sold for £87.

   The shop makes a 45% profit.

   What is the cost price of the camera?

   Choose your answer from the following options.

   A £60   B £56.13   C £47.85   D £39.15

6 In a school 240 students are in Year 10.

   This is 20% of the school population.

   a How many students are there in total in the school?

   b How many students are in all the other years put together at this school?

7 Sarita's pay increased by 15%.

   Her new pay is £172.50.

   What was her pay before the increase?

8 Nine-carat gold is 37.5% pure gold.

   A piece of nine-carat gold jewellery is tested and found to contain 97.5 grams of pure gold.

   What is the total weight of the piece of jewellery?

9 Julia is training for a marathon and she reduces her weight by 5%.

   She weighs 58 kg at the end of her training.

   What did she weigh at the start?

10 In an ultramarathon, 310 runners completed the course within the cut-off time.

   This represents 62% of the runners.

   How many runners started the race?

Checklist of learning and understanding

Review of percentages
- Per cent means 'parts per hundred'.
- To convert a percentage to a fraction, write the percentage with a denominator of 100 and simplify.
- To convert percentages to decimals divide by 100.
- To order a mixture of fractions, decimals and percentages, change them all to percentages or decimals.

Percentage calculations
- To find a percentage of an amount, express the percentage as a fraction over 100 and then multiply the fraction by the amount.
- To express one quantity (quantity A) as a percentage of another quantity (quantity B), make sure the units are the same and then calculate $\dfrac{\text{quantity } A}{\text{quantity } B} \times 100$.

Percentage change
- To increase or decrease an amount by a percentage, find the percentage amount and add or subtract it from the original amount.
- Or, use a multiplier: to increase an amount by $x\%$, the multiplier is $(1 + \frac{x}{100})$; to decrease an amount by $x\%$, the multiplier is $(1 - \frac{x}{100})$.
- To find an original value when you know the percentage increase or decrease and the new amount, make an equation and use reverse percentages to solve for x.

Chapter review

For additional questions on the topics in this chapter, visit GCSE Mathematics Online.

1   **a**   Choose the value that is equivalent to 4.5%.

A $4\frac{5}{100}$ B $\frac{45}{100}$ C $\frac{450}{100}$ D $\frac{45}{1000}$

   b   What is the decimal equivalent of 500%?

Choose from the following options.

A   50 000.0   B   5.0   C   0.05   D   0.005

2   Write the following percentages as fractions in their simplest form.

   a   25%   **b**   30%   **c**   3.5%

3   Express each of these as a percentage.

   a $\frac{1}{20}$ **b** $\frac{1}{8}$ **c** $\frac{8}{15}$

   d   0.5   **e**   1.25   **f**   0.005

4   The value of an investment increased from £120 000 to £124 800.

What percentage increase is this?

Find answers at: cambridge.org/ukschools/gcsemaths-studentbookanswers

5 The population of New Orleans was 484 674 before Hurricane Katrina.

Afterwards, the population was found to have decreased by 53.9%.

What was the population afterwards?

6 The population of England in 2013 was approximately 53 million.

It is predicted that:

the population in 2018 will be 4% more than the population in 2013

and the population in 2023 will be 4% more than the population in 2018.

Work out the predicted population of England in 2023.   *(3 marks)*

© AQA 2013

7 Shaz works 30 hours per week.

She increases this by 12%.

How many hours does she now work per week?

8 Express:

a 3 hours as a percentage of a day

b 750 metres as a percentage of 2 km.

9 The price of a plane ticket was reduced by 8% to £423.20.

What was the original price of the ticket?

10 Niall sold some shares for £1147.50 and made a 35% profit.

What did he pay for the shares?

11 A shop makes a profit of 32% on full-priced computers.

During a promotion, the marked selling prices of computers are reduced by 15%.

What is the cost price of a computer that sells for £980 during the promotion?

14 Powers and roots

In this chapter you will learn how to …

- use integers and fractions to represent numbers in index notation.
- calculate with powers and roots.
- apply the rules for multiplying and dividing indices.

For more resources relating to this chapter, visit GCSE Mathematics Online.

Using mathematics: real-life applications

Financial advisors and investors have to perform calculations involving powers and roots to work out the value of investments over time. They might use computer technology (software programs) to work out different options to help their clients invest their money wisely.

Calculator tip

Make sure you know which buttons to use to evaluate different powers and find different roots of numbers.

"'I have to be able to understand, manipulate and evaluate different formulae to find the best investment. Many of these formulae involve fractional powers and different roots." *(Personal financial adviser)*

Before you start …

Ch 1	You should be able to quickly add and subtract pairs of integers mentally.	**1**	Choose the correct sign: <, = or >. **a** $-3 + -3 \;\square\; 4 + 2$ **b** $6 - 7 \;\square\; 3 - 4$ **c** $4 - (-5) \;\square\; -3 + -6$ **d** $-2 + 6 \;\square\; 9 - 5$

Ch 1	You need to be able to find the squares, cubes, square roots and cube roots of numbers.	**2**	Choose the correct answer.
			 a The area of a square with sides of 3 cm.
			    A $6\,cm^2$ B $9\,cm^2$ C $12\,cm^2$
			 b $\sqrt[3]{27}$
			    A 9 B 5.2 C 3
			 c $\sqrt{810\,000}$
			    A 9 B 90 C 900

Ch 5	You need to be able to find the reciprocal of a number or fraction.	**3**	Find the reciprocal of each number. Choose from the values in the box. **a** $\dfrac{3}{4}$ **b** 12 **c** $1\dfrac{2}{5}$ $\dfrac{12}{1}$ $\dfrac{4}{3}$ $\dfrac{1}{12}$ $\dfrac{7}{5}$ $\dfrac{5}{7}$

Find answers at: cambridge.org/ukschools/gcsemaths-studentbookanswers

Assess your starting point using the Launchpad

STEP 1

1 Write each of these numbers in index notation.

   a $4 \times 4 \times 4 \times 4 \times 4$

   b Eight cubed.

   c Five squared.

   d Nine to the power of seven.

   e The reciprocal of 3 to the power of 4.

   f The reciprocal of 2 to the power of 3.

GO TO
Section 1:
Index notation

STEP 2

2 Evaluate these without a calculator. Give the answer in index form and then work out the answer.

   a $3^3 \times 3^2$ **b** $4^{-2} \times 4^4$ **c** $\dfrac{6^4}{6^4}$

   d $\dfrac{6^5}{6^3}$ **e** $\dfrac{4^5}{4^8}$ **f** $(2^3)^2$

GO TO
Section 2:
The laws of indices
Section 3:
Working with powers and roots

GO TO
Chapter review

Section 1: Index notation

Key vocabulary

index: a power or exponent indicating how many times a base number is multiplied by itself

index notation: writing a number as a base and index, for example 2^3

Tip

Any number to the power of 1 stays as the same number so you don't usually write powers of 1.

You use powers to write repeated multiplications in a shorter form.

For example: $6 \times 6 = 6^2$ and $5 \times 5 \times 5 = 5^3$

The **index** tells you how many times the base number is multiplied by itself.

5^3 This is the index. The index can also be called the power or the exponent.

This is the base.

$4^3 = 4 \times 4 \times 4$

$7^4 = 7 \times 7 \times 7 \times 7$

$9^{12} = 9 \times 9 \times 9 \times 9 \times 9 \times 9 \times 9 \times 9 \times 9 \times 9 \times 9 \times 9$

When you write a number using an index you are using **index notation**.

   7^4 is in index notation.

When you write the multiplication out in full you are using expanded form.

   $7 \times 7 \times 7 \times 7$ is in expanded form.

The plural of index is indices.

Roots

Mathematically, finding the root of a number is the inverse of working out the power of the number.

So $5^2 = 25$ and $\sqrt{25} = 5$, and $2^3 = 8$ and $\sqrt[3]{8} = 2$.

Powers of 2, 3, 4, 5 and 10

It is useful to recognise the first few powers of 2, 3, 4 and 5.

This can help you to work out their roots as well.

It is also useful to know these powers of 10:

$10^3 = 1000$

$10^6 = 1$ million

EXERCISE 14A

1 What is the value of $1^4 + 5^2$?

Choose from the following options.

A 14   B 29   C 11   D 26

2 Draw up a table like this one.

Base \ Index	−3	−2	−1	0	1	2	3	4	5
2	$2^{-3}=\frac{1}{8}$	$2^{-2}=$	$2^{-1}=\frac{1}{2}$	$2^0=1$	$2^1=2$	$2^2=4$	$2^3=$	$2^4=16$	$2^5=$
3									
4									
5									

a Use a calculator to work out the missing values in the table. Some powers of two have been done as an example.

b Compare the positive and negative values for the same index. What do you notice?

c Compare the powers of 2 with the powers of 4. What do you notice?

d How can you decide quickly that a number is **not** a power of 5?

3 Use the table that you completed in question 2 to decide whether each statement is true or false.

a $2^4 = 4^2$

b $2^5 > 3^5$

c $2^0 = 5^0$

d $2^1 = 2^{-1}$

e $3^4 > 4^3$

f $4^4 < 3^4$

g $5^2 = 2^5$

h $3^5 > 5^3$

i $2^{-3} > 3^{-2}$

j $3^{-3} = \dfrac{1}{27}$

k $5^{-1} = 4^{-1}$

l $2(2^{-1}) = 1$

4 Use your table to work these out without using a calculator.

a $\sqrt{25}$

b $\sqrt[3]{8}$

c $\sqrt[4]{256}$

d $\sqrt[3]{125}$

e $\sqrt[5]{243}$

f $\sqrt[3]{64}$

g $\sqrt[3]{8} + \sqrt[4]{625}$

h $\sqrt{2500}$

i $\sqrt[5]{32} + \sqrt[4]{81}$

j $\sqrt[3]{27\,000}$

k $\sqrt[4]{160\,000}$

l $\sqrt[5]{3125} \times \sqrt[4]{625}$

Index notation on your calculator

Most calculators have one key to square a number: $\boxed{x^2}$

Your calculator is also likely to have a key that allows you to enter any other powers quickly and easily. It might be $\boxed{y^x}$ or $\boxed{x^y}$ or $\boxed{a^b}$

To enter 13^4, you press $\boxed{1}\,\boxed{3}\,\boxed{y^x}\,\boxed{4}\,\boxed{=}$

You will get a result of $28\,561$.

EXERCISE 14B

1 Evaluate each expression without using a calculator.

a 2^3

b 6^2

c 1^8

d 8^3

e 10^4

f 10^6

g $2^3 - 1^5$

h $1^6 + 7^2$

i $2^4 \times 2^2$

j $2^4 + 4^2$

k $2^3 \times 2^4$

l $3^3 \times 3^3$

m $2^4 \div 2^3$

n $4^5 \div 4^3$

o $7^2 \times 10^3$

p 7×10^6

q $2 \times 10^2 + 3 \times 10^3$

r $6^2 \times 10^6$

2 Use your calculator to evaluate the following.

a 4^6

b 12^3

c 8^5

d 7^4

e 15^3

f 10^4

g 28^2

h 25^3

3 Use a calculator to find the value of each expression.

a $12^3 - 2^8$

b $20^4 - 15^2$

c $15^3 \times 15^2$

d $3^{12} + 3^4$

e $3^6 + 2^8$

f $35^3 \div 5^3$

4 Copy each statement and fill in < or > to make each one true.

a $4^6 \,\square\, 6^4$

b $10^3 \,\square\, 3^{10}$

c $4^9 \,\square\, 9^4$

d $15^2 \,\square\, 2^{15}$

e $9^8 \,\square\, 8^9$

f $2^{10} \,\square\, 10^2$

Zero and negative indices

In this table, each value is $\frac{1}{10}$ of the value above it.

For example, $10^6 \div 10 = 10^5$

Index notation	Expanded form	Value
10^6	$10 \times 10 \times 10 \times 10 \times 10 \times 10$	$1\,000\,000$
10^5	$10 \times 10 \times 10 \times 10 \times 10$	$100\,000$
10^4	$10 \times 10 \times 10 \times 10$	$10\,000$
10^3	$10 \times 10 \times 10$	$1\,000$
10^2	10×10	100
10^1	10	10
10^0	$10 \div 10$	1
10^{-1}	$1 \div 10$	$\frac{1}{10}$
10^{-2}	$\frac{1}{10} \div 10$	$\frac{1}{100}$
10^{-3}	$\frac{1}{100} \div 10$	$\frac{1}{1000}$
10^{-4}	$\frac{1}{1000} \div 10$	$\frac{1}{10\,000}$

Tip

Remember that you use reciprocals to change fraction divisions into multiplications.
$\frac{1}{10} \div 10 = \frac{1}{10} \times \frac{1}{10} = \frac{1}{100}$

The pattern in the table gives us two very important facts about indices.

Any number with an index of 0 is equal to 1: $a^0 = 1$
(Except for 0^0 that is undefined.)

For example, $5^0 = 1$ and $7^0 = 1$.

Tip

An index can also be a fraction. You will deal with fractional index notation in Section 2 because it is easier to understand how it works when you know the laws of indices.

Any number with a negative index is equal to its reciprocal with a positive index: $a^{-m} = \frac{1}{a^m}$

For example, $4^{-2} = \frac{1}{4^2}$ and $5^{-3} = \frac{1}{5^3}$

EXERCISE 14C

1 How would you write 4^{-2} with a positive index?
Choose from the options below.
A $\frac{2^2}{2}$ B $\frac{2}{2^2}$ C $\frac{1}{4^2}$ D $\frac{4^2}{-1}$

2 Write each of the following using positive indices only.
a 2^{-1} **b** 3^{-1} **c** 4^{-1}
d 3^{-2} **e** 4^{-3} **f** 3^{-5}
g 3^{-4} **h** 6^{-6} **i** 34^{-5}
j x^{-3} **k** m^{-2} **l** $3x^{-4}$

3 Express the following with negative indices.

a $\frac{1}{3}$ **b** $\frac{1}{5}$ **c** $\frac{1}{7}$

d $\frac{1}{3^2}$ **e** $\frac{1}{4^5}$ **f** $\frac{1}{2^6}$

g $\frac{1}{7^2}$ **h** $\frac{1}{10^5}$ **i** $\frac{1}{2^2}$

j $\frac{1}{12^3}$ **k** $\frac{1}{10^4}$ **l** $\frac{1}{3(2)^2}$

m $\frac{1}{x^2}$ **n** $\frac{1}{x^3}$ **o** $\frac{4}{y^2}$

4 Copy each of these statements and fill in = or ≠ to make them true.

a $10^{-1} \square \frac{1}{10}$ **b** $6^0 \square 1$ **c** $6^{-1} \square \frac{1}{6}$

d $10^{-2} \square \frac{2}{10}$ **e** $6^{-3} \square \frac{1}{6^3}$ **f** $10^0 \square 1$

g $6^{-4} \square \frac{1}{6^4}$ **h** $\frac{1}{10^4} \square 10^{-4}$ **i** $\frac{1}{6^3} \square \frac{3}{6}$

j $\frac{1}{4}(x^{-1}) \square 4x$ **k** $\frac{10}{m^5} \square -10m^5$ **l** $0.5x^{-3} \square \frac{1}{2x^2}$

5 Rewrite each expression in the form 2^x.

a 2   **b** 16   **c** 64

d $\frac{1}{8}$ **e** 0.25   **f** 1

g $\frac{1}{32}$ **h** $\sqrt{16}$ **i** $-\sqrt{64}$

Section 2: The laws of indices

The laws of indices are a set of rules that allow you to multiply and divide powers without writing them out in expanded form.

Law of indices for multiplication

To multiply two numbers in index notation you add the indices.

$a^m \times a^n = a^{m+n}$

This law works for all indices, including negative indices.

For example, $2^3 \times 2^{-2} = 2^{3+(-2)} = 2^1 = 2$

Law of indices for division

To divide two numbers in index notation you subtract the indices.

$a^m \div a^n = a^{m-n}$

This law works for all indices, including negative indices.

$2^2 \div 2^4 = 2^{2-4} = 2^{-2}$

You can understand how this works by looking at the expanded notation:

$2^2 \div 2^4 = \dfrac{2 \times 2}{2 \times 2 \times 2 \times 2}$

If you cancel you get $\dfrac{1}{2 \times 2}$

$\dfrac{1}{2^2}$ is equal to 2^{-2}

Law of indices for powers of indices

To find the power of a power you multiply the indices.

$(a^m)^n = a^{mn}$

This law works for all indices, including negative indices.

$(3^2)^3 = 3^{2 \times 3} = 3^6$

$(4^3)^{-4} = 4^{(3)(-4)} = 4^{-12}$

You can understand how this works by looking at the expanded notation:

$(3^2)^3$ means 3^2 to the power of 3, that is $3^2 \times 3^2 \times 3^2$

$3^2 \times 3^2 \times 3^2 = 3 \times 3 \times 3 \times 3 \times 3 \times 3 = 3^6$

> **Tip**
>
> The laws of indices also help to show that $a^0 = 1$
>
> $4^3 \div 4^3 = 4^{3-3} = 4^0$
>
> You already know that any number divided by itself is 1, so $4^3 \div 4^3 = 1$.
>
> But this is also equal to 4^0, so 4^0 must be equal to 1.

EXERCISE 14D

1 Simplify. Leave your answers in index notation.

   a $2^4 \times 2^3$ **b** $10^2 \times 10^5$ **c** $4^3 \times 4^3$

   d 5×5^6 **e** $2^4 \times 2^7$ **f** $3^2 \times 3^{-4}$

   g $2^{-2} \times 2^5$ **h** $3^0 \times 3^2$ **i** $2 \times 2^3 \times 2^{-5}$

   j $3^2 \times 3^2 \times 3$ **k** $10^2 \times 10^{-3} \times 10^2$ **l** $10^0 \times 10^{-2} \times 10^2$

2 Simplify. Leave your answers in index notation.

   a $6^4 \div 6^2$ **b** $10^5 \div 10^2$ **c** $6^5 \div 6^3$

   d $6^3 \div 6^5$ **e** $10^3 \div 10^5$ **f** $3^{10} \div 3^0$

   g $3^8 \div 3$ **h** $10^4 \div 10^4$ **i** $\dfrac{5^4}{5^{-2}}$

   j $\dfrac{10^6}{10^{-4}}$ **k** $\dfrac{3^{-2}}{3^{-3}}$ **l** $\dfrac{2^0}{2^3}$

3 Simplify each expression. Give your answers in index notation.

   a $(2^2)^3$ **b** $(2^3)^3$ **c** $(2^4)^2$

   d $(10^2)^2$ **e** $(10^2)^3$ **f** $(10^4)^2$

   g $(2^4)^{-3}$ **h** $(10^{-2})^2$ **i** $(10^2)^{-3}$

   j $(3^4)^{-2}$ **k** $(2^3)^0$ **l** $(2^2 \times 2^3)^2$

4 Say whether each statement is true or false. If it is false, write the correct answer.

   a $3^3 \times 3^5 = 3^8$ **b** $3^8 \div 3^2 = 3^4$ **c** $10^8 \div 10^2 = 10^6$

   d $(3^3)^2 = 3^6$ **e** $121^0 = 1$ **f** $4^5 \times 4^2 = 4^7$

   g $3^{10} \div 3^2 = 3^5$ **h** $(4^2)^4 = 4^8$ **i** $(3^2)^0 = 1$

Find answers at: cambridge.org/ukschools/gcsemaths-studentbookanswers

Fractional indices

The law of indices for multiplication can be used to explain the meaning of fractional indices.

Read through these examples carefully.

$$3^{\frac{1}{2}} \times 3^{\frac{1}{2}} = 3^{\frac{1}{2}+\frac{1}{2}} = 3^1 = 3 \qquad \text{Add the indices using the law above.}$$

But you also know that $\sqrt{3} \times \sqrt{3} = 3$

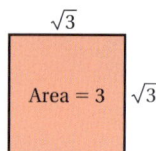

So, $3^{\frac{1}{2}} \times 3^{\frac{1}{2}} = 3$ and $\sqrt{3} \times \sqrt{3} = 3$ · $\quad 3^{\frac{1}{2}}$ must equal $\sqrt{3}$ for this to be the case.

$$\therefore 3^{\frac{1}{2}} = \sqrt{3}$$

Similarly:

$$8^{\frac{1}{3}} \times 8^{\frac{1}{3}} \times 8^{\frac{1}{3}} = 8^{\left(\frac{1}{3}+\frac{1}{3}+\frac{1}{3}\right)} = 8^1 = 8 \qquad \text{Add the indices using the law above.}$$

But you also know that $\sqrt[3]{8} \times \sqrt[3]{8} \times \sqrt[3]{8} = 8$

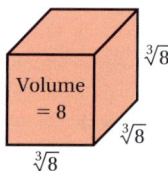

$$lbh = V$$

So, $8^{\frac{1}{3}} \times 8^{\frac{1}{3}} \times 8^{\frac{1}{3}} = 8$ and $\sqrt[3]{8} \times \sqrt[3]{8} \times \sqrt[3]{8} = 8 \quad 8^{\frac{1}{3}}$ must equal $\sqrt[3]{8}$ for this to be the case.

$$\therefore 8^{\frac{1}{3}} = \sqrt[3]{8}$$

From this you can see that $x^{\frac{1}{2}}$ is the square root of x and $y^{\frac{1}{3}}$ is the cube root of y.

This gives us a general rule:

$$\sqrt{x} = x^{\frac{1}{2}} \qquad \text{and} \qquad \sqrt[3]{x} = x^{\frac{1}{3}}$$

So, $\sqrt[n]{x} = x^{\frac{1}{n}}$ $\qquad$ (the nth root of x is the same as x to the power of $\frac{1}{n}$)

Other fractional indices

The general law above applies to fractions where the numerator is 1.

The index law for raising a power to a power can be used to make a general rule for a fraction that does not have a numerator of 1.

$$4^{\frac{2}{3}} = \left(4^{\frac{1}{3}}\right)^2 \qquad \frac{1}{3} \times 2 = \frac{2}{3}$$

$$2^{\frac{3}{4}} = \left(2^{\frac{1}{4}}\right)^3 \qquad \frac{1}{4} \times 3 = \frac{3}{4}$$

A unit fraction gives a root. So you can rewrite these expressions by writing the part inside the bracket as a root, like this:

$$\left(4^{\frac{1}{3}}\right)^2 = (\sqrt[3]{4})^2 \quad \text{and} \quad \left(2^{\frac{1}{4}}\right)^3 = (\sqrt[4]{2})^3$$

So, $4^{\frac{2}{3}} = (\sqrt[3]{4})^2$ and $\quad 2^{\frac{3}{4}} = (\sqrt[4]{2})^3$

In general terms:

$$x^{\frac{m}{n}} = \left(x^{\frac{1}{n}}\right)^m = (\sqrt[n]{x})^m \qquad \text{the nth root of x to the power of m}$$

Tip

It is much simpler to evaluate an expression in root form on your calculator than it is to try and enter $4^{\frac{2}{3}}$.

WORKED EXAMPLE 1

Write in index notation and then work out the value of each expression.

a $27^{\frac{2}{3}}$

$= \left(\sqrt[3]{27}\right)^2$ Rewrite as a power. Remember $\frac{2}{3} = 2 \times \frac{1}{3}$

$= (3)^2$ You should know that the cube root of 27 is 3,
but you can work it out if you need to.

$= 9$

b $5^{\frac{3}{4}}$

$= \left(\sqrt[4]{5}\right)^3$

$= 3.343 \text{ (to 3 dp)}$

💡 Tip

The index laws apply to all indices, including negative and fractional indices.

$2^3 \times 2^{-2} = 2^{3+(-2)} = 2^1 = 2$ and $3^{\frac{1}{2}} \times 3^{\frac{1}{4}} = 3^{\left(\frac{1}{2}+\frac{1}{4}\right)} = 3^{\frac{3}{4}}$

$2^2 \div 2^4 = 2^{2-4} = 2^{-2}$ and $3^{\frac{3}{4}} \div 3^{\frac{1}{2}} = 3^{\left(\frac{3}{4}-\frac{1}{2}\right)} = 3^{\frac{1}{4}}$

$(4^3)^{-4} = 4^{(3)(-4)} = 4^{-12}$ and $\left(2^{\frac{1}{4}}\right)^{\frac{1}{2}} = 2^{\left(\frac{1}{4} \times \frac{1}{2}\right)} = 2^{\frac{1}{8}}$

EXERCISE 14E

1   Rewrite each expression using root signs.

   a $3^{\frac{1}{2}}$ **b** $4^{\frac{1}{3}}$ **c** $5^{\frac{1}{4}}$ **d** $6^{\frac{1}{2}}$

   e $4^{\frac{1}{9}}$ **f** $5^{\frac{2}{3}}$ **g** $4^{\frac{3}{8}}$ **h** $6^{\frac{2}{9}}$

2   Write in index notation:

   a $\sqrt{6}$ **b** $\sqrt[3]{4}$ **c** $\sqrt[3]{11}$ **d** $\sqrt[4]{9}$

   e $\left(\sqrt[3]{3}\right)^4$ **f** $\sqrt[5]{7}$ **g** $\left(\sqrt[3]{7}\right)^2$ **h** $2\left(\sqrt[3]{3}\right)^5$

3   Evaluate:

   a $8^{\frac{1}{3}}$ **b** $32^{\frac{1}{5}}$ **c** $8^{\frac{4}{3}}$

   d $216^{\frac{2}{3}}$ **e** $256^{\frac{3}{4}}$ **f** $256^{-\frac{1}{4}}$

   g $125^{-\frac{4}{3}}$ **h** $\left(\frac{8}{27}\right)^{-\frac{1}{3}}$ **i** $\left(\frac{8}{18}\right)^{-\frac{1}{2}}$

Section 3: Working with powers and roots

Powers and roots are used in many different contexts.

Builders, painters and decorators need to work out areas using square units (powers of 2 and square roots). Volume calculations use cube units (powers of 3 and cube roots).

Calculations dealing with growth rates use different powers and roots and many science formulae rely on being able to work with powers and roots.

In situations involving numbers that are not perfect squares or cubes (or other powers) an estimate of the power or root of a value might be used.

Estimating powers and roots

You can use what you already know about square and cube numbers and their roots to estimate the approximate value of other powers and roots.

For example, you can estimate the square root of a number that is not a perfect square by working out where it lies on a number line in relation to the square number below it and above it.

This example shows how to estimate $\sqrt{98}$.

WORKED EXAMPLE 2

Estimate $\sqrt{98}$.

$\sqrt{81} < \sqrt{98} < \sqrt{100}$
$9 < \sqrt{98} < 10$

First find the perfect squares closest to 98 and write the inequalities.

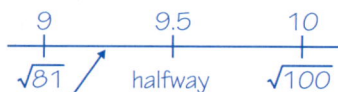

ignore values
<9.5

$\sqrt{98}$ is closer to $\sqrt{100}$
so try 9.9

Use trial and improvement to estimate more accurately.

Check: $9.9 \times 9.9 = 98.01$
As $98.01 \approx 98$, $\sqrt{98} \approx 9.9$

Remember, your estimate might not be an exact value, but it should be close. Usually a value to two decimal places is good enough. If you use a calculator you will see that $\sqrt{98}$ is 9.899, so 9.9 is a fairly accurate estimate.

You can use a similar method using your calculator to find the approximate value of a power by trial and error.

WORKED EXAMPLE 3

If $2^x = 18$, estimate the value of x.

$2^4 = 16 \qquad 2^5 = 32$

So $4 < x < 5$

Use what you know.

16 (18)   32

2^4 2^5

Close to 16, so x must be closer to 4 than to 5.

Try $2^{4.1} = 17.14$ Too small
       $2^{4.2} = 18.37$ Too big

x must be between 4.1 and 4.2

Try $2^{4.15} = 17.75$ Too small
       $2^{4.16} = 17.88$ Too small
       $2^{4.17} = 18.00$ Correct (to 2 dp)

So $x \approx 4.17$

Use trial and improvement starting with an index value slightly larger than 4.

Try values between 4.1 and 4.2

EXERCISE 14F

1   Estimate the following roots. Show your working.

   a $\sqrt{72}$ **b** $\sqrt{33}$ **c** $\sqrt{6}$

   d $\sqrt[3]{29}$ **e** $\sqrt[3]{-200}$ **f** $\sqrt[4]{37}$

2   Use a calculator to find the roots in question 1 to two decimal places. How good were your estimates?

3   Find the value of x in each of the following by trial and improvement. Show your working.

   a $2^x = 25$ **b** $3^x = 36$ **c** $2^x = 280$

   d $x^4 = 1296$ **e** $x^3 = 12$ **f** $x^3 = 7000$

4   Find four different pairs of values for a and m that will satisfy the equation $a^m = 81$.

5   A square has an area of $90\,mm^2$.

   Use trial and improvement to find the length of its sides.

6   A cube has a volume of $800\,mm^3$.

   Find the length of the side of the cube to two decimal places using trial and improvement methods.

Find answers at: cambridge.org/ukschools/gcsemaths-studentbookanswers

Solving problems involving powers and roots

Some problems can seem difficult and confusing because they are so long and wordy.

A good strategy for these problems is to rewrite the problem using only the most important words and numbers.

Problem-solving framework

Steps for solving problems	What you would do for this example
Step 1: Read the problem carefully and highlight the important words and numbers.	Naresh wants to have £5000 saved in three years' time to buy a car. He finds an account that offers an interest rate of 2.9% compounded annually. His sister tells him that you can work out how much you need to put away now to have an amount in the future using the formula Principal amount (P) = Future value (F) × $(1.029)^{-3}$ Use the formula to calculate how much Naresh should put into the account to have £5000 in 3 years' time.
Step 2: Jot down the important words and numbers only.	Future value: £5000 Formula: $P = F(1.029)^{-3}$ We need to find P.
Step 3: Rewrite the problem again in mathematical terms to show what you need to do.	$P = £5000 \times (1.029)^{-3}$ Now you can see that the complicated word problem is really quite a simple substitution problem that you can work out in one step with your calculator.
Step 4: Do the necessary calculation.	$\boxed{5}\boxed{0}\boxed{0}\boxed{0}\boxed{\times}\boxed{1}\boxed{.}\boxed{0}\boxed{2}\boxed{9}\boxed{x^y}\boxed{3}\boxed{+/-}\boxed{=}$ 4589.06 Naresh needs to put £4589.06 into the account now.

Calculator tip

On some calculators you might have to enter

$\boxed{5}\boxed{0}\boxed{0}\boxed{0}\boxed{\times}\boxed{1}\boxed{.}\boxed{0}\boxed{2}\boxed{9}\boxed{x^y}\boxed{-}\boxed{3}\boxed{=}$

Find out how to enter a negative index number on your calculator.

EXERCISE 14G

1 **a** The volume of a cube is $216\,\text{cm}^3$.

What is length of each edge? Choose from the options below.

A 6 cm   B 14.7 cm   C 24 cm   D 72 cm

b A box can hold 24 cuboids of volume $256\,\text{cm}^3$.

What is the volume of the box? Choose from the options below.

A $216\,\text{cm}^3$ B $256\,\text{cm}^3$ C $624\,\text{cm}^3$ D $6144\,\text{cm}^3$

2 The table shows the amount of caffeine (milligrams) per 350 ml drink. You can use the expression $100\left(\frac{1}{2}\right)^{\frac{n}{5}}$ to find the percentage of caffeine still in your system a number of hours (n) after drinking something containing caffeine.

Drink (350 ml)	Amount of caffeine (mg)
Americano coffee	154
Cappuccino	154
Ceylon tea	63
Iced tea	25.5
Cola (the one in the red can)	34
Diet cola (the one in the red can)	45
Cola zero (the one in the red can)	45
Cola (the one in the blue can)	38
Diet cola (the one in the blue can)	38
Cola one (the one in the blue can)	54
Cream soda	29
Energy drink (the one famous for adventure)	120

Marie and Suki apply the formula to find out how many milligrams of caffeine will remain in their system 3 hours after drinking a 350 ml energy drink. This is how each student worked:

a Which answer is correct? Write what the other student did wrong.

b Billy drinks two energy drinks and a cola zero.

How many milligrams of caffeine will be left in his system after 4 hours?

c Karen drinks three cups of Ceylon tea.

How much caffeine will be left in her system $2\frac{1}{2}$ hours later?

d What percentage of caffeine is left in your body $\frac{1}{2}$ hour after drinking any caffeinated drink?

Marie's working

% caffeine $= 100\left(\frac{1}{2}\right)^{\frac{n}{5}}$

$= 100(0.5)^{\frac{3}{5}}$

$= 2.5\%$

2.5% of 120 mg = 3 mg

Suki's working

% C $= 100(0.5)^{\frac{3}{5}}$

$= 65.98\%$

65.98% of 120 mg = 79.18 mg

3 Shamila received an inheritance of £2500.

She invests it for ten years in an account that offers 5% interest.

She works out how much money she will have after the ten years with the formula:

Value of future investment = original amount $\times (1.05)^{10}$

a Work out how much money Shamila will have in the investment after ten years.

b Shamila decides to spend £500 of her inheritance and puts the rest of the money into this investment.

Work out how much she will have after ten years with the new starting amount.

c Rewrite the formula to work out the future value of an investment if the interest rate is 3% and the period of the investment is 18 months.

d Use your formula to find the future value of £3200 invested under these conditions.

4 The time t (seconds) a ball takes to hit the ground after being dropped from a height h (metres) can be found using the formula $t = \sqrt{\dfrac{h}{4.9}}$

a Work out how long it will take a ball dropped from a height of 3.6 metres to hit the ground.

b Matt drops a ball from a height of 2.5 m and Nina drops a ball from a height of 3.6 m.

i Work out whose ball will hit the ground first.

ii Work out how many seconds later the other ball hits the ground.

5 Many measurements in humans and other mammals are in proportion to the mass of the body.

Here are four different formulae that use mass (m) in kilograms to work out other measurements.

Mass of the brain (B) in kilograms	Surface area of the skin (S) in square metres	Resting metabolic rate (C) (Calories consumed at rest)	Time (T) it takes for the blood to circulate in seconds
$B = 0.01m^{\frac{2}{3}}$	$S = 0.0096m^{\frac{7}{10}}$	$C = 70(\sqrt[4]{m})^3$	$T = 17.4\left(\sqrt[4]{m}\right)$

a Work out all of these values based on your own mass in kilograms.

b Compare the circulation time for an elephant with average mass 5000 kg and a human male with average mass 70 kg.

c What is the brain of a 4.5 kg cat likely to weigh?

d Find the surface area of the skin of a mouse of mass 0.3 kg and a cat of mass 4.5 kg.

e How many calories does a 145 kg lion consume while resting?

f Give a reason why all the values found using these formulae are only approximate.

> **Tip**
>
> These formulae are all based on a constant of proportionality (k). You will learn more about this in Chapter 28 when you deal with direct and inverse proportion.

6 Kepler's law can be used to work out the time (T) in Earth days that it takes for a planet to complete an orbit around the sun.

The formula for this is $T = 0.2R^{\frac{3}{2}}$, where R is the mean distance from the planet to the Sun in millions of kilometres.

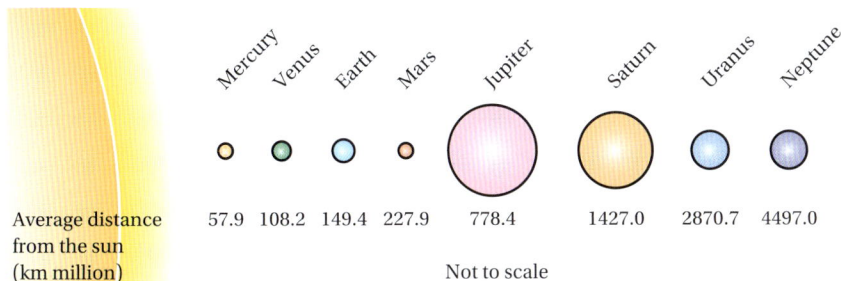

	Mercury	Venus	Earth	Mars	Jupiter	Saturn	Uranus	Neptune
Average distance from the sun (km million)	57.9	108.2	149.4	227.9	778.4	1427.0	2870.7	4497.0

Not to scale

a Use the formula to find the time it takes the Earth to orbit the Sun.

b Which takes longer to orbit the Sun: Jupiter or Uranus?

How much longer does it take?

c Which planet orbits the Sun in the shortest time?

Write down how you know this and then work out how long it takes.

Checklist of learning and understanding

Index notation
- Numbers can be expressed as powers of their factors using index notation.
  - $2 \times 2 \times 2 \times 2$ can be written in index notation as 2^4
  - The 4 is the index (also called the power or the exponent) and it tells us how many times the base (2) must be multiplied by itself.
- Any number to the power of 0 is equal to 1: $a^0 = 1$
- A negative index can be written as a reciprocal fraction with a positive index: $a^{-m} = \frac{1}{a^m}$

Laws of indices
- Multiplication: $a^m \times a^n = a^{m+n}$
- Division: $\frac{a^m}{a^n} = a^{m-n}$
- Raising a power: $(a^m)^n = a^{mn}$

Working with powers and roots
- Finding the root of a number is the inverse of raising the number to a power. For example, $4^2 = 16$ and $\sqrt{16} = 4$
- Powers and roots can be estimated using a number line to locate them in relation to known powers and roots and then finding an accurate estimate by trial and error.
- Many real-life calculations rely on formulae containing integer and fractional indices and roots.

For additional questions on the topics in this chapter, visit GCSE Mathematics Online.

Chapter review

1 Which expression is the smallest?

    A 20^3 B 4^5 C 5^4 D 13^3

2 Write each number in index form.

    a $8 \times 8 \times 8 \times 8 \times 8$ **b** three cubed

    c $\dfrac{1}{64}$ **d** $(\sqrt{5})^3$

3 Put these expressions in order from smallest to largest.

    a $3^4, \sqrt{81}, 10^2, 4^3, 2 \times \sqrt{121}$ **b** $4^5, 5^4, 10^3, 96^0, 3^2, 20^2$

    c $\sqrt[3]{4}, 4^{\frac{3}{2}}, 4^2, \left(\dfrac{1}{4}\right)^{\frac{3}{2}}$

4 Write these numbers with positive indices.

    a 3^{-3} **b** 2^{-10} **c** 5^{-2}

5 Use the laws of indices to simplify each expression and write it as a single power of 4.

    a $4^2 \times 4^2$ **b** $4^6 \times 4^{-3}$ **c** $4^7 \div 4^3$

    d $4^3 \div 4^5$ **e** $(4^3)^2$ **f** $(4^{-2})^2$

6 Evaluate. Check your answers with a calculator.

    a $\sqrt{121}$ **b** $\sqrt{0.25}$ **c** $\sqrt[3]{125}$

    d $\sqrt[5]{32}$ **e** $\sqrt[4]{81}$ **f** $\sqrt{\dfrac{1}{4}}$

    g $9^{\frac{3}{2}}$ **h** $(27)^{\frac{2}{3}}$ **i** $8^{\frac{4}{3}}$

7 Estimate the length of each side of a cube of volume $35\,\text{cm}^3$.

    Show your working.

8 Electricians use the formula $V = \sqrt{PR}$ to work out voltage (V in volts) where P is the power in watts and R is the resistance in ohms.

    Calculate the voltage when $P = 2000$ watts and $R = 24.2$ ohms.

9 The length of time (T seconds) it takes for a pendulum of length L in metres to swing through one complete movement can be calculated using the formula $T = 2\pi\left(\dfrac{L}{9.8}\right)^{\frac{1}{2}}$

    a Work out how long it will take for a pendulum of length $0.25\,\text{m}$ to complete one swing.

    b How does the length of the pendulum affect how long it takes to complete one swing?

    Justify your answer.

10 The radius of a cylindrical container can be found using the formula
$r = \sqrt{\dfrac{V}{\pi h}}$, where V is the volume and h is the height of the container.

Pete has a 12 cm tall cylindrical tin with a volume of 500 cm³.

He wants to use it to store round biscuits of diameter 7 cm. Will they fit?

11 **a** Complete this table.

3^0	3^1	3^2	3^3	3^4	3^5	3^6	3^7
1	3	9			243	729	2187

(2 marks)

b
$$729 \times 2187 = 1594323$$
$$\text{and} \quad 1594323 = 3^x$$

Use the table to work out the value of x. *(1 mark)*

c Use the table, or otherwise, to work out $\dfrac{2187}{9}$

Give your answer as a power of 3. *(1 mark)*

© AQA 2013

15 Standard form

Using mathematics: real-life applications

The study of stars, moons and planets involves huge numbers. Astronomers use standard form to write or type very large quantities. This makes it easier for them to compare the quantities and it allows them to calculate with and without calculators. The Sun has a mass of 1.988×10^{30} kg. This is a number with 27 zeros and it would be clumsy and impractical to have to write it out each time you wanted to use it.

Calculator tip

Make sure you know how your calculator deals with exponents and that you have it in the correct mode to do calculations involving exponents.

"In astronomy we work with very large and very small numbers. There are 100 000 000 000 000 000 000 000 known stars alone! Imagine having to write this number out in full every time you wanted to use it! It is much easier to write 1×10^{23}."

(Astronomy student)

Before you start ...

Ch 6	You should be able to calculate efficiently with decimals.	**1** Evaluate these without using a calculator.
		a $2.9 + 5.8$ **b** $12.5 - 3.8$ **c** 4.5×1.5 **d** $4.5 \div 0.3$
Ch 12	You need to be able to round numbers to a given number of significant figures.	**2** Choose the correct answer.
		a 507 000 000 rounded to 2 sf. A 50 700 B 510 000 000
		b 1.098 rounded to 3 sf. A 1.10 B 1.09
		c 0.00625 rounded to 1 sf. A 0.6 B 0.006
Ch 14	You should know how to apply the laws of indices.	**3** State whether the following are true or false. If the answer is false, work out the correct one.
		a $x^5 \times x^3 = x^8$ **b** $x^{-3} \times x^4 = x$ **c** $\dfrac{x^4}{x^5} = x$ **d** $\dfrac{x^{-4}}{x^2} = x^{-6}$

Assess your starting point using the Launchpad

STEP 1

In questions 1 to 4, choose the correct answer.

1 What is 2.4×10^7 written as an ordinary number?
  A 0.00000024   B 240 000 000   C 0.000000024
  D 24 000 000   E 2 400 000

2 What is 7×10^{-3} written as an ordinary number?
  A 0.0007   B 7000   C 0.007
  D 70 000   E 0.00007

3 What is 23 500 written in standard form?
  A 2.35×10^{-4} B 2.35×10^4 C 235×10^2
  D 23.5×10^3 E 2.35×10^{-2}

4 What is 0.0000231 written in standard form?
  A 23.1×10^{-5} B 2.31×10^5 C 2.31×10^{-4}
  D 2.31×10^4 E 2.31×10^{-5}

GO TO
Section 1:
Expressing numbers in standard form

STEP 2

5 Multiply 2 400 000 × 23 000 giving your answer in standard form.
6 Calculate: $\dfrac{4.6 \times 10^{-3}}{1.84 \times 10^4}$

GO TO
Chapter review

GO TO
Section 2:
Calculators and standard form
Section 3:
Working in standard form

Section 1: Expressing numbers in standard form

Writing out very large or very small numbers takes time and you might make mistakes when doing calculations.

Standard form is a way to write these numbers more simply, using powers of 10.

A number is in standard form when it is written as a product (×) of a number and a power of 10. The number must be greater than or equal to 1 and smaller than 10.

Algebraically, we can say that any number can be expressed in the form:

$A \times 10^n$, where $1 \leqslant A < 10$ and n is an integer.

For example, 2×10^2 and 1.2×10^{-2} are both in standard form.

Find answers at: cambridge.org/ukschools/gcsemaths-studentbookanswers

Consider $3 \times 10^4 = 30\,000$ and $3 \times 10^{-4} = 0.0003$

The index (power of ten) gives you important information.

- Multiplying by 10^4 means you are multiplying by 10 000 so the digits move four places to the left on a place value table.
- Multiplying by 10^{-4} means you are dividing by 10 000 so the digits move four places to the right on a place value table.

Writing a number in standard form

To write a number in standard form:

- Place the decimal point after the first non-zero digit.
- Find the power of 10 needed to move the decimal point back to its original position.
- Write the number as a decimal multiplied by a power of 10.

> ### Tip
>
> In the UK we use the term standard form for numbers in the form $A \times 10^n$, where $1 \leqslant A < 10$. This notation is also called scientific notation.

> ### Tip
>
> As numbers increase in size the digits move left (+) on a place value table and as numbers decrease in size the digits move right (−) on a place value table.

WORKED EXAMPLE 1

a Express 416 000 in standard form.

416 000

④.1 6

④ 1 6 0 0 0.

Find the number between 1 and 10.

Work out how many places the digits need to move to get back to the original number.

$416\,000 = 4.16 \times 10^5$

The digits need to move five places to the left (+), so the power of ten is 5.

Continues on next page . . .

b Express 0.0037 in standard form.

0.0037

3.⑦ ⌣⌣

0.0 0 3 ⑦

| Find the number between 1 and 10.

Work out how many places the digits need to move to get back to the original number.

3.7×10^{-3}

The digits need to move three places to the right (–), so the power of ten is –3.

You can also work like this.

$0.0037 = \dfrac{37}{10\,000}$

Convert the decimal to a fraction.

$= \dfrac{3.7}{1000}$

Divide the top and bottom by 10 to get a numerator between 1 and 10.

$= 3.7 \times 10^{-3}$

Look at the number of zeros in the denominator to find the index. As the original number is less than 1, the index must be negative.

Converting from standard form to ordinary numbers

To convert numbers from standard form to ordinary numbers or decimals you need to look at the powers and move the digits the correct number of places to the left or right.

WORKED EXAMPLE 2

Write as ordinary numbers.

a 3.25×10^5 **b** 2.07×10^{-5}

a 3.25×10^5

⌣⌣⌣⌣⌣ ③.2 5

③ 2 5 0 0 0.

Move the digits 5 places to the left (+).

Fill in the correct number of zeros.

$3.25 \times 10^5 = 325\,000$

b 2.07×10^{-5}

2.0 ⑦ ⌣⌣⌣⌣⌣

0.0 0 0 0 2 0 ⑦

Move the digits 5 places to the right (–).

Fill in the correct number of zeros.

$2.07 \times 10^{-5} = 0.0000207$

Remember to write the 0 before the decimal point as well.

EXERCISE 15A

1 Choose the correct power of 10 to complete the following statement.

$1.25 \times \boxed{} = 0.0125$

A 10   B 10^2 C 10^{-1} D 10^{-2}

2 Express each of the following in standard form.

a 321 000   b 1340   c 40 050

d 3 010 000   e 0.08   f 0.0001

g 32 000 000   h 910 000   i 0.000031255

j 0.00000024152   k 0.00305   l 0.201

m 34 000   n 0.00034   o 0.009

p 2.45   q 0.000426   r 0.426

3 Express each of the following as an ordinary number.

a 1.4×10^2 b 4.8×10^4 c 2.9×10^3

d 3.25×10^2 e 3.25×10^{-1} f 3.67×10^5

g 4.5×10^7 h 2.13×10^{-2} i 3.209×10^4

j 3.46×10^{-3} k 1.89×10^{-4} l 7×10^{-7}

m 1.03×10^{-2} n 1.025×10^{-3} o 2.09×10^{-5}

4 Express each of the following quantities in standard form.

a The population of the Earth is more than 7 000 000 000.

b The distance from the Earth to the Moon is approximately 240 000 miles.

c There are about 37 000 000 000 000 cells in your body.

d Some cells are about 0.0000002 of a metre in diameter.

e The surface area of the Earth's oceans is about 140 million square miles.

f An ångström is a unit of measure. One ångström is equivalent to 0.0000000001 of a metre.

g Humans blink on average about 6 250 000 times per year.

h A dust particle has a mass of about 0.000000000753 kg.

5 Write each quantity out in full as an ordinary number.

a The area of the Atlantic Ocean is 3.18×10^7 square miles.

b The space between tracks on a DVD disc is 7.4×10^{-4} mm.

c The diameter of the silk used to weave a spider's web is 1.24×10^{-6} mm.

d There are 3×10^9 possible ways to play the first four moves in a game of chess.

e A sheet of paper is about 1.2×10^{-4} m thick.

f The distance between the Sun and Jupiter is about 7.78×10^8 km.

g The Earth is about 1.5×10^{11} km from the Sun.

h The mass of an electron is about $9.109\,382\,2 \times 10^{-31}$ kg.

Section 2: Calculators and standard form

You can use a scientific calculator to enter calculations in standard form.

The calculator will also give you an answer in standard form if it has too many digits to display on the screen.

Entering standard form calculations

You will need to use the $\boxed{\times 10^x}$, $\boxed{\text{Exp}}$ or $\boxed{\text{EE}}$ button on your calculator.

These are known as the exponent keys and they all work in the same way, even though they might look different on different calculators.

When you are using the exponent function key of your calculator you don't have to enter the $\times 10$ part. The function automatically includes that part.

Use your own calculator to work through this example. You should get the same result even if your function key is different to the one in the example.

WORKED EXAMPLE 3

Use your calculator to calculate:

a 2.134×10^4 **b** 3.124×10^{-6}

a 2.134×10^4

Enter: $\boxed{2}\boxed{.}\boxed{1}\boxed{3}\boxed{4}\boxed{\times 10^x}\boxed{4}\boxed{=}$

Answer is: $21\,340$

b 3.124×10^{-6}

Enter: $\boxed{3}\boxed{.}\boxed{1}\boxed{2}\boxed{4}\boxed{\text{Exp}}\boxed{+/-}\boxed{6}\boxed{=}$

Answer is: 0.000003124

> Use the correct key for your calculator to enter the negative 6.

Calculator tip

Calculators work in different ways and you need to understand how your own calculator works. Make sure you know what buttons to use to enter standard form calculations, how to read and make sense of the display and how to convert your calculator answer into decimal form.

Making sense of the calculator display

The answer your calculator displays will depend on the calculator you use. Here are two ways in which calculators display answers in standard form:

$5.98\varepsilon{-}06$ This is 5.98×10^{-6}

$2.56\varepsilon24$ This is 2.56×10^{24}

To give the answer in standard form, read the display and write the answer correctly.

To give the answer as an ordinary number, apply the rules you know to convert it from standard form to ordinary form.

Find answers at: cambridge.org/ukschools/gcsemaths-studentbookanswers

EXERCISE 15B

1 Enter each of these numbers into your calculator using the correct function key. Write down what appears on the display.

a 4.2×10^{12} **b** 1.8×10^{-5} **c** 2.7×10^{6}

d 1.34×10^{-2} **e** 1.87×10^{-9} **f** 4.23×10^{7}

g 3.102×10^{-4} **h** 3.098×10^{9} **i** 2.076×10^{-23}

2 A calculator display gives an answer of $\boxed{7.4\text{E}{-}04}$

What is this as an ordinary number? Choose the correct answer below.

A 0.00074   B 74 000   C 0.0074   D 7400

3 Here are ten different calculator displays giving answers in exponential form.

Write each answer correctly in standard form.

a 1.09 05   **b** 2.876 −06   **c** 4.012 09

d 1.89 07   **e** 3.123E13   **f** 2.876E−04

g 9.02E15   **h** 8.076E−12   **i** 8.124E−11

j 5.0234 19

Significant figures

When you work with standard form, you will often be asked to give the answers in standard form to a given number of significant figures.

- 0.003   is to 1 significant figure.
- 0.01   is to 1 significant figure.
- 0.10   is to 2 significant figures.

A zero after a non-zero digit is significant.

Tip

Look back at Chapter 12 if you need to remind yourself about how to round numbers to a given number of significant figures or decimal places.

EXERCISE 15C

1 Write $(0.0125)^5$ in standard form, to three significant figures. Choose from the options below.

A 0.12×10^5 B 0.12×10^{-5} C 3.05×10^{10} D 3.05×10^{-10}

2 Use your calculator to do these calculations. Give your answers in standard form to three significant figures.

a 4216^6

b $(0.00009)^4$

c $0.0002 \div 2500^3$

d $65\,000\,000 \div 0.0000045$

e $(0.0029)^3 \times (0.00365)^5$

f $(48 \times 987)^4$

g $\dfrac{4525 \times 8760}{0.000020}$

h $\dfrac{9500}{0.0005^4}$

i $\sqrt{5.25} \times 10^8$

j $\sqrt[3]{9.1} \times 10^{-8}$

3 Work out the following using your calculator. Give your answers in standard form to five significant figures.

a 4234^5

b $0.0008 \div 9200^3$

c $(1.009)^5$

d $123\,000\,000 \div 0.00076$

e $(97 \times 876)^4$

f $(0.0098)^4 \times (0.0032)^3$

g $\dfrac{8543 \times 9210}{0.000\,034}$

h $\dfrac{9745}{(0.0004)^4}$

i $\sqrt[3]{4.2} \times 10^{-8}$

Section 3: Working in standard form

Writing numbers in standard form allows you to use the laws of indices to calculate quickly without using a calculator.

Multiplying and dividing numbers in standard form

When you multiply powers of ten, you add the indices.

When you divide powers of ten, you subtract the indices.

Tip

Remember:
$$n^x \times n^y = n^{x+y} \qquad \frac{n^x}{n^y} = n^{x-y}$$

WORKED EXAMPLE 4

Do these calculations without using a calculator. Give your answers in standard form.

a $(3 \times 10^5) \times (2 \times 10^6)$ **b** $(2 \times 10^{-3}) \times (3 \times 10^{-7})$ **c** $(2 \times 10^3) \times (8 \times 10^7)$

d $\dfrac{2.8 \times 10^6}{1.4 \times 10^4}$ **e** $\dfrac{4 \times 10^8}{9 \times 10^5}$

a $(3 \times 10^5) \times (2 \times 10^6)$

This is the same as:
$3 \times 2 \times 10^5 \times 10^6$

$= 6 \times 10^{5+6}$ | Add the indices.

$= 6 \times 10^{11}$ | Write the answer in standard form.

b $(2 \times 10^{-3}) \times (3 \times 10^{-7})$

This is the same as:
$2 \times 3 \times 10^{-3} \times 10^{-7}$

$= 6 \times 10^{-3 + -7}$

$= 6 \times 10^{-10}$

c $(2 \times 10^3) \times (8 \times 10^7)$

This is the same as:
$2 \times 8 \times 10^3 \times 10^7$

$= 16 \times 10^{3+7}$

$= 16 \times 10^{10}$ | But 16 is greater than 10 so this is not in standard form.

$= 1.6 \times 10 \times 10^{10}$ | If you think of 16 as 1.6×10 you can change it to standard form.

$= 1.6 \times 10^{11}$

d $\dfrac{2.8 \times 10^6}{1.4 \times 10^4} = \dfrac{2.8}{1.4} \times \dfrac{10^6}{10^4}$

$= 2 \times 10^{6-4}$ | Subtract the indices to divide the powers.

$= 2 \times 10^2$

e $\dfrac{4 \times 10^8}{9 \times 10^5} = \dfrac{4}{9} \times \dfrac{10^8}{10^5}$

$= 0.44 \times 10^3$ | 0.44 is smaller than 1 so this is not standard form.

$= 4.4 \times 10^{-1} \times 10^3$ | If you think of 0.44 as 4.4×10^{-1} you can change it to standard form.

$= 4.4 \times 10^2$

EXERCISE 15D

1 The answer to a calculation is given as 7×10^3.

Which of the following calculations produces this answer?

A $(7 \times 10^5) \div (7 \times 10^3)$ B $(7 \times 10^6) \div (1 \times 10^2)$

C $(1 \times 10^8) \div (7 \times 10^5)$ D $(0.7 \times 10^6) \div (1 \times 10^2)$

2 Simplify, giving the answers in standard form.

a $(2 \times 10^{13}) \times (4 \times 10^{17})$ **b** $(1.4 \times 10^8) \times (3 \times 10^4)$

c $(1.5 \times 10^{13}) \times (1.5 \times 10^{13})$ **d** $(0.2 \times 10^{17}) \times (0.7 \times 10^{16})$

e $(9 \times 10^{17}) \div (3 \times 10^{16})$ **f** $(8 \times 10^{17}) \div (4 \times 10^{16})$

g $(1.5 \times 10^8) \div (5 \times 10^4)$ **h** $(2.4 \times 10^{64}) \div (8 \times 10^{21})$

3 Simplify, giving the answers in standard form.

a $(2 \times 10^{-4}) \times (4 \times 10^{-16})$ **b** $(1.6 \times 10^{-8}) \times (4 \times 10^{-4})$

c $(1.5 \times 10^{-6}) \times (2.1 \times 10^{-3})$ **d** $(11 \times 10^{-5}) \times (3 \times 10^2)$

e $(9 \times 10^{17}) \div (4.5 \times 10^{-16})$ **f** $(7 \times 10^{-21}) \div (1 \times 10^{16})$

g $(4.5 \times 10^8) \div (0.9 \times 10^{-4})$ **h** $(11 \times 10^{-5}) \times (3 \times 10^2) \div (2 \times 10^{-3})$

4 Carry out these calculations without using your calculator. Leave the answers in standard form.

a $(3 \times 10^{12}) \times (4 \times 10^{18})$ **b** $(1.5 \times 10^6) \times (3 \times 10^5)$

c $(1.5 \times 10^{12})^3$ **d** $(1.2 \times 10^{-5}) \times (1.1 \times 10^{-6})$

e $(0.4 \times 10^{15}) \times (0.5 \times 10^{12})$ **f** $(8 \times 10^{17}) \div (3 \times 10^{12})$

g $(1.44 \times 10^8) \div (1.2 \times 10^6)$ **h** $(8 \times 10^{-15}) \div (4 \times 10^{-12})$

5 The speed of light is approximately 3×10^8 metres per second. How far will the light travel in:

a 10 seconds?   **b** 20 seconds?

c 10^2 seconds?   **d** 2×10^3 seconds?

6 An average human being blinks approximately 6.25×10^6 times per year.

a How often does an average human blink in five years? Give your answer in standard form and as an ordinary number.

b There are approximately 7.2×10^9 people on the planet. Calculate the total number of blinks in a year.

Adding and subtracting in standard form

In algebra you can add or subtract like terms and you cannot add or subtract unlike terms. The same rules apply to powers of ten.

You can only add or subtract powers of ten if the powers are identical. This means that you sometimes have to manipulate the expressions to get like terms that you can add or subtract.

For example, you can change 3×10^6 into $3 \times 10^4 \times 10^2$ because $10^4 \times 10^2 = 10^6$.

You can also manipulate the number by multiplying it or dividing it by ten to increase or decrease the powers. For example, you can change 1.6×10^3 into 16×10^2 or into 0.16×10^4.

WORKED EXAMPLE 5

Simplify, giving your answers in standard form.

a $(2.5 \times 10^6) + (3.2 \times 10^8)$ **b** $6 \times 10^{-3} - 3 \times 10^{-4}$

a $(2.5 \times 10^6) + (3.2 \times 10^8)$

$= 2.5 \times 10^6 + 3.2 \times 10^6 \times 10^2$ — Rewrite the second power as its factors to get like powers.

$= 10^6(2.5 + 3.2 \times 10^2)$ — Remove the common factor.

$= 10^6(2.5 + 320)$ — $3.2 \times 10^2 = 320$

$= 10^6(322.5)$ — Add the numbers.

$= 3.225 \times 10^8$ — Rewrite the answer in standard form.

b $6 \times 10^{-3} - 3 \times 10^{-4}$

$= 60 \times 10^{-4} - 3 \times 10^{-4}$ — 6×10^{-3} is the same as 60×10^{-4}

$= 57 \times 10^{-4}$ — This is not yet in standard form.

$= 5.7 \times 10^{-3}$

You can also convert the standard form expressions to ordinary numbers and add or subtract them. You can then write the answer back in standard form.

For example, $6 \times 10^{-3} - 3 \times 10^{-4} = 0.006 - 0.0003 = 0.0057 = 5.7 \times 10^{-3}$

If you do this, remember to write the numbers so the place values line up:

$$\begin{array}{r} 0.0060 \\ -\ 0.0003 \\ \hline 0.0057 \end{array}$$

EXERCISE 15E

1 Carry out these calculations without using a calculator. Give your answers in standard form.

a $(3 \times 10^8) + (2 \times 10^8)$ **b** $(3 \times 10^{-3}) - (1.5 \times 10^{-3})$

c $(1.5 \times 10^5) + (3 \times 10^6)$ **d** $(6 \times 10^7) - (4 \times 10^6)$

e $(4 \times 10^{-4}) + (3 \times 10^{-3})$ **f** $(5 \times 10^{-3}) - (2.5 \times 10^{-2})$

2 A length of 1.5×10^3 mm is cut from a wire 2.5×10^4 mm long.

How much is left? Choose from the options below.

A 1×10^1 mm   B 1×10^7 mm   C 2.35×10^4 mm   D 2.35×10^7 mm

3 The Pacific Ocean has a surface area of approximately 1.65×10^8 km^2.

The Atlantic Ocean has a surface area of approximately 1.06×10^8 km^2.

a State which ocean has the greater surface area.

b Calculate the difference between the surface areas of the two oceans.

c The total surface area of the world's oceans is 361 000 000 km^2.

Work out the combined surface area of the other three oceans (the Indian, Southern and Arctic). Give your answer in standard form.

4 The Earth is approximately 9.3×10^7 miles from the Sun and 2.4×10^5 miles from the Moon.

Work out how much further is it from the Earth to the Sun than from the Earth to the Moon.

5 A scientist studying viruses finds that Virus A has a diameter of 3×10^{-8} m and Virus B has a diameter of 3×10^{-7} m.

a State which virus has the smaller diameter.

b Find the difference in diameter between the two viruses.

c Find the length of their combined diameters in millimetres.

Solving problems using standard form

Standard form is very useful for solving problems involving very large or very small quantities.

Work through this example.

Problem-solving framework

Naresh has a space 0.00000327 m wide, 0.0000002 m long and 0.000116 m high.

He must fit a similarly shaped component with a volume of 8.034×10^{-17} into this space.

Will it fit?

Steps for solving problems	What you would do for this example
Step 1: Work out what you need to do.	Find the volume of the space. Compare it with the volume of the component to see which is bigger.
Step 2: Look for information that will help you.	The dimensions are for length, width and height, so shape must be a cuboid with a volume of $L \times W \times H$. The component volume is given in standard form, so you need the volume in standard form to compare it.
Step 3: What maths can you use?	Convert the dimensions to standard form. 3.27×10^{-6} 2×10^{-7} 1.16×10^{-4} Multiply the numbers (not the powers). $3.27 \times 2 \times 1.16 = 7.5864$ Multiply the powers of ten by adding the indices. $10^{-6} \times 10^{-7} \times 10^{-4} = 10^{-17}$ Combine the results to get 7.5864×10^{-17}
Step 4: Set out the solution clearly, making sure you have answered the original question.	$7.5864 \times 10^{-17} < 8.034 \times 10^{-17}$ $\therefore$ the component will not fit.

EXERCISE 15F

1 Scientists estimate that global sea level is rising 2.9×10^{-3} metres per year on average.

Choose the measurement that is equivalent to this rise.

A 2.9 kilometres   B 2.9 centimetres

C 2.9 millimetres   D 2.9 nanometres

2 Data storage in computers is measured in gigabytes. One gigabyte is 2^{30} bytes.

    a Write 2^{30} in standard form to three significant figures.

    b There are 1024 gigabytes in a terabyte.

       How many bytes is this? Give your answer in standard form to three significant figures.

3 Mobile phone screens can be measured in pixels per inch (ppi).

This is the number of pixels on one side of a square inch. You can see this in the image below.

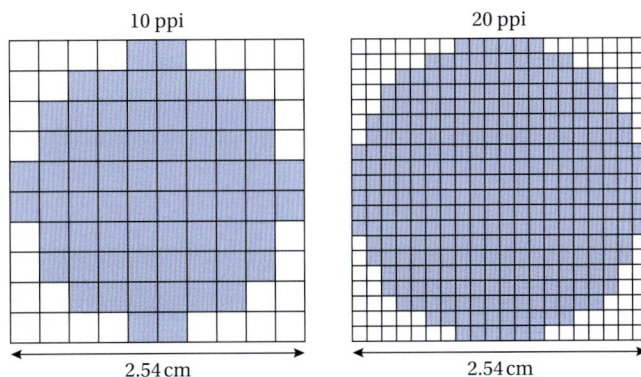

    10 ppi   20 ppi

    2.54 cm   2.54 cm

    a How many pixels are there in a 2.54 cm × 2.54 cm area of the screen on the right?

    b Calculate the area (in cm^2) covered by one pixel at a density of 20 ppi. Give your answer in standard form to three significant places.

    c At a density of 20 ppi, how many pixels would you have on a 4 inch by 3 inch rectangular screen?

On a particular phone, one pixel is 1×10^{-3} cm wide and 4×10^{-5} cm long.

    d Find the area of one pixel on this phone.

    e Calculate the total area of 2.5×10^2 pixels of that size.

4 One nanometer is 1.0×10^{-9} m. Express the following measurements in nanometers.

    a 33 m   **b** 21 mm

Find answers at: cambridge.org/ukschools/gcsemaths-studentbookanswers

5 Light travels at a speed of approximately 3×10^8 metres per second.

The Sun is an average distance of 1.5×10^{11} m from Earth.

Pluto is an average 5.9×10^{12} m from the Sun.

a Work out how long it takes light from the Sun to reach Earth (in seconds). Give your answer in both ordinary numbers and standard form.

b How much longer does it take for the light to reach Pluto? Give your answer in both ordinary numbers and standard form to three significant places.

6 A biologist cultures two sets of bacteria.

Culture X contains 5.8×10^{11} bacterial cells and Culture Y contains 4.8×10^9 bacterial cells.

She combines the two cultures in a flask.

a Calculate the total number of cells in the flask.

b The bacteria numbers double every 8 hours.

Calculate the total number of cells after two days.

7 Use the dimensions given in questions 4 and 5 of Exercise 15A to construct five mixed standard form problems. (Work out the solutions as well.)

Exchange these with another student and try to solve each other's problems.

Checklist of learning and understanding

Standard form

- Very large and very small numbers can be written in standard form by expressing them as the product of a value greater or equal to 1 and less than 10, and a power of 10.
- Positive powers of ten indicate large numbers and negative powers of ten indicate decimal fractions.

Using a calculator

- The exponent function of the calculator allows you to enter calculations in standard form without entering the $\times 10$ part of the calculation.
- When a number has too many digits to display, the calculator will give the answer in exponent form.

Calculations in standard form

- You can multiply and divide numbers in standard form by applying the rules of indices.
- You can add or subtract numbers in standard form without a calculator by writing them out in full.

For additional questions on the topics in this chapter, visit GCSE Mathematics Online.

Chapter review

1 Express the following numbers in standard form.

   a 45 000   **b** 80   **c** 2 345 000

   d 32 000 000 000   **e** 0.0065   **f** 0.009

2 Write the following as ordinary numbers.

   a 2.5×10^3 **b** 3.9×10^4

   c 4.265×10^5 **d** 1.045×10^{-5}

3 Which set of values is arranged in ascending order?

   A $3.5 \times 10^{-2}, 3.5 \times 10^{-3}, 5.3 \times 10^{-3}$

   B $3.5 \times 10^{-3}, 3.5 \times 10^{-2}, 5.3 \times 10^{-3}$

   C $3.5 \times 10^{-3}, 5.3 \times 10^{-3}, 3.5 \times 10^{-2}$

   D $5.3 \times 10^{-3}, 3.5 \times 10^{-3}, 3.5 \times 10^{-2}$

4 Use a calculator and give the answers in standard form.

   a $5 \times 10^4 + 9 \times 10^6$ **b** $3.27 \times 10^{-3} \times 2.4 \times 10^2$

   c $5(8.1 \times 10^9 - 2 \times 10^7)$ **d** $(3.2 \times 10^{-1}) - (2.33 \times 10^{-6})$ (to 3 sf)

   e $\dfrac{4.22 \times 10^7 \times 3.25 \times 10^6}{4 \times 10^5}$ **f** $2.13 \times 10^6 \div (5.67 \times 10^{-5})$

5 Simplify the following without using a calculator and give the answers in standard form.

   a $(1.44 \times 10^7) + (4.3 \times 10^7)$ **b** $(4.9 \times 10^5) \times (3.6 \times 10^9)$

   c $(3 \times 10^4) + (4 \times 10^3)$ **d** $(4 \times 10^6) \div (3 \times 10^5)$

6 **a** Work out $(6.45 \times 10^6) \times (2.5 \times 10^{-4})$

     Write your answer in standard form.   *(2 marks)*

   b Here is a number machine.

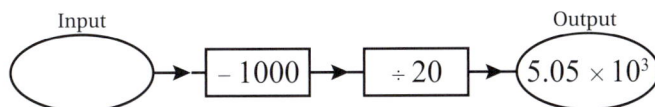

Input → -1000 → $\div 20$ → Output 5.05×10^3

     Work out the input when the output is 5.05×10^3

     Write your answer in standard form.   *(3 marks)*

     © AQA 2013

7 The distance between interconnecting lines on a silicon chip is 4×10^{-8} m.

   Find:

   a twice this distance   **b** a quarter of this distance

   c ten times this distance.

8 The Sun has a mass of approximately 1.998×10^{27} tonnes.

The planet Mercury has a mass of approximately 3.302×10^{20} tonnes.

a State which has the greater mass.

b How many times heavier is the greater than the smaller mass?

9 The diameter of the Earth is approximately 1.27×10^4 km.

a What is the approximate radius of the Earth? Give your answer in standard form.

b Given that $C = 2\pi r$, calculate the approximate distance around the Earth at the equator in kilometres.

c The volume of a sphere is $V = \frac{4}{3}\pi r^3$, where r is the radius.

Calculate the approximate volume of Earth to two decimal places. (The Earth is not a perfect sphere, but assume that it is for your calculation.)

16 Further algebra

In this chapter you will learn how to ...

- expand the product of two or more binomial expressions.
- factorise quadratic expressions of the form $ax^2 + bx + c$.
- simplify and manipulate algebraic fractions.

For more resources relating to this chapter, visit GCSE Mathematics Online.

Using mathematics: real-life applications

Situations that involve motion, including acceleration, stopping distance, velocity and distance travelled (displacement) can be modelled using quadratic expressions and formulae.

"At the site of a crash, I measure the length of the tyre skid marks and apply an equation to work out the speed at which vehicles were moving before the accident."
(Police road accident investigator)

Before you start ...

Ch 7	Check you remember how to simplify expressions.	**1**	**a** Simplify: $5x^2y^2 + 6xy - 11x^2y^2 - 7xy$ **b** Why are terms that are multiples of x^2y^2 and terms that are multiples of xy not 'like' terms?
Ch 7	Make sure you can multiply out brackets.	**2**	Expand and simplify: $3(2x + 3y) + 2(3x - 2y)$
Ch 7	You should be able to recognise an identity.	**3**	Is the identity symbol used correctly in this example? Give reasons why or why not. $3b(3b - 5) - 7b^2 \equiv 2b^2 - 15b$
KS3 Ch 7	You should be able to express situations using algebra.	**4**	The square root of a number (x) is cubed and this is added to 36 divided by a number (y) squared. Write an expression to represent this.
KS3 Ch2, 7	Make sure you remember the rules for multiplying and dividing in algebra.	**5**	Simplify: **a** $6a \times -5a$ **b** $-3y \times -7y^2$ **c** $-2ab \div b$ **d** $-6y \div -5y$ **e** $-2x \times -5x \div -4x$
KS3 Ch 1, 5	Check that you remember how to apply the four operations to fractions.	**6**	Match each calculation to the correct answer: **a** $\frac{1}{3} + \frac{1}{4} = ?$ **b** $\frac{2}{3} - \frac{1}{8} = ?$ **c** $\frac{5}{6} \times \frac{3}{8} = ?$ **d** $\frac{2}{7} \div \frac{1}{14} = ?$ A 4 B $\frac{7}{12}$ C $\frac{13}{24}$ D $\frac{5}{16}$

Find answers at: cambridge.org/ukschools/gcsemaths-studentbookanswers

Assess your starting point using the Launchpad

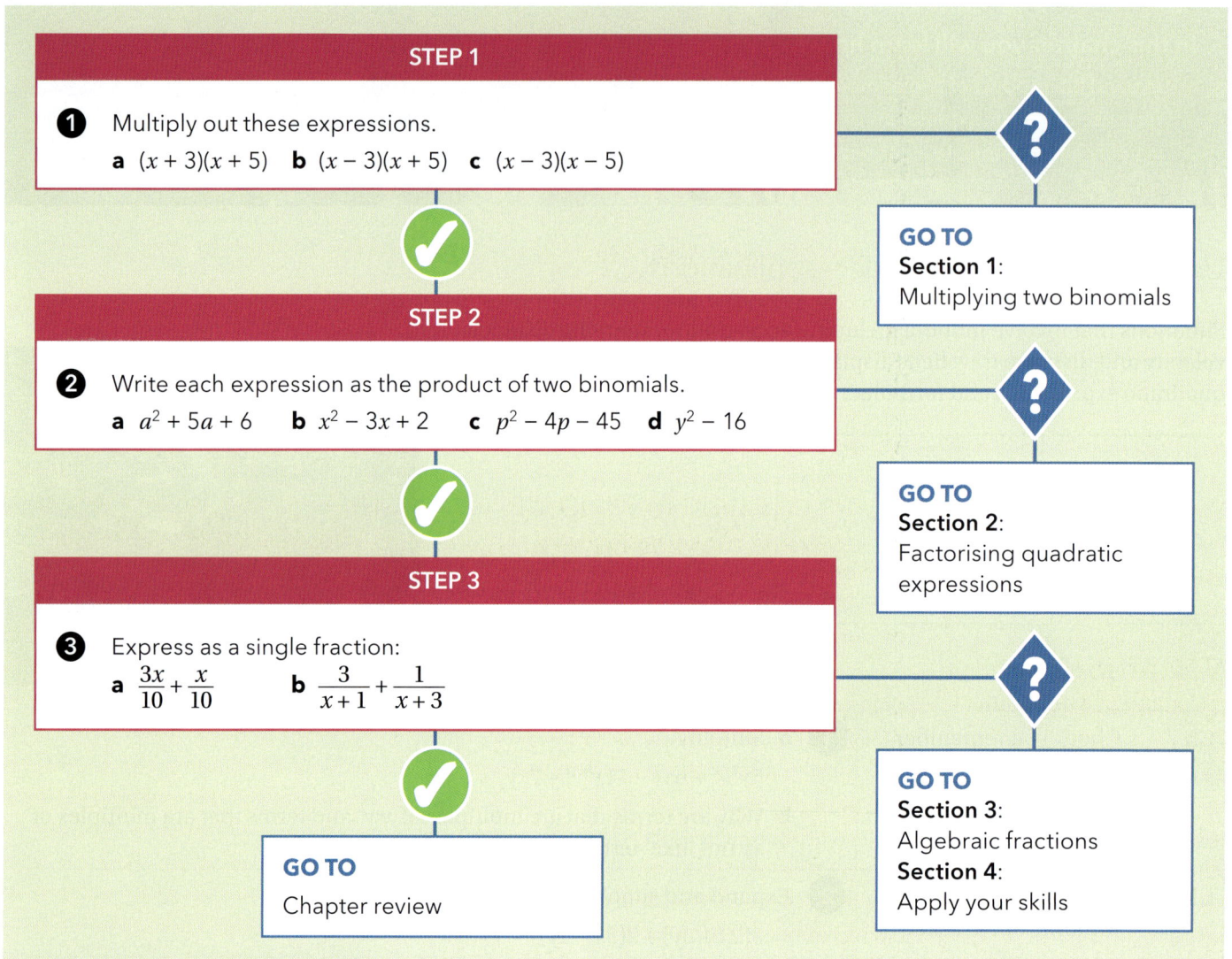

STEP 1

1 Multiply out these expressions.

   a $(x + 3)(x + 5)$ **b** $(x - 3)(x + 5)$ **c** $(x - 3)(x - 5)$

GO TO
Section 1:
Multiplying two binomials

STEP 2

2 Write each expression as the product of two binomials.

   a $a^2 + 5a + 6$ **b** $x^2 - 3x + 2$ **c** $p^2 - 4p - 45$ **d** $y^2 - 16$

GO TO
Section 2:
Factorising quadratic expressions

STEP 3

3 Express as a single fraction:

   a $\dfrac{3x}{10} + \dfrac{x}{10}$ **b** $\dfrac{3}{x + 1} + \dfrac{1}{x + 3}$

GO TO
Section 3:
Algebraic fractions
Section 4:
Apply your skills

GO TO

Chapter review

Key vocabulary

binomial: an expression consisting of two terms

binomial product: the product of two binomial expressions, for example, $(x + 2)(x + 3)$

Tip

Writing numbers in expanded notation to do long multiplication is similar to finding a binomial product.

14×27 can be written as

$(10 + 4) \times (20 + 7)$
$= 10 \times 20 + 10 \times 7 + 4 \times 20 + 4 \times 7$
$= 200 + 70 + 80 + 28 = 378$

Section 1: Multiplying two binomials

A **binomial** is an expression that contains two terms.

For example:

   $x + 2$ $3x^2 + 4$ $2x^2 - 5y^3$

A **binomial product** is the product of two binomials.

To multiply two brackets together each term in the first bracket must be multiplied by each term in the second bracket.

$$ab \quad 6$$
$$(a + 2)(b + 3) \quad ab + 6 + 2b + 3a$$
$$2b$$
$$3a$$

You can also use a grid to make sure you have multiplied all the terms.

×	a	2
b	ab	$2b$
3	$3a$	6

$\left.\right\}\ ab + 2b + 3a + 6$

The product of two binomials gives you four terms.

When you multiply out brackets you need to take care with the minus signs.

$(a - 2)(b + 3)$

×	a	-2
b	ab	$-2b$
3	$3a$	-6

$\left.\right\}\ ab - 2b + 3a - 6$

When the product contains like terms you collect these to simplify the expression.

The expression $x^2 + 8x + 15$ is a **quadratic expression**, because the highest power of x in the expression is x squared (x^2).

The general form of a quadratic equation is

$ax^2 + bx + c = 0$

where a, b and c are real numbers and $a \neq 0$.

The graph of a quadratic is called a parabola.

WORKED EXAMPLE 1

Expand and simplify:

a $(x - 2)(x + 9)$ **b** $(x - 4)(x - 7)$

a $(x - 2)(x + 9) = x^2 + 9x - 2x - 18$ — Notice that you get a positive and a negative like term here.

$= x^2 + 7x - 18$ — Collect like terms.

b $(x - 4)(x - 7) = x^2 - 7x - 4x + 28$ — Notice that the like terms are both negative here.

$= x^2 - 11x + 28$

Perfect squares

A perfect square is any number that is the square of a rational number, and the square root of the square number is a rational number. (A rational number is a whole number or a number that can be written as a fraction.)

When a binomial is multiplied by itself the product is called a **perfect square**.

Expanding and simplifying a perfect square always produces the same pattern.

twice the product of the two terms

twice the product of the two terms

$$(a + b)^2 = a^2 + 2ab + b^2 \qquad (a - b)^2 = a^2 - 2ab + b^2$$

first term squared

second term squared

first term squared

second term squared

Perfect squares produce a pattern that can be used to expand them without doing any working.

EXERCISE 16A

1 Expand and simplify $(2x + 1)(x - 3)$.

Choose from the following options.

A $2x^2 + x - 4$ B $2x^2 + 5x - 3$ C $2x^2 + 4x - 4$ D $2x^2 - 5x - 3$

2 Expand and simplify.

a $(x + 2)(x + 5)$ **b** $(x - 2)(x - 5)$ **c** $(x + 2)(x - 5)$

d $(x - 2)(x + 5)$ **e** $(x + 3)(x - 4)$ **f** $(x + y)(x + y)$

3 Expand and simplify.

a $(2x + 4)(3x + 3)$ **b** $(3x + 4)(5x + 2)$ **c** $(2x - 5)(3x + 1)$

d $(4y - 3)(5y + 1)$ **e** $(3a - 5)(2a - 1)$ **f** $(2b - 5)(b - 3)$

g $(2y - 3)(3y - 5)$ **h** $(2x + 4)(2x - 6)$ **i** $(5x - 3)(4x - 1)$

4 If $A = 3x + 2$ and $B = 2x - 1$, work out:

a AB **b** $A^2 + B^2$ **c** $(A - B)(A + B)$

5 Work out each product.

a $(\frac{2}{x} + \frac{x}{2})^2$ **b** $[2x - (4x + 3y)]^2$ **c** $[2x - (y + z)]^2$

6 What is the value of a if $(2x - 3)$ is a factor of $6x^2 + ax - 12$?

The difference of two squares

Perfect squares produce a pattern that can be used to expand them without doing any working.

Work through the investigation in Exercise 16B to find a shortcut for expanding binomials in the form:

$(a + b)(a - b)$

EXERCISE 16B

1 Expand each of the following binomials:

a $(x + 1)(x - 1)$ **b** $(a + 2)(a - 2)$

c $(2x - 1)(2x + 1)$ **d** $(x - 2y)(x + 2y)$

2 Write down a rule that you can use to quickly find the answer to any similar expansion.

3 In general,

$(x + y)(x - y) \equiv x^2 - y^2$

This is called the difference of two squares identity.

a How can you recognise when a binomial expansion is a difference of two squares?

b Is each of these expressions a difference of squares?

Give reasons why or why not.

i $(3x + 2y)(2x - 3y)$ **ii** $50a^2 - 72b^2$ **iii** $16 - (\sqrt{11})^2$

Expanding more than two binomials

Multiplication is commutative. The order in which you multiply does not change the answer.

You can use this principle to expand three (or more) binomials.

WORKED EXAMPLE 2

Expand $(3x + 2)(2x + 1)(x - 1)$.

$(3x + 2)(2x + 1)(x - 1)$

$= (6x^2 + 4x + 3x + 2)(x - 1)$ — Expand the first two factors.

$= (6x^2 + 7x + 2)(x - 1)$ — Add the like terms.

$= 6x^3 + 7x^2 + 2x - 6x^2 - 7x - 2$ — Expand the remaining two factors.

$= 6x^3 + x^2 - 5x - 2$ — Collect like terms to simplify.

Tip

It is worth doing the multiplication of three or more binomials one step at a time. You are less likely to make sign errors and more likely to get the answer correct.

Tip

To work most efficiently, always check whether some factors are perfect squares or the difference of two squares and expand these first using the rules that you know.

EXERCISE 16C

1 Expand and simplify.

a $(x + 1)(x + 2)(x + 3)$ **b** $(2x - 3)(x - 2)(2x - 1)$

c $(x + 1)(x + 2)(x - 2)$ **d** $(x - 3)(2x + 1)(3x - 2)$

2 **a** $(3x - 4)^3$ **b** $(x + 3)(x^2 - 3x + 9)$

     c $(\frac{1}{5x} + \frac{1}{3y})(\frac{1}{25x^2} - \frac{1}{15xy} + \frac{1}{9y^2})$ **d** $(x^2y^2 + x^2)(xy + x)(xy - x)$

3 The volume of a cuboid can be found using the formula LBH, where L is the length, B is the breadth and H is the height.

Given a cuboid of length $(2x + \frac{1}{2})$ cm, breadth $(x - 2)$ cm and height $(x - 2)$ cm:

a Write an expression for the volume of the cuboid in factor form.

b Expand the expression.

c Give a reason why it is sensible to expand the factors $(x - 2)(x - 2)$ first.

Section 2: Factorising quadratic expressions

Expanding a binomial such as $(x + 3)(x + 4)$ gives you a quadratic expression.

Factorising means 'putting the brackets back into the expression'.

Expanding

$$(x + 3)(x + 4) = x^2 + 7x + 12$$

Factorising

You need to be able to factorise quadratic expressions in the form of $x^2 + bx + c$ as well as those where the x^2 term has a coefficient that is not 0 or 1.

These quadratic expressions are in the form $ax^2 + bx + c$.

Factorising a quadratic expression is the inverse of finding the product of (multiplying) two binomials.

In general:

$$(x + a)(x + b) = x^2 + (a + b)x + ab$$

This pattern can be used to develop a strategy for factorising trinomials.

Work out the signs before you factorise by looking at the signs in the trinomial.

If the **constant is positive**, the brackets will have the same sign.

- If the middle term (the x term) is positive, both brackets will have positive signs.
- If the middle term is negative, both brackets will have negative signs.

Tip

Do you remember how to factorise an expression by taking out a common factor?

Revise that section in Chapter 7 if you are not sure.

If the **constant is negative**, the brackets will have different signs.

- When the signs are different, the middle term is the difference between the two factors.
- The largest number in the factor pair will have the same sign as the middle term in the expression.

Problem-solving framework

Factorise $x^2 - 4x - 12$

Steps for solving problems	What you would do for this example
Step 1: Make two sets of brackets and write an x in each. You can put x in each bracket because to get x^2 you need to multiply x by x. The constant is negative. To get a negative product you have to multiply a negative number by a positive number. This means one bracket will have a negative sign and the other will have a positive sign.	$x^2 - 4x - 12$ $= (x + \square)(x - \square)$
Step 2: The constant is -12. You need factors of 12 that have a difference of 4 to make the middle term $4x$.	Factor pairs of 12 are: $1 \times 12 \qquad 2 \times 6 \qquad 3 \times 4$
Step 3: Which factor pair meets the conditions? (Which factor pair will give you -4 if you add the numbers together and give you -12 if you multiply them?)	There is a difference of 4 between 2 and 6. $-2 + 6 = 4$ $-6 + 2 = -4$ This is the pair you need to satisfy the conditions. $-6 + 2 = -4$ and $-6 \times 2 = -12$ So, the 6 goes in the bracket with the negative sign. The 2 goes in the bracket with the positive sign. $x^2 - 4x - 12 = (x + 2)(x - 6)$
Step 4: Check your answer.	Expand the binomial: $(x + 2)(x - 6) = x^2 - 4x - 12$ Yes, this is the expression you started with.

When you factorise any expression, the first step should be to check for, and remove, common factors.

WORKED EXAMPLE 3

Factorise $4x^2 - 12x - 40$

$4x^2 - 12x - 40$

$4x^2 - 12x - 40 = 4(x^2 - 3x - 10)$ ◁ Take out the common factor of 4.

$4x^2 - 12x - 40 = 4(x - 5)(x + 2)$ ◁ Factorise the expression.

You can always check by multiplying out the brackets.

EXERCISE 16D

1 Factorise:

 a $x^2 + 5x + 6$ **b** $x^2 + 11x + 18$ **c** $x^2 + 7x + 10$

 d $x^2 + 11x + 30$ **e** $x^2 + 9x + 14$ **f** $x^2 + 19x + 90$

2 Factorise:

 a $x^2 - 5x + 6$ **b** $x^2 - 14x + 33$ **c** $x^2 - 17x + 30$

 d $x^2 - 13x + 42$ **e** $x^2 - 15x + 44$ **f** $x^2 - 25x + 100$

3 Factorise fully:

 a $2x^2 + 6x + 4$ **b** $6x^2 - 24x + 18$ **c** $5x^2 - 5x - 10$

 d $2x^2 + 14x + 20$ **e** $2x^2 + 4x - 6$ **f** $3x^2 - 30x - 33$

4 How does $y^2 - 1$ factorise?

Choose from the following options.

 A $(y - 1)(y - 1)$ B $(y - 1)(y + 1)$ C $(y + 1)(y + 1)$ D $(y - \frac{1}{2})(y + \frac{1}{2})$

The difference of two squares

Earlier you saw that multiplying out binomials in the form $(a + b)(a - b)$ gives a product that is the difference of two squares.

$$(a - b)(a + b) = a^2 + ab - ab - b^2$$
$$= a^2 - b^2 \text{ (simplifying)}$$

When you are asked to factorise a quadratic of the form $a^2 - b^2$, you can apply what you know about the difference of two squares to find the factors.

WORKED EXAMPLE 4

Factorise:

a $x^2 - 4$ **b** $x^2 - 36$ **c** $4a^2 - 9$ **d** $5x^2 - 45$ **e** $2(x-1)^2 - 50$ **f** $x^2 - 2$

a $x^2 - 4 = x^2 - (2)^2$

> Express both terms as squares.

$= (x+2)(x-2)$

> Apply the identity:
> $a^2 - b^2 \equiv (a+b)(a-b)$

b $x^2 - 36 = x^2 - (6)^2$
$= (x+6)(x-6)$

c $4a^2 - 9 = (2a)^2 - (3)^2$
$= (2a+3)(2a-3)$

d $5x^2 - 45 = 5(x^2 - 9)$
$= 5(x+3)(x-3)$

> Take out a common factor of 5.

e $2(x-1)^2 - 50 = 2((x-1)^2 - 25))$
$= 2(x-1+5)(x-1-5)$

> Take out a common factor of 2.

$= 2(x+4)(x-6)$

> Add like terms.

f $x^2 - 2 = (x+\sqrt{2})(x-\sqrt{2})$

> The square root of an imperfect square is a surd.

Mathematically a difference of two squares such as $x^2 - 4$ is a special case of the quadratic expression $x^2 + bx + c$.

In a difference of two squares, the coefficient of x is 0, so there is no x term ($x \times 0 = 0$) and the constant (c) is a negative number.

Tip

Some expressions are not a difference of squares until you have removed the common factor. Checking for a common factor should always be the first step when you are factorising.

Using the difference of two squares in number problems

You can use the difference of two squares to subtract square numbers, such as $86^2 - 14^2$ without using a calculator, and without working out the square values, which can be very large numbers.

This method can also be used to find one of the shorter sides in a right-angled triangle.

WORKED EXAMPLE 5

Work out $86^2 - 14^2$

$86^2 - 14^2 = (86 + 14)(86 - 14)$ ◁ Write the subtraction as the product of its factors.

$= 100 \times 72$ ◁ Add and subtract the values in each bracket.

$= 7200$ ◁ Find the product.

WORK IT OUT 16.1

In this right-angled triangle, the hypotenuse measures 13 cm and one of the shorter sides measures 5 cm.

Use the difference of squares and Pythagoras' theorem to calculate the length of the unknown side.

Which of these options is correct?

What mistakes are there in the other options?

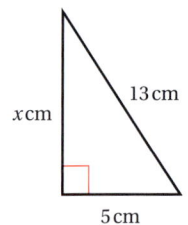

Option A	Option B	Option C
$13^2 - x^2 = 5^2$	$x^2 = 13^2 - 5^2$	$x^2 = 13^2 - 5^2$
$(169 + x)(169 - x) = 25$	$x^2 = (13 + 5)(13 - 5)$	$x^2 = (13 - 5)(13 - 5)$
$169 - x^2 = 25$	$x^2 = 18 \times 8$	$x^2 = 8 \times 8$
$x^2 = 194$	$x^2 = 144$	$x^2 = 64$
$x = \sqrt{194}$	$x = \sqrt{144}$	$x = \sqrt{64}$
$x = 13.9$ cm	$x = 12$ cm	$x = 8$ cm

💡 **Tip**

You should remember Pythagoras' theorem from KS3.

The theorem states that for a right-angled triangle, the square of the length of the hypotenuse (longest side) is equal to the sum of the squares of the lengths of the other two sides.

So in the triangle on the right: $a^2 = b^2 + c^2$

You will need to know the theorem from memory.

See Chapter 37 for more information and practice on Pythagoras' theorem.

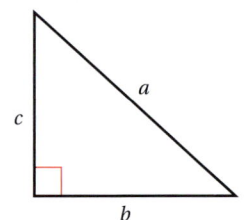

EXERCISE 16E

1 Factorise each of the following.

a $x^2 - 36$ **b** $p^2 - 81$ **c** $w^2 - 16$

d $p^2 - 36q^2$ **e** $144s^2 - c^2$ **f** $64h^2 - 49g^2$

2 Which of the following expressions give the quadratic expression $y^2 - 8y + 3$?

Choose from the following options.

A $(y+4)^2 + 3$ B $(y-4)^2 + 3$ C $(y-4)^2 + 4$ D $(y-4)^2 - 13$

3 Factorise:

a $8x^2 - 2y^2$ **b** $3x^2y^2 - 12z^2$ **c** $1 - (2x-3)^2$

d $3(x+4)^2 - 12$ **e** $7(x-5)^2 - 7y^2$ **f** $(x+5)^2 - (y+3)^2$

4 Using $(a-b)(a+b) = a^2 - b^2$, evaluate the following:

a $100^2 - 97^2$ **b** $50^2 - 48^2$ **c** $639^2 - 629^2$

d $98^2 - 45^2$ **e** $83^2 - 77^2$ **f** $1234^2 - 999^2$

5 Use the difference of two squares method to find the value of a in each triangle.

Leave the answer in square root form.

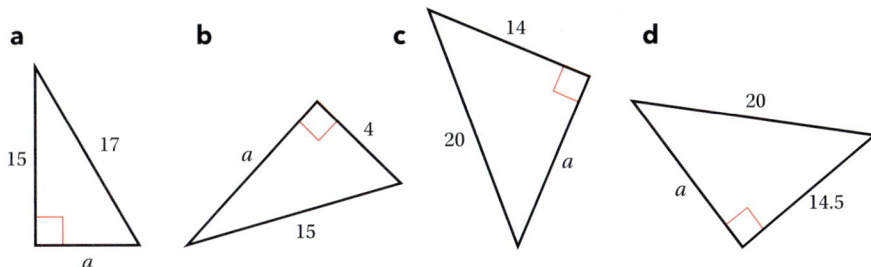

Further quadratics

To factorise quadratic expressions in the form $ax^2 + bx + c$ (where $a \neq 1$) you still need two particular numbers which have a sum equal to b (the coefficient of the x term).

However, the two numbers must now have a product which is equal to ac (rather than just c as before).

There are different methods of finding the correct factors.

You may use any method.

Always check your results by expanding the brackets.

Work through these examples to decide which method you prefer.

WORKED EXAMPLE 6

Factorise:

a $2x^2 + 9x + 4$

There are no common factors.	In this expression $a = 2$, $b = 9$ and $c = 4$.
$ac = 2 \times 4 = 8$	Start by working out ac.
Factors of 8 that add to 9: 8 and 1	Now look for factors of 8 that add up to 9.
$2x^2 + 8x + x + 4$	Write these as the x terms with the correct signs.
$(2x^2 + 8x) + (x + 4)$	Group the terms two by two.
$2x(x + 4) + 1(x + 4)$	Take out any common factors (write the 1 here as a reminder).
$(x + 4)(2x + 1)$	Take out the common factor bracket.

Factorise:

b $5x^2 - 22x + 21$

$5x^2 - 22x + 21$: $ac = 105$	Start by finding ac.
$\dfrac{(5x\ )(5x\ )}{5}$	Make two sets of brackets. Write $5x$ in each bracket. Put the brackets over 5 (i.e. divide by 5).
$\begin{aligned} 105 &= 3 \times 35 \\ &\ 5 \times 21 \\ &\ 7 \times 15 \end{aligned}$	Find the factors of 105 that add up to 22. The correct pair is -7 and -15 as the sum of the x terms is -22.
$\dfrac{(5x - 7)(5x - 15)}{5}$	Write these in the brackets.
$\dfrac{(5x - 7)(5^1x - 15^3)}{5}$	Divide 5 into the product of the two brackets.
$(5x - 7)(x - 3)$	Write the solution.
$\begin{aligned}(5x - 7)(x - 3) &= 5x^2 - 7x - 15x + 21 \\ &= 5x^2 - 22x + 21\end{aligned}$	Check your solution by expanding.

EXERCISE 16F

1 Factorise each quadratic expression fully:

a $2x^2 + 7x + 5$ **b** $3x^2 + 10x + 8$ **c** $2x^2 + 8x - 90$

d $4x^2 + 16x + 15$ **e** $4x^2 - 24x + 27$ **f** $3x^2 - 6x - 105$

g $12x^2 + 9x - 3$ **h** $3x^2 + x - 10$ **i** $2x^2 - 6x - 260$

j $3x^2 - 13x - 10$

2 A rectangle has an area of $(5x^2 - 13x + 6)\,\text{cm}^2$.

Find the length in terms of x if the breadth is $(x - 2)\,\text{cm}$.

3 A triangle has a base $(2x + 8)\,\text{cm}$.

It has an area of $(2x^2 + 11x + 12)\,\text{cm}$.

Use this information to work out an expression for the perpendicular height of the triangle.

4 **a** Show how you could factorise the following expression using substitution.

$3(x + y)^2 + 13(x + y) + 12$

b Apply your method to factorise these expressions:

i $3(x - 3)^2 - (x - 3) - 24$ **ii** $8(5x + 2)^2 - 14(5x + 2) + 3$

Section 3: Algebraic fractions

The rules for simplifying two algebraic fractions are:

Multiplication	$\frac{a}{b} \times \frac{c}{d} = \frac{ac}{bd}$	
Division	$\frac{a}{b} \div \frac{c}{d} = \frac{ad}{bc}$	Remember $\frac{a}{b} \div \frac{c}{d} = \frac{a}{b} \times \frac{d}{c}$
Addition	$\frac{a}{b} + \frac{c}{d} = \frac{ad + bc}{bd}$	$\left.\begin{array}{l} \\ \end{array}\right\} bd$ is the lowest common denominator
Subtraction	$\frac{a}{b} - \frac{c}{d} = \frac{ad - bc}{bd}$	of the two fractions

These rules are explained in the following sections.

Multiplying and dividing fractions

You can simplify algebraic fractions by cancelling terms (using a common factor).

You may need to factorise the numerator and/or the denominator before you can cancel terms.

Tip

You learned how to simplify algebraic terms in the form of fractions by dividing (cancelling) in Chapter 7.

Tip

Remember you cannot cancel out only part of a bracket.

$\frac{(x-2)}{(x-2)}$ can be simplified to give 1.

$\frac{(x-2)}{2}$ cannot be simplified any further.

WORKED EXAMPLE 7

Simplify:

a $\dfrac{8xy^2}{4z} \times \dfrac{yz}{-2x}$

$\dfrac{^2\cancel{8}xy^2}{\cancel{4}z} \times \dfrac{y\cancel{z}}{-2\cancel{x}} = \dfrac{2y^3}{-2} = -y^3$

> Simplify by cancelling down.

b $\dfrac{x^2 + 2x - 3}{x - 1}$

$\dfrac{x^2 + 2x - 3}{x - 1} = \dfrac{(x - 1)(x + 3)}{x - 1}$

> Factorise the numerator
> then cancel the factors $(x - 1)$

$= x + 3$

c $\dfrac{4x^2 - 9}{x + 1} \div \dfrac{2x + 3}{x^2 - 1}$

$\dfrac{4x^2 - 9}{x + 1} \div \dfrac{2x + 3}{x^2 - 1} = \dfrac{4x^2 - 9}{x + 1} \times \dfrac{x^2 - 1}{2x + 3}$

> Rewrite the division as the equivalent
> multiplication by the reciprocal.

$\dfrac{(2x + 3)(2x - 3)}{x + 1} \times \dfrac{(x + 1)(x - 1)}{2x + 3}$

> Factorise the difference of squares.

$\dfrac{(2\cancel{x + 3})(2x - 3)}{\cancel{x + 1}} \times \dfrac{(\cancel{x + 1})(x - 1)}{\cancel{2x + 3}}$

> Cancel common brackets.

$= (2x - 3)(x - 1)$

WORK IT OUT 16.2

Zoey got these three homework questions wrong.

Find her mistakes.

Simplify each fraction correctly.

1	$\dfrac{3x + 2}{2x + 3} = \dfrac{5}{5} = 1$
2	$\dfrac{x^2 - x - 6}{x^2 + 3x + 2} = \dfrac{6}{5}$
3	$\dfrac{^x\cancel{x^2} - 1}{_1\cancel{2x + 4}_1} \times \dfrac{^{2x}\cancel{4x^2} - \cancel{16}^4}{_1\cancel{x + 1}} = \dfrac{(x - 1)(2x - 4)}{4}$

Tip

You may be asked to write an expression as a single fraction.

In that case, you need to find a common denominator and simplify as far as possible.

Adding and subtracting algebraic fractions

To add or subtract fractions you find a common denominator.

WORKED EXAMPLE 8

Type 1: Denominators that are numbers.

a $\dfrac{2x}{5} + \dfrac{x}{3}$

$\dfrac{2x}{5} + \dfrac{x}{3}$

$= \dfrac{6x}{15} + \dfrac{5x}{15}$

> LCD = 15

$= \dfrac{11x}{15}$

Continues on next page …

b $\dfrac{(x+2)}{5} + \dfrac{(x-1)}{4}$

$\dfrac{(x+2)}{5} + \dfrac{(x-1)}{4}$

$= \dfrac{4(x+2)}{20} + \dfrac{5(x-1)}{20}$ LCD = 20

$= \dfrac{4x+8+5x-5}{20}$ Expand the brackets.

$= \dfrac{9x+3}{20}$ Collect like terms.

$= \dfrac{3(3x+1)}{20}$ Take out a common factor.

Type 2: Denominators that are an algebraic expression.

c $\dfrac{4}{x} + \dfrac{3}{2x}$

$\dfrac{4}{x} + \dfrac{3}{2x}$

$= \dfrac{8}{2x} + \dfrac{3}{2x}$ LCD = $2x$

$= \dfrac{11}{2x}$

d $\dfrac{5}{2x^2} + \dfrac{11}{2x}$

$\dfrac{5}{2x^2} + \dfrac{11}{2x}$

$= \dfrac{5}{2x^2} + \dfrac{11x}{2x^2}$ LCD = $2x^2$

$= \dfrac{(5+11x)}{2x^2}$

e $\dfrac{x}{x-2} - \dfrac{3}{x+2}$

$\dfrac{x}{x-2} - \dfrac{3}{x+2}$ LCD = $(x-2)(x+2)$

$= \dfrac{x(x+2) - 3(x-2)}{(x-2)(x+2)}$

$= \dfrac{x^2 + 2x - 3x + 6}{(x-2)(x+2)}$ Expand the brackets.

$= \dfrac{x^2 - x + 6}{(x-2)(x+2)}$ The numerator cannot be factorised.

EXERCISE 16G

1 Simplify:

  a $\dfrac{8x}{10}$ **b** $\dfrac{9x+3}{3x+1}$ **c** $\dfrac{x^2-9}{x+3}$

  d $\dfrac{4x^2-81}{2x-9}$ **e** $\dfrac{(x-3)(x+2)}{(x+4)(x+2)}$ **f** $\dfrac{(2x-5)(x+4)}{(x-4)(5-2x)}$

  g $\dfrac{2x^2-5x+3}{2x^2-x-3}$

2 Simplify $\dfrac{2}{x+1}+\dfrac{3}{x}$

  Choose from the following options.

  A $\dfrac{5}{x(+1)}$ B $\dfrac{5x+3}{x(x+1)}$ C $\dfrac{5}{2x+1}$ D $\dfrac{5x+3}{2x+1}$

3 Express as single fractions:

  a $\dfrac{4x}{5}-\dfrac{2x}{5}$ **b** $\dfrac{2x}{3}+\dfrac{x}{2}-\dfrac{3x}{4}$ **c** $\dfrac{7}{2x}-\dfrac{4}{3x}$

  d $\dfrac{2}{x+1}+\dfrac{1}{x+2}$ **e** $\dfrac{7}{x-2}-\dfrac{4}{x-1}$ **f** $\dfrac{1}{(x-7)^2}-\dfrac{2}{x-7}$

4 Express as single fractions:

  a $\dfrac{x}{x-2}-\dfrac{3}{x+2}$ **b** $\dfrac{x+3}{x+2}-\dfrac{x+2}{x+3}$ **c** $\dfrac{1}{2x-3}+\dfrac{1}{2x+3}$

  d $\dfrac{5}{2p+1}+\dfrac{1}{p}$ **e** $\dfrac{p+2}{p-1}+\dfrac{p-1}{p+2}$ **f** $\dfrac{1}{x-2}-\dfrac{2}{x-1}+\dfrac{1}{x-3}$

Section 4: Apply your skills

Algebraic manipulation is the basis for most mathematics at this level.

You will use the techniques you learned in this chapter regularly to solve problems in many different contexts.

For example, you will use factorising to solve and simplify equations and to sketch curves.

EXERCISE 16H

1 Read each statement and apply what you have learned to decide whether it is true.

  If not, state why not.

  a $2(3b-2)+5(2b-1)=11b+9$ **b** $(3x-2)(4x+7)=12x^2+13x-14$

  c $3x^2+11x+6=(3x+2)(3x+3)$ **d** $9x^2-2=(3x+\sqrt{2})(3x-\sqrt{2})$

  e $x^2+2x-6=(x+1)^2-7$ **f** $\dfrac{5}{x-1}+\dfrac{3}{x+2}=\dfrac{9x+7}{(x-1)(x+2)}$

2 The area of a quadrilateral is expressed as x^2-25.

  Say whether or not this quadilateral can be a square.

3 Use the difference between two squares to simplify the expression $(x+8)^2-(x-8)^2$.

4 Show algebraically that $(x - 1)$ is not a factor of $(-2x^2 - 13x - 15)$.

5 A rectangular slot is $(x - y)$ cm wide and $(x + y)$ cm long.

It is cut out of a square metal plate with sides of $(2x - y)$ cm.

Calculate the area of metal remaining.

6 Given that $A = 2x + 3$ and $B = x - 2$, write each of the following expressions in terms of x in their simplest form:

a AB **b** $A^2 + B^2$ **c** $(A - B)(A + B)$

7 Evaluate the following using $(a + b)^2 \equiv a^2 + 2ab + b^2$ and $(a - b)^2 \equiv a^2 - 2ab + b^2$.

a $(1.01)^2$ **b** $(0.99)^2$ **c** $(4.02)^2$ **d** $(0.98)^2$

8 **a** Find the values of a and b for which:

i $x^2 + 4x + 15 \equiv (x + a)^2 + b$

ii $x^2 + 2x + 15 \equiv (x + a)^2 + b$

b Use your answers to part a to show that:

i $x^2 + 4x + 15 \geqslant 11$

ii $x^2 + 2x + 15 \geqslant 14$

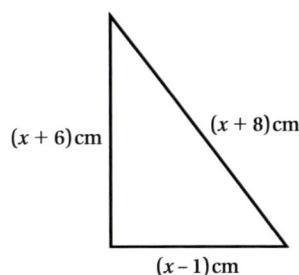

9 The three sides of a triangle are $(x + 8)$ cm, $(x + 6)$ cm and $(x - 1)$ cm.
Show algebraically that the triangle is right-angled when $x = 9$.

$(x + 6)$ cm $(x + 8)$ cm

$(x - 1)$ cm

> **Tip**
>
> The converse of Pythagoras' theorem states that if the square of the longest side of a triangle is equal to the sum of the squares of the other two sides, then the triangle must be right-angled.
>
> You will deal with this in more detail in Chapter 37.

10 **a** A rectangle has a perimeter of 20 cm and width of w cm.

Show that the area, A cm^2, is given by the formula $A = w(10 - w)$.

b Find the values of a and b such that $10w^2 = b - (w+a)^2$.

11 By considering $(\sqrt{x} - \frac{1}{\sqrt{x}})^2$, prove that the sum of a positive number and its reciprocal is greater than or equal to 2.

12 Simplify:

a $\frac{(x^2 - x - 6)}{(x^2 - 8x + 15)}$ **b** $\frac{(9x^2 - 4)}{(12x - 8)}$ **c** $\frac{(a^2 + ab)}{(a^2 - ab)} \times \frac{(ab^2 + b^2)}{(a^3 + a^2b)}$

Checklist of learning and understanding

Expanding expressions

* Expand binomials by multiplying each term in the first bracket by each term in the second bracket.
* The perfect square identity is $(a \pm b)^2 \equiv a^2 \pm 2ab \pm b^2$.
* The difference of squares identity is $(a + b)(a - b) = a^2 - b^2$.

Find answers at: cambridge.org/ukschools/gcsemaths-studentbookanswers

Factorising

- Factorising is the inverse of expanding.
- Check for common factors first, then write expressions as a product of their factors.
- Apply the perfect square and difference of square rules where possible.
- When the terms in a bracket no longer have a factor, number or letter in common, the expression is factorised fully.

Algebraic fractions

- Algebraic fractions can be simplified using the same rules that apply to arithmetic fractions.

For additional questions on the topics in this chapter, visit GCSE Mathematics Online.

Chapter review

1 Expand and simplify:

a $(y+1)^2 + (y+2)^2 + (y+3)^2$ **b** $(x+1)(x+2)(x-3)$

2 Factorise fully and cancel to lowest terms $\dfrac{(y^2 - 6y + 8)}{(y^2 - 4)}$

Choose from the following options.

A $\dfrac{(y+4)}{(y+2)}$ B $\dfrac{(y-4)}{(y+2)}$ C $\dfrac{(y+4)}{(y-2)}$ D $\dfrac{(y-4)}{(y-2)}$

3 Factorise:

a $2x^2 - 11x - 21$ **b** $-6x^2 - 14x - 8$

4 Use the difference of two squares to calculate $1999^2 - 1998^2$.

5 The diagram shows a trapezium.

The lengths of three of the sides of the trapezium are $x - 5$, $x + 2$ and $x + 6$.

All dimensions are in centimetres.

The area of the trapezium is $36\,\text{cm}^2$.

Show that $x^2 - x - 56 = 0$.

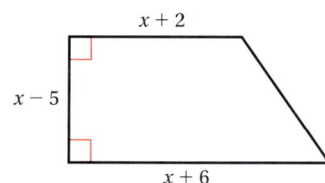

6 **a** Simplify $(2x^5 y^4 z^6) \times (7x^2 y^3 z)$ (3 marks)

b Simplify fully $\dfrac{6(x-5)^2}{3(x-5)(x+4)}$ (2 marks)

c Factorise $(x+1)^2 + 4(x+1)$ (2 marks)

d Factorise fully $2x^2 - 50y^2$ (3 marks)

© AQA 2013

7 Write as single fractions in simplest form:

a $\dfrac{(x+3)}{4} + \dfrac{(x-5)}{3}$ **b** $\dfrac{1}{(x+4)} + \dfrac{2}{(x-4)}$

c $\dfrac{2x}{(3x-3)} \div \dfrac{4y}{(x^2-x)}$ **d** $\dfrac{3}{(4p+q)} + \dfrac{3}{(p-2q)}$

e $\dfrac{1}{x-2} + \dfrac{5}{x-2} + \dfrac{1}{1-3x}$ **f** $\dfrac{2}{x+5} + \dfrac{1}{x-5} + \dfrac{1}{x^2-25}$

17 Equations

In this chapter you will learn how to …

- solve linear equations and apply them in context.
- solve quadratic equations.
- set up and solve simultaneous equations.
- use graphs and iteration methods to find approximate solutions to equations.

For more resources relating to this chapter, visit GCSE Mathematics Online.

Using mathematics: real-life applications

Accounting involves a great deal of mathematics. Accountants set up computer spreadsheets to calculate and analyse data. Programs such as Microsoft Excel® work by applying different equations to values in columns or cells, so you need to know what equations or formulae to use to get the results you need.

"Although the computer does the actual calculations, I have to insert different equations to tell it what operations to perform and in which order to perform them. It is important to check that the equations are producing the correct answers, though." *(Accountant)*

Before you start …

KS3 Ch 7, 16	Apply your skills in using the conventions of algebraic notation to form equations.	**1** Match each statement to the correct equation: **a** y is one half the size of x **b** y is 2 less than x **c** y is the same as x multiplied by x **d** y is the square root of x A $y = x^2$ B $y + 2 = x$ C $y = \pm\sqrt{x}$ D $y = \frac{1}{2}x$	
KS3 Ch 7	Check that you can write an equation to represent a problem mathematically.	**2** Which of the equations below correctly represent this problem? 'I think of a number, multiply it by 6 and add 1. The answer is 37. What is my number?' A $6x + 1 = 37$ B $y \times 6 = 37 + 1$ C $6a = 7$ D $(6x + 1) - 37 = 0$	
KS3 Ch 1	You should be able to recognise and apply inverse operations.	**3** Complete the following statements. **a** $7 + \square = 0$ **b** $\square - 8 = 0$ **c** $-4a + \square = 0$ **d** $5 \times \square = 1$ **e** $\frac{1}{6} \times \square = 1$ **f** $\square \times 12x = x$	
KS3 Ch 16	You need to know how to factorise quadratic expressions.	**4** Match each expression to its factors. **a** $x^2 - 5x + 6$ **b** $x^2 + 3x$ **c** $x^2 - 25$ **d** $x^2 - 5$ A $x(x + 3)$ B $(x + 5)(x - 5)$ C $(x - 2)(x - 3)$ D $(x + \sqrt{5})(x - \sqrt{5})$	

Find answers at: cambridge.org/ukschools/gcsemaths-studentbookanswers

Assess your starting point using the Launchpad

STEP 1

1 Match each equation in the first box to its solution in the second box.

Equations
a $x + 7 = 19$ **b** $x - 6 = 11$ **c** $2x + 5 = 7$
d $8x = -24$ **e** $2 - 3x = 8$

Solutions
A $x = 1$ B $x = 17$ C $x = -2$
D $x = 12$ E $x = -3$

f How can you check whether a solution is correct?

2 Solve.
a $9a - 7 = 7a + 3$ **b** $3(x + 5) = 2(x + 6)$
c $\frac{3a}{2} - 4 = \frac{1}{2}$ **d** $6(5 - 3x) = 5(x^2 - 5)$

3 Is $5x + 3 = 18$ equivalent to $6x + 3 = x + 18$?
How do you know?

4 When 16 is added to twice Jack's age, the answer is 44.
Write an equation to find Jack's age and solve it.

GO TO
Section 1:
Linear equations

STEP 2

5 If $x^2 - 2x - 3 = 0$, which pair of values is the solution?
a $x = 3$ or $x = -1$ **b** $x = -3$ or $x = 1$

6 What are the possible values of x given that $x^2 - 16 = 0$

7 Complete the square for this expression $(x - 3)^2 \bigcirc \square \equiv x^2 - 6x - 2$.

8 Given $x^2 - 6x - 2 = 0$, identify the values of a, b and c in the equation $x = \frac{-b \pm \sqrt{b^2 - 4ac}}{2a}$.

GO TO
Section 2:
Quadratic equations

GO TO
Step 3:
The Launchpad continues on the next page …

Launchpad continued

STEP 3

9 **a** How many whole number solutions can you find for $x + y = 6$?

   b Which of those solutions are correct if $x + y = 6$ and $x - y = 4$?

GO TO
Section 3:
Simultaneous equations

STEP 4

10 A company hires out meeting rooms.

The total cost, y, can be worked out using the equation $y = 15x + 40$, where x represents the number of hours the room is hired for.

The graph of this equation is the straight line shown here.

a Use the graph to find the cost of hiring a meeting room for 4 hours.

b What is the value of x when y is 175?

c What is the value of y when x is 5?

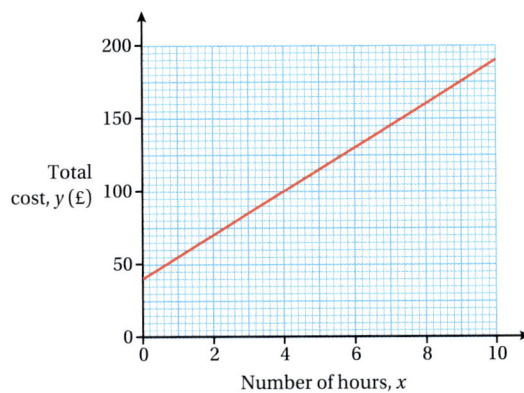

Total cost, y (£)

Number of hours, x

GO TO
Section 4:
Using graphs to solve equations

STEP 5

11 What is the maximum number of solutions a quadratic equation can have?

Can you find an approximate solution to $x^2 - 5x + 2 = 0$ using the iteration $x_{n+1} = 5 - \dfrac{2}{x_n}$ with $x_1 = 4$?

GO TO
Section 5:
Finding approximate solutions by iteration

GO TO
Section 6:
Using equations and graphs to solve problems

GO TO
Chapter review

Find answers at: cambridge.org/ukschools/gcsemaths-studentbookanswers

Section 1: Linear equations

Solving a linear equation involves working out the value (or values) of the unknown letter.

When the highest power of the unknown is 1 the equation is a **linear equation**.

In simple equations like $x + 3 = 7$ where the solution is $x = 4$, you can solve for x without needing to do any working. This is called solving by inspection.

In more complex equations you can find the solution by carrying out inverse operations on both sides of the equation.

> 🔑 **Key vocabulary**
>
> **linear equation**: an equation where the highest power of the unknown is 1, for example $x + 3 = 7$

WORKED EXAMPLE 1

Solve for x.

a $5x - 5 = 3x + 1$ **b** $2y + 17 = 5 - 6y$ **c** $2(3x - 1) = 2(x + 1)$

a
$$5x - 5 = 3x + 1$$
$$5x - 5 - 3x = 3x + 1 - 3x$$
$$2x - 5 = 1$$
$$2x - 5 + 5 = 1 + 5$$
$$2x = 6$$
$$x = 3$$

Subtract $3x$ from each side.

Add like terms.

Add 5 to both sides.

Simplify.

Divide both sides by 2.

$$5 \times 3 - 5 = 3 \times 3 + 1$$
$$10 = 10$$

Check the answer by substitution.

b
$$2y + 17 = 5 - 6y$$
$$2y + 17 + 6y = 5 - 6y + 6y$$
$$8y + 17 = 5$$
$$8y + 17 - 17 = 5 - 17$$
$$8y = -12$$
$$\frac{8y}{8} = \frac{-12}{8}$$
$$y = \frac{-3}{2}$$

Add $6y$ to both sides (this helps you eliminate the negative signs).

Add like terms.

Subtract 17 from both sides.

Simplify.

Divide both sides by 8.

Reduce the fraction to its simplest terms.

c
$$2(3x - 1) = 2(x + 1)$$
$$6x - 2 = 2x + 2$$
$$6x - 2 - 2x = 2x + 2 - 2x$$
$$4x - 2 = 2$$
$$4x - 2 + 2 = 2 + 2$$
$$4x = 4$$
$$x = 1$$

Expand the brackets paying attention to the signs.

Subtract $2x$ from both sides.

Add like terms.

Add 2 to each side.

Divide both sides by 4.

EXERCISE 17A

1 Solve the following equations. Check each answer by substitution.

a $3y + 10 = 5y + 3$ **b** $12x + 1 = 7x + 11$

c $5x - 2 = 3x + 6$ **d** $5x + 12 = 20 - 11x$

e $8 - 8a = 9 - 9a$ **f** $5x + 3 = 2(x + 2)$

2 Solve these equations by expanding the brackets first.

   a $5(t+3)=3(2t+1)$ **b** $7(x+2)=4(x+5)$

   c $4(x-2)+2(x+5)=14$ **d** $3(x+1)=2(x+1)+2x$

   e $-2(x+2)=4x+9$ **f** $4+2(2-x)=3-2(5-x)$

3 Solve this equation in x.

$3(x+1)=4(x-2)$

Choose your answer from the options given.

  A $x=-11$ B $x=-5$ C $x=11$ D $x=5$

Equations containing fractions

When an equation contains fractions, your first steps should be to find a common denominator and multiply each side by it to eliminate the denominators.

WORKED EXAMPLE 2

Solve for x:
$$\frac{x-1}{5}=\frac{2x+1}{4}$$

$\frac{(x-1)}{5}=\frac{(2x+1)}{4}$ As a first step, insert brackets.   Check the answer by substitution:

$20\times\frac{(x-1)}{5}=20\times\frac{(2x+1)}{4}$ Multiply both sides by 20 (the LCD of 4 and 5) and cancel. In this case we could also just cross multiply by 4 and 5.   LHS: $\frac{(-1\frac{1}{2}-1)}{5}$

$4(x-1)=5(2x+1)$ $=\frac{-2\frac{1}{2}}{5}$

                                                           $=-\frac{1}{2}$

$4x-4=10x+5$ Expand the brackets.

$-4=6x+5$ Subtract $4x$ from both sides.   RHS: $\frac{(2(-1\frac{1}{2})+1)}{4}$

                                                           $=\frac{-2}{4}$

$-9=6x$ Subtract 5 from both sides. $=-\frac{1}{2}$

$-\frac{9}{6}=x$ Divide both sides by 6.   LHS = RHS, so the solution is correct.

$x=-\frac{3}{2}$ Cancel by 3 to lowest terms.

EXERCISE 17B

1 Solve for x:

   a $\frac{2x}{3}+\frac{1}{4}=1$ **b** $2x-3x=4x+3$ **c** $3(x-5)=2(4-x)$

   d $\frac{2x-3}{4}=\frac{x+1}{3}$ **e** $\frac{x+20}{9}+\frac{3x}{7}=6$ **f** $\frac{2}{x-1}=\frac{3}{x-4}$

   g $\frac{x}{3}+\frac{x}{2}=10$ **h** $\frac{7x+3}{2}=\frac{18x-16}{8}$ **i** $\frac{-3(4+x)}{2}=-9$

   j $\frac{3x-11}{5}-\frac{3x}{4}=7+4x$

Find answers at: cambridge.org/ukschools/gcsemaths-studentbookanswers

2 Write $\dfrac{x^2 + 2}{x} = \dfrac{-7}{2}$ in the form $ax^2 + bx + c = 0$.

Choose your answer from the options below.

A $x^2 + 7x + 4 = 0$ B $x^2 + 7x - 4 = 0$

C $2x^2 + 7x - 4 = 0$ D $2x^2 + 7x + 4 = 0$

Setting up and solving linear equations

You can use algebra to set up and then solve your own equations.

When you set up an equation you must say what the letters stand for.

When the problem involves a shape it is useful to draw a sketch and label it to help you set up the equation.

WORKED EXAMPLE 3

1 The sum of two numbers is 54. If one number is 14 more than the other number, find the two numbers.

Let x be the value of one unknown

> Let x be the value of one of the unknown numbers.

$\therefore$ value of second number is $x + 14$

> The other number is 14 more than x.

$x + (x + 14) = 54$

> The total of the two numbers is 54.
>
> Use this information to form an equation.

$x + x + 14 = 54$
$2x + 14 = 54$
$2x = 40$
$x = 20$

> Subtract 14 from both sides.
>
> Divide both sides by 2.

If $x = 20$
Value of second number is
$x + 14 = 20 + 14$
$= 34$

> Use the value of $x = 20$ to find the value of $x + 14$.
>
> Check the total is 54.

The two numbers are 20 and 34
Check: $20 + 34 = 54$

> You can solve problems like this without writing equations. However, writing equations will help you to be more efficient.

Continues on next page . . .

2 The length of a rectangle is three times its width.

If the perimeter is 24 centimetres, find the area of the rectangle.

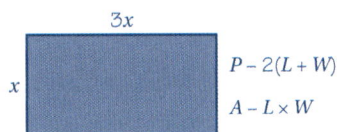

$3x$

x

$P - 2(L + W)$

$A - L \times W$

Draw a sketch and label it.

If x represents the width
Length is $3x$

You need to find the lengths of the sides to work out the area.

Perimeter $= 2(x + 3x) = 24$

Form an equation in x to represent the perimeter.

$2 \times (\text{width} + \text{length}) = 24 \text{ cm}$

$2(x + 3x) = 24$
$x + 3x = 12$
$4x = 12$
$x = 3 \text{ cm}$

Solve for x.

Divide both sides by 2.

Collect like terms.

Divide both sides by 4.

Width $= 3 \text{ cm}$
Length $= 3 \times 3 = 9 \text{ cm}$
Area of rectangle $= 3 \times 9$
$= 27 \text{ cm}^2$

Find the values of width and length given that $x = 3$.

Calculate the area.

Area $=$ width $\times$ length

Make sure to provide the correct units for the answers.

> **Tip**
>
> Make sure you know what the unknown is and state what letter you are using to represent it. We tend to let x be the unknown, but you can choose any letter as long as you define it.

EXERCISE 17C

1 For each of the following, write an equation and solve it to find the unknown number.

a Three times a certain number is 348. What is the number?

b Seven less than a number is –2. What is the number?

c Six greater than a number is –4. What is the number?

d Two less than four times a number is 66, what is the number?

e Two consecutive numbers have a sum of 63. What are the numbers?

f Three less than twice a number is –2. What is the number?

g When $1\frac{1}{2}$ is added to twice a certain number, the result is $4\frac{3}{4}$. What is the number?

2 Form an equation and solve it to answer each question.

a When 16 is added to twice Melissa's age, the answer is 44.

How old is Melissa?

b Stephen buys 8 identical pens.

He receives 80p change from £20.00.

How much does a pen cost?

c Multiplying a number by 2 and then adding 5 gives the same answer as subtracting the number from 23.

What is the number?

d Mustafa is twenty years older than his daughter.

His daughter has worked out that in five years' time, she will be half her dad's age.

How old is she now?

e Gina is 4 years older than her sister.

When their ages are added together the result is 22.

How old is Gina?

f A woman is three times as old as her daughter.

In four years' time she will be only two and a half times as old as her daughter.

What is the woman's present age?

3 A square has sides of $3x$ cm. A parallelogram has sides of $2x$ cm and $(x + 9)$ cm.

a Write an expression for the perimeter of the square.

b Write an expression for the perimeter of the parallelogram.

c The two quadrilaterals have the same perimeter.

Form an equation and solve it to find the length of one side of the square.

4 The area of this rectangle is $10 \, \text{cm}^2$.

Calculate the value of x and use it to find the length and width of the rectangle.

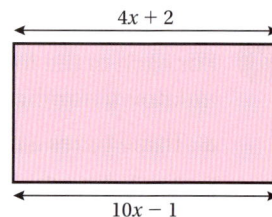

5 In a triangle ABC, angle B is three quarters of angle A.

Angle C is half of angle A.

Find the size of each angle.

6 In a game of netball, the winning team won by 9 goals.

In total, 83 goals were scored in the game.

How many goals did each team score?

7 A cellar contains only bottles of orange, apple, blackcurrant and mango juice.

Of these, $\frac{1}{5}$ of the bottles are orange and $\frac{1}{5}$ are apple.

The cellar contains 15 dozen bottles of blackcurrant and 30 bottles of mango juice.

How many bottles of orange and apple juice does it contain?

8 A stallholder sells articles at either £2 or £5 each.

On a particular day, he sold 101 articles and took £331 in revenue.

How many articles were sold at each price?

9 10 000 tickets were sold for a concert.

Some tickets sold for £80 each and the remainder sold for £60 each.

The total made from selling tickets was £640 000.

How many tickets at each price were sold?

Section 2: Quadratic equations

A quadratic equation has at least one term with a **variable** that is squared (x^2) and no variables with a power higher than 2.

When you square root a number, there is a positive and negative answer.

For example, $\sqrt{9} = 3$ **or** -3. This is written as $\sqrt{9} = \pm 3$

Because you are dealing with a squared variable, quadratic equations have two solutions, known as **roots**. (Some have only one, others have none and in some cases, only one of the roots is valid.)

When you are asked to solve a quadratic equation you need to give a **solution** that contains both roots.

The solution to the equation $x^2 = 9$ is $x = \pm 3$

Look at this diagram showing a graph plotted from a quadratic equation.

It shows why a quadratic can have a maximum of two solutions.

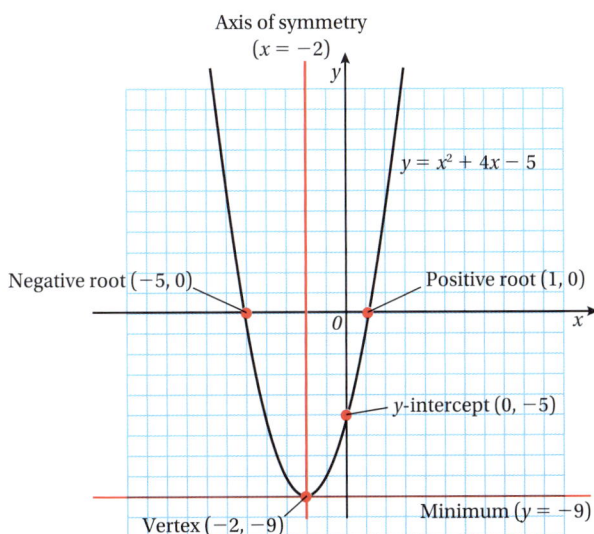

This diagram shows the quadratic function $y = x^2 + 4x - 5$.

It cuts the x-axis in two places marked as the positive root and the negative root.

These are the points at which $y = 0$, so you can solve for x by writing the equation as $0 = x^2 + 4x - 5$.

The general form of a quadratic equation is $ax^2 + bx + c = 0$ (when the coefficient of x^2 is not 0 or 1).

> **Key vocabulary**
>
> **variable**: a letter representing an unknown number
>
> **roots**: the individual values of x in a quadratic equation when $y = 0$
>
> **solution**: all possible values of x in an equation. Depending on the quadratic equation, x can have one, two or possibly no solutions.

> **Tip**
>
> You will deal with graphs of quadratic equations in more detail in Chapter 39.

Tip

Make sure you remember these three methods of factorising quadratic expressions:

$x^2 - 6x \equiv x(x - 6)$
taking out a common factor

$x^2 + 5x + 4 \equiv (x + 1)(x + 4)$
writing a trinomial as a product of binomials

$x^2 - 100 \equiv (x + 10)(x - 10)$
applying the difference of two squares identity.

Read through Chapter 16 again if you have forgotten anything.

Factorising to solve quadratic equations

The general form of a quadratic equation is $x^2 + bx + c = 0$ (when the coefficient of x^2 is 1).

Zero factor principle

The only way to get a product of 0 is to multiply by 0.

For example, if $7 \times a = 0$, then you know that $a = 0$.

This means that if $(x - 1)(x - 2) = 0$ then either $(x - 1) = 0$ or $(x - 2) = 0$.

If $x - 1 = 0$, then $x = 1$.

If $x - 2 = 0$, then $x = 2$.

This is the zero factor principle.

WORKED EXAMPLE 4

Solve

a $9x^2 - 4 = 0$

$(3x + 2)(3x - 2) = 0$ — Factorise using the difference of squares identity.

Either $3x + 2 = 0$ or $3x - 2 = 0$ — Apply the zero factor principle.

Solve the equations

$3x + 2 = 0$
$\therefore x = -\frac{2}{3}$
$3x - 2 = 0$
$\therefore x = \frac{2}{3}$
$x = -\frac{2}{3}$ or $x = \frac{2}{3}$

b $x^2 - 6x = 0$

$x(x - 6) = 0$ — Factorise by taking out a common factor of x.

Either $x = 0$ or $(x - 6) = 0$ — Apply the zero factor principle.

$x - 6 = 0$ — In this case you already have one value for x so you need only solve one equation.

$\therefore x = 6$
$x = 0$ or $x = 6$ — State the solution.

Continues on next page . . .

c $3x^2 - 5x = 2$

$3x^2 - 5x - 2 = 0$ Subtract 2 from each side to get the equation in the general form.
$3x^2 - 6x + x - 2 = 0$

$3x(x - 2) + 1(x - 2) = 0$ Factorise.

$(x - 2)(3x + 1) = 0$

$x - 2 = 0$ or $3x + 1 = 0$ Apply the zero factor principle.

Solve the equations

$x - 2 = 0$

$\therefore x = 2$

$3x + 1 = 0$

$\therefore x = -\dfrac{1}{3}$

$x = 2$ or $x = -\dfrac{1}{3}$ State the solution.

d $x + 5 = \dfrac{14}{x}$ This equation doesn't look like a quadratic until you rearrange it.

$x(x + 5) = 14$ Multiply by x to eliminate the fraction.

$x^2 + 5x = 14$ Expand the brackets. Now you can see the squared variable.

$x^2 + 5x - 14 = 0$ Subtract 14 to get the equation into the general form.

$(x + 7)(x - 2) = 0$ Factorise.

Either $x + 7 = 0$ or $x - 2 = 0$

$\therefore x = -7$ or $x = 2$

e $\dfrac{1}{x - 1} - \dfrac{1}{x + 3} = \dfrac{1}{35}$

$35(x + 3) - 35(x - 1) = (x - 1)(x + 3)$ Multiply to eliminate the denominators.

$35x + 105 - 35x + 35 = x^2 + 2x - 3$ Expand the brackets.

$140 = x^2 + 2x - 3$ Collect like terms.

$x^2 + 2x - 143 = 0$ Rewrite in the general form.

$(x + 13)(x - 11) = 0$ Factorise.

Either $x = -13$ or $x = 11$

After working through these examples you should be able to see a clear set of steps for solving quadratic equations which can be factorised.

Step 1

If necessary, take all the terms to the left-hand side so the right-hand side is 0.

This might involve expanding brackets.

Step 2

Factorise the left-hand side:

- check for common factors
- check for difference of squares
- write trinomials as a binomial product.

Step 3

Write each factor equal to 0.

Solve the equations to find the roots.

Tip

When you are dealing with a difference of two squares you can solve in the following way as well:

$4x^2 - 9 = 0$

$\rightarrow 4x^2 = 9$

$\rightarrow x^2 = \dfrac{9}{4}$

$\rightarrow x = \pm\sqrt{\dfrac{9}{4}}$

$\rightarrow x = \pm\dfrac{3}{2}$

Quadratic equations are very useful for modelling situations in which a parabolic curve would be produced. The parabola is a very naturally occurring curve. You can see it in rainbows, water fountains and in the path followed by the ball in various sports.

EXERCISE 17D

1 For this quadratic equation, choose the correct option for a, b and c.

$-2x^2 - 5x + 12 = 0$

A $a = 2, b = 5, c = 12$

B $a = -5, b = -2, c = 12$

C $a = -2, b = -5, c = 12$

D $a = -2, b = -5, c = -12$

2 Solve the following equations by factorising.

a $x^2 + 12x^2 + 27 = 0$

b $x^2 - x - 30 = 0$

c $6x^2 - 7x - 10 = 0$

d $9x^2 + 4x - 5 = 0$

e $x^2 + 3x = 0$

f $5x^2 - 4x = 0$

g $x^2 - 100 = 0$

h $x^2 - 5 = 0$ (Leave your answer in square root form)

i $x^2 - 6 = 0$ (Leave your answer in square root form)

3 Can you solve the quadratic equation $x^2 + 4 = 0$ by factorising it? Give reasons for your answer.

4 Solve for x:

a $x^2 = 4(x + 8)$

b $(x - 1)(3x + 2) = 2$

c $3x - 8 = \dfrac{x^2}{4}$

d $2(x + 1)^2 = (x + 1)^2 + 9$

e $\dfrac{x + 1}{3} = \dfrac{10}{x}$

f $\dfrac{2}{2x - 3} = \dfrac{x}{4x - 6}$

g $\dfrac{4}{x - 1} - \dfrac{5}{x + 2} = \dfrac{3}{x}$

h $6(4x + 5) + \dfrac{7}{x}(4x + 5) = 0$

Solving quadratic equations by completing the square

If a quadratic equation cannot be factorised, it can be solved by completing the square.

You need to rewrite the quadratic as a square plus a constant.

Then you can solve the equation.

Consider the quadratic equation $x^2 - 6x + 1 = 0$.

Rewrite the LHS as a square plus a constant.

To find the constant term, halve the coefficient of x and then square it.

In the expression $x^2 - 6x + 1 = 0$ the coefficient is 6.

Half of 6 is 3.

3 squared is 9.
So you need to add 9 to this expression to make it a perfect square.

Don't forget to add 9 to the RHS:

$x^2 - 6x + 9 + 1 = 9$

This allows you to solve the equation in x.

$x^2 - 6x + 9 = 8$	Keep the perfect square on the left-hand side. Subtract 1 from both sides.
$(x - 3)^2 = 8$	Factorise the perfect square
$x - 3 = \pm\sqrt{8}$	Take the square root of both sides
So, $x = 3 + \sqrt{8}$ or $x = 3 - \sqrt{8}$	Add 3 to both sides
$x = 5.83$ or $x = 0.17$	Evaluate for x.

If the coefficient of x is an odd number, you will get a fractional value when you halve it.

For example, what is the missing term in the perfect square $x^2 + 3x + \boxed{}$?

Half of 3 is $\frac{3}{2}$ and $(\frac{3}{2})^2 = \frac{9}{4}$.

The perfect square is therefore $x^2 + 3x + \frac{9}{4}$.

> **Tip**
>
> Remember
>
> $(a + b)^2 = a^2 + 2ab + b^2$
>
> $(a - b)^2 = a^2 - 2ab + b^2$

WORKED EXAMPLE 5

Solve: $x^2 + 8x + 7 = 0$

$x^2 + 8x + 7 = 0$

$x^2 + 8x + 16 + 7 = 16$ Add the square of half the coefficient of x to both sides.

$x^2 + 8x + 16 = 9$ Keep the perfect square on the left-hand side and subtract 7 from both sides.

$(x + 4)^2 = 9$ Factorise the perfect square.

$x + 4 = \pm\sqrt{9}$ Take the square root of both sides.

So, $x = -3 - 4$ or $x = 3 - 4$

$x = -7$ or $x = -1$

Find answers at: cambridge.org/ukschools/gcsemaths-studentbookanswers

The quadratic formula

Completing the square results in a formula that can be used to solve quadratic equations.

Consider any quadratic equation $ax^2 + bx + c = 0$.

$ax^2 + bx + c = 0$	
$x^2 + \dfrac{b}{a}x + \dfrac{c}{a} = 0$	Dividing all terms by a
$x^2 + \dfrac{b}{a}x = -\dfrac{c}{a}$	Take $\dfrac{c}{a}$ from both sides
$x^2 + \dfrac{b}{a}x + \dfrac{b^2}{4a^2} = -\dfrac{c}{a} + \dfrac{b^2}{4a^2}$	Complete the square by adding $\dfrac{b^2}{4a^2}$ to both sides
$\left(x + \dfrac{b}{2a}\right)^2 = \dfrac{b^2 - 4ac}{4a^2}$	Factorise the LHS and write the RHS as a single fraction
$x + \dfrac{b}{2a} = \dfrac{\pm\sqrt{b^2 - 4ac}}{2a}$	Take the square root of each side
$x = -\dfrac{b}{2a} \pm \dfrac{\sqrt{b^2 - 4ac}}{2a}$	Make x the subject by subtracting $\dfrac{b}{2a}$
$x = \dfrac{-b \pm\sqrt{b^2 - 4ac}}{2a}$	

This shows that for an equation in the general form $ax^2 + bx + c = 0$, the two roots are:

$$x = \frac{-b + \sqrt{b^2 - 4ac}}{2a} \qquad \text{and} \qquad x = \frac{-b - \sqrt{b^2 - 4ac}}{2a}$$

You need to know the quadratic formula and be able to apply it.

Once you know the formula you can solve any quadratic equation by substituting the values of a, b and c into the formula and evaluating it.

Learn this formula

$$x = \frac{-b \pm \sqrt{b^2 - 4ac}}{2a}$$

Tip

If you are asked to solve a quadratic equation to a given number of decimal places it usually means the roots are irrational and you should apply the quadratic formula to find the solution.

Tip

When you use the quadratic formula it is best to work systematically using a step-by-step approach and paying careful attention to negative values to make sure you get an accurate solution.

WORKED EXAMPLE 6

Solve $3x^2 + 7x - 13 = 0$, giving your answer to two decimal places.

$x = \dfrac{-b \pm\sqrt{b^2 - 4ac}}{2a}$

Start by identifying the values of a, b and c.

In the equation, $a = 3$, $b = 7$, $c = -13$.

$x = \dfrac{-7 \pm\sqrt{7^2 - 4 \times 3 \times (-13)}}{2a}$

$x = \dfrac{-7 \pm\sqrt{49 + 156}}{6}$

$x = \dfrac{-7 \pm\sqrt{205}}{6}$

$x = \dfrac{-7 \pm\sqrt{14.317}}{6}$

Either $x = \dfrac{-7 + 14.317}{6}$ or $x = \dfrac{-7 - 14.317}{6}$

$x = 1.22$ or $x = -3.55$ (to 2 dp)

EXERCISE 17E

1 Complete the square on each expression.

Factorise the resultant expressions.

a $x^2 - 2x + \square$ **b** $x^2 + 2x + \square$ **c** $x^2 + 4x + \square$

d $x^2 + 6x + \square$ **e** $x^2 - \square x + \frac{1}{9}$ **f** $x^2 - \square x + 5$

g $x^2 + \square x + 25$ **h** $x^2 - \square x + 11$ **i** $x^2 + \square x + 7$

j $x^2 - 10x + \square$

2 Complete the square for $y^2 - 7y + 2$.

Choose your answer from the following options.

A $(y - 7)^2 + 2$ B $(y - 3.5)^2 + 2$

C $(y - 3.5)^2 - 12.25$ D $(y - 3.5)^2 - 10.25$

3 Solve each equation by completing the square.

a $x^2 - x - 10 = 0$ **b** $x^2 + 3x - 6 = 0$ **c** $x(6 + x) = 1$

d $2x^2 + x = 98$ **e** $5x = 10 - \frac{1}{x}$ **f** $x - 5 = \frac{2}{x}$

g $(x - 1)(x + 2) - 1 = 0$ **h** $(x - 4)(x - 2) = 5$ **i** $x^2 = x + 1$

4 Solve each of the following equations using the quadratic formula.

Round the answers to three significant figures where necessary.

a $2x^2 - x + 6 = 4x + 5$ **b** $7x^2 - 3x - 6 = 3x - 7$ **c** $x(6x - 3) - 2 = 0$

d $0.5x^2 + 0.8x - 2 = 0$ **e** $(x + 7)(x + 5) = 9$ **f** $\frac{1}{x} + x = 7$

5 Use the quadratic formula to solve each quadratic equation.

Give your answers in simplest surd form.

a $x^2 + 5x + 5 = 0$ **b** $x^2 + 2x - 4 = 0$ **c** $x^2 + 12x + 3 = 0$

d $3x^2 + 2x - 7 = 0$ **e** $5x^2 + 3x - 1 = 0$ **f** $4x^2 - 6x + 1 = 0$

Setting up and solving quadratic equations

As with linear equations, you can set up and solve quadratic equations.

Always define the letters you are using in your equation.

When you use quadratic equations to model real-life situations you might find that one of the solutions is not possible.

For example, if x is the length of the side of a box in metres, and you get the roots $x = 2.5$ or $x = -1.75$ you can ignore the value of -1.75 as this cannot be the length of an object.

Tip

If the problem involves square units then you can probably use a quadratic equation to solve it.

WORKED EXAMPLE 7

A rectangle with an area of 28 cm² has one side 3 cm longer than the other. How long are each of the shorter sides?

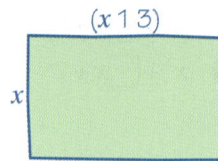

$(x + 3)$

x

Draw a diagram and label the sides.

Shorter side = x
Longer side = $x + 3$

$A = x(x + 3)$

Area of a rectangle is length × breadth.

$x(x + 3) = 28$
$x^2 + 3x = 28$
$x^2 + 3x - 28 = 0$

Use the information in the question.

Expand the brackets.

Subtract 28 from each side to get 0 on the right-hand side to form a quadratic equation equal to zero.

$(x + 7)(x - 4) = 0$
Either $(x + 7) = 0$ or $(x - 4) = 0$
$x + 7 = 0$
$\therefore x = -7$
$x - 4 = 0$
$\therefore x = 4$

Factorise.

Apply the zero factor principle.

Solve the equations.

Subtract 7 from both sides.

Add 4 to both sides.

$x = -7$ or $x = 4$
Length of shorter sides = 4 cm

State the solution to the problem.

In this problem you can ignore the $x = -7$ solution because −7 cm is not a possible length for the side of a rectangle.

EXERCISE 17F

1 Form an equation and solve it to find the unknown numbers.

   a The product of a certain whole number and four more than that number is 140.

     What could the number be?

   b The product of a certain whole number and three less than that number is 108.

     What could the number be?

   c The difference between the square of a number and three times the original number is −10.

     What are possible values of the number?

   d The product of two consecutive positive even numbers is 48.

     What are the numbers?

2 Use Pythagoras' theorem to find the value of x in the diagram below.

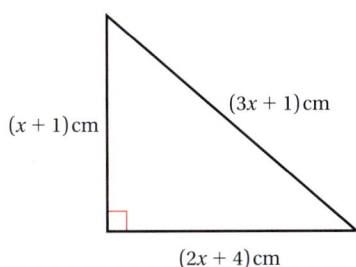

3 A metal sheet is 50 cm wide and 60 cm long.

It has squares cut out of the corners so that it can be folded to form a box with a base area of 1200 cm².

Find the length of the side of the squares.

4 A rectangular lawn is 18 m long and 12 m wide.

The lawn is surrounded by a path of width x m.

The area of the path is equal to the area of the lawn.

Find x.

5 The rectangles shown are equal in area.

Find the value of x and hence the dimensions of each rectangle.

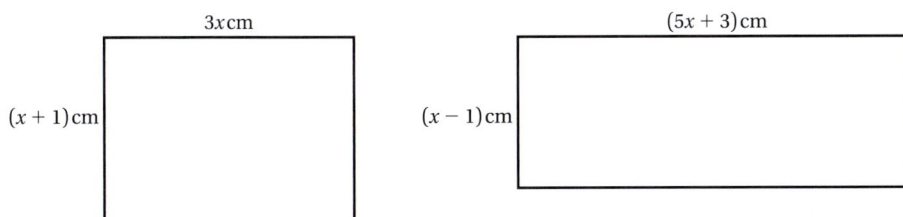

6 The perimeter of a rectangular field is 500 m and its area is 14 400 m².

Find the lengths of the sides.

Section 3: Simultaneous equations

Simultaneous equations are used to solve problems involving two conditions that are met at the same time.

For example, $x + y = 4$ and $3x - y = 2$

This is a pair of equations in two unknowns that are both true.

You can use the fact that both these equations are true to solve them at the same time (simultaneously).

WORKED EXAMPLE 8

There are 30 rose bushes in a nursery. Some are red and others are white.

There are twice as many white rose bushes as red.

How many rose bushes of each colour are there?

Let w = **number** of white rose bushes and r = **number** of red rose bushes
$r + w = 30$
$w = 2r$

> To solve this you need to set up two equations.
> There are 30 rose bushes altogether.
> The number of white bushes is twice the number of red bushes.
> Form two equations.

$r + w = 30$

r	0	10	20	30
w	30	20	10	0

$w = 2r$

r	0	5	10	15
w	0	10	20	30

> Draw up a table for each equation to show some values of r and w.

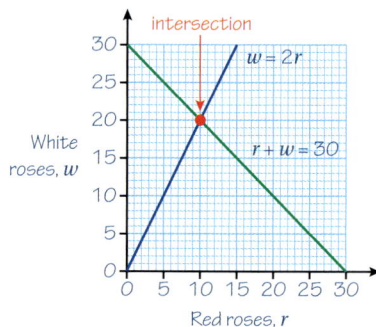

> Draw the graph of each set of values. You get two lines that intersect in one place only.

Point of intersection is (10, 20)
so $r = 10$ and $w = 20$
There are 10 red rose bushes and 20 white rose bushes.
$r + w = 30$
$10 + 20 = 30$
$w = 2r$
$20 = 2 \times 10$

> The point of intersection (r, w) is the simultaneous solution to the two equations.
> State the solution.
> Check the solutions by substitution in both equations.

You can draw graphs to solve simultaneous equations but this method takes a long time and it might not be very accurate, especially if the solution values are fractions.

There are two methods of solving simultaneous equations using algebra: substitution and elimination.

The method you choose depends on how the equations are written.

Solving simultaneous equations by substitution

Problem-solving framework

Solve these simultaneous equations.

$x - 2y + 1 = 0$ and $y + 4 = 2x$

Steps for solving problems	What you would do for this example
Step 1: Number the equations (1) and (2).	$x - 2y + 1 = 0$ (1) $y + 4 = 2x$ (2)
Step 2: Rearrange one equation so x or y is on its own on the left-hand side.	Equation 2 seems simpler, so rearrange it to get: $y = 2x - 4$ (2)
Step 3: Substitute the right-hand side of the rearranged equation into the other equation.	Substitute $(2x - 4)$ in place of y in (1). $x - 2(2x - 4) + 1 = 0$
Step 4: Solve the new equation (which now only has one unknown).	$x - 2(2x - 4) + 1 = 0$ $x - 4x + 8 + 1 = 0$ $-3x + 9 = 0$ $-3x = -9$ $x = 3$
Step 5: Substitute the solution into either of the original equations to find the other unknown.	Substitute $x = 3$ into (2) and solve. $y + 4 = 2(3)$ $y + 4 = 6$ $y = 6 - 4$ $y = 2$
Step 6: Write the solution.	The solution is $x = 3$ and $y = 2$

Tip

This method is suitable when one of the equations already has x or y on its own on one side of the equation or when you can easily rearrange one of the equations to have x or y on its own.

Find answers at: cambridge.org/ukschools/gcsemaths-studentbookanswers

EXERCISE 17G

1 Solve the following pairs of simultaneous equations by substitution. Check that your solutions satisfy **both** equations.

a $y = x - 2$
$y = 3x + 4$

b $y = 2x + 6$
$y = 4 - 2x$

c $y = x + 1$
$x + y = 3$

d $y = x - 2$
$3x + y = 14$

e $y = 2x + 1$
$x + 2y = 12$

f $y = 1 - 2x$
$x + y = 2$

2 Which of the following options is a correct solution for $y = 2x$ and $2x + 3y = 24$?

A $x = 3, y = 2$ B $x = -3, y = 2$ C $x = 3, y = 3$ D $x = 3, y = 6$

3 Solve each pair of simultaneous equations by substitution.

a $y = 3x - 5$
$y = 6x - 11$

b $y = 2x - 3$
$y = 3x - 5$

c $x = 2y - 1$
$2x + y = 11$

4 Solve these simultaneous equations.

a $x + 2y = 11$
$2x + y = 10$

b $x - y = -1$
$2x + y = 4$

c $5x - 4y = -1$
$2x + y = 10$

d $3x - 2y = 29$
$4x + y = 24$

e $3x + y = 6$
$9x + 2y = 1$

f $3x - 2 = -2y$
$2x - y = -8$

Solving simultaneous equations by elimination

In this method you add or subtract the equations to eliminate one of the unknown variables.

You may need to multiply or divide one equation by a factor before you do this.

Problem-solving framework

Solve the simultaneous equations $2x + y = 8$ and $x - y = 1$

Steps for solving problems	What you would do for this example
Step 1: Number the equations (1) and (2).	$2x + y = 8$ (1) $x - y = 1$ (2)
Step 2: Decide whether you can add or subtract to eliminate a variable.	(1) has a variable of y and (2) has a variable of $-y$. If you add the equations, these terms will cancel out. (1) + (2) $2x + y = 8$ $\underline{x - y = 1}$ $3x \quad = 9$
Step 3: Solve the resulting combined equation (which now only has one unknown).	$3x = 9$ $x = 3$
Step 4: Substitute the solution into either of the original equations to find the other unknown.	Substitute $x = 3$ into (2) $3 - y = 1$ $-y = 1 - 3$ $-y = -2$ $y = 2$

Tip

Add if the signs are different and one variable will be eliminated.
Subtract when the signs are the same, including when they are both negative.

Find answers at: cambridge.org/ukschools/gcsemaths-studentbookanswers

In some examples, you will need to form new equations before you can add or subtract to eliminate one variable.

WORKED EXAMPLE 9

Solve this pair of simultaneous equations: $3x - 2y = 5$ $4x + 3y = 18$

$3x - 2y = 5$ (1)
$4x + 3y = 18$ (2)

In this example, you could rewrite one of the equations to make either x or y the subject and use substitution, but this involves introducing fractions into the equations.

The best strategy is to create multiples of these equations, to get one pair of identical coefficients for either x or y.

Multiply (1) by 3 and (2) by 2.

$9x - 6y = 15$ (3)
$8x + 6y = 36$ (4)

This has created a pair of coefficients of -6 and 6.

Adding (3) and (4) eliminates the y terms: $-6y + 6y = 0$

$17x = 51$
$x = 3$

$4 \times 3 + 3y = 18$
$3y = 6$
$y = 2$

Substituting in (2).

So $x = 3$ and $y = 2$ are the solutions that satisfy both equations.

EXERCISE 17H

1 Solve the following pairs of simultaneous equations by elimination.
Check that your solutions satisfy **both** equations.

a $x - y = 2$
$3x + y = 14$

b $2x - 3y = 3$
$x + 3y = 6$

c $3x + y = 4$
$2y - 3x = -10$

d $2x - y = 13$
$5x + y = 13$

e $x + 2y = 14$
$4x - 2y = 14$

f $-x - y = 3$
$x + 5y = -11$

g $x + y = 5$
$3x + y = 9$

h $3x + 4y = 15$
$x + 4y = 13$

i $2x - y = 7$
$4x - y = 15$

2 Solve the following simultaneous equations by elimination.

a $x + y = 2$
$3x - y = 10$

b $2x + y = 5$
$x + y = 2$

c $2x - 3y = 1$
$3x + 3y = 9$

3 Solve each pair of simultaneous equations. Choose the most suitable method for doing this.

a $2x + y = 7$
$3x + 2y = 12$

b $-2x + 8y = 6$
$2x = 3 - y$

c $4x + 2y = 50$
$x + 2y = 20$

d $x + y = -7$
$x - y = -3$

e $y = 1 - 2x$
$5x + 2y = 0$

f $y = 2x - 5$
$y = 3 - 2x$

4 Solve simultaneously:

a $2x + 5y = 10$
$x - 3y = 5$

b $x - 3y = 0$
$2x - 4y = 2$

c $-3x - 2y = 4$
$x + 7y = 5$

d $2x + 3y = 12$
$3x - 4y = -1$

e $5x - 2y = 17$
$4x + 3y = 9$

f $2x + 3y = 1$
$5x + 4y = -1$

Setting up and solving simultaneous equations

Some problems can be described using a pair of simultaneous equations.

Once you have defined the variables and set up the equations you can use algebra to solve them.

Tip

If a problem asks for two different pieces of information then it means there are two unknowns and you will need two equations to solve it.

Problem-solving framework

A field contains a number of goats and chickens.

Altogether there are 60 heads and 200 legs.

How many are there of each type of animal?

Steps for solving problems	What you would do for this example
Step 1: Work out what you have to do. Start by reading the question carefully.	You have to find the number of goats, g, and the number of chickens, c.
Step 2: What information do you need? Have you got it all?	You need to know how many there are altogether. You're not told this, but you can work it out because each goat and each chicken must have one head. $g + c = 60$ Now you need another equation to link the goat and chickens. You've already used the number of heads, so it must be something to do with the legs. Goats have 4 legs each, so the number of goat legs is $4 \times g$. Chickens have 2 legs each, so the number of chicken legs is $2 \times c$. There are 200 legs in total so: $4g + 2c = 200$

Continues on next page …

Step 3: Decide what maths you can use.	There are two unknowns so you should use simultaneous equations.
Step 4: Set out your solution clearly. Check your working and that your answer is reasonable.	Let the number of goats be g and the number of chickens be c. $g + c = 60$ (1) $4g + 2c = 200$ (2) Make g the subject of equation (1). $g = 60 - c$ Substitute $(60 - c)$ for g in (2) and solve: $4(60 - c) + 2c = 200$ $240 - 4c + 2c = 200$ $240 - 2c = 200$ $240 - 200 = 2c$ $40 = 2c$ $20 = c$ Substitute $c = 20$ into equation (1) to find g. $g + 20 = 60$ $g = 40$ Check your result by substituting c and g into original equation (2). $4(40) + 2(20) = 200$ $160 + 40 = 200$ Yes, this works.
Step 5: Check that you've answered the question.	There are 20 chickens and 40 goats.

EXERCISE 17I

1 George and Sanjita both spent £2.20 on sweets.

George bought five fizzers and four toffees.

Sanjita bought two fizzers and six toffees.

Work out the cost of each type of sweet. (You will need to form two new equations to solve by elimination.)

2 A number x is multiplied by 4 and 1 added. This is the same value as the number x multiplied by 2 and 9 added. What is the value of x?

Choose your answer from the following options.

A $x = 9$ B $x = 4$ C $x = 3$ D $x = -4$

3 In a shop, Sam was given £1.65 as change.

The change was made up of 5p coins and 10p coins only.

He was given eighteen coins in total.

How many of each coin did he get?

4 Two children have a total of 264 stickers between them.

One child has 6 fewer stickers than 5 times the other child's stickers.

How many do they each have?

5 The sum of two numbers, a and b, is 120.

When b is subtracted from $3a$, the result is 160.

Find the values of a and b.

6 Two numbers have a sum of 76 and a difference of 48.

What are the numbers?

7 A taxi company charges a flat fee plus a set amount per mile.

A journey of 10 miles costs £7.

A journey of 15 miles costs £9.

What is the cost of a journey of 8 miles?

8 A computer store sold:

4 hard drives and 10 flash drives for £200,

6 hard drives and 14 flash drives for £290.

Find the cost of a hard drive and the cost of a flash drive.

9 A large stadium has 21 000 seats.

The seats are organised in blocks of either 400 or 450 seats.

There are three times more blocks of 450 seats than blocks of 400 seats.

How many blocks of seats are there?

Simultaneous linear and quadratic equations

When the graphs of a linear equation and a quadratic equation are plotted on the same set of axes there are three possible arrangements.

Either the graphs don't intersect at all, or they intersect at one point, or they intersect at two points.

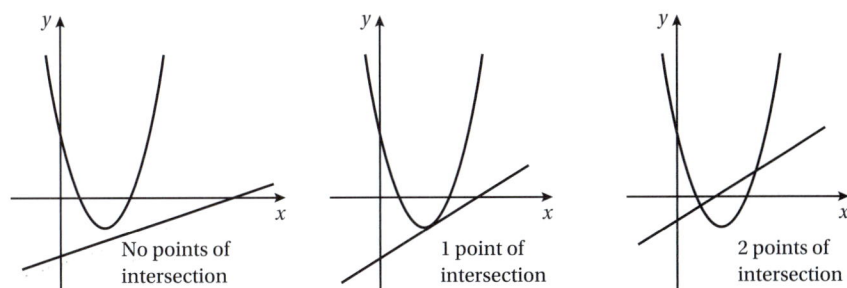

No points of intersection   1 point of intersection   2 points of intersection

If the graphs intersect their equations can be solved simultaneously by substitution or elimination to find the point(s) of intersection.

> **Tip**
>
> You will draw and use graphs to find solutions to equations in Chapters 29 and 39. Here you will focus on algebraic solutions.

WORKED EXAMPLE 10

Work out the point(s) of intersection for the following pairs of equations algebraically:

a $y = x^2 - 1$ (1)

    $y = -x + 5$ (2)

$x^2 - 1 = -x + 5$

> Substituting $(x^2 - 1)$ for y.

$x^2 + x - 6 = 0$

> Arrange the equation to get the general form.

$(x + 3)(x - 2) = 0$

> Factorise.

Either $x = -3$ or $x = 2$

Substituting in (2): $y = -(-3) + 5$ $y = -2 + 5$

                      $y = 8$ $y = 3$

> You are asked to find the points of intersection.
>
> These are given as the ordered pair (x, y) so you cannot simply give values of x and y, you need to give the ordered pairs.

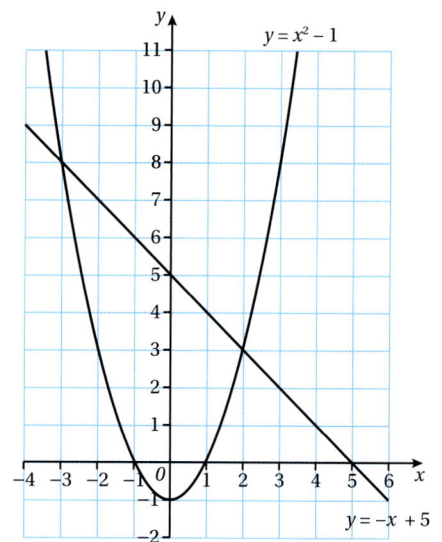

$x = -3$ or 2

$y = 8$ or 3

$\therefore$ the two points of intersection are $(-3, 8)$ and $(2, 3)$.

Substitute to check that the values for x and y satisfy both equations.

Using $(-3, 8)$:   Using $(2, 3)$:

In (1),   LHS $= 8$ In (1),   LHS $= 3$

       RHS $= (-3)^2 - 1 = 9 - 1 = 8$ RHS $= (2)^2 - 1 = 3$

In (2),   LHS $= 8$ In (2),   LHS $= 3$

       RHS $= -(-3) + 5 = 8$ RHS $= -(2) + 5 = 3$

> If you draw the graphs of these equations on the same set of axes, you can see that this solution works.

b $y = x^2 - 3x$ (1)

    $y = x - 4$ (2)

$x - 4 = x^2 - 3x$

> Substitute (2) in (1).

$x^2 - 4x + 4 = 0$

$(x - 2)^2 = 0$

> General form.

$x = 2$

$y = 2 - 4$

$y = -2$

> Substitute x in (2).

The point of intersection is $(2, -2)$.

> In this example there is only one solution, so the graphs will intersect at one point only.
>
> You can always verify this graphically.

EXERCISE 17J

1 Solve each pair of simultaneous equations by substitution:

a $y = x^2$
$y = 2x - 1$

b $y = x^2$
$y = x + 2$

c $y = x^2$
$y = x - 1$

d The graph of $y = x^2$ is a U-shaped parabola that goes through the origin.

Give a reason why there was no possible solution in part **c** above.

2 Find the coordinates of the point(s) of intersection of the following graphs:

a $y = x^2 + 3x + 3$ and $y = x + 2$

b $y = x^2 + 5x + 2$ and $y = x + 7$

c $y = x^2 + 2x + 4$ and $y = x + 6$

d $y = 2x^2 + 3x + 1$ and $y = 2x + 1$

e $y = 3x^2 + x + 2$ and $y = 3x + 3$

f $y = 6x^2 + 9x + 5$ and $y = 2x + 3$

3 Find the points of intersection of $y = -x + 1$ and $y = x^2 - 1$.

Choose your answer from the following options.

A $(-1, 0), (2, 3)$ 　　　　B $(0, -1), (3, -2)$

C $(1, 0), (-2, 3)$ 　　　　D $(1, 0), (-2, -3)$

4 The diagram shows the circular graph plotted from the equation $x^2 + y^2 = 17$ and the graph $x + y = 5$ which cuts the circle in two places.

Find the coordinates of the points of intersection of the graphs.

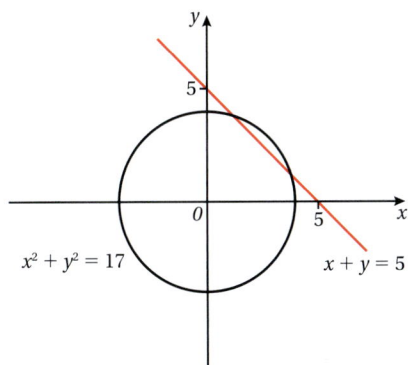

Section 4: Using graphs to solve equations

If you have a graph you can use it to solve an equation or to answer questions based on the equations.

If there are two equations, you need two graphs. In Section 3 you used a pair of graphs to find the solution to a pair of simultaneous equations.

Tip

You will work with graphs and equations again in Chapter 29 and Chapter 39.

WORKED EXAMPLE 11

This is the graph of the equation $4x + y = 2$.

1 Use the graph to estimate the value of y when:

    a $x = 0$ **b** $x = 1$ **c** $x = 2$.

2 What is the value of x when $y = -4$?

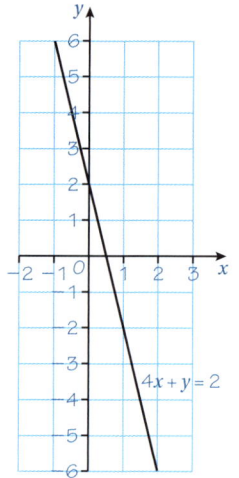

Each point on the graph represents a value of x and y that satisfy this equation.

To find the solutions for different values of x or y, you need to use the value you have been given as one of the coordinates of a point. If you take a line from this point to the graph you can estimate the value of the other coordinate.

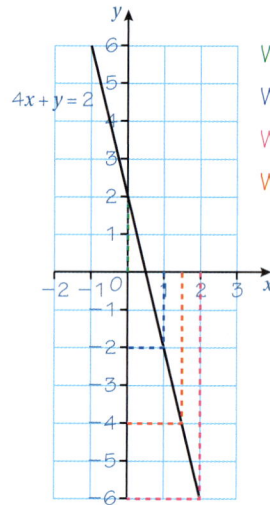

When $x = 0, y = 2$

When $x = 1, y = -2$

When $x = 2, y = -6$

When $y = -4, x = 1\frac{1}{2}$

The solutions are shown on the graph in different colours.

EXERCISE 17K

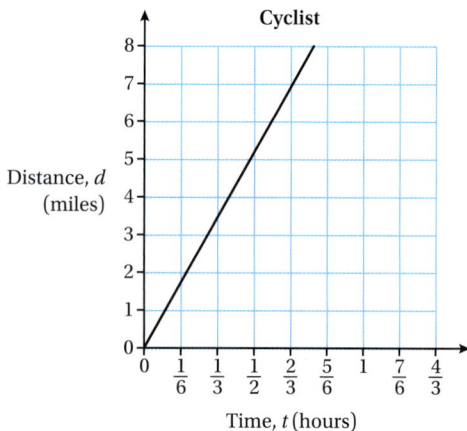

1 This graph represents the distance travelled by a cyclist over time.

    a Use the graph to estimate how far the cyclist has travelled after 30 minutes.

    b How long did it take the cyclist to cover a distance of 8 miles?

    c The equation $s = \dfrac{d}{t}$ can be used to work out the speed, s, of the cyclist. Use values for d and t from the graph to estimate the speed at which the cyclist was travelling.

2 Use this graph of the equation $y = 3x - 2$ to estimate the value of y for the following values.

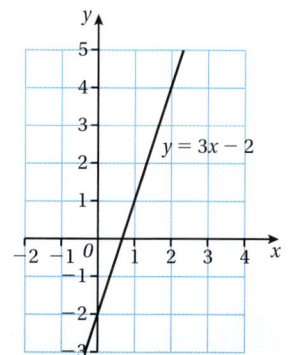

    a $x = 0$ **b** $x = 1$ **c** $x = 2$

3 This graph shows the distance covered over time by a motorist in a car.

  a Estimate how long it took the driver to travel 70 km.

  b How far did the driver travel in the first 20 minutes?

  c By using two points on the graph, estimate the speed at which the driver was travelling.

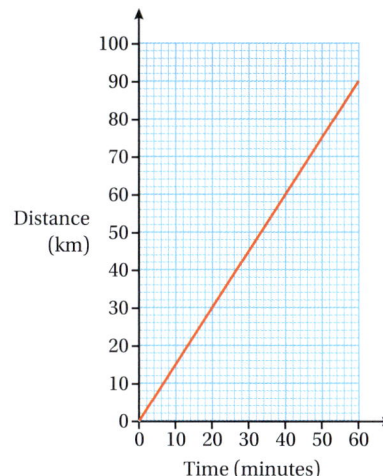

4 This graph shows how water drains from a tank at a constant rate.

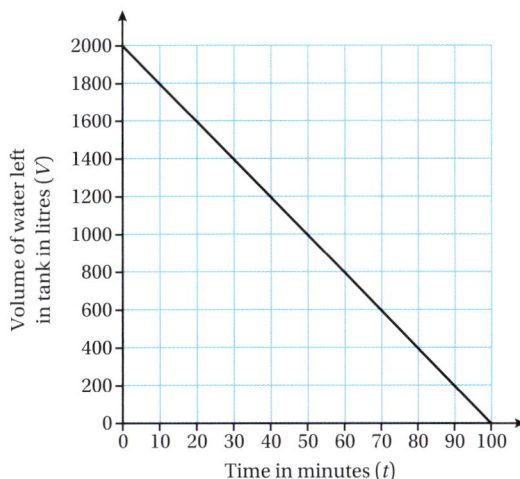

  a How much water was in the tank to start with?

  b How long did it take for the tank to empty?

  c Zena says the equation for this graph is $y = 2000 - 20x$ and Leane says it is $y + 20x = 2000$.

    Show, using different points from the graph, that they are both correct.

5 This graph shows the cost of producing goods and how much money is earned from sales (revenue).

  a Use the graph to estimate the point at which the costs and revenue are equal.

  b The point at which costs and revenue are equal is called the break-even point.

    How does this information help a business owner?

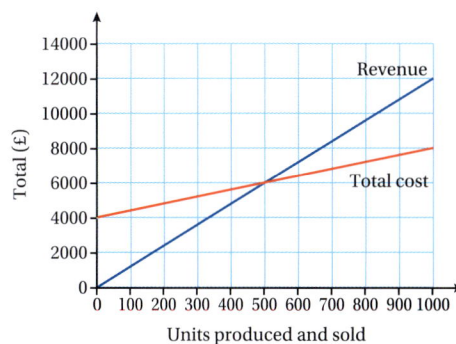

6 This diagram show the graphs of two linear equations $y = 2x$ and $y = -2x + 8$.

Use the graph to find the solution to the two equations.

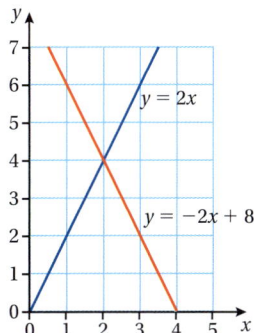

Tip

The solution to a quadratic equation is the value of x when $y = 0$. On a graph, these values are found where the graph intersects the x-axis.

7 This graph of a quadratic equation models a stunt rider's path in the air as he makes a jump.

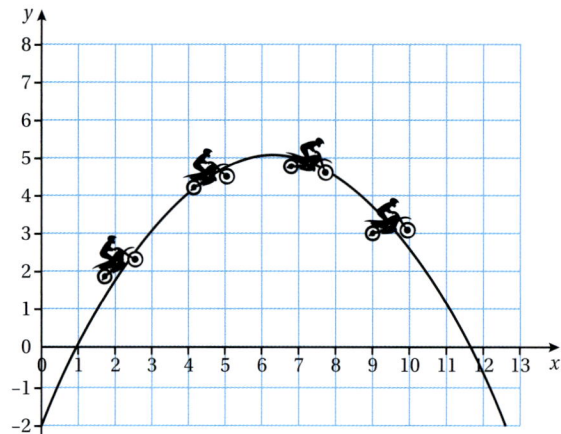

a What do you think the axes represent in this case?

b What values on the horizontal axis represent the rider taking off and landing again?

c Why are these two values useful in terms of the equation?

d Use the graph to estimate the coordinates of the maximum height reached by the rider during this jump.

8 This is the graph of a quadratic equation but the equation is not given.

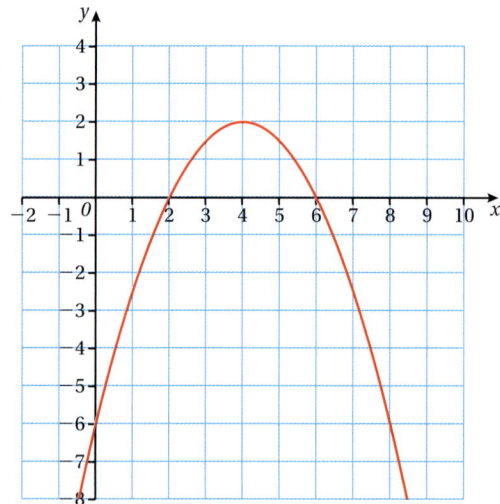

a Write down how you can use the graph to find the roots of the equation even though you don't know what the equation is.

b What are the solutions to the quadratic equation this graph represents?

c What is the quadratic equation of the graph?

9 Two linear graphs are shown here.

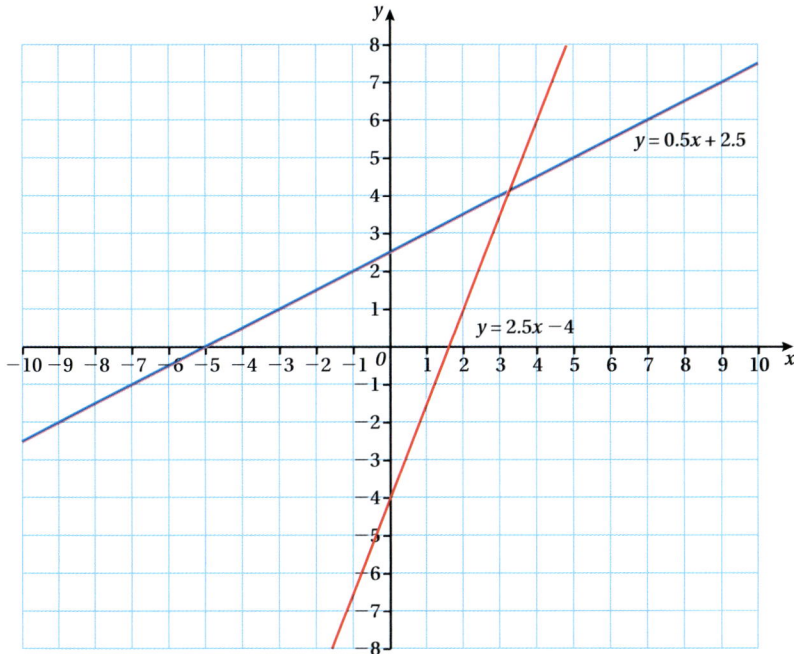

$y = 0.5x + 2.5$

$y = 2.5x - 4$

a Use the graph to estimate the values of x and y that are true for both equations.

b Find the simultaneous solution algebraically.

c What are the limitations of solving a pair of linear simultaneous equations from drawing a graph and finding the point of intersection?

10 The graph shows the bounce height of a ball dropped from different heights.

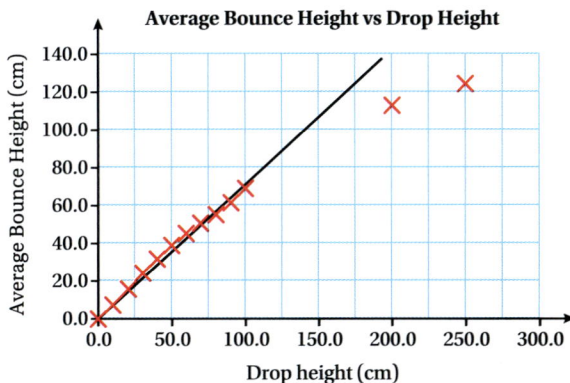

Average Bounce Height vs Drop Height

a Using the line of best fit, estimate the average bounce height for a drop of 150 cm.

b Give an alternative estimate given the results for 200 cm and 250 cm.

c Estimate the average bounce height from a drop of 300 cm.

Find answers at: cambridge.org/ukschools/gcsemaths-studentbookanswers

11 Look at the graph of the final height of a pendulum vs. its mass.

Changing pendulum mass vs final height of the pendulum

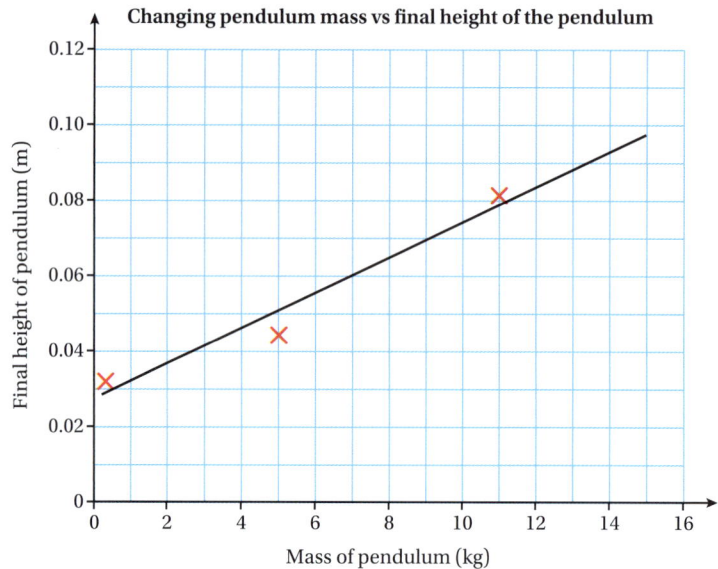

y-axis: Final height of pendulum (m)
x-axis: Mass of pendulum (kg)

a If the height of the swing of the pendulum is 0.07 m, estimate the mass of the pendulum.

b Estimate the height of the swing for a pendulum of mass approximately 6.5 kg.

c Estimate the range of the swing achieved for a pendulum of mass 16 kg.

Section 5: Finding approximate solutions by iteration

Iterate means 'repeat' or 'perform again'.

The process of iteration is a numerical method of solving equations.

It is useful for finding solutions to equations that cannot be solved in any other way.

Iteration provides a method for finding successively better approximations to the roots of the equation for real values.

It can be particularly useful for equations that contain powers of x greater than two, such as cubic graphs where the highest power of x is x^3.

Using an iterative formula

Mathematically, iteration means repeating a series of steps using the 'answer' from the previous step to get an improved 'answer' on the next step.

The starting value of x, x_1, is used to calculate x_2, which in turn is used to calculate x_3, and so on.

i Did you know?

An iterative formula is created by rearranging the original equation you want to solve to make x the subject. Subscript notation is used to indicate that you use the previous approximation of x to generate the next approximation of x.

WORKED EXAMPLE 12

Find the positive root of the quadratic equation $x^2 - 7x - 3 = 0$ to three decimal places given the iterative formula
$x_{n+1} = 7 + \dfrac{3}{x_n}$, where $x_1 = 7$.

By substitution: $x = 7$: $49 - 49 - 3 = -3$ $x = 8$: $64 - 56 - 3 = 5$	If we substitute $x = 7$ in the original equation and then $x = 8$, a change of sign occurs. This means the graph has crossed the x-axis and one of the roots of the equation lies between 7 and 8.
0 lies between -3 and 5, so a value for x lies between 7 and 8.	Remember we solve for factors equal to zero.
$x_1 = 7$ $x_2 = 7 + \dfrac{3}{7}$	Substitute the given starting value for x, $x_1 = 7$ into the iterative formula provided.
$x_3 = 7 + \dfrac{3}{x_2}$	Store the answer on your calculator (or spreadsheet) and substitute it (x_2) back into the iterative formula to get x_3.
The values for each step: $x_1 = 7$ (first estimate) $x_2 = 7.428571429...$ $x_3 = 7.403846154...$ $x_4 = 7.405194805...$ $x_5 = 7.40512101...$ $x_6 = 7.405125047...$ $x_7 = 7.405124826...$	Repeat the process until the values can be estimated with confidence to the required number of decimal places. You can see the value of x converging, and after five calculated values you can see what the value of x is to three decimal places.

$x = 7.405$ (to 3 dp)

$(7.405)^2 - 7 \times 7.405 - 3 \approx 0$

EXERCISE 17L

1 Find an approximate solution to $x^2 - 5x + 2 = 0$ (to three decimal places) using the iteration
$x_{n+1} = 5 - \dfrac{2}{x_n}$ with $x_1 = 4$.

2 Find an approximate solution to the square root of 18 (to four significant figures) using the iteration
$x_{n+1} = \dfrac{1}{2}\left(x_n + \dfrac{18}{x_n}\right)$ with $x_1 = 4$.

3 Find an answer for x (to two decimal places) using the iteration
$x_{n+1} = \dfrac{4}{x_n} + 1$ with $x_1 = 2$.

4 $x^3 - 3x + 1 = 0$
Use the iteration $x_{n+1} = \dfrac{-1}{x_n{}^2 - 3}$ with $x_1 = 0.5$ to approximate a solution for x (to four significant figures).

5 Use the iteration formula $x_{n+1} = \dfrac{2x_n}{3} + \dfrac{4}{x_n{}^2}$, starting with $x_1 = 2$, to find one of the roots of the cubic equation $x^3 - 12 = 0$.
Give your answer to two decimal places.

Find answers at: cambridge.org/ukschools/gcsemaths-studentbookanswers

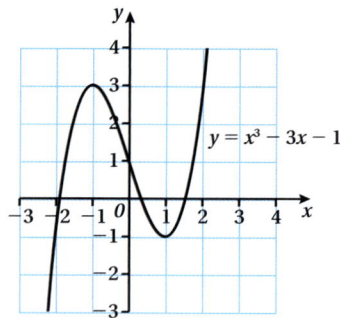

$y = x^3 - 3x - 1$

Looking for the change of sign

In terms of the graph of an equation, the change of sign indicates that the y-value has gone from positive to negative, or negative to positive.

This tells you that the graph has crossed the x-axis, so this is a root of the equation.

Searching the decimals

Here is the graph for the cubic equation $y = x^3 - 3x + 1$.

From the graph you can see that there are three roots, and that the equation does not have integral solutions.

WORKED EXAMPLE 13

Find the largest root of the function $y = x^3 - 3x + 1$ to two decimal places.

From the graph shown previously, the largest root lies between $(1, 0)$ and $(2, 0)$.

$y = x^3 - 3x + 1$

x	$f(x)$
1	−1
1.1	−0.969
1.2	−0.872
1.3	−0.703
1.4	−0.456
1.5	−0.125
1.6	0.96

Record your results in a table, or an ordered list.

y has gone from a negative value to a positive value.

This indicates that the graph has crossed the x-axis.

So, the root lies between $x = 1.5$ and $x = 1.6$

x	$f(x)$
1.5	−0.125
1.51	−0.087
1.52	−0.0482
1.53	−0.0084
1.54	0.03226

Calculate a second table of values with increments of 0.01, starting from $x = 1.5$

y has gone from a negative value to a positive value.

So, the root lies between $x = 1.53$ and $x = 1.54$

x	$f(x)$
1.53	−0.0084
1.531	−0.0044
1.532	−0.0004
1.533	0.00369

Calculate a third table of values with increments of 0.001

y has gone from a negative value to a positive value.

The solution is between 1.532 and 1.533 (the sign changes so the curve crosses the x-axis at the value at which $y = 0$). So, the root lies between $x = 1.532$ and $x = 1.533$

$x = 1.53$ (to 2 dp)

If more decimal places are required then more tables of values could be calculated. Checking the value in the original equation gives $y \approx 0$.

Looking at half-interval sections

You can also look at the values calculated at half-interval sections.

WORKED EXAMPLE 14

Find the root between $x = -1$ and $x = -2$ (to one decimal place) for the cubic function $y = x^3 - 3x + 1$.

For $y = x^3 - 3x + 1$, when
$x = -1, y = 3$
$x = -2, y = -1$

x	y
−1.5	2.125

Take the half interval value between $x = -1$ and $x = -2$: $x = -1.5$
Substitute this value of x into the cubic function.

x	y
−1.75	0.8063

Next substitute in the value of x that is the half interval between $x = -1.5$ and $x = -2$: $x = -1.75$

x	y
−1.875	0.332

Next substitute in the value of x that is the half interval between $x = -1.75$ and $x = -2$: $x = -1.875$

x	y
−1.9375	−0.4607

Next substitute in the value of x that is the half interval between $x = -1.875$ and $x = -2$: $x = -1.9375$

$x = -1.9$ (to 1 dp)

y has gone from a negative value to a positive value.
This indicates that the graph has crossed the x-axis.
So, the root lies between $x = -1.875$ and $x = -1.9375$
The method could continue to produce better accuracy. Checking in the original equation gives $y \approx 0$.

The advantage of these methods is that the solution bounds indicate the interval in which the root lies.

The disadvantage is that an initial search may miss one or more of the roots; for example, when the x-axis is a tangent to the curve or when several roots are very close together.

Tip

You will learn about tangents to the curve in Chapter 39.

EXERCISE 17M

1 Find an approximate solution to $x^3 + 2x - 1 = 0$ using the iteration
$x_{n+1} = \dfrac{1}{x_n^2 + 2}$ with $x_1 = 0.5$

Give the final answer to three decimal places and check by substitution in the original equation.

2 This is the graph of $y = x^3 - 6x - 4$

a Use the decimal search method to find the root of the cubic function $f(x) = x^3 - 6x - 4$ which lies between $(2, 0)$ and $(3, 0)$ (to two decimal places).

b Use the interval bisection method to find the root of the cubic function $f(x) = x^3 - 6x - 4$ which lies between $(0, 0)$ and $(-1, 0)$ (to one decimal place).

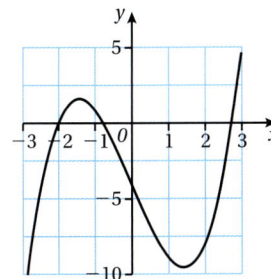

Find answers at: cambridge.org/ukschools/gcsemaths-studentbookanswers

Section 6: Using equations and graphs to solve problems

Work through this mixed exercise to practise and apply your skills.

EXERCISE 17N

1 Read each statement and decide whether it is true or false.

If it is false, give a reason why.

a $\frac{1}{2}(x-3) = \frac{1}{3}(2x+1)$

$x = -11$ is the solution to this equation.

b $10x^2 - 25x + 10 = 0$

$(10x - 5)(x - 2) = 0 \rightarrow x = \frac{1}{2}$ and $x = -2$.

c $30\frac{1}{4}$ must be added to $x^2 - 11x$ to make a perfect square.

d $x = 3 - 4y$ (1)

$7y - 3x = 21$ (2)

Substituting equation (1) in equation (2) $\rightarrow 19y - 9 = 21 \rightarrow y = 2, x = -5$.

e The diagram in the margin shows a pair of simultaneous equations, one linear and one quadratic.

The simultaneous solutions for x are both positive.

2 Solve:

a $4(x - 3) = 3x + 4$ **b** $3(2x - 5) = 2(4x + \frac{3}{2})$

3 A gardener has 60 m of garden edging, which she uses to set out a rectangular garden with its width 5 m less than its length.

If the length of the garden is x metres:

a Find the width of the garden in terms of x.

b Hence, form an equation and solve it to find the length and width of the garden.

4 A father is 28 years older than his daughter.

In six years time, he will be three times her age.

Find their present ages.

5 Find a number such that if 5, 15 and 35 are added separately to it, the product of the first and third results is equal to the square of the second.

6 This diagram consists of two rectangles with dimensions in centimetres. The total area is 95 cm².

a Show that $2y^2 + 6y - 95 = 0$.

b Solve the equation $2y^2 + 6y - 95 = 0$ to three significant figures.

7 Solve the following equations by completing the square:

a $x^2 - 4x - 2 = 0$ **b** $n^2 = 5n + 4$

Tip

→ means 'it follows that'.

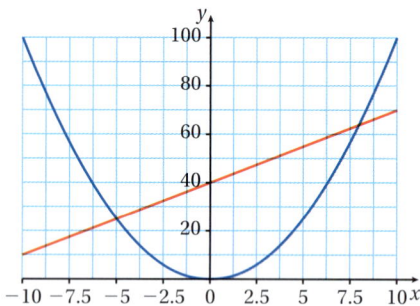

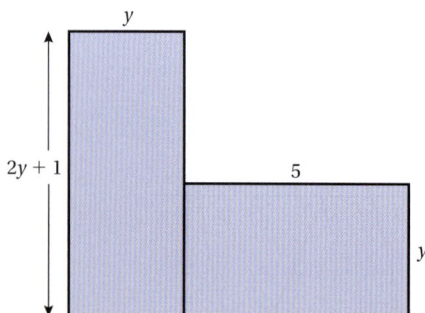

8 **a** Simplify the equation $\dfrac{5}{x+2} = \dfrac{4-3x}{(x-1)}$ to give $3x^2 + 7x - 13 = 0$.

   b Solve the equation $3x^2 + 7x - 13 = 0$ to two decimal places.

9 The base and height of a triangle are $x + 3$ and $2x - 5$.

   If the area of the triangle is 20, find x.

10 For the quadratic equation $ax^2 - 4x + 3 = 0$, find the values of a for which the equation has:

   a one solution   **b** two solutions   **c** no solutions.

11 The sum of two numbers is 112 and their difference is 22.

   Write a pair of simultaneous equations and solve to find the two numbers.

12 A manufacturer of lawn fertiliser produces bags of fertiliser in two sizes, Standard and Jumbo.

   To transport the bags to retail outlets, he uses a van with a carrying capacity of one tonne.

   He discovers that he can transport either 110 Standard bags and 60 Jumbo bags or 50 Standard bags and 100 Jumbo bags at any one time.

   Find the weight of each type of bag in kg.

13 Estimate from the graph the simultaneous solution to $y - 2x = 1$ and $x + y = 10$.

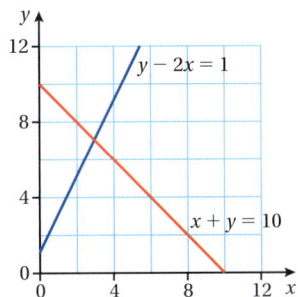

14 **a** Use the graph to estimate the solutions to the two equations.

   b Solve the simultaneous equations $y = x^2 - 5$ and $y = 3x + 7$ algebraically.

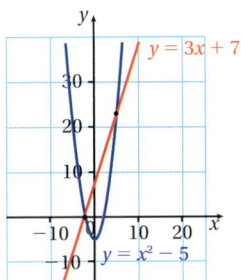

15 The equation $x^3 - 7x + 3 = 0$ has three solutions.

   a Find an approximate solution to $x^3 - 7x + 3 = 0$ in the interval between $(0, 0)$ and $(1, 1)$ using the iteration $x_{n+1} = \dfrac{-3}{x_n^2 - 7}$ with $x^1 = 1$.

     Give your answer to two decimal places.

   b Find a second root that lies between the interval $(2, 0)$ and $(3, 0)$ using the decimal search method.

     Give your answer to two decimal places.

   c Find the third root that lies between the interval $(-3, 0)$ and $(-2, 0)$ using the interval bisection search method.

Checklist of learning and understanding

Linear and quadratic equations

- A linear equation has one unknown and will have one unique value as a solution.
- A quadratic equation has a square as the highest power for the variable.
- Quadratic equations can be solved by factorising, completing the square or using the formula $x = \dfrac{-b \pm \sqrt{b^2 - 4ac}}{2a}$
- Quadratic equations have a maximum of two roots. Sometimes there is only one because the values are the same, and sometimes there is only one because one value doesn't work in a particular context.

Simultaneous equations

- Simultaneous equations are a pair of equations that have solutions that satisfy both equations.
- Simultaneous equations can be solved algebraically by substitution or by elimination.

Iteration

- To solve higher-order equations using the process of iteration, numerical methods are used to find successively better approximations to the real values for the roots of an equation.

Graphs and problems

- Equations are useful for setting up problems mathematically.
- You can find or estimate the solution to equations using graphs
- You need two graphs to solve simultaneous equations. The solution is the point of intersection of the graphs.

For additional questions on the topics in this chapter, visit GCSE Mathematics Online.

Chapter review

1 Solve by the most efficient method.

Leave your answers in square root form when necessary.

a $x^2 - 4x = 21$ **b** $x^2 + 10x = 2x - 12$

c $9 + x^2 + 11x = 2x - 11$ **d** $x^2 + 10x = 5$

e $2x^2 - 4x - 1 = 0$ **f** $3x^2 + 2x = 3$

2 An object is thrown upwards so that its height (h) in metres after a certain time (t) in seconds can be described using the formula $h = 20t - 4t^2$.

   a How long does it take the object to first reach a height of $24\,m$?

   b At what time does it come down to reach this height again?

3 **a** What are the roots of the quadratic equation modelled by this the parabola shown in the margin?

   b Write the equation represented by the graph (think carefully about the shape of the parabola).

   c What does the graph tell you about the selling price?

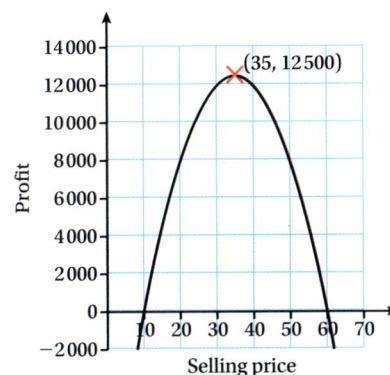

4 Are these two equations a pair of simultaneous equations?

$y = x + 2, 5y = 5x + 10$

5 Solve the simultaneous equations.

$$y = x + 4$$
$$y = 2x^2 + 3x - 1$$

Give your answers to 2 decimal places.   *(6 marks)*

© AQA 2013

6 Solve the simultaneous equations $x^2 + y^2 = 25$ and $y = 3x + 1$.

7 Prove algebraically that the difference between the squares of any two consecutive integers is equal to the sum of these two integers.

8 The product of a number and four less than the number is equal to 16 more than twice the number.

Find the number.

9 **a** Show, by completing the square, that $y = 3x^2 + 6x - 7$ can be written in the form $y = 3(x + 1)^2 - 10$.

   b Solve the equation $3(x + 1)^2 - 10 = 0$, giving your answer to three significant figures.

10 **a** Find an answer (to three decimal places) for x using the iteration $x_{n+1} = \frac{1}{x} + 2$ with a starting value of $x_1 = 2$.

   b Verify that this value of x is the positive solution to the quadratic equation $x^2 - 2x - 1 = 0$.

Find answers at: cambridge.org/ukschools/gcsemaths-studentbookanswers

18 Functions and sequences

For more resources relating to this chapter, visit GCSE Mathematics Online.

Using mathematics: real-life applications

Finding a pattern and working out how the parts of the pattern fit together is important in scientific discovery. Scientists use sequences to model and solve real-life problems, such as estimating how quickly diseases spread.

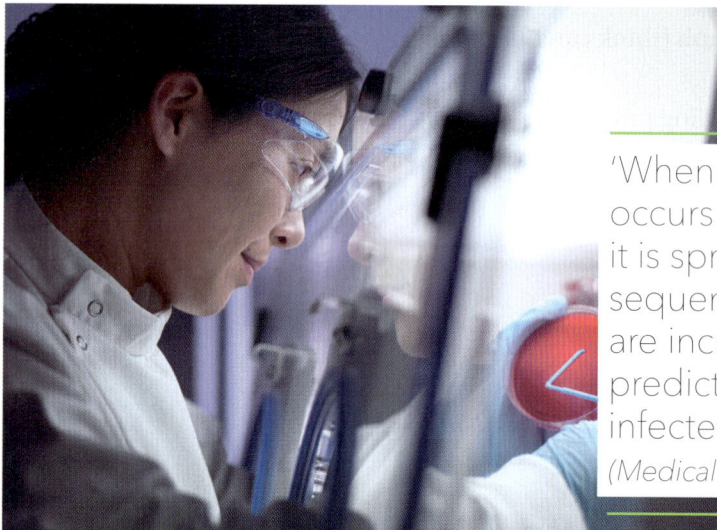

> **Tip**
>
> When you work with sequences you can draw diagrams, flow charts or tables to organise the patterns and make sense of them.

'When a new outbreak of a disease occurs I need to work out how quickly it is spreading. To do this I look at the sequence in which the numbers of victims are increasing. I use the sequence to predict how many people will become infected in a certain length of time.'
(Medical researcher)

Before you start …

KS3 Ch 4	You need to know your times tables and recognise multiples of numbers.	**1**	**a** Write down the first five multiples of 7. **b** Which of these are multiples of 6? 56, 66, 86, 18, 54, 36
KS3 Ch 4	You need to be able to recognise square numbers and cube numbers.	**2**	**a** Which of these are square numbers? 1, 16, 66, 50, 25, 4, 6, 9, 49 **b** Which of these are **not** cube numbers? 9, 15, 27, 64, 1, 8, 125
KS3	You need to be able to spot and describe patterns.	**3**	**a** Describe the rule for continuing the sequence. shape 1 shape 2 shape 3 **b** How many matchsticks are needed for shape 6?

Assess your starting point using the Launchpad

STEP 1

1 The first three terms of a sequence are 23, 35, 47.
  a Write down the next three numbers in the sequence.
  b Write down the rule for this sequence.

GO TO
Section 1:
Sequences and patterns

STEP 2

2 **a** The nth term of a sequence is $3n - 1$.
     Write down the 10th, 20th and 100th terms of the sequence.
  b The first four terms of a sequence are -1, 2, 5, 8.
     Find the nth term of the sequence.

GO TO
Section 2:
Finding the nth term

STEP 3

3 The rule for a sequence is
  'Multiply the input number by 2 and then subtract 4'.
  Draw an input–output diagram for the rule.
4 The rule for a sequence is $y = x + 3$.
  Write down the first five terms in the sequence.
5 Find the inverse function of $x \rightarrow \dfrac{3x}{2} + 1$
6 $gf(x) = 4x + 12$
  $f(x) = x + 3$
  a Find $g(x)$.
  b Which function is applied first?

GO TO
Section 3:
Functions

STEP 4

7 Here is a sequence.
  2, 4, 7, 11, …
  What type of sequence is this?

GO TO
Section 4:
Special sequences

GO TO
Chapter review

Find answers at: cambridge.org/ukschools/gcsemaths-studentbookanswers

Section 1: Sequences and patterns

The term-to-term rule

A **sequence** is an ordered list or pattern.

Terms that follow each other in a sequence are called **consecutive terms**.

The first term in a sequence is called T(1), the second T(2) and so on.

You can find the next term in the sequence by working out what the difference is between each term. This is called the **first difference**.

	Term 1	Term 2	Term 3	Term 4
Value of term	3	5	7	9
Difference	+ 2	+ 2	+ 2	+ 2

The **term-to-term rule** for this sequence is 'add two'.
9 + 2 = 11 so the next term in the sequence is 11.

	Term 1	Term 2	Term 3	Term 4
Value of term	45	42	39	36
Difference	− 3	− 3	− 3	− 3

The term-to-term rule for this sequence is 'subtract three'.

3, 5, 7, 9, ... and 45, 42, 39, 36, ... are both **arithmetic sequences**.
In an arithmetic sequence the terms are generated by adding or subtracting a constant difference.

In a **geometric sequence**, the terms are generated by multiplying or dividing by a constant factor. 3, 6, 12, 24, ... and 1000, 500, 250, 125, ... are both geometric sequences.

	Term 1	Term 2	Term 3	Term 4
Value of term	3	6	12	24
Difference	× 2	× 2	× 2	

	Term 1	Term 2	Term 3	Term 4
Value of term	1000	500	250	125
Difference	÷ 2	÷ 2	÷ 2	

Key vocabulary

sequence: a number pattern or list of numbers following a particular order

term: a combination of letter and/or numbers. Each number in a sequence is called a term.

consecutive terms: terms that follow each other in a sequence

first difference: the result of subtracting a term from the next term

term-to-term rule: operations applied to any number in a sequence to generate the next number in the sequence

Key vocabulary

arithmetic sequence: a sequence where the difference between each term is constant

geometric sequence: a sequence where the ratio between each term is constant

WORKED EXAMPLE 1

'I use term-to-term rules in my job. I know that each row of bricks will have three fewer bricks than the row below it, so I can work out how many bricks I need in each row.'

(Bricklayer)

The first row of the wall has 57 bricks.

a Write down the term-to-term rule.

b Find the number of bricks in the next three rows.

a The term-to-term rule is 'subtract three'.

> The number of bricks decreases by 3 for each new row.

b 57 in the first row
57 – 3 = 54 in the second row
54 – 3 = 51 in the third row
51 – 3 = 48 in the fourth row

> Subtract 3 from 57 to get the next term.
> Continue to do this for the next two terms.

EXERCISE 18A

1 Write down the next three terms of each sequence.
Give a reason for each of your answers.

   a 4, 7, 10, 13, ...   **b** 38, 43, 48, 53, ...   **c** 1, 2, 4, 8, ...
   d 64, 32, 16, ...   **e** 4, 12, 36, ...   **f** 729, 243, 81, ...

2 A sequence begins 3, 9, 15, 21...
The rule for continuing the sequence is 'add 6'.
What are the next three numbers in this sequence?

   A 27, 33, 41, ...   B 26, 32, 38, ...   C 25, 31, 37, ...   D 27, 33, 39, ...

3 This sequence of patterns is made from bricks.

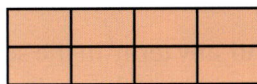
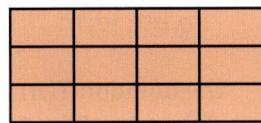

      pattern 1   pattern 2   pattern 3

a How many bricks are needed for pattern 4?

b Describe the rule for continuing the sequence.

Find answers at: cambridge.org/ukschools/gcsemaths-studentbookanswers

4 Write down the term-to-term rule of each sequence.

a 7, 14, 21, 28, ...

b 19, 15, 11, 7, ...

c 2, 8, 32, 128, ...

d 84, 42, 21, ...

5 Write down the term-to-term rule and the next three terms of each sequence.

a 3.5, 5.5, 7.5, ...

b 1.2, 2.4, 4.8, ...

c $1\frac{1}{2}$, 3, $4\frac{1}{2}$, ...

d 8, 5, 2, ...

e 72, 36, 18, ...

f −10, −7, −4, ...

6 A ball is dropped from a height of 96 cm.

Each time it hits the ground it bounces back to half its previous height.

a How high will it bounce on its 4th bounce?

b How many times will it bounce before it bounces to below 1 cm?

7 T(1) of a sequence is 4.

The term-to-term rule is 'add x'.

Find a value for x so that:

a every second term is an integer.

b every third term is a multiple of 4.

c T(2) is smaller than T(1).

Section 2: Finding the nth term

The position-to-term rule

Term-to-term rules are useful for generating the first few terms of a sequence and for finding the next term in a given sequence. They are less useful when you want to find the 50th or 100th term.

A **position-to-term** rule allows you to work out the value of any term in a sequence if you know its position in the sequence.

The sequence 1, 3, 5, 7, ... can be generated using the position-to-term rule 'position number × 2, subtract 1' by substituting the position number into the rule.

To find a sequence using a position-to-term rule, you substitute the term number in place of the variable in the rule.

For example, the tenth term of this sequence is $(2 \times 10) - 1 = 19$.

The nth term

The notation T(n) refers to 'any term' in the sequence, where n is the position of the term. T(n) is known as the 'nth term'.

When given the terms of a sequence, you can use the first difference to help you find the rule for the nth term by comparing the first difference with number patterns you already know.

Problem-solving framework

Find an expression for the nth term of the sequence: 5, 8, 11, 14, 17, ...

Steps for solving problems	What you would do for this example
Step 1: Identify what you have to do.	You are trying to find an expression to work out the value of any term in the sequence.
Step 2: If it is useful, draw a table.	Draw a table showing the position and the term:

n	1	2	3	4	5
$T(n)$	5	8	11	14	17

Step 3: Start working on the problem using what you know.	Label the table with the difference between each term:

n	1	2	3	4	5
$T(n)$	5	8	11	14	17

$+3 \quad +3 \quad +3 \quad +3$

The difference in this sequence is '+ 3'.

Step 4: Connect to other sequences and compare.	(If the difference was '+ 2' you would compare to $2n$; if it was '− 4' you would compare it to $-4n$, and so on.) Add this sequence to your table:

n	1	2	3	4	5
$T(n)$	5	8	11	14	17
Multiples of 3 ($3n$)	3	6	9	12	15

$+2$

Compare the sequence with the sequence for $3n$.

Each term in the sequence is 2 more than $3n$.

So the expression for the nth term of this sequence could be $3n + 2$.

Step 5: Check your working and that your answer is reasonable.	Test for $n = 5$: $(3 \times 5) + 2 = 15 + 2$ $15 + 2 = 17$ The fifth term is 17 so the expression is correct.
Step 6: Have you answered the question?	Yes. The expression for the nth term is $3n + 2$.

Tip

If you are struggling to find the rule for an arithmetic sequence, you can use the following formula: $(a + d(n - 1))$ where a = first term, and d = common difference. The **common difference** is the constant difference between terms.

Find answers at: cambridge.org/ukschools/gcsemaths-studentbookanswers

WORK IT OUT 18.1

A sequence is defined by the rule $n = 3n - 2$.
What are the first 5 terms of the sequence?
Only one answer below is correct. Give reasons why the other two are wrong.

Option A	Option B	Option C
$-2, 1, 4, 7, 10$	$1, 4, 7, 10, 13$	$-1, 1, 3, 5, 7$

The nth term, where u is a sequence, can be written as u_n.

This is read as 'u sub n' and is known as **subscript notation**.

u_1 is used to denote the first term, u_2 is used to denote the second term and so on.

You can use this notation to write term-to-term and position-to-term rules.

For example, the **position-to-term rule** of $3n - 4$ for the sequence u, would be written as:

$u_n = 3n - 4$.

If you want to find the value of the 6th term, substitute 6 into the equation in place of n:

$u_6 = (3 \times 6) - 4$

$u_6 = 14$

The **term-to-term rule** '+2' would be written as: $u_{n+1} = u_n + 2$

The '$n + 1$' indicates that it is the term one more than the current term (u_n).

So, if $u_3 = 7$ then,

$u_4 = u_3 + 2$

$\quad = 7 + 2$

$\quad = 9$

EXERCISE 18B

1 This pattern is made using drinking straws.

pattern 1   pattern 2   pattern 3   pattern 4

    a Which pattern will have 32 straws?

    b How many straws will be in pattern 20?

    c What is the position-to-term rule?

2 The nth term of a sequence is $5n - 1$.
What is the 10th term of the sequence?
Choose from the following options.

A 48   B 49   C 50   D 52

3 The *n*th term of a sequence is $3n - 1$.

   a Write down the first six terms of the sequence.

   b Work out the 20th term.

   c Nathan says, 'The 40th term of the sequence is double the 20th term.' Show that he is wrong.

4 Find the value of the following terms for each position-to-term rule.

   i 1st term   **ii** 2nd term   **iii** 3rd term   **iv** 4th term

   v 10th term   **vi** 20th term   **vii** 100th term

   a $4n + 1$ **b** $4n - 5$ **c** $8n + 2$

   d $5n - \dfrac{1}{2}$ **e** $\dfrac{n}{2} + 1$ **f** $-2n + 1$

5 Here is a sequence.

   4, 11, 18, 25, 32

   What is the expression for the *n*th term of the sequence?

   A $4n + 7$ B $7n + 4$ C $4n - 7$ D $7n - 3$

6 A sequence begins 5, 9, 13, 17...

   Find the *n*th term of the sequence.

7 Find the *n*th term of each sequence.

   a 3, 5, 7, 9, ...   **b** 3, 7, 11, 15, ...   **c** −1, 4, 9, 14, ...

   d 7, 12, 17, 22, ...   **e** −3, 0, 3, 6, ...   **f** −1, 6, 13, 20, ...

8 The first four terms of a sequence are 4, 7, 10, 13.

   What is the rule for this sequence?

   A position number + 3   B 2 × position number

   C 3 × position number + 1

9 Here is a sequence of numbers from a science experiment.

   67, 73, 79, 85, ...

   Find the *n*th term of the sequence.

10 The table shows the heights of a sunflower over a three-week period. The growth rate is constant.

Week	Height
1	4.5 cm
2	6.7 cm
3	8.9 cm

   a How tall will the sunflower be in the *n*th week?

   b How tall will the sunflower be in the 100th week?

   c Give a reason why your answer to part **b** is unlikely to be true.

11 Tammy starts with £100. She saves £4 every week.

   a How much will she have after 52 weeks?

   b How long will it take her to save £400?

12 In a restaurant, tables can be put together in a line to seat different numbers of people.

   a How many people can sit at 6 tables in a line?

   b How many people can sit at 10 tables in a line?

   c Can 31 people be seated at tables arranged in a line? Give a reason for your answer.

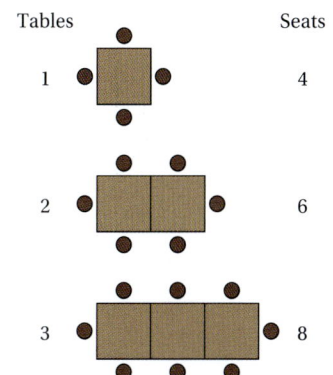

Tables   Seats

1   4

2   6

3   8

Find answers at: cambridge.org/ukschools/gcsemaths-studentbookanswers

Section 3: Functions

A **function** is a rule for changing one number into another.

'Multiply by two', 'add three' and 'divide by 2 and then add 1' are examples of functions.

You can use algebra to write functions, for example 'multiply by 2' can be written as the expression '2n'.

Functions can be expressed in different ways:

$$y = x + 3 \qquad x \rightarrow x + 3 \qquad f(x) = x + 3$$

These all mean the same thing: take any value of x and add 3 to it to get a result.

$f(x)$ is called **function notation**.

input into the function

identifies the expression as a function; it can be any letter but the most commonly used are f, g and h

---

WORKED EXAMPLE 2

$f(x) = 3x - 2$

a Find the value of

   i $f(0)$ **ii** $f(2)$ **iii** $f(-2)$

b Find the value of x for which $f(x) = 16$

a **i** $f(x) = 3x - 2$

$\qquad = (3 \times 0) - 2$

$\qquad = 0 - 2$

$\qquad = -2$

> Substitute the value of 0 in place of x.
> Solve the equation.

   ii $f(x) = 3x - 2$

$\qquad = 6 - 2$

> Substitute the value of 2 in place of x.
> Solve the equation.

   iii $f(x) = 3x - 2$

$\qquad = -6 - 2$

$\qquad = -8$

> Substitute the value of -2 in place of x.
> Solve the equation.

b $f(x) = 3x - 2$

$16 = 3x - 2$

$18 = 3x$

$x = 6$

> Substitute the value of 16 in place of $f(x)$.
> Solve the equation.

The steps you take to work out the value of a function can be shown as a simple flow diagram or function machine.

A function machine shows the input, operation and output for a given rule.

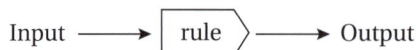

$$\text{Input} \longrightarrow \boxed{\text{rule}} \longrightarrow \text{Output}$$

In a function there is only **one** possible output for each input.

Generating a sequence using a function

You can generate a sequence using a function.

The table shows the outputs when you input the values 1 to 10 into the function $y = 2n + 4$

$$n \longrightarrow \boxed{\times 2} \longrightarrow \boxed{+4} \longrightarrow 2n + 4$$

Input	Function	Output
1	$\times 2 + 4$	6
2	$\times 2 + 4$	8
3	$\times 2 + 4$	10
4	$\times 2 + 4$	12
5	$\times 2 + 4$	14
6	$\times 2 + 4$	16
7	$\times 2 + 4$	18
8	$\times 2 + 4$	20
9	$\times 2 + 4$	22
10	$\times 2 + 4$	24

So the function $y = 2n + 4$ generates the sequence
6, 8, 10, 12, 14, 16, 18 ,20, 22, 24, …

If you know the values of a sequence, you can find the function that generates the sequence by finding the position-to-term rule.

Composite functions

Composite functions are formed by combining two or more functions.

If you have two functions, the composite function is the result of entering the output of the first function as the input of the second function.

Using a function machine, this would look like:

$$\text{Input} \longrightarrow \boxed{\text{Function 1}} \longrightarrow \text{Output of function 1} \longrightarrow \boxed{\text{Function 2}} \longrightarrow \text{Output}$$

Or more simply:

$$\text{Input} \longrightarrow \boxed{\text{Function 1}} \longrightarrow \boxed{\text{Function 2}} \longrightarrow \text{Output}$$

For example, if the first function is $x + 1$, and the second function is $2x$ you would have:

$$x \longrightarrow \boxed{+1} \longrightarrow (x + 1) \longrightarrow \boxed{\times 2} \longrightarrow 2(x + 1)$$

You can also combine two functions **before** entering the input, and still get the same output as applying the functions separately.

To do this, substitute the value of x that would be the output of the first function $(x + 1)$ into the value of x in the second function: $2(x + 1)$

> **Key vocabulary**
>
> **Composite function**: a function created by combining two or more functions

Then multiply out the brackets to write the rule in its simplest form:
$y = 2x + 2$

Function notation can be used to identify different functions within a composite function without needing to draw a function machine.

For example, $f(x)$ can be used to denote one function, and $g(x)$ to denote another function.

For example, you can write a composite function as $fg(x)$ or $gf(x)$.
In $fg(x)$, the output of $g(x)$ is the input of $f(x)$; $g(x)$ is done first.
In $gf(x)$, the output of $f(x)$ is the input of $g(x)$; $f(x)$ is done first.

You can combine the two functions to create a third function.
If $f(x) = 2x$, and $g(x) = x + 1$, then the composite function $fg(x)$ can be written as $h(x) = 2(x + 1)$.
Multiplying out, $h(x) = 2x + 2$.

Inverse functions

Key vocabulary

Inverse function: a function that reverses another function

Every function has an **inverse function**.

You find the inverse of a function by carrying out the inverse operations in the reverse order.

For example, the operation 'times two' can be reversed by 'dividing by two', so the function $x \rightarrow 2x$ has the inverse function $x \rightarrow \dfrac{x}{2}$.

Using function notation, the inversion of the function $f(x)$ is denoted as $f^{-1}(x)$.

WORKED EXAMPLE 3

Find $f^{-1}(x)$ if $f(x) = 3n - 1$.

$n \rightarrow \boxed{\times 3} \rightarrow \boxed{-1} \rightarrow 3n - 1$

First write out the given function using function machines.

$\dfrac{(n + 1)}{3} \leftarrow \boxed{\div 3} \leftarrow \boxed{+ 1} \leftarrow n$

To find the inverse, work in the opposite direction, replacing each rule with the inverse operation.
The inverse operation of 'subtract 1' is 'add 1'.
The inverse operation of 'multiply by 3' is 'divide by 3'.

$f^{-1}(x) = \dfrac{(n + 1)}{3}$

Write out the steps as a function.

Did you know?

$x \rightarrow x$ is called the identify function.
In this function the inverse is the same as the original function.

EXERCISE 18C

1 The numbers 1 to 10 are the input for the function $x \rightarrow x + 3$.
What sequence does this create?

2 The numbers 1 to 10 are input into the function $f(x) = x + 7$ to make a
sequence. What are the last three numbers of the sequence?
Choose your answer from the following options.

   A 8, 9, 10   B 15, 16, 17   C 7, 14, 21   D 56, 63, 70

3 Input the numbers 1 to 10 into each function to generate a sequence.

   a $x \rightarrow x - 5$ **b** $x \rightarrow 3x$ **c** $n \rightarrow n + 7$ **d** $n \rightarrow \dfrac{n}{2}$

4 Input the numbers 21 to 30 into each function to generate a sequence.

   a $y = 2x$ **b** $y = x - 8$ **c** $y = \dfrac{x}{3}$ **d** $y = x + \dfrac{1}{2}$

5 Input the numbers 11 to 20 into each function to generate a sequence.

   a $n \rightarrow 3n + 5$ **b** $n \rightarrow 2n - 7$ **c** $n \rightarrow \dfrac{n}{2} + 4$

   d $n \rightarrow 4n + \dfrac{1}{2}$ **e** $n \rightarrow \dfrac{4}{n} + 4$

6 Three consecutive numbers have been input into the function $f(x) = 3x - 1$.
The sequence created was $-4, -1, 2$.
Which three numbers were inputted into the function?
Choose your answer from the following options.

   A $-1, 0, 1$ B 1, 2, 3   C 0, 1, 2   D 2, 3, 4

7 Write down the inverse of each of the following functions.

   a $x \rightarrow x - 7$ **b** $x \rightarrow 4x$ **c** $x \rightarrow x + 5$ **d** $x \rightarrow \dfrac{x}{3}$

   e $x \rightarrow 2x + 4$ **f** $x \rightarrow 4x - 5$ **g** $x \rightarrow \dfrac{x}{5} + 3$ **h** $x \rightarrow \dfrac{4}{x} - 2$

8 Write down the composite function formed by each of these pairs of functions:

   a $f(x) = 4x$, $g(x) = x - 7$ **b** $f(x) = 2x$, $g(x) = x + 4$
   c $f(x) = 3x$, $g(x) = x - 2$ **d** $f(x) = x^2$, $g(x) = x + 1$

9 **a** Write down the inverse function of $f(x) = 2x$.
   b What is the composite function of $f(x)$ and its inverse function?

Section 4: Special sequences

Some patterns and sequences of numbers are well known.
You need to be able to recognise and use the following patterns

Special sequence	Description
Simple arithmetic progression (or linear sequences)	The **difference** between each term is constant, for example, 3, 5, 7, … or 14, 11, 8, …
Geometric sequences	The **ratio** between each term is constant, for example, 3, 6, 12, 24, …
Triangular numbers	These are made by arranging dots to form equilateral triangles. 1 dot 3 dots 6 dots 10 dots 15 dots
Square numbers	A square number is the product of multiplying a whole number by itself. For example, $3^2 = 3 \times 3 = 9$ 1 4 9 16 25 Square numbers form the sequence: 1, 4, 9, 16, 25, 36, …
Quadratic sequences	These sequences are linked to square numbers. A quadratic sequence has a position-to-term rule that involves squaring one of the variables. For example, $T(n) = n^2 + 3$. | n	1	2	3	4	5
$T(n)$	4	7	12	19	28	 + 3 + 5 + 7 + 9 First different is not constant. + 2 + 2 + 2 Second difference is constant. The second difference is the difference between each term of the first difference.
Cube numbers	A cube number is the product of multiplying a whole number by itself and then by itself again. 64 is a cube number because $4^3 = (4 \times 4 \times 4) = 64$ Cube numbers form the sequence: 1, 8, 27, 64, 125, …
Fibonacci-type sequences	The term-to-term rule for a Fibonacci-type sequence of numbers is 'add the previous two terms together'. The most well-known example (the Fibonacci sequence itself) is: 1, 1, 2, 3, 5, 8, 13, 21, …

Did you know?

Leonard Fibonacci was an Italian mathematician who developed the number pattern 1, 1, 2, 3, 5, 8, 13, 21, … while he was trying to work out how many offspring a pair of rabbits would produce over different generations.

The Fibonacci pattern is found in many natural situations.

In the Fibonacci series, the sequence of numbers is created by adding the 1st and 2nd terms together to make the 3rd term; adding the 2nd and 3rd terms together to make the 4th term and so on.

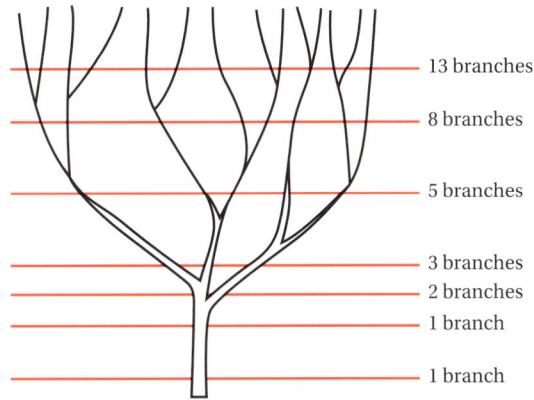

13 branches
8 branches
5 branches
3 branches
2 branches
1 branch
1 branch

EXERCISE 18D

1 a Write down the sequence of the first ten square numbers.
   b How could you use this sequence to find the next two square numbers?

2 a What type of number is shown in the photo? Say how you know this.
   b The picture represents the fifth term in the sequence.
      Write down the first ten numbers in the same sequence.
   c Find the first and second differences between the terms of the sequence.
   d What type of sequence is this?

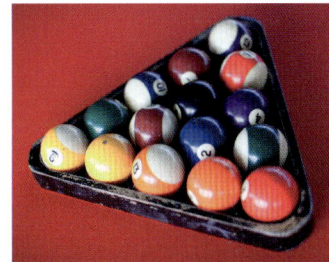

Pattern 5

3 A female bee has a mother and a father.
A male bee has a mother but no father.
The diagram shows the family tree of a male bee.

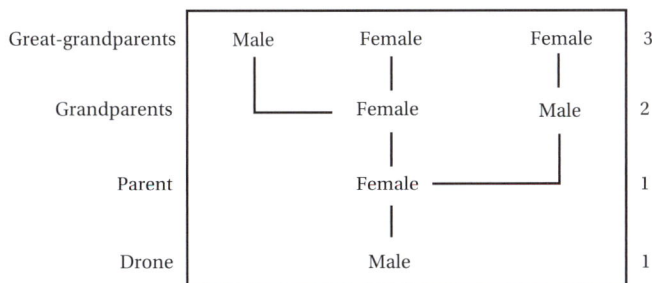

   a How many great-great-grandparents does the male bee have?
   b The family tree shows four generations of bee.
      Copy and complete the tree so that it shows six generations.
      i Write down a sequence for the number of bees in each generation.
      ii How many bees are there in the ninth generation?
      iii Describe the rule for this sequence.
      iv What type of sequence is this?

4 Which of the following pairs of numbers appear in the Fibonacci sequence?

A 22, 34   B 56, 89   C 89, 144   D 256, 357

5 **a** The first two terms of a Fibonacci sequence that follows the rule of 'each term being the sum of the previous two terms' are 3, 4. Write down the first ten terms of the sequence.

b The first two terms of a different Fibonacci sequence are $-2, 3$. Write down the first ten terms of the sequence.

c i The first two terms of another Fibonacci sequence are' 2, -3. Write down the first ten terms of the sequence.

    ii Compare your sequence to the sequence in part **b**. What do you notice?

6 The 6th and 7th terms of a Fibonacci sequence are 31, 50.

What are the first two terms in the sequence?

7 A Fibonacci-type sequence is made by subtracting the second term from double the first term.

a If the first two terms are 6 and 3, what would the 6th and 7th terms be?

b If the first two terms are 3 and 6, what would the 6th and 7th terms be?

c If the 6th and 7th terms are 45 and -83, what would the first two terms be?

8 Find the following terms using each rule for the nth term.

i 1st term   **ii** 2nd term   **iii** 3rd term   **iv** 5th term

v 10th term   **vi** 20th term   **vii** 50th term

a $n^2 + 5$ **b** $n^2 - 3$ **c** $2n^2 + 1$ **d** $2n^2 - 7$

9 The nth term of a sequence is $n^3 + 1$.

Write down the first six terms of the sequence.

10 The nth term of a sequence is $n^2 + n$.

Write down the first ten terms of the sequence.

11 Compare your answer to question 9 with your answer from question 2.

a What is the expression for finding the nth triangular number?

b Find the 10th and 25th triangular numbers.

The nth term of a quadratic sequence

You can find the rule for the nth term of a quadratic sequence in the same way you find the nth term of an arithmetic sequence.

WORKED EXAMPLE 4

Here is a sequence.

4, 7, 12, 19, 28, …

Find the nth term of the sequence.

n	1	2	3	4	5
$T(n)$	4	7	12	19	28

Draw a table showing the position and the term.

n	1	2	3	4	5
$T(n)$	4	7	12	19	28

First difference $\quad +3 \quad +5 \quad +7 \quad +9$

Second difference $\quad +2 \quad +2 \quad +2$

Work out the first difference. It is not constant.

So work out the second difference.

The second difference is constant so it is a quadratic sequence.

n	1	2	3	4	5
$T(n)$	4	7	12	19	28
n^2	1	4	9	16	25

$) +3$

Compare the sequence with the sequence of n^2.

Each term is 3 more than n^2.

The expression could be $n^2 + 3$.

$T(n) = n^2 + 3$

$n = 4$: $(4 \times 4) + 3 = 16 + 3 = 19$ ✓

$n = 5$: $(5 \times 5) + 3 = 25 + 3 = 28$ ✓

Check your answer to see if it works.

Substitute $n = 4$ and $n = 5$ into the nth term.

The general formula for finding the nth term of a quadratic equation is

$$u_n = an^2 + bn + c$$

where the value of a is half the second difference; the value of b depends on the first term and c is the imaginary term before the first term (T_0).

The value of a helps you work out if the sequence involves square numbers or multiples of square numbers.

WORKED EXAMPLE 5

What is the nth term in the sequence 4, 13, 28, 49, … ?

n	1	2	3	4
$T(n)$	4	13	28	49

$+9 \quad +15 \quad +21$ First difference

$+6 \quad +6$ Second difference

Draw a table showing the position, term and first difference. The first difference isn't constant, so find the second differences.

$u_n = an^2 + bn + c$

$a = \dfrac{6}{2} = 3$

Using the general formula, a is half of the second difference.

n	0	1	2	3	4
$T(n)$	1	4	13	28	49

$+9 - 6 = +3 \quad +9 \quad +15 \quad +21$ First difference

$+6 \quad +6 \quad +6$ Second difference

The value of c can be found by working out the value of the imaginary term before the first term (T_0).

Apply inverse operations to count back and find T_0.

$u_n = 3n^2 + bn + 1$

Substitute $a = 3$ and $c = 1$ into the general formula.

$T_1 = 4$, so

$u_1 = 3(1)^2 + b(1) + 1 = 4$

$\qquad 3 + b + 1 = 4$

$\qquad b = 4 - 3 - 1$

$\qquad b = 0$

To work out the value of b you need to substitute the value of T_1 into the formula to solve for b.

If $b = 0$, then $bn = 0$.

The formula for the nth term of the sequence 4, 13, 28, 49 … is therefore $u_n = 3n^2 + 1$.

Substitute b into the general formula to give you the rule for the nth term.

EXERCISE 18E

1 The first four terms of a sequence are 4, 9, 18, 31.

What is the nth term of this sequence?
Choose your answer from the following options.

A $n^2 + n - 3$ B $n^2 + n + 3$

C $2n^2 - 3$ D $2n^2 - n + 3$

2 Find the nth of each of sequence.

   a 3, 8, 15, 24, 35, …   **b** 3, 10, 21, 36, 55, …

   c 7, 22, 45, 76, 115, …   **d** 6, 17, 32, 51, 74, …

   e 1, 8, 21, 40, 65, …   **f** -3, 6, 23, 48, 81, …

   g -2, -8, -18, -32, -50, …   **h** 0, -4, -12, -24, -40, …

3 Here is a sequence. $1, \sqrt{2}, 2, 2\sqrt{2}, \ldots$

Write down the next three terms in the sequence.

4 The nth term of a sequence is $\dfrac{n}{(n+1)}$.

   a Write down the first five terms of the sequence.

   b Write down the 10th term.

5 The nth term of a sequence is $n^2 + 2n - 3$.

   a Write down the first five terms of the sequence.

   b Write down the 15th term.

6 Look at this pattern.

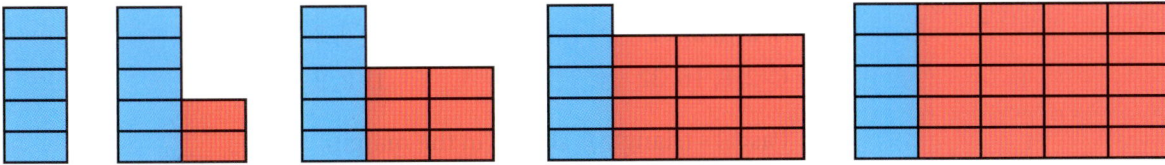

   a How many tiles are there in each shape?

   b How many tiles will there be in the 6th shape?

   c How many tiles will there be in the nth shape?

Checklist of learning and understanding

Sequences

- Sequences can be formed using a term-to-term rule. Each term is generated by applying the same rule to the previous term.

- The position-to-term rule is used to find the value of any term in a sequence using its position in the sequence.

- Subscript notation can be used to describe position-to-term and term-to-term rules.

Functions

- A function is an expression or rule for changing one number (the input) into another number (the output).

- A sequence can be generated by inputting an ordered set of numbers into a function.

- When two or more function are applied one after the other, they make a composite function.

- An example of function notation is f(x) = x + 3. A composite function might be written as fg(x) where the output of the function g(x) is the input of the function f(x).

- A function that reverses the result of another function is called the inverse function. In function notation, the inverse of the function f(x) is denoted by f^{-1}(x).

Find answers at: cambridge.org/ukschools/gcsemaths-studentbookanswers

Special sequences

- It is important to be able to recognise familiar sequences such as square numbers, cube numbers, triangular numbers and Fibonacci numbers.

- In a quadratic sequence the difference between the terms is not constant and the pattern is linked to square numbers.

- It is possible to find an expression for the nth term quadratic sequences by looking at first differences and second differences.

For additional questions on the topics in this chapter, visit GCSE Mathematics Online.

Chapter review

1 Which of the following sequences uses the same rule as the Fibonacci sequence? Choose your answer from the following options.

A 2, 4, 8, 14

B 0, 2, 4, 6, 8

C 2, 8, 16, 32

D 2, 2, 4, 6, 10

2 Pascal's triangle is shown in the margin.

```
            1
          1   1
        1   2   1
      1   3   3   1
    1   4   6   4   1
  1   5   10  10   5   1
```

Each number is the sum of the two numbers above it, except for the edges which are all 1.

a Copy and complete Pascal's triangle to the 10th row.

b i Find the total for each row.

ii Describe the rule for the sequence of totals.

c A sequence of diagonal numbers from Pascal's triangle is highlighted.
1, 3, 6, 10, …

i What is the name for the numbers in this sequence?

ii Find the nth term of the sequence.

3 The table shows the number of people infected by a virus over a four-day period.

Day	1	2	3	4
Number of people infected	8	13	18	23

The infection rate is constant.

a How many people will be infected on day 5?

b How many people will be infected on the nth day?

c There are 126 people.

How long will it be before everyone is infected?

4 The table shows the monthly population of rabbits.

Month	1	2	3
Number of rabbits	9	19	33

The population keeps growing at the same rate and no rabbits die.

a How many rabbits will there be at the end of the year?

b Why is the sequence not likely to reflect the real number of rabbits?

5 The number of hits on a website each day are shown.

Day	1	2	3
Number of hits	13	27	65

The number of hits continues to grow at the same rate.

How many hits will there be on day 20?

6 This sequence of shapes is made from square tiles.

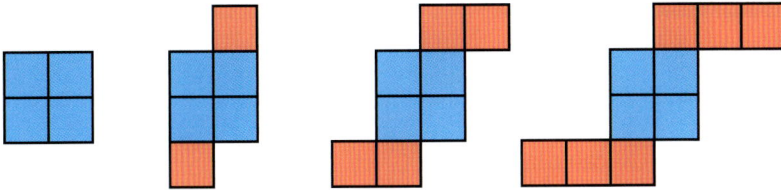

a Write down the number of tiles in each shape as a sequence.

b How many tiles are needed for the fifth shape?

c Complete this function machine for calculating the number of tiles used to make any shape in the pattern:

input $(n) \rightarrow$ ⬡ $\rightarrow$ ⬡ $\rightarrow$ output

d Use your function machine to find the number of tiles needed for the 20th, 25th and nth shape.

7 Tamsyn gets 28 days holiday every year.

She gets an additional half day for each overnight survey.

a How much holiday will she get in 1 year if she does b overnight surveys? Write a function for calculating how much holiday she will get if she does b overnight surveys in a year.

b Tamsyn did 16 overnight surveys last year.
How much holiday did she get?

19 Surds

For more resources relating to this chapter, visit GCSE Mathematics Online.

In this chapter you will learn how to ...

- calculate exactly with surds.
- simplify expressions containing surds.
- manipulate surds.

Using mathematics: real-life applications

Surds are only really used when you are doing mathematical calculations that require exact answers. Surds cannot really be used for practical purposes. You cannot tell a builder to cut a length of steel that is $\sqrt{2}$ metres long, because $\sqrt{2}$ is an irrational number; so you would be more likely to specify an approximate length of 1.41 metres.

"The widths and lengths of A-series rectangular paper were developed using the ratio $1 : \sqrt{2}$ to mathematically construct a rectangle of area $1\,m^2$ (A0 size). In real life paper is cut to exact millimetre sizes, so A0 is $841\,mm \times 1189\,mm$ rather than $841(\sqrt{2})$ which is $1189.353606\ldots mm$." *(Printing works manager)*

Before you start ...

Ch 4	You'll need to be able to write numbers as a product of their factors.	**1** Match the equivalent pairs.	

a 24   **b** 30   **c** 45

A $3^2 \times 5$ B $3 \times 2 \times 5$ C $2^3 \times 3$

KS3	You should remember Pythagoras' theorem.

2 For each triangle, select the correct statement of Pythagoras' theorem.

a

$a^2 = b^2 + c^2$
$b^2 = a^2 + c^2$
$c^2 = a^2 + b^2$
$a^2 + b^2 = c^2$
$a = b^2 + c^2$

b

$z^2 = y^2 - x^2$
$x^2 + z^2 = y^2$
$z^2 + y^2 = x^2$
$x^2 - y^2 = z^2$
$x^2 + y^2 = z^2$

Ch 4, 14	You need know the basic laws of indices.

3 Decide whether each statement is true or false.

a $\dfrac{18x^3}{6x^2} = 3$ **b** $\dfrac{(2y^3)^4}{(4y^6)^2} = y$

Ch 7, 16	You should be able to simplify expressions by collecting like terms.

4 Find the error in each of these answers.

a $5x + 2y - 3x + y = 2x + 2y$ **b** $5x^2 + 2x - 3x^2 = 4x^3$

c $6x - 2y + 5 + y - 2x - 7 = 4x + y - 2$

Assess your starting point using the Launchpad

STEP 1

1 A square has an area of $13\,\text{cm}^2$.

  a What is the length of each side to two decimal places?

  b What is the exact length of each side?

  c Square the values you gave in **a** and **b** and give reasons for your results.

2 How could you construct a line segment of each of these lengths?

  a $\sqrt{25}$ **b** $\sqrt{10}$

GO TO
Section 1:
Approximate and exact values

STEP 2

3 Simplify the following without using a calculator.

  a $\sqrt{3} \times \sqrt{3}$ **b** $\sqrt{\dfrac{32}{2}}$ **c** $\sqrt{4} \times \sqrt{3}$

  d $\sqrt{3} + 2\sqrt{3}$ **e** $\sqrt{12} - \sqrt{3}$

4 Write each expression with a whole number denominator.

  a $\dfrac{2}{\sqrt{5}}$ **b** $\dfrac{5}{2\sqrt{3}}$

GO TO
Section 2:
Manipulating surds
Section 3:
Working with surds

GO TO
Chapter review

Section 1: Approximate and exact values

In mathematics you often have to find the square root of a number that is not itself a perfect square.

For example, you may need to work with **irrational numbers** such as $\sqrt{2}$, $\sqrt{5}$ and $\sqrt{11}$. These are all **surds**.

A surd can only be expressed as an exact value using the root sign ($\sqrt{}$).

The expressions $\sqrt{12}$, $\sqrt{3}$ and $\sqrt[3]{7}$ are all surds. Expressions such as $\sqrt{81}$, $\sqrt{125}$ and $\sqrt[4]{1296}$ are not surds because they have **rational** solutions: $\sqrt{81} = 9$, $\sqrt[3]{125} = 5$ and $\sqrt[4]{1296} = 6$.

The expression $\sqrt[3]{7}$ means the cube root of 7. This is not the same as $3\sqrt{7}$, which means $3 \times \sqrt{7}$.

Key vocabulary

irrational number: a number that cannot be written in the form of $\frac{a}{b}$ or as a terminating or repeating decimal

surd: if $\sqrt[n]{a}$ is an irrational number, then $\sqrt[n]{a}$ is called a surd

rational number: a number that can be expressed in the form of $\frac{a}{b}$ (or as its equivalent as a terminating or repeating decimal)

Find answers at: cambridge.org/ukschools/gcsemaths-studentbookanswers

Approximate values

Approximate values of surds are useful in many situations.

For example, if you want to know the length of a diagonal path across a rectangular 12 m by 7 m field you can use Pythagoras' theorem and rounding to work out that the path is approximately 13.89 m in length.

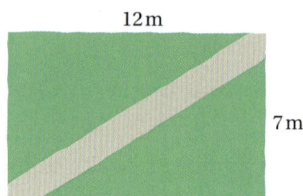

$$h^2 = 12^2 + 7^2$$
$$h^2 = 193$$
$$h = \sqrt{193} \approx 13.89$$

EXERCISE 19A

1 Between which two values does $\sqrt{8}$ lie? Choose the correct option.

A 1 and 2   B 2 and 3   C 3 and 4   D 4 and 5

2 Use a calculator to find the approximate value of each of the following surds. Give your answers to three decimal places.

  a $\sqrt{7}$ **b** $\sqrt{12}$ **c** $\sqrt{51}$

  d $\sqrt{75}$ **e** $-\sqrt{3}$ **f** $-\sqrt{47}$

3 Use a calculator to find the approximate value of each expression to three decimal places.

  a $2\sqrt{2}$ **b** $3\sqrt{5}$ **c** $-3\sqrt{12}$

  d $10\sqrt{2}$ **e** $4(2\sqrt{3})$ **f** $-3(2\sqrt{18})$

4 Find the approximate value of each expression giving your answers to three decimal places.

  a $\sqrt{2} + \sqrt{3}$ **b** $\sqrt{8} - \sqrt{2}$ **c** $\sqrt{2 + 3}$

  d $\sqrt{8 - 2}$ **e** $2\sqrt{3} + 3\sqrt{5}$ **f** $-2\sqrt{3} + 3\sqrt{5}$

Exact values

Values are left as surds when you need to express an answer precisely.

Exact values of surds are used in many technical calculations, such as determining resultant forces and velocities in physics, margins of error in chemistry and peak-to-peak voltages in electronics.

WORKED EXAMPLE 1

Use Pythagoras' theorem to calculate the following exactly.

a Length AC

b Height EG

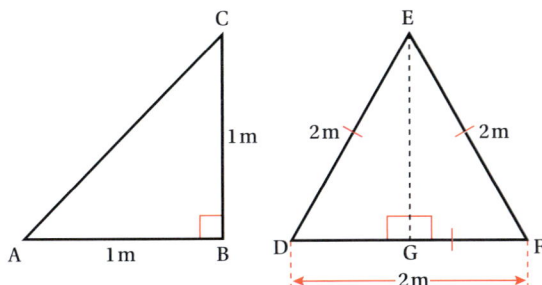

a $(AC)^2 = 1^2 + 1^2$
$(AC)^2 = 1 + 1 = 2$
$AC = \sqrt{2}$

b $(EG)^2 = 2^2 - 1^2$
$(EG)^2 = 4 - 1 = 3$
$EG = \sqrt{3}$

> DG = EF = 1 because EDG and EFG are similar triangles.

Remember to leave the answers in surd form because the question asks for an exact calculation.

Tip

When a question asks for an answer in exact form it means you should leave any surds in root form. Do not use approximate values in either the calculations or the answer.

EXERCISE 19B

1 Find the exact length of a side of a square with area:

a $14\,\text{cm}^2$ **b** $20\,\text{m}^2$ **c** $17\,\text{cm}^2$

2 The area of a square of side a cm is $60\,\text{cm}^2$. Which expression gives the exact length of the diagonal of the square?

A $2a^2$ B $2a$ C $\sqrt{2a^2}$ D $\sqrt{60 - a^2}$

3 What is the exact perimeter of a square of area $40\,\text{cm}^2$? Choose the correct option.

A $4\sqrt{40}$ B 25.298 C $10\,\text{cm}$ D $\sqrt{40}$

4 What is the exact circumference of a coin with a radius of $\sqrt{3}\,\text{cm}$?

5 Find the exact value of $\left(\dfrac{9}{\sqrt{3}}\right)^2$.

6 Two identical square mosaic tiles have a combined area of $14\,\text{cm}^2$.

What is the exact length of the sides of each square?

7 The area of a square plot of land is $50\,\text{m}^2$.

a What is the exact length of each side of the plot?

b What is the exact diagonal distance across the plot?

Tip

Keeping a number in surd form until you get to your final answer means that you don't carry through any approximation or rounding errors that could affect the final answer. This is important for the very small tolerances permitted in structural engineering and other fields.

8 Nico makes square plates of platinum to use in pieces of jewellery.

Each square has a diagonal of 4 cm.

a Find the exact length of each side of such a square.

b Use the exact length to calculate the exact area of the squares.

c Give the length of the sides to:

  i 2 dp   **ii** 3 dp   **iii** 4 dp

d Calculate the area of each square using the approximate values.

e Nico works out the cost of the metal by finding the area of 100 squares and then multiplying this amount by £1245.

Use the exact area as well as the three approximate areas you found to show how the four different values for the area might affect the price of the metal.

f Which value is most beneficial to Nico when he is calculating a selling price? Why?

Section 2: Manipulating surds

When calculating with exact values using surds, you can treat them a bit like variables in algebra.

You can simplify them and rearrange them so you can add and subtract like surds and multiply and divide easily.

Generally you won't need a calculator to work with exact values of surds.

The general rules for working with square roots apply to surds as well.

If x and y represent **positive** integers then, by definition:

$(\sqrt{x})^2 = x$ For example, $(\sqrt{25})^2 = \sqrt{25} \times \sqrt{25} = 5 \times 5 = 25$.

    Similarly, $(\sqrt{3})^2 = \sqrt{3} \times \sqrt{3} = 3$.

$\sqrt{x^2} = x$ For example, $\sqrt{5^2} = \sqrt{25} = 5$.

$\sqrt{x} \times \sqrt{y} = \sqrt{xy}$ For example $\sqrt{9} \times \sqrt{4} = 3 \times 2 = 6$ and $\sqrt{9 \times 4} = \sqrt{36} = 6$.

$\sqrt{x} \div \sqrt{y} = \sqrt{\dfrac{x}{y}}$ For example, $\sqrt{36} \div \sqrt{9} = 6 \div 3 = 2$ and $\sqrt{\dfrac{36}{9}} = \sqrt{4} = 2$.

> **Tip**
>
> It is common to talk about all expressions containing surds as surds even though technically the expression $2\sqrt{5}$ is the product of a whole number and a surd and $\sqrt{3} + \sqrt{5}$ is the sum of two surds.

> **Tip**
>
> Remember that taking a square root and squaring are inverse operations.

WORKED EXAMPLE 2

Is each statement true or false?

$\sqrt{35} = \sqrt{5} \times \sqrt{7}$ $(\sqrt{49})^2 = 49$ $\sqrt{30} \div \sqrt{6} = 5$ $3\sqrt{3} = \sqrt{9} \times \sqrt{3}$

True   True   False   True

$\sqrt{35} = \sqrt{5 \times 7}$ $(\sqrt{49})^2 = (7)^2 = 49$ $\sqrt{30} \div \sqrt{6} = \sqrt{\dfrac{30}{6}} = \sqrt{5}$ $3\sqrt{3} = 3 \times \sqrt{3}$

     $= \sqrt{5} \times \sqrt{7}$ and $3 = \sqrt{9}$

Simplifying surds

A surd is in its simplest form when the number under the root sign is as small as possible.

This means that it has no factors greater than 1 that are perfect squares.

To simplify a surd, you can use the fact that $\sqrt{xy} = \sqrt{x} \times \sqrt{y}$ and write it as the product of two smaller square roots, one of which is a square number. You can see how to do this in the examples below.

WORKED EXAMPLE 3

Simplify the following surds.

a $\sqrt{27}$ **b** $3\sqrt{32}$ **c** $-2\sqrt{320}$ **d** $2\sqrt{12} \times 4\sqrt{3}$

a Factors of 27: 9×3

$\sqrt{27} = \sqrt{9} \times \sqrt{3}$

$\quad = 3 \times \sqrt{3}$

$\quad = 3\sqrt{3}$

Find the factors of the surd.

Write the surd as a product of two smaller roots.

Take the root of the perfect square.

Write the answer using algebraic conventions.

b Factors of 32: 16×2

$3\sqrt{32} = 3 \times \sqrt{16} \times \sqrt{2}$

$\quad = 3 \times 4 \times \sqrt{2}$

$\quad = 12 \times \sqrt{2}$

$\quad = 12\sqrt{2}$

Find the factors of the surd.

Write the surd as a product of two smaller roots.

Take the root of the perfect square.

Multiply the integers.

Write the answer using algebraic conventions.

c Factors of 320: 16×20

Factors of 20: 5×4

$-2\sqrt{320} = -2 \times \sqrt{16} \times \sqrt{20}$

$\quad = -2 \times 4 \times \sqrt{4} \times \sqrt{5}$

$\quad = -2 \times 4 \times 2 \times \sqrt{5}$

$\quad = -16\sqrt{5}$

Find the factors of the surd.

Write the surd as a product of two smaller roots.

Take the root of 16 and factorise 20.

Take the root of 4.

Multiply the integers and write the answer correctly.

d Only 12 can be factorised: 4×3

$2\sqrt{12} \times 4\sqrt{3} = 2 \times \sqrt{4} \times \sqrt{3} \times 4\sqrt{3}$

$\quad = 2 \times 2 \times \sqrt{3} \times 4\sqrt{3}$

$\quad = 16 \times \sqrt{3} \times \sqrt{3}$

$\quad = 16 \times 3$

$\quad = 48$

Find the factors of the surd.

Write $\sqrt{12}$ as product of two smaller roots.

Simplify.

Multiply integers.

Square the surds.

In the examples above the surds can be simplified because the factors that were used included square numbers.

If you choose factors that are not square numbers, you have to do far more work to get to a simplified answer.

For example, $\sqrt{320}$ could be factorised as $\sqrt{8} \times \sqrt{40}$ instead of $\sqrt{16} \times \sqrt{20}$. In that case, you cannot find the roots as both $\sqrt{8}$ and $\sqrt{40}$ are themselves surds and you have to factorise them further before you can simplify the surd.

Tip

Check whether the number in the root sign can be divided by a perfect square (4, 16, 25, 36, 49, 64, 81, 100, …) and if so, use the largest possible square number as one of the factors to make simplification easier.

Find answers at: cambridge.org/ukschools/gcsemaths-studentbookanswers

EXERCISE 19C

1 What is the simplest form of each surd? Choose the correct answer from the given options.

a $\sqrt{28}$

    A $4\sqrt{7}$ B $\sqrt{4} \times \sqrt{7}$ C $2\sqrt{7}$ D $2\sqrt{14}$ E $28\sqrt{1}$

b $\sqrt{12}$

    A $12\sqrt{1}$ B $2\sqrt{3}$ C $3\sqrt{4}$ D $4\sqrt{3}$ E $\sqrt{3} \times \sqrt{4}$

c $\sqrt{72}$

    A $2\sqrt{36}$ B $6\sqrt{2}$ C $\sqrt{36} \times \sqrt{2}$ D $\sqrt{8} \times \sqrt{9}$ E $3\sqrt{8}$

d $5\sqrt{12}$

    A $5\sqrt{4} \times \sqrt{3}$ B $15\sqrt{4}$ C $10\sqrt{3}$ D $3\sqrt{10}$ E $7\sqrt{3}$

e $\sqrt{320}$

    A $\sqrt{16} \times \sqrt{20}$ B $\sqrt{16} \times 4 \times 5$ C $4\sqrt{20}$ D $32\sqrt{10}$ E $8\sqrt{5}$

2 Simplify:

a $\sqrt{8}$ **b** $\sqrt{24}$ **c** $\sqrt{28}$ **d** $\sqrt{45}$

e $\sqrt{54}$ **f** $\sqrt{68}$ **g** $\sqrt{60}$ **h** $\sqrt{126}$

i $\sqrt{90}$ **j** $\sqrt{200}$ **k** $\sqrt{117}$ **l** $\sqrt{243}$

3 Write down how you can tell at a glance that the following surds are already in their simplest form:

    $\sqrt{2}$ $\sqrt{11}$ $\sqrt{13}$ $\sqrt{53}$ $\sqrt{83}$ $\sqrt{101}$

> **Tip**
>
> An entire surd has no rational factors or terms, only a number that is not a perfect square under the root sign. For example $\sqrt{18}$ is an entire surd, but $3\sqrt{2}$ is not. Apply the inverse procedure to get back to an entire surd when you have a whole number and a surd in the expression.

4 Write each surd in its simplest form.

a $3\sqrt{8}$ **b** $-4\sqrt{24}$ **c** $5\sqrt{20}$

d $-5\sqrt{60}$ **e** $3\sqrt{56}$ **f** $-2\sqrt{128}$

g $-4\sqrt{45}$ **h** $-3\sqrt{68}$ **i** $7\sqrt{108}$

5 a Copy and complete the following.

i $2\sqrt{7} = 2 \times \sqrt{7}$	**ii** $-3\sqrt{6} = -3 \times \sqrt{6}$
$= \sqrt{\Box} \times \sqrt{7}$	$= -\sqrt{\Box} \times \sqrt{6}$
$= \sqrt{\Box} \times 7$	$= -\sqrt{\Box} \times 6$
$= \sqrt{\Box}$	$= -\sqrt{\Box}$

  b Give a reason why you leave the minus sign outside the root in part **ii**.

6 Rewrite each of the following in the form $\sqrt{n}$.

a $3\sqrt{2}$ **b** $4\sqrt{3}$ **c** $3\sqrt{6}$

d $4\sqrt{11}$ **e** $-2\sqrt{7}$ **f** $-3\sqrt{3}$

g $-4\sqrt{17}$ **h** $-2\sqrt{11}$ **i** $12\sqrt{3}$

7 **a** Write down what you would need to do to be able to arrange the sets of surds, given below, in order from smallest to largest (without using your calculator).

b Apply your method and arrange the surds in order.

c Compare your answers and your method with a partner. Could you work more efficiently? If so, how?

i $4\sqrt{2}$	$2\sqrt{3}$	$3\sqrt{3}$	**ii** $8\sqrt{3}$	$6\sqrt{7}$	$5\sqrt{7}$
iii $3\sqrt{7}$	$2\sqrt{10}$	$4\sqrt{3}$	**iv** $5\sqrt{6}$	$8\sqrt{2}$	$6\sqrt{3}$

Adding and subtracting surds

You can use algebra to simplify expressions containing surds.

For example, $3\sqrt{5} + 4\sqrt{5}$ can be added because $\sqrt{5}$ is common to both terms.

By factorising, you can take out a common factor of $\sqrt{5}$ to get

$\sqrt{5}\,(3 + 4) = \sqrt{5}\,(7) = 7\sqrt{5}$.

An expression such as $2\sqrt{5} + 4\sqrt{3}$ cannot be added because it has no surds that are common factors. (You can also think about $\sqrt{5}$ and $\sqrt{3}$ as unlike surds.)

As with like terms in algebra, you can only add or subtract terms which have the same surds in them.

Before you add or subtract you may need to express surds in their simplest terms.

WORKED EXAMPLE 4

Simplify this expression: $5\sqrt{2} - 2\sqrt{8}$

$= 5\sqrt{2} - 2 \times \sqrt{4} \times \sqrt{2}$ Use the rule $\sqrt{a} \times \sqrt{b} = \sqrt{ab}$.

$= 5\sqrt{2} - 2 \times 2 \times \sqrt{2}$

$= 5\sqrt{2} - 4\sqrt{2}$

$= \sqrt{2}$

WORK IT OUT 19.1

A teacher gave her class some multiple choice questions for homework. One student's answers are given below. Three of the answers are correct and two are incorrect.

What errors do you think this student made to get the incorrect answers? What are the correct answers for these questions?

Circle the correct answers.

1 $8\sqrt{4} - \sqrt{4} =$

   A $8\sqrt{4}$ B $\boxed{7\sqrt{4}}$ ✓   C 8

   D 0 E 7

2 $7\sqrt{3} + 3\sqrt{2} + 5\sqrt{3} =$

   A $15\sqrt{5}$ B $15\sqrt{8}$ C $12\sqrt{3} + 3\sqrt{2}$

   D $\boxed{12\sqrt{6} + 3\sqrt{2}}$ ✗   E $15\sqrt{3}$

3 $5\sqrt{2} - 2\sqrt{8} =$

   A 1 B 0 C $-3\sqrt{2}$

   D $\boxed{\sqrt{2}}$ ✓   E $3\sqrt{-6}$

4 $4\sqrt{5} - \sqrt{2} + 6\sqrt{5} - 3\sqrt{2} =$

   A $10\sqrt{5} - 3$ B $6\sqrt{3}$ C $\boxed{10\sqrt{5} - 4\sqrt{2}}$ ✓

   D $10\sqrt{10} - 4\sqrt{2}$ E $2\sqrt{5} - 2\sqrt{2}$

5 $\sqrt{27} + 2\sqrt{5} + \sqrt{20} - 2\sqrt{3} =$

   A $\boxed{2\sqrt{8} + \sqrt{47}}$ ✗   B $\sqrt{3} + 4\sqrt{5}$ C $4\sqrt{3} + \sqrt{5}$

   D $5\sqrt{3} - 4\sqrt{5}$ E $-\sqrt{3} + 4\sqrt{5}$

EXERCISE 19D

1 Provide examples using square numbers to show that when x and y are positive integers:

  a $\sqrt{x} + \sqrt{y} \neq \sqrt{x+y}$ **b** $\sqrt{x} - \sqrt{y} \neq \sqrt{x-y}$

2 What is $3\sqrt{8} - 2\sqrt{50} + \sqrt{7}$?
Choose your answer from the following options.

  A $\sqrt{65}$ B $\sqrt{7} - 4$ C $\sqrt{7} - 4\sqrt{2}$ D $4\sqrt{2} + \sqrt{7}$

3 Simplify:

  a $2\sqrt{4} + 3\sqrt{7} + 4\sqrt{4}$ **b** $\sqrt{2} + 3\sqrt{2} + 2\sqrt{5}$

  c $2\sqrt{5} + 3\sqrt{3} + 2\sqrt{5} + 5\sqrt{3}$ **d** $9\sqrt{2} + 2\sqrt{3} - 7\sqrt{2} + 3\sqrt{3}$

  e $4\sqrt{5} - 2\sqrt{2} + 2\sqrt{5} + 5\sqrt{2}$ **f** $4\sqrt{2} + 4\sqrt{3} - 3\sqrt{2} - 6\sqrt{3}$

4 Simplify:

  a $\sqrt{2} + \sqrt{8}$ **b** $\sqrt{28} - \sqrt{7}$ **c** $3\sqrt{6} + \sqrt{24}$

  d $3\sqrt{5} - \sqrt{20}$ **e** $5\sqrt{63} - 7\sqrt{28}$ **f** $4\sqrt{45} - 2\sqrt{20}$

5 Simplify:

a $\sqrt{75} + \sqrt{27} - 2\sqrt{3}$ **b** $-4\sqrt{11} + 8\sqrt{10} - 2\sqrt{11} - 2\sqrt{10}$

c $2\sqrt{75} - \sqrt{45} + 2\sqrt{20}$ **d** $2\sqrt{12} - \sqrt{20} - \sqrt{27} + 2\sqrt{45}$

e $3\sqrt{54} + 4\sqrt{24} - 2\sqrt{96}$ **f** $6\sqrt{50} - 2\sqrt{24} + 4\sqrt{32} + \sqrt{54}$

6 A rectangular component has side dimensions $(3 - \sqrt{3})$ cm by $(3 + \sqrt{48})$ cm.

Calculate the exact perimeter of the component.

Multiplying surds

You've already applied the rules $\sqrt{x} \times \sqrt{y} = \sqrt{xy}$ and $\sqrt{x} \times \sqrt{x} = x$ to simplify surds.

Some expressions will contain both surds and brackets.

To simplify these, you apply the basic rules you know from algebra.

WORKED EXAMPLE 5

Simplify.

a $\sqrt{5} \times \sqrt{7} = \sqrt{35}$

Use the rule $\sqrt{a} \times \sqrt{b} = \sqrt{ab}$.

b $2\sqrt{7} \times 3\sqrt{3} = 2 \times 3 \times \sqrt{7} \times \sqrt{3}$
$= 6\sqrt{21}$

Multiplication can be done in any order.

c $\sqrt{2}(4 - 3\sqrt{2}) = \sqrt{2} \times 4 - \sqrt{2} \times 3\sqrt{2}$
$= 4\sqrt{2} - 3 \times 2$
$= 4\sqrt{2} - 6$

Multiply both terms in the brackets by $\sqrt{2}$ paying attention to the negative sign.

There is now no surd in the second term because $\sqrt{2} \times \sqrt{2} = 2$.

d $(3 + \sqrt{2})(3 - \sqrt{2}) = 3 \times 3 - 3 \times \sqrt{2} + \sqrt{2} \times 3 - \sqrt{2} \times \sqrt{2}$
$= 9 - 3\sqrt{2} + 3\sqrt{2} - 2$
$= 9 - 2$
$= 7$

Use the rules for binomial products.

e $(\sqrt{2} + \sqrt{3})^2 = (\sqrt{2} + \sqrt{3})(\sqrt{2} + \sqrt{3})$
$= \sqrt{2} \times \sqrt{2} + \sqrt{2} \times \sqrt{3} + \sqrt{3} \times \sqrt{2} + \sqrt{3} \times \sqrt{3}$
$= 2 + \sqrt{6} + \sqrt{6} + 3$
$= 5 + 2\sqrt{6}$

Dividing surds

Surds can be divided using the rule $\sqrt{x} \div \sqrt{y} = \sqrt{\dfrac{x}{y}}$

You may need to simplify surds so that you can find common factors and cancel them.

WORKED EXAMPLE 6

Simplify.

a $\sqrt{104} \div \sqrt{13} = \sqrt{\dfrac{104}{13}}$
$= \sqrt{8}$
$= 2\sqrt{2}$

> Apply the rule $\sqrt{x} \div \sqrt{y} = \sqrt{\dfrac{x}{y}}$
> Give your answer in simplest form.

b $\dfrac{3\sqrt{21}}{\sqrt{3}} = 3\sqrt{\dfrac{21}{3}}$
$= 3\sqrt{7}$

> Apply the rule $\sqrt{x} \div \sqrt{y} = \sqrt{\dfrac{x}{y}}$
> Simplify $\sqrt{\dfrac{21}{3}}$

c $\dfrac{6 + 2\sqrt{20}}{2} = \dfrac{6}{2} + \dfrac{2\sqrt{20}}{2}$
$= 3 + \sqrt{20}$
$= 3 + 2\sqrt{5}$

> Remember the rules for dividing fractions.
> Divide both terms by 2.
> Write the surd in simplest form.

Rationalising the denominator

Tip

Look back at Chapter 16 if you need to revise algebraic fractions.

There are many calculations in algebra that are made easier if any surds in a fraction are in the numerator and the denominators are integers.

Removing surds from the denominator of a fraction is called rationalising the denominator and it is done using the same principles as when you make equivalent fractions.

$\dfrac{x}{\sqrt{y}}$ is equivalent to $\dfrac{x}{\sqrt{y}} \times \dfrac{\sqrt{y}}{\sqrt{y}}$ (because $\dfrac{\sqrt{y}}{\sqrt{y}} = 1$).

Multiplying will give you $\dfrac{x\sqrt{y}}{y}$ (because $\sqrt{y} \times \sqrt{y} = y$) and you have removed the surd from the denominator.

WORKED EXAMPLE 7

Rationalise the denominators.

a $\dfrac{5}{\sqrt{7}} = \dfrac{5}{\sqrt{7}} \times \dfrac{\sqrt{7}}{\sqrt{7}} = \dfrac{5\sqrt{7}}{7}$

> Multiply by $\dfrac{\sqrt{7}}{\sqrt{7}}$

b $\dfrac{2\sqrt{5}}{\sqrt{6}} = \dfrac{2\sqrt{5}}{\sqrt{6}} \times \dfrac{\sqrt{6}}{\sqrt{6}}$
$= \dfrac{2\sqrt{30}}{6}$
$= \dfrac{\sqrt{30}}{3}$

> Multiply by $\dfrac{\sqrt{6}}{\sqrt{6}}$
> Multiply.
> Cancel $\dfrac{2}{6} = \dfrac{1}{3}$

EXERCISE 19E

1 Simplify:

a $\sqrt{7} \times \sqrt{3}$ **b** $\sqrt{3} \times \sqrt{5}$ **c** $\sqrt{3} \times \sqrt{12}$

d $2\sqrt{7} \times 3\sqrt{5}$ **e** $-3\sqrt{11} \times 4\sqrt{3}$ **f** $2\sqrt{15} \times 3\sqrt{3}$

g $2\sqrt{13} \times 3\sqrt{13}$ **h** $2\sqrt{6} \times 5\sqrt{3}$ **i** $4\sqrt{2} \times 5\sqrt{3}$

j $\sqrt{27} \times \sqrt{72}$ **k** $\sqrt{48} \times \sqrt{45}$ **l** $2\sqrt{20} \times 3\sqrt{24}$

2 Simplify:

a $\sqrt{14} \div \sqrt{2}$ **b** $\sqrt{26} \div \sqrt{13}$ **c** $\dfrac{\sqrt{5}}{\sqrt{10}}$

d $\dfrac{\sqrt{2}}{\sqrt{20}}$ **e** $\dfrac{\sqrt{45}}{\sqrt{5}}$ **f** $\dfrac{3\sqrt{7}}{3}$

g $\dfrac{5\sqrt{6}}{10}$ **h** $4\sqrt{\dfrac{60}{5}}$ **i** $\dfrac{6\sqrt{22}}{\sqrt{2}}$

j $\dfrac{12\sqrt{12}}{4\sqrt{3}}$ **k** $\dfrac{-3\sqrt{24}}{\sqrt{6}}$ **l** $\dfrac{-2\sqrt{27}}{\sqrt{12}}$

> **Tip**
>
> Simplify the surds first so that you work with smaller numbers.

3 How would you write $\dfrac{3\sqrt{5}}{\sqrt{6}}$ with a rational denominator? Choose the correct answer below.

A $6(3\sqrt{5})$ B $\dfrac{3\sqrt{30}}{3}$ C $\dfrac{\sqrt{30}}{3}$ D $\dfrac{\sqrt{30}}{2}$

4 Which of the following expressions is equivalent to $\dfrac{2\sqrt{14}}{21}$?

A $\dfrac{2\sqrt{6}}{21}$ B $\dfrac{2\sqrt{2}}{3\sqrt{7}}$ C $\dfrac{14\sqrt{2}}{3}$ D $\dfrac{2\sqrt{14}}{3}$

5 Simplify fully:

a $\dfrac{3\sqrt{6} \times 4\sqrt{3}}{4}$ **b** $\dfrac{2\sqrt{5} \times 4\sqrt{6}}{\sqrt{10}}$ **c** $\dfrac{3\sqrt{5} \times 2\sqrt{8}}{6\sqrt{20}}$

d $\dfrac{\sqrt{3} \times \sqrt{15}}{3\sqrt{5}}$ **e** $\dfrac{5\sqrt{6} \times -2\sqrt{5}}{2\sqrt{15}}$ **f** $\dfrac{-\sqrt{12} \times \sqrt{27}}{2\sqrt{6} \times 2\sqrt{2}}$

6 Expand and simplify:

a $\sqrt{5}(\sqrt{3} + 2)$ **b** $2\sqrt{3}(5 - \sqrt{3})$

c $(\sqrt{2} + 1)(\sqrt{6} - 2\sqrt{3})$ **d** $(2\sqrt{5} + \sqrt{7})^2$

e $(\sqrt{2} + 3)(\sqrt{3} + 5)$ **f** $(2 - \sqrt{5})(\sqrt{5} - 1)$

g $(4\sqrt{3} - \sqrt{2})(4\sqrt{3} + \sqrt{2})$ **h** $(\sqrt{7} + \sqrt{2})^2$

i $(\sqrt{3} - \sqrt{5})^2$

7 Express each of the following in simplest form with a rational denominator.

a $\dfrac{5}{\sqrt{3}}$ **b** $\dfrac{1}{\sqrt{5}}$ **c** $\dfrac{-2}{\sqrt{3}}$

d $\dfrac{\sqrt{2}}{\sqrt{3}}$ **e** $4\sqrt{\dfrac{3}{2}}$ **f** $\dfrac{-3}{4\sqrt{7}}$

g $\dfrac{2 + \sqrt{3}}{2\sqrt{3}}$ **h** $\dfrac{2 + \sqrt{5}}{\sqrt{5}}$ **i** $\dfrac{\sqrt{10} - \sqrt{5}}{5\sqrt{10}}$

Section 3 Working with surds

Unless you are asked to give an approximate value, you should leave your answers in exact form.

In maths you generally learn new skills and concepts and then you have to use them to solve problems.

In the case of surds, the problems will generally be similar to those that you have already worked with in algebra or geometry. The only real difference will be that the values are given in surd form.

Problem-solving framework

Steps for solving problems	What you would do for this example
Step 1: Read the question carefully to work out what you have to do.	Find length DE in this figure. Give the answer in the simplest possible exact form.
Step 2 Write down any information that might be useful.	DE = BD − BE BD and BE are sides of right-angled triangles.
Step 3: Decide what method you'll use.	The triangles are right-angled, so use Pythagoras. Find the lengths BE and BD and then subtract.
Step 4: Set out your working clearly.	$BE = \sqrt{14^2 - 13^2}$ Pythagoras $\quad = \sqrt{196 - 169}$ $\quad = \sqrt{27}$ $\quad = 3\sqrt{3}$ $BD = \sqrt{10^2 - 5^2}$ Pythagoras $\quad = \sqrt{100 - 25}$ $\quad = \sqrt{75}$ $\quad = 5\sqrt{3}$ $BD - BE = 5\sqrt{3} - 3\sqrt{3} = 2\sqrt{3}\,\text{cm}$
Step 5: Write an answer and check that it makes sense.	$DE = 2\sqrt{3}\,\text{cm}$

EXERCISE 19F

1 Find the exact area and perimeter of each shape.

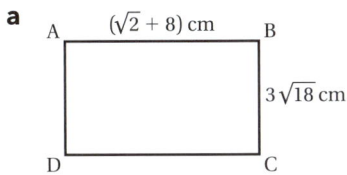

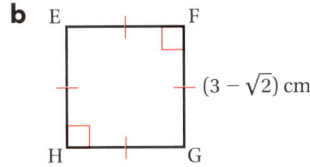

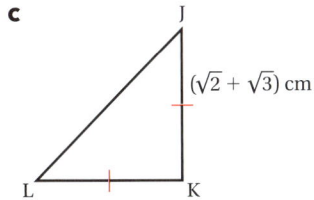

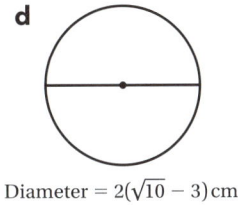

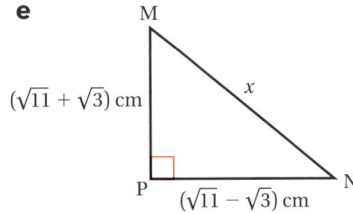

a

A $(\sqrt{2} + 8)$ cm   B

$3\sqrt{18}$ cm

D   C

b

E   F

$(3 - \sqrt{2})$ cm

H   G

c

J

$(\sqrt{2} + \sqrt{3})$ cm

L   K

d

Diameter $= 2(\sqrt{10} - 3)$ cm

e

M

$(\sqrt{11} + \sqrt{3})$ cm x

P   N
$(\sqrt{11} - \sqrt{3})$ cm

2 Find the area of a square of side $(\sqrt{7} + \sqrt{2})$ cm. Choose from the options below.

A $9 - 2\sqrt{14}$ B $9 + 2\sqrt{14}$ C $11\sqrt{14}$ D 9

3 Find the exact area of a parallelogram of height $4\sqrt{6}$ cm and base $\sqrt{2} - \sqrt{3}$. Choose from the options below.

A $4\sqrt{8} - 12\sqrt{2}$ B $8\sqrt{3} - 12\sqrt{2}$ C $8\sqrt{6} - 12\sqrt{2}$ D $4\sqrt{8} - 4\sqrt{18}$

4 Calculate the exact area of a rectangle ABCD with sides of $(6 + \sqrt{5})$ cm and $(6 - \sqrt{5})$ cm.

5 If the area of the front of a circular disk is 12π cm², what is its exact radius?

6 The chart shows the relationship of paper sizes in A-series sheets of paper. The ratio of sides of each sheet is $1 : \sqrt{2}$.

   a Calculate the length of the sides marked x, y and z, giving your answers to the nearest whole millimetre.

   b Size A0 paper is a rectangle of area $1\,\text{m}^2$.

     i Express the area in cm².

     ii Use the ratio of sides $1 : \sqrt{2}$ to work out the length of the diagonal of a sheet of A0 paper given that the width is 841 mm.

   c For any sheet of A-series paper with shorter side of width x, express the length of the diagonal (z) in terms of x.

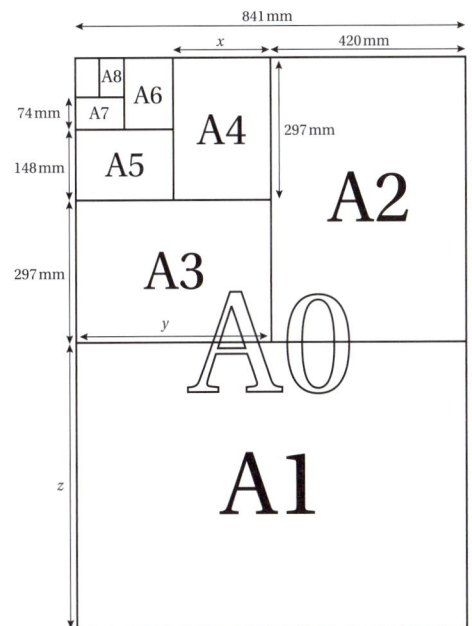

841 mm

x 420 mm

A8   A6

74 mm   A7

A4   297 mm

148 mm   A5

A2

297 mm   A3

A0

y

A1

z

7 A metal cube $(2\sqrt{3} + 4\sqrt{5})$ cm high is to be coated with a rust inhibitor. Calculate the exact area of the surface to be painted.

Determine $\sin A$, leaving your answer in surd form.

8 Given that ABC is a right-angled isosceles triangle with AB = BC, work out $\sin A$, leaving your answer in surd form.

9 If x is a positive integer, simplify $\sqrt{x^3 + 2x^2 + x}$.

10 A square has sides of length $3\sqrt{8}$. Find:

a the area of the square.   **b** the length of a diagonal.

11 Find the exact perimeter of a square of area $150 \, \text{cm}^2$.

Checklist of learning and understanding

Surds are exact values

- Surds can only be expressed exactly using the root sign. Using a calculator to get a decimal value for a surd gives an approximate value.

Surds can be simplified

- Surds can sometimes be simplified by writing them as factors and taking the roots of any factors that are perfect squares.

Adding and subtracting surds

- Expressions containing surds can be simplified by adding or subtracting common factors.

Multiplying and dividing surds

- Surds can be multiplied and divided using the rules:
  - $(\sqrt{x}^2 = x)$
  - $\sqrt{x^2} = x$
  - $\sqrt{x} \times \sqrt{y} = \sqrt{xy}$
  - $\sqrt{x} \div \sqrt{y} = \sqrt{\dfrac{x}{y}}$
- When expanding expressions with brackets, apply the rules of algebra.

Rationalising the denominator

- Fractions with a surd in the denominator can be rewritten as equivalent fractions with an integer denominator.

For additional questions on the topics in this chapter, visit GCSE Mathematics Online.

Chapter review

Two sets of answers to an exercise involving simplifying surds are given below. Do the following for each question:

a Decide whether either of the answers is correct. List the answers that you think are correct.

b If neither answer is correct find the correct answer, showing your working.

Question	Answer A	Answer B
1 $\sqrt{18}$	$\sqrt{6} \times \sqrt{3}$	$3\sqrt{2}$
2 $\sqrt{45}$	$3\sqrt{5}$	$5\sqrt{3}$
3 $3\sqrt{5} + \sqrt{3} + \sqrt{5} - 2\sqrt{3}$	$3\sqrt{5} - \sqrt{3}$	7.2122
4 $\sqrt{14} + \sqrt{8}$	$\sqrt{22}$	$\sqrt{112}$
5 $\sqrt{5} \times \sqrt{5} \times \sqrt{5} \times \sqrt{5}$	25	$4\sqrt{5}$
6 $\sqrt{3} \times \sqrt{3} \times \sqrt{3} + \sqrt{3}$	$4\sqrt{3}$	$3\sqrt{3}$
7 $\dfrac{6\sqrt{35}}{2\sqrt{5}}$	$3\sqrt{30}$	$3\sqrt{7}$
8 $\dfrac{1 + \sqrt{5}}{\sqrt{5}}$	2	$\dfrac{2}{\sqrt{5}} + 1$
9 $\dfrac{10 + 5\sqrt{7}}{5}$	$\sqrt{7} + 2$	$2 + 5\sqrt{7}$

10 **a** Show that $\sqrt{75}$ can be written as $5\sqrt{3}$ *(1 mark)*

  b Rationalise the denominator and simplify $\dfrac{6}{\sqrt{3}}$ *(2 marks)*

  c Work out the mean of the three numbers $\sqrt{75}$, $\sqrt{75}$ and $\dfrac{6}{\sqrt{3}}$

  Give your answer in the form $b\sqrt{3}$ where b is an integer. *(2 marks)*

  © AQA 2013

11 The values $\sqrt[3]{30}$, $\sqrt{20}$, $\sqrt[4]{18}$, $\sqrt[3]{-30}$ and $\sqrt[4]{10}$ are to be arranged in ascending order. Which is the correct ordering?

  A $\sqrt[3]{-30}, \sqrt[4]{10}, \sqrt[4]{18}, \sqrt{20}, \sqrt[3]{30}$ B $\sqrt[3]{-30}, \sqrt[4]{10}, \sqrt[4]{18}, \sqrt[3]{30}, \sqrt{620}$

  C $\sqrt{20}, \sqrt[3]{30}, \sqrt[4]{18}, \sqrt[4]{10}, \sqrt[3]{-30}$ D $\sqrt[4]{10}, \sqrt[4]{18}, \sqrt[3]{-30}, \sqrt[3]{30}, \sqrt{20}$

20 Basic probability

Using mathematics: real-life applications

Software developers use probability when they build applications. Apps such as speech recognition, speech synthesis, keyword spotting and predictive text all rely on probability. In speech recognition, for example, the software analyses the audio input and finds the most likely stream of text based on the audio. So, when you say a name into your phone instead of dialling, the software chooses the most likely name from your contact list.

"Knowing how to use and apply probability was one of the requirements when I was interviewed for this programming job."

(Computer programmer)

Before you start ...

Ch 5, 6, 13	You need to know how to calculate with fractions, decimals and percentages	**1** Choose the correct answer without doing the calculations.	
		a 0.13×0.24 A 0.312 B 0.0312 C 0.00312	
		b $0.82 + 0.18$ A 0.1 B 100 C 1	
		c 0.08% of 50 A 4 B 0.4 C 0.04	
Ch 12	You need to be able to round decimals to 1, 2 or 3 places.	**2** Which answers are rounded incorrectly? Why?	
		a $0.705\,882\,352 \approx 0.706$ **b** $0.316\,666\,6 \approx 0.316$	
		c $0.989\,087 \approx 1.09$	
Ch 5, 6, 13	You should be able to find equivalent fractions, decimals and percentages.	**3** Match the equivalent pairs.	
		$\frac{39}{52}$ 0.25 0.077 $\frac{13}{52}$ 50% $\frac{4}{52}$ $\frac{26}{52}$ 75%	

> **Tip**
>
> Make sure you know how to enter common fractions such as $\frac{17}{23}$ into your calculator and how to convert between fractions and decimals.

Assess your starting point using the Launchpad

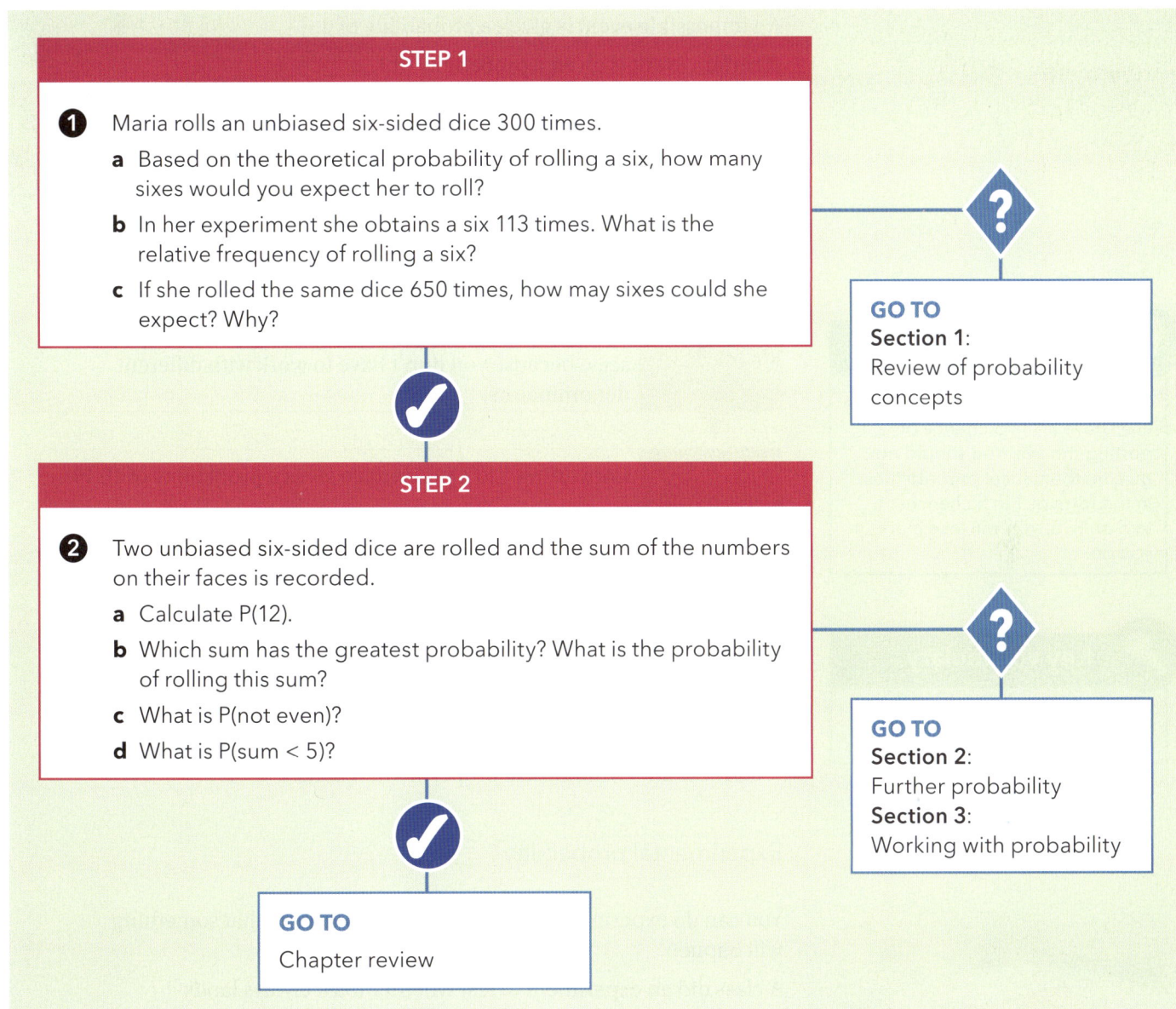

STEP 1

1 Maria rolls an unbiased six-sided dice 300 times.

a Based on the theoretical probability of rolling a six, how many sixes would you expect her to roll?

b In her experiment she obtains a six 113 times. What is the relative frequency of rolling a six?

c If she rolled the same dice 650 times, how may sixes could she expect? Why?

GO TO
Section 1:
Review of probability concepts

STEP 2

2 Two unbiased six-sided dice are rolled and the sum of the numbers on their faces is recorded.

a Calculate P(12).

b Which sum has the greatest probability? What is the probability of rolling this sum?

c What is P(not even)?

d What is P(sum < 5)?

GO TO
Section 2:
Further probability
Section 3:
Working with probability

GO TO
Chapter review

Section 1: Review of probability concepts

Expressions of probability

Each of the following statements indicates the likelihood or probability of an **event** happening.

- I definitely didn't pass that test because I couldn't answer a single question.
- It is unlikely to rain today.
- I'm sure Sarah will be elected captain. Everyone says they will vote for her.

Key vocabulary

event: the thing to which you are trying to give a probability

The likelihood, or chance, of an event can be given more mathematically using the probability scale.

An impossible event is given a probability of 0.

A certain event is given a probability of 1.

All other events are given a probability between 0 and 1.

Probabilities can be expressed as fractions, decimals or percentages.

Fraction	The probability of rolling a six on a dice is $\frac{1}{6}$.
Decimal	Converting $\frac{1}{6}$ to a decimal gives a probability of 0.167 (3 dp). You can quickly compare decimal values on the probability scale because you don't have to work with different denominators.
Percentage	Converting $\frac{1}{6}$ to a percentage gives a probability of 16.7%. Percentages are often used in media reports about probability. For example, 'a probability of $\frac{28}{37}$' is not as clear or easy to read as 'a 76% chance'.

There are two ways of assigning probability:

- Experimental probability – where you do an experiment, observe the **outcome** and record the results.
- Theoretical probability – where you calculate a probability based on fairness and symmetrical properties of results.

Experimental probability

You can do experiments to work out the probability that something will happen.

A class did an experiment to test whether toast always lands butter-side down.

They got 30 volunteers to throw toast into the air and they recorded how many times it landed butter-side facing down.

16 out of 30 times, the toast landed butter-side facing down.

There are two possible outcomes for each trial: butter-side down or butter-side up.

The relative frequency of an outcome is the frequency of the outcome divided by the number of trials.

The relative frequency of butter-side down is $\frac{16}{30} \approx 0.533$

The relative frequency of butter-side up is $\frac{14}{30} \approx 0.467$

This means that the experimental probability of toast landing butter-side down is only slightly higher than it landing butter-side up.

Tip

In real life people often say things like I have a 1 in 5 chance of getting the job. You should not give mathematical probabilities in the form of 1 in 5 chances, 1 to 5 or 1 : 5; you will lose marks if you do.

Key vocabulary

outcome: a single result of an experiment

Tip

In probability questions, a normal (unbiased) dice is a six-sided dice numbered from 1 to 6. Unless specifically stated, assume this is the case.

When you are working with probability problems assume the equipment is fair and unbiased unless you are told differently.

EXERCISE 20A

1 Find the experimental probability of:

a Getting heads with one toss of a coin if the coin landed heads up 96 times in 180 trials.

b Rolling a 6 with a dice. The dice was rolled 300 times, and the frequency of rolling a 6 was 54.

c Getting an even number on a dice when an odd number was rolled 33 times in 60 trials.

2 Two dice were rolled 80 times and the total shown on the faces was recorded.

This table gives the frequency of each outcome.

Total	2	3	4	5	6	7	8	9	10	11	12
Frequency	5	2	8	6	12	14	11	8	7	3	4

a Calculate the relative frequency of getting a total of 7. Give your answer both as a fraction and a decimal.

From this experiment:

b What is the experimental probability of not getting a total of 7?

c What is the experimental probability of rolling two sixes?

d What is the experimental probability of getting a total less than 6?

3 A market-research company did a survey to find out what brand of shampoo people bought most often. The results are given in the table.

Brand	Frequency	Relative frequency
Silk-e-shine	123	
Get knotted	105	
Goldilocks	83	
Bubbly stuff	89	
Total		

a What was the sample size for the survey?

b Calculate the relative frequency of buying each brand.

c Use the results of this survey to estimate the probability that a person chosen at random buys Silk-e-shine shampoo.

4 Mira calls customers who have had their car serviced to check whether they are happy with the service they received.

She kept this record of what happened for 200 calls made one month.

Result	Frequency
spoke to customer	122
phone not answered	44
left message on answering machine	22
phone engaged or out of order	10
wrong number	2

a Calculate the relative frequency of each event as a decimal fraction.

b State whether it is highly likely, likely or unlikely that the following events will occur when Mira makes a call:

i The call will be answered by the customer.

ii The call will be answered by a machine.

iii She will dial the wrong number.

5 The results of a student council election are shown below.

A total of 4000 students voted in the election.

Candidate	Votes
Alexia Adams	1445
Zunaid Darcey	1593
Amitab Smith	483
Nicky Chin	

a Work out how many votes Nicky Chin got.

b What is the probability that a randomly selected student voted for Zunaid Darcey?

c What is the probability that a randomly selected student did not vote for Alexia Adams?

Theoretical probability

When you toss a fair coin there are two possible outcomes: head and tails.

You have the same chance of getting heads as you have of getting tails so the outcomes are **equally likely**.

This does not mean that if you toss a coin six times in a row that you will get three heads and three tails. Although the outcomes are equally likely, they are also **random**.

The more times you toss the coin, the closer you will get to an equal number of heads and tails.

For equally likely outcomes you can calculate the probability using a formula.

Probability of an event $= \dfrac{\text{number of favourable outcomes}}{\text{total number of outcomes}}$

WORKED EXAMPLE 1

A bag of laundry contains 5 blue shirts, 6 red shirts, 7 green shirts and 7 white shirts.

A student takes one shirt at random from the bag.

What is the probability that it is green?

$P(\text{green}) = \dfrac{7}{25}$ Put the values into the formula and calculate the
$\qquad = 0.28$ probability.

EXERCISE 20B

1 Choose the correct probability for each outcome when you roll a dice.

   a P(rolling a 4)

     A $\dfrac{1}{5}$ B $\dfrac{1}{6}$ C $\dfrac{5}{6}$ D 1

   b P(rolling an odd number)

     A 0   B $\dfrac{1}{2}$ C $\dfrac{3}{4}$ D 1

   c P(not getting a 2 or a 3)

     A 0   B $\dfrac{1}{2}$ C $\dfrac{1}{3}$ D $\dfrac{2}{3}$

2 There are 19 girls and 17 boys in a classroom.

The teacher puts their names into a bag and draws one at random.

What is the probability that the name drawn will be a boy?

3 A restaurant has yellow, red and black candles which it chooses to put on tables randomly.

The probability of the chosen candle being yellow is 0.083

A candle is three times as likely to be red as it is to be yellow.

Calculate the probability of the candle being black.

4 A local government agency carried out a census of 500 000 people working in the city.

They collected the following data.

Qualifications	Frequency	Language abilities	Frequency
postgraduate diploma/degree	74 500	English only	123 000
first degree/ diploma	92 350	English and one other language	209 500
no post-school qualifications	333 150	multilingual (English plus at least two other languages)	167 500

If a person included in this census is selected at random, what is the probability that the person:

a has a first degree or a diploma?

b is able to speak English only?

c has some post-school qualification?

d is able to speak a language other than English?

5 Nick and Vijay are playing a game. They take turns to roll two dice with the numbers 1 to 6 on them.

They find the product of the two dice.

If the product is odd, Nick gets a point, if the product is even, Vijay gets a point.

The first person to 20 points wins.

Predict which student is most likely to win. Justify your answer.

6 Is the reasoning in each of these statements correct? Say why or why not.

a Since there are 26 letters in the alphabet, the probability that a name will start with X is $\frac{1}{26}$

b My first three children were boys, so the next one must be a girl.

c There are ten teams in the tournament, so the probability of any team winning is $\frac{1}{10}$

d The probability that a family will go on holiday in August is $\frac{1}{12}$

e This team has won the last four matches, so they are certain to win the next one too.

Section 2: Further probability

Probability is a value that we use to predict what we expect to happen. In reality, there is no guarantee that any particular outcome will occur.

For example, an insurance company may use statistical data to work out that drivers between the ages of 17 and 23 are more likely to have an accident than older drivers. This does not mean that a 19-year-old driver will definitely have an accident.

A good understanding of probability and how it works will help you make sense of chance and risk in daily life.

The probability of an event not happening

All probability situations can be reduced to two possible outcomes. For example, win or not win, heads or not heads, rolling a 6 or not rolling a six.

When you express the outcomes in this way we say they are complementary.

When you add the probability of an event and its complement you get 1.

$P(\text{heads}) + P(\text{not heads}) = \frac{1}{2} + \frac{1}{2} = 1$ Not heads is the same as tails.

$P(\text{six}) + P(\text{not six}) = \frac{1}{6} + \frac{5}{6} = 1$ Not six is the same as rolling 1, 2, 3, 4 or 5.

In general terms, $P(\text{event occurring}) + P(\text{event not occurring}) = 1$

If you rearrange this equation you get:
$P(\text{event not occurring}) = 1 - P(\text{event occurring})$

If $P(E)$ is the probability of an event (E) happening, and $P(E')$ is the probability of that event not happening, then $P(E') = 1 - P(E)$.

WORK IT OUT 20.1

A laboratory tested 500 batches of tablets and found four to be contaminated.

What is the probability that a batch of tablets is:

a contaminated?

b not contaminated?

Which of these options gives the correct answers? What is wrong with the answers in the other option?

Option A	Option B
a $P(\text{contaminated}) = \frac{4}{500} = 0.8\%$	**a** $P(\text{contaminated}) = \frac{4}{500} = 0.008$
b $P(\text{not contaminated}) = \frac{496}{500} = 92\%$	**b** $P(\text{not contaminated}) = 1 - 0.008 = 0.992$

Mutually exclusive events
___

Mutually exclusive events cannot happen at the same time. For example, you cannot get an even number and a three at the same time when you roll a dice.

For example, a bag has 3 red, 2 yellow and 5 green sweets in it. One sweet is chosen at random.

- The probability of choosing a red sweet is $\frac{3}{10}$

- The probability of choosing a yellow sweet is $\frac{2}{10}$ or $\frac{1}{5}$

- The probability of choosing a green sweet is $\frac{5}{10}$ or $\frac{1}{2}$

The sum of probabilities of the three events is 1.

You cannot pick a red sweet and a yellow sweet at the same time, so the events P(red) and P(yellow) are mutually exclusive.

You can, however, work out the probability of choosing **either** a red or a yellow sweet.

There are 3 red and 2 yellow so $\frac{5}{10}$ of the sweets are either red or yellow.

EXERCISE 20C

1 Michelle catches the bus to work. Over a period of 227 working days she did not get a seat on the bus 58 times.

Calculate the experimental probability of her getting a seat on the bus.

2 In an occupational health survey, 8% of the employees suffered from stress, 15% had high cholesterol and 3% suffered from both stress and high cholesterol.

What is the probability that an employee selected at random will either be stressed or have high cholesterol? Choose from the options below.

    A 0.20   B 0.25   C 0.50   D 1.00

3 A set of raffle tickets is numbered 0 to 99 (inclusive).

What is the probability that the number of a raffle ticket drawn at random will be:

  a divisible by 2?   **b** not a multiple 10?

  c a multiple of 8?   **d** not a multiple of 8?

4 The probability of a basketball player missing a goal is given as 0.432

What is the probability that the player will **not** miss?

5 A packet holds 300 sweets in five different flavours.

The probability of choosing a particular flavour is given in the table.

Flavour	strawberry	lime	lemon	blackberry	apple
P(flavour)	0.21	0.22	0.18	0.23	

  a Calculate P(apple).   **b** What is P(not apple)?

  c Calculate the probability of choosing P(neither lemon nor lime).

  d Calculate the number of sweets of each flavour in the packet.

6 Students in a school have five extra-curricular clubs to choose from.

The probability that a student will choose each club is given in the table.

Club	Computers	Sewing	Woodwork	Choir	Chess
P(club)	0.57	0.2	0.2	0.02	0.01

a Calculate P(sewing or woodwork).

b Calculate P(not chess nor choir).

c 55 students choose a club.

How many of these would you expect to choose sewing?

d Four students chose choir.

Calculate how many students chose computers. (Assume the probabilities are correct.)

Organising outcomes – tables and frequency trees

Tables and simple diagrams can be used to record and organise information.

Frequency trees can be useful for doing this as well.

WORKED EXAMPLE 2

A doctor is interested in whether patients know the difference between having a cold and having the flu.

Out of 42 patients, 11 said they had a cold and 31 said they had the flu.

Only 19 of those who said they had the flu actually had flu.

Four of those who said they had a cold actually had the flu.

Construct a two-way table and a frequency tree to show this information.

Two-way table

Actual diagnosis / Self diagnosis	Cold	Flu
Cold	7	4
Flu	12	19

Frequency tree

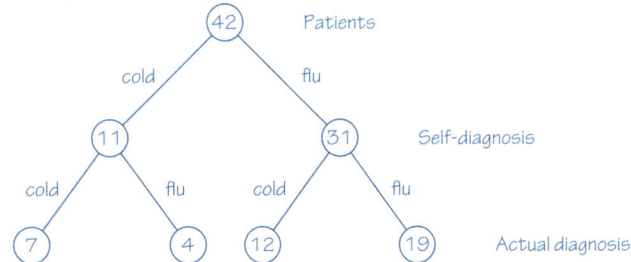

When you have organised data in two different ways, check that the numbers in your two-way table are the same as the numbers at the end of each branch of your frequency table.

Frequency trees

A frequency tree shows the actual frequency of different events.

Frequency trees allow you to understand and make sense of complicated probabilities.

The branches of the tree show the paths or decisions.

The 'leaves' show the actual number of data for each path.

Both the two-way table and the frequency tree in Worked Example 2 show the same information, but the frequency tree is clearer. It shows how many patients thought they had a cold or flu without you having to add the data in the table.

Did you know?

Frequency trees are organisational tools and they are often used in computer programming. (They are sometimes called binary trees.) They are not the same as probability tree diagrams, which you will deal with in Chapter 25.

EXERCISE 20D

1 A hotel chain keeps track of which customers make use of its in-house spa facilities.

Here are the results.

Gender \ Spa Use	Use the spa	Don't use the spa
Female	780	232
Male	348	640

a Copy and complete this frequency tree to show this data.

b Are male or female guests more likely to use the spa? Give reasons for your answer.

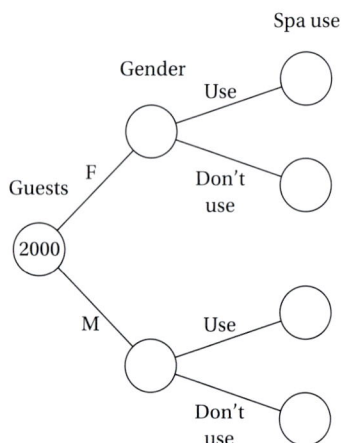

2 Of 60 patients visiting a doctor's rooms, 42 are convinced they will need prescription medication.

The others think they probably won't need a prescription.

Of those who think they will need a prescription, 13 do not actually need one.

Altogether, 36 patients need a prescription.

a Copy and complete the frequency tree to show the actual numbers.

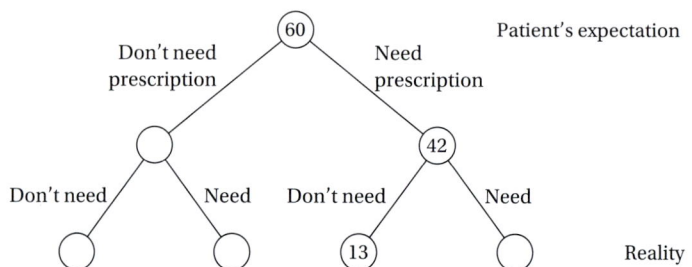

b Assuming this is representative, what is the probability that a patient who thinks they need a prescription will actually need one?

c What percentage of patients who thought they would not need a prescription actually needed one?

3 After completing a multiple-choice test, Andy predicted that he got 16 of the 20 questions correct.

Of the 16 he predicted that he'd answered correctly, he got 3 wrong.

Altogether he got 17 out of 20.

 a Draw a frequency tree to show this information.

 b Comment on how well he predicted the outcomes of the test.

4 80 volunteers take an HIV test to help the medical researchers work out how accurate the test is.

Of the volunteers, 17 people are HIV positive, the others are not.

The results show that one of the HIV-positive people gets a negative result on the test.

Two of the HIV-negative people get a positive result.

Draw a frequency tree to show the actual results.

Section 3: Working with probability

In real life, people tend to use probability informally to explain things and to predict what will happen in the future. For example:

- 'It is never sunny here in February.'
- 'Most people prefer to wear sandals in summer.'
- 'We are only selling 10 000 tickets so you have an excellent chance of winning the car.'
- 'Young people who haven't had a driving licence for very long have more accidents than older drivers.'

These statements are all expressions of probability that make a claim about the future based on experience, patterns or trends.

Each statement can be untrue in individual cases.

Understanding probability allows you to think more critically about statements like the ones above and to work out more accurately what the chance is of different things happening.

WORKED EXAMPLE 3

A series of tests were conducted to work out the average lifetime of a solar garden lamp.

The results of the tests are shown in the table:

Lifetime of solar lamp, L (hours)	$0 \leqslant L < 1000$	$1000 \leqslant L < 2000$	$2000 \leqslant L < 3000$	$3000 \leqslant L$
Frequency	30	75	160	35

a Use the results of the tests to estimate the probability that a solar lamp will last for less than 3000 hours but more than 1000 hours.

$P(1000 \leqslant L < 3000 \text{ hours}) = \frac{75}{300} + \frac{160}{300} = \frac{235}{300} = 0.783$

b A hardware depot orders 2000 solar lamps.

How many of them can they expect to last for more than 3000 hours?

$P(\text{lasts more than 3000 hours}) = \frac{35}{300}$

$\frac{35}{300} \times 2000 = 233$

If these statistics are correct, 233 of the solar lamps should last more than 3000 hours.

Sometimes the way a problem is worded can be confusing, but the actual calculations in probability are generally fairly simple additions or multiplications.

When you have to solve a word problem involving basic probability you can do this by organising your work and following the steps as shown in the example below.

Problem-solving framework

Nick is throwing a ball randomly at a wall on the side of a building.

The side of the building is 2 m high and 10 m wide.

There are three windows on the side of the building, each window is 2 m wide and 1 m high.

What is the probability that Nick will hit a window when he throws the ball at the wall? Express your answer as a percentage.

Step 1: What are you trying to work out?	The probability of hitting any of the windows.
Step 2: What do you need to work out before you can find this?	The area of the wall and the area of the windows. Area of wall = 10 m × 2 m = 20 m^2 Area of windows = 3 × (2 m × 1 m) = 3 × 2 m^2 = 6 m^2
Step 3: Apply the formula and calculate the probability. Convert the answer to a percentage.	$P(\text{hits window}) = \frac{6}{20} = \frac{3}{10}$ $\frac{3}{10} \times 100 = 30\%$ There is a 30% probability that Nick will hit a window.

EXERCISE 20E

1 A coin is tossed 20 times.

Busi claimed the coin was unfair because it landed on tails only 5 out of the 20 times.

She says the probability of getting tails when you toss a coin is 0.5, so if you toss the coin 20 times you should get $20 \times 0.5 = 10$ tails.

Was she correct? Give a reason for your answer.

2 Grey College has a sports tournament against St George's College every year.

The weather on the day of the tournament can be described as sunny and dry, cloudy and humid or rainy.

Grey College keeps a record of the weather on the day and whether the College won or drew the tournament. Here are its results for the past 30 years.

Weather	Wins	Draws	Tournaments played
sunny and dry	4	1	7
cloudy and humid	3	2	10
rainy	3	3	13
Total	10	6	30

a What is the relative frequency of rain on tournament days?

b A student from Grey College says they have a better chance of winning if it is sunny.

Is this a correct statement? Give a reason for your answer.

c A student from St George's says they have an almost even chance of winning the tournament, no matter what the weather.

Is this a correct statement? Give a reason for your answer.

d Calculate the experimental probability that Grey College will draw a tournament.

3 An eight-sided dice has sides coloured red, blue, green, black and white.

If the probability of the dice landing on red is $\frac{1}{4}$, choose the true statement from the following options.

A Four sides are red.

B One out of five sides is red.

C Two sides must be red.

D There are more red sides than black sides.

Find answers at: cambridge.org/ukschools/gcsemaths-studentbookanswers

4 Two coins are tossed 100 times in a trial.

The experimental probability of getting two heads is found to be $\frac{3}{10}$

What does this mean? Choose the correct statement.

A Every third toss resulted in two heads.

B Two heads came up three times.

C Two heads came up 30 times.

D The coins are biased.

5 A local educational authority wants to introduce random drug testing in secondary schools.

It claims the tests have a very small false-positive rate of one half of one per cent.

a Express one half of one per cent as a decimal.

b A school has a total of 800 students.

Some parents claim that four students at the school could incorrectly test positive for drug use.

Are the parents concerns valid? Give a reason why or why not.

c There were 3 831 937 secondary school students included in the drug testing.

How many of them would you expect to be incorrectly accused of being drug users?

6 In a drugs test, 1% of the athletes tested are actually using prohibited drugs.

If an athlete is using prohibited drugs, 90% of the time he or she will fail the drug test.

Of the athletes who are **not** using prohibited drugs, 10% will also fail the drug test even though they are not using drugs.

a Copy and complete this table to show how many athletes will pass or fail the drug test for every 1000 athletes tested.

Status	Test positive (i.e. fail drug test)	Test negative (i.e. pass drug test)	Total
athletes who are using illegal substances			10
athletes who are not using illegal substances			990
Total			1000

b Represent the same information on a frequency tree.

c An athlete tests positive for the illegal substance.

What is the probability that she is not actually using the substance? Give your answer as a percentage.

d Another athlete tests negative for the illegal substance. Is it certain that he is not using them? Give a reason for your answer.

7 Amit designed a round spinner out of plastic to be used in a game.

The spinner was divided into quarters coloured red, green, yellow and white.

His friend Nick said the spinner might be biased because Amit didn't sand it down smoothly.

Amit disagreed, and they decided to test whether it was fair or not by spinning it 1000 times and recording the outcomes. These are the results.

Outcome	red	green	yellow	white
Frequency	295	248	238	219

Does the evidence suggest the spinner is biased? Give a reason for your answer.

8 A shopkeeper did a survey to find out which customers buy fresh fish at his shop every week.

	Females		Males	
	Buy fish	Don't buy fish	Buy fish	Don't buy fish
20–50 years old	23	56	19	25
Over 50 years old	45	26	13	5

a How many people were surveyed?

b How many people over 50 were surveyed?

c A customer from the survey is chosen at random. What is the probability that the customer is:

  i male?   **ii** male or over 50?   **iii** over 50 and buys fish?

d How could this information help the shopkeeper plan advertising and marketing campaigns?

Find answers at: cambridge.org/ukschools/gcsemaths-studentbookanswers

9 There are four main blood groups: A, B, AB and O.

The following data about blood types was collected by a blood bank based on the blood types of 500 blood donors.

Blood type	Number of donors
A	220
B	49
AB	21
O	210

a What percentage of donors belong to group O?

b What is the probability of a donor having blood type AB?

c About 7% of the population are O negative. How many of these donors would you expect to have O negative blood?

d Given these statistics, what is the probability that a baby will be born with blood type AB?

e Why is theoretical probability not very useful for predicting blood type?

10 Eighty people are asked if they can tell the difference between butter and margarine.

The results are: 37 say they can, 24 say no and 19 say they are not sure.

The interviewer then carries out a blind taste test.

Of those who said they could tell the difference, 14 got it wrong.

Of those who said no, 9 got it right.

Of those who said they were not sure, 14 got it wrong.

Draw a frequency tree to show the outcomes of this experiment.

Checklist of learning and understanding

Range of probabilities
- The probability scale ranges from 0 to 1. Impossible events have a probability of 0 and certain events have a probability of 1. It is not possible to have a negative probability (< 0) or a probability greater than 1.
- Probabilities between 0 and 1 can be expressed as fractions, decimals or percentages.

Theoretical probability
- Probability of an event $= \dfrac{\text{number of favourable outcomes}}{\text{total number of outcomes}}$

Sum of probabilities and complementary events
- The sum of probabilities will always total 1.
- The probability of an event happening is equal to 1 minus the probability that the event will not happen. $P(\text{not } E) = 1 - P(E)$.

Experimental probability and relative frequency

- Experimental probability tells you how often a favourable outcome occurs in an experiment.

  Experimental probability = $\dfrac{\text{relative frequency of favourable outcomes}}{\text{number of possible outcomes}}$

- Tables and frequency trees can be used to organise the outcomes of different experiments.

- Statistical data can be used to give relative frequencies of particular events. The relative frequency of an event can be used to predict future outcomes.

Mutually exclusive events

- Mutually exclusive events cannot happen at the same time. For example, you cannot throw a 1 and a 5 at the same time when you roll one dice.

Chapter review

For additional questions on the topics in this chapter, visit GCSE Mathematics Online.

1 The probability of choosing a green sweet from a packet is found to be 0.3. There are 20 identical sweets in the packet. How many of them are green? Choose your answer from the options below.

A 3 B 6 C 6.6 D 30

2 A coin is tossed a number of times giving the following results.

Heads: 4083
Tails: 5917

a How many times was the coin tossed?

b Calculate the relative frequency of each outcome.

c What is the probability that the next toss will result in heads?

d Jess says she thinks the results show that the coin is biased. Do you agree? Give a reason for your answer.

3 A bag contains 10 red, 8 green and 2 white counters.

Each counter has an equal chance of being chosen. Calculate:

a the probability of choosing a red ball

b the probability of choosing a red or a green ball

c the probability of not choosing a white ball

d P(ball is not red).

4 The probability of a person being left-handed is 0.23

How many left-handed people would you expect in a population of 25 000?

5 The probability of a SIM card for a mobile phone being faulty is found to be 0.0265

What percentage of SIM cards are not faulty?

6 Will interviews 64 people to get their opinions about sending texts when in company.

Of those interviewed, 44 say it is rude to send texts in company.

Will then observes the people at a large event.

Of those who said it was rude to send texts in company, 13 sent texts when at the table with others.

Of those who said it was acceptable, 9 did not send texts when in company.

Copy and complete the frequency tree to show this data.

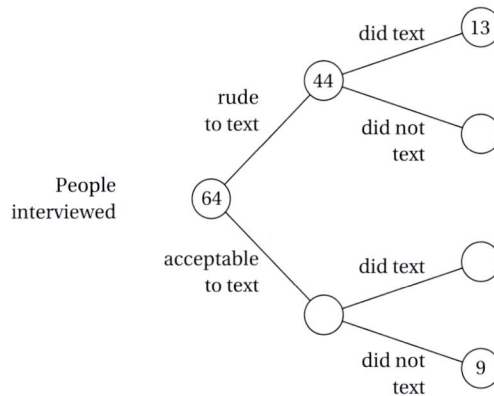

7 150 boys and 160 girls sit an examination.

The table shows some of the probabilities that they came with or without a calculator.

	With calculator	Without calculator
Boy	0.92	0.08
Girl	0.95	

a What is the probability that a girl came without a calculator?

Write your answer in the table. *(1 mark)*

b How many of the 150 boys came with a calculator? *(2 marks)*

© AQA 2013

8 Mina used a computer program to simulate drawing a playing card at random from a shuffled pack.

She recorded the suit of each card drawn. These are her results for 1000 trials.

Suit drawn	hearts	diamonds	spades	clubs
Frequency	238	240	264	258

a Calculate the relative frequency of each outcome.

b Do these results indicate that the simulation is fair and unbiased? Give a reason for your answer.

21 3D objects

In this chapter you will learn how to ...

- apply what you already know about the properties of 3D objects.
- work with 2D representations of 3D objects.
- construct and interpret plans and elevations of 3D objects.

For more resources relating to this chapter, visit GCSE Mathematics Online.

Using mathematics: real-life applications

Buildings, engine parts, vehicles and packaging are all carefully planned and designed before they are built or made. Most design work starts on paper or screen using two-dimensional images to represent the final three-dimensional objects.

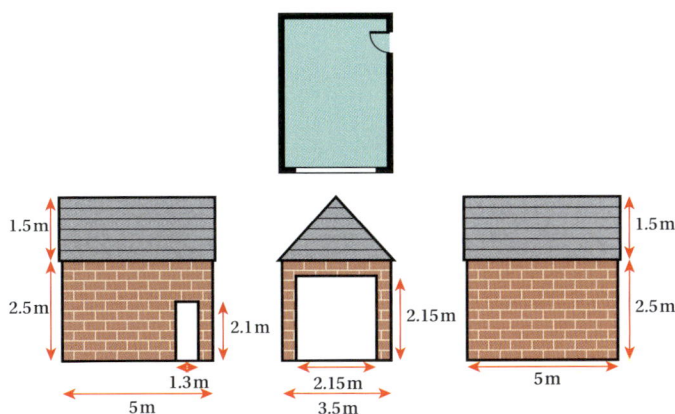

"No one will buy an apartment that isn't built yet if they don't know what it is going to look like. When we sell a development we show people floor plans as well as elevations from all four sides. Sometimes we also have a 3D scale model of the development." *(Estate agent)*

Before you start ...

KS3 Ch 8	You must be able to identify and name some common 3D objects.	**1**	Name each of these 3D objects. **a** **b** **c** **d**
Ch 8	You should know the basic properties of polygons and other 3D objects.	**2**	True or false? Correct the false statements. **a** A cube has 4 faces. **b** A cube has 12 edges. **c** A cuboid has 8 vertices. **d** For any polyhedral, $F + V + E = 2$
KS3 Ch 34	You must be able to accurately construct lines and angles using your ruler and a pair of compasses.	**3**	Construct and bisect a right angle ABC.
		4	Use a pair of compasses to draw a circle of radius 5 cm. Construct a hexagon inside the circle.

Find answers at: cambridge.org/ukschools/gcsemaths-studentbookanswers

385

Assess your starting point using the Launchpad

STEP 1

1 Which solids can be formed from each net?

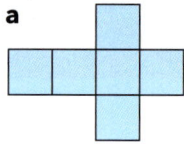

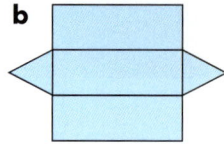

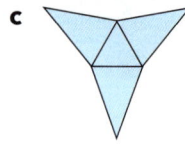

a   **b**   **c**

2 Sketch a possible net for a rectangular box 3 cm long, 2 cm wide and 1 cm high.

GO TO
Section 1:
3D objects and their nets

STEP 2

3 Draw this object on squared paper.

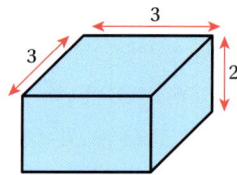

4 Sketch this solid on isometric paper.

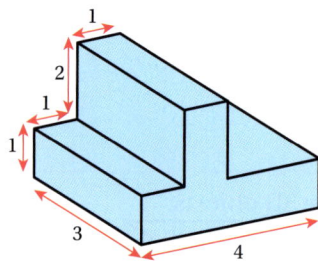

GO TO
Section 2:
Drawing 3D objects

GO TO
Step 3
The Launchpad continues on the next page …

Launchpad continued ...

STEP 3

5 Which is the plan view for this square-based pyramid?

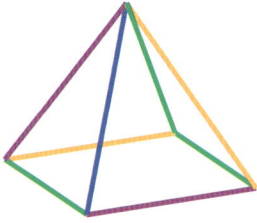

A    B

C 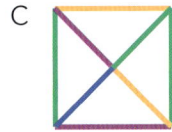   D

6 Draw the plan view, front and right side elevation of each shape on squared paper.

a   b

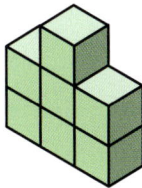   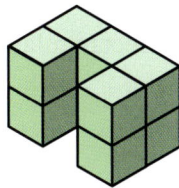

?

GO TO
Section 3:
Plan and elevation views

✓

GO TO
Chapter review

Section 1: 3D objects and their nets

A polyhedron is a 3D shape made up of flat faces. The plural of polyhedron is polyhedra.

The table summarises the main properties of different polyhedra.

Polyhedron	Faces	Vertices	Edges
cube (square prism) 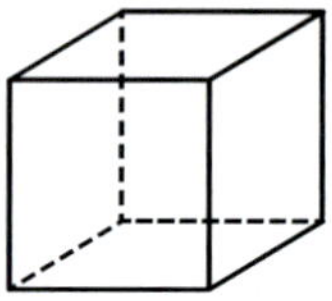	6 square faces	8	12
cuboid (rectangular prism) 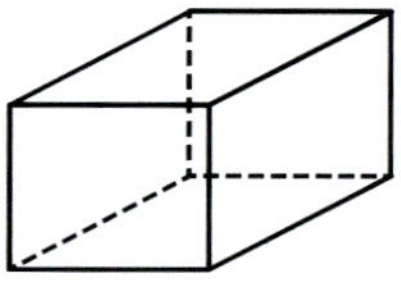	2 congruent rectangular end faces 2 congruent rectangular side faces 2 congruent top and bottom faces	8	12
triangular prism 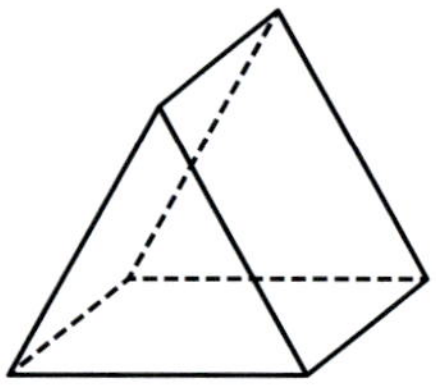	2 congruent triangular end faces 3 rectangular faces	6	9
pentagonal prism 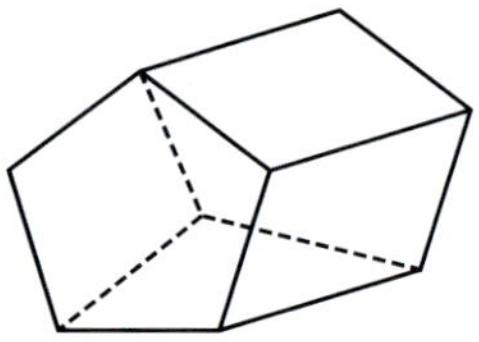	2 congruent pentagonal end faces 5 rectangular faces	10	15
triangular pyramid 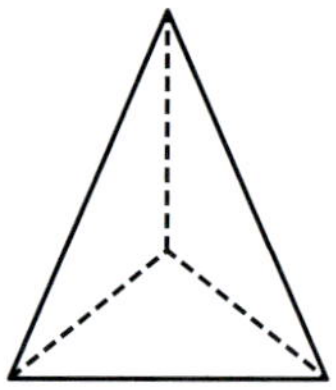	1 triangular base 3 triangular faces that meet at an apex	4	6
square-based pyramid 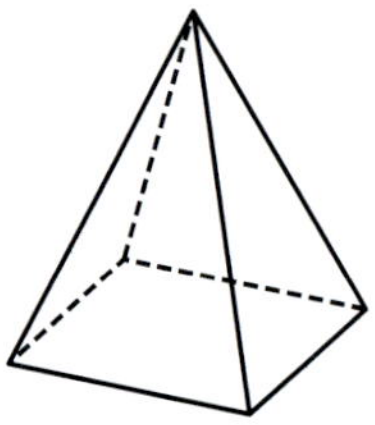	1 square base 4 triangular faces that meet at an apex	5	8

Tip

Shapes are **congruent** if all their corresponding measurements are equal. You will learn more about congruent shapes in Chapter 36.

Tip

Euler's theorem states that $F + V = E + 2$ for any convex polyhedron, where F = number of faces, V = number of vertices, E = number of edges.

Cylinders, cones and spheres are also 3D shapes but they are not classified as polyhedra because they are not formed of flat faces that are polygons.

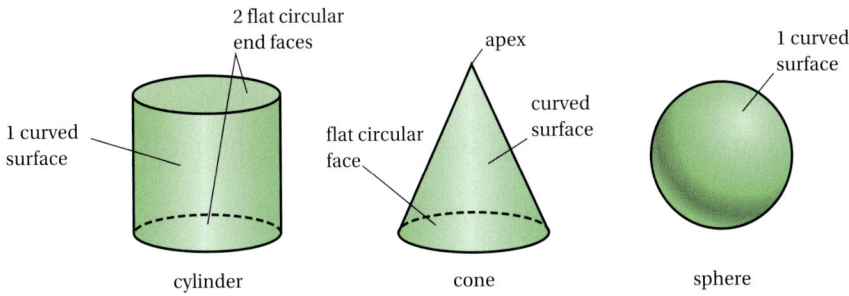

Cylinder labels: 2 flat circular end faces, 1 curved surface — cylinder
Cone labels: apex, curved surface, flat circular face — cone
Sphere labels: 1 curved surface — sphere

Nets of 3D objects

A **net** is a 2D representation of a 3D shape. You can fold up a net to make the 3D shape.

For printed packaging the design is printed on to the net, and then the net is folded up to make the box itself.

A cube has six square faces. There are 11 possible ways of arranging the faces to make the net of a cube.

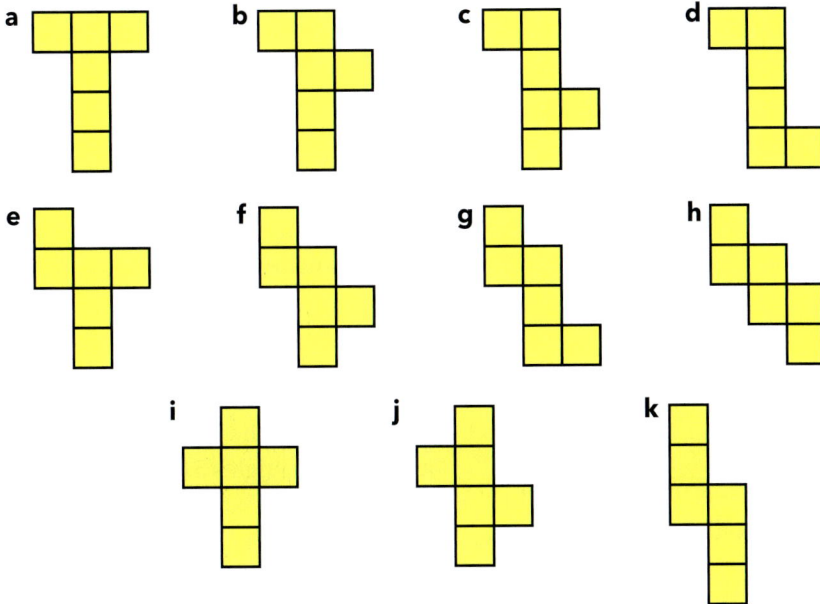

a b c d

e f g h

i j k

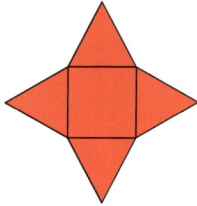

You can use the properties of a 3D shape to help you recognise nets and identify the shapes they will make.

This net shows that the object has one square face and four triangular faces.

It is the net of a square-based pyramid.

When this net is folded up, the triangular faces will meet at a common point.

You can also use the properties to sketch or construct the net of a shape.

Tip

When you draw a net, always start in the middle of the page to give yourself space to construct all the faces.

WORKED EXAMPLE 1

Construct an accurate net of this rectangular prism.

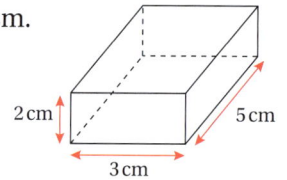

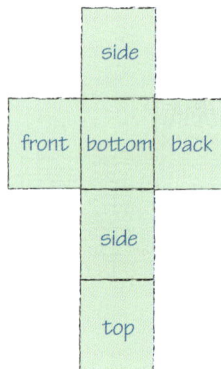

2 cm   3 cm   5 cm

	side	
front	bottom	back
	side	
	top	

You know that a cuboid has six rectangular faces, so your net will have six faces.

Draw a rough sketch to start with.

To construct an accurate net you need to use the measurements given on the diagram.

Use a ruler and pencil to draw the net.

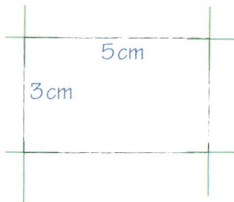

5 cm
3 cm

Draw the bottom face first. This is a rectangle 3 cm wide and 5 cm long.

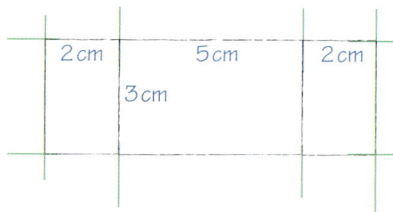

2 cm   5 cm   2 cm
3 cm

Next construct two of the sides that join on to the bottom. These are both rectangles 3 cm long and 2 cm wide.

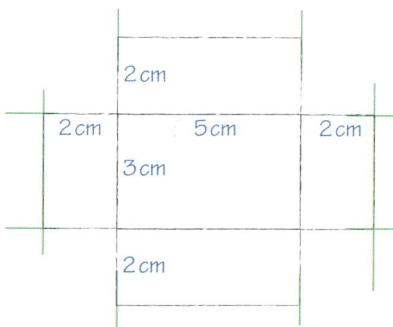

2 cm
2 cm   5 cm   2 cm
3 cm
2 cm

Construct the other two sides that join on to the bottom. These are both rectangles 5 cm long and 2 cm wide.

Continues on next page …

2 cm

2 cm   5 cm   2 cm

3 cm

2 cm

3 cm

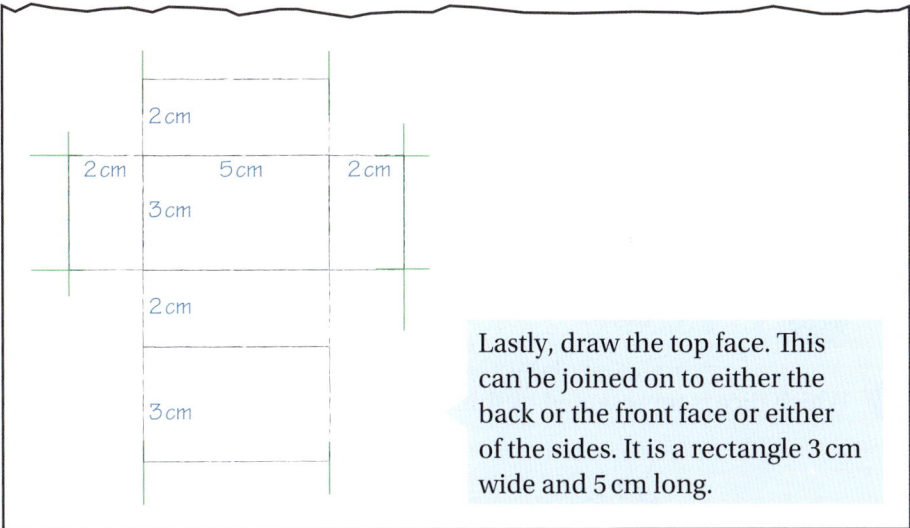

Lastly, draw the top face. This can be joined on to either the back or the front face or either of the sides. It is a rectangle 3 cm wide and 5 cm long.

Tip

More on construction is covered in Chapter 34.

EXERCISE 21A

1 Describe each object fully by referring to its properties. State whether it is a polyhedron or not, giving a reason for your decision.

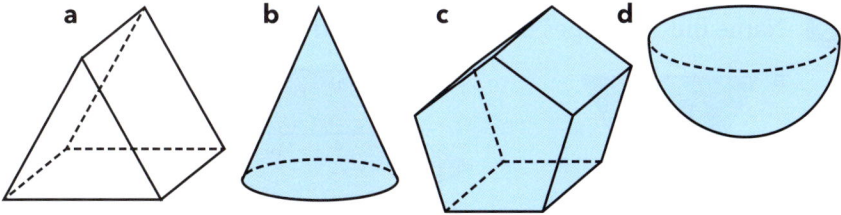

a   **b**   **c**   **d**

2 Which 3D shape can be created from the net shown below? Choose from the options given.

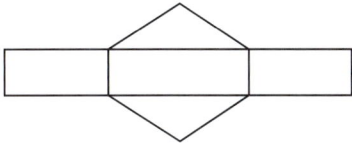

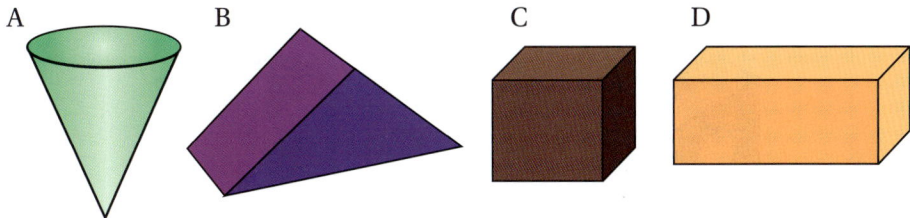

A   B   C   D

3 Which of these nets could be used to make a cylinder? Choose from A, B, C or D.

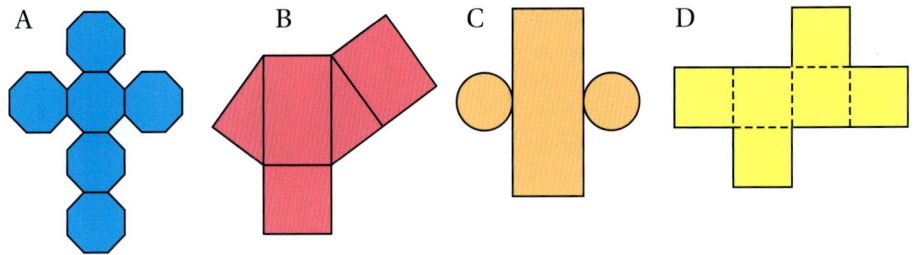

A

B

C

D

> **Tip**
>
> The numbers on the opposite faces of a dice add up to 7.

4 Which dice is represented by this net? Choose from the options given.

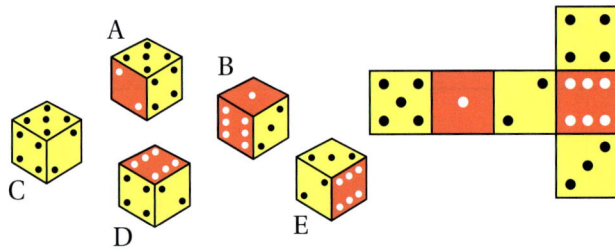

A

B

C

D

E

5 Name the 3D shapes that can be formed from each net.

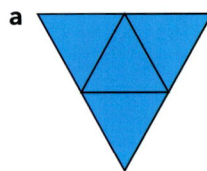

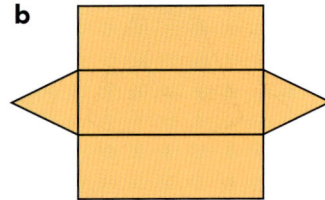

a

b

6 The six faces of a cube are shown.

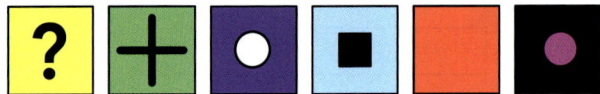

Here are three different views of the cube.

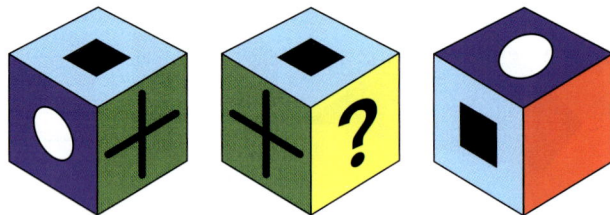

Here is the net of the cube. Only one of the faces has been recorded.

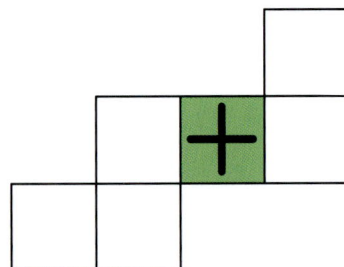

Copy and complete the net.

7 Here are some possible arrangements of five square faces.

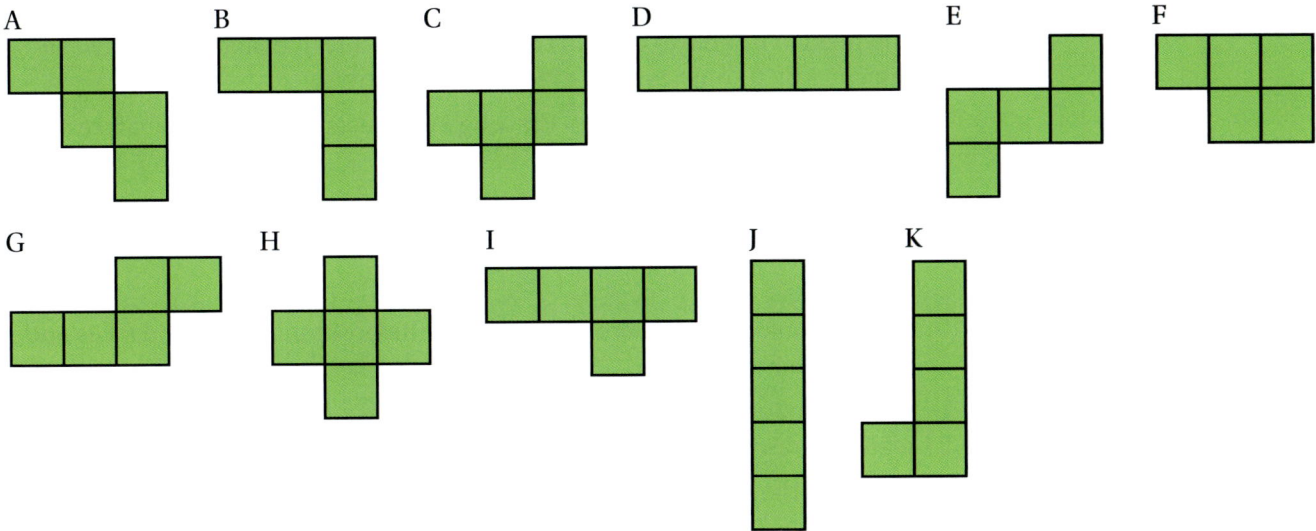

A   B   C   D   E   F

G   H   I   J   K

  a Which of these nets cannot be folded up to form an open box?

  b Draw one more net for an open box. Make sure your net is not just a turned or flipped over version of the ones shown here.

8 A Year 10 class sell popcorn to raise funds. They charge £1.50 per box of popcorn.

The price of popcorn boxes is based on how much material is used to make them.

The more expensive the box, the less profit the class will make.

The diagrams show the three boxes available to them.

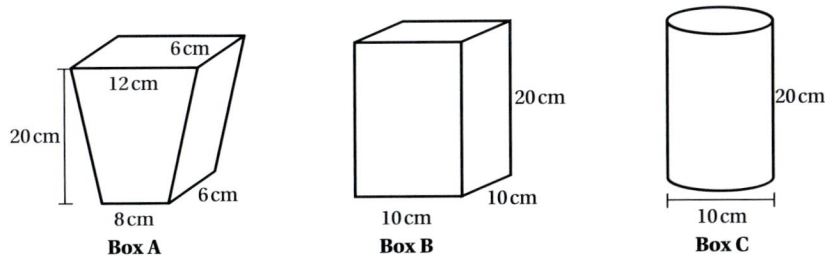

6 cm
12 cm
20 cm
6 cm
8 cm
Box A

20 cm
10 cm
10 cm
Box B

20 cm
10 cm
Box C

  a Sketch the net of each box and label its dimensions.

  b Use the nets to work out the area of cardboard needed to make each box. You can ignore the tabs needed to fold up the box as they all have the same tabs.

  c Which box should the class use? Give reasons for your choice.

Section 2: Drawing 3D objects

You need to be able to draw 3D objects and to interpret and make sense of drawings of 3D objects from different perspectives.

There are a number of ways of drawing 3D objects to show their features in 2D.

Prisms and cylinders using end faces

Draw prisms and cylinders by visualising the position of their end faces and drawing these first.

When you draw a cylinder you use ovals for the faces to get a more realistic drawing.

Then join the end faces by drawing lines to represent the edges.

First draw the two circular end faces by drawing ovals.	Then draw in two lines to join the end faces.	Shading can make the cylinder look more realistic.

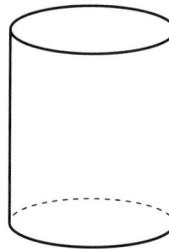

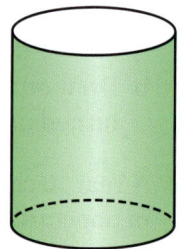

For prisms make sure you match up the corresponding vertices.

To draw a cuboid (rectangular prism):

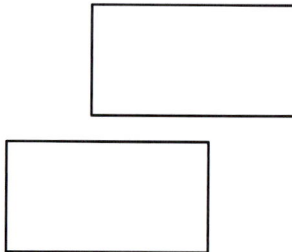

First draw two rectangular faces.	Then draw lines to join the vertices.

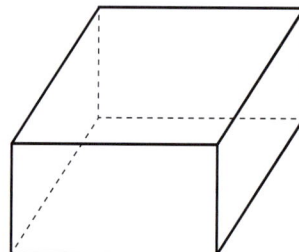

To draw a triangular prism:

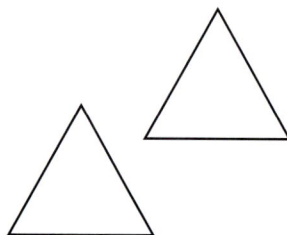

First draw the two triangular end faces.	Then draw lines to join the vertices.

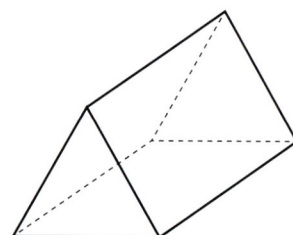

The same process can be used for any shaped prism.

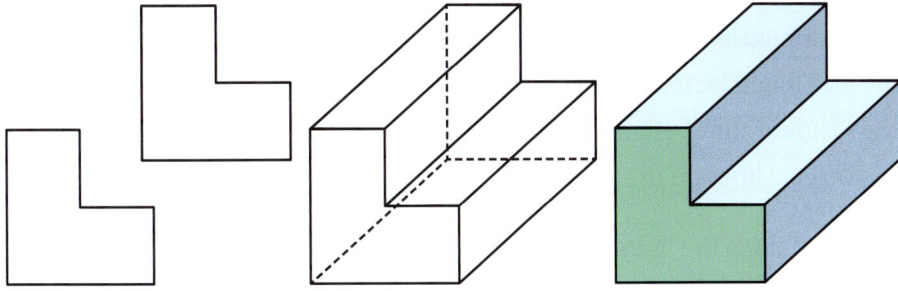

Prisms and pyramids from parallel lines

You can draw square and rectangular prisms and square-based pyramids using two pairs of parallel lines as a starting point.

To draw a prism:

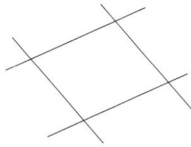

Begin by drawing two pairs of parallel lines that intersect.

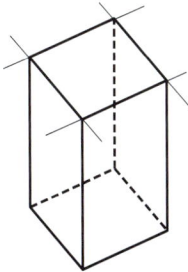

Then draw three lines of equal length down (or up) from the intersections. Complete the shape by joining the ends to make a prism.

To draw a square-based pyramid:

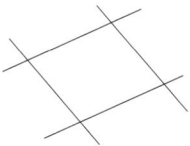

Start by drawing two pairs of parallel lines.

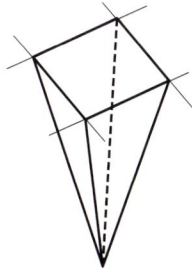

Mark a point and draw lines from three intersections of the parallel lines to the point.

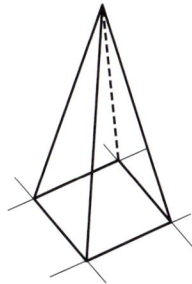

You can also draw the point above (or to the side) of the parallel lines.

Find answers at: cambridge.org/ukschools/gcsemaths-studentbookanswers

Drawing shapes on squared or isometric grids

Three-dimensional (3D) objects can be drawn on squared or isometric grids.

The grid might be made from dots or from faintly printed lines.

The diagram shows a cube and a cuboid drawn on a square grid.

The vertical lines on the grid are used to represent the vertical edges of the 3D object.
You draw along the lines at an angle on the paper to represent the horizontal edges of the 3D object.

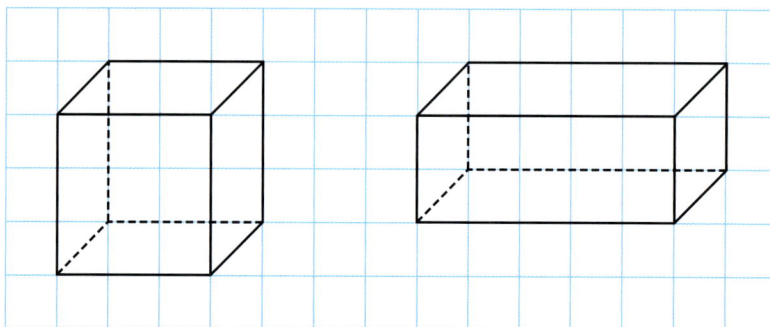

Key vocabulary

isometric grid: special drawing paper based on an arrangement of triangles

This diagram shows the same objects drawn on an **isometric grid**.

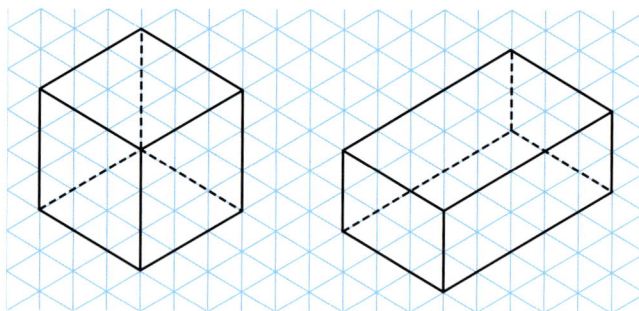

When you draw shapes on both square and isometric grids you use broken lines to show the edges that would not be seen if you viewed the shape from that angle.

You can use squared or isometric grids to draw 3D objects using the end faces or parallel lines method. The grid makes it easier for you to make sure that the end faces are the same size.

The diagrams show a cuboid drawn on a square grid and a hexagonal prism drawn on an isometric grid.

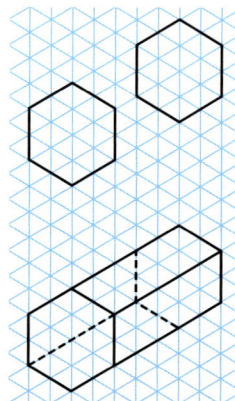

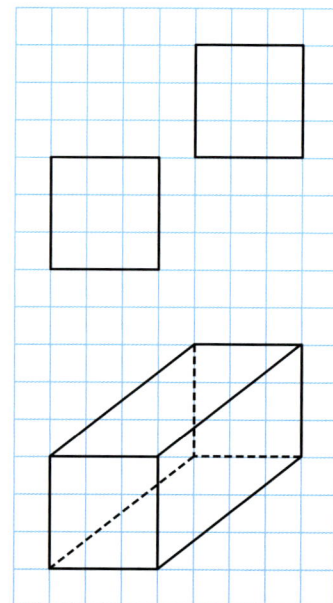

Tip

Be very careful to join up corresponding vertices.

Isometric drawings

Isometric drawings are used to visually represent three-dimensional objects in two dimensions in technical and engineering drawings.

This diagram shows the design of an engineering component on isometric paper.

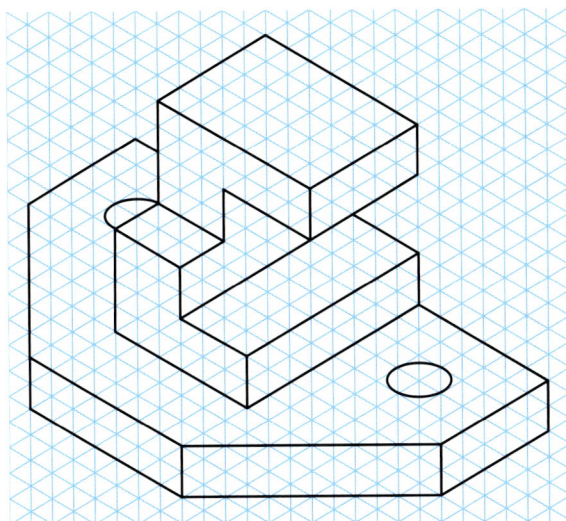

Isometric paper is very useful for drawing solids built from cubes.

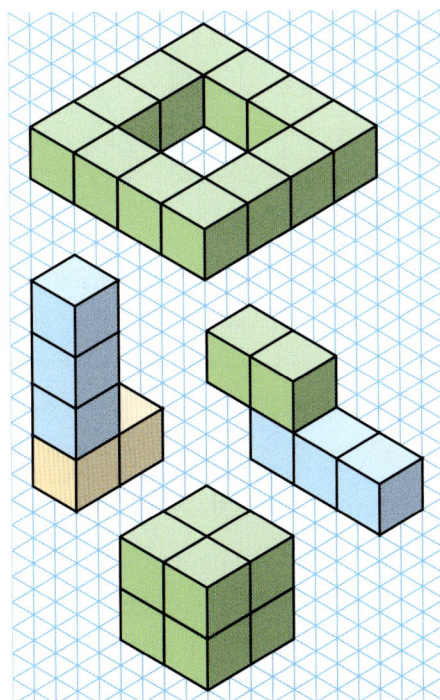

WORK IT OUT 21.1

Students were asked to draw this view of a shape on an isometric grid.

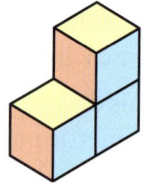

This is how they started their sketches.

| **Student A** | **Student B** | **Student C** |

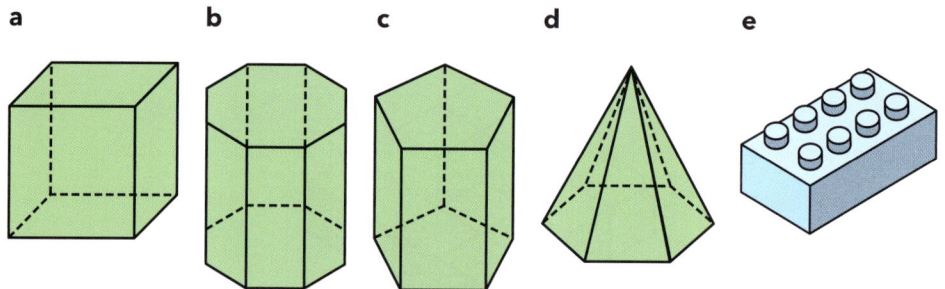

Which student is likely to end up with the correct view of the shape?

What are the others doing incorrectly?

EXERCISE 21B

1 Draw the following objects without using a grid.

a   b   c   d   e

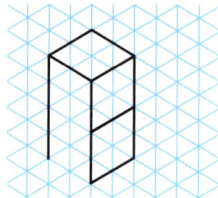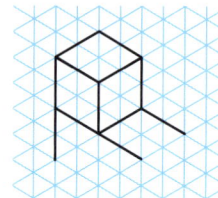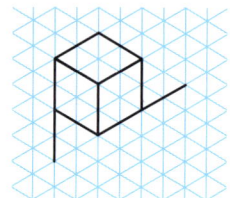

2 The diagram shows one of the parallel end faces of three different prisms.

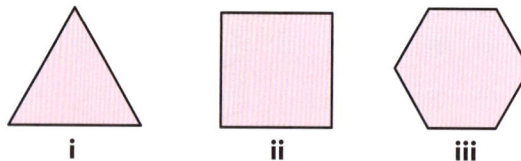

    i   ii   iii

  a Sketch each prism on squared paper.

  b Use isometric paper to draw each prism.

  c Compare the two drawings of each prism. What effect does the grid you use have on your drawing?

3 Draw the following shapes on an isometric grid.

    a   b   c

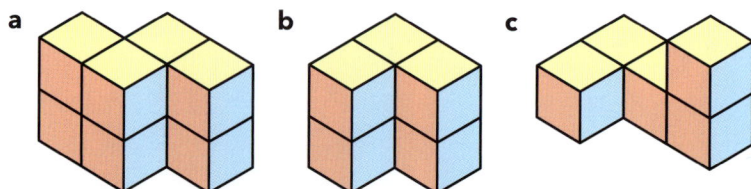

4 The diagrams show different shapes made from cubes. There are no cubes missing from the layers you cannot see.

State how many cubes you need to build each shape.

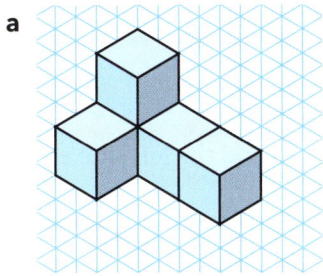

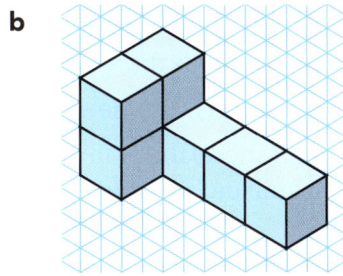

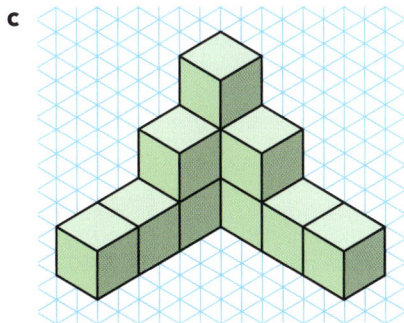

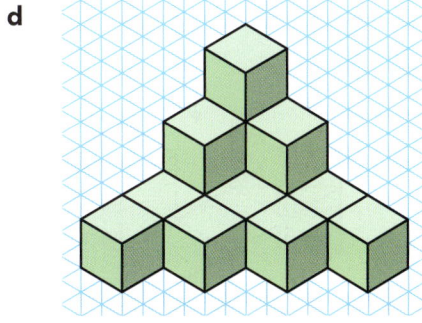

a

b

c

d

5 Shading drawings of 3D objects can create optical illusions like these.

  a Are there six or seven cubes in this diagram?

  b Is this a large cube with a black cube cut out of it or a small black cube in the corner of a large brown cube?

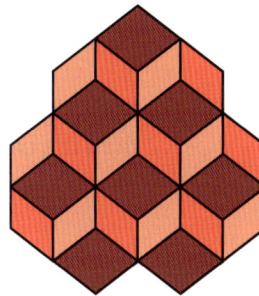

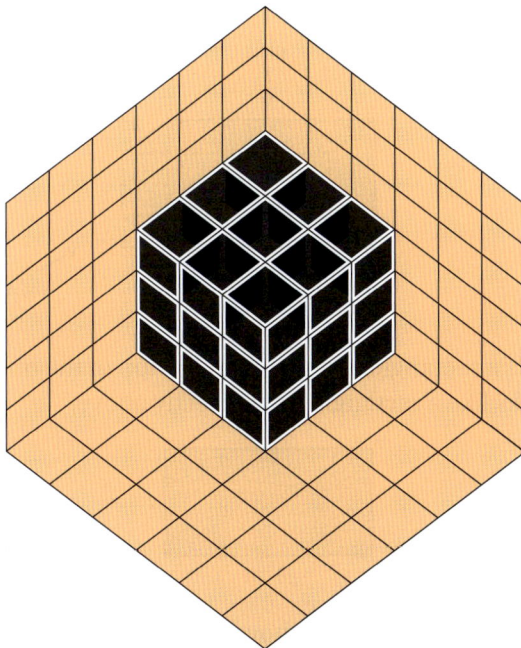

  c Use an isometric grid to reconstruct these diagrams accurately.

  Shade your diagrams to form the illusion.

Find answers at: cambridge.org/ukschools/gcsemaths-studentbookanswers

Section 3: Plan and elevation views

A **plan view** shows a 3D object from directly above.

You can also view objects from the front, sides or back.

The **front elevation** is the view from the front of the object.

The **side elevation** is the view from the side of the object.

This diagram shows the plan view, front elevation and the left side elevation of a shape built out of cubes.

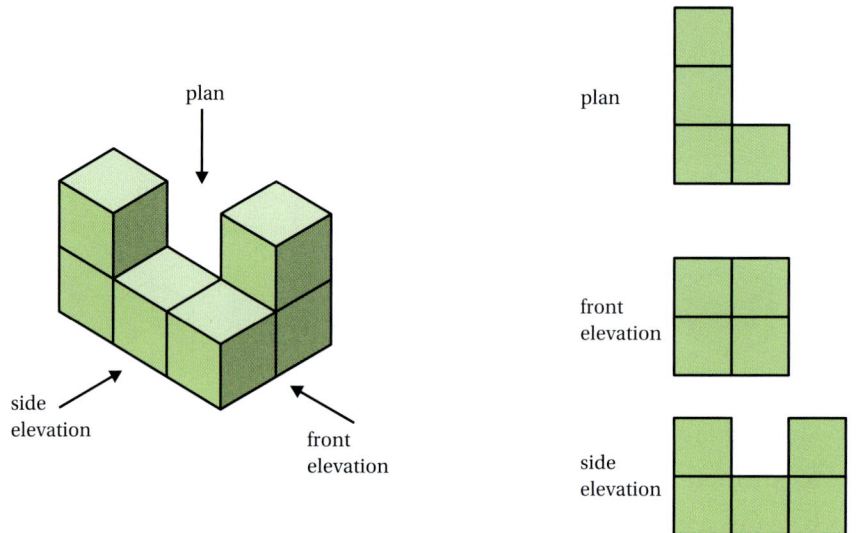

The shape below is a prism with trapezium-shaped ends. The front is higher than the back.

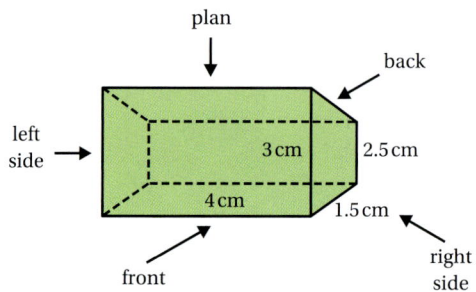

The plan view is a rectangle. Even though the top of the object slopes down to the back, it looks like a rectangle from directly above.

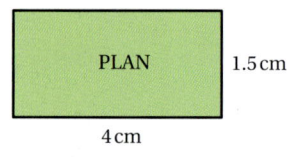

The plan view is normally drawn above the front view because the two views will be the same width.

In a prism, the left and right elevations are reflections of each other. They are drawn on the left side and right side of the front elevation.

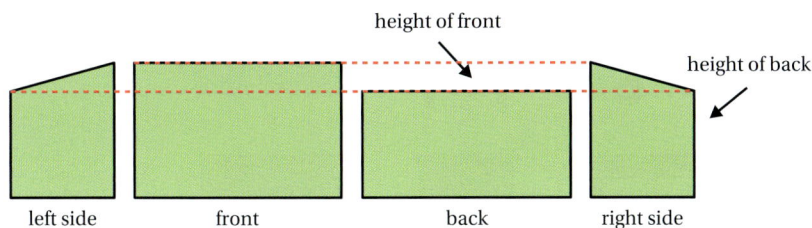

The front elevation is a rectangle.

The back is also a rectangle, but it is not as tall as the front.

You get different information from different views because each one shows two of the three dimensions of the solid.

- The plan view shows the length and width of the solid.
- The front view shows the length and height of the solid.
- The side views show the width and height of the solid.

When you draw plans or elevations you show any changes in height as solid lines. Use dotted lines to indicate any hidden edges.

WORKED EXAMPLE 2

Draw the plan, front and side elevations of this solid.

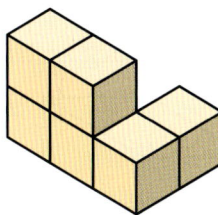

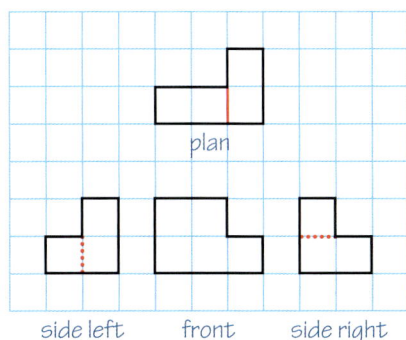

Start by drawing the plan view.

Next, draw the front view below it. It will be same width as the plan view.

Work out what the right side will look like if you view it face on.

Draw it next to the front view. It will be same height.

You can't see the left view, so you have to visualise it.

Draw it in the correct place.

When you draw views of a shape, you have to think quite carefully about what the parts you cannot see clearly will look like.

For example, look at the shape below. It is built from four cubes.

You can only see three cubes. You have to work out that the fourth one is supporting the 'top' cube.

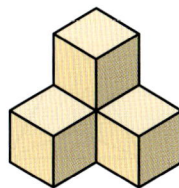

EXERCISE 21C

1 Select the correct plan view of each object from the options given.

a

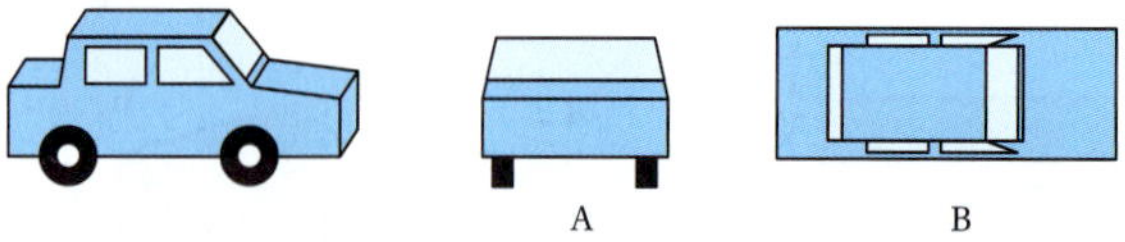

A   B

b

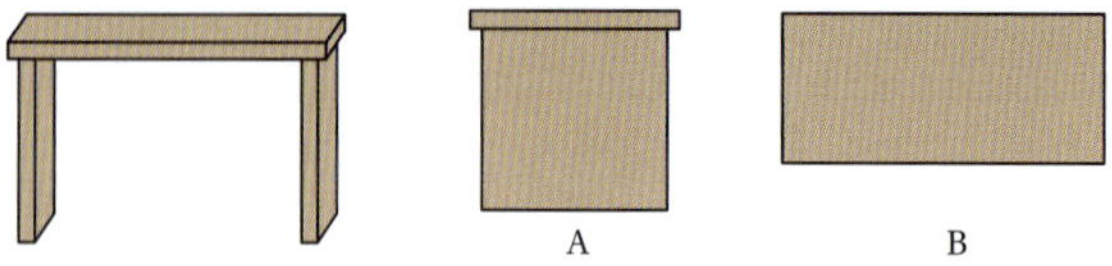

A   B

c

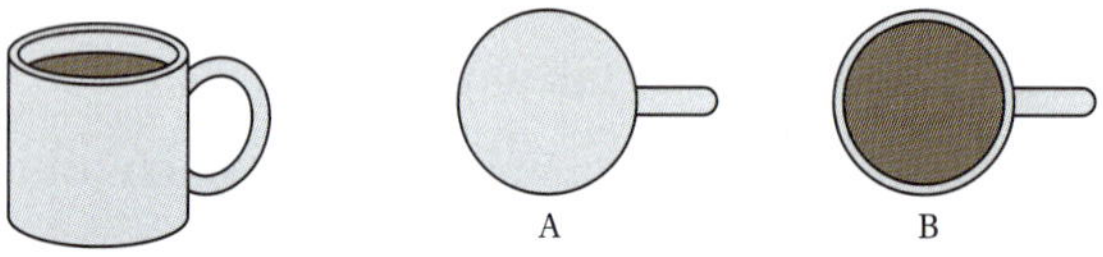

A   B

d

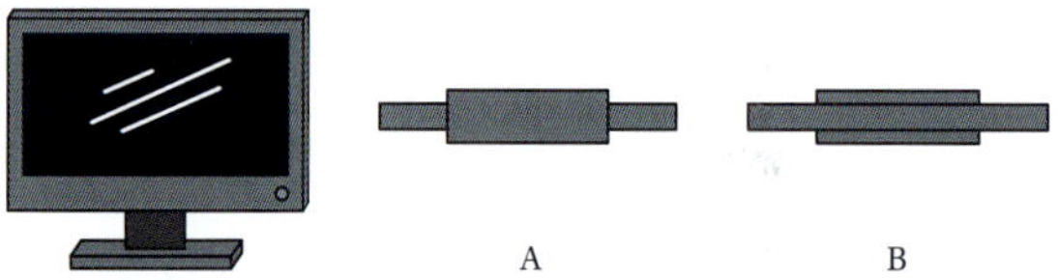

A   B

e

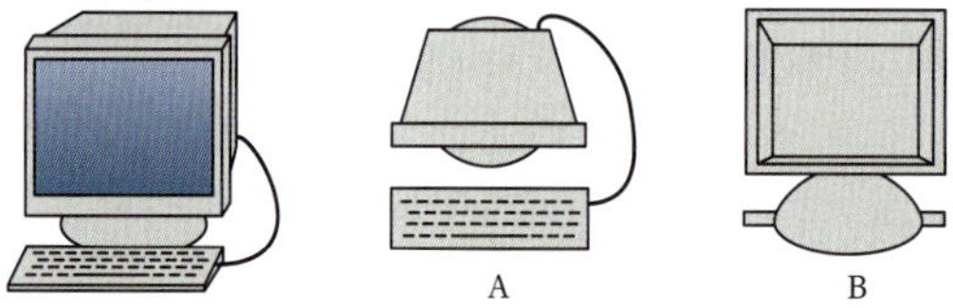

A   B

2 **a** Match each shape to its plan and elevation image.

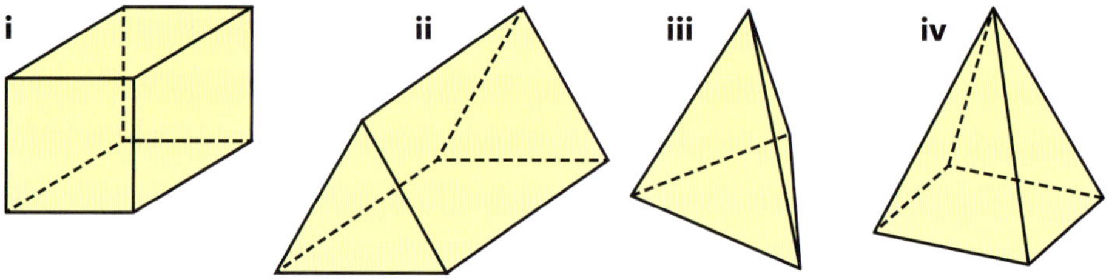

i   ii   iii   iv

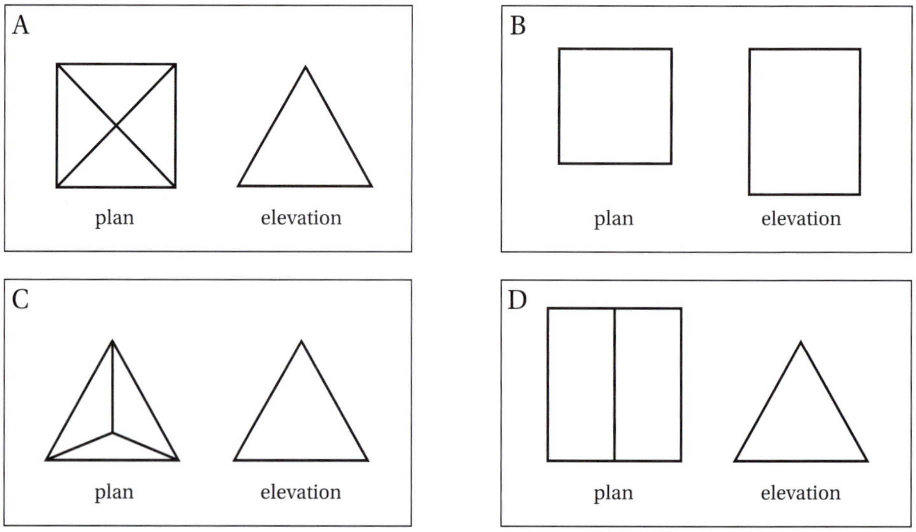

A

plan   elevation

B

plan   elevation

C

plan   elevation

D

plan   elevation

b Sketch and label the elevations that are not shown for each shape.

3 For each coloured set of cubes, draw:

a a plan

b a front elevation

c a right side elevation (from the right-hand side).

4 Draw the plan, the front elevation and the side elevation of the shape below.

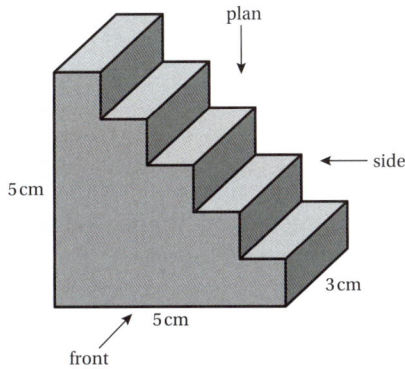

plan

side

5 cm

3 cm

5 cm

front

5 The plan view and elevations of different solids are shown.

Use these to work out what each solid looks like and draw it on an isometric grid.

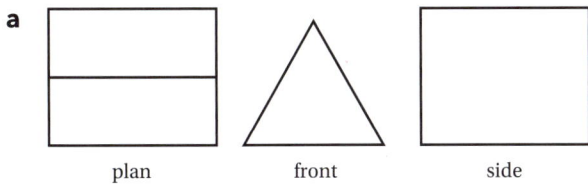

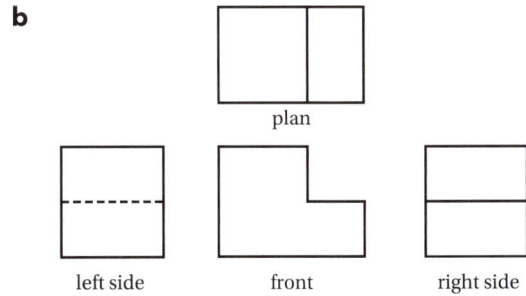

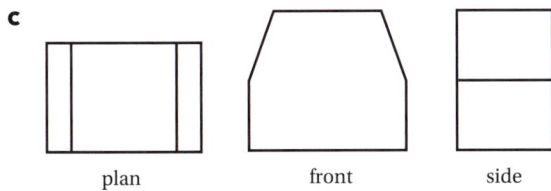

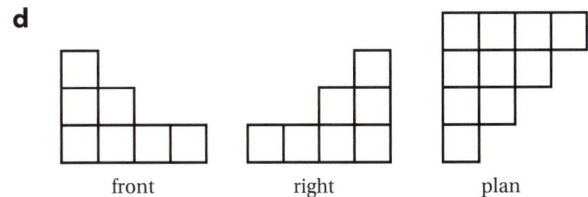

a

plan   front   side

b

plan

left side   front   right side

c

plan   front   side

d

front   right   plan

📎 **Checklist of learning and understanding**

Properties of 3D shapes

- Prisms are shapes with congruent polygonal faces and a regular cross-section.
- Pyramids have a base and triangular sides that meet at an apex.
- Cylinders, cones and spheres are 3D shapes, but they are not polyhedra.
- The number and shape of the faces and the number of edges and vertices can be used to identify and name shapes.

2D representations of 3D shapes

- 3D shapes can be drawn on squared or isometric grids.
- Hidden edges are shown as dotted lines.

Plans and elevations

- A plan is a view from above a shape.
- An elevation is a view from the front, sides or back of a shape.

For additional questions on the topics in this chapter, visit GCSE Mathematics Online.

📁 **Chapter review**

1 The diagram shows the net of a 3D shape. Name the shape, choosing your answer from the options below.

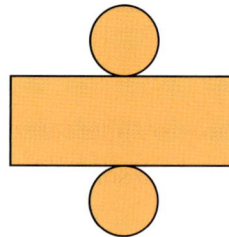

A Sphere	B Cone
C Triangular prism	D Cylinder

2 Give the mathematical name for the 3D object formed from each net.

a

b

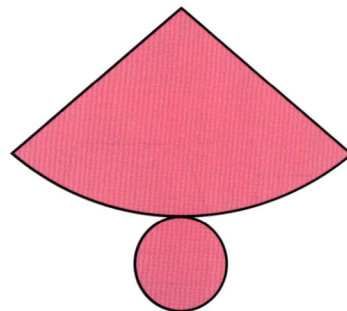

3 **a** Match each block of cubes to the correct plan and elevation.

   b Identify any missing elevations and draw them for each shape.

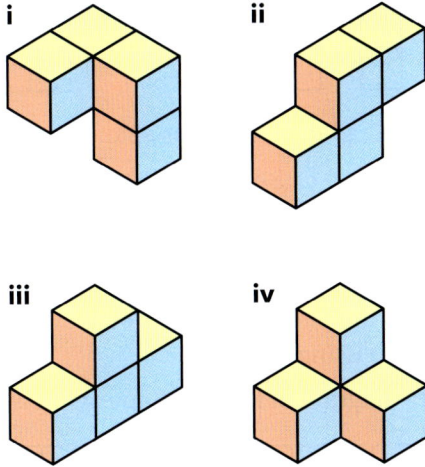

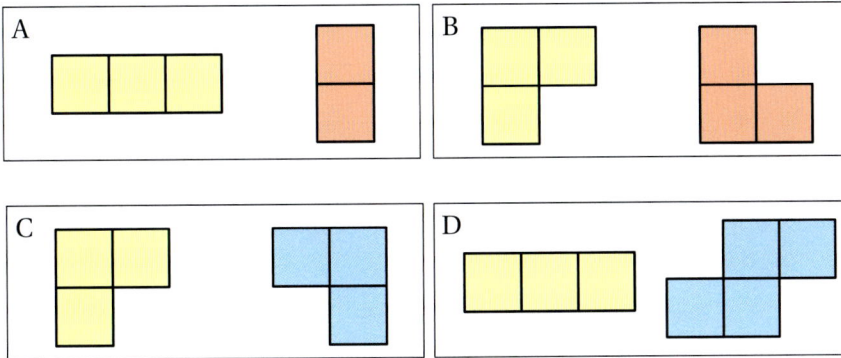

i

ii

iii

iv

A

B

C

D

4 The plan and elevation of a solid built from cubes is shown here. Work out what the solid looks like and sketch it accurately on an isometric grid.

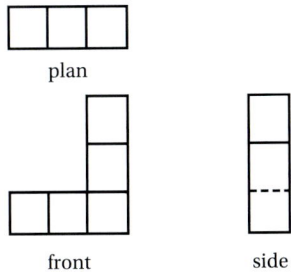

plan

front

side

5 This is the left side and front elevation of a solid built from cubes.

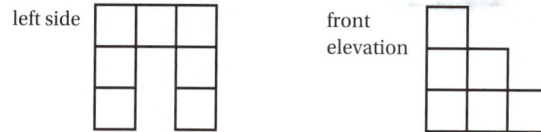

left side

front
elevation

a Draw one possible plan view of this shape.

b Draw a plan view that is not possible for this shape.

c State the least and greatest number of cubes that the shape could be built from to have these elevations.

6 The diagram shows the plan view and front elevation of a computer-generated solid built using 32 cubes.

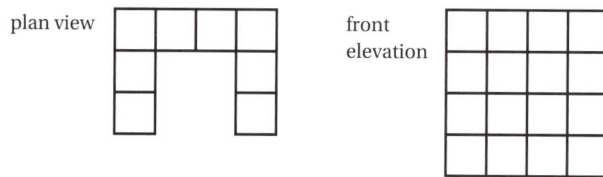

Draw an accurate diagram of the 3D shape on an isometric grid.

plan view

front
elevation

7 This shape is made from five cubes.

Copy these grids and draw what the shape looks like when seen from A, B and C

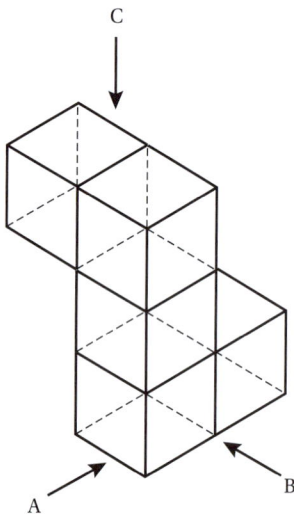

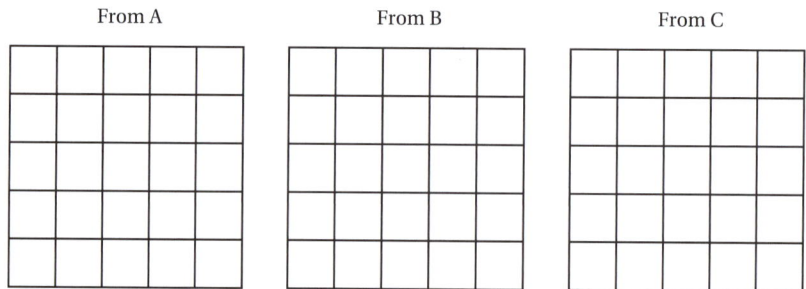

From A

From B

From C

(3 marks)

© AQA 2013

22 Units and measurement

In this chapter you will learn how to …

- work with and convert standard units of measurement.
- use and convert compound units of measurement.
- work with map scales and bearings.
- construct and use scale diagrams to solve problems.

For more resources relating to this chapter, visit GCSE Mathematics Online.

Using mathematics: real-life applications

Measurement has practical applications in many different jobs, but is it also important in everyday activities. Being able to read and work with measurements is important when you make or alter clothes, work out what materials you need to build things and weigh ingredients to make a recipe.

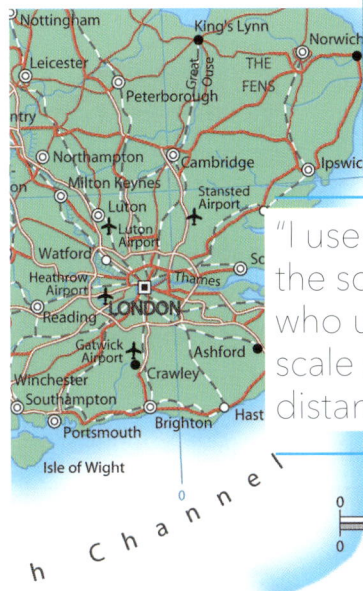

Tip

Think units!

It is important to consider the units in which you are working. Always look back to the original question to decide on the units. With a formula, whatever units you put in must equal the units that come out.

"I use accurate measurements to work out the scale when I draw maps. The people who use maps need to understand the scale so that they can make sense of map distances." *(Cartographer)*

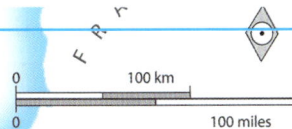

Before you start …

KS3 Ch 6	You must be able to multiply and divide using multiples of 10.	**1**	Work out: **a** 1000×10 **b** $10 \div 1000$ **c** $100 \div 1000$
KS3 Ch 7	You should be able to substitute numbers into a simple formula.	**2**	Use this formula to work out the pay of each person: $p = h \times r$ where p is the pay earned, h is the number of hours worked and r is the rate of pay per hour. **a** Amelia: 20 hours worked at £7 per hour. **b** Billy: 15 hours worked at £6 per hour. **c** Catrin: 40 hours worked at £5.50 per hour.
KS3	You should be able to solve problems involving direct proportion.	**3**	Six pencils cost 90p. Work out the cost of: **a** 12 pencils **b** 1 pencil **c** 4 pencils.

Find answers at: cambridge.org/ukschools/gcsemaths-studentbookanswers

Assess your starting point using the Launchpad

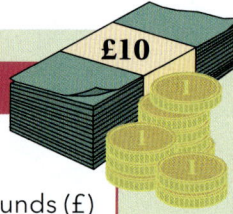

STEP 1

1 Convert:

  a 11 569 grams into kilograms   **c** 123 000 pence into pounds (£)

  b $4\frac{1}{2}$ hours into seconds   **d** 5 cm² into m².

GO TO
Section 1:
Standard units of measurement

STEP 2

2 A car travels 16 kilometres in 20 minutes.

  a What is the average speed of the car in kilometres per hour?

  b Express this speed in m/s.

2 Annie is stuck in traffic.

She works out that her taxi is travelling at an average speed of $6\frac{2}{3}$ m/s.

  a Express that speed in kilometres per hour.

  b How long will it take her to cover a distance of 600 m at this speed?

  c The traffic clears slightly and the average speed increases to 30 km/h.

    How far will she travel in 20 seconds at this speed?

GO TO
Section 2:
Compound units of measurement

STEP 3

4 A helicopter is drawn using a scale of 1 : 100.

On the scale drawing the length of the helicopter blade is 8 cm.

How long is the actual blade?

5 The helicopter takes off from a point X and flies due north for 30 km to reach point Y.

It then flies on a bearing of 150° for 15 km to reach point Z.

  a Use a scale of 1 cm to represent 10 km to make a scale drawing showing the helicopter's journey.

  b Use your diagram to find the bearing from X to Z.

  c Calculate the actual distance directly between X and Z.

GO TO
Section 3:
Maps, scale drawings and bearings

GO TO

Chapter review

Section 1: Standard units of measurement

Standard metric units of measurement are used for recording length, area, volume, capacity, mass, and money.

In the metric system, units of measurement are divided into sub-units.

Each sub-unit is 10 times bigger than the one before it.

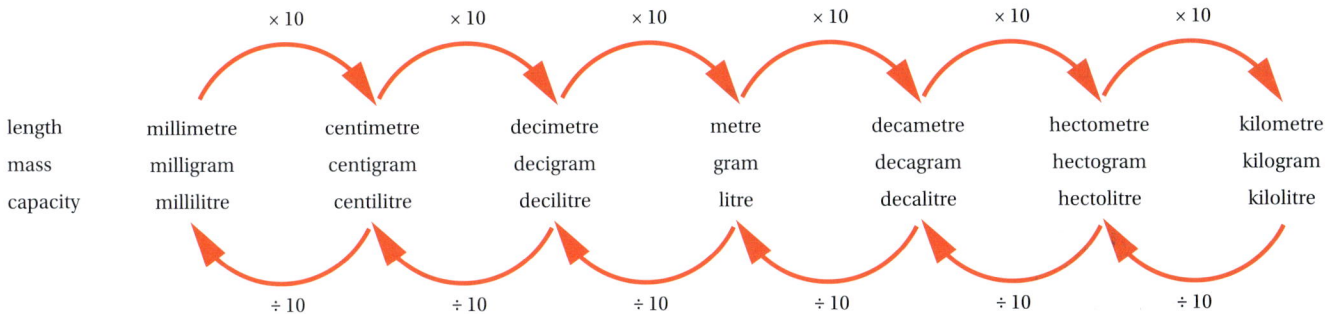

length	millimetre	centimetre	decimetre	metre	decametre	hectometre	kilometre
mass	milligram	centigram	decigram	gram	decagram	hectogram	kilogram
capacity	millilitre	centilitre	decilitre	litre	decalitre	hectolitre	kilolitre

Converting between units

To convert between units in the metric system you need to multiply or divide by powers of 10.

Converting from centimetres to metres is across two sub-units.

So here you have to multiply or divide by $10^2 = 100$.

You will use the following conversions often, so it useful to remember them.

1 centimetre (cm) = 10 millimetres (mm)

1 metre (m) = 100 centimetres (cm)

1 kilometre (km) = 1000 metres (m)

1 kilogram (kg) = 1000 grams (g)

1 tonne (t) = 1000 kilograms (kg)

1 litre (l) = 1000 millilitres (ml)

1 litre (l) = 1000 cubic centimetres (cm^3)

1 cubic centimetre (cm^3) = 1 millilitre (ml)

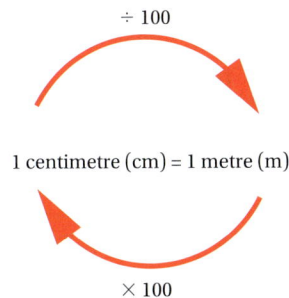

÷ 100

1 centimetre (cm) = 1 metre (m)

× 100

Tip

When you convert from a smaller to a larger unit there are fewer of the larger units, so you divide by a power of 10.
When you convert from a larger to a smaller unit there are more of the smaller units, so you multiply by a power of 10.

WORK IT OUT 22.1

In a sponsored swim the total number of lengths swum is 94.

Each length is 25 metres.

How many kilometres were swum in total?

Which of the answers below is correct?

Option A	Option B	Option C
Total number of metres = 25 × 94 = 2350 metres Conversion: 100 metres = 1 km 2350 ÷ 100 = 23.5 km swum in total	Total number of metres = 25 × 94 = 2350 metres Conversion: 100 metres = 1 km 2350 × 100 = 235 000 km swum in total	Total number of metres = 25 × 94 = 2350 metres Conversion: 1000 metres = 1 km 2350 ÷ 1000 = 2.35 km swum in total

Find answers at: cambridge.org/ukschools/gcsemaths-studentbookanswers

Converting areas and volume

Area is measured in square units, such as mm^2 (square millimetres), cm^2, m^2 or km^2, so any conversion factor also has to be squared.

For example, the two squares below have the same area.

The conversion factor from m^2 to cm^2, and vice versa, is 10 000.

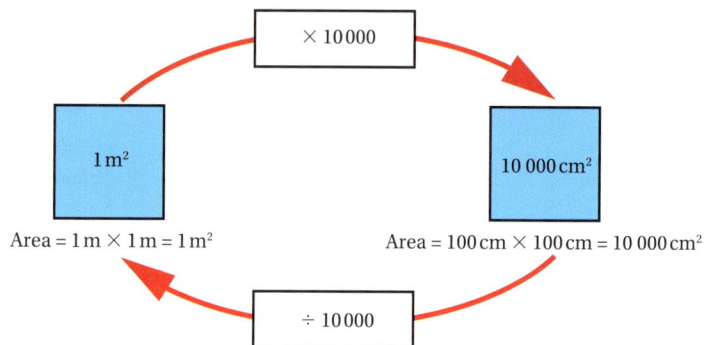

$\times 10\,000$

$1\,m^2$ $10\,000\,cm^2$

$\div 10\,000$

Area = 1 m × 1 m = 1 m^2 Area = 100 cm × 100 cm = 10 000 cm^2

WORKED EXAMPLE 1

Convert each measure to the units given.

a $10\,m^2$ to cm^2 **b** $8.6\,km^2$ to m^2 **c** $3500\,mm^2$ to cm^2

a $10\,m^2$ to cm^2
$= 10 \times 10\,000 = 100\,000\,cm^2$

Conversion factor = 10 000

b $8.6\,km^2$ to m^2
$= 8.6 \times 1\,000\,000 = 8\,600\,000\,m^2$

Conversion factor = 1 000 000

c $3500\,mm^2$ to cm^2
$= 3500 \div 100 = 35\,cm^2$

Conversion factor = 100

Volume is measured in cubic units such as mm^3 (cubic millimetres), cm^3 or m^3 so any conversion factor also has to be cubed.

For example, the two cubes below have the same volume.

The conversion factor from m^3 to cm^3, and vice versa, is 1 000 000.

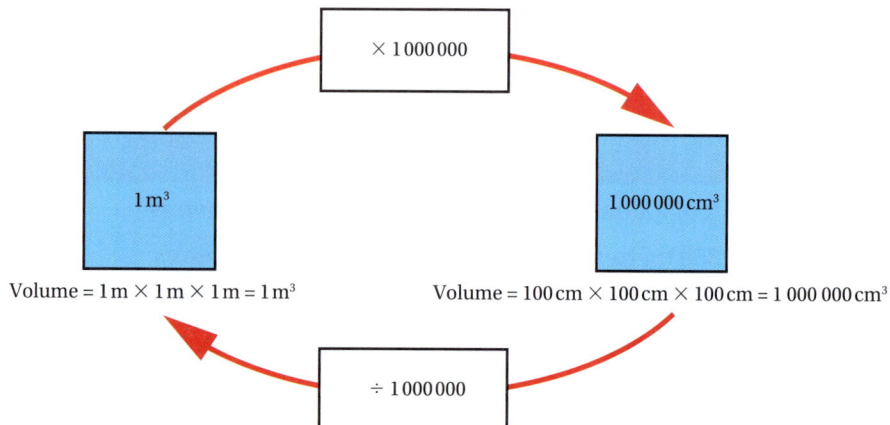

$\times 1\,000\,000$

$1\,m^3$ $1\,000\,000\,cm^3$

$\div 1\,000\,000$

Volume = 1 m × 1 m × 1 m = 1 m^3 Volume = 100 cm × 100 cm × 100 cm = 1 000 000 cm^3

When referring to the volume of liquids, the term capacity is used. Capacity is generally measured in litres or millilitres.

WORKED EXAMPLE 2

Convert each measurement to the units given.

a $6.3\,m^3$ to cm^3 **b** $96\,500\,000\,cm^3$ to m^3 **c** $750\,cm^3$ to mm^3

a $6.3\,m^3$ to cm^3
$= 6.3 \times 1\,000\,000 = 6\,300\,000\,cm^3$

> Conversion factor
> $= 1\,000\,000$.

b $96\,500\,000\,cm^3$ to m^3
$= 96\,500\,000 \div 1\,000\,000 = 96.5\,m^3$

> Conversion factor
> $= 1\,000\,000$.

c $750\,cm^3$ to mm^3
$= 750 \times 1000 = 750\,000\,mm^3$

> Conversion factor
> $= 1000$.

It is easy to make mistakes if you try to calculate with measurements in different units, so it makes sense to convert them all to the same unit before doing any calculations.

WORKED EXAMPLE 3

A builder is putting a cornice around the ceiling of a room. This is a decorative strip that hides the join between the walls and the ceiling.

A plan of the room is drawn on the right.

How many metres of cornice does the builder need?

$80\,cm \div 100 = 0.8\,m$
$700\,mm \div 1000 = 0.7\,m$
Total distance around room:
$2.9 + 4.5 + 3.7 + 3.8 + 0.8 + 0.7 = 16.4\,m$
The builder needs $16.4\,m$ of decorative strip.

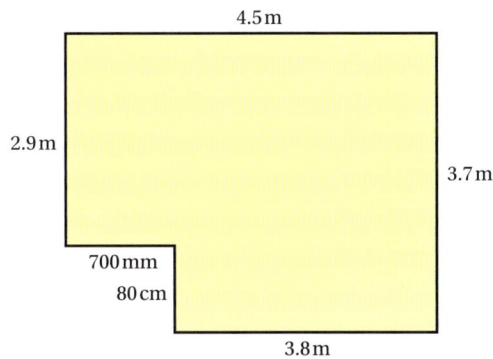

> As the answer needs to be given in metres, it makes sense to convert all the measurements to metres.

(Plan of room showing dimensions: 4.5 m top edge, 2.9 m left edge, 3.7 m right edge, 700 mm and 80 cm on left lower step, 3.8 m bottom edge)

> **Tip**
>
> You will use measurement conversions in Section 3, which covers scale drawings and maps.

EXERCISE 22A

1 How many cm³ are there in 4.5 m³?

Choose your answer from the following options.

A 4500   B 45 000   C 450 000   D 4 500 000

2 Match each measurement on the left to the equivalent measurement on the right.

10 000 mm	10 l
10 000 ml	10 g
10 kg	10 m
0.01 kg	1 mm
0.1 cm	10 000 g

3 Convert the following lengths and masses into the given units to complete the following.

a 2.5 km = ☐ m   **b** 85 cm = ☐ mm   **c** 34 m = ☐ mm

d 1.55 m = ☐ mm   **e** 0.07 m = ☐ cm   **f** 5.4 kg = ☐ g

g 0.9 kg = ☐ g   **h** 102 g = ☐ kg   **i** 14.5 g = ☐ kg

4 Add the following capacities.

Give your answers in the units indicated in brackets.

a 3.5 l + 5 l (ml)   **b** 2.3 l + 450 ml (l)   **c** 20 l + 4.5 l + 652 ml (l)

5 Sadie uses concrete slabs to form a border around a rectangular garden.

The garden is 450 cm wide and 5.5 m long.

a Draw a diagram to represent the garden.

b Calculate the perimeter of the garden in metres.

c The concrete slabs are 120 cm long.

How many will Sadie need to form the border?

d The slabs cost £4.55 each.

Work out how much it will cost Sadie to buy the slabs she needs.

e What is the cost per metre for the concrete border?

6 Convert each of the following into the required units.

a Total mass in kg of 3 bags of flour, each of mass 1200 g.

b The length in cm of a whale 7.763 m long.

c 3567 kg of lead into tonnes.

d Area of 5 m² into mm².

e 96.35 m³ of sand into cm³.

f 345 cm³ of water into litres.

Tip

1 metric tonne is equal to 1000 kg

7 Copy and fill in < or > between the two measurements.

Then calculate the difference between the greater and smaller measurements.

Give your answer in the most appropriate units.

a 5.7 cm ☐ 560 mm   **b** 8 kg ☐ 7900 g

c 590 l ☐ 59 015 cl   **d** 19.3 cm ☐ 189 mm

e 101 cl ☐ 0.99 l   **f** 198 cm ☐ 0.001 99 km

g 145 g ☐ 1.45 kg   **h** 1987 t ☐ 10 987 kg

i 2 m³ ☐ 200 000 cm³

8 The actual dimensions of a new kitchen sink are given on the diagram in millimetres.

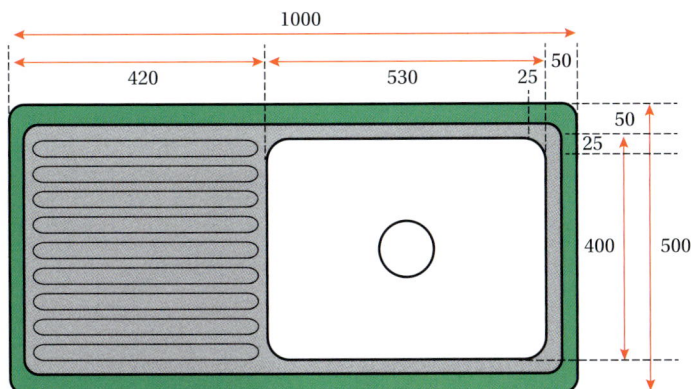

Tip

Volume of a cuboid
= length × breadth × height

a Calculate the total perimeter of the whole sink unit in centimetres.

b What is the area of the draining board section in square millimetres?

c Convert the area of the draining board to square metres.

d The sink is 170 mm deep.

What is the approximate volume or capacity of the sink in:

i cubic millimetres?   **ii** litres?

Time

The units of time we use on a daily basis are not decimal units.

To convert units of time you have to work out how many sub-units there are in the units you are working with.

Time is sometimes given in decimal form, for example 4.8 hours.

You can convert these times back to ordinary units in different ways.

There are 60 minutes in an hour, so

4.8 × 60 minutes = 288 minutes = 4 hours 48 minutes

Or, you can think of this as 4 hours and 0.8 hours.

0.8 × 60 = 48, so the time is 4 hours and 48 minutes

Tip

1 year = 365 days (366 in a leap year)

1 day = 24 hours = 1440 minutes

1 hour = 60 minutes = 3600 seconds

1 minute = 60 seconds

Calculator tip

Modern scientific calculators have a mode that you can use to do sexagesimal calculation (hours, minutes and seconds). Different models work in different ways, so read the manual or check online to see how your calculator works.

Find answers at: cambridge.org/ukschools/gcsemaths-studentbookanswers

In athletics and other timed sporting events the times are often given using decimal fractions of a second.

For example, in August 2009, Usain Bolt ran the 100 m in the world record time of 9.580 seconds.

In the metric system, 1 second = 1000 milliseconds.

9.580 is time recorded exact to $\frac{1}{1000}$ of a second.

This is 9 seconds and 580 milliseconds. You cannot convert it in any other way.

12-hour and 24-hour times

The 12-hour time system uses am to show times from midnight to noon and pm for time from noon till midnight.

The 24-hour time system shows the times 00:00 to 23:59. Midnight is 00:00.

> **Tip**
>
> Add 12 to write a pm time using the 24-hour clock, for example, 10.35 pm + 12 = 22:35.
>
> Subtract 12 to write a time between 13:00 and 23:59 using the 12-hour clock, for example, 15:40 − 12 = 3.40 pm.

Problem-solving framework

Mr Smith is in Moscow.

He needs to return to London.

The flight from Moscow to London takes 3.6 hours.

The local time in Moscow is 3 hours ahead of the UK.

The flight is scheduled for take-off from Moscow at 18:55 local time.

On arrival it takes 45 minutes to get through the airport.

Mr Smith will stop to buy a coffee, sandwich and newspaper for the train.

Trains for central London leave at 5, 27 and 46 minutes past the hour, and the journey will take 29 minutes.

There is a 7-minute walk from the train station to his hotel.

What is the earliest time that Mr Smith can expect to arrive at his hotel?

Give your answer using the 12-hour system of time.

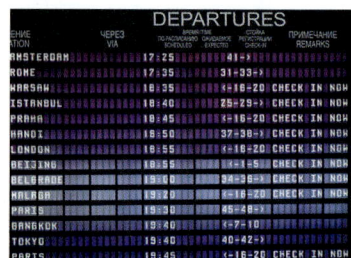

Steps for solving problems	What you would do for this example
Step 1: What have you got to do?	First work out the time of arrival in London and then work out how long it takes from there to the hotel.
Step 2: What information do you need?	Flight departure times: 18:55 (local time) Time difference between London and Moscow: 3 hours Flight time: 3.6 hours Time to get through airport: 45 minutes Train departure times: 5 past, 27 minutes past, 46 minutes past the hour Length of train journey: 29 minutes Walk time: 7 minutes

Continues on next page …

Step 3: What information don't you need?	Assume time to buy a coffee, sandwich and newspaper is negligible
Step 4: What maths can you use?	18:55 minus 3 hours = 15:55 (London time)
	Convert 3.6 from a decimal to time in hours and minutes:
	3 hours and 0.6 × 60 = 3 hours 36 min
	Arrival time in London: 15:55 + 3 hours 36 min = 19:31
	Add on time in customs: 19:31+ 45 min = 20:16
	Next possible train is 20:27
	Time at end of train journey: 20:27 + 29 min = 20:56
	Arrival time at venue following walk: 20:56 + 7 min = 21:03
	21:03 – 12 = 9.03 pm
	Mr Smith can expect to arrive at his hotel at three minutes past nine in the evening at the earliest.
Step 5: Have you used all the information? At this point you should check to make sure you have calculated what was asked of you.	Flight departure time ✓ Time difference ✓ Flight time ✓ Time through customs ✓ Train departure times ✓ Length of train journey ✓ Walk time ✓
Step 6: Is it correct?	Estimate to check: $3\frac{1}{2}$ hours flying + 45 min at airport + 10 min wait + 30 min train + 7 min walk = about 5 hours Take off the time difference leaves 2 hours Leave 7 pm + 2 hours = 9 pm

Tip

When you work with time, treat hours and minutes separately. If you carry over from hours to minutes, remember you are carrying 60 minutes.

Money

£1 = 100p

So the number of £ × 100 gives the number of pence

and the number of pence ÷ 100 gives the number of £.

The rate at which one currency is converted to another is called an **exchange rate**.

If an exchange rate is given as 1 unit of A = x units of B, you can convert currency A to currency B by multiplying by x.

For example, £1 = €1.26

So, £400 = 1.26 × 400 = €504

Currency B can be converted to currency A by dividing by x.

For example, £1 = €1.26

So, €400 = $\frac{400}{1.26}$ = £317.46

EXERCISE 22B

1. The starting pistol for a road race is fired at 12:15:30.

   The first runner crosses the finish line at 14:07:22.

   What was the winning time for the race?

2. How many minutes are there in 10.4 hours?

   Choose your answer from the following options.

   A 64 min   B 604 min   C 624 min   D 640 min

3. Sandra is exactly 16 years old.

   Calculate her age in:

   a weeks   **b** days   **c** hours   **d** seconds.

4. A boat leaves port at 14:35 and arrives at its destination $6\frac{1}{2}$ hours later.

   At what time does the boat arrive?

5. An area of 250 000 cm² needs to be painted.

   A pot of paint can cover an area of 10 m².

   How many pots of paint are needed?

Key vocabulary

exchange rate: a number that is used to calculate the difference in value between money from one country and money from another

6 The table gives the value of the pound (£) against four other currencies in July 2014.

British pound (£)	Euro (€)	US dollar ($)	Australian dollar (AU$)	Indian rupee (Rs)
1	1.26	1.70	1.80	102.28

a Calculate the value of 1 of each of the other currencies in pounds at this rate.

b Convert £125 to US dollars.

c How many Indian rupees would you get if you converted £45 at this rate?

d Dilshaad has 8000 Indian rupees.

What is this worth in pounds at this rate?

e Give a reason why tourists from the UK may find India a cheap place to visit.

f How can a weaker exchange rate affect the economy of a country?

Consider the cost of imports and the value of exports in your answer.

Section 2: Compound units of measurement

Compound measures involve more than one unit of measurement.

For example:

- rate of pay, such as pounds per hour, involves units of money and time
- unit pricing, such as pence per gram, involves units of money and mass (or capacity or volume).

You can simplify compound measures by multiplying or dividing both units by the same factor.

Tip

A forward slash symbol / is often used instead of the word 'per'. So £8.30/hour means the same as £8.30 per hour.

WORKED EXAMPLE 4

Forty litres of petrol cost £52.

a What is the cost in £/litre?   **b** Convert the cost in £/litre to pence per millilitre.

a £$\frac{52}{40}$ = £1.30

The cost is £1.30/litre

> The compound measure £/litre tells you that pounds are the first unit.

b £1.30 = 130 p

1 l = 1000 ml

130 p per 1000 ml

$\frac{130}{1000}$ = 0.13

$\frac{1000}{1000}$ = 1

So 130 p per 1000 ml = 0.13 p/ml

> You want a compound measure comparing pence and millilitres.
>
> Convert pounds to pence.
>
> Convert litres to millilitres.
>
> Compare the two quantities.
>
> You want a rate per **one** millilitre, so divide both quantities by 1000.

Speed

Speed compares the distance travelled to the time taken.

The units of speed depend on the situation.

The speed of a car or train is often given in km/h or mph (kilometres per hour or miles per hour).

An athlete's running speed might be given in m/s (metres per second).

You need to know the formula for calculating speed.

The speed is an average speed because a journey might involve faster and slower speeds over the given period.

The triangle shows the relationship between speed, distance and time.

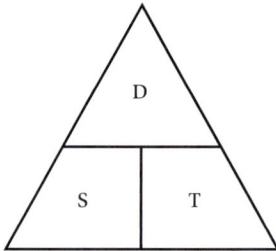

Learn this formula

$$\text{Average speed} = \frac{\text{Distance travelled}}{\text{Time taken}}$$

Tip

- To find distance: cover D with your finger. The position of S next to T tells you to multiply speed by time. Distance = Speed × Time taken
- To find time: cover T with your finger. The position of D over S tells you to divide distance by speed. Time taken = Distance ÷ Speed
- To find speed: cover S with your finger. The position of D over T tells you to divide distance by time. Speed = Distance ÷ Time taken

The units of speed given in a problem usually let you know what units to use.

For example, if the problem talks about km/h, then express distances in kilometres and time in hours to calculate the speed.

WORK IT OUT 22.2

A car travels 330 miles in $5\frac{1}{2}$ hours.

What is the average speed of the car in miles per hour (mph)?

Which of the answers below is correct?

Option A	Option B	Option C
$\text{Speed} = \dfrac{\text{Distance}}{\text{Time taken}}$ $D = 330$ miles $T = 5\frac{1}{2}$ hours = 5.5 hours $S = \dfrac{330}{5.5} = 60$ mph	Speed = Distance × Time taken $D = 330$ miles $T = 5\frac{1}{2}$ hours = 5.5 hours $S = 330 \times 5.5 = 1815$ mph	Speed = Distance − Time taken $D = 330$ miles $T = 5\frac{1}{2}$ hours = 5.5 hours $S = 330 - 5.5 = 324.5$ mph

To convert speeds from one set of units to another, you need to work systematically and take care with the units.

EXERCISE 22C

1 Joe works for a minimum wage of £5.13 per hour.

He works for 14 hours.

How much does he earn in this time?

2 Henry earns £8.75 per hour.

One week he worked 36.5 hours.

Sireta earned £186.50 for working 22 hours.

How much more does Henry earn per hour?

3 A bricklayer lays 680 bricks in four hours.

How many does she lay per minute, to the nearest brick?

4 Bernie cycles 168 km in eight hours.

What is his average speed in kilometres per hour?

5 A car travels 531 km at an average speed of 88 km/h.

Work out the time taken.

6 Usain Bolt set an Olympic Record over 100 m at the London Olympics in 2012 with a time of 9.63 seconds.

  a Express this speed in m/s.

  b How fast is this in kilometres per hour?

  c Usain Bolt is also the world record holder for the 100 m event.

  He set a world record of 9.58 s in August 2009.

  How much faster is the world record speed than the Olympic record speed?

7 A zebra runs at 42 km/h and covers a distance of 6.3 km.

Calculate the time it takes.

8 A train leaves Liverpool Street at 9:37 am and arrives at Norwich at 11:43 am, a distance of 189.9 km.

What is the average speed of the train?

9 A marathon runner starts a 42 km race at 05:54:10 and finishes at 08:12.37.

What was her average speed for the race?

Give your answer in km/h and m/s.

10 A car travelled for 20 minutes at 85 km/h.

It then travelled for another 25 minutes at 100 km/h.

What was the average speed of the car over the whole journey?

Density and pressure

Learn this formula

$$\text{Density} = \frac{\text{Mass}}{\text{Volume}}$$

Density is the ratio between the mass and the volume of an object.

You need to know the formula for calculating the density of an object.

The triangle below helps you see the relationship between density, mass and volume.

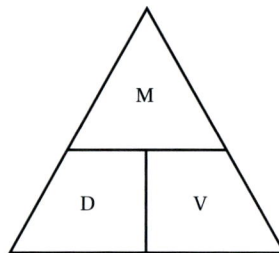

Mass = Density × Volume

$$\text{Volume} = \frac{\text{Mass}}{\text{Density}}$$

The units of density are grams per cubic centimetre (g/cm³) or kilograms per cubic metre (kg/m³).

Express the mass and the volume in the units given when you solve problems involving density.

WORKED EXAMPLE 5

A gold bar has a volume of 725 cm³ and a mass of 14.5 kg.

What is the density of the gold bar in g/cm³?

$$\text{Density} = \frac{\text{Mass}}{\text{Volume}}$$

Write down the formula.

$M = 14.5\,\text{kg} = 14.5 \times 1000$
$\qquad\quad = 14500\,g$
$V = 725\,\text{cm}^3$

Write down the values of mass and volume (the units of density are g/cm³ so the mass must be in g).

$$\text{Density} = \frac{14500}{725} = 20\,g/cm^3$$

The density of the gold bar is 20 g/cm³.

Substitute the values into the formula.

Learn this formula

$$\text{Pressure} = \frac{\text{Force}}{\text{Area}}$$

You also need to know the formula for pressure.

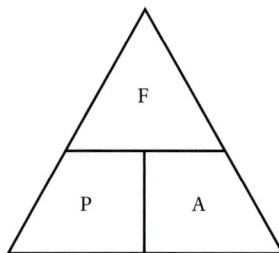

The units given for force and area give you compound units for the pressure.

For example, if force is measured in newtons and area in mm², the compound unit of pressure would be N/mm² (newtons per mm²).

WORKED EXAMPLE 6

A brick exerts a force of 5 N.

a Calculate the pressure exerted on the ground when the brick is in each of the following positions.

i On flat surface

Force = 5 N

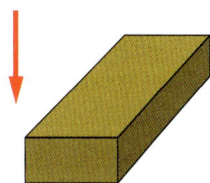

Area of base = 0.03 m²

ii On short edge

Force = 5 N

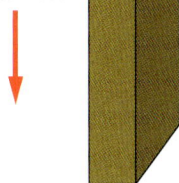

Area of base = 0.015 m²

iii On long edge

Force = 5 N

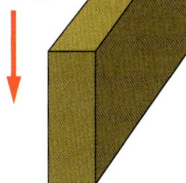

Area of base = 0.02 m²

a **i** $Pressure = \dfrac{5\,N}{0.03\,m^2} = 167\,N/m^2$

ii $Pressure = \dfrac{5\,N}{0.015\,m^2} = 333\,N/m^2$

iii $Pressure = \dfrac{5\,N}{0.02\,m^2} = 250\,N/m^2$

Substitute the values from each diagram into the formula for pressure.

Don't forget to add the compound units for pressure.

b Which brick exerts the strongest pressure? Why?

b The middle brick (B) exerts the strongest pressure.
The force of 5 N is pushing down on a smaller area, so the pressure is greater.

EXERCISE 22D

1 The mass of 1 cm³ of different substances is shown in the diagram.

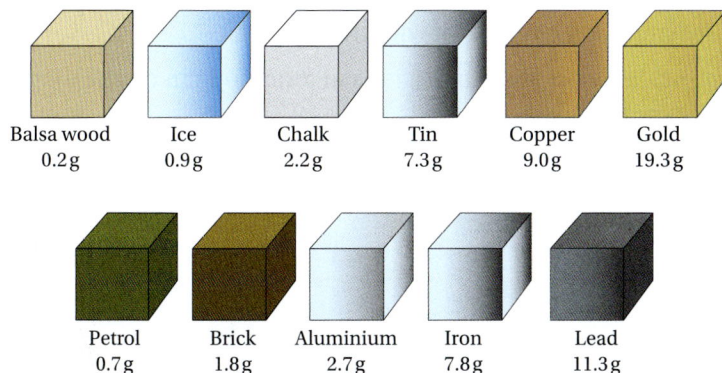

| Balsa wood 0.2 g | Ice 0.9 g | Chalk 2.2 g | Tin 7.3 g | Copper 9.0 g | Gold 19.3 g |

| Petrol 0.7 g | Brick 1.8 g | Aluminium 2.7 g | Iron 7.8 g | Lead 11.3 g |

a Write down the density of each substance in g/cm³.

b Express each density in g/m³ and then convert each to kg/m³.

Find answers at: cambridge.org/ukschools/gcsemaths-studentbookanswers

421

2 The mass of an object is 15 000 kg and its volume is 958 cm³.

What is its density, to two decimal places?

Choose from the following options.

A 15.66 g/cm³   B 15.6 g/cm³   C 15.66 kg   D 15.66 kg/cm³

3 A cube of material with side length 30 mm has a mass of 0.0642 kg.

Calculate the density of the material in g/cm³.

4 Calculate the volume of a piece of wood with a mass of 0.1 kg and a density of 0.8 g/cm³.

5 Two metal blocks both exert a force of 18 N.

Block A is a cube with side 100 cm.

Block B is a cuboid with a base of area 6 m² in contact with the floor.

Calculate the pressure exerted by each block in N/m².

6 A car exerts a force of 6000 N on the road.

Each of the four wheels has an area of 0.025 m² in contact with the road.

What pressure does the car exert on the road?

Section 3: Maps, scale drawings and bearings

A **scale drawing** is a diagram in which measurements are either reduced or enlarged by a scale factor.

The scale tells you by how much the dimensions are reduced or enlarged.

Using the map scale

Maps are scaled representations of areas of the real world.

The scale of a map describes the relationship between lengths in real life and lengths on the map.

Bar scales or **line scales** are useful for finding small distances. You measure the distance and then compare it with the line scale.

On the line scale below, each block is 1 cm long, so 1 cm on the map represents 1 km in real life.

To find a distance in real life:

- measure the map distance using a piece of paper
- make pencil marks on the paper to record the distance
- compare your marked distance with the line scale
- read off the real distance.

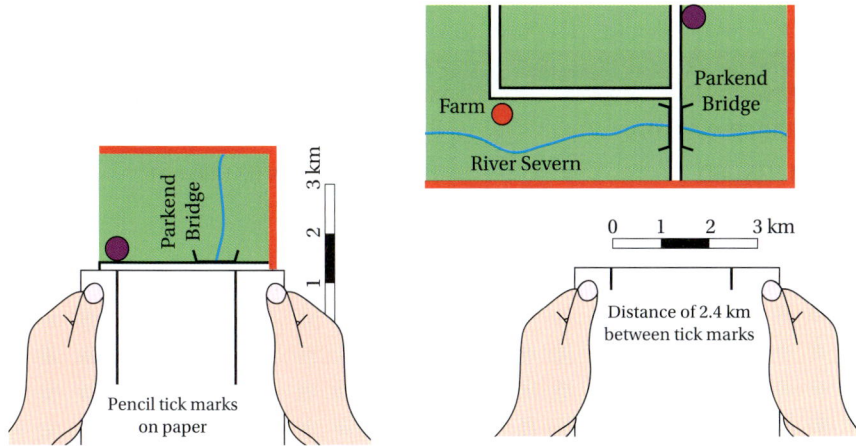

Parkend Bridge

Farm

Parkend Bridge

River Severn

3 km

2

1

Pencil tick marks on paper

0 1 2 3 km

Distance of 2.4 km between tick marks

For bigger distances it is more efficient to use the **ratio scale**. You can convert any distance on a map to a real distance using the following formula:

distance on the map × scale = distance on the ground

× Scale factor

Map

Real life

÷ Scale factor

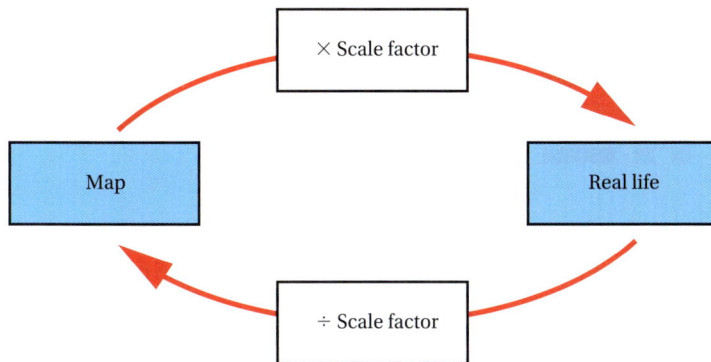

Take care with the units.

When you multiply by the scale your answer will be in the same units that you used to measure on the map.

If the question asks for different units, you will need to convert the measurement to get the units you need.

WORK IT OUT 22.2

The distance between two towns on a 1 : 25 000 map is 3.4 cm.

How many kilometres apart are these towns in reality?

Which student has worked out the correct answer?

What have the other two done incorrectly?

Student A	Student B	Student C
$\dfrac{1}{25\,000} \times \dfrac{3.4}{1}$ $= 0.000136\,\text{cm}$ $= 1.36\,\text{km}$	Map distance = 34 mm Scale = 1 : 25 000 Real distance 34 × 25 000 = 850 000 mm = 8.5 km	3.4 × 25 000 = 85 000 The distance is 85 000 cm ÷ 100 = 850 m ÷ 1000 = 0.85 km

EXERCISE 22E

1   Here are three line scales.

Work out what distance is represented by 1 cm in each case.

a

```
0                                    10km
┌──┬──┬──┬──┬──┐
│  │██│  │██│  │
└──┴──┴──┴──┴──┘
```

b

```
0          50        100km
┌──┬──┬──┬──┐
│██│██│  │  │
└──┴──┴──┴──┘
```

c

```
0  12  24    48    72   96km
┌─┬─┬─┬──┬──┬──┐
│█│ │█│██│  │██│
└─┴─┴─┴──┴──┴──┘
```

2   An Ordnance Survey map has a scale of 1 : 25 000.

The distance between two peaks on the map is 12.5 cm.

How far is the actual distance in kilometres?

Choose your answer from the following options.

A 0.3125 km   B 3.125 km   C 31.25 m   D 312.5 km

3   Work out the real distance (in kilometres) that a map distance of 45 mm would represent at each scale.

a 1 : 120   b 1 : 1200   c 1 : 12 000   d 1 : 120 000

e 1 : 1 200 000   f 1 : 12 000 000   g 1 : 120 000 000

4   Andrew says that a map drawn to a scale of 1 : 15 000 is a larger scale map than one drawn to 1 : 150 000. Is he correct?

Give reasons for your answer.

5 The map below shows several towns.

The map has a scale of 1 : 75 000.

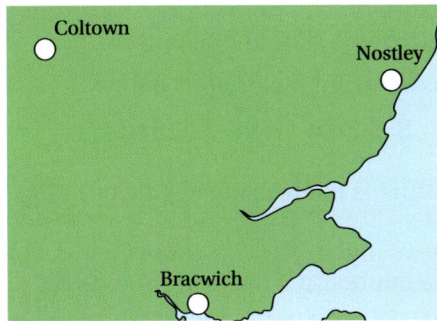

Work out the actual distance directly from Coltown to Bracwich.

6 The red line on the map shows the path of a plane flying from Edinburgh to London.

The flight took 55 minutes.

1 : 10 000 000

a Calculate the distance flown in kilometres.

b What was the plane's average speed on this flight?

7 The length of a skirt made from a sewing pattern is to be 26 cm.

The pattern is drawn to quarter scale which means it is drawn to $\frac{1}{4}$ the size of the object.

What is the length of the skirt on the pattern?

Choose your answer from the options below.

   A 6 cm   B 6.5 cm   C 13 cm   D 104 cm

8 A set of toy furniture is made using a scale of 1 : 50.

Work out:

  a the height of a cupboard if the toy is 5 cm high

  b the width of the toy bed if the actual bed is 1.5 m wide

  c the length of a table if the toy is 2.7 cm long.

9 A model of an F15 fighter jet has a scale of 1 : 32.

The real aircraft is 12.5 m long.

What is the length of the model?

10 A map of Scotland has a scale of 1 : 2 000 000.

  a The distance on the map from Inverness to Glasgow is 90 mm.

    What is the real distance between Inverness and Glasgow?

  b The actual distance by road from Aberdeen to Dundee is 96.5 km.

    How long is this road on the map?

11 Pete has a road map that shows the driving distance from Birmingham to London as 192 km.

He estimates that $2\frac{1}{2}$ cm on the map represents a distance of 50 km.

  a Work out the scale of the map.

  b How long are the roads shown on the map for Pete's journey from Birmingham to London at this scale?

Constructing scale drawings

To make a scaled drawing or simple map you need to:

- find out or measure the real lengths
- decide what size your drawing is going to be so you can work out a scale
- choose an appropriate scale (if you are not given one to use) and work it out from the ratio 'length on drawing : length in real life'
- use the scale to convert the real lengths to ones you need for the scaled drawing.

Tip

You will use scale factors again in Chapter 35 when you deal with similar triangles and enlargements of shapes.

WORKED EXAMPLE 7

Draw a scale plan of a rectangular park that is 115 m long and 85 m wide.

Your plan must fit into a space 7.5 cm long and 5 cm wide.

Step 1: The real measurements are 115 m and 85 m

Check that the measurements are in the same units – if not, convert so that they are.

Step 2: A scale drawing 6 cm long will fit into the given space.

Decide upon a reasonable scale that fits the paper well – not too small so you can't read it.

Step 3: Work out the scale.
Scale = length on drawing : length in real life
= 6 cm : 115 m
= 6 cm : 11 500 cm
= 1 : 1917

Scale is a ratio and should be written as such.

In this case 6 cm : 115 cm

But they must be in the same units.

Convert the metres to centimetres.

Divide both sides by 6 to get 1 on the left.

Most scales are rounded.

1 : 1917 is a clumsy scale so try a scale of 1 : 2000

Step 4: Use the scale to convert the real distances.
Scaled length = $\frac{115}{2000}$ = 0.0575 m = 5.75 cm
Scaled width = $\frac{85}{2000}$ = 0.0425 m = 4.25 cm

Apply the ratio to convert the real distances to the scaled distances.

Draw a 5 cm by 7.5 cm frame.

Use your construction skills to draw an accurate rectangle 4.25 cm by 5.75 cm.

Remember to write the scale you are using on the diagram.

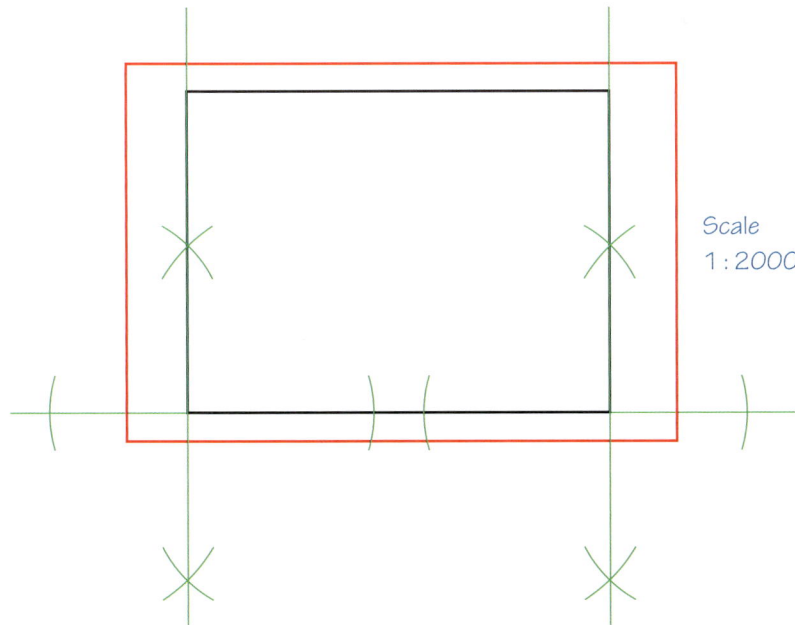

Scale 1 : 2000

To construct each vertical line accurately you need to draw a perpendicular at each corner. To do this:

1 Put your compasses on the corner and mark an arc on the base line to right and left.
2 Widen the arc of your compasses.
3 Put your compasses on one of your marks on the base line and draw an arc above and below the line.
4 Then move your compasses to your other mark on the base line and draw two more arcs above and below the line that intersect your first set.
5 Draw a line through these intersections. It should pass through the corner and be perpendicular to the base line.
6 Repeat for the other corner of the rectangle.

Find answers at: cambridge.org/ukschools/gcsemaths-studentbookanswers

EXERCISE 22F

1 The floor of a school hall is 40 m long and 20 m wide.

Draw scaled diagrams to show what it would look like at each of the following scales.

a 1:50 **b** 1:500 **c** 1:1000

2 Measure the dimensions of your desk in centimetres.

Work out a suitable scale and draw a scaled diagram of your desk, including anything on it.

3 Jules drew this rough plan of a classroom block at her school.

She wrote the actual measurements on the plan.

Use the dimensions on the plan to draw a scaled diagram of this classroom block that fits into the width of your exercise book.

Indicate windows and doors as shown on the plan.

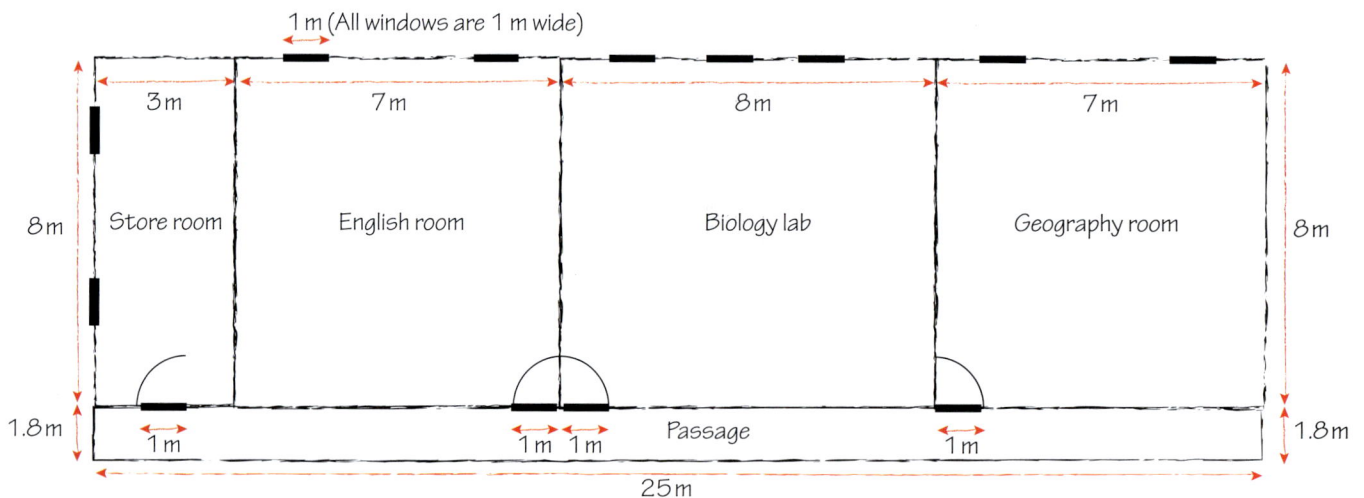

4 A plan of a house is drawn at a scale of 1:80.

The kitchen is 4900 mm by 3800 mm.

A sink unit is 1.2 metres long.

a What are the scaled dimensions of the kitchen?

b Calculate the scaled length of the sink unit.

Bearings

Compass directions can be given using the points shown on a compass rose. The cardinal points are north, east, south and west. The points half way between these cardinal points are north-east, south-east, south-west and north-west, with another set of 8 points defined between these eight, for example north-north-east.

More accurate directions can be given using degrees or bearings.

More accurate directions can be given using degrees or bearings.

Bearings are measured in degrees from 0° (north) around in a **clockwise** direction to 360° (which is back at north).

To measure bearings, you must place the baseline of your protractor in line with the compass direction north. Then you measure the angle from there to the given point.

The direction east written as a three-figure bearing is 090° as the angle from north clockwise is 90°.

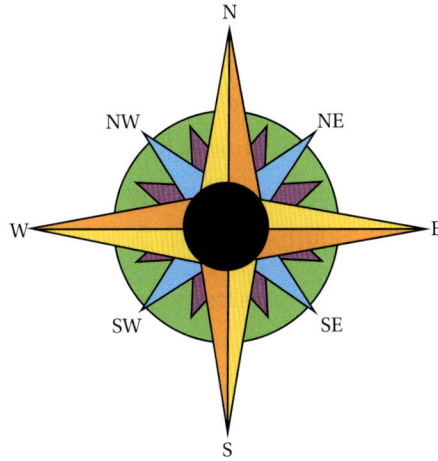

Tip

You might have to draw a perpendicular to a point to make your own north line if it is not on the diagram.

WORKED EXAMPLE 8

In the diagram, find the bearings from:

a A to B   **b** B to A.

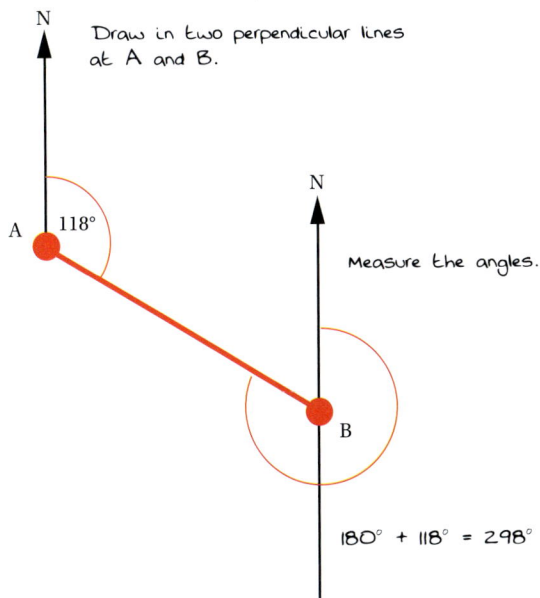

Draw in two perpendicular lines at A and B.

Measure the angles.

There are no north lines on the diagram so you have to draw them on before you can measure the bearings.

180° + 118° = 298°

a Bearing from A to B is 118°.
b Bearing from B to A is 298°.

Find answers at: cambridge.org/ukschools/gcsemaths-studentbookanswers

EXERCISE 22G

1 Write the three-figure bearing that corresponds with each direction.

a Due south   **b** North-east   **c** West

2 Alex is facing north-west. He makes a 270° turn clockwise.

What direction is he now facing?

Choose from the following options.

A South-west   B North-east   C South-east   D West

3 Use a protractor to measure each of the following bearings on the diagram.

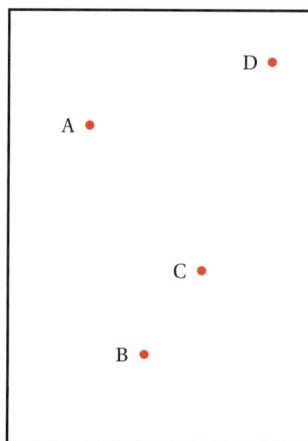

a A to B   **b** B to A   **c** A to C

d B to D   **e** D to A   **f** D to B

4 Beville is 140 km west and 45 km north of Lake Salina.

Draw a scale drawing, with a scale of 1 cm to 20 km, and use it to find:

a the bearing from Lake Salina to Beville

b the bearing from Beville to Lake Salina

c the shortest distance, in kilometres, between the two places.

5 Find the bearing from B to A, if the bearing from A to B is:

a 120°   **b** 045°   **c** 210°

6 Village Q is 7 km from Village P on a bearing of 060°.

Village R is 5 km from Village P on bearing of 315°.

Using a scale of 1 : 100 000, draw a diagram and use it to find:

a the direct distance from Village Q to Village R

b the bearing of Village Q from Village R.

Checklist of learning and understanding

Standard units of measurement

- You can convert between units of length, mass and capacity by multiplying or dividing by powers of ten.
- To convert squared units, you need to square the conversion factors.
- To convert cubed units, you need to cube the conversion factors.
- Units of time are not metric, so you need to use the number of parts in the sub-units when you convert units of time.

Compound units of measurement

- Compound units of measurement involve more than one unit.
- Rates such as £/hour or cost per kilogram are compound units.
- Average speed $= \dfrac{\text{Distance travelled}}{\text{Time taken}}$
- Density $= \dfrac{\text{Mass}}{\text{Volume}}$
- Pressure $= \dfrac{\text{Force}}{\text{Area}}$

Maps, scales and bearings

- The scale of a map or diagram describes how much smaller (or bigger) the lengths on the diagram are compared to the original lengths.
- Real length = map length × scale
- The scale can be written as the ratio 'length on diagram : real length.'
- Bearings are accurate directions given in degrees from 0° to 360°. The bearing of 0° corresponds with north.
- Bearings are measured clockwise from 0° and written using three figures.

Chapter review

For additional questions on the topics in this chapter, visit GCSE Mathematics Online.

1 Match each statement to the correct number in the box below.

| 5 | 475 | 182.5 | 259 200 |

a The number of seconds in 3 days.

b The number of kilometres travelled in $2\frac{1}{2}$ hours by a car travelling at 73 km/h.

c The distance in kilometres in real life of a length of 5 cm on a map with a scale of 1 : 1000.

d The number of litres in 475 000 millilitres.

2 Write down whether the statement in each part is true or false.

   a Tony's fish tank contains 72 litres of water.

     This is 72 000 millilitres.

   b A school is 15 km from a bus stop.

     The bus travels at 40 km/hour.

     It takes half an hour for the bus to get to school.

   c The distance from Liverpool to Manchester is about 55 km.

     The scale of a map is 1 : 25 000.

     The distance on the map would be about 5.2 cm.

3 Convert 60 000 cm^2 to square metres.

4 How many mm^2 are there in 2 m^2?

5 A car is travelling at an average speed of 80 km/h for one hour on a bearing of 120°.

   a Use a scale of 1 cm to 20 km to show this journey.

   b After 45 km, the driver stopped for petrol.

     The stop was after 40 minutes.

     i Mark this spot on your diagram.

     ii Calculate the speed for the part of the journey before the petrol stop.

6 The density of an object is 8 kg/m^3.

   Its volume is 25 m^3.

   Work out the mass of the object.

7 A cyclist travels due east from point A for 10 km to reach point B.

   She then travels 6 km on a bearing of 125° from B to reach point C.

   a Use a scale of 1 cm to 2 km to represent her journey on a scale diagram.

   b Find the bearing from C to A.

   c Find the direct distance from C to A in kilometres.

   d It takes the cyclist $1\frac{1}{2}$ hours to cycle back using the direct route from C to A.

     Find her average speed in:

     i km/h   **ii** m/s.

8 **a** A speed camera takes two photographs of a car.

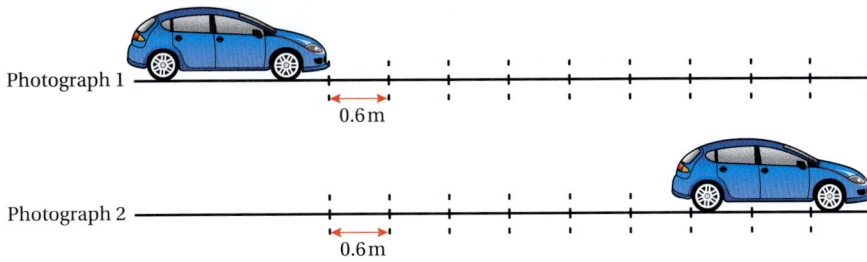

Photograph 1

0.6 m

Photograph 2

0.6 m

Photograph 2 was taken 0.5 seconds after Photograph 1.

Marks on the road are 0.6 metres apart.

Calculate the average speed of the car in m/s. *(3 marks)*

b You are given that

1 kilometre = 1000 metres

and

1 hour = 3600 seconds

A lorry is travelling at 13.6 m/s.

The speed limit is 50 km/h.

Show that the lorry is travelling below the speed limit. *(3 marks)*

© AQA 2013

9 Two motorcyclists set off from point A at the same time.

One travels at 60 km/h on a bearing of 045°.

The other travels at 55 km/h on a bearing of 072°.

Using a scale of 1 cm to 10 km, make a scaled diagram to show their journey.

Work out how far apart they are after $1\frac{1}{2}$ hours.

In this chapter you will learn how to ...

- use formulae to express and solve problems.
- change the subject of a formula.
- substitute numbers into formulae to find the value of the subject.
- understand and use a range of formulae, including kinematics formulae.

For more resources relating to this chapter, visit GCSE Mathematics Online.

Using mathematics: real-life applications

Vets use formulae to make sure they are giving animals the correct dosage of medicines for their age and mass. A poodle weighing 6 kg needs a far smaller dose of medicine than a 35 kg retriever.

"I need to make sure I give the animals I treat the correct amount of medicine. I do this by using formulae that take into account their age, mass and the ratio between any prescribed medicines." *(Veterinary surgeon)*

Did you know?

Einstein's famous formula, $E = mc^2$, looks deceptively simple. It describes the relationship between energy, mass and the speed of light, c. Find out more about this formula and why it is linked to the theory of relativity.

Before you start …

Ch 7, 16	You need to be able to substitute values into expressions.	**1** Evaluate $\dfrac{x + 2y}{z}$ when:	
		a $x = 7$, $y = 4$ and $z = 2$	**b** $x = 7$, $y = -2$ and $z = 2$
		c $x = -7$, $y = 4$ and $z = 4$	**d** $x = -7$, $y = -2$ and $z = 2$
Ch 16	You should be able to solve simple equations.	**2** Solve:	
		a $6x = x + 35$	**b** $5x = 64 - 3x$
		c $2(2x + 3) = x + 7$	**d** $5x - 8 = 3x + 12$
KS3 Ch 7, 11, 16, 17, 22	You should be familiar with some formulae already, and be able to identify the subject, variable(s) and any constants.	**3** Look at these two formulae for finding the area of shapes. $A = \frac{1}{2}bh \qquad A = \pi r^2$ **a** What do the variables represent? **b** What is the constant in each formula? **c** What is the subject of each formula? **d** What tells you that the second formula applies to circles?	

Tip

Formulae often use letters for the variable that relates to the value they represent. For example, in formulae for area, A is often used to represent the value for **a**rea and h to represent the value for **h**eight. Remember the letters represent values (quantities).

Assess your starting point using the Launchpad

STEP 1

1 Match each formula **A–D** with the correct statement **a–d**.

A $y = 180 - x$	**a** y is eight times the square root of one-fifth of x.
B $y = \dfrac{5x}{4}$	**b** A car travelled $80\,\text{km}$ in x hours at an average speed of $y\,\text{km/h}$.
C $y = 8\sqrt{\dfrac{x}{5}}$	**c** x and y are supplementary angles.
D $y = \dfrac{80}{x}$	**d** A car used x litres of petrol on a trip of $80\,\text{km}$ and the fuel consumption was y litres/$100\,\text{km}$.

2 The cooking instructions to cook a leg of lamb are as follows:

Preheat oven to $220\,°\text{C}$ and cook for $45\,\text{min}$ per kg, plus an additional $20\,\text{min}$.

Write a formula relating the cooking time T minutes and weight $w\,\text{kg}$.

GO TO
Section 1:
Writing formulae

STEP 2

3 Given the expression: $\dfrac{x + 2y}{3z}$

if $x = -7$, $y = -2$ and $z = 2$, what is the value of the expression?

4 One of the kinematic equations for motion is: $s = \dfrac{t(u + v)}{2}$

  a How many variables does this equation contain?

  b How many do you need to know to get an answer?

  c If $u = 3.5$, $v = 6.1$ and $t = 9$, what is the value of s?

GO TO
Section 2:
Substituting values into formulae

STEP 3

5 The formula for the area of a circle is: $A = \pi r^2$

  a What do each of the letters represent?

  b Rewrite the formula and make r the subject.

  c Can the value of r ever be a negative value?

GO TO
Section 3:
Changing the subject of a formula
Section 4:
Working with formulae

GO TO
Chapter review

Section 1: Writing formulae

Formulae

A **formula** is a special type of equation that shows the relationship between two or more unknown quantities.

For example, the formula for the area of a triangle is $A = \frac{1}{2}bh$.

To make sense of a formula you need to know what the variables represent. In this example:

- A is the area in square units
- b is the length of the base of the triangle
- h is the perpendicular height of the triangle.

The letters A, b and h are variables. They can be replaced by different values.

In the formula $\frac{1}{2}$ is a constant. No matter what value you use for b, you have to multiply it by $\frac{1}{2}$ in the formula.

A single variable on one side of the formula is called the **subject** of a formula.

The subject is the variable (or quantity) that is being **expressed in terms of** the other variables in the formula.

In $A = \frac{1}{2}bh$, A is the subject of the formula.

Writing formulae to represent real-life situations

You use the same procedures to set up formulae as when you are setting up equations.

- List the quantities involved. Work out whether they represent the subject, a variable, a constant or a coefficient.
- Establish the relationship between each quantity. (What is the subject being expressed in terms of?)
- Write the formula as concisely as possible using algebraic conventions.

Key vocabulary

formula (plural **formulae**): a general rule or equation showing the relationship between unknown quantities

Tip

For a reminder about variables, see Chapter 7.

Key vocabulary

subject: the variable, which is expressed in terms of the other variables or constants. It is the variable is on its own on one side of the equals sign. In the formula $s = \frac{d}{t}$, s is the subject

Problem-solving framework

A group of students are planning to run a day conference.

The local university offers conference rooms for hire at a daily rate.

The students think they will have a maximum of 60 delegates.

They want to offer refreshments costing £4 per delegate.

The largest room they can hire costs £160 for the day.

They want to charge each delegate enough to cover the costs of running the conference.

Write a formula for calculating how much they should charge each delegate.

Steps for solving problems	What you would do for this example
Step 1: If it is useful, draw a diagram.	A diagram is not particularly useful for this question.
Step 2: Identify what you have to do.	Calculate how much to charge each delegate at the conference by writing a formula using the information given.

Continues on next page ...

Step 3: Test the problem with what you already know.	You know a formula is a general rule showing the relationship between quantities.
Step 4: What maths can you use?	**1** List the quantities involved, and establish if they are the subject, a variable, a constant or a coefficient:
	Number of delegates, $d = 60$ (variable, as this can change).
	Cost of refreshments = £4 per delegate (coefficient, as this value is multiplied by how many delegates there are).
	Cost of the room = £160 (constant, this is fixed by the university).
	Cost to charge each delegate = C (subject, this is what we want to find out).
	2 Establish what the relationship is between each quantity.
	The cost to charge each delegate is the same as the cost of having each delegate at the conference, which is the total cost divided by the number of delegates.
	The total cost is equal to the cost of refreshments for each delegate and the cost of the room hire.
	Now put this together using algebra:
	Cost of conference = $4d + 160$
	Cost of one delegate is this value divided by the number of delegates, d.
	So the formula to calculate how much to charge each delegate is:
	$£C = \dfrac{4d + 160}{d}$
	Don't forget to add the units.

EXERCISE 23A

1 Write a formula showing the total number of hours, h, worked in a five-day week for x weeks at y hours a day.

Select the correct formula from the options below.

A $h = 5xy$ B $h = 5x + y$ C $h = \dfrac{5x}{y}$ D $h = 5 + x + y$

2 Simon and Lucy are going to Europe on holiday.

Simon has x euro and Lucy has y euro.

Write an equation for each of these statements:

a Simon and Lucy have a total of 2000 euro.

b Lucy has four times as many euro as Simon.

c If Lucy spent 400 euro she would have three times as many euro as Simon.

d If Lucy gave 600 euro to Simon they would both have the same number of euro.

e Half of Simon's euro are equivalent to two-fifths of Lucy's.

3 When y is the subject and x is an unknown value, write a formula to work out y, when y is:

   a three more than x

   b six less than x

   c ten times x

   d sum of −8 and x

   e the sum of x and the square of x

   f twice x more than x plus 1

   g double x divided by the sum of x and −2

   h half the product of π and the cube root of x divided by 3

4 In general, temperature decreases with height above sea level.

This formula shows how temperature and height above sea level are related:

$$T = \frac{h}{200}$$

where T is the temperature decrease in degrees Celsius and h is the height increase in metres.

   a If the temperature at a height of 500 m is 23 °C, what will it be when you climb to 1300 m?

   b What increase in height would result in a 5 °C decrease in temperature?

5 **a** The population of a town decreases by 2% each year.

     The population was initially P, and is Q after n years.

     What is the formula relating Q, P and n?

   b The population of a town decreases by 5% each year.

     The percentage decrease over a period of n years is a%.

     What is the formula relating a and n?

Section 2: Substituting values into formulae

To find the value of the subject (or any variable) in a formula you need to know the value of all the other variables.

The values are substituted into the formula to work out the missing value.

Substitute means replace the letters with the numbers you have been given.

Evaluate means work out the numerical value of a given calculation.

Key vocabulary

substitute: to replace variables with numbers

evaluate: to calculate the numerical value of something

WORKED EXAMPLE 1

The volume of an object can be found using the formula $V = \frac{1}{3}Ah$.

Find the volume of an object when $A = 30\,\text{cm}^2$ and $h = 6\,\text{cm}$.

$V = \frac{1}{3} \times A \times h$

$V = \frac{1}{3} \times 30 \times 6$

> Find the volume using the formula given:
> $V = \frac{1}{3}Ah$
> Substitute in the values given for A and h in the formula.

$V = \frac{1}{3} \times 30 \times 6$

$\quad = \frac{1}{3} \times 180$

$\quad = 60\,\text{cm}^3$

The volume of the object is $60\,\text{cm}^3$.

> Calculate the value for V.

> Remember to write the correct units.
> Volume is given in cubic units.
> For this example the units required are cm^3.

Tip

It is good practice to show you can correctly substitute values into a formula before calculating the answer. Write down what you need to work out and then calculate the value. Remember to include units when necessary.

WORK IT OUT 23.1

The surface area of a sphere is given by the formula:

$A = 4\pi r^2$

where r is the radius of the sphere.

Calculate the surface area of a sphere of radius 8 cm in exact form.

Which is the correct answer?

What mistakes have been made in the incorrect answers?

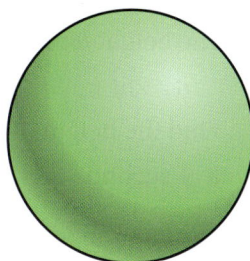

Option A	Option B	Option C
$A = 4 \times \pi \times 8^2$	$A = 256\pi\,\text{cm}^2$	$60\,\text{cm}^3$

Tip

Make sure you include units in an answer when appropriate.

EXERCISE 23B

1 Evaluate these expressions:

a $2a(a - 3b)$ when

 i $a = 2$ and $b = -5$ **ii** $a = -3$ and $b = -2$ **iii** $a = \frac{1}{3}$ and $b = \frac{1}{2}$

b $x^2 - 2y$ when

 i $x = -7, y = 2$ **ii** $x = -\frac{1}{3}, y = \frac{5}{6}$

2 For $x = -\dfrac{a}{2} - \dfrac{b}{c}$, find the exact value of x if:

   a $a = 2$, $b = -2$, $c = -1$ **b** $a = 7$, $b = 3$, $c = -4$

   c $a = -10$, $b = \sqrt{3}$, $c = \sqrt{3}$ **d** $a = \sqrt{2}$, $b = \sqrt{2}$, $c = 4$

   e $a = 0$, $b = 0$, $c = 5$ **f** $a = \pi$, $b = \pi$, $c = 7$

3 For the formula $v = u + at$, find v if $u = 6$, $a = 3$ and $t = 5$.

4 The formula for the volume of the frustum of a cone is given by:

$$V = \frac{1}{3}\pi h(R^2 + Rr + r^2)$$

When $h = 9\,\text{cm}$, $R = 5\,\text{cm}$ and $r = 2$, what is the volume?

Choose your answer from the following options.

   A $117\pi\,\text{cm}^3$ B $\dfrac{117}{3}\pi\,\text{cm}^3$ C 117π D $351\pi\,\text{cm}^3$

5 Given $v^2 = u^2 + 2ax$ and $v > 0$, find the value of v (to one decimal place) when:

   a $u = 0$, $a = 5$ and $x = 10$ **b** $u = 6$, $a = 4$ and $x = 15$

   c $u = 2$, $a = 9.8$ and $x = 22$ **d** $u = 2.3$, $a = 4.9$ and $x = 10.6$

6 Given $\dfrac{1}{f} = \dfrac{1}{u} + \dfrac{1}{v}$, find the value of f when:

   a $u = 2$ and $v = 4$ **b** $u = 2$ and $v = 15$

7 A stone is thrown at $25\,\text{m/s}$.

The height h metres it reaches after t seconds is given by the formula:

$$h = 25t + 4.9t^2$$

Find the height of the stone after:

   a 1 second   **b** 2 seconds.

8 The volume of metal in a tube is found using the formula:

$$V = \pi l\{r^2 - (r - t)^2\}$$

where l is the length of the tube;

r is the radius of the outside surface; and

t is the thickness of the material.

Find V when $l = 40$, $r = 5$ and $t = 0.5$ (leave π in your answer).

9 Find the value of h, to one decimal place, if

$$h = \frac{9gRs}{2v}$$

when $g = 9.8$, $R = 2.5$, $s = 3$ and $v = 7.4$

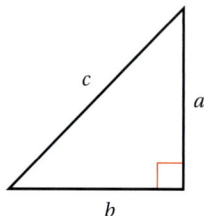

10 The length of the hypotenuse c cm in a right-angled triangle is given by

$$c^2 = a^2 + b^2$$

where a cm and b cm are the lengths of the perpendicular sides, as in the diagram.

Calculate, to the nearest 0.1 cm, the length of the hypotenuse in the right-angled triangle whose perpendicular sides have lengths 14 cm and 25 cm.

11 The time T (in seconds) taken for one complete swing of a pendulum is given to the nearest centimetre by:

$$T = 2\pi \sqrt{\dfrac{L}{g}}$$

where $g = 9.8 \, \text{m/s}^2$ and L is length of the pendulum.

Find, to the nearest centimetre, the length of a pendulum that takes 2 seconds to complete one swing.

Section 3: Changing the subject of a formula

When you need to find the value of a variable that is not the subject of the formula, you need to rearrange it.

A formula is a type of equation, so you can use inverse operations to rearrange the formula to make another variable (letter) the subject.

The rules for solving equations apply to formulae, so whatever you do to one side of the formula you must do to the other.

You can also substitute known values before rearranging the formula.

WORKED EXAMPLE 2

a Given the kinematic formula for acceleration,

$v^2 = u^2 + 2as$

i make s the subject of the formula

$u^2 + 2as = v^2$	Swap the sides to get $2as$ on the left.
$2as = v^2 - u^2$	Subtract u^2 from each side.
$\dfrac{2as}{2a} = \dfrac{(v^2 - u^2)}{2a}$	Divide both sides by $2a$.
$s = \dfrac{v^2 - u^2}{2a}$	You can leave out the brackets because the fraction line acts as a bracket.

ii make u the subject of the formula.

$u^2 + 2as = v^2$	Swap the sides to get u^2 on the left.
$u^2 = v^2 - 2as$	Subtract $2as$ from each side.
$\sqrt{u^2} = \sqrt{(v^2 - 2as)}$	Take the square root of each side to get u on its own.
$u = \sqrt{(v^2 - 2as)}$	

Continues on next page …

> **Tip**
>
> Working quickly and skipping steps can lead to unnecessary mistakes. It is always a good idea to demonstrate your reasoning, especially in tests and exams.

b Given the formula

$$v^2 = u^2 + 2as$$

find the value of s when $u = 8$, $v = 10$ and $a = 3$.

$$v^2 = u^2 + 2as$$

> Rearrange the formula to make s the subject:

$$v^2 - u^2 = 2as$$
$$\frac{v^2 - u^2}{2a} = s$$

> Subtracting u^2 from both sides.
>
> Dividing by 2a.

$$s = \frac{v^2 - u^2}{2a}$$

> The subject is normally written on the left.

$u = 8$, $v = 10$ and $a = 3$

$$s = \frac{10^2 - 8^2}{2 \times 3}$$

> Substitute in the values you know.

$$s = \frac{100 - 64}{6}$$

$$s = \frac{36}{6}$$

$$s = 6$$

> Alternatively, you can substitute the numbers and then solve for s.

$$10^2 = 8^2 + 2 \times 3s$$
$$100 = 64 + 6s$$
$$100 - 64 = 6s$$
$$36 = 6s$$
$$\frac{36}{6} = s$$
$$6 = s$$
$$s = 6$$

Tip

You can substitute numbers into the formula **before** rearranging it, to solve for values other than the given subject of the formula.

EXERCISE 23C

1 Make t the subject of the formula $3t - s = t(s - 6)$.

Choose your answer from the following options.

A $t = \dfrac{9 - s}{s}$ B $t = \dfrac{s}{9 - s}$ C $t = s(9 - s)$ D $t = s(s - 9)$

2 Rearrange each of these formulae to make the letter in the bracket the subject.

a $a(q - c) = d$ (q) **b** $4(p - 2q) = 3p + 2$ (p)

c $5(x - 3) = y(4 - 3x)$ (x) **d** $d = \sqrt{\dfrac{3h}{2}}$ (h)

e $y = \dfrac{2pt}{p - t}$ (t) **f** $a = \dfrac{2 - 7b}{b - 5}$ (b)

g $\dfrac{x}{x + c} = \dfrac{p}{q}$ (x)

3 The formula for the sum S of the interior angles in n-sided polygon is

$$S = 180(n - 2)$$

Rearrange the formula to make n the subject. Use this to find the number of sides in the polygon if the sum of the interior angles is:

a 1080°   **b** 1800°   **c** 3240°

4 The kinetic energy E joules of a moving object is given by

$$E = \frac{1}{2}mv^2$$

where m kg is the mass of the object and v m/s is its speed.

Rearrange the formula to make m the subject. Use this to find the mass of the object when its energy and speed are, respectively:

a 400 joules, 10 m/s   **b** 28 joules, 4 m/s   **c** 57.6 joules, 2.4 m/s

5 The formula for the time T of a swing of a pendulum is $T = 2\pi\sqrt{\dfrac{p}{g}}$.

Make p, the length of the pendulum, the subject of the formula.

Choose your answer from the options below.

A $p = \dfrac{T^2 g}{2\pi}$ B $p = \left(\dfrac{Tg}{2\pi}\right)$ C $p = g\left(\dfrac{T}{2\pi}\right)^2$ D $p = g(2T\pi)^2$

6 The formula for finding the number of degrees Fahrenheit (F) for a temperature given in degrees Celsius (C) is:

$$F = \frac{9}{5}C + 32$$

Rearrange the formula to make C the subject. Use this formula to convert these Fahrenheit temperatures to Celsius temperatures:

a 68 °F   **b** 23 °F   **c** 212 °F

7 The formula for the perimeter P of a rectangle l by w is

$$P = 2(l + w)$$

If $P = 20$ cm and $l = 7$ cm, what is the length of w?

8 The area A cm² enclosed by an ellipse is given by:

$$A = \pi a b$$

Calculate to one decimal place the length a cm if $b = 3.2$ and $A = 25$.

9 An object is shot into the air at a speed of u metres per second.

Its height h metres above the ground and time t seconds of flight are related by:

$$h = ut - 4.9t^2 \quad \text{(ignoring air resistance)}$$

Find the speed at which an object was fired if it reached a height of 30 metres after 5 seconds.

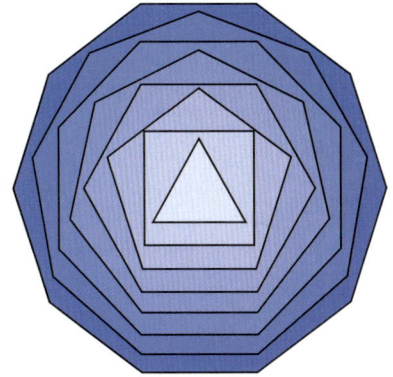

Tip

These are questions where you may decide to rearrange first and then substitute the values given to solve, or substitute the values first and then evaluate.

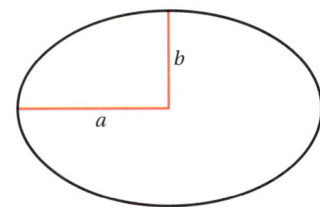

10 For the formula:

$$I = \frac{(180n - 360)}{n}$$

find n when $I = 108$.

11 Given the formula:

$$t = 2\pi \sqrt{\frac{L}{g}}$$

find L given $t = \pi$ and $g = 9.8$

Section 4: Working with formulae

You are now ready to apply your skills at working with formulae to a set of general problems.

Things to remember:

- Substitute in the correct values.
- Include appropriate units in your answer.
- When constructing a formula try some values to make sure it works.
- It can be useful to rearrange a formula to change the subject, but it is not always necessary.

i Did you know?

Formulae and equations are powerful tools to explore and explain the world.

This is an equation from higher-level mathematics:

$Z_{n+1} = Z_n^2 + C$

It is used to explore the amazing patterns called fractals.

You can find out more about fractals and the connection to Chaos Theory, using the Internet or other sources.

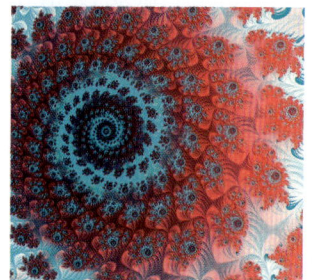

EXERCISE 23D

1 State whether each of the following statements is true or false. Correct any false statements to make them true.

a Using the formula:

$$s = ut + \frac{1}{2}at^2$$

to find the value of s when $u = 4.6$, $a = 9.8$ and $t = 4$, the answer is $s = 96.8$

b The formula:

$$A = \pi r(r + l)$$

rewritten to make l the subject becomes:

$$l = \frac{A - \pi r}{r}$$

c A formula to calculate the number n half way between two numbers x and y can be written as:

$$n = \frac{x + y}{2}$$

d In the formula to calculate the area of a circle:

$$A = \pi r^2$$

π is a constant and A and r are the variables.

e This formula calculates the volume of a triangular prism:

$$V = \pi r^2 h$$

2 The Greek mathematician Hero showed that the area of a triangle with sides a, b and c is given by the formula:

$$A = \sqrt{s(s-a)(s-b)(s-c)}$$

where $s = \frac{1}{2}(a + b + c)$.

Use Hero's formula to find the area of this triangle.

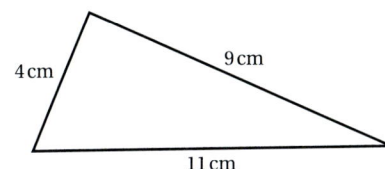

3 Compound interest is calculated by the interest being added to a principal amount at the end of each year.

If P is the principal amount, r is the interest rate over a given period and n is number of years that the interest is compounded:

Total accrued $= P\left(1 + \dfrac{r}{100}\right)^n$

a Find the total accrued when £6000 is borrowed for three years at a rate of 4%. Give your answer to the nearest whole £.

b How much interest was paid? Give your answer to the nearest whole £.

4 What does this formula calculate?

$$x = \frac{-b \pm \sqrt{b^2 - 4ac}}{2a}$$

Why is the sign $\pm$ included in this formula?

5 Given that the general form of a quadratic equation is

$$ax^2 + bx + c = 0$$

use the method of completing the square to obtain the formula in question 4.

6 $n, n^2, \sqrt{n}, 8n, \dfrac{36}{n}, \dfrac{n}{2} + 1$

a If $n = 4$ arrange the above set in order from smallest to largest.

b Arrange the above set in order from smallest to largest if $n = \dfrac{1}{4}$

7 Conversion of a temperature from degrees Fahrenheit to degrees Celsius is worked out using the formula:

$$C = \frac{5(F - 32)}{9}$$

a Gallium is a soft, silvery metal that melts at temperatures above 85.57 °F.

Your normal body temperature is about 37 °C.

Would gallium be likely to melt if you held it in your hand?

Give a reason for your answer.

b Cast iron becomes molten at 1204 °C.

Work out the Fahrenheit equivalent.

Learn this formula

You are expected to know the formula $x = \dfrac{-b \pm \sqrt{b^2 - 4ac}}{2a}$ from memory. See Chapter 16 if you need a reminder.

8 A formula used in life insurance is:

$$Q = \frac{2m}{2+m}$$

a Calculate Q if $m = -0.7$ (to four significant figures).

b Calculate m if $Q = 3$.

9 For a rectangle of length l cm and width w cm, the perimeter P cm is given by:

$$P = 2(l + w)$$

Use this formula to calculate the length of a rectangle which has width 15 cm and perimeter 57 cm.

10 The distance d metres a car takes to stop once the brakes are applied is given by the formula:

$$d = 0.2v + 0.005v^2$$

where v km/h is the speed of the car when the brakes are applied.

Find the distance the car takes to stop if the brakes are applied when it is travelling at each of the speeds given below. Calculate your answers to three decimal places where appropriate.

a 60 km/h   **b** 65 km/h   **c** 70 km/h

d Comment on how stopping distances vary with increasing speed and what this means for road safety.

11 A scientist is calculating how long a Lunar Explorer Vehicle will take to descend towards the surface of the moon.

If u = initial speed and v = speed at time t seconds, then:

$$v = u + at$$

where a is the acceleration and t is the time that has passed.

Rearrange the formula to make a the subject.

12 A headmaster compares the test scores of students across a school.

He has worked out the mean but wants know the spread about the mean to see whether it is representative of the whole school.

He uses this formula for the upper bound b of a class mean:

$$b = \frac{a + \sqrt{3s}}{\sqrt{n}}$$

where s = sample spread about the mean, n = the sample size, a = the school mean and b = the mean maximum value.

Rearrange the formula to make s the subject.

13 An object is shot into the air at a speed of u metres per second.

Its height above the ground h metres and time of flight t seconds are related by:

$$h = ut + 4.9t^2 \quad \text{(ignoring air resistance)}$$

Find the speed at which the object was fired if it reached a height of 272.5 metres after 5 seconds.

14 The general form of a quadratic equation is:

$$ax^2 + bx + c = 0$$

Solve this equation with the formula:

$$x = \frac{-b \pm \sqrt{b^2 - 4ac}}{2a}$$

when $a = 1$, $b = 9$ and $c = 20$.

Checklist of learning and understanding

Writing formulae

- A formula is a general rule or equation showing the relationship between quantities.
- You can use formulae to represent real-life problems as long as you define the variables you are using.

Substituting values into formulae

- To evaluate a formula, you need to know the value of all but one of its variables.
- Substitute the given values into the formula to find the unknown variable.

Changing the subject of a formula

- In any formula we can 'change the subject' by rearranging the formula in the same way as we rearrange equations.

Chapter review

For additional questions on the topics in this chapter, visit GCSE Mathematics Online.

1 A rectangle has a perimeter p and one side of length x.

Choose the correct formula for its area from the options below.

A $A = x\left(\frac{p}{2} - x\right)$ B $A = x(p - x)$ C $A = \frac{x}{2}(p - x)$ D $A = x(p - 2x)$

2 Many of the formulae you learn and prove in mathematics are for finding areas and volumes of standard 3D shapes.

Research any formulae that you will need for the following questions and then do the calculations.

a The side of a cube with a volume of $125\,\text{cm}^3$.

b The length of a cuboid with a total surface area of $157.36\,\text{m}^2$, height $6.5\,\text{m}$ and breadth $2.2\,\text{m}$.

c The formula

$$S = 2\pi r(r + h)$$

represents the total surface area of a cylinder.

Rewrite this formula to make h the subject.

d Find the volume of a sphere if the radius is $\sqrt{3}$. Leave π and any surd values in your answer.

e The curved surface area of a hemisphere is $2\pi r^2$.

Give a reason why the total surface area is $3r^2$.

3 Given the following two formulae:

$A = \pi r(r + 2h)$ and $C = r + h$

create a formula:

a with the subject A, eliminating h.

b with the subject A, eliminating r.

4 The formula for calculating the area of a triangle using the sine of an angle is:

$A = \dfrac{1}{2}ab \sin C$

Given an area of $12.25\,\text{cm}^2$ and $a = 4.4\,\text{cm}$, $b = 6.8\,\text{cm}$, calculate angle C to the nearest degree.

5 A runner completed a 26 km race in 4 hours.

After running 15 km, his average speed decreased by 2 km/h.

Given that $t = \dfrac{d}{s}$, where t is time in hours, d is distance covered in km and s is average speed in km/hr, work out the runner's two speeds for this race.

6 Make t the subject of the formula $w = 3 + \sqrt{t}$ *(2 marks)*

24 Volume and surface area

In this chapter you will learn how to …

- calculate the volume and surface area of cuboids.
- calculate the volume and surface area of prisms.
- calculate the volume and surface area of cylinders.
- solve volume and surface area problems involving composite shapes.

For more resources relating to this chapter, visit GCSE Mathematics Online.

Using mathematics: real-life applications

Freight costs are dependent upon the volume of material being transported. Freight rates are calculated using the container volume measured against the length of the container. The longer the container the higher the freight cost.

"To transport a container full of apples from Felixstowe, England to Le Havre in France, I have to let the freight operator know the volume of apples I have to transport as well as the dimensions of the crates. I am then quoted a transport cost."

(Apple producer)

Before you start …

Ch 8, 21	You need to be able to recognise and identify solid objects.	**1**	Name each object as accurately as possible from the description. **a** A 3D object with six identical square surfaces. **b** A 3D solid with two parallel circular faces. **c** An object with a square base and triangular side faces that meet at an apex. **d** A 3D object with a circular base and one vertex. **e** A 3D object with many flat surfaces that are polygons. **f** A polyhedron with two triangular and three rectangular faces.
Ch 11	You must be able to calculate the area of plane shapes.	**2** **3**	What is the formula for the area of a circle? What is the area of a right-angled triangle with sides of 3 cm, 4 cm and 5 cm?
Ch 8, 21	You should understand and use the properties of solids.	**4**	A shape has 6 faces, 8 vertices and 12 edges. **a** What could it be? **b** What additional information do you need to name the shape more accurately?

Assess your starting point using the Launchpad

STEP 1

❶ Calculate the volume of a cube with side length 5 cm.

❷ What is the volume of this box?

5 cm

12 cm

4 cm

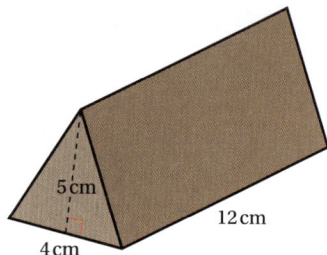

GO TO
Section 1:
Prisms and cylinders

STEP 2

❸ The approximate radius of the Earth at the Equator is 6378.1 km.

Calculate its approximate volume and surface area.

GO TO
Section 2:
Cones and spheres

STEP 3

❹ This pyramid is 21.6 metres high and the base of each triangular face is 35 metres long.

What is the volume of the pyramid?

GO TO
Section 3:
Pyramids

GO TO
Chapter review

Section 1: Prisms and cylinders

A prism is a 3D object with:

- two parallel end faces that are the same size and shape
- a uniform cross-section along its length.

The diagram below shows examples of **right prisms**.

One of the end faces is known as the base of the object. The sides are rectangles perpendicular to the base.

A cube (square prism)   A rectangular prism   A triangular prism

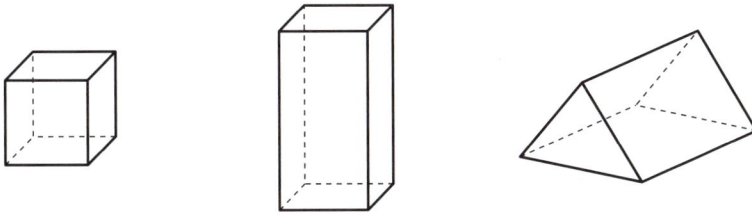

Volume

The volume of an object is the three-dimensional space that it takes up. Volume is given in cubic units, such as mm³, cm³ and m³ (for solids).

You find the volume of any right prism by finding the area of its cross-section (which is the same as its base) and multiplying this by its length. This is the same for a cylinder: you find its volume by multiplying the area of its circular base by its length.

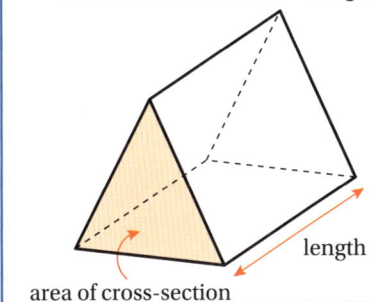

Surface area

Surface area is the total area of the faces of a three-dimensional object.

Sketching a rough net of the object can help you to see what faces to include when you calculate the surface area.

The net of a cuboid shows that the surface area includes the area of six faces.

	base (1)	
side A (1)	side B (1)	side A (2)	side B (2)
	base (2)	

The surface area is calculated by adding the area of each of its faces. The opposite faces match, so

surface area = 2(area of side A) + 2(area of side B) + 2(area of base)

A cube has six identical square faces.
You can use the following formulae for volume and surface area:

Volume of a cube = x^3

Surface area of a cube = $6x^2$

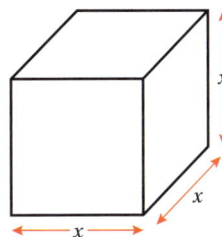

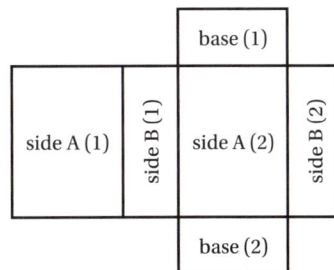

WORKED EXAMPLE 1

Calculate the volume and surface area of this cuboid.

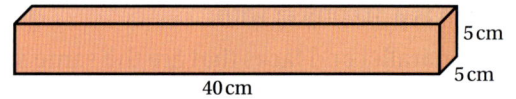

Volume of cuboid = 40 × 5 × 5 = 1000 cm³

> The volume of a cuboid is found using the formula: volume = length × width × depth.
>
> The answer is given as units³ as it has three dimensions.

Surface area of cuboid = 4 × (40 × 5) + 2 × (5 × 5)
$$= 800 + 50$$
$$= 850 \text{ cm}^2$$

> The surface area of a cuboid is the total area of each of its faces.
>
> It has four faces that measure 40 cm × 5 cm and two faces that measure 5 cm × 5 cm.

Prisms with cross sections of other shapes

The same general formula is used to find the volume and the surface area of any prism, or a cylinder.

Volume of a prism = area of cross-section × length

For example, this is a triangular prism. The base is a triangle.

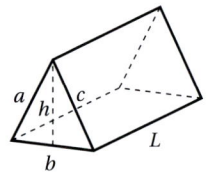

Area of triangle $= \frac{1}{2}bh$

Volume of a prism = area of cross-section × length

Volume of triangular prism $= \frac{1}{2}bh \times L$

Surface area of triangular prism = 2(area of triangular base) + area of three side faces

$$= 2(\frac{1}{2} \times b \times h) + (a \times L) + (c \times L) + (b \times L)$$

Prisms with a trapezium base

Area of trapezium base $= \frac{1}{2}(a + b) \times h$

Volume of prism $= \frac{1}{2}(a + b) \times h \times l$

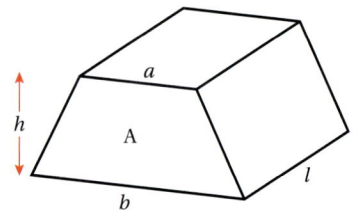

WORK IT OUT 24.1

What is the volume of soil that can be contained in this skip?

Which of the following is the correct calculation?

2 m

1.6 m

2 m

1.4 m

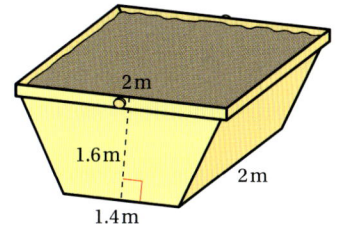

Calculation A	Calculation B	Calculation C
Area of the trapezium	Area of the trapezium	Area of the trapezium:
Area $= \frac{1}{2}(a + b) \times h$	Area $= \frac{1}{2}(a - b) \times h$	Area $= \frac{1}{2} \times b \times h$
Area $= \frac{1}{2} \times 3.4 \times 1.6 = 2.72\,\text{m}^2$	Area $= \frac{1}{2} \times 0.6 \times 1.6 = 0.48\,\text{m}^2$	Area $= \frac{1}{2} \times 1.4 \times 1.6 = 1.12\,\text{m}^2$
Volume =	Volume =	Volume =
area of the trapezium × length	area of the trapezium × length	area of the trapezium × length
Volume $= 2.72 \times 2 = 5.44\,\text{m}^3$	Volume $= 0.48 \times 2 = 0.96\,\text{m}^3$	Volume $= 1.12 \times 2 = 2.24\,\text{m}^3$

Cylinders

Cylinders are not prisms, but you find their volume and surface area in the same way as you do with prisms.

Volume of a cylinder $= \pi r^2 \times h$

The net of a prism shows that the curved surface forms a rectangle when it is flattened out. The length of the rectangle is equivalent to the circumference of the circular base.

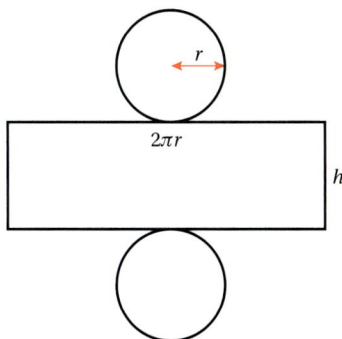

r

$2\pi r$

h

The surface area of a cylinder is calculated using the formula:

$S = 2\pi rh + 2\pi r^2$

WORKED EXAMPLE 2

A road roller has a roller on the front that is filled with water to make it heavy.

The tank of water in the roller has a radius of 0.95 m and a length of 2.4 m.

Find the volume of water in the roller.

Volume of water = area of circle × length

Volume = $\pi r^2 \times l$

Volume of water = 3.14 × 0.95 × 0.95 × 2.4

$\qquad$ = 6.80124 m^3

$\qquad$ = 6.8 m^3 (to 1 dp)

> Try to remember this formula:
>
> volume is the area of the cross-section times the length.

Rearranging the formula

> **Tip**
>
> You will learn more about rearranging formulae in Chapter 23.

You can find the length of a prism if you know the volume and area of the base by changing the subject of the formula.

For example:

The volume of a triangular prism is 100 cm^3 and the area of the end face is 25 cm^2.

How long is the prism?

Volume = area of the triangle × length

so $V \div A = L$

100 ÷ 25 = L = 4 cm

In the same way, you can find the radius or diameter of the base of a cylinder when you know the other dimensions by changing the subject of the formula.

EXERCISE 24A

1 Calculate the volume of a cube of side 10 cm. Choose the correct answer from the options below.

A 10 cm^3 $\qquad$ B 40 cm^3 $\qquad$ C 100 cm^3 $\qquad$ D 1000 cm^3

2 Calculate the volume and surface area of each object. (Each object is a closed object.)

a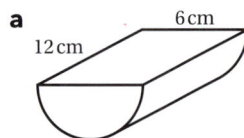

b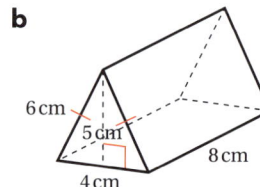

c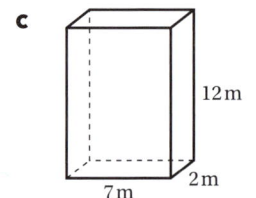

d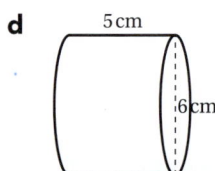

e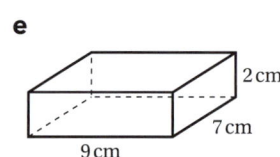

f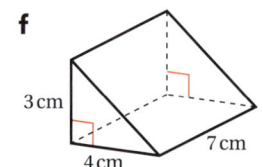

454

3 1 litre = 1000 cm³

What is the capacity, in litres, of the aquarium below?

60 cm

1 m   30 cm

4 The volume of a cube is 144 m³. What is the length of each side? Choose the correct length from the options below.

A 5.24 m   B 12 m   C 36 m   D 576 m

5 The dimensions of a swimming pool are 50 m long and 25 m wide.

The water is 2 m deep.

What is the capacity of water in the swimming pool?

6 What is the volume of this triangular prism? Give your answer to two decimal places.

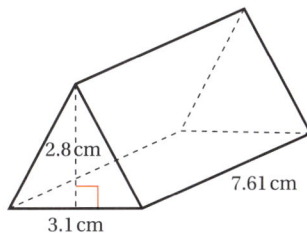

2.8 cm

7.61 cm

3.1 cm

7 A tin can contains oil up to $\frac{3}{4}$ of its full height.

Height of the tin = 45 cm; width = 15 cm; depth = 8 cm.

Show that the volume of oil will be $\frac{3}{4}$ of the volume of the whole tin.

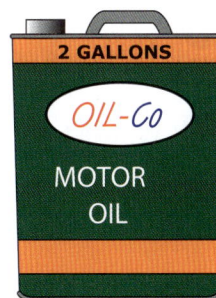

8 A cylindrical water tank with a diameter of 1.2 m and height of 1.6 m is painted around the outside of its curved surface.

Calculate the area of the surface that is painted.

9 Amy makes two types of candle:

one with a radius 4 cm and height 5 cm;

one with a radius of 2 cm and height of 20 cm.

Which candle requires the most candle wax?

Find answers at: cambridge.org/ukschools/gcsemaths-studentbookanswers

10 A length of metal pipe has a hollow radius of 10 cm, an outer radius of 12 cm and a length of 20 cm.

   a Calculate the volume of metal in the length of pipe.

   b Calculate the volume of the hollow centre of the pipe.

11 A cube with side of x cm has a surface area of 150 cm². Calculate x.

12 What is the surface area of one side of this roof?

12 m

5 m

4 m

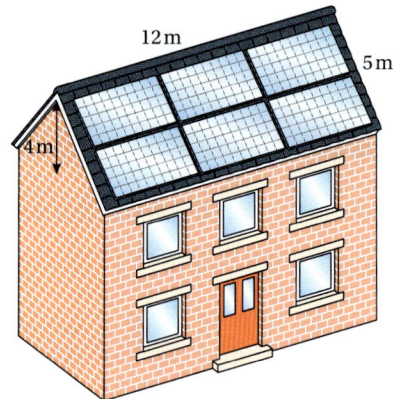

13 Calculate the volume of the object in the diagram.

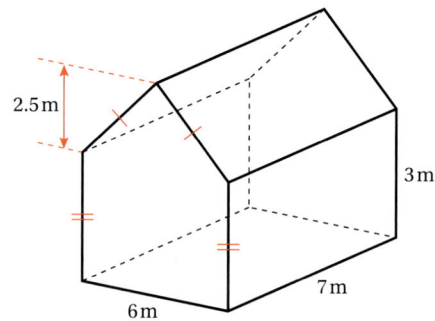

2.5 m

3 m

7 m

6 m

14 A cuboid has sides of length x, $(x + 2)$ and $(x + 3)$.

   Find, in terms of x, the volume and surface area of the cuboid.

15 Write a formula for the volume of a cube with a side equal to $a + b$.

Section 2: Cones and spheres

Cones

The formula for the volume of a cone is

$\frac{1}{3} \times$ area of circular base $\times h$

where h is the perpendicular height from the base to the apex of the cone.

The area of the base can be found using the formula for the area of a circle, πr^2.

Volume of a cone $= \frac{1}{3} \pi r^2 h$

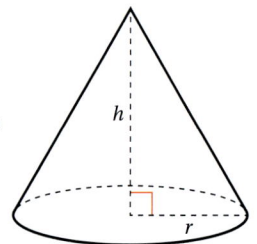

h

r

WORKED EXAMPLE 3

Find the volume of a cone of radius 12 cm with a perpendicular height of 14 cm.

$$\text{Volume} = \frac{1}{3}(\pi r^2)h = \frac{1}{3}(3.14 \times 12 \times 12) \times 14$$
$$= 2110.08\,\text{cm}^3$$

The formula for the volume of a cone is made up of the area of the circle at the end times the height divided by three as there are three cones in the equivalent cylinder. You will remember the formula for the area of a circle which is πr^2.

The area of the curved surface of a cone is πrl, where r is the radius of the base, and l is the **slant height** of the cone.

Therefore, the surface area (S) of the cone is:

S = area of curved surface + area of base

$= \pi rl + \pi r^2$

The slant height of a cone can be calculated using Pythagoras' theorem if the dimensions of the height and base are given. The curved surface area of the cone can also be given by $\pi r\sqrt{r^2 + h^2}$.

Problem-solving framework

You are selling ice creams and need to decide on the price. With two sizes of cone available you have to decide how much to charge for each one. One cone has a radius of 3 cm and is 5 cm long; the other has a radius of 6 cm and is 8 cm long.

You are going to sell strawberry, vanilla and chocolate flavours.

If the price of the first cone is £1.50, prove, through a comparison of the volume of ice cream, that you cannot simply charge double that price for the second cone. Can you recommend a suitable price based upon your findings?

Step 1: What have you got to do?	Compare the volume of the two cones.
Step 2: What information do you need?	The radius and length of the small cone; the radius and length of the large cone; the formula for the volume of a cone: $\frac{1}{3} \times \pi r^2 \times h$.
Step 3: What information don't you need?	The flavours are irrelevant.
Step 4: What maths can you do?	Volume of the small cone $= \frac{1}{3} \times 3.14 \times 3 \times 3 \times 5 = 47.1\,\text{cm}^3$ Volume of the large cone $= \frac{1}{3} \times 3.14 \times 6 \times 6 \times 8 = 301.44\,\text{cm}^3$ Over six times as much ice cream will fit inside.
Step 5: Have you done it all?	Yes, but need to suggest a suitable price.
Step 6: Is it correct?	Yes – double-check made.

Find answers at: cambridge.org/ukschools/gcsemaths-studentbookanswers

Spheres

A sphere is any perfectly round object.

The volume of a sphere is equal to $\frac{4}{3}\pi r^3$, where r is the radius of the sphere.

The surface area of a sphere is equal to $4\pi r^2$, where r is the radius of the sphere.

Many objects include spheres or parts of spheres in their structure.

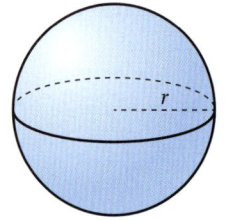

Tip

When working with π (pi), you might be asked to give your answer in terms of π. This means you leave π in your answer but do the other working.

WORKED EXAMPLE 4

The radius of the Earth is approximately 6378.1 km. Give your answers in standard form to four significant figures.

a Find the approximate volume and surface area of the Earth.

b Water covers 70% of the Earth's surface. What is the surface area of land?

a $V = \frac{4}{3} \times \pi \times 6378.1^3$

$= 1\,086\,832\,412\,000\,\text{km}^3$

$= 1.087 \times 10^{12}\,\text{km}^3$ (4 sf)

Surface area $= 4 \times \pi \times 6378.1^2$

$= 511\,201\,962.3\,\text{km}^2$

$= 5.112 \times 10^8\,\text{km}^2$ (4 sf)

The volume of a sphere is given by the formula;

$V = \frac{4}{3}\pi r^3$

The surface area of a sphere is given by the formula: $4\pi r^2$

b 30% of the Earth's surface area is land.

$0.3 \times 511\,201\,962.3$

$= 153\,360\,588.7\,\text{km}^2$

$= 1.534 \times 10^8\,\text{km}^2$ (4 sf)

Once you have found the surface area of the Earth you can find 30% by multiplying the whole by 0.3

Tip

In calculations with such large values answers are usually given in standard form (see Chapter 15).

EXERCISE 24B

1 Calculate the volume and surface area of each object. (The objects are all closed.) Give your answers in terms of π.

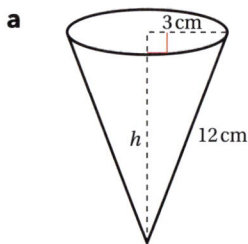

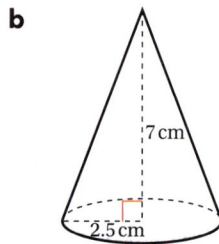

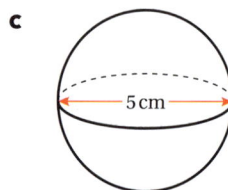

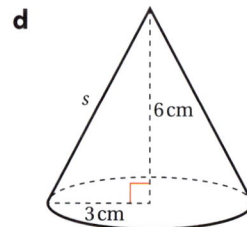

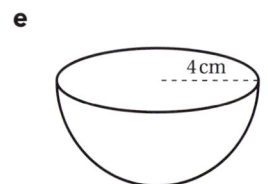

a 3 cm, h, 12 cm

b 7 cm, 2.5 cm

c 5 cm

d s, 6 cm, 3 cm

e 4 cm

2 The Earth's moon has a mean radius of 1738 km.

Find its approximate volume. Take π to be 3.14

3 Find the surface area of a sphere with radius 20 cm. Take π to be 3.14
Choose from the options below.

A 1256 cm²   B 1675 cm³   C 5024 cm²   D 1256 cm³

4 The table below gives some standard diameters of spherical balls used in different sports. Calculate the surface area of each ball. Assume they are round and ignore any dimples on the surface.

	Sport	Standard diameter
a	snooker	52.5 mm
b	tennis	6.35 cm
c	football	15 cm
d	golf	42.7 mm
e	bowling	21.6 cm
f	basketball	25.4 cm
g	hockey	3 cm
h	baseball	74 mm
i	cricket	7 cm

5 A factory needs to calculate the volume and surface area of plastic cones.

The dimensions of the cones are given in the table.

Calculate each volume and surface area.

	Radius, (r cm)	Slant height, (s cm)
a	5	10
b	18	34
c	7	21
d	16	22
e	60	64
f	9	26
g	30	52

6 A conical tent has a circular base with a diameter of 3 m, and a slant height of 3 m.

Calculate the volume of the tent.

Composite solids

> **Tip**
>
> It is useful to use a system for checking that you have included all the surfaces when you are finding the surface area of a composite shape.

In real life, objects are often made up of more than one shape.

This is the winning design for the air traffic control tower at Newcastle airport. The design incorporates cut-off conical shapes around a cuboid-shaped cement tower.	This is the design of the North Gate bus station in Northampton. You can see that many different solids have been used in the design.

To find the total surface area of a composite solid you need to find the area of each part separately then add them together.

The area of some faces will overlap and not form part of the 'outside' area of the solid. You need to be careful to use only the parts of the solid that form the surface area of the shape.

WORKED EXAMPLE 5

Calculate the total volume and surface area of the object shown below. Leave your answer in terms of π.

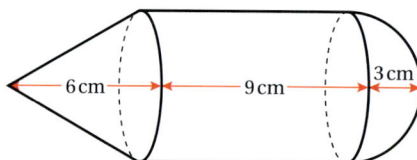

The object consists of a cone, cylinder and half a sphere.

Volume

Volume of cone $= \frac{1}{3}(\pi r^2)h$

$= \frac{1}{3}\pi \times 3^2 \times 6$

$= 18\pi$

Volume of cylinder $= \pi r^2 h$

$= \pi \times 3^2 \times 9$

$= 81\pi$

Surface area

Cone:

S = area of lateral curved surface without the area of base (as this overlaps with the end of the cylinder)

$= \pi r s$

$= \pi r \sqrt{r^2 + h^2}$

$= \pi \times 3 \times \sqrt{3^2 + 6^2}$

$= 9\pi\sqrt{5}$

Cylinder (without top and base):

$S = 2\pi r h$

$= 2\pi \times 3 \times 9$

$= 54\pi$

Continues on next page …

Volume of half sphere $= \frac{2}{3}\pi r^3$

$\qquad = \frac{2}{3}\pi \times 3^3$

$\qquad = 18\pi$

Total volume $= 18\pi + 81\pi + 18\pi$

$\qquad = 117\pi\,cm^3$

Half sphere:

$S = 2\pi r^2$

$\quad = 2\pi \times 3^2$

$\quad = 18\pi$

Total surface area $= 9\pi\sqrt{5} + 54\pi + 18\pi$

$\qquad = 9\pi\sqrt{5} + 72\pi$

$\qquad = 9\pi(8 + \sqrt{5})\,cm^2$

Frustum of a cone

A frustum is what is left if the top of a cone has been removed. It is a truncated cone.

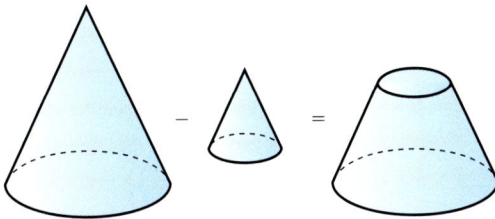

To find the volume of the frustum you find the volume of the whole cone and subtract the part that is missing.

Volume of a cone $= \frac{1}{3}(\pi r^2)h$

You can find the surface area of the frustum of a cone in a similar way. First find the surface area of the whole and subtract the surface area of the part of the cone that is missing.

Surface area of a cone $= = \pi r l + \pi r^2$, where l is the slant height.

Remember to add on the area of the circles at the top and the bottom if needed.

WORKED EXAMPLE 6

Calculate the external surface area and volume of the polystyrene coffee cup in the picture.

The cup is $\frac{2}{3}$ of the height of a cone. Take pi to be 3.14

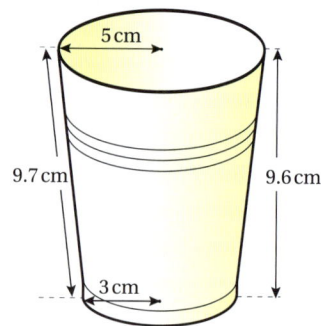

Surface area

Original cone slant height is $9.7 \div 2 \times 3 = 14.55\,\text{cm}$

Surface area of original cone = $\pi r l$

$$= 3.14 \times 5 \times 14.55$$
$$= 228.44\,\text{cm}^2$$

Surface area of cut-off part = $\pi r l$

$$= 3.14 \times 1.5 \times (14.55 - 9.7)$$
$$= 22.84\,\text{cm}^2$$

Surface area of cup = $228.44 - 22.84 = 205.6\,\text{cm}^2$

You divide by $\frac{2}{3}$ because it is $\frac{2}{3}$ of the cone. Remember to find the surface area of the whole and subtract the surface area of the missing part which is $\frac{1}{3}$ of the original part leaving $\frac{2}{3}$.

Volume

Height of cup is $9.6\,\text{cm}$, which is $\frac{2}{3}$ the original cone height

Height of original cone = $9.6 \div 2 \times 3 = 14.4\,\text{cm}$

Volume of original cone = $\frac{1}{3}(\pi r^2)h$

$$= \frac{1}{3} \times 3.14 \times 5^2 \times 14.4$$
$$= 376.8\,\text{cm}^3$$

Height of cut-off part = $14.4 - 9.6 = 4.8\,\text{cm}$

Volume of cut-off part = $\frac{1}{3} \times 3.14 \times 3^2 \times 4.8$

$$= 45.22\,\text{cm}^3$$

Volume of cup = $376.8 - 45.22 = 331.58\,\text{cm}^3$

EXERCISE 24C

1 Find the surface area of each solid. Give your answers to the nearest cm² or mm².

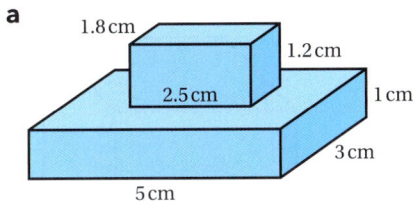

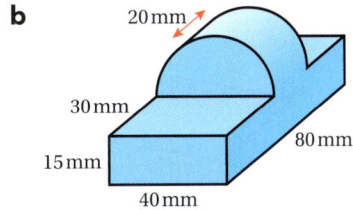

a

1.8 cm
1.2 cm
2.5 cm
1 cm
3 cm
5 cm

b

20 mm
30 mm
80 mm
15 mm
40 mm

2 A flower container as shown in the diagram needs painting with preservative.

The tub can be thought of as part of a full cone with the same top radius.

The slant height of the full cone is 219.3 cm.

90 cm
70.7 cm
50 cm
50 cm

a Calculate the outside surface area of one container, including the base, to the nearest whole number.

b A gardener has five of these flower tubs to preserve.

What preservative coverage will she need to preserve the outside of all five tubs, including the base, at least once?

3 Calculate the volume of this capsule.

2.5 m
1 m

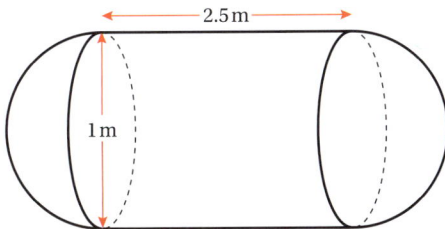

4 Calculate the volume and external surface area of this water tank.

Assume the bottom section is half a cylinder and the top is a right rectangular prism.

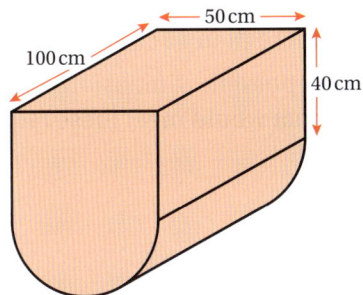

50 cm
100 cm
40 cm

5 These metal blocks have areas cut out of them. For each block, calculate:

a the volume of the metal

b the total surface area to be coated with rust inhibitor.

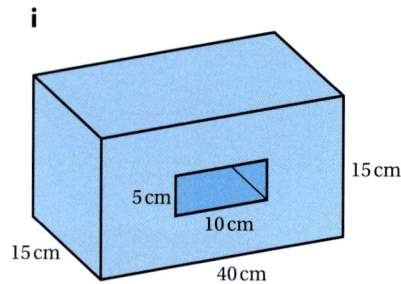

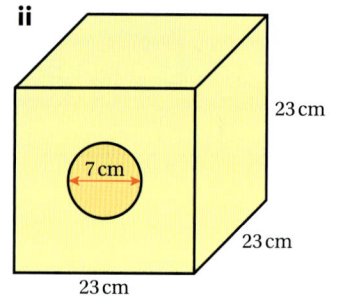

i

ii

6 Work out the volume of water in a swimming pool that is 6 m wide and 30 m long. The shallow end is 2 m deep and the deep end is 3.5 m deep.

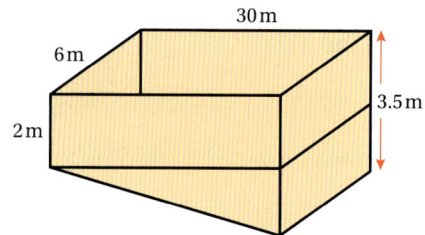

7 A fish tank is in the shape of a regular hexagon with equal sides of 10 cm and a height of 30 cm.

Calculate the volume of the fish tank.

8 Calculate the volume of the prism shown. All measurements are in centimetres. Calculate your answer to one decimal place, if necessary.

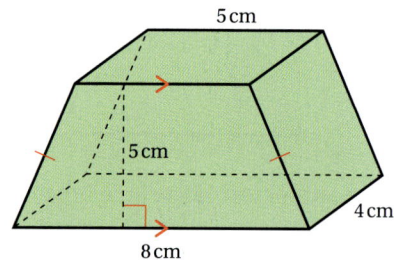

9 A container must have a volume of between 800 ml and 1 litre and the height must be not more than 15 cm.

Draw a table to show possible dimensions of a cylinder, cone and triangular pyramid that would meet these requirements.

Section 3: Pyramids

Pyramids are named according to the shape of their base.

The volume of a pyramid is $\frac{1}{3}$ of the volume of a prism with the same base area and height.

Volume of a pyramid $= \frac{1}{3} \times$ area of base $\times$ perpendicular height

The surface area of a pyramid is the total area of the base plus the area of each triangular side.

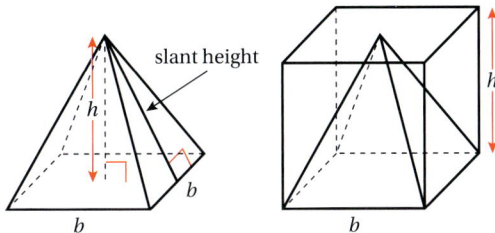

WORKED EXAMPLE 7

Calculate the volume and the surface area of the square-based pyramid.

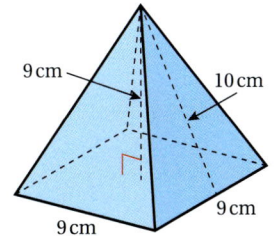

Volume of pyramid $= \frac{1}{3} \times$ area of base $\times h$

$= \frac{1}{3} \times 9 \times 9 \times 9 = 243 \, \text{cm}^3$

Use the formula for the volume of a pyramid and substitute in the given values.

Surface area of pyramid $= b \times b + 4 \times (\frac{1}{2} \times \text{slant height} \times b)$

$= (9 \times 9) + 4 \times (\frac{1}{2} \times 10 \times 9)$

$= 81 + 180 = 261 \, \text{cm}^2$

Surface area of pyramid = area of square base + 4 × area of triangular sides

Height of triangular side is the slant height of 10 cm shown in the diagram.

EXERCISE 24D

1 The six pyramids below have either square or triangular bases.

Calculate the volume and the surface area of each one.

a
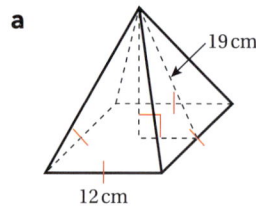
19 cm
12 cm

b
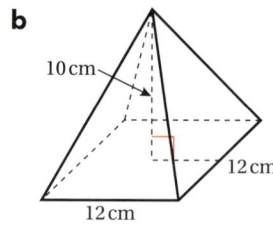
10 cm
12 cm
12 cm

c
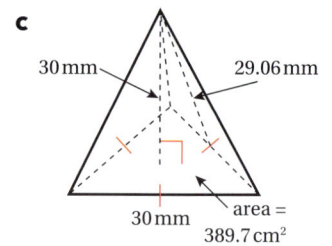
30 mm
29.06 mm
30 mm
area = 389.7 cm²

d
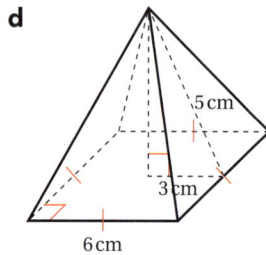
5 cm
3 cm
6 cm

e
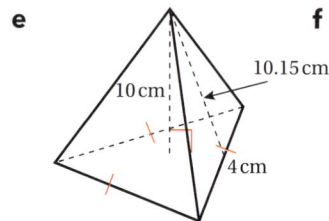
10 cm
10.15 cm
4 cm

f
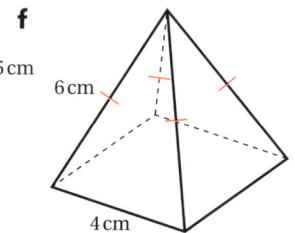
6 cm
4 cm

2 A pyramid is 16 cm tall and has a square base with side 7.5 cm.

Calculate the volume of the pyramid. Choose your answer from the options below.

A 40 cm³   B 300 cm³   C 900 cm³   D 2700 cm³

3 This is a photo of the Great Pyramid.

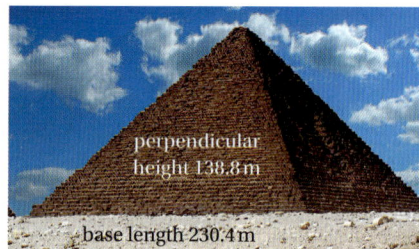
perpendicular height 138.8 m
base length 230.4 m

It has a square base.

Calculate the volume of the Great Pyramid.

4 Pyramid A has a square base of side 6 m and perpendicular height 8 m.

Pyramid B has an equilateral triangle with side 6 m as a base and perpendicular height 8 m.

Find the difference in the volumes of the pyramids.

5 A square-based pyramid has base sides of $6x$ and a perpendicular height of $4x$.

Find, in terms of x, the volume and the surface area of the pyramid.

6 The wooden sculpture shown is a triangular-based pyramid.

The base is an equilateral triangle with side 1 m. The height of the sculpture is 2 m.

Calculate the volume of wood in the sculpture.

7 A regular tetrahedron is a pyramid with four faces that are equilateral triangles.

a A decorative container consists of a closed object with four identical faces.

These faces are equilateral triangles with a side of 3 cm.

Calculate the volume and the surface area of this object.

b Write a formula for the volume and for the surface area of any regular tetrahedron with side x.

8 An obelisk is a square-based column with a pyramidal structure on the top.

Calculate the volume and surface area of the obelisk in the photograph.

It is 30 m high, the square base has an area of 5 m^2 and the pyramid itself is 1.5 m high.

Find answers at: cambridge.org/ukschools/gcsemaths-studentbookanswers

Checklist of learning and understanding

Volume

- Volume is the amount of space a 3D object occupies.
- Volume is calculated in cubic units.
- The volume of a prism and a cylinder is the area of base × length.
- Volume of a cone $= \frac{1}{3} \times$ area of base × height
- Volume of a sphere $= \frac{4}{3}\pi r^3$
- Volume of a pyramid $= \frac{1}{3} \times$ area of base × height

Surface area

- The surface area of a solid is the combined areas of all the external faces.

For additional questions on the topics in this chapter, visit GCSE Mathematics Online.

Chapter review

1 Calculate the area of canvas used to make this tent.

Assume the shape is a triangular prism and that there is no ground sheet.

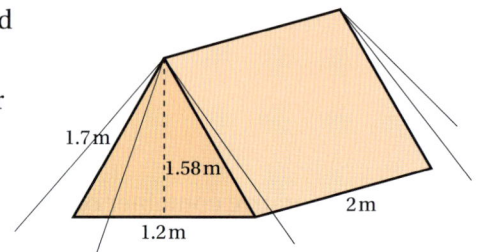

1.7 m, 1.58 m, 1.2 m, 2 m

2 Calculate the volume of the model house in the diagram.

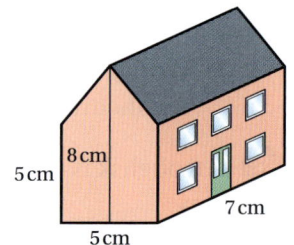

5 cm, 8 cm, 5 cm, 7 cm

3 This sculpture is made of a cube with a cylinder cut out through the middle of it.

Calculate the volume of the sculpture.

3 m

4   Calculate the volume of a room measuring 23 m × 14 m × 13 m.

5   The measurements on this tank are exact.

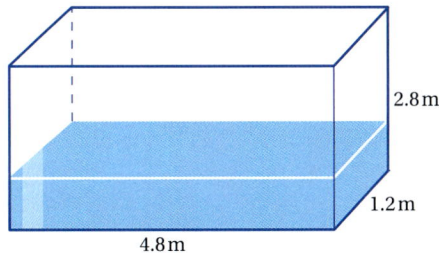

2.8 m

1.2 m

4.8 m

Water is put in the tank to a height of 0.7 m to the nearest tenth of a metre.

The tank is now turned on its side as shown.

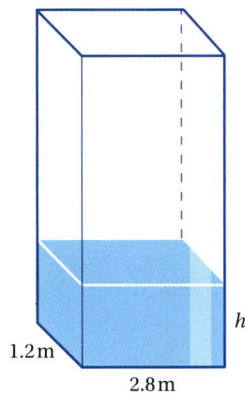

1.2 m

2.8 m

h

Work out the minimum height of water in the tank, marked, h.

Give your answer to 1 decimal place.   *(5 marks)*

© AQA 2013

6   The dimensions of a cube are whole numbers. The volume of the cube is 64 cm³.

Which of the following whole numbers could be a side length?

A 4 cm   B 10 cm   C 8 cm   D 16 cm   E 5 cm

7   Calculate:

a the volume of the tin in the diagram

b the surface area of the printed label.

8 cm

WOOF!

11 cm

DOG FOOD

25 Further probability

Using mathematics: real-life applications

Medical researchers have developed a range of tests to detect drug use, blood-alcohol levels, disease markers and genetic and birth defects in unborn children. The probability that the test results are accurate is very high, but it is seldom 100%.

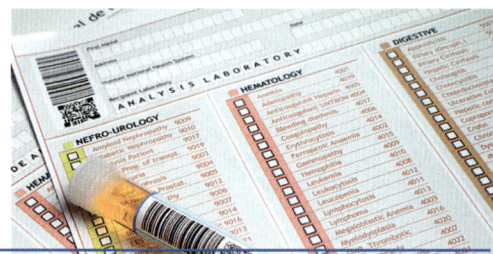

"An incorrect test result can be devastating. People can be convicted of drink-driving or more serious crimes, risk surgery or decide to terminate a pregnancy based on test results, so it is really important to understand the probability of a good test giving a bad result."

(Medical statistician)

Before you start …

Ch 5, 6	You'll need to be able to calculate effectively with fractions and decimals.	**1**	These calculations are all incorrect. What should the answers be? **a** $\frac{1}{8} + \frac{1}{4} = \frac{1}{12}$ **b** $\frac{2}{3} + \frac{1}{5} = \frac{2}{15}$ **c** $1 - \frac{3}{5} = -\frac{2}{5}$ **d** $\frac{2}{3} \times \frac{2}{5} = \frac{2}{15}$ **e** $0.3 \times 0.6 = 1.8$
KS3 Ch 20	You should be familiar with the vocabulary of basic probability.	**2**	Select the correct term from the box for each definition. *event outcomes random sample space relative frequency* **a** The ratio of number of times an event is recorded to the total number of trials conducted. **b** The results of an experiment. **c** An outcome of an experiment, such as getting heads when you toss a coin. **d** Having an equal likelihood of happening. **e** The list of all possible outcomes.
Ch 20	Check that you can list all the possible outcomes of an experiment.	**3**	Copy and c omplete each list of possible outcomes. **a** Two students are to be chosen at random from a group of males and females: FF, FM, … **b** Two coins are to be tossed at the same time: HH, … **c** Two cards are selected from a set of three cards labelled A, B and C and placed next to each other in the order they are drawn: AB, AC, …

Assess your starting point using the Launchpad

STEP 1

1 This spinner is spun twice in a row.

Copy and complete the tree diagram to show all the possible outcomes.

Add the probability of landing on each colour to your tree diagram.

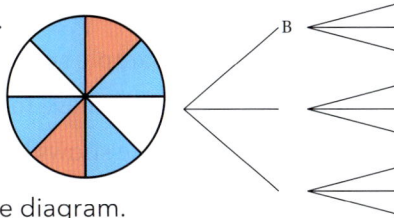

GO TO
Section 1: Combined events

STEP 2

2 The diagram gives the probability of drawing hearts or twos at random from a normal pack of 52 playing cards.

What is the probability that a card drawn at random will be:

a both a heart and a two?

b either a heart or a two?

c not a heart nor a two?

ε = 52 cards

♥ hearts   2 twos

12   1   3

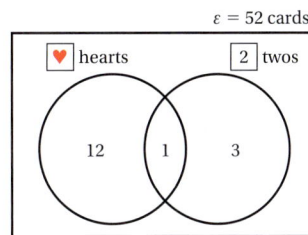

3 A black (B) or white (W) counter is drawn at random from a box.

The counter is replaced before a second counter is drawn.

The possible outcomes and the probabilities of each outcome are shown on the right.

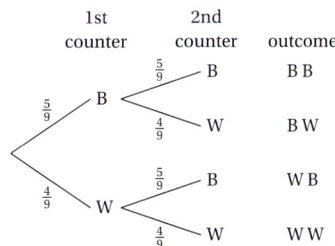

1st counter   2nd counter   outcome

$\frac{5}{9}$ B $\frac{5}{9}$ B → B B

$\frac{4}{9}$ W → B W

$\frac{4}{9}$ W $\frac{5}{9}$ B → W B

$\frac{4}{9}$ W → W W

What is the probability of drawing:

a a black counter on the first draw?

b two counters the same colour?

c a white counter first and a black counter second?

4 a A family has two children. Draw a tree diagram to show the sample space for the genders of the children. Assume each gender is equally likely.

b If the older child is a girl, calculate the probability that the younger child is a boy.

GO TO
Section 2: Theoretical probability of combined events
Section 3: Conditional probability

GO TO
Chapter review

Section 1: Combined events

Lists and tables are useful for showing the sample space (all the possible outcomes) of simple events.

For example, you can list the sample space for rolling a six-sided dice: (1, 2, 3, 4, 5, 6).

For more complex sample spaces, tables are more useful than lists.

In some cases you don't have to list all the possible outcomes.

For example, this table shows how many ways there are to get a total score of 7 when you roll two ordinary dice.

Number on dice	1	2	3	4	5	6
1	2	3	4	5	6	7
2	3	4	5	6	7	
3	4	5	6	7		
4	5	6	7			
5	6	7				
6	7					

Once you get to a sum of 7 you can stop because the next sum will be greater than that.

The table shows there are six ways of getting a score of 7: (1, 6), (2, 5), (3, 4), (4, 3), (5, 2) and (6, 1).

Even though you haven't filled in the empty blocks, you can still see that there are 36 possible outcomes. So the probability of getting 7 is $\frac{6}{36}$ or $\frac{1}{6}$

Tables and grids

WORKED EXAMPLE 1

Represent the sample space for tossing a coin and rolling a dice using:

a a table　　**b** a grid.

a Table

Dice / Coin	1	2	3	4	5	6
Heads	H1	H2	H3	H4	H5	H6
Tails	T1	T2	T3	T4	T5	T6

Draw a two-way table with the numbers on a dice along the top and the sides of a coin down the side.

Then list the possible outcomes in the body of the table.

b Grid

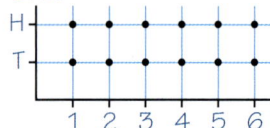

12 possible outcomes

Draw a grid with the numbers on a dice along the bottom and the sides of a coin up the side.

Then mark the possible outcomes as dots where the gridlines cross.

Tree diagrams

A tree diagram is a branching diagram that shows all the possible outcomes (sample space) of one or more activity.

To draw a tree diagram:

- draw a dot to represent the first activity
- draw branches from the dot to show all possible outcomes of that activity only
- write the outcomes at the end of each branch
- draw a dot at the end of each branch to represent the next activity
- draw branches from this point to show all possible outcomes of that activity
- write the outcomes at the end of the branches.

These two diagrams both show the possible outcomes for throwing a dice and tossing a coin at the same time. Both diagrams are correct.

> **Tip**
>
> Tree diagrams show probabilities, not actual responses. This is the main difference between them and the frequency trees you worked with in Chapter 20.

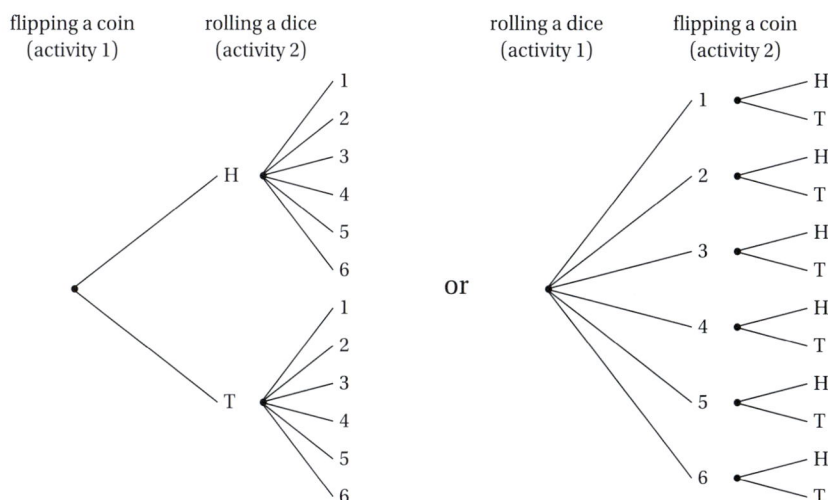

Once you've drawn a tree diagram you can list the possible outcomes by following the paths along the branches.

Listing the combinations lets you work out the probability of different events.

Find answers at: cambridge.org/ukschools/gcsemaths-studentbookanswers

WORKED EXAMPLE 2

Draw a tree diagram to show that when the probability of having a boy or a girl is equal, there are eight possible combinations of boys and girls in a three-child family. Then work out the probability of having three children with the same gender.

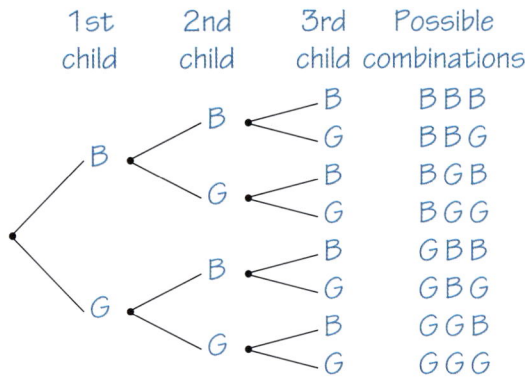

1st child	2nd child	3rd child	Possible combinations
	B	B	B B B
		G	B B G
B		B	B G B
	G	G	B G G
		B	G B B
	B	G	G B G
G		B	G G B
	G	G	G G G

Draw a dot for the first-born child.

Draw and label two branches, one B and one G.

Repeat this at the end of each branch for the second and third child.

List the possible combinations.

You can see from the diagram that there are 8 possible combinations of boys and girls.

There is only one outcome that produces 3 girls so:

$P(3 \text{ girls}) = \frac{1}{8}$

Similarly:

$P(\text{all the same gender}) = \frac{2}{8} = \frac{1}{4}$

You can use the diagram to find different probabilities.

---

i   Did you know?

This tree diagram assumes that a boy or a girl is equally likely for each pregnancy. In reality the probability of having a boy or a girl varies by family and by country.

EXERCISE 25A

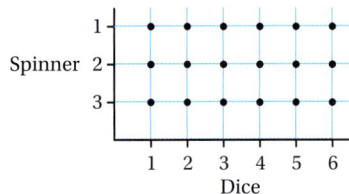

1 The grid represents the possible outcomes when you roll a dice and spin a triangular spinner marked 1, 2 and 3.

Spinner (1, 2, 3) vs Dice (1–6) grid of outcomes

a What is the probability of getting a total of 4? Choose the correct option below.

A 3   B $\frac{1}{6}$ C $\frac{1}{4}$ D 0.4

b What is the probability of getting a score of 4 or higher? Choose the correct option below.

A 1   B $\frac{4}{5}$ C $\frac{7}{9}$ D 0.83

2 Use a grid to represent the sample space for:

a tossing two coins

b choosing a letter at random from the word CAT and tossing a coin

c picking a counter from each of two bags containing one red, one blue and one yellow counter.

3 **a** Draw a table to show:

  i all possible combinations of scores when you roll two dice

  ii the sample space for tossing a coin and spinning a spinner with sectors A, B, C and D.

  b For each table drawn, make up five probability questions that could be answered from the tables. Exchange questions with a partner and answer each other's questions.

4 Draw a tree diagram to show the sample space when three coins are tossed one after the other.

5 Sandy has a bag containing a red, a blue and a green pen.

Copy and complete this tree diagram to show the sample space when she takes a pen from the bag at random, replaces it, and then takes another pen.

R
B
G

6 In a knockout quiz, the winner goes on to the next round.

Hassan takes part in a four-round quiz and he estimates that he has an equal chance of winning or losing each round.

  a Using W to represent win and L to represent lose, draw a tree diagram to show all possible outcomes for Hassan.

  b How many possible outcomes are there?

  c What is the probability that he will win the first round given his own estimate of his chances?

7 The diagram shows two groups of coloured jelly beans.

  a Draw a tree diagram to show the sample space for taking a particular colour of jelly bean at random from each group of jelly beans.

  b Based on this, does any particular combination of colours have a higher probability than another? Is that the reality when you choose jelly beans? What reasons do you give for this?

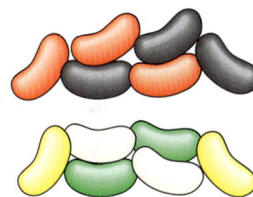

Venn diagrams

Venn diagrams show the mathematical relationships between sets of data.

Different events (sets of outcomes) are represented by circles inside a rectangular frame that in turn represents the sample space (universal set).

The Venn diagram below shows even numbers and multiples of 3 between 1 and 15.

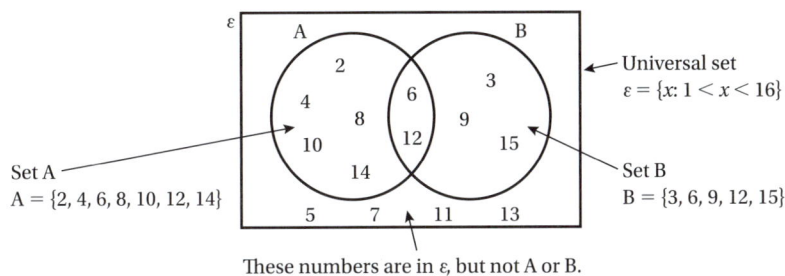

Set A
A = {2, 4, 6, 8, 10, 12, 14}

Universal set
$\varepsilon = \{x: 1 < x < 16\}$

Set B
B = {3, 6, 9, 12, 15}

These numbers are in ε, but not A or B.

ε is the universal set. In this case it the whole numbers between 1 and 15.

Tip

The curly brackets { } are used to show you are describing a set.

The circles A and B represent sets as shown in the diagram.

There are seven elements in set A. This can be written as n(A) = 7, which means 'the number of elements in set A is 7'.

There are five elements in set B, so n(B) = 5.

Elements that are common to both sets are written in the overlapping section of the circles to show that they belong to both sets.

Any elements of the universal set but **not** part of set A or set B are written inside the rectangle but outside the circles.

Intersection, union and complement of sets

Venn diagrams can also represent operations between sets. The three important operations for probability work are shown below.

The shaded area represents the intersection between set A and set B. The intersection of two sets is the elements that are common to (shared by) both sets.

$A \cap B = \{6, 12\}$

$n(A \cap B) = 2$

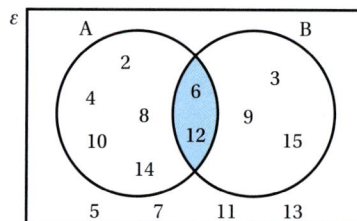

The shaded area here represents the union of set A and set B. This is the combined elements of both sets with no elements repeated.

$A \cup B = \{2, 3, 4, 6, 8, 9, 10, 12, 14, 15\}$

$n(A \cup B) = 10$

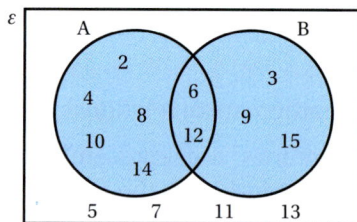

The complement of a set refers to all the elements in the universal set other than the ones in the given set.
The complement of set A is shaded below.

$A' = \{3, 5, 7, 9, 11, 13, 15\}$

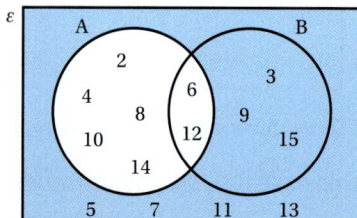

WORKED EXAMPLE 3

Draw a Venn diagram to represent the following information:

ε = {a letter from a to h inclusive}, A = {a, b, c, e} and B = {c, d, e, f, g}.

ε = {a, b, c, d, e, f, g, h}
A = {a, b, c, e}
B = {c, d, e, f, g}

Start by comparing the sets to find the intersection and any elements which are in the universal set but not in A or B (the complement of A and B or $(A \cup B)'$.

c and e are elements of A and B, so A ∪ B = {c, e}
h is not in A or B, so $(A \cap B)' = h$

In other words, h is outside the two circles.

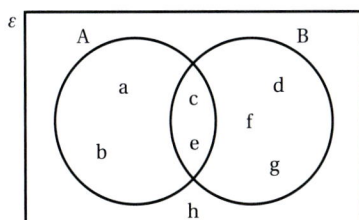

Draw the diagram and label it correctly.

In some problems you might be given information and have to define the sets yourself. In some cases you might not be able to list the separate elements of the sets so you write the number of elements in each set.

WORKED EXAMPLE 4

In a survey, 25 people were asked to say if they liked chocolate and if they liked ice cream.

Fifteen people said they liked ice cream and eighteen said they liked chocolate.

Assuming that everyone surveyed liked chocolate or ice cream or both, draw a Venn diagram and use it to work out the probability that a person chosen at random from this group will like both chocolate and ice cream.

ε = {number of people surveyed}, so, $n(\varepsilon)$ = 25
C = {people who like chocolate}, so, n(C) = 18
I = {people who like ice cream}, so, n(I) = 15
n(C) + n(I) = 18 + 15 = 33
But there were only 25 people surveyed, so 8 people must have said they liked both chocolate and ice cream (since 33 − 25 = 8). This tells you that: $n(C \cap I)$ = 8

Start by defining the sets and writing the information in set language.

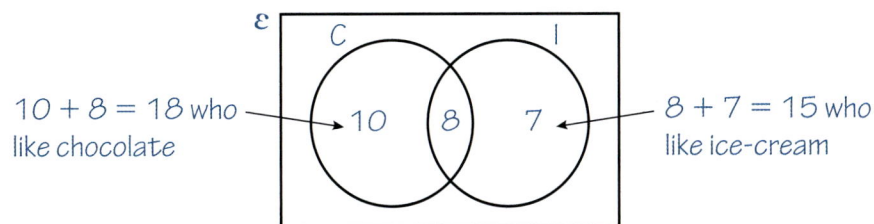

10 + 8 = 18 who like chocolate

8 + 7 = 15 who like ice-cream

Use the figures to draw your Venn diagram.

P(person likes both) = $\frac{\text{number of people who like both}}{\text{number of people surveyed}}$
= $\frac{8}{25}$ = 0.32

Finally, calculate the probability.

EXERCISE 25B

1 Use this Venn diagram to answer the following questions.

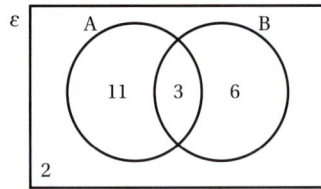

Choose the option to correctly complete the statements given.

a $n(A) = \square$

    A 9   B 6   C 11   D 14

b $n(A \cup B) = \square$

    A 14   B 20   C 22   D 23

c $n(A \cap B) = \square$

    A 2   B 3   C 9   D 20

2 ε = {integers from 1 to 20 inclusive}, A = {6, 7, 8, 9, 10, 11, 12} and B = {factors of 24}.

a Draw a Venn diagram to show this information.

b Use your Venn diagram to find:

    i $A \cap B$ **ii** $A \cup B$ **iii** $n(A)$ **iv** $n(A')$ **v** B'

3 Nadia has 20 pairs of shoes.

Six pairs are sports shoes, four pairs are red. Only one of the pairs of sports shoes is red.

Draw a Venn diagram to show this information.

Work out the probability that a pair of shoes chosen at random from her shoe collection will be neither red nor sports shoes.

4 A factory employs 100 people.

Forty-seven of the employees have to work with moving machinery. If these people have long hair they have to tie it back.

Thirty-five employees have long hair and, of these, some work with moving machinery.

Twenty-three employees neither have long hair nor work with moving machinery.

Draw a Venn diagram to show this information.

Use your diagram to work out the probability of a random employee having to tie his or her hair back at work.

5 Twenty students walked into a classroom.

Of these students, 13 were wearing headphones and 15 were sending texts.

Four students were neither wearing headphones nor sending texts.

Represent this information on a Venn diagram.

State how many students were wearing headphones while sending texts when they walked into class.

6 A group of 200 people were asked about their food preferences.

It was found that 110 people ate red meat, 135 ate chicken and 15 ate neither.

Calculate the probability that a person chosen at random will eat:

a red meat and chicken   **b** only red meat   **c** only chicken.

7 Of 500 customers in a supermarket, 324 bought ready-made meals, 213 shoppers bought fresh produce (fruit or vegetables) and 245 bought dairy products.

237 of the shoppers bought only ready-made meals.

43 of them bought both fresh produce and ready-made meals, but no dairy products.

32 of them bought only ready-made meals and dairy products.

122 of them bought only fresh produce.

Represent this information on a Venn diagram. Use the diagram to find out:

a how many of the shoppers bought all three of the items

b how many bought only fresh produce and dairy products, but no ready-made meals

c how many bought only dairy.

Section 2: Theoretical probability of combined events

You can use sample space diagrams (tables, grids, tree diagrams and Venn diagrams) to find the probabilities of combined events.

Once you have identified all the possible outcomes, you mark the ones that are favourable and use these to find the probability of different outcomes.

You work this out using the formula:

$$P(\text{event happens}) = \frac{\text{number of ways the event can happen}}{\text{number of possible outcomes}}$$

WORKED EXAMPLE 5

Jay has six cards with the numbers 0, 0, 2, 2, 3 and 7 on them.

He picks a number, returns it and then picks another at random.

a Draw a grid to show the sample space.

b Use the grid to find the probability that Jay will pick:

   i two numbers that are the same

   ii two numbers that add up to 7.

a

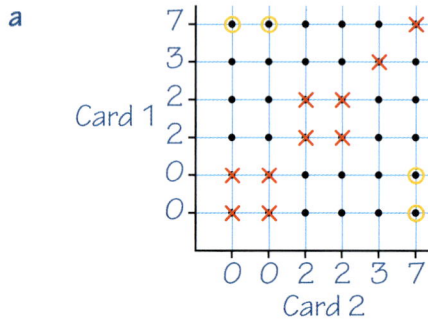

The grid shows there are 36 possible outcomes.

b i $P(\text{two numbers the same}) = \dfrac{10}{36}$

$= \dfrac{5}{18}$

$\text{or } 0.28 \text{ (to 2 dp)}$

The successful outcomes are marked with a cross on the grid.

ii $P(\text{sum of 7}) = \dfrac{4}{36}$

$= \dfrac{1}{9}$

The successful outcomes are circled on the grid.

The product rule for counting

In Worked Example 5 above, the number of possible outcomes is 36.

You can count the dots on the grid, but you can also find the total by multiplying: $6 \times 6 = 36$

WORK IT OUT 25.1

A tube station has two entrance turnstiles and three exit turnstiles.

How many possible options are there to leave and enter the station?

Which answer is correct? List all the possible outcomes to show this.

Option A	Option B
Two entrances = 2 ways in	For each of the two ways in there are three ways out.
Three exits = 3 ways out	$2 \times 3 = 6$ possible options
Total number of ways in and out = $2 + 3 = 5$	

The problem above can also be solved by drawing a tree diagram or grid.

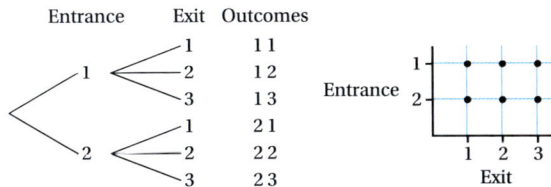

The product rule is useful for quickly solving probability problems like the one above without drawing the sample space.

WORKED EXAMPLE 6

How many three-digit numbers can be made from the digits 2, 3, 4 and 5 without repeating any digits?

Think about the problem like this:

☐ ☐ ☐   I need three digits, so I draw three spaces. There are 4 options for the first digit.

Once, I've chosen the first digit, there are only three options for the second digit and once that is chosen, there are only two options for the third digit.

$4 \times 3 \times 2 = 24$ ways of arranging the digits.

Tip

If the digits can be repeated, then your answer will be $4 \times 4 \times 4 = 64$ as the number of options don't reduce with each new digit.

EXERCISE 25C

1 Sunil has to choose a six-character password for his phone.

He chooses two letters and four numbers, in that order, with no repetition of letters or digits.

How many password options does he have?

2 Anna buys running shoes from a specialist running shop. The choices are:

• either neutral, cushioned or stability shoes

• from three brands

• one of five colours.

How many different shoes can she choose between?

3 A four-digit code number is made from digits 1 to 9. The digits cannot be repeated.

How many combinations are possible?

4 There are five questions in a multiple choice test.

The answers for each are A, B, C or D.

A hacker uses a computer to generate answers.

How many sets of answers must she generate to make sure that one of the sets is 100% correct?

5 A shop sells wraps. There are eight different choices for fillings and customers have three in a wrap.

How many different combinations are there?

Find answers at: cambridge.org/ukschools/gcsemaths-studentbookanswers

Different types of events

The type of event determines whether you add or multiply the probabilities.

Mutually exclusive events and the addition rule

$P(A \text{ or } B) = P(A) + P(B)$, where A and B are mutually exclusive events.

This is called the addition rule for mutually exclusive events.

For example, a bag contains 3 red, 2 yellow and 5 green sweets in it and you choose one sweet at random.

You cannot pick a red sweet and a yellow sweet at the same time, so the events P(red) and P(yellow) are mutually exclusive.

You can work out the probability of choosing *either* a red *or* a yellow sweet.

There are 3 red and 2 yellow sweets, so $\frac{5}{10}$ of the sweets are either red or yellow.

$$P(\text{red or yellow}) = P(\text{red}) + P(\text{yellow}) = \frac{3}{10} + \frac{2}{10} = \frac{5}{10} = \frac{1}{2}$$

Events that are not mutually exclusive

When you list the elements in the union of sets you do not repeat shared elements (those in the intersection).

In set language, we can write this as $n(A \cup B) = n(A) + n(B) - n(A \cap B)$. The elements in the intersection of sets are not mutually exclusive and this affects your probability calculations.

$$P(A \text{ or } B) = P(A) + P(B) - P(A \text{ and } B)$$

> **Tip**
>
> You should remember from Chapter 20 that mutually exclusive events cannot happen at the same time.

> **Tip**
>
> Questions with 'either–or' events usually involve mutually exclusive events so they can be solved by adding the probabilities.

WORKED EXAMPLE 7

The Venn diagram shows the possible outcomes when a six-sided dice is rolled. Set A = {prime numbers} and set B = {odd numbers}. Use the diagram to find the probability of rolling a number that is either odd or prime.

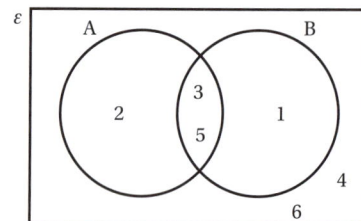

$P(A \text{ or } B) = P(A) + P(B) - P(A \text{ and } B)$

$P(A) = \frac{3}{6}$

$P(B) = \frac{3}{6}$

$P(A \text{ and } B) = \frac{2}{6}$

> The total number of outcomes is the denominator.
>
> It is easier to add and subtract the fractions if you don't simplify the fractions first.

So, $P(A \text{ or } B) = \frac{3}{6} + \frac{3}{6} - \frac{2}{6} = \frac{4}{6} = \frac{2}{3}$

> You can see this is true by looking at the diagram.
>
> The combined elements of A and B are 1, 2, 3 and 5, giving you $\frac{4}{6}$ numbers falling into one or the other of these sets.
>
> We don't want to add the numbers that fall into the intersecting part twice which is why we subtract $n(A \cap B)$ in the formula.

Independent events

When the outcome of one event does not affect the outcome of the others, the events are **independent**.

For example, rolling a dice and tossing a coin are independent events. The score on the dice doesn't affect whether you get heads or tails.

Tree diagrams are useful for solving problems involving independent events. You write the probabilities of the events on the branches.

Here is the tree diagram showing possible outcomes for throwing a dice and tossing a coin at the same time (H is used for a head and T is used for a tail).

> **Key vocabulary**
>
> **independent events**: events that are not affected by what happened before

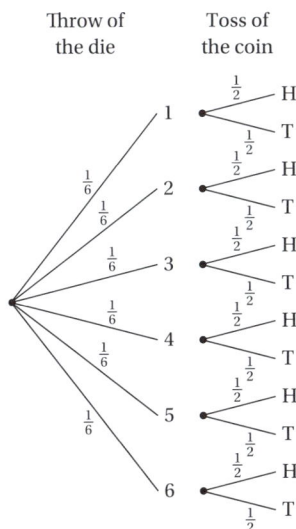

The probability of combined events on a tree diagram

To find the probability of one particular combination of outcomes, multiply the probabilities on consecutive branches.

For example, the probability of throwing a 5 and getting heads is $\frac{1}{6} \times \frac{1}{2} = \frac{1}{12}$

This is called the multiplication rule and it works for independent events only.

$$P(A \text{ and } B) = P(A) \times P(B)$$

> **Tip**
>
> It can be helpful to use a colour to mark the route along the branches to show which events you are dealing with.

Combining the rules

To find the probability when there is more than one favourable combination or when the events are mutually exclusive:

- multiply the probabilities on consecutive branches
- add the probabilities (of each favourable combination) obtained by multiplication,

  for example, throwing 1 or 2 and getting heads is

  $\left(\frac{1}{6} \times \frac{1}{2}\right) + \left(\frac{1}{6} \times \frac{1}{2}\right) = \frac{1}{12} + \frac{1}{12} = \frac{2}{12} = \frac{1}{6}$

WORKED EXAMPLE 8

Two coins are tossed together. Draw a tree diagram to find the probability of getting:

a two tails **b** one head and one tail.

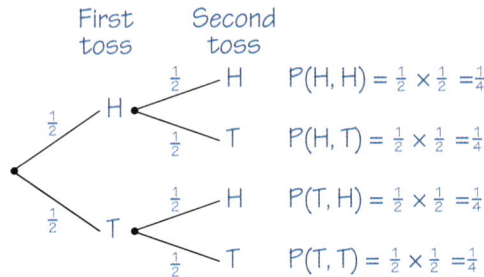

First toss   Second toss

$P(H, H) = \frac{1}{2} \times \frac{1}{2} = \frac{1}{4}$

$P(H, T) = \frac{1}{2} \times \frac{1}{2} = \frac{1}{4}$

$P(T, H) = \frac{1}{2} \times \frac{1}{2} = \frac{1}{4}$

$P(T, T) = \frac{1}{2} \times \frac{1}{2} = \frac{1}{4}$

> Draw the tree diagram first.

a $P(TT) = P(T \text{ on 1st toss}) \times P(T \text{ on 2nd toss})$

$= \frac{1}{2} \times \frac{1}{2} = \frac{1}{4}$

> Multiply the probabilities on consecutive branches.

b $P(HT \text{ or } TH) = P(HT) + P(TH)$

$= \left(\frac{1}{2} \times \frac{1}{2}\right) + \left(\frac{1}{2} \times \frac{1}{2}\right)$

$= \frac{1}{4} + \frac{1}{4} = \frac{1}{2}$

> Add the probabilities obtained by multiplication.

Dependent events

When the outcome of one event affects the outcome of the other, the events are said to be **dependent**.

Here are 4 red and 2 yellow sweets.

One sweet is removed at random before a second sweet is removed. What is the probability of the second sweet being red?

The answer to this depends on what colour the first sweet was. If the first sweet was red then the probability on the second branch that the second sweet was red is $\frac{3}{5}$, because there are only 5 sweets left and only 3 of those are red.

1 red eaten

If the first sweet was yellow then the probability on the second branch that the second sweet was red is $\frac{4}{5}$. There are still only 5 sweets left to choose from, but this time 4 of them are red.

1 yellow eaten

For dependent events you can find the probability by adapting the multiplication rule to accommodate the dependent event.

$P(A \text{ and then } B) = P(A) \times P(B \text{ given that } A \text{ has occurred})$

This example shows how you can use modified tree diagrams to work this out.

WORKED EXAMPLE 9

A box contains three yellow, four red and two purple marbles.

A marble is chosen at random and not replaced before choosing the next one.

Three marbles are chosen (without replacement), what is the probability of choosing:

a three red marbles?   **b** a yellow, a red and a purple marble in that order?

a These are the only outcomes we need

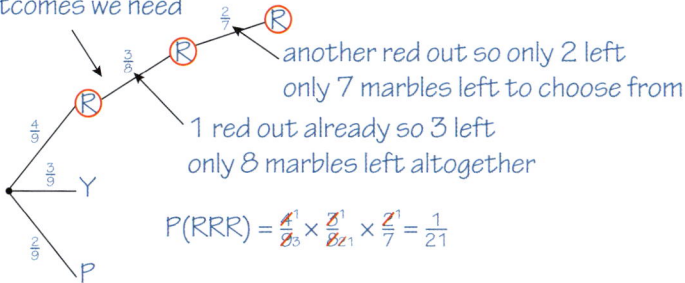

another red out so only 2 left
only 7 marbles left to choose from

1 red out already so 3 left
only 8 marbles left altogether

$$P(RRR) = \frac{4^1}{9_3} \times \frac{3^1}{8_{2_1}} \times \frac{2^1}{7} = \frac{1}{21}$$

Draw only the part of the tree diagram that you need.

Work out the probability by multiplying the probabilities on consecutive branches.

b We need Y/R/P   still 4 red but only 8 to choose from

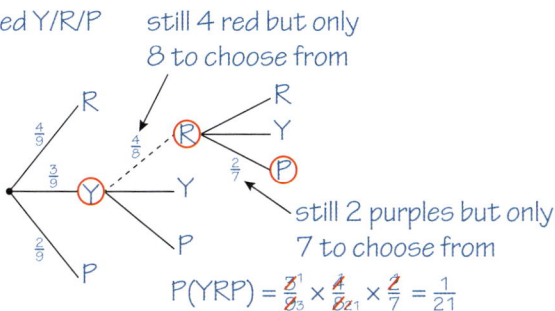

still 2 purples but only 7 to choose from

$$P(YRP) = \frac{3^1}{9_3} \times \frac{4}{8_{2_1}} \times \frac{2}{7} = \frac{1}{21}$$

Draw only the part of the tree diagram that you need.

Work out the probability by multiplying the probabilities on relevant branches.

The product rule for counting is also useful for solving some types of problems without drawing the sample space.

WORKED EXAMPLE 10

Josh has four cards labelled 1, 2, 3 and 4.

He draws two cards at random and lays them on the table to make a 2-digit number, with the first card drawn being used to make the tens digit.

a How many possible outcomes are there?

b What is the probability of making 32?

a ☐☐

4 × 3 = 12 possible outcomes

4 options for the first digit leaves 3 for the second.

b

$$P(32) = \frac{1}{12}$$

Given that the digits don't repeat because Josh can only draw each card once, you should be able to tell straight away that there is only one option.

You can also work this out: P(3 then 2) = P(3) × P(2, given 3 has occurred) = $\frac{1}{4} \times \frac{1}{3} = \frac{1}{12}$

Tip

You need to understand the difference between independent and dependent events to make sense of conditional probability in Section 3.

EXERCISE 25D

1 Nico chooses one consonant and one vowel at random from the names of towns on road signs he passes.

The next road sign is DUNDEE.

a Draw up a sample space diagram to list all the options that Nico has.

b Calculate P(D *and* E).

c Calculate P(D *and* E *or* U).

d Calculate P(*not* (N *and* U)).

2 A bag contains 3 red counters, 4 green counters, 2 yellow counters and 1 white counter.

Two counters are drawn from the bag one after the other, without being replaced.

Calculate:

a P(2 red counters)   b P(2 green counters)

c P(2 yellow counters)   d P(white *and then* red)

e P(white *or* yellow *in any order, but not both yellow*)

f P(white *or* red *in any order, but not both red*)

g P(white *or* yellow *first and then any other colour*).

3 A card is randomly selected from a pack of 52 playing cards and its suit is noted.

The card is not replaced. Then a second card is chosen.

a Draw a tree diagram to represent this situation.

b Use the tree diagram to find the probability that:

  i both cards are hearts.

  ii both cards are not clubs.

  iii the first card is red and the second card is black.

4 Mohammed has four tiles from a word game with the letters A, B, C and D on them.

He draws a letter at random and places it on the table. He then draws a second letter and a third, placing them down next to the previously drawn letter.

a Work out the probability that the letters he has drawn spell the words:

  i cad   ii bad   iii dad

b Work out the probability that he will not draw the letter B.

c Work out the probability of drawing the letters in alphabetical order.

5 In a standard pack of cards, A = {hearts} and B = {kings}. If a card is picked at random, work out:

a P(A)   b P(B)   c P(A *and* B)   d P(A *or* B)

6 During January in Manchester it rained on 16 days. The temperature fell below 6 °C on 25 days in the same period.

Draw a Venn diagram to work out the maximum and minimum possible number of days in January that were below 6 °C and rainy.

Section 3: Conditional probability

Conditional probability is used when you need to work out the probability of one event happening when we already know that another has happened.

The information about the first event changes the sample space and affects the calculation.

For two events A and B, P(B given A has happened) refers to the conditional probability of B happening given that A has already happened.

The way that you work out the conditional probability depends on whether the events are independent or not.

For example, two normal six-sided dice are rolled.

The first dice has already landed on a six. What is the probability of the second dice being a six?

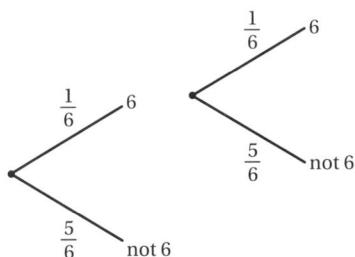

$$P(6 \text{ then } 6) = \frac{1}{6} \times \frac{1}{6} = \frac{1}{36}$$

These two events are independent. The score on the second dice is not affected by the outcome of the first.

If two events A and B are independent, you will find that it is always true that P(B given A has happened) = P(B).

For dependent events, the outcome of the first event affects the probability of the second.

To find the probability of B given that A has happened, use the rule,

$$P(B \text{ given A has happened}) = \frac{P(A \text{ and } B)}{P(A)}.$$

Tip

When the problem states that the items are 'replaced' then the events are independent and the probabilities don't change. When the item is not replaced, the outcome of the second depends on the outcome of the first event and the probabilities change.

WORKED EXAMPLE 11

A card is taken at random from a normal pack of 52 cards. It is not replaced.

A second card is then taken at random.

What is the probability of drawing two queens?

Think about it:

The second probability is dependent on the first. You can only draw two queens if the first and the second card are queens.

The probability that the first card is a queen is $\frac{4}{52}$ or $\frac{1}{13}$

Once you remove a card, there are only 51 cards left to choose from. As the first card was a queen there are only 3 queens left in the pack.

So, $P(A \text{ and } B) = \frac{1}{13} \times \frac{3}{51} = \frac{3}{663} = \frac{1}{221}$

You can also use a partial probability tree to work this out:

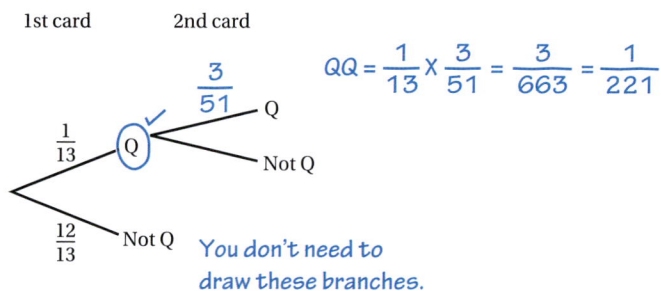

$QQ = \frac{1}{13} \times \frac{3}{51} = \frac{3}{663} = \frac{1}{221}$

You don't need to draw these branches.

For some conditional probability problems it is easier to use Venn diagrams.

Tip

When a problem asks for the probability of at least one event you can either list all the possible outcomes or you can use the fact that
P(at least one happens) = 1 − P(none of the events happen).

WORKED EXAMPLE 12

In a group of 50 students, 36 students work on tablet computers, 20 work on laptops and 12 work on neither of these.

A student is chosen at random. What is the probability that he or she:

a works on a tablet and a laptop computer?

b works on at least one type of computer?

c works on a tablet given that he or she works on a laptop?

d doesn't work on a laptop, given that he or she works on a tablet?

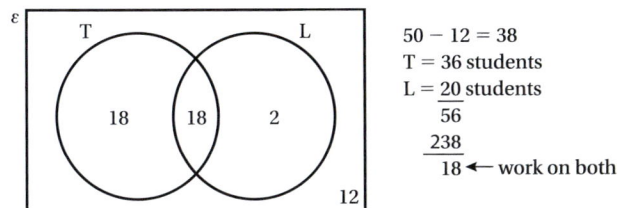

$50 - 12 = 38$
$T = 36$ students
$L = 20$ students
$\overline{}$ 56
$\overline{}$ 238
$\overline{18}$ ← work on both

> Start by investigating the numbers in the question and drawing a Venn diagram.

a $P(\text{works on both}) = P(T \cap L) = \dfrac{18}{50} = \dfrac{9}{25}$

b $P(\text{works on at least one}) = 1 - P(\text{works on neither}) = 1 - \dfrac{12}{50} = \dfrac{38}{50} = \dfrac{19}{25}$

c $P(T \text{ given } L \text{ has happened}) = \dfrac{P(L \text{ and } T)}{P(L)} = \dfrac{18}{20} = \dfrac{9}{10}$

d $P(\text{Not } L \text{ given } T \text{ has happened}) = \dfrac{P(L \text{ and } T')}{P(L)} = \dfrac{18}{36} = \dfrac{1}{2}$

Tip

When starting to answer a problem like this, you will often need to work out which type of diagram and which method or combination of methods is most useful for solving the particular problem.

EXERCISE 25E

1 There are 21 students in a class. 12 are boys and 9 are girls.

The teacher chooses two different students at random to answer questions.

a Draw a tree diagram to represent this information.

b Find the probability that:

i both students chosen are boys

ii both students are girls

iii the second student is a girl given that the first student was a boy.

c The teacher chooses a third student at random. What is the probability that:

i all three students chosen are girls?

ii at least one student is a girl?

iii the third student is a girl, given that the first two students were boys?

2 The labels were accidentally knocked off three students' lockers.

The labels say Raju, Sam and Kerry.

The tree diagram shows the possible ways of replacing the labels.

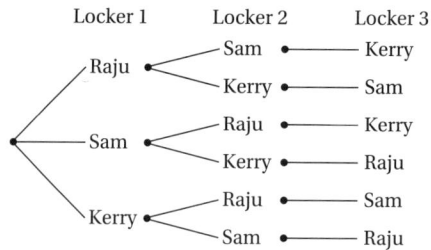

a Copy the diagram and write the probabilities next to each branch.

b Are these events dependent or independent? Give a reason for your answer.

c How many correct ways are there to match the name labels to the lockers?

d How many possible ways are there for the labels to be replaced on the lockers?

e If the labels were randomly stuck back on to the lockers, what is the chance of getting the names correct?

f Work out the probability of getting the labels on lockers 2 and 3 correct given that the first one is correctly labelled Kerry.

3 A climatologist reports that the probability of rain on Friday is 0.21

If it rains on Friday, there is a 0.83 chance of rain on Saturday.

If it doesn't rain on Friday, the chance of rain on Saturday is only 0.3

a Draw a tree diagram to represent this situation.

b Use your diagram to work out the probability of rain on:

i Friday and Saturday   **ii** Saturday given that it was sunny on Friday.

4 In a group of 25 people, 15 like cappuccino (C), 17 like latte (L) and 2 people like neither.

Using an appropriate sample space diagram, calculate the probability that a person will:

a like cappuccino   **b** like cappuccino given that he or she likes latte.

5 100 teenagers went on a summer camp.

80 of them went hiking and 42 went sailing.

Each student did at least one of these activities.

a Draw a Venn diagram to show how many teenagers did both activities.

b A teenager is randomly selected. Find the probability that he or she:

i went hiking but not sailing

ii went sailing given that he or she went hiking.

6 In a group of 120 students, 25 are in the sixth form and 15 attend maths tutorials.

Four of the students are sixth formers who attend maths tutorials.

What is the probability that a randomly chosen student who attends maths tutorials will be a sixth former?

> **Tip**
>
> Think carefully about question 6; it involves conditional probability.

7 A bag contains two red counters and six yellow counters.

Three counters are removed, one at a time.

Find the probability that:

a the three counters are the same colour

b at least one counter is red

c exactly one red counter is removed

d the second counter is red given that the first is yellow.

8 When Nadia takes the train from Monday to Thursday the probability that she gets a seat is 95%.

When she takes the train on a Friday or Saturday, the probability that she gets a seat is 70%.

Assuming that she is equally likely to take the train on any day from Monday to Saturday, work out the probability that:

a she gets a seat   **b** it is Saturday and she gets a seat.

9 **a** Give reasons how you can know whether two events A and B are dependent or independent, given the probability of A and the probability of A given B.

b The probability of drawing a red marble from a bag containing only red and blue marbles is $\frac{1}{8}$

The probability of drawing a blue and then a red marble from a bag is $\frac{2}{15}$

Is the marble returned to the bag after the first draw? Give a reason for your answer.

Checklist of learning and understanding

Representing combined events

- The sample space of an event is all the possible outcomes of the event.
- When an event has two or more stages it is called a combined event.
- Lists, tables, grids, tree diagrams and Venn diagram can be used to represent combined events.

Calculating probabilities for combined events

- For mutually exclusive events, P(A *or* B) = P(A) + P(B)
- For independent events, P(A *and* B) = P(A) × P(B)
- When independent events are mutually exclusive, you need to add the probabilities obtained by multiplication.
- For dependent events, P(A *and then* B) = P(A) × P(B *given that* A *has occurred*)

Conditional probability

- For independent events, P(B given A has happened) = P(B)
- For dependent events, P(B given A has happened) = $\dfrac{P(A \text{ and } B)}{P(A)}$
- For 'at least' problems, P(at least A) = 1 − (not A)

For additional questions on the topics in this chapter, visit GCSE Mathematics Online.

Chapter review

1. Choose the most appropriate method and represent the sample space in each of the following.

   a A coin is tossed and an 8-sided dice, with faces numbered 0 to 7, is rolled at the same time.

   b Boxes A, B and C contain pink and yellow tickets. A box is selected at random and a ticket is drawn from it.

   c The number of ways in which three letters P, A and N might be arranged to form a three-letter sequence.

   d In a class of 24 students, 10 take art, 12 take music and 5 take neither.

2. Two normal six-sided dice are rolled simultaneously. Draw a sample space for this information and hence calculate the probability of rolling:

   a double 2
   b at least one 4
   c a total greater than 9
   d a total of 6 or 7.

3. The letters from the word MANCHESTER are written on cards and placed in a bag.

   a One letter is drawn at random. Work out the probability of drawing a vowel.

   b A letter is drawn from the bag, noted and replaced and then another letter is drawn.

Copy and complete this tree diagram to show all the probabilities.

c Use the tree diagram to work out the probability of drawing:

   i two vowels   **ii** two consonants

   iii a vowel and a consonant   **iv** at least one consonant.

d Give a reason why drawing the letters can be considered independent events in this case.

e How could you change the experiment to make the events dependent?

4 There are 50 students in a year group.

Thirty have brown eyes, nine have fair hair and three have both brown eyes and fair hair.

Represent this information on a Venn diagram.

Use the Venn diagram to work out the probability that a student chosen at random from this group:

a has neither brown eyes nor fair hair

b has brown eyes but not fair hair

c has fair hair given that he or she has brown eyes

d does not have fair hair given that he or she does not have brown eyes.

5 The probability of the sun shining on a given day of the weekend is given as 0.3

What is the probability of it being sunny on both Saturday and Sunday?

Choose from the options below.

A 0.6   B 0.9   C 0.03   D 0.09

6 Find the number of different ways that all the letters in the word PROBABILITY can be arranged.

7 Robin is firing arrows at a target.

The probability that he hits the target on his xth attempt is $\dfrac{x+2}{x+3}$

For example, Probability (hit on his 5th attempt) $= \dfrac{7}{8}$

a Work out the probability that he hits the target with both his 1st and 2nd attempts.   *(3 marks)*

b Work out the probability that he hits the target exactly once on his first two attempts.   *(4 marks)*

                                      © AQA 2013

26 Inequalities

In this chapter you will learn how to …

- use the correct symbols and notation to express inequalities.
- solve linear and quadratic inequalities in one variable and represent the solution set on a number line and in set notation.
- solve linear inequalities in two variables, representing the solution set on a graph.

For more resources relating to this chapter, visit GCSE Mathematics Online.

Using mathematics: real-life applications

Inequalities can be used to model and solve problems where a range of answers are possible rather than specific values. For example, all distances less than 2 m from the edge of a road. Linear programming is used in logistic and project management. It involves graphing complex constraints for a project to find a region of feasibility and identify the best solution.

"Civil engineering projects involve a great deal of planning. We need to work with limits on time and budgets. Inequalities are one way of expressing the ranges of values that have to be met and considered together."

(Civil engineer)

Before you start …

Ch 17	You need to be able to solve linear equations.	**1**	**a** If $3x + 2 = 2x + 5$, $x = ?$ **b** If $4(n + 3) = 6(n - 1)$, $n = ?$ **c** If $6(5 - 3x) = 5(2x - 5)$, $x = ?$ **d** If $\dfrac{3a - 2}{4} = \dfrac{a - 5}{2}$, $a = ?$
Ch 16	You should remember how to solve quadratic equations.	**2**	$x^2 - 2x - 3 = 0$ $x = 3$ is one of the roots of this equation. What is the other root?
KS3	You should be confident using linear graphs.	**3**	The equation of the blue line is $y = -\dfrac{1}{3}x + 1$. **a** What is the gradient of the line that is perpendicular to this line? **b** What is the equation of that line if it cuts the given line at $(3, 0)$?

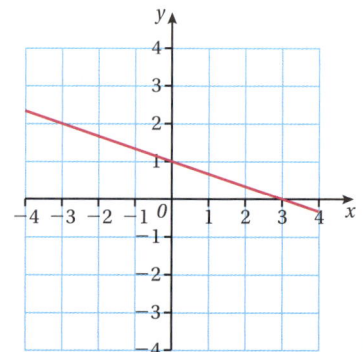

Assess your starting point using the Launchpad

STEP 1

1 Use mathematical symbols to express the following:

    a p is less than 0.45   **b** x is greater or equal to -4

    c y lies between the values of 11 and 18

2 List the whole numbers that satisfy each inequality:

    a $2 < x < 5$ **b** $12 \geqslant x > -2$ **c** $2 \leqslant x - 1 < 5$

GO TO
Section 1:
Expressing inequalities

STEP 2

3 Draw a number line to represent each of the following.

    a $x > -1$ **b** $x \leqslant 2$ **c** $-3 \leqslant x \leqslant 4$

4 State whether each statement is true or false.

    a $x \leqslant -3$ shown on a number line would be a number line starting at and including -3 and pointing in a negative direction.

    b $x > 2\frac{1}{2}$ shown on a number line would be a number line starting at $2\frac{1}{2}$ and including $2\frac{1}{2}$ and pointing in a positive direction.

GO TO
Section 2:
Number lines and set notation

STEP 3

5 Solve, and show the solution graphically:

    a $4x - 5 < 3$ **b** $3(x + 5) \geqslant 9$

GO TO
Section 3:
Solving linear inequalities

STEP 4

6 Solve $x^2 - 4x - 5 = 0$ and express the solution in set notation.

7 Draw a graph of the equation $y = x^2 - 4x - 5$ and represent the solution set for the inequality $x^2 - 4x - 5 > 0$.

Use the graph to identify the range of values that would satisfy this inequality.

GO TO
Section 4:
Solving quadratic inequalities
Section 5:
Graphing linear inequalities

GO TO
Chapter review

Find answers at: cambridge.org/ukschools/gcsemaths-studentbookanswers

Section 1: Expressing inequalities

An **inequality** is a mathematical sentence that uses symbols, such as <, ⩽, > or ⩾, in place of an equals sign.

The expressions on either side of the symbol are not equal.

The most common inequality symbols are:

- \> greater than
- \< less than
- ⩾ greater than or equal to
- ⩽ less than or equal to.

Two inequality symbols are used to give a range of values.

For example,

$2 < x < 6$ means 2 is *less than* x and x is *less than* 6.

Another way to read this statement is to say x lies between 2 and 6.

Addition and subtraction of inequalities

If you add the same number to both sides of an inequality, then the resulting inequality is still true.

If you subtract the same number from both sides of an inequality, then the resulting inequality is still true.

Multiplication and division of inequalities

If you multiply or divide both sides of an inequality by a positive number, then the resulting inequality is still true.

If you multiply or divide both sides of an inequality by a negative number, then you must **reverse** the inequality sign to make the resulting inequality true.

For example:

$7 > 3$

if you multiply both sides by −2 then the result is:

$-14 < -6$

EXERCISE 26A

1 Copy and complete the statements with the correct inequality symbol.

a $7 > 3$, then $4 + 7 \boxed{} 4 + 3$ **b** $8 < 13$, then $8 - 5 \boxed{} 13 - 5$

c $-5 < -1$, then $-5 + 3 \boxed{} -1 + 3$ **d** $-4 > -11$, then $-4 - 6 \boxed{} -11 - 6$

2 Copy and complete the statements with the correct inequality symbol.

a $7 > 3$, then $2 \times 7 \boxed{} 2 \times 3$ **b** $8 < 13$, then $2 \times 8 \boxed{} 2 \times 13$

c $7 > 3$, then $7 \div 2 \boxed{} 3 \div 2$ **d** $8 < 13$, then $8 \div 2 \boxed{} 13 \div 2$

3 Copy and complete the statements with the correct inequality symbol.

   a $7 > 3$, then $(-2) \times 7 \boxed{} (-2) \times 3$ **b** $8 < 13$, then $(-2) \times 8 \boxed{} (-2) \times 13$

   c $7 > 3$, then $7 \div (-2) \boxed{} 3 \div (-2)$ **d** $8 < 13$, then $8 \div (-2) \boxed{} 13 \div (-2)$

4 List the whole number values for x if $x > 6$ and $x \leqslant 8$. Choose from the following options.

   A   6, 7   B   6, 7, 8   C   6, 7   D   7, 8

5 For inequality, list four whole numbers that satisfy the inequality.

   a $x > 14$ **b** $x \geqslant 6$ **c** $x \leqslant -2$

   d $x + 3 \geqslant 7$ **e** $x - 4 \leqslant 5$

6 If $x > 6$ how many values can x take?

7 If $3 < x < 8$, how many whole number (integer) values can x take?

   How many values can x take if you include decimal values or fractions?

8 What whole number values are given by $6 > x > 2$?

Section 2: Number lines and set notation

You can use a **number line** to illustrate an inequality.

When drawing and illustrating values on a number line you use an open dot (small circle) if the starting value is not included. You use a solid dot if the starting point is included.

The expression $x \leqslant 11$ means numbers less than 11 including 11. So a number line representing $x \leqslant 11$ shows values starting from and including 11 with a solid dot at 11.

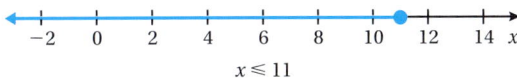

$$x \leqslant 11$$

The expression $x > 11$ means numbers greater than 11. So a number line representing $x > 11$ starts at 11 but the open dot is taken to signify that 11 is not included.

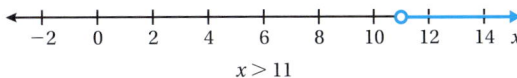

$$x > 11$$

Set notation

Another way to write statements about inequalities and the range of numbers that have been identified is to use **set** notation.

   $x \leqslant 11$ This is the set of numbers that are equal to or less than 11.

   $x > 11$ This is the set of numbers that are greater than 11.

This number line shows the set: $3 \leqslant x < 6$

$$3 \leqslant x < 6$$

> ### 🔑 Key vocabulary
>
> **number line**: line marked with positions of numbers showing the valid values of a variable

> ### 🔑 Key vocabulary
>
> **set**: a collection. The brackets {} are shorthand for 'the set of'. For example, {2, 4, 6, 8} is the set of the numbers 2, 4, 6, 8 which represents the even numbers.

> ### 💡 Tip
>
> Number lines and graphs are a good way of checking you have identified the correct range of numbers in a set. Think carefully about the use of the symbols.

Find answers at: cambridge.org/ukschools/gcsemaths-studentbookanswers

EXERCISE 26B

1 Which set is represented in the diagram?

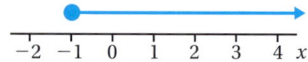

A $x > -1$ B $x < -1$ C $x \geqslant -1$ D $x \geqslant -2$

2 Use set notation to describe the range of values shown on each number line.

a
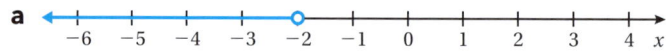

b
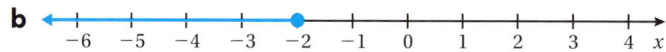

c
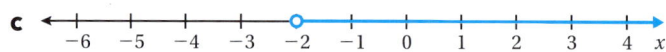

d
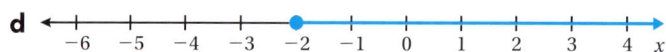

3 Show each set on a number line.

a $x > 8$ **b** $x \leqslant 0$ **c** $x < -5$

d $x > -1$ **e** $x \leqslant 2\frac{1}{2}$

4 Using set notation, write a statement for each set identified in these number lines in two different ways.

a
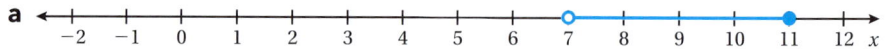

b
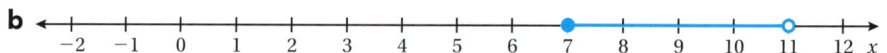

c
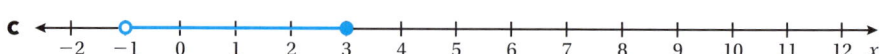

d
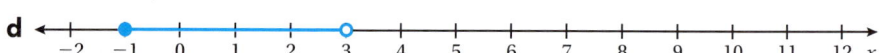

5 Draw a number line for each of the following sets.

a $-5 \leqslant x \leqslant 1$ **b** $6 > x > -1$

Section 3: Solving linear inequalities

Solving a linear inequality means finding all of the values for x that satisfy that inequality.

You can solve inequalities using the same methods that you used for linear equations.

However, you must apply the rules that you learned in Section 1.

WORKED EXAMPLE 1

Solve for x. Show your solutions on a number line.

a $4x - 5 < 3$ **b** $\dfrac{5x - 3}{2} \geqslant 11$ **c** $-5 \geqslant 3x + 4 \geqslant 13$

a $4x - 5 < 3$

$\qquad 4x < 8$

$\qquad\ \ x < 2$

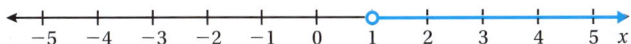

Add 5 to both sides.

Dividing both sides by 4.

Draw a number line.

b $\dfrac{5x - 3}{2} \geqslant 11$

$5x - 3 \geqslant 22$

$\qquad 5x \geqslant 25$

$\qquad\ \ x \geqslant 5$

Multiply both sides by 2 to cancel out the denominator.

Add 3 to both sides.

Divide both sides by 5.

Draw a number line.

c $\qquad -5 \leqslant 3x + 4 \leqslant 13$

$\quad -5 - 4 \leqslant 3x \leqslant 13 - 4$

$\qquad -9 \leqslant 3x \leqslant 9$

$\qquad -3 \leqslant x \leqslant 3$

Subtract 4 from each expression.

Divide all the terms by 3.

Draw a number line.

d $2(5x - 2) > 6$

$\quad 10x - 4 > 6$

$\qquad 10x > 10$

$\qquad\ \ x > 1$

Multiply out the brackets.

Add 4 to both sides.

Divide both sides by 10.

Draw a number line.

> **Tip**
>
> You can substitute your solution into the inequality to check it is correct in the same way you can check solutions to equations.

e $4(7 - x) \leqslant 3$

$\quad 28 - 4x \leqslant 3$

$\qquad 25 \leqslant 4x$

$\qquad 6.25 \leqslant x$

$\qquad\ \ x \geqslant 6.25$

Multiply out the brackets.

Add $4x$ to both sides to remove the negative sign for x and take 3 from both sides.

Divide both sides by 4.

Rearrange the inequality to start with x. Note that the inequality sign will need to change direction. If 6.25 is less than and equal to x then x is greater than and equal to 6.25.

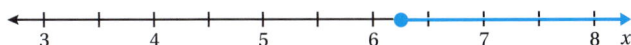

Find answers at: cambridge.org/ukschools/gcsemaths-studentbookanswers

EXERCISE 26C

1 Solve these inequalities, making sure you have the correct symbol in your answer.

   a $4x \leqslant 20$ **b** $-10x \geqslant 130$ **c** $-12x > -42$

   d $\dfrac{-x}{2} \leqslant 5$ **e** $\dfrac{-x}{5} > 4$ **f** $3 - 2x > 5$

2 Which of the options below shows the range of values that the inequality $7 - 2x \leqslant 4x + 10$ can take?

   A $x \leqslant 2$ B $x \geqslant -2$ C $x \leqslant -\dfrac{1}{2}$ D $x \geqslant -\dfrac{1}{2}$

3 Solve each inequality. Leave fractional answers as fractions in their simplest form.

   a $3(h - 4) > 5(h - 10)$ **b** $\dfrac{y + 6}{4} \leqslant 9$

   c $\dfrac{1}{2}(x + 50 \leqslant 2$ **d** $3 - 7h \leqslant 6 - 5h$

   e $2(y - 7) + 6 \leqslant 5(y + 3) + 21$ **f** $6(n - 40) - 2(n + 1) < 3(n + 7) + 1$

   g $5(2v - 3) - 2(4v - 5) \geqslant 8(v + 1)$ **h** $\dfrac{z - 2}{3} - 7 > 13$

   i $\dfrac{3k - 1}{7} - 7 > 7$ **j** $\dfrac{2e + 1}{9} > 7 - 6e$

4 When 5 is added to twice p, the result is greater than 17. What values can p take?

5 When 16 is subtracted from half of q, the result is less than 18. What values can q take?

6 When $2p$ is subtracted from 10, the result is greater than or equal to 4. What values can p take?

7 The sum of $4d$ and 6 is greater than the sum of $2d$ and 18. What values can d take?

8 A number a is increased by 3 and this amount is then doubled. If the result of this is greater than a, what values can a take?

9 In a school, two exams are set.

   The mark out of 100 for the Term 1 exam is added to twice the mark out of 100 for the Term 3 exam.

   The students must get at least 150 marks to achieve a pass grade.

   A student obtains x marks in the Term 1 exam.

   a Write an appropriate inequality to show the mark, y, that the student must obtain in the Term 3 exam in order to pass.

   b Solve this inequality for y when:

      i $x = 35$ **ii** $x = 49$

Section 4: Solving quadratic inequalities

A quadratic inequality contains at least one term with a squared variable and no terms with any powers higher than 2.

You can solve quadratic inequalities using the methods you applied to quadratic equations.

WORKED EXAMPLE 2

Find the values of x that satisfy $x^2 - 4x > 5$

$x^2 - 4x - 5 > 0$

Rewrite the inequality to make the right-hand side 0.

$(x - 5)(x + 1) > 0$

Factorise.

Either both brackets are positive (in other words > 0), **or** both brackets are negative (in other words < 0).

The inequality 'greater than 0' means the product of the brackets is positive.

This could mean two things.

Either $(x - 5) > 0$ and $(x + 1) > 0$
$\rightarrow x > 5$ and $x > -1$: this results in $x > 5$
Or $(x - 5) < 0$ and $(x + 1) < 0$
$\rightarrow x < 5$ and $x < -1$: this results in $x < -1$

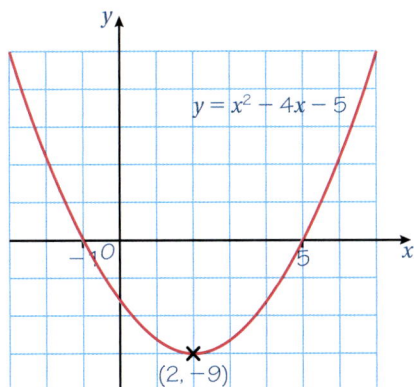

$y = x^2 - 4x - 5$

$(2, -9)$

The graph of $y = x^2 - 4x - 5$ is useful to check this result (it can also be used to find the result).

For $x^2 - 4x - 5 > 0$, this means $y > 0$, this is the parts of the graph **above** the x-axis.

From the graph, you can see that these are the two regions, $x > 5$ or $x < -1$.

WORKED EXAMPLE 3

Find the values of x that satisfy $x^2 - 4x < 5$

Notice that this is similar to Worked Example 2 but the direction of the inequality has been reversed.

$x^2 - 4x - 5 < 0$

> Rewrite the inequality to make the right-hand side 0.

$(x - 5)(x + 1) < 0$

> Factorise.

Either $(x - 5) > 0$ and $(x + 1) < 0$
$\rightarrow x > 5$ and $x < -1$, but this is a contradiction, as x cannot satisfy both conditions at the same time,
or $(x - 5) < 0$ and $(x + 1) > 0$
$\rightarrow x < 5$ and $x > -1$.

> This time the product is less than zero. One of the brackets most be > 0 and the other < 0.

$-1 < x < 5$

> This can be written using set notation.

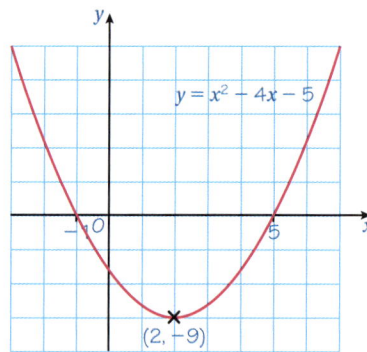

> You can use the same graph as in Worked Example 2 to see this result.
>
> For $x^2 - 4x - 5 < 0$, this means $y < 0$, this is the parts of the graph **below** the x-axis.
>
> From the graph you can see that this is just one enclosed region, $-1 < x < 5$.

Tip

If you are solving a quadratic inequality algebraically be sure to include all the steps involved in the solution to help you apply the correct reasoning.

EXERCISE 26D

1 From the graph estimate:
  a for what values of x is $x^2 - 3x - 3 \geqslant 0$
  b for what values of x is $x^2 - 3x - 3 < 0$

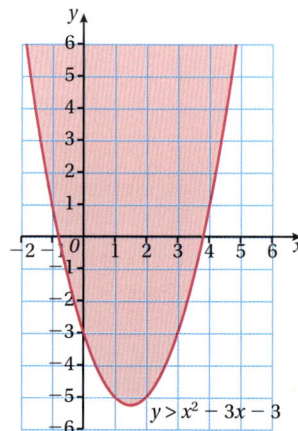

$y > x^2 - 3x - 3$

2　**a**　For what values of x is $-2x^2 + 16x - 24 \geqslant 0$?

　　b　For what values of x is $-2x^2 + 16x - 24 \leqslant 0$?

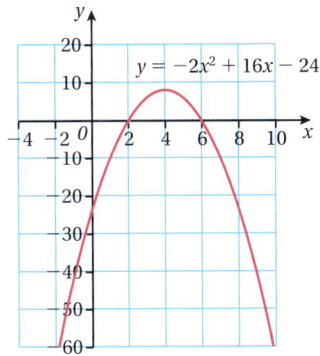

3　Sketch a graph and find all values of x such that:

　　a　$(x-3)(x+2) > 0$　　**b**　$(x+1)(x+4) \leqslant 0$

　　c　$(x-5)(x-2) \geqslant 0$　　**d**　$x(x+3) < 0$

4　Solve for x. Sketch the graphs if you need to.

　　a　$-2x^2 - 5x + 12 > 0$　　**b**　$x^2 - 5x < 0$

　　c　$8 + 2x - x^2 \leqslant 0$　　**d**　$12 - 5x - 2x^2 < 0$

5　Write the quadratic inequalities represented by the values on these number line graphs.

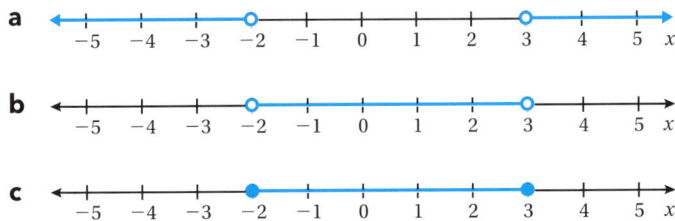

a

b

c

Section 5: Graphing linear inequalities

Inequalities such as $y < x + 1$ have two variables connected to them (x, y).

The solution to such an inequality is a region on a plane.

You can use graphs to find and/or represent the solution to two or more simultaneous inequalities.

Regions on a plane

Simple equations like $y = 3$ and $x = -2$ can also be called **equalities**.

y is equal to 3 and x is equal to -2.

> **Key vocabulary**
>
> **equalities**: having the same amount or value

On a number plane, all the points that satisfy each equality lie on one straight line.

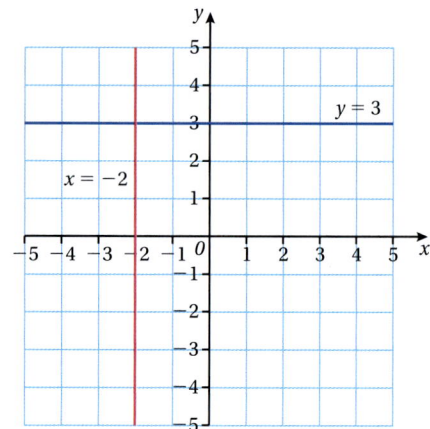

All the points that satisfy the inequality $x > 2$ lie on one side of the line $x = 2$.

The region into which these points fall is shaded on the graph below.

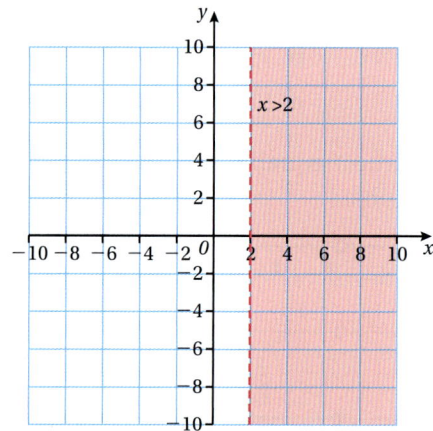

All points on the other side of the line satisfy the inequality $x < 2$.

The line itself is not included in the region $x > 2$, so it is shown as a broken line.

This graph shows the inequality $y \leqslant 2x + 1$.

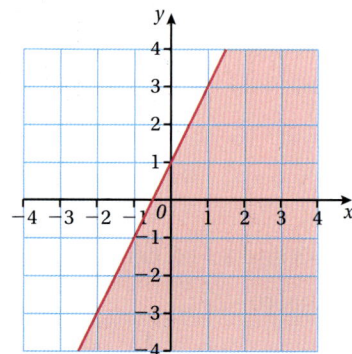

In this case, the points on the line are included in the region so the line is shown as a solid line.

WORKED EXAMPLE 4

Draw a set of x- and y-axes from -4 to 4. Shade the region on the diagram that satisfies both statements $y > 3$ and $x < -2$. Give two points in the identified (shaded) region.

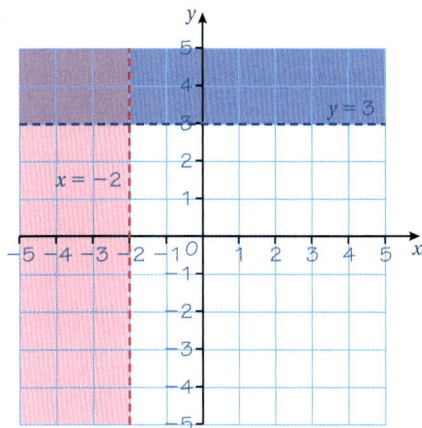

First, draw the lines $y = 3$ and $x = -2$; the lines are dashed because $y = 3$ and $x = -2$ are not included in their respective inequality.

Shade in the graph **above** the line $y = 3$ (you should still see the squared grid through the shading). Shade in the graph to the **left** of the line $x = -2$ in a different colour.

You can choose any two points within the shaded region where the shading will overlap, **except** for those that contain an x-coordinate of -2 or those with a y-coordinate of 3. Two examples are $(-3, 4)$ and $(-5, 5)$.

Verifying solutions

This is the graph of $y = -x + 3$.

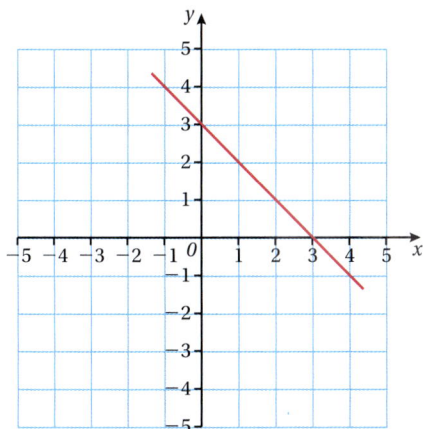

To identify the region that is $y \geqslant -x + 3$, test a point either side of the line.

For example $(-2, 3)$: $3 \geqslant -(-2) + 3$

3 is not greater than or equal to 5.

Try $(2, 2)$ on the other side of the line: $2 \geqslant -2 + 3$, 2 is greater than 1 so the region to the right represents $y \geqslant -x + 3$.

EXERCISE 26E

1 Sketch a graph for each of the following linear equations and shade the region defined by the inequality.

a $y = x + 1, y \geqslant x + 1$ **b** $y = -2x + 4, y \leqslant -2x + 4$

c $y = \frac{1}{2} \times +3, y \geqslant \frac{1}{2} \times +3$

2 Draw the following vertical and horizontal lines on a graph:
$x = -4, x = 1, y = 5$ and $y = -3$.
Shade in the regions defined by the inequalities $x \geqslant 1, y \geqslant 5$.

State the coordinates of two points in the region where the two inequalities overlap.

3 Is the region shaded in this diagram $y \geqslant \frac{1}{3}x - 2$ or $y \leqslant \frac{1}{3}x - 2$?
Give a reason for your answer.

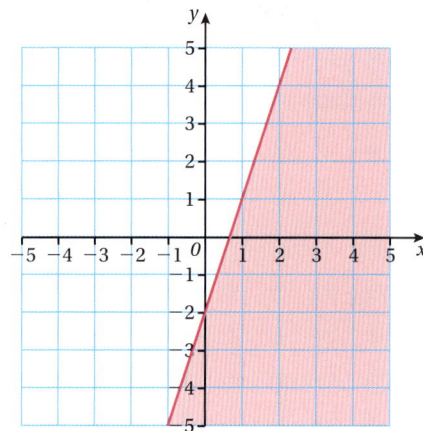

4 For each of the diagrams find the equation of the line and write an inequality to define the shaded region.

a

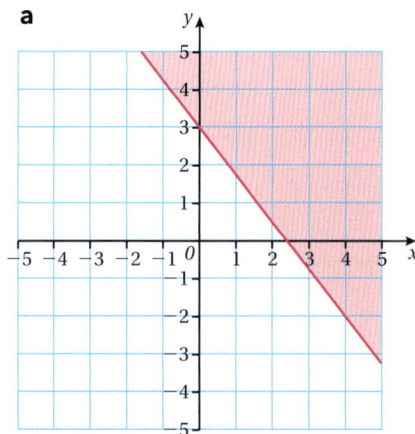

b

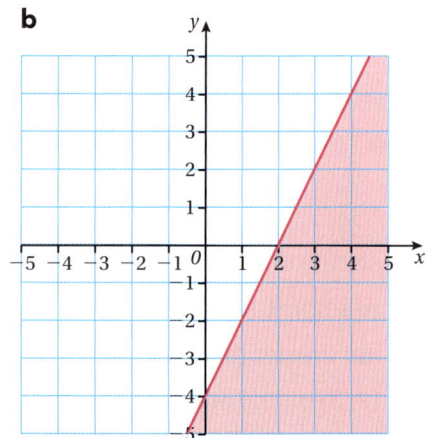

5 Check that the inequalities that define each region of the diagram are correct by substituting a point from the region.

Write a pair of inequalities which define the unshaded region.

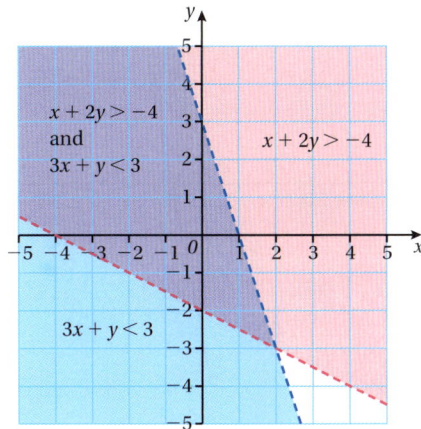

6 Write the equations of the two lines and identify the inequalities that represent the shaded area. Verify your answer with a point in the shaded region.

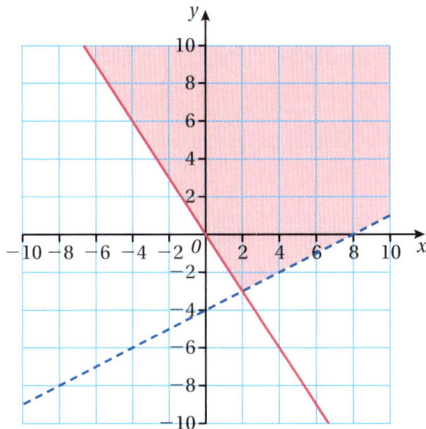

7 Draw a sketch diagram of the two linear equations
$y = -4x + 8$ and $y = x + 1$.

Identify and shade the region satisfied by the inequalities
$y > x + 1$ and $y \leqslant -4x + 8$.

8 **a** Plot the following linear equations:

$y = 2x - 3$

$y = -\dfrac{5}{4}x + \dfrac{5}{2}$

$y = -3$

Identify and shade the region defined by $y \geqslant 2x - 3$, $y > -3$, $y \leqslant -\dfrac{5}{4}x + \dfrac{5}{2}$

b Draw a sketch diagram of the two linear equations
$y = -4x + 8$ and $y = x + 1$.

Identify and shade the region satisfied by the inequalities
$y > x + 1$ and $y \leqslant -4x + 8$.

9 Write the equations of each of the lines in the graph. Write the three inequalities that identify the shaded region.

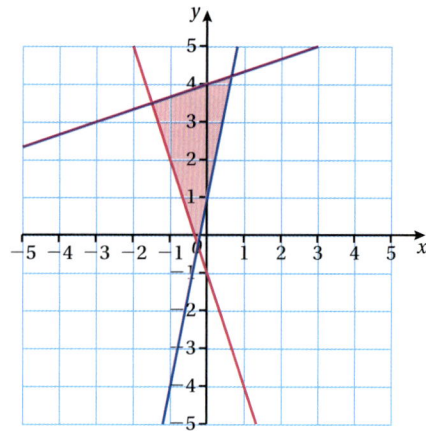

10 List the three inequalities that identify the shaded region and verify your answer with a point in the region.

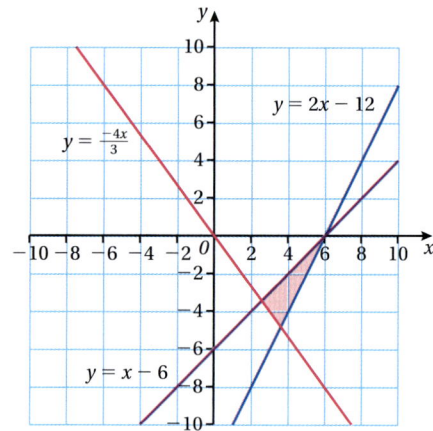

11 Solve this pair of simultaneous equations.

$$4x - 5y = 20$$

$$7x - 2y = 14$$

Draw a sketch graph of the two lines and shade the region defined by $4x - 5y < 20$ and $7x - 2y \geqslant 14$.

Checklist of learning and understanding

Inequalities

- Inequalities indicate a range of values to be considered. For $a \leqslant x \leqslant b$: x is a value that lies between the values of a and b and can be equal to a and b. This statement can also be written in the form $b \geqslant x \geqslant a$.

- An inequality will have a finite number of integer solutions but an infinite number of real solutions. The solutions can be shown on a number line.

Solving inequalities

- Linear inequalities can be solved using techniques similar to those for solving linear equations, but any multiplication or division by a negative will reverse the sign: for example, $4 > 3$ but $-4 < -3$; if $x > y$, then $-x < -y$. If you are not sure, verify by substituting numbers.

- If a solution to an inequality is $3 > x$ you can write this with x on the left-hand side: $x < 3$

- Solutions can be written using set notation: $x < 3$ means the set of numbers x such that the value of x is less than 3. For example, integer solutions for $2 < x \leqslant 5$ are 5, 4, 3.

- Quadratic inequalities are best solved by considering values on a graph. The shaded area in this graph represents the values of x for $y > x^2 - 1$.

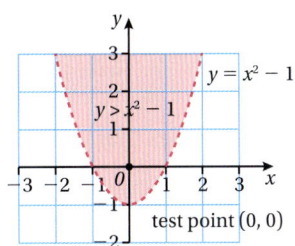

Graphing inequalities

- Problems that require more than one linear inequality can be solved by graphing and identifying the area that is the solution set.

For additional questions on the topics in this chapter, visit GCSE Mathematics Online.

Chapter review

1 List all the prime numbers which satisfy the inequality $3 \leqslant \frac{x}{3} < 7$. Choose from the options below.

   A 3, 5, 7   B 11, 13, 17, 19   C 3, 5, 7, 11, 13, 17   D 11, 13, 15, 17

2 On a graph, identify the three integral values of x and y which satisfy all these four inequalities:

   $4x + 3y < 12$ $y < 3x$ $y > 0$ $x > 0$

3 On a diagram, draw straight lines and use shading to show the region R that satisfies all these three inequalities $x \geqslant 2$ $y \geqslant x$ $x + y \leqslant 6$

4 Write the list of the three inequalities which identify the values in the shaded area.

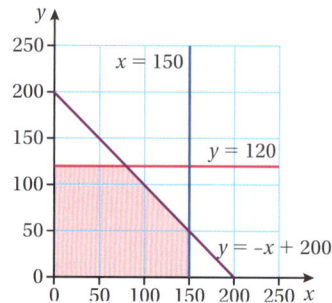

5 Work out the three inequalities that describe the shaded region.

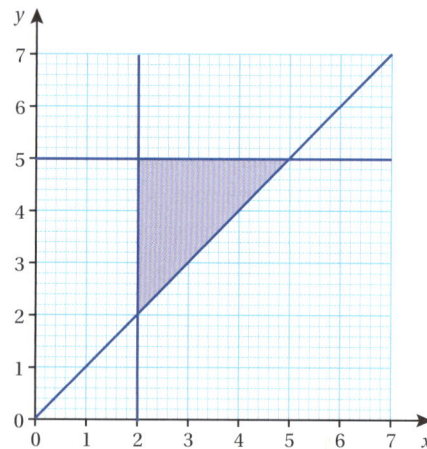

(3 marks)

© AQA 2013

27 Ratio

In this chapter you will learn how to …

- work with equivalent ratios.
- divide quantities in a given ratio.
- identify and work with fractions in ratio problems.
- apply ratio to real contexts and problems, such as those involving conversion, comparison, scaling, mixing and concentrations.

For more resources relating to this chapter, visit GCSE Mathematics Online.

Using mathematics: real-life applications

Ratio is used in many different real-life situations. Converting between different currencies, working out which packet of crisps is the best value for money, mixing large quantities of cement and scaling up a recipe to cater for more people, all involve reasoning using ratios.

"Every day customers bring me paints to match. I have to understand how changing the ratio of base colours affects the colour of the paint and how to scale the quantities up and down for larger or smaller amounts of paint. If I get it wrong, customers will have patches of different colours and their walls will look quite strange."

(Paint technician)

Before you start …

Ch 5	You need to be able to identify and simplify fractions.	**1**	**a** In a class of 35 students, 21 are boys. What fraction of the class are girls? **b** What fraction of this shape is shaded? Write your answer in its simplest form.
Ch 5	You need to be able to find a fraction of a quantity.	**2**	Find $\frac{2}{3}$ of 42.
Ch 5	You need to be able to find an original amount given a fraction.	**3**	There are 51 parents of students in the audience at a school play. These parents make up $\frac{3}{4}$ of the audience. How many people are in the audience?

Find answers at: cambridge.org/ukschools/gcsemaths-studentbookanswers

Assess your starting point using the Launchpad

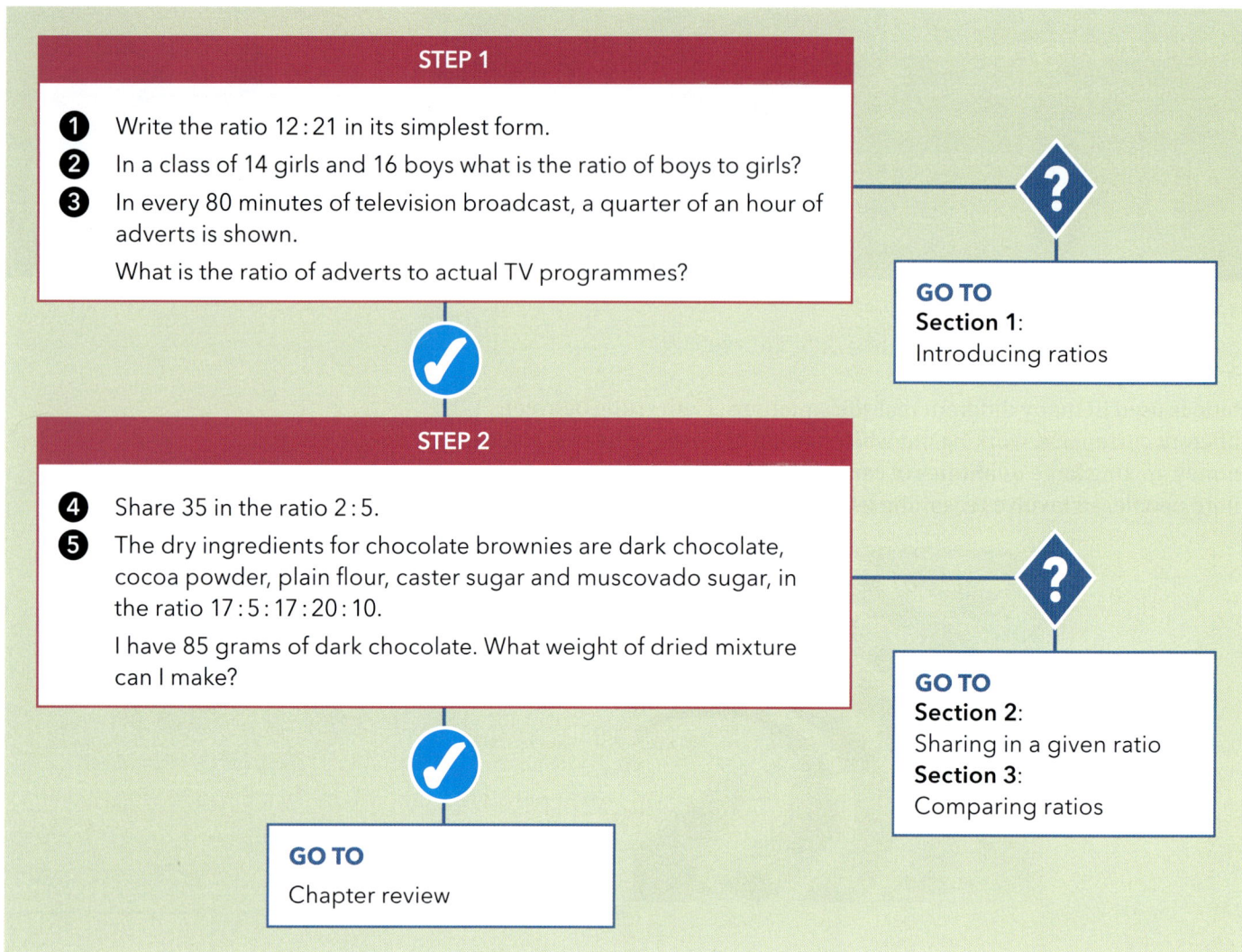

STEP 1

1 Write the ratio 12 : 21 in its simplest form.

2 In a class of 14 girls and 16 boys what is the ratio of boys to girls?

3 In every 80 minutes of television broadcast, a quarter of an hour of adverts is shown.

What is the ratio of adverts to actual TV programmes?

GO TO
Section 1:
Introducing ratios

STEP 2

4 Share 35 in the ratio 2 : 5.

5 The dry ingredients for chocolate brownies are dark chocolate, cocoa powder, plain flour, caster sugar and muscovado sugar, in the ratio 17 : 5 : 17 : 20 : 10.

I have 85 grams of dark chocolate. What weight of dried mixture can I make?

GO TO
Section 2:
Sharing in a given ratio
Section 3:
Comparing ratios

GO TO
Chapter review

Section 1: Introducing ratios

Key vocabulary

ratio: the relationship between two or more groups or amounts, explaining how much bigger one is than another

Ratio describes how parts of equal size relate to each other.

For example, most colours of paint can be mixed from the four base colours: blue, yellow, red and white.

To mix a batch of green paint, you need to know how much of the base colours to mix.

A ratio of yellow to blue paint of 1 : 3 means one unit of yellow for every three units of blue. This would give a very dark green.

A ratio of yellow to blue paint of 5 : 1, means five units of yellow for every one unit of blue. This would give a much lighter green.

The diagram shows a ratio of yellow to blue of $3:9$.

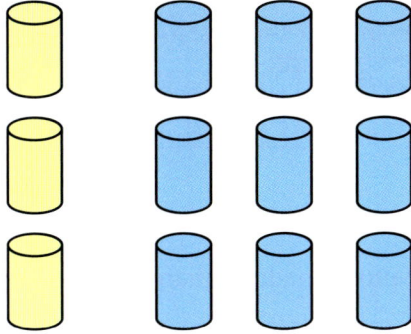

Dividing by three simplifies the ratio of $3:9$ to give $1:3$.

$$\div 3 \left(\begin{array}{ccc} 3 & : & 9 \\ 1 & : & 3 \end{array}\right) \div 3$$

The ratios $3:9$ and $1:3$ are **equivalent** ratios.

The yellow paint makes up the same **proportion** of the mix in both cases.

The difference between ratio and proportion

A ratio compares two or more quantities with each other.

A proportion compares a quantity to the 'whole' of which it is a part.

For example, in the dark green paint mixture, the ratio of yellow paint to blue paints is $3:9$ or $1:3$.

The proportion of yellow paint in the dark green paint mixture is $\frac{3}{12}$ or $\frac{1}{4}$ or 25%.

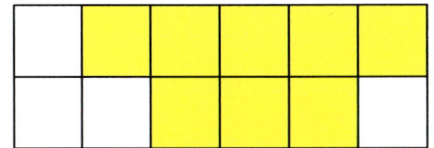

EXERCISE 27A

1 In the diagram, what is the ratio of unshaded to shaded squares in its simplest form?

Choose your answer from the options below.

A $1:3$ B $1:2$ C $4:12$ D $2:1$

2 Three-quarters of the students of a school go on an end-of-year trip to an adventure park.

What is the ratio of those that go to those that do not go?

Choose the correct answer from the options below.

A $3:1$ B $3:4$ C $3:7$ D $4:1$

3 On a school trip, 36 girls and 45 boys went with 9 teachers.

a Write down the ratio of boys to girls.

b Write down the ratio of students to teachers.

c Write down the ratio of students to people on the trip.

d The school policy is that each teacher can be responsible for no more than 10 students.

State whether this requirement has been met on this trip.

4 Write down the ratio of shaded squares to unshaded squares in each diagram.

Write the answers in their simplest form.

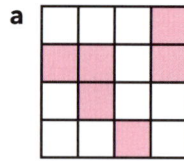

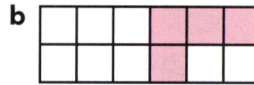

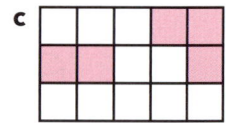

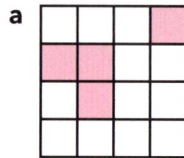

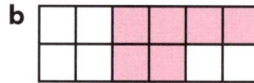

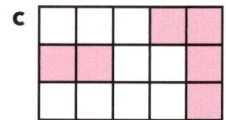

a

b

c

5 Write down the ratio of shaded squares to total squares in each diagram.

Write the answers in their simplest form.

a

b

c

6 The ratio of shaded to unshaded squares in this diagram is $1:3$.

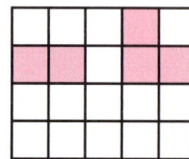

How many more squares need to be shaded to make the ratio $2:3$?

7 The distance between the post office and the bank is represented as 5 cm on a map.

In real life this distance is 20 m. Write the scale of the map as a ratio.

8 On a scale drawing of a cruise ship, a cabin is 8 cm from the restaurant.

On the actual ship the distance is 76 m.

Express the distances as a ratio.

9 A TV programme lasts 90 minutes.

The crew recorded 60 hours of footage.

What is the ratio of used footage to recorded footage?

10 **a** Use the diagram to find the ratio of:

　i side AB to side AC　**ii** side EB to side DC　**iii** side AE to side AD.

b What do these ratios tell you about triangles ABE and ACD?

c What do they tell you about lines EB and DC?

d Write down the ratio of angle AEB to angle ADC.

11 A jam recipe uses 55 g of fruit to make 100 g of jam. The rest is sugar.

Write down the ratio of fruit to sugar.

Tip

Ratios do not include units. To compare measured amounts you need to make sure they are written in the same units.

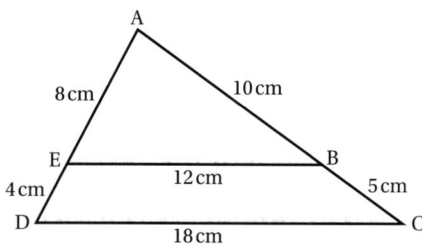

12 An adult ticket for the cinema is one-and-a-half times the price of a child's ticket.

What is the ratio of the price of an adult ticket to the price of a child's ticket?

13 In a school, $\frac{3}{5}$ of sixteen-year-olds have a mobile phone.

What is the ratio of sixteen-year-olds with mobiles to those without?

14 After an increase of 20% in the number of boys in a school, the ratio of boys to girls is 3 : 4.

There are now 630 pupils in the school.

How many boys were there originally?

15 $\frac{1}{5}$ of chocolates in a box are dark chocolate, $\frac{1}{2}$ are milk and the rest are white.

What is the ratio of dark : milk : white chocolate?

Section 2: Sharing in a given ratio

WORKED EXAMPLE 1

Three siblings inherit £32 000 from their mother. In her will she stated that they should receive the money divided according to how many children they each have.

Simon has one daughter, Oliver has three daughters and Lucy four sons.

How should the money be shared between them?

Simon, Oliver and Lucy have children in the ratio 1 : 3 : 4

In total there are 8 boxes, in which we have to share £32 000.

Each box gets $\frac{£32\,000}{8}$ = £4000

So:

Simon receives £4000

Oliver receives 3 × £4000 = £12 000

Lucy receives 4 × £4000 = £16 000

(This method also shows that Simon gets $\frac{1}{8}$ of the total amount, Oliver gets $\frac{3}{8}$ and Lucy gets $\frac{1}{2}$)

£4000 + £12 000 + £16 000 = £32 000

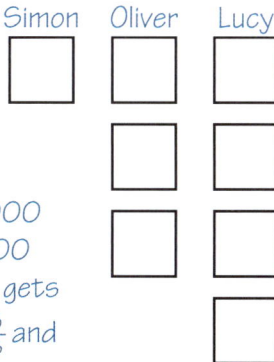

Draw a diagram where each box represents the number of parts of the whole each individual should receive.

Each box has to have the same quantity in it.

Work out the amount that each person receives in the correct ratio.

The final step is to double check that the shared quantities sum to the original amount.

Tip

The box method shown in Worked Example 1 is useful for working out problems on shares in a given ratio.

Find answers at: cambridge.org/ukschools/gcsemaths-studentbookanswers

EXERCISE 27B

1 Share 144 in each of the given ratios.

a $1:3$ b $4:5$ c $11:1$

d $2:3:1$ e $1:2:5$ f $2:7:5:4$

2 A tropical fruit smoothie is made with strawberries, pineapple and banana in the ratio of $3:1:1$.

Using a total of 300 grams of fruit, what weight of strawberries is used?

Choose from the options below.

A 60 g B 100 g C 180 g D 200 g

3 Chocolate butter icing is made using icing sugar, cocoa powder and butter in the ratio of $2:3:1$.

A recipe asks for 120 g of cocoa powder.

How much butter icing will this make?

Choose your answer from the following options.

A 40 g B 80 g C 240 g D 720 g

4 To make mortar you mix sand and cement in the ratio of $4:1$.

a How much sand is needed to make 25 kilograms of mortar?

b What fraction of the mix is cement?

5 The inner disc of a £2 coin is made of copper and nickel in the ratio $3:1$.

The inner disc weighs 6 grams.

How much copper is used to make the centres of ten £2 coins?

6 Flaky pastry is made by mixing flour, margarine and lard in the ratio $8:3:3$.

a How much of each ingredient is needed to make 350 g of pastry?

b What fraction of the pastry is made by the margarine and lard together?

7 The sides of a rectangle are in the ratio of $2:5$.

Its perimeter is 112 cm.

a What are the dimensions of the rectangle?

b Use these dimensions to calculate its area.

8 Orange squash is made by mixing one part cordial to five parts water.

How much squash can you make with 750 ml of cordial?

9 Two-stroke fuel is made by mixing oil and petrol in the ratio of $1:20$.

How much oil needs to be mixed with 10 litres of petrol to make two-stroke fuel?

10 In a recipe for tiffin, the ratio of biscuit to dried fruit to butter to cocoa powder is $5:6:2:2$.

How much of each ingredient is needed to make 600 g of tiffin?

11 In a music college the ratio of flute to oboe to string to percussion players is $7:2:15:1$.

The college has 175 students.

How many students play the oboe?

12 The ratio of red to green to blue to black to white pairs of socks in a drawer is $2:3:7:1:4$.

There are eight pairs of white socks.

How many pairs of socks are there altogether?

13 Potting compost is made by mixing loam, peat and sand in the ratio of $7:3:2$.

A gardener uses 4.5 kg of peat to make potting compost.

How much potting compost does she make?

Section 3: Comparing ratios

When you want to compare ratios, it is often useful to write them in the form $1:n$, where n represents a number.

> 💡 **Tip**
>
> The scale of maps is given as a ratio in the form of $1:n$. For example, $1:25\,000$

WORKED EXAMPLE 2

Red and white paint can be mixed to make pink paint.

Which of the mixes below will give the lightest shade of pink?

Mix A   **Mix B**   **Mix C**

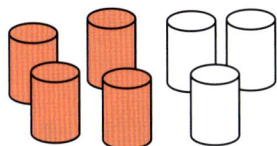 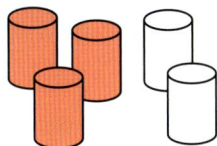 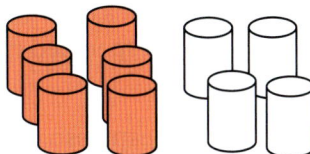

A $4:3$
B $3:2$
C $6:4$

> Work out the ratios of red to white paint for each of the mixes.

A $\frac{4}{4}:\frac{3}{4} = 1:0.75$
B $\frac{3}{3}:\frac{2}{3} = 1:0.67$
C $\frac{6}{6}:\frac{4}{6} = 1:0.67$

> Change these to the form $1:n$ by dividing both parts of the ratio by the first part.
>
> Give the answers as decimals to make the comparison simpler.

Mix A has the greatest amount of white paint per unit of red paint (0.75 tins of white for 1 tin of red), so this will be lightest shade of pink.

> Check that you have answered the question.

Ratios in the form of $1:n$ are also useful for converting from one unit to another.

For example, the ratio of inches to centimetres is $1:2.54$

This means that 1 inch is equivalent to 2.54 cm.

So, 2 inches = 2×2.54 cm and 12 inches = 12×2.54 cm.

This is a linear relationship and it can be shown as a straight-line graph.

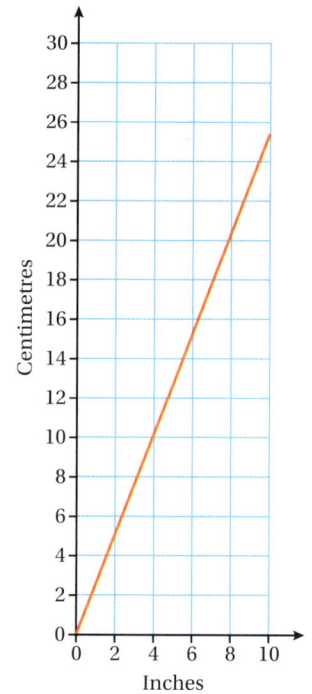

EXERCISE 27C

1 A model car's bonnet is 2.8 cm wide.

In real life the bonnet measures 1.96 m.

What is the ratio of the model to real life in the format $1:n$?

Choose the correct option below.

A $1:0.7$ B $1:196$ C $1:70$ D $1:2.8$

2 Different types of coffee are made by mixing espresso shots, hot water and milk in specified ratios.

Espresso	$1:0:0$
Double espresso	$2:0:0$
Flat white	$1:2:1$
Cappuccino	$1:0:2$
Latte	$1:0:4$

Put the drinks in order of strength of coffee with the weakest first.

3 When Jules was going on holiday he used this graph to convert between pounds and euros.

a What is the ratio of pounds to euros? Express this in the form $1:n$.

b What is the ratio of euros to pounds? Express this in the form $1:n$.

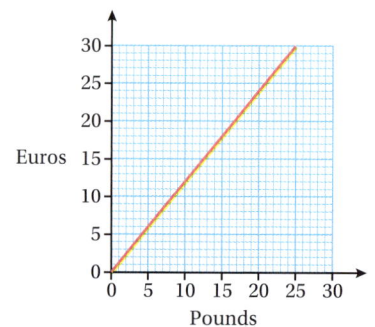

4 This graph shows the relationship between ounces and grams.

  a What is the ratio of ounces to grams?

    Express this in the form $1:n$.

  b What is the ratio of grams to ounces?

    Express this in the form $1:n$.

5 The ratio of fluid ounces to millilitres is $1:28$.

  a Draw a conversion graph to show this relationship.

  b What is the ratio of millilitres to fluid ounces in the form $1:n$?

6 Daisy is aged 5, Patrick is aged 8 and Iona is aged 12.

  They share a packet of sweets in the same ratio as their ages. There are no sweets left over.

  Iona gets 21 more sweets than Daisy.

  a How many sweets were there in the packet to begin with?

  b What fraction of the sweets did Patrick get?

7 The ratio of kilometres to miles is approximately $8:5$.

  A car travels at 45 miles per hour for 20 minutes.

  How many kilometres does it travel?

8 These are the ingredients for a sausage casserole that serves 6 people.

  Find the quantities of ingredients needed to serve sausage casserole to 4 people. Show all the steps in your working.

9 Gill and her sister Bell share a box of chocolates.

  Bell gets $\frac{1}{3}$ of the box.

  Gill shares her chocolates with her best friend Katy in the ratio $4:3$.

  Katy gets 12 chocolates.

  How many chocolates were there in the box?

10 A quarter of a box of chocolates are white chocolates.

  The ratio of dark to milk chocolates is $2:5$.

  There are 7 white chocolates.

  How many more milk chocolates than dark chocolates are there?

11 A, B and C are three pulley wheels.

  For every 3 turns A makes, B makes 4 turns.

  For every 2 turns B makes C makes 3 turns.

  a Write down the ratio of the turns A makes to the turns B makes.

  b Write down the ratio of the turns C makes to the turns B makes.

  c Write down the ratio of the turns A makes to the turns C makes.

  d Pulley wheel A makes 24 turns. How many turns does C make?

  e Pulley wheel C makes 36 turns. How many turns does A make?

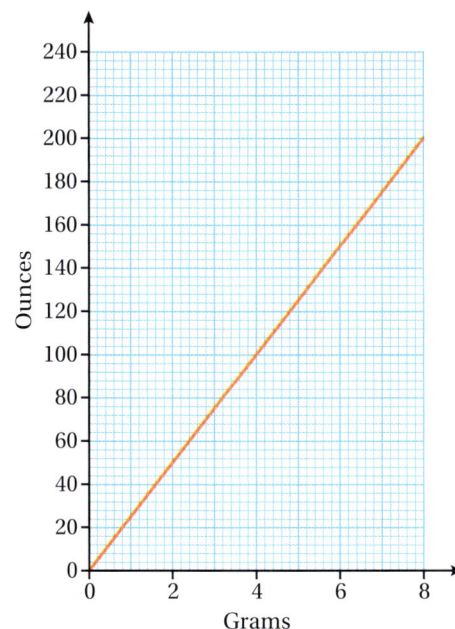

Sausage casserole *(serves 6)*

12 sausages

3 tins of tomatoes

450 g potatoes

9 tsp mixed herbs

600 ml vegetable stock

Find answers at: cambridge.org/ukschools/gcsemaths-studentbookanswers

519

12 A 210 cm ribbon is cut into two sections.

The longer piece is two and a half times the length of the shorter piece.

a What is the ratio of the longer piece to the shorter piece of ribbon?

b Work out the length of each piece.

13 Each month a sunflower's height increases by 40%.

What is the ratio of the height of the sunflower on 1 May to its height on 1 August?

14 A shop sells 325 g jars of chocolate spread for 66p, or a 1 kg tub for £1.99.

Which is the better value for money? Show your working.

15 The ratio of Molly's height at age 3 to her height at age 4 is 15 : 16.

a What percentage increase is this?

b During this time Molly grew 7 cm.

If Molly keeps growing at the same rate, how tall will she be when she is 8?

Golden ratios

The golden ratio has been studied and used for centuries. Artists, including Leonardo da Vinci and Salvador Dali often produced work using this ratio. The ratio can also be seen in buildings, such as the Acropolis in Athens. The golden ratio is said to be the most aesthetically pleasing way to space out facial features.

The diagram shows how the golden ratio can be worked out using the dimensions of a 'golden' rectangle. The large rectangle ACDF is similar to BCDE. Hence the ratio of $a : a + b$ is equivalent to $b : a$.

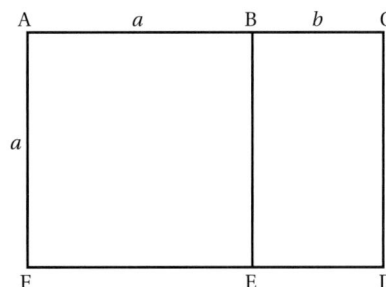

An approximate numerical value for this ratio can be found by measuring.

EXERCISE 27D

How golden are your hands?

Measure the distances A, B and C.

Now calculate these ratios and write them in the form $1:n$.

  Distance B : Distance C

  Distance A : Distance B

  Length of your hand : Distance from your wrist to your elbow

Can you see anything special about these ratios?

The closer your results are to 1.1618 the more golden is your hand!

The Fibonacci sequence follows the golden ratio. If you calculate the ratio of consecutive numbers in the Fibonacci sequence you will find that the ratio gets closer and closer to the actual golden ratio $\dfrac{1+\sqrt5}{2}$ as you get further along the sequence.

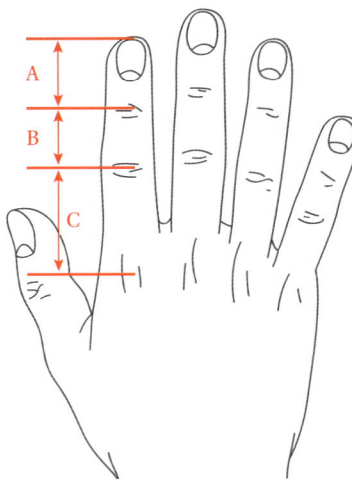

EXERCISE 27E

1. Write the ratio of the diameter of a circle to its circumference in the form $1:n$.

2. The three angles of a triangle are in the ratio $3:3:4$.

   What information can you give about the triangle?

3. The ratio of the five angles in a pentagon are $1:1:1:1:1$.

   What information does this tell you about the pentagon? Give a reason for your answer.

4. The ratio of an exterior angle to an interior angle of a regular polygon is $1:3$.

   Work out how many sides the polygon has.

5. The ratio of the angles in a triangle is $1:2:1$.

   a What information can you give about the triangle?

   b The longest side is 10 cm.

   How long are its other two sides?

6. The ratio of the sides of a rectangle is $3:4$.

   After an enlargement by a scale factor of 5 what is the ratio of the same two sides?

> **Tip**
>
> To answer the questions about triangles, pentagons and rectangles you may need to look again at Chapter 8. For the question on circles, you could refer to Chapter 10, and for the questions on area and volume you may need to look again at Chapters 11 and 24.

7 Gareth and John share a box of chocolates.

Gareth gets $\frac{3}{5}$ of the box.

The ratio of white to milk to dark chocolates in John's share is $1 : 2 : 1$. He gets 4 white and dark chocolates in total.

Gareth gets twice as many white chocolates as John and he has an equal number of dark and milk.

How many of each type of chocolate were in the box?

8 The ratio of the sides of two squares is $3 : 4$. What is the ratio of their areas?

9 The ratio of the edges of two cubes is $5 : 2$.

a What is the ratio of their surface areas?

b What is the ratio of their volumes?

Checklist of learning and understanding

Notation

- The order in which a ratio is written is important. A ratio of $2 : 5$ means 2 parts to 5 parts. Each part is equal in size.

Simplifying ratios

- Two ratios are equivalent if one is a multiple of the other.
- Ratios can be simplified by dividing both parts of the ratio by a common factor.
- Expressing ratios in the form $1 : n$ makes it easy to compare ratios.

Sharing in a given ratio

- The box method can be used to tackle problems that involve sharing a quantity in a given ratio.
  To share quantity Q in the ratio $a : b : c$, divide the quantity evenly into $a + b + c$ boxes.

For additional questions on the topics in this chapter, visit GCSE Mathematics Online.

Chapter review

1 Write down the ratio of vowels to consonants in the English alphabet.

2 Write down the ratio of prime numbers to square numbers between (and including) 1 and 20.

Give your answer in its simplest form.

3 Share 360 in the ratio $3 : 5 : 1$.

4 Using the graph below, express the ratio of miles to kilometres in the form $1:n$.

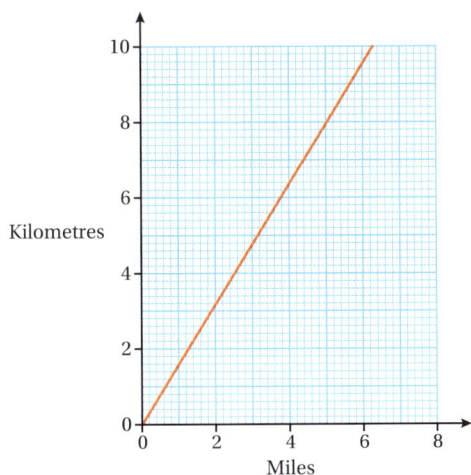

5 A juice drink is made using 2 parts cordial to 4 parts water.

Callum makes up 300 ml of juice drink, but he adds an extra 50 ml of water.

Now what is the ratio of cordial to water?

Choose your answer from the following options.

A 1:2   B 1:3   C 2:5   D 50:300

6 In a car park, cars are silver, blue, red, black or yellow.

Three quarters of the cars are not silver.

The proportion of blue to red to black to yellow cars is $6:2:3:1$.

There are 6 more black cars than yellow cars.

How many cars of each colour are in the car park?

Tip

Don't forget about the silver cars!

7 Jack works eight hours each day.

He is paid £6.50 per hour.

He shares his wages with Kim in the ratio:

Jack : Kim = 4 : 1

Jack saves his share.

How many working days will it take Jack to save £1040?   *(5 marks)*

© AQA 2013

28 Proportion

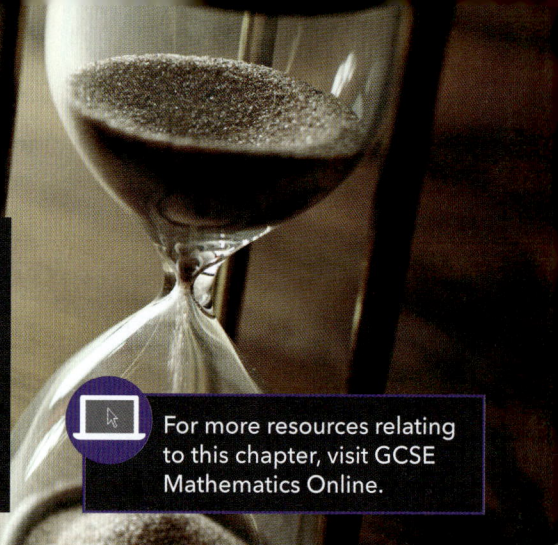

In this chapter you will learn how to …

- understand proportion and the equality of ratios.
- solve problems involving direct and inverse proportion, including using graphs and algebra to do this.
- understand that 'x is inversely proportional to y' is equivalent to 'x is proportional to $\frac{1}{y}$'.
- interpret equations that describe direct and inverse proportion.

For more resources relating to this chapter, visit GCSE Mathematics Online.

Using mathematics: real-life applications

Proportional reasoning is very common in daily life. You use proportional reasoning when you mix ingredients for a recipe, convert between units of measurement or work out costs per unit. It is an area of maths where you can use many different methods to solve particular problems.

Tip

Review the sections in Chapter 27 on equivalent ratios and fractions to prepare for this chapter.

"I test out new dishes on my family. Then I have to scale up the recipes in proportion so that they taste just as good. Sometimes it might be for just a few people at one table in my restaurant; at other times it might be for a whole room of wedding guests." *(Chef and restaurant owner)*

Before you start …

KS3 Ch 5	You need to know how many minutes there are in fractions of an hour.	**1** How many minutes are there in: **a** half an hour? **b** a quarter of an hour? **c** a third of an hour? **d** a fifth of an hour?
KS3 Ch 5	You need to be able to find what fraction of an hour a given time is.	**2** What fraction of an hour is: **a** 5 minutes? **b** 24 minutes? **c** 54 minutes?
KS3 Ch 7, 17	You should know how to substitute values into formulae.	**3** $g = 3b$ **a** What is the value of g when $b = 7$? **b** What is the value of b when $g = 72$? **c** What is b when $g = 1.2$?

Assess your starting point using the Launchpad

STEP 1

1 A recipe for chocolate muffins makes 12 muffins. It uses 180 g of dark chocolate.

How much chocolate is needed to make 30 muffins?

2 A car is travelling at 80 km per hour.

How far would it travel in 75 minutes?

3 €1 = $1.40

How many euros is a T-shirt that costs $24?

GO TO
Section 1:
Direct proportion

STEP 2

4 The cost of carpeting a hallway is proportional to the area of the hall.

One hallway measuring 15 m² costs £97.50.

a Find a formula for the cost, c, of carpeting a hallway with area, a.

b How much would it cost to carpet an area of 32 m²?

c What area can be carpeted for £328.90?

GO TO
Section 2:
Algebraic and graphical representations

STEP 3

5 The cost of putting new soundproofing on a square dance floor is directly proportional to the square of the length of the side of the floor.

A dance floor with a side length of 8 metres costs £976.

a Find a formula for the cost, c, of soundproofing a dance floor with side length s.

b How much would it cost to lay flooring on a dance floor with side length 7.5 m?

c To the nearest 10 centimetres, what size floor can be soundproofed for £645?

GO TO
Section 3:
Directly proportional to the square, square root and other expressions

GO TO
Step 4
Launchpad continues on the next page …

Find answers at: cambridge.org/ukschools/gcsemaths-studentbookanswers

Launchpad continued …

STEP 4

5 Ten people have enough food for a six-day camping trip.

    a How long would the food last if there were only five people?

    b Two more people join the group unexpectedly.

      How long would the food last now?

GO TO
Section 4:
Inverse proportion

GO TO
Chapter review

Section 1: Direct proportion

Key vocabulary

ratio: the relationship between two or more groups or amounts, showing how much bigger one is than another

direct proportion: two values that both increase in the same ratio

When two quantities vary but remain in the same **ratio** they are said to be in **direct proportion**.

A simple example would be the quantity and price of petrol.

The more petrol a driver puts into the car, the more it costs.

In problems involving variables in direct proportion, you might be given a rate such as price per litre.

If not, it might be helpful to find this rate – this is called the unitary method.

Consider the following problem.

A car travels 12 miles in 15 minutes.

a At what speed is the car travelling?

b How far would the car go in 75 minutes?

c How long would it take the car to travel 80 miles?

Think of how you would find the answers to these questions.

One approach is to assume that distance and time are directly proportional to each other, which allows you to develop a **mathematical model** of the problem.

Assuming that distance and time are directly proportional to each other, you can write down a range of combinations of time and distance that would represent the same speed.

Key vocabulary

mathematical model: a representation of a real-life problem; assumptions are used to simplify the situation so that it can be solved mathematically

Then you can use these to answer the questions. The diagram shows some combinations.

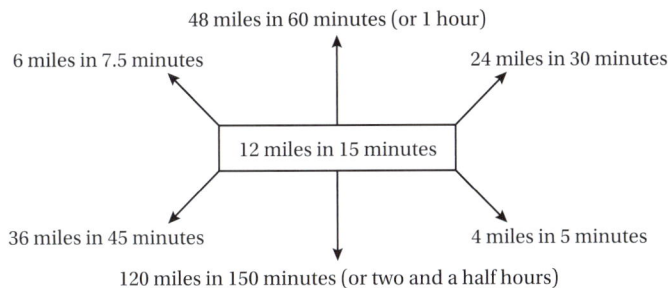

48 miles in 60 minutes (or 1 hour)

6 miles in 7.5 minutes

24 miles in 30 minutes

12 miles in 15 minutes

36 miles in 45 minutes

4 miles in 5 minutes

120 miles in 150 minutes (or two and a half hours)

a Having scaled the quantities up and down, you can see that the car covers 48 miles in an hour so its speed is 48 miles per hour.

b The car would travel 36 miles in 45 minutes and 24 miles in 30 minutes. Therefore it would travel 60 miles in 75 minutes.

c The car would travel 4 miles in 5 minutes. Multiply both of these quantities by 20 to find that it would do 80 miles in 100 minutes (or 1 hour and 40 minutes).

These are not the only combinations you could write down or the only ones that you could use to answer the original questions.

EXERCISE 28A

1 A Bluefin tuna fish can travel 3 km in 20 minutes.

List some other distance–time facts about the fish.

Assume that it always travels at a constant rate.

2 Two dogs eat 120 grams each of dried food twice a day.

How much food is needed to feed the dogs for 10 days?

Choose your answer from the options below.

  A 4.8 kg   B 2.4 kg   C 1.2 kg   D 240 g

3 A lorry travels 48 kilometres in 40 minutes.

At what speed is the lorry travelling?

Choose from the following options.

  A 1.2 km/h   B 48 km/h   C 68 km/h   D 72 km/h

4 Patrick works for four hours and gets paid £22.

What is his rate of pay per hour?

5 Jelly beans cost £1.20 for 100 g.

  a How much would 50 g cost?

  b How much would 300 g cost?

  c How much would 1 kg cost?

  d What weight of jelly beans could you buy with £4.20?

Tip

Very often when working with proportion problems it helps to write down a proportion fact you know and consider what would happen if one side is halved, doubled, tripled, multiplied by 10, and so on.

These notes will often help you to solve the original problem. For example, if you know that six eggs make two cakes, then half the number of eggs, three, will make just one cake.

6. Ben uses his mobile to make a 12-minute international call, costing him £4.20.

   a How much would it cost him to make an international call for 18 minutes?

   Danny makes an international call for 20 minutes and it costs him £6.40.

   b Whose phone is the best value, Ben's or Danny's? Why?

7. The following ingredients for pancakes serves 8 people.

   100 g plain flour   2 eggs   300 ml semi-skimmed milk

   Rakin has 2 litres of milk, 500 g of plain flour and 9 eggs.

   What is the greatest number of people he can serve?

Tip

Calculator allowed.

8. **a** A TGV train travels at 320 kilometres per hour. Assuming that the train is going at its full speed, how far does it travel in:

   i 2 hours?   **ii** 30 minutes?   **iii** 15 minutes?

   iv 1 minute?   **v** 10 seconds?

   b The equator is approximately 40 000 km long.

   If it were possible, how long would it take to travel around it in a TGV train?

9. A cheetah can reach speeds of up to 120 kilometres per hour.

   At this speed, how far would it travel in 15 seconds?

Unitary method

Tip

This is very much like an equivalent ratio problem in Chapter 27.

WORKED EXAMPLE 1

Danny bought a T-shirt in Florida for $18 on his debit card.

When he returned home the charge on Danny's debit card statement was £10.71.

He also bought a pair of jeans for $32.

Assuming the bank uses the same exchange rate, what would this charge appear as on his debit card statement?

From the price of the T-shirt
$18 = £10.71

$$\div 18 \left(\begin{array}{c} \$18 = £10.71 \\ \$1 = 0.595 \end{array} \right) \div 18$$

$$\times 32 \left(\begin{array}{c} \$1 = £0.595 \\ \$32 = £19.04 \end{array} \right) \times 32$$

So the charge on Danny's debit card statement should say £19.04.

In this example scaling up and down is too inefficient so it is better to use the unitary method.

Start by finding the exchange rate of dollars to pounds.

Divide both sides by 18.

Now use this rate to find the cost in pounds of $32.

EXERCISE 28B

1 £1 = $1.68

How many dollars is £25 worth?

Choose from the options below.

A $17   B $42   C $14.88   D $25

2 A tin holding 2.5 litres of paint costs £14.50.

How much would a 750 ml tin cost?

Choose from the options below.

A £43.50   B £8.70   C £5.80   D £4.35

3 Before going to Australia, Finley exchanges £175 into Australian dollars.

He gets an exchange rate of £1 = AU$1.81

How many dollars does he get?

4 Amber exchanges $44 into pounds.

The exchange rate is £1 = $1.68.

How many pounds does she receive?

5 Paint is sold in a variety of tins.

The price per litre remains the same.

Find the cost of tins **a**, **b** and **c**, and the volume of tin **d**.

a 600 ml	b 1 litre	1.5 litres = £18	c 4.5 litres	d __ litres = £585

6 Lucy exchanges £50 for €60.50.

a What is the exchange rate from pounds to euro?

b What is the exchange rate from euro to pounds?

7 When planning a holiday in Switzerland, Ethan compares two resorts.

The exchange rate from pounds to Swiss francs is £1 = CHF1.48.

Which resort is a better deal? State the price difference in pounds.

	Accommodation	Food	Ski rental	Flights
Bun di Scuol	£340	CHF96.20	£300	CHF102.12
Flims-Laax-Falera	CHF444	£100	CHF164.28	£144

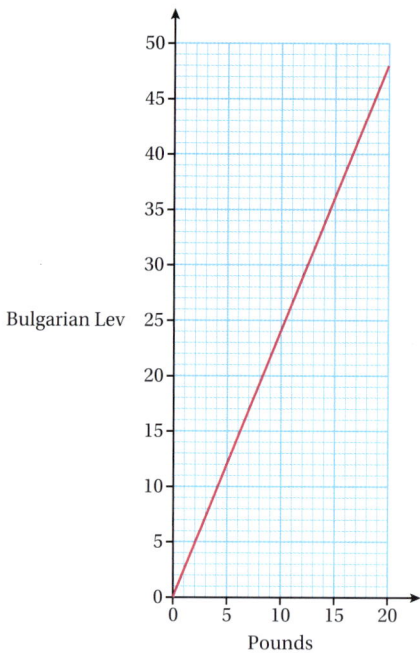

8 The graph shows how to convert between pounds and Bulgarian Lev (ЛВ).

a Work out the exchange rate from pounds to Lev.

b Work out the exchange rate from Lev to pounds.

9 Use the following exchange information to answer the questions below.

UK pounds	Euro	Kenyan shilling	Indian rupee
£1	€1.21	KSh145	Rs 102

Mongolian tughrik	New Zealand dollars	Brazilian real
₮3000	$1.95	R$3.77

a Aaron exchanged £350 into euro.

Work out how many euro he got.

b In Kenya, Aaron went on a safari drive.

He reserved this before going at a cost of £185. He paid in Kenya.

Work out how much it cost in Kenyan shillings.

c When he left India, Aaron exchanged Rs5202 into Mongolian Tughrik.

Work out how many Tughrik he got.

d Aaron paid €11 for a hostel in France, KSh1305 in Kenya, Rs500 in India, ₮6500 in Mongolia, $15 in New Zealand and R$20 in Brazil.

Write these prices in order of expense, cheapest first.

10 In the UK 35 g of saffron can be bought for £2.69. In Spain it costs €11.80 for 125 g.

Which is the better deal, given that £1 = €1.21? Give clear reasons for your answer.

11 What information would you need to collect to compare the 'crowdedness' of two school playing fields?

How would you carry out the comparison?

Section 2: Algebraic and graphical representations

Direct proportion problems can also be represented graphically or generalised through the use of algebra.

This allows you to solve problems concerning the same relationship, either by reading information off a graph or by using an algebraic formula.

WORK IT OUT 28.1

Which of these graphs shows a pair of variables that are directly proportional to each other?

Give a reason for your answer.

Give reasons how you can tell that the variables in the other graphs are not directly proportional to each other.

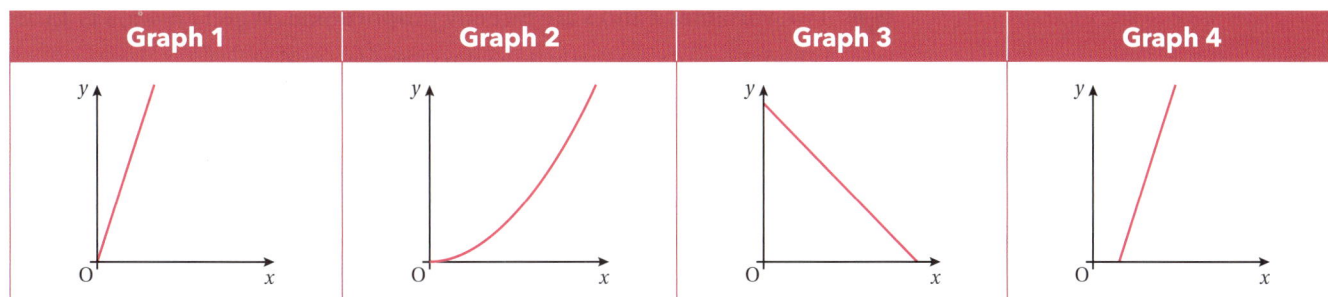

Graph 1	Graph 2	Graph 3	Graph 4

The graph of a directly proportional relationship has a fixed gradient and goes through the origin.

The mathematical symbol $\propto$ means that two values are proportional.

For example, if you pay per minute to use your mobile phone the total time of the call, t, is proportional to the cost of the call, c. Hence $t \propto c$.

This means that for a fixed value k (often called the constant of proportionality), you can write a formula linking the time and cost:

$c = kt$

If you pay 75p for a 15-minute call, you can calculate the value of k by substituting the known values into the formula.

$c = kt$

$75 = k \times 15$

$5 = k$

So the formula linking the cost in pence, c, and time in minutes, t, is $c = 5t$.

Tip

Be careful with units in questions. In this example the cost is in pence and time in minutes. To use the formula you will need to make sure that all the quantities are in pence and minutes and convert any that are not.

WORK IT OUT 28.2

Which of these formulae represent variables that are directly proportional to each other?

For each one give a reason why or why not.

Formula 1	Formula 2	Formula 3	Formula 4
$y = 3x + 5$	$10w = h$	$\dfrac{s}{t} = 7$	$d^2 = 4f$

EXERCISE 28C

1 Two variables r and s are directly proportional. When $r = 4.5$, s is 15.75

Which formula correctly links the variable r and s?

A $r = 3.5s$ B $3.5r = s$ C $r = 70.875s$ D $70.875r = s$

2 This is a distance–time graph for two runners, A and B.

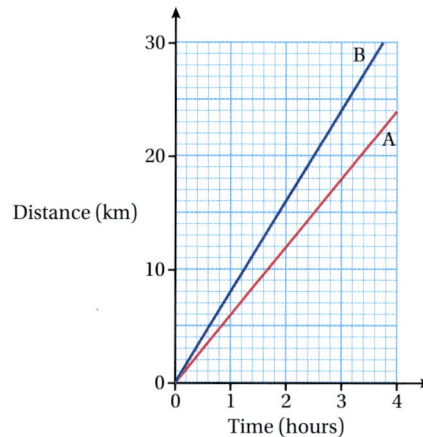

a Write down how far runner A travelled after 30 minutes.

b Write down how long it took runner B to travel 18 km.

c State which runner is going fastest.

d What is the speed of each runner?

e What assumptions have been made when drawing this graph?

3 The graph shows the cost of telephone cable.

Write a formula linking the cost, in pounds (c) and length, in metres, of wire (l).

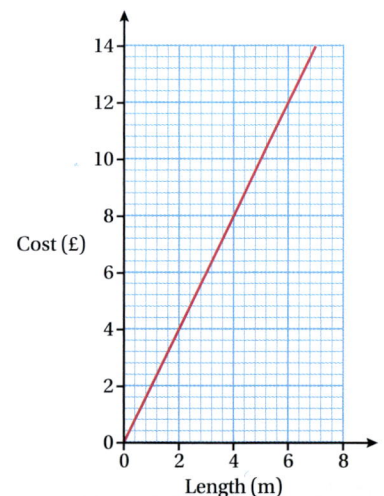

4 The length of an object's shadow is directly proportional to the object's height.

  a Use this diagram to help show why this is true.

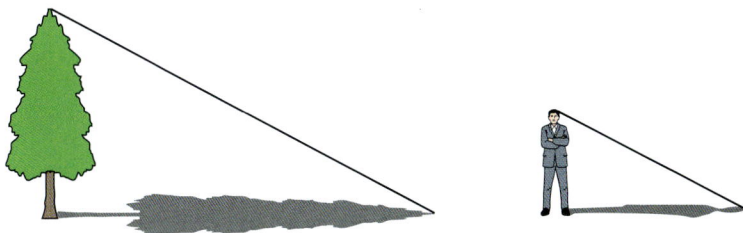

  b At one specific time in the day, a man of height 1.8 m has a shadow of 1.35 m.

    i Write a formula for the length of an object's shadow, s, in terms of its height, h.

    ii The Angel of the North is 20 m tall.

      How long would its shadow be at the same time?

    iii The shadow of a stone at Stonehenge at this time is 502.5 cm.

      How tall is the stone?

5 Two variables p and q are directly proportional. When $p = 6.5$, q is 52.

  a Write a formula for q in terms of p.

  b Find the value of q when p is 3.8

  c Find the value of p when q is 14.8

6 Wheelchair ramps are designed with a specific steepness allowing their safe use.

One such ramp has a horizontal distance of 4 m and a height gain of 60 cm.

Write a formula for the horizontal distance, d, in terms of the height gain, h.

Section 3: Directly proportional to the square, square root and other expressions

In some cases a value is directly proportional to the square, cube or root of another value.

For example, an object dropped from rest doesn't travel at a constant velocity, it accelerates.

Therefore the distance it travels isn't directly proportional to the time it has been falling.

In fact, the distance travelled, d, by an object dropped from rest is proportional to the square of the time, t, for which it has been falling.

So if you double the time, you quadruple the distance travelled; if you triple the time you multiply the distance travelled by 9, and so on.

Find answers at: cambridge.org/ukschools/gcsemaths-studentbookanswers

WORKED EXAMPLE 2

An object is dropped from rest and after 3 seconds has travelled a distance of 44.1 metres.

a How far will it have travelled after 7 seconds?

b How long will it take to travel 100 metres?

a $d \propto t^2$
Hence $d = kt^2$.

d is proportional to t^2

$44.1 = k \times 3^2$
$4.9 = k$

Substituting in the given values

After 7 seconds the object would have travelled 4.9×7^2
$= 240.1$ metres.

So the formula for the distance travelled in terms of the time fallen is
$d = 4.9t^2$

b To travel 100 metres would take
$\sqrt{\dfrac{100}{4.9}} = 4.52$ seconds (2 dp)

To find the time to travel 100 m, make t the subject of the formula and substitute in the value for d.

EXERCISE 28D

1 a is directly proportional to the square root of b.
When $a = 2$, $b = \dfrac{1}{25}$
Which is the correct formula for a in terms of b?
A $a = 10 \times \sqrt{b}$ B $a = 50b$ C $a = 50 \times \sqrt{b}$ D $a = \dfrac{2}{5} \times \sqrt{b}$

2 w is directly proportional to the cube of m. When $m = 3$, $w = 108$.
a Write a formula for w in terms of m.
b Find the value of w when $m = 5$.
c Find the value of m when $w = 62.5$

3 r is directly proportional to the square root of s. When $r = \dfrac{1}{2}$, $s = \dfrac{1}{16}$
a Write a formula for r in terms of s.
b Find the value of r when $s = 20$.
c Find the value of s when $r = 12$.

4 The rate at which a toaster produces heat, j (joules), is proportional to the square of the current, I (amps) in the circuit.
A toaster using 3.5 amps produces 857.5 joules of heat.
a Write a formula for the heat produced, j, in terms of the current, I.
b Another toaster produces 400 joules of heat.
Work out the current this toaster draws.

5 The time it takes a pendulum to complete one full swing (from left to right and back again) is directly proportional to the square root of its length.

A pendulum of length 16 cm takes 1.28 seconds to complete a full swing.

a Write a formula for the time taken, t, in terms of the length of the pendulum, l.

b How long is a pendulum that takes 2 seconds to complete one full swing?

6 The mass of a cube of gold, m, is directly proportional to the cube of its side length, s.

A cube with side length 2 cm has a mass of 154.4 grams.

a Write a formula for the mass of a cube of gold in terms of its side length.

b A gold ingot has a mass of 12.4 kg. What size cube would this bar make?

Section 4: Inverse proportion

In some cases one quantity decreases as the other one increases.

For example, if you increase your speed, the time it takes to travel a fixed distance is reduced.

If you add more workers to a job, the time it takes to complete the job goes down. These types of relationships are inversely proportional.

WORK IT OUT 28.3

A rectangle has a fixed area of 24 cm².

Its length, x, and height, y, can vary.

Which of the graphs below represents this situation?

Give a reason for your answer.

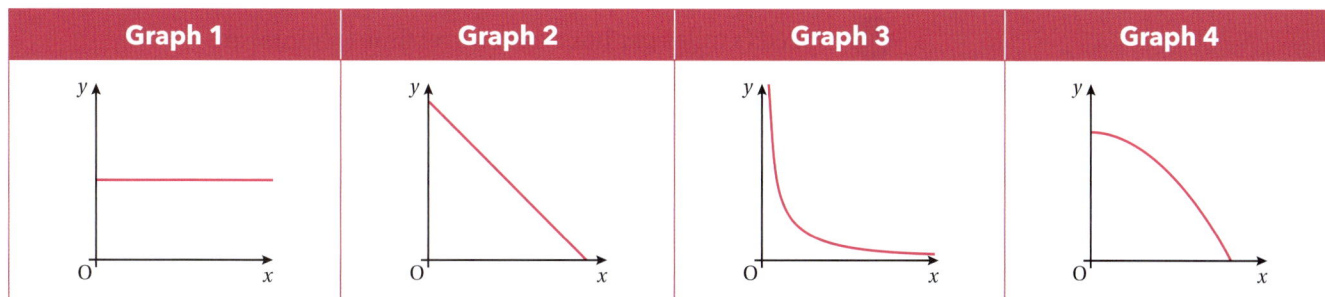

Graph 1	Graph 2	Graph 3	Graph 4

In the example of a rectangle with a fixed area, the length, x, and height, h, are in **inverse proportion**. When one is multiplied the other is divided. Hence:

$$y \propto \frac{1}{x}$$

$$y = \frac{k}{x}$$

An example of a rectangle with area $24\,\text{cm}^2$ is one with a length of $2\,\text{cm}$ and a height of $12\,\text{cm}$.

$$12 = \frac{k}{2} \qquad \text{so } k = 24$$

$$y = \frac{24}{x}$$

EXERCISE 28E

1 It takes 3 builders 4 days to build a wall.

How many builders would take 2 days to build the same wall?

Choose from the options below.

A 12 builders   B 6 builders   C 4 builders   D 3 builders

2 It takes 4 people 3 days to paint the school hall.

  a State the number of person-days this is.

  b Work out how long it would take 2 people to paint the hall.

  c Work out how long it would take 6 people.

  d The job needs to be completed in a day.

    How many people are needed?

  e What assumptions have you made?

3 While on holiday, Karen budgets to buy five souvenirs at $2.40 each.

  a What is the total amount Karen intends to spend on souvenirs?

  b How many souvenirs costing $0.80 each could she buy with her budget?

  c Karen needs eight souvenirs of equal value. How much should she pay for each souvenir to keep within her budget?

4 Speed (s miles per hour) and travel time (t hours) are inversely proportional.

The faster you travel the less time a journey takes.

A journey between Cambridge and Manchester takes 3 hours when travelling at 60 miles per hour.

  a Write a formula for the time taken, h, in terms of the speed travelled, s.

  b It takes James 4 hours to make the journey.

    At what speed is he travelling?

  c How long will it take to do the journey at 75 miles per hour?

  d Megan takes 2 hours 15 minutes to make the journey.

    At what speed is she travelling?

5 A group of friends play a lucky draw game.

The more friends that take part, the more tickets they can buy, but the more people they have to share the prize with.

The graph shows the relationship between the number of people in the group and their share of the winnings.

a If 10 people buy tickets, how much do they win each?

b How much is in the prize fund?

c Write a formula for the winnings, w, in terms of the number of people buying the winning ticket, n.

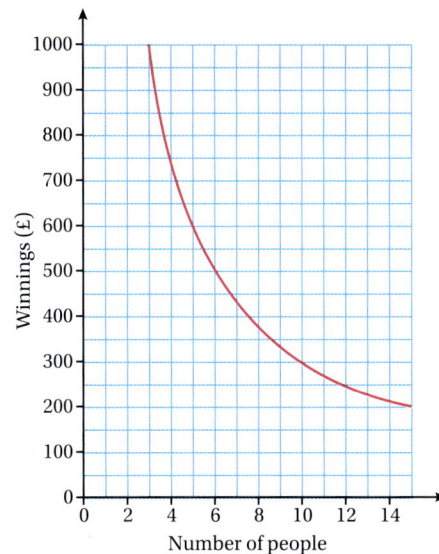

Winnings (£) / Number of people

6 A water tap is running at a constant rate (r litres per minute), filling a pond in m minutes.

The greater the flow of water the less time it takes to fill the pond.

Copy and complete the table. Draw a graph to represent this situation.

m minutes	10	20	30	40	50	60	70	80	90	100
r litres per minute						10				

Write a formula for r in terms of m.

7 The variable a is inversely proportional to the square of b.
When $b = 5$, $a = 2$.

a Write a formula for a in terms of b.

b Find the value of a when $b = 2$.

c Find the value of b when $a = 0.5$

8 The rate, r, at which a gas diffuses is inversely proportional to the square root of its molecular mass, M.

Carbon dioxide diffuses at 1 mol/s (mole per second) and has molecular mass 44 g/mol (gram per mole).

Write a formula for r in terms of M.

9 British driver Andy Green holds the land speed record of 340 metres per second.

Previously, Craig Breedlove had the record at 407 miles per hour.

Find the difference, in minutes, between the times it took the two drivers to travel a mile.

Checklist of learning and understanding

Direct proportion

- Two quantities that are directly proportional to each other increase and decrease at the same rate. For example, if one is tripled so is the other, if one is halved so is the other.

- Direct proportion between two variables x and y can be represented as $y = kx$, where k is the constant of proportionality. The constant of proportionality can be found by substituting known values into the formula.

- The graph of two directly proportional variables is a straight line graph of the form $y = mx$, where m is positive. It looks like the graph on the left.

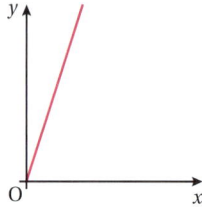

Inverse proportion

- If two quantities are inversely proportional to each other then as one increases the other decreases. For example, if one is tripled the other is divided by three, if one is halved the other is doubled.

- Inverse proportion between two variables x and y can be represented as $y = \dfrac{k}{x}$, where k is the constant of proportionality. The constant of proportionality can be found by substituting known values into the formula.

- The graph of two inversely proportional variables is of the form $y = \dfrac{m}{x}$, where m is positive. It looks like the graph on the left.

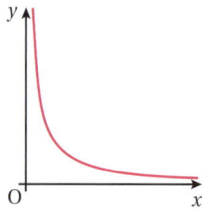

For additional questions on the topics in this chapter, visit GCSE Mathematics Online.

Chapter review

1. Wine gums cost 90p for 200 grams.

   a How much would 800 grams cost?

   b What weight of wine gums would you get for £2.75?

2. This stir-fry recipe serves 6 people.

   120 g chicken

   300 g vegetables

   15 tbsp of soy sauce

   Siobhan has 300 grams of chicken, 500 grams of vegetables and 60 tablespoons of soy sauce.

   What is the greatest number of people she can serve with this recipe?

3. A T-shirt costs £24 or €30.

   Which is the correct exchange rate of euros into pounds?

   A £1 = €1.25   B €1 = £0.80   C £1 = €0.80   D €1 = £1.25

4 The graph shows the cost of buying electrical wire.

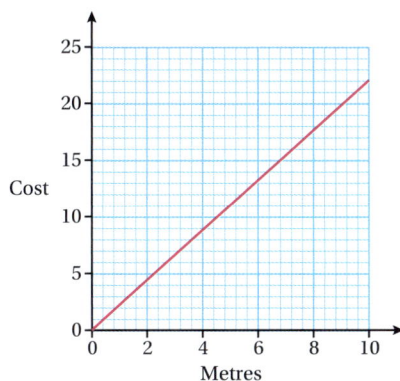

Write a formula for the cost, c, in terms of the number of metres bought, m.

5 F is directly proportional to the cube root of g.

When $g = 64$, $F = 12$.

a Write a formula for F in terms of g.

b Find the value of F when $g = 125$.

c Find the value of g when $F = 21$.

6 It takes three hairdressers an hour to style the hair of models for a fashion show.

How long would it take nine hairdressers?

7 The rate at which water flows into a pond is inversely proportional to the time it takes to fill up.

It takes two hours for the pond to fill when water flows in at a rate of 50 litres an hour.

Write a formula for the time in hours, t, in terms of the flow rate of the water, w.

8 The variable d is inversely proportional to the cube of e.

When $d = 3$, $e = 2$.

a Write a formula for d in terms of e.

b Find the value of d when $e = 3$.

c Find the value of e when $d = 0.5$

9 R is inversely proportional to A.

$R = 12.1$ when $A = 1.5$

a Work out a formula connecting R and A. *(3 marks)*

b Work out the value of R when $A = 4$. *(2 marks)*

© AQA 2013

29 Graphs of linear functions

In this chapter you will learn how to ...

- use a table of values to plot graphs of linear functions.
- identify the main features of straight-line graphs and use them to sketch graphs.
- sketch graphs from linear equations in the form $y = mx + c$.
- find the equation of a straight line using the gradient and points on the line.
- find the equation of a tangent that touches a circle with centre (0, 0).

For more resources relating to this chapter, visit GCSE Mathematics Online.

Using mathematics: real-life applications

This is a photograph of a building nicknamed *The Gherkin*, in London. The curves and lines of the building were designed using complex equations and their graphs. Architecture is just one of many professions in which people plot and use graphs in their work.

> **Tip**
>
> Review the sections in Chapter 27 on equivalent ratios and fractions to prepare for this chapter.

"When designing a new building, I use graphs to help identify and describe the structural properties the building needs to have."

(Architect)

Before you start ...

KS3 Ch 18	You should remember how to generate terms in a sequence using a rule.	**1** Use the rule $T(n) = 3n - 2$ to complete this table.	<table><tr><td>**Term number**</td><td>1</td><td>3</td><td>5</td><td>10</td></tr><tr><td>**Term**</td><td></td><td></td><td></td><td></td></tr></table>
KS3	You should be able to give the coordinates of points on a grid.	**2** Look at the grid below. **a** Write down the coordinates of points A, D and E. **b** What point has the following coordinates? **i** (−2, 2) **ii** (0, −6) **c** What is the name given to the point (0, 0)?	
Ch 17	You must be able to manipulate and solve equations.	**3** Solve for x. **a** $4 - 3x = 13$ **b** $\frac{x}{7} = 6$ **c** $-3(5x + 2) = 0$ **4** If $y = 2x + 5$: **a** find y when $x = -2$ **b** find x when $y = 8$.	
KS3	You should remember how to change the subject of a formula.	**5** Make y the subject of each equation. **a** $-2x - y + 1 = 0$ **b** $2x + 3y = 6$ **c** $x - 2y = -2$	

Assess your starting point using the Launchpad

STEP 1

1 For each function, work out the value of y for each value of x given.

a $x - y = 2$ (for $x = -2, -1, 0, 1$)

b $x + y = 4$ (for $x = -2, 0, 1, 2$)

c $2x + y + 2 = 0$ (for $x = -3, -2, 0, 1$)

d $x - 2y + 2 = 0$ (for $x = -2, 0, 2, 4$)

2 The graphs of two of the functions from question 1 are shown here.

Match each graph to its equation.

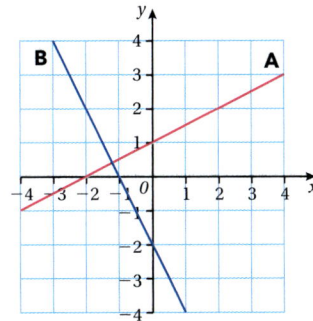

GO TO
Section 1:
Plotting graphs

STEP 2

3 **a** Sketch the graph of $y = 2x + 4$ without plotting a table of values.

b Find the gradient and y-intercept of the resulting straight line.

4 Find the equation of the straight line that passes through the points $(1, 4)$ and $(3, 7)$.

5 A line cuts the x-axis at 4 and the y-axis at 5. What is its gradient?

GO TO
Section 2:
Gradient and intercepts of straight-line graphs

STEP 3

6 Which of these lines are parallel to each other?

A $y = -3x + 3$ B $y = 7 - 3x$ C $y = 3x + 7$

D $y = \frac{1}{3}x + 3$ E $y = 7 - 2x$

7 A line is parallel to the line $y = \frac{1}{2}x$ and passes through the point $(2, 4)$. What is its equation?

8 How do you know $y = \frac{1}{2}x + 3$ crosses the line $y = 5 - 2x$ at right angles?

9 Find the tangent to the circle $x^2 + y^2 = 25$ that passes through $(-3, 4)$.

GO TO
Section 3:
Parallel lines
Section 4:
Working with straight-line graphs

GO TO
Chapter review

Find answers at: cambridge.org/ukschools/gcsemaths-studentbookanswers

Section 1: Plotting graphs

You can draw straight-line and curved graphs to show **functions**.

Cost of hiring a boat

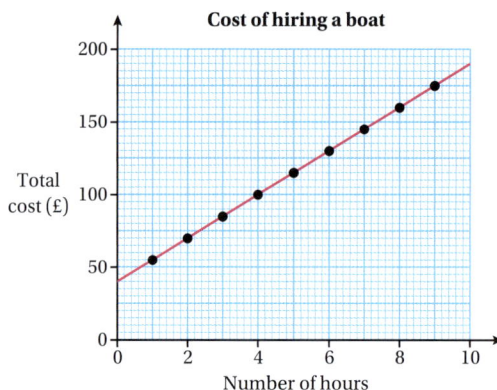

Height of a ball thrown in the air

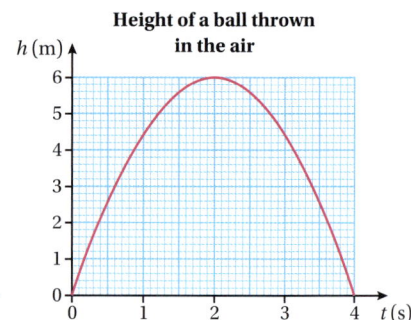

Functions that produce straight lines when you plot matching x- and y-values (or **coordinates**) are called linear functions.

Plotting linear functions

You can plot the graph of a function by drawing up a table of values.

WORKED EXAMPLE 1

Draw a table of values and plot the graph of $y = 2x + 1$.

x	−1	0	1	2
y	−1	1	3	5

Choose some values for x.

Substitute each x-value into the equation to find the matching y-value.

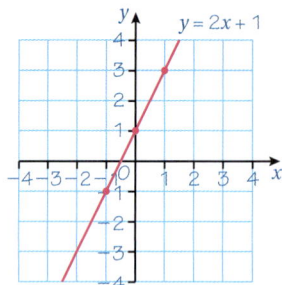

Plot at least three points using the coordinates in the table.

Points (−1, −1), (0, 1) and (1, 3) have been plotted here.

Draw a straight line through the points.

Label the graph with the equation.

EXERCISE 29A

1 Draw a table of values for each function and plot the graph.

a $y = x$
(where x ranges from -2 to 1)

b $y = x + 2$
(where x ranges from -2 to 1)

c $y = 3x - 5$
(where x ranges from 0 to 3)

d $y = 6 - x$
(where x ranges from 0 to 8)

e $y = 2x + 1$
(where x ranges from -2 to 1)

f $y = x - 1$
(where x ranges from -2 to 1)

g $y = -2x + 3$
(where x ranges from -2 to 1)

h $y = 4 - x$
(where x ranges from 0 to 6)

i $y = 3x - 2$
(where x ranges from -1 to 2)

2 What is the minimum number of points you need to plot a straight line accurately?

Give a reason for your answer.

3 Which point lies on the line $y = 3x - 4$?

Choose the correct answer from the options below.

A $(3, -4)$ B $(3, 5)$ C $(3, 4)$ D $(3, -1)$

Section 2: Gradient and intercepts of straight-line graphs

The main characteristics of a straight-line graph are:

- the **gradient**, or slope of the graph
- the **x-intercept** (where it crosses the x-axis)
- the **y-intercept** (where it crosses the y-axis).

You can use these characteristics to sketch graphs without drawing up a table of values.

> ### 🔑 Key vocabulary
>
> **gradient**: a measure of the steepness of a line
> Gradient = $\dfrac{\text{change in } y\text{-values}}{\text{change in } x\text{-values}}$
> **y-intercept**: the point where a line crosses the y-axis when $x = 0$
> **x-intercept**: the point where a line crosses the x-axis when $y = 0$

Gradient

Gradient is a measure of how steep a line is.

On a graph, the gradient is the vertical distance travelled (difference between the y-coordinates) divided by the horizontal distance travelled (difference between the x-coordinates):

Gradient of a line = $\dfrac{\text{change in } y\text{-values}}{\text{change in } x\text{-values}}$

or, more simply,

gradient = $\dfrac{\text{vertical rise}}{\text{horizontal run}}$

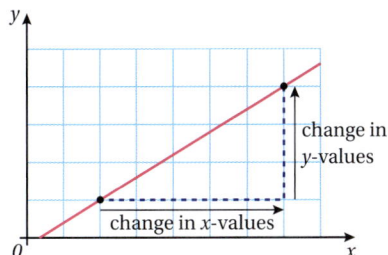

WORKED EXAMPLE 2

Calculate the gradient of each line.

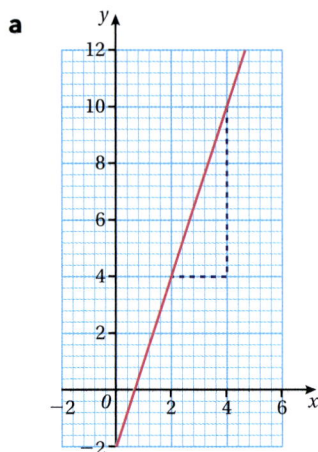

a

b

movement down is negative

movement up is positive

a Gradient $= \dfrac{\text{change in } y\text{-values}}{\text{change in } x\text{-values}} = \dfrac{6}{2} = 3$

Use the formula to work out the gradient.

b Gradient $= \dfrac{\text{change in } y\text{-values}}{\text{change in } x\text{-values}} = \dfrac{-1}{2}$

Notice that the change in y-values is negative in this case.

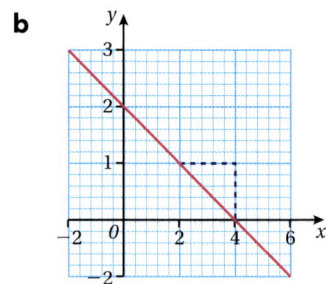

You don't need to draw the graph to find the gradient of a line.

You can calculate the gradient if you know the coordinates of any two points on the line.

WORKED EXAMPLE 3

Calculate the gradient of the line that passes through the points $(1, 4)$ and $(3, 8)$.

$x_1 = 1, x_2 = 3,$
$y_1 = 4, y_2 = 8$

To find the gradient let the coordinates of the two given points be (x_1, y_1) and (x_2, y_2).

$\dfrac{(y_2 - y_1)}{(x_2 - x_1)} = \dfrac{(8 - 4)}{(3 - 1)}$

Gradient $= \dfrac{\text{change in } y\text{-values}}{\text{change in } x\text{-values}}$
Substitute in the values for the two given points.

$= \dfrac{4}{2}$

Calculate the value.

$= 2$

Gradient $= 2$

The value of the gradient of the line that passes through the points $(1, 4)$ and $(3, 8)$.

EXERCISE 29B

1 What is the gradient of the straight line $2y = 6x + 1$?

Choose your answer from the following options.

A 1   B 2   C 3   D 6

2 Calculate the gradient of each line. Leave your answer as a fraction in its lowest terms if necessary.

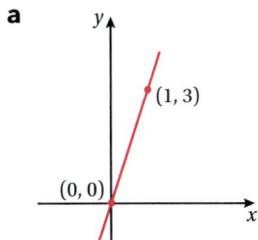

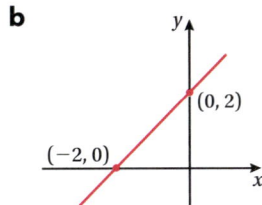

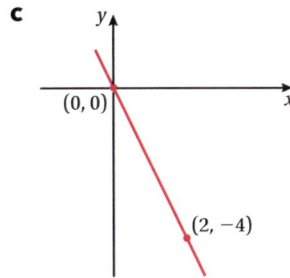

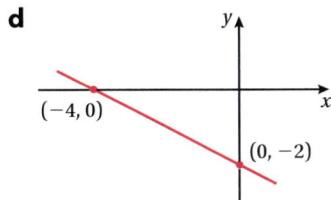

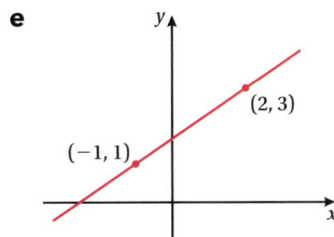

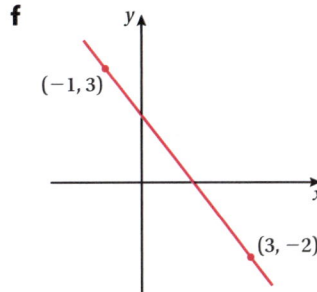

a

b

c

d

e

f

3 Find the gradient of the line that passes through points A and B in each case.

a A(1, 2) and B(3, 8)
b A(0, 6) and B(3, 9)
c A(−1, −4) and B(−3, 2)
d A(3, 5) and B(7, 12)

Using the gradient and y-intercept to sketch graphs

The general form of a linear equation is $y = mx + c$.

In this form, the equation gives you important information about the graph.

The value of the **coefficient** m is the gradient of the graph.

The value of the **constant** c is the y-intercept.

In the equation $y = -x + 2$, the coefficient of x is −1 and the constant is 2.

The gradient is −1 and the line crosses the y-axis at the point (0, 2).

This is the graph of $y = -x + 2$.

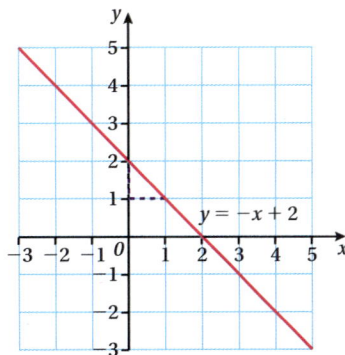

> **Key vocabulary**
>
> **coefficient:** the number in front of a variable in a mathematical expression. In the term $5x^2$, 5 is the coefficient and x is the variable.
>
> **constant:** a number on its own

Tip

When the equation is in the form $y = mx + c$, you can identify the gradient and y-intercept without plotting the graph. If a linear equation is not written in this form you can rearrange it so that it is. More on rearranging formulae is covered in Chapter 23.

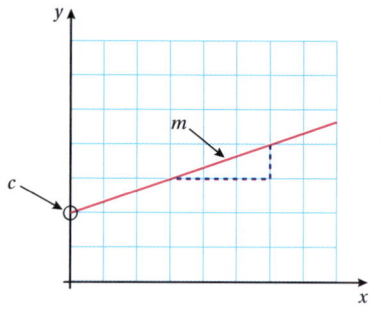

WORK IT OUT 29.1

Find the gradient and y-intercept of the linear function $y = -2x + 4$.

Do not plot a graph. Write down which direction the line moves across the page.

Which of the answers below is correct?

Give a reason why the other one is incorrect.

Option A	Option B
$y = -2x + 4$	$y = -2x + 4$
2 is the coefficient of x.	-2 is the coefficient of x.
4 is the constant.	4 is the constant.
So, the gradient is 2 and the y-intercept is 4.	So, the gradient is -2 and the y-intercept is 4.
The gradient is positive so the graph goes up to the right.	The gradient is negative so the graph goes down to the right.

Using the x-intercept and y-intercept to sketch a graph

Consider these two lines.

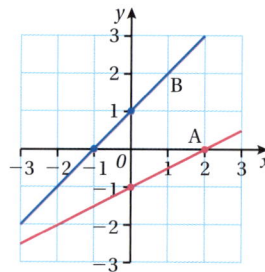

Line A has an x-intercept at $(2, 0)$ and a y-intercept at $(0, -1)$.

Line B has an x-intercept at $(-1, 0)$ and a y-intercept at $(0, 1)$.

When you know where the graph cuts the axes, you can sketch the graph of the line.

You find the x-intercept by substituting $y = 0$ into the equation and you find the y-intercept by substituting $x = 0$ into the equation.

WORKED EXAMPLE 4

Find the x- and y-intercepts and use them to sketch the graph of $y + 2x = 6$.

When $\quad x = 0$
$\quad y + 2(0) = 6$
$\quad\quad\quad y = 6$
$(0, 6)$ is the y-intercept

To find the y-intercept let $x = 0$. This is the point where the line $y + 2x = 6$ cuts the y-axis.

Continues on next page …

Find the *x*- and *y*-intercepts and use them to sketch the graph of $y + 2x = 6$.

When $\quad x = 0$
$\quad y + 2(0) = 6$
$\qquad\quad y = 6$
$(0, 6)$ is the *y*-intercept

> To find the *y*-intercept let $x = 0$.
>
> This is the point where the line $y + 2x = 6$ cuts the *y*-axis.

When $\quad y = 0$
$\quad 0 + 2x = 6$
$\qquad 2x = 6$
$\qquad\ x = 3$
$(3, 0)$ is the *x*-intercept

> To find the *x*-intercept let $y = 0$.
>
> This is the point where the line $y + 2x = 6$ cuts the *x*-axis.

$(3, 0)$ is the *x*-intercept and $(0, 6)$ is the *y*-intercept.

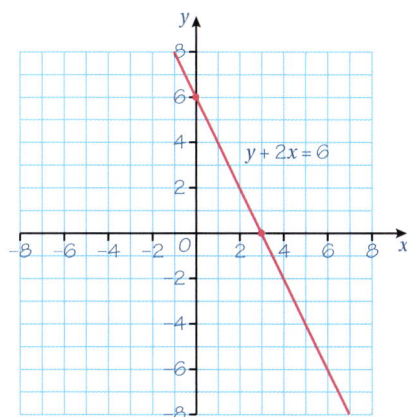

> Plot the two points and join them to draw the graph.
> Label the line.

EXERCISE 29C

1 Plot the graph of each function. Write a description of each one, giving the *y*-intercept and gradient, stating whether this is positive or negative.

a $y = 3x - 2$ **b** $y = -2x + 3$ **c** $y = \frac{1}{2}x - 1$ **d** $y = x - 1$

2 Rearrange each equation so it is in the form $y = mx + c$. Sketch each of the lines.

a $3x - 2y = 6$ **b** $6x + 2y + 10 = 0$ **c** $3y - 6x + 12 = 0$

d $2y - x + 18 = 0$ **e** $6y - 2x + 18 = 0$ **f** $2x - 3y + 12 = 0$

3 Match each graph to the correct linear equation.

a $y = x + 1$ **b** $y = 3 - x$ **c** $y = 9 - 3x$

d $y = x + 4$ **e** $y = -2x + 20$

i

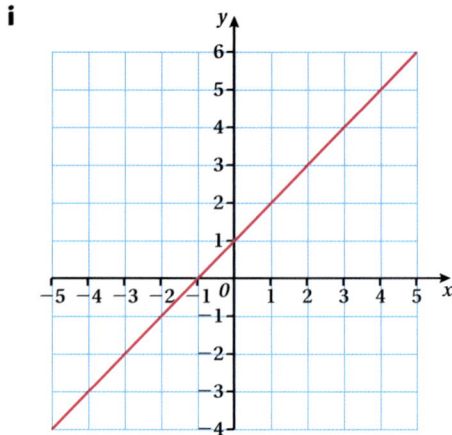

ii

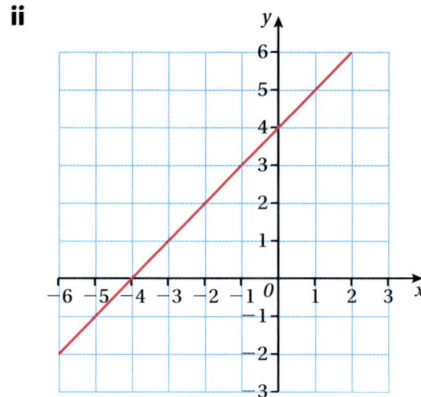

iii

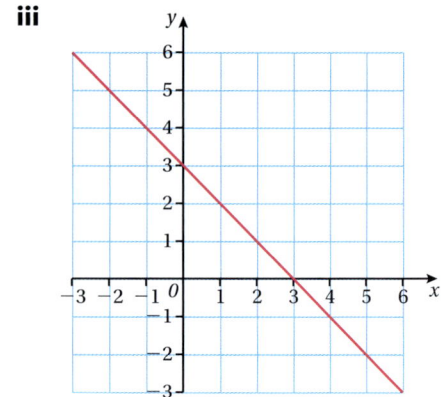

iv

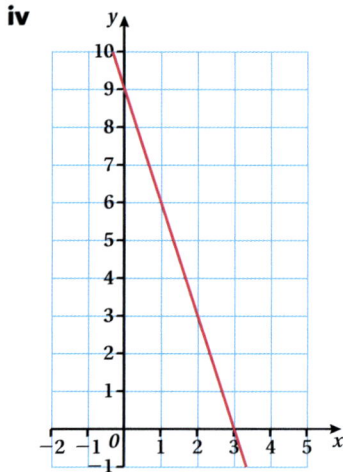

v

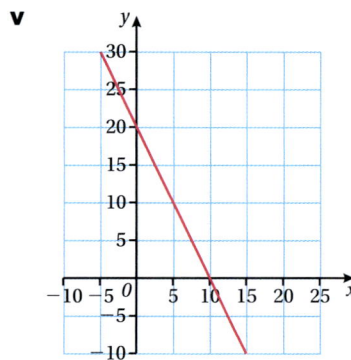

4 Sketch the graph of each line by calculating the coordinates of the x- and y-intercepts.

Write down the gradient of each graph.

a $2x + y = 4$ **b** $3x + 4y = 12$ **c** $x + 2y = 1$ **d** $3x + y = 2$

e $x - y = 4$ **f** $x - y = 1$ **g** $4x - 2y = 8$ **h** $3x - 4y = 12$

Finding the equation of a line using two points on the line

If you have the coordinates of two points on a line you can use them to find the gradient.

Once you have the gradient, you can find the y-intercept by substituting values (x, y) into the equation $y = mx + c$ and solving it to find c.

You can then write the equation of the line in the form: $y = mx + c$.

WORKED EXAMPLE 5

Find the equation of the line passing through points (3, 11) and (6, 7).

$x_1 = 3, x_2 = 6$
$y_1 = 11, y_2 = 7$

Find the gradient of the line first.

Let the coordinates of the two given points be (x_1, y_1) and (x_2, y_2).

$\dfrac{(y_2 - y_1)}{(x_2 - x_1)} = \dfrac{(7 - 11)}{(6 - 3)}$

Gradient $= \dfrac{\text{change in } y\text{-values}}{\text{change in } x\text{-values}}$
Substitute in the values for the two given points.

$\dfrac{7 - 11}{6 - 3} = \dfrac{-4}{3}$
Gradient $= \dfrac{-4}{3}$

Calculate the value of the gradient.

$y = \dfrac{-4}{3}x + c$

The general equation of a straight line is $y = mx + c$, where m is the value of the gradient.

$7 = \dfrac{-4}{3} \times 6 + c$
$7 = -8 + c$
$15 = c$
$y = \dfrac{-4}{3}x + 15$

Substitute one of the given points on the line into the general equation.

(6, 7) is a given point on the line. Substitute in the equation and calculate the value of c, the y-intercept.

$11 = \dfrac{-4}{3} \times 3 + 15$
$11 = -4 + 15$
$11 = 11$

Check that (3, 11) lies on the line.

$y = \dfrac{-4}{3}x + 15$

This is the equation of the line passing through points (3, 11) and (6, 7).

WORKED EXAMPLE 6

Find the equation of a line that has the same gradient as the line
$y = \frac{1}{2}x - 3$ and passes through the point $(-1, 2)$.

Gradient, $m = \frac{1}{2}$

The line has an equation of the form:

$y = \frac{1}{2}x + c$

The general equation of a straight line is $y = mx + c$, where m is the value of the gradient and c is where the line cuts the y-axis, the y-intercept.

The line has the same gradient as the line $y = \frac{1}{2}x - 3$

$y = \frac{1}{2}x + c$

$2 = (\frac{1}{2} \times -1) + c$

$c = 2 + \frac{1}{2}$

$c = \frac{5}{2}$

Substitute the values you know into the equation to find the value of c.

$y = \frac{1}{2}x + \frac{5}{2}$

This is the equation of the new line, that has the same gradient as $y = \frac{1}{2}x - 3$ and passes through the point $(-1, 2)$.

EXERCISE 29D

1 For each equation, find c if the given point is on the line.

a $y = 3x + c$ $\quad$ $(1, 5)$ $\qquad$ **b** $y = 6x + c$ $\quad$ $(1, 2)$

c $y = -2x + c$ $\quad$ $(-3, -3)$ $\qquad$ **d** $y = \frac{3}{4}x + c$ $\quad$ $(4, -5)$

2 Which of the following options is the equation for the line that passes through the points $(0, 3)$ and $(-3, 0)$?

A $y = x + 3$ $\qquad$ B $y = -x - 3$ $\qquad$ C $y = 3x + 1$ $\qquad$ D $y = -x + 3$

3 Find the equation of the line passing through each pair of points.

a $(0, 0)$ and $(6, -2)$ $\qquad$ **b** $(0, 0)$ and $(-2, -3)$

c $(-2, -5)$ and $(-4, -1)$ $\qquad$ **d** $(-2, 9)$ and $(3, -1)$

4 **a** A line passes through the point $(2, 4)$ and has gradient 2.

Find the y-coordinate of the point on the line when $x = 3$.

b A line passes through the point $(4, 8)$ and has gradient $\frac{1}{2}$

Find the y-coordinate of the point on the line when $x = 8$.

c A line passes through the point $(-1, 6)$ and has gradient -1.

Find the y-coordinate of the point on the line when $x = 4$.

Tip

Find the equation of the line before you try to find the coordinates of points on it.

Section 3: Parallel lines

Lines with equal gradients are parallel to each other.

The three lines on the graph are parallel to each other.

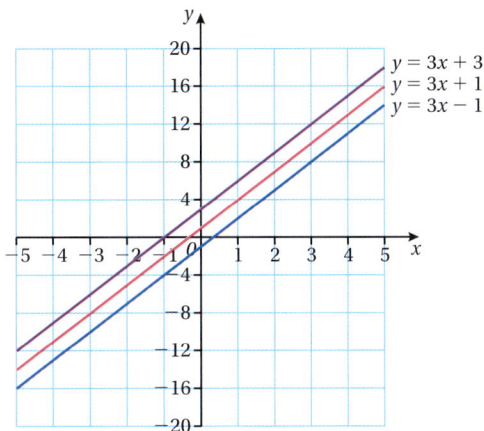

Tip

You learned about parallel and perpendicular lines in Chapter 8.

The equations of the lines show they each have a gradient of 3.

WORK IT OUT 29.2

In which option have parallel lines been correctly grouped together?

Option A	Option B	Option C
$y = 4 - 2x$	$y = \frac{1}{3}x + 1$	$y = x - 1$
$y + 2x = 5$	$3y + x = 1$	$y + x = 1$
$y = -2x + 1$	$y = 3x + 1$	$y = 1 - x$
$y = 3x + 1$	$2y = x + 1$	$x = y + 1$
$y - 3x = -1$	$2y - x = 3$	$x - y = 1$
$y = 2 + 3x$	$y = \frac{1}{2}x - 1$	$x = 1 - y$

If equations written in the form $y = mx + c$ have identical values for m, they have the same gradient. Lines with the same gradient are parallel.

EXERCISE 29E

1 Find the equation of the line that:

a is parallel to the line $y = 2x - 3$ and passes through the point $(1, 5)$

b is parallel to the line $y = 3x - 1$ and passes through the point $(-1, 2)$.

2 **a** The line $y = (2a - 3)x + 1$ is parallel to $y = 3x - 4$.

Find the value of a.

b The line $y = (3b + 2)x - 1$ is parallel to $y = bx - 4$.

Find the value of b.

3 Find the equation of the blue line.

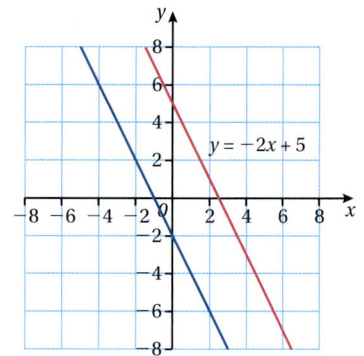

Tip

You learned about the properties of quadrilaterals in Chapter 8.

4 The vertices (corners) of a quadrilateral have coordinates A(1, 6), B(3, 14), C(15, 16) and D(13, 8).

  a Find the gradient of the line AB.

  b Find the equation of the line AB.

  c Prove that ABCD is a parallelogram.

5 Investigate lines that are parallel to the x- and y-axes.

How are the equations for these graphs different to those for sloping graphs?

Give a reason for your answer.

Perpendicular lines

If two lines are perpendicular, the product of their gradients is −1.

Conversely, if the product of their gradients is −1, then two lines are perpendicular.

The graphs of $y = -\frac{1}{3}x + 2$ and $y = 3x - 4$ have been drawn here.

The graphs are perpendicular to each other.

Tip

In order for two graphs to be perpendicular, one must have a negative gradient and the other must have a positive gradient.

Tip

Remember that $\frac{1}{3}$ is the **reciprocal** of 3 and that for any value, $x \times \frac{1}{x} = \frac{x}{x} = 1$.
When one value of x is negative, the product will also be negative.

Key vocabulary

reciprocal: the value obtained by inverting a fraction. Any number multiplied by its reciprocal is 1

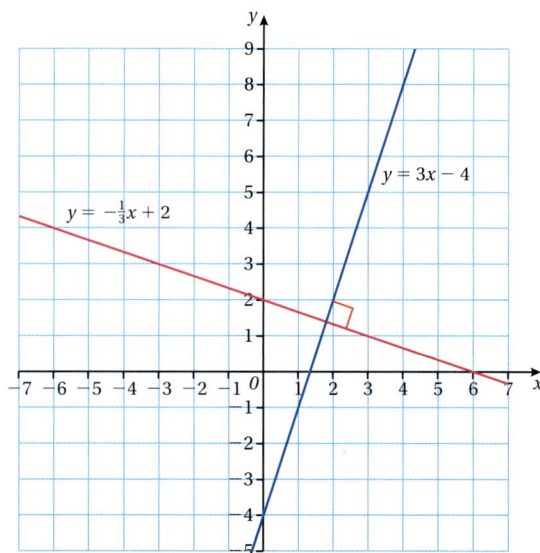

Graph $y = -\frac{1}{3}x + 2$ has negative gradient $m = -\frac{1}{3}$

Graph $y = 3x - 4$ has positive gradient $m = 3$.

The product of the gradients $-\frac{1}{3} \times 3 = -1$.

WORKED EXAMPLE 7

Given that $y = \frac{2}{3}x + 2$, work out the equation of the straight line that is:

a perpendicular to this line and which passes through the origin.

b perpendicular to this line and which passes though the point $(-3, 1)$.

a $y = mx + c$

$m = \frac{-3}{2}$

> Perpendicular gradients have a product of -1.

$c = 0$

> The line passes through the origin.

The equation of the line is $y = \frac{-3}{2}x$.

b $y = \frac{-3}{2}x + c \quad m = \frac{-3}{2}$

Substitute $x = -3$ and $y = 1$

$1 = \frac{-3}{2}(-3) + c$

$1 = \frac{9}{2} + c$

$c = -3\frac{1}{2}$

The equation of the line is $y = \frac{-3}{2}x - 3\frac{1}{2}$.

EXERCISE 29F

1 Which line chosen from the options below is perpendicular to the line $4y + x = -2$?

A $y = 4x$ B $y = 3x + 2$ C $y = x$ D $y = -4x + 3$

2 Show that the line through the points A(6, 0) and B(0, 12) is:

a perpendicular to the line through P(8, 10) and Q(4, 8).

b perpendicular to the line through M(−4, −8) and N(−1, −6½).

3 The equation of a line is $2x + 5y = 20$.

a Write the equation of the line parallel to this one that crosses the y-axis at –2.

b Write the equation of a line that intersects this graph at the x-axis and passes through point (6, −4).

4 Write down the equations of these two lines and prove that the lines are perpendicular.

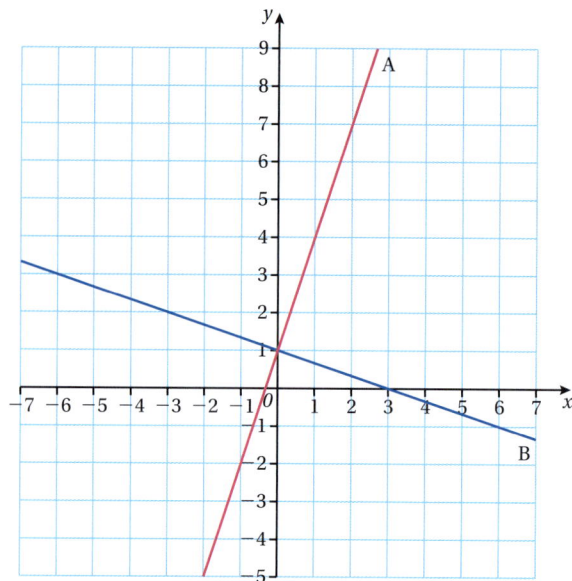

5 Sketch each of the following lines.

a $y = 3x + 2$ **b** $y = -2x - 1$ **c** $2y = x + 8$

d $x - y = -3$ **e** $y + 4 = x$ **f** $3x + 4y = 12$

6 Is the triangle formed by joining P(–1, 3), Q(5, 1) and R(–2, 0) right angled? Justify your answer.

Section 4: Working with straight-line graphs

You need to be able to interpret straight-line graphs.

Interpreting straight-line graphs means you can:

- work out the equation of the line
- calculate the gradient of a line using given information
- use straight-line graphs to model and solve problems, including solving simultaneous equations.

The point of intersection of any two straight-line graphs is the solution to the simultaneous equations (of the lines).

Tip

You learned about simultaneous equations in Chapter 17.

WORKED EXAMPLE 8

a Sketch the graphs of $x + 3y = 6$ and $y = 2x - 5$.

b What are the coordinates of the point of intersection of the two graphs?

c Show, by substitution, that these values of x and y are the simultaneous solution to the two equations

a Sketch the graphs.

$x + 3y = 6$
Let $x = 0$
$3y = 6$
$y = 2$
Let $y = 0$
$x = 6$
Plot $(0, 2)$ and $(6, 0)$.

> Find the x- and y-intercepts for $x + 3y = 6$.

$y = 2x - 5$
y-intercept $= -5$
gradient $= 2$
Plot the line $y = 2x - 5$ using the gradient and the y-intercept.

> Use the equation of the line for $y = 2x - 5$.

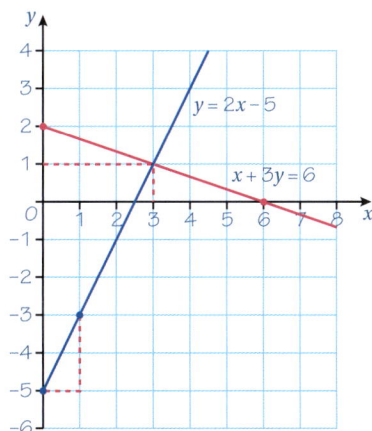

b The point of intersection is $(3, 1)$.

> Read this from the graph.

c Let $x = 3$ and $y = 1$
Substitute in $x + 3y = 6$:
$3 + 3(1) = 6$.
Substitute in $y = 2x - 5$:
$1 = 2(3) - 5$
$1 = 6 - 5$
$1 = 1$
The values of x and y work for both equations, which shows that they are the solution to the simultaneous equations $x + 3y = 6$ and $y = 2x - 5$.

EXERCISE 29G

1 Each table of values has been generated from a function.

i

x	−2	−1	0	1	2	3
y	−4	−3	−2	−1	0	1

ii

x	−2	−1	0	1	2	3
y	4	3	2	1	0	−1

a Which functions would produce each set of values? Choose from the options below.

A $y = -x + 2$　　B $y = 2x - 1$　　C $y = -2x + 4$　　D $y = x - 2$

b Plot the graphs of each function on the same grid.

c Draw a line parallel to each graph that crosses the y-axis at $(0, 3)$ and write its equation.

d Work out the gradient of lines perpendicular to each pair of parallel lines.

2 Write down the equation of the line that has:

a gradient 3 and y-intercept 5　　**b** gradient −1 and y-intercept 4

c gradient $\frac{3}{4}$ and y-intercept −2　　**d** gradient $-\frac{1}{7}$ and y-intercept 0.

3 Find equations that satisfy the following statements.

Write them in the form $y = mx + c$.

a A linear equation that does not pass through the first quadrant.

b Two lines whose gradients differ by 2.

c An equation of a straight line that passes through $(2, 3)$ and has a gradient of 3.

d An equation of a vertical line and a horizontal line.

4 The equations of two lines are $y = x + 3$ and $y = mx - 2$.

a For what values of m will the two lines not intersect?

Choose from the options below.

A −1　　　　B 0　　　　C 1　　　　D 2

b For what values of m will the two lines intersect?

c Given that the lines intersect at $(5, 8)$, find m.

5 Calculate the gradient of the line shown in the diagram.

Write down the equation of the line.

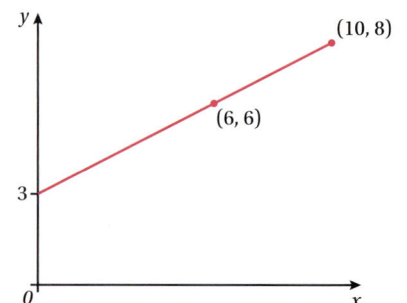

6 Sketch the graph of each equation.

    a $y = 2x - 3$ **b** $y = 3x - 2$ **c** $x + 2y = 4$

    d $2x - y = 1$ **e** $y - 3x = 6$

> **Tip**
>
> Sketch means draw a basic diagram to represent each equation showing the direction and intercept on the y-axis.

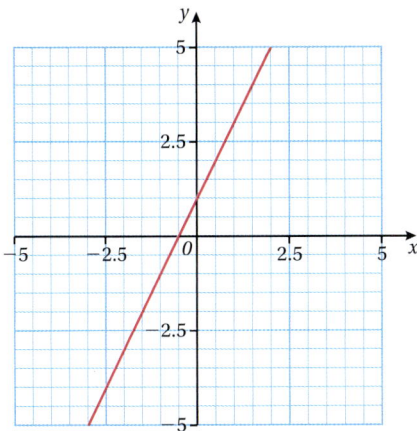

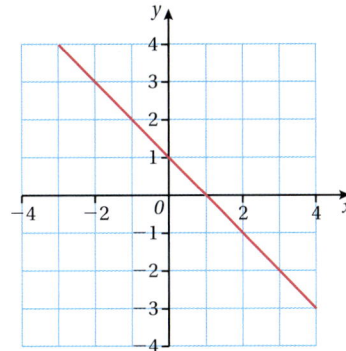

7 Find the equation of the line that passes through each pair of points.

    a $(5, 6)$ and $(-4, 10)$ **b** $(3, 4)$ and $(-2, 8)$ **c** $(-2, 6)$ and $(1, 10)$

8   **a** Find the equation of the line with gradient -4 that passes through the point $(0, -6)$.

    b Find the equation of the line with gradient -4 that passes through the point $(3, 8)$.

    c Find the equation of the line that passes through the points $(-4, 8)$ and $(-6, -2)$.

9 The line passing through the points $(-1, 6)$ and $(4, b)$ has gradient -2. Find the value of b.

10   **a** Is the gradient of this straight line 0.5 or -0.5? Write down the equation of the line.

    b Write down the equation of this line.

11 Find the equations of the four straight lines that would intersect to make this rhombus.

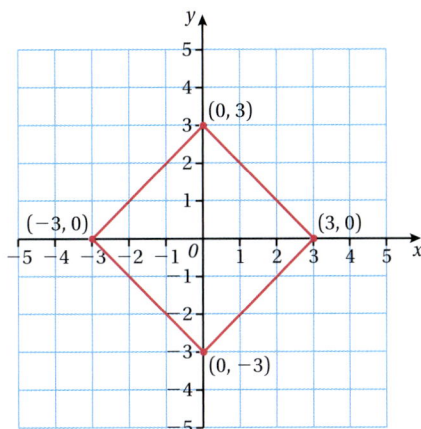

12 Show that the points A(1, 1), B(3, 11) and C(−2, −14) all lie on the same line (are collinear) and find the equation of this line.

13 Given the circle $x^2 + y^2 = 25$, work out the equation of the tangent that touches the circle at $(-1, -2\sqrt{6})$.

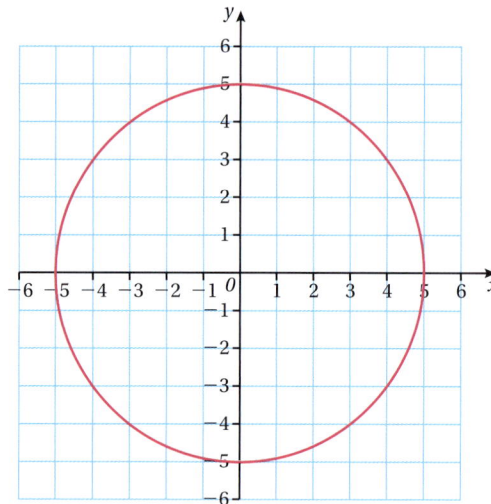

Checklist of learning and understanding

Plotting graphs

- You can use the equation of a line to generate a table of x- and y-values.
- Choose any three (x, y) values, plot them and join the points to draw the graph.

Characteristics of graphs

- The general form of a straight-line graph is represented by $y = mx + c$, where m is the gradient and c is the point where the line cuts the y-axis.
- You can find the equation of a straight line if you have two points on it or one point and the gradient.
- The gradient of a line can be found if you are given two points (x_1, y_1) and (x_2, y_2) that lie on the line:

$$\text{gradient} = \frac{\text{change in } y\text{-values}}{\text{change in } x\text{-values}} = \frac{y_2 - y_1}{x_2 - x_1}$$

- The x-intercept is where a line crosses the x-axis and $y = 0$; the y-intercept is where a line crosses the y-axis and $x = 0$ or the value of c in the general equation $y = mx + c$.
- You can sketch graphs using the gradient and y-intercept or using the x- and y-intercepts.

Parallel graphs

- Parallel lines have the same gradient so the value of m is equal when their equation is written in the form $y = mx + c$.
- The product of the gradients of two perpendicular lines is −1.

Chapter review

1 Draw these lines on the same grid.

a $y = x + 1$ **b** $y = 2x + 5$ **c** $y + 2 = 4x$

2 For each of the following graphs:

i Write the equation of each line.

ii Work out the equation of the line parallel to line **b** passing through point $(0, -1)$.

iii Is the line $2y + 6 = 2x$ perpendicular to graph **d**?

a

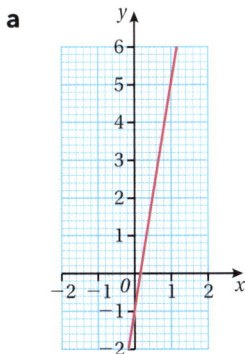

b

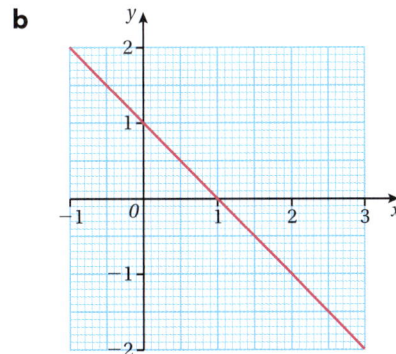

c

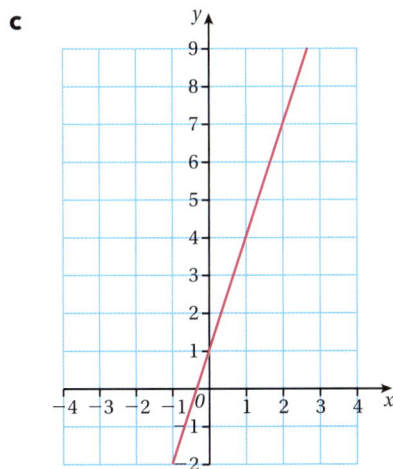

d

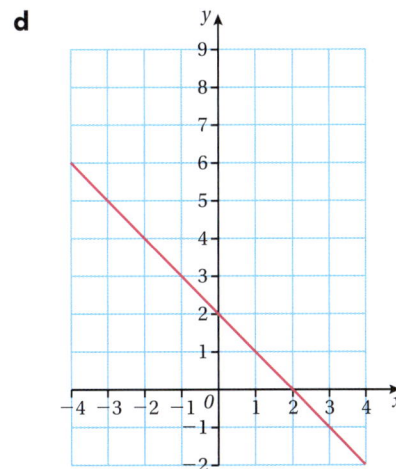

3 Find the equation of the line that passes through the points $(2, 4)$ and $(6, -12)$.

Choose from the following options.

A $y = -4x + 12$ B $y = 4x + 12$ C $y = \frac{2}{3}x + 12$ D $y = -\frac{2}{3}x + 12$

4 a Draw a graph of the two lines $y = 3x - 2$ and $y + 2x = 3$.

Find their point of intersection.

b Show by substitution that this is the simultaneous solution to the two equations.

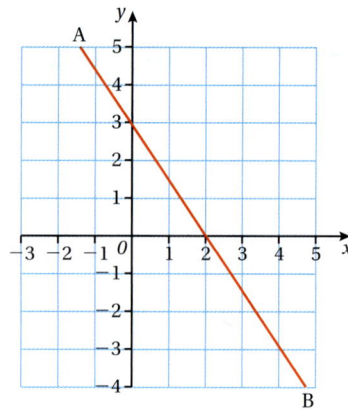

a Work out the equation of line AB. *(3 marks)*

b Work out the equation of the line passing through $(2, -3)$ and parallel to the line $y = 3x + 4$. *(2 marks)*

© AQA 2013

6

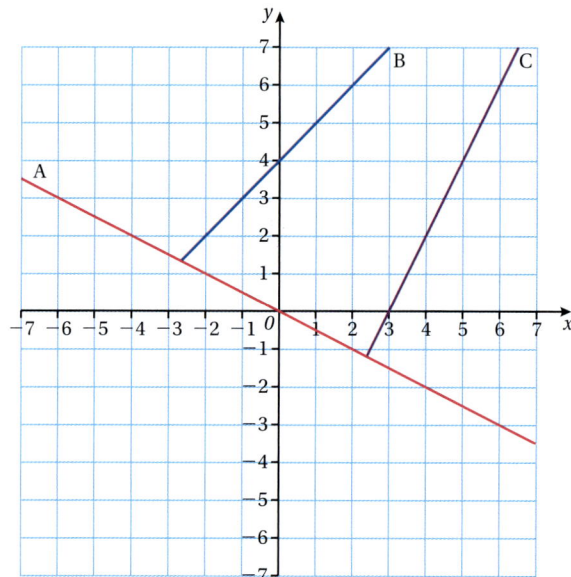

a Find the equation of each line A, B and C.

b Show that $A \perp C$.

c Show that B and C are not parallel.

d Work out the x-intercept of B algebraically.

e Work out the y-intercept of C algebraically.

f Work out the equation of a line passing through $(2, 3)$ such that the four lines on the graph form a trapezium with its base passing through the origin.

30 Interpreting graphs

In this chapter you will learn how to …

- construct and interpret graphs in real-world contexts.
- interpret the gradient of a straight line graph as a rate of change.
- find and interpret the gradient at a point on a curve as the instantaneous rate of change.
- plot and interpret graphs of non-standard functions in real contexts.

For more resources relating to this chapter, visit GCSE Mathematics Online.

Using mathematics: real-life applications

All sorts of information can be obtained from graphs in real-life contexts. The shape of a graph, its gradient and the area underneath it can tell us about speed, time, acceleration, prices, earnings, break-even points or the values of one currency against another, among other things.

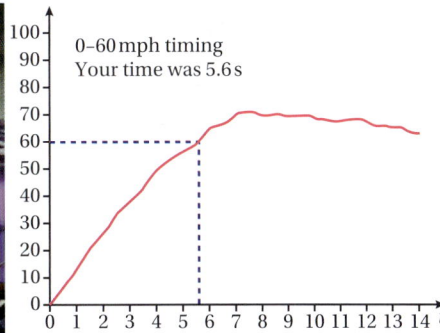

0–60 mph timing
Your time was 5.6 s

"My car needs to perform at its optimum limits. We generate and analyse diagnostic graphs to calculate the slight changes that would increase power, acceleration and top speed."   *(Racing driver)*

Before you start …

Ch 28	You will need to be able to distinguish between direct and inverse proportion.	**1**	Which of these graphs shows an inverse proportion? How do you know this?
Ch 29	You'll need to be able to calculate the gradient of a straight line.	**2**	Calculate the gradient of AB.
Ch 11	You'll need to be able to work with the area of composite shapes.	**3**	ABCD is a rectangle of area 63 cm². Given that CD = 7 cm, work out the area of trapezium EBCD.

Find answers at: cambridge.org/ukschools/gcsemaths-studentbookanswers

Assess your starting point using the Launchpad

STEP 1

1 Describe what is happening in each of the distance–time graphs below. Suggest a possible real-life situation that would result in each graph.

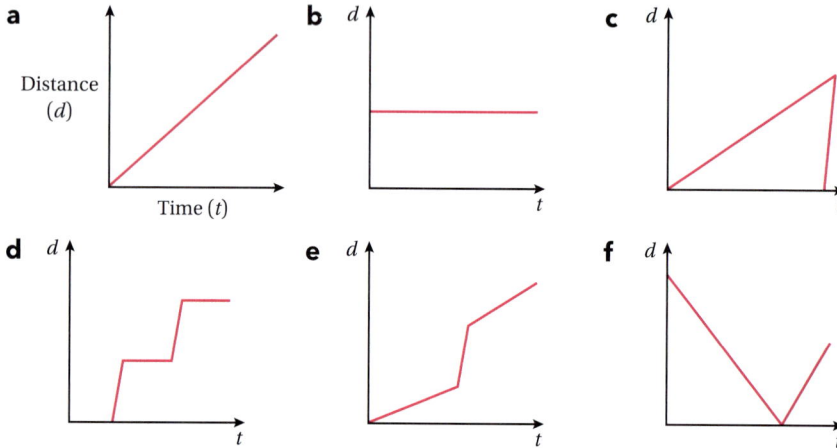

a

Distance (d)

Time (t)

b d

t

c d

t

d d

t

e d

t

f d

t

GO TO
Section 1:
Graphs of real-world contexts

STEP 2

2 Match the graphs below to the scenarios described on the right. Justify your choices.

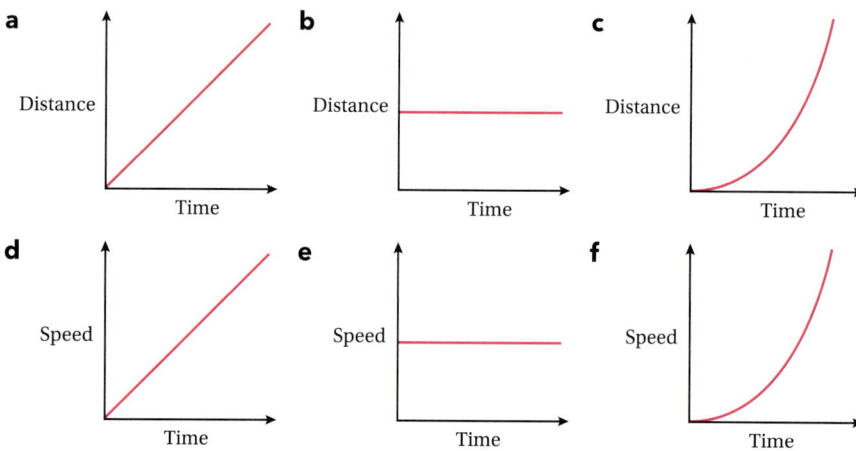

a

Distance

Time

b

Distance

Time

c

Distance

Time

d

Speed

Time

e

Speed

Time

f

Speed

Time

A The car is travelling at a constant speed

B The car is accelerating at a constant rate

C The car's acceleration is increasing

D The car is stationary

GO TO
Section 2:
Gradients

GO TO
Step 3
The Launchpad continues on the next page …

Launchpad continued …

STEP 3

3 The shaded part of one of these graphs represents the amount of water in a swimming pool after four hours. Which graph is it? Give a reason for your answer.

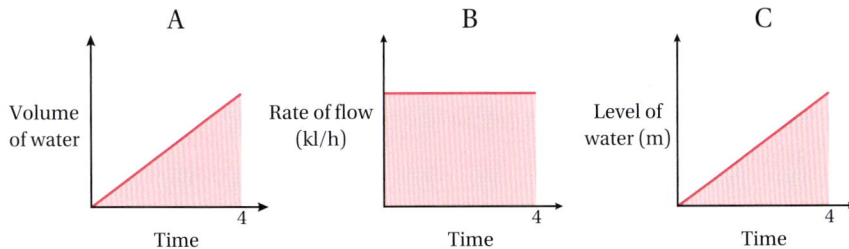

A

Volume of water — Time — 4

B

Rate of flow (kl/h) — Time — 4

C

Level of water (m) — Time — 4

?

GO TO
Section 3:
Areas under graphs

✓

GO TO
Chapter review

Section 1: Graphs of real-world contexts

Graphs are useful for visually representing the relationships between quantities.

For example, a group of people have tickets to see a play at the costs shown in the graph on the right.

The tickets include transport and seats in the theatre.

This graph shows lots of information.

The horizontal axis (or x-axis) shows the number of people attending. The vertical axis (or y-axis) shows the total cost.

The cost depends on the number of people attending. However, there is a cost of £10 for 0 people attending. This is a group charge.

There are six marked points on the graph.

This graph is a linear graph, but it does not show direct proportion because it does not go through the origin.

Read up from 10 people on the x-axis to the straight line. When you reach the line, move across horizontally until you reach the y-axis. The cost is £30. This means that 10 people will need to pay £30 to attend the play.

Graphs are also useful in the real world for reading off values quickly without having to do the whole calculation. They serve as conversion charts.

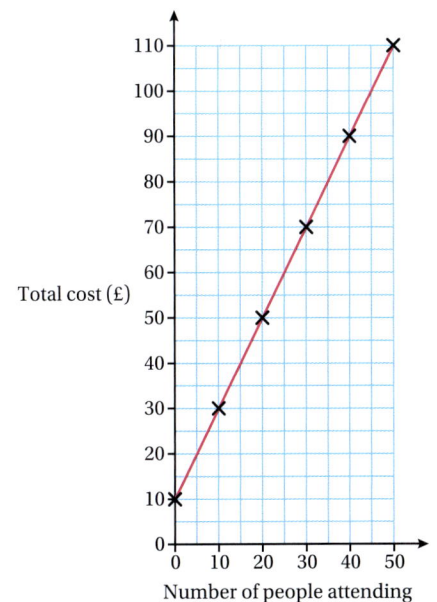

Total cost (£)

Number of people attending

Find answers at: cambridge.org/ukschools/gcsemaths-studentbookanswers

WORKED EXAMPLE 1

This graph shows the amounts of Indian rupees you would get for different amounts of US dollars at an exchange rate of US$1 : Rs 45. This relationship is a direct proportion.

a Use the graph to estimate the dollar value of Rs 250.

b Use the graph to estimate how many rupees you could get for US$9.

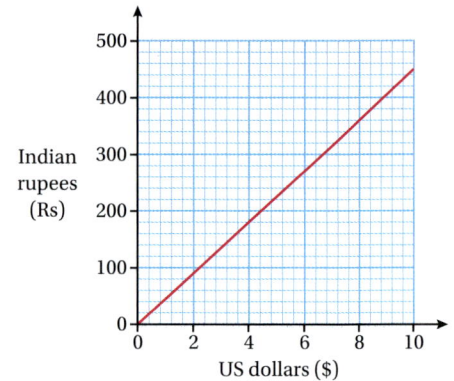

a Rs 250 is worth about $5.50.

b You could get about Rs 400 for US$ 9.

Distance–time graphs

Graphs that show the connection between the distance an object has travelled and the time taken to travel that distance are called distance–time graphs.

Time is normally shown along the horizontal axis and distance on the vertical.

The graphs normally start at the origin because at the beginning no time has elapsed (passed) and no distance has been covered.

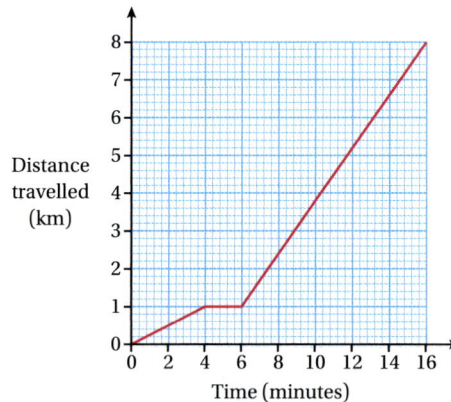

Look at the graph. It shows the following journey:

- a cycle for 4 minutes from home to a bus stop 1 km away
- a 2 minute wait for the bus
- a 7 km journey on the bus that takes 10 minutes.

The line of the graph remains horizontal while the person is not moving (waiting for the bus) because no distance is being travelled.

The steeper the line, the faster the person is travelling.

WORKED EXAMPLE 2

The graph shows the relationship between the length and the breadth of a hall.

Find the formula for this relationship.

Reading the points off the graph, we have $(4, 10)$, $(5, 8)$, $(8, 5)$ and $(10, 5)$.

The area of the hall is constant, at $4 \times 10 = 40 \, m^2$.

This graph shows an inverse proportion.

The formula is length $= \dfrac{40}{breadth}$

Graph of length against breadth

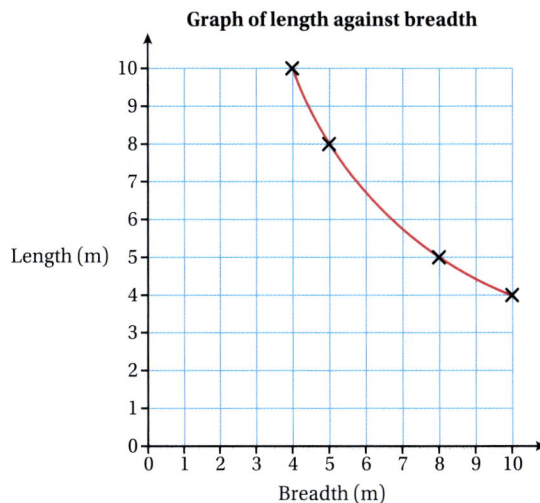

Because it shows a real-world context, the graph in the example above is only valid for that particular range of values.

EXERCISE 30A

1 Choose one of the options below to complete the sentence:

A distance–time graph shows a stationary object. The gradient of this graph is:

A Negative   B Positive   C Zero   D Doesn't exist

2 This graph shows the movement of a taxi in city traffic during a four-hour period.

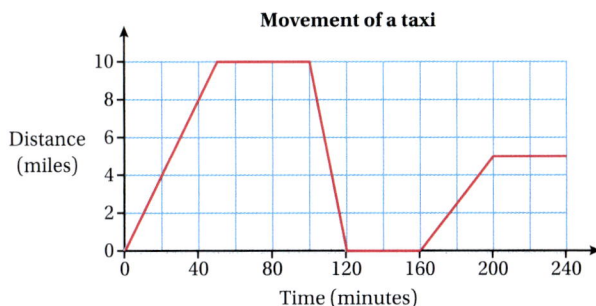

Movement of a taxi

a Using the information from the graph, describe the taxi's journey.

b For how many minutes was the taxi waiting for passengers in this period?

Give a reason how you can tell.

c What was the total distance travelled?

d Calculate the taxi's average speed during:

    i the first 20 minutes   **ii** the first hour

    iii from 160 to 210 minutes   **iv** for the full period of the graph.

3 This distance–time graph represents Monica's journey from home to a supermarket and back again.

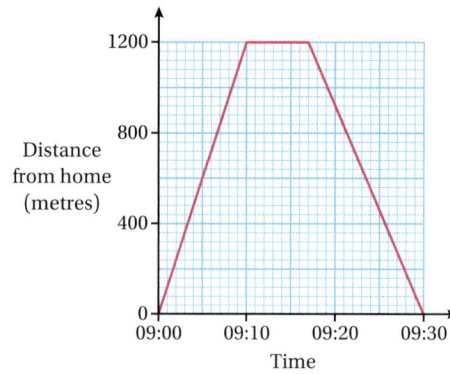

a How far was Monica from home at 09:06 hours?

b How many minutes did she spend at the supermarket?

c At what times was Monica 800 m from home?

d On which part of the journey did Monica travel faster, going to the supermarket or returning home?

4 A swimming pool is 25 m long. Jasmine swims from one end to the other in 20 seconds.

She rests for 10 seconds and then swims back to the starting point.

It takes her 30 seconds to swim the second length.

a Draw a distance–time graph for Jasmine's swim.

b How far was Jasmine from her starting point after 12 seconds?

c How far was Jasmine from her starting point after 54 seconds?

5 A hurricane disaster centre has a certain amount of clean water. The length of time the water will last depends on the number of people who come to the centre.

a Calculate the missing values in this table.

No. of people	120	150	200	300	400
Days the water will last	40	32			

b Plot a graph of this relationship.

Section 2: Gradients

Speed in distance–time graphs

The steepness (slope) of a graph gives an indication of the rate of change.

A straight line graph indicates a constant rate of change.

For distance–time graphs, the rate of change is equivalent to speed.

The steeper the graph is, the greater the speed.

An upward slope and a downward slope represent movement in opposite directions.

The distance–time graph shown is for a person who walks, cycles and then drives for three equal periods of time.

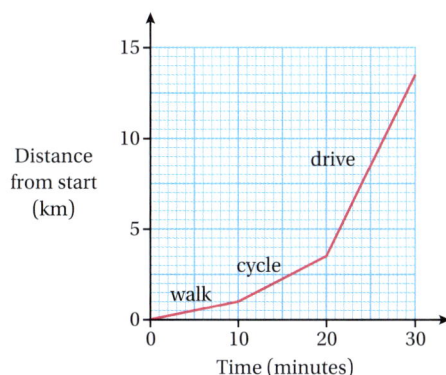

For each period, speed is given by the formula:

$$\text{speed} = \frac{\text{distance travelled}}{\text{time taken}}$$

Acceleration in speed-time graphs

For speed–time graphs, the gradient is equivalent to the acceleration. The steeper the graph is, the greater the acceleration.

In the speed–time graph shown, the speed of the car is increasing uniformly with time because the gradient is constant. This means that the car is accelerating at a constant rate.

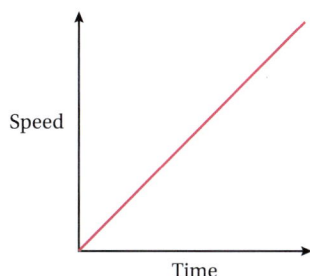

If the line on a speed–time graph is horizontal, the gradient is zero. This means the object moving at constant speed, that is, the acceleration is zero.

If the gradient of a speed-time graph is negative, the object is decelerating.

Using gradient triangles to interpret changing gradients

Looking at the gradient of a graph along with the axis labels gives a large amount of detail – even when, as in this case, there is no scale given.

Consider this graph:

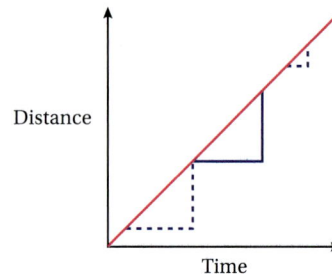

In the distance–time graph , as time moves on the distance covered increases. So the car is moving.

Gradient triangles are drawn on the graph. It doesn't matter where these triangles are drawn, each is similar to the others, so the sides represent the same gradient (rise/run).

This shows that the car is moving at a constant speed.

In the next example, as time moves on the distance covered also increases. So the car is moving.

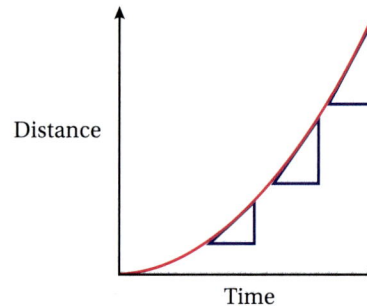

Each gradient triangle drawn on the graph has the same base (unit of time).

You can see by the slope of each triangle's hypotenuse that the speed is changing along the graph.

Moving up the slope, the triangles' hypotenuses are getting steeper. The gradient of the graph is increasing. This shows that the car is speeding up, or accelerating.

EXERCISE 30B

1 The following graphs show what is happening to the level of water in a tank.

Describe what is happening in each case. Justify your answers using gradient triangles.

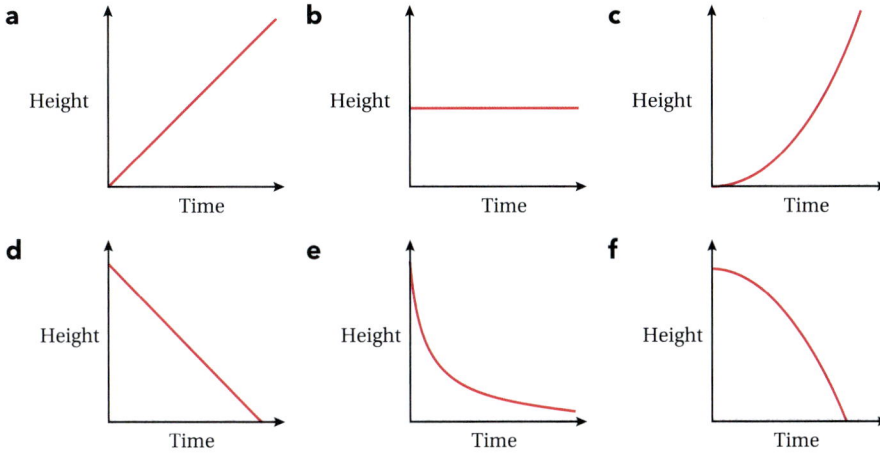

a

Height

Time

b

Height

Time

c

Height

Time

d

Height

Time

e

Height

Time

f

Height

Time

2 The following graphs show what is happening to the price of oil.

Describe what is happening in each case, justifying your answers using gradient triangles.

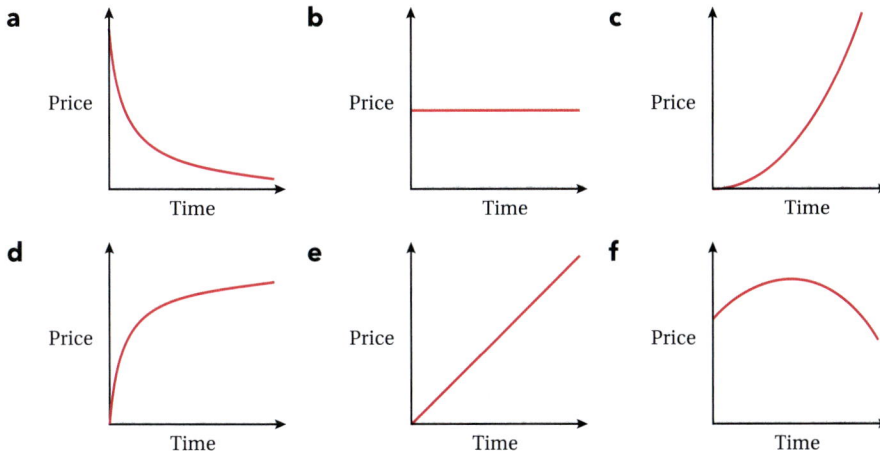

a

Price

Time

b

Price

Time

c

Price

Time

d

Price

Time

e

Price

Time

f

Price

Time

3 The following is a speed–time graph of a parachute jump.

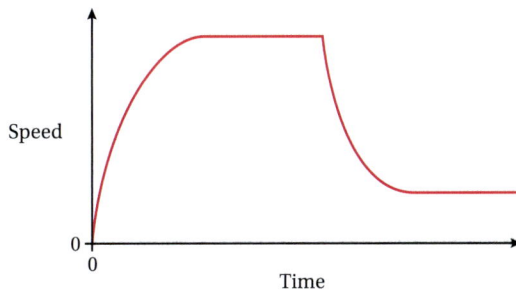

Speed

0

0

Time

Describe what is happening to the speed and acceleration of the parachutist throughout the jump.

Find answers at: cambridge.org/ukschools/gcsemaths-studentbookanswers

Finding the gradient of a curve using a tangent line

This simple graph of height against distance shows the route followed by a mountain biker on a trail.

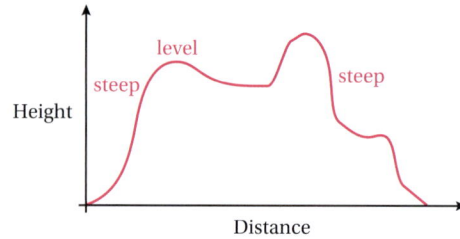

Some parts of the trail have a steep positive gradient, some have a gradual positive gradient. Some parts are level and other parts have a negative gradient.

It is clear from this graph that a curved graph never has a single gradient like a straight line has.

You cannot find the gradient of a whole curve but you can find the gradient at a point on the curve by drawing a tangent to it.

Once you have drawn the tangent to a curve, you can work out the gradient of the tangent just as you would for a straight line gradient:

$$\text{gradient} = \frac{y\,\text{change}}{x\,\text{increase}}$$

Look at the graph below to see how this works. BC is the tangent to the curve at A.

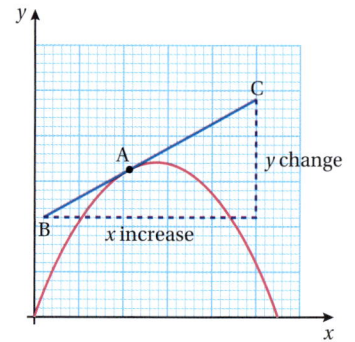

How to draw the tangent

Mark a point on the curve (A).	Place your ruler against the curve so that it touches only at point A.	Position the ruler so that the angle on either side of the point is more or less equal. Use a pencil to draw the tangent.

Calculating the gradient to a tangent

Mark two points, P and Q, on the tangent. Try to make the horizontal distance between P and Q a whole number of units (measured on the *x*-axis scale).

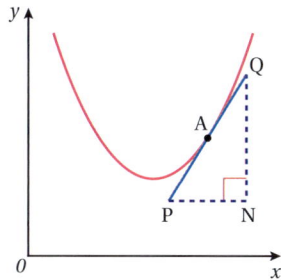

Draw a horizontal line through P and a vertical line through Q to form a right-angled triangle PNQ.

gradient of the curve at A = gradient of the tangent PAQ

$$= \frac{\text{distance NQ (measured on the } y\text{-axis scale)}}{\text{distance PN (measured on the } x\text{-axis scale)}}$$

WORKED EXAMPLE 3

The graph shows the height of a tree (*y* metres) plotted against the age of the tree (*x* years).

Estimate the rate at which the tree was growing when it was four years old.

The rate at which the tree was growing when it was four years old is equal to the gradient of the curve at the point where $x = 4$. Draw the tangent at this point (A).

Gradient at A $= \frac{NQ}{PN} = \frac{22.5}{8} = 2.8$

The tree was growing at a rate of 2.8 metres per year.

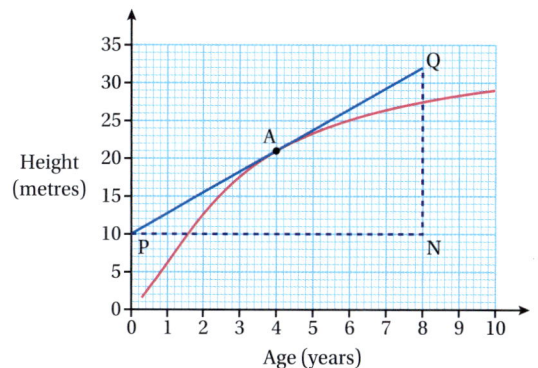

EXERCISE 30C

1. This is a distance–time graph for a drag-racing car.

   a Work out how far the car had travelled after 2 seconds.

   b Work out how long it took the car to travel 50 metres.

   c When was the car going at its fastest speed?

   d How fast was the car going after

   i 0.5 seconds?   ii 3.5 seconds?

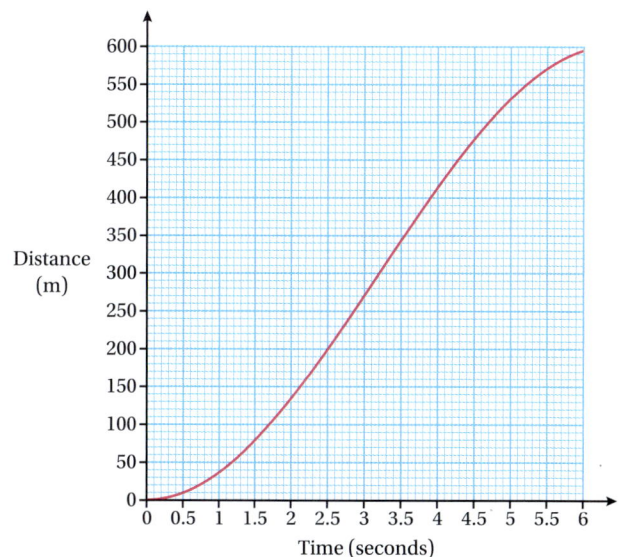

2 The following graph shows the predicted height of the tide at Seahaven.

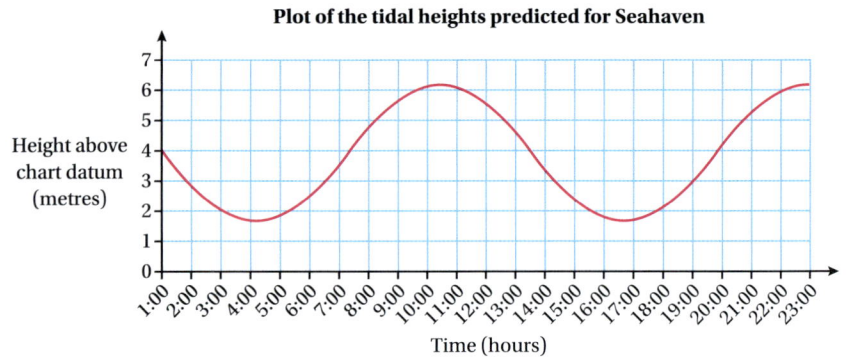

Plot of the tidal heights predicted for Seahaven

Height above chart datum (metres)

Time (hours)

a When is the tide coming in at its fastest rate?

b When is the tide fully in?

c How fast is the tide going out at:

   i 4pm?   **ii** 2pm?

d Give reasons why this kind of information would be useful.

3 The following graph shows the velocity of a car.

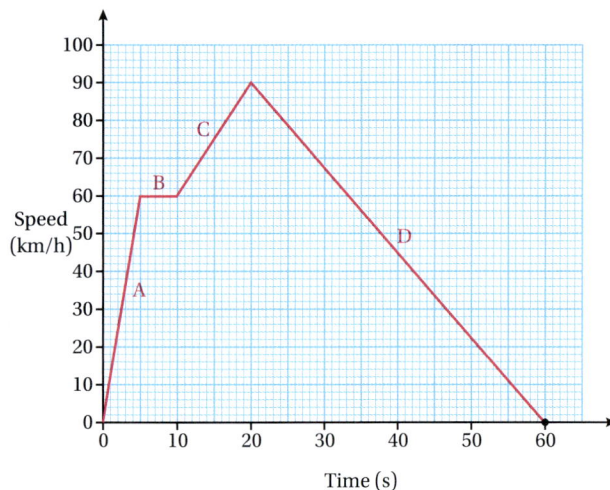

Speed (km/h)

Time (s)

a Describe the motion of this car. Pay particular attention to the four sections of the graph.

b What is the velocity of the car after 15 seconds?

c What is happening after 20 seconds?

d What is the acceleration of the car after 3 seconds?

e At what rate is the car decelerating after 40 seconds?

4 The graph of $y = x^2$ is shown in the diagram.

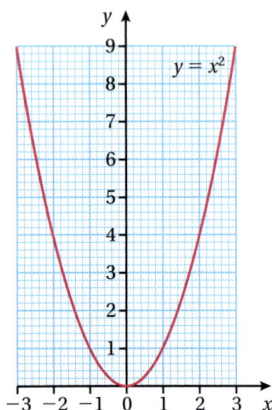

a Copy the graph using tracing paper and find the gradient of the graph at the points:

   i $(2, 4)$ **ii** $(-1, 1)$

b The gradient of the graph at the point $(1.5, 2.25)$ is 3.

Write down the coordinates of the point at which the gradient is -3.

$y = x^2$

572

Section 3: Areas under graphs

WORKED EXAMPLE 4

The graph shows a car travelling at a constant speed of 40 km/h.

Find the area under the graph after 2 hours, 3 hours, 4 hours. What do you notice?

The area under the graph equals the distance travelled.

$Speed = \dfrac{distance}{time}$, *so if you multiply by time you have:*

$speed \times time = \dfrac{distance}{time} \times time = distance$

The same works if the car is accelerating or decelerating.

The area under a speed–time graph is equal to the distance travelled.

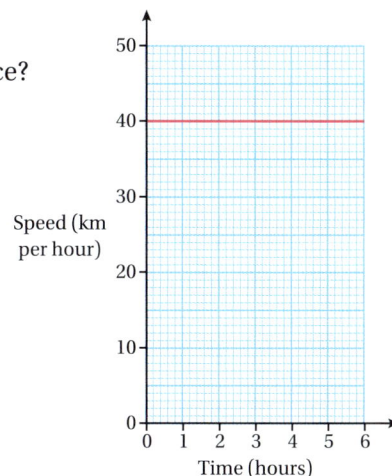

EXERCISE 30D

1 Find the distance travelled for each of the following vehicles in their first four hours:

a

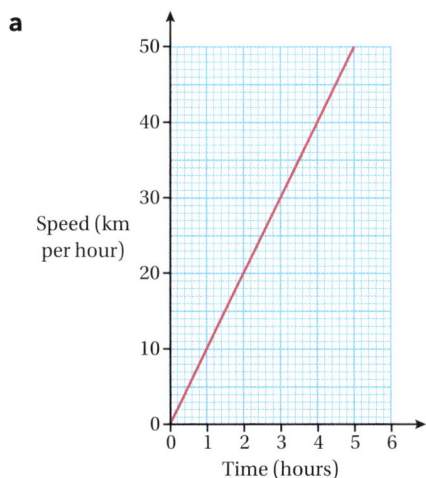

b

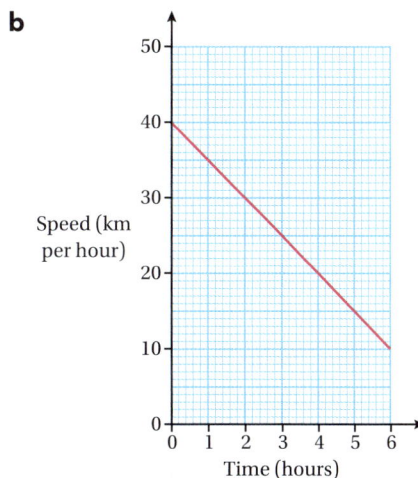

c

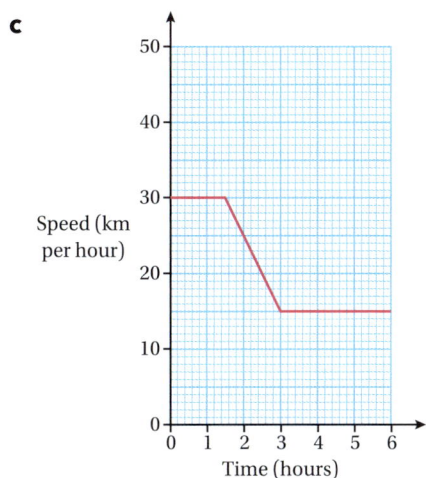

d

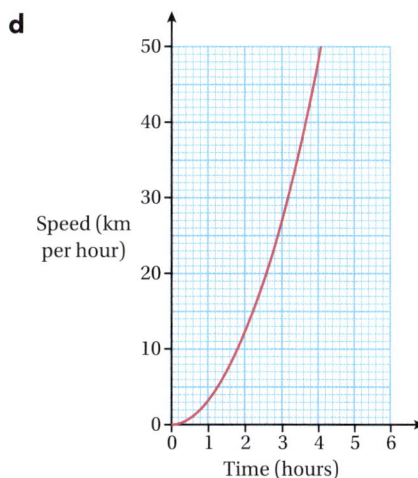

Find answers at: cambridge.org/ukschools/gcsemaths-studentbookanswers

2 The following graph shows the rate of water flow in a river throughout the day.

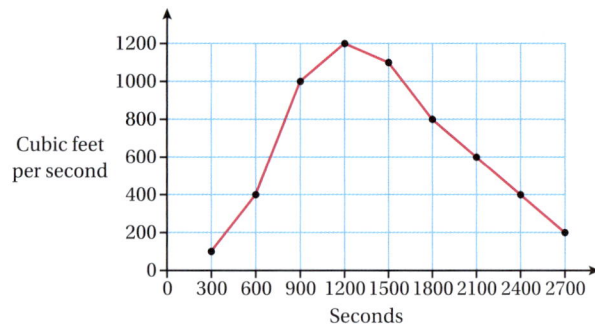

a What does the area under the graph represent?

b How much water had flowed down the river in the first 5 minutes?

c How much flowed between 10 and 15 minutes?

d How much less water flowed between 35 and 40 minutes compared to 15 and 20 minutes?

e Why might a river's flow change like this?

Checklist of learning and understanding

Graphs of real-world contexts

- Real-world graphs show the relationship between variables.

Gradient

- Distance–time graphs show the connection between the distance an object has travelled and the time taken to travel that distance. If speed is constant the gradient is constant.
- Curved graphs have gradients that change along the graph continually.
- Gradient triangles can be used to estimate the changes in the gradient.
- The gradient at a point on a distance–time graph will give the instantaneous speed. This can be calculated by drawing a tangent at the point and finding the gradient of the tangent.

Area under a graph

- The area under a graph can be used to calculate other values. For example, the area under a speed–time graph gives the distance covered.

Chapter review

For additional questions on the topics in this chapter, visit GCSE Mathematics Online.

1 Dan leaves home at 0800.

He drives 60 miles from home in the first 90 minutes.

He stops for 30 minutes.

He then drives home at an average speed of 50 mph.

a Copy the graph axes and draw a distance–time graph to show Dan's journey. *(3 marks)*

b A TV programme starts at 1130.

Does Dan get home in time for the start?

Show how you decide. *(1 mark)*

© AQA 2013

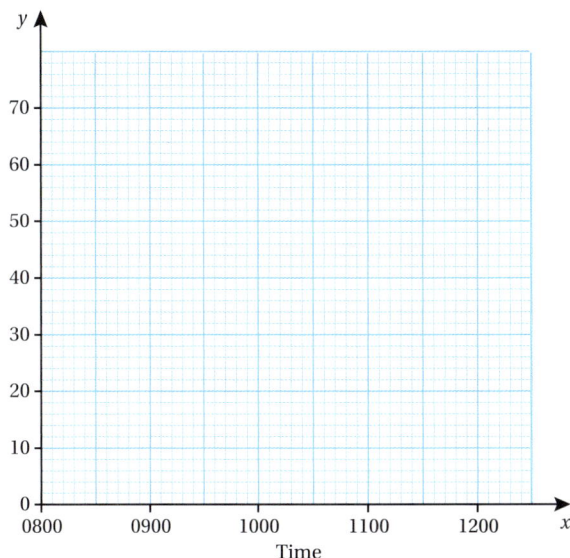

2 The speed–time graph below represents the journey of a train between two stations. The train slowed down and stopped after 15 minutes because of engineering work on the railway line.

a For how long was the train stopped at the place where there was engineering work?

b What was the speed of the train after 19 minutes?

c Calculate the distance the train travelled in the first 15 minutes.

d Calculate the distance between the two stations.

e Calculate the deceleration of the train as it approached the place where there was engineering work.

f Calculate the greatest speed, in km/h, that the train reached.

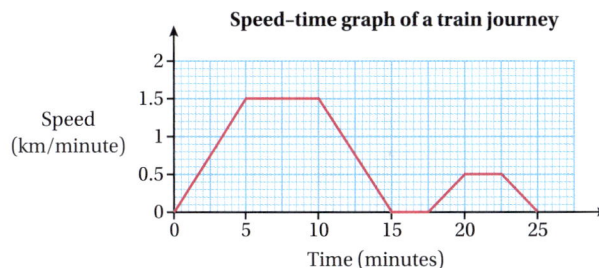

Speed-time graph of a train journey

3 The graph shows how the population of a village has changed since 1930.

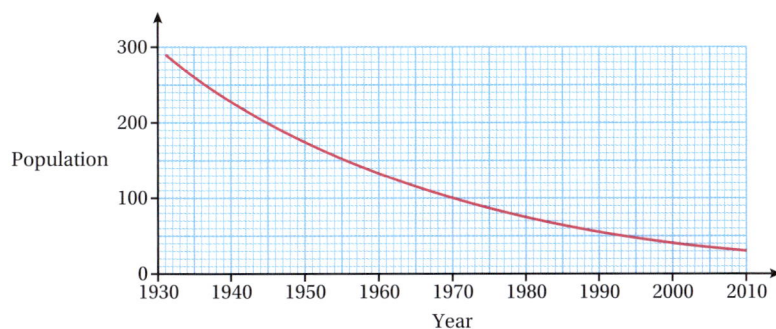

a Copy the graph using tracing paper and find the gradient of the graph at the point (1950, 170).

b What does this gradient represent?

Find answers at: cambridge.org/ukschools/gcsemaths-studentbookanswers

31 Circles

In this chapter you will learn how to …

- use and apply circle definitions and understand their properties.
- prove and apply the standard circle theorems, using them to find related results.

For more resources relating to this chapter, visit GCSE Mathematics Online.

Using mathematics: real-life applications

Circle theorems are a set of proofs that have been developed over hundreds of years by mathematicians who wondered about, and investigated, the properties of circles. Learning about them allows you to appreciate some of the surprising properties of circles and the angles within them.

"I use circle theorems on board the ship to calculate the visible distance to the horizon. I use the tangent properties to give me a right-angled triangle which I then use with Pythagoras' theorem to do my calculations."

(Navigation officer)

Before you start …

Ch 8, 9	You should be able to calculate the sizes of missing angles in geometry problems.	**1** Decide whether each statement is true or false. **a** $c = 120°$ **b** $a = 120°$ **c** $d = b$ **d** $b = c = 60°$	
Ch 9, 10, 11	You should know how to find the circumference and area of circles and parts of circles.	**2** For each of these circle sectors, calculate the length of the arc and the area of the sector: **a** 3 cm, 72° **b** 25 mm, 45° **c** 150°, 12 cm	
KS3 Ch 9	You should be able to use given facts in geometry problems to write proofs.	**3** You need to write a proof that angle BAD = 50°. Which of these proofs is **not** correct? **a** Angle CED = 50° (the sum of angles of a triangle is 180°) Angle BAD = 50° (corresponding angle to angle CED, AB // EC) **b** Angle CEA = 100° (alternate angle to angle ECD) Angle BAD = 50° (180° – 30° – 100° = 50°) **c** Angle DBA = 100° (corresponding angle to angle ECD, AB ∥ EC) Angle BAD = 50° (the sum of angles of a triangle is 180°)	

Assess your starting point using the Launchpad

STEP 1

1 Copy this diagram of a circle and label each part with the appropriate term:

 a chord   **b** radius

 c diameter   **c** circumference

2 If the radius of the Earth is roughly 6378 km, what is its diameter?

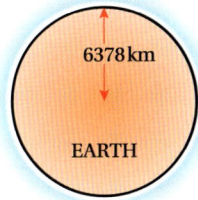

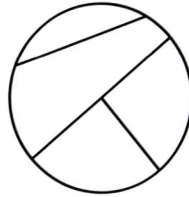

6378 km

EARTH

GO TO
Section 1:
Review of parts of a circle

STEP 2

3 In the diagram, O is the centre of the circle.

 a Find the size of x

 b Prove that APBQ is a rectangle

4 AB is the diameter of a circle. C is the centre. D is any point on the circumference.

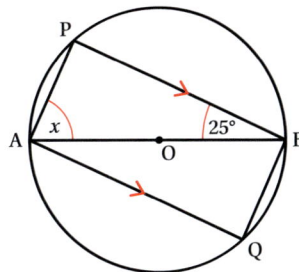

 Find the size of angle ADB.

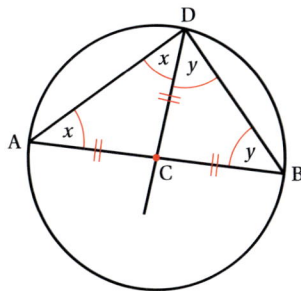

GO TO
Section 2:
Circle theorems and proofs
Section 3:
Applications of circle theorems

GO TO
Chapter review

Find answers at: cambridge.org/ukschools/gcsemaths-studentbookanswers

Section 1: Review of parts of a circle

A circle is the locus of points which are all the same distance from a given point.

That point is the centre of the circle.

Any line drawn from the centre to the circumference is therefore a fixed length called a radius.

If you take any two points on the circumference and join them, you get a line called a chord. If the chord passes through the centre, then it is called the diameter and it is equivalent to two radii ($d = 2r$).

The basic terminology

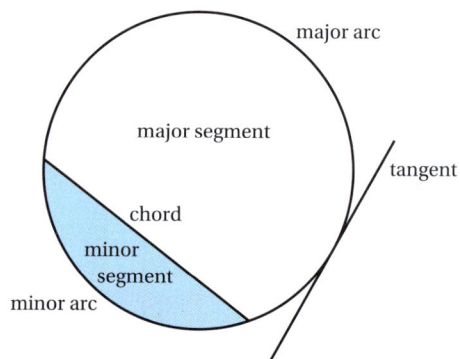

Naming angles in circles

Angles can be formed at the centre of the circle or at the circumference.

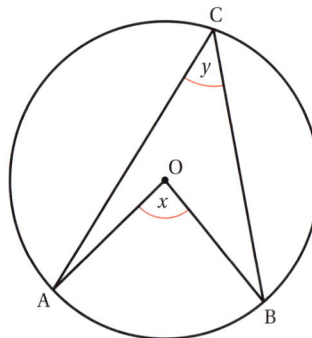

AOB is the angle at the centre.

ACB is the angle at the circumference.

The arms of both these angles are 'standing' on the minor arc AB.

Angles that stand on an arc are said to be **subtended** by the arc.

Angles can also be subtended by a chord.

EXERCISE 31A

1 Match the circle parts to the correct definition.

a half the diameter	A sector
b the larger part of a circle when it is divided into two parts by a chord	B tangent
c formed by two radii and an arc	C minor arc
d a line outside a circle that touches the circumference at one point only	D circle
e the locus of a point at a fixed distance from another point	E radius
f the smaller part of the circumference when a circle is divided by a chord	F major segment

2 In the diagram, O is the centre of both circles. Copy and complete the sentences using the correct mathematical terms.

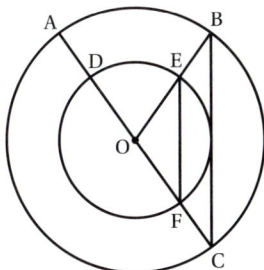

a DF is the _____ of the smaller circle.

b AO is a _____ of the larger circle.

c AC is the diameter of the _____ circle.

d ED is a _____ _____ of the smaller circle.

e ACB is a _____ _____ of the larger circle.

f EF is a _____ of the smaller circle.

g Angle FOE is the angle at the _____ subtended by arc _____.

h Angle ACB is subtended by _____ at the circumference.

3 Look again at the diagram in question 2.

a What can you say about angles OFE and OEF? Give a reason for your answer.

b How can you prove that angle OEF = OFE = OCB = OBC?

4 **a** If the diameter of a circle is 25cm, what is the radius?

b If the radius of a circle is 25cm, what is the diameter?

Section 2: Circle theorems and proofs

Angles subtended at centre and circumference

In the diagram the minor arc DE (or chord DE):

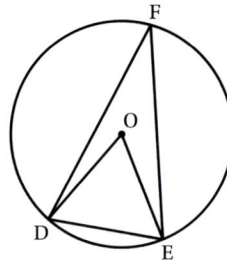

- subtends angle DOE at the centre O
- subtends angle F at point F on the circumference.

The theorem states that the angle subtended by an arc at the centre of a circle is twice the angle subtended by the same arc at the circumference.

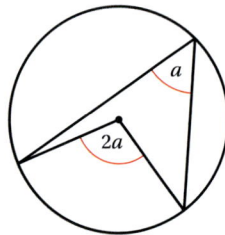

Proof

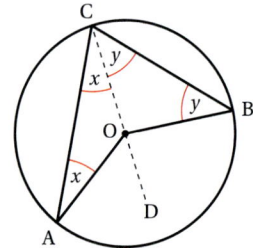

Angle AOB and angle ACB are both subtended by arc AB.

Drawing a line segment joining the centre O to C forms two isosceles triangles: triangle AOC and triangle BOC. The equal sides are the radii of the circle.

The angle ACB = $x + y$

The angle AOC = $(180 - 2x)$ (because the angles in a triangle sum to 180)

The angle BOC = $(180 - 2y)$ (because the angles in a triangle sum to 180)

The angle AOB = $360 - (180 - 2x) - (180 - 2y)$ (because angles at a point sum to 360)

$$= 360 - 180 - 2x - 180 - 2y$$

$$= -2x - 2y$$

$$= 2x + 2y = 2(x + y)$$

$$= 2 \times \text{angle ACB}$$

So the angle subtended by AB at the centre is twice the angle subtended by AB at the circumference.

This theorem will be used in the proof of other theorems. You can accept that it is true when proving other theorems.

Angles in a semicircle

This theorem states that the angle subtended by a diameter at the circumference of a circle is a right angle. This follows from the first theorem.

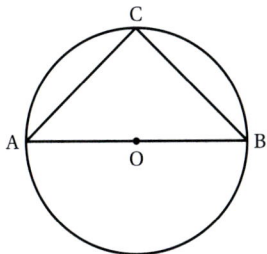

In this diagram, AB is a diameter, and C is called an angle in a semicircle.

Arc AB subtends an angle of 180° at the centre (a straight line), and it subtends angle C on the circumference.

Using the first theorem, you know that the angle subtended at the centre is twice the angle subtended by the same arc at the circumference.

So angle $C = \frac{1}{2} \times 180° = 90°$

'The angle in a semicircle is always a right angle' is another fact that you can use in other proofs.

Tip

Simply write 'angle in a semicircle' as a reason in your proofs.

Angles in the same segment

This theorem states that two angles in the same segment are equal. This theorem also follows from the first theorem.

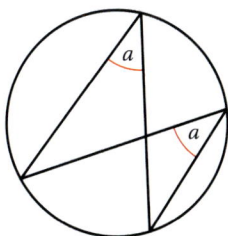

Two angles in the same segment refers to two angles at the circumference that are subtended by the same arc or chord.

Proof

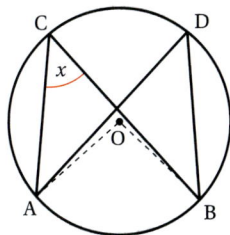

Angles C and D are in the same segment, because they are both subtended at the circumference by arc AB.

You are given that angle $C = x$.

The arc AB also subtends angle AOB at the centre.

AOB = 2x, using the result of our first theorem.

You can state the reason as 'angles subtended at centre and circumference'.

Angle D is equal to x, using the same reason: angles subtended at centre and circumference.

So angle C = angle D = x.

This is another fact that you can use in other proofs.

EXERCISE 31B

1 The angle at the centre of a circle is 170°.

What is the size of the angle made at the circumference? Choose from the following options.

A 85°　　　　　　B 90°　　　　　　C 170°　　　　　　D 340°

2 Prove that angle COB = 2(angle CAB).

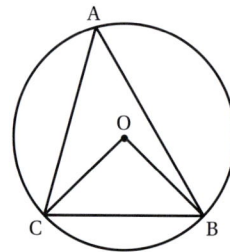

3 Prove that angle Y is a right angle.

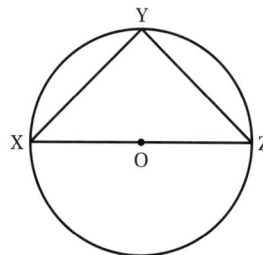

4 Prove that $y = 25°$.

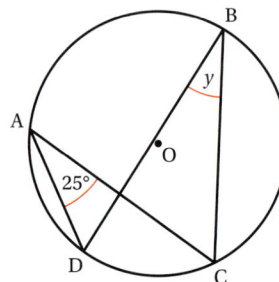

5 What size is the angle at POQ?

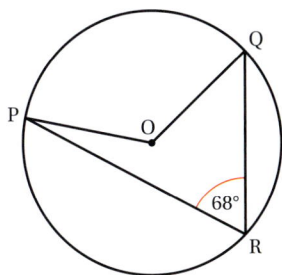

6 What is the size of angle BAC?

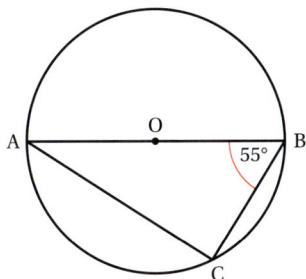

7 What is the size at angle BCD?

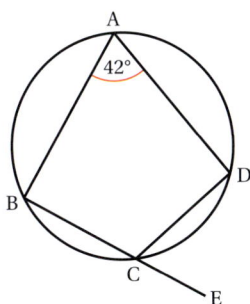

8 The angle CAB is twice the angle at CBA.
What are the sizes of both angles?

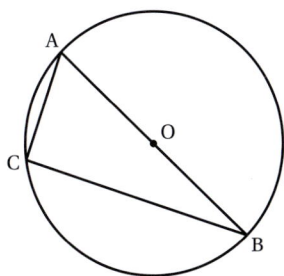

Find answers at: cambridge.org/ukschools/gcsemaths-studentbookanswers

Angle between radius and chord

This theorem states that a radius or diameter bisects a chord if it is perpendicular to the chord.

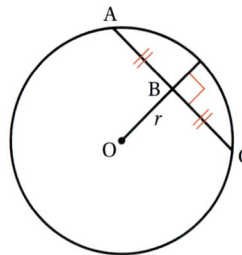

In other words, if the radius r in the diagram is perpendicular to the chord AC, then it bisects the chord and AB = BC.

The radius does not bisect the chord if it is not perpendicular to the chord.

So you have two facts that we can use from this theorem.

Proof

Circle with centre O and with chord AB. OM is perpendicular to AB.

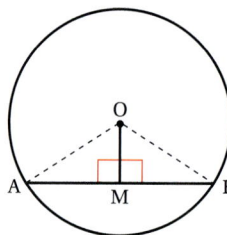

Prove that AM = MB.

First show that triangle OMA and triangle OMB are congruent, because:

OA = OB (they are radii of the circle).

They have a common side OM.

OM is perpendicular to AB, so angle M_1 = angle M_2 = 90°.

AM = MB (because the triangles are congruent).

Tip

This fact is useful when solving geometry problems. State it in short as 'angle between radius and chord'.

Angle between the radius and tangent

This theorem states that for a point P on the circumference, the radius or diameter through P is perpendicular to the tangent at P.

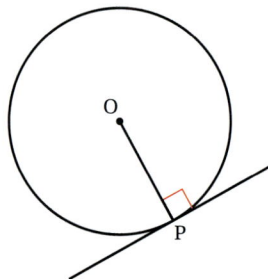

If the line is a tangent, it touches the circle at a single point.

If the radius did not meet the tangent at a right angle, then the line would not be a tangent.

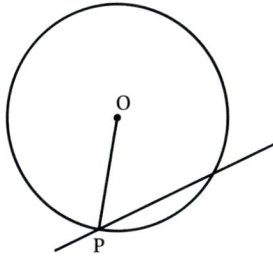

This kind of proof is called a proof by contradiction.

It shows that the only way that the line can be a tangent is if the angle at the point where it touches the circle is at a right angle to the radius drawn at that point.

> **Tip**
>
> When you use this theorem in a geometry problem, write 'angle between radius and tangent' as a reason.

Two tangent theorem

This theorem states that two tangents from a given point outside of the circle are equal in length.

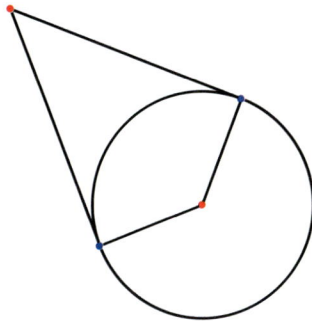

Proof

Here is a circle with centre O and tangents TA and TB touching the circle at A and B. Prove that TA = TB.

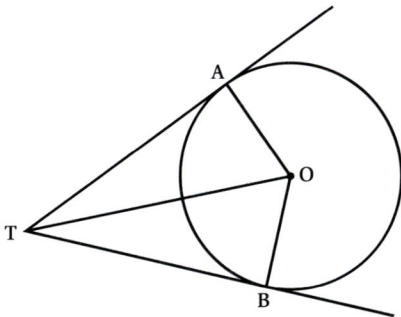

Draw radii OA and OB. Join OT.

Triangle OAT is congruent to triangle OBT for the following reasons:

Angle A_1 = angle B_1 = 90° (the tangent is perpendicular to the radius)

They both have the same side, TO.

OA and OB are radii, so OA = OB.

So triangle OAT is congruent to triangle OBT and therefore TA = TB.

EXERCISE 31C

1 PQ is a chord of a circle centre O.

Radius OS ⊥ PQ, and cuts PQ at R.

Radius OQ = 25 units and PQ = 48 units.

Calculate the length of SR.

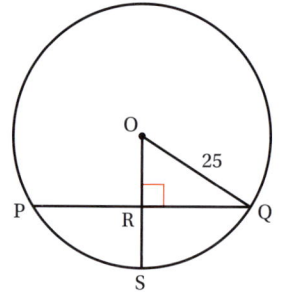

2 The diagram shows a circle with centre O and chord PQ.

OR ⊥ PQ.

OR = 6 units and PQ = 16 units.

Calculate the length of OQ.

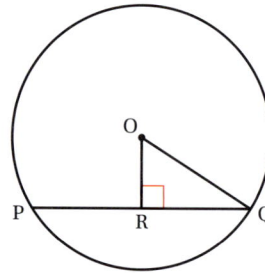

3 In the diagram, NT is parallel to CD. Given that angle NAC is 66°, what is the size of angle ECD?

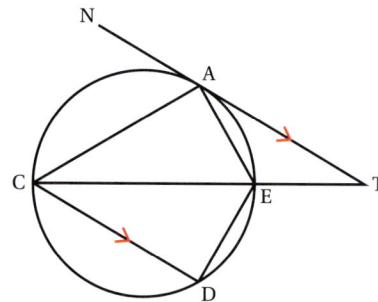

4 What is the size of angle x in the diagram? Give a reason for your answer.

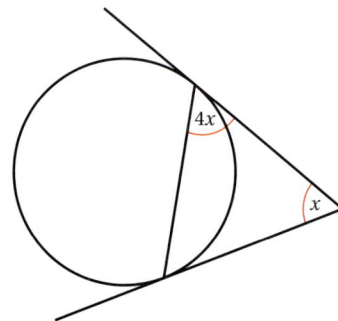

4 The diagram shows a circle with centre O and tangents LM and LP.

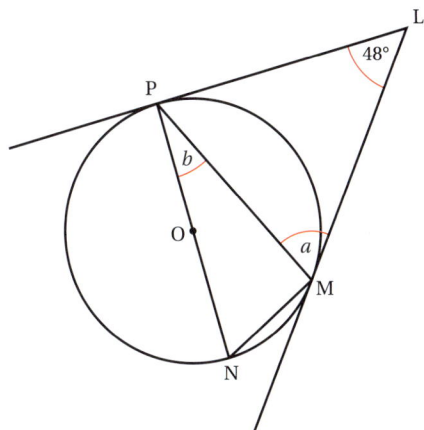

Find the size of the angles marked *a* and *b*.

Alternate segment theorem

This theorem states that for a point P on the circumference, the angle between the tangent and a chord through P equals the angle subtended by the chord in the alternate segment.

You need to think carefully about this theorem so that you can work out when it is needed to solve a problem.

A chord divides a circle into a minor segment and a major segment. So this theorem is used when you have a tangent, one angle in a minor segment and one angle in the major segment.

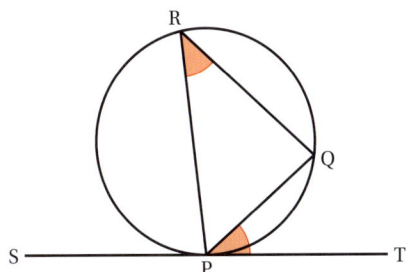

Proof

This circle has centre O and a tangent at P.

PR is a chord with W on the minor arc and Q on the major arc.

Prove that angle SPR = PQR and also that angle TPR = PWR.

Draw diameter VP. Join points V and Q.

1 Angle PQV = 90° (VP is the diameter, so angle PQV is the angle in a semicircle)

Angle SPV = 90° (angle between the radius and tangent)

So Angle PQV = angle SPV

But angle RPV = angle RQV (angles in the same segment)

So angle SPR = PQR

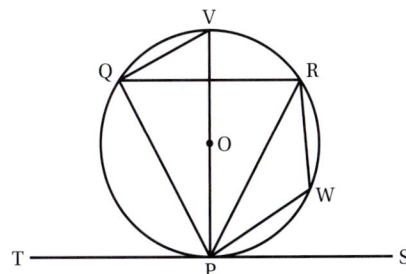

2 Join line segment VW.

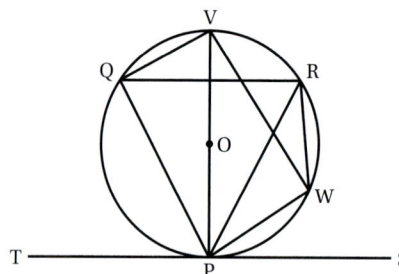

Angle TPV = 90° (angle between radius and tangent)

Angle PWV = 90° (angle in a semicircle)

Now notice that angle RPV = RWV (angles in the same segment subtended by VR)

angle TPV + RPV = angle PWV + RWV

So angle TPR = PWR.

Angles in cyclic quadrilaterals

Key vocabulary

cyclic quadrilateral: any quadrilateral with all four vertices on the circumference of a circle

A **cyclic quadrilateral** has all four vertices touching the circumference of a circle.

This theorem states that the opposite angles in a cyclic quadrilateral add up to 180°.

Proof

ABCD is a cyclic quadrilateral.

BO and DO are radii of the circle.

Tip

ABCO is not a cyclic quadrilateral.

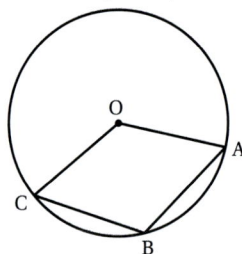

For a quadrilateral to be a cyclic quadrilateral all four vertices must sit on the circumference. Make sure you check this carefully when you are applying the theorems.

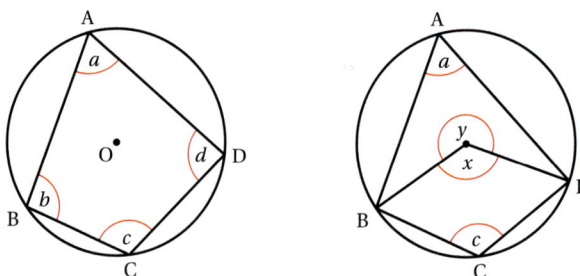

$x = 2a$ (angle at centre theorem, minor arc BD)

$y = 2c$ (angle at centre theorem, major arc BD)

$\therefore x + y = 2a + 2c$

But $x + y = 360°$ (angles at a point add to 360°)

$\therefore 2a + 2c = 360°$

$\therefore a + c = 180°$

EXERCISE 31D

1 Opposite angles in a cyclic quadrilateral have special properties.

Which is the correct statement?

a Opposite angles are corresponding and are therefore equal.

b Opposite angles add to 180°.

c Opposite angles are equal as they are vertically opposite.

d Opposite angles are alternate angles and are therefore equal.

2 In the diagram, TAN is a tangent to the circle. Angle TAC = angle BAN.

Prove that:

a CB is parallel to TN

b AC = AB

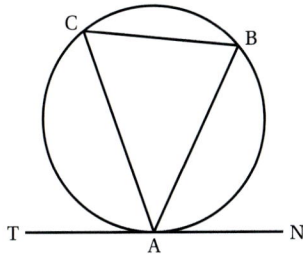

3 Given: APB is a tangent at P to circle centre S. Angle APR = x.

Write the following angles in terms of x:

a angle Q **b** angle QSP   **c** angle RSP

d angle RPS   **e** angle QPB

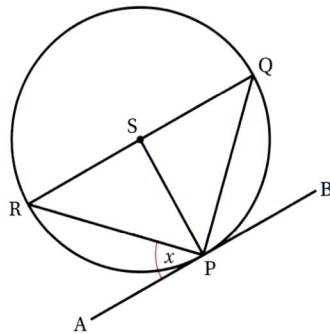

4 In each of the following examples, calculate the values of the variables. Give reasons for your statements.

a

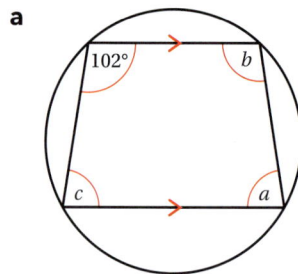

b

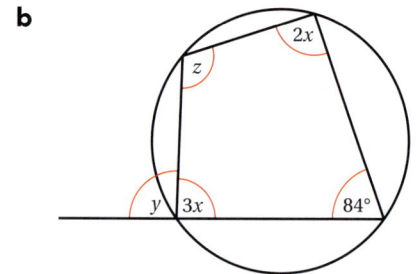

c

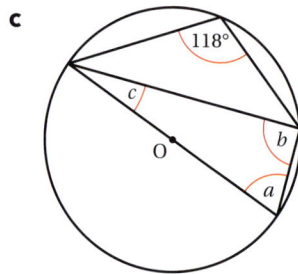

d

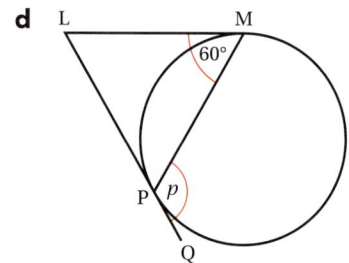

Section 3: Applications of circle theorems

To solve problems in geometry, you need to apply your knowledge correctly. You might not see the solution immediately, but you can start to identify a pathway towards the final solution by building on the information step by step. It is useful to follow these steps:

Problem-solving framework

Steps for solving problems	What you would do for this example
Step 1: Read the question carefully to decide what you have to find.	Look at the diagram below. AOB and COD are diameters of circle O. Angle ACD = 33°. Calculate the sizes of: **a** angle AOD **b** angle D **c** angle B 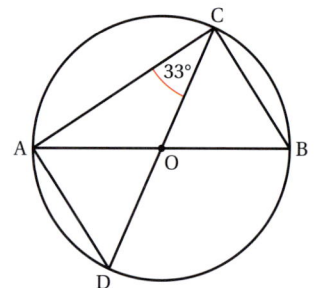
Step 2: Draw a diagram if you have not been given one. Mark all the information on the diagram.	

Continues on next page …

Step 3: Analyse where you can work out additional information and fill it in.	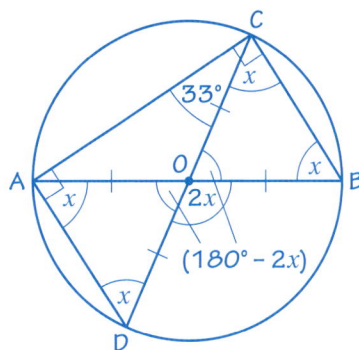
Step 4: Use this information to decide what method you will use. This might not be obvious immediately. You might need to spend some time studying the problem.	Think: I have marked that angle ACB and DAC are right angles. Call angle OCB x. Four angles are equal to x because of angles in the same segment and isosceles triangles formed by radii. x is $90° - 33° = 57°$
Step 5: When you can see a way to find the solution, write down all the steps.	**a** angle ACB = 90° (angle in a semicircle) angle OCB = 90° − 33° = 57° angle DAO = angle OCB = 57° (angles in the same segment) angle ODA = angle DAO = 57° (triangle OAD is isosceles triangle) angle AOD = 180° − 2(57°) = 66° (sum of angles in a triangle) **b** angle D = 57° (already proved) **c** angle B = angle OCB = 57° (triangle OBC is isosceles)
Step 6: Give reasons for each step. You can use the theorems as accepted facts. You can also use facts that you have proved.	

WORK IT OUT 31.1

Rose needs to solve the following problem.

P, Q and T are points on the circumference of a circle, centre O.

The line ATB is the tangent to the circle at T.

PQ = TQ.

Angle ATP = 48°.

Calculate the size of angle OTQ.

Give a reason for each stage in your working.

Which of her answers below is the correct answer?

Where have her other answers gone wrong?

Not to scale

Option A	Option B	Option C
angle PQT = 48° (angles in alternate segments)	angle PQT = 48° (angles in alternate segments)	angle PQT = 48° (angles in alternate segments)
angle OTQ = angle PQT (radii of circle are equal, isosceles triangle)	Triangle QPT is isosceles (QP = QT) So angle QPT = angle QTP	Triangle QPT is isosceles (QP = QT)
angle OTQ = 48°	angle QTP = $\frac{1}{2} \times (180° - 48°)$ (the sum of angles in a triangle is 180°) angle QPT = 66°	angle QPT = angle OTQ (triangle QPT is isosceles)
	angle OTA = angle OTB = 90° (angle between radius and tangent)	angle OTQ = $\frac{1}{2} \times (180° - 48°)$ (the sum of angles in a triangle is 180°)
	OTP = 90° − 48° = 42°	angle OTQ = $\frac{1}{2} \times 132°$
	QTP − OTP = angle OTQ OTQ = 66° − 42° = 24°	angle OTQ = 66°

EXERCISE 31E

1 AB is a chord of a circle centre P, with D the midpoint of AB.

PA = 50 units and AB = 96 units.

Calculate the lengths of:

a PD **b** DE

c DF **d** BF

e BE

2 AC is a tangent to a circle with centre O at B. FOB is a diameter. GF // BD, EH = HD and angle ABG = 62°.

Write down the sizes of the following angles. Give reasons in each case.

a angle EHO   **b** angle GFB   **c** angle GBF

d angle FEG   **e** angle DBF   **f** angle GEH

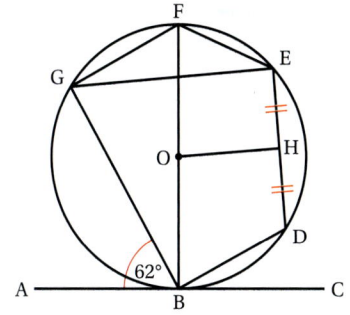

3 Find the size of angle *L* in terms of *x*.

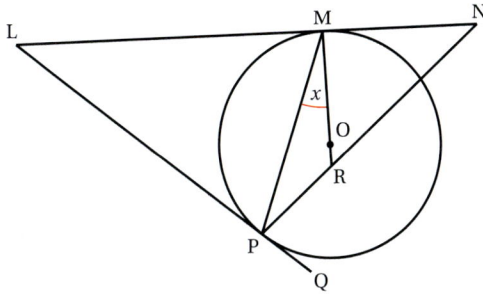

4 In the diagram, TA and TB are the tangents from T to the circle with centre O. AC is a diameter of the circle and ACB = *x*.

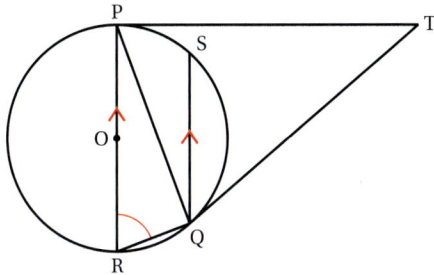

a Find CAB in terms of *x*.

b Find ATB in terms of *x*.

c The point P on the circumference of the circle is such that BP is parallel to CA.

Express PBT in terms of *x*.

5 What is the size of the three missing angles?

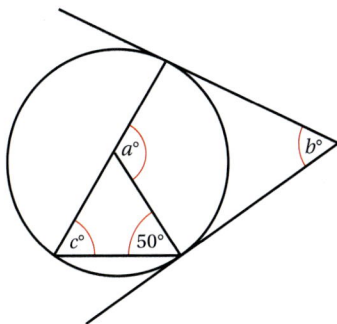

Find answers at: cambridge.org/ukschools/gcsemaths-studentbookanswers

📎 **Checklist of learning and understanding**

Circle theorems

- The angle subtended by an arc at the centre is twice the angle at the circumference.
- The angle on the circumference subtended by a diameter is a right angle.
- Two angles in the same segment are equal.
- A radius or diameter bisects a chord if and only if it is perpendicular to the chord.
- For a point P on the circumference, the radius or diameter through P is perpendicular to the tangent at P.
- Two tangents from a given point outside of the circle are equal in length.
- For a point P on the circumference, the angle between the tangent and a chord through P equals the angle subtended by the chord in the opposite segment.
- The opposite angles of a cyclic quadrilateral are supplementary.

🖥️ For additional questions on the topics in this chapter, visit GCSE Mathematics Online.

📂 **Chapter review**

1 PR is the diameter of a circle with centre O.

PT and QT are tangents to the circle.

If angle SQP is 32°, what is the size of angle QRP?

Choose from the following options.

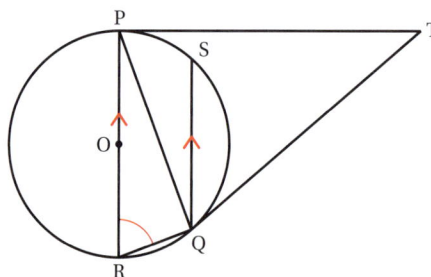

A 32°   B 58°   C 60°   D 122°

2 In the diagram, A, B, C and D are points on the circumference of a circle, centre O.

Angle BAD = 70°. Angle BOD = x. Angle BCD = y.

a Work out the value of x. Give a reason for your answer.

b Work out the value of y.

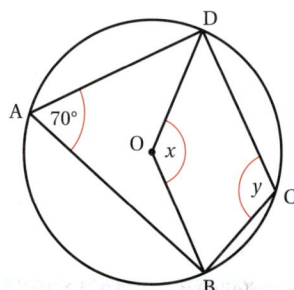

Not to scale

594

3 A, B, C and D are points on the circumference of a circle.
Angle ABD = 54°. Angle BAC = 28°.

Find the size of angle ACD. Give a reason for your answer.

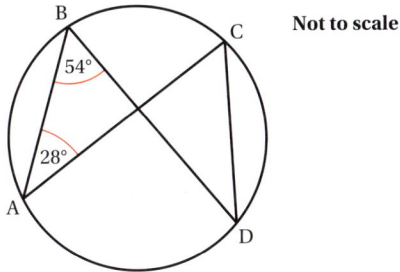

Not to scale

4 The diagram shows a circle with centre O and ABT is a straight line.
Angle AOB = 80° and angle CBT = 102°.

Find the size of the labelled angles.

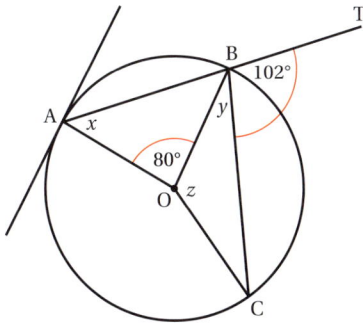

5 The diagram shows a circle, centre O.

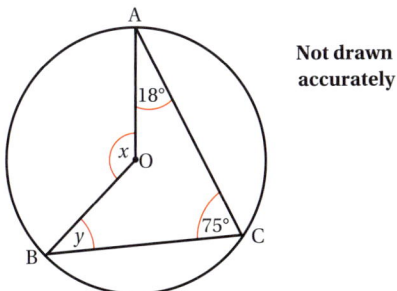

Not drawn
accurately

a Work out the size of angle x.   *(1 mark)*

b Work out the size of angle y.   *(3 marks)*

© *AQA 2013*

32 Vector geometry

In this chapter you will learn how to ...

- represent vectors as a diagram or column vector.
- add and subtract vectors.
- multiply vectors by a scalar.
- use vectors to construct geometric arguments and proofs.

For more resources relating to this chapter, visit GCSE Mathematics Online.

Using mathematics: real-life applications

Vectors are used in navigation to make sure that two ships don't crash into each other. They are used to model objects sliding down slopes with varying amounts of friction. They can be used to work out how far an object can tilt without tipping over, and much more.

"When landing at any airport I have to consider how the wind will blow me off course. Over a set amount of time I expect to travel along a particular vector but I have to add on the effect the wind has on my flight path. If I don't do this accurately I would struggle to land the plane safely." *(Pilot)*

Before you start ...

KS3	You need to be able to plot coordinates in all four quadrants.	**1**	Draw a set of axes going from -6 to 6 in both x- and y-directions. Plot the points A(2, 3), B(-3, 4) and C(-2, -3).
KS3	You need to be able to add, subtract and multiply negative numbers.	**2**	Calculate. **a** $3 - 7$ **b** $-4 + 11$ **c** $-5 - 18$ **d** -4×7 **e** -3×-9
KS3 Ch 17	You need to be able to solve simple linear equations.	**3**	Solve. **a** $12 = 4m - 36$ **b** $2k + 15 = 7$ **c** $-6 + 5d = -41$
KS3 Ch 17	You need to be able to solve simultaneous linear equations.	**4**	Solve. $3x + 2y = 8$ and $4x - 3y = 5$

Assess your starting point using the Launchpad

STEP 1

1 Write down the column vector for $\overrightarrow{HG}$.

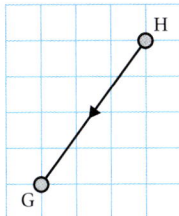

2 Draw the triangle ABC where

$$\overrightarrow{AB} = \begin{pmatrix} 3 \\ -5 \end{pmatrix} \text{ and } \overrightarrow{CA} = \begin{pmatrix} 2 \\ 7 \end{pmatrix}$$

GO TO
Section 1:
Vector notation and representation

STEP 2

3 $\mathbf{j} = \begin{pmatrix} -1 \\ 3 \end{pmatrix}$ $\mathbf{k} = \begin{pmatrix} 2 \\ 1 \end{pmatrix}$ $\mathbf{l} = \begin{pmatrix} -4 \\ -2 \end{pmatrix}$

Write the following as single vectors.
a $\mathbf{j} + \mathbf{k}$ **b** $2\mathbf{k} - \mathbf{l}$

4 Find the values of f and g.
$$\begin{pmatrix} 10 \\ g \end{pmatrix} - 4 \begin{pmatrix} f \\ -3 \end{pmatrix} = \begin{pmatrix} -2 \\ 18 \end{pmatrix}$$

5 In the diagram:
$$\overrightarrow{AC} = \begin{pmatrix} 14 \\ 2 \end{pmatrix} \text{ and } \overrightarrow{AB} = \begin{pmatrix} 9 \\ 12 \end{pmatrix}$$
Find:
a $\overrightarrow{CA}$ **b** $\overrightarrow{CA} + \overrightarrow{AB}$

6 Which of these vectors are parallel?

$$\begin{pmatrix} -3 \\ 4 \end{pmatrix} \begin{pmatrix} 9 \\ 16 \end{pmatrix} \begin{pmatrix} 15 \\ -20 \end{pmatrix} \begin{pmatrix} -3 \\ 2 \end{pmatrix}$$

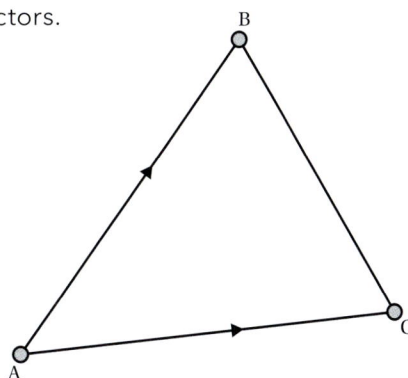

GO TO
Section 2:
Vector arithmetic

STEP 3

7 ABCD is a square.
$\overrightarrow{AB} = \mathbf{j}$, $\overrightarrow{BC} = \mathbf{k}$

If the ratio of AB : AE is 1 : 2, find:
a $\overrightarrow{BE}$ **b** $\overrightarrow{AF}$

M is the midpoint of EF.
c Find $\overrightarrow{AM}$

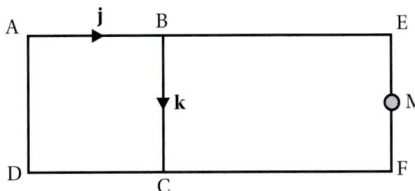

GO TO
Section 3:
Using vectors in geometric proofs

GO TO
Chapter review

Find answers at: cambridge.org/ukschools/gcsemaths-studentbookanswers

Section 1: Vector notation and representation

A **vector** describes movement from one point to another, it has a direction and a magnitude (size).

Vectors can be used to describe many different kinds of movement. For example: **displacement** of a shape following translation, displacement of a boat during its journey, the velocity of an object and the acceleration of an object.

A vector that describes the movement from A to B can be represented by:

- an arrow in a diagram

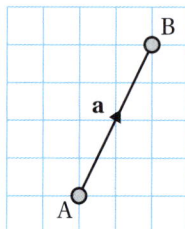

- $\overrightarrow{AB}$ (arrow indicates direction)

- **a** (if handwritten this would be underlined, <u>a</u>)

- a column vector $\begin{pmatrix} x \\ y \end{pmatrix}$

If you were to travel along this vector in the opposite direction, from B to A, you would represent this vector as:

- $\overrightarrow{BA}$

- **−a**

- $\begin{pmatrix} -2 \\ -4 \end{pmatrix}$

Column vectors

In a column vector, **x** represents the **horizontal** movement; **y** represents the **vertical** movement.

	Movement	
	x	**y**
Positive	right	up
Negative	left	down

In the diagram, $\overrightarrow{AB} = \begin{pmatrix} 2 \\ 4 \end{pmatrix}$

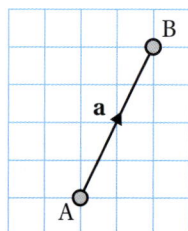

EXERCISE 32A

1 Match up equivalent representations of the vectors.

1 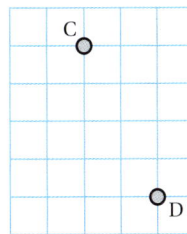	**2** 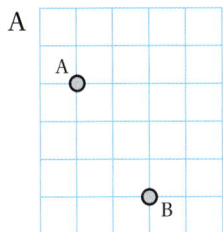	**3** 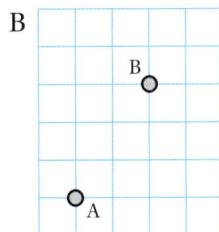	**4** 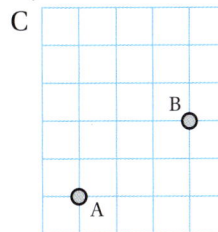	**5** 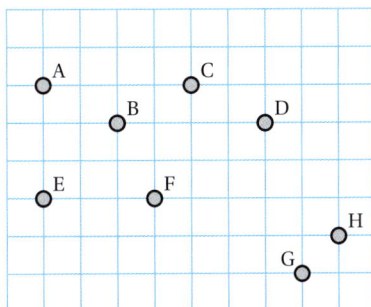
A $\begin{pmatrix} -4 \\ -2 \end{pmatrix}$	**B** $\begin{pmatrix} 4 \\ 2 \end{pmatrix}$	**C** $\begin{pmatrix} 2 \\ -4 \end{pmatrix}$	**D** $\begin{pmatrix} 3 \\ 0 \end{pmatrix}$	**E** $\begin{pmatrix} 0 \\ -4 \end{pmatrix}$
i $\overrightarrow{FE}$	**ii** $\overrightarrow{HG}$	**iii** $\overrightarrow{EF}$	**iv** $\overrightarrow{GH}$	

2 Use the diagram to find the column vector, $\overrightarrow{DC}$.
Choose your answer from these options.

A $\begin{pmatrix} 4 \\ -2 \end{pmatrix}$ B $\begin{pmatrix} 2 \\ -4 \end{pmatrix}$

C $\begin{pmatrix} -4 \\ 2 \end{pmatrix}$ D $\begin{pmatrix} -2 \\ 4 \end{pmatrix}$

3 Which of the following diagrams represents $\overrightarrow{BA} = \begin{pmatrix} -3 \\ -2 \end{pmatrix}$?

A   B   C

4 Use the diagram to answer the following questions.

a Write the column vector for:

  i $\overrightarrow{AB}$ **ii** $\overrightarrow{DC}$ **iii** $\overrightarrow{BC}$

  iv $\overrightarrow{DF}$ **v** $\overrightarrow{HF}$ **vi** $\overrightarrow{BH}$

b What do you notice about $\overrightarrow{AB}$ and $\overrightarrow{DC}$?

c What do you notice about $\overrightarrow{AB}$ and $\overrightarrow{BH}$?

Find answers at: cambridge.org/ukschools/gcsemaths-studentbookanswers

5 Draw a pair of axes going from -8 to 8 in both x- and y-directions.

Plot the point A $(2, -1)$.

Then plot points B, C, D, E, F and G where:

$$\overrightarrow{AB} = \begin{pmatrix} 2 \\ 7 \end{pmatrix} \qquad \overrightarrow{AC} = \begin{pmatrix} -3 \\ 7 \end{pmatrix} \qquad \overrightarrow{AD} = \begin{pmatrix} -6 \\ 3 \end{pmatrix}$$

$$\overrightarrow{AE} = \begin{pmatrix} 5 \\ 3 \end{pmatrix} \qquad \overrightarrow{AF} = \begin{pmatrix} -3 \\ -1 \end{pmatrix} \qquad \overrightarrow{AG} = \begin{pmatrix} 2 \\ -1 \end{pmatrix}$$

6 **a** A is the point with coordinates $(3, -4)$.

B is the point with coordinates $(-1, 2)$.

Find the column vector that describes the movement from A to B.

b Give the coordinates of two more points E and F where the vector from E to F is the same as $\overrightarrow{AB}$.

7 **a** K is the point with coordinates $(-2, -1)$.

L is the point with coordinates $(-8, 9)$.

Find the column vector that describes the movement from K to L.

b Use your answer to find the coordinates of the midpoint of KL.

8 These vectors describe how to move between points A, B, C and D.

$$\overrightarrow{AB} = \begin{pmatrix} 2 \\ 1 \end{pmatrix} \qquad \overrightarrow{BC} = \begin{pmatrix} 1 \\ 0 \end{pmatrix} \qquad \overrightarrow{DA} = \begin{pmatrix} -1 \\ 2 \end{pmatrix}$$

Draw a diagram showing how the points are positioned to form the quadrilateral ABCD.

9 In a game of chess, different pieces move in different ways.

- A king can move one square in any direction (including diagonals).
- A bishop can move any number of squares diagonally.
- A knight moves two squares horizontally and one square vertically or two squares vertically and one horizontally.

A chessboard is eight squares wide and eight squares long.

What vectors can the following pieces move?

a Bishop   **b** King   **c** Knight

10 How would you find the length (magnitude) of a vector?

How could you describe its direction?

Use these diagrams, and your knowledge of Pythagoras' theorem and trigonometry, to help design a method.

Vector $\begin{pmatrix} 2 \\ -4 \end{pmatrix}$ Vector $\begin{pmatrix} 3 \\ 5 \end{pmatrix}$

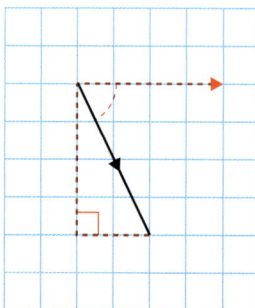

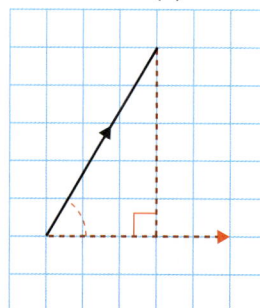

> **Tip**
>
> You will need to think algebraically for part **a** of question 9.

> **Tip**
>
> See Chapter 37 on Pythagoras' theorem and Chapter 38 on trigonometry if you need a reminder.

Section 2: Vector arithmetic

Addition and subtraction

The diagram shows $\overrightarrow{AB} = \begin{pmatrix} 2 \\ 4 \end{pmatrix}$, $\overrightarrow{BC} = \begin{pmatrix} 4 \\ -2 \end{pmatrix}$, and $\overrightarrow{AC} = \begin{pmatrix} 6 \\ 2 \end{pmatrix}$

Moving from A to B and then from B to C is the same as moving directly from A to C. In other words, you can take a 'shortcut' from A to C by adding together $\overrightarrow{AB}$ and $\overrightarrow{BC}$.

$\overrightarrow{AC}$ is known as the **resultant** of $\overrightarrow{AB}$ and $\overrightarrow{BC}$.

$$\overrightarrow{AB} + \overrightarrow{BC} = \overrightarrow{AC}$$

$$\begin{pmatrix} 2 \\ 4 \end{pmatrix} + \begin{pmatrix} 4 \\ -2 \end{pmatrix} = \begin{pmatrix} 6 \\ 2 \end{pmatrix}$$

The diagram shows $\overrightarrow{AB}$ and $\overrightarrow{CB}$.

To find $\overrightarrow{AC}$ you need to travel along $\overrightarrow{CB}$ in the opposite direction.

So, **subtract** $\overrightarrow{CB}$.

$$\overrightarrow{AB} - \overrightarrow{CB} = \overrightarrow{AC}$$

$$\begin{pmatrix} -4 \\ 1 \end{pmatrix} - \begin{pmatrix} 2 \\ 5 \end{pmatrix} = \begin{pmatrix} -4-2 \\ 1-5 \end{pmatrix} = \begin{pmatrix} -6 \\ -4 \end{pmatrix}$$

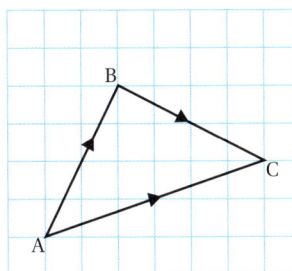

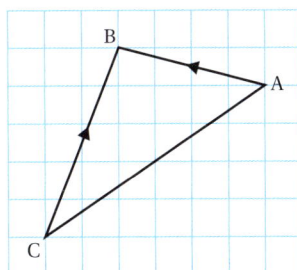

Multiplying by a scalar

Multiplying a vector by a **scalar** results in repeated addition.

This is the same as multiplying the x-component by the scalar, k, and the y-component by the same scalar, k.

$$\overrightarrow{AB} = \begin{pmatrix} 4 \\ -1 \end{pmatrix} \text{ and } \overrightarrow{CD} = \begin{pmatrix} 12 \\ -3 \end{pmatrix}$$

$$\overrightarrow{CD} = 3\overrightarrow{AB}$$

Key vocabulary

scalar: a numerical quantity (it has no direction)

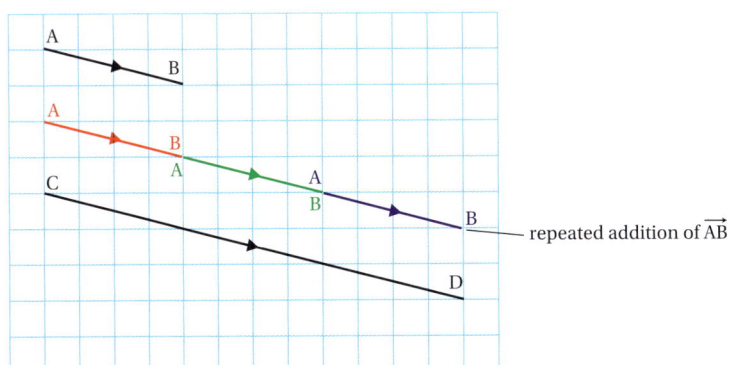

$$3 \times \begin{pmatrix} 4 \\ -1 \end{pmatrix} = \begin{pmatrix} 4 \\ -1 \end{pmatrix} + \begin{pmatrix} 4 \\ -1 \end{pmatrix} + \begin{pmatrix} 4 \\ -1 \end{pmatrix}$$ — repeated addition

$$= \begin{pmatrix} 3 \times 4 \\ 3 \times -1 \end{pmatrix}$$ — multiplying the x-component by the scalar k

multiplying the y-component by the scalar k

$$= \begin{pmatrix} 12 \\ -3 \end{pmatrix}$$

Multiplying a vector by a scalar, k, results in a **parallel vector** with a magnitude multiplied by k.

Vectors are parallel if one is a multiple of the other.

Key vocabulary

parallel vectors: occur when one vector is a multiple of the other. When drawn next to each other they are parallel lines, even if they go in opposite directions.

Find answers at: cambridge.org/ukschools/gcsemaths-studentbookanswers

WORK IT OUT 32.1

Which of the following vectors are parallel?

$$\mathbf{a} = \begin{pmatrix} 3 \\ -1 \end{pmatrix} \qquad \mathbf{b} = \begin{pmatrix} 4 \\ -3 \end{pmatrix} \qquad \mathbf{c} = \begin{pmatrix} 9 \\ -3 \end{pmatrix} \qquad \mathbf{d} = \begin{pmatrix} 6 \\ 2 \end{pmatrix} \qquad \mathbf{e} = \begin{pmatrix} -6 \\ 2 \end{pmatrix}$$

Option A	Option B	Option C
Vectors **a** and **c**	Vectors **d** and **e**	Vectors **a**, **c** and **e**

EXERCISE 32B

1 Which pair of the following four vectors are parallel? Choose your answer from the options below.

$$\mathbf{p} = \begin{pmatrix} -1 \\ 2 \end{pmatrix} \qquad \mathbf{q} = \begin{pmatrix} -2 \\ -4 \end{pmatrix} \qquad \mathbf{r} = \begin{pmatrix} 4 \\ 8 \end{pmatrix} \qquad \mathbf{s} = \begin{pmatrix} 0 \\ 3 \end{pmatrix}$$

   A **p** and **q**   B **r** and **s**   C **p** and **s**   D **q** and **r**

2 $$\mathbf{p} = \begin{pmatrix} -3 \\ 2 \end{pmatrix} \qquad \mathbf{q} = \begin{pmatrix} 5 \\ -1 \end{pmatrix} \qquad \mathbf{r} = \begin{pmatrix} -3 \\ -2 \end{pmatrix} \qquad \mathbf{s} = \begin{pmatrix} 4 \\ -7 \end{pmatrix}$$

  a Write each of these as a single vector.

     i **p** + **q**   **ii** **s** − **r**   **iii** 4**p**

     iv −3**s**   **v** **p** + **q** + **r**   **vi** 2**p** + **q** − 2**s**

  b Which of the results from parts **i** to **vi** are parallel to the vector $\begin{pmatrix} 3 \\ -2 \end{pmatrix}$?

3 Give three vectors parallel to $\begin{pmatrix} 2 \\ -3 \end{pmatrix}$.

4 Find the values of x, y, z and t in each of the following vector calculations.

  a $\begin{pmatrix} x \\ 3 \end{pmatrix} + \begin{pmatrix} 5 \\ y \end{pmatrix} = \begin{pmatrix} 9 \\ 3 \end{pmatrix}$ **b** $\begin{pmatrix} 10 \\ y \end{pmatrix} - \begin{pmatrix} x \\ -3 \end{pmatrix} = \begin{pmatrix} -2 \\ 8 \end{pmatrix}$ **c** $\begin{pmatrix} x \\ -3 \end{pmatrix} + \begin{pmatrix} -6 \\ y \end{pmatrix} = \begin{pmatrix} 11 \\ -8 \end{pmatrix}$

  d $z\begin{pmatrix} x \\ 12 \end{pmatrix} = \begin{pmatrix} 7 \\ -24 \end{pmatrix}$ **e** $z\begin{pmatrix} -12 \\ y \end{pmatrix} = \begin{pmatrix} 3 \\ -8 \end{pmatrix}$ **f** $\begin{pmatrix} 2 \\ -4 \end{pmatrix} + z\begin{pmatrix} 5 \\ y \end{pmatrix} = \begin{pmatrix} 17 \\ 14 \end{pmatrix}$

  g $\begin{pmatrix} x \\ -4 \end{pmatrix} - z\begin{pmatrix} -5 \\ -3 \end{pmatrix} = \begin{pmatrix} 20 \\ 5 \end{pmatrix}$ **h** $z\begin{pmatrix} 3 \\ 4 \end{pmatrix} + t\begin{pmatrix} 2 \\ -2 \end{pmatrix} = \begin{pmatrix} 18 \\ 10 \end{pmatrix}$

5 In the diagram, $\overrightarrow{AB} = \begin{pmatrix} 20 \\ 16 \end{pmatrix}$

The ratio of AC : CB is 1 : 3

  a Find $\overrightarrow{AC}$.

  b Find $\overrightarrow{BC}$.

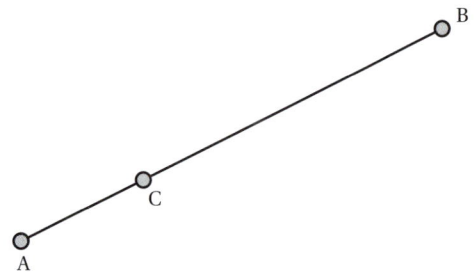

> **Tip**
>
> You can multiply a vector by a fractional scalar if you need to divide. If you need a reminder on fractions see Chapter 5; if you need a reminder of how to calculate ratios, see Chapter 27.

6 The four vertices of a quadrilateral are labelled E, F, G and H.

The following vectors describe how to move between some of the vertices.

$$\overrightarrow{EF} = \begin{pmatrix} 3 \\ -1 \end{pmatrix} \qquad \overrightarrow{HG} = \begin{pmatrix} 6 \\ -2 \end{pmatrix} \qquad \overrightarrow{EH} = \begin{pmatrix} 0 \\ 1 \end{pmatrix}$$

  a What can you say about sides EF and HG?

  b Predict what kind of quadrilateral EFGH is.

  c Draw the quadrilateral and find $\overrightarrow{GF}$.

7 ABCD is a quadrilateral.

$\overrightarrow{AB} = \overrightarrow{DC}$ and $\overrightarrow{DA} = \overrightarrow{CB}$

What kind of quadrilateral is ABCD? How do you know this?

Section 3: Using vectors in geometric proofs

Vectors can be used to prove geometric results.

You can use them to:

- identify parallel lines
- find midpoints
- share lines in a given ratio.

For example, in this triangle $\overrightarrow{AB} = -\mathbf{a} + \mathbf{b}$
$$= \mathbf{b} - \mathbf{a}$$

M is the midpoint of AB.

The ratio of ON : NA is 1 : 2

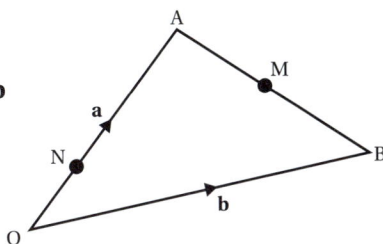

- You can use what you know about vectors to find $\overrightarrow{AM}$.

  You know that AM is half of AB, so it follows that $\overrightarrow{AM}$ is half of the journey from A to B, so
  $$\overrightarrow{AM} = \tfrac{1}{2}(\mathbf{b} - \mathbf{a})$$

- You can use what you know about the effect of scalars on vectors to calculate $\overrightarrow{ON}$.

  You know that the ratio of ON : NA is 1 : 2

  So, you know that the point N is such that $2\overrightarrow{ON} = \overrightarrow{NA}$, so
  $$\overrightarrow{ON} = \tfrac{1}{3}\mathbf{a}$$

WORKED EXAMPLE 1

OACB is a parallelogram.

M is the midpoint of AC, and N is the midpoint of BC.

Prove that $\overrightarrow{MN}$ is parallel to $\overrightarrow{AB}$.

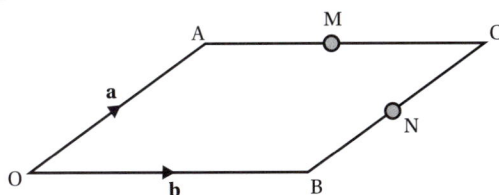

$\overrightarrow{AB} = \mathbf{b} - \mathbf{a}$

$\overrightarrow{MN} = \overrightarrow{MA} + \overrightarrow{AO} + \overrightarrow{OB} + \overrightarrow{BN}$

$\quad = -\tfrac{1}{2}\mathbf{b} - \mathbf{a} + \mathbf{b} + \tfrac{1}{2}\mathbf{a}$

$\quad = \tfrac{1}{2}(\mathbf{b} - \mathbf{a})$

Since $\overrightarrow{MN}$ is a multiple of $\overrightarrow{AB}$, they are parallel.

Tip

If you're struggling with a question, highlight sides that are labelled with vectors or that are parallel to any given vectors. Then identify the journey between your two points by using these highlighted lines.

Find answers at: cambridge.org/ukschools/gcsemaths-studentbookanswers

WORKED EXAMPLE 2

In the regular hexagon shown, $\overrightarrow{EF} = \mathbf{e}$ and $\overrightarrow{JI} = \mathbf{j}$.

It is possible to move between any two vertices of the regular hexagon using combinations of vectors $\mathbf{e}$ and $\mathbf{j}$.

Find the vector that describes each of the following:

a $\overrightarrow{EG}$ **b** $\overrightarrow{HJ}$ **c** $\overrightarrow{EJ}$

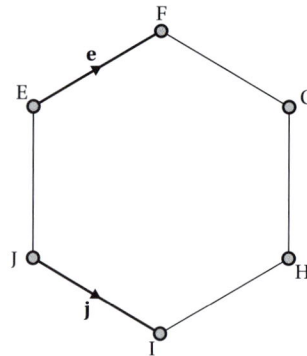

> **Tip**
>
> Opposite sides of a regular hexagon are parallel.

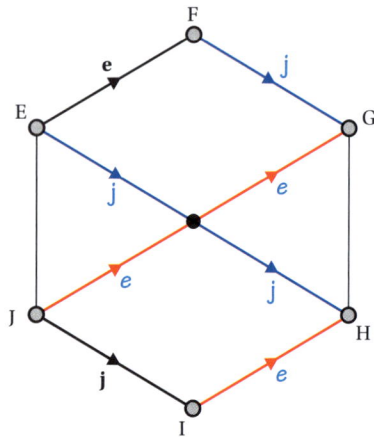

> Drawing a few additional lines parallel to the vectors given can help you to see a solution.
>
> Write these in terms of $\mathbf{e}$ and $\mathbf{j}$.

a $\overrightarrow{EG} = \overrightarrow{EF} + \overrightarrow{FG}$

> Using addition of vectors, $\overrightarrow{EG}$ is the resultant vector.

$\overrightarrow{FG} = \mathbf{j}$
$\overrightarrow{EG} = \mathbf{e} + \mathbf{j}$

> Using the properties of a regular hexagon, the line FG is parallel to JI. Parallel vectors are a multiple of each other, in this case the scalar is 1.

b $\overrightarrow{HJ} = \overrightarrow{HI} + \overrightarrow{IJ}$

> Using addition of vectors, $\overrightarrow{HJ}$ is the resultant vector.

$\overrightarrow{HI} = -\mathbf{e}$

> Using the properties of a regular hexagon, the line IH is parallel to EF. Parallel vectors are a multiple of each other, in this case the scalar is 1. We are travelling from H to I, in the opposite direction of $\mathbf{e}$, so need the negative of $\mathbf{e}$.

$\overrightarrow{HJ} = \mathbf{e} - \mathbf{j}$

> $\overrightarrow{IJ}$ is the opposite direction of $\overrightarrow{JI}$.

c $\overrightarrow{EJ} = \overrightarrow{EH} + \overrightarrow{HI} + \overrightarrow{IJ}$

> Using addition of vectors, $\overrightarrow{EJ}$ is the resultant vector

$\overrightarrow{EH} = 2\mathbf{j}$

> Using the helpful additional lines, EH is parallel to IJ and twice its length. It is moving in the same direction.

$\overrightarrow{HI} = -\mathbf{e}$

> $\overrightarrow{HI}$ is the opposite direction to $\overrightarrow{IH}$.

$\overrightarrow{IJ} = -\mathbf{j}$

> $\overrightarrow{IJ}$ is the opposite direction to $\overrightarrow{JI}$.

$\overrightarrow{EH} = 2\mathbf{j} - \mathbf{e} - \mathbf{j} = \mathbf{j} - \mathbf{e}$

EXERCISE 32C

1 In triangle OEF, $\overrightarrow{OE} = \mathbf{e}$ and $\overrightarrow{OF} = \mathbf{f}$.

The ratio of OP to PF is 4 : 3

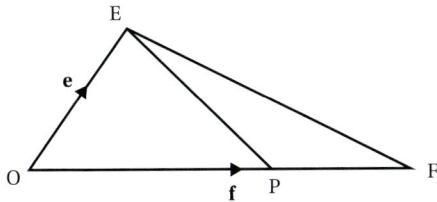

What is the vector from P to E?

A $\mathbf{e} - \mathbf{f}$ 　　　 B $\mathbf{e} - \frac{4}{3}\mathbf{f}$ 　　　 C $\mathbf{e} - \frac{3}{4}\mathbf{f}$ 　　　 D $\mathbf{e} - \frac{4}{7}\mathbf{f}$

2 In the diagram, $\overrightarrow{AC} = \begin{pmatrix} 10 \\ 2 \end{pmatrix}$ and $\overrightarrow{AB} = \begin{pmatrix} 8 \\ 14 \end{pmatrix}$ and M is the midpoint of BC.

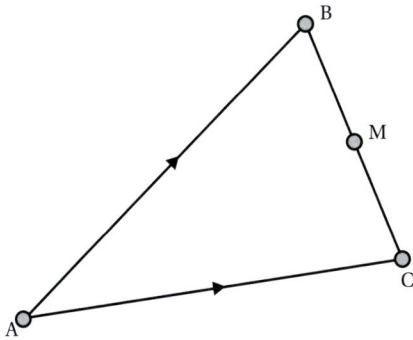

> **Tip**
>
> Remember that the line CM is half the length of the line CB. What does this mean about the journey from C to M?

Find:

a $\overrightarrow{CA}$ 　　　 **b** $\overrightarrow{CA} + \overrightarrow{AB}$ 　　　 **c** $\overrightarrow{CM}$

3 Two triangles have vertices ABC and DEF:

A(0,0), B(3,2), C(2, 5)

D(1,1), E(7,5), F(5,11)

a Compare the vectors:

i $\overrightarrow{AB}$ and $\overrightarrow{DE}$

ii $\overrightarrow{AC}$ and $\overrightarrow{DF}$

b What does this tell you about the triangles ABC and DEF?

4 MNOP is a square.

Find the following vectors. Give reasons for your answers.

a $\overrightarrow{NO}$ 　　　　　　 **b** $\overrightarrow{OP}$

c $\overrightarrow{MO}$ 　　　　　　 **d** $\overrightarrow{PN}$

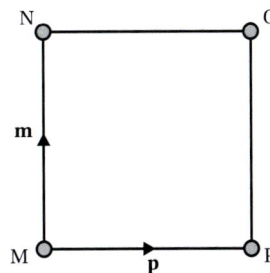

5 The vector from A to B is $\begin{pmatrix} 1 \\ 3 \end{pmatrix}$

The vector joining C to D is parallel to $\overrightarrow{AB}$.

D is three times the distance from C as B is from A.

What is the vector from C to D? Choose your answer from these options.

A $\begin{pmatrix} 4 \\ 6 \end{pmatrix}$ 　　　　 B $\begin{pmatrix} -1 \\ -3 \end{pmatrix}$ 　　　　 C $\begin{pmatrix} 1 \\ 9 \end{pmatrix}$ 　　　　 D $\begin{pmatrix} 3 \\ 9 \end{pmatrix}$

Find answers at: cambridge.org/ukschools/gcsemaths-studentbookanswers

6 ABCD is a parallelogram.

M is the midpoint of side BC, N the midpoint of CD.

$\overrightarrow{AB} = \mathbf{p}$ and $\overrightarrow{BM} = \mathbf{q}$

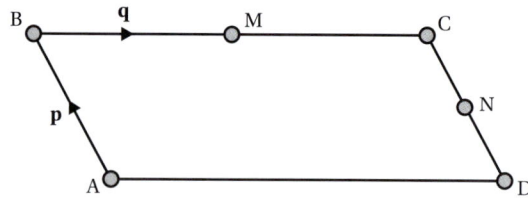

a Find the vectors. Explain your answers.

i $\overrightarrow{AC}$ **ii** $\overrightarrow{DB}$ **c** $\overrightarrow{MD}$

b Show that $\overrightarrow{NM}$ is parallel to $\overrightarrow{DB}$.

Tip

Congruent shapes are exactly the same shape and size. You will learn more about congruency in Chapter 36.

7 The diagram shows four congruent triangles forming a tessellating pattern, and vectors **m** and **n**.

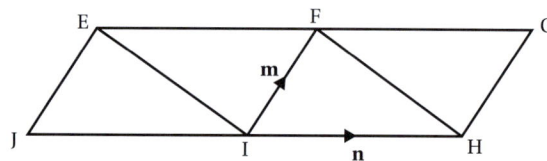

Find the vectors:

a $\overrightarrow{IJ}$ **b** $\overrightarrow{EJ}$ **c** $\overrightarrow{JF}$ **d** $\overrightarrow{EH}$

8 EFG is an equilateral triangle.

Points H, I and J are the midpoints of each side.

$\overrightarrow{EF} = \mathbf{e}$ and $\overrightarrow{EG} = \mathbf{g}$

a Find the vectors

i $\overrightarrow{EH}$ **ii** $\overrightarrow{JE}$ **iii** $\overrightarrow{FG}$

iv $\overrightarrow{HI}$ **v** $\overrightarrow{IJ}$

b What can you say about triangle HIJ?

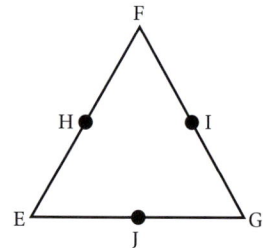

9 EFG is an equilateral triangle.

Points H and I are the midpoints of sides EF and FG.

JI is a straight line with midpoint H.

$\overrightarrow{EF} = \mathbf{e}$ and $\overrightarrow{EG} = \mathbf{g}$

Find the vectors:

a $\overrightarrow{FH}$ **b** $\overrightarrow{IG}$ **c** $\overrightarrow{HI}$ **d** $\overrightarrow{JI}$ **e** $\overrightarrow{JE}$

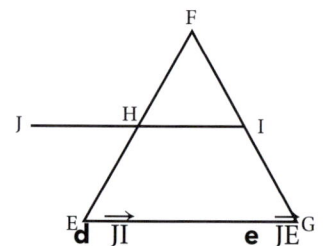

10 In the diagram, V is the midpoint of TR and W is the midpoint of RS.

The ratio of TU : US is 1 : 4

$\overrightarrow{SR} = \mathbf{R}$ and $\overrightarrow{TU} = \mathbf{T}$

Find the vectors:

a $\overrightarrow{TS}$ **b** $\overrightarrow{UR}$ **c** $\overrightarrow{VR}$ **d** $\overrightarrow{WV}$

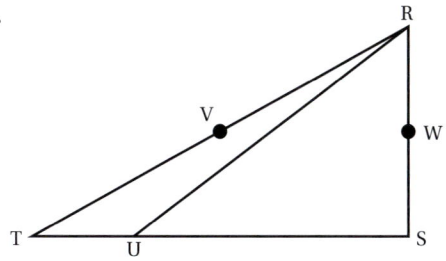

11 In the diagram, the ratio of PM : MQ is 3 : 1

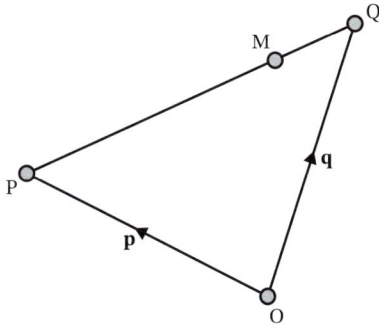

a Find $\overrightarrow{PQ}$ **b** Find $\overrightarrow{PM}$ **c** Show $\overrightarrow{OM} = \frac{1}{4}(3\mathbf{q} + \mathbf{p})$

12 A river runs from east to west at 3 m every second.

The river is 12 m wide.

James can swim at 1.5 m every second.

He sets off to cross the river.

a How far off course is he when he reaches the other river bank?

b How far does he actually swim?

Checklist of learning and understanding

Notation

- Vectors can be written in a variety of ways: $\overrightarrow{AB}$, $\mathbf{a}$, $\begin{pmatrix} 1 \\ 2 \end{pmatrix}$

Addition and subtraction

- To add or subtract vectors simply add or subtract the x- and y-components.

$$\begin{pmatrix} 3 \\ 2 \end{pmatrix} + \begin{pmatrix} 2 \\ -4 \end{pmatrix} = \begin{pmatrix} 5 \\ -2 \end{pmatrix} \qquad \begin{pmatrix} -1 \\ 4 \end{pmatrix} - \begin{pmatrix} 5 \\ -6 \end{pmatrix} = \begin{pmatrix} -6 \\ 10 \end{pmatrix}$$

Multiplication by a scalar

- To multiply by a scalar you can use repeated addition; or multiply the x-component by the scalar and the y-component by the scalar.

$$3\begin{pmatrix} -2 \\ 1 \end{pmatrix} = \begin{pmatrix} -2 \\ 1 \end{pmatrix} + \begin{pmatrix} -2 \\ 1 \end{pmatrix} + \begin{pmatrix} -2 \\ 1 \end{pmatrix} = \begin{pmatrix} -6 \\ 3 \end{pmatrix}$$

$$3\begin{pmatrix} -2 \\ 1 \end{pmatrix} = \begin{pmatrix} -6 \\ 3 \end{pmatrix}$$

- Multiplying a vector by a scalar quantity produces a parallel vector; you can identify that vectors are parallel if one vector is a multiple of the other. Parallel vectors can be part of the same line and described using a ratio.

Using vectors in geometric proofs

- You can use vectors to identify parallel lines, find midpoints and share lines in a given ratio.

For additional questions on the topics in this chapter, visit GCSE Mathematics Online.

Chapter review

1 What is the difference between coordinate $(-2, 3)$ and vector $\begin{pmatrix} -2 \\ 3 \end{pmatrix}$?

2 Match the parallel vectors.

$$\mathbf{a} = \begin{pmatrix} -6 \\ 2 \end{pmatrix} \qquad \mathbf{b} = \begin{pmatrix} 1 \\ 3 \end{pmatrix} \qquad \mathbf{c} = \begin{pmatrix} 3 \\ -1 \end{pmatrix} \qquad \mathbf{d} = \begin{pmatrix} 7 \\ 21 \end{pmatrix}$$

$$\mathbf{e} = \begin{pmatrix} -2 \\ 4 \end{pmatrix} \qquad \mathbf{f} = \begin{pmatrix} -6 \\ 12 \end{pmatrix} \qquad \mathbf{f} = \begin{pmatrix} -1 \\ 2 \end{pmatrix}$$

3 Calculate.

a $\begin{pmatrix} 1 \\ -2 \end{pmatrix} + \begin{pmatrix} -2 \\ -1 \end{pmatrix}$
b $\begin{pmatrix} 0 \\ -3 \end{pmatrix} - \begin{pmatrix} -2 \\ 4 \end{pmatrix}$
c $-3\begin{pmatrix} 2 \\ -1 \end{pmatrix}$

4 In triangle OEF, N is the mid-point of EF and M the mid-point of ON.

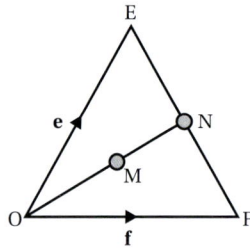

$$ON = \mathbf{e} + \frac{1}{2}(-\mathbf{e} + \mathbf{f})$$

What is the vector from E to M?

A $-\frac{3}{4}\mathbf{e} + \frac{1}{4}\mathbf{f}$
B $\mathbf{e} + \mathbf{f}$
C $\frac{1}{2}(\mathbf{f} - \mathbf{e})$
D $\frac{1}{4}(\mathbf{f} - \mathbf{e})$

5 EFG is a straight line.

EF : FG = 2 : 3

Find:

a $\overrightarrow{EG}$

b $\overrightarrow{FG}$

c $\overrightarrow{OF}$

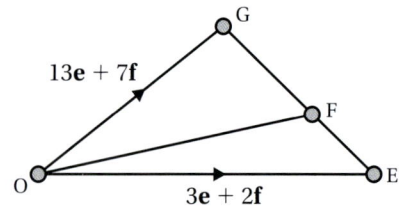

6 The points G and H lie on line EF.

$$\overrightarrow{EF} = 12\mathbf{e} - 18\mathbf{f}$$

The ratio of EG : GH : HF is 1 : 3 : 2

a Draw a sketch of this situation.

b Find the vectors:

i $\overrightarrow{GH}$
ii $\overrightarrow{HE}$

33 Transformations in a plane

In this chapter you will learn how to …

- carry out rotations, reflections and translations.
- identify and describe rotations, reflections and translations.
- describe translations using column vectors.
- perform multiple transformations on a shape and describe the results.

For more resources relating to this chapter, visit GCSE Mathematics Online.

Using mathematics: real-life applications

You can see examples of reflections, rotations, and translations all around you. Patterns in wallpaper and fabric are often translations, images reflected in water are reflections and the blades of a wind turbine are a good example of rotation.

Tip

Tracing paper is very useful for work with transformations. Don't be afraid to ask for it in an exam.

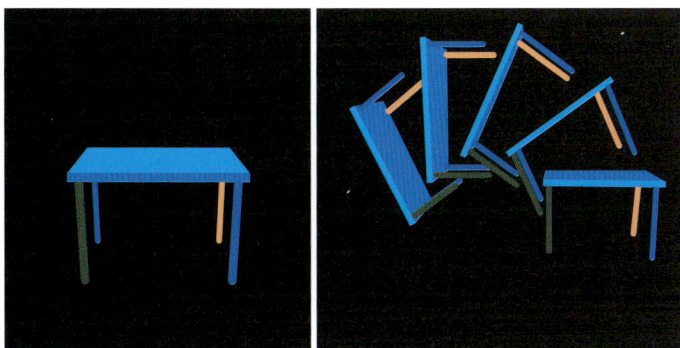

"I use transformations all the time when I program computer graphics. Transformations allow me to position objects, shape them and change the view I have of them. I can even change the type of perspective that is used to show something." *(Computer programmer)*

Before you start …

KS3 Ch 9	You need to know what angles of 90°, 180° and 270° look like and also the directions clockwise and anticlockwise.	**1** How many degrees is each angle? State whether each arrow is showing clockwise or anticlockwise movement. **a** **b** **c**
Ch 29	You need to know how to plot straight-line graphs in the form $x = a$, $y = a$ and $y = x$.	**2** Find the equation of each of these lines. **a** **b** **c** **d**
Ch 32	You need to know what a vector is and how they describe movement.	**3** **a** What is the difference between the coordinate (3, 2) and the vector $\binom{3}{2}$? **b** What is the difference between the vectors $\binom{-1}{3}$ and $\binom{3}{1}$?

Find answers at: cambridge.org/ukschools/gcsemaths-studentbookanswers

Assess your starting point using the Launchpad

STEP 1

1 Reflect the given shape in the mirror line.

2 What is the equation of the mirror line?

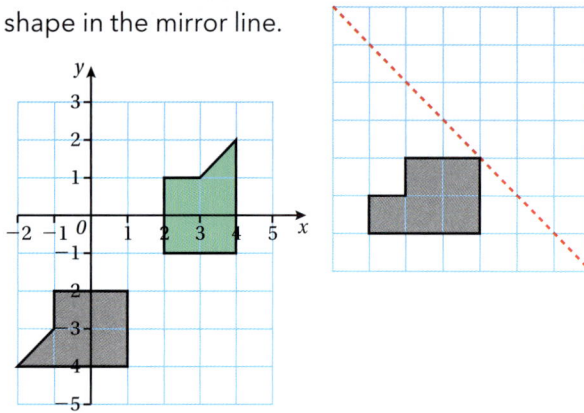

GO TO
Section 1:
Reflections

STEP 2

3 Translate the shape through the vector $\begin{pmatrix} 3 \\ 2 \end{pmatrix}$

4 Describe the translation of this object to its image.

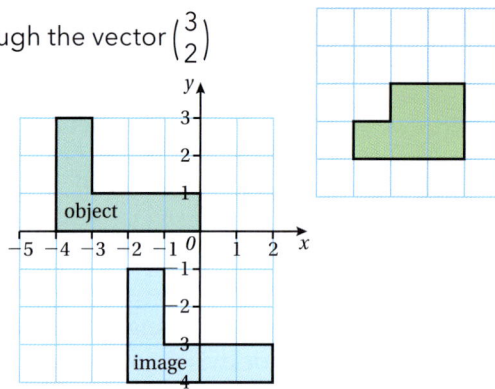

GO TO
Section 2:
Translations

STEP 3

5 Rotate the shape 90° anticlockwise around (1, 1).

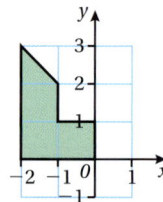

GO TO
Section 3:
Rotations
Section 4:
Combined transformations

GO TO

Chapter review

Section 1: Reflections

A transformation is a change in the position of a point, line or shape.

When you transform a shape you change its position or its size.

The original point, line or shape is called the **object**, for example, triangle ABC.

The transformation is called the **image**. The symbol ′ is used to label the image. For example, the image of a triangle with vertices ABC is a triangle with vertices A′B′C′.

Reflection, rotation and transformation change the position of an object, but not its size.

Under these three transformations an object and its image will be **congruent**.

You can see the reflection of clouds and trees in the photograph.

If you draw a line horizontally across the centre of the image and fold it, the top half will fit exactly on to the bottom half.

The fold line is called a **mirror line**.

Mathematically, when a shape is reflected it is reversed over a mirror line to give its image.

EXERCISE 33A

1 The shape below is reflected in the line $y = -x$.

Which diagram shows the correct reflection?

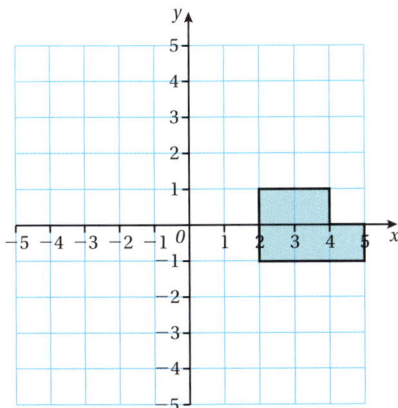

A
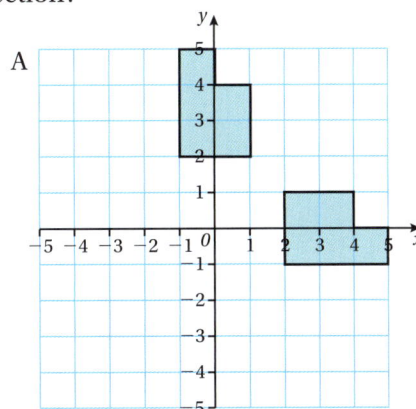

B
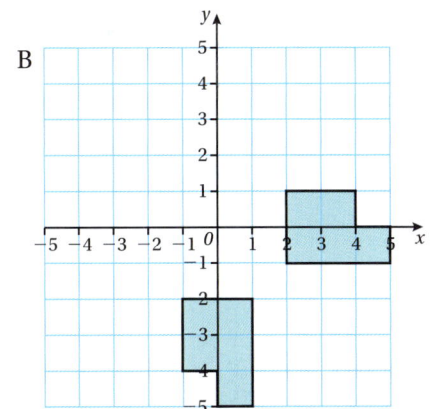

C
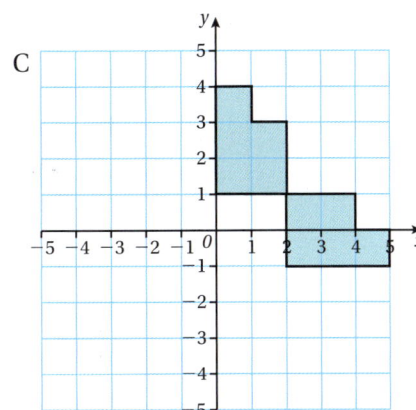

D
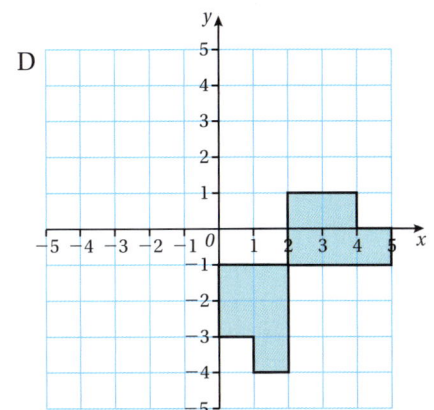

2 Copy the grid. Reflect the triangle in the line $x = 1$.

Then reflect both the triangle and the resultant image in the line $y = -1$.

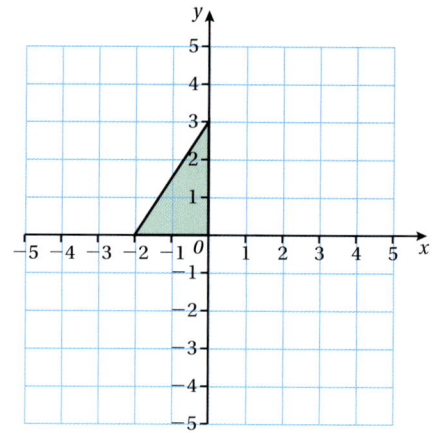

3 Copy each grid and reflect this shape in the line $y = x$.

Then reflect the shape and the resultant image in the line $y = 1 - x$.

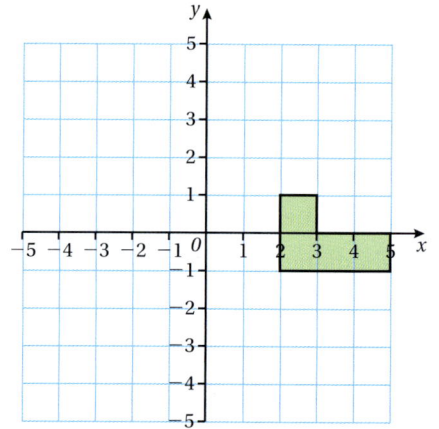

4 Copy the grid. Carry out the ten reflections listed below to reveal the picture.

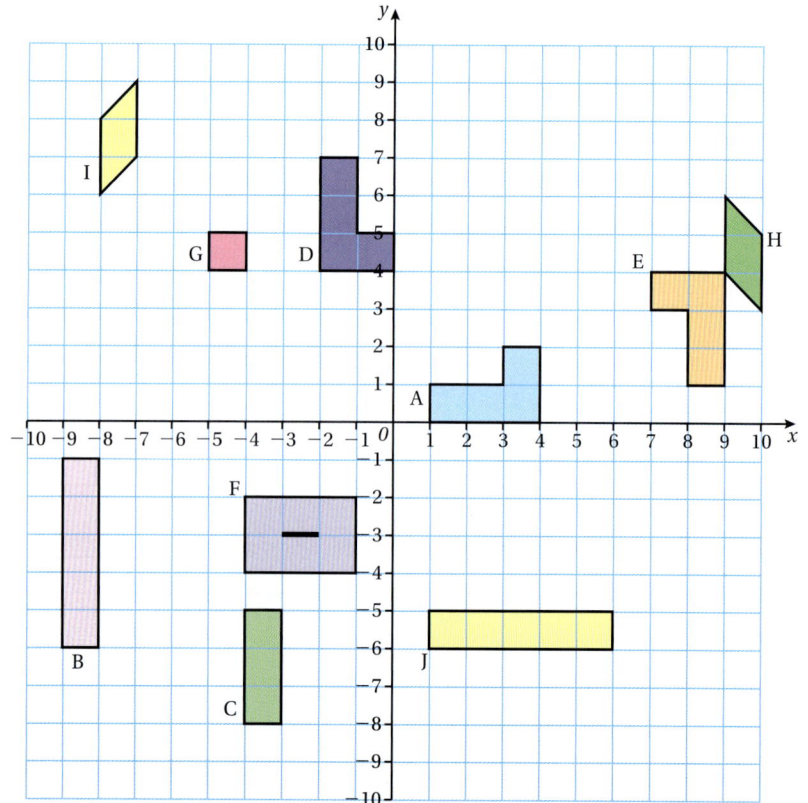

a Shape A in the line $y = x$

b Shape B in the x-axis

c Shape C in the line $y = -2$

d Shape D in the line $y = 4$

e Shape E in the line $x = 7$

f Shape F in the line $y = -x$

g Shape G in the line $x = -4$

h Shape H in the line $x = 1.5$

i Shape I in the line $y = 6$

j Shape J in the line $y = x$

5 Draw a pair of axes going from -10 to 10 in both directions.

Draw two line segments, the first with ends at $(0, 0)$ and $(1, 1)$, and the second with ends at $(1, 1)$ and $(2, 1)$.

Show how this shape can be made into:

a a hexagon with two successive reflections.

b an octagon with three successive reflections.

6 Make up your own reflection puzzle for another student to solve.

In a reflection, the object and the image are the same distance from the mirror line.

If you join a pair of corresponding points the line formed is cut in half by the mirror line and they meet at 90°.

The mirror line is the **perpendicular bisector** of the line joining any pair of corresponding points.

Key vocabulary

perpendicular bisector: a line perpendicular to another that also cuts it in half

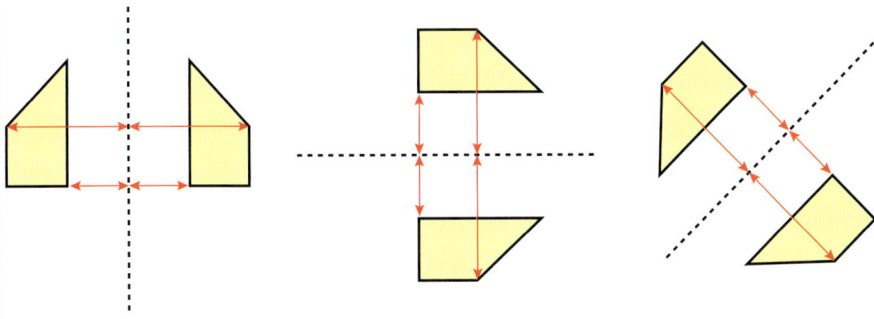

Tip

You can turn your book around so that diagonal mirror lines look vertical or horizontal. Often our brains find this easier than working diagonally.

WORK IT OUT 33.1

This Z shape is reflected in the line $y = -1$. What is its image?

Which one of these answers is correct?

What has gone wrong in each of the others?

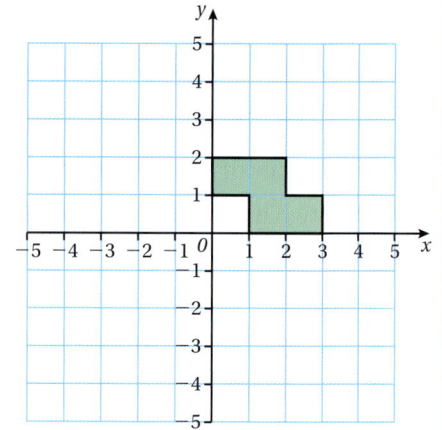

Option A	Option B	Option C
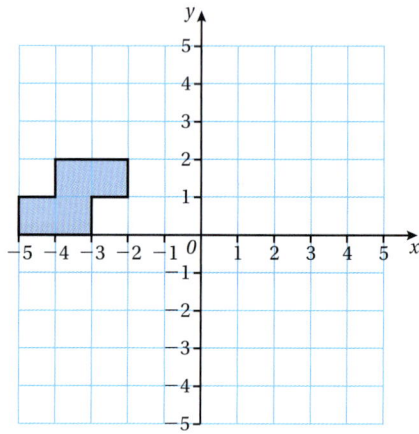	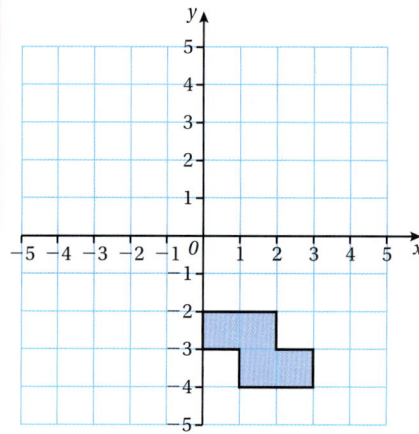	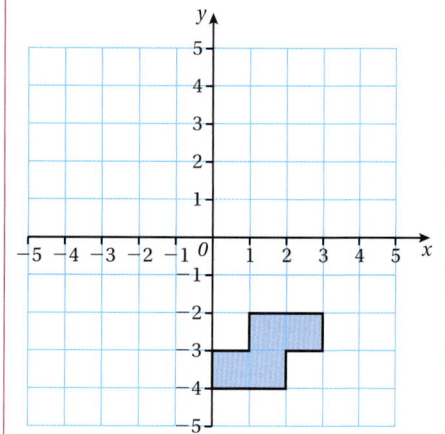

Describing reflections

You need to be able to draw a mirror line on a diagram.

When describing reflections, you must give the equation of the mirror line when the reflection is shown on a coordinate grid.

The mirror line is the perpendicular bisector of two corresponding points in a reflection.

So if you can't 'spot' a mirror line, you can join two corresponding points and construct the perpendicular bisector to find it.

Tip

To check a reflection, trace the **object**, the **image** and the mirror line. If you fold the tracing paper along the mirror line, the shapes should match up exactly.

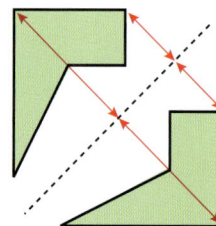

EXERCISE 33B

1 What is the equation of the mirror line in the reflection below?

Choose from the following options.

A $x = -2$ B $x = 2$ C $y = -2$ D $y = 2$

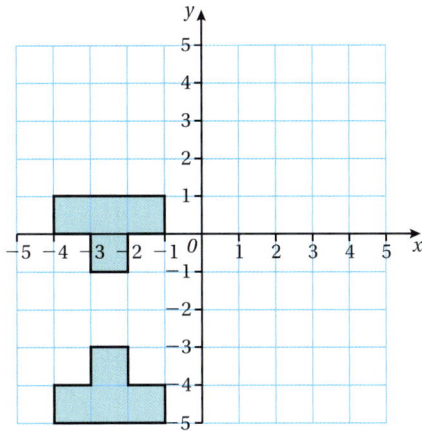

2 Find the equation of the mirror line in each reflection.

a

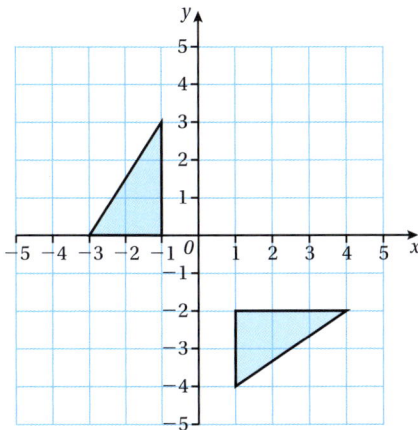

b

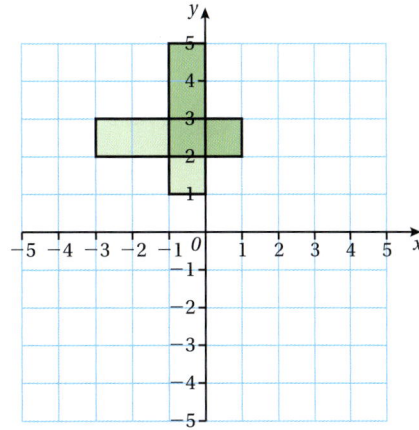

c

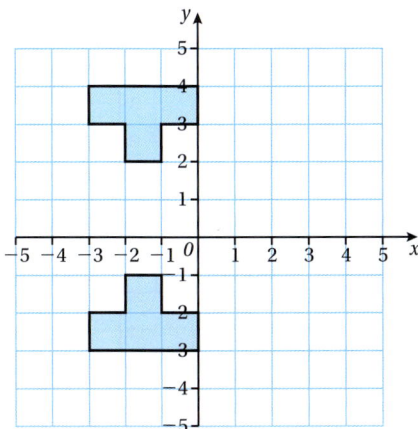

d

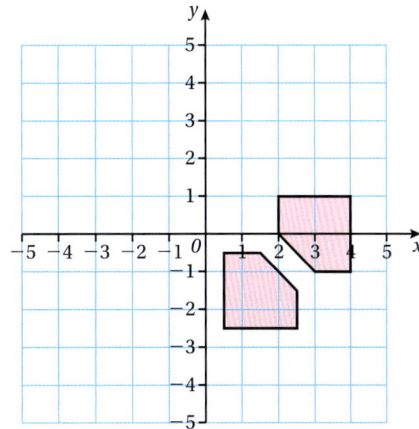

Find answers at: cambridge.org/ukschools/gcsemaths-studentbookanswers

3 **a** Fully describe each of the following reflections.

    i Shape A to shape E

    ii Shape C to shape G

    iii Shape G to shape E

    iv Shape B to shape F

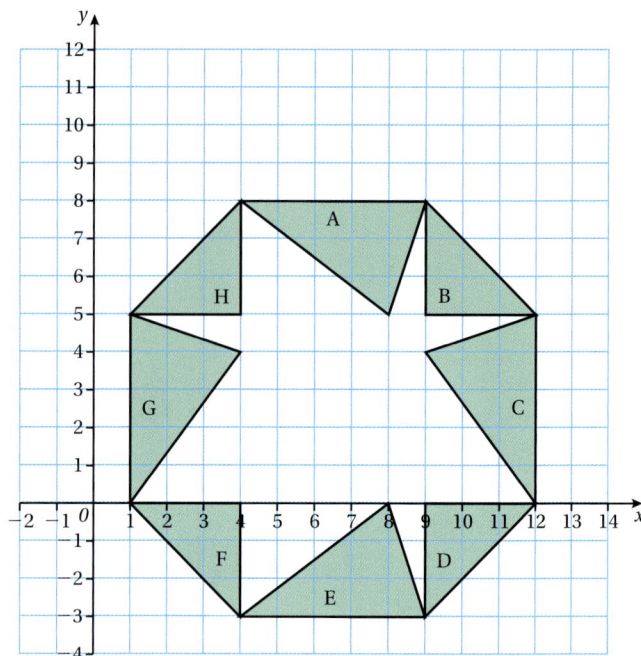

b Challenge another student to describe a reflection of two triangles you choose from the diagram.

4 Trace each pair of shapes and construct the mirror line for the reflection.

  a   **b**   **c**

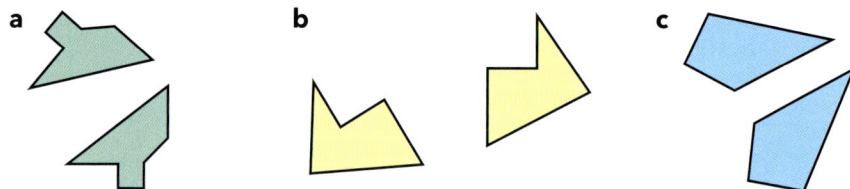

5 **a** In each diagram below, describe the multiple reflections that take the original shaded shape to its image.

  i   **ii**

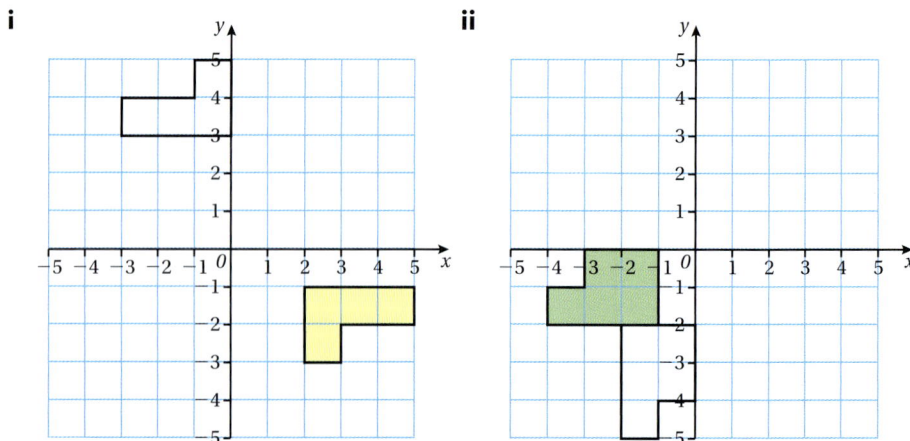

b Is there more than one possible answer to part **a**?

c Does the order of the reflections matter?

d Is there any easy way to tell the minimum number of reflections needed?

Section 2: Translations

A translation is a slide along a straight line. (Think about pushing a box across a floor.)

The translation can be from left to right (horizontal), up or down (vertical) or both (horizontal and vertical).

The image is in the same **orientation** as the object and every point on the shape moves exactly the same distance in exactly the same direction. Translated shapes are congruent to each other.

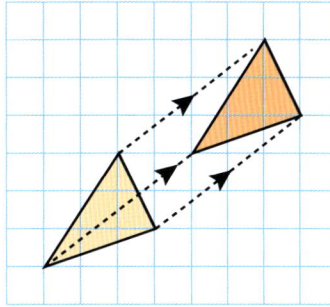

Translations are described on a coordinate grid using column vectors.

A column vector shows horizontal displacement over vertical displacement.

WORKED EXAMPLE 1

Describe the translation ABC to A′B′C′ by means of a column vector.

Look at point C and point C′.

Take any point on the object and find the corresponding point on the image.

To get from C to C′ move:
2 units to the right = +2
and
1 unit down = −1

Work out how the point has been translated horizontally and vertically.

The translation is $\begin{pmatrix} 2 \\ -1 \end{pmatrix}$

Write this as a vector.

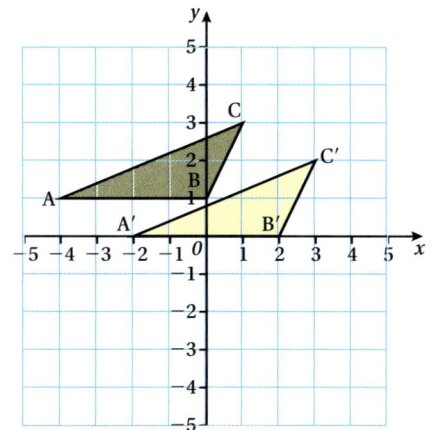

Tip

Drawing on a grid to show the movements of a shape can help you to avoid unnecessary mistakes.

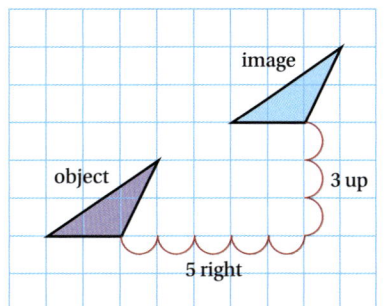

image

object

3 up

5 right

WORK IT OUT 33.2

This T shape is translated through a vector of $\binom{-2}{4}$. Draw its image.

Which one of these answers is correct?

What has gone wrong in each of the others?

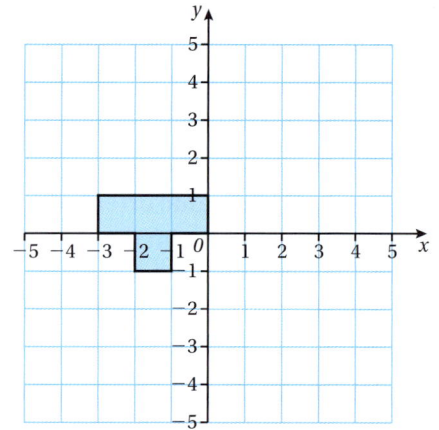

Option A	Option B	Option C
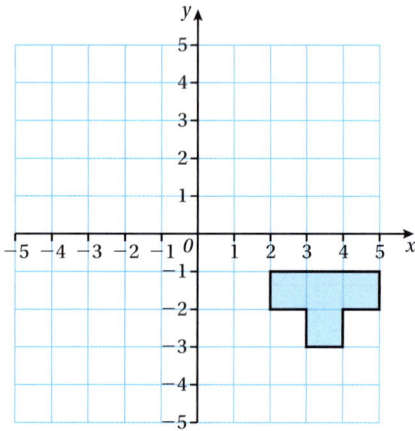	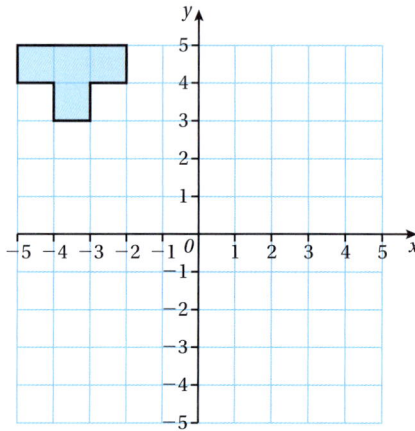	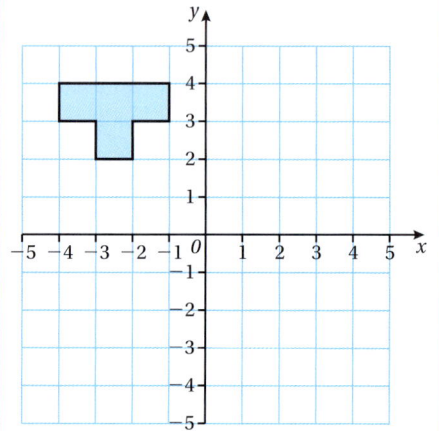

EXERCISE 33C

1 Copy and translate each shape using the given vector.

a $\binom{3}{-2}$

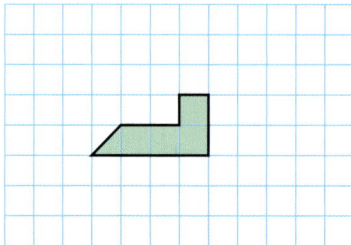

b $\binom{-1}{2}$

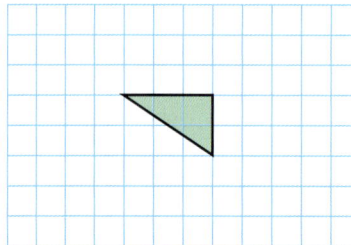

c $\binom{0}{4}$

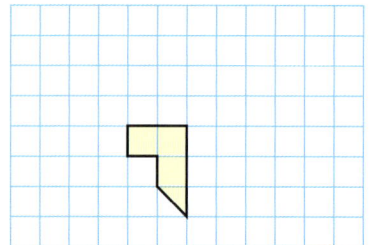

2   **a** Copy and translate each shape by the given vector.

   i Translate shape A $\begin{pmatrix} -1 \\ -3 \end{pmatrix}$ **ii** Translate shape B $\begin{pmatrix} 1 \\ 5 \end{pmatrix}$

   iii Translate shape C $\begin{pmatrix} 2 \\ -1 \end{pmatrix}$

   b Give the name of the shape you have put together.

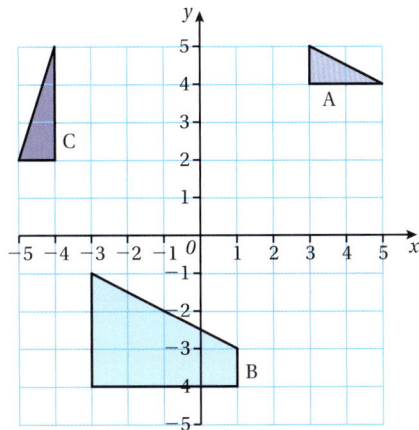

3   Copy and translate each piece of this jigsaw using the vectors on the right.

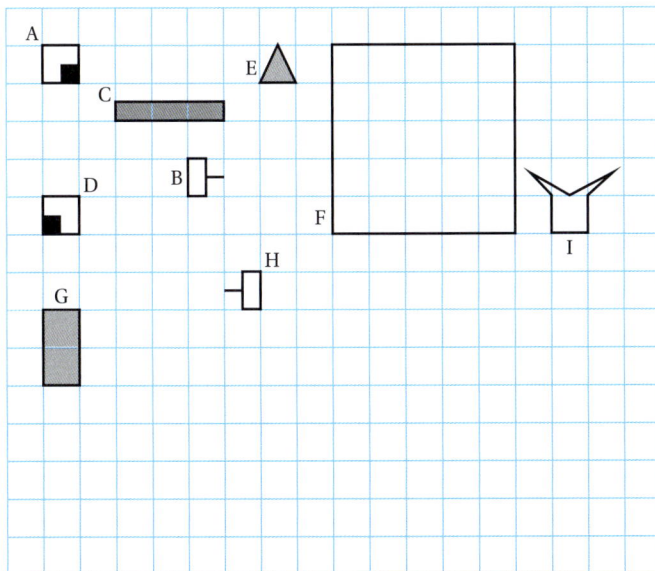

A $\begin{pmatrix} 12 \\ -8 \end{pmatrix}$

B $\begin{pmatrix} 12 \\ -5 \end{pmatrix}$

C $\begin{pmatrix} 10 \\ -9 \end{pmatrix}$

D $\begin{pmatrix} 14 \\ -4 \end{pmatrix}$

E $\begin{pmatrix} 7 \\ -9 \end{pmatrix}$

F $\begin{pmatrix} 3 \\ -7 \end{pmatrix}$

G $\begin{pmatrix} 13 \\ -5 \end{pmatrix}$

H $\begin{pmatrix} 5 \\ -2 \end{pmatrix}$

I $\begin{pmatrix} -1 \\ -2 \end{pmatrix}$

Describing translations

You should be able to use vectors to describe a translation. Remember to count between corresponding points on the two shapes.

WORK IT OUT 33.3

Which transformations below are reflections and which are translations?

How did you make your decision?

Transformation A

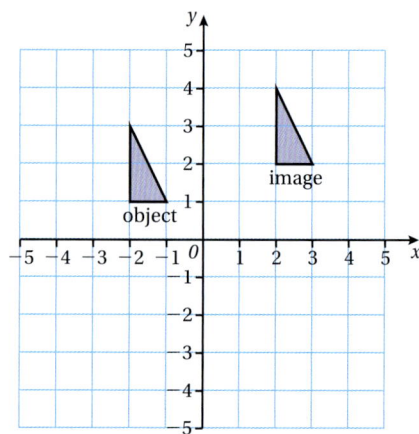

Transformation B

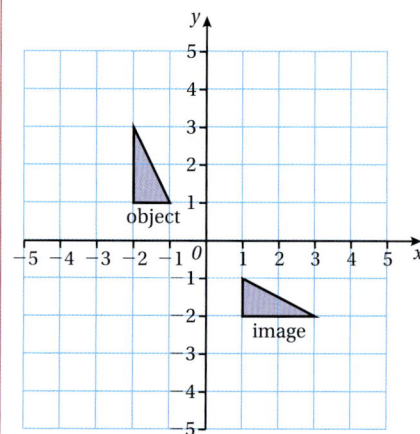

Transformation C

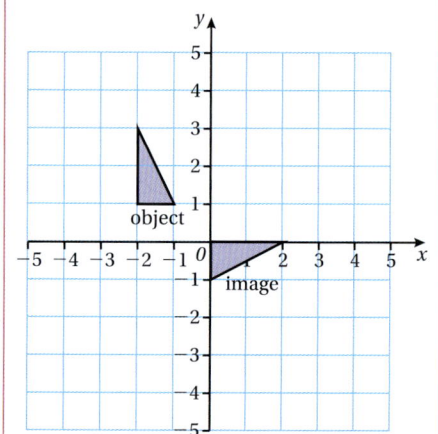

Transformation D

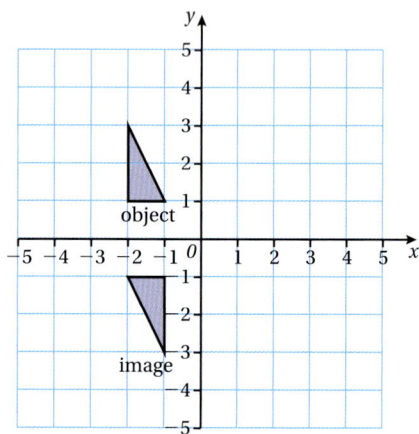

Transformation E

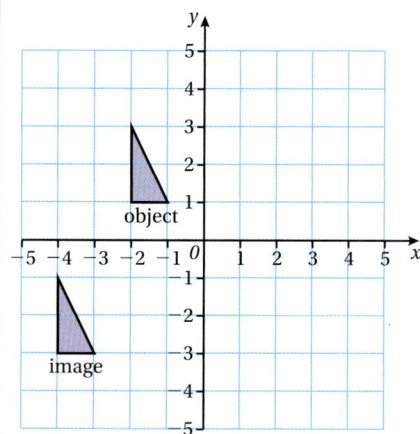

Transformation F

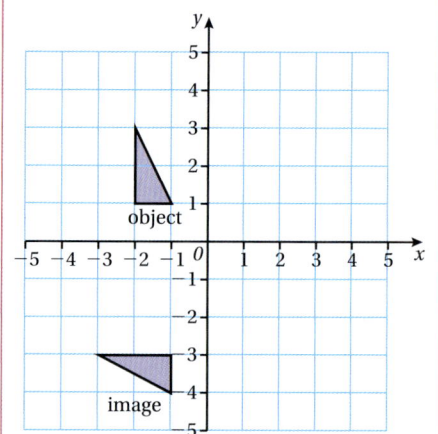

EXERCISE 33D

1 Which vector correctly describes the translation from shape B to shape A shown in the grid in the margin?

A $\begin{pmatrix} 2 \\ -4 \end{pmatrix}$ B $\begin{pmatrix} -4 \\ 2 \end{pmatrix}$ C $\begin{pmatrix} 4 \\ -2 \end{pmatrix}$ D $\begin{pmatrix} -2 \\ 4 \end{pmatrix}$

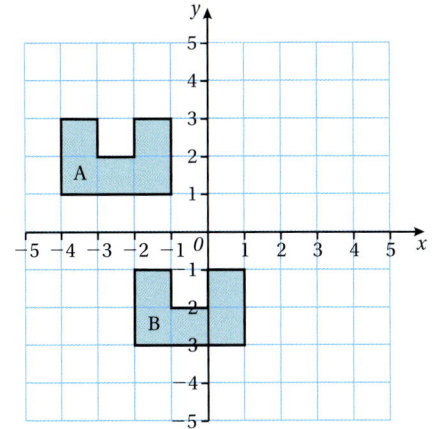

2 Here are some completed translations.

The objects are shown in grey and the images are in colour.

Write column vectors to describe the translation from each object to its image.

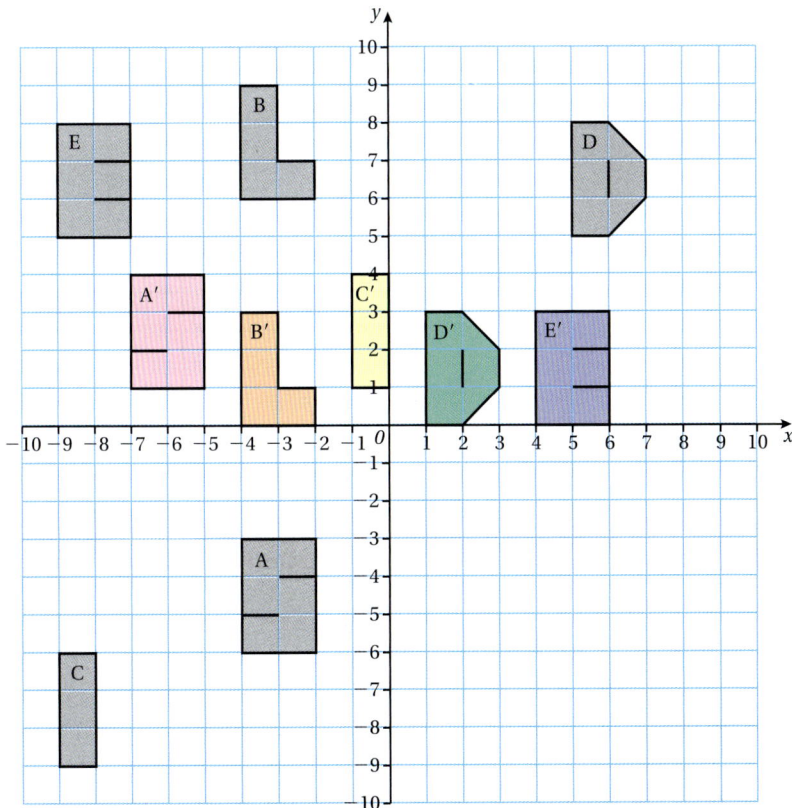

3 Work on a grid.

In any position on your grid, draw the four objects A, B, C and D that have been used to make up the image shown on the right.

Make up translation instructions for moving the four objects into position to form the image.

Exchange with a partner and perform the translations to make sure their instructions are correct.

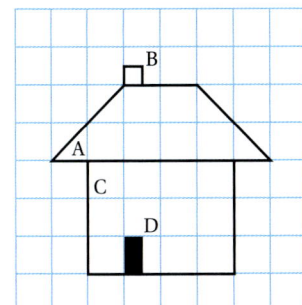

Find answers at: cambridge.org/ukschools/gcsemaths-studentbookanswers

Section 3: Rotations

A rotation is a turn. An object can turn clockwise or anticlockwise around a fixed point called the centre of rotation.

The centre of rotation might be inside, on the edge of or outside the object.

A rotation changes the orientation of a shape, but the object and its image remain congruent.

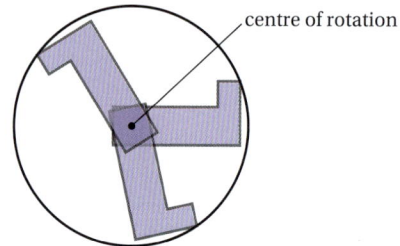

centre of rotation

To carry out a rotation you need to know the centre of rotation as well as the angle and direction of rotation.

In this book, all rotations will be in multiples of 90°.

WORK IT OUT 33.4

This L shape is rotated anticlockwise, with centre of rotation (0, 1) through an angle of 90°. What is its image?

Which one of these answers is correct?

What has gone wrong in each of the others?

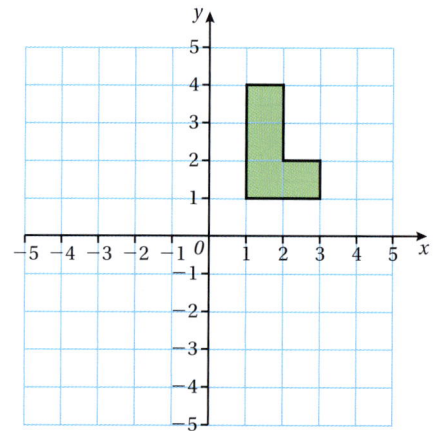

Option A	Option B	Option C
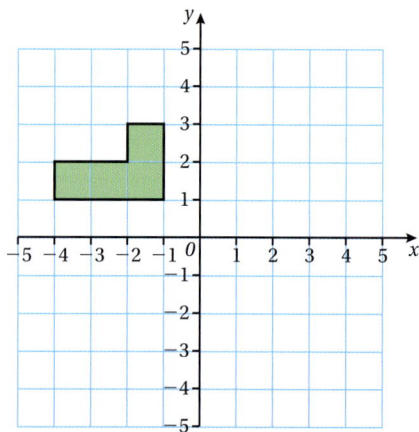	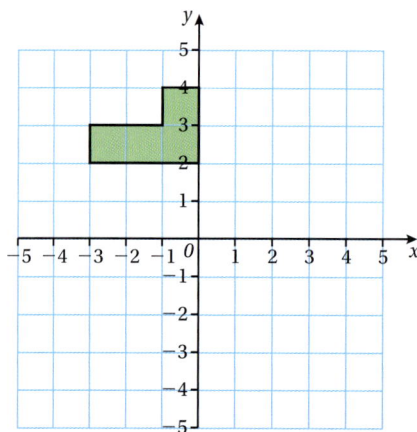	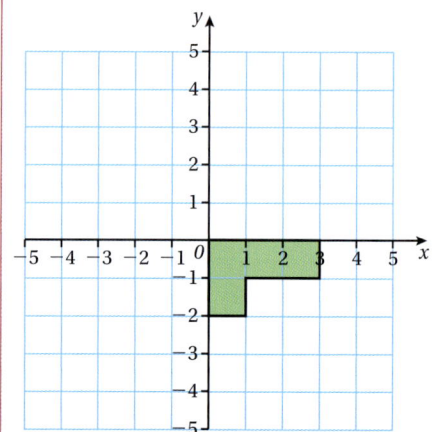

EXERCISE 33E

1 Which of the following diagrams shows a rotation?

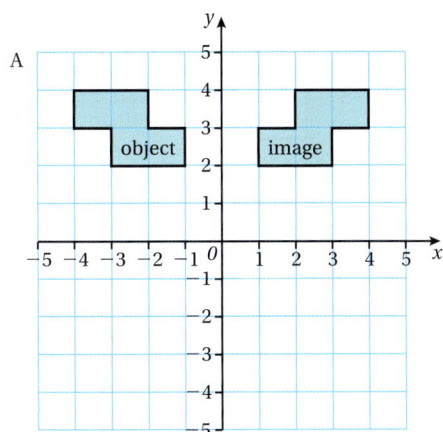

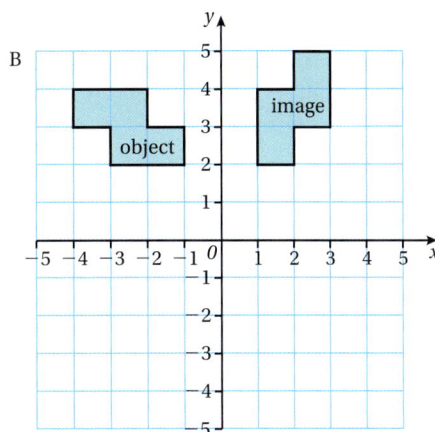

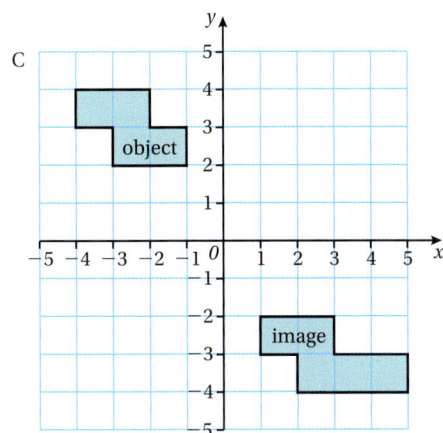

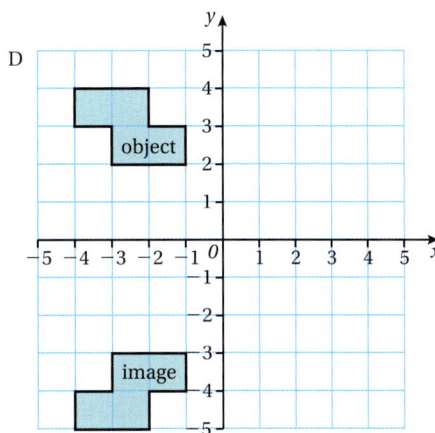

A

B

C

D

2 Copy and rotate the triangle 180° about the origin.

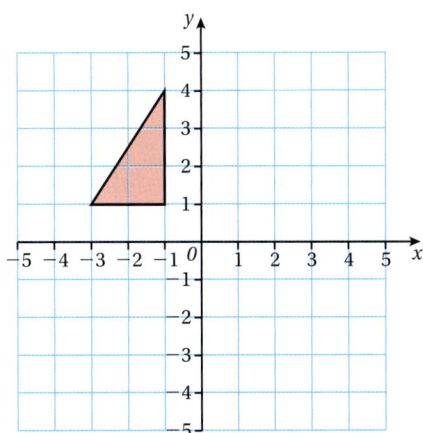

3 Copy and rotate the shape 90° clockwise around the point (1, 1).

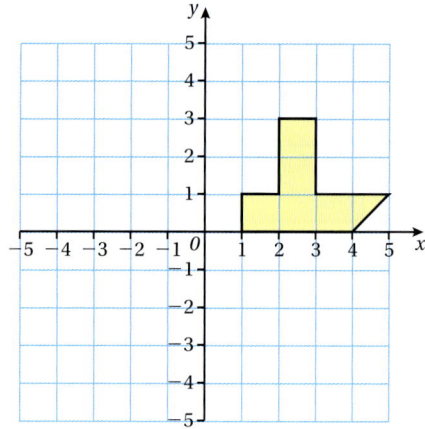

4 Copy and rotate the shape 90° anticlockwise around the point (−2, 1).

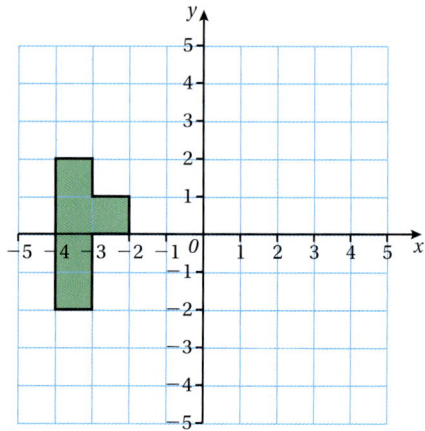

5 Copy and rotate the shape 90° anticlockwise around the point (2, 1).

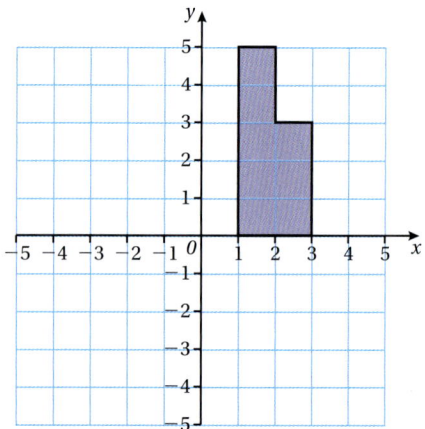

6 Copy the grid. Rotate each shape as directed.

Shape A: 90° anticlockwise around the point (−1, −1).
Shape B: 180° around the point (2, 3).
Shape C: 90° clockwise around the point (1, 0). Label this new shape D.
Shape D: 180° around the point (−3.5, 2).
Shape E: 180° around the point (3, 1).

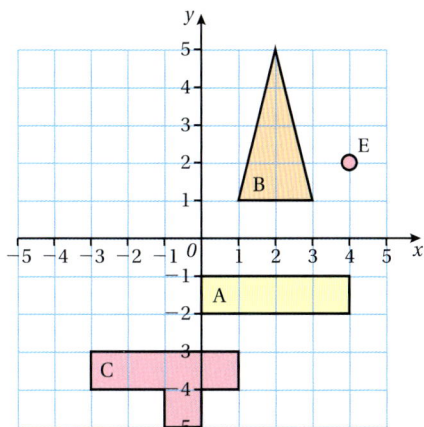

7 The following image was designed by drawing a triangle and rotating this around the origin in multiples of 90°.

What do you notice about the coordinates of the vertices of the triangle?

Would this work if you rotated an image around a different point? Give reasons why.

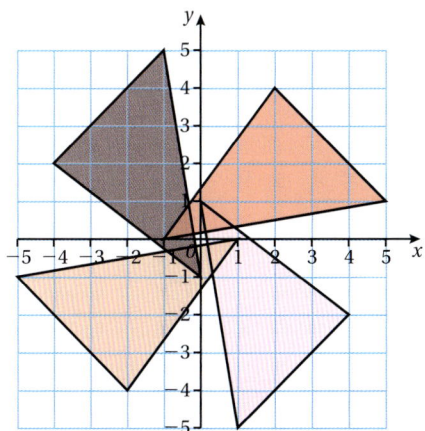

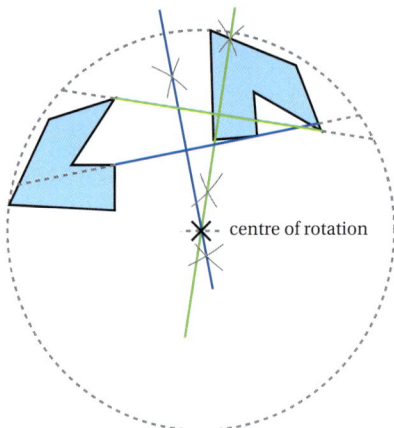

centre of rotation

Describing rotations

To describe a rotation you give a centre of rotation, angle and direction.

You can find the centre of rotation using tracing paper and trial and error.

Trace the object and rotate the tracing paper using different centres of rotation.

Spotting the centres of rotation improves with practice.

You can use construction to find the centre of rotation.

Corresponding points on an object and its image under rotation lie on the circumference of a circle.

If you join these to make a chord, its perpendicular bisector will go through the centre of the circle. So by drawing two perpendicular bisectors you can determine the centre.

WORK IT OUT 33.5

Which of these transformations are reflections, which are rotations and which are translations?

How did you make your decision?

Transformation A

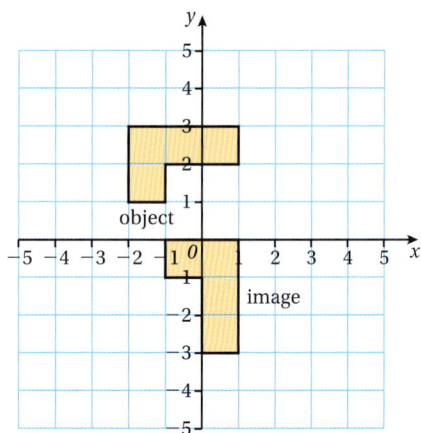

Transformation B

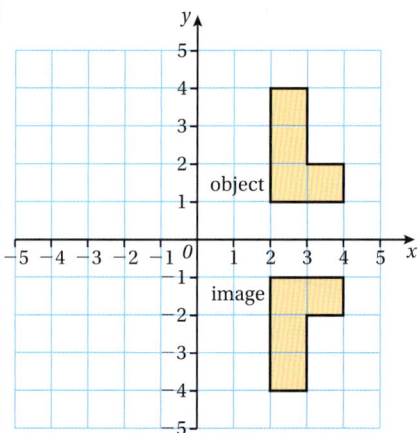

Transformation C

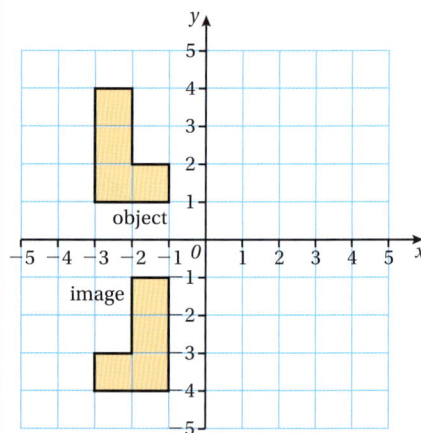

Transformation D

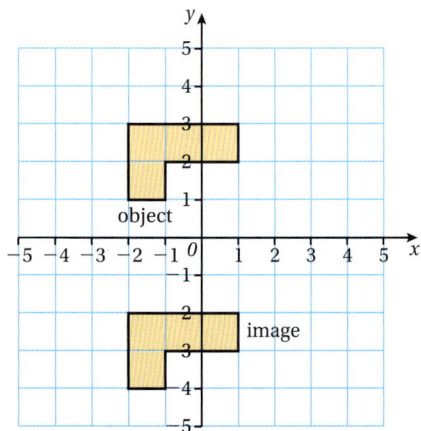

Transformation E

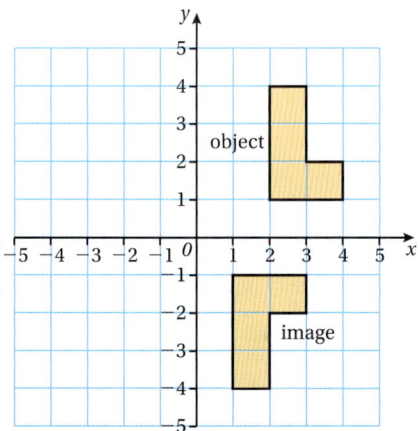

Transformation F

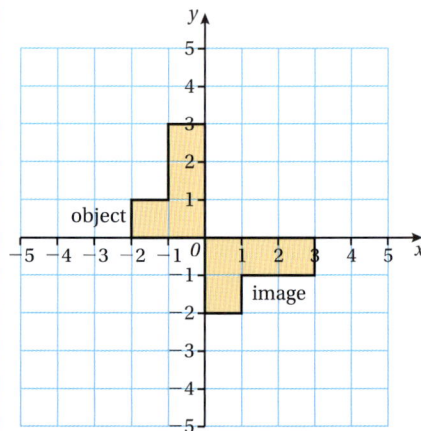

EXERCISE 33F

1 Which of the following correctly describes the rotation in the diagram?

A Rotation of 90° anticlockwise, centre (0, 4).

B Rotation of 180°, centre (0, 4).

C Rotation of 90° anticlockwise, centre (0, 5).

D Rotation of 90° clockwise, centre (0, 5).

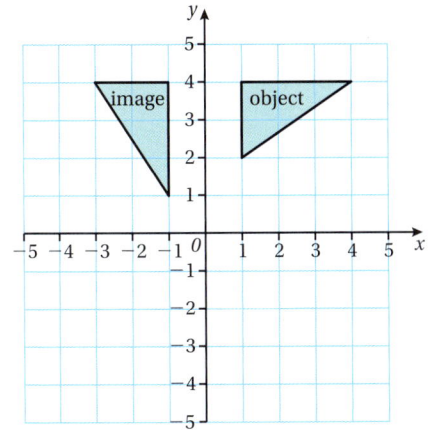

2 Describe each of the following rotations.

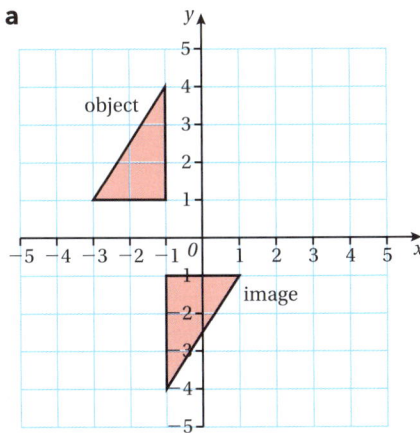

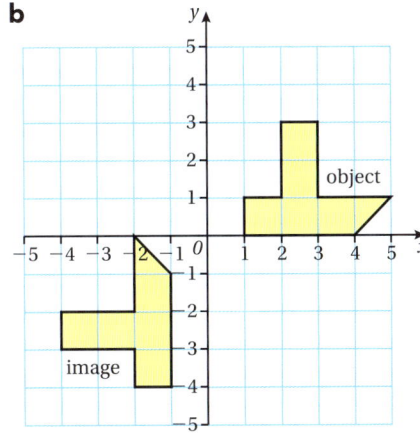

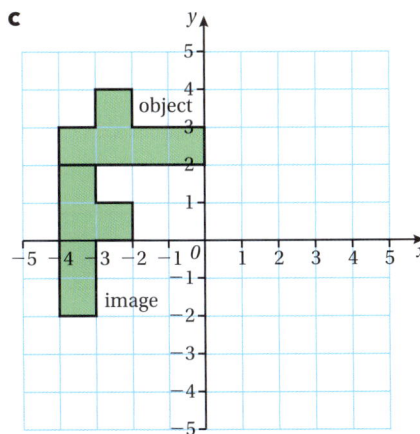

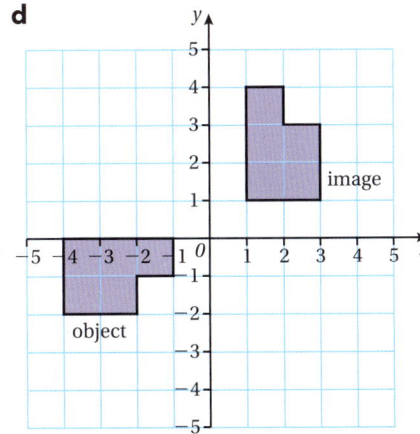

a

b

c

d

3 This section of wallpaper has been designed using rotations.

A coordinate grid is overlaid on top of the pattern.

Identify and describe as many different rotations as you can.

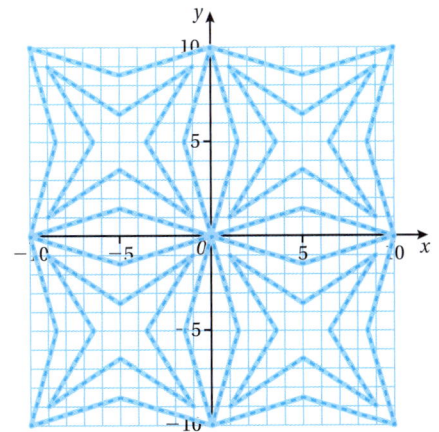

4 Trace each pair of shapes and use construction to locate the centres of rotation for each pair.

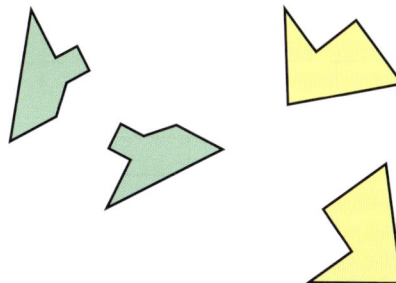

Find answers at: cambridge.org/ukschools/gcsemaths-studentbookanswers

Section 4: Combined transformations

An object can undergo two (or more) transformations in a row.

For example, it could be reflected in the line $y = 0$ and then rotated clockwise through 90° about a vertex.

A combined transformation can be described by a single, equivalent, transformation.

EXERCISE 33G

1. The following shape is rotated through 90° clockwise around the point (0, 1) and then reflected in the x-axis.

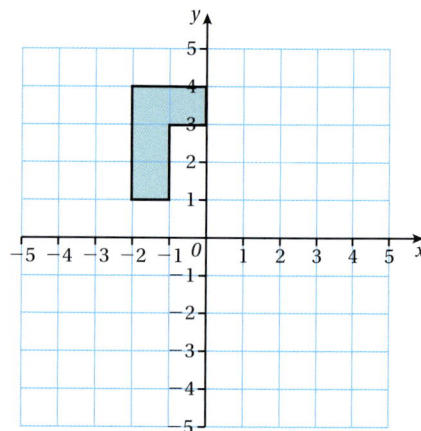

Which diagram shows the result of these combined transformations?

A

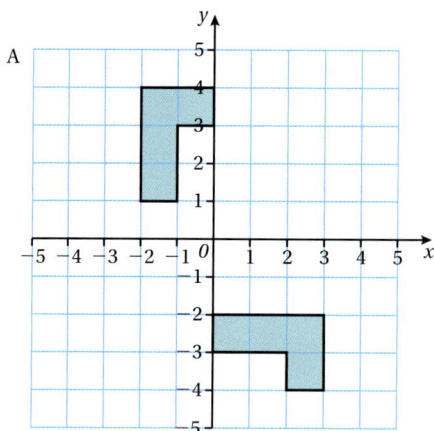

B

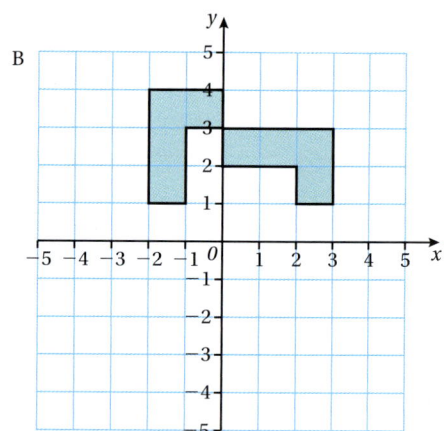

C

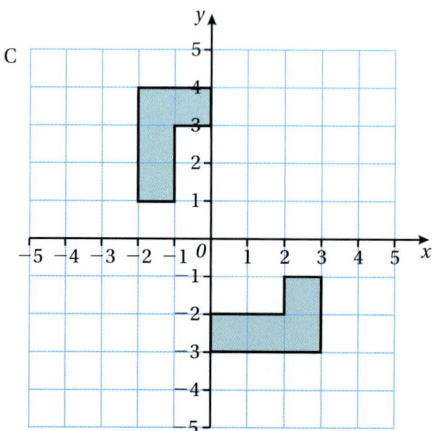

D

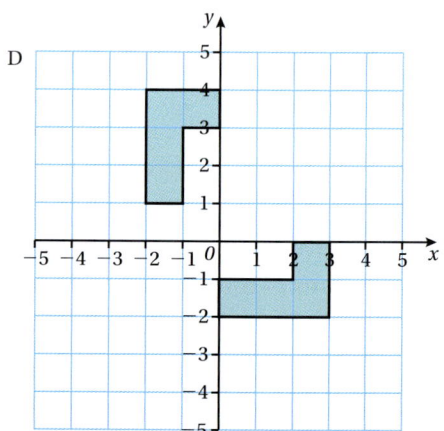

2 Make a copy of this diagram. Reflect the object A in the line $x = 2$ and label it A'.

Rotate shape A' 90° anti-clockwise around the point $(2, -2)$ and label it A'.

Describe the single transformation that maps shape A to shape A'.

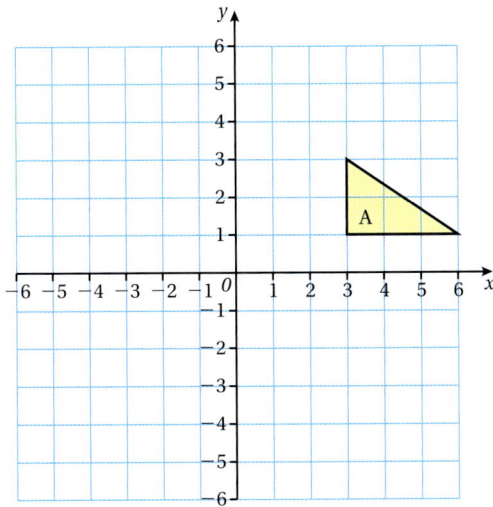

3 Make a copy of this diagram. Translate F through a vector of $\begin{pmatrix} -3 \\ 2 \end{pmatrix}$ and label it F'.

Rotate F' 180° around the point $(-3, 0)$ and label it F''.

Describe the single transformation that maps shape F onto to shape F''.

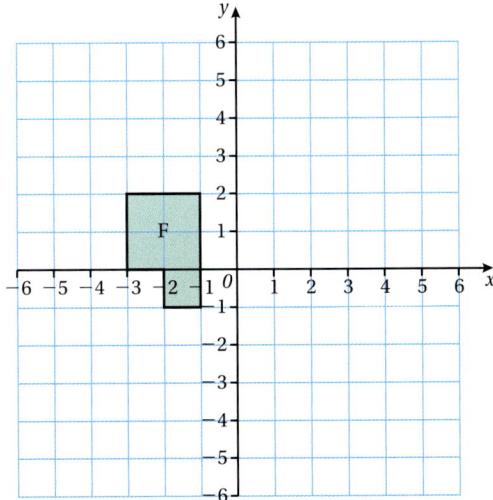

Find answers at: cambridge.org/ukschools/gcsemaths-studentbookanswers

4 Make a copy of this diagram. Reflect K in the y-axis and label it K′.

Rotate K′ 90° clockwise around the point $(2, -1)$ and label it K″.

Reflect K″ in the line $x = 0$ and label it K‴.

Describe the single transformation that maps shape K onto shape K‴.

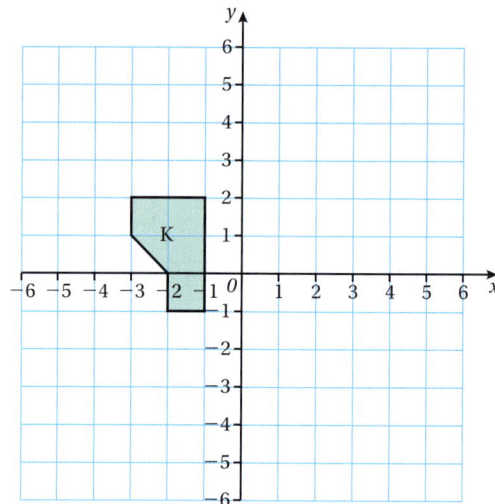

5 **a** Describe fully the combined transformations from shape A to A′.

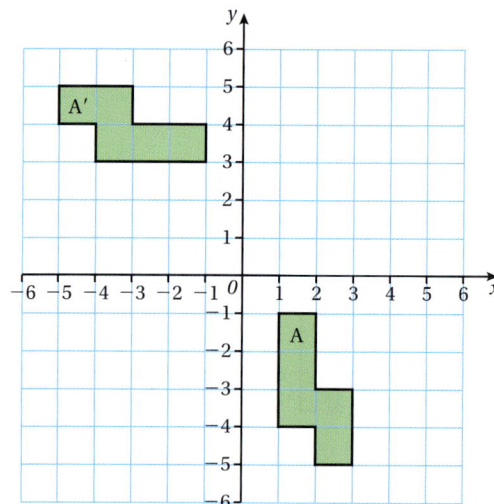

b Does the order of the transformations matter?

c Find another solution.

6 A shape is transformed by carrying out a reflection in the x-axis followed by a reflection in the y-axis.

What single transformation has the same effect?

7 What two transformations would have the same effect as rotating the following shape 90 degrees anticlockwise around the point (−2, 0)?

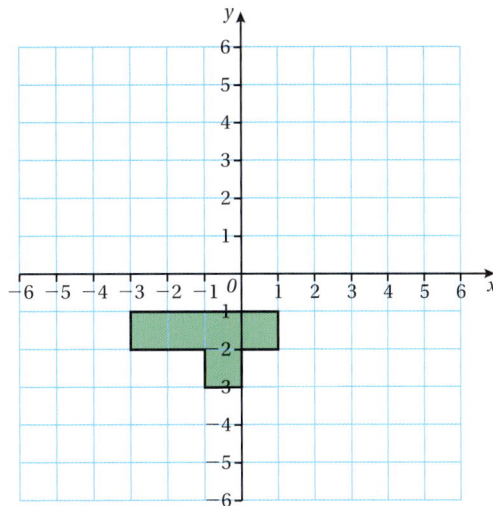

Checklist of learning and understanding

Reflections
- Reflections change the orientation of a shape or object but the image remains congruent.
- To describe a reflection the equation of the mirror line must be given.
- The mirror line is the perpendicular bisector of any two corresponding points on the image and the object.

Translations
- Translations leave the orientation of the shape unchanged but move it horizontally and/or vertically.
- Translations are described using vectors.

Rotations
- A rotation is a turn around a centre of rotation. Rotations are described by giving the coordinates of the centre of rotation, and the angle and direction of the rotation.

Combined transformations
- Transformations can be combined by completing one after another.

Chapter review

For additional questions on the topics in this chapter, visit GCSE Mathematics Online.

1 Which of the following statements are true?

Write down your reasoning.

a The images constructed by reflecting, rotating or translating are congruent with the objects.

b The images constructed by reflecting, rotating or translating are similar to the objects.

c The images constructed by reflecting, rotating or translating are in the same orientation to the objects.

d The images constructed by reflecting, rotating or translating have the same angles as the objects.

Find answers at: cambridge.org/ukschools/gcsemaths-studentbookanswers

2 Describe fully the transformation from:

  a shape A to shape B

  b shape B to shape C

  c shape C to shape A.

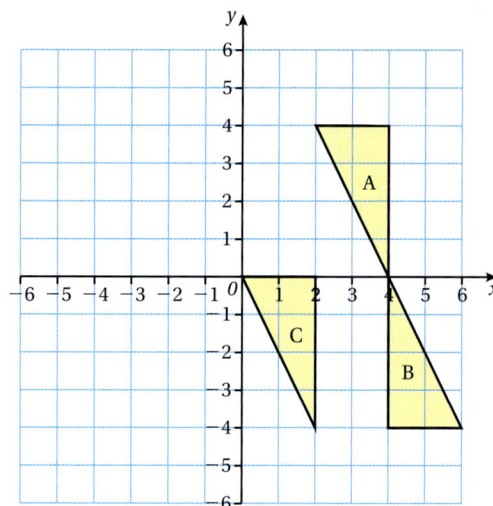

3 The triangle below is used to create a tessellating pattern.

The pattern is produced using multiple translations and one rotation.

Write down how this could be done.

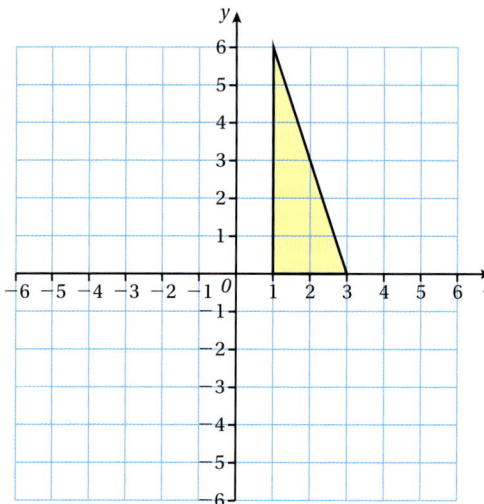

4 Rotate shape A, 90° clockwise around the point (1, 2). Label it B.

Reflect shape B in the line $y = x$. Label it C.

Translate shape C through the vector $\begin{pmatrix} -1 \\ 1 \end{pmatrix}$. Label it D.

Describe the single transformation that maps shape A onto shape D.

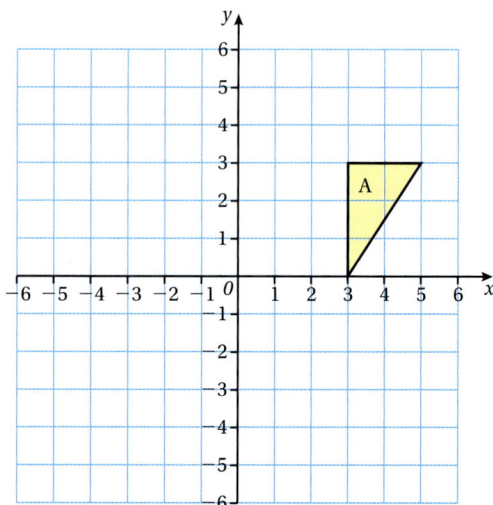

5 **a** Translate the shape by the vector $\begin{pmatrix} 2 \\ 3 \end{pmatrix}$ *(2 marks)*

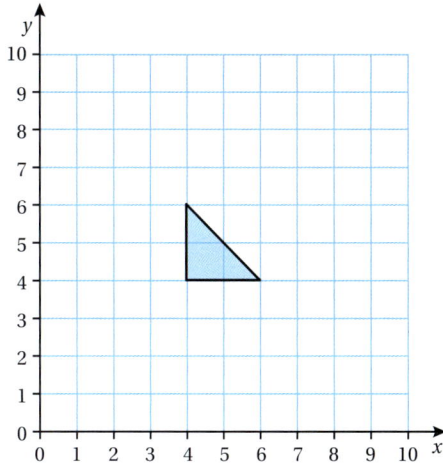

b Describe fully the single transformation that takes shape A to shape B. *(3 marks)*

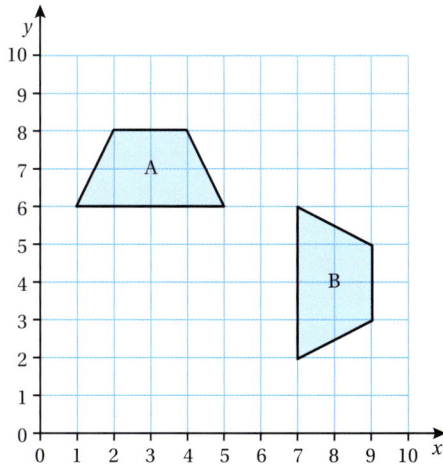

6 Describe how the figure in the diagram can be drawn using only transformations of shapes A, B, C and D.

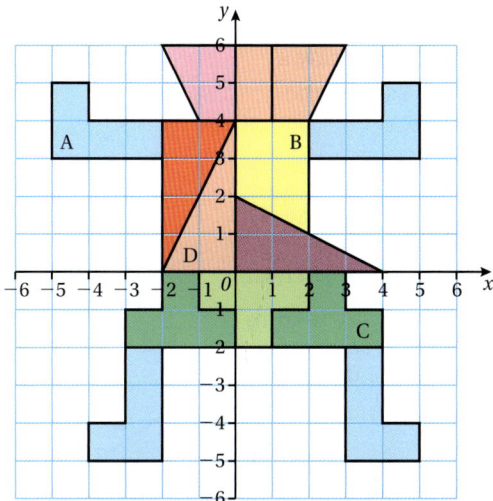

Find answers at: cambridge.org/ukschools/gcsemaths-studentbookanswers

In this chapter you will learn how to …

- use a ruler, protractor and pair of compasses effectively.
- use a ruler and a pair of compasses to bisect lines and angles and construct perpendiculars.
- use construction skills to construct geometrical figures.
- construct accurate diagrams to solve problems involving loci.

For more resources relating to this chapter, visit GCSE Mathematics Online.

Using mathematics: real-life applications

Draughtspeople and architects need to draw accurate scaled diagrams of the buildings and other structures they are working on. Although the drawings are complicated, they still use ordinary mathematical instruments like pencils, rulers and pairs of compasses to draw them.

"I prepare technical drawings and plans that are given to me by an architect. I use a CAD program, but I always start with a drawing board and plans that I draw using my ruler, set squares and pair of compasses."

(Draughtsperson)

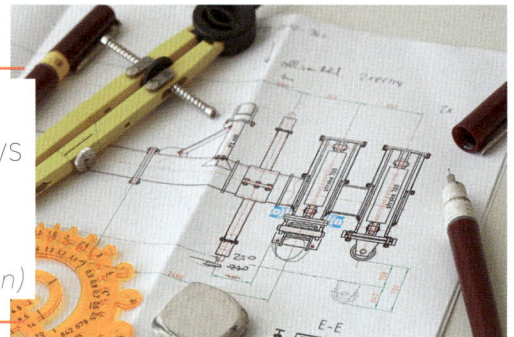

Before you start …

KS3	You need to be able to measure and draw angles accurately using a protractor.	**1**	Read the correct measurement for each angle. **a** **b** **2** Use a ruler and a protractor to draw a reflex angle the same size as this one.
KS3	You should be able to convert between units of length.	**3**	Choose the correct answers. **a** 1 m is equivalent to: A 10 mm B 100 mm C 1000 mm **b** Half of 8.7 cm is: A 43 mm B 435 mm C 43.5 mm
KS3 Ch 8	You must know and be able to use the correct names for parts of shapes, including circles.	**4**	Match the letters **a** to **e** on the diagrams with the correct mathematical names from the box below. vertex centre radius side diameter

Assess your starting point using the Launchpad

STEP 1

① Which of the following statements are true of this angle?

A It is an acute angle.

B It measures 120°.

C It is called QRP.

D If you extend arm QR, the size of the angle will increase.

② Which of the following statements are **not** true of this circle?

A It has a radius of 5 cm.

B It has a diameter of 5 cm.

C OC ⊥ AB

D OC = $\frac{1}{2}$(AB)

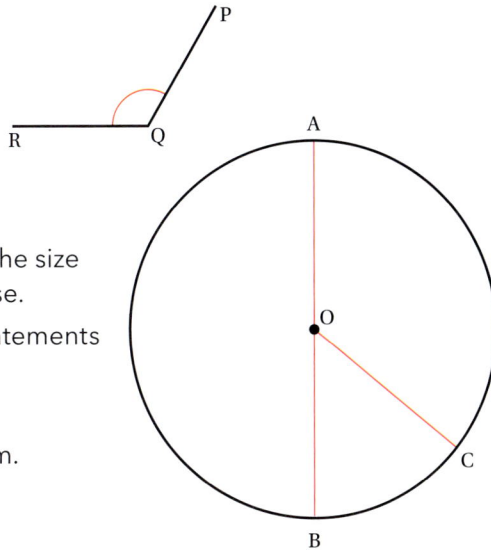

GO TO
Section 1:
Geometrical instruments

STEP 2

③ Niresh did the construction shown here.

a What is the mathematical name for the line BR?

b What did Niresh do to produce the line BR?

c Given that angle ABC = 48°, state the size of angle ABR without measuring it.

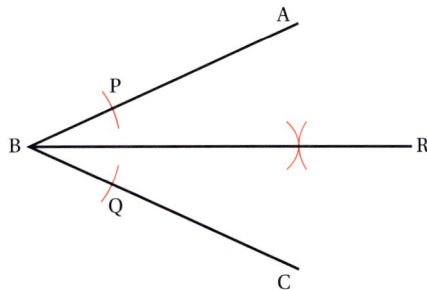

GO TO
Section 2:
Ruler and compass constructions

GO TO
Step 3
The Launchpad continues on the next page …

Find answers at: cambridge.org/ukschools/gcsemaths-studentbookanswers

Launchpad continued …

STEP 3

4 Simone wants a campsite that is less than 50 m from the river and no further than 50 m from the showers.

She drew this diagram to help her decide where to camp.

Copy the diagram and shade the area that satisfies Simone's conditions to show where she should camp.

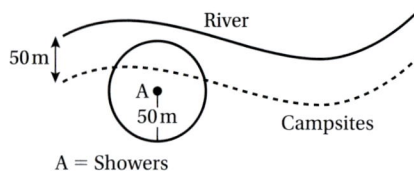

River

50 m

A

50 m

Campsites

A = Showers

GO TO

Section 3:
Loci
Section 4:
Applying your skills

GO TO

Chapter review

Tip

Always measure and draw as accurately as you can. At this level you are expected to draw lengths correct to the nearest millimetre and angles correct to the nearest degree.

Section 1: Geometrical instruments

Measuring and drawing angles

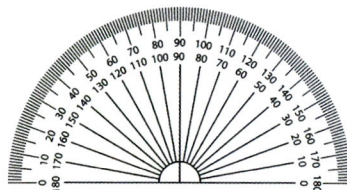

Protractors like the one in the diagram have two scales.

These are for measuring angles facing different directions.

To avoid measuring on the wrong scale, estimate the size of the angle before you measure.

Use your knowledge of acute, right and obtuse angles to estimate as accurately as possible.

WORKED EXAMPLE 1

a Estimate and then measure the size of each marked angle. **i** A **ii**

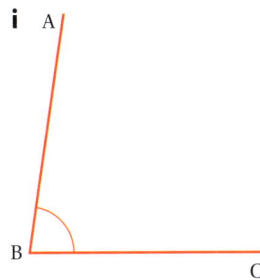

B   C   D   E   F

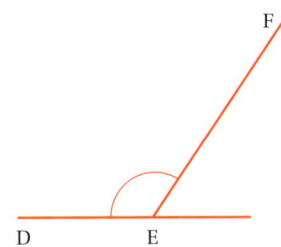

a i Estimate about 80°.

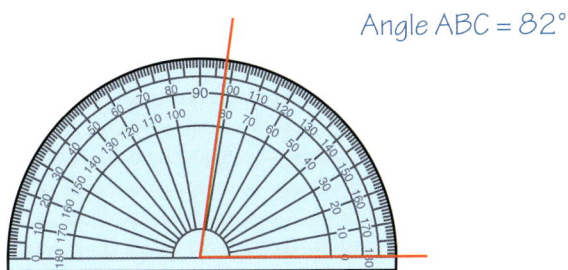

Angle ABC = 82°

This is an acute angle but it is close to 90°.

Use the inner scale to measure because this is the scale that has 0 on the arm of the angle.

ii Estimate about 130°.

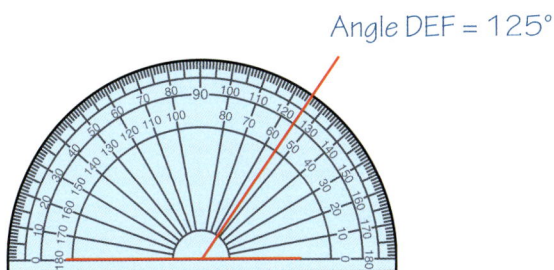

Angle DEF = 125°

This is an obtuse angle. It is about one-third bigger than a right angle.

Use the outer scale to measure because this is the scale that has 0 on the arm of the angle.

b Use your protractor to draw angle ABC = 76°.

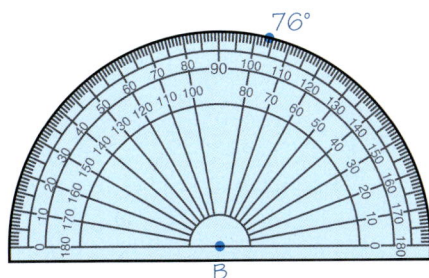

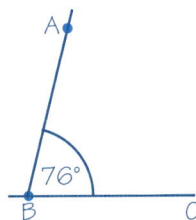

b B

76°

A

76°

B   C

Draw a line using your ruler.

Mark B, the vertex in angle ABC.

Place your protractor with its centre on B and baseline on the line you drew.

Measure and mark 76°.

Remove the protractor.

Draw a line from B through the 76° marking.

Label the angle correctly.

Tip

If the arms of the angle are too short to read the scale correctly use a ruler and a pencil to extend them. This doesn't change the size of the angle but it allows you to read the measurement more accurately. If you cannot draw on the angle (because it is in a book) you can extend the arm with the straight edge of a sheet of paper.

Find answers at: cambridge.org/ukschools/gcsemaths-studentbookanswers

Parts of a circle

🔑 **Key vocabulary**

radius (plural **radii**): distance from the centre to the circumference of a circle. One radius is half of the diameter of the circle.

circumference: distance around the outside of a circle

semicircle: half of a circle

chord: a straight line that joins one point on the circumference of a circle to another point on its circumference. The diameter is a chord that goes through the centre of the circle.

Make sure you know the names of the parts of a circle as you will need to use them in your work on construction.

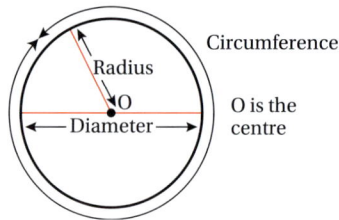

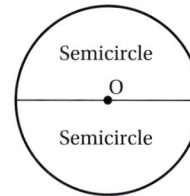

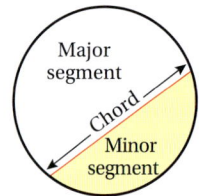

WORKED EXAMPLE 2

a Draw a circle with a **radius** of 4.5 cm.

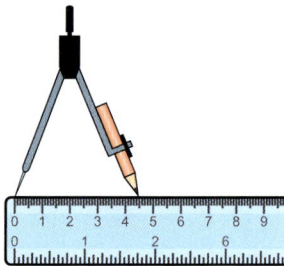

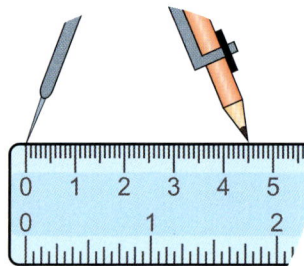

Place the pair of compasses alongside a ruler and open it to 4.5 cm.

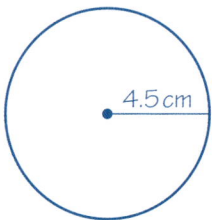

Draw a circle.

4.5 cm

b Make an accurate copy of this figure.

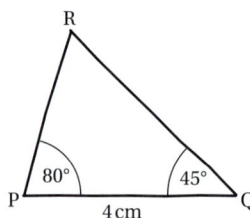

R

80°   45°

P   4 cm   Q

P ————— 4 cm ————— Q

First draw the base line of 4 cm and label this PQ.

Continues on next page …

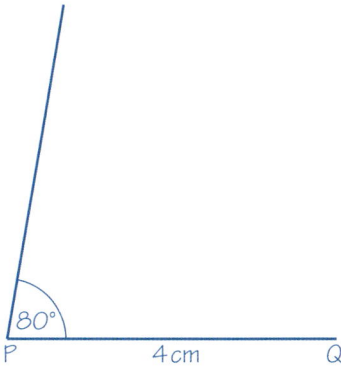

Use the protractor to measure the angle 80° from point P and draw a line.

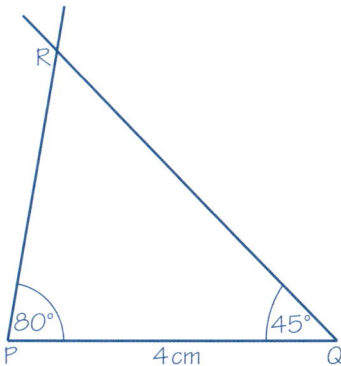

80°
P   4 cm   Q

From point Q measure the angle 45° and draw a line from Q extending out so that is crosses the other line.

Where the two lines cross is point R. This is the apex of the triangle.

R
80°   45°
P   4 cm   Q

c Construct an equilateral triangle with side lengths 6 cm.

A   6 cm   B

First draw the base line of 6 cm with a ruler and label it AB.

Then set your compasses to 6 cm and draw an arc above that line, setting the point of your compasses at A.

A   6 cm   B

Repeat this from the other side at point B.

A   6 cm   B

Continues on next page …

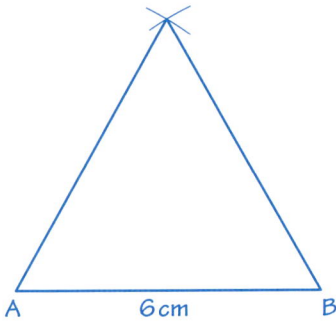

Where the two arcs join is the apex of the triangle. Use this point to complete the triangle.

This process has constructed a triangle with three equal side lengths and subsequently has three equal angles of 60°.

Tip

Leave the construction markings (arcs made using your pair of compasses) on your diagrams as this shows the method you used to construct them.

The method in Worked Example 2c can be used for triangles with sides of different lengths by setting your pair of compasses to whatever the lengths of the sides are.

EXERCISE 34A

1 The diameter of a circle is 15 cm.

What is the radius of the circle?

Choose from the following options.

A 7.5 cm   B 10 cm   C 15 cm   D 30 cm

2 Use a ruler and protractor to draw and label the following angles.

a PQR = 25°   **b** DEF = 149°   **c** XYZ = 90°

3 Write down the steps that you would follow to use a protractor marked from 0° to 180° to measure an angle of 238°.

4 **a** Draw a line MN that is 8.4 cm long.

    i At M, measure and draw angle NMP = 45°.

    ii At N, measure and draw angle RNM = 98°.

  b Give a reason why the lengths of MP and NR do not matter in this diagram.

5 Use a pair of compasses to construct:

  a a circle of radius 4 cm

  b a circle of diameter 12 cm

  c a circle of diameter 2 cm, that shares a centre, O, with another circle of radius 5 cm.

6 Draw a line AB that is 70 mm long.

Construct the circle for which this line is the diameter.

7 Draw a circle of radius 3.5 cm and centre O.

Use a ruler to draw any two radii of the circle. Label them OA and OB.

Join point A to point B to form triangle AOB.

Measure angles AOB, OBA and BAO.

Write the measurements on your diagram.

8 Accurately copy the following diagrams using only a ruler and pair of compasses.

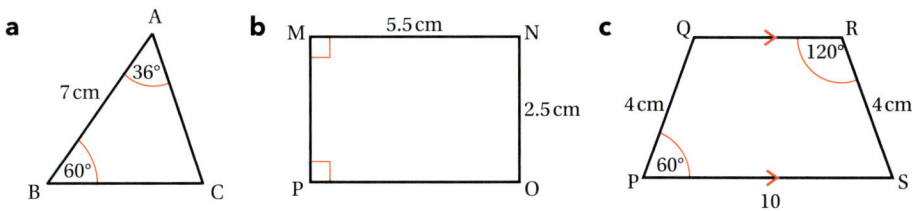

a

A, 36°, 7 cm, 60°, B, C

b

M, 5.5 cm, N, 2.5 cm, P, O

c

Q, 120°, R, 4 cm, 60°, 4 cm, P, 10, S

9 Write a step-by-step set of instructions for using only a ruler and a pair of compasses to construct:

a an equilateral triangle ABC with sides of 6.4 cm

b a semicircle with a radius of 30 mm.

10 Use a ruler, a pair of compasses and a protractor to construct one ninth of a circle of diameter 82 mm.

Section 2: Ruler and compass constructions

Bisecting a line

You can use a ruler and a pair of compasses to **bisect** any line without measuring it.

WORKED EXAMPLE 3

Bisect a line AB by construction.

Draw a line and mark points A and B on it.

Open the pair of compasses to any width that is greater than half the line.

Place the point of the compasses on A and draw arcs above and below the line.

Keep the compasses open to the same width and place the point on B.

Draw arcs above and below the line so that they cut the first set of arcs.

Use a ruler to join the points where the arcs intersect.

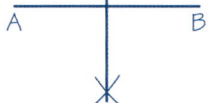

Tip

Remember that perpendicular means 'at right angles to'.

The point where the constructed line cuts AB is called the **midpoint** of AB.

The distance from A to this point is equal to the distance from B to this point.

The constructed line is perpendicular to AB, so it is called the **perpendicular bisector** of AB. All points along the constructed line will be an equal distance from both point A and point B.

Constructing perpendiculars

You can use your pair of compasses to construct a line perpendicular to any point on a given line or to construct a perpendicular line from a point above or below a given line.

Construct a perpendicular at a given point on a line

WORKED EXAMPLE 4

Construct XY ⊥ AB at a point X on a line.

Draw a line about 12 cm long and label it AB.

Open your compasses to a width of about 4 cm.

Mark on a point, X.

Place the point of your compasses on X.

Draw two arcs to cut AB on either side of X.

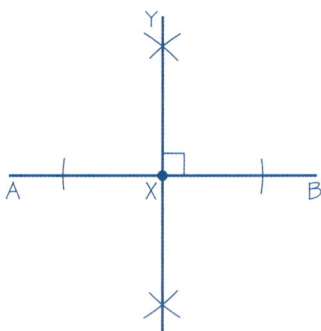

Construct the perpendicular bisector of the line segment between the arcs.

Draw a line through the intersecting arcs.

Label one end of it Y to produce XY and mark the right angle.

Construct a perpendicular from a point to a line

Construct PX perpendicular to line AB from point P.

•P

A ——————————— B

•P

A ——————————— B

•P

Place the point of your compasses on P.
Draw an arc that cuts AB in two places.

Label these points of intersection C and D.

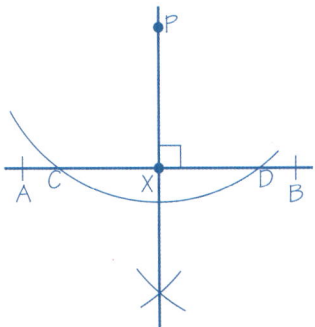

Open the pair of compasses to a width more than half the distance between C and D.

Place the point on C and draw an arc on the opposite side of the line to point P.

Place the point on D and draw an arc that intersects the one you just drew. Draw a line from the intersecting arcs to P.

Label PX and mark the right angle.

💡 **Tip**

You should remember from your work on parallel and perpendicular lines in Chapter 8 that the shortest distance from any point to a line is a perpendicular from the point to the line.

Bisecting an angle

An angle bisector divides any angle into two equal halves.

WORKED EXAMPLE 6

Use a protractor to draw an angle PQR of 70°.

Construct the angle bisector of this angle without measuring.

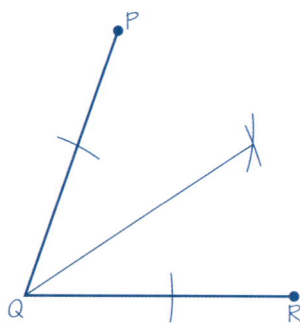

First draw the 70° angle using a protractor.

Label it PQR.

Place the pair of compasses on the vertex of the angle, Q.

Open your compasses a few centimetres and draw arcs that cut each arm of the angle.

Place the point of your compasses on each arc where it cuts the arm of the angle, and keeping the width the same, draw arcs between the arms of the angle.

Draw a line from the vertex of the angle through the intersection of the arcs.

This is the angle bisector.

Tip

Remember if you bisect a 90° angle you will then have two angles of 45°.

EXERCISE 34B

1 Define the term 'bisect'.

Choose from the options below.

A To draw a perpendicular line.   B To double.

C To find the midpoint.   D To cut into two halves.

2 Draw each of the following line segments.

Find the midpoint of each line segment by construction.

a AB = 9 cm   b MN = 48 mm   c PQ = 6.5 cm

3 a Draw any three acute angles. Bisect each angle without measuring.

b How could you check the accuracy of your constructions?

4 Measure and draw the angles shown.

Using only a ruler and a pair of compasses, bisect each angle.

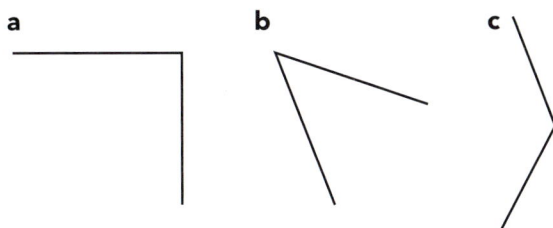

a   b   c

5 Draw any triangle ABC.

   a Construct the perpendicular bisector of each side of the triangle.

   b Draw a circle with its centre where the perpendicular bisectors meet.
Use the distance to vertex A as the radius.

   c What do you notice about this circle?

6 Construct equilateral triangle DEF with sides of 7 cm.

   a Bisect each angle of the triangle by construction. Label the point
where the angle bisectors meet as O.

   b Measure DO, EO and FO. What do you notice?

7 Draw MN = 80 mm. Insert any point A above MN.

   a Construct $AX \perp MN$.

   b Draw AB // MN.

8 Draw any two line segments PQ and ST that intersect at point O.

   a Bisect SOQ.

   b Is the angle bisector of SOQ also the bisector of POT?
Give a reason for your answer.

9 Draw any two circles and use a ruler to draw in any two chords of each.

   a Construct the perpendicular bisector of each chord.

   b Describe where they meet.

   c What can you deduce from this?

Section 3: Loci

A **locus** is a set of points that all meet a given condition or set of conditions.

All points in the locus must meet the conditions and all points that do meet
the conditions must be included in the locus.

The locus can be a single point, a line, a curve or a shaded region of points
that overlap because they meet the same conditions in a particular area.

The locus of points at a given distance from a fixed point forms a
circular path.

Key vocabulary

locus (plural **loci**): a set of points
that satisfy the same rule

You can use a pair of compasses to construct this locus.

WORKED EXAMPLE 7

A tap is located at point X.

Draw the locus of points that are exactly 50 metres from the tap.

Your diagram does not need to be to scale.

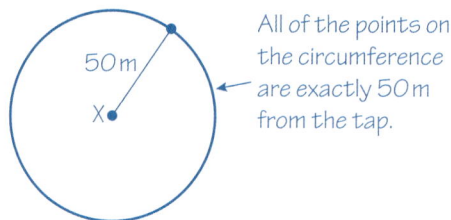

50 m

X

All of the points on the circumference are exactly 50 m from the tap.

Tip

If a line is included in the locus you draw it as a solid line. If the line is not included, but just shows the edge of the locus you draw it as a broken, or dashed, line.

In Worked Example 7, the locus of points that are less than 50 m from the tap is the region inside the circle.

If you are asked to construct this type of locus, you should shade the interior of the circle.

This shows that all the points inside the circumference meet the conditions of the locus.

You should show the circumference as a broken line to indicate that it is **not** included in the locus.

> The locus of a point at distance, r, from a fixed point, O, is a circle with centre O and radius r.

WORKED EXAMPLE 8

India lives at point A. Joby lives at point B.

They want to meet exactly midway between their homes.

Draw a diagram to show where they could meet.

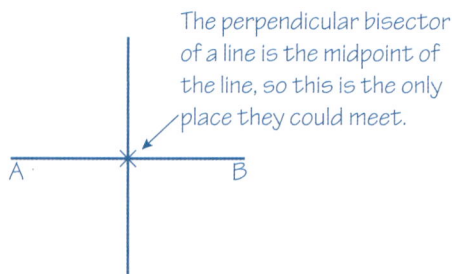

The perpendicular bisector of a line is the midpoint of the line, so this is the only place they could meet.

A   B

Draw a line to join the points.

Construct the perpendicular bisector of this line.

The point where the lines cross is exactly midway between their homes.

In Worked Example 8 any point on the perpendicular bisector is the same distance from A and B.

If India and Joby wanted to meet at a point that was the same distance from their home, they could meet anywhere along that line.

However, the question asked you to find the point exactly midway between A and B.

The midpoint of line AB is the only point that meets that condition.

> The locus of points equidistant from two fixed points is the perpendicular bisector of the line joining the two points.

> The locus of points a fixed distance, d, from a line is the pair of parallel lines that are d cm away from the given line.

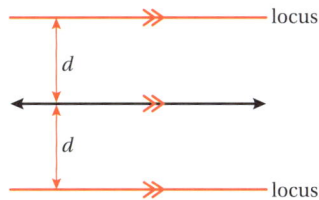

Tip

Remember a line continues to infinity in both directions, so it has no end points.

> The locus of points at a fixed distance, d, from a line segment is a pair of parallel lines d cm away from the line segment, as well as the semicircles of radius d cm at the ends of the line segment.

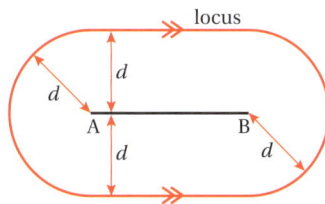

> The locus of points that is equidistant from two intersecting lines is their angle bisector. (the line BP in the diagram below)

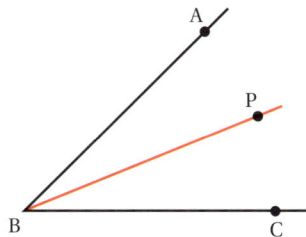

EXERCISE 34C

1 Loci are common in architecture and also in the line markings on sports fields.

Identify and describe some of the loci in the two photographs.

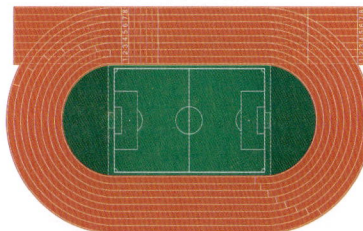

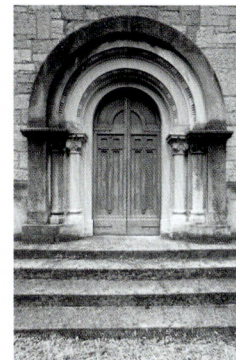

Find answers at: cambridge.org/ukschools/gcsemaths-studentbookanswers

2 A tractor is used to trim the hedge around the perimeter of a rectangular field.

The tractor drives at a constant distance of 2 m from the hedge.

Describe the shape produced by the locus of the tractor's path.

Choose your answer from the options below.

A Circle　　　　B Rectangle with rounded corners

C Rectangle　　D Square

3 In words, describe the point, path or area that each locus will produce.

a Points that are 200 km from a shop at point X.

b Points that are more than 2 km but less than 3 km from a straight fence 1 km long.

c Points that are equidistant from the two baselines of a tennis court.

d Points that are equidistant from the four corners of a soccer field.

e Points that are within 1 km of a railway line.

4 Accurately construct the locus of points 4 cm from a point D.

5 Draw angle MNO = 50°.

Accurately construct the locus of points equidistant from MN and NO.

6 Draw line PQ of length 4 cm long.

Construct the locus of points 1 cm from PQ.

7 PQ is a line segment of 5 cm.

X is a point exactly 4 cm from P and exactly 2.5 cm from Q.

Show by construction the possible locations of point X.

8 Draw a rectangle ABCD with AB = 6 cm and BC = 4 cm.

a Construct the locus of points that are equidistant from AB and BC.

b Shade the locus of points that are less than 1 cm from the centre of the rectangle.

c Construct the locus of points that are exactly 1 cm outside the perimeter of the rectangle.

9 MNOP is a square with sides of 5 cm.

Show by construction the locus of all points that are less than 1 cm from the sides of the square.

10 Draw a diagram to show:

a the locus of the valve on the rim of a bicycle wheel as it moves along a flat road surface.

b the locus of the centre of the same wheel as it moves along the road.

Section 4: Applying your skills

You need to be able to combine the construction techniques you have learned to construct accurate diagrams of shapes and to construct loci to show different situations.

In many cases you will need to decide which construction technique to use.

Many of the loci problems that you will have to solve will be presented in context.

You might be asked to draw scaled diagrams to solve these problems.

The scale might be given, for example, 1 cm : 10 km.

If you are not given a scale, always state the scale that you have used.

Problem-solving framework

A, B and C represent three towns.

A mobile phone tower is to be erected in the area.

The tower is to be equidistant from towns A and B and within 30 km of town C.

Show by accurate construction on a scale diagram all possible sites for the tower.

Use a scale of 1 cm : 10 km.

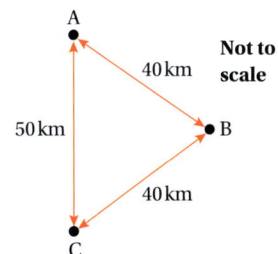

Steps for solving problems	What you would do for this example
Step 1: Work out what you have to do. Start by reading the question carefully.	You have to find the locus of points equidistant from A and B and the locus of points that are less than 30 km from C. The solution is where these loci overlap.
Step 2: What information do you need? Have you got it all?	You have to draw a scale diagram. The distances and the scale are given. The conditions for the loci are given.
Step 3: Decide what maths you can use.	First work out the lengths you have to construct using the scale. The scale is 1 cm : 10 km. So: $\dfrac{40\,\text{km}}{10}$ is represented by 4 cm $\qquad$ $\dfrac{50\,\text{km}}{10}$ is represented by 5 cm Next use these lengths to construct a triangle using your ruler and pair of compasses. Once you have the triangle you can find the loci by construction.
Step 4: Set out your solution clearly. Check your working and that your answer is reasonable.	The tower could be built at any position along the thick red line.
Step 5: Check that you've answered the question.	You have shown the overlapping loci and written a statement to answer the question.

Find answers at: cambridge.org/ukschools/gcsemaths-studentbookanswers

EXERCISE 34D

1 A scale drawing is made of a town.

The scale is 10 m : 1 cm.

The post office is 54 m from the nursery.

What is the distance between the two on the scale drawing?

Choose your answer from the options below.

A 0.54 cm   B 5.4 cm   C 54 cm   D 5.4 m

2 Draw line AB of length 5.2 cm.

Construct the perpendicular bisector of AB, which crosses AB at E.

Mark the point D 44 mm along the perpendicular bisector from E.

Mark point F on DE such that DF = FE = 22 mm.

Construct MN // AB and passing through point F.

3 Construct a parallelogram with sides of 46 mm and 28 mm and a longest diagonal of length 60 mm.

Measure and write in the length of the other diagonal.

4 Accurately construct a square of side 45 mm.

5 Construct a quadrilateral ABCD such that angle ABC = 90°, AB = DC = 2.2 cm and AD = BC = 5 cm.

What kind of quadrilateral is this?

6 On a map, the position of buried treasure is known to be 10 metres from point Y and 12 metres from point Z.

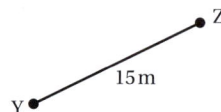

Y and Z are 15 metres apart.

Draw a scale diagram and mark with an X all the places where the treasure might be buried.

Use a scale of 1 cm to 2 m.

7 A monkey is in a rectangular enclosure that is 10 m by 17.5 m.

The monkey is able to stretch through the fence around its enclosure and reach a distance of 25 cm.

a Draw a scale diagram to show the locus of points that the monkey can reach outside its enclosure.

b Show on your diagram where you should place a safety barrier to make sure that visitors cannot touch the monkey.

Give a reason for your answer.

8 A garden has a semicircular lawn surrounded by fencing.

The semicircle has a diameter of 10 m.

The distance from the lawn to the fence is consistently 1 m.

Draw an accurate scaled diagram of the lawn and fence.

9 MNOP is a rectangular field 150 m by 400 m.

A fence is built across the field so that it is equidistant from points M and O.

Draw a scaled plan of the field and indicate on it the position in which the fence is built.

10 A museum installs motion sensors at points A and B as shown in the diagram.

Each sensor covers 270°.

Each sensor picks up any movement within a range of 8 m as long as the distance is a straight line.

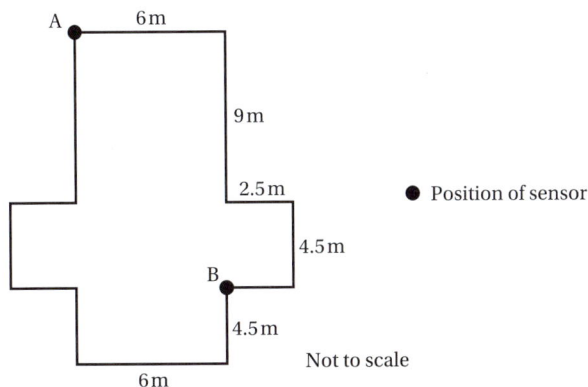

Not to scale

a Work out by scale drawing and construction any areas not protected by the motion sensors.

b Are these the best positions for the sensors?

If not, suggest where they might be located to ensure better coverage.

Checklist of learning and understanding

Geometry constructions

- A protractor is used to measure and draw angles.
- You can use a ruler and a pair of compasses to construct perpendicular lines and to bisect lines and angles.
- The perpendicular bisector of any line cuts the line at its midpoint.
- The shortest distance from a point to a line is always the perpendicular distance.

Loci

- A locus is a set of points that meet the same conditions.
- The locus of points can be a single point, a line, a curve or a shaded area.
- Loci can be used to solve problems involving equal distances and overlapping areas.

Find answers at: cambridge.org/ukschools/gcsemaths-studentbookanswers

For additional questions on the topics in this chapter, visit GCSE Mathematics Online.

Chapter review

1 **a** Use a protractor to measure angles *a* and *b* on this clockface.

  b Draw two angles that are the same size as *a* and *b*.

  c Bisect the two angles you have drawn by construction.

2 Draw a line AB of length 6.5 cm.

  a Find its midpoint by construction.

  b Indicate the locus of points that are equidistant from A and B on your diagram.

3 Town X is due north of town Y.

  They are 20 km apart.

  Town Z is 25 km from town X and 35 km from town Y.

  a Draw a scale diagram to show the location of town Z in relation to the other two towns.

  Use a scale of 1 cm : 5 km.

  b A railway runs between towns X and Y such that it is equidistant from both towns.

  Indicate the position of the railway on your diagram.

  c The electricity supply from town X is carried on a cable that is the same distance from XZ and XY along its length.

  Indicate on your diagram where this cable would be.

  d Salman wants to live within 10 km of town Y, but no more than 30 km from town Z.

  Show by shading the area that meets these conditions.

4 The scale drawing shows a post that is 1.5 metres from the fence.

Drawn
to scale

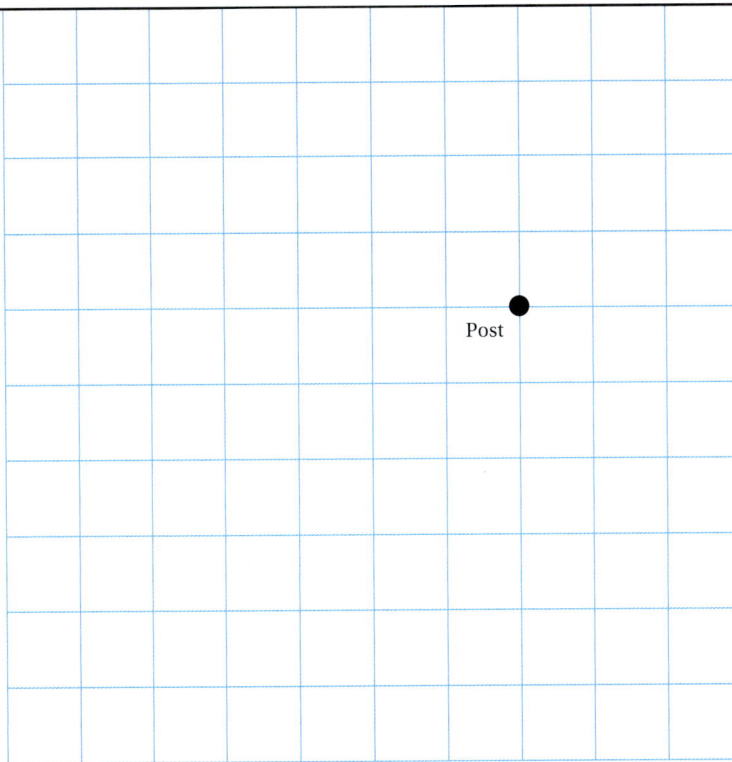

Wall

Post

Fence

a How far is the post from the wall? *(1 mark)*

b A pony is tied to the post by a rope.

The pony can reach 2.5 metres from the post.

On a copy of the scale drawing, show accurately the area that the
pony can reach. *(2 marks)*

c Work out the scale of the drawing as a ratio.

Give your answer in its simplest form. *(3 marks)*

© AQA 2013

5 Make an accurate drawing to show the loci of all points that are within
1 cm of the circumference of a circle of radius 2.5 cm.

6 Construct a parallelogram with diagonals 46 mm and 80 mm and one
side of 60 mm.

Measure and fill in the sizes of the internal angles and the length of the
other side.

35 Similarity

In this chapter you will learn how to …

- identify similar triangles and prove that two triangles are similar.
- work with positive, fractional and negative scale factors to enlarge shapes on a grid.
- find the scale factor and centre of enlargement of a transformation.
- understand the relationship between lengths, areas and volumes of similar objects.

For more resources relating to this chapter, visit GCSE Mathematics Online.

Using mathematics: real-life applications

When you enlarge a photo, project an image on to a screen or make scaled models you are dealing with similarity. Many toys and other objects are scaled, but similar, versions of larger objects from real life.

"I work with scale drawings and scale models all the time. The models are mathematically similar to the real aircraft so the clients can see what they are buying. We made these scale models to display at an international air show."

(Aircraft designer)

Before you start …

Ch 9	You need to be able to label angles correctly.	**1** **a** Which angle is a right angle? **b** What size is angle DOA? **c** What size is angle BOD?
KS3	You need to know the criteria for when two triangles are congruent.	**2** Prove that the triangles below are congruent, giving reasons.
Ch 17	You need to know how to solve simple equations using inverse operations.	**3** Solve: **a** $3x = 24$ **b** $15 = 6h$ **c** $6.25 = 25k$

Before You Start continues on next page …

Before you start continued …

Ch 27	You need to be able to recognise numbers in equivalent ratios.	④ Which pairs of numbers are in the same ratio as 3:2? A 6:5 B 4:6 C 0.15:0.1 ⑤ Given that $\dfrac{x}{15} = \dfrac{4}{90}$, find x.
Ch 1, 4, 14	You need to be able to find powers of whole numbers, fractions and decimals.	⑥ Calculate the following: a $\left(\dfrac{1}{2}\right)^3$ b 4.5^2 c 15^3

Assess your starting point using the Launchpad

STEP 1

① Which of the following pairs of shapes are similar? Give a reason for your decisions.

a Any two rectangles.

b Triangles ACE and BCD in the diagram.

② The diagram shows two similar triangles. Find the lengths of AC, BC and AE.

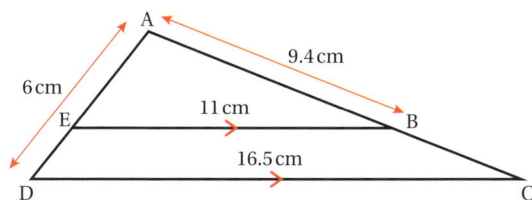

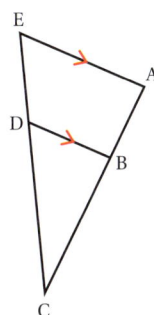

GO TO
Section 1:
Similar triangles

STEP 2

③ Copy the grid and enlarge the triangle by a scale factor of 2.5 and a centre (−1, −4).

④ Describe this enlargement.

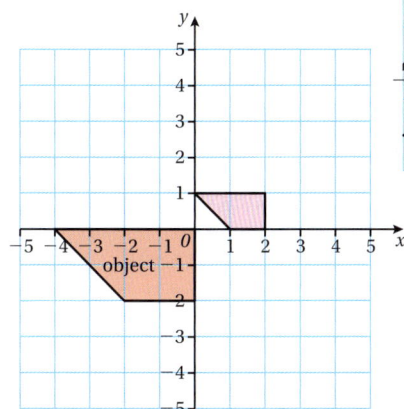

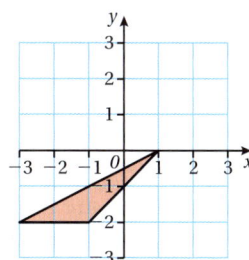

GO TO
Section 2:
Enlargements

GO TO
Step 3
The Launchpad continues on the next page …

Find answers at: cambridge.org/ukschools/gcsemaths-studentbookanswers

Launchpad continued ...

STEP 3

5 Are these two quadrilaterals similar? Give reasons for your answer.

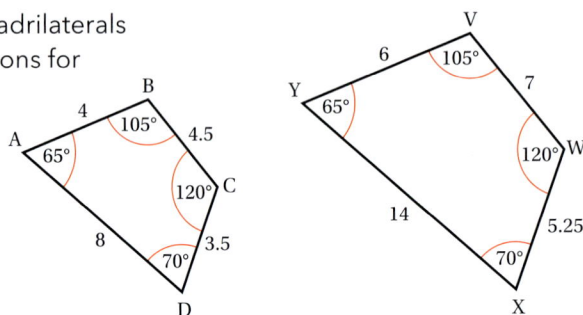

6 The shapes on the right are similar.

Given that:
the area of ABCD = 48 cm²
the area of PQRS = 108 cm²
find the length of diagonal AC in ABCD.

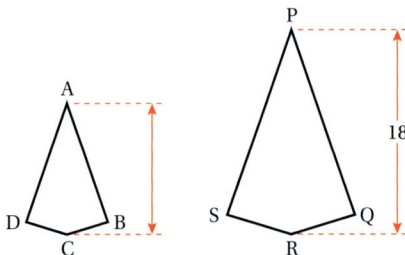

?

GO TO
Section 3:
Similar shapes and objects

✓

GO TO
Chapter review

Section 1: Similar triangles

Two shapes are mathematically similar if they have the same shape and proportions but are different in size.

To prove that two triangles are similar, you have to show that one of these statements is true:

- all the corresponding angles are equal
- the three sides are in proportion
- two sides are in proportion and the included angles (between these two sides) are equal.

You must name triangles with the corresponding vertices in the correct order when you state facts about similarity.

WORKED EXAMPLE 1

Show that the triangles ABC and RTS are similar.

State which angles are equal and which sides are in proportion.

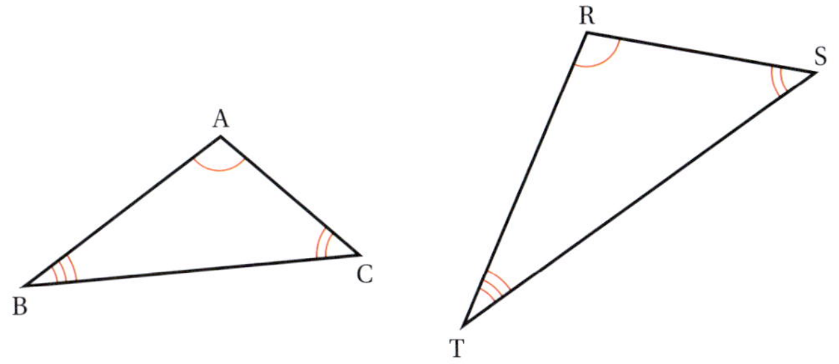

Triangle ABC is similar to triangle RTS because angle A = angle R, angle B = angle T and angle C = angle S.
The three sides are in proportion, so $\frac{AB}{RT} = \frac{AC}{RS} = \frac{BC}{TS}$

Finding unknown lengths using proportional sides

In similar triangles the lengths of any pair of corresponding sides are in the same ratio.

You can use the ratio of corresponding sides to find the lengths of unknown sides in similar figures.

Problem-solving framework

In the diagram, triangle ABC is similar to triangle QRP.
Find the length of x.

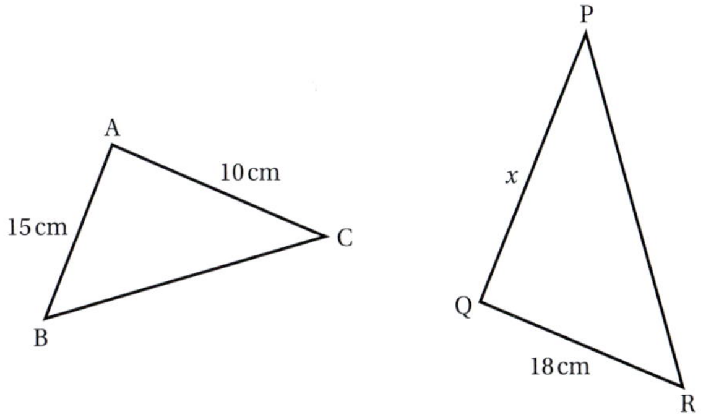

Steps for solving problems	What you would do for this example
Step 1: Identify the similar triangles in the problem and write them down with the vertices in the correct order.	Triangle ABC is similar to triangle QRP.

Continues on next page ...

Find answers at: cambridge.org/ukschools/gcsemaths-studentbookanswers

Step 2: Write down what you know.	That the triangles are similar. Two sides of triangle ABC. One side of triangle QRP.
Step 3: Find the ratio between the sides.	AB corresponds to QR, so the ratio is 15 : 18.
Step 4: Write a proportion with the unknown side.	$\dfrac{AC}{QP} = \dfrac{15}{18} = \dfrac{10}{x}$
Step 5: Solve the proportion.	$x = \dfrac{18 \times 10}{15} = 12\,\text{cm}$
Step 6: Have you answered the question?	$x = 12\,\text{cm}$

EXERCISE 35A

1 Each diagram below contains a pair of similar triangles.

Identify the matching angles and the sides that are in proportion.

Write down your reasoning using the correct angle vocabulary.

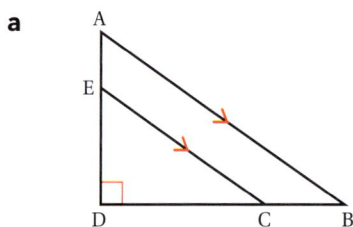

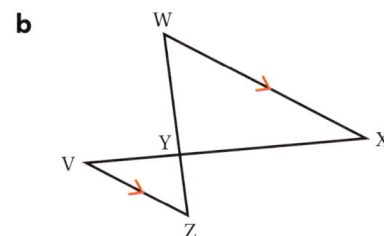

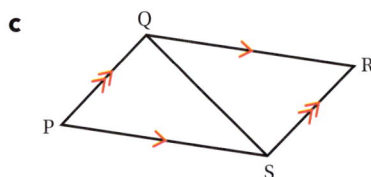

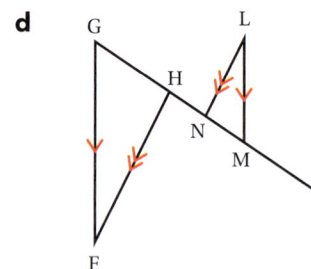

a

b

c

d

2 Which of the following statements does not prove that two triangles are mathematically similar?

A There are three equal corresponding angles.

B There are two angles that are equal.

C The three pairs of sides are in the same ratio.

D Two sides are in proportion and the included angles are equal.

3 Are the following pairs of triangles similar? Give reasons for your answers.

a

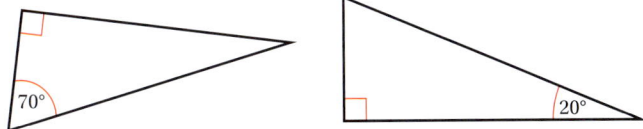

b

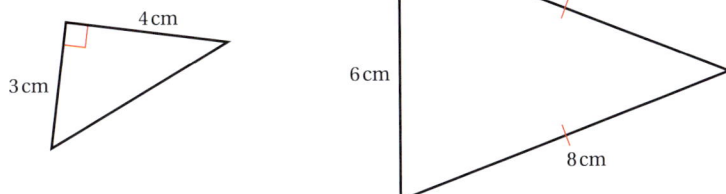

c

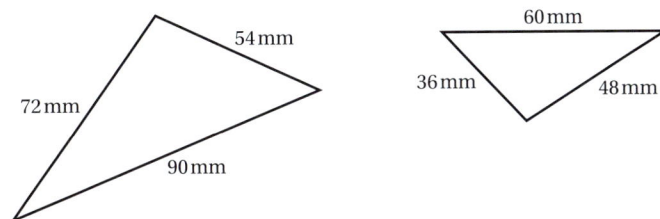

4 State whether each of the statements below is true or false.

Write down your reasoning and give a counter-example for any statement you believe is false

a All isosceles triangles are similar.

b All equilateral triangles are similar.

c All right-angled triangles are similar.

d All right-angled triangles with an angle of 30° are similar.

e All right-angled isosceles triangles are similar.

f No pair of scalene triangles are ever similar.

5 Each diagram below contains three similar triangles.

Identify the matching angles and sides in each group of triangles.
Write down your reasoning.

a

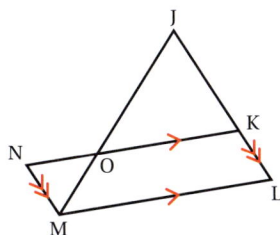

b

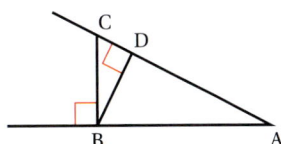

6 The two shapes below are similar.
Find the missing lengths *c* and *d*.

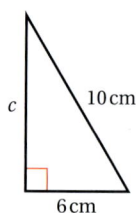 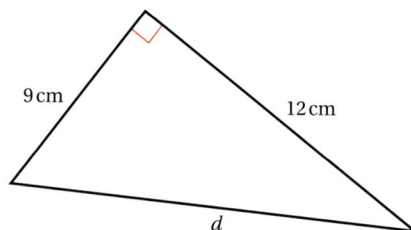

7 The two shapes below are similar.
Find the missing lengths *e* and *f*.

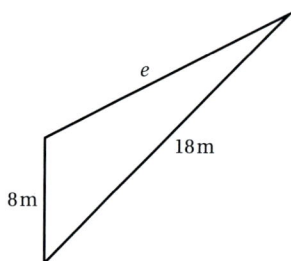 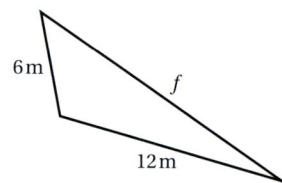

8 Find the lengths of AE, CE and AB.

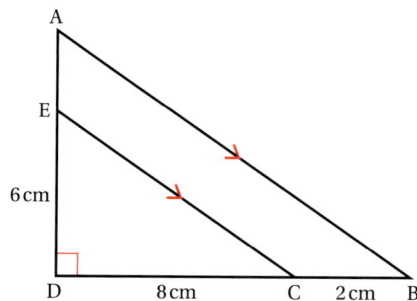

9 Find the lengths of YZ and XY.

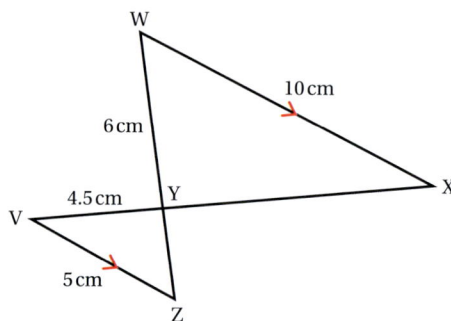

10 The diagram shows part of a children's climbing frame.

Find the length of BC.

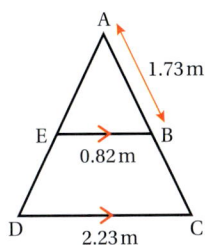

11 The diagram shows that a swimmer A and boat B are 80 m apart.

The boat B is 1200 m from the lighthouse C.

The height of the boat is 12 m and the swimmer can see the top of the lighthouse at the top of the boat's mast when her head lies at sea level.

Work out the height of the lighthouse.

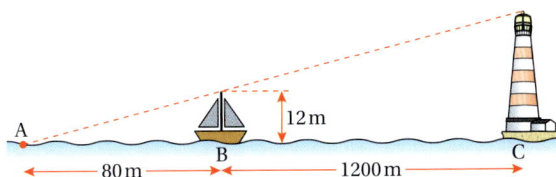

Section 2: Enlargements

An enlargement is a transformation that changes the position of a shape as well as its size.

Under enlargement, an object and its image are similar shapes, because their angles remain unchanged.

In mathematics, you use the word enlargement for all transformations that produce similar images even if the image is smaller than the original object.

To construct an enlargement of a shape, you multiply the length of each side by the scale factor.

Before you enlarge a shape, consider its new dimensions.

Has it got bigger?
Has it stayed the same size?
Has it got smaller?

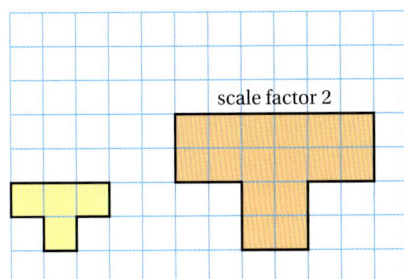

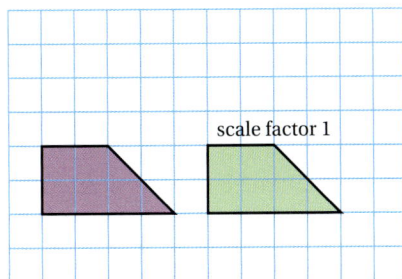

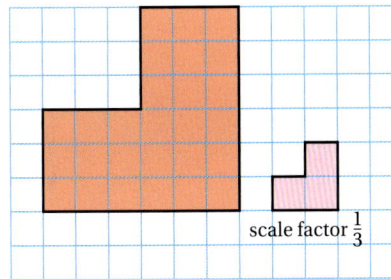

WORKED EXAMPLE 2

Draw an enlargement of triangle ABC by a scale factor of 2.

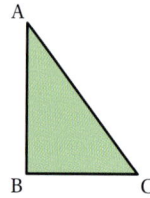

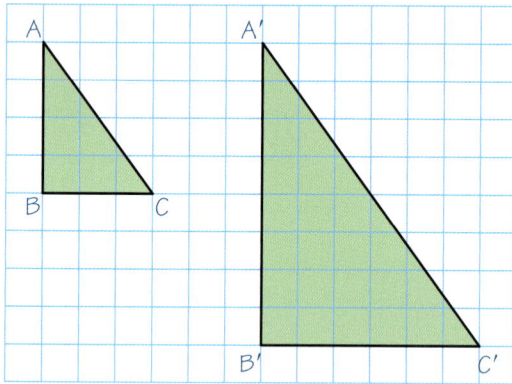

The image of triangle ABC is triangle A′B′C′.

The length of A′B′ is twice the length of AB, the length of A′C′ = 2AC and length of B′C′ = 2BC.

Notice that triangle ABC is similar to triangle A′B′C′ and that the sides are in proportion

EXERCISE 35B

1 Enlarge each shape by the scale factor given.

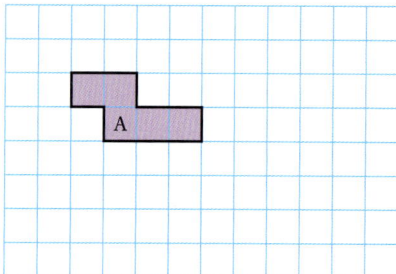

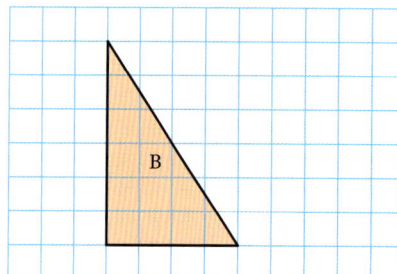

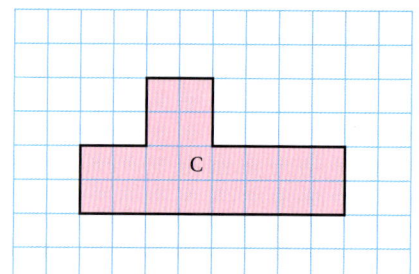

a Enlarge A by a scale factor of 3.

b Enlarge B by a scale factor of 0.5

c Enlarge C by a scale factor of $1\frac{1}{2}$

The centre of enlargement

You need two pieces of information to accurately draw an enlargement: the scale factor and the centre of enlargement.

The centre of enlargement is the point from where the enlargement is measured.

When you use a centre of enlargement, you draw the enlargement in a certain position in relation to the original object.

The table below shows you how to enlarge a shape from a given centre of enlargement by a scale factor of 2.

Step 1: Find the distance from the centre of enlargement to a point on the object. You can draw a ray from the centre to the point.

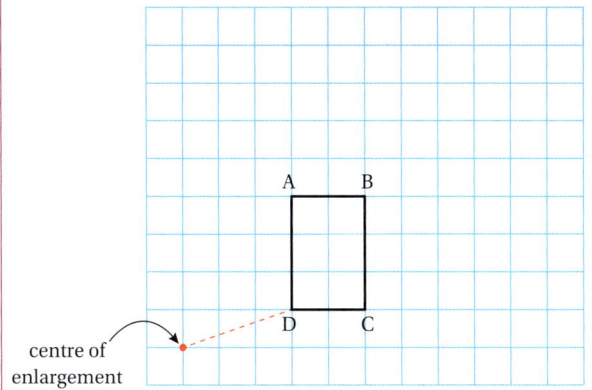

centre of enlargement

Step 2: The original ray is three units to the right and one unit up. Double the distance of the ray to find the image of point D. Label it D′.

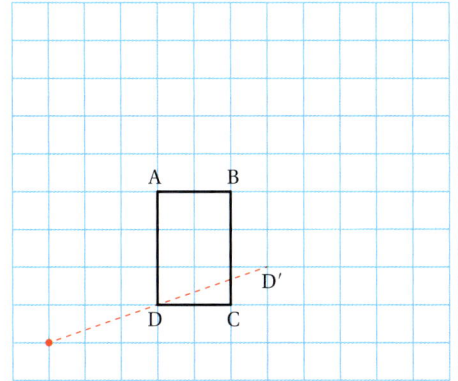

Step 3: Follow the same process of drawing rays and extending them to find the images of all the vertices ABCD. Label them A′B′C′D′.

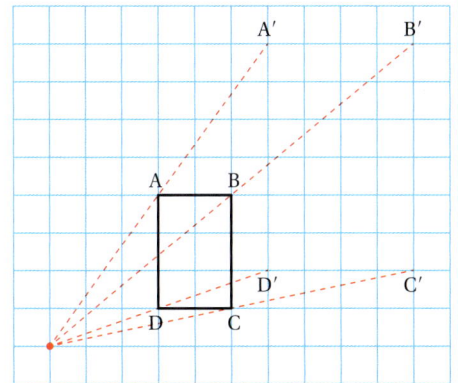

Step 4: Draw in the image. Check that the lengths of the image are correct.

Note that lines from the corresponding vertices of the object and its image will meet at the centre of enlargement.

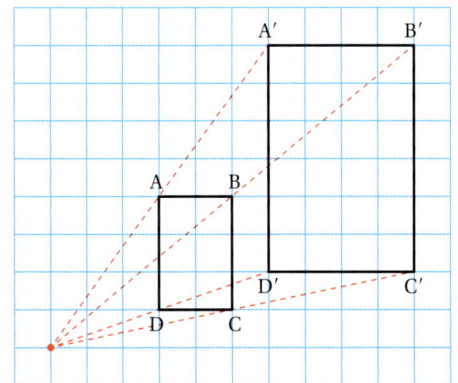

The procedure is the same for a centre of enlargement in any position, even for a centre of enlargement inside the shape itself.

WORK IT OUT 35.1

This triangle is enlarged from centre (−3, 4) with a scale factor of 2. Draw its image.

Which one of these answers is correct?

Why are the others wrong?

How many marks would you give the incorrect answers if you were the teacher? Why?

Option A	Option B	Option C

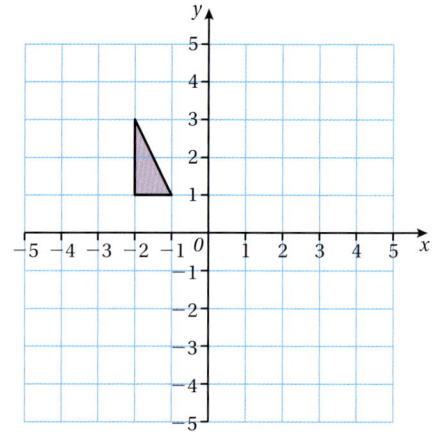

Tip

Sketch the new shape before you construct the enlargement. Draw one ray to identify the new position of the shape. After drawing the enlargement add in additional rays to check that it is in the correct position.

Fractional scale factors

If the scale factor is a fraction, the image will be smaller than the object.

WORKED EXAMPLE 3

Enlarge the triangle on the grid by a scale factor of $\frac{1}{2}$ through the given centre of enlargement.

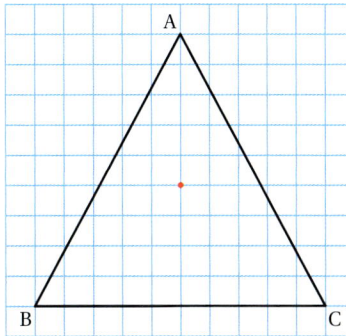

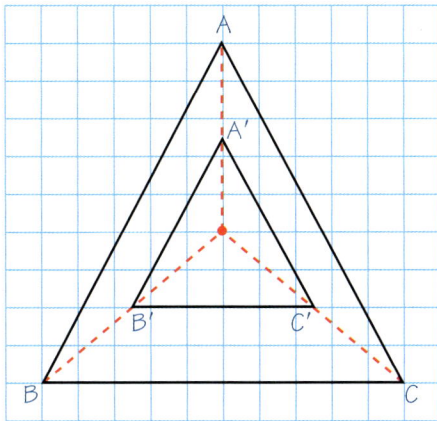

In this case, the rays from each vertex of the object are halved to find the position of the image.

EXERCISE 35C

1 Enlarge each shape as directed.

Use the point C as the centre of enlargement.

  a Enlarge shape R by a scale factor of 3.

  b Enlarge shape S by a scale factor of 2.

  c Enlarge shape T by a scale factor of $\frac{1}{2}$

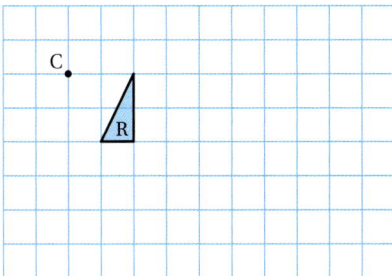

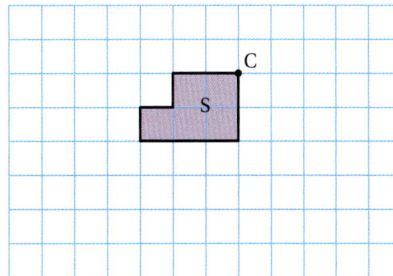

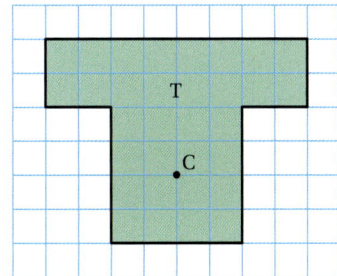

Find answers at: cambridge.org/ukschools/gcsemaths-studentbookanswers

2 Enlarge the given shape by a scale factor of 3.
Use the origin as the centre of enlargement.

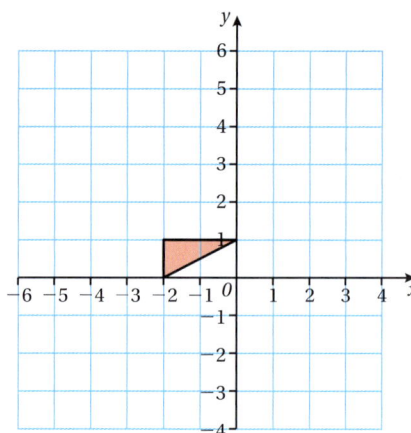

3 Enlarge the given shape by a scale factor of 2.
Use (−4, 3) as the centre of enlargement.

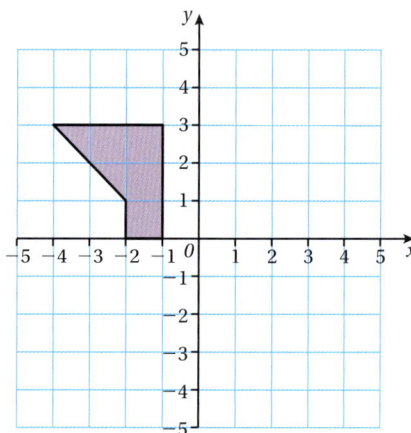

4 Enlarge the given shape by a scale factor of $\frac{1}{3}$
Use (−5, 2) as the centre of enlargement.

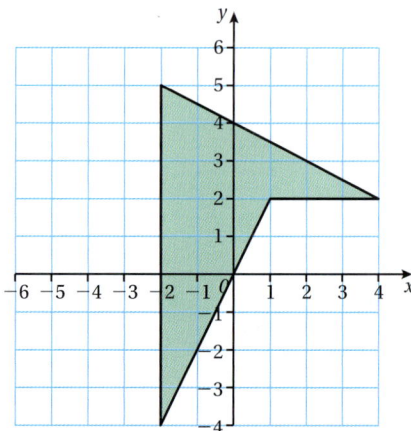

5 Enlarge the given shape by a scale factor of $1\frac{1}{2}$

Use $(0, 1)$ as the centre of enlargement.

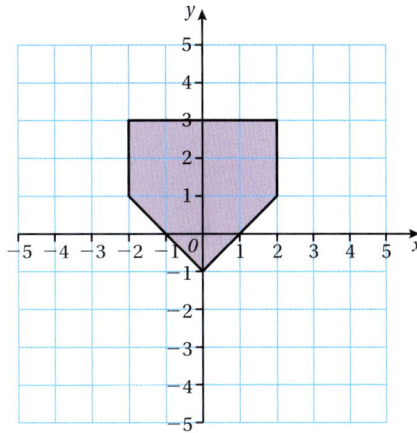

Negative scale factors

A negative scale factor has additional effects on the image.

The points of the image remain on their ray but they are located on the other side of the centre of enlargement in an inverted position.

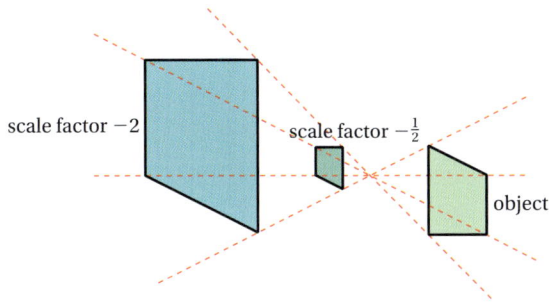

scale factor -2 scale factor $-\frac{1}{2}$ object

WORKED EXAMPLE 4

Enlarge the rectangle PQRS by a scale factor of -2.

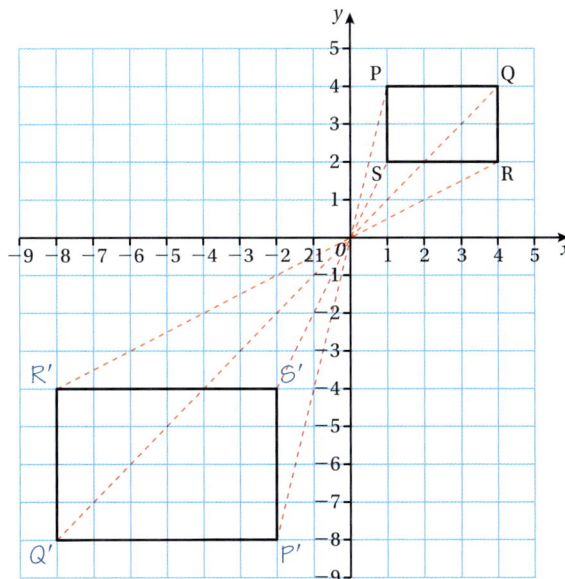

For each vertex, the coordinates are multiplied by -2 to find the image of the point.

EXERCISE 35D

1 Enlarge the given shape by a scale factor of –1.

Use the origin as the centre of enlargement.

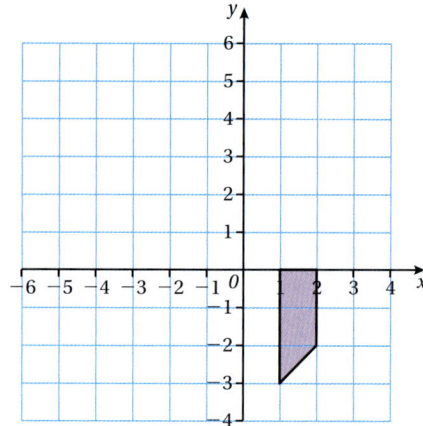

2 Enlarge the given shape by a scale factor of –2.

Use (–2, 2) as the centre of enlargement.

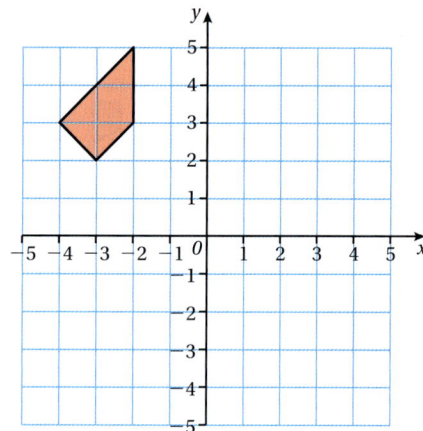

3 Enlarge the given shape by a scale factor of $-\frac{1}{2}$

Use (–3, 0) as the centre of enlargement.

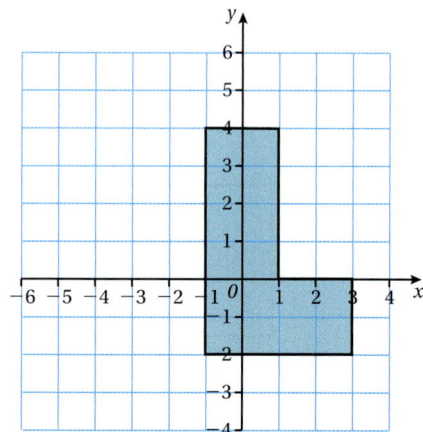

4 Enlarge the given shape by a scale factor of $-1\frac{1}{2}$

Use $(-1, 1)$ as the centre of enlargement.

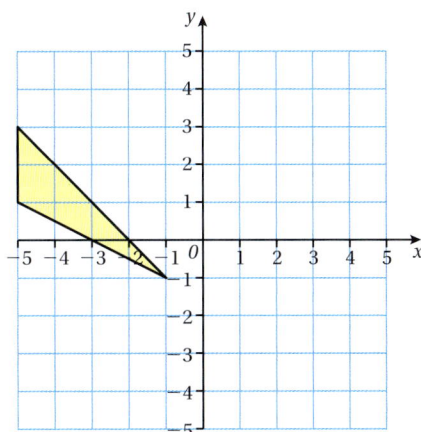

Properties of enlargements

You need to remember the following properties of an enlargement.

- The centre of enlargement can be anywhere: inside the object, on a vertex or side of the object or outside the object.
- A scale factor greater than 1 will enlarge the object. A scale factor smaller than 1 will reduce the size of the object although this is still called an enlargement.
- The object and its image are similar under enlargement. Sides are in the ratio $1 : k$, where k is the scale factor.
- The area of an object and its image will be in the ratio $1 : k^2$, where k is the scale factor.
- An object and its image have the same angles.
- For positive scale factors an object and its image have the same orientation.

Describing enlargements

To describe an enlargement you need to give:

- the scale factor
- the centre of enlargement.

The ratio of sides gives the scale factor.

To find the centre of enlargement you need to draw lines from corresponding vertices of the object and its image to find the point where they meet.

WORK IT OUT 35.2

What scale factors have been used to enlarge this shape?

Which one of these students' answers is correct?

What feedback would you give each student to make sure they don't make the same mistakes again?

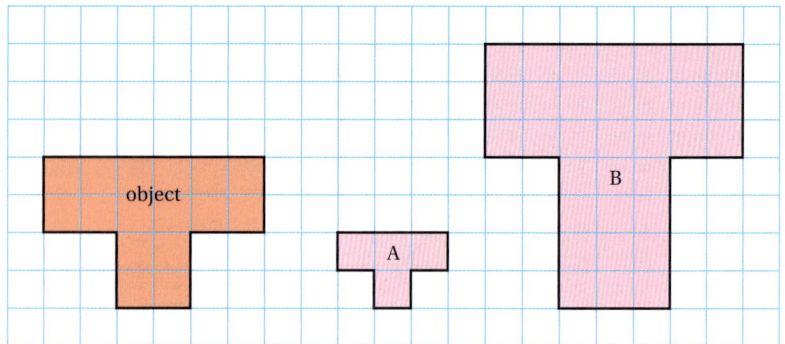

Student A	Student B	Student C
A scale factor of 2 has been used to produce shape A.

The top of shape A is 3 squares across, multiply this by 2 to get 6, the length of the top of the object.

B can't be an enlargement. Its top is 7 squares and the object is 6. You can't do that using multiplication. Maybe it's 1? | Since the sides have halved in length to get A, the scale factor is $\frac{1}{2}$

Shape B isn't an enlargement. The sides have been increased by different numbers of squares. | To get shape A you have to take away one square along the bottom and along each side edge. So the scale factor is -1.

Shape B is a scale factor of $1\frac{1}{2}$ because 2 squares have become 3 squares. |

EXERCISE 35E

1 Triangle ABC is enlarged to give triangle A′B′C′. Angle BCA is 80°. What is angle B′C′A′?

Choose from the following options.

A 40°   B 80°   C 160°

D It is impossible to say.

2 Which of the houses shown on the grid are enlargements of house A?

For each enlargement state the scale factor.

3 These diagrams each show an object and its image after an enlargement.

Describe each of these enlargements by giving both the scale factor and the coordinates of the centre of enlargement.

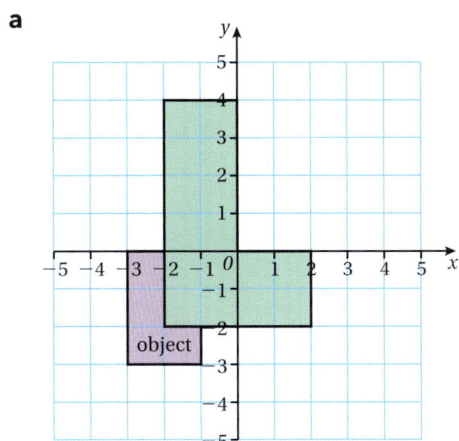

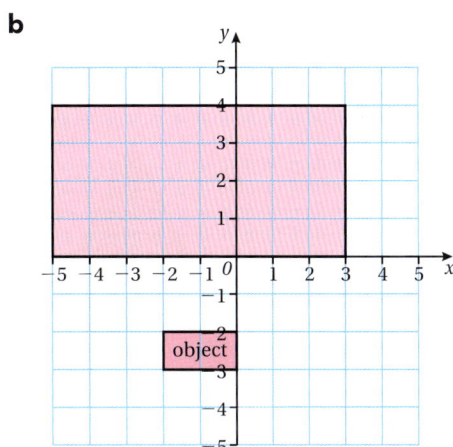

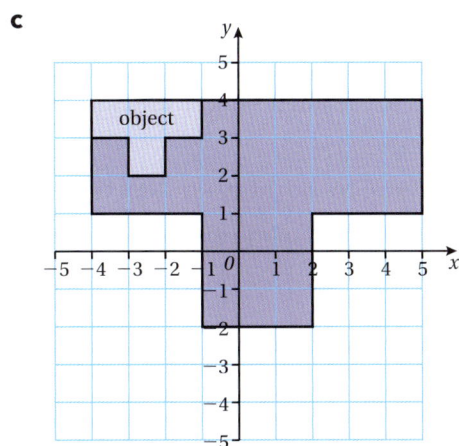

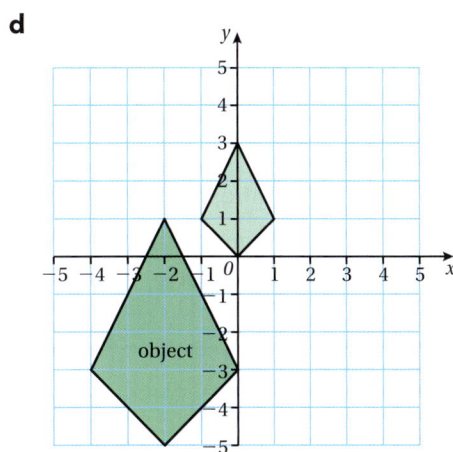

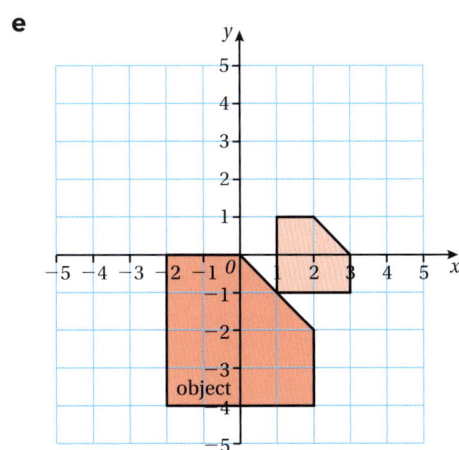

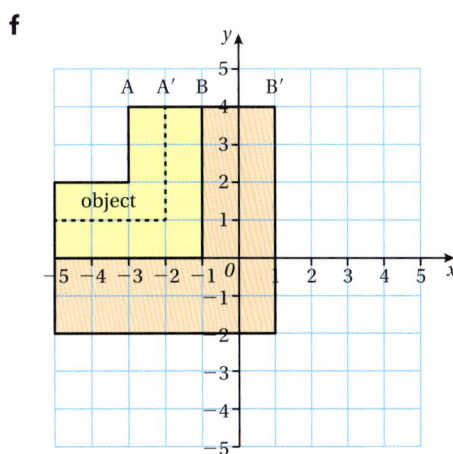

a

b

c

d

e

f

4 Describe each of these enlargements. In each case the object is labelled.

a

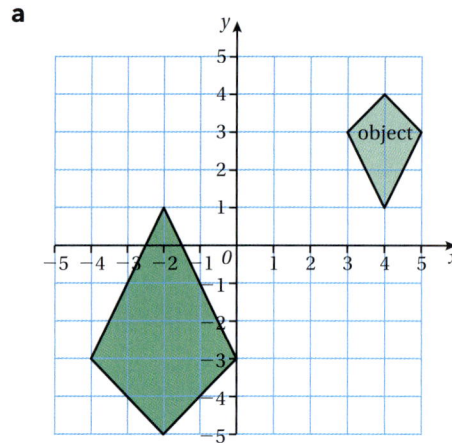

b

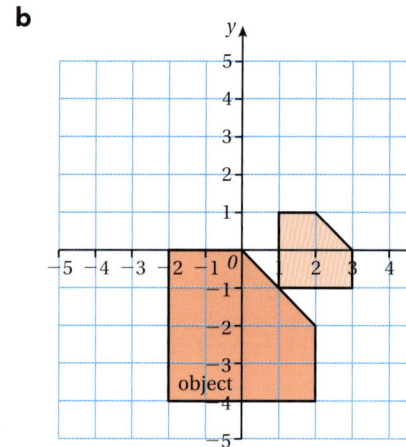

Section 3: Similar shapes and objects

Two polygons are similar if:

* the angles in one polygon are equal to the angles in the other polygon

and

* the ratios of the sides from one polygon to the other are kept the same.

For polygons other than triangles, equal angles alone are not sufficient to prove similarity.

WORKED EXAMPLE 5

Which of the quadrilaterals, B to D, are similar to A?

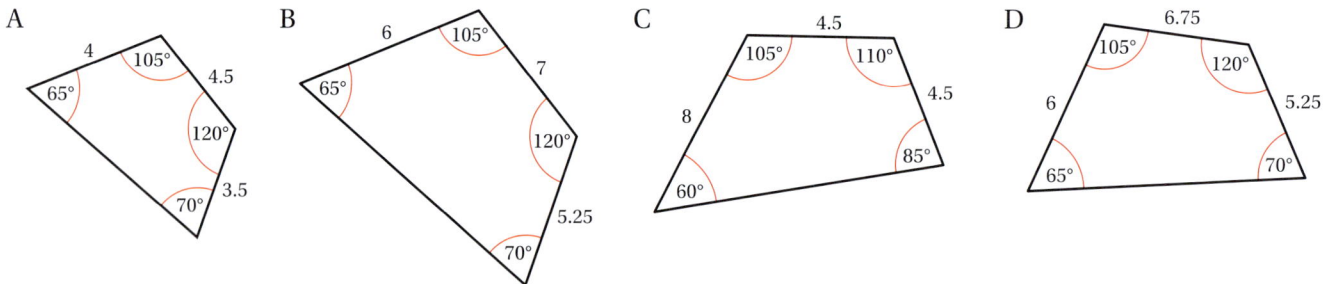

B has the same size angles as A, but the sides are not in proportion.

For example, $\frac{4}{6} \neq \frac{4.5}{7}$. So B is not similar to A.

The angles in C are different to the angles in A, so C is not similar to A.

D has corresponding angles equal to those in A.

Test to see whether the sides are in the same proportion:

$$\frac{4}{6} = \frac{4.5}{6.75} = \frac{3.5}{5.25}$$

D is similar to A.

D is an enlargement of A with a scale factor of 1.5

Similar areas and volumes

If two shapes are similar their corresponding sides are in the same ratio, and their corresponding angles are equal.

If a 2D shape is enlarged and the scale factor is a, then the ratio of the area of the image to the area of the original shape will be a^2.

If a 3D object is enlarged by a scale factor of a, then the ratio of the volume of the enlarged object will be a^3.

Consider the following set of similar triangles.

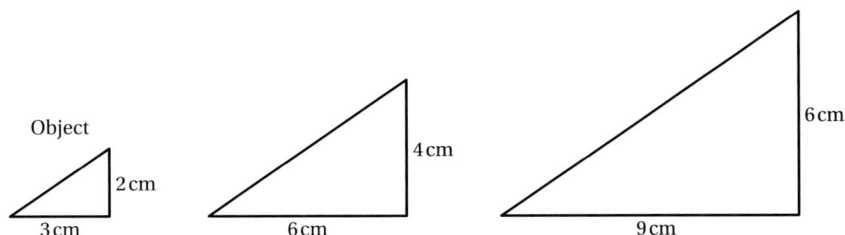

Object		
3 cm, 2 cm	6 cm, 4 cm	9 cm, 6 cm
enlargement scale factor 1	enlargement scale factor 2	enlargement scale factor 3
area = 3 cm^2	area = 12 cm^2	area = 27 cm^2

You should notice the following:

Scale factor 2   area scale factor $2^2 = 4$

Scale factor 3   area scale factor $3^2 = 9$

Scale factor n area scale factor n^2

Consider the following set of similar cuboids.

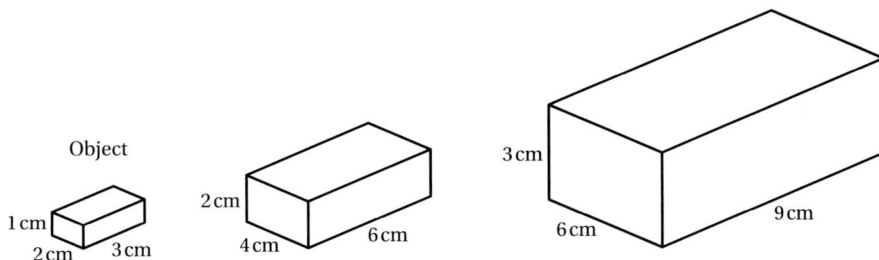

Object		
1 cm, 2 cm, 3 cm	2 cm, 4 cm, 6 cm	3 cm, 6 cm, 9 cm
enlargement scale factor 1	enlargement scale factor 2	enlargement scale factor 3
volume = 6 cm^3	volume = 48 cm^3	volume = 162 cm^3

You should notice the following:

Scale factor 2   volume scale factor $2^3 = 8$

Scale factor 3   volume scale factor $3^3 = 27$

Scale factor n volume scale factor n^3

EXERCISE 35F

1 A triangle with side lengths 3 cm, 4 cm and 5 cm is enlarged.

Which of the following could be this enlarged shape's side lengths?

A 5 cm, 12 cm, 13 cm   B 4 cm, 6 cm, 5 cm

C 6 cm, 8 cm, 15 cm   D 15 cm, 9 cm, 12 cm

2 State whether each statement below is true or false.

Write down your reasoning.

a All squares are similar.

b All hexagons are similar.

c All rectangles are similar.

d All regular octagons are similar.

3 Sketch the following pairs of shapes and decide if they are similar.

Write down your reasoning.

a Rectangle ABCD with AB = 5 cm and BC = 3 cm

Rectangle EFGH with EF = 10 cm and FG = 6 cm

b Rectangle ABCD with AB = 5 cm and BC = 3 cm

Rectangle EFGH with EF = 10 cm and GH = 9 cm

c Square ABCD with AB = 4 cm

Square EFGH with EF = 6 cm

4 Joseph is an architect.

He uses these scale diagrams to tell his builders that *a* is 8 m, and *b* is 10 cm.

What has he done wrong?

What are the correct lengths?

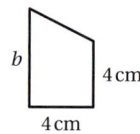
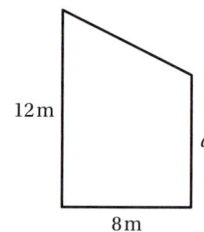

5 The two shapes below are similar.

Find the missing lengths of the sides in the second shape.

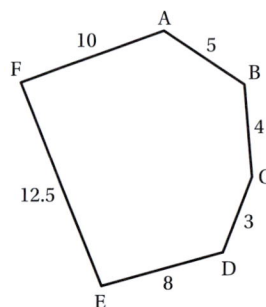
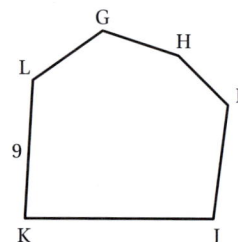

6 Joe makes jewellery out of wire.

He has made a model ABCDEF.

The model will be enlarged by a scale factor of 1.5 when he makes the real item GHIJKL.

AB = 5 cm and BC = 7 cm

What length of wire will Joe need to make the real item?

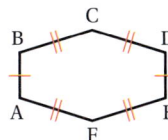

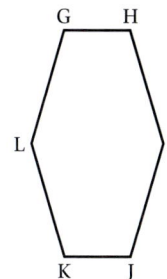

7 The original surface area of a triangular prism is 144 cm². It is enlarged.

Its new surface area is 9 cm². Its new volume is 2.5 cm³.

What was its original volume? Choose from the options below.

A 160 cm³   B 40 cm³   C 6 cm³   D 0.16 cm³

8 Two similar shapes have volumes in the ratio 1:512.

Susan thinks the ratio of their surface areas is 1:8.

Say why she is wrong.

9 Triangles A and B are similar.

Triangle A has an area of 48 square units.

Triangle B has an area of 588 square units.

a What is the scale factor of enlargement?

b Triangle A has a base of 8 units. Work out the dimensions of Triangle B.

10 A canned food producer makes tins of radius 2.5 cm, and similar tins that have a radius of 7 cm.

The smaller tin has a volume of 157 ml (or 157 cm³).

a Calculate the height of the smaller tin.

b Work out the height and the volume of the larger tin.

11 A cone has a radius of 4 cm and a height of 8 cm.

a Calculate the volume and surface area of the cone.

b Each measurement is increased by a factor of 3.

Calculate the new volume and surface area.

12 A company making beach balls uses 196π cm² of material to make a ball with a diameter of 14 cm.

a What is the volume of the ball?

They also make a giant ball that is larger by a scale factor, k.

b If the company needs 3136π cm² to make the giant ball, what is k?

c What is the volume of the giant ball?

📎 **Checklist of learning and understanding**

Similar triangles

- Two triangles are similar if all three corresponding angles are equal. Similar triangles are the same shape and their corresponding sides are in proportion.
- The proportion between corresponding sides of similar triangles can be used to solve problems in geometry.

Enlargements

- An enlargement is a transformation that changes the position and size of a shape.
- Enlargements are described by a scale factor and centre of enlargement.

Similar shapes

- If shapes are enlarged, similar shapes are created with all their sides in proportion. The proportionality between lengths can be used to solve geometry problems.
- If a 2D shape is enlarged, a similar shape is created. All of the dimensions of the image will be enlarged by the same scale factor. If the scale factor is a, then the ratio of the area of the image to the area of the original shape will be a^2.
- If a 3D object is enlarged by a scale factor of a, then the ratio of the volume of the enlarged object to the volume of the original object will be a^3.

For additional questions on the topics in this chapter, visit GCSE Mathematics Online.

📁 **Chapter review**

1. Which of the following are always similar?

   A Isosceles triangles   B Equilateral triangles

   C Right-angled triangles   D Scalene triangles

2. **a** Prove that triangle VWX is similar to triangle VYZ.

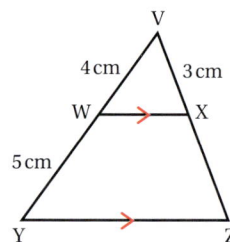

   b Find the length of XZ.

3 A tree is 3 m high and its shadow has a length of 7.5 m.

At the same time of day, a building casts a shadow that is 16.25 m long.

Use similar triangles to calculate the height of the building.

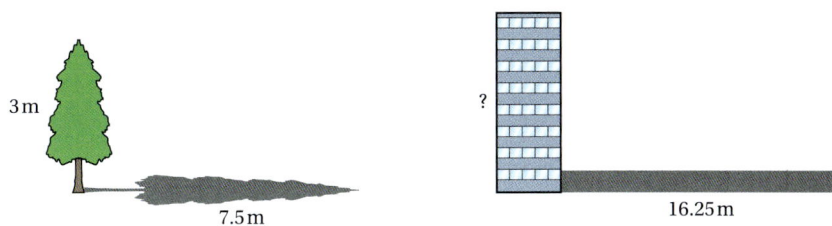

4 Draw an enlargement of ABCD by $\frac{1}{3}$

Use the given point as the centre of enlargement.

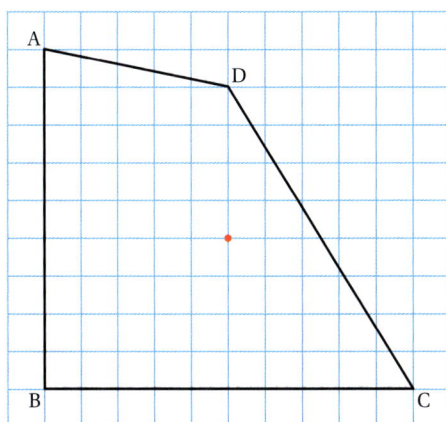

5 Draw an enlargement of the shape by a scale factor of 1.5

Use the origin as the centre of enlargement.

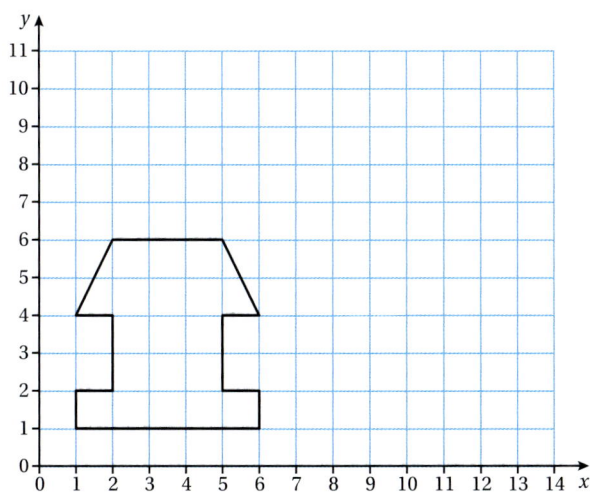

Find answers at: cambridge.org/ukschools/gcsemaths-studentbookanswers

6 Are any two regular hexagons similar shapes?

Give reasons for your answer.

7 Are any two rhombuses similar shapes?

Give reasons for your answer.

8 Two similar shapes have areas of 90 cm² and 62.5 cm².

The perimeter of the smaller shape is 40 cm.

What is the perimeter of the larger shape?

9 A square-based pyramid has a base length of 10 cm and a perpendicular height of 12 cm.

The pyramid is enlarged by a factor of $\frac{1}{2}$

Calculate the new volume.

10 A and B are two similar solids.

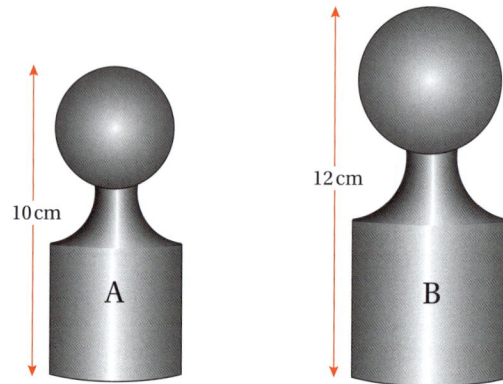

The volume of A is 500 cm³.

Work out the volume of B.

(3 marks)

© AQA 2013

11 David says this is an enlargement by a scale factor of $\frac{1}{2}$.

He is wrong.

Say why.

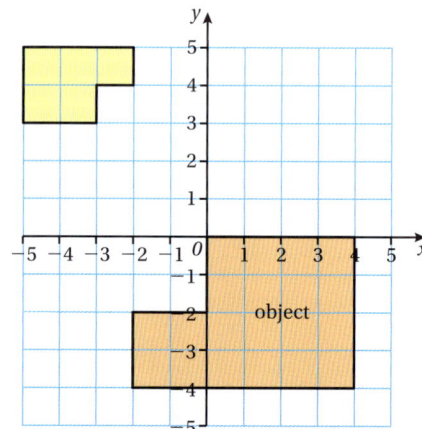

36 Congruence

In this chapter you will learn how to …

- prove that two triangles are congruent using the cases SSS, ASA, SAS, RHS.
- apply congruency in calculations and simple proofs.

For more resources relating to this chapter, visit GCSE Mathematics Online.

Using mathematics: real-life applications

Congruent triangles are used in construction to reinforce structures that need to be strong and stable.

"When designing any bridge I have to allow for reinforcement. This ensures that the bridge stays strong and doesn't collapse under heavy traffic. Any bridge I design has many congruent triangles." *(Structural engineer)*

Before you start …

Ch 8	You need to know how to label angles and shapes that are equal.	**1**	Here are two identical triangles. **a** Write down a pair of sides that are equal in length. **b** What angle is equal in size to angle BAC? **c** Write down another pair of angles that are equal in size.
Ch 9	You need to know basic angle facts.	**2**	Match up the correct statement with the correct diagram. **a** Vertically opposite angles are equal. **b** Alternate angles are equal. **c** Corresponding angles are equal.
Ch 8, 9	You should be able to apply angle facts to find angles in figures and to justify results in simple proofs.	**3**	Decide whether each statement is true or false. **a** Angle DBE = 40° (alternate to angle ADB) **b** Angle BEC = 50° (complementary to angle ADB) **c** Triangle ABD, triangle BDE and triangle BCE are equilateral. **d** Angle BDE = angle BED = 70°

Before You Start continues on next page …

Before you start continued …

Ch 8	You need to know and be able to apply the properties of triangles and quadrilaterals.	**4** What is the value of *x*? Choose the correct answer. A 60° B 30° C 45° D 50° 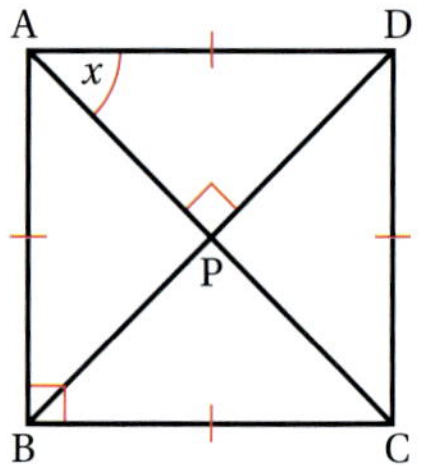

Assess your starting point using the Launchpad

STEP 1

1 Identify which pairs of triangles are congruent.

Give reasons for your decisions.

a

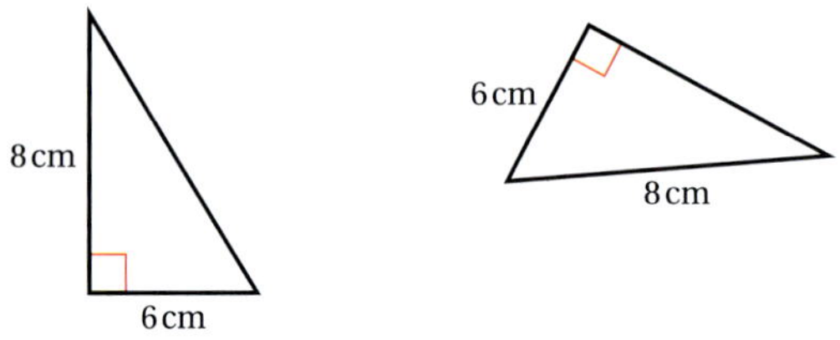

b

c

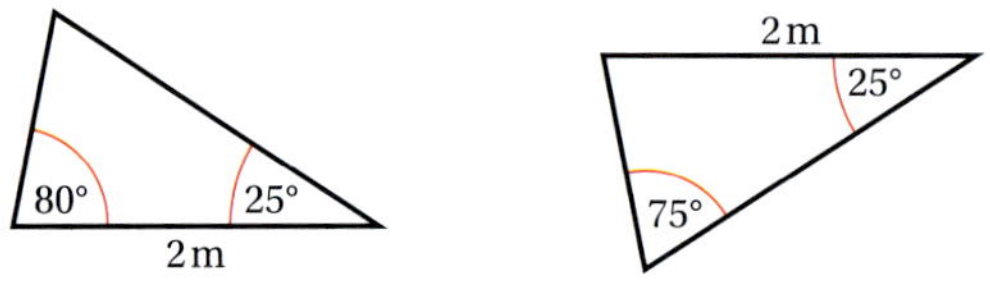

GO TO

Section 1:
Congruent triangles

STEP 2

2 Quadrilateral ABCD is a kite.

   a Prove that triangle ACD is congruent with triangle ACB.

   b Prove that angle ADC = angle ABC.

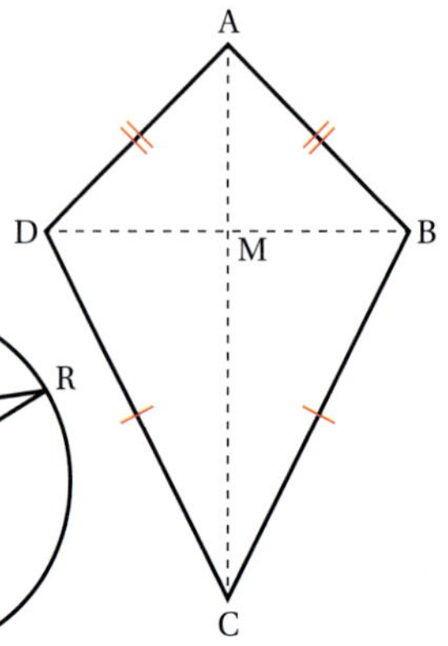

3 O is the centre of a circle.

Prove that OQP = OQR = 90°.

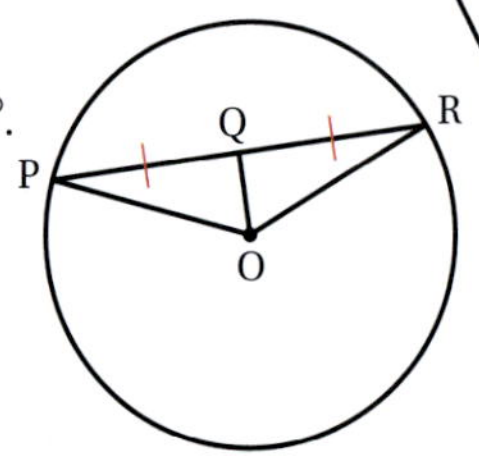

GO TO

Section 2:
Applying congruency

GO TO

Chapter review

Section 1: Congruent triangles

Congruent triangles are identical in shape and all corresponding measurements are equal.

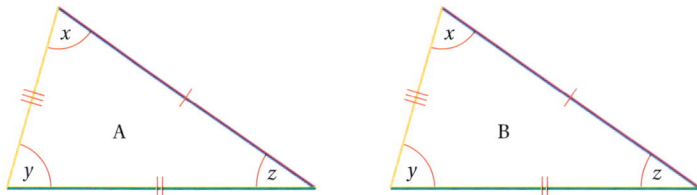

Key vocabulary

congruent: identical in shape and size

When the triangles are in different orientations you need to think carefully about the corresponding sides and angles.

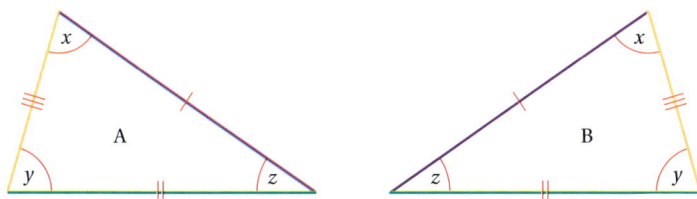

Tip

You worked with congruent shapes in different orientations when you dealt with reflections and rotations in Chapter 33.

Tip

If you place two congruent triangles on top of each other the angles and sides will match up. The matching sides and angles are the corresponding sides or angles.

Two triangles are congruent if one of the following sets of conditions is true.

Side Side Side or **SSS:** the three sides of one triangle are equal in length to the three sides of the other triangle.	
Angle Side Angle or **ASA**: two angles and one side of one triangle are equal to the corresponding two angles and the corresponding side of the other triangle. **Angle, Angle, Side** or **AAS**: the two equal sides in the triangles are opposite the corresponding angles.	

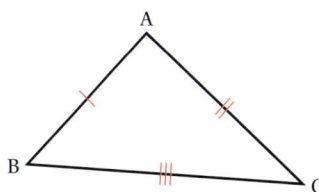

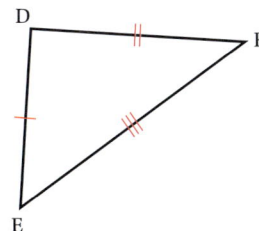

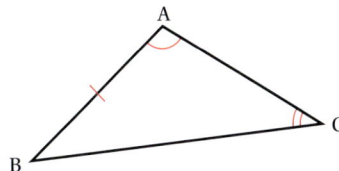

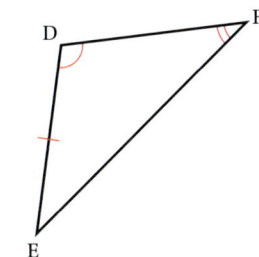

Side Angle Side or **SAS**: two sides and the included angle of one triangle are equal to two sides and the included angle of the other triangle.

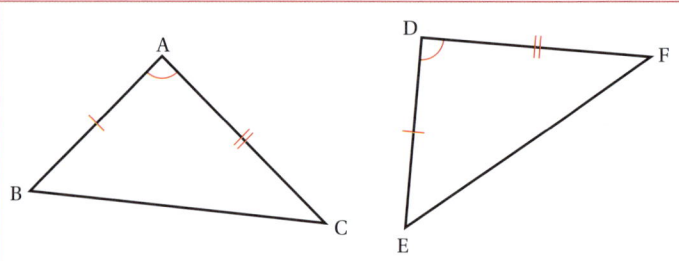

Right angle Hypotenuse Side or **RHS**: the hypotenuse and one other side of a right-angled triangle are equal to the hypotenuse and one other side of the other right-angled triangle.

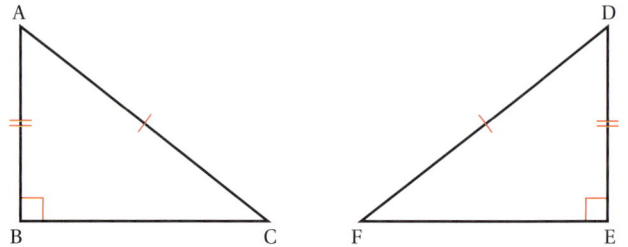

Tip

It is important to write the letters of the vertices of the two triangles in the correct order.

When we write that triangle ABC is congruent to triangle DEF, it means that:

angle A = angle D, angle B = angle E, angle C = angle F

and

AB = DE, AC = DF and BC = EF.

The conditions in the table above and on the preceding page are the minimum conditions for proving that triangles are congruent. No other combinations of side and angle facts are sufficient to tell you whether a triangle is congruent or not.

For example, the triangles in each pair in the table below are not congruent.

Two triangles with all their angles equal can still be very different sizes.

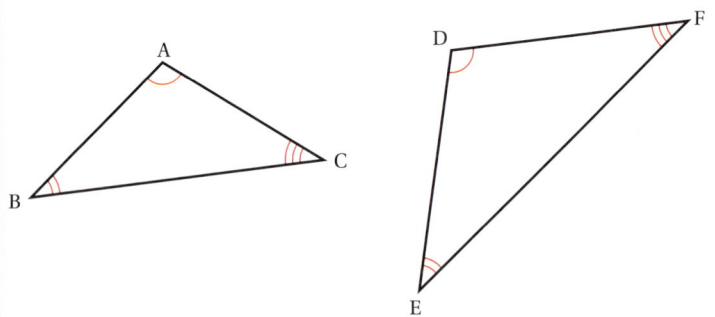

The condition Side Angle Side (SAS) must be the included angle (between the two sides). Otherwise, you do not know if they are congruent or not. The third side might have a different length in each of the triangles.

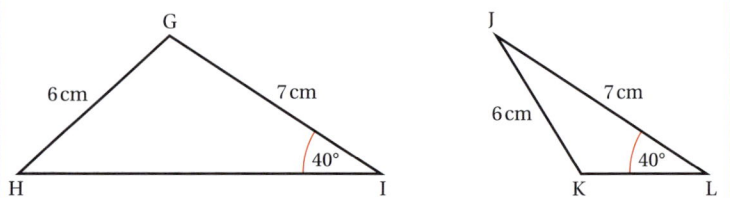

Although a pair of triangles with one of these sets of information might still be congruent, the conditions given are not sufficient proof that they are.

WORK IT OUT 36.1

Here are three proofs for congruence for the pair of triangles.

Which one uses the correct reasoning?

Why are the others incorrect?

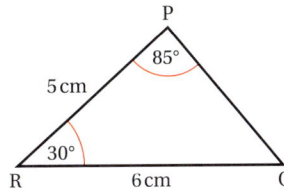 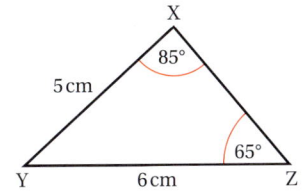

Option A	Option B	Option C
In triangle PQR and triangle XYZ:	In triangle PRQ and triangle XYZ:	In triangle PRQ and triangle XYZ:
PR = XY = 5 cm	In triangle PRQ, angle Q = 65° (sum of angles in a triangle)	PR = XY = 5 cm
angle P = angle X = 85°	angle Q = angle Z = 65°	RQ = YZ = 6 cm
RQ = YZ = 6 cm	RQ = YZ	In triangle XYZ, angle Y = 30° (sum of angles in a triangle),
so triangle PQR is congruent to triangle XYZ (SAS).	so the triangles are congruent.	so triangle PRQ is congruent to triangle XYZ (SAS).

EXERCISE 36A

1 Match up each of the congruency descriptions (SSS, ASA, SAS, RHS) with each pair of triangles below:

a

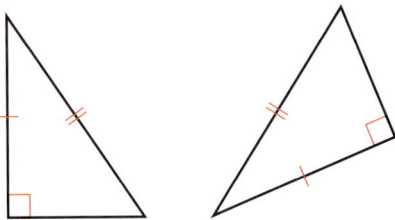

b

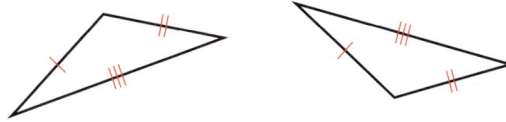

c

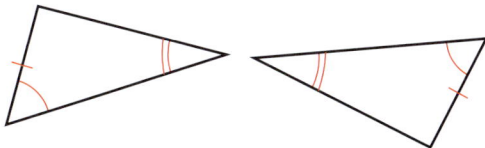

d

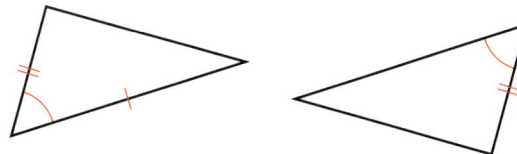

2 Triangles ABC and EFG are congruent.

Angle ABC = 35° and angle FGE = 90°

What is angle CAB?

Choose from the options below.

A 35°   B 55°   C 90°   D It's impossible to say.

3 State whether each pair of triangles is congruent or not.

For those that are, state the conditions that make them congruent.

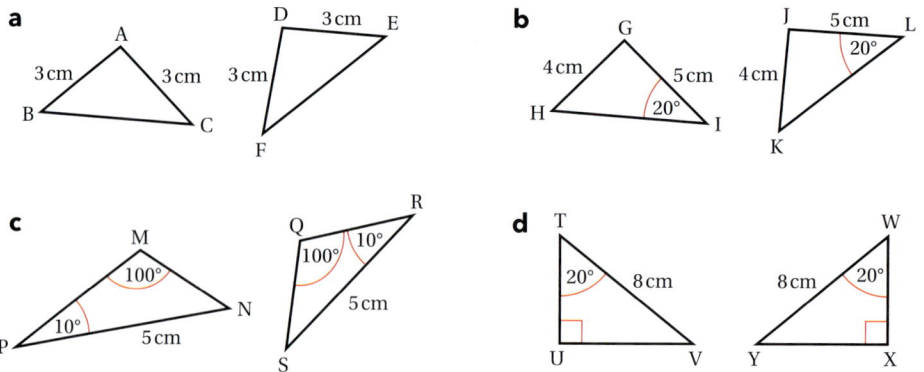

a

b

c

d

4 Prove that triangle ABC is congruent to triangle DCE.

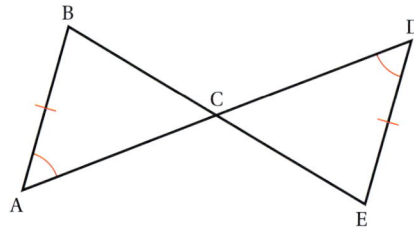

5 Write down two different proofs for congruence of triangles DEF and DGF.

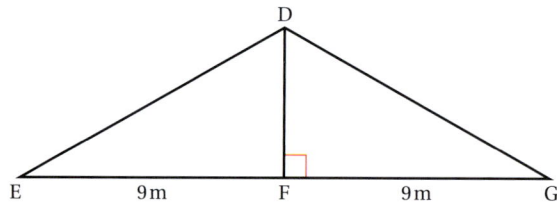

6 In the diagram, PQ is parallel to SR and QT = TR = 2 cm.

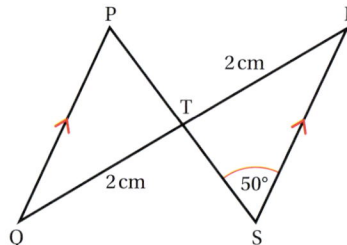

Prove that triangle PQT is congruent to triangle SRT.

7 Prove that triangles ABE and CBD in the figure are congruent, giving full reasons.

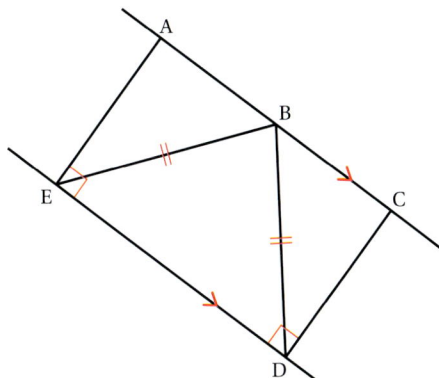

8 Triangle ABD is isosceles.

AC is the perpendicular height.

Prove that triangle ABC is congruent to triangle ADC.

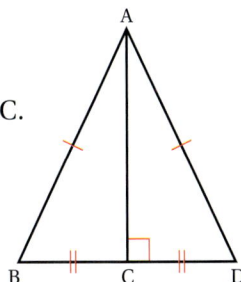

9 In the figure below, PR = SU and RTUQ is a kite.

Prove that triangle PQR is congruent to triangle SQU.

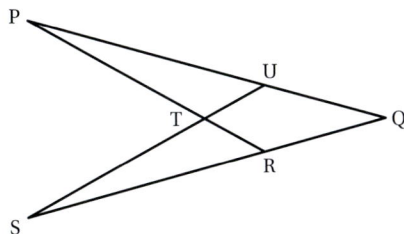

10 ABCD in the figure is a kite.

Prove that:

a triangle ADB is congruent to triangle CDB

b triangle AED is congruent to triangle CED.

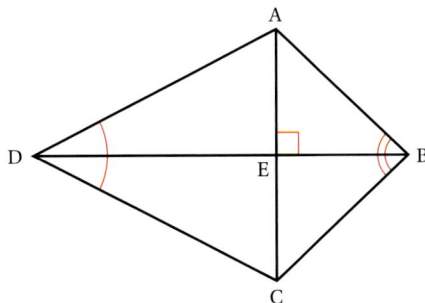

11 Quadrilateral ABCD is a rhombus.

Write down three sets of congruent triangles in this diagram. Give the reasons why they are congruent.

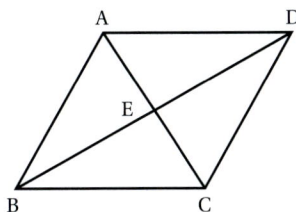

Find answers at: cambridge.org/ukschools/gcsemaths-studentbookanswers

12 O is the centre of two concentric circles.

Prove that triangle MPO is congruent to triangle NQO giving reasons.

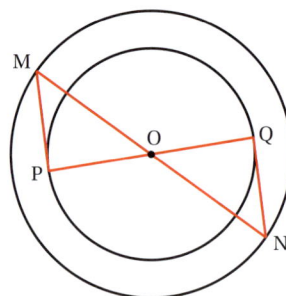

Section 2: Applying congruency

Problem-solving framework

In a problem-solving situation, you will need to combine what you have learnt previously with your new skills to solve problems.

The following steps are useful for solving geometry problems.

Steps for solving problems	What you would do for this example
Step 1: Read the question carefully to decide what you have to find.	In the diagram, AM = BM and PM = QM. **a** Prove that triangle AMP is congruent to triangle BMQ. **b** Prove that AP // BQ.
Step 2: Write down any further information that might be useful.	The two triangles also have vertically opposite angles, that are equal.
Step 3: Decide what method you will use.	You are given two pairs of equal sides and you can see that the included angle is also equal, so use SAS to prove congruence.
Step 4: Set out your working clearly.	**a** In triangles AMP and BMQ: AM = BM (given) PM = QM (given) Angle AMP = angle BMQ (vertically opposite angles are equal at M) So triangle AMP is congruent to triangle BMQ (SAS). **b** Angle APM = angle BQM (matching angles of congruent triangles). Hence APM and BQM are alternate angles and AP // BQ.

WORKED EXAMPLE 1

In the diagram, triangle DEF is divided by GF into two smaller triangles.

Prove that FG is perpendicular to DE.

In triangle FGD and triangle FGE, side FG
is common to both triangles.
DG = GE
DF = EF
So the triangles are congruent (SSS).
Angle DGF = angle EGF and the two
angles lie on a straight line.
So each angle = 90°, and FG is
perpendicular to DE.

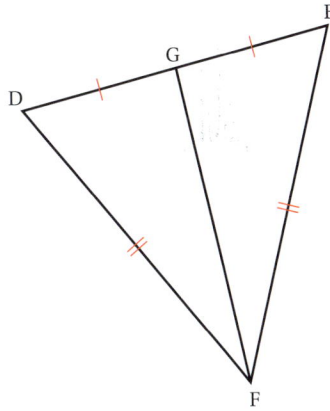

EXERCISE 36B

1 In the diagram below, prove that KL = ML.

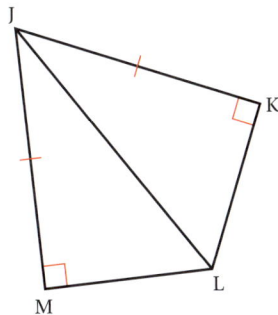

2 Use the facts given in the diagram to:

a prove that angle ABE = angle EDC

b prove that quadrilateral ABCD is a parallelogram.

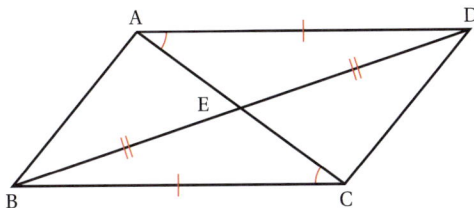

3 In the quadrilateral, SP = SR and QP // RS. Angle QRP = 56°.

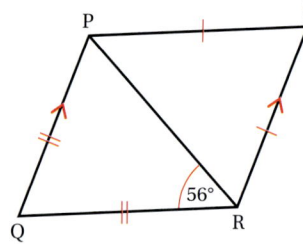

Calculate the size of angle PSR and give your reasons.

4 In the diagram, PQ = PT and QR = TS.

Prove that triangle PRS is isosceles.

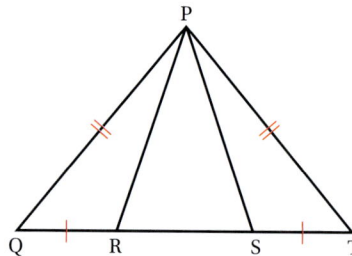

5 In the figure below, prove that angle EAD = angle ECD.

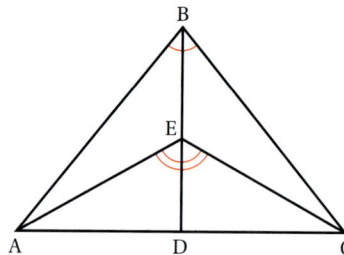

6 Prove that the diagonals of a rectangle are equal in length.

Use the diagram below to help.

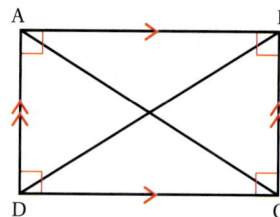

7 In the parallelogram ABCD, the points X and Y are on the diagonal such that DX = DA and BY = BC.

Angle ADX = 40°

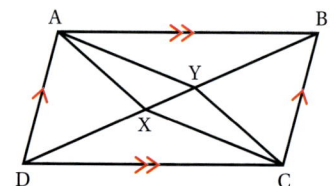

a Find angle XYC.

b Prove that AY = CX.

c Prove that triangles AYX and CXY are congruent.

d Prove that AYCX is a parallelogram.

8 ABCD is a straight line such that AB = BC = CD.

BCPQ is a rhombus.

The lines produced through AQ and DP meet at R.

Prove that angle ARD is a right angle.

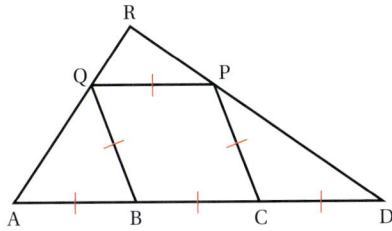

9 The trapezium ABCD has angle BCD = 70° and CDA = 50°.

a Find the other two angles in the trapezium.

b The perpendicular distance between the two parallel sides of the trapezium is 5 cm.

Side CD is 15 cm.

Using your knowledge of right-angled trigonometry, find the area of the trapezium.

> **Tip**
>
> There is more on trigonometry in Chapter 38.

10 AC and BD are the diagonals of a quadrilateral ABCD.

AC and BD are perpendicular, meeting at M.

Name the quadrilateral(s) if:

a M is the midpoint of AC and BD

b M is the midpoint of AC and BD and AB = BC

c M is the midpoint of AC.

11 a The points P and Q lie on the diagonal BD of the square ABCD.

BP = DQ

i Prove that the triangles ABP, CBP, ADQ and CDQ are all congruent.

ii Hence prove that APCQ is a rhombus.

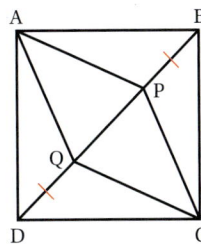

b In triangle ABC below, MA is the bisector of angle BAC.

The line MF is parallel to BA. The line MG is parallel to CA.

Prove that AFMG is a rhombus.

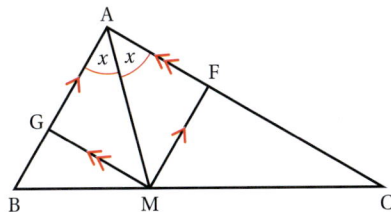

12 Prove that the quadrilateral below is **not** a trapezium.

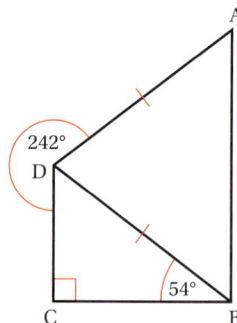

Checklist of learning and understanding

Congruent triangles

- You can prove that two triangles are congruent using one of the four cases of congruence:
  - Side Side Side or SSS: the three sides of one triangle are equal in length to the three sides of the other triangle.
  - Angle Side Angle or ASA: two angles and one side of one triangle are equal to the corresponding two angles and one side of the other triangle.
  - Side Angle Side or SAS: two sides and the included angle of one triangle are equal to two sides and the included angle of the other triangle.
  - Right angle Hypotenuse Side or RHS: the hypotenuse and one side of a right-angled triangle are equal to the hypotenuse and one side of the other right-angled triangle.

For additional questions on the topics in this chapter, visit GCSE Mathematics Online.

Chapter review

1 State whether these pairs of triangles are congruent.

Give reasons for your answers.

a

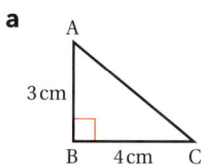

b

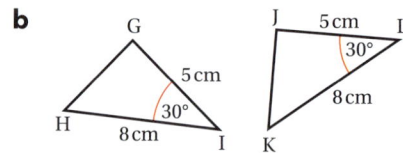

c

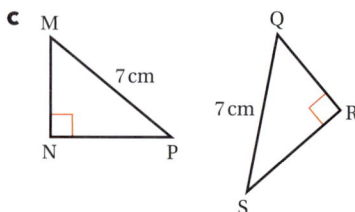

d

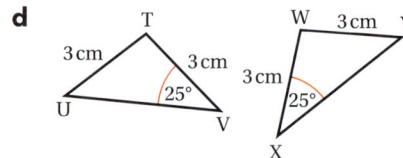

2 These two triangles are congruent.

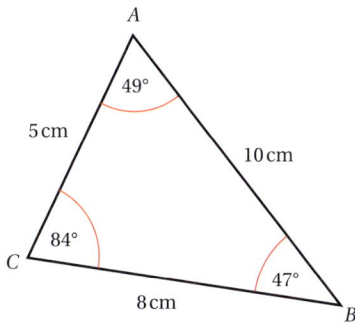

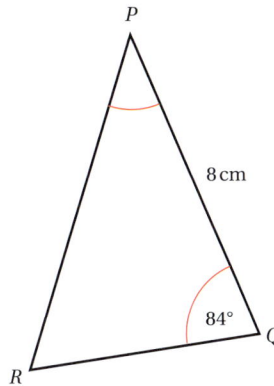

Not drawn accurately

a What is the size of angle P?

Choose your answer from the following options.

A 47°   B 49°   C 84°   D None of these

(1 mark)

b What is the length of PR?

Choose your answer from the following options.

A 5 cm   B 8 cm   C 10 cm   D None of these

(1 mark)

© AQA 2013

3 In the figure below, prove that angle QTS = angle QRP.

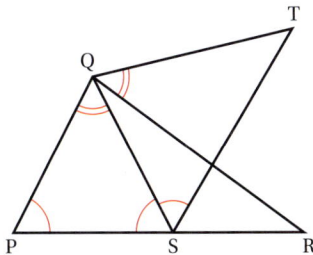

4 Prove that angle EBC = angle ECB in the diagram below. Note that ABCD is a straight line.

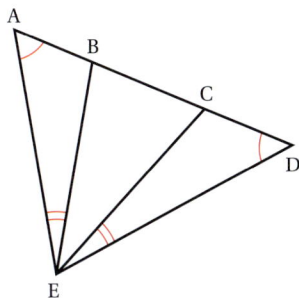

5 In the figure below, triangle ABD lies between two parallel lines.
BC = CA = AD

Prove that angle EAD = 2 × angle ABC.

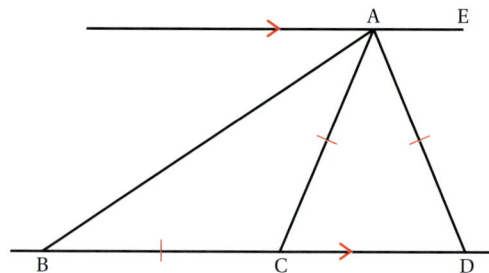

6 Triangle UVW is congruent to triangle UZY.

Prove that quadrilateral UWXY is a kite.

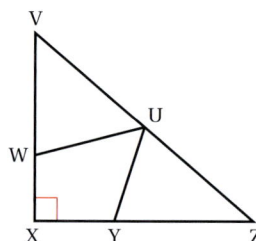

7 Triangle MNP is congruent to triangle NPQ.

Prove that quadrilateral MNPQ is a square.

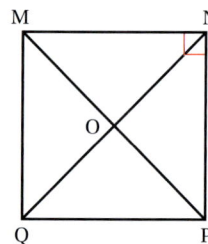

37 Pythagoras' theorem

In this chapter you will learn how to …

- develop full knowledge and understanding of Pythagoras' theorem.
- apply Pythagoras' theorem in 2D and 3D contexts.
- link the maths to real-life skills for industry.

For more resources relating to this chapter, visit GCSE Mathematics Online.

Using mathematics: real-life applications

Builders, carpenters, garden designers, and navigators all use Pythagoras' theorem in their jobs. It is a method based on right-angled triangles which helps them to work out unknown lengths and find right angles.

"I use Pythagoras' theorem to help me prepare floor plans and do calculations for footings and heights of buildings. Any building surveyor will have a range of tools to help them make check calculations on site." *(Building surveyor)*

Calculator tip

Make sure you know how to work with surds on your calculator and that you can round numbers to given levels of accuracy using decimal places and significant figures.

Before you start …

Ch 19	You must be able to work with exact and approximate values of surds.	**1** **a** Which are correct? **i** $\sqrt{19} = \pm 4.36$ (2 dp) **ii** $\sqrt{19} = \pm 361$ **iii** $\sqrt{361} = \pm 19$ **iv** $19^2 = 361$ **b** Which are correct? **i** $1.95^2 = 3.8025 = 3.80$ (2 dp) **ii** $\sqrt{7} = 2.645751311\ldots = \pm 2.64$ (2 dp) **iii** $\sqrt{3} = 1.732050808\ldots = 1.73$ (2 dp) **iv** $3.14^2 = 9.8596 = 9.86$ (2 dp)		
Ch 9	You need to recognise and define different types of angle.	**2** Which is a right angle? Identify the other angles. **a** **b** **c** **d** **e**		
Ch 8	You'll need to apply the properties of different types of triangle to solve problems.	**3** What is the area of triangle ABC? **4** What do you know about angles x and y in this triangle?		

Find answers at: cambridge.org/ukschools/gcsemaths-studentbookanswers

Assess your starting point using the Launchpad

STEP 1

1 A crane can reach a distance of 12 m.

The operator sits 8 m away from the load before it is lifted.

How long is the cable?

12 m

8 m

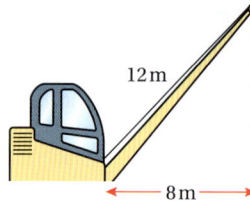

GO TO
Section 1:
Understanding Pythagoras' theorem

STEP 2

2 **a** A garden designer wants to build some triangular decking that fits against a corner fence.

Do the measurements in this design produce a right-angled corner?

b An isosceles triangle has one side of length 10 cm and a perpendicular height of 10 cm.

The other two sides are equal.

How long are they?

3.1 m

5.3 m

4.2 m

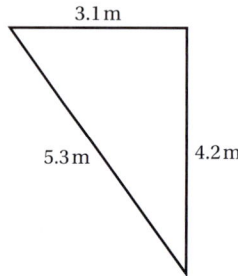

GO TO
Section 2:
Using Pythagoras' theorem

STEP 3

3 What is the longest length of steel rod that can be transported in the container?

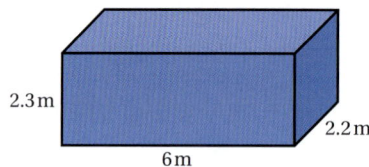

2.3 m

6 m

2.2 m

GO TO
Section 3:
Pythagoras' theorem in three dimensions
Section 4:
Using Pythagoras' theorem to solve problems

GO TO
Chapter review

Section 1: Understanding Pythagoras' theorem

What is Pythagoras' theorem?

Pythagoras' theorem describes the relationship between the lengths of the sides of a right-angled triangle.

The **theorem** states:

In a right-angled triangle, the square of the length of the **hypotenuse** *is equal to the sum of the squares of the two shorter sides.*

For this triangle, the theorem can be expressed using the formula:

$a^2 + b^2 = c^2$

If you know the lengths of any two sides of a right-angled triangle, you can use them to find the length of the third side.

In the formula $a^2 + b^2 = c^2$, c is always the hypotenuse and a and b are the two shorter sides.

The formula can be rearranged to make a or b the subject of the formula.

$a^2 = c^2 - b^2$

$b^2 = c^2 - a^2$

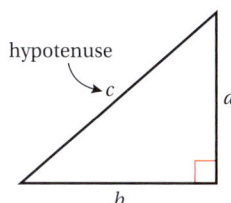

🔑 Key vocabulary

theorem: a statement that can be demonstrated to be true by accepted mathematical operations

hypotenuse: the longest side of a right-angled triangle; the side opposite the 90° angle

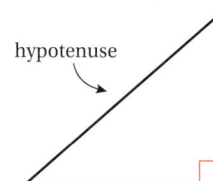

💡 Tip

Naming conventions for a right-angled triangle:

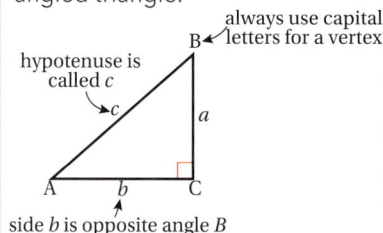

hypotenuse is called c

always use capital letters for a vertex

side b is opposite angle B

WORK IT OUT 37.1

This is the design of an access ramp for the front entrance step to a building.

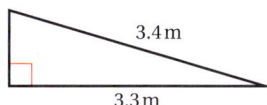

What is the vertical height of the step?

Which of these calculations is correct for this design?

Why are the others wrong?

Calculation A	Calculation B	Calculation C
$c^2 - b^2 = a^2$	$c^2 - b^2 = a^2$	$c^2 - b^2 = a^2$
$3.4^2 - 3.3^2 = a^2$	$3.3^2 + 3.4^2 = c^2$	$3.4^2 - 3.3^2 = a^2$
$3.4 \times 2 = 6.8$	$3.3 \times 3.3 = 10.89$	$3.4 \times 3.4 = 11.56$
$3.3 \times 2 = 6.6$	$3.4 \times 3.4 = 11.56$	$3.3 \times 3.3 = 10.89$
$6.8 - 6.6 = a^2$	$10.89 + 11.56 = c^2$	$11.56 - 10.89 = a^2$
$0.2 = a^2$	$22.45 = c^2$	$a^2 = 0.67$
$a = \dfrac{0.2}{2}$	$a = \sqrt{22.45}\,\text{m} = 4.74\,\text{m}$	$a = \sqrt{0.67}\,\text{m} = 0.82\,\text{m}$
$a = 0.1\,\text{m}$	(to two decimal places)	(to two decimal places)

EXERCISE 37A

1 In the triangle ABC, what is the length AC?
Choose your answer from the following options.

A 10 cm   B 100 cm

C $\sqrt{6} + \sqrt{8}$ D $8^2 - 6^2$

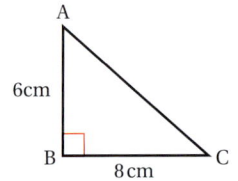

Tip

The four rules for success when working with Pythagoras' theorem

- Always write the formula.
- Always include a sketch of the problem.
- Show full workings.
- Show the final answer to a given degree of accuracy. This could be two decimal places or several significant figures, depending on the detail of the problem.

2 Find the length of the hypotenuse in each of the following triangles:

a

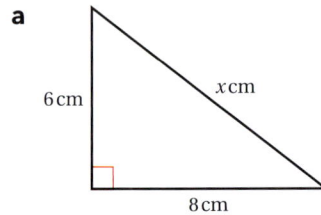

b

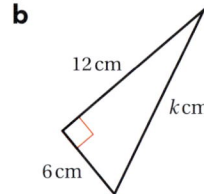

c

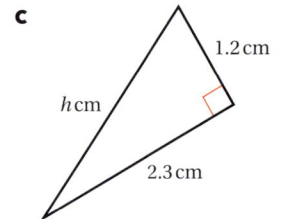

d

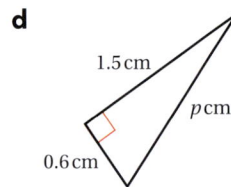

e

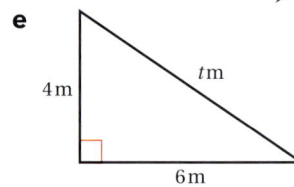

3 Find the length of the missing side in each of these triangles.

a

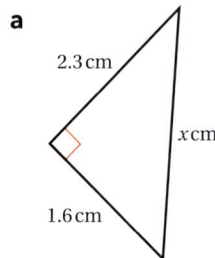

b

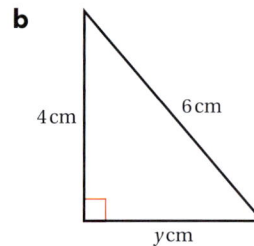

c

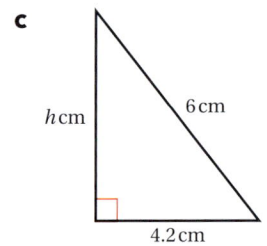

d

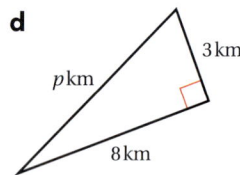

e

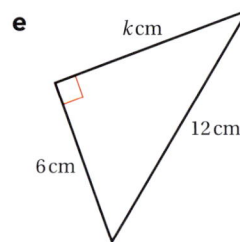

f

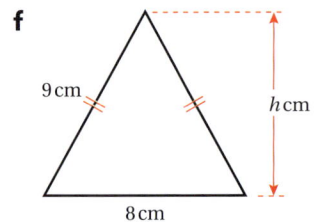

4 Points A, B and C are markers on a building site, at ground level.

Point B is 35 m east of point A. Point C is due north of point A and 100 m from point B.

Calculate the distance AC, giving your answer to two decimal places.

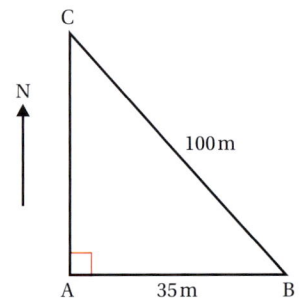

5 Find the value of x in each of the following triangles to two decimal places:

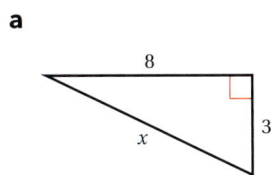

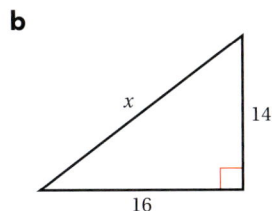

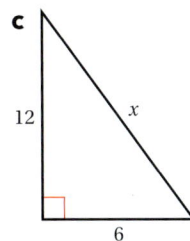

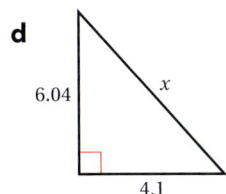

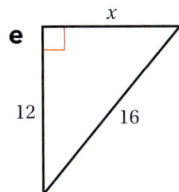

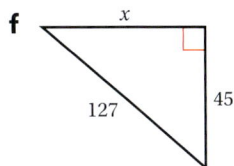

a

8

3

x

b

x

14

16

c

12

x

6

d

6.04

x

4.1

e

x

12

16

f

x

127

45

Section 2: Using Pythagoras' theorem

"I use 'Pythagorean triples' in my job. I measure 3 units up and 4 across the corner of a frame and check that the line that joins the end points is 5 units long. If the rule applies, then I know the frame is a right angle and that the window will fit properly." *(Window fitter)*

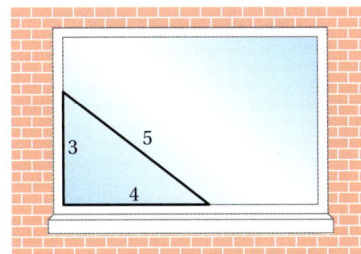

3   5   4

Pythagorean triples

If a triangle contains a right angle, then both sides of Pythagoras' theorem will be equal, $a^2 + b^2$ will equal c^2.

This fact is crucial to many people in their jobs.

For example, carpenters need to make rectangular window frames.

If the sides of the triangle at the corner of the frame have lengths in the ratio of $3 : 4 : 5$, then the angle is a right angle because $3^2 + 4^2 = 5^2$.

Many people know this as the '3, 4, 5 rule.'

Any set of three whole numbers that satisfy Pythagoras' theorem are called **Pythagorean triples**.

One such triple is 3, 4, 5; so are any multiples of that, for example, 6, 8, 10 and 9, 12, 15. Other common triples are 5, 12, 13 and 7, 24, 25.

Key vocabulary

Pythagorean triple: three non-zero positive integers, (a, b, c) for which $a^2 + b^2 = c^2$

The converse of Pythagoras' theorem

The converse of Pythagoras' theorem states that:

If the square on the longest side of any triangle is equal to the sum of the squares of the other two sides, then the triangle is right-angled.

WORK IT OUT 37.2

Is this triangle right angled?

Which of these answers is correct?

Where have the others gone wrong?

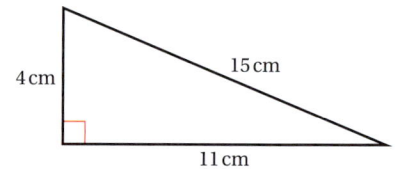

Option A	Option B	Option C
$4 + 11 = 15$ So $a^2 + b^2 = c^2$ Yes, the triangle is right angled.	$a^2 + b^2 = 4^2 + 11^2$ $ = 4 \times 2 + 11 \times 2$ $ = 8 + 22 = 30$ $c^2 = 15^2 = 15 \times 2 = 30$ $a^2 + b^2 = c^2$ Yes, the triangle is right angled.	$a^2 + b^2 = 4^2 + 11^2$ $ = 16 + 121$ $ = 137$ $c^2 = 15 \times 15 = 225$ $a^2 + b^2 \neq c^2$ No, the triangle is not right angled.

EXERCISE 37B

1 Work out which of these sets of lengths are Pythagorean triples.

a 6, 8, 10 **b** 24, 45, 51 **c** 10, 16, 18

d 20, 48, 52 **e** 9, 40, 41 **f** 12, 35, 37

2 Give a reason why 3, 4, 5 is the smallest possible whole number Pythagorean triple.

3 Is there a limit to the number of Pythagorean triples there are? Give a reason for your answer.

4 Which of the following triangles are right angled?

a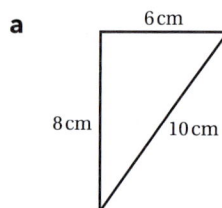

b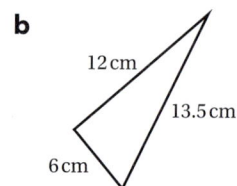

c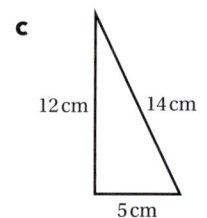

d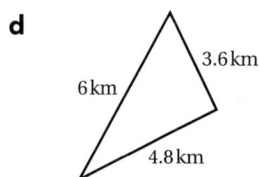

e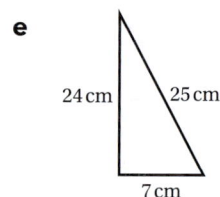

5 Work out which of the following are rectangles:

a

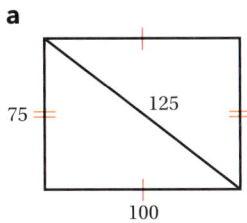

b

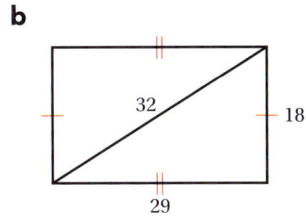

c

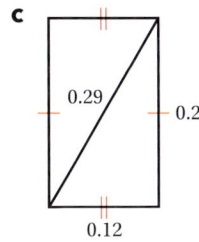

Pythagoras' theorem in polygons

Pythagoras' theorem is very useful for solving many geometrical problems involving polygons and composite figures, particularly when you need to find the lengths of unknown sides.

WORKED EXAMPLE 1

1 Find the length of side x and then calculate the perimeter of this composite shape.

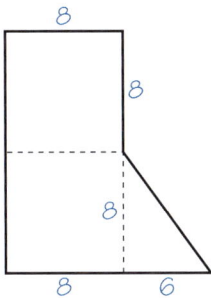

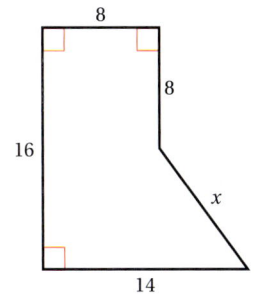

> Divide the shape up to make a right-angled triangle.

> Now you can use Pythagoras' theorem to find x.

$$8^2 + 6^2 = x^2$$
$$64 + 36 = x^2$$
$$100 = x^2$$
$$x = 10\,cm$$
$$\text{Perimeter} = 16 + 14 + 8 + 8 + 10 = 56\,cm.$$

2 Rhombus ABCD has diagonals BD = 12 cm and AC = 8 cm that intersect at E. What is the exact side length of the rhombus? Give your answer in simplified surd form.

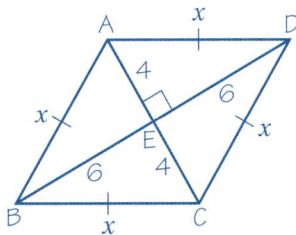

> Start by doing a rough sketch and marking what you know.
>
> AE = 4 cm and BE = 6 cm (diagonals of a rhombus bisect at right angles)

$$x^2 = 4^2 + 6^2$$
$$x^2 = 52$$
$$x = \sqrt{52}$$
$$x = 2\sqrt{13}$$

Find answers at: cambridge.org/ukschools/gcsemaths-studentbookanswers

EXERCISE 37C

1 An equilateral triangle has side length 5 cm.
Work out the perpendicular height.

2 An isosceles triangle has side length 8 cm and base length 6 cm.
Work out the perpendicular height.

3 Calculate the length of the sides in this square.

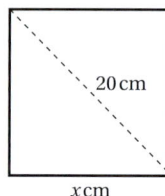

4 A scalene triangle has sides of length 14 cm, 10.5 cm and 17.5 cm.
State whether this is a right-angled scalene triangle.

Tip

Note that there are different types of right-angled triangle:

Scalene right-angled triangle
- one right angle
- two other unequal angles
- no equal sides

Isosceles right-angled triangle
- one right angle
- two other equal angles, always 45°
- two equal sides

You can apply Pythagoras' theorem to both types of right-angled triangle.

5 **a** Show that the length of the hypotenuse of this triangle is 10.0 cm to one decimal place.

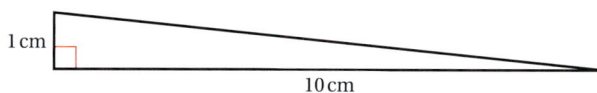

b Work out whether it an isosceles triangle.

6 Find the length of AD in this figure.

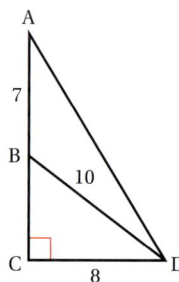

7 Calculate the length of:

a AC

b BC

c EC

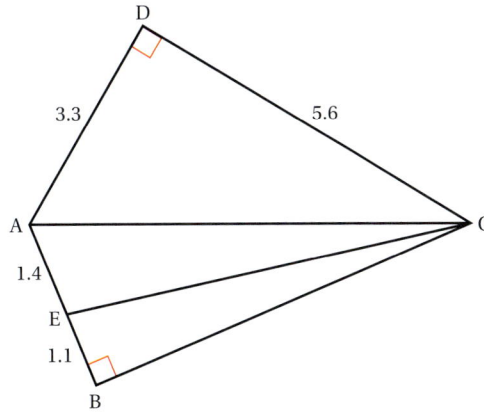

8 Find the area of trapezium ABCD.

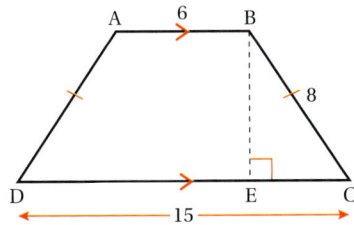

9 Find the length of side AD and calculate the perimeter of this shape.

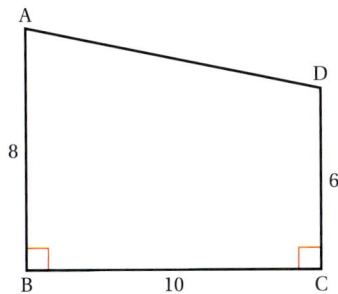

10 The area of square ACDE is $50\,\text{mm}^2$.

Work out the length of AB.

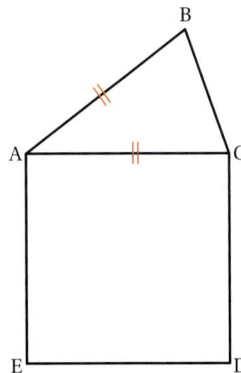

11 Find the value of x using Pythagoras' theorem.
Leave your answer as a surd in simplified form.

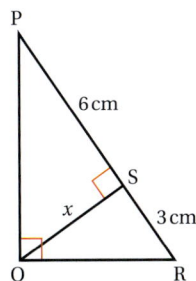

12 Prove that in this figure, $BN^2 + CM^2 = 5BC^2$.

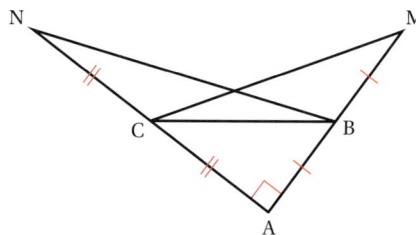

Section 3: Pythagoras' theorem in three dimensions

The first step in working with three-dimensional objects is to find the right-angled triangle in the plane that has the length you need to work out.

Once you've identified the correct triangle, you can draw it on its own and add all the necessary information.

When you work with three-dimensional shapes it is important to draw careful diagrams. In most cases, you will need to separate out triangles to work with them.

WORKED EXAMPLE 2

The height of a box is 7 cm, its length is 4 cm and its depth is 3 cm. Find the length of the diagonal SB.

Find the length of the diagonal QS first.

It is the hypotenuse of right-angled triangle QRS on the base of the box.

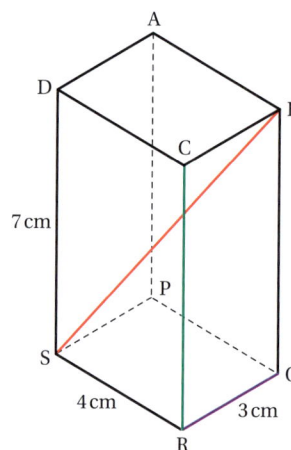

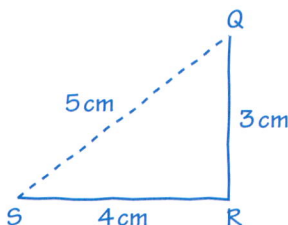

$QS = \sqrt{4^2 + 3^2} = \sqrt{25} = 5$ cm.

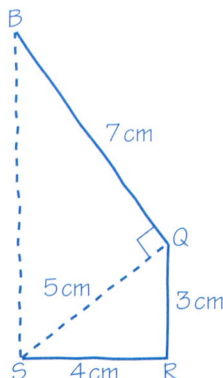

Draw the upright right-angled triangle with a base of 5 cm.
Find SB, the hypotenuse of this triangle.

$SB = \sqrt{5^2 + 7^2} = \sqrt{74} = 8.60$ cm (2 dp)

EXERCISE 37D

1 This symmetrical pyramid has a rectangular base.

Find the perpendicular height of the pyramid.

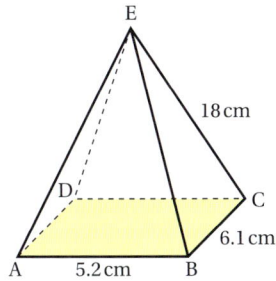

2 The diagram shows a wedge used to get trolleys through a doorway.

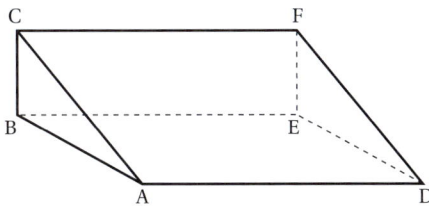

The face ABED is a rectangle and is at right angles to CBEF, which is another rectangle.

AB = 50 cm, AF = 65 cm and BE = 30 cm

Calculate whether the wedge will fit under the lip of a door measuring 30.5 cm high.

3 An office block is the shape of a cuboid with a rectangular-based pyramid fitting exactly on the top.

Calculate how tall the building is.

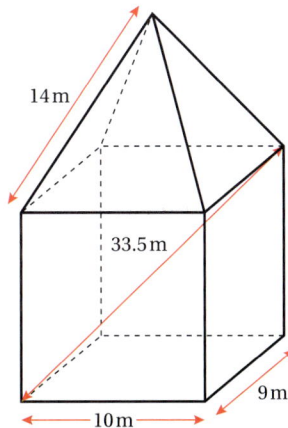

4 A spaghetti jar is the shape of a cylinder with a radius of 8 cm and a height of 0.35 m.

Some dried spaghetti is 40 cm.

Work out whether the spaghetti will fit into the jar.

5 The slant height of a cone with a circular base is 100 mm.

The diameter of its base is 60 mm.

Work out the perpendicular height of the cone.

Find answers at: cambridge.org/ukschools/gcsemaths-studentbookanswers

Section 4: Using Pythagoras' theorem to solve problems

Pythagoras' theorem is very useful for solving a range of problems involving real-life contexts.

Shortest and longest route problems are a good example:

Problem-solving framework

Sally wants to cross a 100 metre by 60 metre rectangular football field diagonally from one corner to the other. There is a game playing so she has to go round the edge.

Calculate how much further she has to walk.

If you get a question like this you can use the following steps to approach it:

Steps for solving problems	What you would do for this example
Step 1: If it is useful to have a diagram. Sketch one and add the information. This might help you visualise the problem.	
Step 2: Identify what you have to do.	Find the difference between the length of the diagonal and the length of the two sides added together.
Step 3: Test the problem with what you know. Can you use a ruler? What type of angle is it?	You could use a ruler, but you would have to draw a very accurate diagram to scale. As you have a right-angled triangle and side lengths you can use Pythagoras' theorem.
Step 4: What maths can you use?	Use Pythagoras' theorem to work out the length of the diagonal: $100^2 + 60^2 = c^2$ $10\,000 + 3600 = c^2$ $13\,600 = c^2$ $c = \sqrt{13\,600} = 116.6\,\text{m}$ If she walked straight across the diagonal the distance would be 116.6 m. She has to go round the outside which is $100 + 60 = 160\,\text{m}$, so she must walk $160 - 116.6 = 43.4\,\text{m}$ further.
Step 5: Check your workings and that your answer is reasonable.	A diagonal pitch length of 116.6 m seems reasonable given the sides are 60 m and 100 m.
Step 6: Have you answered the question?	You were asked to find how much further she would have to walk. You have found this to be 43.4 m.

EXERCISE 37E

1 Computer gaming designers use *x*- and *y*-coordinates to place characters or objects in a game.

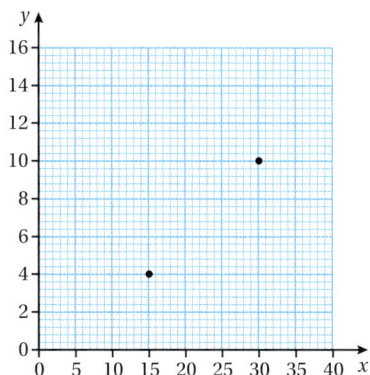

One player is at coordinate (30, 10) and the other at (15, 4).

Work out how far apart the two players are.

2 Zoe is going to buy a new television. It is an 80-inch television (measured along its diagonal length).

Her current television has a 52-inch screen.

Both are the same height, 40 inches.

a How much wider is Zoe's new television than her current one?

b Zoe needs to place the television in a 58 inch gap between the chimney and wall.

Will the new television fit in this space?

3 A rectangular shed measures 6 metres by 4 metres by 3 metres.

Work out whether a boat mast 7 metres long would fit inside.

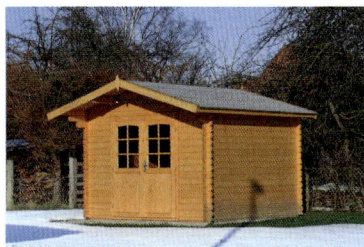

4 In which of these storage boxes can you fit the longest pole?

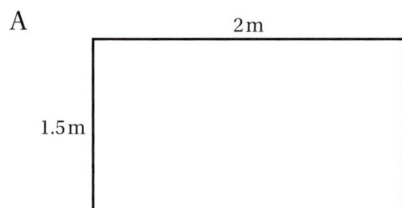

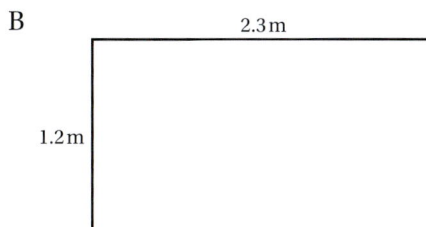

A 2 m 1.5 m

B 2.3 m 1.2 m

5 Find the length of the hypotenuse of the largest triangle.

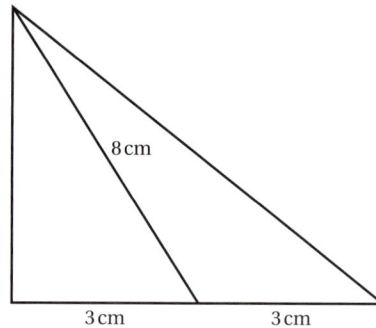

8 cm

3 cm   3 cm

6 Here is a square box with a diagonal brace across it.

Is it constructed correctly as a perfect square, within reasonable bounds?

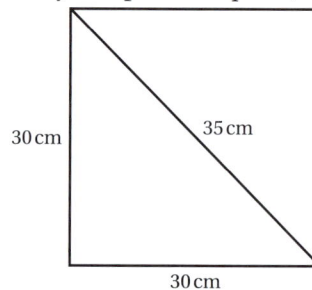

30 cm   35 cm

30 cm

7 Calculate the length of AB in this trapezium.

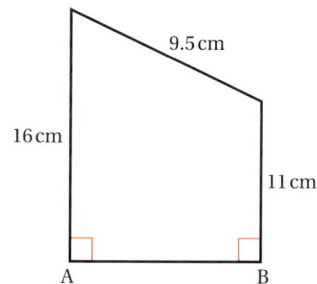

9.5 cm

16 cm

11 cm

A   B

8 A plumber carries piping on the
roof of his van in a cylindrical
canister that is 4.6 metres long.

The longest pipe the tube can
carry is 4.65 m.

Work out the diameter of the
tube, in centimetres. Give your
answer to two decimal places.

9 A hotel has a square courtyard with sides 12 metres long.

The hotel owners want to construct a circular fountain with diameter
1.2 m in the middle of the courtyard.

a What is the length of each of the courtyard's diagonals?

b How many metres along each diagonal should the fountain be
placed?

10 A rectangular horse paddock has a diagonal of 20 m and a shorter side of 10 m.

   a Work out the perimeter and the area of the paddock.

   b How many laps of the paddock would a horse have to trot to cover a kilometre, to the nearest whole lap?

11 A plumber is tiling a bathroom.

   The tiles are isosceles triangles of side length 15 cm and base 10 cm.

   a Calculate the height of 10 rows of tiles.

   b Work out how many rows of tiles would fit below a shelf that sits 90 cm from the floor.

12 A piece of artwork is made of three right-angled triangles welded together, as shown in the diagram.

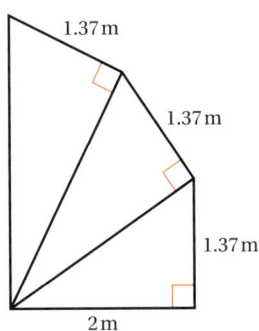

The hypotenuse of the top triangle is perpendicular to the ground.

Work out if it will fit under an archway that is 3 m high.

Checklist of learning and understanding

Pythagoras' theorem

- Pythagoras' theorem only applies to right-angled triangles.
- The theorem is that the square of the hypotenuse of a right-angled triangle equals the sum of the squares of the other two sides. It can be written as:
  $$a^2 + b^2 = c^2$$
- Rearrange the formula to find either of the other two sides:
  $$a^2 = c^2 - b^2$$
  $$b^2 = c^2 - a^2$$
- You can use the theorem to find the length of the hypotenuse (the longest side). The theorem can also be used to prove there is a right angle within a triangle or to find a missing length within a right-angled triangle.
- Always draw a diagram and label it; also write out the formula you are using to fully explain what you have done.
- Pythagorean triples are three lengths that satisfy the formula and therefore prove you have a right angle; learn the common ones, such as 3, 4, 5 and 5, 12, 13.

Find answers at: cambridge.org/ukschools/gcsemaths-studentbookanswers

Chapter review

1 Find the length of x and y in this figure, giving your answers to two decimal places.

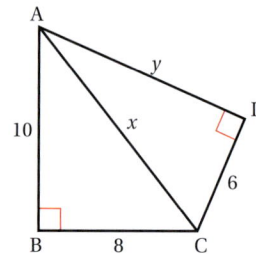

2 Is this a right-angled triangle?

Not drawn accurately

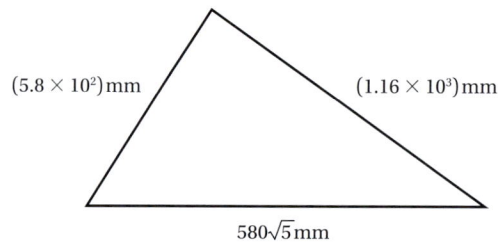

You must justify your answer.

(4 marks)

© AQA 2012

3 Work out the perimeter of this kite.

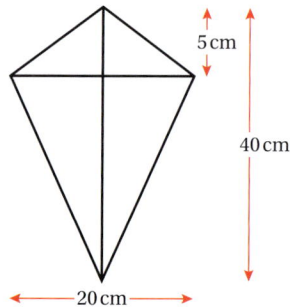

4 Find the length of FG.

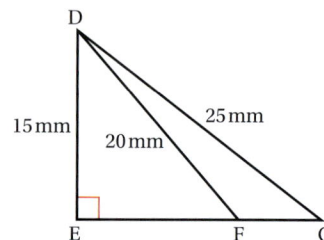

5 A pyramid has a height of 1.6 m. Its base is a square with a diagonal of 2.4 m.

Calculate the length of the sloping edge of the pyramid.

38 Trigonometry

In this chapter you will learn how to ...

- Use trigonometric ratios to find lengths and angles in right-angled triangles.
- Find and memorise exact values of important trigonometric ratios.
- Use the sine and cosine rules to calculate unknown sides or angles in any triangle.
- Use the area rule to calculate the area of a triangle.
- Solve trigonometry problems in two- and three-dimensional figures.

For more resources relating to this chapter, visit GCSE Mathematics Online.

Using mathematics: real-life applications

Trigonometry means 'triangle measurements' and it is very useful for finding the lengths of sides and sizes of angles of triangles. Trigonometry is used to work out lengths and angles in navigation, surveying, astronomy, engineering, construction and even in the placement of satellites and satellite receivers.

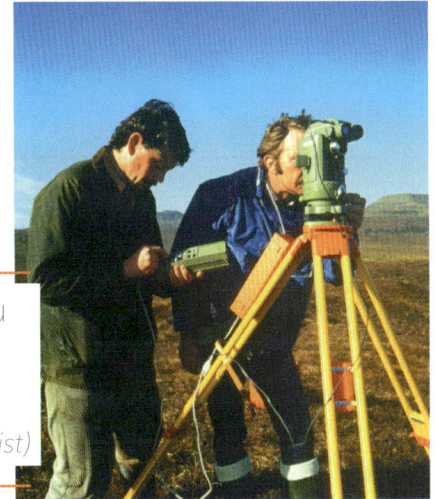

"I use a theodolite to work out the height of mountains. You basically point it at the top of the mountain. The theodolite uses the principles of trigonometry to measure angles and distances."

(Geologist)

Before you start ...

Ch 37	You should be able to use Pythagoras' theorem to find lengths in triangles.	**1**	Find the length of x in each triangle: **a** (triangle with sides 7, 16, and hypotenuse x) **b** (triangle with sides 7, 5, and x)
Ch 12	You must be able to work with approximate values and round to a specified number of places.	**2** **3**	What is $\sqrt{53}$, to two decimal places? If $c^2 = 94.34$, what is c to three significant figures?
Ch 27, 28	You need to be able to use ratio and proportion to calculate sides in similar triangles.	**4**	Find the length of AC if the ratio of sides $\dfrac{AB}{AC} = \dfrac{5}{3}$ and AB = 35 cm.

Find answers at: cambridge.org/ukschools/gcsemaths-studentbookanswers

Assess your starting point using the Launchpad

STEP 1

1 Find the length of the diagonal x in this rectangle.

2 A wheelchair ramp is 90 cm long.

One end is placed on a step 24 cm above the horizontal floor.

Calculate the angle of the ramp to the floor at the other end.

Give your answer to two decimal places.

3.4 cm

x

36°

90 cm

24 cm

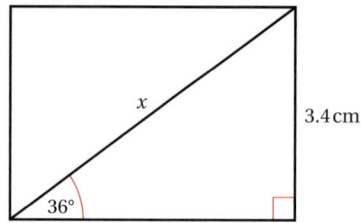

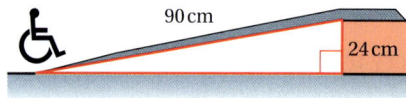

GO TO
Section 1:
Trigonometry in right-angled triangles

STEP 2

3 Write down the exact value of:

  a sin 45°   **b** cos 0°   **c** tan 60°

4 Without using a calculator, show that $(\sin 60)^2 + (\cos 60)^2 = 1$

GO TO
Section 2:
Exact values of trigonometric ratios

STEP 3

5 What is angle C if $c = 4$ cm, $B = 46°$ and b is 7 cm?

6 In triangle PQR, $R = 100°$, PR = 8 cm and PQ = 5 cm

  a Calculate the length of PQ.

  b Calculate, to the nearest degree, the sizes of angles P and Q.

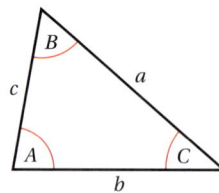

B

a

c

A C

b

GO TO
Section 3:
The sine, cosine and area rules

GO TO
Step 4
The Launchpad continues on the next page …

Launchpad continued …

STEP 4

7 A girl is standing looking at a chimney.

Use the dimensions in the diagram to find the height of the chimney.

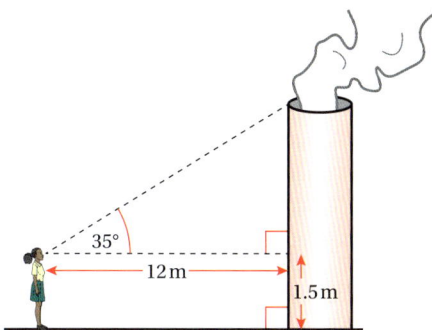

8 A pyramid, VPQRS, has a square base, PQRS, with sides of length 8 cm. Each sloping edge is 9 cm long.

  a Calculate the perpendicular height of the pyramid.

  b Calculate the angle the sloping edge VP makes with the base.

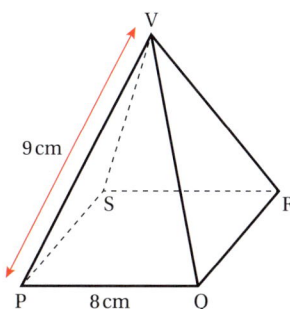

GO TO
Section 4:
Using trigonometry to solve problems

GO TO
Chapter review

Section 1: Trigonometry in right-angled triangles

Pythagoras' theorem is used in right-angled triangles to find missing sides when two sides are known.

The ratio of corresponding pairs of sides in similar triangles is always the same.

These facts are important in understanding and using trigonometry.

Naming the sides of right-angled triangles

The hypotenuse is the longest side of a right-angled triangle, opposite the right angle.

The other two (shorter) sides are named in relation to the acute angles (marked θ) in the triangle.

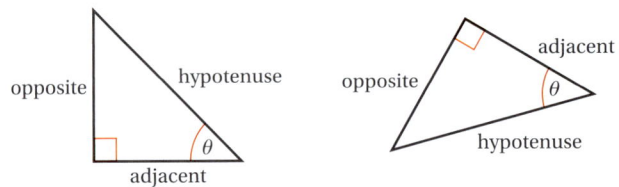

This system of naming the sides is fundamental to working with trigonometry.

Make sure you understand how it works for triangles in any orientation before moving on.

The trigonometric ratios

This diagram shows three similar right-angled triangles.

The green sides are opposite angle θ and the blue sides are adjacent to it.

The ratio of $\frac{\text{opposite}}{\text{adjacent}}$ sides is $\frac{1}{2}$ for all these similar triangles.

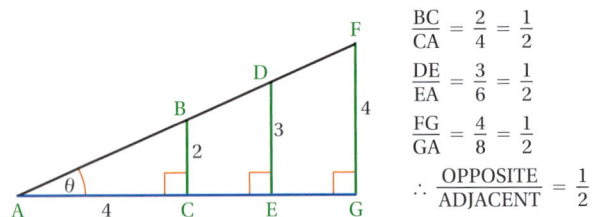

$$\frac{BC}{CA} = \frac{2}{4} = \frac{1}{2}$$
$$\frac{DE}{EA} = \frac{3}{6} = \frac{1}{2}$$
$$\frac{FG}{GA} = \frac{4}{8} = \frac{1}{2}$$
$$\therefore \frac{\text{OPPOSITE}}{\text{ADJACENT}} = \frac{1}{2}$$

In similar triangles like the set above, the ratios $\frac{\text{opposite}}{\text{hypotenuse}}$, $\frac{\text{adjacent}}{\text{hypotenuse}}$ and $\frac{\text{opposite}}{\text{adjacent}}$ are equal in all the triangles.

These ratios are called the trigonometric ratios (shortened to trig. ratios) and they are named as follows:

- the sine ratio, $\sin \theta$, is the ratio of the side opposite to the angle to the hypotenuse
- the cosine ratio, $\cos \theta$, is the ratio of the side adjacent to the angle to the hypotenuse

- the tangent ratio, tan θ, is the ratio of the side opposite the angle to the side adjacent to the angle

$$\sin\theta = \frac{a}{c} = \frac{\text{opposite}}{\text{hypotenuse}}$$

$$\cos\theta = \frac{b}{c} = \frac{\text{adjacent}}{\text{hypotenuse}}$$

$$\tan\theta = \frac{a}{b} = \frac{\text{opposite}}{\text{adjacent}}$$

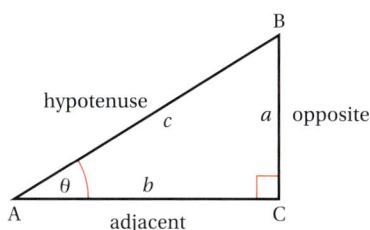

Calculator tip

Make sure you know how to use the trig. function keys on your calculator.

Sin⁻¹   cos⁻¹   tan⁻¹

sin   cos   tan

The three ratios have the same value for a particular angle no matter how long the sides are.

For example, $\sin 30°$ is $\frac{1}{2}$ or 0.5 for any right-angled triangle. This means that the length of the opposite side is half the length of the hypotenuse if the angle you are working with is 30°.

You can find the ratio for any angle using your calculator.

WORKED EXAMPLE 1

1 For triangle ABC, find the value of:

a $\sin A$

b $\cos A$

c $\tan A$

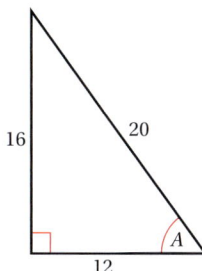

a $\sin A = \frac{\text{opposite}}{\text{hypotenuse}} = \frac{16}{20} = \frac{4}{5}$

Identify the trigonometric ratio to use and then substitute in the lengths given.

b $\cos A = \frac{\text{adjacent}}{\text{hypotenuse}} = \frac{12}{20} = \frac{3}{5}$

Identify the trigonometric ratio to use and then substitute in the lengths given.

c $\tan A = \frac{\text{opposite}}{\text{adjacent}} = \frac{16}{12} = \frac{4}{3}$

Identify the trigonometric ratio to use and then substitute in the lengths given.

2 Use your calculator to find the value of each of these trig. ratios.

Give your answers to three significant figures where necessary.

a $\cos 32°$ **b** $\sin 18°$ **c** $\tan 80°$

a $\cos 32° = 0.848$

Check you know how to find the cos of an angle and the inverse of it using your calculator.

b $\sin 18° = 0.309$

With each of these three ratios, enter the angle given and press sin, cos or tan.

c $\tan 80° = 5.67$

Check to make sure you round appropriately to the given degree of accuracy.

Find answers at: cambridge.org/ukschools/gcsemaths-studentbookanswers

Finding unknown sides

Finding unknown sides or angles is called solving the triangle.

You can use the three trigonometric ratios to do this.

If you know an angle (other than the right angle) and one side in a right-angled triangle, you can use trig. ratios to form an equation. You can then solve it to find the missing lengths.

You will not be told which ratio to use. You have to pick the right one based on the information that you have about the triangle.

You can remember the ratios using the mnemonic SOH-CAH-TOA and the formula triangles:

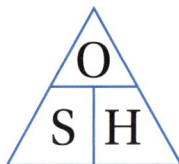

Tip

If you have two sides of a right-angled triangle you can find the other side using Pythagoras' theorem.

SOH: $\text{Sin } x = \dfrac{\text{Opposite}}{\text{Hypotenuse}}$ CAH: $\text{Cos } x = \dfrac{\text{Adjacent}}{\text{Hypotenuse}}$ TOA: $\text{Tan } x = \dfrac{\text{Opposite}}{\text{Adjacent}}$

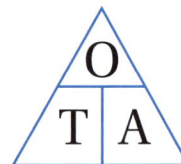

Tip

Draw a sketch of the triangle in the question. Circle the angle you are working with and mark the sides H, A and O to help you see which values you have and which you need.

WORKED EXAMPLE 2

a In triangle ABC, angle $B = 90°$, $AC = 15$ cm and angle $C = 35°$.

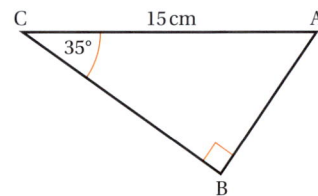

Calculate the length of AB to one decimal place.

Given: angle $C = 35°$
AB is opposite angle C
CA = 15 cm and is the hypotenuse

$\sin 35° = \dfrac{\text{opp}}{\text{hyp}}$

$\sin 35° = \dfrac{AB}{15}$

> Use the ratio with opposite and hypotenuse.
>
> sine ratio = $\dfrac{\text{opp}}{\text{hyp}}$

$AB = \sin 35° \times 15$

> Multiply both sides by 15 to get AB on its own.

$AB = 8.6$ cm

> Use your calculator to find the value of $\sin 35°$.

Continues on next page ...

b In triangle XYZ, angle Z is a right angle and angle X = 71°. Side YZ = 7.9 cm

Calculate the length of XZ to one decimal place.

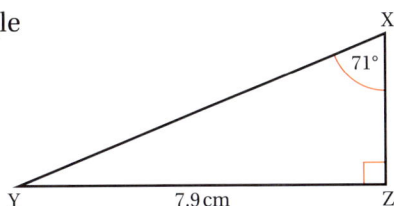

Given: angle X = 71°
YZ = 7.9 cm = opposite side
XZ is the adjacent side

> Identify the information you have been given.

Use the ratio with opposite and adjacent, which is TOA.

> Identify the trig. ratio that uses the information you have been given.

$\tan 71° = \dfrac{\text{opp}}{\text{adj}}$

$\tan 71° = \dfrac{7.9}{XZ}$

> Fill in the information you know.

$XZ \times \tan 71° = 7.9$

> Multiply both sides by XZ to deal with the fraction.

$XZ = \dfrac{7.9}{\tan 71°}$

> Divide by tan 71° to get XZ on its own.

$XZ = 2.7$ cm (to 1 dp)

> Complete the calculation on your calculator.
> Give your answer to the appropriate degree of accuracy.

EXERCISE 38A

1 Which of the following angles is tan of 0.475, to 2 dp?

    A 61.64°   B 28.36°   C 25.41°   D 0.008°

2 Use your calculator to give the value of each ratio. Give your answers to three decimal places where necessary.

    a sin 32°   **b** cos 90°   **c** tan 24°

    d sin 30°   **e** tan 87°   **f** cos 49°

    g sin 0°   **h** cos 32°   **i** tan 45°

Find answers at: cambridge.org/ukschools/gcsemaths-studentbookanswers

3 Select the correct trigonometric ratio and use it to find the length of the side marked with a variable in each triangle.

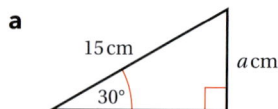

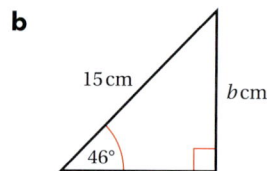

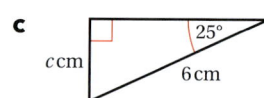

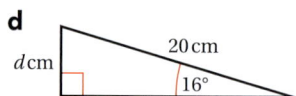

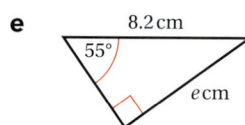

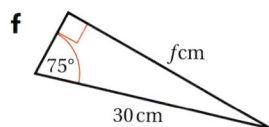

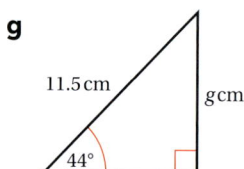

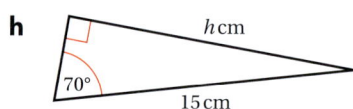

a
15 cm
a cm
30°

b
15 cm
b cm
46°

c
25°
c cm
6 cm

d
d cm
20 cm
16°

e
8.2 cm
55°
e cm

f
75°
f cm
30 cm

g
11.5 cm
g cm
44°

h
h cm
70°
15 cm

4 Work out the length of the marked side in each triangle. Give your answers to two decimal places.

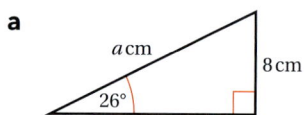

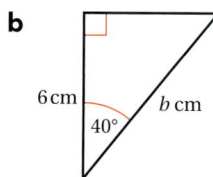

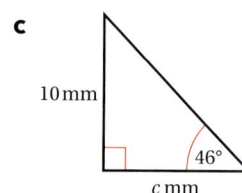

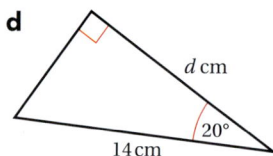

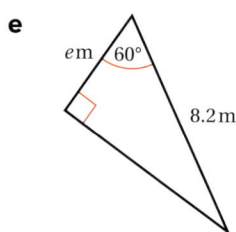

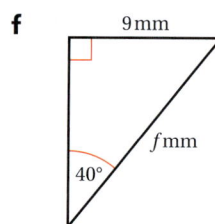

a
a cm
8 cm
26°

b
6 cm
b cm
40°

c
10 mm
46°
c mm

d
d cm
20°
14 cm

e
e m 60°
8.2 m

f
9 mm
f mm
40°

Finding unknown angles

To find the size of unknown angles using the trigonometric ratios you need to use the inverse function of each ratio.

On most calculators these are the second functions of the sin, cos and tan buttons.

They are usually marked sin⁻¹, cos⁻¹ and tan⁻¹. You may need to use the SHIFT key to get these functions.

WORKED EXAMPLE 3

1 Given that tan x is 5, what is the size of angle x?

Using calculator:

[SHIFT] [tan] [5] [=]

> Identify on your calculator which key combination will produce the angle size.

[78.69006753]

> The answer will be given in full to a varying degree of decimal places according to the size of angle.

Angle x is 78.7°

> Round the final answer to an appropriate degree of accuracy.

2 Find the size of angle x in each triangle.

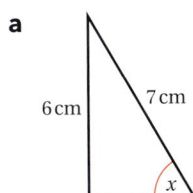

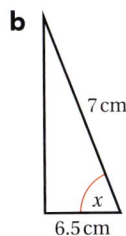

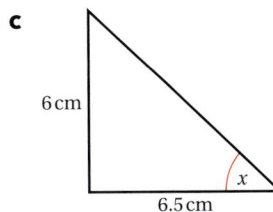

a
6 cm · 7 cm · x

b
7 cm · x · 6.5 cm

c
6 cm · x · 6.5 cm

a $\sin x = \dfrac{opp}{hyp}$

> Identify which trig. ratio to use.

$\sin x = \dfrac{6}{7} = 0.857$

> Fill in the information you are given.

$\sin^{-1} 0.857 = x = 59°$

> Identify on your calculator which key combination will find the size of angle from the ratio.

b $\cos x = \dfrac{adj}{hyp}$

> Identify which trig. ratio to use.

$= \dfrac{6.5}{7} = 0.929$

> Fill in the information you are given.

$\cos^{-1} 0.929 = x = 21.8°$

> Identify on your calculator which key combination will find the size of angle from the ratio.

c $\tan x = \dfrac{opp}{adj}$

> Identify which trig. ratio to use.

$= \dfrac{6}{6.5} = 0.923$

> Fill in the information you are given.

$\tan^{-1} 0.923 = x = 42.7°$

> Identify on your calculator which key combination will find the size of angle from the ratio.

Find answers at: cambridge.org/ukschools/gcsemaths-studentbookanswers

WORK IT OUT 38.1

For a ladder to be safe it must be inclined at between 70° and 80° to the ground.

The diagram shows a ladder resting against a wall.

Is the ladder positioned safely?

Which of these calculations gives you the answer that you need?

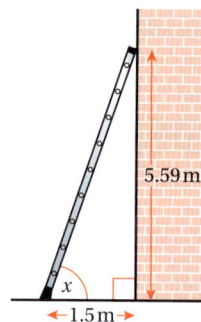

Not to scale

5.59 m

x

←1.5 m→

Option A	Option B	Option C
$\sin x = \dfrac{1.5}{5.59} = 0.268$ $\sin^{-1} 0.268 = 15.56°$	$\cos x = \dfrac{1.5}{5.59} = 0.268$ $\cos^{-1} 0.268 = 74.43°$	$\tan x = \dfrac{5.59}{1.5} = 3.73$ $\tan^{-1} 3.73 = 74.98°$

EXERCISE 38B

1 Work out, to one decimal place:

   a $\sin^{-1} 0.7$ **b** $\cos^{-1} 0.713$ **c** $\tan^{-1} 0.1$

   d $\sin^{-1} 0.732$ **e** $\cos^{-1} 0.1234$ **f** $\tan^{-1} 12$

2 Find the size of θ, to one decimal place.

   a $\sin \theta = 0.682$ **b** $\cos \theta = 0.891$

   c $\tan \theta = 2.4751$ **d** $\sin \theta = 0.2588$

   e $\tan \theta = 3.9469$ **f** $\cos \theta = 0.7847$

3 Calculate the size of each marked angle.

Give your answers to one decimal place.

a
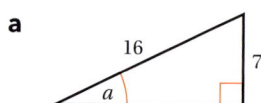

b
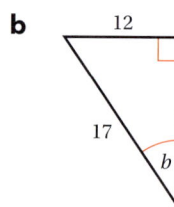

c
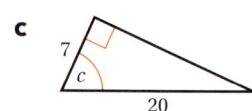

d
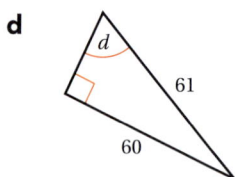

e
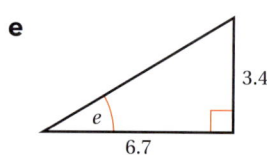

f
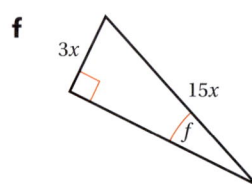

4 PQR is a right-angled triangle.

PQ = 11 cm and QR = 24 cm

Calculate the size of angle PRQ.

Not to scale

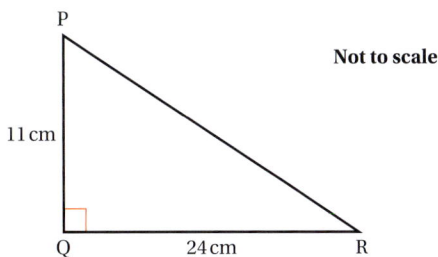

5 What is the size of angle x?

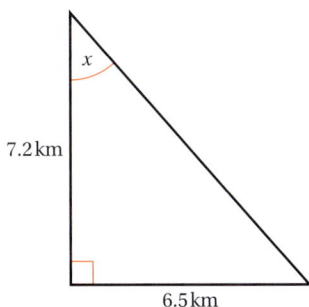

6 For each triangle, draw a sketch and calculate the missing value.

a In triangle ABC, angle $B = 90°$, BC = 45 units and angle $C = 23°$.

Calculate the length of AB.

b In triangle PQR, angle $R = 90°$, PQ = 12.2 cm and angle $P = 57°$.

Calculate the length of QR.

c In triangle EFG, angle $G = 90°$, EG = 8.7 cm and angle $E = 49°$.

Calculate the length of FG.

d In triangle XYZ, angle $Y = 90°$, XZ = 36 units and angle X is 25°.

Calculate the lengths of:

i XY   **ii** YZ

Section 2: Exact values of trigonometric ratios

The sides of right-angled triangles are not always perfect squares. When you work out trigonometric ratios on your calculator you often get approximate (or truncated) values.

However, some values of sin, cos and tan can be calculated exactly.

You need to know the exact values of the sin, cos and tan ratios for 0°, 30°, 45° and 60° angles, as well as the values of sin and cos for 90°. There is no tan ratio for 90°.

Sine, cosine and tangent ratios for 30° and 60°

The diagram shows an equilateral triangle of side 2 cm.

Angle $y = 60°$ (angles of equilateral triangle are equal).

Angle DEF is bisected by EG, so $z = 30°$.

EG is the perpendicular bisector of the base.
So, DG and GF are each 1 cm long.

Using Pythagoras' theorem, you can find the length of EG.

$$2^2 - 1^2 = EG^2$$
$$4 - 1 = EG^2$$
$$3 = EG^2$$
$$EG = \sqrt{3}$$

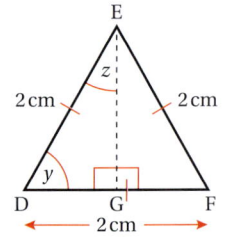

The square root of 3 is not an exact value so you leave it in surd form as this is easier to work with.

This gives us the right-angled triangle below:

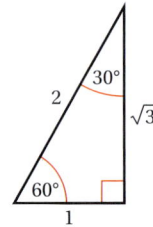

$$\sin 30° = \frac{\text{opposite}}{\text{hypotenuse}} = \frac{1}{2} \qquad \sin 60° = \frac{\text{opposite}}{\text{hypotenuse}} = \frac{\sqrt{3}}{2}$$

$$\cos 30° = \frac{\text{adjacent}}{\text{hypotenuse}} = \frac{\sqrt{3}}{2} \qquad \cos 60° = \frac{\text{adjacent}}{\text{hypotenuse}} = \frac{1}{2}$$

$$\tan 30° = \frac{\text{opposite}}{\text{adjacent}} = \frac{1}{\sqrt{3}} \qquad \tan 60° = \frac{\text{opposite}}{\text{adjacent}} = \frac{\sqrt{3}}{1} = \sqrt{3}$$

Sine, cosine and tangent ratios for 45°

The diagram shows a right-angled isosceles triangle with the two equal sides 1 cm long.

The hypotenuse is $\sqrt{2}$ cm (by Pythagoras).

The base angles, x, are each 45°.

$$\sin 45° = \frac{\text{opposite}}{\text{hypotenuse}} = \frac{1}{\sqrt{2}}$$

$$\cos 45° = \frac{\text{adjacent}}{\text{hypotenuse}} = \frac{1}{\sqrt{2}}$$

$$\tan 45° = \frac{\text{opposite}}{\text{adjacent}} = \frac{1}{1} = 1$$

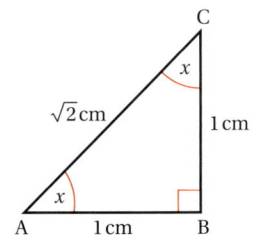

You need to know these exact values of special angles.

You can always draw the triangles to find them if you forget.

EXERCISE 38C

1 Copy and complete the table. Use it to memorise the exact values of the trigonometric ratios for the different angles.

Angle θ	$\sin \theta$	$\cos \theta$	$\tan \theta$
0°			
30°			
45°			
60°			
90°			tan 90° is undefined

2 Without using your calculator, find:

a $\sin 30° + \cos 60°$ **b** $\sin 45° + \cos 45°$ **c** $\cos 30° + \sin 60°$

d Give reasons for your results. Think about complementary angles.

3 Find the exact value of the variable(s) in each triangle.

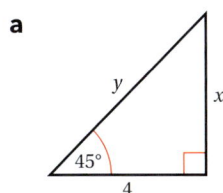

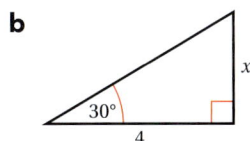

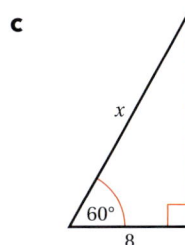

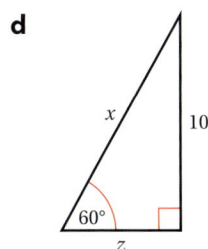

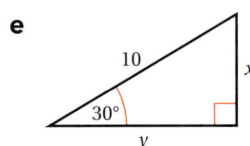

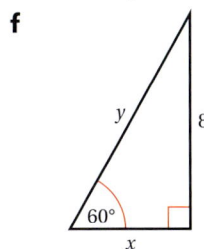

Section 3: The sine, cosine and area rules

Trigonometry can be used to solve any triangle, not just right-angled triangles.

There are two important formulae for finding lengths and angles in any triangle: the sine rule and the cosine rule.

Find answers at: cambridge.org/ukschools/gcsemaths-studentbookanswers

The sine rule

In triangle CAX the sine of the base angle at A = $\dfrac{h}{b}$

Rearranged, this becomes $h = b \sin A$

In triangle CBX the sine of base angle at B = $\dfrac{h}{a}$

Rearranged, this becomes $h = a \sin B$

Therefore $b \sin A = a \sin B$

This can be rearranged to:

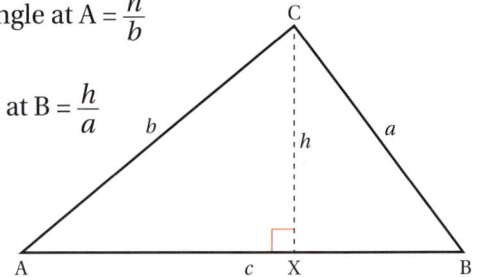

Learn this formula

$$\frac{a}{\sin A} = \frac{b}{\sin B} = \frac{c}{\sin C}$$

This is the sine rule.

This rule means that any side of the triangle divided by the sine of its opposite angle is equal to any other side divided by the sine of its opposite angle. So, the rule actually shows three possible relationships.

This version of the sine rule, with the sine ratios as the denominator, is usually used to calculate lengths.

You can invert the ratios to calculate the size of unknown angles:

$$\frac{\sin A}{a} = \frac{\sin B}{b} = \frac{\sin C}{c}$$

Tip

The sine rule is used when you are dealing with pairs of opposite sides and angles.

Tip

You can use the sine rule to find missing angles as long as you know the length of one side and the size of the angle opposite it.

WORKED EXAMPLE 4

1 Calculate length AB.

$$\frac{a}{\sin A} = \frac{b}{\sin B} = \frac{c}{\sin C}$$

$$\frac{7}{\sin 35°} = \frac{c}{\sin 105°}$$

$$\frac{7}{0.574} = \frac{c}{0.96}$$

$$12.2 = \frac{c}{0.96}$$

$$12.2 \times 0.96 = c = 11.71 \text{ cm}$$

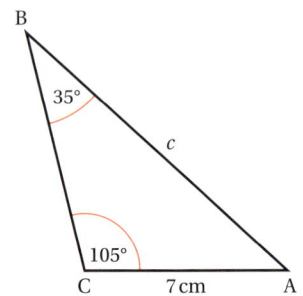

2 Find the size of angle θ to the nearest degree.

$$\frac{8}{\sin \theta} = \frac{12}{\sin 75°}$$

Apply the sine rule to the triangle.

$$\frac{\sin \theta}{8} = \frac{\sin 75°}{12}$$

Take the reciprocal of both sides to make your calculation simpler.

$$\sin \theta = \frac{8 \sin 75°}{12} = 0.6439\ldots$$

Use $\sin^{-1}$ to find the angle.

$$\therefore \theta = 40° \text{ (to the nearest degree)}$$

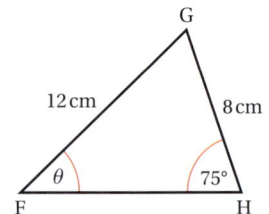

EXERCISE 38D

1 Find the value of x in each of the following equations.

a $\dfrac{x}{\sin 50°} = \dfrac{9}{\sin 38°}$ **b** $\dfrac{x}{\sin 235°} = \dfrac{20}{\sin 100°}$ **c** $\dfrac{20.6}{\sin 50°} = \dfrac{x}{\sin 70°}$

2 Find the length of the side marked x in each triangle.

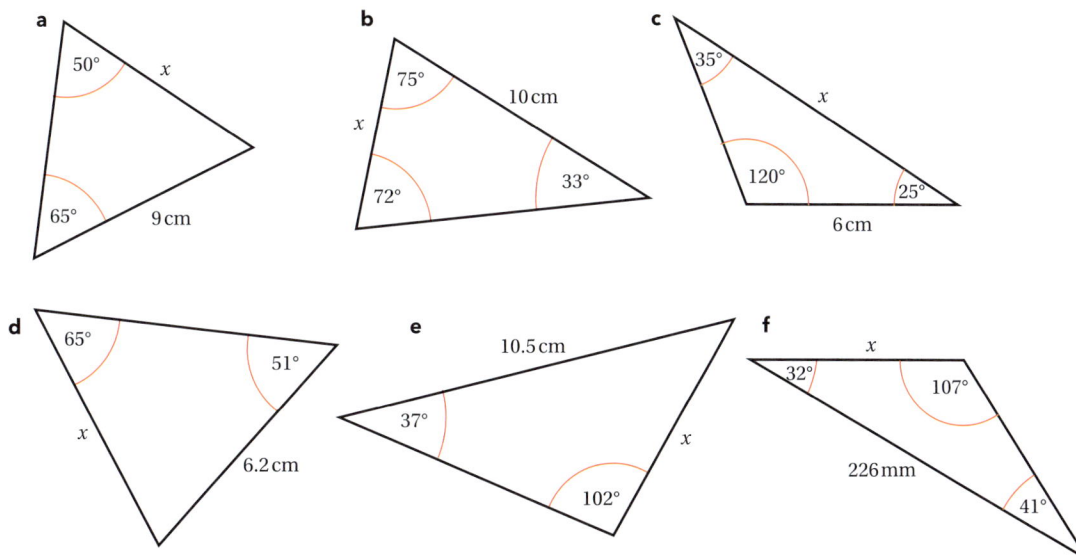

3 Find the size of the angle marked θ in each triangle.

Give your answers to one decimal place.

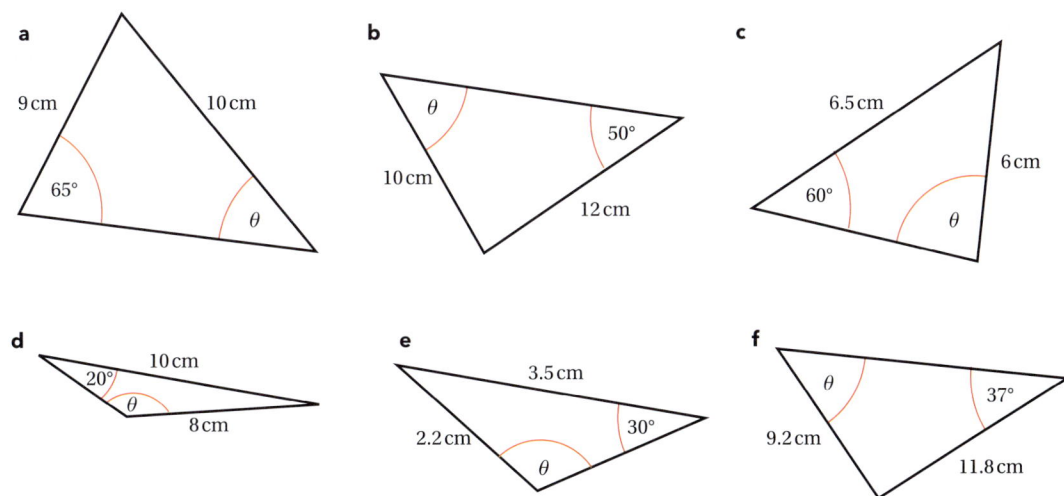

4 In triangle XYZ, angle $X = 40°$, XZ = 12 cm and YZ = 15 cm

a Give a reason why angle Y must be less than 40°.

b Calculate the size of angle Y and angle Z.

c Work out the length of side XY.

5 ABCD is a parallelogram with AB = 32 mm and AD = 40 mm.

Angle BAC = 77°

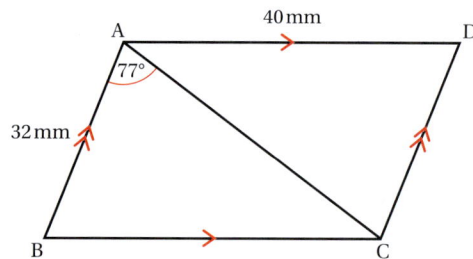

a Find the size of angle BCA to the nearest degree.

b Find the size of angle ABC to the nearest degree.

c What is the length of the diagonal AC in this figure? Give your answer to two decimal places.

The cosine rule

You can use the sine rule when you know the size of an angle and the length of the side opposite the angle. If you don't have this information, you might be able to use another formula called the cosine rule.

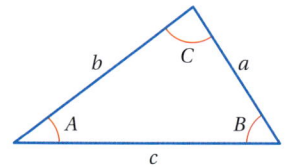

The cosine rule is based on Pythagoras' theorem and it applies to any triangle.

The cosine rule states that:

Learn this formula

$$a^2 = b^2 + c^2 - 2bc \cos A$$

Notice that all three sides are used in the cosine rule but only one angle.

The side whose square is used as the subject of the formula is opposite the known angle. This form of the cosine rule is used to find unknown sides.

The formula can be rearranged to make the square of any side the subject.

$$b^2 = a^2 + c^2 - 2ac \cos B \qquad\qquad c^2 = a^2 + b^2 - 2ab \cos C$$

You can also make the cosine ratio the subject of the formula in order to calculate unknown angles.

WORKED EXAMPLE 5

1 In triangle ABC, angle $B = 50°$, AB = 9 cm and BC = 18 cm.

Find the length of AC to three significant figures.

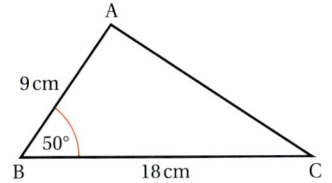

$b^2 = a^2 + c^2 - 2ac \cos B$
$b^2 = 9^2 + 18^2 - (2 \times 9 \times 18 \times \cos 50°)$
$b^2 = 81 + 324 - (208.2631...)$
$b^2 = 196.7368...$
$b = \sqrt{196.7368...}$
$b = 14.0262$
$AC = 14.0 \text{ cm (3 sf)}$

> AC = b and you know that $B = 50°$, so use this form of the cosine rule.

2 Calculate the size of angle C.

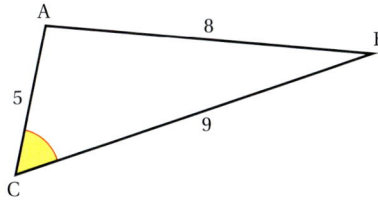

$a^2 + b^2 - 2ab \cos C = c^2$
$9^2 + 5^2 - 2 \times 9 \times 5 \cos C = 64$
$81 + 25 - 90 \cos C = 64$
$106 - 64 - 90 \cos C = 0$
$42 - 90 \cos C = 0$
$42 = 90 \cos C$
$\frac{42}{90} = \cos C$
$0.467 = \cos C$
$\cos^{-1} 0.467 = C$
Angle $C = 62.1°$

EXERCISE 38E

1 Find the length of the side marked x in each triangle. Give your answers to three significant figures.

a

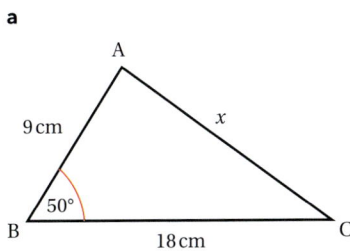

b

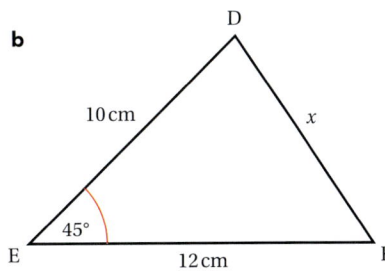

c

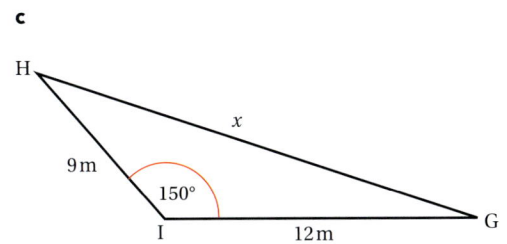

2 In triangle PQR, PQ = 11 cm, QR = 9 cm and RP = 8 cm

Find the size of angle RPQ, giving your answer to three significant figures.

Find answers at: cambridge.org/ukschools/gcsemaths-studentbookanswers

3 In triangle STU, angle $S = 95°$, ST = 10 m and SU = 15 m

  a Calculate the length of TU.

  b Find the size of angles U and T.

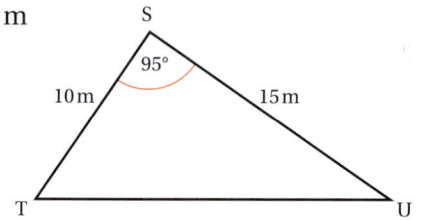

4 Work out the size of each angle in this triangle.

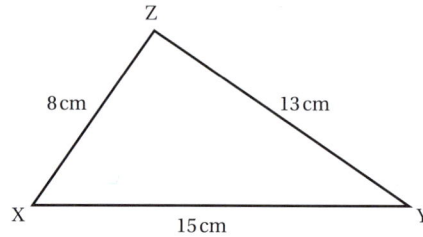

5 A boat sails in a straight line from Aardvark Island on a bearing of 060°. When the boat has sailed 8 km, it reaches Beaver Island and it turns to sail on a bearing of 150°.

The boat remains on this bearing until it reaches Crow Island, 12 km from Beaver Island.

From Crow Island, the boat sails directly back to Aardvark Island.

Calculate:

  a the length of the return journey

  b the bearing on which the boat must sail to return directly to Aardvark Island.

The area rule

If you don't have the length of the base or the perpendicular height you can calculate the area of any triangle using trigonometry.

Look at triangle ABC.

The perpendicular height (h) creates a right-angled triangle BMC.

In triangle BMC, the height (h) is the side opposite angle C and the hypotenuse is side a.

Using the sine ratio, $\sin C = \dfrac{h}{a}$, so $h = a \sin C$.

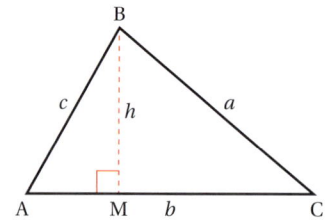

This means that you have a way of determining the perpendicular height and you can use it with the base length to find the area.

$$\text{Area} = \frac{1}{2} \times \text{base} \times \text{height}$$
$$= \frac{1}{2}b \times a \sin C$$

This gives a formula for finding the area of any triangle.

Learn this formula

Area $= \frac{1}{2}ab \sin C$

To use the area formula you need two sides and their included angle.

When you find the area of a triangle, you can use any side as the base. This means that the formula can be rearranged to suit the information you have.

Area $= \frac{1}{2}ac \sin B$ Area $= \frac{1}{2}bc \sin A$

Problem-solving framework

Calculate the area of the triangle ABC, angle $A = 48°$, $c = 5$ cm and $b = 7$ cm.

Give your answer to two decimal places.

Steps for solving problems	What you would do for this example
Step 1: What information have you been given?	We have been given the measurements of two sides and the included angle and so we can use the area rule.
Step 2: Draw a diagram to show the information.	
Step 3: Choose the formula and write it down correctly.	Since we are given the size of the angle at A, we will use the formula area of triangle ABC $= \frac{1}{2}bc \sin A$
Step 4: Do the calculation.	$= \frac{1}{2} \times 7 \times 5 \sin 48°$ $= 13.01 \text{ cm}^2$
Step 5: Check the answer.	You can do this on your calculator by checking that $\sin^{-1}\left(\frac{2 \times 13.01}{5 \times 7}\right) = 48$

EXERCISE 38F

1 Calculate the area of each triangle.

Give your answers to two decimal places.

a

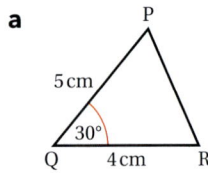

b

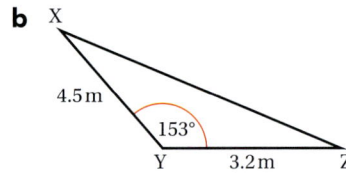

c

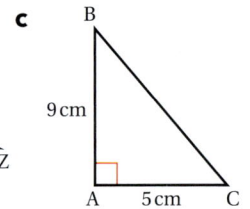

d

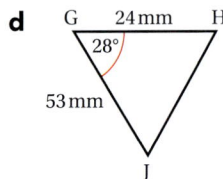

e

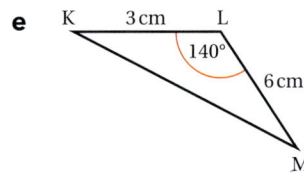

f

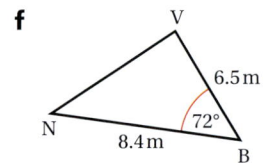

2 Calculate the area of each triangle ABC with the following measurements.

a $a = 3$ cm, $b = 6$ cm and angle $C = 65°$

b $b = 5.2$ cm, $c = 7.7$ cm and angle $A = 105°$

c $a = 6.1$ cm, $c = 5.3$ cm and angle $B = 98°$

d $b = 8$ cm, $c = 12$ cm and angle $A = 39°$.

3 Triangle XYZ has an area of 500 cm².

Calculate the length of YZ.

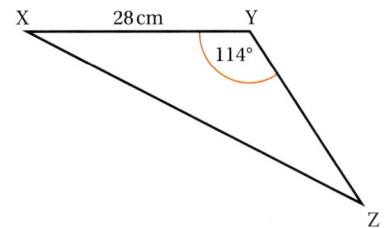

Section 4: Using trigonometry to solve problems

The trigonometric ratios together with the sine, cosine and area rules can be applied to many different types of measurement problems in both two- and three-dimensional figures.

If the question does not include a sketch, it is useful to draw one.

Make it large and clear and mark what you know on it. This will help you to identify the correct ratio to use to solve the problem.

Angles of elevation and depression

Many trigonometry problems involve lines of sight. (In other words, looking at an object from a distance away.)

Problems that involve looking up to an object can be described in terms of an **angle of elevation**. This is the angle between an observer's line of sight and a horizontal line.

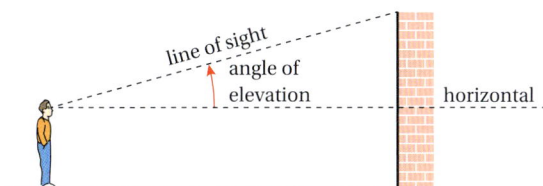

When an observer is looking down, the **angle of depression** is the angle between the observer's line of sight and a horizontal line.

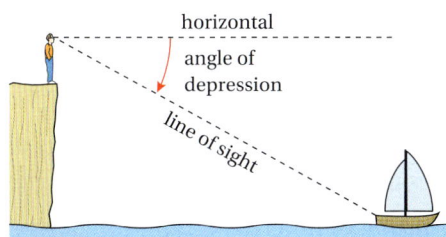

🔑 Key vocabulary

angle of elevation: when looking up, the angle between the line of sight and the horizontal

angle of depression: when looking down, the angle between the line of sight and the horizontal

Problem-solving framework

A ship is laying cable along the sea bed.

The angle of the cable to the sea bed is 40° and the length of cable to the sea bed is 40 metres.

The ship is 50 miles offshore and travelling north-west.

What is the depth of the sea bed?

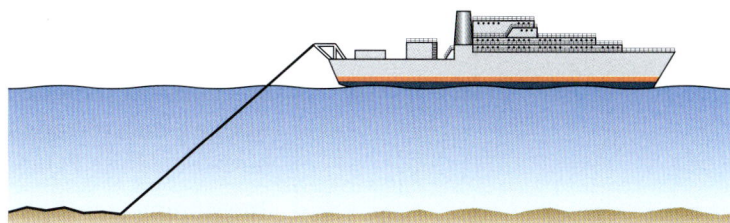

Steps for solving problems	What you would do for this example
Step 1: What have you got to do?	Use Pythagoras' theorem or trigonometry to find the depth of water.
Step 2: What information do you need?	Angle 40° and length of cable as the hypotenuse is 40 m.
Step 3: What information don't you need?	50 miles offshore and the direction of travel.

Continues on next page …

Step 4: What maths can you use?	Use a right-angled triangle.
	Cannot use Pythagoras' theorem as you do not know two lengths, so use trig. ratios.
	Decide which trigonometric function to use: sin, cos or tan?
	One angle and the hypotenuse are known so need to find the opposite length.
	$\sin 40° = \dfrac{\text{opp}}{\text{hyp}} = \dfrac{\text{opp}}{40}$
	$0.643 \times 40 = \text{opposite length} = 25.72\,\text{m}$
	The sea bed is 25.7 metres deep (to 3 sf).
Step 5: Have you done it all?	Yes, the question has been answered and the correct units have been used in the answer.
Step 6: Is it correct?	Yes, double-checked and estimated. The depth must be less than 40 m.
	$\sin 30° = 0.5$ so half of 40 m would be 20 m.

Three-dimensional problems

To solve problems related to three-dimensional objects you need to visualise two different flat planes and how they meet at right angles.

Then you think of the problem in terms of 2D triangles.

One of the 2D triangles will give you the information you need to solve the other.

> **Tip**
>
> It often helps to sketch the 2D triangles from a 3D problem. Then solve each triangle in turn.

WORKED EXAMPLE 6

The diagram shows a door wedge with a rectangular horizontal base PQRS.

The sloping face PQTU is also rectangular.

PQ = 3.8 cm and angle TQR = 6°

The height TR is 2.5 cm.

What is the length of the diagonal PT?

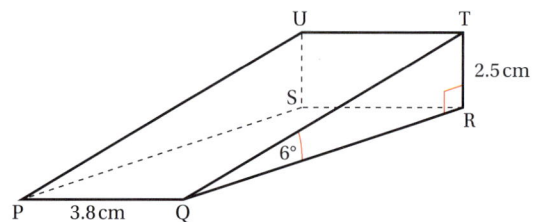

$\sin 6° = \dfrac{2.5}{QT}$

$0.105 = \dfrac{2.5}{QT}$

$QT = \dfrac{2.5}{0.105} = 23.81\,cm$

Using trigonometry in triangle TQR.

$PQ^2 + QT^2 = PT^2$

$3.8^2 + 23.81^2 = PT^2$

$14.44 + 566.92 = PT^2$

$581.36 = PT^2$

$PT = \sqrt{581.36} = 24.11\,cm$

Using Pythagoras' theorem for triangle PQT.

EXERCISE 38G

1 Calculate the angle marked x in the diagram.

Choose your answer from the options below.

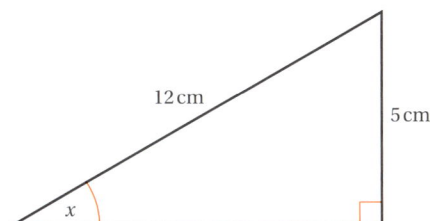

A 24.62°   B 2.4°   C 0.416°   D 65.38°

2 A child's playground slide is 4.2 m long and makes an angle of 63° with the horizontal.

Calculate the height of the slide.

3 Carol is in a hot-air balloon at point C in the sky.

CG is the vertical height of the hot-air balloon above the ground.

David is standing on the ground at point D.

The distance between points D and G is 27 m.

The angle of elevation from David to the hot-air balloon is 53°.

Calculate the length of CG.

4 Two boats are sailing a distance of 25 m apart.

The angle of depression from the top of a lighthouse to one boat is 35° and to the other boat is 55°.

How tall is the lighthouse?

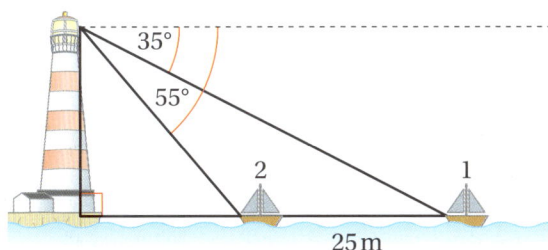

5 Mike is standing 15 m away from a flagpole.

The angle of elevation from his line of sight to the top of the flagpole is 60°.

a Calculate the height of the flagpole if Mike's eye is 1.6 m above ground level.

b Mike moves another 10 m further away from the flagpole.

How will the angle of elevation from his line of sight to the top of the flagpole change?

Find answers at: cambridge.org/ukschools/gcsemaths-studentbookanswers

6 Two observers in different positions at A and B are watching a rare bird on a tree at C.

The angle of elevation from A to C is 56° and the angle of elevation from B to C is 25°.

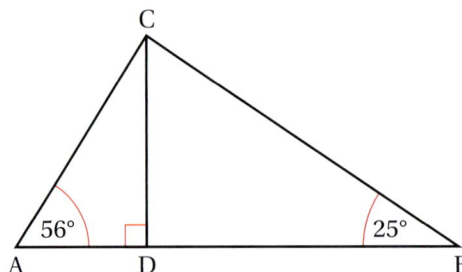

a Person B is standing 15 m from D (the base of the tree).

Calculate the height of the bird above the ground (the length CD).

b Calculate the distance of person A from D.

7 Paolo is standing at a point P, 30 m away from a mobile phone signal tower.

The angle of depression from the top of the tower to P is 56°.

Calculate the height of the tower.

8 A tree surgeon measures the angle of elevation from her point of view to the top of a tree as 20°.

She is standing 10 m away from the tree.

a If she assumes that the tree is perfectly perpendicular, how would she calculate the height of the tree?

b To check her calculation, she moves another 10 m away from the tree in a straight line, and measures the angle of elevation again.

What should the angle measurement be now if her first measurement and calculation were correct?

9 The sketch represents a field PQRS on level ground.

The sides PQ and SR run due east.

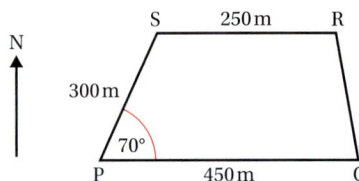

a Work out the bearing of S from P.

b Calculate the shortest distance between SR and PQ.

c Calculate the area of the field in square metres.

10 Find the area of a regular pentagon with sides $2a$ metres long.

11 The diagram shows a room in the shape of a cuboid.

AB = 6 m, AD = 4 m and AP = 2 m

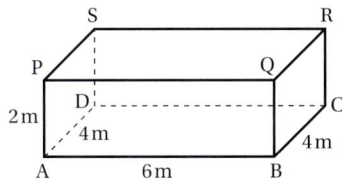

Calculate the angle between the diagonal BS and the floor ABCD.

12 ABCDE is a square-based pyramid.

AB = BC = CD = AD = 5.6 cm

N is the centre of the square ABCD. E is directly above N.

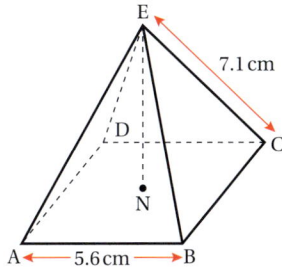

a Calculate the distance BD.

b Calculate angle EBN.

13 The Great Pyramid in Egypt has a square base with sides of 232.6 m long.

The distance from the top of the pyramid to each corner of the base was originally 221.2 m.

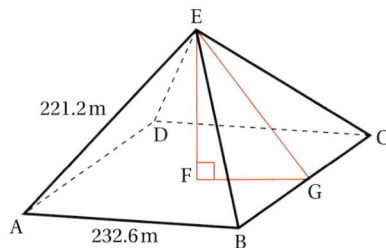

a Work out the angle each face makes with the base.

b Work out the size of the apex angle of a face of the pyramid (angle BEF).

Trigonometric ratios

- In a right-angled triangle, the longest side is the hypotenuse. For a given angle, θ, the other two sides can be labelled opposite (to angle θ) and adjacent (to angle θ).
- The sine, cosine and tangent ratios can be used to find unknown sides and angles in right-angled triangles.
  - $\sin\theta = \dfrac{\text{opposite}}{\text{hypotenuse}}$
  - $\cos\theta = \dfrac{\text{adjacent}}{\text{hypotenuse}}$
  - $\tan\theta = \dfrac{\text{opposite}}{\text{adjacent}}$
- You can find the value of a ratio using the sin, cos and tan buttons on your calculator.
  To find the size of an angle, use the inverse functions $\sin^{-1}$, $\cos^{-1}$ and $\tan^{-1}$.

Exact values

- You can find the exact values of sin, cos and tan for special angles. Some exact values contain square roots.

Angle θ	$\sin\theta$	$\cos\theta$	$\tan\theta$
0°	0	1	0
30°	$\dfrac{1}{2}$	$\dfrac{\sqrt{3}}{2}$	$\dfrac{1}{\sqrt{3}}$
45°	$\dfrac{1}{\sqrt{2}}$	$\dfrac{1}{\sqrt{2}}$	1
60°	$\dfrac{\sqrt{3}}{2}$	$\dfrac{1}{2}$	$\sqrt{3}$
90°	1	0	tan 90° is undefined

Sine, cosine and area rules

- The sine and cosine rules can be used to calculate unknown sides and angles in triangles that are not right-angled.
- The sine rule is used for calculating an angle from another angle and two sides, or a side from another side and two known angles. The sides and angles must be arranged in opposite pairs.
- The cosine rule is used for calculating an angle from three known sides, or a side from a known angle and two known sides.
- You can calculate the area of any triangle by using the sine ratio (the area rule).

For additional questions on the topics in this chapter, visit GCSE Mathematics Online.

Chapter review

1 What is the value of cos 45°?

Choose from the following options.

A $\frac{1}{\sqrt{2}} = 0.707$ B $\frac{1}{\sqrt{3}} = 0.577$ C 1   D 0.5

2 The diagram shows a triangle ABC.

Angle $A = 20°$, angle $C = 90°$ and $AB = 32\,m$

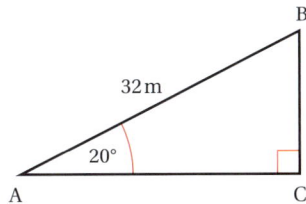

Calculate the height BC.

3 A ladder leans against the side of a house.

The ladder is 4.5 m in length and makes an angle of 74° with the ground.

How high up the wall will it reach? (This length is marked x in the diagram.)

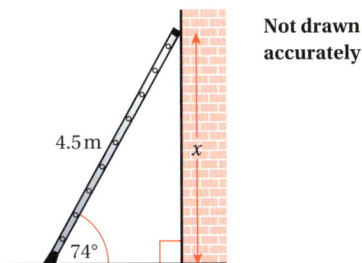

Not drawn accurately

4 The ladder from question 3 is placed 0.9 m away from the side of the house.

What angle does the ladder now make with the ground? (This angle is marked y in the diagram.)

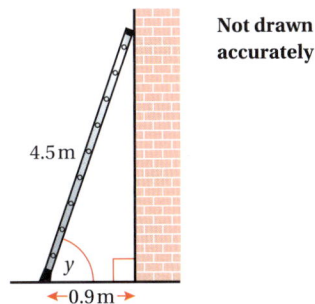

Not drawn accurately

Find answers at: cambridge.org/ukschools/gcsemaths-studentbookanswers

5 The dimensions of the lean on the Leaning Tower of Pisa are shown below.

From the information given, what is the actual height of the tower?

6 Triangles ABC and PQR are similar.

AC = 3.2 cm, AB = 4 cm and PR = 4.8 cm

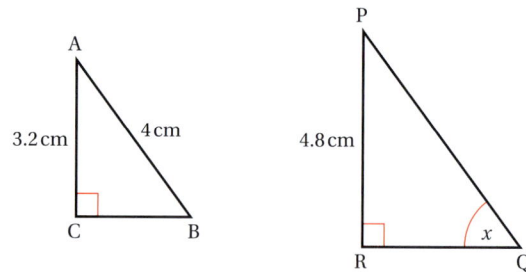

Give a reason why sin x = 0.8.

7 Calculate the perimeter of this triangle, to the nearest mile.

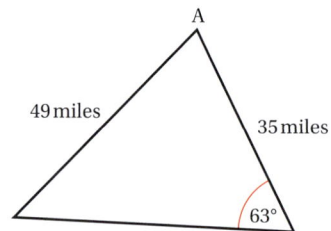

8 Work out the size of angle A.

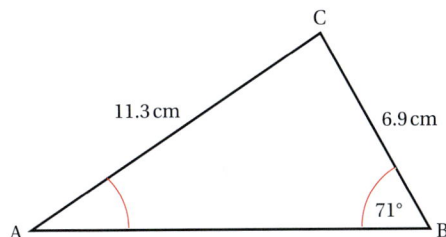

Not drawn
accurately

Give your answer to a suitable degree of accuracy.

(4 marks)

© AQA 2013

9 An equilateral triangle has an area of $24\,cm^2$.

Work out the length of a side of the triangle, giving your answer to one decimal place.

10 The area of triangle FGH is $804\,cm^2$.

FG = 43.2 cm and GH = 38.7 cm

Calculate two possible values for angle G to one decimal place.

11 The area of triangle ABC is $18\,cm^2$.

Angle $B = 30°$ and AB = 8 cm

Calculate the length of BC.

39 Graphs of other functions and equations

In this chapter you will learn how to …

- plot and sketch graphs of linear and quadratic functions.
- identify the main features of graphs of quadratic functions and equations.
- plot and sketch other polynomials and reciprocal functions.
- recognise and sketch graphs of exponential and trigonometric functions.
- recognise and use the equation of a circle with centre at the origin.

For more resources relating to this chapter, visit GCSE Mathematics Online.

Using mathematics: real-life applications

Graphs are used to process information, make predictions and generalise patterns from sets of data. The nature of the data and the relationship between values leads to the shape and form of the graph.

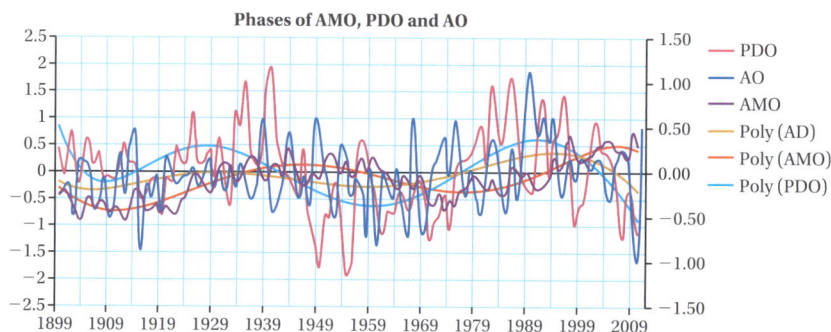

Phases of AMO, PDO and AO

"I study the Earth using gravity, magnetic, electrical and seismic methods. I used this graph in a study of the Pacific and Atlantic Oceans. I need to be able to understand equations and recognise the features of graphs to understand and interpret it." *(Geophysicist)*

Before you start …

Ch 29	You should be able to interpret equations of linear graphs.	**1**	For the graph $y = 3x + 1$: **a** identify the gradient of the graph **b** give the coordinates of the y-intercept **c** find the value of x when $y = -14$ **d** show that it is parallel to the graph $2y - 6x = -4$.
Ch 29	You must be able to generate a table of values from a function.	**2**	Given $y = 3x^2 + 1$, copy and complete the table of values: <table><tr><td>x</td><td>-2</td><td>-1</td><td>0</td><td>1</td><td>2</td></tr><tr><td>y</td><td></td><td></td><td></td><td></td><td></td></tr></table>
Ch 17	You need to be able to find the roots of a quadratic equation algebraically.	**3**	What are the roots of: **a** $x^2 + 2x - 8 = 0$? **b** $x^2 + 5x = -4$? **4** Complete the square to find the solution of $x^2 + 4x - 6 = 0$.

Assess your starting point using the Launchpad

STEP 1

1 How many points do you need to calculate to plot the graph of a linear equation?

2 Sketch the graph of the linear equation $y = 2x + 1$.

?

GO TO
Section 1:
Review of linear graphs

✔

STEP 2

3 **a** Is this the graph of $y = x^2 + 1$ or $y = -x^2 + 1$?

b How can you tell?

c Is the turning point a maximum or a minimum?

d What are the coordinates of the vertex?

e For what values of x is $y = 0$?

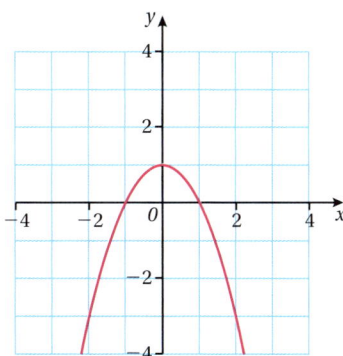

?

GO TO
Section 2:
Quadratic functions

✔

STEP 3

4 **a** What type of equation is $y = x^3$?

b How many points do you need to calculate to plot the graph of $y = x^3$?

5 Given $y = \frac{1}{x}$

a what happens when $x = 0$?

b what happens to the value of y as the value of x increases?

c when $x = 60$, what is the value of y?

?

GO TO
Section 3:
Other polynomials and reciprocals

✔

GO TO
Step 4
The Launchpad continues on the next page …

Find answers at: cambridge.org/ukschools/gcsemaths-studentbookanswers

Launchpad continued …

6 Sketch the graph of $y = 2^x$

7 Which of these graphs is $y = \sin x$ and which one is $y = \cos x$?

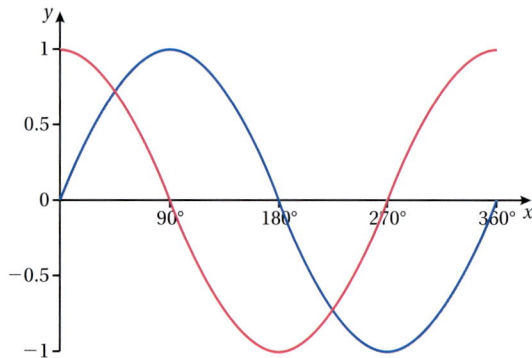

GO TO
Section 4:
Exponential and trigonometric functions
Section 5:
Circles and their equations

GO TO
Chapter review

Section 1: Review of linear graphs

Graphs in the form of $y = mx$

In the equation $y = mx + c$, the value of c tells you where the graph cuts the y-axis.

When there is no value of c in the equation you get a graph in the form of $y = mx$.

WORK IT OUT 39.1

These are three linear functions.

$$y = 3x \qquad y = -3x \qquad y = \frac{1}{3}x$$

There is a common point that all the graphs pass through.

What is that point? How do you know?

Option A	Option B	Option C
(0, 3)	(−3, 0)	(0, 0)

Any linear equation of the form $y = mx$ passes through the origin with a gradient of m.

The graphs of $y = mx$ and $y = -mx$ are shown here.

If $m = 1$, the equation is written as $y = x$. If $m = -1$, the equation is written as $y = -x$.

$y = x$ is the line that passes through the origin from left to right going up at an angle of 45° (as the axis scales are equal).

$y = -x$ is the line that passes through the origin from left to right going down at an angle of 45°.

Sketching $y = ax$ ...	Examples	Notes
if a is greater than 1	$y = 3x$ $y = 7x$	The line still passes through the origin but it is steeper than $y = x$.
if a is a value between 0 and 1	$y = \frac{1}{2}x$ $y = \frac{1}{5}x$	The line still passes through the origin but it is less steep than $y = x$.
if a is a negative value	$y = -3x$ $y = -\frac{1}{2}x$	The line still passes through the origin but it will go down from left to right like $y = -x$.

Vertical and horizontal lines

The equations of some lines are in the form of $x = a$ or $y = b$, where a and b are constant values. Equations of this form tell you that the value of x or y never changes.

For example, the graph of the equation $x = 7$ passes through the point $(7, 0)$. It also passes through all points on the grid with an x-coordinate of 7. Some of these points are $(7, -4)$, $(7, -1)$, $(7, 3)$ and $(7, 50)$.

Another example is the graph of the equation $y = 7$, that would need to pass through the point $(0, 7)$ and all other points with a y-coordinate of 7.

The graphs of $x = 7$ and $y = 7$ are shown here.

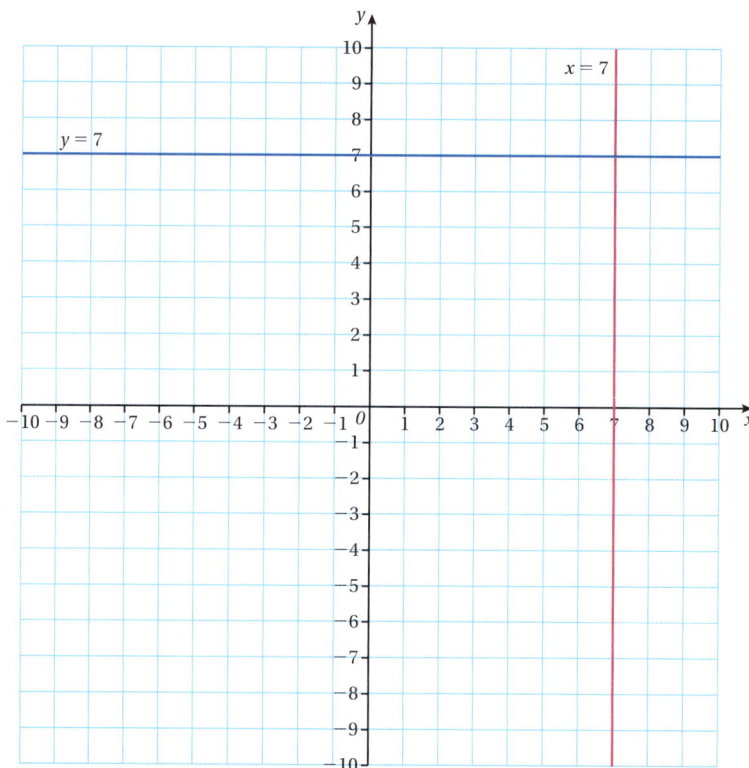

In general:

- any graph in the form of $x = a$ is parallel to the y-axis and passes through a on the x-axis
- any graph in the form of $y = b$ is parallel to the x-axis and passes through b on the y-axis
- the values of a and b in $x = a$ and $y = b$ can be positive or negative.

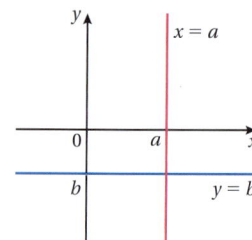

The axes themselves can be described using equations.

The x-axis is the line $y = 0$ and the y-axis is the line $x = 0$.

Tip

You should be able to recognise and sketch the graphs of any line in the form $x = a$ or $y = b$.

EXERCISE 39A

1 Which of the following points lies on the line $y = -2x + 3$?

    A $(1, 2)$ B $(1, 1)$ C $(1, 5)$ D $(-1, 1)$

2 Write down which of the graphs on the grid above can be described in each of the following ways.

    a The x-coordinate of each point is equal to the y-coordinate.

    b The gradient is negative.

    c The general form of the graph is $y = mx$.

    d The y-coordinate is 6 times the x-coordinate.

    e The y-coordinate is 6 less than the x-coordinate.

3 Give the equation of each line on the grid in question 2.

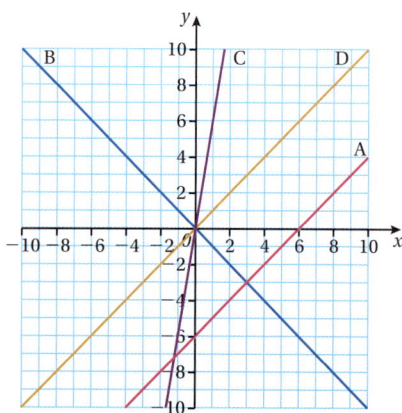

4 a Write down the equation of each of the lines A to F.

b Work out the equation of the line parallel to D that passes through point (0, 7).

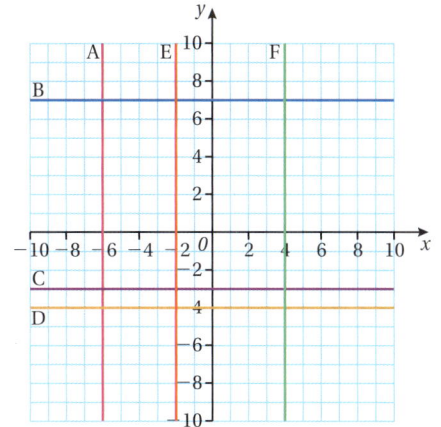

5 Draw the following graphs on a grid numbered from –6 to 6 on each axis.

a $x = -3$ **b** $y = 5$ **c** $y = -3$ **d** $x = 5$

6 Name the type of quadrilateral enclosed by the four lines you drew in question 5.

Give reasons for your answer.

7 a Write down the equations of two lines that divide the quadrilateral formed in question 5 into two identical rectangles.

b Which line divides shapes into two identical halves?

Choose from the options below.

A Mirror line   B Perpendicular bisector   C Line of best fit

c It is possible to draw two other lines that divide the quadrilateral into two equal halves.

i Draw these lines on your diagram.

ii Work out the equation of each line.

8 Sketch the graph of each linear equation.

a $y = 2x$ **b** $y = -8x$ **c** $y = -\frac{1}{4}x$

d $y = x + 7$ **e** $y = -2x - 1$

Section 2: Quadratic functions

A **quadratic** expression has the form $ax^2 + bx + c$, where $a \neq 0$.

Two quadratic expressions are $2x^2 + 4x - 1$ and $3x^2 + 7$, but $2x - 1$ is a linear expression as it has no x^2 term.

The graph of a quadratic function is a curve called a **parabola**.

Key vocabulary

quadratic: an expression with a variable to the power of 2 but no higher power

parabola: the symmetrical curve produced by the graph of a quadratic function

Tip

In Chapter 17 you learnt how to solve quadratic equations by writing them as the product of two factors equal to 0. Revise that chapter if you have forgotten how to do this.

Find answers at: cambridge.org/ukschools/gcsemaths-studentbookanswers

The path of moving objects such as this basketball can be modelled as a parabola.

The simplest equation of a parabola is $y = x^2$.

This is the graph of $y = x^2$.

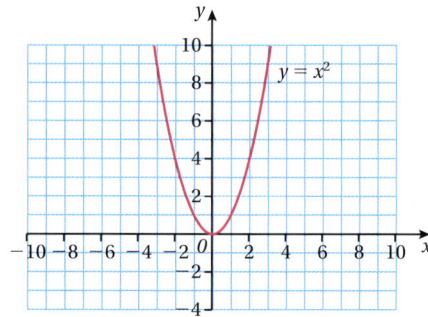

> **Tip**
>
> The shape of a parabola can extend upwards to a maximum point or downwards to a minimum point. The equation of the graph tells you which of these shapes it will be.

You can plot the graph of a quadratic function by drawing up a table of values.

WORKED EXAMPLE 1

Plot the graph of $y = x^2 - 2x - 8$.

x	-3	-2	-1	0	1	2	3	4	5
y	7	0	-5	-8	-9	-8	-5	0	7

Draw a table of points that satisfy the equation $y = x^2 - 2x - 8$.

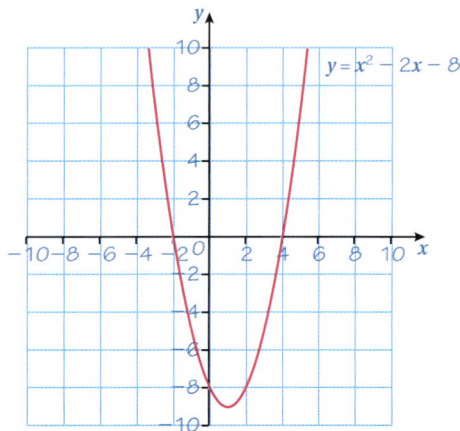

Plot all these points to draw the graph and produce a smooth curve drawing through and beyond the points calculated.

Don't forget to label the curve you have drawn.

EXERCISE 39B

1 $y = -2x^2 + 3$. State the value of y when $x = -5$.

Choose from the options below.

    A $y = 53$ B $y = -47$ C $y = -53$ D $y = 47$

2 Plot the graph of each of these equations for $-3 \leqslant x \leqslant 3$ on the same grid.

    a $y = x^2$ **b** $y = -x^2$ **c** $y = x^2 + 1$ **d** $y = x^2 - 4$

3 Plot the graph of each quadratic equation for whole number values of x in the given range:

    a $y = x^2 + 2x - 3$ $-4 \leqslant x \leqslant 2$ **b** $y = x^2 + x - 2$ $-3 \leqslant x \leqslant 2$

    c $y = x^2 + 3x$ $-4 \leqslant x \leqslant 1$

4 Plot some graphs to help you answer these questions.

    a If the coefficient of x^2 is greater than 1 what effect does it have on the shape of the parabola compared with when the coefficient of x^2 equals 1?

    b If the coefficient of x^2 is a value between 1 and 0, what effect does it have on the shape of the parabola compared with when the coefficient of x^2 equals 1?

    c What happens to the graph of the parabola if a constant value is added?

    Consider the difference between the graph of an equation such as $y = ax^2$ and $y = ax^2 + b$.

    d How does the graph of the parabola differ from the basic $y = x^2$ graph when the coefficient of x^2 is negative?

5 Plot the graph of $y = x^2 - x - 2$ for $-2 \leqslant x \leqslant 3$.

    a Solve the equation $x^2 - x - 2 = 0$.

    b How would you read the solution to the equation $x^2 - x - 2 = 0$ from the graph?

Features of graphs of quadratic equations

Quadratic graphs have characteristics that you can use to sketch and interpret them.

The main features of a parabola are:

- the axis of symmetry – a line which divides the parabola into two symmetrical halves.
- the y-intercept where the curve cuts the y-axis – a parabola can only have one y-intercept.
- the turning point or vertex of the graph – this is the point at which the graph changes direction.
- the x-intercepts where the graph cuts the x-axis – a parabola can have 0, 1 or 2 x-intercepts depending on the position of the graph.

The graph either has a minimum turning point or a maximum turning point.

If the x^2 term is positive, the graph will go down to a minimum turning point (this is the lowest point of the graph and is called the minimum).

If the x^2 term is negative, the graph will go up to a maximum turning point (this is the highest point of the graph and is called the maximum).

The diagram shows the main features of a parabola drawn from the equation $y = x^2 + 4x - 5$.

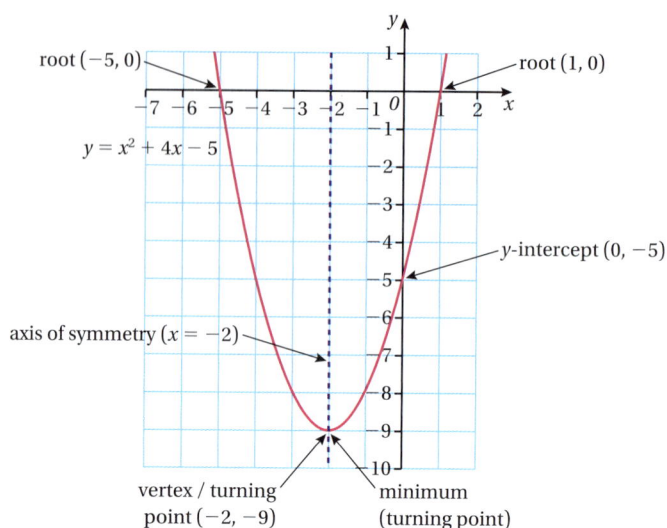

The curve is symmetrical and the axis of symmetry is $x = -2$ (the x-value of the vertex).

The y-intercept, where the graph cuts the y-axis, is the point $(0, -5)$.

The vertex is $(-2, -9)$ and is a minimum turning point.

The curve cuts the x-axis at the points $(-5, 0)$ and $(1, 0)$.

The values of x for which the quadratic function equals 0 are known as the roots of the quadratic equation.

These are the points where the graph crosses the x-axis (when $y = 0$).

In the example above, the roots of the equation are $x = -5$ and $x = 1$.

This information can also be established algebraically by solving $x^2 + 4x - 5 = 0$.

The y-intercept can also be found algebraically. It is the value of y when $x = 0$:

$y = x^2 + 4x - 5$
$= 0^2 + (4 \times 0) - 5 = -5$

So the y-intercept is the point $(0, -5)$.

Identifying the turning point

You can complete the square of an equation to find the turning point algebraically.

For example:

Completing the square for $y = x^2 + 4x - 5$, gives $y = x^2 + 4x - 5 = (x + 2)^2 - 9$.

$(x + 2)^2 \geqslant 0$, so the minimum value of y is when $(x + 2)^2 = 0$.

This is when $x = -2$, and $y = -9$. So the turning point, is the point $(-2, -9)$.

The axis of symmetry goes through the turning point. So the axis of symmetry of this graph is the line $x = -2$.

All parabolas are symmetrical and will have an axis of symmetry.

Not all parabolas will cross the x-axis and have real roots.

WORK IT OUT 39.2

What are the main features of this parabola?

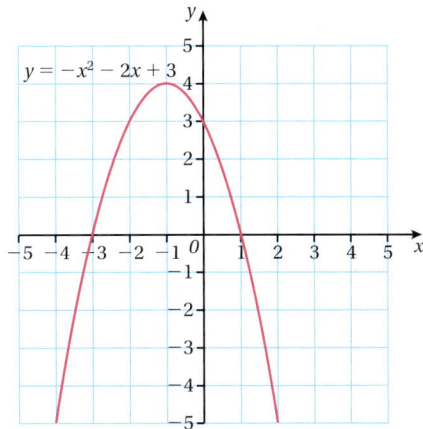

$y = -x^2 - 2x + 3$

Option A	Option B	Option C
y-intercept $(0, 3)$	y-intercept $(0, 3)$	y-intercept $(0, 3)$
vertex $(-1, -4)$ is a minimum turning point.	vertex $(-1, 4)$ is a maximum turning point.	vertex $(-1, 4)$ is a maximum turning point.
axis of symmetry $x = 1$	axis of symmetry $x = 1$	axis of symmetry $x = -1$
x intercepts: $(-3, 0)$ and $(1, 0)$	x intercepts: $(-3, 1)$ and $(1, 1)$	x intercepts: $(-3, 0)$ and $(1, 0)$

x-intercepts and roots of a quadratic equation

The x-intercepts of a parabola are the roots of the quadratic equation that defines the graph.

You can find the roots graphically by reading their values off the graph.

You can also solve the quadratic equation to find its roots. The roots are the points at which its graph crosses the x-axis (or the x-intercepts). This is useful when you have to sketch the graph.

EXERCISE 39C

1 For each parabola work out:

i the turning point and whether it is a minimum or maximum

ii the axis of symmetry

iii the y-intercept

iv the x-intercepts

v the roots of the equation used to generate the graph.

a

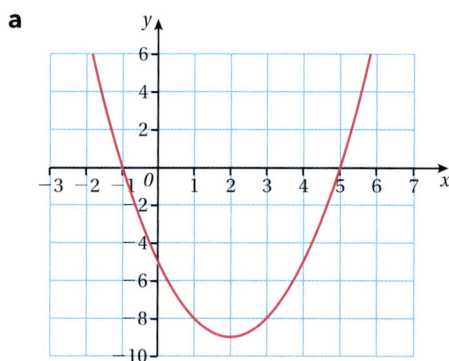

b

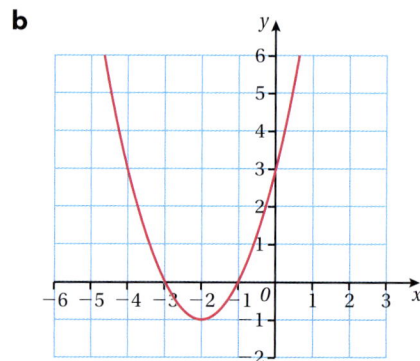

c

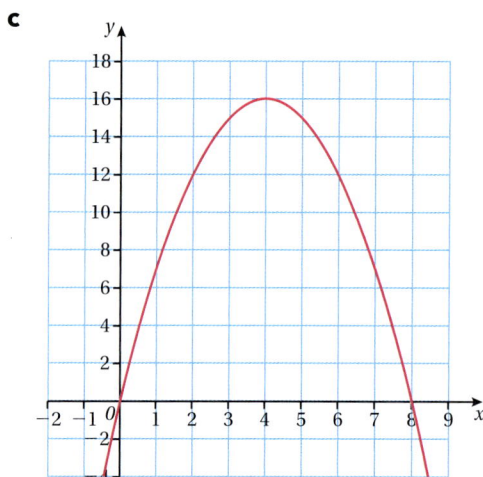

d

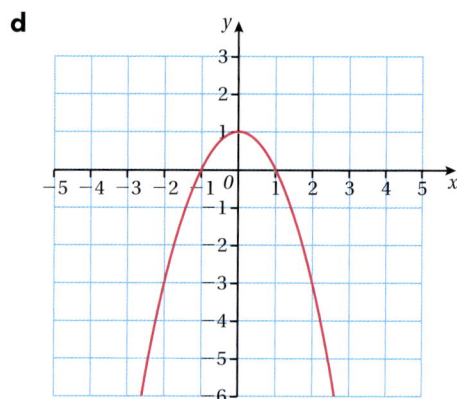

2 Rewrite the equation $y = 3x^2 + 6x + 3$ in the form $y = a(x - h)^2 + k$.

a Work out the y-intercept.

b Find the axis of symmetry and the vertex.

c Work out the x-intercepts.

d Sketch the graph of the equation, labelling the main features.

Sketching quadratic graphs

You can use the characteristics of a parabola to sketch graphs without drawing up a table of values.

A sketch shows the general features of a graph but it does not have to be drawn on graph paper.

How to sketch a parabola:

- Make sure the equation is in the general form $y = ax^2 + c$, where a is the **coefficient** of x and c is a constant.
- Check the sign of a to work out whether the graph goes up to a maximum turning point (negative) or down to a minimum turning point (positive).
- Work out the y-intercept. This is given by c in the equation.
- Calculate the x-intercepts by substituting $y = 0$ and solving for x. If there are no x-intercepts or only one when the graph touches the x-axis, find the coordinates of one point on the graph. This will help you draw an accurate sketch.
- Mark the y-intercept and x-intercepts (if they exist) and use the shape of the graph as a guide to draw a smooth curve.
- Label your graph.

> 🔑 **Key vocabulary**
>
> **coefficient**: the number in front of a variable in a mathematical expression. In the term $5x^2$, 5 is the coefficient and x is the variable.

WORKED EXAMPLE 2

Sketch the graph of $y = 3x^2$

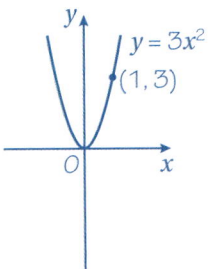

Coefficient of x is 3, which is positive, so graph goes down to a minimum turning point.

There is no constant, so graph goes through the origin (0, 0).

When $y = 0$, $x = 0$. There is only one solution for x, so find another point on the graph.

When $x = 1$, $y = 3(1)^2 = 3$

So, (1, 3) is a point on the curve.

Sketch and label the graph.

> 💡 **Tip**
>
> Draw a smooth curve to join the points and try to make your graph as symmetrical as possible.

WORKED EXAMPLE 3

Sketch the graph of $y = -x^2 + 4$

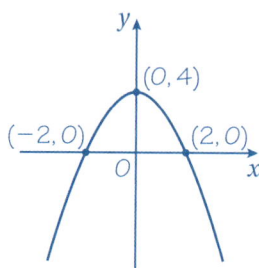

Coefficient of x is -1, so graph goes up to a maximum turning point.

Constant is 4, so y-intercept is $(0, 4)$.

x-intercepts when $y = 0$

$$0 = -x^2 + 4$$

$$\therefore x^2 - 4 = 0$$

This is a difference of two squares.

$$(x + 2)(x - 2) = 0$$

$$x + 2 = 0 \text{ or } x - 2 = 0$$

$$x = -2 \text{ or } x = 2$$

So, intercepts are $(-2, 0)$ and $(2, 0)$.

Sketch and label the graph.

EXERCISE 39D

1 Noor sketched these graphs but she didn't write the equations on them.
Use the features of each graph to work out what the correct equations are.

a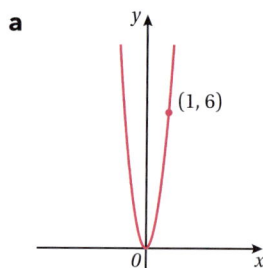

b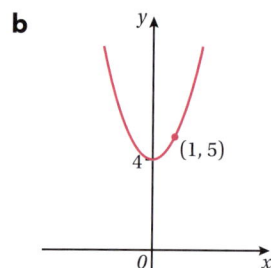

c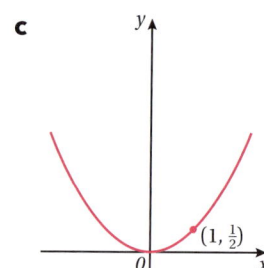

d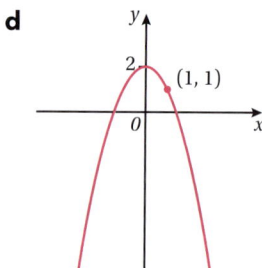

e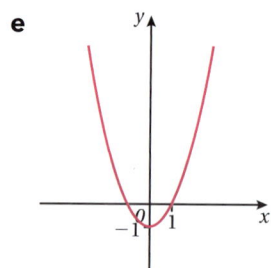

f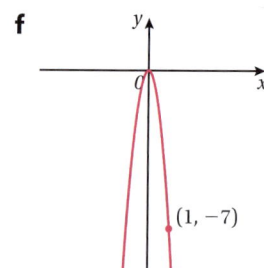

2 Sketch the graph of each of these quadratic equations on the same grid.

A $y = x^2$ B $y = x^2 + 2$ C $y = 3x^2$ D $y = \frac{1}{2}x^2 - 2$ E $y = -x^2 + 2$

3 For each equation, work out:

i   the y-intercept   **ii**   the x-intercept(s)

iii   the axis of symmetry   **iv** the turning point.

Use the results to sketch and label each graph.

a $y = x^2 + 2x - 3$ **b** $y = 2x^2 + 4x + 3$

c $y = 4x - x^2$ **d** $y = x^2 + 2x - 8$

e $y = x^2 - 8x + 12$ **f** $y = -x^2 - 6x - 10$

g $y = 2(x - 3)(x + 5)$ **h** $y = 4x^2 + 16x + 7$

i $x^2 + 3x - 6 = y$ **j** $2x^2 + x = 8 + y$

Section 3: Other polynomials and reciprocals

A **polynomial** is an expression with many terms.

If the highest power of x is 3, the expression is called a cubic expression.

For example, $2x^3$ and $2x^3 + x^2 + 3$ are both cubics.

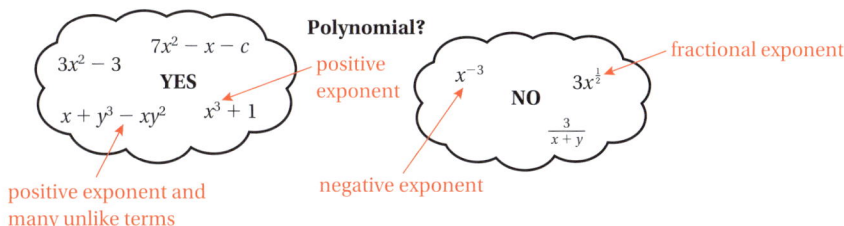

You can use a table of values to plot the graph of a cubic equation. The simplest equation of a cubic graph is $y = x^3$.

All cubic graphs have a similar shape. The diagram shows the basic shape of cubic graphs in the form of $y = ax^3$.

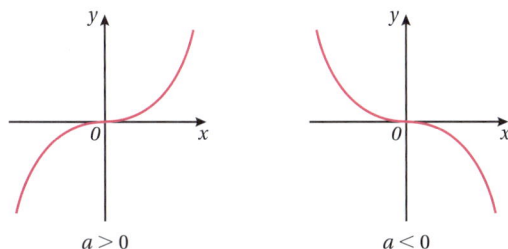

The shape on the left occurs when a is positive. This is called an increasing curve.

The shape on the right occurs when a is negative. This is called a decreasing curve.

The larger the value of a, the steeper the curve.

This is a table of values for $y = x^3$ for values of x from -3 to 3.

x	-3	-2	-1	0	1	2	3
y	-27	-8	-1	0	1	8	27

Key vocabulary

polynomial: an expression made up of many terms with positive powers for the variables

exponent: the number that says how many times a letter or number is multiplied by itself. It is another name for power or index.

Tip

Remember that when you cube a negative number you will get a negative result.

For example, $(-1)^3 = -1 \times -1 \times -1$
$= -1$

Find answers at: cambridge.org/ukschools/gcsemaths-studentbookanswers

To draw an accurate graph you plot all of the calculated points and draw a smooth curve through and beyond them.

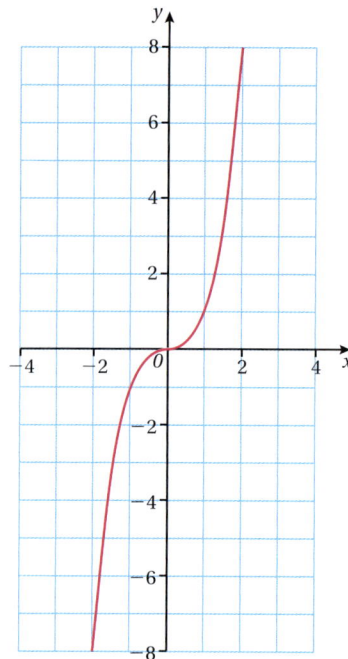

Note that the curve passes through the origin but it is not symmetrical.

For more complicated cubic equations with two or more terms you should work out whole number and half number values to make sure you plot the graph as accurately as possible.

You might find it easier to evaluate each term separately in the table and add them to find y-values.

WORKED EXAMPLE 4

Draw the graph of the equation $y = x^3 - 6x$ for $-3 \leqslant x \leqslant 3$

Work out whole number values first.

x	-3	-2	-1	0	1	2	3
x^3	-27	-8	-1	0	1	8	27
$-6x$	18	12	6	0	-6	-12	-18
y	-9	4	5	0	-5	-4	9

Construct a separate table for in-between values of x.

x	-2.5	-1.5	-0.5	0.5	1.5	2.5
x^3	-15.625	-3.375	-0.125	0.125	3.375	15.625
$-6x$	15	9	3	-3	-9	-15
y	-0.625	5.625	2.875	-2.875	-5.625	0.625

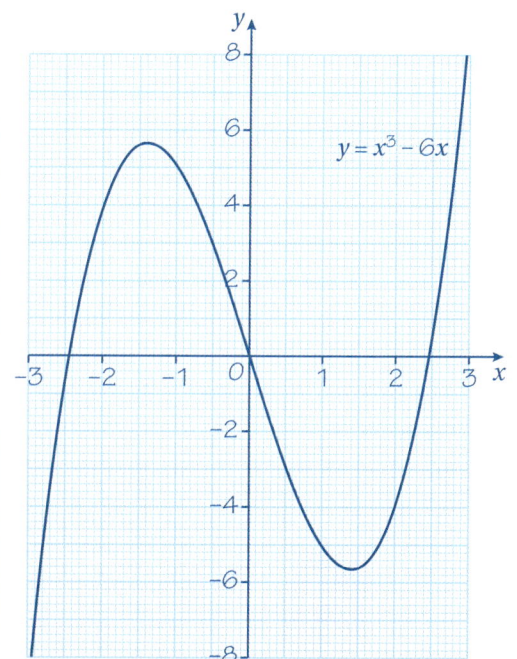

$y = x^3 - 6x$

Plot the points against the axes and join them with a smooth curve.

EXERCISE 39E

1 Write down a table of values for whole number values of x from -3 to 3 for the graph $y = -x^3$.

Write down how this graph differs from the graph of $y = x^3$.

2 Use a table of values to sketch the following pairs of cubic graphs.

Plot each pair on the same grid, but use a separate grid for each pair.

a $y = -2x^3$ and $y = 2x^3$ **b** $y = \frac{1}{2}x^3$ and $y = -\frac{1}{2}x^3$

3 Work with a partner to compare the pairs of graphs you drew in question 2.

Discuss how you could sketch the graph of $y = -4x^3$ if you were given the graph of $y = 4x^3$.

4 Complete a table of values for whole number values of x from -3 to 3 for these equations.

Draw a graph of each curve.

a $y = x^3 + 1$ **b** $y = x^3 - 2$

5 Look at the graphs and their equations in question 4.

What information does the constant give you about the graph?

6 The red line is the graph $y = x^3$.

Write down the equations of graphs A and B.

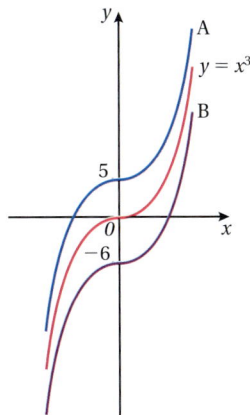

7 Plot the graph of each cubic equation for the given values of x.

a $y = x^3 + 3x^2$ $-3 \leqslant x \leqslant 3$

b $y = x^3 - 3x + 1$ $-3 \leqslant x \leqslant 4$

Reciprocal functions

The product of a number and its **reciprocal** is 1.

For example:

$$8 \times \frac{1}{8} = 1 \qquad \frac{2}{5} \times \frac{5}{2} = 1$$

Every number has a reciprocal except for 0, as $\frac{1}{0}$ cannot be defined.

The reciprocal of a is $\frac{1}{a}$

$$a \times \frac{1}{a} = 1$$

The general equation of a reciprocal function is $y = \frac{a}{x}$, where a is a constant value.

This equation can be rearranged to give $xy = a$.

The graphs of reciprocal functions have a characteristic shape. Each graph is made up of two curves that are mirror images in opposite quadrants of the grid.

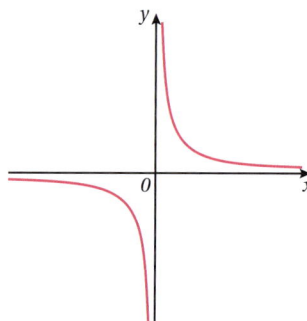

This is the table of values for the equation of $y = \frac{1}{x}$

x	−3	−2	−1	$-\frac{1}{2}$	$-\frac{1}{3}$	0	$\frac{1}{2}$	$\frac{1}{2}$	1	2	3
y	$-\frac{1}{3}$	$-\frac{1}{2}$	−1	−2	−3	undefined	2	3	1	$\frac{1}{2}$	$\frac{1}{3}$

In order to draw a reciprocal graph accurately you need to work with some non-integer values of x.

There is no y-value when $x = 0$ because division by 0 is undefined.

To draw the graph:

* plot the (x, y) values from the table
* join the points with a smooth curve
* write the equation on both parts of the graph.

Note that as the value for x gets bigger, the value for y gets closer and closer to 0 but the graph never actually meets the x-axis.

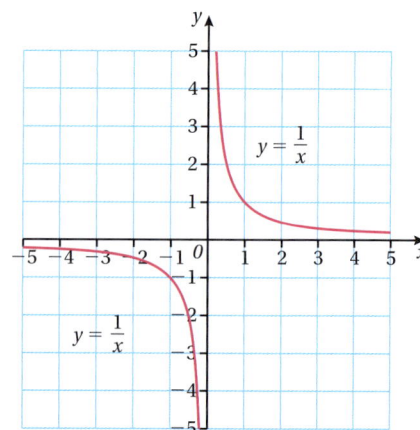

EXERCISE 39F

1 Copy and complete each table for the given values of x. Plot the graphs on the same grid.

a $y = \frac{2}{x}$

x	−4	−2	−1	1	2	4
y						

b $y = \frac{6}{x}$

x	−6	−3	−1	1	3	6
y						

c $xy = -12$

x	−10	−8	−6	−4	−2	2	4	6	8
y									

d $y = \frac{8}{x}$

x	−8	−6	−4	−2	1	2	4	6	8
y									

2 Compare the graphs that you have drawn for question 1. How does the value of the constant in the equation affect the position of the graph?

3 Plot each of the following graphs on the same grid using x-values from −5 to 5.

a $y = \frac{1}{x}$ **b** $y = \frac{1}{x} + 1$ **c** $y = \frac{1}{x} + 3$

4 Use your graphs from question 3 to describe how the constant c in the equation $y = \frac{a}{x} + c$ changes the reciprocal graph of $y = \frac{a}{x}$

5 Neo says that the line $y = x$ is the line of symmetry of the graph $y = \frac{1}{x}$ Is he correct?

Give reasons for your answer.

6 Plot the graphs for each of the reciprocal equations for the given values of x.

a $y = \frac{5}{x}$ $-5 \leqslant x \leqslant 4$

b $y = \frac{3}{x + 2}$ $x = -16, -12, -8, -4, 0, 4, 8, 12, 16$

c $y = \frac{1}{x - 2}$ $-4 \leqslant x \leqslant 6$

7 Use what you now know about the shape of the graphs of the basic cubic and reciprocal from questions 1 and 2 to sketch diagrams of these equations:

a $y = x^3 + 2$

b $y = -x^3$

c $y = \dfrac{2}{x}$

d $y = \dfrac{1}{x} - 1$

e $y = -\dfrac{1}{x}$

f $y = \dfrac{1}{x} + 2$

Use ICT to check your answers and try some more versions of a basic cubic and a reciprocal by changing the value of the constant numbers in the equations.

8 The equation of the first diagram is $y = \dfrac{1}{x}$

What is the equation of the second graph?

a

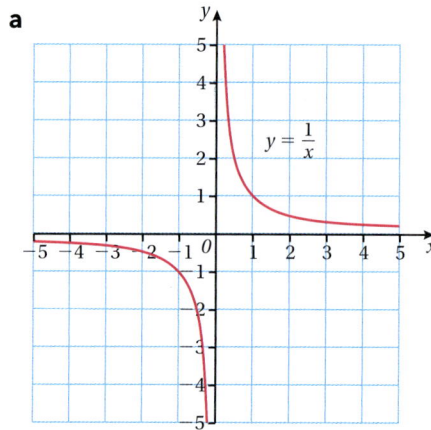

$y = \dfrac{1}{x}$

b

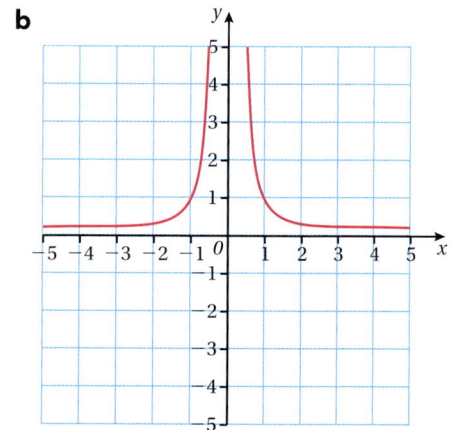

Section 4: Exponential and trigonometric functions

Exponential functions are used to model situations involving rapid growth or decay.

An **exponential function** has a number as the base and a variable as the **exponent**.

For example $y = 2^x$

Key vocabulary

exponential function: a function of the form $y = k^x$

Population growth and compound interest are both examples of exponential growth.

The general form of the exponential function $y = k^x$ (where k is positive) produces a graph called an exponential curve.

WORKED EXAMPLE 5

Complete a table of values for $y = 2^x$ for $-4 \leqslant x \leqslant 4$ and draw the graph.

x	-4	-3	-2	-1	0	1	2	3	4
y	$\frac{1}{16}$	$\frac{1}{8}$	$\frac{1}{4}$	$\frac{1}{2}$	1	2	4	8	16

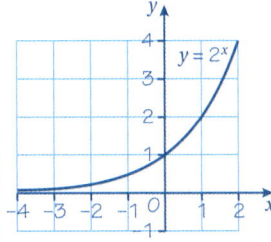

Plot all of the calculated points and draw a smooth curve through and beyond the points plotted.

This example shows the typical shape of graphs of exponential growth. The curve rises rapidly.

As the values of x decrease the curve gets closer and closer to the x-axis without ever touching it. This is because there is no defined value for x when $y = 0$.

The curve has a y-intercept at $(0, 1)$. When $x = 0$, $y = k^0 = 1$, so all graphs in the form $y = k^x$ will pass through the point $(0,1)$.

Exponential curves do not pass through the origin and they are not symmetrical.

If $k = 1$ we get $1^x = 1$ and the equation becomes $y = 1$ which is a straight line.

k cannot be a negative value because the y-value might not be defined.

Because k^x is always positive, the curve will never extend below the x-axis.

The graph $y = k^{-x}$ is the reciprocal of $y = k^x$

Graphing $y = 2^{-x}$ produces a reflection of the graph $y = 2^x$ about the y-axis.

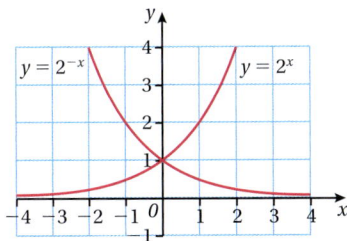

$y = 2^{-x}$ is equivalent to $y = \left(\frac{1}{2}\right)^x$. If x is negative then $0 < k < 1$ (k is a fractional value).

Whether the curve slopes up to the right (increases) or down to the right (decreases) depends on the value of k.

Where $k > 1$, the graph is increasing.

Where $0 < k < 1$, the graph is decreasing. Similarly, where the equation has an exponent of $-x$, it means that the value of the base is a fraction.

Tip

Remember that any value raised to a power of 0 is equal to 1. $k^0 = 1$.

Find answers at: cambridge.org/ukschools/gcsemaths-studentbookanswers

The value of k affects the steepness of the curve. The graphs of $y = 2^x$, $y = 3^x$ and $y = 5^x$ are shown here on the same grid.

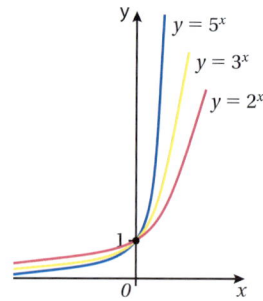

They all have a y-intercept at $(0, 1)$ and they all approach the x-axis to the left. The graph of $y = 5^x$ is much steeper than $y = 2^x$ and $y = 3^x$ because powers of 5 (5, 25, 125, 625) increase in value faster than powers of 2 and 3.

WORKED EXAMPLE 6

Plot a table of values and draw the graphs of A $y = 3^x$, B $y = \frac{1}{2} \times 3$ and C $y = 2 \times 3^x$ on the same grid.

x	-2	-1	0	1	2
3^x	$\frac{1}{9}$	$\frac{1}{3}$	1	3	9
$\frac{1}{2} \times 3^x$	$\frac{1}{18}$	$\frac{1}{6}$	$\frac{1}{2}$	$\frac{3}{2}$	$\frac{9}{2}$
2×3^x	$\frac{2}{9}$	$\frac{2}{3}$	2	6	18

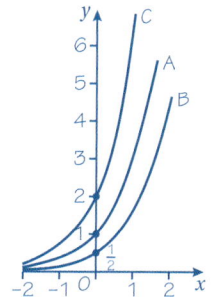

EXERCISE 39G

1 Produce a table of values and draw the graph of each equation for the given values of x.

Draw each set of graphs on the same axes.

    a i $y = 3^x$ **ii** $y = 1.1 \times 3^x$ **iii** $y = 2.5 \times 3^x$ values: $-2 \leqslant x \leqslant 3$

    b i $y = 5^x$ **ii** $y = 2 \times 5^x$ **iii** $y = \frac{1}{2} \times 5^x$ values: $-1 \leqslant x \leqslant 2$

2 **a** Plot the graph of the equation $y = 2^x$ on a grid.

    Use the table of values from Worked Example 5 to do this.

  b Sketch the graphs of $y = 4^x$ and $y = 2^{-x}$ in relation to $y = 2x$.

3 Complete a table of values, plot the points and draw the graph for $y = \left(\frac{1}{4}\right)^x$ for $-3 \leqslant x \leqslant 3$.

4 Draw a sketch graph of the following equations.

a $y = 3^x$ 　　　　　**b** $y = 1^x$

5 Consider the equation $P = 5 \times (0.85)^t$

a Will this equation result in an increasing or decreasing curve? Give a reason for your answer.

b Where will this graph cut the y-axis?

c Use the information to draw a sketch of this graph.

Trigonometric functions

Trigonometric graphs are **periodic graphs** because the same y-values repeat at regular intervals.

Consider what happens to one capsule on the London Eye as it rotates through 360°.

As the Eye turns, the angle of the capsule and its distance above the ground changes.

Each time the capsule passes the same point, it will be at the same angle and the same height again.

The graph of this movement has a wave shape.

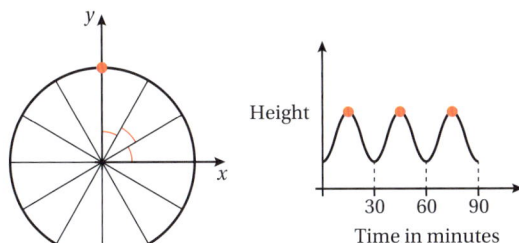

Position of capsule
during one rotation
at 30° intervals
(i.e. every 2.5 minutes)

The sin function ($y = \sin x$)

The table of values below shows the positive values of $y = \sin x$ for angles from 0° to 360°.

x	0°	30°	90°	180°	270°	360°
$y = \sin x$	0	$\frac{1}{2}$	1	0	−1	0

The x-axis for this graph needs to be labelled in degrees because the values of the x-coordinates are angles.

Plotting these values produces this graph.

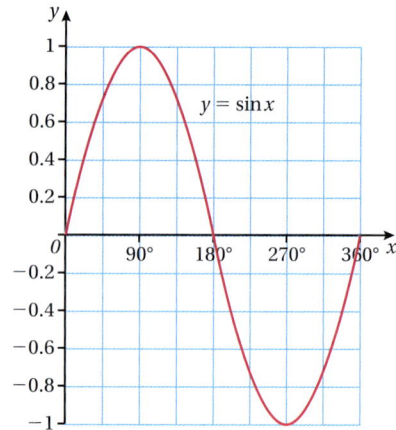

This graph only shows the values of $y = \sin x$ between $0°$ and $360°$ but the graph is not restricted to these values. Working out values from $-270°$ to $720°$ would produce this graph.

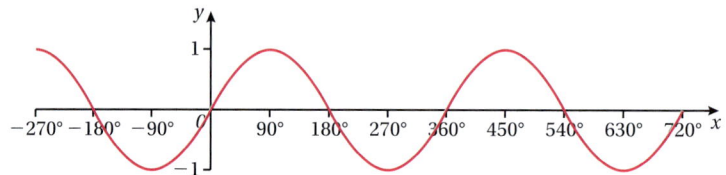

The graph repeats itself every $360°$ and it intercepts the x-axis every $180°$.

The cos function ($y = \cos x$)

The graph of $y = \cos x$ can be generated from a table of values. This is the resulting graph for $-360 \leqslant x \leqslant 360$.

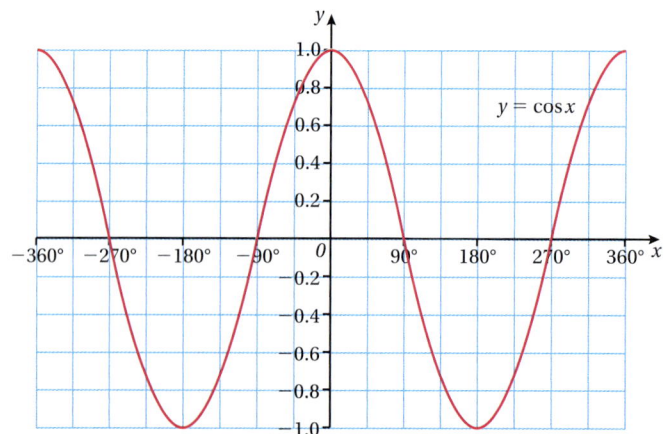

The graph of $y = \cos x$ has the same shape as the graph of $y = \sin x$ with minimum and maximum values at -1 and 1. However, it does not go through the origin because $\cos 0° = 1$.

The graph repeats every $360°$ and it intercepts the x-axis every $180°$ after $90°$.

The tan function ($y = \tan x$)

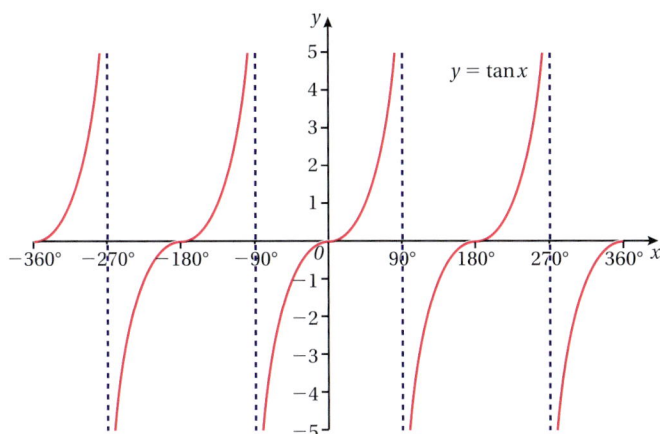

The tan function is periodic, repeating every 180°, but it is not a wave function.

The graph is discontinuous and it has no minimum or maximum turning points.

The tan function approaches but never crosses the lines $x = -270$, $x = -90$, $x = 90$ and $x = 270$. The function $\tan x$ is undefined for these values.

EXERCISE 39H

1 Plot the graphs of $y = \sin x$, $y = \cos x$ and $y = \tan x$ for $-360 \leqslant x \leqslant 360$.

  a Label the minimum and maximum (if it exists) on each graph and state the period over which it repeats.

  b Use the graphs to work out the value of x for which $\sin x = \cos x$ between 0° and 90°?

2 Graph A shows how voltage varies over time in mains electricity.

Graph B shows what happens when an AC signal is added to a DC voltage source.

Which trigonometric function does each graph most resemble? Give reasons for your answer.

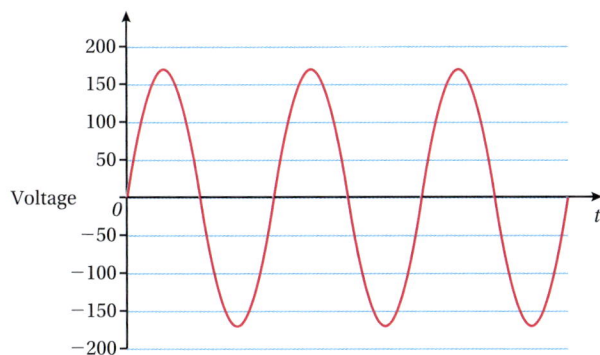

Graph A

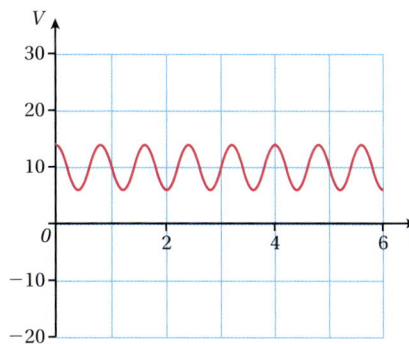

Graph B

Tip

You will learn more about graphs of trigonometric functions when you deal with transformation of curved graphs in Chapter 41.

Tip

These graphs are useful for solving trigonometric equations.

Section 5: Circles and their equations

The equation of a circle is based on the fact that every point on the circumference is the same distance from the centre.

Any circle that has its centre on the origin and a radius of r can be defined by the equation:

$x^2 + y^2 = r^2$

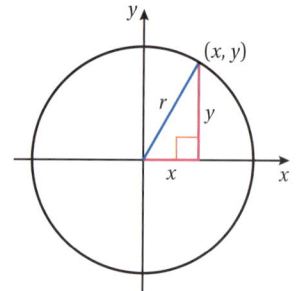

WORK IT OUT 39.3

What is the equation of a circle, centre the origin, with a radius of 4 units?

Option A	Option B	Option C
$(x + y)^2 = 4$	$x^2 + y^2 = 16$	$x^2 + y^2 = 4$

EXERCISE 39I

1 $x^2 + y^2 = 25$ is a circle, centre the origin.

  a Write down the value of the radius.

  b Verify that the following points lie on the circle: $(3, 4)$, $(-3, 4)$

  c List the coordinates of four other points that would also lie on this circle.

2 Sketch the graph of each circle, marking the intercepts on each of the axes.

  a $x^2 + y^2 = 25$ **b** $x^2 + y^2 = 1$ **c** $x^2 + y^2 = 2$

  d $x^2 + y^2 = \dfrac{9}{4}$ **e** $x^2 = 5 - y^2$

3 **a** Which of these points lie on the circle $x^2 + y^2 = 100$?

  $(6, 8)$ $(10, 10)$ $(20, 80)$ $(-6, 8)$ $(5\sqrt{2}, 5\sqrt{2})$ $(10, 0)$

  b Which of these points lie on the circle $x^2 + y^2 = 169$?

  $(5, 12)$ $(100, 69)$ $(-5, -12)$ $(-5, 12)$ $(-13\sqrt{2}, 13\sqrt{2})$ $(0, 13)$

4 Write the equation of each of the circles in this diagram.

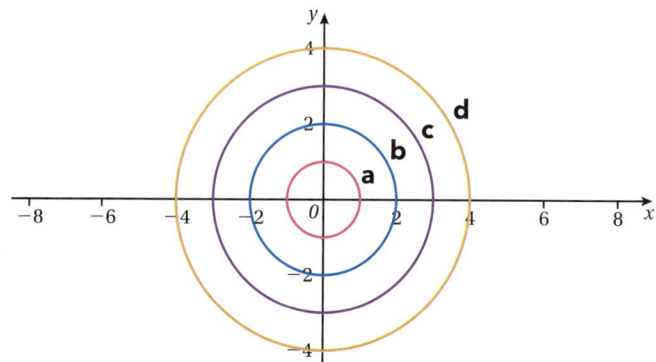

Finding the equation of a tangent to a circle

A **tangent** to a circle will meet the radius at a right angle.

The radius is perpendicular to the tangent at the point where the tangent meets the circle.

Key vocabulary

tangent: a line that makes contact with a curve at one point; it does not cut the curve, it just touches the curve

Tip

Circle theorems were covered in Chapter 31.

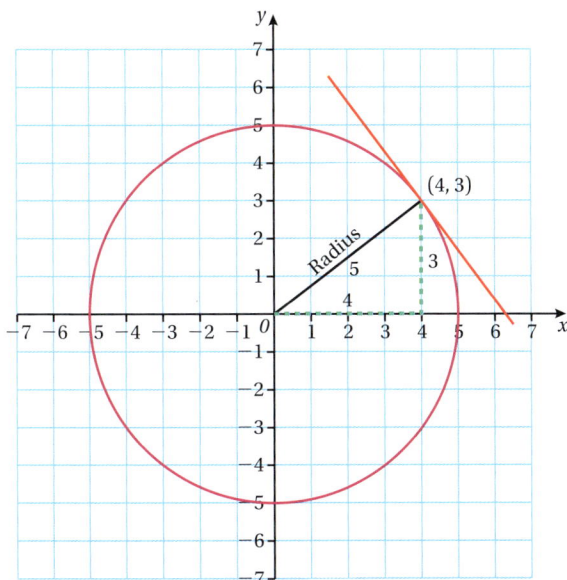

In the diagram, a tangent touches the circle at the point (4, 3).

There is a relationship between the gradient of the radius and the gradient of the tangent at the point (4, 3).

The product of the gradients of perpendicular lines is –1, and we know that the tangent is perpendicular to the radius.

So, we know that $m_{tangent} \times m_{radius} = -1$.

We can use this to calculate the gradient of the tangent.

The gradient of the radius is $\frac{3}{4}$. So you can find the gradient of the tangent.

$$m_{tangent} \times m_{radius} = -1$$
$$m_{tangent} \times \frac{3}{4} = -1$$
$$m_{tangent} = \frac{-4}{3}$$

This is gradient of the tangent. To work out the equation of the tangent, you need the y-intercept.

Substitute the values into the gradient-intercept equation of a line, $y = mx + c$.

The tangent passes through the point (4, 3). So, $y = 3$ when $x = 4$.

$$3 = 4 \times \frac{-4}{3} + c$$
$$c = 3 + \frac{16}{3} = \frac{25}{3}$$

The equation of the tangent to the circle at (4, 3) is $y = \frac{16}{3}x + \frac{25}{3}$

This is better expressed as $3y = -4x + 25$

EXERCISE 39J

1 This diagram shows a circle defined by the equation $x^2 + y^2 = 25$.

The tangent touches the circle at $(3, -4)$.

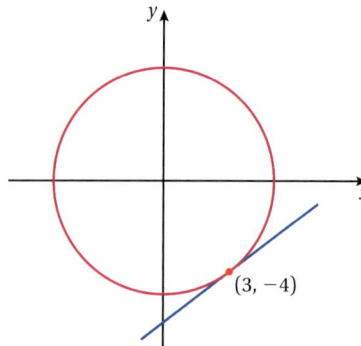

(3, −4)

   a Copy the diagram. Draw in a radius from $(0, 0)$ to the point $(3, -4)$.

   b What is the gradient of the line of this radius?

   c What is the gradient of the tangent to the circle at point $(3, -4)$?

   d Find the equation of this tangent.

2 The point at which a tangent touches each circle is given.

Work out the equation of each tangent.

   a $x^2 + y^2 = 5$ $(2, 1)$

   b $x^2 + y^2 = 80$ $(-4, 8)$

   c $x^2 + y^2 = 90$ $(3, 9)$

3 The circle $x^2 + y^2 = 81$ has tangents at the points $(0, 9)$ and $(9, 0)$.

Work out the equations of the tangents.

Checklist of learning and understanding

Linear functions

- Linear functions produce straight-line graphs.
- The general form of the linear function is $y = mx + c$.
- Graphs $x = a$ are vertical lines parallel to the y-axis.
- Graphs $y = b$ are horizontal lines parallel to the x-axis.
- Lines of the form $y = mx$ go through the origin.

Quadratic functions

- Graphs of quadratic equations, such as $y = ax^2$, $y = ax^2 + c$ and $ax^2 + bx + c$, are called parabolas.
- When a is positive, the graph goes down to a minimum point. When a is negative, the graph goes up to a maximum point. The y-intercept is given by c.
- Parabolas have a turning point, that can be a minimum or maximum depending on the shape of the graph.

Polynomials and reciprocals

- To draw graphs of polynomials, first calculate a table of values that satisfy the equation for a range of values of x.
- A cubic function is a curve defined by $y = ax^3$.
- A reciprocal function is a graph made up of two curves in opposite quadrants defined by $y = \frac{a}{x}$ or $xy = a$.

Other curved graphs

- A cubic function is a curve defined by $y = ax^3$.
- A reciprocal function is a graph made of two curves in opposite quadrants defined by $y = \frac{a}{x}$ or $xy = a$.
- An exponential function is a steeply increasing or decreasing curve defined by $y = k^x$.
- The graphs of trigonometric functions are periodic graphs with particular shapes and characteristics.
- Any circle with a centre of $(0, 0)$ and radius r, can be defined by $x^2 + y^2 = r^2$.
- A tangent to a circle touches it at one point only. The gradient of a tangent is $m_{\text{tangent}} \times m_{\text{radius}} = -1$. Once you have this, you can find the equation of the tangent by substitution.

Chapter review

For additional questions on the topics in this chapter, visit GCSE Mathematics Online.

1 Draw the graphs of the straight lines $y = 2x - 5$ and $2y - x = 5$.

What is the point of intersection of these two lines?

2 **a** What are the roots of the quadratic equation represented by this graph?

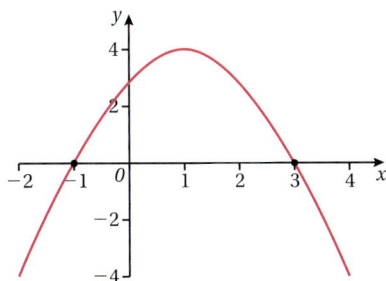

b Show that the equation of the graph is $y = -x^2 + 2x + 3$.

c Complete the square for $x^2 - 2x - 3 = 0$ to find the coordinates of the turning point and the axis of symmetry for the graph of $y = -x^2 + 2x + 3$.

3 **a** Identify and give the equations of the red and blue curves on this grid.

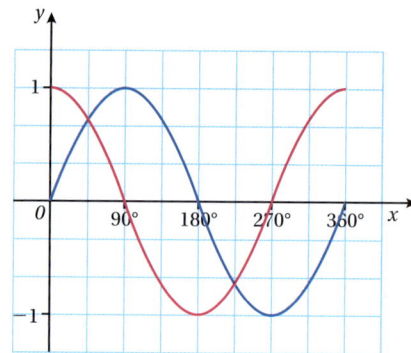

b For what values of x in the range $0° \leqslant x \leqslant 270°$ are the values of $\sin x$ and $\cos x$ equal?

4 **a** Draw a 4-quadrant xy grid and make a sketch of $y = x^3$ *(1 mark)*

b Draw another 4-quadrant xy grid and make a sketch of $y = \dfrac{1}{x}$ *(1 mark)*

© *AQA 2012*

5 Draw a sketch diagram of the circle $x^2 + y^2 = 25$.

On the same diagram sketch the two linear functions represented by the equations $y = 2x - 2$ and $y = -\frac{3}{4}x + 6\frac{1}{4}$ to verify that one of the lines will intersect with the circle at two points and the other line will be a tangent to the circle.

What are the coordinates of the point of contact of the tangent with the circle?

6 Work out the equation of each graph using what you know about the features of different graphs.

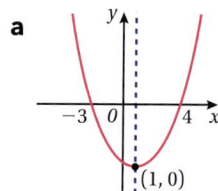

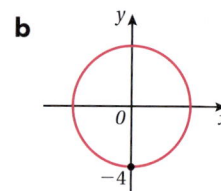

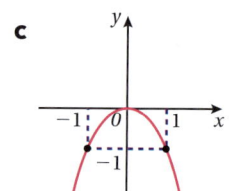

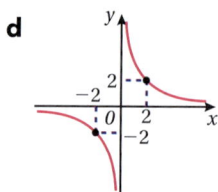

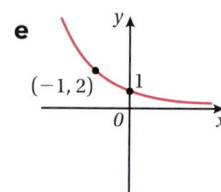

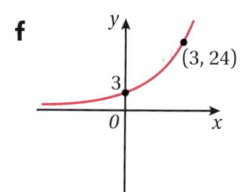

40 Growth and decay

In this chapter you will learn how to …

- set up and solve problems involving growth and decay, including simple and compound interest.
- express exponential growth or decay as a formula.

For more resources relating to this chapter, visit GCSE Mathematics Online.

Using mathematics: real-life applications

Many real-life situations involve growth (increase) or decay (decrease) as time passes. Population numbers, growth of bacteria, disease infection rates, world temperature patterns and the value of money or possessions might all increase or decrease over time.

"My computer program calculates interest on a daily basis. This means whatever is in the account gains interest, not just the initial investment." *(Investment broker)*

Before you start …

Ch 6, 13	You must be able to convert percentages to decimals.	**1** Write each of the following as a decimal:	
		a 5%	**b** 190%
		c 0.4%	**d** 12.5%
Ch 13	You must be able to increase or decrease a quantity by a given percentage by multiplying by a suitable decimal.	**2** Carry out the following increases and decreases using only multiplication:	
		a increase \$44 by 22%	**b** increase £35 by 5.5%
		c decrease £13 by 44%	**d** decrease \$170 by 8%
Ch 39	You should remember how to plot and interpret functions in the form of $y = ab^x$	**3** The graph shows the growth rate of bacteria in cheese. **a** How many bacteria were there to start with? **b** What happens to the number of bacteria each hour? **4** The function for this graph is $n = 100(2)^t$, where n is the number of bacteria and t is the time period in hours. **a** Write down where the constant value of 100 comes from. **b** Why does $b = 2$?	 Number of bacteria (*n*) vs Time in hours (*t*)

Find answers at: cambridge.org/ukschools/gcsemaths-studentbookanswers

Assess your starting point using the Launchpad

STEP 1

❶ £500 is invested at a compound interest rate of 3.5%.

  a Work out how much will be in the account after 4 years.

  b Write an expression to show how much would be in the account after n years.

  c How long would it take to get a total increase of more than 20%?

GO TO
Section 1:
Simple and compound growth

STEP 2

❷ Food manufacturers are reducing the sodium levels in processed food by 2.5% each year.

  a A pre-prepared pizza currently contains 4 grams of sodium. How much should it contain in 10 years?

  b How many years until the amount of sodium in the pizza is below 2 grams?

  c Write an expression to show how much sodium would be in the pizza after n years.

GO TO
Section 2:
Simple and compound decay

GO TO
Chapter review

Section 1: Simple and compound growth

Simple interest

The original amount of money you invest or borrow is called the principal.

Simple interest is interest paid on the principal. The same interest is paid for each time period.

For example:

£1000 is borrowed at an interest rate of 5% per year.

Each year the interest charged is 5% × £1000 = £50.

In other words, the interest will be £50 for each year of the loan period.

Simple interest can be worked out using a formula:

$I = PRT$

where P is the principal amount, R is the rate of interest as a percentage and T is the time period over which the interest is calculated.

Compound interest

When using compound interest, you calculate the interest on the principal amount plus any interest that has been added to the capital.

So using our previous example, after the first loan period, the bank would work out the interest you owe based on £1050 (principal plus interest) not £1000.

Compound interest can be calculated by considering the increase as a series of simple interest calculations.

WORKED EXAMPLE 1

Fatima deposits £500 into a savings account for six years.

The bank pays interest on the savings at 5% per year.

Compare the amount each year when the interest is calculated using simple interest to the amount when the interest is compounded annually.

Year	Simple interest	Compound interest
1	£500 + 5% = £525	£500 + 5% = £525
2	£525 + (5% of £500) = £550	£525 + 5% = £551.25
3	£575	£578.81
4	£600	£607.75
5	£625	£638.14
6	£650	£670.05

The table shows the value of the investment over the six years when using both simple interest and compound interest.

WORK IT OUT 40.1

Three students attempt the question below.

Decide who has got the correct answer and also who has used the most efficient method to find it.

The population of Europe is growing at a rate of 0.2% per year.

The current population is 739 million.

What will the population be in three years' time?

Student A	Student B	Student C
Find 0.2%: 0.2% of 739 000 000 $= 0.002 \times 739\,000\,000$ $= 1\,478\,000$ The same growth for 3 years: $3 \times 1\,478\,000 = 4\,434\,000$ Add it on: $739\,000\,000 + 4\,434\,000$ $= 743\,434\,000$	Year 1: Find 0.2% of 739 000 000 $= 0.002 \times 739\,000\,000$ $= 1\,478\,000$ Add it on: 740 478 000 Year 2: Find 0.2% of 740 478 000 $= 0.002 \times 740\,478\,000$ $= 1\,480\,956$ Add it on: 741 958 956 Year 3: Find 0.2% and add it on $1\,483\,918 + 741\,958\,956$ $= 743\,442\,874$	Increase by 0.2% means there is 100.2%, do this three times in a row. $739\,000\,000 \times 1.002 \times 1.002 \times 1.002$ $= 739\,000\,000 \times 1.002^3$ $= 743\,442\,874$

Tip

Always show your working for these types of questions so that your teacher can see how you have calculated your answer. Write down what you enter into the calculator so you can check it several times.

Working with compound interest and growth rates is like working with function machines.

Each time an output is produced it goes back to becoming an input and the process is repeated.

This kind of process is called iterative. This means it iterates or repeats.

For example, the population of starlings in a park is 80 and it increases at a rate of 10%. Predict how many starlings there will be after five years.

To increase a quantity by 10% we multiply by 1.1 (100% + 10% = 110% or 1.1).

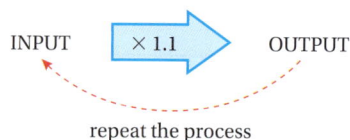

INPUT → × 1.1 → OUTPUT

repeat the process

The first input is 80.

$80 \times 1.1 = 88$

$88 \times 1.1 = 96.8$

Notice that if our model was to stop here you would round sensibly. However, you use the unrounded value to ensure the following year's prediction is more accurate.

$96.8 \times 1.1 = 106.48$

$106.48 \times 1.1 = 117.128$

$117.128 \times 1.1 = 128.8408$

So we would predict that there will be 129 starlings after five years.

This could be re-written as:

$80 \times 1.1 \times 1.1 \times 1.1 \times 1.1 \times 1.1$ or 80×1.1^5

We can generalise this for this example for n years:

80×1.1^n

Exponential growth

When a quantity increases (grows) in a fixed proportion (normally a percentage) at regular intervals the growth is called exponential growth.

Exponential functions produce curved graphs that slope steeply up to the right.

The general function for these graphs is $y = ka^x$, where k, the original value, is greater than zero ($k > 0$) and a, the growth factor, is greater than one ($a > 1$).

This function can be used to express compound growth as a formula:

$y = k(1 + r)^n$

where k is the principal (original value),

r is the growth rate (expressed as a decimal)

n is the number of time periods.

Tip

You learned about exponential graphs in Chapter 39.

WORKED EXAMPLE 2

£100 is invested at a compound interest rate of 8% per annum. Find the value of the investment after a period of 15 years.

Value $= k(1 + r)^n$

$= 100(1.08)^{15}$

$= 317.2169114$

Value is £317.22 (to the nearest penny).

EXERCISE 40A

1 £300 is invested in an account for three years with interest compounded annually at a rate of 2%.

Calculate how much is in the account after:

a 1 year   b 3 years   c 8 years   d n years.

Find answers at: cambridge.org/ukschools/gcsemaths-studentbookanswers

2 £400 is invested at a compound interest rate of 4%.

How much interest (to the nearest penny) will be earned in 3 years?

Choose from the following options.

A £449.95　　　B £448　　　C £49.95　　　D £48

3 A company grows in size each year by 10%.

In 2014 the company employs 726 people.

How many did it employ in 2012?

Choose from the following options.

A 580　　　B 588　　　C 600　　　D 660

4 Copy and complete this table. The interest is compounded annually.

Investment	Interest rate	1 year	2 years	$5\frac{1}{2}$ years	n years
£250	2%				
£1500	4.5%				
	3%	£51.50			

5 £1000 is invested subject to compound interest at a rate of 3% per annum.

Plot a graph showing how much money is in the account over the first 10 years of the investment.

6 A colony of bacteria grows by 4% every hour.

At first the colony has 100 bacteria.

a Assuming the rate of growth stays the same, work out how many bacteria there will be after 24 hours.

b Write a formula to calculate the number of bacteria after n hours.

7 The population of Ireland is growing at an annual rate of 1.7%.

In 2014 the population was 4.6 million.

a Assume this growth rate remains constant and predict how many people will be living in Ireland in 2024.

b How many new inhabitants are there in 2024?

c Use this model to show how many people there were in Ireland in 2012.

d Comment on whether your answers for parts **a** and **c** are likely to give the actual population values for these years..

8 The Bank of England's target inflation rate is 2%.

This tells you how much the cost of living, food, fuel and rent is likely to go up each year.

In 2015 a month's rent is given as £450.

a Assuming that the Bank's targets are correct, predict how much a month's rent is likely to be twenty years later.

b What will rent be in n years' time?

9 Gavin is saving for a new bike.

The model he wants cost £255. So far he has saved £200.

Gavin's dad has offered to pay him 8% interest each month on this amount.

How long is he going to have to wait for the bike? Show clear working as part of your answer.

10 Population growth models help predict the spread of invasive species. Zebra mussels are one such species.

Their population can increase by 1900% each year.

Two zebra mussels are found in a freshwater lake.

Should biologists be worried that this will have a significant impact over the next 10 years? Give detailed reasoning in your answer.

11 Two investors are investing for 5 years and have a choice.

They can either have 6% simple interest or 5.5% compound interest.

a Which should they choose?

b Would the answer change if they were investing for 4 years?

12 Copy and complete this table:

Investment	Rate	1 year	2 years	3 years	n years
					$\$600 \times 1.015^n$
£500		£530			
$6000			$7260		
£750				£1296	

13 Jenny is saving for her first car. She needs a deposit of £2775.

Each month she saves £200 in an account offering 1% interest a month.

a Work out if Jenny will have enough money after a year to buy a car.

b If not, how much extra money does she need?

c How many more months will this take her to save?

14 Between 1980 and 2010 the price of a chocolate bar went from 25p to 65p.

a By what percentage did the cost rise?

b Assume the cost keeps increasing at the same rate. Predict how much the bar will cost in 2040.

c Predict how much the bar will cost in 2070.

d What is the annual percentage increase?

e In what year does the chocolate bar first cost more than £1?

15 £100 000 is invested at a rate of 5% for 10 years.

a How much more money is earned using compound interest compared to simple interest?

b What simple interest rate would be needed to achieve the same earnings?

16 A two-bedroomed house cost £195 000 last year and now costs £216 450.

Assuming the price keeps rising at the same rate, how much will this house cost in three years' time?

17 Which of the following investment models gives the highest earnings?

Model A	Model B	Model C
Year 1: 5% interest	Years 1–3:	Years 1–3:
Year 2: 4% interest	4% compound interest	4.1% simple interest
Year 3: 3% interest		

18 A colony of bacteria grows by 5% every hour.

How long does it take for the colony to double in size?

Section 2: Simple and compound decay

When the value of something goes down it has depreciated.

For example, a brand new car will show a **depreciation** in value of about 30% in the first year of ownership alone.

Key vocabulary

depreciation: the loss in value of an object over a period of time

---

WORKED EXAMPLE 3

A new computer depreciates by 30% per year.

It cost £1200 new.

What will it be worth in two years' time?

Method 1
Value after 1 year = £1200 – (30% of £1200)
= £1200 – £360
= £840
Value after 2 years = £840 – (30% of £840)
= £840 – £252
= £588

Each year the value decreases by 30%.

Method 2
Value after 1 year = 70% of £1200 = £840
Value after 2 years = 70% of £840 = £588

Each year its new value is 70% (100% – 30%) of its value in the previous year.

When the number of items in a population declines over time, it is called decay rather than depreciation.

For example, if the population of squirrels is in decay, it means that each year there are fewer and fewer animals in the population.

If the rate of decline is 10%, each year 10% of the squirrels disappear, leaving 90%. So at the end of each year, the number of animals is $n \times 0.9$, where n is the number of animals at the start of that year.

WORK IT OUT 40.2

Three students attempt the question below.

Decide who has got the correct answer and also who has used the most efficient method to find it.

For every 1000 m you go up in the Earth's atmosphere, the atmospheric pressure decreases by 12%. This is called the lapse rate.

The sea-level atmospheric pressure is 100 300 pascal (Pa).

What is the atmospheric pressure for a skydiver at an altitude of 4000 metres?

Student A	Student B	Student C
12% of 100 300	Decrease by 12% leaves 88%	Decrease by 12% leaves 88%, do this four times in a row.
$= 0.12 \times 100\,300$	88% of 100 300	$100\,300 \times 0.88 \times 0.88 \times 0.88 \times 0.88$
$= 12\,036$	$= 0.88 \times 100\,300$	$= 100\,300 \times 0.88^4$
$4 \times 12\,036 = 48\,144$	$= 88\,264$	$= 60\,149.444608 \text{ Pa}$
$100\,300 - 48\,144$	88% of 88 264	60 149.4 Pa (to 1 dp)
$= 52\,156 \text{ Pa}$	$= 77\,672.32$	
	88% of 77 672.32	
	$= 68\,351.6416$	
	88% of 68 351.6416	
	$= 60\,149.444608 \text{ Pa}$	

Exponential decay

When a quantity decreases by a fixed percentage over regular periods of time it is called exponential decay.

The graph of exponential decay is a curve that slopes down steeply towards the right.

The general function of such decreasing exponential graphs is $y = ka^x$, where k, the original value, is greater than zero ($k > 0$) and a, the decay factor, is between zero and one ($0 < a < 1$). In other words a is a fractional quantity.

The general formula for exponential decay is therefore:

$$y = k(1 - r)^n$$

where k is the original value/quantity

r is the rate of decay (as a decimal)

n is the number of time periods.

Find answers at: cambridge.org/ukschools/gcsemaths-studentbookanswers

EXERCISE 40B

1 A computer depreciates in value by 3% every six months.

Originally the computer cost £799.

How much is it worth, to the nearest penny, 24 months later?

Choose your answer from the options below.

A £719.10   B £727.09   C £729.22   D £707.35

2 After losing 15% of its value a car is worth £4250.

What was it worth originally?

Choose your answer from the options below.

A £5000   B £4887.50   C £4265   D £3612.50

3 A car depreciates in value each year by 8%.

A new compact car costs £11 000.

How much will it be worth in:

a 1 year?   **b** 3 years?   **c** 8 years?   **d** n years?

4 Copy and complete this table:

Initial cost	Depreciation rate	1 year	2 years	6 years	n years
£400	2%				
£2500	15%				
£50 000	3.5%				

5 A pesticide is absorbed by the soil (i.e. it decays) at a rate of 7% a year.

A farmer used 2 kg of pesticide on a field in 2000.

a Work out how much pesticide remains in the field in 2014.

b Will there ever be 0 g of pesticide left in the field? Give reasons for your answer.

6 The height of the water in a tank reduces by 15% every 5 minutes.

Which of the following graphs shows this?

A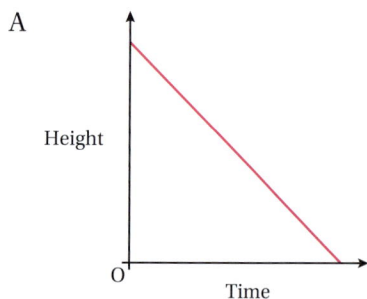

B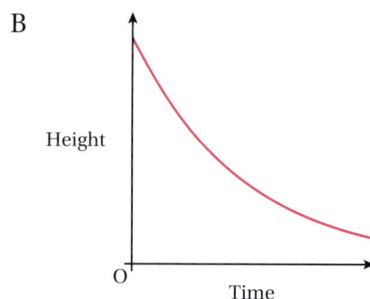

C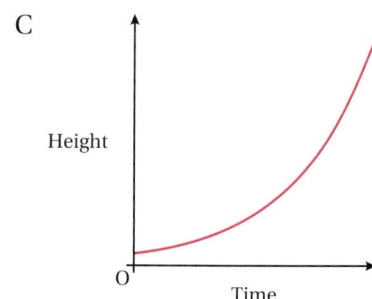

7 At the start of an experiment there are 8000 bacteria in a population.

A lethal pathogen is introduced to the population causing a reduction of 1600 in an hour.

  a What is the percentage decrease in population?

  b Assuming the same rate of decrease, how many bacteria would you expect to be alive after 8 hours?

  c How long will it be until fewer than 100 bacteria are alive?

8 For every 1000 m higher that you climb, the atmospheric pressure decreases by 12%.

The sea-level atmospheric pressure is 100 300 pascal (Pa).

Work out the pressure at a height of 39 km above sea level.

9 The population of Bulgaria is decreasing at a rate of 0.6% per year.

In 2014, the population was 7.4 million people.

  a How many people are expected to be living in Bulgaria in 2020?

  b How many years until the population gets to below 7 million?

10 Copy and complete this table:

Initial cost	Depreciation rate	1 year	2 years	6 years	n years
					$\$7500 \times 0.925^n$
£650		£617.50			
	11%	$\$30\,260$			
£12 million			£10 267 500		

11 The cost of mobile phones has been falling.

Three years ago the latest model cost £400.

Today the latest model costs £342.95.

Assuming the price keeps falling at this rate, how long will it be until the current model costs less than two-thirds of today's price?

Checklist of learning and understanding

Simple and compound growth
- Simple growth, such as interest, is a fixed rate of growth, calculated on the original amount.
- The formula $I = PRT$ can be used to calculate simple interest.
- Compound growth, such as compound interest, is calculated on the principal for the first period and then compounded by calculating it on the principal plus any interest paid or due for each previous period.
- You can work out compound growth using a multiplier for each period or by applying the formula: $y = k(1 + r)^n$

Find answers at: cambridge.org/ukschools/gcsemaths-studentbookanswers

Simple and compound decay

- A drop in value of an object over time is called depreciation.
- A decline in a population is called decay.
- Simple and compound decay can be found by repeated subtraction, by working out the percentage remaining, or by applying the formula for compound decay: $y = k(1 - r)^n$

For additional questions on the topics in this chapter, visit GCSE Mathematics Online.

Chapter review

1 A camera has a cash price of £850.

Nasief buys it on credit and pays a 10% deposit, with the balance to be paid over two years at a simple interest rate of 10%.

Calculate:

a the amount of his deposit

b the balance owing after deducting the deposit

c the amount of interest paid in total over two years

d the monthly payment amount for 24 equal monthly instalments

e the difference between the cash price and what Nasief actually paid in the end.

2 Salma invests £2300 in an account that pays 6% interest compounded half-yearly.

Work out how much money she will have after two years.

3 A car valued at £8500 depreciates by 30% in the first year, 20% in the second year and a further 12% in the third year.

Calculate how much is it worth after three years.

4 Each year the education department arranges a quiz.

There are 140 students in the competition to start with.

During each round, half of the quiz contestants are eliminated.

How many students are still participating after Round 4?

5 £1800 is invested at 4% compound interest per year.

How many years will it take for the investment to be worth £2000?

(4 marks)

© AQA 2013

6 The population of elephants in a park increased exponentially from 40 elephants in 1963 to 640 elephants in 2013.

Work out the growth rate r of the elephant population.

41 Transformations of curves

In this chapter you will learn how to ...

- identify translations and reflections of a given graph.
- sketch the graphs of transformations.

For more resources relating to this chapter, visit GCSE Mathematics Online.

Using mathematics: real-life applications

Many people study the graphs of curves in the course of their work. Sound engineers are a good example. They mix and balance sounds by looking at curves made by sound waves.

Lower pitch

Higher pitch

"Sound engineers in today's music industry need to be talented in both the arts and the sciences."

(Sound engineer)

Before you start ...

Ch 29, 39	Recognise the graphs of standard functions: $y = mx + c$ $y = x^2$ $y = ax^2 + bx + c$ $y = \frac{1}{x}$	**1**	Which of these functions would result in a graph as a curve and which would produce a graph as a line? **a** $y = x^2 + 9$ **b** $5y + x = 10$ **c** $y = \frac{2}{x}$ **d** $y = (x + 7)^2 - 2$ Sketch each function to show its general shape.
Ch 39	Be able to sketch the trigonometric functions: $y = \sin x$ $y = \cos x$ $y = \tan x$	**2**	Which trigonometric functions are represented by these graphs? **a** **b** **c** Sketch and label the third trigonometric function.
Ch 17	You should be able to complete the square on a quadratic equation.	**3**	Rewrite $y = 3x^2 + 6x + 7$ in the form $a(x - h)^2 + k$

Assess your starting point using the Launchpad

STEP 1

1 This is a graph of $y = x^2$.

Sketch:

a $y = x^2 + 2$

b $y = x^2 - 2$

c Write the equation of the reflection of this graph about the x-axis.

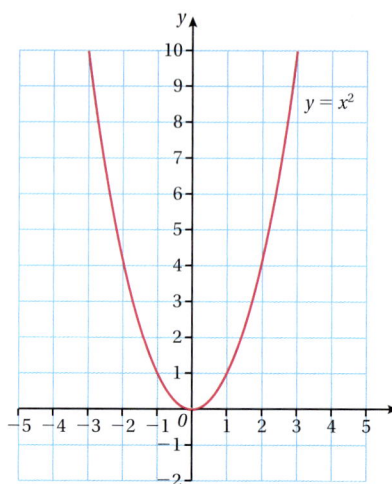

$y = x^2$

GO TO

Section 1:
Quadratic functions and parabolas

STEP 2

2 **a** What are the values of sin 90° and cos 90°?

For what values of θ does cos $\theta = 1$?

b Sketch graphs of $y = \sin x + 2$ and $y = \cos(x + 90°)$

GO TO

Section 2:
Trigonometric functions

STEP 3

3 **a** What is the equation of this function, $y = x^3$ or $y = -x^3$?

b Draw its reflection about the x-axis and give the equation of the function.

c Sketch the graph of $y = \dfrac{1}{x}$

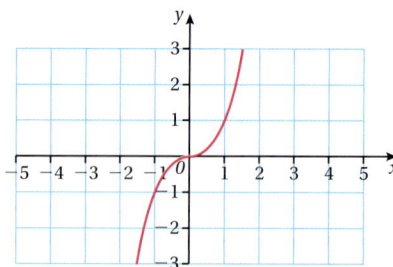

GO TO

Section 3:
Other functions

Section 4:
Translation and reflection problems

GO TO

Chapter review

Section 1: Quadratic functions and parabolas

The general form of a quadratic function is:

$y = ax^2 + bx + c$

The graph of a quadratic equation is called a parabola.

If you change the equation of a parabola, this results in a reflection and/or a translation of the curve.

WORK IT OUT 41.1

Quadratic equations can have two different solutions, a single solution or no solutions. Look at these three graphs of quadratic equations.

Identify the equation that has two solutions.

What can you say about the other two equations based on the graphs?

Graph A	Graph B	Graph C
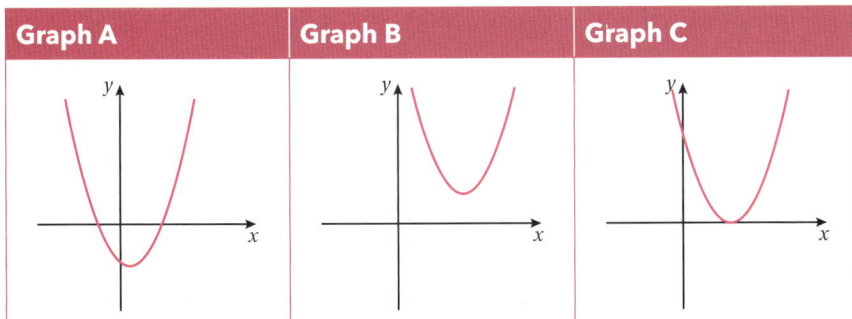		

Tip

Look back at Chapters 16 and 17 to make sure you understand the main features of quadratic equations. You should be able to solve quadratic equations and understand what is meant by the terms turning point, vertex and roots.

Find answers at: cambridge.org/ukschools/gcsemaths-studentbookanswers

Vertical translations

This is a graph of the function $f(x) = x^2$.

The axis of symmetry is the y-axis (or $x = 0$).

The minimum turning point is the origin $(0, 0)$. This is called the vertex of the function $f(x) = x^2$.

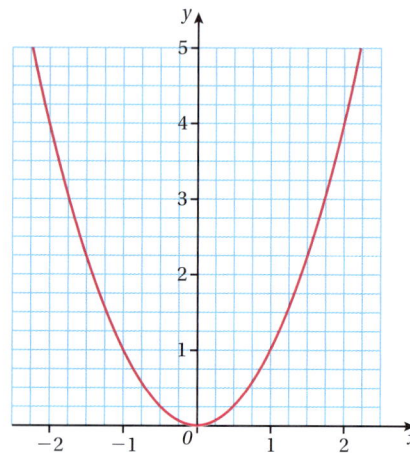

Consider what happens to the graph $y = x^2$ if we add 3 units to the function and get $y = x^2 + 3$.

For $y = x^2$ the vertex is $(0, 0)$, also known as the turning point. But if $y = x^2 + 3$, the vertex moves up three positions and the graph cuts the y-axis at $(0, 3)$.

Adding the constant $(+3)$ to the equation therefore translated the graph 3 units upwards (in the positive direction).

If the constant is negative, the graph is translated downwards (in the negative direction).

The diagram below shows the graph of $y = x^2$ in red.

The graphs of $y = x^2 + 5$, $y = x^2 + 12$ and $y = x^2 - 8$ are shown too.

Note that these graphs are all translations of $y = x^2$.

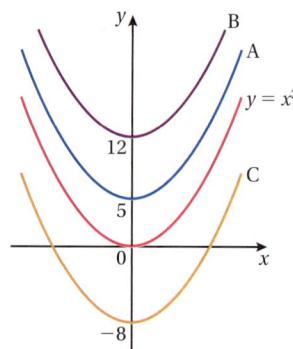

EXERCISE 41A

1 What is the vertex of the graph of this quadratic function $y = x^2 - 7$?
Choose from the following options.

A $(7, 0)$ B $(7, 7)$ C $(0, 7)$ D $(0, -7)$

2 Sketch the graphs of the following quadratic functions and state the coordinates of the vertex:

a $y = x^2 + 1$ **b** $y = x^2 - 1$ **c** $y = x^2 - 4$

d $y = x^2 + 2$ **e** $y = x^2 - 3$ **f** $y = x^2 + 3$

3 Sketch the graph of $y = -x^2$. This is an image of the graph $y = x^2$.

Describe the type of transformation.

4 Using your sketch for $y = -x^2$, copy and complete this sentence:

As x increases and decreases in value, y …

5 Draw a sketch graph for each of the quadratic functions in question 2 if x^2 is now replaced by $-x^2$.

Describe the types of transformation to the original curves.

Tip

In mathematics you refer to families of lines or curves that have a main feature in common. How would you describe the family of parabolas you have just investigated?

Horizontal translations

Graphs can also be translated in a horizontal direction. The result is a shift to the left or right.

Look at this graph carefully.

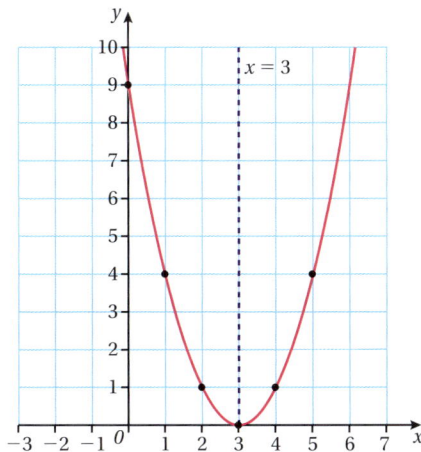

Every point on the basic parabola $y = x^2$ has coordinates (p, p^2).

If the parabola translates three units to the right, then the vertex $(0, 0)$ goes to $(3, 0)$.

The axis of symmetry, $x = 0$, goes to $x = 3$.

For a horizontal translation of three units, the general point (p, p^2) goes to the point $(p + 3, p^2)$ as we move along the x-axis.

If $x = p + 3$, then $p = x - 3$.

And as $y = p^2$, substituting for p gives

$y = (x - 3)^2$

So a translation of 3 units to the right results in the function $y = (x - 3)^2$.

If you translate 3 units to the left, a similar argument would produce the result $y = (x + 3)^2$.

The axis of symmetry for $y = (x + 3)^2$ is $x = -3$.

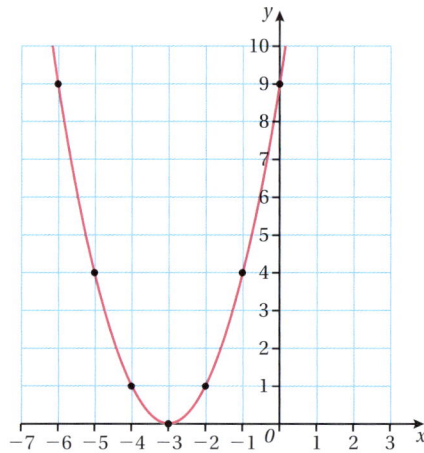

The table summarises the general case for translating a parabola.

	Equation of translated curve	Axis of symmetry	Vertex
Vertical translations	$y = x^2 + a$	$x = 0$	$(0, a)$
	$y = x^2 - a$	$x = 0$	$(0, -a)$
Horizontal translations	$y = (x + a)^2$	$x = -a$	$(-a, 0)$
	$y = (x - a)^2$	$x = a$	$(a, 0)$

Tip

In order to draw a sketch of a graph from a translation of a quadratic function, you need to check for vertical and horizontal moves. Identify the axis of symmetry and the vertex (the turning point).

WORKED EXAMPLE 1

Sketch $y = (x - 2)^2 - 4$.

The graph of $y = (x - 2)^2 - 4$ is obtained by translating the graph of $y = x^2$ two units to the right and four units down.

The axis of symmetry is $x = 2$. The vertex is at $(2, -4)$.

When $x = 0$, $y = (-2)^2 - 4 = 0$, so the y-intercept is $(0, 0)$, the origin.

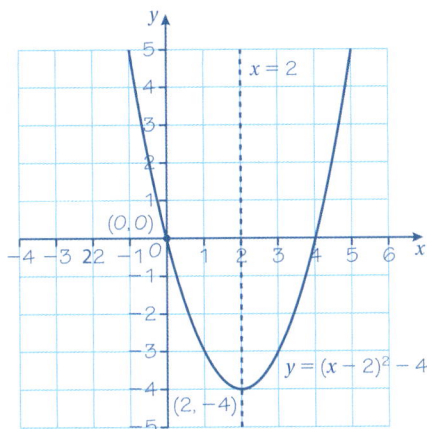

Tip

Learning rules can be useful but it is always best if these rules are based on understanding, so that you can go back and establish the rule if you forget it.

EXERCISE 41B

1 Write down what happens to the following graphs when $(x \pm 2)^2$ is replaced by $-(x \pm 2)^2$.

a $y = (x + 2)^2 + 3$ **b** $y = (x + 2)^2 - 3$

c $y = (x - 2)^2 + 3$ **d** $y = (x - 2)^2 - 3$

Check using ICT that the graphs produced are images of the original graphs reflected in the horizontal line that passes through the vertex.

Give the equation of the line of reflection in each case.

2 If a quadratic equation has real roots (solutions) the graph will either cut the x-axis in two places or touch the x-axis (the axis is a tangent to the curve at the point of contact.)

Which of the equations in question 1 will not have real roots?

3 Sketch the graphs of:

a $y = (x - 5)^2$ **b** $y = (x - 1)^2 - 3$ **c** $y = (x + 2)^2 + 3$

d $y = (x - 4)^2 - 3$ **e** $y = (x - 1)^2 + 6$ **f** $y = (x - 4)^2 - 4$

Find answers at: cambridge.org/ukschools/gcsemaths-studentbookanswers

Sketching quadratic functions

In a negative quadratic function $y = -ax^2 + bx + c$ (where $a > 0$), the vertex becomes a maximum turning point and not a minimum turning point.

The graph of the equation $y = -x^2$ is the image of $y = x^2$ reflected in the x-axis.

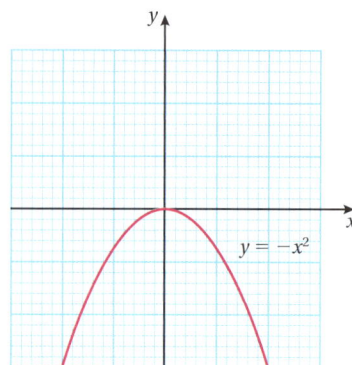

> **Tip**
>
> Look back at the section on completing the square in Chapter 17.

WORKED EXAMPLE 2

Sketch the parabola $y = -x^2 - 6x + 7$.

Rewrite this in the form $y = a(x - b)^2 + c$.

$$y = -x^2 - 6x + 7 = -(x + 3)^2 + 16$$

This equation has an axis of symmetry of $x = -3$, the y-intercept is 7 and the vertex is $(-3, 16)$.

To find the x-intercepts, solve the equation:

$$-(x + 3)^2 + 16 = 0$$
$$-(x + 3)^2 = -16$$
$$(x + 3)^2 = 16$$
$$(x + 3) = \pm 4$$

So $x = 1$ or $x = -7$: the parabola crosses the x-axis at $(1, 0)$ and $(-7, 0)$.

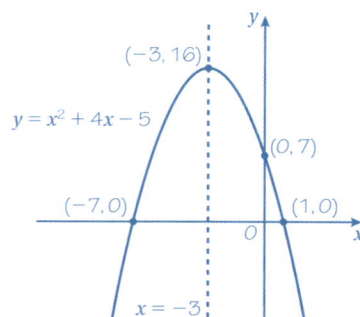

> **Tip**
>
> Rewriting quadratic expressions by completing the square provides the information you need for a sketch. Remember that some parabolas will not cut the x-axis at all.

EXERCISE 41C

1 Complete the square for the quadratic function $y = x^2 + 6x - 3$. Choose the correct answer from the following options.

    A $(x + 6)^2 + 3$ B $(x + 3)^2 + 3$ C $(x + 3)^2 - 12$ D $(x + 3)^2 + 12$

2 Complete the square to find the information you need to sketch the following graphs.

    a $y = x^2 + 6x - 5$ **b** $x^2 + 8x + 4 = y$

    c $y = x^2 - 4x + 2$ **d** $(x - 1)(x + 2) - 1 = y$

3 Complete the square to sketch each parabola.

Show the y-intercept, axis of symmetry, vertex and x-intercepts.

    a $y = -x^2 + 3$ **b** $y = -x^2 - 2x$ **c** $y = -x^2 + 6x + 13$

    d $y = -x^2 + 8x - 7$ **e** $y = -x^2 + 8x + 7$

Section 2: Trigonometric functions

This diagram show the graphs of $y = \sin x$ and $y = \cos x$ for a range of values for angles from 0° to 360°.

The maximum and minimum values of the two functions are 1 and −1 respectively.

The graphs are called wave functions and continue in both directions repeating the same pattern at set intervals.

> **Tip**
>
> Revise the section on trigonometric functions in Chapter 39 if you have forgotten the features of these graphs.

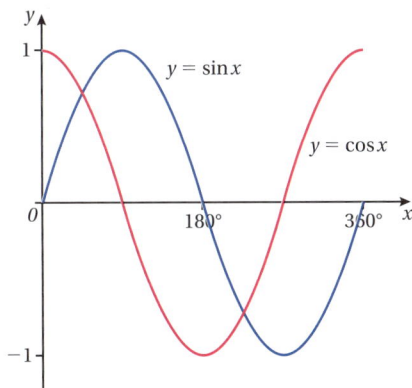

In the next exercise, you will investigate transformations of these functions so that we can produce some generalised findings.

To do this, make sure you can generate these functions using ICT. It might be useful to work with another student on these questions so that you can both check your findings.

EXERCISE 41D

1 Investigate these graphs using ICT and write an explanation of what you find.

    a $y = \sin x + 2$, $y = \sin x - 2$ **b** $y = \cos x + 2$, $y = \cos x - 2$

2 Investigate these graphs using ICT and write an explanation of what you find.

    a $y = \sin(x + 90°)$, $y = \sin(x - 90°)$ **b** $y = \cos(x + 90°)$, $y = \cos(x - 90°)$

3 Without using ICT describe the following transformations of the trigonometric functions.

    a $y = \sin x + 1$ **b** $y = \sin(x + 45°)$

    c $y = \cos(x - 45°)$ **d** $y = \cos x - 1$

4 What happens to the graph of $y = -\sin x$ and what is its relationship to $y = \sin x$?

5 What happens to the graph of $y = -\cos x$ and what is its relationship to $y = \cos x$?

Transformations of trigonometric functions

Your investigation in Exercise 41D should have helped you reach these conclusions.

Action	Transformation	Resultant image
Adding or subtracting a numerical value to a trigonometric function Example: $y = \sin x + a$	Vertical translation	The graph of the transformed function follows a parallel path to the original.
Adding or subtracting an angle to the argument of a trigonometric function Example: $y = \sin(x + a°)$	Horizontal translation	The graph of the transformed function moves left for an addition to the angle and right for a subtraction.
Taking the negative of a trigonometric function Example: $y = -\sin x$	Reflection	The graph of the transformed function is a reflection of the original in the x-axis ($y = 0$).

Section 3: Other functions

You can apply what you have learned about transformations of curves to some of the other functions you have studied in this course.

In the next exercise you can use ICT to produce graphs of the functions, but use the findings from earlier in the chapter to predict what you expect to see before you do so.

Again, it might be useful to work with another student to finalise your conclusions.

EXERCISE 41E

1 This is the graph of the basic cubic equation (highest power of x is 3).

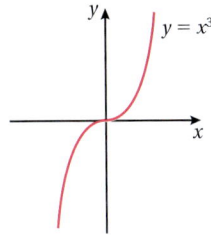

Sketch:

a $y = x^3 + 2$ and $y = x^3 - 2$

b $y = (x + 2)^3$ and $y = (x - 2)^3$

c $y = -x^3$

About what line is $y = x^3$ reflected to become $y = -x^3$?

2 Which equation translates $y = x^3$ by a horizontal move of 2 units left and 1 unit up? Choose from the following options.

A $y = x^3 + 3$ B $y = (x - 2)^3 + 1$

C $y = (x + 2)^3 + 1$ D $y = 2x^3 + 1$

3 This is a graph of a hyperbolic function.

a Give a reason why it has two sections. What happens when $x = 0$? Why?

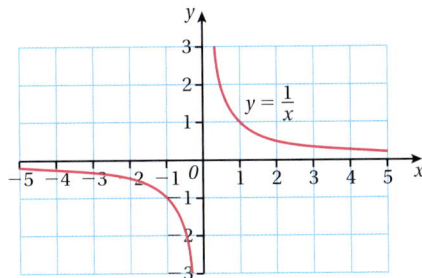

b Sketch:

i $y = \dfrac{1}{x} + 3$ **ii** $y = \dfrac{1}{x} - 3$ **iii** $y = -\dfrac{1}{x}$

4 This is an exponential function.

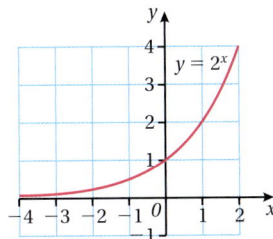

Sketch these exponential functions:

a $y = -2^x$ **b** $y = 2^x + 3$ **c** $y = 2^{-x}$

Find answers at: cambridge.org/ukschools/gcsemaths-studentbookanswers

Section 4: Translation and reflection problems

Changing the parameters of a function can change the position and orientation of a graph.

In this section you are going to use the general principles you learned to solve problems related to shifting graphs.

EXERCISE 41F

1 Sketch the parabola $y = (x + 3)^2 - 8$. What is the equation of the resulting image if it is:

a translated 8 units up and 3 units to the right?

b translated 2 units to the left and 3 units down?

2 The graph of the function $y = (x + a)^2 - b$ has a vertex of $(-3, 5)$.

Which of the following options are the correct values of a and b?

A $a = -3, b = 5$ B $a = 3, b = 5$ C $a = 3, b = -5$ D $a = -3, b = -5$

3 Consider the parabola $y = (x - 1)^2 + a$. Find the value of a if the y-intercept is:

a 1   **b** 3   **c** 0   **d** -7

Sketch the graph in each case.

4 Sketch the graph of each quadratic. Clearly label the x- and y-intercepts, the axis of symmetry and the vertex.

a $y = x^2 - 6x + 5$ **b** $y = x^2 - 4x - 12$

5 Describe the translation of $y = \sin x$ that would result in $y = \sin x$ merging with $y = \cos x$.

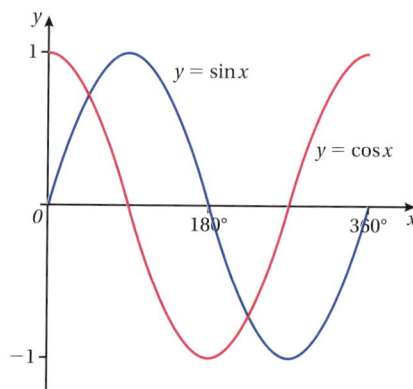

6 Draw a sketch of:

a $y = x^3 + 2$

b the reflection of $y = x^3 + 2$ about the y-axis and about the x-axis.

7 The diagram shows the graph of $y = 2^x$ shifted horizontally to the right.

What is the equation of the image?

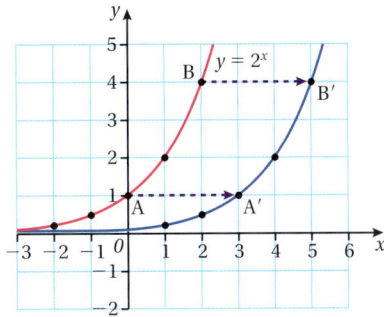

8 A basic curve has been shifted to form each of the graphs below.

Decide how the graph was shifted and write the equation of the graph shown.

Substitute the coordinates of the given points into the equation to check that your answers are correct.

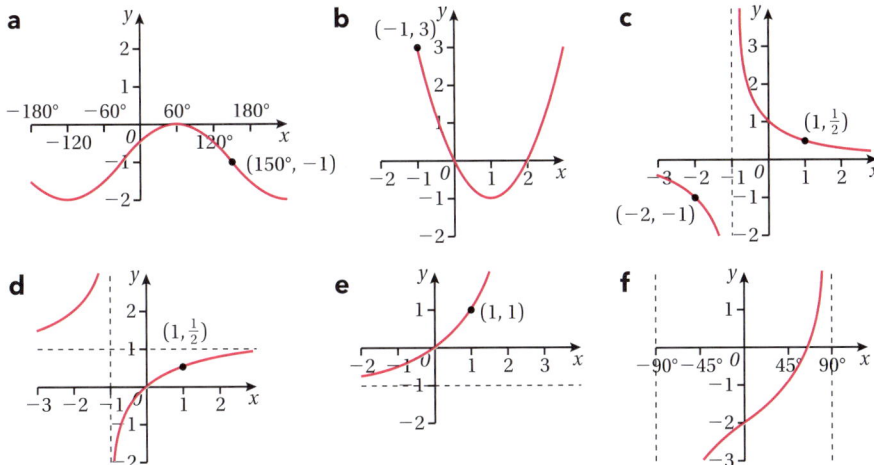

a

b

c

d

e

f

9 If you shift the graph of $y = \sin x$ to the right by 40° and down by 2 units, what will the equation of the new graph be?

Checklist of learning and understanding

Quadratic functions

- Vertical translations of the basic parabola $y = x^2$ are represented by the family of curves $y = x^2 \pm a$. The vertex is $(0, \pm a)$ and the axis of symmetry is the y-axis, $x = 0$.
- $y = -x^2 \pm a$ represents the family of curves with a maximum turning point, which are reflections of the curves $y = x^2 \pm a$ about the x-axis.
- Horizontal translations of $y = x^2$ are represented by $y = (x \pm a)^2$.
- The axis of symmetry for $y = (x + a)^2$ is $x = -a$ and the vertex is $(-a, 0)$.
- The axis of symmetry for $y = (x - a)^2$ is $x = a$ and the vertex is $(a, 0)$.

Find answers at: cambridge.org/ukschools/gcsemaths-studentbookanswers

- Completing the square: $y = (x + a)^2 \pm b$ gives the axis of symmetry $x = -a$, vertex $(-a, \pm b)$, y-intercept $(0, a^2 \pm b)$

Trigonometric functions

- $y = \sin x \pm a$ and $y = \cos x \pm a$ represent vertical translations of the functions $y = \sin x$ and $y = \cos x$.

- $y = \sin(x \pm a°)$ and $y = \cos(x \pm a°)$ represent a horizontal translation of the functions $y = \sin x$ and $y = \cos x$, $+a°$ to the left and $-a°$ to the right.

For additional questions on the topics in this chapter, visit GCSE Mathematics Online.

Chapter review

1 Which of these equations represents a reflection of the function $y = 2^x$ about the y-axis? Choose from the following options.

A $y = -2^x$ B $y = 2^{-x}$ C $y = \dfrac{1}{2^x}$ D $y = \dfrac{1}{-2^x}$

2 **a** Sketch the graphs **i** to **iv** on the same set of axes.

     i $y = x^2$ **ii** $y = x^2 - 5$ **iii** $y = -x^2$ **iv** $y = (x - 5)^2$

     b Describe the transformation that changes graph **i** to graphs **ii**, **iii** and **iv**.

3 **a** What translation of the trigonometric function $y = \sin x$ has resulted in this shift to the right?

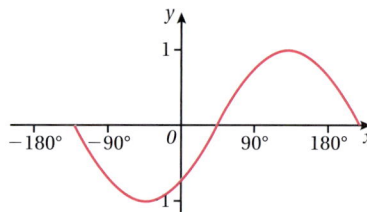

     b Draw a sketch of:

     i $y = \sin(x - 90°) + 1$ **ii** $y = \cos(x - 45°)$

4 **a** Copy this grid and draw the graph of $y = 1 + \sin x$ for values of x from 0° to 360°.

The graph of $y = \sin x$ has been drawn to help you. *(1 mark)*

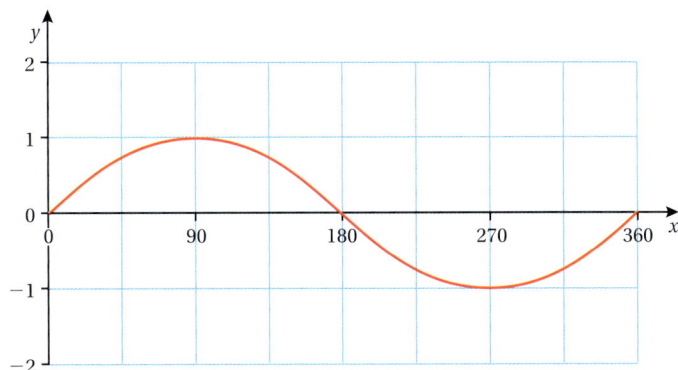

b Copy this grid and draw the graph of $y = 2\sin x$ for values of x from 0° to 360°.

The graph of $y = \sin x$ has been drawn to help you. *(1 mark)*

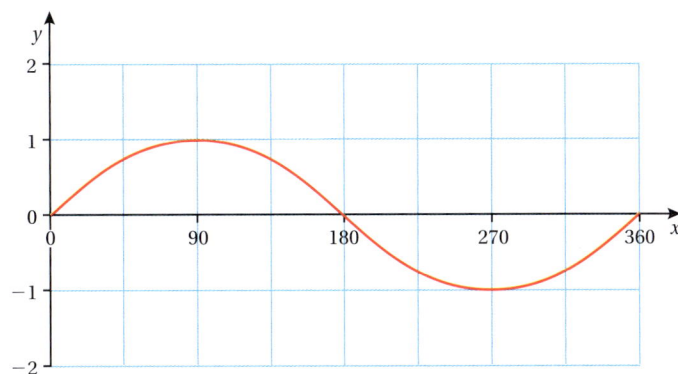

© AQA 2013

5 Sketch the graph of:

a $y = \dfrac{1}{x} - 1$

b $y = 2^x$ reflected in the line $y = 0$

6 The reciprocal function $y = \dfrac{1}{x} + 2$ is changed and the new function is $y = \dfrac{1}{x+1} + 2$.

What effect would this change have on the graph?

Glossary

A

Adjacent: next to each other. In shapes, sides that intersect each other are adjacent.

Alternate angles: the angles on parallel lines on opposite sides of a transversal

Angle of depression: when looking down, the angle between the line of sight and the horizontal

Angle of elevation: when looking up, the angle between the line of sight and the horizontal

Arithmetic sequence: a sequence where the difference between each term is constant

B

Binomial: an expression consisting of two terms

Binomial product: the product of two binomial expressions, for example, $(x + 2)(x + 3)$

Bisect: to divide exactly into two halves

Bivariate data: data that is collected in pairs

C

Chord: a straight line that joins one point on the circumference of a circle to another point on its circumference. The diameter is a chord that goes through the centre of the circle

Circumference: distance around the outside of a circle

Class intervals: the sizes of the groups that data has been grouped into

Coefficient: the number in front of a variable in a mathematical expression. In the term $5x^2$, 5 is the coefficient and x is the variable.

Co-interior angles: the angles within the parallel lines on the same side of the transversal

Combined events: one event followed by another event producing two or more outcomes

Common denominator: a number into which all the denominators of a set of fractions divide exactly

Composite function: a function created by combining two or more functions

Congruent: identical in shape and size

Conjugate: binomial expressions with the same terms but opposite signs

Consecutive: following each other in order, for example 1, 2, 3 or 35, 36, 37

Consecutive terms: terms that follow each other in a sequence

Constant: a number on its own

Continuous data: data that can have any value

Conversion factor: the number that you multiply or divide by to convert one measure into another smaller or larger unit

Coordinates: an ordered pair (x, y) identifying a position on a grid

Correlation: a relationship or connection between data items

Corresponding angles: angles that are created at the same point of the intersection when a transversal crosses a pair of parallel lines

Cumulative frequency: the sum total of all the frequencies up to a given value

Cyclic quadrilateral: any quadrilateral with all four vertices on the circumference of a circle

D

Degree of accuracy: the number of places to which you round a number

Dependent events: events in which the outcome is affected by what happened before

Dependent variable: the variable that is being measured in an experiment

Depreciation: the loss in value of an object over a period of time

Direct proportion: two values that both increase in the same ratio

Discrete data: data that can be counted and that can only have certain values

Discrete values: countable values where you only count certain values

Displacement: a change in position

E

Elevation view: a view of an object from the front, side or back

Error interval: the difference between the upper and lower bounds

Equalities: having the same amount or value

Equally likely: having the same probability of occurring

Equivalent: having the same value. Two ratios are equivalent if one is a multiple of the other

Estimate: an approximate answer or rough calculation

Evaluate: to calculate the numerical value of something

Event: the thing to which you are trying to give a probability

Exchange rate: a number that is used to calculate the difference in value between money from one country and money from another

Expanding: multiplying out an expression to get rid of the brackets

Exponent: the number that says how many times a letter or number is multiplied by itself. It is another name for power or index

Exponential function: a function of the form $y = kx$

Expression: a group of numbers and letters linked by operation signs

Exterior angles: angles produced by extending the sides of a polygon

F

First difference: the result of subtracting a term from the next term

Formula: a general rule or equation showing the relationship between unknown quantities

Function: a set of instructions for changing one number (the input) into another number (the output)

G

Geometric sequence: a sequence where the ratio between each term is constant

Gradient: a measure of the steepness of a line

Gradient = $\dfrac{\text{change in } y\text{-values}}{\text{change in } x\text{-values}}$

Grouped data: data that has been put into groups

H

Histogram: a bar chart in which the area of each bar is proportional to the frequency of a variable and its width equal to the class interval

Hypotenuse: the longest side of a right-angled triangle; the side opposite the 90° angle

I

Identity: an equation that is true no matter what values are chosen for the variables

Image: the new shape (after the object has been transformed)

Independent events: events that are not affected by what happened before

Index: a power or exponent indicating how many times a base number is multiplied by itself

Index notation: writing a number as a base and index, for example 2^3

Inequality: a mathematical sentence in which the left side is not equal to the right side

Integers: whole numbers in the set $\{\dots -3, -2, -1, 0, 1, 2, 3, \dots\}$; when they have a negative or positive sign

Interior angles: angles inside a two-dimensional shape at the vertices or corners

Inverse function: a function that reverses another function

Inverse proportion: a relation between two quantities such that one increases at a rate that is equal to the rate that the other decreases

Irrational number: a number that cannot be written in the form of $\dfrac{a}{b}$ or as a terminating or repeating decimal

Irregular polygon: a polygon that does not have equal sides and equal angles

Isometric grid: special drawing paper based on an arrangement of triangles

L

Line of symmetry: a line that divides a plane shape into two identical halves, each the reflection of the other

Linear equation: an equation where the highest power of the unknown is 1, for example $x + 3 = 7$

Locus (plural **loci**): a set of points that satisfy the same rule

Lower bound: the smallest value that a number (given to a specified accuracy) can be

M

Mathematical model: a representation of a real-life problem; assumptions are used to simplify the situation so that it can be solved mathematically

Midpoint: the centre of a line; the point that divides the line into two equal halves

Mirror line: a line equidistant from all corresponding points on a shape and their reflections

Mutually exclusive: events that cannot happen at the same time

N

Number line: a line marked with positions of numbers showing the valid values of a variable

O

Object: the original shape (before it has been transformed)

Orientation: the position of a shape relative to the grid

Outcome: a single result of an experiment

Outlier: data value that is much larger or smaller than others in the same data set

P

Parabola: the symmetrical curve produced by the graph of a quadratic function

Parallel vectors: occur when one vector is a multiple of the other. When drawn next to each other they are parallel lines, even if they go in opposite directions

Perfect square: a binomial product of the form $(a \pm b)^2$

Periodic graph: a graph that repeats itself in a regular way

Perimeter: the distance around the boundaries (sides) of a shape

Perpendicular bisector: a line perpendicular to another that also cuts it in half

Plan view: the view of an object from directly above

Plane shape: a flat, two-dimensional shape

Polygon: a closed plane shape with three or more straight sides

Polyhedron: a solid shape with flat faces that are polygons

Polynomial: an expression made up of many terms with positive powers for the variables

Population: the name given to a data set

Position-to-term rule: operations applied to the position number of a term in a sequence in order to generate that term

Prime factor: a factor that is also a prime number

Proportion: the number or amount of a group compared to the while, often expressed as a fraction, percentage or ratio

Pythagorean triple: three non-zero positive integers (a, b, c) for which $a^2 + b^2 = c^2$

Q

Quadratic: an expression with a variable to the power of 2 but no higher power

Quadratic expression: an expression in which the highest power of x is x^2

R

Radius (plural **radii**): distance from the centre to the circumference of a circle. One radius is half of the diameter of the circle.

Random: not predetermined

Ratio: the relationship between two or more groups or amounts, explaining how much bigger one is than another

Rational number: a number that can be expressed in the form of $\frac{a}{b}$ (or as its equivalent as a terminating or repeating decimal)

Reciprocal: the value obtained by inverting a fraction. Any number multiplied by its reciprocal is 1.

Reflection: an exact image of a shape about a line of symmetry (mirror line)

Regular polygon: a polygon with equal straight sides and equal angles

Representative sample: a small quantity of data that represents the characteristics of a larger population

Right prism: a prism with sides perpendicular to the end faces (base)

Roots: the individual values of x in a quadratic equation

Rotation symmetry: symmetry by turning a shape around a fixed point so that it looks the same from different positions

Round to significant figures: round to a specified level of accuracy from the first significant figure

Rounding: writing a number with zeros in the place of some digits

S

Sample: a small set of data from a population

Sample space: a list or diagram that shows all possible outcomes from two or more events

Scalar: a numerical quantity (it has no direction)

Scale factor: a number that scales a quantity up or down

Second difference: the difference between each term in the first difference

Semicircle: half of a circle

Sequence: a number pattern or list of numbers following a particular order

Set: a collection. The brackets { } are shorthand for 'the set of'. For example, {2, 4, 6, 8} is the set of the numbers 2, 4, 6, 8, which represents the even numbers.

Significant figure: the first non-zero digit when you read a number from left to right

Simultaneous equations: a pair of equations with two unknowns that can be solved at the same time

Solution: all possible values of x in an equation. Depending on the quadratic equation, x can have one, two or possibly no solutions.

Subject: the variable which is expressed in terms of other variables or constants. It is the variable on its own on one side of the equals sign. In the formula $s = \frac{d}{t}$, s is the subject

Substitute: to replace variables with numbers

Supplementary angles: two angles are supplementary angles if they add up to 180°

Surd: if $\sqrt[n]{a}$ is an irrational number, then $\sqrt[n]{a}$ is called a surd

T

Tangent: a line that makes contact with a curve at one point; it does not cut the curve, it just touches the curve

Term: a combination of letters and/or numbers. Each number in a sequence is called a term

Term-to-term rule: operations applied to any number in a sequence to generate the next number in the sequence

Theorem: a statement that can be demonstrated to be true by accepted mathematical operations

Transversal: a straight line that crosses a pair of parallel lines

Trinomial: an expression with three terms

Truncation: cutting off all digits after a certain point without rounding

U

Unknown: part of an equation which is represented by a letter

Upper bound: the largest value that a number (given to a specified accuracy) can be

V

Variable: a letter representing an unknown number

Vector: a quantity that has both magnitude and direction. For example, displacement (30 m south), velocity (30 m/s forwards) or acceleration due to gravity (9.8 m/s² down).

Vertically opposite angles: angles that are opposite one another at an intersection of two lines. Vertical in this context means 'of the same vertex or point' and not up and down.

X

x-intercept: the point where a line crosses the x-axis when $y = 0$

Y

y-intercept: the point where a line crosses the y-axis when $x = 0$

Index